THE GENEVA BIBLE

PILGRIM CLASSIC COMMENTARIES

EDITED BY GERALD T. SHEPPARD

Volume 1 The Geneva Bible

the Geneva Bible

The Annotated New Testament

1602 Edition

Edited by
Gerald T. Sheppard

Introductory Essays by
Gerald T. Sheppard
Marvin W. Anderson
John H. Augustine
Nicholas W. S. Cranfield

The Pilgrim Press
Cleveland, Ohio

Dedicated to
Brevard S. Childs,
Holmes Professor of Old Testament Interpretation and Criticism,
Yale University

The Pilgrim Press, Cleveland, Ohio 44115

The 1607 New Testament is reproduced
by permission of the British and Foreign Bible Society
from a copy in their collection at
Cambridge University Library.

 Published 1989
Printed in Mexico on acid-free paper

97 96 95 5 4 3

Library of Congress Cataloging-in-Publication Data
Bible. N.T. English. Geneva. 1602.
The Geneva Bible.

(Pilgrim classic commentaries; v.1)
Includes bibliographies.
1. Bible. N.T.—Commentaries—Early works to 1800.
I. Sheppard, Gerald T., 1946- . II. Bible. N.T.
English. Geneva. 1988. III. Title. IV. Series.
BS2070 1602 225.5'201 88-28891
ISBN 0-8298-0789-6
ISBN 0-8298-0785-3 (pbk.)

Contents

Editor's Note vii

INTRODUCTORY ESSAYS

The Geneva Bible and English Commentary, 1600–1645
Gerald T. Sheppard 1

The Geneva (Tomson/Junius) New Testament Among Other English Bibles of the Period
Marvin W. Anderson 5

"Cleared by Faith": The Use of Scriptural Precedent in English Protestant Defenses of Poetry
John H. Augustine 18

From England to New England: The Protestant and "Puritan" Movement, 1600–1645
Nicholas W. S. Cranfield 27

THE NEW TESTAMENT OF OUR LORD JESUS CHRIST

Editor's Note

My interest in the history of translation and commentary on the Bible derives chiefly from a doctoral seminar taught by Prof. Brevard Childs at Yale Graduate School many years ago. One of the contributing editors, John H. Augustine, similarly studied with Professor Childs at Yale. We dedicate this volume to Dr. Childs in order to recognize his contribution to New Testament studies, to Christian theology, and to the history of interpretation. His contributions to these fields have been far more than token, including a large book on the subject of *The New Testament as Canon: An Introduction* (Philadelphia: Fortress Press, 1984). In that volume he states: "The traditional Christian form of viewing the New Testament within the framework of dogmatic theology emerged in the post-Reformation period as the result of a variety of doctrinal controversies in the late sixteenth and seventeenth centuries" (p. 5). The Geneva New Testament is the best single witness to that tradition, providing a standard by which to measure the innovations and heterodoxies of the modern period.

A few words cannot do justice to the help I gained from the consulting editors, who each wrote an introductory essay. I have come late to disciplines they have mastered. Their patience with me and sound advice underlie anything of value here. I also owe much appreciation to my family. Anne, my wife, has been a priceless adviser and intellectual companion on such projects. Our children—David, Elisabeth, and Stephen—have helped in some wonderful ways I hope they will some day understand.

Behind the scenes of this series is the Senior Editor at The Pilgrim Press, who improved the quality of our work without recognition. Marion M. Meyer exemplifies the best of what The Pilgrim Press has represented from its inception. She has supported controversial books and contributed incisively to their formation. Likewise, the director of the Press, Dr. Larry E. Kalp, recognized the value of this series and had the courage to pursue it.

I and my consulting editors thank Cambridge University and particularly Allen F. Jesson, the Bible Society's librarian at the university. We value his help in selecting the 1607 text for reproduction. This facsimile edition is reproduced by permission of the Bible Society Trustees. We also express our thanks to Gerald Bye, the Cambridge University photographer, for providing the negative copy for this Pilgrim Press edition.

Finally, I thank the Rev. Garland C. Brooks of the United Church of Canada for a generous grant in support of this volume, based on its significance for the history of preaching. I am further grateful for encouragement from my colleagues within the Toronto School of Theology and especially Principal Douglas Jay of Emmanuel College within Victoria University of the University of Toronto.

GERALD T. SHEPPARD

The Geneva Bible and English Commentary, 1600–1645

GERALD T. SHEPPARD

This edition of the Geneva (Tomson-Junius) New Testament inaugurates a series titled "Pilgrim Classic Commentaries," facsimile reprints of rare commentaries from the period 1600–1645. Introductory essays accompany each volume of these works, which constituted the first English-language commentaries and have the stamp of the continental Reformation. Moreover, these volumes are essential sources for the study of seventeenth-century English and American literature. The marginal notes in the Geneva Bible and in the biblical commentaries of the subsequent publications provide the background for the Westminster Confession of 1945. Consequently, these books represent the early English heritage of many major denominational groups, including the United Presbyterian Church and the United Church of Christ. For this reason The Pilgrim Press, the publishing house of the United Church of Christ, is now reprinting the very books that the first presses in America imported from the greater presses of England and made available to the learned clergy of puritan New England.

The basis of the current volume is an unusually well-preserved 1607 printing of the third edition (1602) of the "Geneva" New Testament. The marginal annotations are those of Laurence Tomson based on Theodore Beza's 1574 Latin translation of the Bible with notes, together with the notes by Franciscus Junius on Revelation, which had by that time replaced those of Beza in this edition. Here is presented the last of the three major forms of the Geneva Bible and the most indicative of the climate of opinion among Puritans in the first half of the seventeenth century. From the inception of the Geneva Bible, the aim of the annotations was clearly expressed in a preface by its first translator, William Whittingham (1557): "so that by this meanes both they which have not abilitie to by the Commentaries upon the Newe testament, and they also which have not opportunitie and leasure to reade them because of their prolixitie may use this book in stede therof. . . ." The effect of the Geneva Bible was to safeguard the advance of the Reformation by placing text and commentary together.

The Geneva Bible became the most popular Bible in England and America and remained so until about 1640, when the less popular King James Version (1611) finally gained wide acceptance. Contemporary reprints have consistently omitted these extremely important annotations. Theodore Beza (1519–1605) succeeded Calvin as theological interpreter of the Reformation in Geneva. Because of the rare combination of competence in Greek and of practical theological insight in Beza's notes, the notes became extremely popular among several generations of English Protestants. For exam-

Gerald T. Sheppard, Ph.D., is associate professor of Old Testament studies at Emmanuel College of Victoria University of the University of Toronto.

ple, the doctrine of "limited atonement," prevalent in Calvinism, although not originally found explicitly in the teaching of John Calvin, is attributed to Beza. As the first continental theologian to make the doctrine of predestination the central feature of a "supralapsarian" system, Beza viewed the Bible with a persistent focus on divine election and predestination. This slant in his orientation toward the biblical text found great affinity among most Protestant biblical commentators who placed special emphasis on one's ability to discern from scripture the hand of God steering the course of both individual lives and nations. The Roman Catholic interpreters naturally objected to such a refraction in the Christian vision of scripture, for it effectively discouraged the possibility of other readings of the biblical text integral to Catholic faith but outside the domain of a Calvinistic perspective.

Although a 1560 Geneva Bible has already been reprinted, this current volume is required for understanding English biblical commentary of this early period. Whereas the notes in the 1560 edition reflect more strongly the influence of Calvin and the "common Protestant" opinion of Marian exiles, those of 1602 mirror the more separatistic puritan heritage of the next generation of Calvinism. Junius' notes on the book of Revelation, which replaced those of Tomson, contained in the 1576 edition, display a robust millenarian impulse together with unrestrained polemics with Roman Catholic positions. The Geneva Bible—reprinted here—became familiar to most of the English commentators of the period, who frequently interacted with its marginal notes and often, for the purpose of "interpreting scripture with scripture," relied on the resonances of word and imagery inherent in Tomson's translation.

The scholarly significance of publishing the Geneva Bible with its annotations and selected commentaries from the seventeenth century is far ranging. The "Pilgrim Classic Commentaries" series provides an unparalleled resource for studies in English Protestant and puritan social and political history, the Reformation in England and its legacy in New England, history of biblical interpretation, and assessments of Westminster Assembly and Confession. It also provides specific sources for the study of the renaissance heritage of Protestant poetics. A reprint series of this scope has not been undertaken since the well-known Nicholas series in the mid-nineteenth century.

In Sydney E. Ahlstrom's *A Religious History of the American People,* the late Yale historian argued persuasively that the inheritance from seventeenth-century England in America had not been adequately recognized. Ahlstrom calls for greater attention to ways in which "the Reformation was being carried out of Great Britain," precisely because from this heritage "come the colonial impulses—imperial, commercial, and evangelistic—which would form the chief foundations—political, economic, and religious—of the American tradition." A stridently Protestant America, with little regard for the massive Catholic presence in its midst, grew out of this "Protestant synthesis," giving rise to the Great Puritan Epoch that Ahlstrom thinks came to a close only in the 1960s. English Protestant religious themes of election and predestination of a chosen people composing a "New Israel" took on a powerful political thrust in the milieu of the colonies, further fueled by the Great Awakening and the American Revolution in the century that followed. What emerged was a uniquely American form of Evangelical Protestantism as spontaneously political as it was religious. Because of this profound connection between England and New England, with a history of persistent influence from the English Protestant Reformation, this series concentrates specifically on commentaries that passed from England to New England, playing a definitive role in the perception of religion and society both in the history of the United States and in some parts of eastern Canada.

Unlike biblical commentaries in the twentieth century, their antecedents in seventeenth-century England and New England pervasively influenced every level of intellectual, artistic, social, and political life. Books such as Jeremiah, Hosea, and Jonah challenge the assumption of God's continuous covenantal relationship with Israel: English Protestant commentators on these same books sought to know under what circumstances England (or New England) might be a nation chosen like Israel or similarly rejected by God. Every aspect of social and political life invited a critique from a divine point of view—the role of the king in church affairs, the propriety of owning slaves, the use of East Indians as sources of cheap labor, the pros and cons of tobacco, and so forth. In this "Golden Age of Preaching," the commentaries fully reflected the vibrancy of the lecture hall and pulpit. Those who did not read commentaries heard them quoted, praised, or condemned. "Search the scriptures" (John 5:39) was the rallying cry of the English Protestant Reformation. Because the Bible represented, at least rhetorically, the fulcrum on which the fate of the world rested, biblical commentaries covered a vast range of contemporary issues and often wedded the highest aesthetic gifts to pragmatic concerns of daily life and politics.

These Protestant commentaries belong among the first English contributions to Reformation literature, and the Geneva Bible provided the text that most of them interpreted. Encouraged and supported by John Calvin, the Geneva Bible illustrates the dependence of the Reformation in England on continental resources. Although the original edition of this popular Bible was reprinted in 1969, only this series provides an opportunity for scholars to examine the English translation of Beza's marginal notes that accompany the Geneva Bible—notes that seventeenth-century commentators frequently discuss.

When considering commentaries during this period, the editors are aware that the milieu is still largely that of a Latin church. Older Latin commentaries, including many contemporary Roman Catholic volumes, continued to be treasured by many Protestants alongside the new English contributions. Moreover, the task of selecting which works to include in this collection was complicated by an awareness of the popularity of some continental Reformation commentaries (for example, those on Isaiah, Jeremiah, and the Gospels), which explains the tendency of English expositors to neglect certain major biblical books. In many cases a choice was made in favor of the more original contributions rather than the compilations because they better reflect an indigenous appropriation of continental Reformation themes, cast in uniquely English forms.

Because these commentaries antedate the full impact of the Enlightenment and its modern critical approach to history, they remain among the few extant English works that sustain the biblical text as a literary and coherent whole. At the same time, the seventeenth century was not, by and large, an age of sermons or of interpretations of scripture for any but controversial and polemical purposes. Rather than resolve inner-biblical tensions or contradictions by a speculative appeal to different and autonomous authors/editors, the commentators more often found in these instances an opportunity to understand the equally perplexing tensions and contradictions of their own daily and national life. By means of this vision of a canonical text, English Protestant commentators sought to discover within the past tense of Christian scripture a realistic and pragmatically compelling present tense, ripe with implications for their own time.

Accordingly, these works warrant a distinct place in the history of English commentary and prove particularly provocative to scholars concerned with a post-modern literary interpretation of the Bible or how it was read as canonized "scripture" within Christian faith.

Theological students will find in these commentaries a primary source for understanding the implications of the famous Westminster Assembly. Many of these same volumes were collected at Union Theological Seminary in New York City by Old Testament scholar Charles Briggs, at the end of the nineteenth century. Briggs drew on them for his defense in his historic heresy trial as a minister in the Presbyterian Church. Relying on these commentaries and a copy of the *Westminster Annotations,* Briggs argued that the Westminster Confession did not deny the value of modern historical-critical investigations of biblical texts. The close association in the commentaries between exposition of biblical claims and the value placed on the illumination of historical inquiry confirmed for Briggs that the Westminster Divines were at most "pre-critical" rather than "anti-clerical" or fundamentalistic in their approach. In the current foment over Bible and history, these volumes mark a pivotal moment in Christian interpretation.

The influence of these commentaries on English literature remains seriously underestimated. For example, when John Milton defends a controversial point in the *Tetrachordon,* he can confidently assert that "I say we conclude no more than what *the common expositors* themselves give us, both in that which I have recited, and much more hereafter." Most English Protestant commentaries did not bury the biblical text under the debris of arcane historical details or linguistic minutiae. Artistic and literary features were central elements within their style. As part of their commenting on scripture, the expositors often rendered the scriptural text in the form of a poetic paraphrase, transforming the alien traces of Hebrew poetry into the familiar register of rhyme and meter of the great English poets. In this way the aesthetic circle was complete. As the Bible influenced the poets and great prose artists, so the Bible was itself paraphrased to meet the approval of a fastidious cultural idea of literary beauty. Without the aid of the Bible and the guide of these commentaries, English literature in this period is easily distorted.

For literary scholars these commentaries have drawn increasing attention to the long-neglected influence of Reformed theology on English and American literature and culture. Students of the seventeenth century are often hampered by a lack of primary source materials. This "Pilgrim Classic Commentary" series provides precisely the materials necessary to study biblical typology, English Protestant defenses of poetry, the art of biblical translation and paraphrase, the "plain style," the complex manner in which the Bible affords a literary model for Protestant poetry and prose, as well as the intertextual nature of the commentaries themselves. Literary scholars conversant with the great literature and poetry in the seventeenth century will be particularly interested in this series, for it provides essential background material that will bring precision to studies of how Reformed theology directly influenced the poetry and prose of the period.

The Geneva (Tomson/Junius) New Testament Among Other English Bibles of the Period

MARVIN W. ANDERSON

The purpose of this essay is to set the various editions of the Geneva Bible in perspective, in the context of prior English translations of the Bible. Some consideration also will be given to the Roman Catholic reaction in the two editions of the Rheims New Testament up to 1600. Less concern will be given to the 1560 Geneva Bible than to illustrations of the differences introduced by Tomson's revision of it in 1576, and by the Tomson/Junius edition (1607) here reprinted, which appeared as puritanism intensified religious opinions in the 1580s.[1]

A Brief Historical Overview

English translations of the Bible began to appear in the reign of Henry VIII (1509–47), nearly four decades before the circulation of the first Geneva Bible of 1560. From this earliest period onward the continental Reformation had inspired and often strongly influenced the content of these translations. Erasmus, who came to teach at Cambridge from 1509 to 1514, provided a stimulus for Bible translation and study undeterred by Henry VIII's subsequent public objections to Martin Luther and the German Reformation. Later, injunctions by Edward VI in 1547 and Elizabeth I in 1559 required that each church post a copy of the paraphrases of Erasmus so that all parishioners could read it. For the Geneva Bible the decisive events transpired after the death of Henry's successor, Edward VI (1553).

The new monarchy under Queen Mary Tudor proceeded vigorously to lay claim to the earlier Catholicism of Henry that had earned him the title "Defender of the Faith" from Pope Leo X in 1521. During the year after Edward's death, the queen wedded the Roman Catholic Philip of Spain. She then appointed Reginald Pole as Cardinal of England and induced the Parliament to vote in favor of recognizing papal authority. On November 30, 1554, Cardinal Pole granted the nation papally recognized absolution from heresy. The resulting persecution of Protestants accounts for the exile of gifted English Protestant scholars throughout the continent. A number settled in Calvin's Geneva, where large portions of "The Geneva Bible" were translated and brought back to England when the Marian exiles returned in the year of the accession of Elizabeth I (1558). The Geneva Bible derives out of these circumstances. An excellent overview of

Marvin Anderson, Ph.D., is professor of church history at Bethel Theological Seminary, St. Paul, Minnesota.

these events is available in Lloyd E. Berry's introduction to the 1560 facsimile edition of the Geneva Bible published by the University of Wisconsin Press, 1969.

Although the climate of Elizabethan England (1558-1603) was less hostile to Protestantism, the Geneva Bible remained controversial and not without its rival alternatives. The Marian exiles originally dedicated it to Queen Elizabeth, "our Zurubbabal," affirming that she had a divine mandate to rebuild the nation just as did the governor who accompanied the ancient Israelites' return to Jerusalem from exile in Babylon.[2] Nonetheless, Elizabeth, as well as her successor, James I (1603–25), expressed strong reservations regarding the Geneva Bible and its annotations. Elizabeth chose to lend her support to the Bishop's Bible (1568), translated by Archbishop Parker, whom she had appointed. In direct reference to the Geneva Bible, Parker swore "to make no bitter notis uppon any text, or yet to set downe any determinacion in places of controversy."

King James I openly objected to the Geneva Bible at Hampton Court in 1604. He complained that these notes were seditious and entirely biased. As examples, James cited the note to Exodus 1:19, which allowed for disobedience of certain royal demands, and the following annotation to 2 Chronicles 15:16, chiding King Asa for not putting his wicked queen mother to death: "herein he shewed yt he lacked zeale: for she oght to have dyed bothe by the couenant, and by Lawe of God: but he gaue place to foolish pitie, & wolde also seme after a sorte to satisfie the Lawe." His "Authorized Version" (King James Bible) of 1611 was never officially imposed on the churches. Slowly it began to replace the Bishop's Bible in churches, since the latter ceased to be reprinted. Bishops in this period commonly used the Geneva Bible for sermons, and it was the version brought over on the *Mayflower* to the New World by the Pilgrims. Only by the 1640s did the Authorized Version become dominant, although dissenting Protestants and Puritans often still continued to prefer the Geneva in the ensuing decades. Ironically, in 1642 a King James Version began to be printed, accompanied by the New Testament annotations of the same Geneva (Tomson/Junius) Bible here reprinted.

English Precedents to the Geneva Bible

Tudor Translations

Vernacular English versions of scripture appeared in Tudor times under humanist and Protestant auspices. The former impulse gained inspiration from the popular translations of Erasmus' *Paraclesis* to his 1516 New Testament and the preface to his *Paraphrase of St. Matthew*. Both of his *Exhortacyons* (1533/34) depict scripture as a moral and active philosophy—"a lyfe, rather then a disputacyon."[3] Each contains the familiar images of the ploughman singing the psalms in his mother tongue and the weaver at work singing of the gospel.

Protestant translators refer to scripture as the root of faith (Coverdale) or the charter of neighbor love (Tyndale/Oecolampadius).[4] So the *Vom alten und nüen Gott* in its 1534 English edition reads: "euery man may often tymes rede the byble namely ye gosapelles . . . so moche the better . . . to vnderstande Chryste . . . & theyre charyte is somoche the more excited and styrred vp towardes theyre neyghbor."[5] Tyndale himself follows this Basel advice in his own 1528 *Obedience of a Christian*. Although his enemies may do their worst to take away his goods and name, "yet as long as Christ remaineth in my heart, so long I love thee not a whit the less."[6] Whether viewed as a norm of moral philosophy or as a charter of neighborly love, English vernacular scripture continued to play a central role in the Reformation.

Regarding the style of English New Testaments, all the translations from 1534 to 1560 rely heavily on Tyndale's poetic prose.[7] The most recent study underscores Tyndale's "even, grave rhythm, familiar words" and bold figures.[8] His crisp use of everyday language is illustrated, for example, in his 1534 translation of Matthew 6:28–34:

> Considre the lylies of the felde, how they growe. They labour not nether spynne. And yet for all that I saye vnto you, that euen Salomon in all his royalte was not arayed lyke vnto one of these. Wherfore yf God so clothe the grasse, which ys to daye in the felde, and to morowe shalbe caste into the fournace: shall he not moche more do the same vnto you, o ye of lytle fayth? . . . But rather seke yefyrst the kyngdome of heuen and the rightwisenes therof, and all these thynges shalbe ministred vnto you. Care not then for the morow, but let the morow care for it selfe: for the daye present hath ever ynough ofhis awne trouble.[9]

The saliency and potency of such expressions moved Sir Thomas More to warn his readers: "Let not therfore Tyndall (good reader) wyth his gay gloryouse wordes carye you so fast & so far away, but that you remember to pull hym bakke/ by the sleve a lytle."[10] Translators in later periods would often find Tyndale's phrases both difficult to shake from the memories of English readers and not easily surpassed.

Tyndale/Coverdale

Tyndale's first printed English New Testament of 1525 relies on Luther's Wittenberg New Testament as a pattern. The "Prologge" cites sixty lines from Luther; the Genealogy of Matthew is set up one generation per line as in Luther; marginal comments use Luther's marginalia; and the order of books is identical in number and sequence to Luther's. The biblical text itself is not that of Luther, but Erasmus' third Greek edition of 1522. In Matthew 6, Tyndale highlights the poetic force of the text by punctuation and the spacing of lines:

> No man can serve two masters. For other he shall hate the one/and love the other: or els he shall lene to the one/and despise that other. Ye cannott serve god and mãmon. . . . Ys not the lyfe more worth then meate? and the boddy moare of value then ryament? Beholde the foules of the aier:
>
> for they sowe not nether reepe. noer yet cary into the barnes/and yett youre hevenly father fedeth them. Are ye nott better than they?

All that has survived of this Cologne quarto of Matthew/Mark is a portion of Matthew in the unique British Library copy. Although Tyndale revised this edition and removed the marginal notes for his 1526 Worms octavo, the same elements of style continue to appear in his widely known revised New Testament of 1534. Before his death Tyndale had completed from the Old Testament a translation of only the Pentateuch, the Former Prophets, and the book of Jonah.

Tyndale's translations were taken over by Miles Coverdale, who finished translating the Old Testament and published the first English Bible in 1535. The Coverdale Bible is a small folio edition, printed in Schwabacher black-letter type with two columns and fifty-seven lines to a full page. It was "prynted in the yeare of oure Lorde M.DXXXV. and fynished the fourth daye of October."[11] All the recorded copies are incomplete. The main argument of the dedication includes Coverdale's purpose for translation.

> Seynge then that the scripture of God teacheth us euery thynge sufficiently, both what we oughte to do, and what we oughte to leaue undone: whome we are bounde to obey, and whome we shulde not obeye: therfore (I saye) it causeth all prosperite, and setteth euery thyng in frame: and where it is taught and knowen, it lygteneth all darkenesses, comyforteth all sory hertes, leaueth no poore man unhelped, suffreth nothynge amysse unamended, letteth no prynce be disobeyed, permytteth no heresie to be preached: but refourmeth all thinges, amendeth that is amysse, and setteth euery thynge in order.[12]

When his bishops carped at several flaws in the translated text, Henry VIII asked the crucial question "But are there any heresies maintained thereby?" When the bishops could specify none, the king retorted: "If there be no heresies then in God's name let it go abroad among our people."[13] Therefore, his first printed English Bible effectively promoted Tyndale's New Testament, which circulated with official help. Behind these events lies the influence of Thomas Cromwell, architect of the state policy, who sought to implement a social/humanistic program through parliamentary statutes and their popular appeal.

Great Bible

Coverdale also caused Tyndale's New Testament to be widely known through his incorporation of it in the seven Great Bible editions of 1539–1541. The first edition of the Great Bible was finished in April of 1539. The second printing and the second edition both appeared in April of 1540. This has been called Cranmer's Bible, from the preface that the archbishop contributed to the Whytchurche edition (John Rylands Library, Manchester, has Richard Grafton on the title page).

The prologue made by the "Prymate of Englande, Thomas Archbiyshop of Canturbury," expressed well the tension that public access to the Bible may lead to heresy rather than to a true understanding of the gospel. The opening paragraph affirms the ancient English custom to read the scriptures in a common-speech translation. Cranmer quotes from John Chrysostom, the great preacher of Antioch and Constantinople, who urged his hearers to study the Bible between sermons. After references to English custom and patristic precedent, the prologue concludes its first half with a sweeping lesson for several classes of society. The last half warns against misuse of scripture by citing from Gregory of Nazianzus how not everyone should address high questions of divinity. "Let us keep us in our boundes," wrote Cranmer, "and nether let us go farre on thone syde, lest we retorne into Egypte, nether to farre over ye other, leste we be caried awaye to Babylon."[14] The third Great Bible appeared in July 1540 with Cranmer's Prologue.[15]

Although the royal order that set up Bibles in every parish church was never rescinded, another proclamation of July 8, 1546, ordered that after August 31, 1546, no person should have "the text of the New Testament of Tyndale's or Coverdale's translation in English."[16] The Great Bible, which incorporated their best work, was—miracle of miracles—exempt from this royal decree. It is significant that Tyndale's New Testament, in its 1534 revision, became the pattern for the text of the Geneva Bible from 1560.[17]

Geneva Bible

William Whittingham's 1557 Translation

A contemporary of this Marian exile claims that Whittingham collaborated with Miles Coverdale, Christopher Goodman, Anthony Gilby, Thomas Sampson, and William Cole in the translation of the 1560 Geneva Bible.[18] Most of the work was done by the date of the February 10, 1559, dedicatory letter to Elizabeth I in *The Boke of Psalmes,* and many returned to England after Elizabeth's accession on November 17, 1558. Whittingham seems to have supervised the New Testament and Anthony Gilby, the Old Testament.[19] The 1557 version is the prototype for the 1560 edition in verse divisions, roman type, and vocabulary selection. More than 80 percent of the text common to all four New Testament English versions is Tyndale (1534), reflecting the dominant position of the printed Erasmian biblical text over that of Luther for this translation. Nonetheless, one is overwhelmed by the permanence of the Tyndale version and its literary impact on the Genevan New Testament, which appeared first in 1560, and on the more than 150 reprints up to 1644.[20]

A specific comparison of Matthew 6:24–26 in Tyndale's 1534 text with its form in the 1560 Geneva text shows the high degree of dependence and subtle differences.

Tyndale (1534)	*Geneva* (1560)
No man can serve two masters	No man can serve two masters:
For ether he shall hate the one	for either he shal hate the one,
and love the other: or els he	and love the other, or els he
shall lene to the one and despise	shal leane to the one and despise
the other: ye can not serve	the other. Ye cannot serve
God and mammon. . . .	God and riches. . . .
ys not the lyfe more worth	Is not the life more worth
then meate, and the body	then meat? and the bodie
more of value then rayment?	then raiment?
Beholde the foules of the ayer:	Beholde the foules of the heauen:
for they sowe not, nether reepe,	for they sowe not, neither reape,
nor yet cary in to the barnes:	nor carie into the barnes:
and yet youre hevenly father	yet your heauenlie Father
fedeth them. Are ye not	feedeth them. Are ye not
moche better then they?	mouche better then they?

"Mammon" becomes "riches," "ayer" becomes "heauen," and "more of value" is dropped, as well as the words "yet" and "and." Seventy-eight of the eighty-five words cited above are carried over into the Geneva Bible, which, in this selection, is 91.76 percent Tyndale, despite Coverdale, Matthew, Taverner, the Great Bible, and Whittingham printings, which occur between 1535 and 1557.

1560 New Testament Text and Notes

It is already apparent that the 1557 Genevan New Testament in English was the prototype for the 1560 text. Analysis of Acts 12 and 1 Peter 1:1–25 confirms the impression that has been derived from the 43.24 percent common vocabulary changes in Matthew

6:24–33, John 14:1–7, Romans 8:31–39, and James 4:1–17. Results of the Acts 12 comparison are as follows: At verse 19 Whittingham and Geneva have "punished." Verse 20 has "intended to make warre against them," whereas the Tyndale Bible and the Great Bible have "was displeased with them." Acts 12 shows a high correlation between Tyndale (1534), the Great Bible (1539), Whittingham (1557), and Geneva (1560). The text in all three versions is 95 percent set by Tyndale.

1 Peter 5:2–3 is taken directly from Whittingham rather than from the Tyndale Bible or the Great Bible. The three versions are listed below.

Great Bible (1539)	*Whittingham* (1557)	*Geneva* (1560)
(2): Fede ye Christes flocke as moch as lyeth in you takynge the ouersyght of them not as compelled therto	Feed the flocke of God which dependeth vpon you caring for it not as though ye were compelled therto	Fede the flocke of God which dependeth vpon you caring for it not by constraint
but wyllyngly (after a godly sorte) not for the desyre of fylthy lucre but of a good mynde	but wyullingly not for the desire of filthy lucre lust of a good mynde	but willingly not for filthie lucre lust of a readie minde
(3): not as though ye were lordes ouer the parrishes but that ye be an ensample to the flocke (and that wyth good wyll)	Not as thogh ye wer lordes ouer Gods heritage but that ye be ensamples to the flocke	Not as thogh ye were lords ouer Gods heritage but that ye may be ensamples to the flocke

"Ouer the parrishes" derives from Tyndale and survives in the Great Bible version. Our limited random sample from six separate sections of the New Testament indicates that the translators used both the Great Bible and Whittingham in their revision. These samples suggest that the 1557 New Testament is the prototype for the 1560 version, with the underlying literary core that of Tyndale as retained in the Great Bible.

The 1560 notes are exegetical for the most part, with several cross-references to other sections of the New Testament more prominent than the notes themselves. Some notes are explicitly Protestant in tone, such as the comment on John 20:30, "It is finished." The note adds: "Mans salvation is perfected by the onlie sacrifice of Christ: & all ye ceremonies of the Law are ended." For the most part this first set of notes provides a lexical aid to the reader. For example, the statement in Luke 15:8 that the pieces of silver are "drachmae" gains the explanation "which is some what more in value then fyue pence of olde sterling money, & was equal with a Romaine penie."

Even the notes to Romans 9–11 are mild in tone, given the Genevan setting of this enterprise. The word election is mentioned only twice in the annotations to this *locus classicus* for a doctrine of predestination. At Galatians 2:20 the expression "Thus I live yet" provokes the comment "Not as I was once, but regenerat, and changed into a new creature, in qualitie, & not in substance."

The descriptive rather than dogmatic tone of this translation shines forth in the "arguments" to several of the New Testament letters. There is one summary for the four Gospels and none for 2 or 3 John, making twenty-two arguments in all. The summary to 1 Peter is a good example of this modesty:

> He exhorteth the faithful to denie them selues, and to condemne the worlde, that being deliuered from all carnal affections and impediments, they may more spedely atteine to the heauenlie kingdome of Christ, whereunto we are called by the grace of God reueiled to vs in his Sonne, and haue already receued it by faith, possessed it by hope, and are therein confirmed by holines of life.

Tomson/Junius Edition: Text and Annotations

The first edition of 1560 was altered by Tomson's translation of L'Oiseleur's notes on the Gospels (Camerarius) and Epistles (Beza) in 1576 and in 1602 with Junius' notes on Revelation.

Theodore Beza made a complete Latin translation of the New Testament for Robert Estienne's Latin Bible of 1556/57. Opposite the Vulgate text Beza's translation was printed in the upper half of the left-hand page with his annotations on the lower half. This five-year effort on Beza's part was used in the 1560 Geneva New Testament. When Beza finished his Greek text of 1565, the annotations were altered beneath the Greek and opposite the Vulgate. More substantial changes were made in the 1582 edition. The fourth edition of 1589 and fifth of 1598 contain minor revisions. Backus identifies the 1565 notes as L'Oiseleur's base for translation and the 1589/98 editions as the source of final revisions in the King James Version of 1611. Thus Beza left his mark on both versions.[21]

The most popular "Black Letter" quartos of the 1560 edition, such as that of 1594, had Calvin's "The Summe of the whole Scripture" taken from the French Geneva Bible, which was added at the front of the New Testament, together with Beza's "Questions and Answers on the Doctrine of Predestination and the Use of God's Word and Sacraments."[22] These additions, as well as the summaries of each New Testament book, are dropped in the Geneva/Tomson/Junius "Roman Letter" folio editions, including Beza's special summary of Revelation that accompanied the "Black Letter" quartos. There were twelve editions of Geneva/Tomson and twenty-four Geneva/Tomson/Junius complete Bibles. Separate New Testament editions of Geneva/Tomson number twenty-seven and Geneva/Tomson/Junius, three. There were, moreover, at least sixty-six editions of the Geneva New Testament with part or all of the 1560 notes replaced. The 1607 edition is quite representative of the Geneva/Tomson/Junius genre.

Changes in the translation are infrequent in printing of the Geneva New Testament after 1560. Some occur as words like "enter in" are shortened to "enter," as in Matthew 25:23. Other changes alter a metaphor such as "stand in doute" at Luke 12:29 to "hang you in suspense." In the Gospels an occasional change seems more than stylistic. The text and note of Luke 22:25 is one such alteration.

1560	*1607*
they that beare rule over thē, are called Gracious lords.	they that beare rule over them, are called bountifull.

The 1560 note reads: "Meaning yt thei have vaine & flattering titles given them, for asmuche as they are nothing less then their names do signifie." In 1607 it reads: "Have great titles, for so it was the custome to honour Princes with some great titles." Irena Backus comments on these notes by L'Oiseleur: "On seeing that Beza's content was sometimes expressed much more concisely in Camerarius, he would quite likely copy the latter, thereby saving himself the labour of cutting Beza's lengthy notes."[23] In this instance, however, a more positive attitude toward magistrates comes from the Lutheran Camerarius.

John 9:1 has no note in 1560. The text reads: "And as Jesus passed by, he sawe a man which was blinde from his birth." The Camerarius note reads: "Sin is the beginning euen of all bodily diseases, & yet doth it not folow, yt God alway respecteth their sinnes, whō he most sharply punisheth." Both Osiander and Beza held that the plague was God's judgment for sin. The context of John 9:1–3 precludes sin as the origin of this blindness. Thus the note is added to remind readers that their common reference to passages such as Deuteronomy 28:21 does not pertain to this case, even though sin is the source of all bodily disease.[24]

The Gospel of John has some new notes in chapter three. Verse 1 describes Nicodemus in a note contrasting learning with wisdom. "There are none sometimes more vnlearned, then the learned; but as well the learned as the vnlearned must desire wisedome of Christ onely." At Psalm 111:10, that "the beginning of wisedome is the feare of the Lord," the unaltered 1560 note reads: "They onely are wise, that feare God, and none have vnderstanding, but they that obey his word."

At John 14:1 Tyndale, followed by Whittingham and Geneva 1560, reads: "And he sayde unto his disciples." Beza omitted these words and began with "Let not your heart be troubled." This change is made in the Tomson text at John 14:1. Backus reminds us as well that Beza used Camerarius in preparing his notes on the Gospels.[25] Such textual changes may have the double endorsement of Camerarius and Beza.

At 1 Corinthians 14:29 the Tomson edition adds a note that defines the manner of prophesying:

> Let two or three propound, and let the other iudge of that that is propounded, whether it be agreeable to the word of God or no: If in this examination the Lord give any man ought to speake. Let every man be admitted to prophecie, severally and in his order, so farre forth as it is requisite for the edifying of the Church: Let them be content to be subject each to others iudgement.

This interpretation supported a well-known practice for evaluating preaching among the English Puritans, which Elizabeth I suspended along with Archbishop Grindal in 1577.[26] For instance in Zurich in June 1525 every day except Sunday and Friday at 7 A.M. students and pastors gathered in the cathedral. One person read the Old Testament text for the day in Latin, another gave the Hebrew, and a third read aloud the Greek of the Septuagint and explained the passage. A fourth person described how one should preach from the passage, and another, sometimes Zwingli himself, would preach (in German) on the carefully studied text. In England similar sessions were conducted in a variety of ways.[27]

Beza's notes on Romans 9 and Ephesians 1 replace the textual comments of the 1560 edition. They demonstrate the growing influence in England of Beza's predestinarian views. Even today Beza's views fuel a debate over the central doctrine in Calvin's *Institutes*.[28] For example, the note on Ephesians 1:4, "As he hath chosen vs in him, before the foundation of the world," used Aristotelian causes to explain election, and the note on verse 5, "Who hath predestinate vs," states that no reason is to be sought here for our election, "but in the free mercie of God, neither is faith which God forsaw, the cause of our predestination, but the effect."

Beza had defended the use of Aristotle in the Genevan Academy. Beza saw Pierre Ramus as the false dialectician, going on to defend the dialectic of the Academy in his famous letter of July 1, 1572, to Joachim Camerarius.[29] That Beza so uses Aristotle does not necessarily argue that Beza was a Protestant scholastic in the sense of investigating commonplace questions about the nature of God.[30] That paradigmatic shift in Reformed theology from scriptural questions to more speculative ones occurs with Jerome Zanchi's double knowledge of God in 1591 and Francis Turretin at Geneva in the seventeenth century.

Romans 9:24 attracts from Beza a comment that the doctrine of the eternal reprobate and elect is not to be sought "in the secret counsel of God, but by the vocation which is made manifest . . . that the doctrine may be better perceived." Both Jill Raitt and Roland Bainton are helpful in showing how Beza focuses on vocation.[31] For instance, the note to Romans 9:31 claims that "the pride of men is the cause that they contemne vocation, so that the cause of their damnation neede not be sought for any other where but in themselves." On the positive side the faithful seek the purpose of God not "in the bottomlesse counsell of God but rather in the manifestation of it, namely in his vocation by the Word and Sacraments."[32]

Apocalypse/Junius

Franciscus Junius (1545–1602) studied oriental language and theology at the Geneva Academy (1562–65). Serving for a short time as a reformed minister in Antwerp (1565–67), he fled from the Netherlands to the Palatinate, where he pastored the French-speaking congregation of Schonau (1567-73). Junius then joined Immanuel Tremellius at Heidelberg to assist in the Latin translation of the Old Testament (1575–79). From 1578 to 1584 he held a chair of theology at Neustadt, where he taught Hebrew and Old Testament exegesis, interrupted by a stint back in the parish ministry. In 1584 Junius became a professor at Heidelberg, which post he exchanged for the principal chair of theology at Leiden, where he died of the plague in 1602.[33]

The 1560 notes to Revelation derive from Bale and Bullinger. John Bale's *The Image of bothe churches* went through several editions, and its framework was incorporated into the 1560 Geneva Bible as well as into John Foxe's *Actes and Monuments*.[34] Junius' *A brief commentary upon the Revelation of St. John* appeared in 1592 and was reprinted in 1594, 1596, and 1600.[35] The 1592 edition was eighty-eight pages in octavo, which replaced Tomson's text in some versions from 1598.[36] The 1599 date is probably untrue in most cases because it was a date used by Barker for editions published at different times in Amsterdam and Dort. Some copies bear both the 1599 imprint and 1633 by Stam of Amsterdam.[37]

The note to Revelation 9:4 comments that "God guardeth the godly and elect by his decree. Not even the papal example of Pope Gregory VII shall trouble those sealed by the will of God." This Gregory VII is labeled "a most monstrous Necromancer, . . . the most wicked firebrand of the world." His successors are "most expert cut-throats," who came to ruin by setting "cities, Common-weales, and whole kingdomes . . . by the eares amongst themselves . . . while they miserably wounded one another."

At Revelation 12:14 the "time, and times, and halfe a time" for the woman with the wings of a great eagle is calculated from Nero's reign in the first century. The time is three and a half years, as in Daniel 7:25. The note cites Josephus and Hegesippus.

In chapter 13 the ideology is more complex, with two parts to describe the meaning of the beast risen from the abyss—the one being Imperial Rome and the other, ecclesiastical Rome or the Papacy. The latter comes under attack in these notes by Francis Junius. The notes claim that the *Decretals, Clementines,* and *Extravagants* are full of papal pretension. Pope Sixtus IV is singled out for having posted a verse on the gates of Rome to celebrate his pageant of entry to his seat of rule. The blasphemous verse reads:

By oracle of thine owne voyce,
the world thou gouernest all,
And worthily a God on earth,
men thinke and doe thee call.

The infamous number of the beast in Revelation 13:18 calls forth a papal application of the "sixe hundreth three score and sixe." The series of sixes, which are in unities, tens, and hundreds, speaks of the hierarchical pattern of the papacy. When Boniface VIII commended six books of decretals, he marked himself with the number of that beast. Junius does not agree with the common interpretation of this number, preferring his own pattern as described earlier. "It seemeth vnto mee neither profitable, nor like to be true, that the number of the beast, or the name of the beast shold be taken as the common sort of interpreters doe take it."

The common interpreters are reflected in the original note to Revelation 13:18, which used the Greek letters of the small number that makes up 666 and signifies Lateinas or Latin (i.e., the language of the papal Antichrist). This came from Heinrich Bullinger's Latin commentary of 1557, in which the Zurich reformer added 666 years to the reign of Domitian, who was Emperor of Rome when the book of Revelation was written. This placed the reader at the reign of Pepin the Short, king of the Franks, who was anointed in A.D. 754 by Pope Stephen II with the title of Roman patrician. Pepin used the Donation of Constantine to grant lands to the papacy known as the Pentapolis and the Exarchate of Ravenna. Bullinger's commentary was translated into English in 1561, making such a historical application more prominent among the readers of the Geneva Bible.

John Foxe worked out a whole scheme in his *Actes and Monuments* (1563), using the Lateinas to argue against Nicholas of Lyra that the 666 was not the Turk who established supremacy about A.D. 666, but was the papacy instead. In Foxe's commentary on the Apocalypse of 1587 he preferred Romanus ("a man of Rome"), which would produce the number 666 whether written in Greek or Hebrew.[38] Political (Pepin III), pestilential (Turk), and papal (Boniface VIII) interpretations of Romans 13 circulated among the readers of the two Genevan versions of the Apocalypse in the late 1590s and beyond. Henoch Clapham, in 1609, made the 666 of Revelation 13:18 into "Vicarius generalis dei in terris." This common identity of the Roman bishop as Antichrist provoked an English Catholic response. In 1613, in his first part and again in the 1614 second part, Michael Walpole defended Rome in his *A Treatise of Antichrist.* That interchange requires further comment on the fate of these bitter Protestant notes.

Recusant Rejection

Religious controversies of the Elizabethan age raged after the first return of the Marian exiles in 1559. The English Catholic community occupies a central role in such controversy, fueled by another group of exiles who also produced a Bible—this time at Rheims rather than Geneva. The leader of these exiles was William, Cardinal Allen, whose "articles of the catholicke faith" (1567) escalated the rhetorical interchange with the English Protestant community. The English Catholic New Testament symbolizes the continuing quarrel over a vernacular Bible that, since 1408, had been the vehicle of heretical opinion. Its four editions from 1582 to 1633 amply document this contention.

Martin's translation of the Rheims New Testament in 1582 with Bristow's polemical notes more often than not had Beza's version in view. John Keltridge preached sermons in the Tower that make this explicit. The sermons were preached on May 7 and 21, 1581. The "Bezites" teach that "white" shall be "black" and "chalk" shall be "cheese": "and al this their euident false translation, must be to our miserable deceiued poore soules, the holy Scripture and Gods word."[39] Bristow and Allen had revised Martin's English New Testament, for which Bristow prepared the notes.[40]

One annotation will suffice to illustrate the polemical purpose of the translation that would be unnecessary in times more obedient to the Roman bishop, when printed Protestant Bibles were not in general circulation. The example is taken from 1 Corinthians 4:4, in which Paul speaks about the certainty of salvation that comes not from a clear conscience, but from God's judgment. Bristow could not restrain himself at this point in the Pauline discourse. The phrase reads, "But not iustified."

> The Heretikes are certaine that they be in Gods grace, but S. Paul though guiltie of no crime in his conscience, durst not assure him self that he was iustified, neither could take vpon him to be iudge of his owne hart and cogitations, whether they were pure or no: but the trial therof he left onely to Gods iudging day.[41]

A second edition of the Rheims New Testament came from the Antwerp press of Daniel Vervliet in 1600. A notable addition is a *Table of Heretical Corruptions* summarized from Martin's *Discouerie* (1582). The longer title reveals the polemical intent of this insertion made by Richard Gibbons, a Jesuit.[42] It reads: "A table of certaine places of the New Testament corruptly translated in favour of heresies of these dayes in the English Editions: especially of the years 1562, 77, 79 and 80."[43]

The charge is that the Protestants, under the pretense of offering a translation directly from the Greek text, have instead corrupted it. 1 Peter 1:25 becomes an example, in which they add to the word evangelized the qualification "by the Gospel is preached." That addition introduces the heresy "that there is no other word of God, but the written word only."[44] The fresh notes to 2 Thessalonians 2:3 call Protestants and Calvinists "near forerunners of Antichrist" and insert a six-page discussion of the term Antichrist. The note charges Protestants with confusion, since Calvin "and his fellowes and followers Illyricus and Beza, and the rest are . . . so contrarie to him, that it is horrible to see their confusion, and a pitieful case that any reasonable man will follow such companians to evident perdition."[45]

It is clear that controversy marked the circulation of the translations prepared by the two English exiled communities, the Marian exiles, who produced the Geneva Bible, and the English recusants, who responded with the Rheims New Testament some two decades later.[46] Neither party trusted the bare text to circulate among those for whom it was intended—English readers who saw either papist or Puritan as the Antichrist of Revelation 13. Such apocalyptic language was endemic to the religious controversies of the Tudor and Stuart period. The Geneva/Tomson/Junius New Testament is a primary document from that volatile time.

NOTES

1. Patrick Collinson, *From Iconoclasm to Iconophobia: The Cultural Impact of the Second English Reformation* (Reading: University of Reading, 1986), p. 25. On the wider challenge see Peter G. Lake, "Calvinism and the English Church 1570–1635," *Past & Present* 114:32–76, 1987.

2. J. Leonard Trinterud, ed., *Elizabethan Puritanism* (New York: Oxford University Press, 1971), pp. 213–14.

3. John F. McDiarmid, "Humanism, Protestantism, and English Scripture, 1533–1540," *Journal of Medieval and Renaissance Studies* 14:124, 1984.

4. Ibid., pp. 130–32.

5. Ibid., p. 132.

6. *Obedience of a Christian Man* (Antwerp: Johannes Hoochestraten, October 2, 1528), sig. Qv[r].

7. See Peter Auksi, "So rude and simple style': William Tyndale's Polemical Prose," *Journal of Medieval and Renaissance Studies* 8:235–56, 1978.

8. Ibid., p. 238, citing Norman Davis, *William Tyndale's English of Controversy* (London: 1971).

9. N. Hardy Wallis, *The New Testament Translated by William Tyndale 1534* (Cambridge: Cambridge University Press, 1938).

10. Louis A. Schuster, "Thomas More's Polemical Career, 1523–1533," in *The Confutation of Tyndales Answer, The Complete Works of St. Thomas More* (New Haven, CT: Yale University Press, 1973), Vol. 8, Pt. I, p. 48.

11. *The Coverdale Bible 1535, Holkham Copy British Library Facsimile Edition* (Folkestone: Wm. Dawson & Sons, Ltd., 1974), colophon.

12. Ibid., p. 36.

13. William Fulke, *Defence of the Translations of the holy scriptures into the English tongue* (1583), cited in J.F. Mozley, *Coverdale and His Bibles* (London: Lutterworth, 1953), p. 113.

14. A.S. Herbert, *Historical Catalogue of Printed Editions of The English Bible 1525–1961* (London: British and Foreign Bible Society, 1968), p. 30.

15. Mozley, p. 252.

16. *The Acts and Monuments of John Foxe,* ed. George Townsend and Stephen Cattley (London: R.B. Seeley and W. Burnside, 1833), vol. 5, p. 565.

17. On its contribution from 1560 see Dan G. Danner, "The Contributions of the Geneva Bible of 1560 to the English Protestant Tradition," *Sixteenth Century Journal* 12:5–18, 1981.

18. Peter Lorimer, *John Knox and the Church of England* (London: Henry S. King & Co., 1875), appendix.

19. Lloyd E. Berry, "Introduction to the Facsimile Edition," *The Geneva Bible* (Madison: University of Wisconsin Press, 1969), pp. 9–10.

20. Examples taken from *The English Hexapla* (London: Samuel Bagster & Sons, 1841).

21. Irena D. Backus, *The Reformed Roots of the English New Testament*(Pittsburgh: Pickwick Press, 1980), pp.43–93 (Gospels), 109–39 (Pauline epistles).

22. Maurice S. Betteridge, "The Bitter Notes: The Geneva Bible and Its Annotations," *Sixteenth Century Journal* 14:44–46, 1983.

23. Backus, p. 22.

24. Andreas Osiander, *A Godly and Learned Sermon, Vpon the 91. Psalme* (London: Edward White, 1603), sig. A3[v].

25. Backus, p. 23.

26. Patrick Collinson, "Lectures by Combination," *Godly People* (London: Hambledon Press, 1983), pp. 467–88. See appendix on p. 563 of some eighty-five locations.

27. Stanford E. Lehmberg, "Archbishop Grindal and the Prophesyings," *Historical Magazine of the Protestant Episcopal Church* 34:87–145, 1965.

28. Charles Partee, "Calvin's Central Dogma Again," *Sixteenth Century Journal* 18:191–200, 1987; Jill Raitt, "Beza, Guide for the Faithful Life," *Scottish Journal of Theology* 39:83–107, 1986.

29. Beza, *Correspondance* X (1569), p. 174.

30. Marvin Anderson, "Theodore Beza: Savant or Scholastic?" *Theologische Zeitschrift* 43:320–32, 1987.

31. Roland Bainton, "Calvin, Beza and the Protestant Work Ethic," *Reformed Journal* 32:20–21, 1982.

32. Loc. cit. from *Questions and Responses.*

33. C. De Jonge, "Franciscus Junius (1545–1602) and the English Separatists at Amsterdam," in *Reform and Reformation: England and the Continent C.1500–C.1750,* ed. Derek Baker (Oxford: Basil Blackwell, 1979), pp. 165-66. See also John Platt, *Reformed Thought and Scholasticism* (Leiden: E.J. Brill, 1982), pp. 131–43.

34. Paul Christianson, *Reformers and Babylon* (Toronto: University of Toronto Press, 1978), pp. 40–46.

35. *S.T.C.*2 2988–91, 7296–97.

36. Herbert, pp. 107 (no. 214), 110 (no. 224), 115 (no. 247). But see his contradictory statement about the 1602 edition on p. 121 (no. 272). It was inserted after the text of Revelation in issues of 1598 and 1601 and in some copies of 1600.

37. Ibid., pp. 116–17 (no. 252).

38. David Brady, *The Contribution of British Writers between 1560 and 1830 to the Interpretation of Revelation 13:16–18* (Tübingen: J.C.B. Mohr, 1983), p. 40. See also Peter Lake, "The Significance of the Elizabethan Identification of the Pope as Antichrist," *Journal of Ecclesiastical History* 31:161–78, 1980, and David Brady, "1666: The Year of the Beast," *Bulletin of the John Rylands Library* 61:314–36, 1979.

39. John Keltridge, *Two Godlie and Learned Sermons* (London: J. Charlewood and R. Jhones, 1581), sig. G4.

40. "Bristow, Richard," *Dictionary of National Biography,* vol. 2, pp. 1264–65.

41. Ibid., sig. Ii^{r} (433).

42. Harry R. Hoppe, "The Copyright-Holder of the Second Edition of the Rheims New Testament (Antwerp, 1600), Richard Gibbons, S.J.," *The Library,* Fifth Series, 6:116–20, 1951.

43. *The New Testament* (Antwerp: Daniel Vervliet, 1600), sig. di^{r}.

44. Ibid., sig. d.iij^{r}.

45. Ibid., sig. Aaaiij^{v}.

46. Thomas Clancy, "Papist-Protestant-Puritan: English Religious Taxonomy 1565–1665," *Recusant History* 13:227–53, 1976.

"Cleared by Faith"
The Use of Scriptural Precedent in English Protestant Defenses of Poetry

JOHN H. AUGUSTINE

In the years immediately after World War II the declining popularity of the King James Bible, together with a historicist zeal for correct translations, coincided with the isolation of biblical studies from the broader disciplines of literary interpretation within the university. Conversely, in the past few decades, renewed debate in the areas of literary method, comparative literature, aesthetics, and intertextuality has resulted in contributions concerned with the Bible from every source. The recent work on the Bible by scholars of English literature, such as Northrop Frye, Frank Kermode, and Robert Alter, complements an avalanche of books and articles from biblical scholars on topics including narrative, metaphor, irony, the nature of poetry, and other related topics.

The Geneva Bible represented more than a "Protestant" version of Christian scripture, preoccupied with the plain or literal sense. The poetic sensitivity used in rendering the biblical text into English made important doctrines memorable in a way that further ensured subtle levels of influence on new literature and even on the English language itself. The Geneva Bible well deserves the popular ascription "the Bible of Shakespeare." In fact, Barbara Lewalski has the Geneva Bible, among others, in mind when she writes that "Protestant poets of the sixteenth and seventeenth centuries looked to the Bible and its commentators both for genre theory and for generic models for the religious lyric" (31).* However, the purpose of this essay is to focus less on the verbal influence of the Geneva Bible in the seventeenth century than on the provenance of scripture in sixteenth-century defenses of poetry as a "divine art."

Calvin and the Marian exiles responsible for the Geneva Bible by no means offered an uncritical assessment of the aesthetic dimension of scripture. Calvin claimed that "we are captivated with admiration for Scripture more by grandeur of subjects than by grace of language" (82; bk. 1, ch. 8, sec. 1). Still, Reformed Protestants recognized the literary qualities of the Bible and argued that these qualities established an authoritative precedent for the use of poetry elsewhere. A number of Elizabethan writers, such as Peter Martyr, Thomas Lodge, and Sir Philip Sidney, initiated the English defense of poetry from the perspective of the Reformed doctrine of scripture. They developed a theological explanation for the place of poetry—whether fiction or verse—in a fallen world that

John H. Augustine received his theological education (M.Div.) in religion and literature at Yale University Divinity School.

*When no superscripted number is used, see author listed in "Works Cited" at end of essay.

relied on the precedent set by the Bible's use of poetry.[1] These Protestant writers often wrote in the form of a *laudatio,* the rhetorical form used to praise an art. Curtius surveys the history of this form and lists four customary motifs: "1. human and divine discoverers of the art; 2. its moral and political use; 3. encyclopedic knowledge and philosophy as preliminaries to the art; 4. catalog of heroes" (547). The discoverer motif, the one most often used in Elizabethan defenses of poetry, included a discussion of the biblical origin of poetry. The "use of poetry" motif often included, among other things, a description of the teachings of biblical poetry. The list of heroes included famous Christian poets or Church Fathers who praise poetry. The *laudatio* form was so pervasive, according to Curtius, that even brief discussions of poetry frequently followed its pattern.

Peter Martyr's *Common Places* (1581–82, tr. 1583) provides an important example of a *laudatio* of an art written from the perspective of Reformed Protestant theology. Martyr considers the religious origins of verse and discusses its moral use as well as its supporters. He bases this poetics largely on the authoritative example of scripture understood by Elizabethan Protestants to be the living Word of God. The Italian Reformer was invited to England by Thomas Cranmer in 1547 and appointed Regius Professor of Divinity at Oxford in 1548. Patrick Collinson claims that Martyr's *Common Places* is of singular importance to the understanding of Elizabethan theology. He suggests that "if we were to identify one author and one book which represented the centre of theological gravity of the Elizabethan Church it would not be Calvin's *Institutes* but the *Common Places* of Peter Martyr, described by his translator, Anthony Marten, as 'a verie Apostle'" ("England and International Calvinism: 1558–1640," p. 214). Martyr's work is often neglected by literary scholars in discussions of religion and literature in sixteenth-century England, but it can qualify our understanding of the role of Reformed doctrine in the justification of poetry and the flowering of poetry in the seventeenth century.

Martyr's primary discussion about poetry occurs in a section titled "Of Musicke and Miter" (311–314; pt. 3, ch. 13, secs. 25–28), in which he announces that he plans to write of the use of music "so far as concerneth pietie" (311). He then summarizes the contents of the section by listing, "first, from whence they are instituted; secondlie, whether they may be reteined in the churches; lastlie, what maner of songs and measures belong unto our profit and saluation" (311). Martyr claims that poetry had a religious origin, for "the men in old time, both when they should giue thanks unto God, and also when they intended to obteine anie thing at his hands, were wont with one consent to use certeine solemne verses" (311). Orpheus, Linus, Pindar, Horace, and "such other harping poets, wrote the most part of their hymnes for these uses" (311). Poetry was also used to praise "famous men" (312). These poems, according to Martyr, were designed to "warne them that were present, to imitate their noble acts, and to detest the vices which did wrestle with their vertues" (312). Poetry enhances these examples, for singing, "although it do of it selfe delight mens minds," becomes more pleasant and persuasive when "there is added a speech that standeth upon numbers, and is bound to certeine feet (as we see it to be in versifieng)" (312).

Martyr's most significant claim in his discussion of music and poetry, and the foundation for his appeal, is the identification of poetry as a divine gift: "And undoubtedlie poetrie had first his originall from hence; and that it was the gift of God" (312). He wishes, however, that this gift be more "chastlie reteined amongst men" because certain writers have abused the gift, shamefully converting "songs and verses unto lewd lust, and to euerie dishonest act" (312). Although elegant, these verses are "unworthie of Christian eares" (312).

On the positive side, Peter Martyr provides numerous examples in scripture as proof of "a great use of holie songs among the godlie" (312). He cites Moses, Solomon, and even Christ, who sang a hymn at the Last Supper. Martyr claims, alluding to Elisha, "that godlie Musicke hath power to frame the affections of the mind" (312), when he alludes to 2 Kings 3:15: "And it came to pass, when the minstrel played, that the hand of the Lord came upon him [AV]." Another, similar example cited by Martyr is David, who "in praieng upon the harpe, suppresseth the violence of the ill spirit, which vexed him" (312). In addition, he praises Paul's use of rhetoric in his *Common Places:*

> This oration of *Paule* they thinke to be so notable & excellent, as they suppose that neither *Cicero,* nor *Demosthenes* could euer haue spoken more eloquentlie; not indeed that the holie Ghost hath need of these ornaments; but bicause he sometimes vouchsafeth to abase himselfe unto these things, when they may serue for our commoditie. Which I therefore thought good to giue warning of, bicause young men might understand, that this force of eloquence perteineth unto the gifts of God; and that they must endeuour to get the same in time, that the holie Ghost may use it, when it shall serue for the commoditie of the church. (281; pt. 3, ch. 12, sec. 13)

The marginal title adjacent to these sentences summarizes Martyr's argument: "The art of eloquence is the gift of God, and must not be contemned of young men."

Martyr's purpose is to justify the use of music and hymns in church by appealing directly to the teaching and example of scripture. His position is further supported, he claims, by Saint Augustine and Saint Ambrose. Martyr discusses, in a later section (28), the value, as well as the dangers, of ecclesiastical music. Three primary issues stand at the center of his comments. His first and foremost concern is that the use of music and poetry not be considered redemptive in itself, and he challenges the Catholic Church in this regard:

> For almost euerie where in popish religion, they thinke that they haue in the churches fullie worshipped God; when they haue a great while and a great deale sung and bellowed. Further, we must take heed that we put no merit nor remission of sinnes therein. (314)

Second, he insists, in characteristic Reformed fashion, that "singing be not so much occupied in the church, as there be almost no time left for to preach the word of GOD, and holie doctrine" (314). English Protestants would all agree that in some sense, the Bible expressed the Word of God, for, as Knott points out in *The Living Word* (1980), "they were people of the book who took their stand on Scripture in rejecting the authority of Rome and who continued to practice a strongly scriptural religion, whether this was given its shape by the Book of Common Prayer or by the vigorous preaching of the Word" (39). Martyr's comments on the importance of preaching stem from an important Reformation doctrine formulated by Johann Heinrich Bullinger (1504–75) that the preaching of the Word is the Word.[2] In other words, "The letter of Scripture," writes Knott, "had to be animated by the Spirit, and the Spirit was most likely to be conveyed by lively preaching" (38).

Third, Martyr requires that the words be intelligible "bicause measures and singing were brought in for the words sake, and not words for musicke sake" (313). He stresses the importance of the scriptural origin of these words: "Heed must be taken, that in the churches nothing be sung without choise, but onelie those things which be conteined in the holie Scriptures, or which are by iust reasons gathered out of them, and do exactlie agree with the word of God" (314). Martyr's reference to "iust reasons" gathered out of scripture that "do exactlie agree with the word of God" states a generally accepted principle of biblical interpretation in sixteenth- and seventeenth-century England based on Romans 12:6. In this passage Paul writes about serving the church through gifts of the Spirit: "Having then gifts differing according to the grace that is given to us, whether prophecy, *let us prophecy* according to the proportion of faith [AV]." In the seventeenth century, William Perkins sought to define the idea of a proportion or "analogy of faith" in his *Arte of Prophesying* (1607). It involved, for Perkins, "a certain *abridgement* or *summe* of the Scriptures, collected out of the most manifest and familiar places" and evaluated according to the principles of faith and love (*Workes* 652). George Herbert later expresses the same principle in *A Priest to the Temple* (1652). He suggests that the country parson interpret the Bible by a

> diligent Collation of Scripture with Scripture. For all Truth being consonant to it self, and all being penn'd by one and the self-same Spirit, it cannot be, but that an industrious, and judicious comparing of place with place must be of singular help for the right understanding of the Scriptures. To this may be added the consideration of any text with the coherence therof, touching what goes before, and what follows after, as also the scope of the Holy Ghost. (229)

Dennis Quinn traces the development of this idea from Augustine's *De Doctrina Christiana.*

Yet Martyr warns his readers of the consequence of audible but empty words. To avoid empty "fables and trifles" (314), music and poetry must be based in scripture rightly understood to "exactlie agree with the word of God" (314). Martyr assumes a distinction between the Bible as written word, and the living Word of God conveyed by the Spirit through preaching and verse. Heinrich Heppe in *Reformed Dogmatics* (tr. 1950) quotes Martyr, Calvin, and many other Reformers in his description of the history of this distinction between the Word of God and the Bible (12–41). Both Calvin and Luther maintain a close relation between scripture and the Word of God.[3] They claim that the literal sense is intimately related to the meaning of a text, that is, to Christ, yet the meaning of a text is not exhausted by the literal sense. As Calvin puts it in his *Commentary upon Acts* (tr. 1585), "the gospel loseth his whole authority, unless we know and be also fully persuaded that Christ being alive, speaketh to us from the heavens" (36). Georgia B. Christopher explains that "God's word in the first two centuries after the Reformation was *not* equated with the lexical surface of the Bible, nor with the exact wording of any particular passage" (15).

This doctrine is important to poetics in Elizabethan England, for another reason that poetry—in this case sacred poetry in particular rather than poetry generally—could be considered a divine gift was that it was based on the words of scripture understood as the Word of God. When scripture is thus properly understood, it becomes the living Word of God, whether versified, preached, or sung.[4] Like a "windowe opened unto the inuentions of men" (314), these words, writes Martyr, are capable of stirring up "true faith" (314) in those who hear them. Consequently, "the Holy Spirit's work, formally considered, was that of rhetorical expertise," as Christopher aptly puts it (7). "In a very important sense," she goes on to explain, "faith became a 'poetic' activity—a passionate reading of a divine text (in which the figures were identified and read aright) followed by a reading of experience through this text" (7). For Luther and Calvin, religious experience, to an overwhelming degree, became accessible through the text of scripture.

Like significant portions of Martyr's *Common Places,* Thomas Lodge's *Reply to Gosson* (1579) takes the form of a *laudatio* of an art. He responds to Stephen Gosson's attack on poetry in the *School of Abuse* (1579). Lodge's praise of poetry primarily includes a list of heroes and the discoverer motif. His heroes are the Church Fathers, who santioned the use of poetry in their work by recognizing the authoritative use of poetry in scripture. Lodge dismisses Gosson's ideas, and develops a number of theological arguments for supporting fiction and verse. Poetry, Lodge asserts, deserves honor and respect because it "proceedeth from the Scripture" (1.71):

> Among the precise Iewes you shall find Poetes; and for more maiestie Sibilla will prophesie in verse. Beroaldus can witnes with me that Dauid was a poet, and that his vayne was in imitating (as S. Ierom witnesseth) Horace, Flaccus, and Pindarus; sometimes his verse runneth in an Iambus foote, anone he hath recourse to a Saphic vaine, and *aliquando semipede ingreditur.* Ask Iosephus, and he wil tel you that Esay, Iob, and Salomon voutsafed poetical practises, for (if Origen and he fault not) theyre verse was Hexameter and pentameter. Enquire of Cassiodorus, he will say that all the beginning of Poetrye proceeded from the Scripture. (1.71)

Lodge affirms the idea that "poetry is a heavenly gift, a perfit gift" (1.75), and develops it further than Martyr. The greatness of poetry, asserts Lodge, derives from its origin in heaven: "Poetrye commeth from aboue, from a heauenly seate of a glorious God, vnto an excellent creature man" (1.71). Even the legends about how Aeneas and Hesiod became poets actually indicate that poetry comes "from nature and from aboue" (1.72). The heavenly origin of poetry explains why poets themselves have had such a significant role in human affairs, for "Poetes were the first raysors of cities, prescribers of good lawes, mayntayners of religion, disturbors of the wicked, aduancers of the wel disposed, inuentors of laws, and lastly the very fot-paths to knowledge and vnderstanding" (1.75).

Unlike Lodge, Sidney's response to Gosson, *An Apology for Poetry* (1595), is philosophical. In terms of the *laudatio* topics, he examines explicitly the human and divine discoverers of the art, and the "use of poetry" motif. Furthermore, he pays close attention to how the role of poetry in scripture, informed by the Protestant interpretation of scripture, authorizes its use outside of scripture. Sidney begins with the discoverer motif, a characteristic argument of theologically oriented poetics in Elizabethan England: "Let learned Greece in any of her manifold sciences be able to show me one book before Musaeus, Homer, and Hesiod, all three nothing else but poets" (96). But he gives the motif an unusual turn by arranging it as a demonstration that poetry was "the first light giver to ignorance," and by introducing a comparison with other arts. "Nay, let any history," he writes, "be brought that can say any writers were there before them, if they were not men of the same skill, as Orpheus, Linus, and some other are named, who, having been the first of that country that made pens deliverers of their knowledge to their posterity" (96). Ancient philosophy and history were written in the form of poetry, notes Sidney, and "truly even Plato whosoever well considereth shall find that in the body of his work, though the inside and strength were Philosophy, the skin as it were and beauty depended most of Poetry" (97). Sidney's reference to the Roman title for poets, *vates,* or "prophet," is also part of the discoverer motif. The Roman title reflects their discovery of poetry's divine attributes, for "so heavenly a title did that excellent people bestow upon this heart-ravishing knowledge" (98).

Sidney's primary concern is to establish that David's prophecy

> is merely poetical. For what else is the awaking his musical instruments, the often and free changing of persons, his notable *prosopopeias,* when he maketh you, as it were, see God coming in His majesty, his telling of the beasts' joyfulness, and hills leaping, but a heavenly poesy, wherein almost he showeth himself a passionate lover of that unspeakable and everlasting beauty to be seen by the eyes of the mind, only cleared by faith? (99)

This method of reading scripture contrasted sharply with the allegorical construals of the medieval conception of biblical exegesis according to four levels of images: the literal, the tropological, the analogical, and the anagogical. The traditional medieval scheme sought to exploit various levels of spiritual meaning apart from the literal sense. By acknowledging the text's poetic form, readers approached a single meaning through the rhetorical figures.

Most Protestant biblical commentaries in Elizabethan England followed the method of interpretation exemplified by Sidney's description of David's psalms. William Whitaker states the policy of the Church of England on scriptural interpretation in *A Disputation on Holy Scripture* (1588), disclaiming the enumeration of "mystical senses" (1610 ed.; 403) and any separation of the letter from the spirit of the text:

> We concede such things as allegory, anagoge, and tropology in scripture; but meanwhile we deny that there are many and various senses. We affirm that there is but one true, proper and genuine sense of scripture, arising from the words rightly understood, which we call the literal: and we contend that allegories, tropologies, and anagoges are not various senses, but various collections from one sense, or various applications and accommodations of that one meaning. (404)

Later, in his more detailed comments to expositors of scripture, Whitaker directs readers to distinguish between words that "are proper, and [those] which [are] figurative and modified":

> For, when words are taken figuratively, they should not be expounded strictly. "It is," says Augustine, in his books of Christian Doctrine, "a wretched bondage of the soul, when signs are taken for things"; that is, when what is spoken figuratively is expounded as if spoken strictly. (470)

Although Calvin and Luther do not always share the same ideas about scriptural interpretation, they do share this view of the all-embracing literal sense. Brevard S. Childs summarizes Calvin's principles of interpretation that, Childs notes, "held together the historical and theological meaning":

> Calvin spoke of the *verus scripturae sensus* which is both literal and spiritual, the single true sense of the text. Above all, Calvin's approach focused on the text itself, not trying to penetrate through it in a search for something behind it, because for him the text was the faithful vehicle for communicating the oracles of God. Calvin does not therefore need to add a secondary or spiritual meaning to the text because the literal sense is its own witness to God's divine plan. (87)

Gordon W. O'Brien relates the proper understanding of the poetry of scripture to attempts by Elizabethan poets to achieve what Sidney claims for David. He first discusses Sidney's claim that poets are uniquely qualified to "inform those regions that lie beyond the sensible with life and invest beatitude with such dimensions as the imagination can compass and feeling cope with" (xvi). Yet some poets fail, O'Brien notes, to provide more than "the abstraction unwedded to the image" (xvi), for these poets "failed to distinguish between metered exposition (frequently, it is true, vitiated and distorted by the most wretchedly ill-suited allegories, tropes, and symbols) and the employment of such exposition as the basis of image making" (xvi–xvii). At the same time, O'Brien praises the efforts of Elizabethan poets who, like Sidney's depiction of the psalmist, rely on the specific, literal image.[5]

While discussing Martyr's *Common Places,* I mentioned the presence of a dialectic between the living Word of God and the text of scripture, which also relates to this statement by Sidney. Scripture and gospel are for the Reformers inseparably bound yet not identical. Scripture exists for the sake of Christ; yet Christ is not accessible apart from scripture. This dynamic depends on what Calvin calls "the inward testimony of the Spirit" (79; bk. 1, ch. 7, sec. 4), for the witness of the Holy Spirit authenticates this scripture that "sprung from heaven, as if the living words of God were heard" (1.74; bk. 1, ch. 7, sec. 1).[6] The Holy Spirit also illumines the hearts and minds of readers of scripture:

> For as God alone is a fit witness of himself in his Word, so also the Word will not find acceptance in men's hearts before it is sealed by the inward testimony of the Spirit. The same Spirit, therefore, who has spoken through the mouths of the prophets must penetrate into our hearts to persuade us that they faithfully proclaimed what had been divinely commanded. (79; bk. 1, ch. 7, sec. 4)

Thus interpreting scripture is not only a human work; it depends on faith and the work of the Spirit, as well as a knowledge of the text and its language. Scripture becomes God's Word when read under the direction of the Holy Spirit. Whitaker claims, following Calvin, that scripture generates its own light for those who look with the "eyes of faith" (290).

Sidney uses a similar metaphor to indicate a relation between an individual's spiritual life and the enjoyment of the aesthetic dimensions of the psalmist's poetry. He writes "that unspeakable and everlasting beauty" can be "seen by the eyes of the mind, only cleared by faith" (99). For Sidney, a life of faith cannot be separated from an awareness of beauty and truth.

The Geneva Bible was forged in a sixteenth-century climate in which poetry was considered a high, even a divine, art. On the basis of this biblically oriented defense of English poetry in the sixteenth century, the biblical interpreters of the seventeenth century relied on texts of scripture as examples of various styles and genres and did not hesitate to offer poetic paraphrases of the Bible before their commentary on it. The works of William Perkins and other commentators in the seventeenth century reflect the precedent established by the literary qualities of scripture. These ideas of the art of the Bible and the complementary art of commentary prevailed at least until the middle of the seventeenth century.

NOTES

1. Lewalski refers briefly to a similar idea at the beginning of *Protestant Poetics.* She suggests that "the new focus on scripture occasioned by the Protestant Reformation promoted in six-

teenth- and seventeenth-century England a specifically biblical poetics, which revived and further developed these ancient assumptions under the impetus of Protestant theology and the new literary and philological interests of the period. I suggest further that this biblical poetics is itself the most important component of an emerging Protestant aesthetics." (8) This theory of poetry that Lewalski has called "biblical poetics" provides a basis for her study of how particular biblical texts function as literary models for seventeenth-century poets. However, Lewalski attributes the term biblical poetics to Curtius (7), who uses the phrase in connection with Jerome's "substantially enlarg[ing] the concept of poetry by teaching that certain books of the Bible were written partly or wholly in verse" (447). It included an account of poetry's origins, a reconciliation of ancient literature and scriptural revelation, as well as a defense of the art of versification by an appeal to the metrical form of the Bible (215–21, 550–51).

2. Leith discusses Bullinger's principles of interpretation (342).

3. For Luther, scripture *is* one form of the Word. Preaching and Christ, the second person of the Trinity, are the other forms. The forms of the Word are distinguishable but inseparable. See Lotz (262–64), Frei (19), and Pelikan, *Luther the Expositor* (67–69), on Luther; Kraus, on Calvin.

4. The scripture is "properly understood" through the work of the Holy Spirit. Yet the Spirit's work of illumination is always consistent with its work of inspiring the authors of the biblical text. Thus correct interpretation requires careful philological work. Nevertheless, the individual texts invariably point to Christ, although in different ways. Frei explains at greater length the relation between the Word of God and the scriptural text in Reformed theology.

5. Lynch makes this same link between principles of Reformation biblical interpretation and poetry. For Lynch, Christ symbolizes poetic attempts "to enter the finite as the only creative and generative source of beauty," and Apollo stands for "that kind of fantasy beauty which is a sort of infinite, which is easily gotten everywhere, but which will not abide the straitened gates of limitation that lead to stronger beauty" (xii). Like O'Brien, he notes the potential distortion of ill-suited allegories, tropes, and symbols, but Lynch relates this problem in the use of metaphor explicitly to the medieval, fourfold method of biblical exegesis: "For I am convinced that according to its terms it is undoubtedly true that there are four levels of insight, the literal, moral, allegorical, and analogical, but that, even more importantly, there is also only one, and that the literal, which has been brought to complete illumination by the minds marching through all its possibilities, by marching indeed through a finite, according to the whole thesis of this book" (155).

6. Willis describes how Calvin relates the Holy Spirit to interpretation of the biblical text.

WORKS CITED

Alter, Robert. *The Art of Biblical Narrative*. New York: Basic Books, 1985.

———. *The Art of Biblical Poetry*. New York: Basic Books, 1981.

Alter, Robert, and Frank Kermode, eds. *The Literary Guide to the Bible*. Cambridge: Harvard University Press, 1987.

Calvin, John. *The Commentaries of M. Iohn Calvin upon the Acts of the Apostles*. Trans. Christopher Fetherstone. Edinburgh: Calvin Translation Society, 1859.

———. *The Institutes of the Christian Religion*. 2 vols. Trans. Ford Lewis Battles. Ed. John T. McNeil. The Library of Christian Classics, 20. Philadelphia: Westminster Press, 1960.

Childs, Brevard S. "The Sensus Literalis of Scripture: An Ancient and Modern Problem." *Beitrage zur Alttestamentlichen Theologie Festschrift fur Walther Zimmerli zum 70. Geburtstag*. Ed. H. Donner. Göttingen, West Germany: Vandenhoeck & Ruprecht, 1978, pp. 80–93.

Christopher, Georgia B. *Milton and the Science of the Saints*. Princeton: Princeton University Press, 1982.

Collinson, Patrick. "England and International Calvinism: 1558–1640." *International Calvinism: 1541–1715*. Ed. Menna Prestwick. Oxford: Clarendon Press, 1985, pp. 197–223.

Curtius, Ernst R. *European Literature and the Latin Middle Ages*. Trans. Willard R. Trask. London: Routledge & Kegan Paul, 1953.

Frei, Hans. *The Eclipse of Biblical Narrative*. New Haven: Yale University Press, 1974.

Frye, Northrop. *The Great Code: The Bible and Literature*. New York: Harcourt Brace Jovanovich, 1982.

Gosson, Stephen. *The School of Abuse*. 1579. London: Reprinted for the Shakespeare Society, 1841. New York: AMS Press, 1970.

Heppe, Heinrich. *Reformed Dogmatics: Set Out and Illustrated from the Sources*. Trans. G.T. Thomson. Ed. Ernst Bizer. London: George, Allen and Unwin, 1950; Grand Rapids: Baker, 1978.

Herbert, George. *The Works of George Herbert*. Ed. E.F. Hutchinson. Oxford: Clarendon Press, 1941.

Kermode, Frank. *The Genesis of Secrecy: The Interpretation of Narrative*. Cambridge: Harvard University Press, 1979.

Knott, John R. *The Sword of the Spirit: Puritan Responses to the Bible*. Chicago: University of Chicago Press, 1980.

Kraus, Hans-Joachim. "Calvin's Exegetical Principles." *Interpretation* 31: 8–18, 1977.

Leith, John H. "John Calvin: Theologian of the Bible." *Interpretation* 25: 329–44, 1971.

Lewalski, Barbara K. *Protestant Poetics and the Seventeenth-Century Religious Lyric*. Princeton: Princeton University Press, 1979.

Lodge, Thomas. *The Complete Works*. 4 vols. Glasgow: Hunterian Club, 1879.

Lotz, David W. "*Sola Scriptura:* Luther on Biblical Authority." *Interpretation* 35: 258–73, 1981.

Lynch, William F. *Christ and Apollo: The Dimensions of the Literary Imagination*. Notre Dame: University of Notre Dame Press, 1975.

Martyr, Peter. *The Common Places of the most famous and renowned Divine Doctor Peter Martyr*. Trans. A. Marten. 3 vols. London, 1583.

O'Brien, Gordon W. *Renaissance Poetics and the Problem of Power*. Chicago: Institute of Elizabethan Studies, 1956.

Pelikan, Jaroslav. *Luther's Works*. Companion Volume. St. Louis: Concordia Publishing House, 1959.

Perkins, William. *The Arte of Prophecying. Or a Treatise Concerning The Sacred and Onely True Manner and Methode of Preaching*. 1609.

Quinn, Dennis. "Donne's Christian Eloquence." *ELH* 27: 276–97, 1960.

Sidney, Sir Philip. *An Apology for Poetry*. Ed. Geoffrey Shepherd. London: Nelson, 1965.

Whitaker, William. *A Disputation on Holy Scripture: Against the Papists, Especially Bellarmine and Stapleton*. Trans. William Fitzgerald. Parker Society Publications 46. Cambridge: Cambridge University Press, 1849.

Willis, E. David. "Rhetoric and Responsibility in Calvin's Theology." *The Context of Contemporary Theology*. Ed. Alexander McKelway and E. David Willis. Atlanta: John Knox Press, 1974, pp. 43–63.

From England to New England

The Protestant and "Puritan" Movement, 1600–1645

NICHOLAS W. S. CRANFIELD

This essay will study the appearance of English biblical commentaries in the later Elizabethan and Stuart church and their use by Puritans in New England. The Puritans found in England a people and a country ripe for repentance, but when such a call to the nation failed and went unheard in the recently established Church of England, many felt betrayed; they left England for the comparatively liberal shelter afforded by Holland and by the unknown freedoms of North America. Like another chosen people, they crossed the Red Sea, traveling out of bondage and captivity to the Promised Land, a second Canaan. The arrival of biblical commentaries in the fledgling colonies of New England evidences the social and political ends that many of their compilers espoused. Before examining puritan biblical exegesis it is necessary to summarize the availability of a hermeneutic tradition in the church and something of its tradition.

The absence of any major concern for the study of hermeneutics in the Western tradition, at least until recently, is the more remarkable given the plethora of exegetical and expository material available to the church in successive ages.[1] Pre-Christian Jews had developed a complex and often elaborate system of exegesis. The first known biblical commentary on the Old Testament is to be found among the literary remains of Qumran. This system, familiar to some of the later New Testament writers, who used a similar form of interpretation when citing prophetic fulfillments from the Old Testament, was inherited by the church. The earliest Christian commentary exists in the works of Hippolytus of Rome.[2] The Church Fathers became renowned for their exegetical work: Origen, Basil, Athanasius, Gregory Nazianzen, Cyril of Alexandria, and John Chrysostom foremost among the Greek Church Fathers; Ambrose, Jerome, Augustine, and Gregory among the Latins. The energy with which these scholars wrote was in part informed by a need for definition; the interest in biblical exegesis ran parallel to the gradual establishment of the scriptural canon.[3]

Thereafter, despite some Byzantine exegetical scholars,[4] the tradition of exposition lapsed in favor of compilers of *catenae,* a habit that continued throughout the Medieval church.[5] It would be wrong to assume that biblical commentary had ceased in the period, but the patristic authors dominated the field. Where the catenists were answered it was often by impressive scholarship. The *Postillae* of Nicholas of Lyra drew on existing Hebraic commentaries and showed the importance to the early Franciscans of rigid

Nicholas W. S. Cranfield is a doctoral student in theology at Oxford University.

A shorter form of this paper was given at Professor Conrad Russell's graduate seminar in the Institute of Historical Research, at University College, London, in February 1987.

scholarship.[6] Lyra's works, together with the earlier glosses of Anselm of Laon (d. 1117), became the standard works of the high Middle Ages. With the coming of the Renaissance, textual criticism as we know it became possible. An opportunity arose for the comparison of texts with the superfluity of classical documents and early copy texts. Literary and biblical scholarship flourished. Both John Rainolds, later dean of Lincoln and president of Corpus Christi College at Oxford, and a Cambridge contemporary, William Fulke, urged the study of the biblical languages on their pupils. In 1577 Rainolds drew his pupils' attention to the importance of reading Greek and Hebrew.[7] Fulke often used his knowledge of Hebrew to answer the polemical claims of the Romanists.[8]

The impetus of Renaissance scholarship and the dissemination of the New Learning had come largely from the invention of the printing press and of movable type. The first complete edition of the Greek New Testament was printed for Erasmus by Froben at Basel in 1516.[9] Within the next three years the Aldine Press at Venice had published the whole Bible in Greek, and in 1516/17 there had appeared the first edition of the rabbinical Bible, printed by Daniel Bomberg and edited by a convert Jew, Felix Pratensis. Those who wanted to learn the grammatical tools for the reading of the Greek versions were served by the scholarship of Erasmus, who published Theodore of Gaza's grammar in 1516, and of the great Paris printer Robert Estienne and his son, Henri.[10] From 1531 to 1543 Estienne Père produced his *Thesaurus Linguae Latinae,* and in 1572 his son's Greek dictionary appeared at Geneva.

How much such scholarship prompted, or was prompted by, the technological advances of the age cannot easily be determined.[11] More than any other development in 1500 years of Christianity, the invention of the printing press made possible widespread—international by the understanding of the age—evangelization and raised education to levels undreamed of in the earlier history of the church. The phenomenon that the reprinting of these seventeenth-century biblical commentaries highlights, therefore, is that of a new science that draws on printed works, published little more than a century after Caxton had set up his London press and dispatched to a continent that had only newly become known to the Europeans. The novelty of both experiences must contribute to our understanding of the impact that such works could have had at the time and of their importance for any historical study of hermeneutics and homiletics.[12]

It has been convincingly argued that the real inheritance of seventeenth-century England in America has been underplayed.[13] The way in which the Reformed tradition was carried out of Great Britain into North America was not simply an accident. The "Protestant synthesis," which so dominates and determines American social forms, derived from several colonial interests, largely imperial and commercial, but also evangelistic and doctrinal. The themes of election and predestination taken up by the English took on a new dynamic for the history of a chosen people who compared the land of their settlement with that of a New Israel.[14] It was also necessary for the new colonists to propagate the faith among the peoples they encountered.[15] The English Reformation had, on God's behalf, restored "the cleare and sunne-shine light of his Glorious Gospell unto these parts of Europe."[16] God had not lacked for "golden trumpets" or for "golden candlesticks" when it came to shedding light on his message: Luther, Melanchthon, Bucer, Oeclampadius, Calvin, Bullinger, Zwingli, Peter Martyr Vermigli, and Zanchius were among the Reformed scholars and writers whose works informed the early Elizabethan church in England.[17] Of the Reformed authors in England we can single out Whittaker, Fulke, Rainolds, Willett, and Perkins, as well as the Scot Richard Rollock. It was the hermeneutical perspective and exegetical ability of these men that formed the background to the Stuart church.

It is difficult to assess how widespread the influence of such English commentators and biblical scholars may have been in the contemporary church. The age was still marked by the study of Latin, and the triumph of the old culture continued for a century after the Reformation. Scholars, and those who were trained by them in the universities at Oxford and Cambridge, were initially hesitant to put their learned expositions in the vernacular.

Although it has not been possible to draw on all the libraries and private collections housing Renaissance materials in Great Britain, an examination of several institutional libraries confirms the impression that the English commentaries were not readily acceded to library collections until later in the seventeenth century.[18] Under the successive presidencies of William Laud and William Juxon (1612–33), the library at St. John's College in Oxford received some 224 works, few of which were Reformed works of commentary. Rather, the college acquired more modern editions of the patristic authors, many of them from the presses of Paris, Basel, and Frankfurt.[19] The earlier Oxford foundation of Corpus Christi College bought works of controversy and at the death of Richard Cobbe in 1597 was notably strong in modern theology. In the next decade, under the presidency of the noted Calvinist John Rainolds, the library added several works of commentary, all of them, however, works of continental authors with the single exception of the works of Richard Rollock. Even these had been published abroad, at Geneva and Herborn.[20]

Something of a contrast is to be found in the library gift of Bishop John Williams to his former Cambridge college. Williams was bishop of Lincoln from 1621 and in 1641 became archbishop of York, a post that he held to his death in 1650. In 1632 he made a generous presentation to St. John's College of some 600 works of biblical exposition and exegesis, nearly 400 of them works relating to the Old Testament.[21] Although only twenty-five of these volumes are still at St. John's, the survival of the 1632 inventory makes it possible to see the range of his generosity.[22] Excluding the patristic authors in this collection, the most popular commentators were Calvin, Luther, Cornelius a Lapide, Nicholas Heminge, Lorinus, Musculus, Pererius, and Johannes Piscator. Among the English authors are works by Henry Ainsworth, William Perkins, Andrew Willett, John Dod, Thomas Cartwright, Henry Broughton, and William Fulke. These works suggest the puritan bias of John Williams, but it remains clear that despite a large number of English writers, the field of biblical exegesis was still dominated by the Latin scholarship of continental Europe.

Williams' library bequest is by far the most substantial and extensive in the period, and its size has to be considered when its range is under discussion. Certainly other episcopal libraries do not appear to have the range and degree of material made available by Williams, and they remain traditionally biased to the non-English authorities. The volumes left to the citizens of Colchester by Samuel Harsnett, an earlier bishop of Chichester, Norwich, and archbishop of York, included works of controversy but few of commentary. Of the commentaries only one was in English.[23] The library of another archbishop of York, Tobie Matthew, who died in 1628, formed the core of the post-Reformation Minster Library at York. No record of the books in the bequest seems to exist, but the 3,000 volumes listed in the 1638 *Catalogus librorum* include his collection.[24] Among the English works of commentary may be found the much reprinted commentary on the Decalogue by John Dod and Robert Cleaver, a work of popular commentary that is the only such volume among the books recorded by Joseph Mead at Cambridge in his accounts for 1614–37.[25]

The paucity of English commentary from these libraries and bequests, and the overriding preponderance of continental scholarship and of works in Latin, argue that in the church and the universities there was an initial reluctance to accommodate the vernacular. Conversely, the association of puritan scholarship with the use of English in educated circles undoubtedly contributed to the official disregard of such helps to divinity and the belief that such works might corrupt the minds of young scholars.

Thus, at Oxford, in his attempt to silence the pulpit quarrels in the universities in the middle of the 1610s, when the prevailing Calvinist consensus at court was first seriously challenged by "Arminian" teachers in the university, James I had issued a series of pertinent directives.[26] These included an injunction that young students in divinity "be diverted to study pure bookes as bee most agreeable in Doctrine and discipline to the Church of England."[27] By this James intended to insist on the use of the Church Fathers, Councils, Schoolmen, histories, and controversies rather than the easier approach of using *compendia* and abbreviators, a practice increasingly identified with the Puritans. The insistence would naturally concentrate the scholarship of the Stuart church on the primary texts and on the received tradition. The commentaries themselves could be disparaged as aids to the less able preacher.

At Cambridge, Richard Holdsworth, who became Master of Emmanuel College in 1637 after years of being a successful London preacher and professor of divinity at Gresham College, drew up a series of directions for university students that significantly did not commend the vernacular. Instead, the Bible was to be understood of itself and the practice of reading three chapters a day was to be adopted.[28] Yet it was as aids to the preaching minister and lecturer that the commentaries became popular.

According to Thomas Taylor, it became possible, by the exact interpretation of the scriptures, "to draw out both the true *sence,* and the true *use* of them (which are the two proper parts of interpretation) seeing so many things are to us hard to understand," a view that echoes the magisterial commands with which William Perkins ended his much circulated discourse on preaching, a work that had itself first appeared in Latin.[29] The most prolific commentator on the Pentateuch, Henry Ainsworth, when faced with the Hebrew tradition of Moses, similarly argued that,

> the litteral sense of Moses Hebrew (which is the tongue wherein he wrote the Law), is the ground of all interpretation, and that Language hath figures and proprieties of speech, different from ours: these therefore in the first place are to be opened that the natural meaning of the Scripture, being knowen, the mysteries of godlynes therein implyed, may be better discerned.[30]

Study of the original language was by no means readily acceptable as of necessity even when the scholarship and ability were available. Thus, in 1593, Lancelot Andrewes defended the use of the three languages of the cross during a sermon he preached at St. Giles, Cripplegate.[31] The use of both Greek and Hebrew was attacked by Robert Browne, who regarded it as yet another way of showing off false knowledge, deriding such linguistics as the "maidens of the bishops."[32] It was a proper, informed understanding of the scriptures, which must include some textual awareness and critical scholarship,

> that maketh ministers to be fruitfull preachers: that maketh private persons to be profitable hearers: that yeeldeth matter of wholesome meditation to the minde: that putteth vigour of good affection in the heart.[33]

Thomas Westfield, preaching thirty years before he was elevated to the episcopate, regarded it as the minister's first duty to study and his second to preach "painfullie." For the minister to study proficiently, Westfield urged that he should read not only the Book of Books, but also "ye writings of ye auncient, & most learned fathers of ye primitive Churche, before those of latter times, they being not so subiect to error, as some of ye other."[34] Scholars, preachers, and the godly alike had to be enabled to study early Christianity *ad fontes*. The commentaries, despite the royal proclamation to the contrary, thus supplied a real need. In effect they often reproduced a course of lectures or sermons that had been greeted with public acclaim at the time of their first delivery.

Of these series perhaps the best known were those lectures delivered by John King, later bishop of London, at York on the book of Jonah. King served Archbishop Piers of York as one of his domestic chaplains and in 1594 delivered a course of lectures in which he matched the tribulations faced by Jonah to those of England in his own day.[35] In his lectures he called publicly for God to choose out England for God's special care. As Jonah went to Nineveh, God had only three days in which to convert England and save it.[36] Nor were such lectures always given in a short series. John Rainolds' study of the book of Haggai never got beyond Haggai 2:15, and although the series had begun at least as early as 1584, it was still unfinished fifteen years later.[37]

Such studies, if undertaken carefully and with proper regard for scholarship,

> prepareth a way for faith, for repentance, and all internall graces, and externall obedience to the whole man. The want hereof is the cause why the words of God are so much by some perverted publikely to such purposes, as the holy Ghost never intended, both presses and pulpits (which is with teares to be lamented) sending out so many erroneous writings, and sayings, for the confirmation of separation, superstition, iniustice, sensuall lusts, and all manner of licentiousness.[38]

The principal end of such study was to enable the preacher. Even more than by their doctrinal position, Puritans were to be distinguished by their insistence on and their manner of preaching expository sermons.[39]

In 1602 the vice-chancellor of Oxford University used the occasion of a university sermon, preached on Accession Day, to denounce those who preferred preaching to praying: the *oratoria* had become mere *auditoria,* while the proper cult of God, using a defined liturgy and the calendar of the established order, had been set aside.[40] This opinion was not new, and Howson had himself urged it before.[41] In this case he was using the full weight of his authority to admonish the godly who stayed away from the university sermons and the proper devotions of the college chapels in the university. Within a few months his command of authority had been seriously called into account by the redoubtable head of The Queen's College, Henry Airay. This dispute over factious preaching in the university was brought to the attention of the Privy Council, suggesting the degree of seriousness with which such matters were to be treated.[42] Even though the court sermons of Lancelot Andrewes and John Donne were popular with more literate readers, the real acclaim was reserved for those of a puritan cast of mind, who turned their attention to less literary and more biblical subjects. In this regard the traditions of Oxford were preserved and fostered by John Rainolds and Henry Airay, whose commentary on Philippians eschewed elegance of words and all affectation of language in order to open faithfully "the naked and naturall sense of his holy Text."[43]

It was to be this more plain method of preaching that characterized the approach and the preferences of the founders of American Christianity, Roger Williams and John Cotton. In the twenty articles of John Davenport's *Credo,* which became the ecclesiological framework and theological justification for so much of New England, the first article gives the preeminence of scripture. The nature of the Godhead and the divinity of Christ, and the articles associated with more conformed accounts of religion, are relegated to secondary positions. The scripture is by divine inspiration and "is profitable for doctrine, for reproof, for correction, for instruction in righteousness, that the man of God may be perfect, thoroughly furnished unto all good works."[44] Luther would have been proud that his insistence on the Bible would bear such fruit in the New World.

Preachers in subsequent generations have had a range of homiletic aids that have helped them in the pulpit. Such varied works were not allowed or available to the early Stuart church, although it would appear that the later medieval habit of circulating *florilegia* continued, albeit on a much reduced scale. Henry King, son of Bishop King and himself a later bishop (he was the first bishop to be consecrated after Parliament had suspended the right of bishops to sit in the House of Lords [February 1642], shortly before the abolition of the order of bishops in the Church of England), kept a commonplace book in which he listed suitable texts to preach at ordination services.[45] Such a collection did not list the suitable expositors of individual texts. This need was met by something of a later seventeenth-century growth industry: the more immediate precursors of the expositors Philip Doddridge, John Darling, and William Orme were John Wilkins, future bishop of Chester in the post-Restoration Church of England; William Crowe; and Bishop William Chappell.

Writing in 1646, Wilkins discoursed on the homiletic art and included an index of available texts and commentaries. Citing Francis Bacon, the disgraced Jacobean lord chancellor, Wilkins averred that assembling the observations of all those who had preached in English "would be the best worke in Divinity that has been written since the Apostles time."[46] He felt certain that the ability and genius of such English divines as Henry Ainsworth, William Ames, Nicholas Byfield, Thomas Cartwright, William Perkins, and Andrew Willett raised the state of biblical scholarship above the standards of many other writings.[47] In addition to a contemporary list of commentaries available—which is a major source for showing that as late as the 1640s there were no works in English to be met with on the Four Gospels, the Catholic epistles, and the letters to Timothy—Wilkins provided a cross-reference for writers who could be of most use in defending controversies.

A generation later William Crowe's work catalogued scriptural writers who were of special value to the preacher.[48] Acknowledging that he had first been prompted by the existence of a hand list for the Bodleian Library, devised in 1637 by Jean Verneuil, Crowe had assembled his expositors and annotators for each text. The mammoth compilation, which was arranged subalphabetically and was further expanded five years later by some 3,000 or 4,000 additions, was the work of some twenty or thirty assistants.[49] As a venture, this compilation deserves to rank alongside the joint project that brought into existence the Authorized Version of 1611.[50]

Between both ventures there appeared in 1656 an episcopal contribution to the art of preaching, which listed in a dozen pages the tracts and commentaries "as may in some measure tend to make a skilful laborer in the Lords vineyard."[51] This work was the posthumous translation of his Latin work that had appeared anonymously in London in 1648. Like its forerunner, the *Methodus Concionandi,* this work listed the available commentaries, indexed according to the books of the Bible. It also listed "elaborate sermons," as well as a series of books on the *Pater Noster, Credo,* and the Decalogue and works on the sacraments, death, sin, grace, hell, prayer, the reading of scripture, and other subjects. As a compendium, Bishop Chappell's volume holds further interest because it appeared at a time when the old established order of the Church of England had been swept away, to be replaced by a presbyterian order that had been set up in the period 1643–45 by the Westminster Assembly and ultimately became the legal order for the English church until 1660. Chappell had himself suffered during the period and died in quiet isolation in 1649.[52]

These three preaching tools attest to the plethora of post-Reformation material available that needed to be collated and in some ways made more accessible to the preacher in the pulpit. It would be naive to suggest that the emphasis on preaching was simply or wholly a puritan one, and that its criticism was inevitably the Anglican response.[53] It can be suggested that such works would be of more use to the nonconformists than to the established clergy, but the importance of preaching, as a teaching vehicle, also had a beneficial effect on the required levels of education among the clergy.

How rapidly did such volumes reach New England? It will be helpful first to remind ourselves of the salient dates in the early history of North America. The first "pilgrims" arrived in Plymouth by way of Holland in 1620, and in 1629 a charter was granted to the settlement of Massachusetts Bay. The next year John Cotton gave his farewell address, "God's promise to his plantations," to John Winthrop and his puritan colleagues on the *Arbella.* Meanwhile, in England, William Laud became archbishop of Canterbury at the death of George Abbott (August 1633), and within ten years civil war had broken out in England. Shortly after the political execution of Charles I (1649) the Society for the Propagation of the Gospel in New England was established in England to raise funds to support missionary endeavor among "the Indians."[54]

For the earliest settlers New England might have appeared to be a haven from the prosecuting justices of England, but it also brought with it new risks and dangers resulting from the encounters with the native people.[55] The biblical allegory of a wilderness was interchangeable with images of a remote and earthly paradise as well as with those of a place of trial and hardship.[56] The tenacity with which the settlers survived depredations and real hardship evidences their commitment to the experiment and their belief in their destiny. Further, it reminds us that adversity itself was not simply to be seen as a sign of God's disfavor. Roger Williams argued from a typological position that many of the saints had been tested in their day; the ultimate ideal must be the search for spiritual affluence rather than temporal sufficiency.[57] One of the first discernible tensions in the New England community arose from those who held their stomachs in too high a regard and practiced commercial exploitation at the cost of the Calvinist injunctions to serve society.[58]

It was into such a world that the commentaries first made their appearance. Among the first libraries are those of the Mathers, which began around 1610 and included a list of books acquired in April 1629, and those of Thomas Jenner and of Thomas Weld.[59] Jenner settled in Massachusetts in 1635 and spent fifteen years in New England, while Thomas

Weld reached Boston in 1632, where he became a pastor at Roxbury. At his excommunication by Bishop Laud in 1631 Weld had decided to leave his parish appointment in Essex. He was never fully integrated into the life of the new colony, and when he returned to England in 1649 he became a minister in Newcastle. Other substantial colonial libraries are to be found in the collection of William Brewster at Plymouth Bay and in the foundation library of Harvard College.[60]

Survival of such records has often been haphazard, and it is not possible to suggest how widespread the acquisition and knowledge of English imprints may have been at any one time. Thus the list of books owned by Thomas Jenner is that of books that were sold to the Society for the Propagation of the Gospel and purchased for Thomas Mayhew in 1651 as he worked among the native peoples of Martha's Vineyard and Nantucket. Thomas Weld was instrumental in gaining the first endowment to be given to Harvard by a woman, Lady Moulson. Another early library that enriched Harvard was that of Solomon Stoddard.[61] Records for books purchased by the Virginia Company suggest that colonial Puritans found in commentaries a genre that was for public readership as much as for private devotion.[62]

Almost certainly such lists are not exhaustive. With this caveat in mind, it is possible to examine at least some of the volumes that occur most often, works of commentary that had found their way across "the streights of the Redd Sea" to New England and that helped to form the ecclesiological and theological mind of the earliest colonists.[63] In turn, these books would influence the patterns adopted in society and the prevailing social forms; as a democratic order the society claimed to hold land that it had gained by "lawful war," by free purchase or gift of the natives, or by *vacuum domicilium*.[64] Into that land the Puritans introduced a social order based on the scriptures that continues to shape the nation-states of North America to this day.

Of the 200 volumes in the Jenner library, the preponderance of Reformed authors remained those of continental writers. Thus, in addition to the *Institutio Christianae Religionis,* the library held no fewer than fifteen exegetical works by Calvin, including his commentaries on the Pentateuch, the Minor Prophets, Synoptics, and Ephesians. It also contained fifteen works by Benedictus Aretius on the books of the New Testament, which had been published in the last quarter of the sixteenth century. The puritan exegesis of mainland Britain was well represented, and among Jenner's books were a dozen volumes by Rollock, several of which had been published on the continent; works by Paul Baynes and Thomas Wilson; the 1618 *Philippians* of Henry Airay, which had been dedicated posthumously to Archbishop Abbott; Nicholas Byfield's *Colossians* of 1614, a work that was widely reprinted; and Thomas Taylor's definitive commentary on Titus (1612), which derived from his preaching to an auditory in which there were as many "young Titusses" preparing for ministry as there were "ordinarie Christians."[65] Jenner owned David Dickson's explanation of Hebrews, which John Harvard also had bequeathed to his college.[66] Faced with a canonical book that was likened to "a piece of hard meate," Dickson had sought help from the godly of his acquaintances. In effect, the commentary was a compendium of opinions current in puritan circles.[67] For all that he professed brevity as a virtue much looked to by the reader, it is a substantial volume, comprising more than 300 octavo pages. Among the works on the Old Testament that Jenner had owned were the widely encountered writings of Henry Ainsworth (his commentaries on Genesis and Exodus); Richard Rogers' *Judges,* in which Rogers admitted how much more difficult it was to write commentaries than sermons; Edward

Topsell's popular *Lectures on Ruth,* which ran to four editions between 1596; the Authorized Version of the Bible in 1611; and William Pemble's work on Zachariah.[68]

Thomas Weld's library is rather more that of a theologian than of an expositor; for instance, it included works of contemporary polemic such as William Ames' 1613 *De Arminii sententia* and the Synod of Dort's report, *Iudicium Synodi Nationalis,* which appeared in 1619, but nonetheless held Daniel Dyke's notable work on Philemon, which was dedicated after his death to the puritan countess of Bedford.[69] The libraries of the Mathers contain a wide range of puritan commentary and, in addition to Ainsworth's influential works, include Dod and Cleaver on the ten commandments, a work that appeared no fewer than nineteen times between 1603 and 1635; Pemble on Ecclesiastes and Zachariah; and William Greenhill's serial exposition of Ezekiel.[70] Among the works on the New Testament are to be found the Stoke Newington lectures of Thomas Manton on the book of James and Thomas Brightman's convoluted interpretation of the Apocalypse, which had first appeared, in Latin, at Frankfurt (1609) and in English at Amsterdam six years later.[71]

The other available library lists suggest that there was great interest in commentaries in the colonies. For example, Ainsworth's *Hexapla* on the books of Moses is found in Elder Brewster's library at Plymouth Bay and in the libraries both of the Massachusetts Company and of John Harvard, as well as in the collections of the Mathers and Jenner, as has been seen. The popularity of Dod and Cleaver on the Decalogue clearly reached across the Atlantic, and copies appear widely. Besides the *Short and Sweet Exposition . . . of Zachary,* already noted in the collections of the Mathers and Jenner, John Harvard gave a copy of William Pemble's other works to his college. The Accomoc County records in colonial Virginia indicate Byfield's commentary on 1 Peter, which was also owned by William Brewster. The widespread transmission of such works as those furnished by puritan biblical commentaries clearly met a real need and a demand for spiritual nourishment.

Not that it should be uncritically argued that the New England settlers wholly absorbed the puritan theology that derived from different contextual difficulties in England. Views on the puritan use of Calvinism from England have been much debated.[72] It is certainly apparent that there were often marked distinctions between individual writers in New England. The controversy between John Cotton and Roger Williams is perhaps the best known.[73] The availability of material from across the Atlantic and the frequency with which it is encountered suggests the importance of biblical commentaries in the age on both sides of the water. Nor was the discipline ever regarded as only a barren academic pursuit. John Barlow of Plymouth and Chester, in England, defended his decision to publish his sermons on 2 Timothy in order "that *sinne* might be mortified, *holinesse* vivified, *God our Master* after the best manner served; and both *speaker* and *hearer* at the last day saved."[74] There is no reason to think that the pious readers of New England entertained any serious doubts that salvation itself was at issue. The task of providing for God's saving action in the world called up "hundreds more of Zion-builders choice."[75]

Such an undertaking was a method by which the knowledge of Jesus Christ might be proclaimed throughout the world as the "onely knowledge that preserved the soule and makes it to live for ever." For that reason alone, Rollock continued, "this science is to be sought, praised, and preferred to all others in all respects . . . other sciences were invented by men: but God himselfe is the Author of this science."[76] Fifty years later another Scot, James Fergusson, the minister at Kilwinning, believed that expositions "may prove a profitable help to propagate the knowledge of the Gospel."[77]

How much more important would this work become among the native people of the New World? Those settlers who had failed to find in England a country willing to be converted but had rather uncovered less encouraging biblical paradigms of a nation split by party, could not hope of realizing salvation among "the Indians."[78] The alternative to Israel was not Assyria, but rather a new Israel. The presence of Jesuits in Canada gave further justification to the need for missionary zeal.[79]

It is the consensus of this opinion that makes the study of puritan biblical scholarship such an important area of previous neglect. Within the constraints of English society, and under the law, the godly had had "to gad up and down to heare the word preached, as they cal it."[80] The greater liberty afforded by the settlements of New England enabled them to choose for themselves a religion of salvation in which preaching and the proper understanding of the scriptures would be paramount. Nor was such a consideration simply the expression of a pietistic notion of devotional life. Rather, it was a proclamation that the Bible held unassailable truths for the living standards of the people of God. Joseph Hall's serviceable commentary on the books of Proverbs and Ecclesiastes was intended as an analytical study of commonwealths and the ethics and politics that govern the way in which human society can be ordered and rightly governed.[81] The establishment of a liberal democracy in New England gave many of the early colonists the opportunity to found for themselves the kingdom of salvation promised to God's chosen people. The wilderness was a safe haven, a sanctuary of God's presence. Richard Rogers was in no doubt that the value of his commentary on *Judges* was that "apt and fit instructions should bee drawne out, with the application to the present state, need, and use of the hearers."[82]

The seventeenth-century use of the Bible and of biblical commentary in North America originates in a profound shift in the emphasis of hermeneutics, which has to be appreciated if the importance of the works in this series is to be grasped. It had long been the case that the medieval church found in each biblical passage a fourfold sense: the literal, the allegorical, the moral, and the anagogical.[83] Such a tradition had developed as a result of a combination of interests in the work of biblical interpreters. At the Reformation this principle was thrown over, and there had emerged a concentrated focus on the literal.

This transition, which had occurred with the work of Luther and Calvin, insisted that the key to scripture lay within the text itself, except where its sense could be shown to run counter to Christ.[84] So the writings of Moses were to be understood by reference to Paul and could not stand on their own. Even where it can be demonstrated that such a doctrine of the "analogy of faith" and the much vaunted principle of *sola scriptura* ran directly counter to each other, the Reformation transition had fundamentally altered the way in which exegetes and biblical commentators could set about their task.[85] For it exalted a christological methodology to the point at which Christ was to be found prefigured in all things, however darkly.

In tackling a commentary on Job, "fuller of difficultie than all the other books of Adams tongue," Hugh Broughton observed that "God would have this book as a jewel hid in the ground, not seen playn without paines." The gem that was to be uncovered was nothing less than the commandments of God, revealed in the holiness of Jesus Christ for "the eternal testified of *Abraham,* how he would teach his house to keep holy wayes. That hath story in Job's book: where . . . five of his house, shew Gods wayes for Christ."[86] Such a conviction in the Old Testament as scriptures of prefiguration led to the growth in importance of the study of the books of the people of Israel and to the familiar "mythological" reading of the Judaic revelation. To the late Elizabethan and early Stuart church, as to the churches of Reformed Europe, the Old Testament contained a myth of a new creation, of a lost paradise, and of a promised land, themes magisterially surveyed by John Milton in his great works *Paradise Lost* and *Samson Agonistes*. Further, the scriptures held accounts of the myths of the exodus, of a messianic figure as the suffering servant, of the kingdom in which a godly ruler represents God on earth, and of a new Jerusalem. Such a christological emphasis enabled the settlers to proclaim the godliness of their experiment as part of the continuation of salvation history.

The primary purpose of this essay has been to argue that the displaced Puritans of New England continued to make use of biblical commentaries that spoke to their condition. The closer study of the sources and languages of the Bible had generated a more widely informed reading of it and had opened it up to the more searching critic, who had access to the historical and literary sources. The hermeneutical principles forged by Luther and by Calvin, and transmitted by them to the churches of Europe, have characterized much subsequent scholarship.

The Hebrews of the Exodus, flung out of a foreign land into the desert wastes of the Negev, and the puritan settlers of the New England colonies, fugitives from an increasingly rigid ecclesial-centric power, together form the earlier contexts that have given rise to similar aspirations and theologies of liberation, which today draw so deeply on the christological pattern.

NOTES

1. For this period, studies of sermons and homiletics abound at the expense of any methodological study of hermeneutics. See, for instance, A.F. Herr, *The Elizabethan Sermon* (Philadelphia, 1940); W.F. Mitchell, *English Pulpit Oratory from Andrewes to Tillotson* (London, 1932); H. Davies, *Worship and Theology in England, 1534–1965*, 5 vol. (Princeton: Princeton University Press: 1961–75), vol. 2, pp. 133–84.

2. It has been suggested that the fragment of "Papias' Exposition of the Lord's Oracles" (Eusebius, *Historia Ecclesiae*, III, xxxix) is a commentary, in which case it would predate Hippolytus. See *The Cambridge History of the Bible*, ed. S.L. Greenslade et al. (Cambridge: Cambridge University Press, 1963–70), vol. 3, p. 531.

3. H. von Campenhausen, *The Formation of the Christian Bible* (Philadelphia: Fortress Press, 1972; K.L. Carroll, "The Earliest New Testament," *Bulletin of the John Rylands Library* 38: 45–57, 1955–56; R.P.C. Hanson, *Tradition in the Early Church* (London, 1962).

4. Most notably Oecumenius.

5. An individual study of the methods used by medievalists may be found in H. Caplan, "Four Senses of Scriptural Interpretation," *Speculum* 4: 282–90, 1929.

6. G. Lloyd Jones, *The Discovery of Hebrew in Tudor England: A Third Language* (Manchester, 1983), p. 12.

7. J. Rainolds, *Motives to Godly Knowledge* (London, 1613), sig., A5.

8. Jones, pp. 151ff.

9. Subsequent editions (1518, 1522, 1527, 1536) greatly improved on the misprints that Oeclampadius, employed as the youthful proofreader, had let slip. S.P. Tregelles, *An Account of the Printed Text of the Greek New Testament* (London, 1854), pp. 19–29.

10. Initially, Greek was disregarded; it was thought to be the language of heretical schismatics.

11. See, for instance, M.V. Chrisman, *Lay Culture, Learned Culture, Books and Social Change in Strasbourg, 1480–1599* (New Haven: Yale University Press, 1982).

12. The earliest chartered colony was Virginia (1606). It was not until 1629 that Massachusetts was incorporated.

13. S.E. Ahlstrom, *A Religious History of the American People* (New Haven: Yale University Press, 1972), p. 1090.

14. P. Collinson, *The Religion of Protestants* (Oxford: Oxford University Press, 1982), pp. 252ff.

15. H. Broughton, *A Revelation of the Holy Apocalyps* (n.p., 1610), p. 141.

16. W. Perkins, *A godlie and learned exposition upon the whole epistle of Jude* (London, 1601), "To the Christian Reader." Perkins had preached sixty-six sermons on Jude at Cambridge, which were published posthumously by Thomas Taylor. Perkins remained one of the most highly regarded commentators of his day. Even before the establishment of any organization for the spreading of the faith among "the Indians" his phrases found an echo in tracts supporting a missionary collection; see, for example, the anonymous work *The Day-breaking if not the Sun-rising of the Gospell with the Indians in New England* . . . (London: 1647), and T. Shepard, *The Clear Sun-shine of the Gospel breaking forth upon the Indians in New-England* . . . (London, 1648). In 1653 Humphrey Chetham of Manchester left a thousand pounds for the provision of a public library, of which £200 was assigned to "godly English Bookes, such as Calvins, Prestons, and Perkins workes, comments or annotacions uppon the Bible or some parts thereof." Cited in A.C. Snape, "Seventeenth-century Book Purchasing in Chetham's Library, Manchester," *Bulletin of the John Rylands Library* 67: 783–96, 1984–85.

17. Perkins, loc. cit.

18. A complete listing may be found in S.R. Jayne, *Library Catalogues of the English Renaissance* (Berkeley, 1956; revised ed., London, 1983).

19. J.F. Fuggles, "A history of the library of S. John's College, Oxford, from the foundation of the College to 1660," unpublished B.Litt. thesis, Oxford University, 1975.

20. J.R. Liddell, "The Library of Corpus Christi College, Oxford," unpublished B.Litt. thesis, Oxford University, 1933.

21. St. John's College, Cambridge, MS, V.5.

22. Six hundred two works are listed, including several works that are joint volumes with other works. There were 393 works on the Old Testament, 209 on the New Testament, including partial commentaries.

23. G. Goodwin, *Catalogue of the Harsnett Library at Colchester* (London, 1888). Harsnett died in 1631.

24. C.B.L. Barr, "The Minster Library," in *A History of York Minster,* ed. G.E. Aylmer and R. Cant (Oxford: Oxford University Press, 1977), pp. 487–539, 500–501.

25. J. Dod and R. Cleaver, *A treatise or exposition upon the Ten Commandments, grounded upon the Scriptures canonical* (London, 1603). The commentary was revised and reprinted ten times by 1632. See H.F. Fletcher, *The Intellectual Development of John Milton,* 2 vols. (Urbana: University of Illinois Press, 1956–61), vol. 2, pp. 553–622.

26. See, for example, the examinations of William Laud and John Howson, both later bishops, before the king in June 1615; Public Record Office, London, SP/14/80/124 and SP/14/80/113. Both documents are printed for the first time in "John Howson's answers to Archbishop Abbott's accusation at his 'trial' before James I at Greenwich, 10 June 1615," ed. N.W.S. Cranfield and K.C. Fincham, in Camden Miscellany XXIX, fourth series, 34: 323, 328–41, 1987.

27. These articles were sent to the university in January 1617. Oxford University Archive/NEP Supra/Register f.33.

28. Emmanuel College, Cambridge, MS.1.2.27(1), p. 28. "Directions for a student in the Universitie." Printed in Fletcher, vol. 2, pp. 623–24.

29. T. Taylor, *A Commentarie upon the epistle of S. Paul written unto Titus* . . . (n.p., 1612, sig., ¶¶ 2r. W. Perkins, *The Arte of Prophesying: or a treatise of preaching* . . . , trans. T. Tuke (London, 1607). The work first appeared fifteen years earlier in Latin. *Prophetica, sive de sacra et unica ratione concionandi* (Cambridge, 1592).

30. H. Ainsworth, *Annotations upon the first book of Moses called Genesis* . . . (Amsterdam, 1616), Preface, second page.

31. L. Andrewes, *Works,* ed. J.P. Wilson and J. Bliss, 11 vols. (Oxford, 1841–43), vol. 5, p. 61.

32. *The Writings of Robert Harrison & Robert Browne,* ed. A. Peel and L.H. Carlson (London, 1953), p. 173.

33. R. Cleaver, *A Briefe explanation of the Whole Booke of the Proverbs of Salomon* (London, 1615), sig., A3v.

34. British Library, London, MS. Egerton 2877, F. 64. T. Westfield, sermon, May 6, 1611.

35. J. King, *Lectures upon Jonas, Delivered at Yorke In the yeare of our Lorde 1594* . . . (Oxford, 1597).

36. M. McGiffert, "God's Controversy with Jacobean England," *American Historical Review* 88:1155–56, 1983.

37. J. Rainolds, *The Prophecie of Haggai, interpreted and applyed in sundry sermons* . . . , ed. E. Leigh (London, 1649), sig., II; H. Airay, *Lectures upon the whole epistle of St. Paul to the Philippians Delivered in St. Peters Church in Oxford* . . . , ed. C. Potter (London, 1618), sig., Ar.

38. Cleaver, sig., A3v.

39. W. Haller, *The Rise of Puritanism* (New York: Harper & Row, 1938), pp. 19ff.

40. J. Howson, *A Sermon preached at St. Maries in Oxford in Defence of the Festivities of the Church of England* (Oxford, 1602) sig., A3v.

41. J. Howson, *A second sermon preached at Paules Crosse, the 21, of May, 1598. Upon the 21 of Math the 12, and 13, verses: concluding a former sermon preached the 4, of December 1597 upon the same Text* (London, 1598), pp. 40–44.

42. Oxford University Archive/NEP Supra/Register M ff. 71v–72r.

43. J. Rainolds, *The Prophecie of Haggai, interpreted and applyed* . . . (London, 1649).

44. J. Cotton, *The Covenant of God's Free Grace* (London, 1645), Appendix.

45. Bodleian Library, MS. Rawlinson D. 399, see also 181–91, 219–38.

46. J. Wilkins, *Ecclesiastes or A discourse concerning the Gift of Preaching as it falls under the Rules of Art* (London, 1646), p. 44. Wilkins had in mind Bacon's *Advancement of Learning* (London, 1605). Thirty years later the comprehensiveness of Wilkins' project was acknowledged by Richard Baxter in his own attempt to list suitable books for the Christian's library. R. Baxter, *A Christian Directory* (London, 1678), p. 198.

47. Wilkins, p. 34.

48. W. Crowe, *An exact collection or Catalogue of our English Writers on the Old & New Testament, either in whole or in part* . . . (London, 1663).

49. W. Crowe, *The Catalogue of our English Writers on the Old & New Testament either in Whole or in part* . . . (London, 1668).

50. D. Daiches, *The King James Version of the English Bible* . . . *with special reference to the Hebrew Tradition* (Chicago, 1941), esp., pp. 139–66.

51. W. Chappell, *The Preacher, or the Art and Method of Preaching* . . . (London, 1656).

52. Chappell became bishop of Cork in November 1638. In 1640 the political turmoil in Ireland made it impossible for him to remain in his see and he returned to England, where he was later imprisoned (1641).

53. Tobie Matthew was a notable preacher: "He was seldom a hearer, if he could get to preach, but when he did hear others inferior to him in age or place, he is very candid in censuring." British Library, MS. Additional 4460 f.28. H. Samson, "The Preaching Bishop or Some Memorialls of the Life & Death of . . . Dr. Tobie Matthewes . . ." Such an impression is confirmed by Matthew's own diary, Borthwick Institute of Historical Research, York, MF.8.

54. W. Kellaway, "The Collection for the Indians of New England, 1649–1660," *Bulletin of the John Rylands Library* 39: 444–62, 1956–57

55. See C. Bridenbaugh, *Vexed and Troubled Englishment: 1590–1642* (New York: Oxford University Press, 1968); P.N. Carroll, *Puritanism and the Wilderness: The Intellectual Significance of the New England Frontier* (New York: Columbia University Press, 1969), esp. pts. II and III.

56. G.H. Williams, *Wilderness and Paradise in Christian Thought* (New York: Harper & Row, 1962); A. Williams, *The Common Expositor. An Account of the Commentaries on Genesis 1527–1633* (Chapel Hill: University of North Carolina Press, 1948), chs. 3–11.

57. E.S. Morgan, *Roger Williams: The Church and the State* (New York: Harcourt, Brace & World, 1967), p. 113.

58. C.M. Segal and D.C. Stinebeck, *Puritans, Indians and Manifest Destiny* (New York: G.P. Putnam's Sons, 1977), pp. 41–49; W.S. Hudson, "Puritanism and the Spirit of Capitalism," *Church History* 18: 3–17, 1949.

59. J.H. Tuttle, "The Libraries of the Mathews," *Proceedings of the American Antiquarian Society,* n.s., 20: 269–356, 1910. Bodleian Library, MS, Rawlinson C 934. See also 32–38, printed in C.F. Robinson and R. Robinson, "Three Early Massachusetts Libraries," *Publications of the Colonial Society of Massachusetts, Transactions* 28: 107–75, 1935.

60. T.G. Wright, *Literary Culture in Early New England, 1620–1730* (New Haven: Yale University Press, 1920), pp. 254–93.

61. N.S. Fiering, "Solomon Stoddard's Library at Harvard in 1664," *Harvard Library Bulletin* 20: 255–69, 1972.

62. D.S. Quinn, "A List of Books Purchased for the Virginia Company," *Virginia Magazine of History and Biography* 77: 347–60, 1969.

63. J. Winthrop, *Winthrop Papers,* ed. A.B. Forbes, 5 vols. (Boston, 1929–47), vol. 2, p. 219. John Winthrop to his wife, March 10, 1630.

64. Segal and Stinebeck, pp. 75–79.

65. *Ephesians* (1590) and *John* (1599). T. Wilson, *A Commentarie upon the most Divine Epistle of S. Paul to the Romanes* (London, 1614). Wilson urged his readers especially to "looke for these termes, coherence, scope, sum, parts, interpretation, Doctrines &c", ibid., sig., A3v; N. Byfield, *An exposition upon the Epistle to the Colossians* . . . (London, 1614). It was reprinted in 1617, 1627, and 1638; T. Taylor, ¶¶ 2v.

66. D. Dickson, *A short explanation of the Epistle of Paul to the Hebrewes* (London, 1635).

67. Ibid., sig., ¶ 4.

68. R. Rogers, *A commentary upon the whole book of Judges preached first and delivered in sundrie lectures* (London, 1615).

69. D. Dyke, *Two Treatises. The one a most fruitfull exposition upon Philemon; the other the school of Affliction* (London, 1618).

70. W. Greenhill, *An exposition of the first five chapters of the Prophet Ezekiel* . . . (London, 1645). Successive volumes appeared in 1649, 1654, and 1658.

71. T. Brightman, *A revelation of the revelation . . . opened clearly with a logicall resolution and expoosition etc.* (Amsterdam, 1615). See also K.R. Firth, *The Apocalyptic Tradition in Reformation Britain 1530–1645* (Oxford: Oxford University Press, 1979), pp. 164–76, and P. Christianson, *Reformers and Babylon* (Toronto: University of Toronto Press, 1978), pp. 100–106.

72. P.G.E. Miller, *Orthodoxy in Massachusetts, 1630–1650* (Magnolia, MA: Peter Smith, 1933); *New England Mind: The Seventeenth Century* (Cambridge: Harvard University Press, 1939).

73. S. Bercovitch, "Typology in Puritan New England: The Williams-Cotton Controversy Reassessed," *American Quarterly* 19: 166–91, 1967; M.I. Lowance, "Typology and the New England Way: Cotton Mather and the Exegesis of Biblical Types," *Early American Literature* 4: 15–37, 1969.

74. J. Barlow, *An Exposition of the First and Second Chapters of the Latter Epistle of the Apostle Paul to Timothie* (London, 1625), epistle dedicatory.

75. Dr. Francis Hering, a medic, composed a poem of nine stanzas saluting the work of commentators who brought forth the grace of God and revealed it in the world. J. Calvin, *A Commentary upon the prophecie of Isaiah . . . Translated out of the french by c.c.* (London, 1609), prefatory poem, stanza 5, line 3.

76. R. Rollock, *Lectures upon the first and second epistles of Paul to the Thessalonians* (Edinburgh, 1606), sig., A3v.

77. J. Fergusson, *A brief exposition of the Epistles of Paul to the Philippians and Colossians* (London, 1656), sig., A3r.

78. McGiffert, pp. 1166–77.

79. S.E. Morison, *Builders of the Bay Colony* (Boston: Houghton Mifflin, 1930), p. 26.

80. J. Howson, 1602 sermon, sig., A3v.

81. J. Hall, *Salomons Divine Arts of 1 Ethickes 2 Politickes 3 Oecumenciks* (London, 1609).

82. Rogers, sig., B3 IIv.

83. H. Caplan, fn. 5 supra.

84. This exception is a major qualification and guided Luther's thought as regards canonical revision. He found the text of James particularly difficult to reconcile with the Pauline emphases. It was made in the course of his Disputation thesis *De Fide,* September 1535 (M. Luther, *Works, Weimarer Ausgabe,* 39/1, pp. 47, 3f., 19f., 23f.).

85. D.P. Fuller, "Biblical Theology and the Analogy of Faith," *Unity and Diversity in New Testament Theology,* ed. R. Guelick (Grand Rapids: Wm. B. Eerdmans, 1978), pp. 195–213.

86. H. Broughton, *IOB to the King. A Colon-Agrippina studie of one moneth: for the metricall translation: But of many yeres for Ibrew difficulties* (n.p., 1610), sig., A2r.

THE NEW TESTA- MENT OF OVR Lord Iesus Christ, Translated out of Greeke by *Theod. Beza.*

WHEREVNTO ARE ADIOYNED briefe Summaries of doctrine vpon the Euangelists and Acts of the Apostles, together with the methode of the Epistles of the Apostles, by the said THEOD. BEZA.

And also short Expositions on the phrases and hard places, taken out of the large Annotations of the foresaid Author and Ioach. Camerarius, by P. Lo. Villerius.

Englished by L. Tomson.

¶ *Together with the Annotations of* FR. IVNIVS *vpon the Reuelation of* S. IOHN.

IMPRINTED AT LON DON BY ROBERT BARKER, *Printer to the Kings most Excellent Maiestie.* 1607.

¶ *Cum priuilegio.*

THE PRINTER TO THE DILIGENT READER.

*Eare Christian Reader, to the intent thou mightest the better enioy the benefit of these notes or expositions vpon the new Testament: I thought it not amisse to declare vnto thee the vse of the same. And first, forasmuch as the quotations or citing of places of the Scriptures in the margent which direct to other places, containing like Phrase or sense, haue bin so placed, that none without great labour could finde out the texts alleadged, I haue made this marke *, and haue set it as well in the margent, as in the text, so that thou mayest easily find that which thou desirest. For example, in the first word of the first Chapter of Matthew is placed this first marke *, looke out the like marke in the margent, and there thou shalt find, Luke 3.23. which place agreeth to this of Matthew, and so likewise thou shalt find in the residue. But if many quotations belong to one place, word or sentence, the first is onely marked, and those that follow vnmarked appertaine to the same.*

The Notes which are directed by figures of Arithmeticke, as 1.2.3.4.&c. *throughout the Euangelists and Acts, declare the effect or summe of the doctrine conteined betweene one of the said figures, and the next that followeth: as for example, from the figure* 1. *in the first line and first word of Matthew vnto the figure* 2. *in the* 18. *verse of the same Chapter, the doctrine there gathered is set downe in the margent in this sort,* 1. Iesus came of Abraham of the tribe of Iuda, and of the stocke of Dauid, as God promised.

And in the Epistles in like sort they declare the methode and arte which the Apostles vse, and how euery argument or reason dependeth one vpon another: these figures are begun againe at the beginning of euery Chapter. Lastly, the notes which goe by order of the letters of the Alphabet placed in the text, with the like answering vnto them in the margent, serue to expound and lighten the darke words and Phrases immediatly following in them. As in the first line and second word, the letter a, *being referred vnto* a, *directly against him in the margent, sheweth that this word, Booke, signifieth* A rehearsall, as the Hebrewes vse to speake: as Gene.5.1. The booke of the generations. *These letters begin at the beginning of euery Chapter, continuing vnto* z, *and so beginning againe with* a, *if there be so many Notes that they doe exceed in number the letters of one Alphabet. This haue I faithfully done for thy commoditie, reape thou the fruit, and giue the praise to God.*

Farewell.

The deſcription of the Holy Land, containing the places mentioned in the foure Euangeliſts, *with other places about the Sea Coaſts, wherein* may be ſeene the wayes and iourneyes of CHRIST and his Apoſtles in Iudea, Samaria, and Galile: for into theſe three parts this Land is diuided.

The Places ſpecified in the Map, with their Situation by the Obſeruation of their degrees concerning *their length and breadth.*

Aſcalon	65,24: 31,32.
Azot	65,35: 32.
Bethlehem	65,55: 31,51.
Bethphage	68,31,58.
Bethſaida	66,51: 32,29.
Bethabara	66,34: 32,1.
Bethania	66,31,58.
Cana of Galile	66,52: 32,48.
Capernaum	66,53: 32,29.
Carmel mount	66,31: 32,50.
Ceſarea Straton	66,16: 32,25.
Ceſarea Philippi	67,39: 33,5.
Coraſim	66,53: 32,29.
Dan, one of the fountaines whence Iordan ſpringeth	67,25: 33,8.
Ennon	66,40: 32,18.
Emmaus	65,54: 31,59.
Ephen	66,8,32.
Gadara or Gazara	66,48: 32,29.
Gaza	65,10: 31,40.
Iericho	66,10: 32,1.
Ieruſalem	66,31,55.
Ioppe	65,40: 32,5.
Ior, the other fountaine whence Iordan ſpringeth	67,31: 33,7.
Magdalon, called alſo Damanutha	66,48: 32,28.
Naim	66,35: 32,33.
Nazareth	66,56: 32,42.
Ptolemais	66,50: 32,58.
Samaria the citie	66,22: 32,19.
Sidon	67,15: 33,30.
Silo	66,27: 32,19.
Tyrus	67,33,20.
Tiberias	66,44: 32,26.

THE

THE HOLY GOSPEL OF IESVS CHRIST, ACCORDING TO S. MATTHEW.

CHAP. I.

1 *That Iesus is that Messias, the Sauiour promised to the Fathers.* 18 *The Natiuitie of Christ.*

* *Luke 3.23.*
1 Iesus Christ came of Abraham of the tribe of Iuda, and of the stocke of Dauid, as God promised.
a *Rehearsall: As the Hebrewes vse to speake: as Gene.5.1. The booke of the generations.*
b *Of the ancesters of whom Christ came.*
c *Which Christ is also the sonne of Abraham.*
* *Gen.21.2.* * *Gen.25.24.* * *Gen.29.35.* * *Gen.38.27.* * *1.Chron.2.5.* *Ruth.4.18,19.* * *Ruth 4.21.*

HE *1 a Booke of the
b generation of IESVS
CHRIST, the sonne of
Dauid, the c sonne of
Abraham.
2 *Abraham begate
Isaac. *And Isaac be-
gate Iacob. And *Ia-
cob begate Iudas and his brethren.
3 *And Iudas begate Phares, and Zara of
Thamar. And *Phares begate Esrom. And
Esrom begate Aram.
4 And Aram begate Aminadab. And A-
minadab begate Naasson. And Naasson begate
Salmon.
5 And Salmon begate Booz of Rachab.
And *Booz begate Obed of Ruth. And Obed
begate Iesse.
6 And *Iesse begate Dauid the King. And
*Dauid the King begate Salomon of her that
was *the wife* of Vrias.

* *1.Sam.16.1. and 17.12.* * *2.Sam.12.24.*

7 And *Salomon begate Roboam. And
Roboam begate Abia. And Abia begate Asa.

* *1.King.11.43. 1.chro.3.10,11.*

8 And Asa begate Iosaphat. And Iosaphat begate Ioram. And Ioram begate Hozias.
9 And Hozias begate Ioatham. And Ioatham begate Achaz. And Achaz begate Ezekias.
10 And *Ezekias begate Manasses. And
Manasses begate Amon. And Amon begat Iosias.

* *2.King.20.21. and 21.18. 1.chron.3.13,14,15.*

11 And *Iosias begate Iakim. And Iakim
d begate Iechonias and his brethren, about the
time they were caried away to Babylon.
12 And after they were caried away into
Babylon, *Iechonias begate Salathiel. *And
Salathiel begate Zorobabel.
13 And Zorobabel begate Abiud. And A-
biud begate Eliacim. And Eliacim begate A-
zor.
14 And Azor begate Sadoc. And Sadoc
begate Achim and Achim begate Eliud.

* *2.King.23.34. and 24.1,6. 2.chron.36.4,9.*
d *That is, the captiuitie fell in the dayes of Iakim and Iechonias: for Iechonias was borne before their carying away into captiuitie.*
* *1.Chron.3.16.* * *1.Chron 3.17. Ezra 3.2. and 5.2*

15 And Eliud begate Eleazar. And Eleazar begate Matthan. And Matthan begate
Iacob.
16 And Iacob begate Ioseph the husband
of Marie, of whome was borne IESVS, that is
called Christ.
17 So e all the generations from Abraham
to Dauid, *are* fourteene generations. And from
Dauid vntill they were caried away into Babylon, fourteene generations: & after they were
caried away into Babylon vntill Christ, foure-
teene generations.

e *All these which are reckoned vp in this pedigree of Dauids stocke, as they begate one another orderly in their degrees.*

18 ¶ Now the birth of 2 IESVS Christ
was thus, When as his mother Mary was
* betrothed to Ioseph, before they came together, she was found with childe of the holy
Ghost.
19 Then Ioseph her husband being a iust
man, and not willing to * make her a publique example, was minded to put her away secretly.
20 But whiles he thought these things, beholde, the Angel of the Lord appeared vnto
him in a dreame, saying, Ioseph the sonne of
Dauid, feare not to f take Mary thy g wife: for
that which is h conceiued in her, is of the holy
Ghost.

2 Christ the true Immanuel, and therefore, Iesus (that is, Sauiour) is conceiued in the Virgine by the holy Ghost as it was foretold by the Prophets.
* *Luke 1.72.* * *Deut.24.1.*
f *Receiue her at her parents and kinsefolkes handes.*
g *Which was promised and made sure to thee to bee thy wife.*
h *Of the mothers substance by the holy Ghost.*

21 And she shall bring 3 forth a sonne, and
thou shalt * call his Name IESVS: for he shall
* i saue his people from their sinnes.
22 And all this was done that it might be fulfilled, which is spoken of the Lord by the Pro
phet, saying,
23 *Behold, a k virgine shall be with child,
and shall beare a sonne, and they shall call his
name Emmanuel, which is by interpretation,
God with vs.
24 ¶ Then Ioseph, being raised from sleepe,
did as the Angel of the Lord had inioyned him,
and tooke his wife.
25 But he knew her not, l til she had brought
forth her first borne sonne, and hee called his
name IESVS.

3 Christ is borne of the same virgine which neuer knew man: and is called Iesus of God himselfe, by the Angel.
* *Luke 1.31.* * *Acts 4.12.*
i *Deliuer, and this sheweth vs the meaning of this Name Iesus.*
* *Esai 7.14.*
k *There is in the Hebrewe and Greeke text, an article added, to point out the woman, and set her forth plainely: as you would say, That Virgine, or a certaine Virgine.*
l *This little word Till, in the Hebrew tongue, giueth vs to vnderstand also, that a thing shall not come to passe in time to come: as Michol had no children Till her deaths day, 2 Sam.6.23. And in the last Chapter of this Euangelist: Behold, I am with you Till the ende of the world.*

CHAP. II.

The wiſe men, who are the firſt fruits of the Gentiles, worſhip Chriſt. 14 Ioſeph fleeth into Egypt with Ieſus and his mother. 16 Herod ſlayeth the children.

WHen *[1] IESVS then was borne at
Beth-leem in [a] Iudea, in the dayes of
Herod the King, beholde, there came [b] Wiſe
men from the Eaſt to Hieruſalem,
2 Saying, Where is that King of the Iewes
that is borne? for we haue ſeene his ſtarre in the
Eaſt, and are come to worſhip him.
3 When King Herod heard *this*, hee was
[c] troubled, and all Ieruſalem with him.
4 And gathering together all the [d] chiefe
Prieſts and [e] Scribes of the people, he asked of
them, where Chriſt ſhould be borne.
5 And they ſaide vnto him, At Beth-leem in Iudea: for ſo it is written by the Prophet,
6 *And thou Beth-leem in the land of Iuda, art not the [f] leaſt among the Princes of Iuda: For out of thee ſhall come the gouernour
that [g] ſhall feed that my people Iſrael.
7 Then Herod priuily called the Wiſemen, *and* diligently inquired of them the time
of the ſtarre that appeared,
8 And ſent them to Beth-leem, ſaying,
Goe, and ſearch diligently for the Babe: and
when yee haue found him, bring mee word
againe, that I may come alſo and worſhippe
him.
9 ¶ So when they had heard the King,
they departed: and loe, the ſtarre which they
had ſeene in the Eaſt, went before them, till it
came and ſtood ouer *the place* where the Babe
was.
10 And when they ſaw the ſtarre, they reioyced with an exceeding great ioy,
11 And went into the houſe, and found the
babe with Mary his mother, and [h] fell downe,
and worſhipped him, and opened their [i] trea-
ſures, and preſented vnto him gifts, *euen* gold,
and frankincenſe, and myrrhe.
12 And after they were [k] warned of God in
a dreame, that they ſhould not goe againe to
Herod, they returned into their countrey another way.
13 ¶ [2] After their departure, beholde, the
Angel of the Lord appeareth to Ioſeph in a
dreame, ſaying, Ariſe, and take the Babe and
his mother, and flee into Egypt, and bee there
till I bring thee word: for Herod will ſeeke
the Babe to deſtroy him.
14 So he aroſe, and tooke the Babe and his
mother by night, and departed into Egypt,
15 And was there vnto the death of Herod, that that might be fulfilled, which is ſpoken of the Lord by the *Prophet, ſaying, Out
of Egypt haue I called my ſonne.
16 ¶ Then Herod, ſeeing that he was mocked of the Wiſemen, was exceeding wroth, and
ſent forth, and ſlew all the male children that
were in Beth-leem, and in all the coaſts thereof, from two yeere old and vnder, according to
the time which he had diligently ſearched out
of the Wiſemen.
17 Then was that fulfilled which is ſpoken
[l] by the Prophet Ieremias, ſaying,
18 *In Rhama was [m] a voyce heard, mourning, and weeping, and great howling: [n] Rachel weeping for her children, and would not
be comforted, becauſe they were not.
19 [3] And when Herod was dead, behold, an
Angel of the Lord appeareth in a dreame to
Ioſeph in Egypt,
20 Saying, Ariſe and take the Babe and his
mother, and go into the land of Iſrael: for they
are dead which ſought the Babes life.
21 Then hee aroſe vp and tooke the Babe
and his mother, and came into the lande of Iſrael.
22 But when hee heard that Archelaus did
reigne in Iudea in ſtead of his father Herod, he
was afraid to goe thither: yet after he was warned of God in a dreame, hee turned aſide into
the parts of Galile,
23 And went and dwelt in a citie called Nazareth, that it might bee fulfilled which was
ſpoken by the Prophets, *which was,* That hee
ſhould be called a Nazarite.

CHAP. III.

1 Iohn preacheth. 4 His apparell and meate. 5 He baptizeth. 8 The fruits of repentance. 10 The axe at the root of the tree. 12 The fan and the chaffe. 13 Chriſt is baptized.

ANd in [a] thoſe dayes, [1] Iohn the Baptiſt
came and preached in the [b] wilderneſſe
of Iudea,
2 And ſaid, [c] Repent: for the [d] kingdome
of heauen is at hand.
3 For this is hee of whome it is ſpoken
by the Prophet Eſaias, ſaying, *The voyce
of him that crieth in the wilderneſſe, Prepare
yee the way of the Lord: [e] make his pathes
ſtraight.
4 *And this Iohn had his garment of camels haire, and a girdle of a ſkinne about his
loynes: his meat alſo was [f] locuſts and wilde
honie.
5 *Then went out to him [g] Ieruſalem
and all Iudea, and all the region round about
Iordan.
6 *And they were baptized of him in Iordan, [h] confeſſing their ſinnes.
7 [2] Now when he ſaw many of the Phariſes, and of the Sadduces come to his baptiſme, hee ſaide vnto them, *O generations

* *Luke 2.6.*
1 Chriſt a poore child, laid down in a crib, and nothing ſet by of his owne people, receiueth notwithſtanding a noble witneſſe of his diuinitie from heauen, & of his kingly eſtate, of ſtrangers: which his owne alſo vnwittingly allow of, although they doe not acknowledge him.
a For there was another in the tribe of Zabulon.
b Wiſe and learned men: It is a Perſian worde which they vſe in good part.
c Was much moued, for he was a ſtranger and came to the kingdome by force: and the Iewes were troubled: for wickedneſſe is mad and raging.
d The chiefe Prieſts, that is, ſuch as were of Aarons familie, which were diuided into foure and twentie orders 1.Chro.24.5. and 2.Chro.36.14.
e They that expound the Lawe to the people: for the Hebrewes take this word of another which ſignifieth as much as to expound and declare.
* *Mica.5.2. iohn 7.42.*
f Though thou be a ſmall towne, yet ſhalt thou be very famous and noble through the birth of the Meſſias, who ſhall be borne in thee.
g That ſhall rule and gouerne: for Kings are fitly called feeders and ſhepheards of the people.
h A kind of humble and lowly reuerence.
i The rich and coſtly preſents, which they brought him.
k God warned and told them of it, when as they asked it not.
2 Chriſt being yet ſcarce borne, beginneth to be crucified for vs, both in himſelfe, and alſo in his members.
* *Hoſe.11.1.*
l For God ſpeaketh by the mouth of the Prophets.
* *Iere.31.15.*
m A voyce of lamenting, weeping and howling.
n That is to ſay, All that compaſſe about Beth-lehem: for Rachel Iaakobs wife, who died in childbed, was buried in the way that leadeth to this towne, which is alſo called Ephrata, becauſe of the fruitfulneſſe of the ſoyle, and plentie of corne.
3 Chriſt is brought vp in Nazareth, after the death of the tyrant by Gods prouidence: that by the very name of the place, it might plainely appeare to the world, that he is the Lords true Nazarite.
* *Marke 1.4. luke 3.3.*
a Not when Ioſeph went to dwell at Nazareth, but a great while after, about the ſpace of fiue and twentie yeeres: for in the thirtieth yeere of his age was Ieſus baptized of Iohn: therefore by thoſe dayes, is meant, at that time that Ieſus remained as yet an inhabitant of the towne of Nazareth.
1 Iohn who through his ſingular holineſſe and rare auſtereneſſe of life, cauſed all men to caſt their eyes vpon him, prepareth the way for Chriſt following faſt on at his heeles, as the Prophet Eſai foretold, and deliuereth the ſumme of the Goſpel, which in ſhort ſpace after ſhould be deliuered more fully. *b In an hilly countrey, which was notwithſtanding inhabited, for Zacharie dwelt there: Luke 1.40. and there was Ioabs houſe, 1.King.2.34. and beſides theſe, Ichoſhua maketh mention of ſixe townes that were in this wilderneſſe, chap.15.61. c The word in the Greeke tongue, ſignifieth a changing of our minds & hearts from euill to better. d The Kingdome of Meſſias, whoſe gouernement ſhall be heauenly, and nothing but heauenly. * Eſai 40.3. mar.1.3. luke 3.4. ioh.1.23. e Make him a plaine and ſmooth way. * Mar.1 6. f Locuſts were a kinde of meat, which certaine of the Eaſt people vſe, which were therefore called deuourers of locuſts. Euſt.in Ode.9. * Mar.1.5.luke 1.7. g The people of Ieruſalem. h Acknowledging that they were ſaued onely by free remiſſion and forgiueneſſe of their ſinnes.* 2 There is nothing that ſtoppeth vp the way of mercie and ſaluation againſt vs ſo much as the opinion of our owne righteouſneſſe doeth.
* *Chap.12.34.*

of vipers, who hath forewarned you to flee
from the anger to come?
8 [3]Bring foorth therefore fruite worthie
amendment of life.
9 [4]And [i] thinke not to say [k] with your
selues, *Wee haue Abraham to *our* father: for
I say vnto you, that God is able euen of these
stones to raise vp children vnto Abraham.
10 And now also is the axe put to the roote
of the trees: *therefore euery tree which bringeth not foorth good fruite, is hewen downe,
and cast into the fire.
11 *[5]In deede I baptize you with water to
[l]amendment of life, but he that commeth after me, is mightier then I, whose shooes I am
not worthie to beare: he will baptize you with
the holy Ghost, and with fire.
12 [6]Which hath his fanne in his hand, and
will [m] make cleane his floore, and gather his
wheate into his garner, but will burne vp the
chaffe with vnquenchable fire.
13 ¶ *[7]Then came Iesus from Galile to
Iordan vnto Iohn, to be baptized of him.
14 But Iohn earnestly put him backe, saying, I haue neede to be baptized of thee, and
commest thou to me?
15 Then Iesus answering, sayde to him,
Lee bee nowe: for thus it becommeth vs to
fulfill [n] all righteousnesse. So hee suffered
him.
16 And Iesus when he was baptized, came
straight out of the water. And loe, the heauens
were opened vnto [o] him, and *Iohn* saw the Spirit of God descending like a doue, and ligh-
ting vpon him.
17 [8]And loe, a voice *came* from heauen,
saying, *This is my beloued Sonne, in whome
I am [p] well pleased.

3 True repentance, is an inward thing, which hath it seate in the mind and heart.
4 The faith of the fathers auaileth the vnbeleeuing children nothing at all: and yet for all that, God playeth not the liar, nor dealeth vnfaithfully in his league which he made with the holy fathers.
i *Thinke not that you haue any cause to be proud of Abraham.*
k *In your hearts.*
*Iohn 8.39. actes 13.26.
*Chap. 7.19.
*Marke 1.8. luke 3.16. iohn 1.26. actes 1.5. & 2.4. & 8.17. & 19.4.
5 We may neither dwell vpon the signes which God hath ordeined as meanes to leade vs vnto our saluation, neither vpon them that minister them: but we must clime vp to the matter it selfe, that is to say, to Christ, who inwardly worketh that effectually, which is outwardly signified vnto vs.
l *The outward signe putteth vs in minde of this, that we must change our liues and become better, assuring vs as by a seale, that wee are ingraffed into Christ, whereby our old man dieth, and the new man riseth vp, Roman. 6* 6 The triumphs of the wicked shall ende in euerlasting torment. *m* *Will cleanse it throughly, and make a full riddance.* *Marke 1.9. luke 3.21. 7 Christ sanctifieth our baptisme in himselfe. *n* *All such things as he hath appointed vs to keepe.* *o* *To Iohn.* 8 Christes full consecration and authorizing to the office of the Mediatourship, is shewed by the Fathers owne voice, and a visible signe of the holy Ghost. *Coloss. 1.13. 2.pet. 1.17. *p* *The Greeke word betokeneth a thing of great account, and such as highly pleaseth a man. So then the Father sayth, that Christ onely is the man, whom when he beholdeth, looke what opinion he had conceiued of vs, he layeth it cleane aside.*

CHAP. IIII.

1 Christ is tempted. 4 Hee vanquisheth the deuill with Scripture. 11 The Angels minister vnto him. 12 Hee preacheth repentance, and that himselfe is come. 18 The calling of Peter, Andrew, 21 Iames and Iohn. 23 Hee preacheth the Gospel, and healeth the diseased.

THen *was [1]Iesus ledde aside of the Spirit
into the wildernesse, to bee tempted of
the deuill.
2 And when hee had fasted [a]fortie dayes,
and fortie nights, he was afterward hungrie.
3 Then came to him the tempter, and said,
If thou be the Sonne of God, command that
these stones be made bread.
4 But hee answering, said, It is written,
*Man shall not liue by bread onely, but by e-
uery word that proceedeth out of the mouth
of God.

*Marke 1.12. luke 4.1.
1 Christ was tempted all manner of waies, and still ouercommeth, that wee also through his vertue, may ouercome.
a *Full fortie dayes.*
*Deut. 8.3.

5 Then the deuill tooke him vp into the
holy Citie, and set him on a [b] pinacle of the
Temple,
6 And said vnto him, If thou be the Sonne
of God, cast thy selfe downe: for it is written,
*that hee will giue his Angels charge ouer
thee, and with their hands they shall lift thee
vp, lest at any time thou shouldest dash thy
foote against a stone.
7 Iesus sayd vnto him, It is written a-
gaine, *Thou shalt not [c] tempt the Lord thy
God.
8 Againe the deuill tooke him vp into an
exceeding high mountaine, and shewed him
all the kingdomes of the world, and the glory
of them,
9 And said to him, All these will I giue
thee, if thou wilt fall downe and worship me.
10 Then said Iesus vnto him, Auoid Satan: for it is written, * Thou shalt worship
the Lord thy God, and him onely shalt thou
serue.
11 *Then the deuill left him: and behold,
the Angels came, and ministred vnto him.
12 ¶ *[2]And when Iesus had heard that
Iohn was committed to prison, he returned into Galile.
13 And leauing Nazareth, went and dwelt
in [d]Capernaum, which is neere the sea in the
borders of Zabulon and Nephthalim,
14 That it might bee fulfilled which was
spoken by Esaias the Prophet, saying,
15 *The land of Zabulon, and the land of
Nepththalim *by* the way of the [e]sea, beyond
Iordan, [f] Galile of the Gentiles:
16 The people which sate in darkenesse,
sawe great light: and to them which sate in the
region, and shadow of death, light is risen vp.
17 *From that time Iesus began to preach,
and to say, Amend your liues: for the kingdome of heauen is at [g] hand.
18 ¶ [3]And Iesus walking by the sea of Galile, saw two brethren, Simon, which was called Peter, and Andrew his brother, casting a
net into the sea (for they were fishers)
19 *And hee said vnto them, Follow me,
and I will make you fishers of men.
20 And they straightway leauing the nets,
followed him.
21 And when hee was gone foorth from
thence, hee saw other two brethren, Iames *the*
sonne of Zebedeus, and Iohn his brother in a
ship with Zebedeus their father, mending their
nets, and he called them.
22 And they without tarying, leauing the
ship and their father, followed him.
23 So [4]Iesus went about all Galile, teaching in [h] their [i] Synagogues, and preaching the
Gospel of the [k] kingdome, and healing [l] euery
sicknes, and euery [m] disease among the people.

b *The battlement wherewith the flat roofe of the Temple was compassed about, that no man might fall downe: as was appointed by the law, Deut. 22.8.*
*Psal. 91.11.
*Deut. 6.16.
c *Word for word, Thou shalt not goe on still in tempting.*
*Deut. 6.13. and 10.20.
*Marke 1.13. luke 4.13.
*Marke 1.14. luke 4.14. iohn 4.43.
2 When the Heralds mouth is stopped, the Lord reueileth himselfe & bringeth full light into the darknes of this world, preaching free forgiuenesse of sinnes to them that repent.
d *Which was a towne a great deale more famous then Nazareth was.*
*Esai 9.1.
e *Of Tiberias, or because that countrey bended toward Tyrus, which standeth vpon the sea that cutteth the midst of the world.*
f *So called, because it bordered vpon Tyrus and Sidon, & because Salomon gaue the king of Tyrus twentie cities in that quarter, 1 King. 9.11.*
*Marke 1.15.
g *Is come to you.*
3 Christ thinking by time, that he should at length depart from vs, euen at the beginning of his preaching getteth him disciples after an heauenly sort, men indeede poore, and vtterly vnlearned, and therefore such as might be least suspected witnesses of the trueth of those things which they heard and saw.
*Marke 1.16. 1.cor. 1.27.
4 Christ assureth the hearts of the beleeuers of his spirituall and sauing vertue, by healing the diseases of the body.
h *Their, that is, the Galileans.*

i *Synagogues, that is, the Iewes Churches.* *k* *Of Messias.* *l* *Diseases of all kindes, but not euery one: that is, as wee say, some of euery one.* *m* *The word signifieth properly, the weakenesse of the stomacke: but here it is taken for those diseases which make men faint and weare away, that haue them.*

n The word signifieth properly the stone wherewith gold is tried: and by a borrowed kind of speech, is applied to all kinde of examination by torture, when as by rough dealing and torments, we goe about to draw out the trueth of men, which otherwise they would not

24 And his fame spread abroad thorow
all Syria: and they brought vnto him all sicke
people, that were taken with diuers diseases
and [n] torments, and them that were possessed
with deuils, and those which were [o] lunaticke,
and those that had the [p] palsie: and hee healed
them.
25 And there followed him great multitudes out of Galile, and Decapolis, and Ierusalem, and Iudea, and from beyond Iordan.

confesse: and in this place it is taken for those diseases, which put sicke men to great woe. o Which at euery full Moone, or the changes of the Moone, are shrewdly troubled and diseased. p Weake and feeble men, who haue the parts of their body loosed, and so weakened, that they are neither able to gather them vp together, nor put them out as they would.

CHAP. V.

1 *Who are blessed.* 13 *The Apostles are the salt and light of the world.* 14 *The citie set on an hill.* 15 *The candle.* 16 *Good workes.* 19 *The fulfilling of Christes commandements.* 21 *What killing is.* 23 *Reconciliation is set before sacrifice.* 27 *Adulterie.* 29 *The plucking out of the eye.* 30 *Cutting off the hand.* 31 *The bill of diuorcement.* 33 *Not to sweare.* 43 *To loue our enemies.* 48 *Perfectnesse.*

1 Christ teacheth that the greatest ioy and felicitie is not in the commodities and pleasures of this life, but is laid vp in heauen for them that willingly rest in the good will and pleasure of God, and endeauour to profit all men, although they be cruelly vexed and troubled of the worldlings, because they will not fashion themselues to their manners.
* *Luke 6.20.*
a Vnder the name of pouertie, are all such miseries meant, as are ioyned with pouerty.
b Whose mindes and spirits are brought vnder, and tamed, and obey God.
* *Esai 61.2,3. luke 6.21.*
* *Psal 37.11.*
* *Esai 65.13.*
* *Psal.24.4.*
c Fitly is this word, Pure, ioyned with the heart, for as a bright and shining resemblance or image may be seene plainely in a cleare and pure looking glasse, euen so doeth the face (as it were) of the euerlasting God, shine foorth, and clearely appeare in a pure heart.

AND when he saw the multitude, he went
vp into a mountaine: and when hee was
set, his disciples came to him.
2 [1] And he opened his mouth, and taught
them, saying,
3 *Blessed *are* the [a] poore in [b] spirit, for
theirs is the kingdome of heauen.
4 *Blessed *are* they that mourne: for they
shall be comforted.
5 *Blessed *are* the meeke: for they shall
inherite the earth.
6 * Blessed *are* they which hunger and
thirst for righteousnesse: for they shall bee
filled.
7 Blessed *are* the mercifull: for they shall
obtaine mercie.
8 Blessed *are* the * [c] pure in heart: for they
shall see God.
9 Blessed *are* the peacemakers: for they
shalbe called the children of God.
10 Blessed *are* they * which suffer persecution for righteousnesse sake: for theirs is the
kingdome of heauen.
11 * Blessed shall yee be when men reuile
you, and persecute *you*, and say all manner of
euill against you for my sake, falsely.
12 Reioyce and be glad, for great is your
reward in heauen: for so persecuted they the
Prophets which were before you.
13 * Yee [2] are the salt of the [d] earth: but if
the salt haue lost his sauour, wherewith shall it
bee [e] salted? It is thencefoorth good for nothing, but to be cast out, and to be troden vnder foot of men.
14 Yee are the [f] light of the world. A citie
that is set on an hill, cannot be hid.
15 * Neither doe men light a candle, and
put it vnder a bushel, but on a candlesticke, and
it giueth light vnto all that are in the house.
16 * Let your light so shine before men,
that they may see your good workes, and glorifie your Father which is in heauen.
17 [3] Thinke not that I am come to destroy
the Lawe, or the Prophets. I am not come to
destroy them, but to [g] fulfill them.
18 * For truely I say vnto you, Till heauen
and earth perish, one iote or one title of the
Law shall not scape, till all things be fulfilled.
19 * [4] Whosoeuer therefore shall breake
one of these least commandements, and teach
men so, he shalbe called the [h] least in the kingdome of heauen: but whosoeuer shall obserue
and teach *them*, the same shalbe called great in
the kingdome of heauen.
20 For I say vnto you, Except your righteousnes * exceed the *righteousnes* of the Scribes
and Pharises, yee shall not enter into the kingdome of heauen.
21 [5] Yee haue heard that it was sayd vnto them of olde time, * Thou shalt not kill:
for whosoeuer killeth, shall bee culpable of
iudgement.
22 But I say vnto you, whosoeuer is angry
with his brother vnaduisedly, shalbe [i] culpable
[k] of iudgement. And whosoeuer sayth vnto
his brother, Raca, shall be worthy to be punished by the [l] Council. And whosoeuer shall
say, Foole, shalbe worthy to be punished with
[m] hell [n] fire.
23 [6] If then thou bring thy gift to the [o] altar, and there remembrest that thy brother hath
ought against thee,
24 Leaue there thine offering before the
altar, and goe thy way: first be reconciled to
thy brother, and then come and offer thy
gift.
25 * [p] Agree with thine aduersarie quickly,
whiles thou art in the way with him, lest thine
aduersarie deliuer thee to the Iudge, and the
Iudge deliuer thee to the sergeant, and thou
be cast into prison.
26 Verely I say vnto thee, thou shalt not

* *Marke 4.21. luke 8.16. and 11.33.*
* *1.Pet.2.12.*
3 Christ came not to bring any new way of righteousnesse and saluation into the world, but to fulfill that in deed, which was shadowed by the figures of the Law, by deliuering men through grace from the curse of the Law: and moreouer to teach the true vse of obedience, which the Law appointeth, and to graue in our hearts the force of obedience.
g That the prophecies may be accomplished.
* *Luke 16.17.*
* *Iames 2.10.*
4 He beginneth with the true expounding of the Law, and setteth it against the olde (but yet false) gloses of the Scribes: So farre is he from abolishing the least commandement of his Father.
h He shall haue no place in the Church.
* *Luke 11.39.*
5 The true meaning of the sixt commandement.
* *Exod.20.13. deut 5.17.*
i He speaketh of the iudgement of God, and of the difference of sins, and therefore applyeth his words to the forme of ciuill iudgements, which were then vsed.
k Of that iudgement which was ruled by three men, who had the hearing and deciding of money matters, and such other small causes. l By that iudgement which stood of three and twentie Iudges, who had the hearing and deciding of weightie affaires, and matters of life and death: as the highest Iudges of all were, to the number of seuentie and one, which had the hearing of most weightie affaires, as the matter of a whole Tribe, or of an high Priest, or of a false prophet. m Whereas we reade here, Hell, it is in the Text it selfe, Gehenna, which is an Hebrew word made of two, and is as much to say, as the valley of Hinnon, which otherwise the Hebrewes called Topheth: it was a place where the Israelites were woont most cruelly to sacrifice their children to false gods, whereupon it was taken for a place appointed to torment the reprobates in, Ierem.7.31. n The Iewes vsed foure kindes of punishments, before their gouernment was taken away by Herode, hanging, beheading, stoning, and burning: this is it that Christ shot at, because burning was the greatest punishment, therefore in that he maketh mention of a iudgement, a Councill, and a fire, he sheweth that some sinnes are worse then other some, but yet they are all such, that we must giue an account for them, and shall be punished for them. 6 The couetous Pharises taught, that God was appeased by the sacrifices appointed in the Lawe, which they themselues deuoured. But Christ on the contrary side denyeth, that God accepteth any mans offering, vnlesse hee maketh satisfaction to his brother whome hee hath offended: and sayth moreouer, that these stubburne and stiffe-necked despisers of their brethren, shall neuer escape the wrath and curse of God, before they haue made full satisfaction to their brethren. *o He applyeth all this speech, to the state of his time, when as there was an Altar standing in Ierusalem: and therefore they are very foolish, that gather hereupon, that we must build Altars, and vse Sacrifices: but they are more fooles, which drawe that to purgatorie, which is spoken of peace making and atonement one with another.* * *Luke 12.58.* *p Cut off all cause of enmitie.*

* *1.Corinth.14.33. 1.pet.3.14.* * *Actes 5.41. 1.pet.5.14.* * *Marke 9.50. luke 14.34.* 2 The ministers of the word especially (vnlesse they will bee the most caitifes of all) must needs lead other both by word and deede to this greatest ioy and felicitie. *d Your doctrine must be very sound and good, for if it be not so, it shalbe nought set by, and cast away as a thing vnsauorie and vaine. e What shall you haue to salt withall? And so are fooles in the Latine tongue called saltlesse, as you would say, men that haue no salt, or sauour and taste in them. f You shine and giue light, by being made partakers of the true light.*

come out thence, till thou hast [q] payed the vtmost farthing.

27 ¶ [7] Yee haue heard that it was said to them of olde time, * Thou shalt not commit adulterie.

28 But I say vnto you, that whosoeuer looketh on a woman to lust after her, hath committed adulterie with her alreadie in his heart.

29 * Wherefore if thy [r] right eye cause thee [s] to offend, plucke it out, and cast it from thee, for better it is for thee, that one of thy members perish, then that thy whole body should be cast into hell.

30 Also if thy right hand make thee to offend, cut it off, and cast it from thee: for better it is for thee, that one of thy members perish, then that thy whole body should be cast into hell.

31 It hath beene said also, * Whosoeuer shall put away his wife, let him giue her a bill of diuorcement.

32 But I say vnto you, whosoeuer shall put away his wife (except it be for fornication) causeth her to commit adulterie: and whosoeuer shall marrie her that is diuorced, committeth adulterie.

33 [8] Againe, ye haue heard that it was said to them of old time, * Thou shalt not forsweare thy selfe, but shalt performe thine othes to the Lord.

34 But I say vnto you, Sweare not at all: neither by heauen, for it is the throne of God:

35 Nor yet by the earth: for it is his footstoole: neither by Ierusalem: for it is the citie of the great King.

36 Neither shalt thou sweare by thine head, because thou canst not make one haire white or blacke.

37 * But let your communication be [t] Yea, yea: Nay, nay. For whatsoeuer *is* more then these, commeth of [u] euill.

38 ¶ [9] Ye haue heard that it hath been said, An * eye for an eye, and a tooth for a tooth.

39 But I say vnto you, * Resist not euill: but whosoeuer shall smite thee on the right cheeke, turne to him the other also.

40 And if any man will sue thee at the law, and take away thy coate, let him haue thy cloke also.

41 And whosoeuer will compell thee *to goe* a mile, goe with him twaine.

42 * Giue to him that asketh, and from him that would borrow of thee, turne not away.

43 Yee haue heard that it hath beene said, * Thou shalt loue thy neighbour, and hate thine enemie.

44 But I say vnto you, * Loue your enemies: blesse them that curse you: doe good to them that hate you, * and pray for them which hurt you, and persecute you,

q Thou shalt be dealt withall, to the vtmost extremitie.

7 He is taken for an adulterer before God whatsoeuer he be, that coueteth a woman: and therfore we must keepe our eyes chaste, and all the members we haue, yea and we must eschew all occasions, which might mooue vs to euill, how deare soeuer it cost vs.

* *Exod.* 20.14. *rom.* 13.9.

* *Chap.* 18.8,9. *marke* 9.47.

r He nameth the right eye and the right hand, because the parts of the right side of our bodie are the chiefest, and readiest to commit any wickednesse.

s Word for word, doe cause thee to offend: for sinnes are stumbling blockes as it were, that is to say, rockes which we are cast vpon.

* *Chap.* 19.7. *deut.* 24.1. *marke* 10.4. *luke* 16.18. 1.*cor.* 7.10.

8 The meaning of the third commandement against the froward opinion & iudgement of the Scribes, which excused by-othes or indirect formes of swearing.

* *Exod* 20.7. *leuit.* 19.12. *deut.* 5.11.

* *Iam.* 5.12.

t Whatsoeuer you vouch, vouch it barely, and whatsoeuer you denie, denie it barely without any more words.

u From an euill conscience, or from the deuill.

9 He sheweth cleane contrarie to the doctrine of the Scribes, that the summe of the second Table must be so vnderstood, that we may in no wise render euill for euil, but rather suffer double iniurie, and doe well to them that are our deadly enemies

* *Exod.* 21.24. *leuit.* 24.20. *deut.* 19.21.

* *Luke* 6.29. *rom.* 12.17. 1.*corinth.* 6.7.

* *Deut.* 15.8.

* *Leuit.* 19.8.

* *Luke* 6.27. * *Luke* 23.34. *actes* 7.60. 1.*corinth.* 4.13.

45 [10] * That ye may be the children of your father that is in heauen: for hee maketh his sunne to arise on the euill, and the good, and sendeth raine on the iust, and vniust.

46 For if yee loue them, which loue you, what reward shall you haue? Do not the Publicanes euen the same?

47 And if yee be friendly to your brethren onely, what singular thing doe ye? doe not euen the [x] Publicanes likewise?

48 Yee shall therefore be perfite, as your Father which is in heauen, is perfite.

10 A double reason: the one is taken of the relatiues, The children must be like their father: the other is taken of comparisons, The children of God must be better then the children of this world.

* *Luke* 6.35.

x They that were the tolle masters, and had the ouersight of tributes and customes: and a kinde of men that the Iewes hated to death, both because they serued the Romanes in those offices (whose yokefull bondage they could hardly away withall) and also because these toll-masters are for the most part giuen to couetousnesse.

CHAP. VI.

1 Almes. 5 Prayers. 14 Forgiuing our brother. 16 Fasting. 19 Our treasure. 20 We must succour the poore. 24 God and riches. 25 Carefull seeking for meate and drinke, and apparell, forbidden. 33 The kingdom of God and his righteousnesse.

Take heede that yee giue not your [1] almes before men, to be seene of them, or else ye shall haue no [a] reward of your Father which is in heauen.

2 * Therefore when thou giuest thine almes, thou shalt not make a trumpet to bee blowen before thee, as the [b] hypocrites doe in the Synagogues and in the streetes, to be praised of men. Verely I say vnto you, they haue their reward.

3 But when thou doest thine almes, let not thy left hand knowe what thy right hand doeth,

4 That thine almes may be in secret, and thy Father that seeth in secret, hee will reward thee openly.

5 [2] And when thou prayest, be not as the hypocrites: for they loue to stand, and pray in the Synagogues, and in the corners of the streetes, because they would be seene of men. Verely I say vnto you, they haue their reward.

6 But when thou prayest, enter into thy chamber: and when thou hast shut thy doore, pray vnto thy Father which is in secret, and thy Father which seeth in secret, shall reward thee openly.

7 Also when ye pray, vse no [c] vaine repetitions as the heathen: for they thinke to bee heard for their much babling.

8 Be ye not like them therefore: for your Father knoweth whereof ye haue neede, before ye aske of him.

9 [3] After this manner therefore pray yee, * Our Father which art in heauen, hallowed be thy Name.

10 Thy kingdome come. Thy will be done euen in earth, as *it is* in heauen.

11 Giue vs this day our [d] daily bread.

12 And forgiue vs our debts, as we also forgiue our debters.

13 And lead vs not into tentation, but deliuer vs * from [e] euill: for thine is the kingdome, and the power, and the glory for euer. Amen.

14 * [4] For

1 Ambition maketh almes vaine.

a This word, Reward, is alwayes taken in the Scriptures for a free recompense, and therefore the schoolemen doe fondly set it to be answerable to a deseruing, which they call, merite.

* *Rom.* 12.8.

b Counterfeits, for hypocrites were players that played a part in a play.

2 He reprehendeth two foule faults in prayer, ambition, and vaine babling.

c Long prayers are not condemned, but vaine, needlesse, and superstitious.

3 A true summe and forme of all Christian prayers.

* *Luke* 11.2.

d That that is meete for our nature for our daily food, or such as may suffice our nature and complexion.

* *Chap.* 13.19.

e From the deuill, or from all aduersitie.

* *Marke* 11.25.
4 They that forgiue wrongs, to them sinnes are forgiuen, but reuenge is prepared for them that reuenge.

5 Against such as hunt after a name of holines by fasting.
f They suffer not their first hue to be seene, that is to say, they marre the naturall colour of their faces, that they may seeme leane and pale faced.

6 Those mens labors are shewed to be vaine, which passe not for the assured treasure of euerlasting life, but spend their liues in scraping together fraile and vaine riches.
* *Luke* 12.33. 1.*tim*.6.19.
* *Luke* 11.34.
7 Men doe maliciously & wickedly put out euen the little light of nature that is in them.
g The iudgement of the mind: that as the body is with the eyes, so our whole life may be ruled with right reason, that is to say, with the spirit of God wherewith we are lightned.
* *Luke* 16.13.
8 God will be worshipped of the whole man.
h Which be at iarre together, for if two agree, they are as one.
i This word is a Syrian word, and signifieth all things that belong to money.
* *Luke* 12.22. *phil*.4.6. 1.*tim*. 6.8. 1.*pet*.5.7. *psal*.53.23.
9 The froward carking carefulnesse for things of this life, is corrected in the children of God by an earnest thinking vpon the prouidence of God.
k Of the ayre, or that liue in the ayre: for in all tongues almost this word Heauen, is taken for the ayre.
l He speaketh of care which is ioyned with thought of mind, and hath for the most part distrust yoked with it.
m By labour.

14 * [4]For if yee doe forgiue men their trespasses, your heauenly Father will also forgiue
you.
15 But if ye doe not forgiue men their trespasses, no more will your father forgiue *you*
your trespasses.
16 [5]Moreouer, when yee fast, looke not
sowre as the hypocrites: for they [f] disfigure
their faces, that they might seeme vnto men to
fast. Verely I say vnto you, that they haue their
reward.
17 But when thou fastest, annoint thine
head, and wash thy face,
18 That thou seeme not vnto men to fast,
but vnto thy Father which is in secret: and thy
Father which seeth in secret, will reward thee
openly.
19 ¶ [6]Lay not vp treasures for your selues
vpon the earth, where the moth and canker
corrupt, and where theeues digge thorow and
steale.
20 *But lay vp treasures for your selues in
heauen, where neither the moth nor canker
corrupteth, and where theeues neither digge
thorow nor steale.
21 For where your treasure is, there will
your heart be also.
22 ¶ *[7]The light of the bodie is the eye:
if then thine [g] eye be single, the whole body
shalbe light.
23 But if thine eye be wicked, then all thy
bodie shall bee darke. Wherefore if the light
that is in thee, be darkenesse, how great is that
darkenesse?
24 *[8]No man can serue [h] two masters: for
either he shall hate the one, and loue the other,
or else he shall leane to the one, and despise the
other. Ye cannot serue God and [i] riches.
25 * [9] Therefore I say vnto you, Be not
carefull for your life, what ye shall eat, or what
ye shall drinke: nor yet for your body, what ye
shall put on. Is not the life more worth then
meate? and the body then raiment?
26 Behold the fowles of the [k] heauen: for
they sowe not, neither reape, nor carie into the
barnes: yet your heauenly Father feedeth
them. Are ye not much better then they?
27 Which of you by [l] taking care is able to
adde one cubite vnto his stature?
28 And why care yee for raiment? Learne
how the lilies of the field doe grow: they [m] are
not wearied, neither spin.
29 Yet I say vnto you, that euen Salomon
in all his glorie was not arayed like one of
these.
30 Wherefore if God so cloth the grasse of
the field which is to day, and to morow is cast
into the ouen, shall he not *doe* much more vnto you, O ye of little faith?
31 Therefore take no thought, saying,
What shall wee eate? or what shall we drinke?
or wherewith shall we be clothed?
32 (For after all these things seeke the Gentiles) for your heauenly Father knoweth, that
ye haue neede of all these things.
33 But seeke ye first the kingdome of God,
and his righteousnes, and all these things shall
be ministred vnto you.
34 Care not then for the morowe: for the
morow shall care for it selfe: the day hath
enough with his owne griefe.

CHAP. VII.

1 We may not giue iudgement of our neighbour, 6 nor cast that which is holy to dogges. 13 The broad and straight way. 15 False prophets. 18 The tree and fruite. 24 The house built on a rocke, 26 And on the sand.

IVdge [1] not, that ye be not iudged.
2 For with what * iudgement ye iudge,
ye shalbe iudged, and with what * measure ye
mete, it shalbe measured to you againe.
3 And why seest thou the mote that is in
thy brothers eye, and perceiuest not the beame
that is in thine owne eye?
4 * Or how sayest thou to thy brother,
Suffer me to cast out the mote out of thine eye,
and behold, a beame is in thine owne eye?
5 Hypocrite, first cast out that beame out
of thine owne eye, and then shalt thou see
clearely to cast out the mote out of thy brothers eye.
6 ¶ [2]Giue yee not that which is holy to
dogges, neither cast ye your [a] pearles before
swine, lest they tread them vnder their feet, and
turning againe, all to rent you.
7 ¶ * [3]Aske, and it shall bee giuen you:
seeke, and ye shall finde: knocke, and it shalbe
opened vnto you.
8 For whosoeuer asketh, receiueth: and he
that seeketh, findeth: and to him that knocketh, it shall be opened.
9 For what man is there among you,
which if his sonne aske him bread, would giue
him a stone?
10 Or if he aske fish, will he giue him a serpent?
11 If ye then, which are euill, can giue to
your children good gifts, how much more shal
your Father which is in heauen, giue good
things to them that aske him?
12 *[4]Therefore whatsoeuer ye would that
men should doe to you, euen so doe ye to
them: for this is the [b] Law and the Prophets.
13 ¶ *[5]Enter in at the straight gate: for
it is the wide gate, and broad way that leadeth
to destruction: and many there be which goe
in thereat.
14 Because [c] the gate is straite, and the way
narrow that leadeth vnto life, and few there be
that finde it.
15 ¶ [6]Beware of false prophets, which
come to you, in sheepes clothing, but inwardly they are rauening wolues.
16 Yee shall know them by their fruites,
*Doe men gather grapes of thornes? or figs of
thistles?

1 We ought to finde fault one with another, but we must beware we doe it not without cause, or to seem holier then they, or in hatred of them.
* *Luke* 6.37,38. *rom*.2.1. 1.*cor*.4.3. *Marke* 4.24. *luke* 6.38.
* *Luke* 6.41.
2 The stiffe necked and stubborne enemies of the Gospel, are vnworthie to haue it preached vnto them.
a A pearle hath his name among the Grecians, for the orient brightnesse that is in it: and a pearle was in ancient time in great estimation among the Latines: for a pearle that Cleopatra had, was valued at two hundred and fifty thousand crownes: and the word is now borrowed from that, to signifie the most precious heauenly doctrine.
* *Chap*.21.22. *marke* 11.24. *luke* 11.9.*iohn* 14.13.*and* 16.23.*iames* 1.5.
3 Prayers are a sure refuge in all miseries.
* *Luke* 6.31. *iohn* 4.16.
4 A rehearsall of the meaning of the second table.
b That is to say, The doctrine of the Law aad Prophets.
* *Luke* 13.24.
5 Example of life must not be taken from a multitude.
c The way is strait and narrow: we must passe thorow this rough way, and suffer, and endure, and be changed, and so enter into life.
6 False teachers must be taken heede of: and they are knowen by false doctrine and euill liuing.
* *Luke* 6.44.

17 So

17 So euery good tree bringeth foorth
good fruit, and a corrupt tree bringeth foorth
euill fruite.
18 A good tree cannot bring foorth euill
fruite, neither can a corrupt tree bring foorth
good fruite.
19 *Euery tree that bringeth not foorth
good fruite, is hewen downe, and cast into the
fire.
20 Therefore by their fruits ye shall know
them.
21 ¶ [7] Not euery one that sayth vnto me,
Lord, Lord, shall enter into the kingdome of
heauen, *but hee that doeth my Fathers will
which is in heauen.
22 *Many will say to me in that day, Lord,
Lord, haue we not by thy [d] Name prophesied?
and by thy Name cast out deuils? and by thy
Name done many [e] great workes?
23 And then will I professe to them, *[f] I
neuer knew you: *depart from me, [g] yee that
worke iniquitie.
24 [8] Whosoeuer then heareth of mee these
wordes, *and doeth the same, I will liken him
to a wise man, which hath builded his house on
a rocke.
25 And the raine fell, and the floods came,
and the winds blew, and beat vpon that house,
and it fell not: for it was grounded on a rocke.
26 But whosoeuer heareth these my words,
and doeth them not, shall bee likened vnto a
foolish man, which hath builded his house vpon the sand:
27 And the raine fell, and the floods came,
and the winds blew, and beat vpon that house,
and it fell, and the fall thereof was great.
28 ¶ *And it came to passe, when Iesus
had ended these words, the people were astonied at his doctrine.
29 For hee taught them as one hauing authoritie, and not as the Scribes.

*Chap.3.10.
7 Euen the best gifts that are, are nothing without godlinesse.
*Rom.2.13.
*Iames 1.22.
d By Name here, is meant that mightie working power of God, which euery man witnesseth that calleth vpon him.
e Properly, powers: Now these excellent workes wrought, are called Powers, by occasion of those things which they bring to passe, for by them we vnderstand how mightie the power of God is.
*Luke 13.27.
f This is not of ignorance, but because he will cast them away.
*Psal.6.8.
g You that are giuen to all kinde of wickednesse, and seeme to make an arte of sinne.
8 True godlinesse resteth onely vpon Christ, and therefore alwayes remaineth inuincible.
*Luke 6.47,48.
*Marke 1.22. luke 4.32.

CHAP. VIII.

1 The leper clensed. 5 The Centurions faith. 11 The calling of the Gentiles, 12 and casting out of the Iewes. 14 Peters mother in lawe healed. 19 A Scribe desirous to follow Christ. 23 The tempest on the sea. 28 Two possessed with deuils, cured. 32 The deuils go into the swine.

NOw when he was come downe from the
mountaine, great multitudes followed him.
2 *[1] And loe, there came a leper, and worshipped him, saying, Master, if thou wilt, thou
canst make me cleane.
3 And Iesus putting foorth his hand, touched him, saying, I will, be thou cleane: and
immediatly his leprosie was cleansed.
4 Then Iesus said vnto him, See thou tell
no man, but goe, *and* shewe thy selfe vnto the
Priest, and offer the gift that *Moses commanded, for a witnesse to them.
5 ¶ *[2] When Iesus was entred into Capernaum, there came vnto him a Centurion,
beseeching him,
6 And said, Master, my seruant lieth sicke
at home of the palsie, and is grieuously pained.
7 And Iesus sayd vnto him, I will come
and heale him.
8 But the Centurion answered, saying,
Master, I am not worthy that thou shouldest
come vnder my roofe: but speake the word
onely, and my seruant shalbe healed.
9 For I am a man also vnder the authoritie
of another, and haue souldiers vnder mee: and
I say to one, Goe, and hee goeth: and to another, Come, and he commeth: and to my seruant, Doe this, and he doeth it.
10 When Iesus heard *that*, hee marueiled,
and said to them that followed *him*, Verely, I
say vnto you, I haue not found so great faith,
euen in Israel.
11 But I say vnto you, that many shall
come from the East and West, and shall [a] sit
downe with Abraham, and Isaac, and Iacob,
in the kingdome of heauen.
12 And the children of the kingdome shall
be cast out into [b] vtter *darknesse: there shall
be weeping and gnashing of teeth.
13 Then Iesus said vnto the Centurion,
Goe thy way, and as thou hast beleeued, so be
it vnto thee. And his seruant was healed the
same houre.
14 ¶ *[3] And when Iesus came to Peters
house, hee sawe his wiues mother laid downe,
and sicke of a feuer.
15 And hee touched her hand, and the feuer left her: so shee arose, and ministred vnto
them.
16 *When the Euen was come, they
brought vnto him many that were possessed
with deuils: and he cast out the spirits with *his*
word, and healed [c] all that were sicke,
17 That it might be fulfilled, which was
spoken by *Esaias the Prophet, saying, Hee
tooke our infirmities, and bare *our* sicknesses.
18 ¶ *And when Iesus sawe great multitudes of people about him, hee commanded
them to goe [d] ouer *the water*.
19 [4] Then came there a certaine Scribe,
and said vnto him, Master, I will follow thee
whithersoeuer thou goest.
20 But Iesus said vnto him, The foxes haue
holes, and the birds of the heauen haue [e] nests,
but the Sonne of man hath not whereon to
rest his head.
21 ¶ [5] And another of his disciples said vnto him, Master, suffer me first to goe, and bury
my father.
22 But Iesus said vnto him, Follow me, and
let the dead bury their dead.
23 ¶ *[6] And when he was entred into the
ship, his disciples followed him.
24 And behold, there arose a great tempest
in the sea, so that the shippe was couered with
waues: but he was asleepe.

25 Then

*Marke 1.40. luke 5.12.
1 Christ in healing the leprous with the touching of his hand, sheweth that he abhorreth no sinners that come vnto him, be they neuer so vncleane.
*Leuit.14.3,4.
*Luke 7.1.
2 Christ by setting before them the example of the vncircumcised Centurion, and yet of an excellent faith, prouoketh the Iewes to emulation, and together forewarneth them of their casting off, and the calling of the Gentiles.

a A metaphore taken of bankets, for they that sit downe together, are fellowes in the banquet.
b Which are without the kingdome: For in the kingdome is light, and without the kingdome darkenesse.
*Chap.22.13.
*Marke 1.29. luke 4.38.
3 Christ, in healing diuers diseases, sheweth that he was sent of his Father, that in him onely we should seeke remedie in all our miseries.
*Marke 1.32. luke 4.40.
c Of all sorts.
*Esai 53.4. 1.pet.2.24.
*Luke 9.57,58.
d For Capernaum was situate vpon the lake of Tiberias.
4 The true disciples of Christ must prepare themselues to all kind of miseries.
e Word for word, shades made with boughes.
5 When God requireth our labour, we must leaue off all dutie to men.
*Marke 4.37. luke 8.23.
6 Although Christ seemeth often times to neglect his, euen in most extreme dangers, yet in time conuenient he asswageth all tempests, and bringeth them to the hauen.

25 Then his disciples came and awoke him
saying, Master, saue vs: we perish.
26 And he said vnto them, Why are ye fearefull, O ye of litle faith? Then he arose, and rebuked the windes and the sea: and *so* there was
a great calme.
27 And the men marueiled, saying, What
man is this, that both the windes and the sea o-
bey him!
28 ¶ *[7] And when he was come to the o-
ther side into the countrey of the Gergesenes,
there met him two possessed with deuils which
came out of the graues very fierce, so that no
man might goe by that way.
29 And behold, they cryed out, saying, Iesus the sonne of God, what haue we to do with
thee? Art thou come hither to torment vs before the time?
30 Now there was [f] a farre off from them,
a great heard of swine feeding.
31 And the deuils besought him, saying, If
thou cast vs out, suffer vs to goe into the heard
of swine.
32 And he said vnto them, Goe. So they
went out and departed into the heard of swine:
and beholde, the whole heard of swine ranne
headlong into the sea, and died in the water.
33 Then the heardmen fled: & when they
were come into the citie, they told all things,
and what was become of them that were possessed with the deuils.
34 And beholde, all the citie came out to
meete Iesus: and when they saw him, they besought him to [g] depart out of their coasts.

*Marke 5.1,2. luke 8.26,27.
7 Christ came to deliuer men from the misera-ble thraldome of Satan: but the world had rather lacke Christ, then the vilest and least of their commodities.
f On an hill, as Marke and Luke witnesse: Now Gedera as Ioseph recordeth, booke 17 chap. 13. liued after the order of the Grecians, and therefore we may not marueile if there were swine there.
g Where men liue as swine, there doeth not Christ tarie, but deuils.

CHAP. IX.

1 One sicke of the palsie is healed. 5 Remission of sinnes. 9 Matthew is called. 10 Sinners. 17 New wine. 18 The rulers daughter raised. 20 A woman healed of a bloodie issue. 28 Two blinde men by faith receiue sight. 32 A dumbe man possessed is healed. 37 The haruest and workemen.

THen he [1] entred into a ship, and passed o-
uer, and came into his [a] owne citie.
2 And *loe, they brought to him a man
sicke of the palsie, laid on a bed. And Iesus [b] seeing their faith, saide to the sicke of the palsie,
Sonne, be of good comfort: thy sinnes are forgiuen thee.
3 And behold, certaine of the Scribes said
with themselues, This man [c] blasphemeth.
4 But when Iesus saw their thoughts, hee
said, Wherefore thinke ye euill things in your
hearts?
5 For whether is it easier to say, Thy sinnes
are forgiuen thee, or to say, Arise, and walke?
6 And that ye may know that the Sonne of
man hath authoritie in earth to forgiue sinnes,
(then said hee to the sicke of the palsie,) Arise,
take vp thy bed, and goe to thine house.
7 And he arose, and departed to his owne
house.
8 So when the multitude saw it, they marueiled, & glorified God, which had giuen such
authoritie to men.

1 Sinnes are the causes of our afflictions, and Christ onely forgiueth them if we beleeue.
a Into Capernaum, for as Theoph. saith, Bethleem brought him foorth, Nazareth brought him vp, and Capernaum was his dwelling place.
*Marke 2.3. luke 5.18.
b Knowing by a manifest signe.
c To blaspheme, signifieth amongst the Diuines, to speake wickedly: and amongst the more eloquent Grecians, to slander.

9 ¶ *[2] And as Iesus passed foorth from
thence, hee saw a man sitting at the [d] custome,
named Matthew, and said to him, Follow me.
And he arose, and followed him.
10 And it came to passe, as Iesus sate at
meate in *his* house, behold, many Publicanes
and [e] sinners, that came *thither*, sate downe at
the table with Iesus and his disciples.
11 And when the Pharises sawe that, they
said to his disciples, Why eateth your master
with Publicanes and sinners?
12 Now when Iesus heard it, hee said vnto
them, The whole neede not a Physician, but
they that are sicke.
13 But goe yee and learne what this is, *I
will haue mercie, and not sacrifice: for I am
not come to call the righteous, but the * sinners to repentance.
14 ¶ *[3] Then came the disciples of Iohn
to him, saying, Why doe wee and the Pharises
fast oft, and thy disciples fast not?
15 And Iesus said vnto them, Can the [f] children of the mariage chamber mourne as long
as the bridegrome is with them? But the dayes
will come, when the bridegrome shalbe taken
from them, and then shall they fast.
16 Moreouer no man pieceth an olde garment with a piece of [g] new cloth: for that that
should fill it vp, taketh away from the garment,
and the breach is worse.
17 Neither doe they put new wine into old
vessels: for then the vessels would break, and
the wine would be spilt, and the vessels should
perish: but they put new wine into new vessels, and *so* are both preserued.

*Marke 2.14. luke 5.17.
2 Christ calleth the humble sinners vnto him, but he contemneth the proud hypocrites.
d At the Customers table, where it was receiued.
e The Customers fellowes which were placed by the Romanes, after that Iudea was brought into the forme of a prouince, to gather the customes, and therefore of the rest of the Iewes they were called sinners, that is to say, very vile men.
*Hose. 6.6. chap. 12.7.
*1. Tim. 1.15.
*Marke 2.18. luke 5.33.
3 Against naughtie emulation in matters indifferent.
f An Hebrewe kind of speech, for they that are admitted into the mariage chamber, are as the neerest about the bridegrome.
g Raw, which was neuer put to the fuller.

18 ¶ *[4] While hee thus spake vnto them,
behold, there came a certaine ruler, and worshipped him, saying, My daughter is now deceased, but come and lay thine hand on her,
and shee shall liue.
19 And Iesus arose, and followed him with
his disciples.
20 (And behold, a woman which was diseased with an issue of blood twelue yeeres,
came behinde him, and touched the hemme of
his garment.
21 For shee said in her selfe, If I may touch
but his garment onely, I shalbe whole.
22 Then Iesus turned him about, and seeing her, did say, Daughter, be of good comfort:
thy faith hath made thee whole. And the woman was made whole at that same moment.)
23 [5] Now when Iesus came into the rulers
house, and saw the [h] minstrels and the multitude making noise,
24 He said vnto them, Get you hence: for
the maide is not dead, but sleepeth. And they
laughed him to scorne.
25 And when the multitude were put
foorth, he went in and tooke her by the hand,
and the maid arose.
26 And this bruite went throughout all
that land.

*Marke 5.22. luke 8.41.
4 There is no euill so olde, and incurable, which Christ cannot heale by and by if he be touched with true faith but lightly as it were with the hand.
5 Euen death it selfe giueth place to the power of Christ.
h It appeareth that they vsed minstrels at their mournings.

27 [6] And

6 By healing these two blind Christ sheweth that he is the light of the world.

27 [6]And as Iesus departed thence, two blind
men followed him, crying, and saying, O sonne
of Dauid, haue mercie vpon vs.
28 And when he was come into the house,
the blind came to him, & Iesus said vnto them,
Beleeue yee that I am able to doe this? And
they said vnto him, Yea, Lord.
29 Then touched he their eyes, saying, According to your faith be it vnto you.
30 And their eyes were opened, and Iesus
gaue them great charge, saying, See that no
man know it.
31 But when they were departed, they
spread abroad his fame throughout all the land.

* *Luke* 11.14.
7 An example of that power, that Christ hath ouer the deuill.

32 ¶ * [7] And as they went out, behold, they
brought to him a dumme man possessed with a
deuill.
33 And when the deuill was cast out, the
dumme spake: then the multitude marueiled,
saying, The like was neuer seene in Israel.

* *Chap.* 12.24. *marke* 3.22. *luke* 11.15.
* *Marke* 6.6. *luke* 13.22.

34 But the Pharises said, * Hee casteth out
deuils, through the prince of deuils.
35 ¶ And * Iesus went about all cities and
townes, teaching in their Synagogues, and
preaching the Gospel of the kingdome, and
healing euery sicknesse and euery disease among
the people.

8 Although the ordinary pastors cease, yet Christ hath not cast off the care of his Church.
* *Marke* 6.34.
* *Luke* 10.2. *iohn* 4.35,36.

36 [8]But * when he saw the multitude, hee
had compassion vpon them, because they were
dispersed, and scattered abroad, as sheepe hauing no shepheard.
37 Then said hee to his disciples, * Surely
the haruest *is* great, but the labourers *are* few.

i *Word for word, cast them out: for men are very slow in so holy a worke.*

38 Wherefore pray the Lord of the haruest,
that hee would [i] send foorth labourers into his
haruest.

CHAP. X.

1 *The gift of healing giuen to the Apostles.* 5 *They are sent to preach the Gospel.* 13 *Peace.* 14 *Shaking off the dust.* 16 *Affliction.* 22 *Continuance vnto the ende.* 23 *Flying from persecution.* 28 *Feare.* 29 *Two sparowes.* 30 *Haires of our head.* 32 *To acknowledge Christ.* 34 *Peace and the sword.* 35 *Variance.* 37 *Loue of parents.* 38 *The crosse.* 39 *To lose the life.* 40 *To receiue a preacher.*

1 The Apostles are sent to preach the Gospel in Israel.
* *Mark.* 3.13,14,15. *luke* 9.1,2.

AND [1] * he called his twelue disciples vnto
him, and gaue them power against vncleane spirits, to cast them out, and to heale e-
uery sicknesse, and euery disease.
2 Now the names of the twelue Apostles
are these. The [a] first *is* Simon, called Peter, and
Andrew his brother: Iames *the sonne* of Zebedeus, and Iohn his brother.

a *Theophylact saith that Peter and Andrew are called the first, because they were first called.*

3 Philip and Bartlemew: Thomas, and
Matthew that Publicane: Iames *the sonne* of
Alpheus, and Lebbeus whose surname was
Thaddeus.

b *A man of Keriot. Now Kerioth was in the tribe of Iudah, Iosh.* 15.25.

4 Simon the Cananite, and Iudas [b] Iscariot, who also betrayed him.
5 These twelue did Iesus send foorth, and
commanded them, saying, Go not into the way
of the Gentiles, and into the cities of the Samaritanes enter yee not.

* *Luke* 10.9,11.

6 But goe rather * to the lost sheepe of the
house of Israel.

* *Act.* 13.46.
2 The summe of the Gospel, or preaching of the Apostles.
3 Miracles are dependances of the word.
* *Marke* 6.8,9. *luk.* 9.3.& 22.35
4 The ministers of the word must cast away all cares that might hinder them the least wise that might be.
c *For this iourney, to wit, both that nothing might hinder them, and also that they might feele some taste of Gods prouidence: for at their returne backe, the Lord asketh of them, whether they lacked any thing by the way, Luke* 22.35.
* 1.*Tim.* 5.15.
d *God will prouide you meate.*

7 * [2] And as yee goe, preach, saying, The
kingdome of heauen is at hand.
8 [3] Heale the sicke, clense the leapers: raise
vp the dead: cast out the deuils. Freely he haue
receiued, freely giue.
9 * [4] Possesse [c] not gold nor siluer, nor money in your girdles,
10 Nor a scrippe, for the iourney, neither
two coates, neither shoes, nor a staffe: * for the
workman is worthy of his [d] meate.
11 [5] And into * whatsoeuer citie or towne
ye shall come, enquire who is worthy in it, and
there abide till yee goe thence.
12 And when yee come in into an house, salute the same.
13 And if the house bee worthy, let your
[e] peace come vpon it: but if it bee not worthy,
let your peace returne to you.
14 * And whosoeuer shall not receiue you,
nor heare your words, when yee depart out of
that house, or that citie, * shake off the dust of
your feete.

5 Happie are they that receiue the preaching of the Gospel: and vnhappie are they that refuse it.
* *Luke* 10.8.
e *It is a maner of speach taken from the Hebrewes, whereby they meant all kind of happinesse.*
* *Marke* 6.11. *luke* 9.5.
* *Actes* 13.51.
* *Luke* 10.3.
6 Christ sheweth how the ministers must behaue themselues vnder the crosse.
f *You shall be in great danger.*
g *You shall not so much as reuenge an iniurie: and by the mixing of these beasts natures together, he will not haue our wisedome to be malicious, nor our simplicitie mad, but a certaine forme of good nature as exquisitely framed of both them, as may be.*
h *For in the cause of religion men are wolues one to another.*

15 Truely I say vnto you, it shall bee easier
for them of the land of Sodom and Gomorrah
in the day of iudgement, then for that citie.
16 ¶ * [6] Behold, I send you as [f] sheepe in the
mids of the wolues: be yee therfore wise as serpents, and [g] innocent as doues.
17 But beware of [h] men, for they will deliuer you vp to the Councils, and will scourge
you in their Synagogues.
18 And yee shall be brought to the gouernours and Kings for my sake, in witnesse to
them, and to the Gentiles.
19 * But when they deliuer you vp, take no
thought how or what ye shall speake: for it shal
be giuen you in that houre, what yee shall say.
20 For it is not yee that speake, but the spirit of your father which speaketh in you.
21 And the * brother shall betray the brother to death, and the father the sonne, and the
children shall rise against *their* parents, and shal
cause them to die.
22 And yee shall be hated of all men for my
Name: * but he that endureth to the end, hee
shall be saued.
23 And when they persecute you in this citie, flee into another: for verily I say vnto you,
yee shall not [i] goe ouer *all* the cities of Israel, till
the sonne of man be come.
24 * The disciple is not aboue his master,
nor the seruant aboue his Lord.
25 It is enough for the disciple to bee as his
master *is*, and the seruant as his Lord. * If they
haue called the master of the house [k] Beel-ze-
bub, how much more them of his houshold?
26 [l]Feare them not therefore: * for there is
nothing couered, that shal not be disclosed, nor
hid, that shall not be knowen.
27 What I tell you in darknesse, that speake

* *Marke* 13.11. *luke* 12.11.
* *Luke* 21.16.
* *Marke* 13.13.
i *Bring to an ende, that is, you shall not haue gone through all the cities of Israel, and preached in them.*
* *Luke* 6.40. *iohn* 13.16. *and* 15.20.
* *Chap.* 12.24.
k *It was the Idoll of the Acaronites, which wee call the god of flies.* l *Trueth shall not alwayes bee hid.*
* *Marke* 4.22. *luke* 8.17. *and* 12.2.

yee in light: and what ye heare in the eare, that preach yee on the [m] houses.

m Openly, and in the highest places. For the tops of their houses were so made, that they might walke vpon them, Act.10.9.

28 And [n] feare yee not them which kill the body, but are not able to kill the soule: but rather feare him, which is able to destroy both soule and body in hell.

n Though tyrants be neuer so raging and cruell, yet we may not feare them.

29 Are not two sparrowes sold for a [o] farthing, and one of them shall not fall on the ground without your father?

o The fourth part of an ounce.

30 * Yea, and all the haires of your head are numbred.

** 1.Sam. 14 45. 2.sam.14.11. actes 27 34.*

31 Feare ye not therefore, yee are of more value then many sparrowes.

32 [7] * Whosoeuer therefore shall confesse me before men, him will I confesse also before my father which is in heauen.

7 The necessitie and reward of open confessing Christ.

** Marke 8.38. luke 6.26. & 11. 8 2.tim 2.12.*

33 But whosoeuer shall denie mee before men, him will I also denie before my Father which is in heauen.

34 * [8] Thinke not that I am come to send peace into the earth: I came not to send peace, but the sword.

** Luke 12.51.*

8 Ciuill dissentions follow the preaching of the Gospel.

35 For I am come to set a man at variance against his father, and the daughter against her mother, and the daughter in law against her mother in law.

** Micah.7.6.*

36 * And a mans enemies *shalbe* they of his owne houshold.

** Luke 14 26.*

37 * [9] Hee that loueth father or mother more then me, is not worthy of me. And hee that loueth sonne or daughter more then me, is not worthy of me.

9 Nothing without exception is to be preferred before our duetie to God.

38 * And he that taketh not his crosse, and followeth after me, is not worthy of me.

** Chap.16.24. marke 8 34. luke 9.23. and 14 27.*

39 * Hee that will [p] find his life, shall lose it: and hee that loseth his life for my sake, shall find it.

** Iohn 12.25.*

p They are said to find their life, which deliuer it out of danger: and this is spoken after the opinion of the people, which thinke them cleane lost that die, because they thinke not of the life to come.

40 [10] He that receiueth you, receiueth me: and hee that receiueth me, receiueth him that hath sent me.

10 God is both Authour and reuenger of his holy Ministerie.

** Luke 10.16. iohn 13 20*

41 * [11] He that receiueth a Prophet in [q] the name of a Prophet, shall receiue a Prophets reward: and he that receiueth a righteous man, in the name of a righteous man, shall receiue the reward of a righteous man.

11 We shal lose nothing that we bestow vpon Christ.

q As a Prophet.

42 * And whosoeuer shall giue vnto one of these [r] little ones to drinke a cup of cold water onely, in the name of a disciple, verily I say vnto you, he shall not lose his reward.

** Marke 9.41.*

r Which in the sight of the world are vile and abiect

CHAP. XI.

2 Iohn sendeth his disciples to Christ. 7 Christs testimonie of Iohn. 13 The Law and the Prophets. 18 Christ and Iohn. 21 Chorazin, Bethsaida. 25 The Gospel reueiled to children. 28 They that are wearie and laden.

AND [1] it came to passe that when Iesus had made an end of [a] commanding his twelue disciples, hee departed thence to teach and to preach in [b] their cities.

1 Christ sheweth by his works that he is the promised Messias

a Of instructing the with precepts.

b The Disciples cities, that is to say, in Galile, where many of them were borne, act 2 7.

2 ¶ * And when Iohn heard in the prison the workes of Christ, hee sent two of his disciples, and said vnto him,

** Luke 7.18.*

3 Art thou hee that should come, or shall we looke for another?

4 And Iesus answering, said vnto them, Goe, and shew Iohn, what things yee heare, and see.

5 The blind receiue sight, and the halte doe walke: the lepers are clensed, and the deafe heare, the dead are raised vp, * and the poore receiue the Gospel.

** Esai 61.1. luke 4.18.*

6 And blessed is he that shall not be offended in me.

7 [2] And as they departed, Iesus began to speake vnto the multitude, of Iohn, What went yee out into the wildernesse to see? a reed shaken with the wind?

2 What agreement and what difference is betwixt the ministerie of the Prophets, the preaching of Iohn, and the ful light of the Gospel, which Christ hath brought.

8 But what went yee out to see? A man clothed in soft raiment? Behold, they that weare soft clothing, are in Kings houses.

9 But what went yee out to see? A Prophet? Yea, I say vnto you, and more then a Prophet.

10 For this is he of whom it is written, * Behold, I send my messenger before thy face, which shall prepare thy way before thee.

** Malach.3.1. luke 7.28.*

11 Verily, I say vnto you, among them which are begotten of women, arose there not a greater then Iohn Baptist: notwithstanding, he that is the least in the [c] kingdome of heauen, is greater then he.

c In the new state of the Church where the true glorie of God shineth: the persons are not compared together, but the kinds of doctrines, the preaching of Iohn with the Law and the Prophets: and againe, the most cleare preaching of the Gospel with Iohns.

12 And from * the time of Iohn Baptist hitherto, the kingdome of heauen suffereth violence, and the violent take it by force.

** Luke 16.16.*

13 For all the Prophets and the Law [d] prophecied vnto Iohn.

d They prophecied of things to come, which are now present, and clearely and plainly seene.

14 And if yee will receiue it, this is * that Elias, which was to come.

** Mal.4.5.*

15 ¶ Hee that hath eares to heare, let him heare.

16 * [3] But whereunto shall I liken this generation? [e] It is like vnto little children which sit in the markets, and call vnto their fellowes,

** Luke 7.31.*

3 There are none more stout and stubborne enemies of the Gospel, then they to whom it ought to be most acceptable.

e He blameth the forwardnesse of this age, by a prouerbe, in that they could be mooued neither with rough, nor gentle dealing.

17 And say, We haue piped vnto you, and yee haue not daunced, we haue mourned vnto you, and yee haue not lamented.

18 For Iohn came neither eating nor drinking, and they say, He hath a deuill.

19 The sonne of man came eating and drinking, and they say, Behold a glutton and a drinker of wine, a friend vnto Publicanes and sinners: [4] but [f] wisedome is iustified of her children.

4 That which the most part refuse, the elect and chosen embrace.

f Wise men doe acknowledge the wisedome of the Gospel, when they receiue it.

20 ¶ [5] * Then began he to vpbraide the cities, wherein most of his great workes were done, because they repented not.

5 The proude reiect the Gospel offered vnto them, to their great hurt and smart, which turneth to the saluation of the simple.

** Luke 10.13.*

21 Woe *be* to thee, Chorazin: Woe *be* to thee Bethsaida: for if the great workes which were done in you, had bene done in Tyrus and Sidon, they had repented long agone in sackecloth and ashes.

22 But I say to you, It shall bee easier for Tyrus and Sidon at the day of iudgement, then for you.

23 And thou, Capernaum, which art lifted vp vnto heauen, shalt be brought downe to hell:

hell: for if the great workes, which haue beene done in thee, had beene done among them of Sodom, they had remained to this day.

24 But I say vnto you, that it shalbe easier for them of the land of Sodom in the day of iudgement, then for thee.

25 * At that time Iesus answered, and said, I giue thee thankes, O Father, Lord of heauen and earth, because thou hast hid these things from the wise and men of vnderstanding, and hast [g] opened them vnto babes.

26 It is [h] so, O Father, because thy [i] good pleasure was such.

27 * [6] All things are giuen vnto mee of my father: and * no man knoweth the sonne, but the father: neither knoweth any man the Father, but the Sonne, and he to whom the sonne will reueile *him*.

28 Come vnto me, all yee that are wearie and laden, and I will ease you.

29 Take my yoke on you, and learne of me that I am meeke and lowly in heart: and yee shall find * rest vnto your soules.

30 * For my yoke is [k] easie, and my burden light.

* Luke 10.21.
g Through the ministerie of Christ, who onely sheweth the trueth of all things perteining to God.
h This word sheweth that he contenteth himselfe in his Fathers counsell.
i Gods will is the onely rule of righteousnesse.
* Iohn 3.35.
6 There is no true knowledge of God, nor quietnesse of minde, but onely in Christ alone.
* Iohn 6.46.
* Iere. 6.16.
* 1. Iohn 5 3.
k May easily be borne. For his commandements are not grieuous, for all that is borne of God ouercommeth the world, 1. Iohn 5 4.

CHAP. XII.

1 The disciples plucke the eares of corne. 6 Mercie, sacrifice. 10 The withered hand is healed. 12 Wee must doe good on the Sabbath. 22 The possessed is holpen. 25 A kingdome diuided. 31 Sinne, blasphemie. 33 The good or euill tree. 34 Vipers. 41 The Nineuites. 42 The Queene of Saba. 48 The true mother and brethren of Christ.

At [1] * that time Iesus went on a Sabbath day through the corne, and his disciples were an hungred, and began to plucke the eares of corne, and to eate.

2 And when the Pharises saw it, they said vnto him, Behold, thy disciples doe that * which is not lawfull to doe vpon the Sabbath.

3 But hee said vnto them, * Haue yee not read what Dauid did when he was an hungred, and they that were with him?

4 How hee entred into the house of God, and did eate the [a] shew-bread, which was not lawfull for him to eat, neither for them which were with him, but onely for the * Priests?

5 Or haue yee not read in the Law, how that on the Sabbath dayes the Priests in the Temple * [b] breake the Sabbath, and are blamelesse?

6 But I say vnto you, that here is one greater then the Temple.

7 Wherefore if yee knew what this is, * I will haue mercie, and not sacrifice, yee would not haue condemned the innocents.

8 For the sonne of man is Lord, *euen* of the Sabbath.

9 * [2] And he departed thence, and went into their Synagogue:

10 And behold, there was a man which had *his* hand dried vp. And they asked him, saying, Is it lawfull to heale vpon a Sabbath day? that they might accuse him.

1 Of the true sanctifying of the Sabbath, and the abrogating of it.
* Marke 2.23. luke 6.1.
* Deut. 23 25.
* 1. Sam. 21.6.
a The Hebrewes call it bread of faces, because it stood before the Lord all the weeke vpon the golden table appointed to that seruice, Leuit. 24.6.
* Exod. 29.33. leui 8.31. & 24 9
* Num. 28 9.
b When the Priests doe Gods seruice vpon the Sabbath day, yet they breake not the Law: much lesse doth the Lord of the Sabbath breake the Sabbath.
* Hose 6.7. chap 9.13.
* Marke 3.1. luke 6.6.
2 The ceremonies of the Law are not against the loue of our neighbour.

11 And he said vnto them, What man shall there be among you, that hath a sheepe, and if it fall on a Sabbath day into a pit, doth not take it and lift it out?

12 How much more then is a man better then a sheepe? therefore, it is lawfull to doe well on the Sabbath day.

13 Then said he to the man, Stretch foorth thine hand. And he stretched it foorth, and it was made whole as the other.

14 [3] Then the Pharises went out and consulted against him, how they might destroy him.

15 But when Iesus knew it, hee departed thence, and great multitudes followed him, and he healed them all,

16 And charged them in threatning wise, that they should not make him knowen,

17 That it might bee fulfilled, which was spoken by Esaias the Prophet, saying,

18 * Behold my seruant whom I haue chosen, my beloued in whom my soule delighteth: I will put my Spirit on him, and hee shall shew [c] iudgement to the Gentiles.

19 He shall not striue, nor crie, neither shal any man heare his voice in the streetes.

20 A bruised reede shall he not breake, and smoking flaxe shal he not quench, til he [d] bring forth iudgement vnto victorie.

21 And in his Name shall the Gentiles trust.

22 ¶ * [4] Then was brought to him one possessed with a deuill, *both* blind, and dumme, and he healed him, so that hee *which was* blind and dumme, both spake and saw.

23 And all the people were amased and said, Is not this that sonne of Dauid?

24 But when the Pharises heard it, they said, * This man casteth the deuils no otherwise out, but through Beelzebub the prince of deuils.

25 [5] But Iesus knewe their thoughtes, and said to them, Euery kingdome diuided against it selfe, is brought to nought: and euery citie or house, diuided against it selfe, shall not stand.

26 So if Satan cast out Satan, hee is diuided against himselfe: how shall then his kingdome endure?

27 Also if I through Beelzebub cast out deuils, by whom doe your children cast them out? Therefore they shall be your iudges.

28 But if I cast out deuils by the Spirite of God, then is the kingdome of God come vnto you.

29 Else how can a man enter into a strong mans house and spoile his goods, except he first bind the strong man, and then spoile his house.

30 Hee that is not with me, is against mee: and he that gathereth not with me, scattereth.

31 * Wherefore I say vnto you, euery sinne and blasphemie shalbe forgiuen vnto men: but the blasphemie *against* the holy Ghost shal not be forgiuen vnto men.

3 How farre and in what respect we may giue place to the vnbridled rage of the wicked.
* Esai. 42.1.
c By iudgement is meant a setled state, because Christ was to publish true religion among the Gentiles, and to cast out superstition, which thing wheresoeuer it is done, the Lord is said to reigne and iudge there, that is to say, to gouerne and rule matters.
d He shall pronounce sentence and iudgement, maugre the world and Satan, and shew himselfe conquerour ouer all his enemies.
* Luke 11.14.
4 A trueth, be it neuer so manifest, is subiect to the slaunder of the wicked: yet notwithstanding it ought to be auouched stoutly.
* Chap. 9.34. marke 3.22. luke 11.15.
5 The kingdome of Christ and the kingdome of the deuill cannot consist together.
* Marke 3.28, 29. luke 12.10 1. iohn. 5. 16

32 And whosoeuer shall speake a word a-
gainst the Sonne of man, it shall bee forgiuen
him: [6]but whosoeuer shall speake against the
holy Ghost, it shall not bee forgiuen him, neither in this world, nor in the world to come.

6 Of blaspheme against the holy Ghost.

33 Either make the tree good, and his fruit
good: or else make the tree euill, and his fruit
euill: for the tree is knowen by the fruit.
34 [7]O generations of vipers, how can you
speake good things, when yee are euill? For
of the * abundance of the heart the mouth
speaketh.

7 Hypocrites at the length bewray themselues euen by their owne mouth.
* *Luke 6.45.*

35 A good man out of the good treasure of
his heart bringeth forth good things: and an e-
uill man out of an euill treasure bringeth foorth
euill things.
36 But I say vnto you, that of euery [e] idle
word that men shall speake, they shall giue accompt thereof at the day of Iudgement.

e Vaine and vnprofitable trifles, which the most part of men spend their liues in.

37 For by thy words thou shalt bee iustified, and by thy words thou shalt bee condemned.
38 ¶ [8] * Then answered certaine of the
Scribes and of the Pharises, saying, Master, we
would see a signe of thee.
39 But hee answered and said to them, An
euil and [f]adulterous generation seeketh a signe,
but no signe shall bee giuen vnto it, saue that
signe of the Prophet Ionas.
40 *For as Ionas was three dayes and three
nights in the whales belly: so shall the Sonne
of man bee three dayes and three nights in the
heart of the earth.

8 Against froward desires of miracles.
* *Chap.16.1. luke 11.29. 1.cor.1.22.*
f Bastard, which fell from Abrahams faith, or forsooke the true worship of God.
* *Ionas 1.17.*

41 [9]The men of Nineue shall rise in iudgement with this generation, and condemne it:
for they * repented at the preaching of Ionas:
and behold, a greater then Ionas *is* here.
42 * The Queene of the [g] South shall rise
in iudgement with this generation, and shall
condemne it: for shee came from the [h] vtmost
parts of the earth to heare the wisedome of Salomon: and behold, a greater then Salomon
is heere.
43 ¶ * Now when the vncleane spirit is
gone out of a man, he walketh throughout drie
places, seeketh rest, and findeth none.
44 Then hee saith, I will returne into mine
house from whence I came: and when hee is
come, hee findeth it emptie, swept & garnished
45 Then hee goeth, and taketh vnto him seuen other spirits worse then himselfe, and they
enter in, and dwell there: * and the end of that
man is worse then the beginning, Euen so shall
it be with this wicked generation.

9 Christ teacheth by the sorrowfull example of the Iewes, that there are none more miserable then they which put out the light of the Gospel, which was kindled in them.
* *Ionas 3.5.*
* *1.King.10.1. 2.chro.9.1.*
g He meaneth the Queene of Saba: whose countrey is South in respect of the land of Israel, 1.King.10.
h For Saba is situate in the vtmost coast of happie Arabia vpon the mouth of the Arabian sea.
* *Luke 11.24.*
* *Heb.6.4,5. and 10.26. 2.pet.2.20.*

46 ¶ [10] *While he yet spake to the multitude, behold, his mother, and his brethren stood
without, desiring to speake with him.
47 Then one said vnto him, Behold, thy
mother and thy brethren stand without, desiring to speake with thee.
48 But hee answered, and said to him that
told him, Who is my mother? and who are
my brethren?

10 Christ teacheth by his owne example, how that all things ought to be set apart, in respect of Gods glorie.
* *Marke 3.31. luke 8.20.*

49 [11] And hee stretched foorth his hand toward his disciples, and said, Behold my mother
and my brethren.
50 For whosoeuer shall doe my Fathers wil
which is in heauen, the same is my brother and
sister and mother.

11 None are more neere vnto vs, then they that are of the houshold of faith.

CHAP. XIII.

1 The parable of the sower. 11 and 34 Why Christ spake in parables. 18 The exposition of the Parable. 24 The parable of the tares. 31 Of the mustard seed. 33 Of the leauen. 44 Of the hidden treasure. 45 Of the Pearle. 47 Of the draw net cast into the sea. 53 Christ is not receiued of his countrey men the Nazarites.

THe * same day went Iesus out of the
house, and sate by the sea side.
2 [1]And great multitudes resorted vnto
him, so that hee went into a shippe, and sate
downe: and the whole multitude stood on
the shore.
3 Then hee spake many things to them in
parables, saying, Behold, a sower went foorth
to sowe.
4 And as hee sowed, some fell by the way
side, and the foules came & deuoured them vp.
5 And some fel vpon stony ground, where
they had not much earth, and anon they sprung
vp, because they had no depth of earth.

* *Marke 4.1. luke 8.4,5.*
1 Christ sheweth in putting forth this parable of the sower, that the seede of life which is sowen in the world commeth not on so well in one as in another, and the reason is for that men for the most part, either doe not receiue it, or suffer it not to ripen.

6 And when the Sunne was vp, they were
parched, and for lacke of rooting withered
away.
7 And some fell among thornes, and the
thornes sprung vp, and choked them.
8 Some againe fell in good ground, and
brought foorth fruit, one *corne* an hundreth
fold, some sixtie fold, and another thirtie fold.
9 Hee that hath eares to heare, let him
heare.
10 ¶Then the disciples came, and said to
him, Why speakest thou to them in parables?
11 [2]And hee answered, and said vnto them,
Because it is giuen vnto you to know the secrets of the kingdome of heauen, but to them it
is not giuen.
12 *For whosoeuer hath, to him shalbe giuen, and he shall haue abundance: but whosoeuer hath not, for him shall bee taken away, e-
uen that he hath.

2 The gift of vnderstanding and of faith is proper to the elect, and all the rest are blinded through the iust iudgement of God.
* *Chap.25.29.*

13 Therefore speake I to them in parables,
because they seeing, doe not see: and hearing,
they heare not, neither vnderstand.
14 So in them is fulfilled the prophecie of
Esaias, which *prophecie* saith, * By hearing, yee
shall heare, and shall not vnderstand, and seeing
yee shall see, and shall not perceiue.
15 For this peoples heart is waxed fat, and
their eares are dull of hearing, and with their
eyes they haue winked, lest they should see
with their eyes, and heare with their eares, and
should vnderstand with their hearts, and should
returne, that I might heale them.
16 [3]But blessed *are* your eyes, for they see:
and your eares, for they heare.
17 *For verily I say vnto you, that many
Prophets, and righteous men haue desired to

* *Esai.6.9. marke 4.12 luke 8.10. iohn 12.40. actes 28.26. rom.11.8.*
3 The condition of the Church vnder and since Christ, is better then it was in the time of the fathers vnder the Law.
* *Luke 10.24.*

see

see those things which yee see, and haue not
seene *them*, and to heare those things, which
yee heare, and haue not heard *them*.

* *Marke* 10.24. *luke* 8.11.

18 ¶ * Heare yee therefore the parable of
the sower.
19 Whensoeuer any man heareth the
word of that kingdome, and vnderstandeth
it not, that euill one commeth, and catcheth
away that which was sowen in his [a] heart: and
this is hee which hath receiued the seede by the
way side.
20 And he that receiued seede in the stonie
ground, is he which heareth the word, and incontinently with ioy receiueth it,
21 Yet hath hee no roote in himselfe, and
dureth but a season: for assoone as tribulation
or persecution commeth because of the word,
by and by he is offended.
22 And hee that receiued the seede among
thornes, is hee that heareth the word: but
the care of this world, and the deceitfulnesse
of riches choke the word, and hee is made vnfruitfull.
23 But he that receiued the seed in the good
ground, is hee that heareth the word, and vnderstandeth it, which also beareth fruite and
bringeth foorth, some an hundreth fold, some
sixtie fold, and some thirtie fold.

a Though there be mention made of the heart, yet this sowing is referred to hearing without understanding. For whether the seede be receiued in the heart or no, yet he that soweth, soweth to the heart

24 ¶ [4] Another parable put hee foorth vnto them, saying, The kingdome of heauen
is like vnto a man which sowed good seede in
his field.
25 But while men slept, there came his e-
nemy, and sowed tares among the wheate, and
went his way.
26 And when the blade was sprung vp,
and brought foorth fruit, then appeared the
tares also.
27 Then came the seruants of the housholder,
der, and said vnto him, Master, sowedst not
thou good seed in thy field? from whence then
hath it tares?
28 And hee said to them, Some enuious
man hath done this. Then the seruants said vnto him, Wilt thou then that we goe and gather
them vp?
29 But hee said, Nay, least while yee goe a-
bout to gather the tares, ye plucke vp also with
them the wheate.
30 Let both grow together vntill the haruest, and in time of haruest I will say to the reapers, Gather yee first the tares, and bind them
in sheaues to burne them: but gather the wheat
into my barne.

4 Christ sheweth in an other parable of the euill seede mixt with the good, that the Church shall neuer be free and quit from offences, both in doctrine and maners, vntill the day appointed for the restoring of all things do come, and therefore the faithfull haue to arme themselues with patience and constancie.

* *Marke* 4.30. *luke* 13.19.

31 ¶ * [5] Another parable he put forth vnto
them, saying, The kingdome of heauen is like
vnto a graine of mustard seed, which a man taketh and soweth in his field:
32 Which in deede is the least of all seedes:
but when it is growen, it is the greatest
among herbes, and it is a tree, so that the
birds of heauen come and build in the branches thereof.

5 God beginneth his kingdome with very small beginnings to the end that by the growing on of it beside the expectation and hope of all men, his mightie power and working may be the more set forth.

33 ¶ * Another parable spake hee to them,
The kingdome of heauen is like vnto leauen,
which a woman taketh and hideth in three
peckes of meale till all be leauened.

* *Luke* 13.21.

34 ¶ * All these things spake Iesus vnto the
multitude in parables, and without parables
spake he not to them,
35 That it might bee fulfilled, which was
spoken by the Prophet, saying, * I wil open my
mouth in parables, and will vtter the things
which haue beene kept secret from the foundation of the world.

* *Mar.* 4.33, 34.

* *Psal.* 78.2.

36 Then sent Iesus the multitude away, and
went into the house. And his disciples came
vnto him, saying, Declare vnto vs the parable
of the tares of that field.
37 [6] Then answered hee, and said to them,
Hee that soweth the good seede, is the Sonne
of man.
38 And the field is the world, and the good
seed are the children of the kingdome, and the
tares are the children of that wicked one.
39 And the enemy that soweth them, is the
deuil, * and the haruest is the end of the world,
and the reapers be the Angels.
40 As then the tares are gathered and
burned in the fire, so shall it bee in the ende of
this world.
41 The Sonne of man shall send foorth his
Angels, and they shall gather out of his kingdome all things that offend, and them which
doe iniquitie,
42 And shal cast them into a fornace of fire.
There shalbe wailing and gnashing of teeth.
43 * Then shall the iust men shine as the
sunne in the kingdome of their Father. He that
hath eares to heare, let him heare.

6 He expoundeth the former parable of the good and euill seede.

* *Ioel* 4.13. *reuel.* 13.14.

* *Dan.* 12.3.

44 ¶ [7] Againe, the kingdome of heauen is
like vnto a treasure hid in the field, which when
a man hath found, hee hideth it, and for ioy
thereof departeth, and selleth all that hee hath,
and buyeth that field.
45 ¶ Againe, the kingdome of heauen is
like to a merchant ma[illegible], that seeketh good
pearles,
46 Who hauing foun[illegible]arle of great price,
went and sold all that he h[illegible]and bought it.

7 Fewe men vnderstand how great the riches of the kingdome of heauen are, and no man can bee partaker of them, but he that redeemeth them with the losse of of all his goods.

47 ¶ [8] Againe, the kingdome of heauen is
like vnto a draw net cast into the sea, that gathereth of all kinds of *things*.
48 Which, when it is full, men drawe to
land, and sit and gather the good into vessels,
and cast the bad away.
49 So shall it bee at the end of the world.
The Angels shall goe foorth, and seuer the bad
from among the iust,
50 And shal cast them into a fornace of fire:
there shalbe wailing, and gnashing of teeth.

8 There are many in ẏ Church which notwithstanding are not of the Church, and therefore at length shall be cast out: but the full and perfect clensing of them is deferred to the last day.

51 ¶ [9] Iesus said vnto them, Vnderstand
yee all these things? They said vnto him, Yea,
Lord.
52 Then said hee vnto them, Therefore e-
uery Scribe which is taught vnto the king-

9 They ought to be diligent, which haue not onely to be wise for themselues, but to dispence the wisedome of God to other.

dome of heauen, is like vnto an housholder,
which bringeth forth out of his treasure things
both new and old.
53 ¶And it came to passe, that when Iesus
had ended these parables, he departed thence,

* *Marke* 6.1. *luke* 4.16.
10 Men doe not onely sinne of ignorance, but also wittingly and willingly lay stumbling blockes in their owne wayes, that when God calleth them, they may not obey, and so most plainely destroy, and cast away themselues.
* *Iohn* 6.42.
* *Marke* 6.4. *luke* 4.24. *iohn* 4.44.

54 * [10] And came into his owne countrey,
and tauth them in their Synagogue, so that
they were astonied, and said, Whence commeth this wisedome and great workes vnto
this man?
55 Is not this the carpenters sonne? Is not
his mother called Mary, * and his brethren
Iames and Ioses, and Simon and Iudas?
56 And are not his sisters all with vs?
Whence then hath he all these things?
57 And they were offended with him. Then
Iesus said to them, * A Prophet is not without
honour, saue in his owne countrey, and in his
owne house.
58 And he did not many great works there
for their vnbeliefes sake.

CHAP. XIIII.

1 Herods iudgement of Christ. 3 Wherefore Iohn was bound, 10 And beheaded. 13 Iesus departeth. 18 Of the fiue loaues, &c. 23 Christ prayeth. 24 The Apostles tossed with the waues. 27 Faith. 30 Peter in ieopardie. 36 The hemme of Christes garment.

* *Marke* 6.14. *luke* 9.7.
1 Here is in Iohn, an example of an inuincible courage, which all faithfull ministers of Gods word ought to follow: in Herod, an example of tyrannous vanitie, pride, and crueltie, and to bee short, of a courtly conscience, and of their miserable slauerie, which haue once giuen themselues ouer to pleasures: in Herodias and her daughter, an example of whorelike wantonnes, and womanly crueltie.
a *By workes, he meaneth that force and power, whereby workes are wrought, and not the workes, as is seene oft before.*
* *Marke* 6.17. *luke* 3.12.
* *Leuit.* 18.16. *and* 20.21.
* *Chap.* 21.26.
b *There were three Herodes: the first of them was Antipaters sonne, who is also called Ascalonius, in whose reigne Christ was borne, and he it was that caused the children to be slaine. The second was called Antipas, Magnus his sonne, whose mothers name was Malthaca or Martaca, and this was called Tetrach, by reason of enlarging his dominion, when Archelaus was banished to Vienna in France. The third was Agrippa, Magnus his nephew by Aristobulus, and he it was that slew Iames.*

AT * [1] that time Herod the Tetrarch heard
of the fame of Iesus,
2 And said vnto his seruants, This is that
Iohn Baptist, hee is risen againe from the dead,
and therefore great [a] workes are wrought
by him.
3 * For Herod had taken Iohn, and bound
him, and put him in prison for Herodias sake,
his brother Philips wife.
4 For Iohn said vnto him, It is not * lawfull
for thee to haue her.
5 And when hee would haue put him to
death, hee feared the multitude, because they
counted him as a * Prophet.
6 But when Herods birth day was kept,
the daughter of Herodias daunced before
them, and pleased [b] Herod.
7 Wherefore shee promised with an oath,
that he would giue her whatsoeuer shee would
aske.
8 And shee being before instructed of her
mother, said, Giue me here Iohn Baptists head
in a platter.
9 And the King was sorie: neuerthelesse
because of the oath, & them that sate with him
at the table, he commanded it to be giuen *her*,
10 And sent, and beheaded Iohn in the
prison.
11 And his head was brought in a platter,
and giuen to the maide, and shee brought it vnto her mother.
12 And his disciples came, and tooke vp
the bodie, and buried it, and went, and tolde
Iesus.

* *Marke* 6.23. *luke* 9.10.

13 * And when Iesus heard it, he departed
thence by ship into a desert place apart. And
when the multitude had heard it, they followed him on foote out of the cities.

2 Christ refresheth a great multitude with fiue loaues and two little fishes, shewing thereby that they shall want nothing, which lay all things aside, and seeke the kingdome of heauen.
* *Marke* 6.35. *luke* 9.12. *iohn* 6.5.

14 [2] And Iesus went foorth and saw a great
multitude, and was mooued with compassion
toward them, and he healed their sicke.
15 ¶And when euen was come, * his disciples came to him, saying, This is a desert
place, and the time is already past, let the multitude depart, that they may go into the towns,
and buy them vitailes.
16 But Iesus said to them, They haue no
neede to goe away: giue yee them to eate.
17 Then said they vnto him, We haue here
but fiue loaues and two fishes.
18 And he said, Bring them hither to me.
19 And he commanded the multitude to sit
downe on the grasse, and tooke the fiue loaues
and the two fishes, and looked vp to heauen,
and blessed, and brake, and gaue the loaues to
his disciples, and the disciples to the multitude.
20 And they did all eate, and were sufficed,
and they tooke vp of the fragments that remained, twelue baskets full.
21 And they that had eaten, were about
fiue thousand men, beside women and little
children.
22 ¶And straightway Iesus compelled his
disciples to enter into a ship, and to goe ouer
before him, while he sent the multitude away.

* *Mar.* 6.45, 46, 47. *iohn* 6.16, 17, 18.
3 Wee must saile euen through mightie tempests, and Christ will neuer forsake vs, so that we go whither hee hath commanded vs.
c *By the fourth watch is meant the time neere to day breaking: for in olde time they diuided the night into foure watches in which they scouted.*
d *A spirit, as it is here taken, is that which a man imagineth to himselfe vainely in his mind, perswading himselfe that he seeth something, and seeth nothing.*
4 By faith we tread vnder our feete euen the tempests themselues but yet by the vertue of Christ, which helpeth that vertue, which he of his mercie hath giuen.

23 And assoone as he had sent the multitude
away, hee went vp into a mountaine alone to
pray: and * when the euening was come, he was
there alone.
24 [3] And the ship was now in the middes of
the sea, and was tossed with waues: for it was a
contrarie wind.
25 And in the [c] fourth watch of the night,
Iesus went vnto them, walking on the sea.
26 And when his disciples saw him walking
on the sea, they were troubled, saying, It is a
[d] spirit, and cried out for feare.
27 But straightway Iesus spake vnto them,
saying, Bee of good comfort, It is I: bee not a-
fraide.
28 [4] Then Peter answered him, and said, Master, if it bee thou, bid me come vnto thee, on
the water.
29 And hee said, Come. And when Peter
was come downe out of the ship, he walked on
the water, to goe to Iesus.
30 But when he saw a mightie wind, he was
afraid: and as hee began to sinke, he cried, saying, Master, saue me.
31 So immediatly Iesus stretched foorth his
hand, and caught him, & said vnto him, O thou
of little faith, wherefore diddest thou doubt?
32 And assoone as they were come into the
ship, the wind ceased.
33 Then they that were in the ship, came
and worshipped him, saying, Of a trueth thou
art the Sonne of God.

34 ¶ * And

34 ¶ *And when they were come ouer,
they came into the land of [e] Gennezaret.
35 [5] And when the men of that place knew
him, they sent out into all that countrey round
about, and brought vnto him, all that were sick,
36 And besought him that they might touch
the hemme of his garment onely: and as many
as touched it, were made whole.

*Marke 6.54.
e This Gennezareth was a lake nigh to Capernaum, which is also called the sea of Galile, & Tiberias, so that the countrey it selfe grew to be called by that name.
5 In that that Christ healeth the sicke, we are giuen to vnderstand, that we must seeke remedie for spirituall diseases at his hands: and that we are bound not onely to runne our selues, but also to bring others vnto him.

CHAP. XV.

3 The commandements and traditions of men. 12 Offence. 13 The plant which is rooted vp. 14 Blinde leading the blind. 18 The heart. 22 The woman of Canaan. 26 The childrens bread: whelps. 28 Faith. 32 Foure thousand men fed. 36 Thankesgiuing.

THen [1] came to Iesus the Scribes and Pharises, which were of Ierusalem, saying,
2 *Why do thy disciples transgresse the tra-
dition of the Elders? for they [a] wash not their
hands when they eate bread.
3 [2] But hee answered and sayd vnto them,
Why doe yee also transgresse the commaundement of God by your tradition?
4 *For God hath commanded, saying, [b] Honour thy father and mother: *and he that curseth father or mother, let him die the death.
5 But yee say, [c] whosoeuer shall say to father or mother, By the gift that is *offred* by me,
thou mayest haue profite,
6 Though he honour not his father or his
mother, *shall be free*: thus haue yee made the
commandement of God of no [d] authoritie by
your tradition.
7 [3] O hypocrites, Esaias prophecied well
of you, saying,
8 *This people draweth neere vnto mee
with their mouth, and honoureth me with the
lips, but their heart is farre off from me.
9 But in vaine they worship me, teaching
for doctrines mens precepts.
10 [4] Then he called the multitude vnto him,
and said to them, Heare and vnderstand.
11 *That which goeth into the mouth, defileth not the man, but that which commeth
out of the mouth, that defileth the man.
12 ¶ Then came his disciples, and sayd vnto him, Perceiuest thou not, that the Pharises
are offended in hearing *this* saying?
13 But he answered and said, *Euery plant
which mine heauenly Father hath not planted,
shall be rooted vp.
14 Let them alone, they be the *blind lea-
ders of the blinde: and if the blinde leade the
blinde, both shall fall into the ditch.
15 ¶ *Then answered Peter, and sayd to
him, Declare vnto vs this parable.
16 Then sayd Iesus, Are yee yet without
vnderstanding?
17 Perceiue yee not yet, that whatsoeuer
entreth into the mouth, goeth into the belly,
and is cast out into the draught?
18 But those things which proceede out of
the mouth, come from the heart, and they defile the man.
19 For out of the heart *come euil thoughts,
murders, adulteries, fornications, thefts, false testimonie, slanders.
20 These are the things, which defile the
man: but to eate with vnwashen hands, defileth not the man.
21 *And Iesus went thence, and departed
into the [e] coastes of Tyrus and Sidon.
22 And beholde, a woman a [f] Cananite
came out of the same coastes, and cried, saying
vnto him, Haue mercie on mee, O Lord, the
sonne of Dauid: my daughter is miserably
vexed with a deuill,
23 [5] But he answered her not a word. Then
came to him his disciples, and besought him,
saying, Send her away, for she crieth after vs.
24 But hee answered, and sayd, I am not
sent but vnto the *lost sheep of the [g] house of
Israel.
25 Yet she came, and worshipped him, saying, Lord, helpe me.
26 And hee answered, and sayd, It is not
good to take the childrens bread, and to cast it
to whelps.
27 But she said, Trueth, Lord: yet indeede
the whelps eate of the crummes, which fal from
their masters table.
28 Then Iesus answered, and sayd vnto
her, O woman, great is thy faith: bee it to thee,
as thou desirest. And her daughter was made
whole at that houre.
29 ¶ [6] So Iesus *went away from thence,
and came neere vnto the sea of Galile, and went
vp into a mountaine and sate downe there.
30 And great multitudes came vnto him,
*hauing with them, halt, blind, dumbe, [h] mai-
med and many other, and cast them downe at
Iesus feete, and he healed them.
31 Insomuch that the multitude wondered,
to see the dumbe speake, the maimed whole,
the halt to goe, and the blind to see: and they
glorified the God of Israel.
32 *[7] Then Iesus called his disciples vnto
him, and sayd, I haue compassion on this multitude, because they haue [i] continued with me
already three dayes, and haue nothing to eate:
and I will not let them depart fasting, lest they
faint in the way.
33 And his disciples said vnto him, Whence
should we get so much bread in the wildernes,
as should suffice so great a multitude!
34 And Iesus sayd vnto them, How many
loaues haue yee? And they sayd, Seuen, and a
few little fishes.
35 Then hee commanded the multitude to
[k] sit downe on the ground,
36 And tooke the seuen loaues, and the
fishes, and gaue thankes, and brake *them*, and

gaue

1 None commonly are more bold contemners of God, then they whom God appointed keepers of his law.
*Marke 7.1.
a Which they receiued of their ancesters from hand to hand, or their elders allowed, which were the gouernors of the Church.
2 Their wicked boldnesse in corrupting the commandements of God, and that vpon pretence of godlinesse, and vsurping authoritie to make lawes, is here reproued.
*Exod. 20.12. deut. 5.16 ephe. 6.2.
b By honour is meant all kind of duetie which children owe to their parents.
*Exo. 21.17. leu. 20 9. pro. 20.20.
c The meaning is this: whatsoeuer I bestowe vpon the temple, is to thy profite, for it is as good as if I also gaue it thee, for (as the Pharises of our time say) it shalbe meritorious for thee, for vnder this colour of religion they raked all to themselues, as though that hee that had giuen any thing to the temple, had done the duetie of a child.
d You made of it no power and authoritie as much as lay in you: for otherwise the commandements of God stand fast in the Church of God, in despite of the world and Satan.
3 The same men are condemned for hypocrisie & superstition, because they made the kingdome of God to stand in outward things.
* Esai. 29 13. 4 Christ teacheth vs, that hypocrisie of false teachers which deceiue our soules is not to be borne withall, no not in indifferent matters, and there is no reason why their ordinary vocation should blind our eyes: otherwise we are like to perish with them. *Matth. 7.18. *Iohn 16.2. *Luke 6.39. *Mark. 7.17.

*Gen 6.5. and 8. 21. mar. 7.21.
*Mar. 7.24, 25.
e Coastes which were next to Tyre and Sidon, that is in that quarter where Palestina bendeth toward Phenice, and the sea of Syria.
f Of the stocke of the Canaanites, which dwelled in Phenicia.
5 In that that Christ doeth sometimes as it were stoppe his eares against the prayers of his saints, he doeth it for his gloy, and our profit.
* Chap. 10.6.
g Of the people of Israel, which people was diuided into tribes, but all those tribes came of one house.
6 Christ ceaseth not to be beneficiall euen there where he is contemned, and in the middest of wolues hee gathereth together and fostereth his flocke.
*Marke 7.31.
*Esai. 35.5.
h Whose members were weakened with the palsey, or by nature, for afterward it is said, he healed them. Now Christ was wont to heale in this wise, that such members as were weake, he restored to health, and yet he could easily if he had would, haue giuen them hands and feete and other members which wanted them.
*Marke 8.1.
7 By doing againe this miracle, Christ sheweth that he will neuer be wanting to them that follow him, no not in the wildernesse.
i Goe not from my side.
k Word for word, to lie downe backward, as rowers do in rowing they drawe their oares to them.

gaue to his disciples, and the disciples to the
multitude.
37 And they did all eate, and were sufficed: and they tooke vp of the fragments that
remained, seuen [l] baskets full.
38 And they that had eaten, were foure
thousand men, beside women, and little children.
39 Then *Iesus* sent away the multitude,
and tooke shippe, and came into the parts of
Magdala.

CHAP. XVI.

4 The signe of Ionas. 6 The leauen of the Pharises, 12 for their doctrine. 13 The peoples opinion of Christ. 17 Faith commeth of God. 18 The rocke. 19 The keyes. 21 Christ foresheweth his death. 24 The forsaking of ones selfe, and the crosse. 25 To lose the life.

THen [1] * came the Pharises and Sadduces,
and did [a] tempt *him*, desiring him to shew
them a signe from heauen.
2 But he answered, and sayd vnto them,
When it is euening, yee say, Faire weather:
for the skie is red.
3 * And in the morning, *yee say*, To day
shall be a tempest: for the skie is red and low-
ring. O hypocrites, yee can discerne the [b] face
of the skie, and can ye not *discerne* the signes of
the times?
4 * The wicked generation, and adulterous seeketh a signe, but there shall no signe be
giuen it, but [c] that signe of the Prophet * Ionas:
so he left them, and departed.
5 ¶ [2] And when his disciples were come
to the other side, they had * forgotten to take
bread *with them*.
6 Then Iesus sayd vnto them, Take heed
and beware of the leauen of the Pharises and
Sadduces.
7 And they reasoned among themselues,
saying, *It is* because we haue brought no bread.
8 But Iesus [d] knowing it, said vnto them, O
ye of litle faith, why reason ye *thus* among your
selues, because yee haue brought no bread?
9 Doe yee not yet perceiue, neither remember the [e] fiue loaues, when there were * fiue
thousand *men*, and how many baskets tooke
yee vp?
10 Neither the seuen loaues when there
were * foure thousand *men*, and how many baskets tooke ye vp?
11 Why [f] perceiue yee not that I [g] sayde
not vnto you concerning bread, that ye should
beware of the leauen of the Pharises and
Sadduces?
12 Then vnderstoode they that he had not
sayd that they should beware of the leauen of
bread, but of the doctrine of the Pharises, and
Sadduces.
13 ¶ * [3] Now when Iesus came into the
coasts of [h] Cesarea Philippi, he asked his disci-

l A kind of vessel wrought with twigs.

1 The wicked which otherwise are at defiance one with another, agree well together against Christ, but doe what they can, Christ beareth away the victorie, and triumpheth ouer them.

**Chap.12.38. marke 8.11.*

a To trie whether he could doe that which they desired, but their purpose was naught for they thought to find some thing in him by that meanes, whereupon they might haue iust occasion to reprehend him, or els distrust and curiositie mooued them so to doe, for by such meanes also is God said to be tempted, that is to say, prouoked to anger, as though men would striue with him.

**Luke 12.54.*

b The outward shew and countenance as it were of all things, is called in the Hebrew tongue, a face.

**Chap.12.39.*

c The article sheweth the notablenesse of the deede.

**Ionas 1.17.*

2 False teachers must be taken heed of.

**Marke 8.14. luke 12.1.*

d Not by others, but by vertue of his diuinitie.

e That fiue thousand men were filled with so many loaues?

**Chap.14.17. iohn 6.9.*

**Chap 15.34.*

f A demaund or question ioyned with admiration.

g Said, for commaunded.

**Mar.8.27 luke 9.18.* 3 There are diuers iudgements and opinions of Christ, notwithstanding he is knowen of his alone. *h There were two Cesareas, the one called Stratonis vpon the sea Mediterranie, which Herod built sumptuously in the honour of Octauius, Ioseph lib.15. the other was Cesarea Philippi, which Herod the great the Tetrarches sonne by Cleopatra, built in the honour of Tiberius at the foote of Lebanon, Ioseph.lib.15.*

ples, saying, Whome doe men say that I, the
sonne of man, am?
14 And they sayd, Some *say*, [i] Iohn Baptist:
and some, Elias: and others, Ieremias, or one of
the Prophets.
15 He sayd vnto them, But whom say yee
that I am?
16 Then Simon Peter answered, and sayd,
* Thou art that Christ, the sonne of the liuing God.
17 [4] And Iesus answered, and said to him,
Blessed art thou Simon, the sonne of Ionas: for
[k] flesh and blood hath not reuealed it vnto thee,
but my Father which is in heauen.
18 [5] And I say also vnto thee, that thou
art * [l] Peter, and vpon this rocke I will build
my Church: and the [m] gates of hell shall not o-
uercome it.
19 [6] And I * will giue vnto thee the [n] keyes
of the kingdome of heauen, and whatsoeuer
thou shalt [o] binde vpon earth, shall be bound in
heauen: and whatsoeuer thou shalt loose on
earth, shall be loosed in heauen.
20 [7] Then hee charged his disciples, that
they should tell no man that he was Iesus that
Christ.
21 ¶ [8] From that time foorth Iesus began
to shewe vnto his disciples, that hee must goe
vnto Hierusalem, and suffer many things of the
[p] Elders, and of the hie Priests, and Scribes, and
be slaine, and be raised againe the third day.
22 Then Peter [q] took him aside, and began
to rebuke him, saying, Master, pitie thy selfe:
this shall not be vnto thee.
23 [9] Then he turned backe, and said vnto
Peter, Get thee behinde me, [r] Satan: thou art
an offence vnto mee, because thou [s] vnderstandest not the things that are of God, but the
things that are of men.
24 [10] Iesus then said to his disciples, * If
any man will follow mee, let him forsake him
selfe, and take vp his crosse, and follow me.
25 For * whosoeuer will saue his life, shall
lose it: and whosoeuer shall lose his life for my
sake, shall [t] find it.
26 * For what shall it profit a man though

i As Herod thought.

**Iohn 6.69.*

4 Faith is of grace, not of nature.

k By this kinde of speach is meant mans naturall procreation vpon the earth, the creature not being destroyed which was made, but deformed through sinne: So then this is the meaning: this was not reuealed to thee by any vnderstanding of man, but God shewed it thee from heauen.

5 That is true faith, which confesseth Christ, the vertue whereof is inuincible.

**Iohn 1.42.*

l Christ spake in the Syrian tongue, and therefore vsed not this descanting betwixt Petros, which signifieth Peter, and Petra, which signifieth a rocke, but in both places vsed this word Cepha: but his minde was that wrote in Greeke, by the diuers termination to make a difference betweene Peter, who is a piece of the building, and Christ the Petra, that is, the rocke and foundation: or els he gaue his name Peter, because of the confession of his faith, which is the Churches as well as his, as the old fathers witnesse, for so saith Theoph. That confession which thou hast made, shall be the foundation of the beleeuers.

m The enemies of the Church are compared to a strong kingdome, and therefore by Gates, are meant cities which are made strong with counsaile and fortresses, and this is the meaning, whatsoeuer Satan can doe by counsaile or strength. So doeth Paul, 2.Cor.10.4. call them strong holds. 6 The authoritie of the Church is from God. **Iohn 20.21.* *n A metaphore taken of stewards which carie the keyes: and here is set forth the power of the ministers of the word, as Esa.22.22. and that power is common to all ministers, as Chap.18.18. and therefore the ministerie of the Gospel may rightly bee called the key of the kingdome of heauen.* *o They are bound whose sinnes are reteined, heauen is shut against them, because they receiue not Christ by faith: on the other side, how happie are they, to whom heauen is open, which imbrace Christ, and are deliuered by him, and become fellow heires with him?* 7 Men must first learne, and then teach. 8 The minds of men are in time to be prepared and made ready against the stumbling blocke of persecution. *p It was a name of dignitie and not of age: and it is put for them which were the Iudges, which the Hebrewes call Sanhedrim.* *q Tooke him by the hand and led him aside, as they vse to do, which meane to talke familiarly with one.* 9 Against a preposterous zeale. *r The Hebrews call him Satan, that is to say an aduersary, whom the Grecians call diabolos, that is to say, slanderer, or tempter: but it is spoken of them, that either of malice, as Iudas, Ioh.6.70. or of lightnesse and pride resist the will of God.* *s By this worde wee are taught that Peter sinned through a false perswasion of himselfe.* 10 No men do worse prouide for themselues, then they that loue themselues more then God. **Chap.10.38. mar.8.34. luk.9.22. and 14.27.* **Chap.10.39. marke 8.35,36. luke 9.24, 25,26. and 17.33.* *t Shall gaine him selfe: And this is his meaning, they that denie Christ to saue themselues, doe not onely not gaine that which they looke for, but also lose the thing they would haue kept, that is, themselues, which losse is the greatest of all: but as for them that doubt not to die for Christ, it fareth farre otherwise with them.* **Iohn 12.25.*

he should winne the whole world, if he lose his
owne soule? or what shall a man giue for recompence of his soule?
27 For the sonne of man shall come [u] in the
glory of his Father, with his Angels, and
* then shall he giue to euery man according to
his deedes.
28 *Verely I say vnto you, There be some
of them that stand here, which shall not taste of
death, till they haue seene the Sonne of man
come in his [x] kingdome.

CHAP. XVII.

2 The transfiguration of Christ. 5 Christ ought to be heard 11 Elias. 13 Iohn Baptist. 17 The vnbeliefe of the Apostles. 20 The power of faith. 21 Prayer and fasting. 22 Christ foretelleth his passion. 24 He payeth tribute.

AND *1 [a] after sixe dayes, Iesus tooke Peter, and Iames, and Iohn his brother, and
brought them vp vnto an high mountain apart,
2 And was [b] transfigured before them:
and his face did shine as the Sunne, and his
clothes were white as the light.
3 And behold, there appeared vnto them
Moses, and Elias, talking with him.
4 Then answered Peter, and sayd to Iesus,
Master, it is good for vs to be here: if thou wilt,
let vs make here three Tabernacles, one for
thee, and one for Moses, and one for Elias.
5 While hee yet spake, beholde, a bright
cloud shadowed them: and behold, there *came*
a voice out of the cloude, saying, *This is [c] that
my beloued Sonne, in whom I am well pleased:
heare him.
6 And when the disciples heard that, they
[d] fell on their faces, and were sore afraid.
7 Then Iesus came and touched them, and
said, Arise, and be not afraid.
8 And when they lifted vp their eyes, they
saw no man, saue Iesus onely.
9 ¶ And as they came downe from the
mountaine, Iesus charged them, saying, Shew
the [e] vision to no man, vntill the Sonne of man
rise againe from the dead.
10 *And his disciples asked him, saying,
Why then say the Scribes that * Elias must first
come?
11 And Iesus answered, and sayd vnto
them, Certainely Elias must first come, and
restore all things.
12 But I say vnto you that Elias is come already, and they knew him not, but haue done
vnto him whatsoeuer they would: likewise shal
also the Sonne of man suffer of them.
13 Then the disciples perceiued that hee
spake vnto them of Iohn Baptist.
14 ¶ * 2 And when they were come to the
multitude, there came to him a certaine man,
and [f] fell downe at his feete,
15 And sayd, Master, haue pitie on my
sonne: for he is [g] lunaticke, and is sore vexed:

u Like a King, as Chap. 6. 29.
Psal. 62. 12. rom. 2. 6.
Marke 9. 1. luke 9. 27.
x By his kingdom is vnderstood the glorie of his ascension, and what followeth thereof, Eph 4. 10 or the preaching of the Gospel, Mar. 9. 1.
Marke 9 2. luke 9. 28.
1 Christ is in such sort humble in the Gospel, that in the mean season he is Lord both of heauen and earth.
a Luke reckoneth eight dayes, conteining in that number the first and and last, and Matthew speaketh but of them that were betwixt them.
b Changed into another hue.
Chap 3. 17. 2. pet. 1. 17.
c The article or the word, That, seuereth Christ from other children. For hee is Gods naturall sonne, we by adoption, therefore he is called the first begotten among the brethren, because that although he bee of right the onely sonne, yet is hee chiefe among manie, in that he is the fountaine and head of the adoption.
d Fell downe flat on their faces and worshipped him, as Chap. 2. 11.
e Which they saw, otherwise the word vsed in this place is properly spoken of that which is seene in a dreame.
Mark. 9. 11, 12. Mala. 4. 5. chap. 11. 14.
Mar. 9. 14. luke 9. 38.
2 Men are vnworthy of Christ his goodnes, yet notwithstãding hee regardeth them.
f As men that make supplications vse to doe.
g They that at certaine times of the moone are troubled with the falling sickenesse, or any other kind of disease: but in this place, we must so take it, that besides the naturall disease he had a deuilish frensie.

for oft times hee falleth into the fire, and oft
times into the water.
16 And I brought him to thy disciples, and
they could not heale him.
17 Then Iesus answered, and sayd, O generation faithlesse, and crooked, how long nowe
shal I be with you! how long now shall I suffer
you! bring him hither to me.
18 And Iesus rebuked the deuill, and hee
went out of him: and the childe was healed at
that houre.
19 3 Then came the disciples to Iesus apart,
and sayd, Why could not we cast him out?
20 And Iesus sayd vnto them, Because of
your vnbeliefe: for * verely I say vnto you, if
ye haue faith *as much* as *is* a graine of mustard
seed, ye shall say vnto this mountaine, Remoue
hence to yonder place, and it shall remoue: and
nothing shall be vnpossible vnto you.
21 4 Howbeit this kinde goeth not out, but
by [h] prayer and fasting.
22 ¶ 5 And they *being in Galile, Iesus
sayd vnto them, The sonne of man shall be deliuered into the hands of men,
23 And they shal kill him, but the third day
shall he rise againe: and they were very sory.
24 ¶ 6 And when they were come to Capernaum, they that receiued poll money, came
to Peter, and sayd, Doeth [i] not your Master
[k] pay poll [l] money?
25 He sayd, Yes. And when hee was come
into the house, Iesus preuented him, saying,
What thinkest thou, Simon? Of whom do the
Kings of the earth take tribute or poll money?
of their [m] children, or of strangers?
26 Peter sayde vnto him, Of strangers.
Then sayde Iesus vnto him, Then are the
children free.
27 Neuerthelesse, lest wee should offend
them, goe to the sea, and cast in an angle, and
take the first fish that commeth vp, and when
thou hast opened his mouth, thou shalt finde a
[n] piece of twenty pence: that take, and giue it
vnto them for me and thee.

3 Incredulitie and distrust, hinder and breake the course of Gods benefits.
Luke 17. 6.
3 The remedie against distrust.
h To giue vs to vnderstand the watchfulnesse and diligence of earnest prayer, which cannot be without sobrietie.
5 Our mindes must be prepared more and more against the offence of ye crosse.
Chap 20. 17. mar. 9. 31. luke 9. 44. and 7. 24.
6 In that that Christ doth willingly obey Cesars edicts, hee sheweth that ciuil policie is not taken away by the Gospel.
i He denieth not, but he asketh.
k Ought he not to pay?
l They that were from twenty yeeres of age to fiftie, payed halfe a sicle of the Sanctuary, Exod 30. 13. This was an Atticke didrachme which the Romanes exacted after they had subdued Iudea.
m By children we must not vnderstand subiects which pay tribute, but naturall children.
u The worde here vsed, is stater, which is in value foure didrachmes, euery drachme is about fiue pence.

CHAP. XVIII.

1 The greatest in the kingdome of God. 5 To receiue a little childe. 6 To giue offence. 7 Offences. 9 The pulling out of the eye. 10 The Angels. 12 The lost sheepe. 15 The telling of one his fault. 17 Excommunication. 21 We must alwayes pardon the brother that repenteth. 23 The parable of the King that taketh an account of his seruants.

THE *same time the disciples came vnto
Iesus, saying, Who is the greatest in the
kingdome of heauen?
2 1 And Iesus called a [a] little childe vnto
him, and set him in the mids of them,
3 And said, Verely I say vnto you, except ye
be * [b] conuerted, and become as little children,
ye shal not enter into the kingdome of heauen.
4 Whosoeuer therefore shall humble himselfe as this little childe, the same is the greatest
in the kingdome of heauen.
5 And whosoeuer shall receiue one such
little

Mark. 9. 34. luke 9. 46.
1 Humblenesse of minde is the right way to preeminence.
a A childe in yeeres.
Chap. 19. 14. 1. cor. 14 20.
b A kinde of speach taken from the Hebrewes, and it is as much as, repent.

little childe in my name,receiueth me.
6 * [2]But whosoeuer shall offend one of
these little ones which beleeue in mee, it were
better for him, that a milstone were hanged a-
bout his necke, and that hee were drowned in
the depth of the sea.
7 [3]Woe *be* vnto the world because of offences: for it must needs be that [c]offences shall
come,but woe *be* to that man by whom the offence commeth.
8 *Wherefore, if thy hand or thy foote
cause thee to [d]offend, cut them off, and cast
them from thee: it is better for thee to enter into life, halt, and maymed, then hauing two
hands,or two feete, to bee cast into euerlasting
fire.
9 And if thine eye cause thee to offend,
plucke it out,and cast it from thee: it is better
for thee to enter into life with one eye,then hauing two eyes to be cast into hell fire.
10 [4]See that yee despise not one of these
little ones: for I say vnto you, that in heauen
their * Angels alwayes behold the face of my
Father which is in heauen.
11 For *the Sonne of man is come to saue
that which was lost.
12 How thinke yee? * If a man haue an
hundreth sheepe, and one of them be gone a-
stray, doeth he not leaue ninetie and nine, and
goe into the mountaines, and seeke that which
is gone astray?
13 And if so be that he finde it, verely I say
vnto you, hee reioyceth more of that sheepe,
then of the ninetie and nine which went not
astray:
14 So is it not the will of your Father
which is in heauen, that one of these little ones
should perish.
15 ¶ * [5]Moreouer, if thy brother trespasse
against [e]thee, goe and tell him his fault betweene thee and him alone: if hee heare thee,
thou hast wonne thy brother.
16 But if hee heare thee not, take yet with
thee one or two, that by the * [f]mouth of two
or three witnesses euery word may bee [g]con-
firmed.
17 [6]And if he [h]refuse to heare them, tell it
vnto the [i]Church: and if he refuse to heare the
Church also, let him bee vnto thee as [k]an heathen man,and a Publicane.
18 Verely I say vnto you, * Whatsoeuer ye
binde on earth, shall be bound in heauen: and
* whatsoeuer yee loose on earth, shall be loosed in heauen.
19 Againe, verely I say vnto you, that
if two of you shall [l]agree in earth vpon any
thing, whatsoeuer they shall desire, it shall be
giuen them of my Father which is in heauen.

*Marke 9.42. luke 17.2.
2 We ought to haue great respect to our brethren be they neuer so base: and he that doeth otherwise shalbe sharpely punished.
3 A good man cannot but goe thorow the mids of offences,yet he must cut off all occasion of offences.
c Lets and hinderances which stop the course of good workes. The Greeke word importeth thus much, things which we stumble at.
* *Chap.* 5.20,30. *mark.*9.45.
*d Looke afore, chap.*5.29.
4 The weaker that a man is, the greater care we ought to haue of his saluation,as God teacheth vs by his own example.
**Psal.* 34.8.
* *Luke* 19.10.
**Luke* 15 4.
**Leu.* 19.7 *luke* 17.3.*iam.*5.19.
5 We must labor for concord, not to reuenge iniuries.
e If his offence be such, that thou onely knowest thy brothers offence.
**Deut.* 19.15. *iohn* 8.17. 2.*cor.*13.1. *heb* 10.28.
f That is,by the worde and witnesse, the mouth is sometime taken for the word or speach,Num. 3.16. *and also for a still witnesse, to wit, when the matter speaketh of it selfe, as beneath,chap.* 21. 16.
g Sure and certaine.
6 He that contemneth the iudgement of the Church, contemneth God.
h Worde for word,doe not vouchsafe to heare,or make as though he did not heare.
i He speaketh not of any kinde of policie,but of an ecclesiasticall assembly,for he speaketh afterward of the power of loosing and binding, which belonged to the Church, and hee hath regard to the order vsed in those dayes, at what time the Elders had the iudgement of Church matters in their hands,Iohn 9.22. *and* 12.42.*&* 16.2.*and vsed casting out of the Synagogue for a punishment, as wee doe now excommunication. k Prophane,and voide of religion: such men, the Iewes called Gentiles: whose company they shunned, as they did the Publicanes.*
* 1 *Cor.*5.4. 2.*thess.*3.14. **Iohn* 20.23. *l This worde is translated from the body to the minde, for it belongeth properly to song.*

20 For where two or three are gathered
together in my Name, there am I in the mids
of them.
21 [7]Then came Peter to him, & sayd,Ma-
ster,how oft shall my brother sinne against me,
and I shall forgiue him? * vnto seuen times?
22 Iesus sayd vnto him, I say not vnto thee,
Vnto seuen times, but, Vnto seuentie times
seuen times.
23 Therefore is the kingdome of heauen
likened vnto a certaine King,which would take
an account of his seruants.
24 And when hee had begunne to reckon,
one was brought vnto him, which ought him
[m]ten thousand talents.
25 And because he had nothing to pay, his
Lord commanded him to be sold, and his wife,
and *his* children,and all that he had,and *the debt*
to be payd.
26 The seruant therefore fell downe, and
[n]worshipped him,saying,Lord,[o]refraine thine
anger toward me,and I will pay thee all.
27 Then that seruants Lord had compassion,and loosed him,and forgaue him the debt.
28 But when the seruant was departed, hee
founde one of his fellow seruants, which ought
him an hundred pence, and he layd handes on
him,and thratled him,saying, Pay me that thou
owest.
29 Then his fellow seruant fell downe at
his feete, and besought him, saying, Refraine
thine anger towards me, and I will pay thee all.
30 Yet hee would not, but went, and cast
him into prison, till he should pay the debt.
31 And when his *other* fellowe seruants
sawe what was done, they were very sorie,and
came, and declared vnto their Lord all that
was done.
32 Then his Lord called him vnto him,
and sayd to him,O euill seruant, I forgaue thee
all that debt, because thou prayedst me.
33 Oughtest not thou also to haue had pitie on thy fellow seruant, euen as I had pitie
on thee?
34 So his Lord was wroth, and deliuered
him to the tormentors, till hee should pay all
that was due vnto him.
35 So likewise shall mine heauenly Father
do vnto you, except yee forgiue from your
hearts,each one to his brother their trespasses.

CHAP. XIX.

2 The sicke are healed. 3 and 7 A bill of diuorcement. 12 Eunuches. 13 Children brought to Christ. 17 God onely good. The commaundements must be kept. 21 A perfect man. 23 A rich man. 26 Saluation commeth of God. 27 To leaue all and follow Christ.

AND *it came to passe, that when Iesus had
finished these sayings, hee [a]departed
from Galile,and came into the coastes of Iudea
beyond Iordan.
2 And great multitudes followed him,
and he healed them there.
3 ¶ [1]Then came vnto him the Pharisees tempting him, and saying to him, Is it
lawfull

7 They shall finde God seuere,and not to bee pleased, which doe not forgiue their brethren although they haue been diuersly and grieuously iniured by them.
**Luke* 17.4.
m Heere is set down a very great summe of threescore hundred thousand crownes, and a small sum of ten crownes, that the difference may be the greater,for there is no proportion betweene them.
n This was a ciuil reuerence which was very vsuall in the East.
o Yeeld not too much to thine anger against me: so is God called in the Scripture, slow to anger, that is to say,gentle, and one that refraineth the storming of his mind, Psal 86 5 *patient and of great mercy.*
* *Marke* 10.1.
a Passed ouer the water out of Galile into the borders of Iudea.
1 The band of mariage ought not to be broke, vnlesse it be for fornication.

lawfull for a man to [b]put away his wife vpon
euery occasion.
4 And hee answered and sayd vnto them,
Haue ye not read, *that he which made *them* at
the beginning, made them male and female,
5 And said, *For this cause shal a man leaue
father and mother, and [c] cleaue vnto his wife,
and they which were [d] two shall be one flesh?
6 Wherefore they are no more twaine,
but one flesh. Let not man therefore put asunder that, which God hath [e] coupled together.
7 [2]They sayd to him, Why did then * Moses command to giue a bill of diuorcement, and
to put her away?
8 He sayd vnto them, Moses, [f]because of
the hardnesse of your heart, [g]suffered you to
put away your wiues: but from the beginning
it was not so.
9 I say therefore vnto you, * that whosoeuer shall put away his wife, except *it bee* [h]for
whoredome, and marrie another, committeth
adulterie: and whosoeuer marrieth her which
is diuorced, doeth commit adulterie.
10 *Then* sayde his disciples to him, If the
[i]matter be so betweene man and wife, it is not
good to marrie.
11 [3]But he said vnto them, All men cannot
[k]receiue this thing, saue they to whõ it is giuen.
12 For there are some [l]eunuches, which
were so borne of *their* mothers belly: and there
bee some eunuches which bee gelded by men:
and there be some eunuches, which haue [m] gelded themselues for the kingdom of heauen. He
that is able to receiue *this*, let him receiue it.
13 ¶[4]*Then were brought to him little
children, that he should put *his* hands on them,
and pray: and his disciples rebuked them.
14 But Iesus sayd, Suffer the little children,
and forbid them not to come to me: for of such
is the kingdome of heauen.
15 And when he had put his hands on them,
he departed thence.
16 ¶[5]*And behold, one came and sayd
vnto him, Good Master, what good thing shall
I doe, that I may haue eternall life?
17 And he sayd vnto him, Why callest thou
me good? there is none good but one, euen
God: but if thou wilt enter into life, keepe the
commandements.
18 He sayd to him, Which? And Iesus said,
*These, Thou shalt not kill: Thou shalt not
commit adulterie: thou shalt not steale: Thou
shalt not beare false witnesse.
19 Honour thy father and mother: and,
Thou shalt loue thy neighbour as thy selfe.
20 The yong man sayd vnto him, I haue
obserued all these things from my youth: what
lacke I yet?

b To send her a booke of diuorcement, afore chap. 1.19.
**Gene. 1.27.*
**Gene. 2.24. 1. cor. 6.16. ephes. 5.31.*
c The Greeke word importeth to be glewed vnto, whereby is signified that streight knot, which is betweene man and wife, as though they were glewed together.
d They which were two, become as it were one: and this word flesh, is by a figure take for the whole man, or the body after the maner of Hebrewes.
e Hath made them yokefellowes, as the mariage it selfe is by a borowed kinde of speech called a yoke.
2 Because politike lawes are constrained to beare with some things, it followeth not by and by that God alloweth them.
**Deut. 24.1.*
f Being occasioned by reason of the hardnesse of your hearts.
g By a politike lawe, not by the morall lawe: for this lawe is a perpetual law of Gods iustice, the other boweth and bendeth as the carpenters Beuel.
**Chap. 5.32. mar. 10.11. luke 16.18. 1. cor 7.11.*
h Therefore in these dayes the lawes, that were made against adulterers, were not regarded: for they should haue needed no diuorcement, if mariage had been cut asunder with punishment by death.
i If the matter stand so betweene man and wife, or in mariage.
3 The gift of continencie is peculiar, and therfore no man can set a lawe to himselfe of perpetuall continencie.
k Receiue and admit, as by translation we say, that a streight and narrow place, is not able to receiue many things.
l The word Eunuch is a generall word, & hath diuers kindes vnder it, as gelded men and burstenmen. *m Which absteine from marriage, and liue continently through the gift of God.* 4 Infants and little children are conteined in the free couenant of God. **Marke 10.13. luke 18.15. chap. 18.3.* 5 They neither know themselues nor the Lawe, that seeke to bee saued by the Lawe. **Marke 10.17. luke 18.18.* **Exodus 20.13. deuteronom. 5.16. romanes 13.9.*

22 Iesus said vnto him, If [n] thou wilt be perfite, goe sell that thou hast, and giue it to the
poore, and thou shalt haue treasure in heauen,
and come and follow me.
22 And when the yong man heard that saying, he went away sorrowfull: for he had great
possessions.
23 [6]Then Iesus sayd vnto his disciples, Verely I say vnto you, that a rich man can hardly
enter into the kingdome of heauen.
24 And againe I say vnto you, It is [o] easier
for a [p] camell to goe through the eye of a needle, then for a rich man to enter into the kingdome of God.
25 And when his disciples heard it, they
were exceedingly amazed, saying, Who then
can be saued?
26 And Iesus beheld them, and sayd vnto
them, With men this is vnpossible, but with
God all things are possible.
27 ¶ * Then answered Peter, and sayd to
him, Behold, we haue forsaken all, and followed
thee: what therefore shall wee haue?
28 [7]And Iesus said vnto them, Verely I say
to you, that when the Sonne of man shall sit in
the throne of his maiesty, ye which folowed me
in the [q] regeneration, *shal sit also vpon twelue
thrones and iudge the twelue tribes of Israel.
29 And whosoeuer shall forsake houses, or
brethren, or sister, or father, or mother, or wife,
or children, or lands, for my Names sake, hee
shall receiue an hundred fold more, and shal inherite euerlasting life.
30 [8]*But many that are first, shall bee last,
and the last *shall be* first.

n The yong man did not answere truely in saying that he had kept all the commandements: and therefore hee layeth out an example of true charitie before him, to shew the disease that lay lurking in his minde.
6 Rich men haue need of a singular gift of God to escape out of the snares of Satan.
o Worde for word, it is of lesse labour.
p Theophylact noteth, that by this word is meant a cable rope, but Caninius alleadgeth out of the Thalmudists, that it is a prouerb and the worde, Camel, signifieth the beast it selfe.
**Marke 10.28. luke 18.28.*
7 It is not lost, that is neglected for Gods sake.
q The regeneration is taken for that day, wherein the elect shall begin to liue a new life, that is to say, when they shall enioy the heauenly inheritance, both in bodie and soule.
**Luke 22.29.*
8 To haue begun wel, and not to continue vnto the end, doth not onely not profit, but also hurteth very much. **Cha. 20.16. mar. 10.31. luk. 13.30.*

CHAP. XX.

1 *Labourers hired into the vineyard.* 15 *The euill eye.* 17 *He foretelleth his passion.* 20 *Zebedeus sonnes.* 22 *The cup.* 28 *Christ is our minister.* 30 *Two blind men.*

FOr the kingdome of heauen is like vnto a
certaine [1] housholder, which went out at
the dawning of the day to hire labourers into
his vineyard.
2 And he [a]agreed with the labourers for
a penie a day, and sent them into his vineyard.
3 And he went out about the third houre,
& saw other standing idle in the market place,
4 And sayd vnto them, Goe yee also into
my vineyard, and whatsoeuer is right, I wil giue
you: and they went their way.
5 Againe he went out about the sixt and
ninth houre, and did likewise.
6 And he went about the [b] eleuenth houre,
and found other standing idle, and sayd vnto
them, Why stand ye here all the day idle?
7 They sayd vnto him, Because no man
hath hired vs. He said to them, Go ye also into
my vineyard, and whatsoeuer is right, that shall
ye receiue.
8 ¶And when euen was come, the master
of the vineyard sayd vnto his steward, Call the
labourers, and giue them their hire, beginning
at

1 God is bound to no man, and therefore he calleth whomsoeuer and whensoeuer he listeth. This onely euery man ought to take heed of, and hereupon bestow his whole indeuour, that he goe forward & come to the marke without al stopping or staggering, and not curiously to examine other mens doings, or the iudgements of God.
a Word for word, fell in time: it is a kind of speach taken from song.
b The last houre: for the day was twelue houres long, and the first houre began at the sun rising.

at the last,till *thou come* to the first.
9 And they *which were hired* about the e-
leuenth houre, came and receiued euery man a
penie.
10 Now when the first came,they supposed
that they should receiue more, but they likewise receiued euery man a peny.
11 And when they had receiued it, they
murmured against the master of the house,
12 Saying, These last haue wrought but
one houre,and thou hast made them equall vnto vs,which haue borne the burden and heat of
the day.
13 And he answered one of them, saying,
Friend,I doe thee no wrong: didst thou not a-
gree with me for a peny?
14 Take that which is thine owne, and go
thy way: I will giue vnto this last, as much as
to thee.
15 Is it not lawfull for mee to doe as I will
with mine owne? Is thine eye [c] euill, because I
am good?
16 *So the last shalbe first, and the first last:
for many are called, but few chosen.
17 *[2] And Iesus went vp to Hierusalem,
and took the twelue disciples apart in the way,
and said vnto them,
18 [3]Behold,we go vp to Hierusalem,& the
Sonne of man shal be deliuered vnto the chiefe
Priests,and the Scribes, & they shal condemne
him to death,
19 [4]And *shall deliuer him to the Gentiles,
to mocke, and to scourge, and to crucifie *him*,
but the third day he shall rise againe.
20 *[5] Then came to him the mother of Zebedeus children with her sonnes, worshipping
him,and desiring a certaine thing of him.
21 And he sayd vnto her, What wouldest
thou? She said to him,Grant that these my two
sonnes may sit, the one at thy right hand, and
the other at thy left hand in thy kingdome.
22 And Iesus answered and sayd, Ye know
not what ye aske. Are ye able to [d]drinke of the
cup that I shal drinke of,& to be baptized with
the [e] baptisme that I shall bee baptized with?
They said to him,We are able.
23 And he said vnto them,Yee shall drinke
indeed of my cup,and shalbe baptized with the
baptisme that I am baptized with,but to sit at
my right hand,and at my left hand,is [f]not mine
to giue: but *it shalbe giuen* to them for whom
it is prepared of my Father.
24 * And when the *other* tenne heard this,
they disdained at the two brethren.
25 Therefore Iesus called them vnto him,
& said, Ye know that the lords of the Gentiles
haue [g]domination ouer them,and they that are
great,exercise authority ouer them.
26 But it shall not bee so among you: but
whosoeuer will be great among you,let him be
your seruant.
27 And whosoeuer will bee chiefe among
you,let him be your seruant.

c Naught,that is to say,doest thou enuie at my goodnes towards them? for the Hebrewes by an euill eye, meane enuie, because such dispositions appeare chiefly in the eyes, as aboue chap.6. 23. It is set to answere the worde single,and it is taken there for corrupt: for whereas he said there afore, vers 22 If thine eye be single,hee addeth in the 23. but if thine eye be wicked,or corrupt, the word being the same in that place,as it is here.

*Chap.19.30. and 22.14. marke 10.31. luke 13.30.

*Marke 10.32. luke 18.31.

2 Christ goeth to the Crosse necessarily, but yet willingly.

3 They that least ought,are the greatest persecuters of Christ.

4 The ignominie of the crosse, is the sure way to the glory of euerlasting life.

*Iohn 18.32.

* Marke 10.35.

5 The maner of the heauenly kingdome is quite contrary to the earthly kingdome.

d This is spoken by a figure, taking the cup, for that which is conteined in the cup, And againe,the Hebrewes vnderstand by this word Cup, sometime the the maner of punishment which is rendred to sinne, as Psal.11.6 or the ioy that is giuen to the faithful, as Psal.23.5. and sometime a lot or condition, as Psal 16.5.

e That is applied to afflictions, as Dauid commonly vseth.

f The almightinesse of Christ his diuinitie is not shut out by this, but it sheweth the debasing of himselfe by taking mans nature vpon him.

*Marke 10.41. luke 22 25.

g Somewhat sharply and roughly.

28 *Euen as the Sonne of man came not to
bee serued, but to serue, and to giue his life for
the ransome of many.
29 ¶*[6]And as they departed from Iericho,
a great multitude followed him.
30 And behold, two blinde men, sitting by
the way side, when they heard that Iesus passed
by,cried,saying, O Lord, the Sonne of Dauid,
haue mercy on vs.
31 And the multitude rebuked them,be-
cause they should hold their peace: but they
cried the more, saying, O Lord, the Sonne of
Dauid,haue mercy on vs.
32 Then Iesus stoode still, and [h] called
them, and said,What will ye that I should doe
to you?
33 They sayd to him, Lord, that our eyes
may be opened.
34 And Iesus moued with compassion,tou-
ched their eyes,and immediatly their eyes receiued sight,and they followed him.

CHAP. XXI.

1 *Christ rideth on an asse into Ierusalem.* 12. *He casteth out the sellers.* 13 *The house of prayer.* 19 *The withered figgetree.* 25 *Iohns Baptisme.* 28 *Who doe the will of God.* 30 *Publicanes. Harlots.* 33 *Gods vineyard. The Iewes.* 38 *The sonne killed of the husbandmen.* 42 *The corner stone.*

AND *[1] when they drew neere to Hierusalem, and were come to Bethphage, vnto
the mount of Oliues, then sent Iesus two disciples,
2 Saying to them, Goe into the towne
that is ouer against you, and anon ye shall find
an asse bound, and a colt with her: loose them,
and bring them vnto me.
3 And if any man say ought vnto you, say
ye,that the Lord hath need of them,& straightway [a] he will let them goe.
4 All this was done that it might be fulfilled, which was spoken by the Prophet,saying,
5 ¶*Tell yee the [b] daughter of Sion, Behold,thy King commeth vnto thee,meeke,and
sitting vpon an asse, and a colt, the foale of an
asse vsed to the yoke.
6 So the disciples went, and did as Iesus
had commanded them,
7 And brought the asse & the colt, and put
on them their [c] clothes,and set him [d] thereon.
8 And a great multitude spred their garments in the way: and other cut downe branches from the trees, and strawed them in the
way.
9 Moreouer,the people that went before,
and they also that folowed,cried,saying, *Hosanna to the Sonne of Dauid. [f]Blessed *be* hee
that commeth in the Name of the Lord, Hosanna *thou which art* in the highest *heauens*.
10 * And when hee was come into Hierusalem, [g] all the citie was mooued, saying, Who
is this?
11 And the people sayd, This is Iesus,that
Prophet of Nazareth in Galile.
12 ¶ And Iesus went into the Temple
of

* *Phil.2.7.*

* *Mar.10.46. luke 18.35.*

6 Christ by healing these blind men with an onely touch, sheweth that he is the only light of the world.

h Himselfe,not by other mens meanes.

* *Mar.11.1. luke 19.29.*

1 Christ by his humilitie,triumphing ouer the pride of this world,ascendeth to true glory by ignominie of the crosse.

a He that shall say any thing to you shall let them goe,to wit,the asse and the colt.

* *Esa.62.11 zac.9 9 ioh.12.15.*

b The citie of Sion. An Hebrew kind of speach, common in the Lamentations of Ieremie.

c Their vppermost garment.

d Vpon their garments,not vpon the asse and the colt.

e This was an ancient kind of crying, which they vsed in the feast of Tabernacles,when they caried boughs according as God commanded, Leu. 23.40. And the word is corruptly made of two, for we should say, Hoshiang-na, which is as much to say, as, Saue I pray thee.

f Wel be it to him that commeth in the Name of the Lord, that is to say, whom the Lord hath giuen vs for our King.

* *Marke 11.11. luke 19.45. iohn 2.13.*

g That is, all the men of Hierusalem were moued.

of God, and cast out all them * that solde and
bought in the Temple, and ouerthrew the tables of the money changers, and the seates of
them that sold doues,
13 And said to them, It is written, * My
house shall be called the house of prayer : but
ye haue made it a denne of theeues.
14 Then the blinde, and the halt came to
him in the Temple, and he healed them.
15 [2] But when the chiefe Priests & Scribes
saw the marvailes that he did, and the children
crying in the Temple, and saying, Hosanna to
the Sonne of Dauid, they disdained,
16 And said vnto him, Hearest thou what
these say? And Iesus said vnto them, Yea : read
ye neuer, * By the mouth of babes & sucklings
thou hast [h] made perfit the prayse?
17 ¶ [3] So he left them, and went out of the
citie into Bethania, and lodged there.
18 [4] And * in the morning, as he returned
into the citie, he was hungry,
19 And seeing a figge tree in the way,
came to it, and found nothing thereon, but
leaues onely, and said to it, Neuer fruit growe
on thee henceforwards. And anon the fig tree
withered.
20 And when his disciples sawe it, they
marueiled, saying, How soone is the fig tree
withered!
21 [5] And Iesus answered and saide vnto
them, Verily I say vnto you, if ye haue faith,
and [i] doubt not, ye shall not onely doe that,
which I haue done to the figge tree, but also if
yee say vnto this mountaine, Take thy selfe
away, and cast thy selfe into the sea, it shall be
done.
22 * And whatsoeuer ye shall aske in prayer, if ye beleeue, ye shall receiue it.
23 ¶ * [6] And when hee was come into the
Temple, the chiefe Priests, and the Elders of
the people came vnto him, as he was teaching,
and said, By what authoritie doest thou these
things? and who gaue thee this authoritie?
24 Then Iesus answered & said vnto them,
I also will aske of you [l] a certaine thing, which
if you tell me, I likewise will tell you by what
authoritie I doe these things.
25 The [m] baptisme of Iohn, whence was it?
from [n] heauen, or of men? Then they [o] reasoned among themselues, saying, If we shall say,
From heauen, he will say vnto vs, Why did yee
not then beleeue him?
26 And if we say, Of men, wee feare the
multitude, * for all hold Iohn as a Prophet.
27 Then they answered Iesus, and saide,
We cannot tell. And he said vnto them, Neither tell I you by what authoritie I doe these
things.
28 ¶ [7] But what thinke yee? A *certaine*
man had two sonnes, and came to the elder,
and said, Sonne, goe and worke to day in my
vineyard.
29 But he answered, and said, I will not:

*Deut. 14.25.
* *Esai.* 56.6.
* *Iere.* 7.11. *mar.* 11.17. *luk.* 19.46
2 Such as should be masters of godlinesse, are they that doe most enuie the glory of Christ: but in vaine.
* *Psal.* 8.2.
h Thou hast made most perfit. We read in Dauid, Thou hast established or grounded, and if the matter be considered well, it is all one that the Euangelist saith, for that is stable and sure, which is most perfit.
3 Christ doeth so forsake the wicked, that he hath a consideration and regard of his Church.
4 Hypocrites shall at length haue their maskes discouered, and vizards plucked from their faces.
* *Marke* 11.13.
5 How great the force of faith is.
* *Chap.* 17.20.
i The Greeke word signifieth a sticking or wauering of mind, so that we cannot tell which way to take.
* *Chap.* 7.7. *iohn* 15.7. 1. *iohn* 5.14.
* *Mar* 11.27,28 *luke* 20.1,2.
6 Against them which ouerslipping the doctrine, binde the calling and vocation to an ordinarie succession, going about by that false pretext, to stoppe Christs mouth.
k Or by what power.
l One word, that is to say, I will aske you one in word
m Iohn his preaching is called by figure, Baptisme, because he preached the baptisme of repentance, &c. Marke 1.4. *acts* 19.3
n From God, and so it is plainely seene, howe these are set one against another.
o Beate their heads about it, and mused, or laid their heads together.
* *Chap* 14.5. *marke* 6.20.
7 It is no new thing to see them to be the worst of al men, which ought to shewe the way of godlines to others.

yet afterward he repented himselfe, and went.
30 Then came he to the second, and saide
likewise. And he answered, and saide, I will,
Sir: yet he went not.
31 Whether of them twaine did the will
of the father? They saide vnto him, The first.
Iesus said vnto them, Verily I say vnto you, that
the Publicanes and the harlots [p] go before you
into the kingdome of God.
32 For Iohn came vnto you in the [q] way of
righteousnesse, and ye beleeued him not: but
the Publicanes, and the harlots beleeued him,
and ye, though yee sawe it, were not mooued
with repentance afterward, that ye might beleeue him.
33 ¶ [8] Heare another parable, There was a
certaine housholder, * which planted a vineyard, and hedged it round about, and made a
winepresse therein, and built [r] a tower, and let
it out to husbandmen, and went into a strange
countrey.
34 And when the time of the fruit drewe
neere, he sent his seruants to the husbandmen
to receiue the fruits thereof.
35 And the husbandmen took his seruants,
and beat one, and killed another, and stoned a-
nother.
36 Againe he sent other seruants, moe then
the first: and they did the like vnto them.
37 But last of all hee sent vnto them his
owne sonne, saying, They will reuerence my
sonne.
38 But when the husbandmen sawe the
sonne, they said among themselues, * This is
the heire: come, let vs kill him, and let vs [s] take
his inheritance.
39 So they tooke him, and cast him out of
the vineyard, and slew him.
40 When therefore the Lord of the vineyard shall come, what will he doe to those husbandmen?
41 They said vnto him, Hee will [t] cruelly
destroy those wicked men, and will let out his
vineyard vnto other husbandmen, which shall
deliuer him the fruits in their seasons.
42 Iesus said vnto them, Read yee neuer in
the Scriptures, * The stone which the [u] builders
refused, the same is [x] made the [y] head of the corner? [z] This was the Lords doing, and it is marueilous in our eyes.
43 Therfore I say vnto you, The kingdom
of God shall be taken from you, and shall bee
giuen to a nation, which shall bring foorth the
[a] fruits thereof.
44 * And whosoeuer shall fall on this stone,
he shall be broken: but on whomsoeuer it shall
fall, it will [b] dash him in pieces.
45 And when the chiefe Priestes and Pharisees had heard his parables, they perceiued that
he spake of them.
46 [9] And they seeking to lay hands on him,
feared the people, because they tooke him as a
Prophet.

p They make haste to the kingdome of God, and you slacke: so that at least wise you should haue followed their example. Marke then that this word, goe before, is improperly taken in this place, wheras no man followeth.
q Liuing vprightly, being of a good and honest conuersation: For the Hebrewes vse this word, Way, for life and maners.
8 Those men often times are the cruellest enemies of the Church, to whose fidelitie it is committed: But the vocation of God, is neither tied to time, place, nor person.
* *Esai.* 5.1. *ierem.* 2.21. *marke* 12.1 *luke* 20.9.
r Made the place strong: for a towre is the strongest place of a wall.
* *Chap.* 26.3,4. *and* 27.1. *iohn* 11.53.
s Word for word, let vs hold it fast.
t A kinde of prouerbe, shewing what ende the wicked are worthy of.
* *Psal.* 118.22. *acts* 4.11. *rom.* 9.33.
u Master builders, which are chiefe builders of the house, that is of the Church.
x Began to be.
y The chiefest stone in the corner is called the head of the corner: which beareth vp the couplings or ioints of the whole building.
z That matter (in that the stone which was cast away is made the head) is the Lords doing which we behold and greatly marueile at.
a They bring forth the fruits of the kingdome of God, which bring forth the fruits of the spirit, and not of the flesh, Gal. 5.
* *Esai* 8.14
b As chaffe vseth to be scattered with the wind, for he vseth a word which signifieth properly, to separate the chaffe frō the corne with winnowing, and to scatter it abroad.
9 The wicked can doe nothing but what God will.

CHAP. XXII.

2 The parable of the mariage. 9 The calling of the Gentiles. 11 The wedding garment, faith. 16 Of Cesars tribute. 23 The question with Christ touching the resurrection. 32 God is of the liuing. 36 The greatest commandement. 37 To loue God. 39 To loue our neighbour. 42 Iesus reasoneth with the Pharises touching the Messias.

THen * [1] Iesus answered, and spake vnto
them againe in parables, saying,
2 The Kingdome of heauen is like vnto a
certaine King which maried his sonne,
3 And sent forth his seruants, to call them
that were bid to the wedding, but they would
not come.
4 Againe he sent forth other seruants, saying, Tell them which are bidden, Beholde, I
haue prepared my dinner: mine oxen and my
fatlings are [a] killed, and all things are ready:
come vnto the mariage.
5 But they made light of it, & went their
wayes, one to his farme, and another about his
marchandise.
6 And the remnant tooke his seruants, and
intreated them sharpely, and slew them.
7 [2] But when the King heard it, hee was
wroth, and sent forth his warriours, & destroyed those murtherers, and burnt vp their citie.
8 Then said he to his seruants, Truely the
[b] wedding is prepared: but they which were
bidden, were not worthy.
9 [3] Goe yee therefore out into the high
wayes, and as many as ye find, bid them to the
mariage.
10 So these seruants went out into the *high*
wayes, & gathered together all that euer they
found, both good and [c] bad: so the wedding
was furnished with guests.
11 [4] Then the King came in, to see the guests,
and saw there a man which had not on a wedding garment.
12 And he said vnto him, Friend, how camest thou in hither, and hast not on a wedding
garment? And he was [d] speechlesse.
13 Then saide the King to the [e] seruants,
Binde him hand and foot: take him away, and
cast him into vtter darkenesse: * there shall bee
weeping and gnashing of teeth.
14 * For many are called, but fewe chosen.
15 ¶ * Then went the Pharises and tooke
counsell how they might [f] tangle him in talke.
16 And they sent vnto him their disciples
with the [g] Herodians, saying, Master, we know
that thou art true, and teachest the way of God
[h] truely, neither carest for any man: for thou
considerest not the [i] person of men.
17 [5] Tell vs therfore, how thinkest thou? Is
it lawfull to giue [k] tribute vnto Cesar, or not?

** Luke 14.16. reuel. 19.6.*
1 Not all the whole companie of them that are called by the voice of the Gospel, are the true Church before God: for the most part of them had rather follow the commodities of this life: and some do most cruelly persecute those that call them: but they are the true Church, which obey when they are called, such as for the most part they are, whome ŷ world despiseth.
a The word here vsed is commonly vsed in sacrifices, and is by translation vsed for other feasts also: For feasts & banquets were wont to be begun with sacrifices.
2 A dreadfull destruction of them that contemne Christ.
b The mariage feast.
3 God doth first call vs, when we thinke nothing of it.
c The generall calling offereth the Gospel to all men: but their life is examined that enter in.
4 In the small number which come at the calling, there are some cast awayes which doe not confirme their faith with newnesse of life.
d Worde for word, haultered, that is to say, he held his peace, as though he had had a bridle or an halter about his necke.
e To them that serued the ghests.
** Chap 8.12. and 13.42. & 25.30*
** Chap. 20.16.*
** Marke 12.13. luke 20.20.*
f Snare him in his words or talke. The Greeke word is deriued of snares which hunters lay. *g They which with Herode made a new religion, patched together of the heathenish and of the Iewish religion.* *h Truely and sincerely.* *i Thou art not moued with any appearance and outward shew.* 5 The Christians must obey their Magistrates, although they be wicked and extortioners, but so farre foorth as the authoritie that God hath ouer vs may remaine safe vnto him, and his honour be not diminished. *k The word that is vsed here, signifieth a valewing and rating of mens substance, according to the proportion whereof they payed tribute in those prouinces, which were subiect to tribute, and it is here taken for the tribute it selfe.*

18 But Iesus perceiued their wickednesse,
and said, Why tempt ye me, ye hypocrites?
19 Shew me the tribute money. And they
brought him a [l] penie.
20 And hee said vnto them, Whose is this
image and superscription?
21 They said vnto him, Cesars. Then said he
vnto them, * Giue therefore to Cesar, the things
which are Cesars, and giue vnto God, those
things which are Gods.
22 And when they heard it, they marueiled, and left him, and went their way.
23 ¶ [6] * The same day the Sadduces came
to him (which say that there is no resurrection)
and asked him,
24 Saying, Master, * Moses said, If a man
die, haue no [m] children, his brother shall marrie
his wife by the right of alliance, and raise vp
seed vnto his brother.
25 Now there were with vs seuen brethren,
and the first maried a wife, & deceased: and hauing no issue, left his wife vnto his brother.
26 Likewise also the second, and the third,
vnto the seuenth.
27 And last of all the woman died also.
28 Therefore in the resurrection, whose
wife shall she be of the seuen? for all had her.
29 Then Iesus answered, & said vnto them,
Ye are deceiued, not knowing the Scriptures,
nor the power of God.
30 For in the resurrection they neither marie wiues, nor wiues are bestowed in marriage,
but are as the [n] Angels of God in heauen.
31 And concerning the resurrection of the
dead, haue ye not read what is spoken vnto you
of God, saying,
32 * I am the God of Abraham, & the God
of Isaac, and the God of Iacob? God is not the
God of the dead, but of the liuing.
33 And when the multitude heard it, they
were astonied at his doctrine.
34 ¶ * [7] But when the Pharises had heard
that he had put the Sadduces to silence, they
assembled together.
35 And [o] one of them, *which was* an expounder of the Law, asked him a question, tempting
him, and saying,
36 Master, which is the great commandement in the Law?
37 Iesus said to him, * Thou shalt loue the
Lord thy God with all thine heart, with all thy
[p] soule, and with all thy minde.
38 This is the first and the great commandement.
39 And the second is like vnto this, * Thou
shalt loue thy [q] neighbour as thy selfe.
40 On these two commandements hangeth the whole Law, and the Prophets.
41 ¶ [8] * While the Pharises were gathered
together, Iesus asked them,

l Before, Chap. 17.24 there is mention made of a didrachme, and here of a peny, whereas a didrachme is more by the seuenth part then a peny: so that there seemeth to be a iarre in these two places: but they may easily be accorded thus: The penie was payed to the Romanes for tribute, according to the proportion they were rated at, the drachme was payed of euery one to the Temple, which also the Romanes tooke to themselues when they had subdued Iudea.
** Marke 12.17. luke 20.25. rom 13.7.*
6 Christ voucheth the resurrection of the flesh against the Sadduces.
** Mar. 12.18. luke 20.27. actes 23.8.*
** Deut. 25.5.*
m Under which name are daughters also comprehended, but yet as touching the familie and name of a man, because he that left daughters was in no better case, then if he had left no children at all, (for they were not reckoned in the familie) by the name of children are sonnes vnderstood.
n He saith not that they shalbe without bodies, for then they should not bee men any more, but they shall be as Angels, for they shall neither marrie nor be married.
** Exod. 3.6. marke 12.27.*
** Marke 12.28.*
7 The Gospel doeth not abolish the precepts of the Lawe, but doeth rather confirme them.
o A Scribe, so saith Marke 12.28. now what a Scribe is, looke Chap. 2.4.
** Deut. 6.5.*
p The Hebrew text readeth, Deut. 6.5. with thine heart, soule, and strength: and in Marke 12.30. and Luke 10.27. we reade, with soule, heart, strength & thought. ** Mar 12.31. rom. 13.9. gal. 5.24 iam. 2.8*
q Another man. 8 Christ prooueth manifestly that he is Dauids sonne, according to the flesh, but otherwise Dauids Lord, and very God. ** Mar. 12.35. luke 20.41.*

42 Saying,

42 Saying, What thinke yee of Christ?
[r] whose sonne is hee? They said vnto him, Dauids.
43 He said vnto them, How then doeth Dauid in spirit call him Lord, saying,
44 *The Lord said vnto my Lord, Sit at my
right hand, till I make thine enemies thy footstoole?
45 If then Dauid call him Lord, how is he
then his sonne?
46 And none could answere him a word,
neither durst any from that day forth aske him
any moe questions.

r Of whose stocke or familie: for the Hebrewes call a mans posteritie, sonnes.

* *Psal.110.1.*

CHAP. XXIII.

2 How the Scribes, teaching the people the Law of Moses, behaue themselues. 5 Their Phylacteries, and Fringes. 7 Greetings. 8 We are brethren. 9 The Father. 10 The seruant. 13 To shut the kingdome of heauen. 14 To deuoure widowes houses. 15 A Proselyte. 16 To sweare by the Temple. 23 To tithe mynt. 25 To clense the outside of the cup. 27 Painted sepulchres. 33 Serpents, vipers. 37 The Henne.

THen spake Iesus to the multitude, and to
his disciples,
2 [1] Saying, The * Scribes and the Pharises
[a] sit in Moses seat.
3 [b] All therefore whatsoeuer they bid you
obserue, that obserue and doe: but after their
works doe not: for they say, and doe not.
4 *[2] For they binde heauie burdens, and
grieuous to be borne, and lay them on mens
shoulders, but they themselues will not mooue
them with *one* of their fingers.
5 [3] All their works they doe for to be seene
of men: for they make their [c] phylacteries
broad, and make long [d] the * fringes of their
garments,
6 * And loue the chiefe place at feasts, and
to haue the chiefe seats in the [e] assemblies,
7 And greetings in the markets, and to be
called of men Rabbi, [f] Rabbi.
8 *[4] But be not ye [g] called, Rabbi: for [h] one
is your doctour, *to wit,* Christ, and all yee are
brethren.
9 And * call no man your [i] father vpon the
earth: for there is but one, your father which is
in heauen.
10 Be not called [k] doctors: for one is your
doctour, *euen* Christ.
11 But he that is greatest among you, let
him be your seruant.

1 We ought to heare whatsoeuer any wicked teachers teach vs purely out of the word of God, yet so that wee eschew their euil maners.

* *Nehem.8.4.*

a Because God appoynted the order, therefore the Lord would haue his word to be heard euen from the mouth of hypocrites and hirelings.

b Prouided alwayes, that they deliuer Moses his doctrine which they professe, which thing the Metaphore of the seat sheweth, which they occupied as teachers of Moses his learning.

* *Luke 11.46. actes 15.10.*

2 Hypocrites for the most part are most seuere exactors of those things, which they themselues chiefly neglect.

3 Hypocrites are ambitious.

c It was a thread, or ribband of blue silke in the fringe of a corner, the beholding whereof made them to remember the lawes and ordinances of God: and therefore was it called a phylacterie, as ye would say, a keeper, Numbers 15. 38. deuteronmie 6.8, which order the Iewes afterward abused, as they doe now a dayes, which hang Saint Iohns Gospel about their necks: a thing condemned many yeeres agoe in the Councill of Antioch. d Word for word, Twisted tassels of thread which hanged at the nethermost hemmes of their garments. * *Numbers 15.38. deut.22.12. marke 12.38.* * *Luke 11.43. and 20.46. e When assemblies and Councils are gathered together. f This word Rab, signifieth one that is about his fellowes, and is as good as a number of them: and wee may see by the repeating of it, how proud a title it was. Now they were called Rabbi, which by laying on of hands were vttered and declared to the world to be wise men.* * *Iames.3.1.* 4 Modestie is a singular ornament of Gods ministers. *g Seeke not ambitiously after it: for our Lord doeth not forbid vs to giue the Magistrate and our masters the honour that is due to them, Augustinus de sermone verbi Domini ex Matth. cap.11. h Hee seemeth to allude to a place of Esaias, chap. 54. 13. and Ieremie 31. 34.* * *Malachi 1.6. i Hee shooteth at a fashion which the Iewes vsed, for they called the Rabbins our fathers. k It seemeth that the Scribes did very greedily hunt after such titles, whome verse 16. he calleth blinde guides.*

12 * For whosoeuer [l] will exalt himselfe,
shall bee brought lowe: and whosoeuer will
humble himselfe, shall be exalted.
13 ¶ [5] Woe therefore *be* vnto you, Scribes
and Pharises, [m] hypocrites, because yee shut vp
the kingdome of heauen before men: for yee
your selues goe not in, neither suffer yee them
that would [n] enter, to come in.
14 * [6] Woe *be* vnto you, Scribes and Pharises, hypocrites: for ye deuoure widowes houses, euen [o] vnder a colour of long prayers:
wherefore ye shall receiue the greater damnation.
15 Woe *be* vnto you, Scribes and Pharises,
hypocrites: for ye compasse sea and [p] lande to
make one of your profession: and when hee is
made, ye make him two fold more the child of
hell, then your selues.
16 Woe *be* vnto you blind guides, which
say, Whosoeuer sweareth by the Temple, it is
nothing: but whosoeuer sweareth by the gold
of the Temple, he [q] offendeth.
17 Ye fooles and blinde, whether is greater, the golde, or the Temple that [r] sanctifieth
the gold?
18 And whosoeuer sweareth by the altar, it
is nothing: but whosoeuer sweareth by the offering *that is* vpon it, offendeth.
19 Ye fooles and blinde, whether is greater, the offering, or the altar which sanctifieth
the offering?
20 Whosoeuer therfore sweareth by the altar, sweareth by it, and by all things thereon.
21 * And whosoeuer sweareth by the Temple, sweareth by it, and by him that dwelleth
therein.
22 * And he that sweareth by heauen, sweareth by the [s] throne of God, and by him that
sitteth thereon.
23 ¶ [7] * Woe *be* to you, Scribes and Pharises, hypocrites: for ye tithe mint and annise,
and cummin, and leaue the weightier matters
of the Law, *as* iudgement, and mercie and [t] fidelitie. These ought ye to haue done, and not
to haue left the other.
24 Yee blinde guides, which straine out a
gnat, and swallow a camell.
25 ¶ [8] Wo *be* to you, * Scribes & Pharises,
hypocrites: for ye make cleane the vtter side of
the cup, and of the platter: but within they are
full of briberie and excesse.
26 Thou blinde Pharise, clense first the inside of the cup and platter, that the outside of
them may be cleane also.
27 Woe *bee* to you, Scribes, and Pharises, hypocrites: for yee are like vnto whited
tombes, which appeare beautifull outward,
but are within full of dead mens bones, and all
filthinesse.
28 So are ye also: for outward ye appeare
righteous vnto men, but within yee are full of
hypocrisie and iniquitie.
29 ¶ [9] Woe *be* vnto you, Scribes and Pharises,

* *Luke 14.11. and 18.14.*

l He seemeth to allude to the name of the Rabbins, for Rab signifieth one that is aloft.

5 Hypocrites can abide none to be better then themselues.

m Christ when hee reproueth any man sharpely, vseth this word, to giue vs to vnderstand that there is nothing more detestable then hypocrisie and falshood in religion.

n Which are euen at the doore.

* *Marke 12.40. luke 20.47.*

6 It is a common thing amongst hypocrites to abuse the pretence of zeale to couetousnesse and extortion.

o Word for word, vnder a colour of long praying. And this word, Euen, noteth a double naughtines in them: the one, that they deuoured widowes goods: the other, that they did it vnder a colour of godlines.

p The drie part: now that part of the earth is called drie, which the Lord hath giuen vs to dwell vpon.

q Is a debter. Sinnes are called in the Syrian tongue, Debts, and it is certaine that Christ spake in the Syrian tongue.

r Causeth the gold to be counted holy, which is to be dedicate to an holy vse.

* *1.King.8.13. 2.chron 6.2.*

* *Chap.5.34.*

s If heauen be Gods throne, then he is no doubt aboue al this world.

7 Hypocrites are carefull in trifles, and neglect the greatest things of purpose.

* *Luke 11.42.*

t Faithfulnesse in keeping of promises.

8 Hypocrites are too much carefull of outward things, and the inward they vtterly cõtemne.

* *Luke 11. 39.*

9 Hypocrites when they goe most about to couer their wickednesse, then doe they by the iust iudgement of God, shame themselues.

riſes, hypocrites: for yee build the tombes of
the Prophets, and garniſh the ſepulchres of the
righteous,
30 And ſay, If we had bene in the dayes of
our fathers, we would not haue beene partners
with them in the blood of the Prophets.
31 So then ye be witneſſes vnto your ſelues,
that ye are the children of them that murthered the Prophets.
32 [u] Fulfill ye alſo the meaſure of your fathers.
33 O ſerpents, the generation of vipers,
how ſhould ye eſcape the damnation [x] of hell!
34 [10] Wherefore beholde, I ſend vnto you
Prophets, and wiſe men, and Scribes, and of
them ye ſhal kill and crucifie: and of them ſhal
ye ſcourge in your Synagogues, and perſecute
from citie to citie,
35 [11] That vpon you may come all the
righteous blood that was ſhed vpon the earth,
* from the blood of Abel the righteous, vnto
the blood of Zacharias the ſonne of [y] Barachi-
as, * whom ye ſlew betweene the Temple and
the altar.
36 Verely I ſay vnto you, all theſe things
ſhall come vpon this generation.
37 [12] * Hieruſalem, Hieruſalem, which kil-
leſt the Prophets, and ſtoneſt them which are
ſent to thee, how often would I haue [z] gathered thy children together, as the henne gathereth her chickins vnder her wings, & ye would
not!
38 Behold, your habitation ſhall be left vnto you deſolate,
39 For I ſay vnto you, ye ſhall not ſee mee
henceforth, till that ye ſay, Bleſſed *is* hee that
commeth in the Name of the Lord.

u A prouerbe vſed of the Iewes, which hath this meaning, Goe ye on alſo, and followe your anceſters, that at length your wickedneſſe may come to the full.
x Looke Chap. 5. verſe 22.
10 Hypocrites be cruell.
11 The end of them which perſecute the Goſpel, vnder the pretence of zeale.
** Gen. 4.8.*
y Of Ioiada, who was alſo called Barach-iah, that is, bleſſed of the Lord.
** 2. Chro. 24 22.*
12 Where the mercie of God was greateſt, there was greateſt wickednes and rebellion, and at length the moſt ſharpe iudgements of God.
** Luke 13.34.*
z He ſpeaketh of the outward miniſterie, and as he was promiſed for the ſauing of this people, ſo was he alſo carefull for it, euen from the time that the promiſe was made to Abraham.

CHAP. XXIIII.

2 The deſtruction of the Temple. 4 The ſignes of Chriſtes comming. 12 Iniquitie. 23 Falſe Chriſts. 29 The ſignes of the ende of the world. 31 The Angels. 32 The figge tree. 37 The dayes of Noe. 42 Wee muſt watch. 45 The ſeruant.

AND * Ieſus went out, and departed from
the Temple, & his diſciples came to him,
to ſhew him the building of the Temple.
2 [1] And Ieſus ſaid vnto them, See ye not all
theſe things? Verely I ſay vnto you, * there
ſhall not be here left a ſtone vpon a ſtone, that
ſhall not be caſt downe.
3 And as hee ſate vpon the mount of O-
liues, his diſciples came vnto him apart, ſaying,
Tell vs when theſe things ſhall bee, and what
ſigne *ſhall be* of thy comming, and of the ende
of the world.
4 [2] And Ieſus anſwered, & ſaid vnto them,
* Take heed that no man deceiue you.
5 For many ſhall come in my Name, ſaying, I am Chriſt, and ſhall deceiue many.
6 And ye ſhall heare of warres, and rumours of warres: ſee that ye be not troubled:
for all theſe things muſt come to paſſe, but the
[a] end is not yet.

** Marke 13.1. luke 21,5,6.*
1 The deſtruction of the citie, and eſpecially of the Temple is foretold.
** Luke 19 44.*
2 The Church ſhall haue a continuall conflict with infinite miſeries and offences, and that more is, with falſe prophets, vntill the day of victorie and triumph commeth.
** Epheſ. 5.6. coloſſ. 2.18.*
a That is, when thoſe things are fulfilled, yet the ende ſhall not come.

7 For nation ſhall riſe againſt nation, and
realme againſt realme, and there ſhall bee famine, and peſtilence, and earthquakes in [b] diuers places.
8 All theſe are but the beginning of [c] ſo-
rowes.
9 * Then ſhall they deliuer you vp to bee
afflicted, and ſhall kill you, and ye ſhall be hated of all nations for my Names ſake.
10 And then ſhall many be offended, and
ſhall betray one another, and ſhall hate one a-
nother.
11 And many falſe prophets ſhall ariſe, and
ſhall deceiue many.
12 And becauſe iniquitie ſhall be increaſed,
the loue of many ſhall be cold.
13 * [3] But he that endureth to the ende, he
ſhall be ſaued.
14 And this [d] Goſpel of the kingdom ſhall
be preached thorow the whole [e] world for a
witneſſe vnto all nations, and then ſhall the
end come.
15 ¶ [4] When ye * therefore ſhall ſee the
[f] abomination of deſolation ſpoken of by * Daniel the Prophet, ſet in the holy place (let him
that readeth conſider it.)
16 Then let them which be in Iudea, flee
into the mountaines.
17 Let him which is on the houſe top, not
come downe to fetch any thing out of his
houſe.
18 And he that is in the field, let not him
returne backe to fetch his [g] clothes.
19 And woe *ſhalbe* to them that are with
childe, and to them that giue ſucke in thoſe
dayes.
20 But pray that your flight bee not in the
winter, neither on the * [h] Sabbath *day*.
21 For then ſhall be great tribulation, ſuch
as was not from the beginning of the world to
this time, nor ſhall be.
22 And except [i] thoſe dayes ſhould be ſhortned, there ſhould no [k] fleſh be ſaued: but for
the elects ſake thoſe dayes ſhall be ſhortned.
23 * Then if any ſhall ſay vnto you, Loe,
here is Chriſt, or there, beleeue it not.
24 For there ſhall ariſe falſe Chriſts, and
falſe prophets, and [l] ſhall ſhew great ſignes and
wonders, ſo that if it were poſſiible, they ſhould
deceiue the very elect.
25 Behold, I haue told you before.
26 Wherefore if they ſhall ſay vnto you,
Beholde, he is in the deſert, goe not foorth:
Behold, hee is in the ſecret places, beleeue
it not.
27 For as the lightning commeth out of the
Eaſt, and is ſeene into the Weſt, ſo ſhall alſo the
comming of the Sonne of man be.
28 * [5] For whereſoeuer a dead [m] carkeis is,
thither will the Egles be gathered together.

b Euery where.
c Word for word, of great torments, like vnto women in trauell.
** Chap. 10.17. luke 21.12. iohn 15.20. and 16.2.*
** 2. Theſſ 3.13. 2. tim. 2.5.*
3 The Goſpel ſhalbe ſpread abroad, rage the world and the deuill neuer ſo much: and they which doe conſtantly beleeue, ſhall be ſaued.
d Ioyfull tidings of the kingdome of heauen.
e Through all that part that is dwelt in.
4 The kingdom of Chriſt ſhall not be aboliſhed when the citie of Hieruſalem is vtterly deſtroyed, but ſhall be ſtretched out euen to the ende of the world.
** Marke 13. 14. luke 21.20.*
f The abomination of deſolation, that is to ſay, which all men deteſt and cannot abide, by reaſon of the foule and ſhamefull filthineſſe of it: and he ſpeaketh of the idoles that were ſet vp in the Temple, or as other thinke, he meant the marring of the doctrine in the Church.
** Dan. 9.27.*
g This betokeneth the great feare that ſhalbe.
** Acts 1.12.*
h It was not lawfull to take a iourney on the Sabbath day, Ioſeph booke 13.
i Thoſe things which befell the people of the Iewes in the 34. yeeres, when as the whole land was waſted, and at length the citie of Hieruſalem taken, and both it and their Temple deſtroyed, are mixed with thoſe which ſhall come to paſſe before the laſt comming of the Lord.
k The whole nation ſhould vtterly be deſtroyed: and this worde, Fleſh, is by a figure taken for man, as the Hebrewes vſe to ſpeake. ** Mar. 13.21. luke 17.23.* *l Shall openly lay forth great ſignes for men to behold.* ** Luk. 17.37.* 5 The only remedie againſt the furious rage of the world, is to be gathered and ioyned to Chriſt. *m Chriſt, who will come with ſpeede, and his preſence wil be with a maieſtie, to whom all ſhall flocke euen as Egles.*

29 *6 And

29 *6 And immediatly after the tribulation of those dayes, shall the sunne be darkened,
and the moone shall not giue her light, and the
starres shall fall from heauen, and the powers
of heauen shall be shaken.
30 And then shal appeare the n signe of the
Sonne of man in heauen: and then shall all the
o kinreds of the earth p mourne,* and they shal
see the Sonne of man q come in the cloudes of
heauen with power and great glory.
31 * And he shall send his Angels with a
great sound of a trumpet, and they shal gather
together his elect from the r foure windes, *and*
from the one ende of the heauens vnto the o-
ther.
32 7 Now learne the parable of the figge
tree: when her bough is yet s tender, and it
putteth foorth leaues, ye know that Summer *is*
neere.
33 So likewise yee, when ye see all these
things, know that *the Kingdom of God* is neere,
euen at the doores.
34 Verely I say vnto you, this t generation
shall not passe, till all these things be done.
35 *8 Heauen and earth shall passe away:
but my words shall not passe away.
36 9 But of that day and houre knoweth no
man, no not the Angels of heauen, but my Father onely.
37 But as the dayes of Noe *were,* so likewise shal the comming of the Sonne of man be.
38 *For as in the dayes *before* the flood,
they did u eate and drinke, marrie, and gaue in
mariage, vnto the day that Noe entred into the
Arke,
39 And knew nothing till the flood came,
and tooke them all away, so shall also the comming of the Sonne of man be.
40 10 *Then two shall be in the fields, the
one shall bee receiued, the other shall bee refused.
41 x Two women shall bee grinding at the
mill: the one shall be receiued, and the other
shall be refused.
42 11 *Watch therefore: for ye know not
what houre your master will come.
43 * Of this be sure, that if the good man
of the house knewe at what watch the thiefe
would come, he would surely watch and not
suffer his house to be digged through.
44 Therefore be ye also ready: for in the
houre that ye thinke not, will the Sonne of man
come.
45 *Who then is a faithfull seruant & wise,

* *Marke 13.24. luke 21.25. esai. 13.10. eze. 32.7. ioel 2.31. and 3.15.*
6 Euerlasting damnation shall be the end of the securitie of the wicked, and euerlasting blisse, of the miseries of the godly.
n *The exceeding glory and maiestie, which shall beare witnesse, that Christ the Lord of heauen and earth draweth neere to iudge the world.*
o *All nations, and he alludeth to the dispersion which we reade of, Gene. 10. and 11. or to the diuiding of the people of Israel.*
p *They shalbe in such sorow, that they shall strike themselues: and it is transferred to the mourning.*
* *Reue. 1.7. dan. 7.13.*
q *Sitting vpon the cloudes, as he was taken vp into heauen.*
* *1. Cor. 15.52. 1. thess. 4.16.*
r *From the foure quarters of the world.*
7 If God hath prescribed a certain order to nature, much more hath he done so to his eternall iudgements, but the wicked vnderstand it not, or rather make a mocke at it: but the godly doe marke it, and wait for it.
s *When his tendernes sheweth that the sappe which is the life of the tree, is come from the root into the barke.*
t *This age: this word Generation or Age, being vsed for the men of this age.*
* *Marke 13.31.*
8 The Lord doeth now begin the iudgement, which he wil make an end of in the latter day.
9 It is sufficient for vs to know that God hath appoynted a latter day for the restoring of all things, but when it shall be, it is hidden from vs all, for our profit, that we may be so much the more watchful, that we be not taken, as they were in old time in the flood. * *Luke 17.26. gene. 7.1. 1. pet. 3.20.* u *The word which the Euangelist vseth, expresseth the matter more fully then ours doeth: for it is a worde which is proper to bruit beasts: and his meaning is, that in those dayes men shall be giuen to their bellies like vnto bruit beasts: for otherwise it is no fault to eate and drinke.* 10 Against them that perswade themselues that God will bee mercifull to all men, and do by that meanes giue ouer themselues to sinne, that they may in the meane while liue in pleasure, void of all care. * *Luke 17.36.* x *The Greeke women and the Barbarians did grinde and bake, Plutarch, booke Problem.* 11 An example of the horrible carelesnesse of men in those things whereof they ought to bee most carefull. * *Marke 13.35.* * *Luke 12.39 1. thess. 5.2. reuel. 16.15.* * *Luke 12.42.*

whome his master hath made ruler ouer his
houshold, to giue them meate in season?
46 Blessed *is* that seruant, whom his master
when he commeth, shall find so doing.
47 Verely I say vnto you, he shal make him
ruler ouer all his goods.
48 But if that euill seruant shall say in his
heart, My master doeth deferre his comming,
49 And begin to smite his fellowes, and to
eate, and to drinke with the drunken,
50 That seruants master will come in a day,
when he looketh not for him, and in an houre
that he is not ware of,
51 And will y cut him off, and giue him his
portion with hypocrites: * there shall be weeping and gnashing of teeth.

CHAP. XXV.

1 *The Virgins looking for the Bridegrome.* 13 *Wee must watch.* 14 *The talents deliuered vnto the seruants.* 24 *The euill seruant.* 30 *After what sort the last iudgement shalbe.* 41 *The cursed.*

THen 1 the Kingdome of heauen shall bee
likened vnto tenne virgins, which tooke
their lamps, and a went forth to meet the bridegrome.
2 And fiue of them were wise, & fiue foolish.
3 The foolish tooke their lamps, but tooke
none oyle with them.
4 But the wise tooke oyle in their vessels
with their lamps.
5 Now while the bridegrome taried long,
all b slumbred and slept.
6 And at midnight there was a crie made,
Behold, the bridegrome commeth: goe out to
meet him.
7 Then all those virgins arose, and trimmed
their lamps.
8 And the foolish said to the wise, Giue vs
of your oyle, for our lamps are out.
9 But the wise answered, saying, *Not so,* lest
there will not be ynough for vs and you: but
goe ye rather to them that sel, and buy for your
selues.
10 And while they went to buy, the Bridegrome came: and they that were ready, went
in with him to the wedding, and the gate was
shut.
11 Afterwards came also the other virgins,
saying, Lord, Lord, open to vs.
12 But he answered, and said, Verely I say
vnto you, I know you not.
13 *Watch therefore: for ye know neither
the day, nor the houre, when the sonne of man
will come.
14 * 2 For *the Kingdome of heauen is* as a
man that going into a strange countrey, called
his seruants, and deliuered to them his goods.
15 And vnto one he gaue fiue talents, and
to another two, to another one, to euery man
after his owne c habilitie, and straightway went
from home.
16 Then hee that had receiued the fiue ta-

Hhhh 3 lents,

y *To wit from the rest, or will cut him into two parts, which was a most cruell kind of punishment: wherewith as Iustine martyr witnesseth, Esai the Prophet was executed by the Iewes: the like kinde of punishment we read of, 1. Sam. 15.33. and Dan. 3 29.*
* *Chap. 13.42. and 25.30.*
1 We must desire strength at Gods hand which may serue vs as a torch while we walke through this darkenesse, to bring vs to our desired end: otherwise if we become slouthfull and negligent as wearie of our paines and trauell, we shalbe shut out of the doores.
a *The pompe of bridedeales was wont for the most part to be kept in the night seasons, and that by damsels.*
b *Their eyes being heauy with sleepe.*
* *Chap. 24.42. mar. 13.35.*
* *Luke 19.12,13*
2 Christ witnesseth that there shall be a long time, betweene his departure to his Father, and his comming againe to vs, but yet notwithstanding that, he will at that day take an account not onely of the rebellious & obstinate, how they haue bestowed that which they receiued of him, but also of his houshold seruants, which haue not through slouthfulnesse employed those gifts which he bestowed vpon them.
c *According to the wisedome and skill in dealing, which was giuen them.*

lents, went and occupied with them, and gained other fiue talents.
17 Likewise also, he that *receiued* two, he
also gained other two.
18 But he that receiued that one, went and
digged it in the earth, and hid his masters money.
19 But after a long season, the master of
those seruants came, and reckoned with them.
20 Then came he that had receiued fiue talents, and brought other fiue talents, saying,
Master, thou deliueredst vnto me fiue talents:
behold, I haue gained with them other fiue talents.
21 Then his master said vnto him, It is well
done good seruant and faithfull, Thou hast bin
faithfull in little, I will make thee ruler ouer
much: [d] enter into thy masters ioy.
22 Also hee that had receiued two talents,
came, and saide, Master, thou deliueredst vnto
mee two talents: behold, I haue gained two o-
ther talents more.
23 His master said vnto him, It is well done
good seruant, and faithfull, Thou hast beene
faithful in litle, I wil make thee ruler ouer much:
enter into thy masters ioy.
24 Then he which had receiued the one talent, came, and said, Master, I knewe that thou
wast an hard man, which reapest where thou
sowedst not, and gatherest where thou straw-
edst not:
25 I was therefore afraide, and went, and
hid thy talent in the earth: beholde, thou hast
thine owne.
26 And his master answered, and said vnto
him, Thou euill seruant, and slouthfull, thou
knewest that I reape where I sowed not, and
gather where I strawed not.
27 Thou oughtest therefore to haue put my
money to the [e] Exchangers, & then at my comming should I haue receiued mine owne with
vantage.
28 Take therefore the talent from him, and
giue it vnto him which hath ten talents.
29 *For vnto euery man that hath, it shall
bee giuen, and he shall haue abundance, and
from him that hath not, euen that he hath, shall
be taken away.
30 Cast therefore that vnprofitable seruant
into vtter * darkenesse: there shall be weeping
and gnashing of teeth.
31 ¶ [3] And when the Sonne of man commeth in his glorie, and all the holy Angels
with him, then shall hee sit vpon the throne of
his glory,
32 And before him shall be gathered all nations, and he shall separate them one from another, as a shepheard separateth the sheepe from
the goats.
33 And hee shall set the sheepe on his right
hand, and the goats on the left.
34 Then shall the King say to them on his
right hand, Come yee [f] blessed of my father:
take the inheritance of the Kingdome prepared
for you from the foundation of the world.
35 *For I was an hungred, and ye gaue me
meat: I thirsted, and ye gaue me drinke: I was
a stranger, and ye tooke me in vnto you.
36 *I was* naked, and ye clothed me: I was
* sicke, and ye visited me: I was in prison, and
ye came vnto me.
37 Then shall the righteous answere him,
saying, Lord, when sawe we thee an hungred,
and fed thee? or a thirst, and gaue thee drinke?
38 And when sawe we thee a stranger, and
tooke thee in vnto vs? or naked, and clothed
thee?
39 Or when saw we thee sicke, or in prison,
and came vnto thee?
40 And the King shall answere, and say vnto them, Verily I say vnto you, in as much as ye
haue done it vnto one of the least of these my
brethren, ye haue done it to me.
41 Then shall he say vnto them on the left
hand, *Depart from me ye cursed, into euerlasting fire, which is prepared for the deuill and
his angels.
42 For I was an hungred, and ye gaue me
no meat: I thirsted, and ye gaue me no drinke:
43 I was a stranger, and ye tooke me not in
vnto you: *I was* naked, and ye clothed me not:
sicke, and in prison, and ye visited me not.
44 Then shall they also answere him, saying, Lord, when saw wee thee an hungred, or
athirst, or a stranger, or naked, or sicke, or in
prison, and did not minister vnto thee?
45 Then shall he answere them, and say,
Verely I say vnto you, in as much as yee did
it not to one of the least of these, yee did it not
to me.
46 * And these shall goe into euerlasting
paine, and the righteous into life eternall.

d *Come and receiue the fruit of my goodnes: now the Lords ioy is doubled, Iohn 15.11. that my ioy may remaine in you, and your ioy be fulfilled.*

e *Table mates which haue their shop bulks or tables set abroad, where they let out money to vsurie.*

* *Chap.* 13.12. *marke* 4.25. *luke* 8.18. *and* 19.26.

* *Chap.* 8.12. *and* 22.13.

3 A liuely setting forth of the euerlasting iudgment which is to come.

f *Blessed and happie, vpon whom my Father hath most abundantly bestowed his benefits.*

* *Esai.* 58.7. *ezech.* 18.7.

* *Ecclus* 7.35.

* *Psal* 6.8. *chap.* 7.23. *luke* 13.27.

* *Daniel* 12.2. *iohn* 5.29.

CHAP. XXVI.

3 The consultation of the Priests against Christ. 6 His feet are anointed. 15 Iudas selleth him. 26 The institution of the Supper. 34 and 69 Peters deniall. 38 Christ is heauie. 47 He is betrayed with a kisse. 56 He is lead to Caiaphas. 64 He confesseth himselfe to be Christ. 67 They spit at him.

AND * [1] it came to passe, when Iesus had
finished all these sayings, he said vnto his
disciples,
2 [2] Ye knowe that after two dayes is the
Passeouer, and the Sonne of man shall be deliuered to be crucified.
3 * Then assembled together the chiefe
Priests, and the Scribes, and the Elders of the
people into the hall of the hie Priest called Caiaphas:
4 And consulted together that they might
take Iesus by subtiltie, and kill him.
5 But they said, Not on the [a] feast *day*, lest
any vproare be among the people.

* *Marke* 14.1. *luke* 22.1.

1 Christ witnesseth by his voluntarie going to death, that he wil make full satisfaction for the sinne of Adam, by his obedience.

2 God himselfe and not men, appointed the time that Christ should be crucified in.

* *Iohn* 11.47.

a *By this word Feast, is meant the whole feast of vnleauened bread: the first and eight day whereof, were so holy, that they might doe no manner of worke therein, though the whole companie of the Sandhedrin determined otherwise: And yet it came to passe through Gods prouidence, that Christ suffered at that time, to the end that all the people of Israel might be witnesses of his euerlasting sacrifice.*

6 ¶ * [3] And

6 ¶ *[3] And when Iesus was in Bethania,
in the house of Simon the leper,
7 [b] There came vnto him a woman, which
had a [c] boxe of very costly ointment, and powred it on his head, as he sate at the table.
8 And when his [d] disciples sawe it, they
had indignation, saying, What needed this
[e] waste?
9 For this ointment might haue beene
solde for much, and been giuen to the poore.
10 [4] And Iesus knowing it, said vnto them,
Why trouble yee the woman? for shee hath
wrought a good worke vpon me.
11 *[5] For yee haue the poore alwayes with
you, but me shall ye not haue alwayes.
12 For [f] in that she powred this oyntment
on my body, she did it to burie me.
13 Verely I say vnto you, Wheresoeuer
this Gospel shalbe preached thorowout all the
world, there shall also this that she hath done,
be spoken of for a memoriall of her.
14 ¶ *Then one of the twelue, called Iudas Iscariot, went vnto the chiefe Priests,
15 And said, What will yee giue me, and I
will deliuer him vnto you? and they appointed
vnto him thirtie *pieces* of siluer.
16 And from that time, hee sought opportunitie to betray him.
17 ¶ *[6] Now [g] on the first *day* of the feast
of vnleauened bread the disciples came to Iesus, saying vnto him, Where wilt thou that we
prepare for thee to eate the Passeouer?
18 And hee said, Goe yee into the citie to
such a man, and say to him, The Master sayth,
My time is at hand: I will keepe the Passeouer
at thine house with my disciples.
19 And the disciples did as Iesus had giuen
them charge, and made readie the Passeouer.
20 *So when the euen was come, hee [h] sate
downe with the twelue.
21 And as they did eate, hee said, *Verely
I say vnto you, that one of you shall betray me.
22 And they were exceeding sorowful, and
began euery one of them to say vnto him, Is it
I, Master?
23 And hee answered, and said, *Hee that
[i] dippeth his hand with me in the dish, he shall
betray me.
24 Surely the Sonne of man goeth his way,
as it is written of him: but woe *be* to that man,
by whome the Sonne of man is betrayed: it
had beene good for that man, if he had neuer
beene borne.
25 Then Iudas [k] which betrayed him, answered and said, Is it I, master? Hee said vnto
him, Thou hast said it.
26 ¶ [7] *And as they did eate, Iesus tooke
the bread, and when he had [l] blessed, he brake
it, and gaue it to the disciples, and said, Take,
eate: [m] this is my body.
27 Also he tooke the cup, and when he had
giuen thankes, he gaue it them, saying, Drinke
ye [n] all of it.
28 [o] For this is my blood of the [p] newe Testament, that is shed for many, for the remission of sinnes.
29 I say vnto you, that I will not drinke
hencefoorth of this fruite of the vine vntill that
day, when I shall drinke it new with you in my
Fathers kingdome.
30 And when they had sung [q] a Psalme,
they went out into the mount of Oliues.
31 ¶ [8] *Then said Iesus vnto them, All ye
shall be offended by mee this night: for it is
written, I *will smite the shepheard, and the
sheepe of the flocke shalbe scattered.
32 But *after I am risen againe, I will goe
before you into Galile.
33 But Peter answered, and said vnto him,
Though that all men should be offended by
thee, yet will I neuer be offended.
34 *Iesus said vnto him, Verely I say vnto
thee, that this night, before the cocke crowe,
thou shalt denie me thrice.
35 Peter said vnto him, Though I should
die with thee, I wil in no case denie thee. Likewise also said all the disciples.
36 ¶ *[9] Then went Iesus with them into a
place which is called Gethsemane, and sayd
vnto his disciples, Sit ye here, while I goe, and
pray yonder.
37 And hee tooke vnto him Peter, and the
two sonnes of Zebedeus, and began to waxe
sorowfull, and [r] grieuously troubled.
38 [10] Then said Iesus vnto them, My soule
is very heauie, *euen* vnto the death: tarie yee
here, and watch with me.
39 So hee went a little further, and fell on
his face, and prayed, saying, O my Father, if it
be possible [s] let this [t] cup passe from me: neuerthelesse, not as I will, but as thou wilt.
40 [11] After, he came vnto his disciples, and
found them asleepe, and said to Peter, What?

* *Marke 14.3. iohn 11.2.*

3 By this sudden worke of a sinfull woman, Christ giueth the guests to vnderstand of his death and buriall which was nigh: the sauour whereof shall bring life to all sinners which flee vnto him. But Iudas taketh an occasion here by to accomplish his wicked purpose and counsell.

b *For these things were done before Christ came to Hierusalem: and yet some thinke that the Euangelists recite two histories.*

c *These boxes were of alabaster, which in old time men made hollow to put in oyntments: for some write, that alabaster keepeth oyntment without corruption, Plinie booke 13. chap. 1.*

d *This is a figure called Synecdoche: for it is said but of Iudas that he was mooued thereat, Iohn 12.14.*

e *Vnprofitable spending.*

4 We ought not rashly to condemne that which is not orderly done.

* *Deut. 15.11.*

5 Christ who was once anointed in his owne person, must alwayes be anointed in the poore.

f *In that she powred this oyntment vpon my body, she did it to bury me.*

* *Mark. 14.10.*

* *Marke 14.12. luke 22.7.*

6 Christ verely purposing to bring vs into our countrey out of hand, and so to abrogate the figure of the Law, fulfilleth the Law, neglecting the contrary tradition and custome of the Iewes: and therewithall sheweth that all things shall so come to passe by the ministerie of men, that the secret custome of God shall gouerne them. g *This was the fourteenth day of the first moneth: and the first day of vnleauened bread should haue beene the fifteenth, but because this dayes euening (which after the manner of the Romanes was referred to the day before) did belong by the Iewes manner to the day following, therefore it is called the first day of vnleauened bread.* * *Luke 22.14.* h *Because the Lawe appointed them to be shod, and haue their staues in their hands, as though they were in haste, thereby it is to be gathered, that they sate not downe when they did eate the Passeouer, but stood, for otherwise when they went to meate, they put off their shooes: therefore he speaketh here in this place, not of the Passeouer, but of the Supper, which was celebrated after that the Passeouer was solemnely done.* * *Marke 14.18. iohn 13.21.* * *Psalm. 41.9.* i *That is to say, whome I vouchsafed to come to my table, alluding to the place, Psal. 41.10. which is not so to be vnderstood, as though at the selfe same instant that the Lord spake these words, Iudas had had his hand in the dish (for that had beene an vndoubted token) but it is meant of his tabling and eating with him.*

k *Whose head was about nothing els but to betray him.*

7 Christ minding forthwith to fulfill the promises of the olde couenant, instituteth a newe couenant with new signes.

* *1. Cor. 11.24.*

l *Marke sayth, Had giuen thankes: and therefore blessing is not a consecrating, with a coniuring kind of murmuring and force of words: and yet the bread and the wine are changed, not in nature but in qualitie, for they become vndoubted tokens of the body and blood of Christ, not of their owne nature or force of words, but by Christ his institution, which must be recited and laid foorth, that faith may finde what to lay hold on, both in the word and in the elements.*

m *This is a figuratiue speech, which is called Metonymia: that is to say, the putting of one name for another: so calling the bread his body, which is the signe and sacrament of his body: and yet notwithstanding, it is so a figuratiue and changed kind of speech, that the faithfull do receiue Christ in deed with all his gifts (though by a spirituall means) & become one with him.*

n *Therefore they which tooke away the cup from the people, did against Christ his institution.*

o *To wit, this cup or wine, is my blood sacramentally, as Luke 22.20.*

q *Or, couenant, that is to say, whereby the new league and couenant is made, for in making of leagues, they vsed powring of wine and shedding of blood.* q *When they had made an end of their solemne singing, which some thinke was sixe Psalmes, beginning at the 112. to the 117.* 8 Christ being more carefull of his disciples then of himselfe, forewarneth them of their flight, and putteth them in better comfort. * *Mark. 14.27. iohn 16.32. and 18.8.* * *Zech. 13.7.* * *Mar. 14.28. & 16.7.* * *Ioh. 13.38. mar. 14.30.* 9 Christ hauing regard to the weaknesse of his disciples, leauing all the rest in safety, taketh with him but three to be witnesses of his anguish, and goeth of purpose into the place appointed to betray him in. r *The word which he vseth, signifieth great sorow, and marueilous and deadly griefe: which thing, as it betokeneth the trueth of mans nature, which shunneth death as a thing that entred in against nature, so it sheweth that though Christ were void of sinne, yet he susteined this horrible punishment, because he felt the wrath of God kindled against vs for sinnes, which he reuenged and punished in his person.* 10 Christ a true man, going about to suffer the punishment which was due vnto vs, for forsaking of God, is forsaken of his owne: hee hath a terrible conflict with the horror & feare of the curse of God: out of which he escaping as conquerour, causeth vs not to be any more afraid of death. s *Let it passe me, and not touch me.* t *That is, which is at hand, and is offered and prepared for me: a kinde of speech which the Hebrewes vse, for the wrath of God, and the punishment hee sendeth: aboue Chap. 20.22.* 11 An example of the carefulnesse of man.

could

could ye not watch with me one houre ?
41 Watch, and pray, that ye enter not into
tentation : the spirit in deede is ready, but the
flesh is weake.
42 Againe he went away the second time,
and prayed, saying, O my Father, if this cuppe
cannot passe away from me, but that I must
drinke it, thy will be done.
43 And hee came, and found them asleepe
againe, for their eyes were heauie.
44 So he left them, and went away againe,
and prayed the third time, saying the same
wordes.
45 Then came hee to his disciples, and said
vnto them, Sleepe hencefoorth, and take your
rest : behold, the houre is at hand, & the Sonne
of man is giuen into the hands of sinners.
46 [12] Rise, let vs goe : behold, he is at hand
that betrayeth me.
47 * And while he yet spake, loe Iudas one
of the twelue came, and with him a great multitude with swords and staues, [u] from the high
Priests and Elders of the people.
48 Now hee that betrayed him, had giuen
them a token, saying, Whomsoeuer I shall
kisse, that is he, lay hold on him.
49 And foorthwith hee came to Iesus, and
said, God saue thee, Master, and kissed him.
50 [13] Then Iesus said vnto him, [x] Friend,
wherefore art thou come? Then came they,
and laid hands on Iesus, and tooke him.
51 And behold, one of them which were
with Iesus, stretched out *his* hand, and drewe
his sword, and stroke a seruant of the hie Priest,
and smote off his eare.
52 [14] Then said Iesus vnto him, Put vp thy
sword into his place : * for all that [y] take the
sword, shall perish with the sword.
53 [15] Either thinkest thou, that I cannot
now pray to my Father, and hee will giue me
moe then twelue legions of Angels?
54 [z] How then should the * Scriptures be
fulfilled, *which say*, that it must be so?
55 The same houre said Iesus to the multitude, Ye be come out as *it were* against a thiefe,
with swords and staues to take me : I sate daily teaching in the Temple among you, and yee
tooke me not.
56 But all this was done, that the Scriptures
of the Prophets might be fulfilled. * Then all
the disciples forsooke him, and fled.
57 ¶ * [16] And they tooke Iesus, and led him
to [a] Caiaphas the hie Priest, where the Scribes
and the Elders were assembled.
58 And Peter followed him afarre off vnto the high Priests [b] hall, and went in, and sate
with the seruants to see the end.
59 Now * the chiefe Priests and the Elders,
and all the whole Councill sought false witnesse against Iesus, to put him to death.
60 But they found none, and though many
false witnesses came, yet found they none : but
at the last came two false witnesses,

12 Christ offereth himselfe willingly to be taken, that in so obeying willingly, he might make satisfaction for the wilful fall of man.
* Marke 14.43. luke 22.47. iohn 18.3.
u *Sent from the high Priests.*
13 Christ is taken, that wee might be deliuered.
x *Christ reprehendeth Iudas tantingly, and rebuketh him sharply, for he knewe well enough for what cause he came.*
14 Our vocation must be the rule of our zeale.
* Gen. 9.6. reuel. 13.10.
y *They take the sword to whom the Lord hath not giuen it, that is to say, they which vse the sword, and are not called to it.*
15 Christ was taken, because he was willing to be taken.
z *By this questioning, he answereth a slie obiection, for they might haue asked him, why he did not in this his great extremity of danger, call to his Father for aid : but to this he answereth by a question.*
* Isa 35.10.
* Verse 31.
* Marke 14.53. luke 12.54. iohn 18.14.
16 Christ being innocent is condemned of the high Priest for that wickednesse whereof we are guiltie.
a *From Annas to Caiaphas, before whom the multitude was assembled, Iohn 18.13.*
b *The word here vsed, signifieth properly an open large roume before an house, as we see in Kings palaces and noble mens houses : we call it a court, for it is open to the aire, and by a figure Synecdoche, is taken for the house it selfe.*
* Marke 14.55.

61 And said, This man sayd, * I can destroy
the Temple of God, and build it in three dayes.
62 Then the chiefe Priest arose, and said to
him, Answerest thou nothing? [c] What is the
matter that these men witnesse against thee?
63 But Iesus held his peace. Then the chiefe
Priest answered, and said to him, I charge thee
sweare vnto vs by the liuing God, to tell vs, If
thou be that Christ the Sonne of God, *or no.*
64 * Iesus sayd to him, Thou hast said it :
neuerthelesse I say vnto you, [d] hereafter shall
yee see the Sonne of man, sitting [e] at the right
hand of the power *of God*, and come in the
[f] clouds of the heauen.
65 Then the high Priest [g] rent his clothes,
saying, Hee hath blasphemed, what haue we
any more neede of witnesses? behold, now ye
haue heard his blasphemie.
66 What thinke yee? They answered, and
said, He is guiltie of death.
67 * Then spet they in his face, and buffeted him, and other smote him with rods,
68 Saying, Prophecie to vs, O Christ, Who
is he that smote thee?
69 ¶ * [17] Peter [h] sate without in the hall,
and a maid came to him, saying, Thou also wast
with Iesus of Galile :
70 But hee denied before them all, saying,
I wote not what thou sayest.
71 And when he went out into the porch,
another *maide* sawe him, and sayd vnto them
that were there, This man was also with Iesus
of Nazareth.
72 And againe he denied with an othe, saying, I know not the man.
73 So after a while, came vnto him they
that stood by, and said vnto Peter, Surely thou
art also one of them : for euen thy speech be-
wrayeth thee.
74 Then began hee to [i] curse *himselfe*, and
to sweare, saying, I knowe not the man. And
immediatly the cocke crew.
75 Then Peter remembred the wordes of
Iesus, which had said vnto him, Before the
cocke crowe thou shalt denie me thrice. So he
went out, and wept bitterly.

* Iohn 2.19.
c *How commeth it to passe that these men witnesse against thee?*
* Chap. 16.27. rom 14.10. 1. thess. 4.14.
d *This word distinguisheth his first comming from the latter.*
e *Sitting with God in like and equall honour at the right hand of his power, that is, in greatest power : for the right hand signifieth among the Hebrewes, that that is mightie and of great power.*
f *Clouds of heauen, Looke afore, Chap. 24.30.*
g *This was an vsuall matter among the Iewes : for so were they bound to do, when they heard any Israelite to blaspheme God, and it was a tradition of their Talmude in the booke of the Magistrates, in the title, of the foure kindes of death.*
* Esai 50.6.
* Marke 14.66. luke 22.55. iohn 18.29.
17 Peter by the wonderfull prouidence of God, appointed to be a witnesse of all these things, is prepared to the example of singular constancie, by the experience of his owne incredulitie.
h *That is, without the place where the Bishop sate, but not without the house, for afterward he went from thence into the porch.*
i *He swore and cursed himselfe.*

CHAP. XXVII.

2 Hee is deliuered bound to Pilate. 5 Iudas hangeth himselfe. 19 Pilates wife. 20 Barabbas is asked. 24 Pilate washeth his hands. 29 Christ is crowned with thorne. 34 He is crucified, 40 Reuiled. 50 Hee giueth vp the ghost. 57 He is buried. 62 The souldiers watch him.

WHen * the morning was come, all the
chiefe Priests, and the Elders of the
people tooke counsell against Iesus, to put
him to death,
2 And ledde him away bound, and deliuered him vnto Pontius Pilate the gouernour.
3 ¶ [1] Then when Iudas which betrayed
him, saw that he was condemned, he repented
himselfe, and brought againe the thirtie *pieces*
of siluer to the chiefe Priests and Elders,
4 Saying, I haue sinned, betraying the
innocent

* Marke 15.1. luke 22.66. iohn 18.28.
1 An example of the horrible iudgement of God, as well against them which sel Christ, as against them which buy Christ.

innocent blood. But they said, What is that to
vs? see thou to it.
5 And when he had cast downe the siluer
pieces in the Temple, he [a] departed, and went,
* and hanged himselfe.
6 And the chiefe Priests tooke the siluer
pieces, and said, It is not lawfull for vs to put
them into the [b] treasure, because it is the price
[c] of blood.
7 And they tooke counsell, and bought
with them a potters field, for the buriall of
[d] strangers.
8 Wherefore that field is called, * The
field of blood, vntill this day.
9 (Then was fulfilled that which was spoken by [e] Ieremias the Prophet, saying, * [f] And
they tooke thirtie siluer *pieces*, the price of him
that was valued, whom *they* of the children of
Israel valued.
10 And they gaue them for the Potters
field, as the Lord appointed me.)
11 ¶ [2] * And Iesus stood before the gouernour, and the gouernour asked him, saying, Art
thou the King of the Iewes? Iesus said vnto
him, Thou sayest it.
12 And when he was accused of the chiefe
Priests and Elders, he answered nothing.
13 Then said Pilate vnto him, Hearest thou
not how many things they lay against thee?
14 But hee answered him not to one word,
in so much that the Gouernour marueiled
greatly.
15 [3] Now at the feast, the gouernour was
woont to deliuer vnto the people a prisoner
whom they would.
16 And they had then a notable prisoner
called Barabbas.
17 When they were then gathered together, Pilate sayd vnto them, Whether will yee
that I let loose vnto you Barabbas, or Iesus
which is called Christ?
18 (For hee knew well, that for enuie they
had deliuered him.
19 Also when hee was set downe vpon the
iudgement seate, his wife sent to him, saying,
Haue thou nothing to doe with that iust man:
for I haue suffered many things this day in a
dreame by reason of him.)
20 * But the chiefe Priests and the Elders
had perswaded the people that they should
aske Barabbas, and should destroy Iesus.
21 Then the gouernour answered, and said
vnto them, Whether of the twaine will yee
that I let loose vnto you? And they said, Barabbas.
22 Pilate said vnto them, What shall I doe
then with Iesus, which is called Christ? They
all said to him, Let him be crucified.
* 23 Then said the gouernour, But what euill
hath he done? Then they cried the more, saying, Let him be crucified.
24 [4] When Pilate sawe that hee auailed nothing, but that more tumult was made, hee

a Out of mens sights.
* *Actes 1.18.*
b The treasure of the temple.
c Of life and death.
d Strangers and guests, whome the Iewes could not abide to be ioyned vnto, no not after they were dead.
* *Actes 1.19.*
e Seeing this prophecie is read in Zach.11.12. it cannot be denyed but Ieremies name crept into the text either through the Printers fault, or by some others ignorance: it may be also that it came out of the margine, by reason of the abbreuiation of the letters, the one being Iou, the other Zou, which are not much vnlike: But in the Syrian text the Prophets name is not set downe at all.
* *Zach. 11.12.*
f The Euangelist doeth not follow the Prophets words, but his meaning, which he sheweth to be fulfilled.
2 Christ holdeth his peace when he is accused, that we may not be accused: acknowledging our guiltinesse, and therewithall his owne innocencie.
* *Marke 15.2. luke 23.3. iohn 18.33.*
3 Christ is first quitted of the same Iudge, before he be condemned, that we might see how the iust died for the vniust.
* *Marke 15.11. luke 23.18. iohn 18.40. actes 3.14.*
4 Christ being quit by the testimonie of the Iudge himselfe, is notwithstanding condemned by the same, to quit vs before God.

tooke water and [g] washed his hands before the
multitude, saying, I am innocent of the [h] blood
of this iust man: looke you to it.
25 Then answered all the people, and said,
[i] His blood *be* on vs, and on our children.
26 Thus let he Barabbas loose vnto them,
and scourged Iesus, and deliuered him to bee
crucified.
27 ¶ * Then the souldiers of the gouernour
tooke Iesus into the common hall, and gathered about him the whole band,
28 [5] And they stripped him, and [k] put about
him a [l] skarlet robe,
29 And platted a crowne of thornes, and
put it vpon his head, and a reede in his right
hand, and bowed their knees before him, and
mocked him, saying, God saue thee king of the
Iewes,
30 And spitted vpon him, and tooke a
reede, and smote him on the head.
31 Thus when they had mocked him, they
tooke the robe from him, and put his owne
raiment on him, and ledde him away to crucifie him.
32 * And as they came out, they found a
man of Cyrene, named Simon: him they
[m] compelled to beare his crosse.
33 * [6] And when they came vnto the place
called Golgotha, (that is to say, the place of
dead mens skulles)
34 [7] They gaue him vineger to drinke, mingled with gall: and when hee had tasted thereof, he would not drinke.
35 ¶ [8] And when they had crucified him,
they parted his garments, and did cast lottes,
that it might be fulfilled, which was spoken by
the Prophet, * They diuided my garments
among them, and vpon my vesture did cast
lottes.
36 And they sate, and watched him there.
37 ¶ [9] They set vp also ouer his head his
cause written, THIS IS IESVS THE KING
OF THE IEVVES.
38 ¶ [10] And there were two theeues crucified with him, one on the right hand, and another on the left.
39 [11] And they that passed by, reuiled him,
wagging their heads,
40 And saying, * Thou that destroyest the
Temple, and buildest it in three dayes, saue thy
selfe: if thou be the Sonne of God, come down
from the crosse.
41 Likewise also the high Priests mocking
him, with the Scribes, and Elders, and Pharises, said,
42 Hee saued others, *but* hee cannot saue
himselfe: if hee be the King of Israel, let him
now come downe from the crosse, and we will
beleeue in him.

g It was a maner in olde time, when any man was murthered and in other slaughters, to wash their hands in water, to declare themselues guiltlesse.
h Of the murder, an Hebrew kinde of speech.
i If there be any offence committed in slaying him, let vs and our posteritie smart for it.
* *Marke 15.16. iohn 19.2.*
5 Christ suffereth that reproch which was due to our sinnes, notwithstanding in the meane time by the secret prouidence of God, he is intituled king by them which did him that reproch.
k They cast a cloake about him, and wrapped it about him, for it lacked sleeues.
l Iohn and Marke make mention of a purple robe, which is also a very pleasant redde. But these prophane and malapert saucie souldiers clad Iesus in this aray, to mocke him withall, who was in deede a true King.
* *Marke 15.21. luke 23.26.*
m They compelled Simon to beare his burdensome crosse, whereby it appeareth that Iesus was so sore handled before, that he fainted by the way, and was not able to beare his crosse thorow: for Iohn writeth that hee did beare the crosse, to wit, at the beginning.
* *Marke 15.22. iohn 19.17.*
6 He is led out of the citie that we might be brought into the heauenly kingdome.
7 Christ found no comfort any where, that in him we might be filled with all comfort.
8 He is made a curse, that in him we may be blessed: he is spoiled of his garments, that we might be enriched by his nakednesse.
* *Psal. 22.18. marke 15.24.*
9 Hee is pronounced the true Messias, euen of them of whom hee is reiected. 10 Christ began then to iudge the world, when after his iudgement, hee hung betweene two theeues. 11 To make full satisfaction for vs, Christ suffereth and ouercommeth not onely the torments of the bodie, but also the most horrible torments of the minde.

*Iohn 2. 19.
*Psal.22.9.
n This is spoken by the figure Synecdoche, for there was but one of them that did reuile him.

43 *Hee trusted in God, let him deliuer him now, if he will haue him: for he said, I am the Sonne of God.

44 The selfe same thing also the [n] theeues which were crucified with him, cast in his teeth.

12 Heauen it selfe is darkened for very horror, and Iesus cryeth out frō the depth of hel, and in the meane while he is mocked.

45 [12]Now from the sixt houre was there darkenesse ouer all the land, vnto the ninth houre.

*Psal.28.1.

46 And about the ninth houre Iesus cryed with a loude voice, saying, *Eli, Eli, lamasabachthani? that is, My God, my God, why hast thou [o] forsaken me?

o To wit, in this misery: And this crying out is proper to his humanity, which notwithstanding was voyd of sinne, but yet it felt the wrath of God, which is due to our sinnes.

47 And some of them that stood there, when they heard it, sayd, This man calleth [p] Elias.

p They allude to Elias name, not for want of vnderstāding the tongue, but of a prophane impudency and saucinesse, and he repeated those words, to the ende that this better harping vpon the name, might be vnderstood.

48 And straightway one of them ranne, and tooke * a sponge, and filled it with vineger, and put it on a reede, and gaue him to drinke.

*Psal. 69. 22.

49 Other said, Let be: let vs see, if Elias will come and saue him.

13 Christ after he had ouercome other enemies, at lēgth prouoketh and setteth vpon death it selfe.

50 [13] Then Iesus cryed againe with a loude voice, and yeelded vp the ghost.

14 Christ when he is dead, sheweth himselfe to be God Almighty, euen his enemies confessing the same.

51 [14] And behold, *the [q] vaile of the Temple was rent in twaine, from the toppe to the bottome, and the earth did quake, and the stones were clouen.

*2. Chron.3.14.
q Which diuided the holiest of all.

52 And the [r] graues did open themselues, and many bodies of the Saints, which slept, arose,

r That is to say, the stones claue in sunder, and the graues did open themselues, to shew by this token that death was ouercome: and the resurrection of the dead followed the resurrection of Christ, as appeareth by the next verse following.

53 And came out of the graues after his resurrection, and went into the holy citie, and appeared vnto many.

54 When the Centurion, and they that were with him watching Iesus sawe the earthquake, and the things that were done, they feared greatly, saying, Truely this was the Sonne of God.

55 ¶And many women were there, beholding him afarre off, which had followed Iesus from Galile, ministring vnto him.

56 Among whom was Mary Magdalene, and Mary the mother of Iames, and Ioses, and the mother of Zebedeus sonnes.

13 Christ is buried, not priuily or by stealth, but by the Gouernors consent, by a famous man, in a place not farre distant, in a new sepulchre, so that it cannot bee doubted of his death.

*Marke 15.42. luke 23.50. iohn 19.38.

57 ¶[15] *And when the euen was come, there came a rich man of Arimathea, named Ioseph, who had also himselfe beene Iesus disciple.

58 He went to Pilate, and asked the bodie of Iesus. Then Pilate commanded the bodie to be deliuered.

59 So Ioseph tooke the body, and wrapped it in a cleane linnen cloth,

60 And put it in his new tombe, which hee had hewen out in a rocke, and rolled a great stone to the doore of the sepulchre, and departed.

61 And there was Mary Magdalene, & the other Mary sitting ouer against the sepulchre.

16 The keeping of the sepulchre is committed to Christs owne murtherers, that there might be no doubt of his resurrection.

62 ¶[16] Now the next day that followed the Preparation *of the Sabbath*, the hie Priests and Pharises assembled to Pilate,

63 And sad, Sir, wee remember that that deceiuer said, while hee was yet aliue, Within three dayes I will rise.

64 Commaund therefore, that the sepulchre be made sure vntill the third day, lest his disciples come by night, and steale him away, and say vnto the people, Hee is risen from the dead: so shall the last errour be worse then the first.

65 Then Pilate said vnto them, Yee haue a [s] watch: goe, and make it sure as ye know.

s The souldiers of the garison which were appointed to keepe the Temple.

66 And they went, and made the sepulchre sure with the watch, and sealed the stone.

CHAP. XXVIII.

1 The women goe to the sepulchre. 2 The Angel. 9 The women see Christ. 18 Hee sendeth his Apostles to preach.

*Marke 16.5. iohn 20. 11.

1 Christ hauing put death to flight in the sepulchre, riseth by his owne power, as straightway the Angel witnesseth.

a At the going out of the Sabbath, that is, about day breake after the Romanes count, which reckon the naturall day from the sunne rising to the next sunne rising: and not as the Hebrews, which count from euening to euening.

b When the morning of the first day after the Sabbath beganne to dawne: and that first day is the same, which we now call Sunday, or the Lords day.

NOw *in [1] the [a] end of the Sabbath, when the first *day* of the weeke [b] beganne to dawne, Mary Magdalene, and the other Mary came to see the sepulchre,

2 And behold, there was a great earthquake: for the Angell of the Lord descended from heauen, and came and rolled backe the stone from the doore, and sate vpon it.

3 And his [c] countenance was like lightening, and his raiment white as snow.

c The beames of his eyes, and by the figure Synechdoche, for the countenance.

4 And for feare of him, the keepers were astonied, and became as dead men.

5 But the Angel answered, and said to the women, Feare [d] yee not: for I know that yee seeke Iesus which was crucified:

d The word (Ye) is spoken with force to confirme the women, now that the souldiers were afraid.

6 Hee is not here, for he is risen, as hee sayd: come, see the place where the Lord was laid,

7 And goe quickely, and tell his disciples, that he is risen from the dead: and behold, hee goeth before you into Galile: there ye shall see him: loe, I haue told you.

8 So they departed quickly from the sepulchre, with feare and great ioy, and did runne to bring his disciples word.

2 Christ appeareth himselfe after his resurrection, and sending the women to his disciples, sheweth that he hath not forgotten them.

9 [2]And as they went to tell his disciples, beholde, Iesus also met them, saying, God saue you. And they came, and tooke him by the feet and worshipped him.

10 Then sayd Iesus vnto them, Bee not afraid. Goe, *and* tell my brethren, that they goe into Galile, and there shall they see me.

3 The more the sunne shineth, the more are the wicked blinded.

11 ¶[3]Now when they were gone, behold, some of the watch came into the city, & shewed vnto the hie Priests all the things that were done.

12 And they gathered them together with the Elders, and tooke counsell, and gaue large money vnto the souldiers,

13 Saying, Say, His disciples came by night and stole him away while we slept.

14 And if this matter [e] come before the gouernour to bee heard, wee will perswade him, and so vse the matter that you shall not neede to care.

e For it was to be feared, that it would be brought to the Gouernours eares.

15 So they tooke the money, and did as
they were taught: and this saying is noised a-
mong the Iewes vnto this day.
16 ¶[4] Then the eleuen disciples went into
Galile, into a mountaine where Iesus had appointed them.
17 And when they saw him, they worshipped him: but some doubted.
18 And Iesus came, and spake vnto them,
saying, *All power is giuen vnto me, in heauen, and in earth.
19 *[5] Goe therefore, and teach all nations,
baptizing them [f] in the Name of the Father,
and the Sonne, and the holy Ghost,
20 Teaching them to obserue all things,
whatsoeuer I haue commanded you: and loe,
*I am with you [g] alway, vntill the end of the
world, Amen.

4 Christ appeareth also to his disciples, whom he maketh Apostles.

* Heb.1.2.chap.11.27.ioh.17 2.

* Marke 16.15. 5 The summe of the Apostleship, is the publishing of the doctrine receiued of Christ throughout all the world, and the ministring of the Sacraments: the efficacie of which things, hangeth not of the ministers, but of the Lord. *f Calling vpon the Name of the Father, the Sonne, and the holy Ghost.* * Iohn 14.16. *g For euer: and this place is meant of the manner of the presence of his Spirit, by meanes whereof hee maketh vs partakers both of himselfe, and of all his benefites, but is absent from vs in bodie.*

THE HOLY GOSPEL OF IESVS CHRIST, ACCORDING TO S. MARKE.

CHAP. I.

4 Iohn baptizeth. 6 His apparell and meate. 9 Iesus is baptized. 12 He is tempted. 14 He preacheth the Gospel. 21 and 39 He teacheth in the Synagogues. 23 He healeth one that had a deuill. 29 Peters mother in lawe. 32 Many diseased persons. 40 The Leper.

THe beginning of the Gospel
of Iesus Christ, the Sonne of
God:
2 [1] As it is written in the
[a] Prophets, *Behold, [b] I send
my messenger [c] before thy
face, which shall prepare thy way before thee.
3 *The voice of him that cryeth in the
wildernesse, *is*, Prepare the way of the Lord:
make his pathes straight.
4 [2]* Iohn did baptize in the wildernesse,
and preach the [d] baptisme of amendment of
life, for remission of sinnes.
5 And all the countrey of Iudea, and they
of Ierusalem went out vnto him, and were all
baptized of him in the riuer Iordan, confessing
their sinnes.
6 *Now Iohn was clothed with camels
haire, and with a girdle of a skinne about his
loines, and hee did eate *locusts and wilde
honie,
7 *[3] And preached, saying, A stronger
then I commeth after me, whose shoes latchet
I am not worthie to [e] stoupe downe, and vnloose.
8 Trueth it is, I haue [f] baptized you with
water: but he will baptize you with the holy
Ghost.
9 ¶*[4] And it came to passe in those dayes,
that Iesus came from Nazareth, a *citie* of Galile, and was baptized of Iohn in Iordan.
10 [5] And assoone as [g] hee was come out of
the water, *Iohn* sawe the heauens clouen in
twaine, and the holy Ghost descending vpon
him like a doue.
11 Then there was a voice from heauen,
saying, Thou art my beloued sonne, in whome
I am [h] well pleased.
12 *[6] And immediatly the spirit [i] driueth
him into the wildernesse.
13 And he was there in the wildernesse fortie dayes, and was tempted of Satan: hee was
also with the wilde beasts, and the Angels ministred vnto him.
14 ¶*[7] Now after that Iohn was committed *to prison*, Iesus came into Galile, preaching
the Gospel of the kingdome of God,
15 And saying, The time is fulfilled, and the
kingdome of God is at hand: repent and beleeue the Gospel.
16 ¶*[8] And as hee walked by the sea of
Galile, hee sawe Simon and Andrew his brother, casting a net into the sea, (for they were
fishers)
17 Then Iesus said vnto them, Follow me,
and I will make you to be fishers of men.
18 And straightway they forsooke their
nets, and followed him.
19 [9] And when he had gone a little further
thence, hee saw Iames *the sonne* of Zebedeus,
and Iohn his brother, as they were in the ship,
mending their nets.
20 And anon hee called them: and they
left their father Zebedeus in the shippe with
his hired seruants, and went their way after
him.
21 ¶ So *they entred into [k] Capernaum,
and straightway on the Sabbath day he entred
into the Synagogue, and taught.
22 And they were astonied at his doctrine,
*for he taught them as one that had authority,
and not as the Scribes.
23 ¶[10] And there was in their Synagogue,
a man [l] in whome was an vncleane spirit, and
he cryed out,
24 Saying, Ah, what haue we to doe with
thee, O [m] Iesus of Nazareth? Art thou come
to

1 Iohn goeth before Christ as it was forespoken by the Prophets.
a This is the figure Metonymia, whereby is meant the bookes of the Prophets, Malachie and Esay.
* Mal.3.1.
b The Prophet vseth the present tense, when hee speaketh of a thing to come, being as sure of it, as if he saw it.
c A Metaphore taken from the vsage of Kings, which vse to haue vshers goe before them.
* Isa 40.3.luke 3.4.ioh.1.15.
2 The summe of Iohns doctrine, or rather Christs, is remission of sinnes and amendment of life.
* Mat.3.1.
d The Iewes vsed many kindes of washings: but here is spoken of a peculiar kinde of washing, which hath all the parts of true baptisme, amendment of life, and forgiuenesse of sinnes.
* Matth.3.4.
* Leuit.11.21.
* Mat.3.11.luke 3.16.iohn 1.26.actes 1.5.and 2.4 and 11.16.and 19.4.
3 Iohn and all ministers cast their eyes vpon Christ the Lord. *e The Euangelist his meaning was to expresse the condition of the basest seruant.* *f He sheweth that all the force of baptisme proceedeth from Christ, who baptizeth within.* * Matth.3.13.luke 3.21.iohn 1.33. 4 Christ doeth consecrate our baptisme in himselfe. 5 The vocation of Christ from heauen, as head of the Church. *g Iohn that went downe into the water with Christ.*

h Looke Mat.3.17.
* Mat.4.1.luke 4.1 heb.2.18.
6 Christ being tempted ouercommeth.
i Here is no violent and forcible driuing out meant: but the diuine power claddeth Christ (who had liued vntill this time as a priuate man) with a new person, and prepareth him to the combate that was at hand, and to his ministerie.
* Mat 4.12.luke 4. 4.iohn 4.43.
7 After that Iohn is taken, Christ sheweth himselfe fully.
* Matth.4.18.luke 5.2.
8 The calling of Simon and Andrew.
9 The calling of Iames and Iohn.
* Mat.4.13.luke 4 31.
k From the citie Nazareth.
* Mat.7.28.luke 4.32.
10 He preacheth that doctrine, by which alone Satan is driuen out of the world, which also he confirmeth by a miracle.
l Word for word, a man in an vncleane spirit, that is to say, possessed with an euill spirit.
m He was borne in Bethlehem but through the errour of the people, he was called a Nazarean, because hee was brought vp in Nazareth.

to destroy vs? I know thee what thou art, *euen*
that [n] Holy one of God.
25 And Iesus rebuked him, saying, Holde
thy peace, and come out of him.
26 And the vncleane spirit [o] tare him, and
cryed with a loude voice, and came out of
him.
27 And they were all amazed, so that they
demaunded one [p] of another, saying, What
thing is this? what new doctrine is this? for
hee [q] commandeth euen the foule spirits with
authoritie, and they obey him.
28 And immediatly his fame spread a-
broad throughout all the region [r] bordering on
Galile.
29 ¶ *[11] And assoone as they were come
out of the Synagogue, they entred into the
house of Simon and Andrew, with Iames and
Iohn.
30 And Simons wiues mother lay sicke of
a feuer, and anon they told him of her.
31 And he came and tooke her by the hand,
and lifted her vp, and the feuer forsooke her by
and by, and she ministred vnto them.
32 And when euen was come, at what time
the sunne setteth, they brought to him all that
were diseased, and them that were possessed
with deuils.
33 And the whole citie was gathered together at the doore.
34 And he healed many that were sicke of
diuers diseases: and hee cast out many deuils,
and [s] suffered not the deuils to say that they
knew him.
35 And in the morning very earely before
day, *Iesus* arose and went out into a solitarie
place, and there prayed.
36 And Simon, and they that were with
him, followed carefully after him.
37 And when they had found him, they
said vnto him, All men seeke for thee.
38 Then he said vnto them, Let vs go into
the [t] next townes, that I may preach there also: for I came out for that purpose.
49 And he preached in their Synagogues,
throughout all Galile, and cast the Deuils
out.
30 ¶ *[12] And there came a leper to him,
beseeching him, and kneeled downe vnto him,
and sayd to him, If thou wilt, thou canst make
me cleane.
41 And Iesus had compassion, and put
forth his hand, and touched him, and sayd to
him, I will: be thou cleane.
42 And assoone as he had spoken, immediatly the leprosie departed from him, and he
was made cleane.
43 And after hee had giuen him a straite
commaundement, hee sent him away foorthwith,
44 [13] And sayd vnto him, See thou say
nothing to any man, but get thee hence, and
shew thy selfe to the [u] * Priest, and offer for

n He alludeth to that name that was written in the golden plate which the high Priest wore, Exod. 28. 36.
o Looke beneath chap. 9. 20.
p As men amased.
q By his owne authoritie, or as a lord.
r Not onely into Galile, but also into the countries bordering vpon it.
* Mat. 8. 14. luke 4. 38.
11 By healing of diuers diseases, he sheweth that hee hath brought true life into the world.
s For it belongeth not to the deuils to preach the Gospel, Actes 16. 18.
t Villages which were as cities.
* Mat. 8. 2. luke 5. 12.
12 By healing the leprous, he sheweth that he came for this cause to wipe out the sinnes of the world with his touching.
13 He witnesseth that he was not moued with ambition, but with the onely desire of his fathers glorie, and loue towards poore sinners.
u All the posteritie of Aaron might iudge of a Leper.
* Leuit. 14. 4.

thy cleansing these things, which Moses commaunded, for a testimoniall vnto them.
45 But when he was departed, * he began
to tell many things, and to publish the matter:
so that Iesus could no more openly enter into
the citie, but was without in desart places: and
they came to him from euerie quarter.

CHAP. II.

3. and 4. One sicke of the palsie, hauing his sinnes forgiuen him, is healed. 14 Mathew is called. 19 Fastings and afflictions are foretold. 23 The disciples plucke the eares of corne. 26 The shew-bread.

AFter *[1] *a fewe* dayes, he entred into Capernaum againe, and it was noised that he
was in the [a] house.
2 And anon, many gathered together, in
so much that the [b] places about the dore could
not receiue any more: and he preached the
word vnto them.
3 And there came vnto him, that brought
one sicke of the palsie, borne of foure men.
4 And because they could not come neere
vnto him for the multitude, they vncouered
the roofe of the house where hee was: and
when they had broken it open, they [c] let
downe the [d] bed, wherein the sicke of the palsie lay.
5 Now when Iesus saw their faith, he said
to the sicke of the palsie, Sonne, thy sinnes are
forgiuen thee.
6 And there were certaine of the Scribes
sitting there, and [e] reasoning in their hearts,
7 Why doeth this man speake such blasphemies? * who can forgiue sinnes, but God
onely?
8 And immediatly when Iesus perceiued
in his spirite, that thus they reasoned with
themselues, he said vnto them, Why reason ye
these things in your hearts?
9 Whether is it easier to say to the sicke of
the palsie, Thy sinnes are forgiuen thee? or to
say, Arise, and take vp thy bed, and walke?
10 But that ye may know, that the sonne
of man hath authoritie in earth to forgiue sins,
(he sayd vnto the sicke of the palsie.)
11 I say vnto thee, Arise, and take vp thy
bed, and get thee hence into thine owne house.
12 And by and by hee arose, and tooke vp
his bed, and went foorth before them all, in
so much that they were all [f] amazed, and
glorified God, saying, We neuer sawe such a
thing.
13 ¶ [2] Then he went foorth againe toward
the sea, and all the people resorted vnto him,
and he taught them.
14 * And as Iesus passed by, he saw [g] Leui
the sonne of Alpheus sit at the receite of custome, and sayd vnto him, Follow mee. And he
arose and followed him.
15 ¶ And it came to passe, as Iesus sate at
table in his house, many Publicanes and sinners sate at table also with Iesus, and his disciples: for there were many that followed him.

* *Luke 5. 13.*
* Matth. 9. 1. luke 5. 18.
1 Christ sheweth by healing this man which was sicke of the palsie, that men recouer in him through faith onely, all their strength which they haue lost.
a In the house where he vsed to remaine: for he chose Capernaum to dwell in, and left Nazareth.
b Neither the house nor the entrie was able to hold them.
c They brake vp the vpper part of the house, which was plaine, and let downe the man that was sicke of the palsie into the lower part where Christ preached, for they could not otherwise come into his sight.
d The word signifieth the worst kind of bedde, whereupon men vse to lay downe themselues at noontide, and such other times to refresh themselues: we call it a couch.
e In their mindes disputing vpon that matter, on both sides.
* *Iob 14. 4. isa 43. 25.*
f Word for word, past themselues, or out of their wits.
2 The Gospel offendeth the proud, and saueth the humble.
* *Matth. 9. 9. luke 5. 27.*
g Matthew, an other name.

16 And when the Scribes and Pharises
sawe him eate with the Publicanes and sinners, they said vnto his disciples, How is it
that hee eateth and drinketh with Publicanes
and sinners?
17 Now when Iesus heard it, hee said vnto
them, The whole haue no need of the Physici-
on, but the sicke. *I came not to call the righteous, but the sinners to repentance.
18 *[3] And the disciples of Iohn, and the
Pharises did fast, and came and said vnto him,
Why doe the disciples of Iohn, and of the Pharises fast, and thy disciples fast not?
19 And Iesus said vnto them, Can the children of the marriage chamber fast, whiles the
bridegrome is with them? as long as they haue
the bridegrome with them, they cannot fast.
20 But the dayes wil come, when the bridegrome shall be taken from them, and then shall
they fast in those dayes.
21 And no man soweth a piece of new cloth
in an old garment: for else the new piece that
filled it vp, taketh away *somewhat* from the old,
and the breach is worse.
22 Likewise no man putteth new wine into olde vessels: for else the new wine breaketh
the vessels, and the wine runneth out, and the
vessels are lost: but new wine must be put into
new vessels.
23 ¶ *[4] And it came to passe as hee went
through the corne on the [h] Sabbath day, that
his disciples, as they went on their way, began
to plucke the eares of corne.
24 And the Pharises said vnto him, Behold,
why doe they on the Sabbath day that which is
not lawfull?
25 And hee said to them, Haue yee neuer
read what *Dauid did when hee had need, and
was an hungred, *both* hee, and they that were
with him?
26 How he went into the house of God, in
the dayes of [i] Abiathar the hie Priest, and did
eate the shew bread, which was not lawfull to
eate, but for the *Priests, and gaue also to them
which were with him?
27 And hee said to them, The Sabbath was
made for man, and not man for the Sabbath.
28 Wherefore the sonne of man is Lord,
euen of the [k] Sabbath.

* 1.Tim.1.13.
* Matth.9.14. luke 5.33.
3 The superstitious and hypocrites doe rashly put the summe of godlinesse in things indifferent, and are here for three causes reprehended. First, for that not considering what euery mans strength is able to beare, they rashly make all maner of lawes concerning such things, without all discretion.
* Matth.12.1. luke 6.1.
4 Secondarily, for that they make no difference betweene the lawes which God made concerning the same things, and lawes that are made of things which are vtterly vnlawfull.
h Word for word, on the Sabbaths, that is, on the holy dayes.
* 1.Sam.21.6.
i 1.Sam.21.1. *he is called Achimelech and his sonne Abiathar, but by conference of other places, it is plaine that both of them had two names, Looke 1.Chron.24.6. 2.Sam.8.17 and 15.29. 1.King.2.26. 2.King.25.18.*
* Exod.29.33. leuit.8.31. and 24.9.
k Hath the Sabbath day in his power, and may rule it as him listeth.

CHAP. III.

1 The withered hand is healed. 6 The Pharises consult with the Herodians. 10 Many are healed by touching Christ. 11 At his sight the deuils fall downe before him. 14 The twelue Apostles. 24 The kingdome diuided against it selfe. 29 Blasphemie against the holy Ghost. 33 Christs parents.

1 And *[1] hee entred againe into the Synagogue, and there was a man which had a
[a] withered hand.
2 And they watched him, whether hee
would heale him on the Sabbath day, that they
might accuse him.
3 Then hee said vnto the man which had
the withered hand, Arise: *stand foorth* in the
middes.
4 And he said to them, Is it lawfull to doe
a good deede on the Sabbath day, or to doe e-
uill? to saue the [b] life, or to kill? But they held
their peace.
5 Then hee looked round about on them
[c] angerly, mourning also for the [d] hardnesse
of their hearts, and said to the man, Stretch
forth thine hand. And he stretched it out: and
his hand was restored, as whole as the other.
6 ¶ [2] And the Pharises departed, and
straightway gathered a councill with the [e] Herodians against him, that they might destroy him.
7 But Iesus auoided with his Disciples to
the sea: and a great multitude followed him
from Galile, and from Iudea,
8 And from Ierusalem, and from Idumea,
and [f] beyond Iorden: and they that dwelled a-
bout Tyrus and Sydon, when they had heard
what great things hee did, came vnto him in
great number.
9 And hee commaunded his Disciples,
that a little shippe should [g] waite for him,
because of the multitude, lest they should
throng him.
10 For he had healed many, insomuch that
they preased vpon him to touch him, as many
as had [h] plagues.
11 And when the [i] vncleane spirits saw him,
they fell downe before him, and cried, saying,
Thou art the sonne of God.
12 And hee sharply rebuked them, to the
end they should not vtter him.
13 ¶ *Then he went vp into a mountaine,
and called vnto him whom he would, and they
came vnto him.
14 [3] And hee [k] appointed twelue, that they
should bee with him, and that hee might send
them to preach,
15 And that they might haue power to
heale sicknesses, and to cast out deuils.
16 And the first *was* Simon, and hee named
Simon, Peter.
17 Then Iames *the sonne* of Zebedeus, and
Iohn Iames brother (and surnamed them Boa-
nerges, which is, the sonnes of thunder,)
18 And Andrew, and Philip, and Bartlemew,
and Matthew, and Thomas, and Iames *the sonne*
of Alpheus, and [l] Thaddeus, and Simon the
Cananite,
19 And Iudas Iscariot, who also betrayed
him, and they came [m] home.
20 And the multitude assembled againe, so
that they could not so much as eate bread.
21 [4] And when his [n] kinsfolkes heard of it,
they went out to lay hold on him: for they said
that he was beside himselfe.
22 ¶ *And the Scribes which came downe

* Matth.12.9. luke 6.6.
1 Thirdly, for that they preferred the ceremoniall lawe (which was but an appendant to the morall law) before the morall law. Whereas contrariwise, they should haue learned out of this, the true vse of the ceremoniall law.
a That is, vnprofitable and dead.
b A figuratiue speach, by the figure Synecdoche. For this kind of saying, To saue the life, is as much as to saue the man.
c Men, when they haue wrong done vnto them, are angrie, but not without vice: but Christ is angrie without vice, neither is he firie so much for the iniurie that is done to his owne person, as for their wickednesse: and therefore he had pitie vpon them, and for that cause is he said to haue mourned.
d As though their heart had beene so closed vp, and growen together, that wholesome doctrine could preuaile no more with them.
2 The more the trueth is kept vnder, the more it commeth out.
e Looke Matth.22.16.
f Which Iosephus calleth stonie or rockie.
g Should alwayes be ready for him.
h Diseases wherewith God scourgeth men as it were with whips.
i In them whom they had entred into: or by the figure called Metonymia, for them which were vexed with the vncleane spirits.
* Chap.6.7. matth.10.1. luke 9.1.
3 The twelue Apostles are set apart to be trained vp to the office of the Apostleship.
k Chose and appointed out twelue to be familiar and conuersant with him.
l Whom Luke also calleth Iudas: and for difference sake, the other Iudas is called Iscariot.
m The disciples whom Christ had taken to be of his traine and liue with him, come home to his house, to be with him alwayes after.
4 None are worse enemies of the Gospel, then they that left ought.
n Word for word, they that were of him, that is, his kinsfolks: for they that were mad were brought to their kinsmen.
* Matth.9.34. and 12.24. luke 11.15.

from Hierusalem, said, Hee hath Beelzebub,
and through the prince of the deuils he casteth
out deuils.
23 But hee called them vnto him, and said
vnto them in parables, How can Satan driue
out Satan?
24 For if a kingdome bee diuided against it
selfe, that kingdome cannot stand.
25 Or if a house bee diuided against it selfe,
that house cannot continue.
26 So if [o] Satan make insurrection against
himselfe, and be diuided, he cannot endure, but
is at an end.

o Satans imps or band.

27 No man can enter into a strong mans
house, and take away his goods, except hee
first binde that strong man, and then spoyle his
house.
28 ¶ * [5] Verily I say vnto you, all sinnes
shall be forgiuen vnto the children of men, and
blasphemies, wherewith they blaspheme:
29 But he that blasphemeth against the holy Ghost, shall neuer haue forgiuenesse, but is
culpable of eternall damnation.
30 [p] Because they said, He had an vncleane
spirit.

**Matth.18.31. luke 12.10. 1.iohn 5.16.*
5 They onely are without hope of saluation, which doe maliciously oppugne Christ, whom they know.
p These are the words of the Euangelist.

31 ¶ * Then came his [q] brethren and mother, and stood without, and sent vnto him, and
called him.
32 And the people sate about him, and they
said vnto him, Behold, thy mother, and thy brethren seeke for thee without.
33 But hee answered them, saying, Who is
my mother and my brethren?
34 [6] And he looked round about on them,
which sate in compasse about him, and said, Behold my mother and my brethren.
35 For whosoeuer doeth the will of God,
hee is my brother, and my sister, and my mother.

** Matth.12.46. luke 8.19.*
q Under this name Brother, the Hebrewes vnderstand all that are of the same stocke and kinred.
6 The spirituall kinred is farre otherwise to be accounted of, then the carnall or fleshly.

CHAP. IIII.

4 The parable of the sower, 14 And the meaning thereof. 18 Thornes. 22 The candle. 26 Of him that sowed, and then slept. 31 The graine of mustard seede. 38 Christ sleepeth in the ship.

AND * hee began againe to teach by the
[a] sea side, and there gathered vnto him a
great multitude, so that hee entred into a ship,
and sate [b] in the sea, and all the people was by
the sea side on the land.
2 And hee taught them many things in
parables, and said vnto them in his doctrine,
3 [1] Hearken: Behold, there went out a
sower to sow.
4 And it came to passe as hee sowed, that
some fell by the way side, and the foules of the
heauen came, and deuoured it vp.
5 And some fell on stonie ground, where it
had not much earth, and by and by sprang vp,
because it had not depth of earth.
6 But assoone as the sunne was vp, it was
burnt vp, and because it had not roote, it withered away.
7 And some fell among the thornes, and
the thornes grew vp, and choked it, so that it
gaue no fruit.

** Matth.13.1. luke 8.4.*
a Sea side of Tyberias.
b In a ship which was launched into the sea.
1 The selfe same doctrine of the Gospel is sowen euery where, but it hath not like successe in deed through the fault of man, but yet by the iust iudgment of God.

8 Some againe fell in good ground, and
did yeeld fruit that sprong vp, and grew, and it
brought foorth, some thirtie fold, some sixtie
fold, and some an hundreth fold.
9 Then hee said vnto them, Hee that hath
eares to heare, let him heare.
10 And when hee was [c] alone, they that
were [d] about him with the twelue, asked him of
the parable.
11 And he said vnto them, To you it is giuen to know the mysterie of the kingdome of
God: but vnto them that are [e] without, al things
be done in parables,
12 * That they seeing, may see, and not discerne: and they hearing, may heare, and not vnderstand, least at any time they should turne,
and their sinnes should be forgiuen them.

c Word for word, solitarie.
d They that followed him at the heeles.
e That is to say, to strangers, and such as are none of ours.
** Esai 6.9. matth. 13.14. luke 8.10 iohn 12.40. actes 28.26. rom. 11.8.*

13 Againe he said vnto them, Perceiue yee
not this parable? how then should yee vnderstand all *other* parables?
14 The sower soweth the word.
15 And these are they that *receiue the seede*
by the wayes side, in whom the word is sowen:
but when they haue heard it, Satan commeth
immediatly, and taketh away the word that
was sowen in their hearts.
16 And likewise they that receiue the seed
in stonie ground, are they, which when they
haue heard the word, straightwayes receiue it
with gladnesse.
17 Yet haue they no roote in themselues,
and endure but a time: *for* when trouble and
persecution ariseth for the word, immediatly
they be offended.
18 Also they that receiue the seede among
the thornes, are such as heare the word:
19 But the cares [f] of this world, and the
* deceitfulnesse of riches, and the lusts of other
things enter in, and choke the word, and it is
vnfruitfull.
20 But they that haue receiued seede in
good ground, are they that heare the word,
and receiue it, and bring foorth fruite: one
corne thirtie, another sixtie, and some an hundreth.

f Which pertaine to this life.
** 1.Tim.6.17.*
2 Although the light of the Gosple be reiected of the world, yet it ought to be lighted, if it were for no other cause then this, that the wickednesse of the world might be made manifest.

21 ¶ [2] Also hee said vnto them, * Commeth the candle in, to bee put vnder a bushell,
or vnder the bed, and not to bee put on a candlesticke?
22 * For there is nothing hid, that shall not
be opened: neither is there a secret, but that it
shall come to light.
23 If any man haue eares to heare, let him
heare.
24 [3] And hee said vnto them, Take heede
what yee heare. * With what measure ye meete
it shall bee measured vnto you: and vnto you
that heare, shal more be giuen.
25 * For vnto him that hath, shall be giuen,
and from him that hath not, shall bee taken a-
way, euen that he hath.

** Matth.4.15. luke 8.16. and 11.33.*
** Matth.10.26. luke 8.17. and 12.2.*
3 The more liberally that we communicate such gifts as God hath giuen vs with our brethren, the more bountifull will God be toward vs.
** Matth.7.2. luke 6.38.*
** Matth.13,12. and 25.29. luke 8.18. and 19.26.*

26 ¶ [4] Also hee said, So is the kingdome
of God, as if a man should cast seede in the
ground,
27 And [g] should sleepe, and rise vp night
and day, and the seede should spring and grow
vp, he [h] not knowing how.
28 For the earth bringeth foorth fruit [i] of it
selfe, first the blade, then the eares, after that
full corne in the eares.
29 And assoone as the fruit sheweth it selfe,
anon he putteth in the sickle, because the haruest is come.
30 ¶ * [5] Hee said moreouer, Whereunto
shall wee liken the kingdome of God? or with
what comparison shall we compare it?
31 *It is* like a graine of mustard seed, which
when it is sowen in the earth, is the least of all
seedes that be in the earth:
32 But after that it is sowen, it groweth vp,
and is greatest of all herbes, and beareth great
branches, so that the foules of heauen may
build vnder the shadow of it.
33 And * with many such parables he preached the word vnto them, [k] as they were able
to heare it.
34 And without parables spake he nothing
vnto them: but he [l] expounded all things to his
disciples apart.
35 ¶ * Now the same day when euen was
come, he said vnto them, Let vs passe ouer vnto
the other side.
36 And they left the multitude, and tooke
him as hee was in the ship, and there were also
with him other little ships.
37 [6] And there arose a great storme of wind,
and the waues dashed into the ship, so that it
was now full.
38 And hee was in the sterne a sleepe on a
pillow: and they awoke him, and said to him,
Master, carest thou not that we perish?
39 And hee rose vp, and rebuked the wind,
and said vnto the sea, Peace, and be still. So the
wind ceased, and it was a great calme.
40 Then he said vnto them, [m] Why are yee
so fearefull? how is it that yee haue no faith?
41 And they feared exceedingly, and said
one to another, Who is this, that both the wind
and sea obey him?

4 The Lord soweth and reapeth after a maner vnknowen to men.

g That is, when he hath done sowing, should passe the time both day and night, nothing doubting but that the seede should spring, which groweth both by day and night.

h It is the part of the ministers, to labour the ground with all diligence, and commend the successe to God: for that mightie working whereby the seede commeth to blade and eare is secret, and is only knowen by the fruit

i By a certaine power which moueth it selfe.

* *Matth. 13.31. luke 13 19.*

5 God farre otherwise then men vse, beginneth with the least, and endeth with the greatest.

* *Matth. 13.34.*

k According to the capacitie of the hearers.

l Word for word, Loosed, as you would say, reade them the hard riddles.

* *Matth 8.23. luke 8.22.*

6 They that saile with Christ, although he seeme to sleepe neuer so soundly when they are in danger, yet they are preserued of him in time conuenient, being awaked.

m How commeth it to passe that you haue no faith?

CHAP. V.

2 One possessed is healed. 7 The deuil acknowledgeth Christ. 9 A legion of deuils 13 entreth into swine. 22 Iairus daughter. 25 A woman healed of a bloodie issue. 26 Physitians. 34 Faith. 39 Sleepe.

And * [1] they came ouer to the other side
of the sea into the countrey of the [a] Gadarens.
2 And when he was come out of the ship,
there met him incontinently out of the graues,
a man [b] which had an vncleane spirit:
3 Who had his abiding among the graues,
and no man could binde him, no not with
chaines.

* *Matth. 8.28. luke 8.26.*

1 Many haue the vertue of Christ in admiration, and yet they will not redeeme it with the losse of the least thing they haue.

a Looke Mat. 8.30

b Word for word, in an vncleane spirit: now they are said to be in the spirit, because the spirit holdeth them fast locked vp, and as it were bound.

4 Because that when hee was often bound
with fetters & chaines, he plucked the chaines
asunder, and brake the fetters in peeces, neither
could any man tame him.
5 And alwayes both night and day he cried
in the mountaines, and in the graues, & strooke
him selfe with stones.
6 And when hee saw Iesus a farre off, hee
ranne, and worshipped him,
7 And cried with a lowde voice, and said,
What haue I to doe with thee, Iesus the sonne
of the most high God? I [c] will that thou sweare
to me by God, that thou torment me not.
8 (For he said vnto him, Come out of the
man, thou vncleane spirit.)
9 And hee asked him, What is thy name?
and he answered, saying, My name *is* Legion:
for we are many.
10 And hee [d] prayed him instantly, that
hee would not send them away out of the
countrey.
11 Now there was there in the [e] mountaines
a great heard of swine, feeding.
12 And all the deuils besought him, saying,
Send vs into the swine, that we may enter into
them.
13 And incontinently Iesus gaue them
leaue. Then the vncleane spirits went out, and
entred into the swine, and the heard ran headlong from the high banke into the [f] sea (and
there were about two thousand swine) and
they were choked vp in the sea.
14 And the swineheards fled, and told it in
the citie, and in the countrey, and they came
out to see what it was that was done.
15 And they came to Iesus, and sawe him
that had bene possessed with the deuill, and had
the legion, sit both clothed, and in his right
mind: and they were afraid.
16 And they that saw it, told them, what
was done to him that was possessed with the
deuill, and concerning the swine.
17 Then they began to pray him, that hee
would depart from their coasts.
18 And when hee was come into the ship,
he that had bene possessed with the deuill, praied him that he might be with him.
19 Howbeit, Iesus would not suffer him,
but said vnto him, Goe thy way home to thy
friends, and shew them what great things the
Lord hath done vnto thee, and *how* he hath had
compassion on thee.
20 So he departed, and began to publish in
Decapolis, what great things Iesus had done
vnto him: and all men did maruaile.
21 ¶ And when Iesus was come ouer againe
by ship vnto the other side, a great multitude
gathered together to him, and hee was neere
vnto the sea.
22 * And [g] behold, there came one of the
rulers of the Synagogue, whose name was
Iairus: and when he saw him, hee fell downe at
his feete,

c That is, assure me by an oath, that thou wilt not vexe me.

d The deuill that plaied the messenger for his fellowes.

e This whole countrey is for the greater part of it very hilly, for the mountaines of Galaad runne through it.

f Strabo in the sixteenth booke saith that in Gadaris there is a standing poole of very naughtie water, which if beastes taste so, they shead their haire, nayles, or houes and hornes.

* *Matth. 9.18. luke 8.41.*

g The whole companie assembled not disorderly, but in euery Synagogue there were certaine men which gouerned the people.

23 And besought him instantly, saying,
My little daughter lieth at point of death: *I
pray thee* that thou wouldest come and lay
thine hands on her, that shee may bee healed,
and liue.
24 Then hee went with him, and a great
multitude followed him, and thronged him.
25 ([2] And there was a certaine woman,
which was diseased with an issue of blood
twelue yeeres,

2 Iesus being touched with true faith, although it be but weake, doeth heale vs by his vertue.

26 And had suffered many things of many
physicions, and had spent all that shee had, and
it auailed her nothing, but shee became much
worse.
27 When shee had heard of Iesus, shee
came in the presse behind, and touched his garment.
28 For shee said, If I may but touch his clothes, I shalbe whole.
29 And straightway the course of her blood
was dried vp, and shee felt in her body, that she
was healed of that plague.
30 And immediatly when Iesus did know
in himselfe the vertue that went out of him, hee
turned him round about in the preasse, and said,
Who hath touched my clothes?
31 And his disciples said vnto him, Thou
seest the multitude throng thee, & saiest thou,
Who did touch me?
32 And hee looked round about, to see her
that had done that.
33 And the woman feared and trembled:
for shee knew what was done in her, and shee
came and fell downe before him, and told him
the whole trueth.
34 And he said to her, Daughter, thy faith
hath made thee whole: goe in peace, and bee
whole of thy plague.)
35 While he yet spake, there came from the
same ruler of the Synagogues house *certaine*
which said, Thy daughter is dead: why diseasest thou the Master any further?
36 [3] Assoone as Iesus heard that word spoken, hee said vnto the ruler of the Synagogue,
Be not afraid: onely beleeue.

3 Fathers apprehend by faith, the promises of life euen for their children.

37 And hee suffered no man to follow him
saue Peter and Iames, and Iohn the brother of
Iames.
38 So hee came vnto the house of the ruler
of the Synagogue, and saw the tumult, and
them that wept and wailed greatly.
39 And hee went in, and said vnro them,
Why make yee this trouble, and weepe? the
child is not dead, but sleepeth.
40 [4] And they laught him to scorne: but
hee put them all out, and tooke the father,
and the mother of the childe, and them
[h] that were with him, and entred in where the
child lay,

4 Such as mock and scorn Christ are vnworthy to be witnesses of his goodnesse.
h The three disciples.

41 And tooke the child by the hand, and said
vnto her, Talitha cumi, which is by interpretation, Maiden, I say vnto thee, arise.
42 And straightway the maiden arose, and
walked: for she was of the age of twelue yeres,
and they were astonied out of measure.
43 And hee charged them straitly that no
man should know of it, and commaunded to
giue her meate.

CHAP. VI.

2 Christ preaching in his countrey, his owne contemne him. 6 The vnbeliefe of the Nazarits. 7 The Apostles are sent. 13 They cast out deuils: they anoint the sicke with oile. 14 Herods opinion of Christ. 18 The cause of Iohns imprisonment. 22 Dauncing. 27 Iohn beheaded, 29 Buried. 30 The Apostles returne from preaching. 34 Christ teacheth in the desert. 37 Hee feedeth the people with fiue loaues. 48 The Apostles are troubled on the sea. 56 The sicke that touch Christs garment are healed.

AND * [1] he departed thence, and came into
his owne countrey, and his disciples followed him.
2 And when the Sabbath was come, hee
began to teach in the Synagogue, and many
that heard him, were astonied, and said, From
whence hath this man these things? and what
wisedome is this that is giuen vnto him, that
euen such [a] great workes are done by his
hands?

* *Matth. 13.54. luke 4.16.*
1 The faithlesse world doeth no whit at all diminish the vertue of Christ, but wittingly and willingly depriued it selfe of the efficacie of it being offered vnto them.
a The word signifieth powers or vertues, whereby are ment those wonderfull workes that Christ did, which shewed and set forth the vertue and power of his Godhead to all the world, Matth. 7.22.

3 Is not this that carpenter Maries sonne,
the brother of Iames and Ioses, and of Iuda and
Simon? and are not his [b] sisters here with vs?
And they were offended in him.
4 And Iesus said vnto them, A * Prophet
is not without [c] honour, but in his owne countrey, and among his owne kindred, and in his
owne house.

b After the maner of the Hebrewes, who by brethren and sisters, vnderstand all their kinsfolkes.
* *Matth. 13.57. luke 4.24. iohn 4.44.*

5 And he [d] could there do no great works,
saue that hee laide his hands vpon a fewe sicke
folke, and healed *them*.
6 And he marueiled at their vnbeliefe * and
went about by the townes on euery side, teaching.
7 ¶ * [2] And he called vnto him the twelue,
and began to send them forth two and two, and
gaue them power ouer vncleane spirits,

c Not onely that hath that honour which of right is due to him taken from him, but is also euill spoken of and misreported.
d That is, hee would not: for we must needes haue faith if we will receiue the workes of God.
* *Matth. 4.23. luke 13.22.*
* *Chap. 3.14. matth. 10.1. luke 9.1.*
2 The disciples are prepared to that generall Apostleship, by a peculiar sending foorth.

8 [3] And commanded them that they should
take nothing for *their* iourney, saue a staffe only: neither scrip, neither bread, neither money
in their girdles:
9 But that they should bee shod with
* [e] sandals, and that they should not put on
[f] two coates.
10 And hee said vnto them, Wheresoeuer
yee shall enter into an house, [g] there abide till
yee depart thence.
11 * [4] And whosoeuer shal not receiue you,
nor heare you, when yee depart thence, * shake
off the dust that is vnder your feete, for a witnesse vnto them. Verily I say vnto you, It shall
be easier for Sodom, or Gomorrha at the day of
iudgement, then for that citie.
12 ¶ And they went out, and preached, that
men should amend their liues.
13 And they cast out many deuils: and they

3 Faithfull Pastours ought not to haue their minds set, no not on things that are necessarie for this life, if they may be an hinderance vnto them, be it neuer so little.
* *Actes 12.8.*

e The word signifieth properly womens shooes. f That is, they should take no change of garments with them, that they might bee lighter for this iourney, and make more speede. g That is, change not your Innes in this short iourney. * *Mat. 10.14. luke 9.5.* 4 The Lord is a most seuere reuenger of his seruants. * *Actes 13.51. and 18.6.*

* [h] anoynted

*[b] anoynted many that were sicke, with oyle,
and healed *them.*
14 ¶ *[5] Then King Herod heard *of him* (for
his name was made manifest) and said, Iohn
Baptist is risen againe from the dead, and therefore great [i] workes are wrought by him.
15 Other said, It is Elias, and some said, It
is a Prophet, or as one of [k] those Prophets.
16 * So when Herod heard it, hee said, it is
Iohn whome [l] I beheaded: he is risen from the
dead.
17 For Herod himselfe had sent foorth, and
had taken Iohn, and bound him in prison for
Herodias sake, which was his brother Philips
wife, because he had married her.
18 For Iohn said vnto Herod, * It is not
lawfull for thee to haue thy brothers wife.
19 Therefore Herodias [m] laide waite a-
gainst him, and would haue killed him, but shee
could not.
20 For Herod feared Iohn, knowing that
he *was* a iust man, and an holy, and reuerenced
him, and when hee heard him, hee did many
things, and heard him [n] gladly.
21 But the time being conuenient, when
Herod on his birth day made a banket to his
princes and captaines, and chiefe estates of
Galile:
22 And the daughter [o] of the same Herodias came in, and daunced, and pleased Herod,
and them that sate at table together, the King
said vnto the maide, Aske of mee what thou
wilt, and I will giue it thee.
23 And hee sware vnto her, Whatsoeuer
thou shalt aske of mee, I will giue it thee, *euen*
vnto the halfe of my kingdome.
24 * So [p] shee went foorth, and said to her
mother, What shall I aske? And shee said, Iohn
Baptists head.
25 Then shee came in straightway with
haste vnto the king, and asked, saying, I would
that thou shouldest giue mee euen now in a
charger the head of Iohn Baptist.
26 Then the King was very sorie: *yet* for
his oaths sake, and for their sakes which sate at
table with him, he would not refuse her.
27 And immediatly the king sent the [q] hang-
man, and gaue charge that his head should bee
brought in. So hee went and beheaded him in
the prison,
28 And brought his head in a charger, and
gaue it to the maide, and the maide gaue it to
her mother.
29 And when his Disciples heard it, they
came and tooke vp his bodie, and put it in a
tombe.
30 ¶ * And the Apostles gathered themselues together to Iesus, and tolde him all
things, both what they had done, and what
they had taught.
31 [6] And hee said vnto them, Come yee a-
part into the wildernesse, and rest a while: for
there were many commers and goers, that

* *Iames 5.14.*
b That oyle was a token and a signe of his merueilous vertue: and seeing that the gift of healing is ceased a good while since, the ceremonie which is yet retained of some, is to no purpose.
* *Matth.14.1. luke 9.7.*
5 The Gospel confirmeth the godly, and vexeth the wicked.
i The word signifieth Powers, whereby is meant the power of working miracles.
k Of the olde Prophets.
* *Luke 3.19.*
l Commanded to be beheaded.
* *Leuit. 18.16. and 20.21.*
m Sought all meanes to doe him hurt.
n The tyrant was very well content to heare sentence pronounced against him, but the seede fell vpon stonie places.
o Which the same Herodias had not by Herodes Antipas, and by Philip, and Iosephus called her Salome.
* *Matth.14.8.*
p For women vsed not to sit at table with men.
q The word signifieth one that beareth a dart, and the Kings garde was so called, because they did beare dartes.
* *Luke 9.10.*
6 Such as follow Christ shall want nothing, no not in the wildernesse, but shall haue abundance. And how wicked a thing is it, not to looke for this transitorie life at his hands, who giueth euerlasting life?

they had no leasure to eate.
32 * So they went by ship out of the way
into a desert place.
33 But the people saw them when they departed, and many knew him, and ranne a foote
thither out of all cities, and came thither before
them, and assembled vnto him.
34 * Then Iesus went out, and sawe a great
multitude, and had compassion on them, because they were like sheepe which had no
shepheard: * and he began to teach them many things.
35 * And when the day was now farre spent,
his disciples came vnto him, saying, This is a
desert place, and now the day is farre passed.
36 Let them depart, that they may goe into
the countrey and townes about, and buy them
bread: for they haue nothing to eate.
37 But hee answered, and said vnto them,
Giue ye them to eate. And they said vnto him,
[r] Shall we goe, and buy [s] two hundreth penie
worth of bread, and giue them to eate?
38 * Then hee said vnto them, How many
loaues haue yee? goe and looke. And when
they knew it, they said, Fiue, and two fishes.
39 So hee commanded them to make them
all sit downe by [t] companies vpon the greene
grasse.
40 Then they sate downe by [u] rowes, by
hundreds, and by fifties.
41 And hee tooke the fiue loaues, and the
two fishes, and looked vp to heauen, and gaue
thankes, and brake the loaues, and gaue them
to his disciples to set before them, and the two
fishes he diuided among them all.
42 So they did all eate, and were satisfied.
43 And they tooke vp twelue baskets ful of
the fragments, and of the fishes.
44 And they that had eaten, were aboue
fiue thousand men.
45 ¶ [7] And straightway he caused his disciples to goe into the ship, and to goe before vnto the other side vnto Bethsaida, while he sent
away the people.
46 Then assoone as he had sent [x] them away,
he departed into a mountaine to pray.
47 * And when euen was come, the shippe
was in the middes of the Sea, and hee alone on
the land.
48 And hee saw them troubled in rowing,
(for the wind was contrarie vnto them) and a-
bout the fourth watch of the night, he came vnto them walking vpon the sea, and would haue
passed by them.
49 And when they saw him walking vpon
the sea, they supposed it had beene a spirit, and
cried out.
50 For they all sawe him, and were sore
afraid: but anon he talked with them, and said
vnto them, Be of good comfort: it is I, bee not
afraide.
51 Then hee went vp vnto them into the
ship, and the wind ceased, and they were [y] much

* *Matth.14.13. luke 9.10*
* *Matth.9.36. and 14.14.*
* *Luke 9.11.*
* *Matth.14.15.*
r This is a kind of demand and wondring, not without a priuie mocke, which men doe commonly vse, when beginning to be in a fume, they denie to doe a thing.
s Which is about twentie crownes, which is fiue pound.
* *Matth.14.17. luke 9.13. iohn 6.9.*
t Word for word, by bankets, after the maner of the Hebrewes, who haue no distributiues, as Chap.6.7. Now he calleth the rowes of the sitters bankets.
u The word signifieth, the beds in a garden, and it is word for word, by beds and beds, meaning thereby that they sate downe in rowes one by another, as beds in a garden.
7 The faithfull seruants of God after their little labour, are subiect to a great tempest, which Christ doth so moderate, being present in power, although absent in body, that he bringeth them to an happy hauen, at such time and by such meanes as they looked not for: A liuely image of the Church tossed to and fro in this world.
x His disciples.
* *Matth.14.23. iohn 6.15.*
y They were so farre from leaning to be amased, when they knew that it was no spirit, that they were much more astonished then euer they were before, when they saw the wind & the seas obey his commandement.

more amased in themselues, and marueiled.
52 For they had not [z] considered *the matter* of the loaues, because their heartes were
hardned.
53 ¶ * And they came ouer, and went into
the land of Gennesaret, and arriued.
54 [8] So when they were come out of the
ship, straightway they knew him,
55 And ran about throughout all that region
round about, *and* began to carie hither and
thither in couches all that were sicke, where
they heard that he was.
56 And whithersoeuer hee entred into
townes, or cities or villages, they laide their
sicke in the streetes, and prayed him that they
might touch at the least the edge of his garment.
And as many as touched [a] him, were
made whole.

z Either they perceiued not, or had not well considered that miracle of the fiue loaues, insomuch that that vertue of Christ was no lesse strange to them, then if they had not beene present at that miracle which was done but a litle before.
* Marke 14.34.
8 Christ being reiected in his owne countrey, and arriued vpon a sudden amongst them of whom he was not looked for, is receiued to their great profit.
a Or, the hemme of the garment.

CHAP. VII.

2 The Apostles are found fault with, for eating with vnwashen hands. 4 The Pharises traditions about washings. Hypocrites. 8 Mans traditions more set by then Gods. 10 Parents must bee honoured. 14 The things that doe in deede defile a man. 25 The woman of Chanane. 32 The deafe dumme man is healed.

THen * [1] gathered vnto him the Pharises,
and certaine of the Scribes which came
from Hierusalem.
2 And when they saw some of his disciples
[a] eate meate with [b] common hands, (that is to
say, vnwashen) they complained.
3 (For the Pharises, and all the Iewes, except
they wash their hands oft, eate not, [c] holding
the tradition of the Elders.
4 And *when they come* from the [d] market,
except they wash, they eate not: and many other
things there bee, which they haue taken
vpon them to obserue, *as* the washing of cups,
and [e] pots, and of brasen vessels, and of beds.)
5 Then asked him the Pharises and Scribes,
Why [f] walke not thy disciples according to the
tradition of the Elders, but eate meate with vnwashen
hands?
6 [2] Then he answered and said vnto them,
Surely * Esay hath prophecied well of you, hypocrites,
as it is written, This people honoureth
me with lips, but their heart is farre away
from me.
7 [3] But they worship me in vaine, teaching
for doctrines the commandements of men.
4 [4] For ye lay the commandement of God
apart, and obserue the tradition of men, *as* the
washing of pots and of cups, and many other
such like things yee doe.
9 [5] And he said vnto them, Well, yee reiect
the commandement of God, that yee may obserue
your owne tradition.
10 For Moses said, * Honour thy father and

* Matth. 15.2.
1 None do more resist the wisedome of God then they that should be wisest, and that vpon a zeale of their owne traditions: for men doe not please themselues more in any thing then in superstition, that is to say, in a worship of God fondly deuised of themselues.
a Word for word, eate bread: a kind of speech which the Hebrewes vse, taking bread for all kind of foode.
b For the Pharises would not eat their meate with vnwashed hands, because they thought that their hands were defiled with common handling of things, Matth 15.11, 12.
c Obseruing diligently.
d That is to say, from ciuill affaires and worldly, they goe not to meate, vnlesse they wash themselues first.
e By these words are vnderstood all kindes of vessels, which are appointed for our daily vse.
f Why liue they not? a kind of speach taken from the Hebrewes: for amongs them, the way is taken for trade of life.
2 Hypocrisie is alwayes ioyned with superstition.
* Isai 29.14.
3 The more earnest the superstitious are, the more they are mad, in promising themselues Gods fauour by their deserts.
4 The deuises of superstitious men doe not onely not fulfill the Law of God (as they blasphemously perswaded themselues) but also doe vtterly take it away.
5 True religion, which is cleane contrarie to superstition, consisteth in spirituall worship: and all enemies of true religion, although they seeme to haue taken deepe roote, shall be pluckt vp.
* Exod. 20.12. deut. 5.16. ephes. 6.2.

thy mother: and * Whosoeuer shall speake euil
of father or mother, let him [g] die the death.
11 But yee say, If a man say to father or mother,
Corban, *that is*, By the gift that is *offered*
by mee, thou maiest haue profit, *hee shall
be free*.
12 So yee suffer him no more to doe any
thing for his father, or his mother,
13 Making the word of God of none authoritie,
by your tradition which yee haue ordeined:
and yee doe many such like things.
14 Then he called the whole multitude vnto
him, and said vnto them, Hearken you all
vnto me, and vnderstand.
15 There is nothing without a man, that
can defile him, when it entreth into him: but
the things which proceede out of him, are they
which defile the man.
16 If any haue eares to heare, let him heare.
17 And when he came into an house, *away*
from the people, his disciples asked him concerning
the parable.
18 And he said vnto them, What? are yee
without vnderstanding also? Doe ye not know
that whatsoeuer thing from without entreth
into a man, cannot defile him,
19 Because it entreth not into his heart,
but into the belly, and goeth out into the
draught which is the [h] purging of all meates?
20 Then he said, That which commeth out
of man, that defileth man.
21 * For from within, *euen* out of the heart
of men, proceede euill thoughts, adulteries,
fornications, murthers,
22 Thefts, [i] couetousnesse, wickednesse, deceite,
vncleannesse, a [k] wicked eye, backbiting,
pride, foolishnesse.
23 All these euill things come from within,
and defile a man.
24 ¶ * [6] And from thence hee arose, and
went into the [l] borders of Tyrus and Sidon,
and entred into an house, and would that no
man should haue knowen: but hee could not
bee hid.
24 For a certaine woman, whose litle daughter
had an vncleane spirit, heard of him, and
came, and fell at his feete,
26 (And the woman was a [m] Greeke, a
[n] Syrophenissian by nation) and shee besought
him that he would cast out the deuill out of her
daughter.
27 But IESVS said vnto her, Let the
children first bee fed: for it is not good to
take the childrens bread, and to cast it vnto
[o] whelpes.
28 Then shee answered, and said vnto
him, [p] Trueth Lord, yet in deede the
whelpes eate vnder the table of the childrens
crummes.
29 Then hee sayd vnto her, For this saying
goe thy way: the deuill is gone out of thy
daughter.
30 And when shee was come home to her
house,

* Exod. 21.17. leuit. 20.9. prouerb 20.20.
g Without hope of pardon, he shall be put to death.
* Matth. 15.10.
h For that that goeth into the draught, purgeth all meates.
* Gene. 6.5. and 8.21.
i Al kind of craftinesse whereby men profit themselues by other mens losses.
k Cankered malice.
* Matth. 15.21.
6 That which the proud doe reiect when it is offered vnto them, that same doe the modest and humble sinners as it were violently wring out.
l Into the vttermost coasts of Palestine, which were next to Tyrus and Sidon.
m By profession, prophane.
n Neighbour or neere to Damascus.
o He vseth this word Whelpes rather then the word Dogs, that he may seeme to speake more contumeliously.
p As if shee said, It is as thou sayest Lord, for it is enough for the whelpes, if they can but gather vp the crummes that are vnder the table: therefore I craue the crummes and not the childrens bread.

house, shee found the deuill departed, and her
daughter lying on the bed.

7 As the Father created vs to this life in the beginning in his onely sonne so doeth he also in him alone renew vs vnto euerlasting life.

q It was a little countrey, and so called of tenne cities, which the foure gouernments do runne betweene and compasse, Plinie, booke 3. chap. 8.

31 ¶ [7] And hee departed againe from the
coastes of Tyrus and Sidon, and came vnto
the sea of Galile, through the middes of the
coasts of [q] Decapolis.
32 And they brought vnto him one that
was deafe, and stammered in his speach, and
prayed him to put his hand vpon him.
33 Then he tooke him aside from the multitude, and put his fingers in his eares, and did
spit and touched his tongue.
34 And looking vp to heauen, hee sighed,
and sayd vnto him, Ephphata, that is, Bee o-
pened.
35 And straightway his eares were opened,
and the string of his tongue was loosed, and hee
spake plaine.
36 And hee commanded them that they
should tell no man: but how much soeuer hee
forbade them, the more a great deale they
published it,
37 And were beyond measure astonied,
saying, * He hath done all things well: he maketh both the deafe to heare, and the dumbe
to speake.

** Gene. 1. 31. eccles. 39. 21.*

CHAP. VIII.

1 The miracle of the seuen loaues. 11 The Iewes seeke signes. 15 To beware of the leauen of the Pharises. 22 A blind man healed. 27 The peoples sundry opinions of Christ. 29 The Apostles acknowledge Christ. 31 Hee foretelleth his death. 33 Peter, Satan. 35 To saue and lose the life. 38 To be ashamed of Christ.

**Matth. 15. 32.*

In * those dayes, when there was a verie
great multitude, and had nothing to eate,
Iesus calleth his disciples to him, and sayd vnto them,
2 I haue compassion on the multitude, because they haue now continued with me three
dayes, and haue nothing to eate.
3 And if I send them away fasting to their
owne houses, they would [a] faint by the way:
for some of them came from farre.

a Word for word, they wil fall in sunder, or e dissolued, for when men fall in a sound, their synewes fall one from another.

4 Then his disciples answered him, Whence
can a man satisfie these with bread here in the
wildernesse?
5 And hee asked them, How many loaues
haue ye? And they sayd, Seuen.
6 Then he commanded the multitude to
sit downe on the ground: and he tooke the seuen loaues, and gaue thankes, brake *them*, and
gaue to his disciples to set before *them*, and
they did set *them* before the people.
7 They had also a fewe small fishes: and
when he had giuen thankes, hee commaunded
them also to be set before *them*.
8 So they did eate, and were sufficed, and
they tooke vp of the broken meate that was
left, seuen baskets full.
9 (And they that had eaten, were about
foure thousand) so he sent them away.
10 ¶ * And anon he entred into a ship with
his disciples, and came into the parts of Dal-
manutha.

**Matth. 15. 39.*

11 * [1] And the Pharises [b] came foorth, and
began to dispute with him, seeking of him a
signe from heauen, and tempting him.
12 Then hee [c] sighed deepely in his spirit,
and sayd, Why doeth this generation seeke a
signe? Verily I say vnto you, [d] A signe shall
not be giuen vnto this generation.
13 ¶ So hee left them, and went into the
ship againe, and departed to the other side.
14 ¶ * And they had forgotten to take
bread, neither had they in the ship with them
but one loafe.
15 [2] And hee charged them, saying, Take
heede, and beware of the leauen of the Pharises, and of the leauen of Herod.
16 [3] And they reasoned among themselues,
saying, *It is*, because we haue no bread.
17 And when Iesus knew it, hee sayd vnto
them, Why reason you *thus*, because ye haue no
bread? perceiue ye not yet, neither vnderstand?
haue ye your hearts yet hardened?
18 Haue hee eyes, and see not? and haue ye
eares and heare not? and doe yee not remember?
19 * When I brake the fiue loaues among
fiue thousand, how many baskets full of broken meate tooke yee vp? They sayd vnto him,
Twelue.
20 And when *I brake* seuen among foure
thousand, how many baskets of the leauings
of broken meate tooke yee vp? And they said,
Seuen.
21 Then he said vnto them, [e] How *is it* that
ye vnderstand not?
22 [4] And hee came to Bethsaida, and they
brought a blind man vnto him, and desired him
to touch him.
23 Then he tooke the blinde by the hand,
and led him out of the towne, and spat in his
eyes, & put his hands vpon him, and asked him,
if he saw ought.
24 And he looked vp, and said, I [f] see men:
for I see them walking like trees.
25 After that, hee put his hands againe vpon his eyes, and made him [g] looke againe. And
hee was restored to his sight, and sawe euery
man afarre off clearely.
26 [5] And hee sent him home to his house,
saying, Neither goe into the towne, nor tell it
to any in the towne.
27 ¶ * [6] And Iesus went out, and his disciples into the townes of Cesarea Philippi. And
by he way hee asked his discipes, saying vnto
them, Whom doe men say that I am?
28 And they answered, *Some say*, Iohn
Baptist: and some, Elias: and some, one of the
Prophets.
29 And he sayd vnto them, But whom say
ye that I am? Then Peter answered, and sayd
vnto him, Thou art that Christ.

** Matth. 16. 1.*

1 The stubborn enemies of the doctrine of the Gospel, giuing no credit to the miracles already done, require new: but Christ being angrie with them, doth vtterly forsake them.

b A common kinde of speach, which the Hebrewes vse, whereby is meant that the Pharises went from their houses of purpose to encounter with him.

c These sighes came euen from his heart roote, for the Lord was very much mooued with these mens so great infidelitie.

d Word for word, If a signe be giuen: It is a cutted kind of speach very common among the Hebrewes: wherein some such wordes as these must bee vnderstood, Let mee be taken for a liar, or some such like. And when they speake out the whole, they say, The Lord do thus and thus by mee.

**Matth. 16. 5.*

2 We must especially take heede of them which corrupt ẏ word of God, what degree soeuer they be of, either in the Church, or in ciuill policie.

3 They that haue their minds fixed on earthly things, are vtterly blinde in heauenly things, although they be neuer so plainly set forth vnto them.

**Iohn 6. 11.*

e How commeth it to passe, that you vnderstand not these things which are so plain and euident?

4 A true image of our regeneration, which Christ, separating vs from the world, worketh and accomplisheth by little and little in vs.

f He perceiued some moouing of men when he could not discerne their bodies.

g Hee commanded him againe, to trie in deede, whether he could see well or no.

5 Christ will not haue his miracles to be separated from his doctrine. **Matth. 16. 13. luke 9. 18.* 6 Manie prayse Christ, which yet notwithstanding spoyle him of his prayse.

30 [7] And

7 Christ hath appointed his times to ÿ preaching of the Gospel & therefore here deferreth it to a more commodious time, lest sudden haste should rather hinder then further the mystery of his cōming.
8 Christ suffred all that he suffered for vs, not vnwillingly, neither vnawares, but foreknowing it, & willingly.
9 None are more mad then they that are wise beside the word of God.
h This is not godly, but worldly wisedome.
10 The disciples of Christ must beare stoutly, what burdē soeuer the Lord layeth vpō them, & subdue the affections of ÿ flesh.
*Mat. 10.38. & 16.24. luke 9.23 and 14 27.
*Mat. 10.39. & 16.25. luke 9.24 and 17.33.
11 They are the most foolish of all men, which purchase the enioying of this life, with the losse of euerlasting blisse.
*Mat 10.33. luke 9.26. and 12.9.

30 [7] And hee sharpely charged them, that
concerning him they should tell no man.
31 [8] Then he began to teach them that the
Sonne of man must suffer many things, and
should be reprooued of the Elders, and of the
hie Priests, and the Scribes, and bee slaine, and
within three dayes rise againe.
32 [9] And he spake that thing boldly. Then
Peter tooke him aside, and began to rebuke
him.
33 Then he turned backe, and looked on his
disciples, and rebuked Peter, saying, Get thee
behinde me Satan: for thou vnderstandest not
the things that are of God, but the things that
are of men.
34 ¶ [10] And he called the people vnto him
with his disciples, and sayd vnto them, * Whosoeuer
will follow me, let him forsake himselfe,
and take vp his crosse, and follow me.
35 For whosoeuer will *saue his life, shall
lose it: but whosoeuer shall lose his life for my
sake and the Gospels, he shall saue it.
36 [11] For what shall it profite a man,
though he should winne the whole world, if he
lose his soule?
37 Or what exchange shall a man giue for
his soule?
38 *For whosoeuer shall bee ashamed of
me, and of my wordes among this adulterous
and sinfull generation, of him shall the
Sonne of man bee ashamed also, when he commeth
in the glorie of his Father with the holy
Angels.

CHAP. IX.

2 Christs transfiguration. 7 Christ must be heard. 11 Of Elias and Iohn Baptist. 14 The possessed is healed. 23 Faith can doe all things. 31 Christ foretelleth his death. 33 Who is greatest among the Apostles. 36 Christ taketh a childe in his armes. 42 To offend 50 Salt. Peace.

*Mat. 6.28. luke 9.27.
a When hee shall begin his kingdom through the preaching of the Gospel: that is to say, after the resurrection.
*Matth. 17.1. luke 9.28.
1 The heauenly glory of Christ, which should within a short space be abased vpon the crosse, is auouched by visible signes, by the presence and talke of Elias & Moses, & by the voice of the Father himselfe, before three of his disciples, which are witnesses against whom lyeth no exceptiō.
d Did sparkle as it were.
e They were beside themselues for feare.
*Matth. 3.17. and 17.5. chap. 1.11.

AND * hee sayd vnto them, Verely I say
vnto you, that there be some of them that
stand here, which shall not taste of death till
they haue seene the [a] kingdome of God come
with power.
2 * [1] And sixe dayes after, Iesus taketh
vnto him Peter, and Iames, and Iohn, and
carieth them vp into an hie mountaine out of
the way alone, and his shape was changed before
them.
3 And his rayment did [b] shine, *and was*
very white as snowe, so white as no fuller can
make vpon the earth.
4 And there appeared vnto them Elias
with Moses, and they were talking with Iesus.
5 Then Peter answered, and sayd to Iesus,
Master, it is good for vs to bee here: let vs
make also three tabernacles, one for thee, and
one for Moses, and one for Elias.
6 Yet he knew not what he sayd: for they
were [c] afraid.
7 And there was a cloude that shadowed
them, and a voice came out of the cloud, saying,
* This is my welbeloued Sonne: heare him.

8 And suddenly they looked round about,
and sawe no more any man saue Iesus
onely with them.
9 [2] * And as they came downe from the
mountaine, he charged them that they should
tell no man what they had seene, saue when the
Sonne of man were risen from the dead againe.
10 So they [d] kept the matter to themselues,
and [e] demanded one of another, what the rising
from the dead againe should meane?
11 [3] Also they asked him, saying, Why say
the Scribes, that * Elias must first come?
12 And hee answered, and sayd vnto them,
Elias verely shal first come, and restore all
things: and * as it is written of the Sonne of
man, hee must suffer many things, and be set at
nought.
13 But I say vnto you, that Elias is come,
(and they haue done vnto him whatsoeuer they
would) as it is written of him.
14 ¶ * [4] And when he came to *his* disciples,
he saw a great multitude about them, and the
Scribes disputing with them.
15 And straightway all the people, when
they beheld him, were amased, and ranne to
him, and saluted him.
16 Then hee asked the Scribes, What dispute
you among your selues?
17 And one of the company answered, and
sayd, Master, I haue brought my sonne vnto
thee, which hath a dumbe spirit:
18 And wheresoeuer hee taketh him, hee
[f] teareth him, and he fometh, and gnasheth his
teeth, and pineth away: and I spake to thy disciples,
that they should cast him out, and they
could not.
19 Then hee answered him, and sayd, O
faithlesse generation, how long now shall I
be with you! how long now shall I suffer you!
Bring him vnto me.
20 So they brought him vnto him: and assoone
as the spirit [g] saw him he tare him, and he
fel down on the ground wallowing & foming.
21 Then hee asked his father, How long
time is it since he hath been thus? And he said,
Of a childe.
22 And oft times hee casteth him into the
fire, and into the water to destroy him: but if
thou canst doe any thing, helpe vs, and haue
compassion vpon vs.
23 And Iesus sayd vnto him, If thou canst
beleeue it, [h] all things are possible to him that
beleeueth.
24 And straightway the father of the child
crying with teares, sayd, Lord, I beleeue: helpe
my vnbeliefe.
25 When Iesus sawe that the people came
running together, hee rebuked the vncleane
spirit, saying vnto him, Thou dumbe and deafe
spirit, I charge thee, come out of him, and enter
no more into him.
26 [5] Then the spirit cried, and rent him
sore, and came out, and he was as one dead, in
so

2 The Lord hath appointed his times for the publishing of the Gospel.
*Matth. 17.9.
d Euen very hardly as it were.
e They questioned not together touching the generall resurrection, which shall be in the latter day, but they vnderstood not, what he meant by that which hee spake of his owne peculiar resurrection.
3 The foolish opinion of the Rabbines is here refelled touching Elias cōming, which was that either Elias should rise againe, from the dead, or that his soule should enter into some other body.
*Mala. 4.5.
*Esai 53.4.
*Matth. 17.14. luke 9.38.
4 Christ sheweth by a miracle euen to the vnworthy, that hee is come to bridle the rage of Satan.
f Vexeth him inwardly, as the cowlicke vseth to doe.
g So soone as Iesus had looked vpon the boy that was brought vnto him, the deuill began to rage after this maner.
h There is nothing but Christ can and will do it, for them that beleeue in him.
5 The neerer that the vertue of Christ is the more outragiously doth Satan rage.

so much that many sayd, He is dead.
27 But Iesus tooke his hand, and lift him vp,
and he arose.

6 We haue need of faith, & therfore of prayer & fasting, to cast Satan out of his olde possession.

28 [6] And when he was come into the house,
his disciples asked him secretly, Why could not
we cast him out?
29 And hee said vnto them, This kinde can
by no other meanes come foorth, but by prayer
and fasting.

*Matth 17.22. luke 9.22. i He and his disciples together. 7 Christ forewarneth vs with great diligence, to the end wee should not bee oppressed with sudden calamities, but ẏ slothfulnesse of man is wonderfull.

30 ¶ * And they departed thence & [i] went
together through Galile, and hee would not
that any should haue knowen it.
31 [7] For hee taught his disciples, and sayd
vnto them, The Sonne of man shall be deliuered into the hands of men, and they shall kill
him, but after that he is killed, hee shall rise a-
gaine the third day.
32 But they vnderstood not that saying,
and were afraid to aske him.

*Matth. 18.1. luke 9.46. 8 Onely humilitie doth exalt. k Where he was wont to make his abode.

33 * [8] After, hee came to Capernaum: and
when hee was in the [k] house, hee asked them,
What was it that yee disputed among you by
the way?
34 And they held their peace: for by the
way they reasoned among themselues, who
should be the chiefest.
35 And he sate down, and called the twelue,
and sayde to them, If any man desire to bee
first, the same shall bee last of all, and seruant
vnto all.
36 And he tooke a little childe, and set him
in the middes of them, and tooke him in his
armes, and sayd vnto them,
37 Whosoeuer shall receiue one of such
little children in my Name, receiueth me: and
whosoeuer receiueth me, receiueth not [l] mee,
but him that sent me.

l He doeth not onely receiue me, but also him that sent me. *Luke 9.49. 9 God, who is the author of an ordinary vocation, worketh also extraordinarily so oft as it pleaseth him. But an extraordinarie vocation is tried by the doctrine and the effects. *1.Cor. 11.3. *Matth. 10.42.

38 ¶ * [9] Then Iohn answered him, saying, Master, wee sawe one casting out deuils by
thy Name, which followeth not vs, and wee
forbade him, because he followeth vs not.
39 * But Iesus sayd, Forbid him not: for
there is no man that can doe a miracle by my
Name, that can lightly speake euill of me.
40 For whosoeuer is not against vs is on
our part.
41 * And whosoeuer shall giue you a cup
of water to drinke for my Names sake, because
ye belong to Christ, verely I say vnto you, hee
shall not lose his reward.

*Matth. 11.6. luke 17.1. 10 God is so seuere a reuenger of offences, that it is better to suffer any losse, then to be an occasion of offence vnto any. *Matth. 5.29. and 18.8.

42 * [10] And whosoeuer shall offend one of
these little ones that beleeue in me, it were better for him rather, that a milstone were hanged about his necke, and that he were cast into
the sea.
43 * Wherefore, if thine hand cause thee
to offend, cut it off: it is better for thee to enter
into life, maimed, then hauing two handes, to
goe into hell, into the fire that neuer shall be
quenched,

*Esa. 66.24. m Their worme which shall be cast into that flame.

44 * Where their [m] worme dieth not, and
the fire neuer goeth out.
45 Likewise, If thy foote cause thee to offend, cut it off: it is better for thee to goe halt
into life, then hauing two feete, to be cast into
hell, into the fire that neuer shall be quenched,
46 Where their worme dieth not, and the
fire neuer goeth out.
47 And if thine eye cause thee to offend,
plucke it out, it is better for thee to goe into
the kingdome of God with one eye, then hauing two eyes, to be cast into hell fire,
48 Where the worme dieth not, and the fire
neuer goeth out.
49 [11] For euery man shall bee [n] salted with
fire: & * euery sacrifice shall be salted with salt.
50 * Salt is good: but if the salt be vnsauorie, wherewith shall it be seasoned? haue salt in
your selues, and haue peace one with another.

11 We must be seasoned and powdred by God, both that we may bee acceptable sacrifices vnto him, and also, that we being knit together, may season one another. n That is, shall be consecrate to God, being seasoned with the incorruptible word. *Leuit 2.13. *Matth 5.13. luke 14.34.

CHAP. X.

9 The wife onely for fornication is to be put away. 13 Little children are brought to Christ. 17 A rich man asketh Iesus how he may possesse eternall life. 28 The Apostles forsooke all things for Christs sake. 33 Christ foresheweth his death. 35 Zebedeus his sonnes request. 46 Blinde Bartimeus healed.

*Matth. 19.1. a That is to say, departed and went from thence: for in the Hebrewe tongue sitting and dwelling are all one, and so are rising and going foorth.

AND * he [a] arose from thence, and went into the coasts of Iudea by the farre side of
Iordan, & the people resorted vnto him againe,
and as he was wont, he taught them againe.
2 Then the Pharises came and asked him,
if it were lawfull for a man to put away *his* wife,
and tempted him.
3 And he answered, and sayd vnto them,
What did * Moses command you? *Deut. 24.1.
4 And they sayd, Moses suffered to write
a bill of diuorcement, and to put her away.

1 God did neuer allow those diuorces which the Lawe did tolerate. b Looke Mat. 19. For Moses gaue them no commandement to put away their wiues, but rather made a good prouiso for the wiues against the stubborn hardnesse of their husbands. *Gen. 1.27. matth. 19.4. *Gen. 2.24. 1.cor. 6.16. ephes. 5.31. *1.Cor. 7.10. *Matth. 5.32. and 19.9. luke 16.18. c Whom he putteth away, for he is an adulterer by keeping company with another.

5 [1] Then Iesus answered, and sayd vnto
them, For the hardnesse of your heart he wrote
this [b] precept vnto you.
6 But at the beginning of the creation
* God made them male and female:
7 * For this cause shall man leaue his father and mother, and cleaue vnto his wife.
8 And they twaine shall be one flesh: so
that they are no more twaine, but one flesh.
9 * Therefore, what God hath coupled together, let not man separate.
10 And in the house his disciples asked him
againe of that matter.
11 And hee sayd vnto them, * Whosoeuer
shall put away his wife and marrie another,
committeth adultery [c] against her.
12 And if a woman put away her husband,
and bee married to another, shee committeth
adulterie.

*Matth 19.13. luke 18.15. 2 God of his goodnesse comprehendeth in the couenant not only the fathers, but ẏ children also: and therefore hee blesseth them.

13 ¶ * [2] Then they brought little children
to him, that he should touch them, and his disciples rebuked those that brought them.
14 But when Iesus saw it, hee was displeased, and sayd to them, Suffer the little children
to come vnto me, and forbid them not: for of
such is the kingdome of God.

3 We must in malice become children if we will enter into the kingdome of heauen.

15 Verely I say vnto you, Whosoeuer shall
not receiue the kingdome of God [3] as a little
childe, he shall not enter therein.
16 And hee tooke them vp in his armes,
and

and put *his* hands vpon them, and blessed them.
17 ¶ [4] And when hee was gone out on the
way, there came one * running, and kneeled
to him, and asked him, Good Master, what shall
I doe that I may possesse eternall life?
18 Iesus said to him, Why callest thou mee
good? there is none good but one, euen God.
19 Thou knowest the commaundements,
* Thou shalt not commit adultery. Thou shalt
not kill. Thou shalt not steale. Thou shalt not
beare false witnesse. Thou shalt [d] hurt no *man*.
Honour thy father and mother.
20 Then he answered, and said to him, Master, all these things I haue obserued from my
youth.
21 And Iesus looked vpon him, and loued
him, and sayd vnto him, One thing is lacking
vnto thee. Goe *and* sell all that thou hast, and
giue to the poore, and thou shalt haue treasure
in heauen, and come, followe mee, and take vp
the crosse.
22 But he was sad at that saying, and went
away sorrowfull: for he had great possessions.
23 And Iesus looked round about, and said
vnto his disciples, How hardly doe they that
haue riches enter into the kingdome of God!
24 And his disciples were afraide at his
wordes. But Iesus answered againe, and sayd
vnto them, Children, how hard is it for them
that trust in riches, to enter into the kingdome
of God!
25 It is easier for a camell to goe through
the eye of a needle, then for a rich man to enter into the kingdome of God.
26 And they were much more astonied, saying with themselues, Who then can be saued?
27 But Iesus looked vpon them, and sayd,
With men *it is* impossible, but not with God:
for with God all things are possible.
28 ¶ * [5] Then Peter began to say vnto
him, Loe, wee haue forsaken all, and haue followed thee.
29 Iesus answered, and sayd, Verely I say
vnto you, there is no man that hath forsaken
house, or brethren, or sisters, or father, or
mother, or wife, or children, or lands for my
sake and the Gospels,
30 But he shall receiue an [e] hundred folde,
now at this present, houses, and brethren, and
sisters, and mothers, and children, and landes
[f] with persecutions, and in the world to come,
eternall life.
31 * But many *that are* first, shall bee last,
and the last, first.
32 ¶ * [6] And they were in the way, going
vp to Hierusalem, and Iesus went before them
and they were troubled, and as they followed,
they were afraid, and Iesus tooke the twelue a-
gain, and began to tel them what things should
come vnto him,
33 *Saying*, Behold, we go vp to Hierusalem,
and the Sonne of man shall bee deliuered vnto
the hie Priests, and to the Scribes, and they
shall condemne him to death, and shall deliuer him to the Gentiles.
34 And they shall mocke him, and scourge
him, and spit vpon him, and kill him: but the
third day he shall rise againe.
35 ¶ * [7] Then Iames and Iohn the sonnes
of Zebedeus came vnto him, saying, Master,
[g] we would that thou shouldest doe for vs that
we desire.
36 And he said vnto them, What would ye
I should doe for you?
37 And they sayd to him, Graunt vnto vs,
that we may sit, one at thy right hand, and the
other at thy left hand in thy glory.
38 But Iesus sayd vnto them, Yee knowe
not what yee aske, Can yee drinke of the cuppe
that I shall drinke of, and be baptized with the
baptisme that I shall bee baptized with?
39 And they sayd vnto him, We can. But
Iesus sayd vnto them, Yee shall drinke in deed
of the cuppe that I shall drinke of, and bee baptized with the baptisme wherewith I shall bee
baptized:
40 But to sit at my right hand and at my
left, is not mine to giue, but *it shall bee giuen*
to them for whom it is prepared.
41 And when the ten heard that, they began to disdaine at Iames and Iohn.
42 [8] But Iesus called them vnto him, and
said to them, * Yee knowe that [h] they which
are princes among the Gentiles, haue domination ouer them, and they that be great among
them, exercise authoritie ouer them.
43 But it shall not bee so among you: but
whosoeuer will be great among you, shall bee
your seruant.
44 And whosoeuer will be chiefe of you,
shall be the seruant of all.
45 For euen the Sonne of man came not
to be serued, but to serue, and to giue his life
for the ransome of many.
46 ¶ * [9] Then they came to Iericho: and
as hee went out of Iericho with his disciples,
and a great multitude, Bartimeus the sonne
of Timeus, a blinde man, sate by the wayes
side, begging.
47 And when he heard that it was Iesus of
Nazareth, he began to crie, and to say, Iesus the
Sonne of Dauid, haue mercie on me.
48 And many rebuked him, because hee
should hold his peace: but he cried much more,
O Sonne of Dauid, haue mercie on me.
49 Then Iesus stood still, and commaunded him to be called: and they called the blind,
sayd vnto him, Be of good comfort: arise, he
calleth thee.
50 So he threw away his cloke, and arose,
and came to Iesus.
51 And Iesus answered, and sayd vnto him,
What wilt thou that I doe vnto thee? And
the blinde sayd vnto him, Lord, that I may receiue sight.
52 Then Iesus sayd vnto him, Goe thy
way:

4 Two things are chiefly to be eschewed of them which earnestly seek eternal life: that is to say an opinion of their merits or deseruings, which is not only vnderstood, but condemned by the due consideration of the Lawe: and the loue of riches, which turneth aside many from that race wherin they ran with a good courage.

*Matth. 19.16. luke 18.18.

*Exod. 20.13.

d *Neither by force nor deceit, nor any other meane whatsoeuer.*

*Matth. 19.27. luke 18.28.

5 To neglect all things in comparison of Christ, is a sure way vnto eternall life, so that we fall not away by the way.

e *An hundreth fold as much, if we looke to the true vse and commodities of this life, so that wee measure them after the will of God, and not after the wealth it selfe, and our greedy desire.*

f *Euen in the mids of persecutions.*

*Matth. 19.30. luke 13.30.

*Matth. 20.17. luke 18.31.

6 The disciples are again prepared to patience not to be ouercome by the foretelling vnto them of his death, which was at hand, and therewithall of life, which should most certainly follow.

*Matth. 20.20.

7 We must first striue before we triumph.

g *We pray thee.*

8 The Magistrates according to Gods appointment rule ouer their subiects: but the Pastors are not called to rule, but to serue according to the example of the Sonne of God himselfe, who went before them, forsomuch as he also was a Minister of his Fathers will.

*Luke 22.25.

h *They to whom it is decreed and appointed.*

*Matth. 20.29. luke 18.35.

9 Christ onely, being called vpon by faith, healeth our blindenesse.

way : thy faith hath saued thee. And by and by
he receiued *his* sight, and followed Iesus in the
way.

CHAP. XI.

1 Christ entreth into Hierusalem riding on an asse. 13 The fruitlesse figge tree is cursed. 15 Sellers and buyers are cast out of the Temple. 23 The force of faith. 24 Faith in prayer. 25 The brothers offences must bee pardoned. 27 The Priests aske by what authoritie he wrought those things that he did. 30 Whence Iohns baptisme was.

*Matth.21.1. luke 18.29.
1 A liuely image of the spirituall kingdome of Christ on earth.

AND * [1] when they came neere to Hierusalem, to Bethphage and Bethania vnto
the mount of Oliues, he sent foorth two of his
disciples,
2 And sayd vnto them, Go your wayes into that towne that is ouer against you, and assoone as ye shall enter into it, yee shall find a
colte tied, whereon neuer man sate : loose him,
and bring him.
3 And if any man say vnto you, Why doe
yee this? Say that the Lord hath neede of him,
and straightway he will send him hither.
4 And they went their way, and found a
colt tied by the doore without, in a place where
two wayes met, and they loosed him.
5 Then certaine of them that stood there
said vnto them, What do ye loosing the colt?
6 And they said vnto them, as Iesus had
commanded them : So they let them goe.

*Iohn 12.14.

7 ¶ * And they brought the colt to Iesus,
and cast their garments on him, and he sate vpon him.
8 And many spread their garments in the
way : other cut downe branches off the trees,
and strawed them in the way.
9 And they that went before, and they that
followed, cried, saying, Hosanna : [a] blessed *bee*
he that commeth in the Name of the Lord.
10 [b] Blessed *bee* the kingdome that commeth in the Name of the Lorde of our father
Dauid : Hosanna, *O thou which art* in the
highest *heauens*.

a Wel be it to him that commeth to vs from God, or that is sent of God.
b Happie and prosperous.

*Matth.21.10. luke 19.45.

11 * So Iesus entred into Ierusalem, and
into the Temple : and when hee had looked
about on all things, and nowe it was euening, hee went foorth vnto Bethanie with the
twelue.

*Matth. 21.19.

12 * And on the morrow when they were
come out from Bethania, he was hungrie.
13 [2] And seeing a figge tree a farre off, that
had leaues, hee went *to see* if he might find any
thing thereon : but when hee came vnto it, hee
found nothing but leaues : for the time of figs
was not yet.

2 An example of that vengeance which hangeth ouer the heads of hypocrites.

14 Then Iesus answered, and sayd to it, Neuer man eate fruit of thee hereafter while the
world standeth : and his disciples heard it.
15 ¶ [3] And they came to Hierusalem, and
Iesus went into the Temple, and beganne to
cast out them that solde and bought in the
Temple, and ouerthew the tables of the money changers, and the seates of them that sold
Doues.
16 Neither would hee suffer that any man

3 Christ sheweth in deede that he is the true King and high Priest, and therfore the reuenger of the diuine seruice of the Temple.

should carie a [c] vessell through the Temple.
17 And hee taught, saying vnto them, Is it
not written, * Mine house shall bee [d] called the
house of praier vnto all nations? * but you haue
made it a denne of theeues.
18 And the Scribes and high Priests heard
it, and sought how to destroy him : for they feared him, because the whole multitude was astonied at his doctrine.

c That is, any prophane instrument of which those fellowes had a number, that made the Court of the Temple a market place.
*Isa.56.7.
d Shall openly be so accompted and taken.
*Ierem.7.11.

19 But when euen was come, *Iesus* went
out of the citie.
20 ¶ * [4] And in the morning as they iourneyed together, they saw the figge tree dried
vp from the rootes.
21 Then Peter remembred, and sayd vnto
him, Master, behold, the figge tree which thou
cursedst, is withered.

*Matth.21.19.
4 The force of faith is exceeding great, and charitie is euer ioyned with it.

22 And Iesus answered, and said vnto them,
Haue [e] the faith of God.
23 For verily I say vnto you, that whosoeuer shall say vnto this mountaine, Bee thou taken away, and cast into the Sea, and shall not
wauer in his heart, but shall beleeue that those
things which he saith, shal come to passe, whatsoeuer he sayth, shall be *done* to him.
24 * Therefore I say vnto you, Whatsoeuer ye desire when yee pray, beleeue that [f] yee
shall haue it, and it shall be *done* vnto you.
25 * But when [g] yee shall stand, and pray,
forgiue, if ye haue any thing against any man,
that your Father also which is in heauen, may
forgiue you your trespasses.
26 For if ye will not forgiue, your Father
which is in heauen, will not pardon you your
trespasses.

e The faith of God is that assured faith and trust which we haue in him.
*Matth.7.7. luke 11.9.
f Word for word, that you receiue it, speaking in the time that now is, to shewe the certaintie of the thing, and the performance in deede.
*Matth.6.14.
g When you shall appeare before the altar.

27 ¶ * [5] Then they came againe to Hierusalem : and as he walked in the Temple, there
came to him the hie Priests, and the Scribes,
and the Elders,
28 And sayd vnto him, By what authoritie
doest thou these things? and who gaue thee
this authoritie, that thou shouldest doe these
things?
29 Then Iesus answered, and sayd vnto
them, I will also aske of you a certaine thing,
and answere ye me, and I will tell you by what
authoritie I doe these things.
30 The baptisme of Iohn, was it from heauen, or of men? answere me.
31 And they thought with themselues, saying, If we shall say, From heauen, hee will say,
Why then did ye not beleeue him?
32 [6] But if wee say, Of men, wee feare the
people : for all men counted Iohn, that he was
a Prophet in deede.
33 Then they answered, and sayd vnto Iesus, We cannot tell. And Iesus answered, and
sayd vnto them, Neither will I tell you by what
authoritie I doe these things.

*Matth.21.23. luke 20.1.
5 The Gospel haue been assaulted long time since, vnder the pretence of an ordinary succession.
6 A reward of an euill conscience to be afraid of those, of whō they should and might haue been feared.

CHAP. XII.

1 Of the vineyard. 10 Christ the stone refused of the Iewes. 13 Of tribute to be giuen to Cesar. 18 The Sadduces denying the resurrection. 28 The first commandement. 31
To

To loue God and thy neighbour, is better then sacrifices. 36 Christ Dauids sonne. 38 To beware of the Scribes and Pharises. 42 The poore widowe.

1 The calling of God is not tied either to place, person, or time without exception.

a This word parable, which the Euangelists vse, doeth not onely signifie a comparing of things together, but also darke speaches and allegories.

**Esai. 5.1. ier. 2.2 matth. 21.33. luke 20.9.*

b When the fruits of the ground vse to be gathered.

AND [1] hee began to speake vnto them in
[a] parables, * A *certaine* man planted a
vineyard, and compassed it with an hedge, and
digged a pit for the winepresse, and built a
tower in it, and let it out to husbandmen, and
went into a strange countrey.
2 [b] And at the time, he sent to the husbandmen a seruant, that he might receiue of the husbandmen of the fruit of the vineyard.
3 But they tooke him, and beat him, and
sent him away emptie.
4 And againe he sent vnto them an other
seruant, and at him they cast stones, and brake
his head, & sent him away shamefully handled.
5 And again he sent another, and him they
slew, and many other, beating some, and killing
some.
6 Yet had he one sonne his deare beloued:
him also he sent the last vnto them, saying, They
will reuerence my sonne.
7 But the husbandmen sayd among themselues, This is the heire: come, let vs kill him,
and the inheritance shall be ours.
8 So they tooke him, and killed him, and
cast him out of the vineyard.
9 What shall then the Lord of the vineyard doe? He will come and destroy these husbandmen, and giue the vineyard to other.
10 Haue ye not read so much as this Scripture? *The stone which the builders did refuse, is made the head of the corner.
11 This was done of the Lord, and it is marueilous in our eyes.
12 Then they went [c] about to take him,
but they feared the people: for they perceiued
that he spake that parable against them: therefore they left him, and went their way.
13 ¶ * [2] And they sent vnto him certaine of
the Pharises, and of the Herodians that they
might take him in *his* talke.
14 And when they came, they sayd vnto
him, Master, we knowe that thou art true, and
carest for no man: for thou [d] considerest not the
person of men, but teachest the [e] way of God
truely, Is it lawfull to giue tribute to Cesar,
or not?
15 Should wee giue it, or should wee not
giue it? but he knew their hypocrisie, and sayd
vnto them, Why tempt ye me? Bring me a penie, that I may see it.
16 So they brought it, and hee sayd vnto
them, Whose is this image and superscription? and they said vnto him, Cesars.
17 Then Iesus answered, and sayd vnto
them, * Giue to Cesar the things that are Cesars, and to God, those that are Gods: and they
marueiled at him.
18 ¶ [3] * Then came the Sadduces vnto
him, (which say there is no resurrection) and
they asked him, saying,

**Psal. 118.22. isai. 28.16. matt. 21.42. acts 4.11. rom. 9.33. 1 pet. 2.8.*

c They were greedie and verie desirous.

**Matth. 22.15. luke 20.20.*

2 The Gospel ioyneth the authoritie of the Magistrate with the seruice of God.

d Thou doest not so iudge by outward appearance, that the trueth is thereby darkened any whit at all.

e The way whereby wee come to God.

**Rom. 13.7.*

3 The resurrection of the bodie is auouched against the foolish ignorance and malice of the Sadduces.

Matth. 22.23. luke 20.27.

19 Master, * Moses wrote vnto vs, If any
mans brother die, and leaue *his* wife, and leaue
no children, that his brother should take his
wife, and raise vp seede vnto his brother.
20 There were seuen brethren, and the
first tooke a wife, & when he died, left no issue.
21 Then the second tooke her, and he died,
neither did hee yet leaue issue, and the third
likewise:
22 So those seuen had her, and left no issue:
last of all the wife died also.
23 In the resurrection then, when they shal
rise againe, whose wife shall she be of them?
for seuen had her to wife.
24 Then Iesus answered, and sayd vnto
them, Are yee not therefore deceiued, because
ye know not the Scriptures, neither the power
of God?
25 For when they shall rise againe from
the dead, neither men marrie, nor wiues are
married, but are as the Angels which are in
heauen.
26 And as touching the dead, that they shal
rise againe, haue yee not read in the booke of
Moses, how in the bush God spake vnto him,
saying, I * am the God of Abraham, and the
God of Isaac, and the God of Iacob?
27 God is not the God of the dead, but the
God of the liuing. Ye are therefore greatly deceiued.
28 ¶ * [4] Then came one of the Scribes
that had heard them disputing together, *and*
perceiuing that hee had answered them well,
hee asked him, Which is the first commaundement of all?
29 Iesus answered him, The first of all
the Commandements *is*, * Heare, Israel, The
Lord our God is the onely Lord.
30 Thou shalt therefore loue the Lord thy
God with all thine heart, and with al thy soule,
and with all thy minde, & with all thy strength:
this is the first Commandement.
31 And the second *is* like, that is, * Thou
shalt loue thy neighbour as thy selfe. There is
none other Commaundement greater then
these.
32 Then the Scribe sayd vnto him, Well,
Master, thou hast sayd the trueth, that there is
one God, and that there is none but he.
33 And to loue him with all the heart, and
with all the vnderstanding, and with all the
soule, and with all the strength, and to loue *his*
neighbour as himselfe, is more then all the
whole burnt offerings and sacrifices.
34 Then when Iesus sawe that he answered
discreetly, he sayd vnto him, Thou art not farre
from the kingdome of God. And no man after
that durst aske him any question.
35 ¶ * [5] And Iesus answered, and sayd teaching in the Temple, How say the Scribes that
Christ is the Sonne of Dauid?
36 For Dauid himselfe sayd by [f] the holy
Ghost, * The Lord sayd to my Lord, Sit at my
right

**Deut. 25.5. matth. 22.24.*

**Exod. 3.6. matth. 22.32.*

**Matth. 22.35.*

4 Sacrifices and outward worship neuer pleased God, vnlesse such necessary dueties as wee owe to God and our neighbours went afore.

**Deut. 6.4.*

**Leuit. 19.18. mat. 22.39. rom. 13.9. gal. 5.14. iames 2.8.*

**Matth. 22.41. luke 20.41.*

5 Christ proueth his Godhead euen out of Dauid himselfe, of whom he came according to the flesh.

f Word for word, in the holy Ghost, & there is a great force in this kinde of speach, whereby is meant, that it was not so much Dauid, as the holy Ghost that spake who did in a maner possesse Dauid.

**Psal. 110.1.*

right hand, till I make thine enemies thy footstoole.
37 Then Dauid himselfe calleth him Lord:
by what meanes is he then his sonne? & much
people heard him gladly.
38 *6 Moreouer he said vnto them in g his
doctrine, Beware of the Scribes which loue to
goe in h long robes, and *loue* salutations in the
markets,
39 And the chiefe seats in the Synagogues,
and the first roomes at feasts,
40 Which * deuoure widowes houses, euen
vnder a colour of long prayers. These shall receiue the greater damnation.
41 *7 And as Iesus sate ouer against the treasurie, he behelde how the people cast i money
into the treasurie, and many rich men cast in
much.
42 And there came a certaine poore widowe, and she threw in two mites, which make
a quadrin.
43 Then he called vnto him his disciples,
and said vnto them, Verily I say vnto you, that
this poore widowe hath cast more in, then all
they which haue cast into the treasurie.
44 For they all did cast in of their superfluitie: but she of her pouertie did cast in all that
she had, *euen* all her liuing.

*Marke 23.6. luke 11.43. and 20.43.
6 The maners of Ministers are not rashly to be followed as an example.
g Whiles hee taught them.
h The word is a stole, which is a kind of womans garment, long euen downe to the heeles, and is taken generally, for any garment made for comelinesse, but in this place it seemeth to signifie that fringed garment mentioned in Deut. 22. 11.
* *Matth. 23. 14. luke 20 47.*
7 The doing of our dueties, which God alloweth, is not esteemed according to the outward value, but to the inward affects of the heart.
* *Luke 21. 1.*
i Money of any kind of mettall, as the Romanes vsed, who in the beginning did stampe or coine brasse, and after vsed it for currant money.

CHAP. XIII.

1 Of the destruction of Ierusalem. 9 Persecutions for the Gospel. 10 The Gospel must be preached to all nations. 26 Of Christs comming to iudgement. 33 We must watch and pray.

AND * 1 as hee went out of the Temple,
one of his disciples saide vnto him, Master, see what maner stones, and what manner
buildings *are here*.
2 * Then Iesus answered and saide vnto
him, Seest thou these great buildings? there
shall not be left one stone vpon a stone, that
shall not be throwen downe.
3 And as he sate on the mount of Oliues,
ouer against the Temple, Peter, and Iames, and
Iohn, and Andrew asked him secretly,
4 Tell vs, when shall these things be? and
what *shalbe* the signe when all these things shal
be fulfilled?
5 And Iesus answered them, and began to
say, *Take heed lest any man deceiue you.
6 For many shall come in my Name, saying, I am *Christ*, and shall deceiue many.
7 Furthermore, when yee shall heare of
warres, and rumours of warres, be ye not troubled: for *such things* must needs bee: but the
end *shall* not *be* yet.
8 For nation shall rise against nation, and
kingdome against kingdome, and there shalbe
earthquakes in diuers quarters, and there shall
be famines and troubles: these *are* the beginnings of sorowes.
9 But take ye heed to your selues: for they
shall deliuer you vp to the Councils, and to the

* *Matth. 24. 1. luke 21. 5.*
1 The destruction of the Temple, citie, and whole nation is aforetold, and the troubles of the Church: but yet there are annexed many comforts, and last of all, the ende of the world is described.
* *Luke 19. 43.*
* *Ephes. 5. 6. 1. thes. 2. 3.*

Synagogues: ye shall be beaten, and brought
before rulers and kings for my sake, for a a testimoniall vnto them.
10 And the Gospel must first be published
among all nations.
11 * But when they leade you, and deliuer
you vp, b be ye not careful before hand, neither
c studie what ye shal say: but what is giuen you
at the same time, that speake: for it is not yee
that speake, but the holy Ghost.
12 Yea, and the brother shall deliuer the
brother to death, and the father the sonne, and
the children shall rise against their parents, and
shall cause them to die,
13 And ye shal be hated of all men d for my
Names sake: but whosoeuer shall endure to
the end, he shall be saued
14 * Moreouer, when ye shall see the abomination of desolation (spoken of by * Daniel
the Prophet) e set where it ought not, (let him
that readeth, consider it) then let them *that be*
in Iudea, flee into the mountaines,
15 And let him that is vpon the house, not
come downe into the house, neither enter therin, to fetch any thing out of his house.
16 And let him that is in the field, not turne
backe againe to take his garment.
17 Then woe *shall be* to them that are with
child, & to them that giue sucke in those dayes.
18 Pray therefore that your flight be not in
the winter.
19 For f those dayes shall be such tribulation, as was not from the beginning of the creation which God created vnto this time, neither
shall be.
20 And except that the Lord had shortned
those dayes, no flesh should be saued: but for
the elects sake, which he hath chosen, hee hath
shortened those dayes.
21 Then * if any man say to you, Loe, here
is Christ, or loe, *he is* there, beleeue it not.
22 For false Christs shall rise, and false prophets, and shall shew signes and wonders, to
deceiue if it were possible the very elect.
23 But take ye heed: behold, I haue shewed
you all things before.
24 ¶ Moreouer in those dayes, after that
tribulation, * the sunne shall waxe darke, and
the moone shall not giue her light,
25 And the starres of heauen shall fall: and
the powers which are in heauen, shall shake.
26 And then shal they see the Sonne of man
comming in the cloudes, with great power and
glory.
27 * And he shall then send his Angels, and
shall gather together his elect from the foure
windes, *and* from the vtmost part of the earth
to the vtmost part of heauen.
28 Now learne a parable of the figge tree.
When her bough is yet tender, and it bringeth
forth leaues, ye know that summer *is* neere.
29 So in like manner when yee see these
things come to passe, knowe that *the kingdome*

a The hearing of you preaching, shall be a most euident witnesse against them, so that they shall not be able to pretend ignorance.
* *Matth. 10. 19. luke 12. 11. and 21. 14.*
b We are not forbidden to thinke before hand, but pensiue carefulnesse whereby men discourage themselues, which proceedeth from distrust, and want of confidence and sure hope of Gods assistance, that carefulnesse we are willed to beware of, Looke Matth. 6. 27.
c By any kinde of artificious and cunning kinde of tale what to speake
d For me.
* *Mat. 24. 14. luke 21. 20.*
* *Dan. 9. 27.*
e When the heathen and prophane people shall not onely enter into the Temple, and defile both it, and the citie, but also cleane destroy it.
f This is a kinde of speach which the Hebrewes vse, and it hath a great force in it, for it giueth vs to vnderstand that in all that time one miserie shall so follow vpon another, as if the time it selfe were very miserie it selfe. So the Prophet Amos 5. 20 saith that the day of the Lord shall be darkenesse.
* *Matth. 24. 23. luke 17. 23. and 21. 8.*
* *Isa. 13. 10. ezek. 32. 7. ioel 2. 10. and 3. 15.*
* *Mat. 24. 31.*

of God is neere, *euen* at the doores.
30 Verely I say vnto you, that this generation shall not passe, till all these things bee
done.
31 Heauen and earth shall passe away, but
my words shall not passe away.
32 [2] But of that day and houre knoweth no
man, no, not the Angels which are in heauen,
neither the Sonne himselfe, but the Father.
33 * Take heede: watch, and pray: for ye
know not when the time is.
34 *For the Sonne of man is* as a man going
into a strange countrey, and leaueth his house,
and giueth authoritie to his seruants, and to
euery man his worke, and commaundeth the
Porter to watch.
35 Watch ye therefore, (for ye knowe not
when the master of the house will come, at e-
uen, or at midnight, at the cocke crowing, or
in the dawning,)
36 Lest if he come suddenly, hee should
finde you sleeping.
37 And those things that I say vnto you, I
say vnto all men, Watch.

2 The latter day is not curiously to be searched for, which the Father alone knoweth: but let vs rather take heed, that it come not vpon vs vnware.
**Matth.24.13.*

CHAP. XIIII.

1 *The Priestes conspiracie against Christ.* 3 *The woman powring oyle on Christs head.* 12 *The preparing of the Passeouer.* 22 *The institution of the Supper.* 41 *Christ deliuered into the handes of men.* 43 *Iudas betrayeth him with a kisse.* 55 *Christ is before Caiaphas.* 66 *Peters deniall.*

AND * [1] two dayes after followed *the feast
of* the Passeouer, & of vnleauened bread:
and the high Priests, and Scribes sought how
they might take him by craft, and put him to
death.
2 But they said, Not in the feast *day*, lest
there be any tumult among the people.
3 * And when he was in Bethania, in the
house of Simon the leper, as he sate at table,
there came a woman hauing a boxe of oyntment of spikenard, very costly, and shee brake
the boxe, and powred it on his head.
4 [2] Therefore some disdained among them
selues, and said, To what ende is this waste of
oyntment?
5 For it might haue bene solde for more
then [a] three hundreth pence, and bin giuen vnto
the poore, and they murmured against her.
6 But Iesus said, Let her alone: why trouble ye her? she hath wrought a good worke on
me.
7 [3] For yee haue the poore with you alwayes, and when ye will yee may doe them
good, but me ye shall not haue alwayes.
8 [4] She hath done that she could: she came
afore hand to anoint my body to the burying.
9 Verely I say vnto you, wheresoeuer this
Gospel shalbe preached throughout the whole
word, this also that she hath done, shall be spoken of in remembrance of her.
10 ¶ * [5] Then Iudas Iscariot, one of the
twelue, went away vnto the high Priestes, to
betray him vnto them.

**Matth.26.2. luke 22.1.*
1 By the will of God, against the counsell of men, it came to passe that Christ should be put to death vpon the solemne day of the Passeouer, that in all respects the trueth might agree to the figure.
**Matth.26.6. iohn 12.2.*
2 Rash iudgements are frustrate before God.
a Which is about fixe pounds English.
3 Christ suffered himselfe to be anointed once or twise for certaine considerations: but his will is to be daily anoynted in the poore.
4 This woman by the secret instinct of the spirit, anointing Christ, setteth before mens eyes, his death & buriall which were at hand.
**Matth. 26.14. luke 22.4.*
5 Couetousnes cloked with a zeale of charitie, is an occasion to betray and crucifie Christ.

11 And when they heard it, they were glad,
and promised that they would giue him mony:
therefore he sought how he might conueniently betray him.
12 ¶ * [6] Now the first day of vnleauened
bread, [b] when [c] they sacrificed the [d] Passeouer,
his disciples saide vnto him, Where wilt thou
that we goe and prepare, that thou mayest eate
the Passeouer?
13 Then he sent forth two of his disciples,
and said vnto them, Goe ye into the citie, and
there shall a man meet you bearing a pitcher of
water: follow him.
14 And whithersoeuer he goeth in, say ye
to the good man of the house, The Master
saith, Where is the lodging where I shall eate
the Passeouer with my disciples?
15 And he will shew you an [e] vpper chamber *which is* large, trimmed and prepared: there
make it ready for vs.
16 So his disciples went forth, and came to
the citie, and found as he had said vnto them,
and made ready the Passeouer.
17 ¶ And at euen he came with the twelue.
18 * [7] And as they sate at table and did eat,
Iesus said, Verely I say vnto you, that one of
you shall betray me, which eateth with me.
19 Then they began to be sorowfull and to
say to him one by one, Is it I? and another, Is
it I?
20 And he answered and said vnto them, *It
is* one of the twelue that [f] dippeth with me in
the platter.
21 Truely the Sonne of man goeth his way,
as it is written of him: * but woe *be* to that
man, by whom the Sonne of man is betrayed:
it had bene good for that man, if he had neuer
bene borne.
22 * And as they did eate, Iesus tooke the
bread, and when he had giuen thanks, he brake
it and gaue it to them, and said, Take, eate, this
is my body.
23 Also he tooke the cup, and when he had
giuen thankes, gaue it to them: and they all
dranke of it.
24 And hee said vnto them, This is my
blood of that newe Testament which is shedde
for many.
25 Verely I say vnto you, I will drinke no
more of the fruit of the vine vntill that day, that
I drinke it new in the kingdome of God.
26 And when they had sung a Psalme, they
went out to the mount of Oliues.
27 ¶ * [8] Then Iesus saide vnto them, All
ye shall be offended by me this night: for it is
written, * I will smite the shepheard, and the
sheepe shall be scattered.
28 But after that I am risen, I will goe into
* Galile before you.
29 [9] And Peter said vnto him, Although
all men should be offended at thee, yet would
not I.
30 Then Iesus saide vnto him, Verily I say
vnto

**Matth.26.17. luke 22.8.*
6 Christ being made subiect to the Lawe for vs, doeth celebrate the Passeouer according to the Lawe: and therewithall by a miracle sheweth that notwithstanding he in the flesh shall straightway suffer, yet that he is God.
b That is, vpon which day, and at the euening of the same day, which was the beginning of the fifteenth, Looke Matth.26.17.
c They vsed to sacrifice.
d That is, spoken thus, by the figure Metonymia, which is vsuall in Sacraments, and by the Passeouer is meant the Paschall lambe.
e The Greeke word signifieth that part of the house that is highest from the ground, to what vse soeuer it be put, but because they vsed to sup in that part of the house, they called it a supping chamber.
**Psal 41.10. mat.26.20,23. luke 22.14. iohn 13.18,21.*
7 The figure of the law which is by and by to be fulfilled, is abrogated: and in place thereof are put figures of the new couenant answerable vnto them, which shal continue to the worlds end.
f That vseth to eate meate with me.
**Acts 1.16.*
**Mat.26.26. 1.cor.11.24.*
**Iohn 16.32.*
8 Christ foretelleth how he shal be forsaken of his, but yet that he will neuer forsake them.
**Zach.13.7.*
**Chap.16.7.*
9 Here is set forth in an excellent person a most sorowfull example of mans rashnesse and weakenesse.

vnto thee, this day, *euen* in this night, before
the Cocke crowe twise, thou shalt denie mee
thrise.
31 But he said [g] more earnestly, If I should
die with thee, I will not denie thee: likewise
also said they all.
32 ¶ * [10] After, they came into a place named Gethsemane: then he said to his disciples,
Sit ye here, till I haue prayed.
33 And he tooke with him Peter, & Iames,
and Iohn, and he began to be troubled, and in
great heauinesse,
34 And saide vnto them, My soule is very heauie, *euen* vnto the death: tarie here, and
watch.
35 So he went forward a litle, & fell downe
on the ground, and prayed, that if it were possible, that houre might passe from him.
36 And he saide, [h] Abba, Father, all things
are possible vnto thee: take away this cup from
me: neuerthelesse not that I wil, but that thou
wilt, *be done*.
37 [11] Then he came, and found them sleeping, and said to Peter, Simon, sleepest thou?
couldest not thou watch one houre?
38 ¶ Watch ye, and pray, that yee enter
not into tentation: the spirit indeed is readie,
but the flesh is weake.
39 And againe he went away, and prayed,
and spake the same words.
40 And hee returned, and found them a-
sleepe againe: for their eyes were heauie: neither knew they what they should answer him.
41 And he came the third time, and saide
vnto them, Sleepe hencefoorth, and take your
rest: it is ynough: the houre is come: Behold,
the Sonne of man is deliuered into the hands of
sinners.
42 Rise vp: let vs goe: loe, he that betrayeth me, is at hand.
43 * [12] And immediatly while he yet spake,
came Iudas that was one of the twelue, and
with him a great multitude with swords and
staues from the hie Priestes, and Scribes, and
Elders.
44 And hee that betrayed him, had giuen
them a token, saying, Whomsoeuer I shal kisse,
he it is: take him and leade him away [i] safely.
45 And assoone as he was come, hee went
straightway to him, and said, Haile Master, and
kissed him.
46 Then they laid their hands on him, and
tooke him.
47 And [k] one of them that stood by, drewe
out a sword, and smote a seruant of the high
Priest, and cut off his eare.
48 And Iesus answered and saide to them,
Ye be come out as against a thiefe with swords
and with staues, to take me.
49 I was dayly with you teaching in the
Temple, and ye tooke me not: but *this is done*
that the Scriptures should be fulfilled.
50 Then they [l] all forsooke him, and fled.

g That doubling of words setteth out more plainly Peters vehement affirmation.
* *Matth. 26.36. luke 22.39.*
10 Christ suffering for vs, in that flesh which he tooke vpon him for our sakes, the most horrible terrours of the curse of God, receiueth the cup at his fathers hands, which he being iust, doeth straight way drinke off for the vniust.
h This doubling of the word, was vsed in those dayes when their languages were so mixed together: for this word Abba, is a Syrian word.
11 An horrible example of sluggishnes of men, euen in the disciples whome Christ had chosen.
* *Mat. 26.47. luke 22.47. iohn 18.3.*
12 As men did willingly spoyle God their Creator of his praise, in forsaking and betraying him: so Christ willingly going about to make satisfaction for this ruine, is forsake of his own, and betrayed by one of his familiars as a theefe, that the punishment might be agreeable to the sinne, and we who are very traitours, forsakers & sacrilegers, might be deliuered out of the deuils snare.
i So diligently, that he escape not out of your hands.
k That is, Peter.
l All his disciples.

51 [13] And there followed him a certaine
yong man, clothed in [m] linnen vpon his bare
bodie, and the yong men caught him.
52 But he left his linnen cloth, and fled from
them naked.
53 * So they ledde Iesus away to the high
Priest, and to him came [n] together all the high
Priests, and the Elders, and the Scribes.
54 Then Peter followed him afarre off e-
uen into the hall of the high Priest, and sate
with the seruants, and warmed *himselfe* at the
fire.
55 [14] And the * high Priests, & all the Councill sought for witnesse against Iesus to put him
to death, but found none.
56 For many bare false witnesse against
him, but their witnesse agreed not together.
57 Then there arose certaine, and bare
false witnesse against him, saying,
58 We heard him say, * I will destroy this
Temple made with handes, and within three
dayes I will builde another made without
hands.
59 But their witnesse yet agreed not together.
60 Then the hie Priest stoode vp amongst
them, and asked Iesus, saying, Answerest thou
nothing? What is the matter that these beare
witnesse against thee?
61 But he held his peace, and answered nothing. Againe the hie Priest asked him, and said
vnto him, Art thou that Christ the sonne of the
[o] Blessed?
62 And Iesus said, I am *he*, * and yee shall
see the Sonne of man sit at the right hande of
the power *of God*, and come in the cloudes of
heauen.
63 Then the high Priest rent his clothes,
and said, What haue we any more need of witnesses?
64 Yee haue heard the blasphemie: what
thinke ye? And they all condemned him to be
worthy of death.
65 [15] And some began to spit at him, and to
couer his face, and to beat him with fists, and to
say vnto him, Prophesie. And the sergeants
smote him with *their* rods.
66 [16] * And as Peter was beneath in the
hall, there came one of the maides of the high
Priest.
67 And when she saw Peter warming *himselfe*, she looked on him, and said, Thou wast
also with Iesus of Nazareth.
68 But he denied it, saying, I knowe him
not, neither wote I what thou sayest. Then he
went out into the porch, and the cocke crew.
69 * Then [p] a maid saw him againe, and began to say to them that stood by, This is *one* of
them.
70 But he denied it againe: and anon after,
they that stood by saide againe to Peter, Surely
thou art *one* of them: for thou art of Galile,
and thy speech is like.

13 Vnder pretence of godlines, all things are lawfull to such as doe violence against Christ.
m Which he cast about him, when he hearing that sturre in the night suddenly ranne forth: whereby we may vnderstand with how great licentiousnesse these villaines violently set vpon him.
* *Matth. 26.57. luke 22.54. iohn 18.24.*
n The highest Councill was assembled, because Christ was accused as a blasphemer and a false prophet: for as for the other crime of treason, it was forged against him by the Priests, to enforce Pilate by that meanes to condemne him.
14 Christ, who was so innocent that hee could not be oppressed, no not by false witnesses, is at length, for confessing God to be his father, condemned of impietie before the high Priest: that we, who denied God and were in deede wicked, might be quit before God.
* *Matth. 26.59.*
* *Iohn 2.19.*
o Of God, who is most worthy of all prayse?
* *Matth. 24.39.*
15 Christ suffering all kinde of reproch for our sakes, getteth euerlasting glory to them that beleeue in him.
* *Marke 26.69. luke 22.55. iohn 18.25.*
16 An heauy example of ÿ frailnesse of man together with a most comfortable example of the mercy of God, who giueth the spirit of repentance and faith to his elect.
* *Mat. 26.71.*
p If we compare the Euangelists diligently together, we shall perceiue that Peter was knowen of many through the maidens report: yea, and in Luke when the second deniall is spoken of, there is a man seruant mentioned, and not a maid.

71 And he began to curſe, and ſweare, *ſay-*
ing, I know not this man of whom ye ſpeake.

* *Matth.26.75. iohn 13.38.*

72 *Then the ſecond time the cocke crew,
and Peter remembred the word that Ieſus had
ſaid vnto them, Before the cocke crowe twiſe,
thou ſhalt denie mee thriſe, and waying that
with himſelfe, he wept.

CHAP. XV.

15 Of the things that Chriſt ſuffred vnder Pilate. 11 Barabbas is preferred before Chriſt. 15 Pilate deliuereth Chriſt to be crucified. 17 He is crowned with thorne. 19 They ſpit on him and mocke him. 21 Simon of Cyrene carieth Chriſts croſſe. 27 Chriſt is crucified betweene two theeues. 29 He is railed at. 37 He giueth vp the ghoſt. 43 Ioſeph burieth him.

* *Matth.27.1. luke 22.66. iohn 18.19.*

1 Chriſt being bound before the iudgement ſeat of an earthly Iudge, in open aſſembly is condemned as guiltie vnto the death of the croſſe, not for his owne ſinnes, (as appeareth by the Iudges own words) but for all ours, that we moſt guiltie creatures being deliuered from the guiltineſſe of our ſinnes, might be quitted before the iudgement ſeat of God, euen in open aſſemblie of the Angels.

a It was not lawfull for them to put any man to death, for all cauſes of life and death were taken away from them, first by Herod the great, and afterward by the Romanes, about fortie yeeres before the deſtruction of the Temple, and therefore they deliuer Ieſus to Pilate.

AND* [1] anon in the dawning, the high
Prieſts helde a Councill with the Elders,
and the Scribes, and the whole Council, and
bound Ieſus, and led him away, and [a] deliuered
him to Pilate.

2 Then Pilate asked him, Art thou the
King of the Iewes? And he anſwered, and ſaid
vnto him, Thou ſayeſt it.

3 And the high Prieſts accuſed him of many things.

4 * Wherefore Pilate asked him againe,
ſaying, Anſwereſt thou nothing? behold how
many things they witneſſe againſt thee.

* *Matth 27.12. luke 23.3. iohn 18.35.*

5 But Ieſus anſwered no more at all, ſo
that Pilate marueiled.

6 Now at the feaſt, Pilate [b] did deliuer a
priſoner vnto them, whomſoeuer they would
deſire.

b Vſed Pilate to deliuer.

7 Then there was one named Barabbas,
which was bound with his fellowes, that had
made inſurrection, who in the inſurrection had
committed murther.

8 And the people cried aloud, and began
to *deſire that he would doe* as he had euer done
vnto them.

9 Then Pilate anſwered them, and ſaide,
Wil ye that I let looſe vnto you the King of the
Iewes?

10 For he knew that the high Prieſtes had
deliuered him of enuie.

11 But the high Prieſts had moued the people *to deſire* that he would rather deliuer Barabbas vnto them.

12 And Pilate anſwered, and ſayd againe
vnto them, What will ye then that I doe *with*
him, whom ye call the King of the Iewes?

13 And they cryed againe, Crucifie him.

14 Then Pilate ſaid vnto them, But what
euil hath he done? and they cried the more feruently, Crucifie him.

15 So Pilate willing to content the people,
looſed them Barabbas, and deliuered Ieſus,
when he had ſcourged him, that hee might be
crucified.

16 Then the ſouldiers led him away into the
hall, which is the common hall, and called together the whole band,

17 [2] And clad him with purple, and platted
a crowne of thornes, and put it about *his head*,

2 Chriſt going about to take away the ſinnes of men, who went about to vſurpe ye throne of God himſelfe, is condemned as one that hunted after the kingdome and mocked with a falſe ſhew of a kingdome, that wee on the other ſide, who ſhall indeed be eternal kings, might receiue the crowne of glory at Gods owne hand.

18 And began to ſalute him, *ſaying*, Haile
King of the Iewes.

19 And they ſmote him on the head with a
reed, and ſpat vpon him, and bowed the knees,
and did him reuerence.

20 And when they had mocked him, they
tooke the purple off him, and put his owne
clothes on him, and led him out to crucifie him.

21 * And they [3] compelled one that paſſed
by, *called* Simon of Cyrene (which came out of
the countrey, and was father of Alexander and
Rufus) to beare his croſſe.

* *Matth. 27.32. luke 23.26.*

3 The rage of the wicked hath no meaſure, but in the meane ſeaſon, euen ye weakneſ of Chriſt, being in paine vnder the heauie burden of the croſſe, doeth manifeſtly ſhewe that a lamb is led to be ſacrificed.

22 *[4] And they brought him to a place named Golgotha, which is by interpretation, the
place of *dead mens* skulles.

* *Matth.27.33. luke 23.33. iohn 19.17.*

4 Chriſt is led out of the wals of the earthly Ieruſalem, into a foule place of dead men carkaſes, as a man moſt vncleane, not touching himſelfe, but touching our ſinnes, which were laid vpon him, to the end that we being made cleane by his blood, might be brought into the heauenly Sanctuarie.

23 And they gaue him to drink wine mingled with myrrhe: but he receiued it not.

24 *[5] And when they had crucified him,
they parted his garments, caſting lots for them
what euery man ſhould haue.

* *Luke 23.24.*

5 Chriſt hangeth naked vpon the croſſe, and as the wickedeſt caitiſe that euer was, moſt vilely reproued: that we being clothed with his righteouſneſſe, and bleſſed with his curſes and ſanctified by his onely oblation, may be taken vp into heauen.

25 And it was the third houre, when they
crucified him.

26 And the title of his cauſe was written a-
boue, THAT KING OF THE IEVVES.

27 They crucified alſo with him two theeues,
the one on the right hand, and the other on his
left.

28 Thus the Scripture was fulfilled, which
ſaith, *And he was counted among the wicked.

* *Eſai.53.12.*

29 And they that went by, railed on him,
wagging their heads, and ſaying, *Hey, thou
that deſtroyeſt the Temple, and buildeſt it in
three dayes,

* *Iohn 2.19.*

30 Saue thy ſelfe, and come downe from the
croſſe.

31 Likewiſe alſo euen the hie Prieſts mocking, ſaid among themſelues with the Scribes,
Hee ſaued other men, himſelfe hee cannot
ſaue.

32 Let Chriſt the King of Iſrael now come
downe from the croſſe, that we may ſee, and beleeue. They alſo that were crucified with him,
reuiled him.

33 ¶ Now when the ſixt houre was come,
[6] darkeneſſe aroſe ouer [c] all the land vntill the
ninth houre.

6 How angry God was againſt our ſinnes, which he puniſhed in our ſuretie his ſonne, it appeareth by this horrible darkeneſſe.

c By this word land, he meaneth Paleſtina: ſo that the ſtrangeneſſe of the wonder, is ſo much the more ſet forth in that, that at the feaſt of the Paſſeouer, and in the full moone, whe͂ the Sunne ſhined ouer all the reſt of the world, and at mid-day, that corner of the world, wherein ſo wicked an acte was committed, was ouercouered with moſt groſſe darkeneſſe.

34 And at the [7] ninth houre Ieſus cried with
a loud voyce, ſaying, *Eloi, Eloi, lamma-ſa-
bachthani? which is by interpretation, My God,
my God, why haſt thou forſaken me?

35 And ſome of them that ſtood by, when
they heard it, ſaid, Behold, he calleth Elias.

36 And one ranne and filled a * ſpunge full
of vineger, and put it on a reede, and gaue him
to drinke, ſaying, Let him alone: let vs ſee if E-
lias will come, and take him downe.

7 Chriſt ſtriuing mightily with Satan, with ſinne and with death, all three armed with the horrible curſe of God, grieuouſly tormented in body hanging vpon the croſſe, and in ſoule plunged in the depth of hell, yet hee riddeth himſelfe, crying with a mightie voyce: and notwithſtanding the wound which hee receiued of death, in that hee died, yet by ſmiting both things aboue, and things beneath, by renting of the vaile of the Temple, and by the Teſtimonie wrung out of the which murdered him, he ſheweth euidently vnto the reſt of his enemies which are as yet obſtinate, and mocke at him, that he ſhall be knowen out of hand to be conquerour and Lord of all. * *Pſal.22.1. matth.27.46.* * *Pſal.69.22.*

37 And

37 And Iesus cryed with a loude voyce,and
gaue vp the ghost.
38 And the vaile of the Temple was rent in
twaine from the top to the bottome.
39 Now when the Centurion,which stood
ouer against him, saw that he thus crying gaue
vp the ghost, he said, Truely this man was the
Sonne of God.

8 Christ to the great shame of men which forsooke the Lord, chose women for his witnesses, which beheld all this whole action.
* *Luke 8.2.*

40 ¶ [8] There were also women, which beheld afarre off, among whom was Mary Magdalene, and Mary (the mother of Iames the
lesse,and of Ioses) and Salome,
41 Which also when he was in Galile, *followed him, and ministred vnto him, and many
other women which came vp with him vnto
Hierusalem.

* *Matth.27.57.*

42 * And now when the night was come
(because it was the day of preparation that is
before the Sabbath)

* *Luke 23.50. iohn 19.38.*
d A man of great authoritie,of the councell of the Sanhedrin,or els taken into counsell by Pilate.
e If we consider what danger Ioseph cast himselfe into,we shall perceiue how bolde he was.

43 *Ioseph of Arimathea, an [d] honourable
counseller,which also looked for the kingdome
of God,came,and went in [e] boldly vnto Pilate,
and asked the body of Iesus.
44 And Pilate marueiled, if he were alreadie dead, and called vnto him the Centurion,
and asked of him whether hee had beene any
while dead.
45 And when hee knewe *the trueth* of the
Centurion, he gaue the body to Ioseph:
46 Who bought a linnen cloth, and tooke
him downe, and wrapped him in the linnen
cloth, and laid him in a tombe that was hewen
out of a rocke,and rolled a stone vnto the doore
of the sepulchre:
47 And Mary Magdalene, and Mary Ioses
mother,beheld where he should be laid.

CHAP. XVI.

1 Of Christs resurrection. 9 He appeareth to Mary Magdalene and others. 15 Hee sendeth his Apostles to preach. 19 His ascension.

* *Luke 24.1. iohn 20.1.*

AND * when the Sabbath day was past,
Mary Magdalene, and Mary the *mother*
of Iames,& Salome, bought sweet oyntments,
that they might come and anoint him.
2 Therefore earely in the morning,the first
day of the weeke, they came vnto the Sepulchre, when the Sunne was now risen.

a When they cast their eyes toward the Sepulchre.
* *Matth.28.1. iohn 20.12.*
b Into the caue, wherein the sepulchre was cut out.

3 And they said one to another,Who shall
rolle vs away the stone from the doore of the
sepulchre?
4 And when they [a] looked, they saw that
the stone was rolled away (for it was a very
great one)
5 *So they went into the [b] Sepulchre,and
saw a yong man sitting at the right side,clothed
in a long white robe: and they were sore troubled.
6 Be he said vnto them,Be not so troubled:
ye seeke Iesus of Nazareth, which hath beene
crucified: he is risen,he is not here: behold the
place where they put him.
7 But goe your way, and tell his disciples,
and Peter, that hee will goe before you into
Galile: there shall ye see him, * as he said vnto you.
8 And they went out quickly, and fledde
from the sepulchre: for they trembled, & were
amased: neither saide they any thing to any
man: for they were afraid.
9 ¶ [1] And when Iesus was risen againe,
earely the first day of the weeke, he appeared
first to Mary Magdalene,* out of whom he had
cast seuen deuils:
10 And she went and tolde them that had
bene with him, which mourned and wept.
11 And when they heard that hee was a-
liue, and had appeared to her, they beleeued it
not.
12 ¶ * [2] After that, he appeared vnto two
of them in another forme, as they walked and
went into the countrey.
13 And they went, and told it to the remnant,neither beleeued they them.
14 ¶ * [c] Finally hee appeared vnto the eleuen as they sate together,and reproched them
for their vnbeliefe and hardnesse of heart, because they beleeued not them which had seene
him,being risen vp againe.
15 [3] And he said vnto them, *Goe ye into
all the world,and preach the Gospel to [d] euery
creature.
16 He that shall beleeue and be baptized,
shall be saued: *but he that will not beleeue,
shall be damned.
17 And these tokens shall follow them that
beleeue, *In my Name they shall cast out deuils,and *shall speake with [e] new tongues,
18 *And they shall take away serpents,and
if they shall drinke any deadly thing,it shal not
hurt them: * they shall lay their hands on the
sicke, and they shall recouer.
19 * [4] So after the Lord had spoken vnto
them, he was receiued into heauen, and sate at
the right hand of God.
20 And they went foorth, and preached e-
uery where. And the * Lord wrought with
them, and confirmed [f] the worde with signes
that followed. Amen.

* *Chap.14.28. matth.26.32.*
1 Christ himselfe appeareth to Mary Magdalene to vpbraid the disciples incredulitie
* *Iohn 20.16. luke 8.2.*
* *Luke 24.13.*
2 Christ appeareth to two other disciples, and at length to the eleuen.
* *Luke 24.36. iohn 20.19.*
c The Euangelist considered not the order of the time, but the course of his history,which he diuided into three parts: The first sheweth how he appeared to the women, the second to his Disciples, the third to his Apostles,& therefore he saith finally.
3 The Apostles are appoynted, and their office is limited vnto them, which is to preach that, which they heard of him, and to minister the Sacraments, which Christ hath instituted, hauing besides power to doe miracles.
* *Matth.28.19.*
d Not to the Iewes onely,nor in Iudea onely, but to all men,and euery where: and so must all the Apostles doe.
* *Iohn 12.48.*
* *Acts 16.18.*
* *Act.2.4.and 10.46*
e Strange tongues such as they knewe not before.
* *Acts 28.5.*
* *Acts 28.8.*
* *Luke 24.51.*
4 Christ hauing accomplished his office on earth, ascendeth into heauen,from whence (the doctrine of his Apostles being confirmed with signes) he will gouerne his Church,vnto the worlds ende.
* *Hebr.2.4.*
f To wit,the doctrine: therefore doctrine must goe before,and signes must follow after.

THE HOLY GOSPEL OF IESVS CHRIST, ACCORDING TO S. LVKE.

CHAP. I.

1 Lukes preface. 5 Zacharias and Elizabet. 15 What an one Iohn ſhould be. 20 Zacharias ſtrooken dumbe, for his incredulitie. 26 The Angel ſaluteth Mary, and foretelleth Chriſts natiuitie. 39 Mary viſiteth Elizabet. 46 Maries ſong. 68 The ſong of Zacharias, ſhewing that the promiſed Chriſt is come. 76 The office of Iohn.

Orasmuch as [1] many haue [a] taken in hand to ſet foorth the ſtory of thoſe things, whereof we are fully perſwaded,

2 [b] As they haue deliuered them vnto vs, which from the beginning ſaw them themſelues, and were miniſters of the word,

3 It ſeemed good alſo to me ([c] moſt noble Theophilus) aſſoone as I had ſearched out perfectly all things [d] from the beginning, to write vnto thee thereof from poynt to poynt,

4 That thou mighteſt [e] acknowledge the certainetie of thoſe things, whereof thou haſt beene inſtructed.

5 IN [2] the [f] time of [g] Herod King of Iudea, there *was* a certaine Prieſt named Zacharias, of the * [h] courſe of Abia: and his wife *was* of the daughters of Aaron, and her name *was* Elizabet.

6 Both were [i] iuſt before God, and [k] walked in all the [l] commandements and ordinances of the Lord, [m] without reproofe.

7 And they had no childe, becauſe that Elizabet was barren: and both were well ſtriken in age.

8 And it came to paſſe, as he executed the Prieſts office before God, as his courſe came in order,

9 *According to the cuſtome of the Prieſts office, his lot was to burne incenſe, when hee went into the [n] Temple of the Lord.

10 And the whole multitude of the people were without in prayer, *while the incenſe was burning.

11 Then appeared vnto him an Angel of the Lord ſtanding at the right ſide of the altar of incenſe.

12 And when Zacharias ſawe *him*, he was troubled, and feare fell vpon him.

13 But the Angel ſaid vnto him, Feare not, Zacharias: for thy prayer is heard, and thy wife Elizabet ſhal beare thee a ſonne, and thou ſhalt call his name Iohn.

14 And thou ſhalt haue ioy and gladneſſe, and many ſhall reioyce at his birth.

15 For he ſhall be great in the [o] ſight of the Lord, and ſhal neither drinke wine, nor [p] ſtrong drinke: and hee ſhall bee filled with the holy Ghoſt, euen from his mothers wombe.

16 * And many of the children of Iſrael ſhall he [q] turne to the Lord their God.

17 *For hee ſhall goe [r] before him [ſ] in the ſpirit and power of Elias, to turne the [t] hearts of the fathers to the children, and the diſobedient to the [u] wiſedome of the iuſt men, to make ready a people prepared for the Lord.

18 Then Zacharias ſaide vnto the Angel, Whereby ſhall I knowe this? for I am an olde man, and my wife is of a great age.

19 And the Angel anſwered, and ſaid vnto him, I am Gabriel [x] that ſtand in the preſence of God, and am ſent to ſpeake vnto thee, and to ſhew thee theſe good tidings.

20 And behold, thou ſhalt be dumbe, and not be able to ſpeake, vntill the day that theſe things be done, becauſe thou beleeuedſt not my wordes, which ſhall bee fulfilled in their ſeaſon.

21 Now the people waited for Zacharias, and marueiled that hee taried ſo long in the Temple.

22 And when he came out, hee could not ſpeake vnto them: then they perceiued that he had ſeene a viſion in the Temple: For hee made ſignes vnto them, and remained dumbe.

23 And it came to paſſe, when the dayes of his office were fulfilled, that he departed to his owne houſe.

24 And after thoſe dayes, his wife Elizabet conceiued, and hid her ſelfe fiue moneths, ſaying,

25 Thus hath the Lord dealt with mee, in the dayes wherein he loked on *me*, to take from me my rebuke among men.

23 ¶ [3] And in the ſixt moneth, the Angel Gabriel was ſent from God vnto a citie of Galile, named Nazareth,

27 *To a virgin affianced to a man whoſe name *was* Ioſeph, of the [y] houſe of Dauid, and the virgins name *was* Mary.

28 And the Angel went in vnto her, and ſaid, Haile thou *that art* [z] freely beloued: the Lord *is* with thee: [a] bleſſed *art* thou among women.

29 And

---

1 Luke commendeth the witneſſes that ſawe this hiſtorie.
a Many tooke it in hand, but did not performe: Luke wrote his Goſpel before Matthew and Marke.
b Luke was not an eye witneſſe, and therefore it was not hee, to whom the Lord appeared when Cleopas ſaw him: & he was taught not onely by Paul, but by others of the Apoſtles alſo.
c It is moſt mightie, and therfore Theophilus was a very honourable man, and in place of great dignitie.
d Luke beganne his Goſpel a great deale farther off, then the other did.
e Haue fuller knowledge of thoſe things, which before thou kneweſt but meanely.
2 Iohn who was another Elias, and appointed to be herault of Chriſt, comming of the ſtocke of Aaron, and of two famous & blameleſſe parents, hath ſhewed in his conception, which was againſt the courſe of nature, a double miracle, to the end that men ſhould be more readily ſtirred vp to the hearing of his preaching, according to the forewarning of the Prophets.
f Word for word, in the dayes: ſo ſpeake the Hebrewes, giuing vs to vnderſtand, how ſhort and fraile a thing the power of princes is. g Herod the great. * *1. Chr. 24. 1. h For the poſteritie of Aaron was diuided into courſes. i The true marke of righteouſneſſe is, to bee liked and allowed of in the iudgement of God. k Liued, ſo ſpeake the Hebrewes, for our life is as a way, wherein wee muſt walke, vntill wee come to the marke. l In all the morall and ceremoniall Lawe. m Whome no man could iuſtly reprooue: now ſo it is, that the fruits of iuſtification are ſet forth here, and not the cauſe, which is faith onely, and nothing els.* * *Exod. 30. 7. n The Temple was one, and the Court another, for Zacharias went out of the Court, or outward roome, where all the people were, and therefore are ſaid to be without, into the Temple.* * *Leuit. 16. 17.*

o So ſpeake the Hebrewes, when is ſignified a rare kind of excellencie: ſo it is ſaid of Nemrod, Gene. 10. 9. He was a valiant hunter before God.
p Any drink that may make drunkẽ.
* *Malac. 4. 5.*
q Shalbe a means to bring many to repentance, and turne themſelues to the Lord, from whom they fell.
* *Matth. 11. 14.*
r As they vſe to goe before kings, and when you ſee them, you know the king is not farre off.
ſ This is ſpoken by the figure Metonymie, taking the ſpirit, for the gift of the ſpirit, as you would ſay, the cauſe for that that commeth of the cauſe.
t By the figure Synecdoche, he ſheweth that he ſhall take away all kindes of enmities, which vſe to breed great troubles and turmoiles amongſt men.
u Wiſedome and goodneſſe are two of the chiefeſt cauſes which make men to reuerence, and honour their fathers.
x That appeare, for ſo the Hebrewes vſe this word (to ſtand) meaning that they are ready to do his commandement.
3 The Angel ſeruing the Lord which ſhould be borne, is ſent to the Virgin Mary, in whom the ſon of the moſt high promiſed to Dauid, is conceiued by the vertue of the holy Ghoſt.
* *Mat. 1. 18.*
y As much is to be ſaid of Mary, otherwiſe Chriſt had not bene of the ſtocke, nor the ſonne of Dauid.
z It might bee rendred word for word, full of fauour and grace, and he ſheweth ſtraight after, laying out plainely vnto vs, what that fauour is, in that he ſaith, The Lord is with thee.
a Of God.

29 And when she saw *him*, she was [b] troubled at his saying, and thought what maner of
salutation that should be.
30 Then the Angel said vnto her, Feare
not, Marie: for thou hast [c] found fauour with
God.
31 *For loe, thou shalt conceiue in thy
wombe, and beare a sonne, *and shalt call his
name IESVS.
32 Hee shall be great, and shall be [d] called
the Sonne of the most High, and the Lord God
shall giue vnto him the throne of his father
Dauid.
33 *And hee shall reigne ouer the House
of Iacob for euer, and of his kingdome shall
be none end.
34 Then said Mary vnto the Angel, [e] How
shall this be, seeing [f] I know not man?
35 And the Angel answered, and said vnto her, The holy Ghost [g] shal come vpon thee,
and the power of the most High shall ouersha-
dow thee: therfore also that [h] holy thing which
shalbe borne of thee, shalbe [i] called the Sonne
of God.
36 And behold, thy [k] cousin Elizabet, shee
hath also conceiued a sonne in her olde age:
and this is her [l] sixt moneth, which was called
barren.
37 For with God shall nothing be vnpossible.
38 Then Mary said, Behold the seruant of
the Lorde: be it vnto mee according to thy
word. So the Angel departed from her.
39 ¶ [4] And Mary arose in those dayes, and
went into the [m] hill *countrey* with haste to a
[n] citie of Iuda,
40 And entred into the house of Zacharias,
and saluted Elizabet.
41 And it came to passe, as Elizabet heard
the salutation of Mary, the babe [o] sprang in
her belly, and Elizabet was filled with the holy Ghost.
42 And shee cryed with a loud voice, and
said, Blessed art thou among women, because
[p] the fruit of thy wombe is blessed.
43 And whence *commeth* this to mee,
that the mother of my Lorde should come
to me?
44 For loe, assoone as the voice of thy salutation sounded in mine eares, the babe sprang
in my belly for ioy.
45 And blessed *is* shee that beleeued: for
those things shall be performed, which were
tolde her from the Lord.
46 [5] Then Mary said, My soule magnifieth
the Lord,

b Mooued at the strangenesse of the matter.
c So spake the Hebrewes, saying that men haue found fauour, which are in fauour.
**Esai 7.14.*
**Chap.2.21. matth.1.21.*
d He shalbe declared so to be, for hee was the Sonne of God from euerlasting, but was made manifest in the flesh in his time.
**Dan.7.14,27. mich.4.7.*
e The greatnesse of the matter causeth the virgin to aske this question, not that she distrusteth any whit at all, for she asketh onely of the maner of the conceiuing, so that it is plaine, shee beleeued all the rest.
f So speake the Hebrewes, signifying by this modest kind of speech the company of man and wife together, and this is the meaning of it: how shall this be, for seeing I shall be Christ his mother, I am very sure, I shall not know any man: for the godly virgin had learned by the Prophets, that the Messias should be borne of a virgine.
g That is, the holy Ghost shall cause thee to conceiue by his mightie power.
h That pure thing and void of all spot of vncleannesse: for he that was to take away sinne, must needs be void of sinne.
i Declared and shewed to the world to bee the Sonne of God.
k Though Elizabet were of the tribe of Leui, yet shee might be Maries cousin: for whereas it was forbidden by the Law, for maidens to be maried to men of other tribes, this could not let, but that the Leuites might take them wiues out of any Tribe: for the Leuites had no portion allotted them, when the land was diuided among the people. *l This is now the sixt moneth from the time when she conceiued.* 4 Elizabet being great with childe of Iohn, and Mary with Christ, by the inspiration of the holy Ghost, doe reioyce ech for other. *m Which is on the South side of Hierusalem.* *n That is to say, Hebron: which was in times past called Cariatharbe: which was one of the townes that were giuen to the Leuites, in the Tribe of Iuda, and is said to be in the mountaines of Iuda, Iosh.14.15. and 21.11.* *o This was no ordinarie nor vsuall kinde of mouing.* *p Christ is blessed in respect of his humanitie.* 5 Christ the redeemer of the afflicted, and reuenger of the proud, of long time promised to the fathers, is now at length exhibited indeed.

47 And my spirit reioyceth in God my Sauiour.
48 For he hath [q] looked on the [r] poore degree of his seruant: for behold, from hencefoorth shall all ages call me blessed,
49 Because hee that is mightie, hath done
for me great things, and holy *is* his Name.
50 And his mercie *is* from generation to
generation on them [s] that feare him.
51 *Hee hath shewed strength with his
[t] arme: *he hath [u] scattered the proud in the
[x] imagination of their hearts.
52 *Hee hath [y] put downe the mightie
from *their* seates, and exalted them of [z] lowe
degree.
53 *He hath filled the [a] hungry with good
things, and sent away the rich emptie.
54 [b] *Hee hath vpholden Israel his seruant
to be mindfull of *his* mercie,
55 (*As hee hath [c] spoken to our fathers,
to wit, to Abraham, and his seede) for euer.
56 ¶ And Marie abode with her about
three moneths: after she returned to her owne
house.
57 ¶ [6] Now Elizabets time was fulfilled,
that she should be deliuered, and she brought
foorth a sonne.
58 And her neighbours and cousins heard
tell how the Lord had shewed his great mercy
vpon her, and they *reioyced with her.
59 And it was so that on the eight day they
came to circumcise the babe, and called him
Zacharias after the name of his father.
60 But his mother answered, and said, Not
so, but he shall be called Iohn.
61 And they said vnto her, There is none
of thy kinred, that is named with this name.
62 Then they made signes to his father,
how he would haue him called.
63 So hee asked for writing tables, and
wrote, saying, His name is Iohn, and they marueiled all.
64 And his mouth was opened immedi-
atly, and his tongue, || and he spake and praised
God.
65 Then feare came on all them that dwelt
neere vnto them, and all [d] these wordes were
noised abroad throughout all the hill *countrey*
of Iudea,
66 And all they that heard them, [e] layd
them vp in their hearts, saying, What manner
childe shall this be! and the [f] hand of the Lord
was with him.
67 [7] Then his father Zacharias was filled
with the holy Ghost, and prophecyed, saying,
68 Blessed *bee* the Lorde God of Israel,
because hee hath [g] visited *and [h] redeemed his
people,

q Hath freely and graciously loued.
r Word for word, My basenesse, that is, my base estate: so that the virgine vaunteth not her deserts, but the grace of God.
s To them that liue godly and religiously, so speake the Hebrewes.
**Esai 51.9. psal.33.10.*
t This is an heaping vp of words more then needs, which the Hebrewes vse very much, and the arme is taken for strength.
**Esai 29.15.*
u Euen as the winde doeth the chaffe.
x He hath scattered them, and the imagination of their hearts: or by and through the imagination of their owne hearts: so that their wicked counsell turned to their owne destruction.
**1.Sam.2.6.*
y The mightie and rich men.
z Such as none account is made of, and are vile in mens eyes, which are in deede the poore in spirit, that is, such as challenge nothing to themselues in the sight of God.
**Psal.34.10.*
a Them that are brought to extreme pouertie.
b He hath holpen vp Israel with his arme, being cleane cast downe.
**Esai 30.18. and 41.8. and 54.5. ierem. 31.3,20.*
**Gen.17.19. and 22.17. psal. 132.11.*
c Promised.
6 Iohns natiuitie is set out with new miracles.
**Verse 14.*
|| Was restored to it former state, *is read in some copies.*
d All this that was sayd and done.
e Thought vpon them diligently and earnestly, and as it were, printed them in their hearts.
f That is, the present fauour of God, and a singular kinde of vertue appeared in him. 7 Iohn yet scarce borne, by the authoritie of the holy Ghost, is appointed to his office. *g That hee hath shewed himselfe mindfull of his people, in so much that hee came downe from heauen himselfe to visite vs in person, and to redeeme vs.* **Chap.2.30. matth.1.21.* *h Hath payd the ransome, that is to say, the price of our redemption.*

69 *And

69 *And hath raised vp the [i] horne of saluation vnto vs, in the house of his seruant
Dauid,
70 *As he spake by the mouth of his holy
Prophets, which were since the world began,
saying,
71 *That he would send vs* deliuerance from
our enemies, and from the handes of all that
hate vs,
72 That hee might shewe mercie towards
our fathers, and [k] remember his holy couenant,
73 * *And* the othe which hee sware to our
father Abraham.
74 *Which was*, that hee would grant vnto
vs, that wee being deliuered out of the hands
of our enemies, should serue him without
feare,
75 All the dayes our life, in * holinesse and
righteousnesse [l] before him.
76 And thou [m] babe, shalt be called the
Prophet of the most High: for thou shalt goe
before the face of the Lorde, to prepare his
wayes,
77 *And* to [n] giue knowledge of saluation
vnto his people, by the [o] remission of their
sinnes,
78 Through the tender mercie of our God,
whereby * the [p] day spring from an high hath
visited vs,
79 To giue light to them that sit in darkenesse, and in the shadow of death, and to guide
our feete into the [q] way of peace.
80 And the childe grew, and waxed strong
in spirit, and was in the wildernesse, till the
day came that hee should shewe himselfe vnto
Israel.

* *Psal.132.18.*
i This word horne, in the Hebrew tongue signifieth might, and it is a metaphore, taken from beasts, that fight with their hornes: And by raising vp the might of Israel, is meant, that the kingdome of Israel was defended, and the enemies thereof layd on the ground, euen then when the strength of Israel seemed to be vtterly decayed.
* *Ierem.23.6. and 30.10.*
k Declare indeed that he was mindfull.
* *Gen.22.16 iere.31.33.heb.6.13, 17.*
* *1.Pet.1.15.*
l To Gods good liking
m Though thou be at this present neuer so little.
n Open the way.
o Forgiuenesse of sinnes, is the means whereby God saueth vs, Rom.4.7.
* *Zach.3.8. and 6.12. mal.4.2.*
p Or, budde, or branch, he alludeth vnto the places in Ier.23.5. zach.3.8. and 6.12. and he is called a bud from an high, that is sent from God vnto vs, and not as other buds which bud out of the earth
q Into the way which leadeth vs to true happinesse.

CHAP. II.

1 Augustus Cesar taxeth all the world. 7 Christ is borne. 13 The Angels song. 21 Christ is circumcised. 22 Marie purified. 28 Simeon taketh Christ in his armes. 29 His song. 39 Anna the Prophetesse. 40 The childe Christ. 46 Iesus disputeth with the doctours.

AND [1] it came to passe in those dayes, that
there came a decree from Augustus Cesar, that all the [a] world should be [b] taxed.
2 (This first taxing was made when Cy-
renius was gouernour of Syria.)
3 Therefore went all to bee taxed, euery
man to his owne citie.
4 And Ioseph also went vp from Galile
out of a citie called Nazareth, into Iudea, vnto
the citie of * Dauid, which is called Bethlehem
(because hee was of the house and linage of
Dauid,)
5 To be taxed with Marie that was giuen
him to wife, which was with child.
6 ¶ And so it was, that while they were
there, the dayes were accomplished that shee
should be deliuered.

1 Christ the sonne of God, taking vpon him the forme of a seruant, and making himselfe of no reputation, is poorely borne in a stable: and by the meanes of Augustus the mightiest prince in the world, (thinking nothing lesse) hath his cradle prepared in Bethlehem, as the Prophets fore warned.
a So farre as the Empire of the Romanes did stretch.
b That is, the inhabitants of euery citie should haue their names taken, and their goods rated at a certaine value, that the Emperour might vnderstand how rich euery countrey, citie, family, and house was. *c Which Dauid was borne, and brought vp in.* * *Iohn 7.42.*

7 And she brought foorth her first begotten sonne, & wrapped him in swadling clothes,
and laid him in a cratch, because there was no
roume for them in the Inne.
8 ¶ [2] And there were in the same countrey
shepheards, [d] abiding in the field, and keeping
watch by night ouer their flocke.
9 And loe, the Angel of the Lord [e] came
vpon them, and the glory of the Lord shone a-
bout them, and they were sore afraid.
10 Then the Angel said vnto them, Be not
afraid: for behold, I bring you glad tidings of
great ioy, that shall be to all the people,
11 *That is*, that vnto you is borne this day
in the citie of Dauid, a Sauiour, which is Christ
the Lord.
12 And this *shall be* a signe to you, Ye shall
finde the babe swadled, and laid in a cratch.
13 And straightway there was with the Angel [f] a multitude of heauenly souldiours, praising God, and saying,
14 Glory *be* to God in the hie *heauens*, and
peace in earth, and towards men [g] good will.
15 And it came to passe when the Angels
were gone away from them into heauen, that
the shepheards said one to another, Let vs goe
then vnto Beth-leem, and see this thing that
is come to passe which the Lord hath shewed
vnto vs.
16 So they came with haste, and found both
Mary and Ioseph, & the babe laid in the cratch.
17 And when they had seene it, they published abroad the thing, that was tolde them of
that childe.
18 And all that heard it, wondered at the
things which were told them of the shepherds.
19 But Mary kept all those sayings, and
pondered *them* in her heart.
20 And the shepheards returned glorifying
and praysing God, for all that they had heard
and seene, as it was spoken vnto them.
21 ¶ * [3] And when the eight dayes were accomplished, that they should circumcise the
child, his name was then called * Iesus, which
was named of the Angel, before he was conceiued in the wombe.
22 * [4] And when the daies of [h] her purification after the Law of Moses were accomplished, they brought him to Hierusalem, to present
him to the Lord,
23 (As it is written in the Lawe of the
Lord, * Euery man child that *first* openeth the
wombe, shalbe called holy to the Lord)
24 And to giue an oblation, * as it is commanded in the Lawe of the Lord, a paire of
turtle doues, or two yong pigeons.
25 [5] And behold, there was a man in Hierusalem, whose name was Simeon: this man
was iust, and feared God, and waited for the
consolation of Israel, and the [i] holy Ghost was
vpon him.
26 And it was declared to him from God
by the holy Ghost, that he should not see
death,

2 The Angels themselues declare to poore shepheards (nothing regarding the pride of the mightie) the Godhead and office of the childe lying in the crib.
d Lodging without doores, and open in the aire.
e Came suddenly vpon them, when they thought of no such matter.
f Whole armies of Angels, which compasse the Maiestie of God round about, as it were souldiers.
g Gods readie, good, infinite, and gracious fauour towards men.
* *Gen.17.12. leuit.12.3. iohn 7.22.*
3 Christ the head of the Church, made subiect to the Law, to deliuer vs from the curse of the Law (as the Name of Iesus doeth well declare) being circumcised, doeth ratifie and seale in his owne flesh, the circumcision of the fathers.
* *Chap.1.31. matth.1.21.*
* *Leuit.12.6.*
4 Christ vpon whom all our sinnes were laid, being offered to God, according to the law, doth purifie both Mary, and vs all, in himselfe.
h This is meant for the fulfilling of the Law: for otherwise the virgine was not defiled, nor vncleane, by the birth of this childe.
* *Exod.13.2. num.8.16.*
* *Leuit.12.6.*
5 Simeon doth openly in the Temple foretell the deafe, of the comming of Messias, of the casting out of the greatest part of Israel, and of the calling of the Gentiles.
i He was endued with the gifts of the holy Ghost, and this is spoken by the figure Metonymia.

death, before hee had seene that Anointed of
the Lord.
27 And hee came by *the motion* of the spirit
into the Temple, and when the [k] parents
brought in the babe Iesus, to doe for him after
the custome of the Law,
28 Then hee tooke him in his armes, and
praised God, and said,
29 Lord, now [l] lettest thou thy seruant depart in peace, according to thy [m] word.
30 For [n] mine eyes haue seene thy [o] saluation,
31 Which thou hast prepared [p] before the
face of all people,
32 A light to be reueiled to the Gentiles,
and the glory of thy people Israel.
33 And Ioseph and his mother marueiled
at those things, which were spoken touching
him.
34 And Simeon blessed them, and said vn-
to Mary his mother, Behold, this *childe* is [q] appointed for the * [r] fall and rising againe of many in Israel, and for a [s] signe which shalbe spoken against,
35 (Yea and a sword shall [t] pierce through
thy soule) that the thoughts of many hearts
may be opened.
36 [6] And there was a Prophetesse, one Anna the daughter of Phanuel, of the Tribe of
Aser, which was of a great age, after shee had
liued with an husband seuen yeeres from her
virginitie:
37 And shee *was* widow about fourescore
and foure yeres, and went not out of the Temple, but serued *God* with fastings and prayers
night and day.
38 Shee then comming at the same instant
vpon them, confessed likewise the Lord, and
spake of him to all that looked for redemption
in Hierusalem.
39 And when they had perfourmed all
things according to the Law of the Lord, they
returned into Galile to their owne citie Nazareth.
40 And the childe grew, and waxed strong
in Spirit, [u] and was filled with wisedome, and
the grace of God was with him.
41 ¶ [7] Now his parents went to Hierusalem euery yeere, *at the feast of the Passeouer.
42 And when he was twelue yeere old, and
they were come vp to Hierusalem, after the
custome of the feast,
43 And had finished the dayes *thereof*, as
they returned, the child Iesus remained in Hierusalem, & Ioseph knew not, nor his mother.
44 But they supposing, that hee had beene
in the companie, went a dayes iourney, and
sought him among *their* kinsfolke, and acquaintance.
45 And when they found him not, they
turned backe to Hierusalem, and sought him.
46 And it came to passe three dayes after,
that they found him in the Temple, sitting in

k Ioseph & Mary: and so he speaketh as it was commonly taken.

l Lettest me depart out of this life, to be ioyned to my fathers.

m As thou promisedst me.

n That is, for I haue seene with my very eyes: for he saw before in mind, as it is said of Abraham, He saw my day, and reioyced.

o That, wherein thy saluation is conteined.

p As a signe set vp in an hie place, for all men to looke vpon.

q Is appointed, and set of God for a marke.

* *Esai 8.14. rom.9.32. 1.pet.2.8.*

r Fall of the reprobate, which perish through their owne default: and for the rising of the elect, vnto whom God shall giue faith to beleeue.

s That is, a mark, which all men shal striue earnestly to hit.

t Shall wound and grieue most sharpely.

6 An other witnesse beside Simeon, against whom no exception may be brought, inuiting all men to the receiuing of the Messias.

u As Christ grew vp in age, so the vertue of his Godhead shewed it selfe more and more.

7 The Scribes and Pharises are stirred vp to heare the wisedome of Christ in his time, by an extraordinarie deede.

* *Deut.16.1.*

the middes of the doctors, both hearing them,
and asking them questions:
47 And all that heard him, were astonied
at his vnderstanding and answeres.
48 [8] So when they saw him, they were amazed, and his mother sayd vnto him, Sonne,
why hast thou thus dealt with vs? behold, thy
father and I haue sought thee with very heauie
hearts.
49 Then said hee vnto them, How is it that
ye sought me? knew yee not that I must goe a-
bout my Fathers businesse?
50 But they vnderstood not the word that
he spake to them.
51 [9] Then hee went downe with them, and
came to Nazareth, and was subiect to them:
and his mother kept all these sayings in her
heart.
52 And Iesus increased in wisedome, and
stature, and in fauour with God and men.

8 All dueties which we owe to men, as they are not to be neglected, so are they according to our vocation, not to be preferred before the glory of God.

9 Christ verie man is made like vnto vs in all things, except sinne.

CHAP. III.

4 Iohn exhorteth to repentance. 15 His testimony of Christ. 20 Herod putteth him in prison. 21 Christ is baptized. 23 His pedegree.

NOw [1] in the fifteenth yeere of the reigne
of Tiberius Cesar, Pontius Pilate being
gouernour of Iudea, and Herode being Tetrarch of Galile, & his brother Philip Tetrarch
of Iturea, and of the countrey of Trachonitis,
and Lysanias the Tetrarch of Abilene,
2 (* When [a] Annas and Caiaphas were
the high Priests) the word of God came vnto
Iohn the sonne of Zacharias in the wildernesse.
3 * And he came into all the coasts about
Iordan, preaching the baptisme of repentance
for the remission of sinnes,
4 As it is written in the booke of the sayings of Esaias the Prophet, which sayth, * The
voice of him that cryeth in the wildernesse *is*,
Prepare yee the way of the Lord: make his
paths straight.
5 Euery valley shall bee filled, and euery
mountaine and hill shall be brought lowe, and
crooked things shall be made straight, and the
rough wayes *shall be made* smoothe.
6 And all flesh shall see the saluation of
God.
7 Then said hee to the people that were
come out to be baptized of him, * O generations of vipers, who hath forewarned you to flee
from the wrath to come?
8 Bring foorth therefore fruites worthy
amendment of life, and begin not to say with
your selues, We haue Abraham to *our* father:
for I say vnto you, that God is able of these
stones to raise vp children vnto Abraham.
9 Now also is the axe laid vnto the roote
of the trees: therefore euery tree which bringeth not foorth good fruite, shall bee hewen
downe, and cast into the fire.
10 ¶ Then the people asked him, saying,
What shall we doe then?

1 Iohn commeth at the time foretold of the Prophets, and layeth the foundation of the Gospel which is exhibited vnto vs, setting forth the true obseruing of the law, and free mercie in Christ, which commeth after him, vsing also baptisme the effectuall signe both of regeneration, and also forgiuenesse of sinnes.

* *Actes 4.6.*

a Iosephus calleth him Ananus.

* *Matth.3.1. marke 2.4.*

* *Esai 40.3. iohn 1.23.*

* *Matth.3.7.*

11 And

11 And hee answered, and said vnto them, *Hee that hath two coates, let him part with him that hath none: and he that hath meat, let him doe likewise.

*Iames 2.15. 1.iohn 3.17.

12 Then came there Publicanes also to be baptized, and said vnto him, Master, what shall we doe?

13 And hee said vnto them, Require no more then that which is [b] appointed vnto you.

b Require no more then that summe, that is appointed for the tribute money.

14 The souldiers likewise demanded of him, saying, And what shall we doe? And hee said vnto them, Doe violence to no man, neither accuse any falsely, and bee content with your [c] wages.

c Which was paid them partly in money, and partly in victuall.

15 [2] As the people waited, and all men mused in their hearts of Iohn, if hee were not that Christ,

16 Iohn answered, and said to them all, *In deede I baptize you with water, but one stronger then I, commeth, whose shooes latchet I am not worthy to vnloose: he will baptize you with the holy Ghost, and with fire.

2 If we will rightly, & fruitfully receiue the Sacraments, we must neither rest in the signes, neither in him that ministreth the signes, but lift vp our eyes to Christ, who is the authour of the Sacraments, and the giuer of that which is represented by the Sacraments.

*Mat.3.11. mar.1.8. iohn.1.26. acts 1.5. and 8.4 and 11.16. and 19.4.

17 [3] Whose fanne *is* in his hand, and he will make cleane his floore, and will gather the wheate into his garner, but the chaffe will hee burne vp with fire that neuer shalbe quenched.

3 The Gospel is the fanne of the world.

18 Thus then exhorting with many other things, he preached vnto the people.

19 * [4] But when Herod the Tetrarch was rebuked of him, for Herodias his brother Philips wife, and for all the euils which Herod had done,

*Matth.14.3. marke 6.32.

4 Iohns preaching is confirmed with his death.

20 He added *yet* this aboue all, that he shut vp Iohn in prison.

21 * [5] Now it came to passe, as all the people were baptized, and that Iesus was baptized and did pray, that the heauen was opened:

*Matth.3.13. marke 1.9. iohn.1.32.

22 And the holy Ghost came downe in a bodily shape like a doue vpon him, and there was a voice from heauen, saying, Thou art my beloued sonne: in thee I am well pleased.

5 Our baptisme is sanctified in the head of the Church, and Christ also is pronounced, by the voice of the Father, to be our euerlasting king, Priest, and Prophet.

23 ¶ [6] And Iesus himselfe began to be about thirtie yeere of age, being as men supposed the sonne of Ioseph, *which was the sonne* of Eli,

6 The stocke of Christ according to the flesh, is brought by order euen to Adam, and so to God, that it might appeare, that he onely it was, whom God promised to Abraham and Dauid, & appointed from euerlasting to his Church, which is gathered together of all sorts of men.

24 *The sonne* of Matthat, *the sonne* of Leui, *the sonne* of Melchi, *the sonne* of Ianna, *the sonne* of Ioseph,

25 *The sonne* of Mattathias, *the sonne* of Amos, *the sonne* of Naum, *the sonne* of Esli, *the sonne* of Nagge,

26 *The sonne* of Maath, *the sonne* of Mattathias, *the sonne* of Simei, *the sonne* of Ioseph, *the sonne* of Iuda,

27 *The sonne* of Ioanna, *the sonne* of Rhesa, *the sonne* of Zorobabel, *the sonne* of Salathiel, *the sonne* of Neri,

28 *The sonne* of Melchi, *the sonne* of Abdi, *the sonne* of Cosam, *the sonne* of Elmodam, *the sonne* of Er,

29 ¶ *The sonne* of Iose, *the sonne* of Eliezer, *the sonne* of Iorim, *the sonne* of Matthat, *the sonne* of Leui,

30 *The sonne* of Simeon, *the sonne* of Iuda, *the sonne* of Ioseph, *the sonne* of Ionan, *the sonne* of Eliacim,

31 *The sonne* of Melea, *the sonne* of Mainan, *the sonne* of Mattatha, *the sonne* of Nathan, *the sonne* of Dauid,

32 *The sonne* of Iesse, *the sonne* of Obed, *the sonne* of Booz, *the sonne* of Salmon, *the sonne* of Naasson,

33 *The sonne* of Aminadab, *the sonne* of Aram, *the sonne* of Esrom, *the sonne* of Phares, *the sonne* of Iuda,

34 *The sonne* of Iacob, *the sonne* of Isaac, *the sonne* of Abraham, *the sonne* of Thara, *the sonne* of Nachor,

35 *The sonne* of Saruch, *the sonne* of Ragau, *the sonne* of Phalec, *the sonne* of Eber, *the sonne* of Sala,

36 *The sonne* of Cainan, *the sonne* of Arphaxad, *the sonne* of Sem, *the sonne* of Noe, *the sonne* of Lamech,

37 *The sonne* of Mathusala, *the sonne* of Enoch, *the sonne* of Iared, *the sonne* of Maleleel, *the sonne* of Cainan,

38 *The sonne* of Enos, *the sonne* of Seth, *the sonne* of Adam, *the sonne* of God.

CHAP. IIII.

1 Of Christes temptation, and fasting. 16 He teacheth in Nazareth to the great admiration of all. 24 A Prophet that teacheth in his owne countrey is contemned. 33 One possessed of the deuill is cured. 38 Peters mother in Law healed, 40 and diuers sicke persons are restored to health. 41 The deuils acknowledge Christ.

And [1] Iesus full of the holy Ghost returned from Iordan, and was ledde by that Spirit into the wildernesse,

1 Christ being caried away (as it were out of the world) into the desart, after the fast of forty dayes, and the ouercomming of Satan thrice, comming as it were suddenly from heauen, beginneth his office.

2 * And was *there* fourtie dayes tempted of the deuill, and in those dayes hee did eate nothing: but when they were ended, he afterward was hungrie.

*Matth.4.1. marke 1.12.

3 [2] Then the deuill sayd vnto him, If thou be the Sonne of God, command this stone that it be made bread.

2 Christ being stirred vp of Satan, first to distrust in God, secondly to the desire of riches and honour, and lastly to a vaine confidence of himselfe, ouercommeth him thrice by the word of God.

4 But Iesus answered him, saying, It is written, *That man shall not liue by bread only, but by euery word of God.

*Deut.8.3. matth.4.4.

5 Then the deuill tooke him vp into an high mountaine, and shewed him all the kingdomes of the world, in the twinkling of an eye.

6 And the deuill said vnto him, All this [a] power will I giue thee, and the glory of those *kingdomes*: for that is deliuered to me: and to whomsoeuer I will, I giue it.

7 If thou therefore wilt worship me, they shall be all [c] thine.

8 But Iesus answered him, and said, Hence from me, Satan: for it is written, *Thou shalt worship the Lord thy God, and him alone thou shalt serue.

9 Then hee brought him to Hierusalem,

a By this word power, are the kingdomes themselues meant, which haue the power: and so it is spoken by the figure Metonymie. b That is sure so, for he is prince of the world, yet not absolutely, and as the soueraigne of it, but by sufferance, and way of intreatie, and therefore hee sayeth not true, that hee can giue it to whome hee will. c Out of an high place, which had a goodly champion countrey underneath it, hee shewed him the situation of all countreys. *Deut.6.13. and 10.20.

and set him on a pinacle of the Temple, and
said vnto him, If thou be the Sonne of God,
cast thy selfe downe from hence,

* Psal.91.12.

10 For it is written, *That he will giue his
Angels charge ouer thee to keepe thee:
11 And with *their* hands they shall lift thee
vp, lest at any time thou shouldest dash thy
foote against a stone.
12 And Iesus answered, and said vnto him,
It is said, *Thou shalt not tempt the Lord thy
God.

* Deut.6.16.

13 And when the deuill had ended all the
tentation, hee departed from him for a little
season.
14 ¶ And Iesus returned by the power of
the spirit into Galile: and there went a fame of
him throughout all the region round about.
15 For he taught in their Synagogues, and
was honoured of all men.
16 *3 And he came to Nazareth where he
had been brought vp, and (as his custome was)
went into the Synagogue on the Sabbath day,
and stood vp to reade.

* Matth.13.52. marke 6.1. iohn 4.43.
3 Who Christ is, and wherefore he came, he sheweth out of the Prophet Esai.

17 And there was deliuered vnto him the
booke of the Prophet Esaias: and when he had
[d] opened the booke, he found the place, where
it was written,

d Their bookes in those dayes were rolled vp as scrolles vpon a ruler: and so Christ vnrolled, or vnfolded it, which is here called opened.

18 *The Spirit of the Lord *is* vpon me, because hee hath annointed mee, that I should
preach the Gospel to the poore: hee hath sent
me, that I should heale the broken hearted, that
I should preach deliuerance to the captiues,
and recouering of sight to the blinde, that I
should set at libertie them that are bruised:

* Esai 61.1.
4 Familiaritie causeth Christ to be contemned, and therefore he oftentimes goeth to strangers.

19 And that I should preach the acceptable yeere of the Lord.
20 And he closed the booke, and gaue it a-
gaine to the minister, and sate downe: and the
eyes of all that were in the Synagogue were
fastened on him.
21 Then hee began to say vnto them, This
day is this Scripture fulfilled in your eares.
22 4 And all [e] bare him witnesse, and [f] wondered at the [g] gracious words, which proceeded out of his mouth, and said, Is not this Iosephs sonne?

e Approued those things, which hee spake, with common consent and voice: for this word, witnesse, signifieth in this place, and many other, to allow and approoue a thing with open confession.

f Not onely the doctours, but also the common people were present at this conference of the Scriptures: and besides that, their mother tongue was vsed, for else how could the people haue wondred? Paul appointed the same order in the Church at Corinth, 1.Cor.14.

g Words full of the mighty power of God, which appeared in all his doings, as well, and allured men maruellously vnto him, Psal.45.2. grace is powred into thy lips.

23 Then he said vnto them, Yee will surely
say vnto me this prouerbe, Physician, heale thy
selfe: whatsoeuer we haue heard done in Capernaum, doe it heere likewise in thine owne
countrey.
24 And he said, Verely I say vnto you, *No
Prophet is accepted in his owne countrey.

* Iohn 4.44.

25 But I tel you of a trueth, many widowes
were in Israel in the dayes of * Elias, when
heauen was shut three yeres and sixe moneths,
when great famine was throughout all the
[h] land:

* 1.King.17.9. iames 5.17.
h Lord of Israel, Look matt.15.38.

26 But vnto none of them was Elias sent,
saue into Sarepta, *a citie of* Sidon, vnto a certaine widow.
27 Also many lepers were in Israel, in the
time of *Elizeus the Prophet: yet none of them
was made cleane, sauing Naaman the Syrian.

* 2.King.5.14.

28 5 Then all *that were* in the Synagogue,
when they heard it, were filled with wrath,

5 The more sharpely the world is rebuked, the more it rageth openly: but the life of the godly is not simply subiect to the pleasure of the wicked.

29 And rose vp, and thrust him out of the
citie, and ledde him vnto the edge of the hill,
whereon their citie was built, to cast him down
headlong.
30 But hee passed through the middes of
them, and went his way,
31 ¶ * And came downe into Capernaum
a citie of Galile, and there taught them on the
Sabbath dayes.

* Matt.4.13. marke 1.21.

32 * And they were astonied at his doctrine: for his word was with authoritie.

* Matt.7.29. marke 1.22.

33 * And in the Synagogue there was a
man which had a spirit of an vncleane deuill,
which cryed with a loud voice,

* Marke 1.23.

34 6 Saying, Oh, what haue we to doe with
thee, thou Iesus of Nazareth? art thou come
to destroy vs? I know who thou art, *euen* the
holy One of God.

6 Christ astonisheth not onely men, but they neuer so blockish, but euen the deuils also whether they will or not.

35 And Iesus rebuked him, saying, Holde
thy peace, and come out of him. Then the deuill throwing him in the middes *of them*, came
out of him, and hurt him nothing at all.
36 So feare came on them all, & they spake
among themselues, saying, What thing is this?
for with authoritie and power he commandeth
the foule spirits, and they come out.
37 And the fame of him spread abroad thorowout all the places of the countrey round a-
bout.
38 ¶ *7 And hee rose vp, and came out of
the Synagogue, and entred into Simons house.
And Simons wiues mother was taken with a
great feuer, and they required him for her.

* Matth.8.14. marke 1.30.
7 In that, that Christ healeth the diseases of the body with his word only, he prooueth that hee is God Almightie, sent for mans saluation.

39 Then hee stood ouer her, and rebuked
the feuer, and it left her, and immediatly shee
arose, and ministred vnto them.
40 Now at the sunne setting, all they that
had sicke *folks* of diuers diseases, brought them
vnto him, and hee laid his hands on euery one
of them, and healed them.
41 *8 And deuils also came out of many,
crying, and saying, Thou art that Christ that
Sonne of God: but he rebuked them, and suffered them not to say, that they knew him to
be that Christ.

* Marke 1.35.
8 Satan, who is a continual enemie to the truth, ought not to be heard, no not then, when hee speaketh the trueth.

42 9 And when it was day, hee departed,
and went foorth into a desert place, and the
people sought him, and came to him, and kept
him that he should not depart from them.

9 No colour of zeale ought to hinder vs in the race of our vocation.

43 But hee said vnto them, Surely I must
also preach the kingdome of God to other cities: for therefore am I sent.
44 And he preached in the Synagogues of
Galile.

CHAP. V.

1 Christ teacheth out of the shippe. 6 Of the draught of fish. 12 The Leper. 16 Christ prayeth in the desart. 18 One sicke of the palsie. 27 Leui the Publicane. 34 The fastings and afflictions of the Apostles after Christs ascension. 36. 37. 38 Faint hearted and weake disciples are likened to olde bottels and worne garments.

Then

1 Chriſt aduertiſeth the foure diſciples, which he had taken vnto him, of the office of the Apoſtleſhip, which ſhould hereafter be committed vnto them.
* Matt.4.18. marke 1.10.
a Did as it were lie vpon him, ſo deſirous they were both to ſee him, and heare him, and therefore he taught them out of a ſhip.

THen [1] *it came to paſſe, as the people [a] preaſſed vpon him to heare the word of God, that he ſtood by the lake of Gennesaret,

2 And ſaw two ſhippes ſtand by the lakes ſide, but the fiſhermen were gone out of them, and were waſhing their nets.

3 And he entred into one of the ſhippes, which was Simons, and required him that hee would thruſt off a little from the land: and hee ſate downe, and taught the people out of the ſhippe.

4 ¶ Now when he had left ſpeaking, hee ſaid vnto Simon, Lanch out into the deepe, and let downe your nets to make a draught.

b The word ſignifieth him that hath rule ouer any thing.

5 Then Simon anſwered, and ſayd vnto him, [b] Maſter, we haue trauailed ſore all night, and haue taken nothing: neuertheleſſe at thy word I will let downe the net.

6 And when they had ſo done, they encloſed a great multitude of fiſhes, ſo that their net brake.

7 And they beckened to their parents, which were in the other ſhip, that they ſhould come and helpe them, who came then, and filled both the ſhips, that they did ſinke.

8 Now when Simon Peter ſaw it, hee fell downe at Ieſus knees, ſaying, Lord, goe from me: for I am a ſinnefull man.

9 For he was vtterly aſtonied, and all that were with him, for the draught of fiſhes which they tooke.

* Matth.8.2. marke 1.40.
2 Chriſt by healing the leper with his onely touch, and ſending him to the Prieſt, witneſſeth that it is he, thorow whom and by whom, apprehended by faith, all wee which are vncleane, according to the law, by the witneſſe of God himſelfe, are pronounced to be pure and cleane.
* Leuit.14.4.
3 Chriſt had rather to be famous by his doctrine, then by miracles, & therefore he departeth from them that ſeeke him, as a Phyſician of the body, and not as the author of ſaluatiō.
4 Chriſt, in healing him that was ſicke of the palſie, ſheweth the cauſe of all diſeaſes, and the remedie.
c The mightie power of Chriſts Godhead, ſhewed it ſelfe in him at that time.
* Matth.9.2. marke 2.3.

10 And ſo was alſo Iames and Iohn the ſonnes of Zebedeus, which were companions with Simon. Then Ieſus ſaid vnto Simon, Feare not: from henceforth thou ſhalt catch men.

11 And when they had brought the ſhips to land, they forſooke all, and followed him.

12 ¶ *[2] Now it came to paſſe, as hee was in a certaine citie, behold, *there was* a man full of leproſie, and when he ſaw Ieſus, hee fell on his face, and beſought him, ſaying, Lord, if thou wilt, thou canſt make me cleane.

13 So he ſtretched forth his hand, and touched him, ſaying, I will, be thou cleane. And immediatly the leproſie departed from him.

14 And he commanded him that he ſhould tell it to no man: but goe, *ſayth he*, and ſhewe thy ſelfe to the Prieſt, and offer for thy cleanſing, as *Moſes hath commanded, for a witnes vnto them.

15 [3] But ſo much more went there a fame abroad of him, and great multitudes came together to heare, and to be healed of him of their infirmities.

16 But hee kept himſelfe apart in the wilderneſſe, and prayed.

17 ¶ [4] And it came to paſſe on a certaine day, as hee was teaching, that the Phariſes and doctours of the Law ſate by, which were come out of euery towne of Galile, and Iudea, and Hieruſalem, and the power of the Lord [c] was *in him* to heale them.

18 *Then behold, men brought a man lying in a bedde, which was taken with a palſie, and they ſought meanes to bring him in, and to lay him before him.

19 And when they could not finde by what way they might bring him in, becauſe of the preſſe, they went vp on the houſe, and let him downe through the tiling, bedde and all, in the mids before Ieſus.

20 And when hee ſawe their faith, he ſayd vnto him, Man, thy ſinnes are forgiuen thee.

21 Then the Scribes and the Phariſes began to reaſon, ſaying, Who is this that ſpeaketh blaſphemies? who can forgiue ſinnes, but God onely?

22 But when Ieſus perceiued their reaſoning, hee anſwered and ſaid vnto them, What reaſon ye in your hearts?

23 Whether is eaſier to ſay, Thy ſinnes are forgiuen thee, or to ſay, Riſe and walke?

24 But that yee may know that the Sonne of man hath authoritie to forgiue ſinnes in earth, (hee ſaid vnto the ſicke of the palſie) I ſay to thee, Ariſe: take vp thy bed and goe to thine houſe.

25 And immediatly he roſe vp before them, and tooke vp *his bed* whereon hee lay, and departed to his owne houſe, praiſing God.

26 And they were all amazed, and praiſed God, & were filled with feare, ſaying, Doubtleſſe we haue ſeene ſtrange things to day.

* Matth.9.9. marke 2.14.
5 The Church is a company of ſinners through the grace of Chriſt repentant, which banket with him, to the great offence of the proud and enuious worldlings.

27 ¶ *[5] And after that, he went foorth, and ſaw a Publicane named Leui, ſitting at the receit of cuſtome, and ſaid vnto him, Follow me.

28 And hee left all, roſe vp, and followed him.

29 Then Leui made him a great feaſt in his owne houſe, where there was a great company of Publicanes, and of other that ſate at table with them.

30 But they that were Scribes and Phariſes among them, murmured againſt his diſciples, ſaying, Why eate yee and drinke ye with Publicanes and ſinners?

31 Then Ieſus anſwered, and ſayde vnto them, They that are whole, neede not the Phyſician, but they that are ſicke.

32 *I came not to call the righteous, but ſinners to repentance. * 1.Tim.1.15.

* Matt.9.14. marke 2.18.
6 It is the point of hypocrites and ignorant men, to put an holineſſe in faſting, and in things indifferent.
7 Lawes generally made without any conſideratiō of circumſtances, for faſting and other things of like ſort, are not onely tyrannous, but very hurtfull in the Church.

33 ¶ *[6] Then they ſaid vnto him, Why doe the diſciples of Iohn faſt often, and pray, and the *diſciples* of the Phariſes alſo, but thine eate and drinke?

34 [7] And he ſaid vnto them, Can yee make the children of the wedding chamber to faſt, as long as the bridegrome is with them?

35 But the dayes will come, euen when the bridegrome ſhall bee taken away from them: then ſhall they faſt in thoſe dayes.

36 Againe he ſpake alſo vnto them a parable, No man putteth a piece of a newe garment into an olde veſture: for then the new renteth it, and the piece *taken* out of the newe, agreeth not with the olde.

37 Alſo

37 Also no man powreth new wine into old
vessels: for then the new wine will breake the
vessels, and it will run out, and the vessels will
perish:
38 But new wine must be powred into new
vessels: so both are preserued.
30 Also no man that drinketh olde wine,
straightway desireth new: for he saith, The old
is more profitable.

CHAP. VI.

1 The disciples pull the eares of corne on the Sabbath. 6 Of him that had a withered hand. 13 The election of the Apostles. 20 The blessings and curses. 27 Wee must loue our enemies. 46 With what fruit the word of God is to be heard.

AND *[1] it came to passe on a second solemne Sabbath, that he went thorow the
corne fields, and his disciples [a] plucked the
eares of corne, and did eate and rubbe them in
their hands.
2 And certaine of the Pharises saide vnto
them, Why doe ye that which is not lawfull to
doe on the Sabbath dayes?
3 Then Iesus answered them, and said,
*Haue ye not read this, that Dauid when hee
himselfe was an hungred, and they which were
with him,
4 How hee went into the house of God,
and tooke, and ate the shewbread, and gaue
also to them which were with him, which
was not lawfull to eate, but for the *Priestes
onely?
5 And he said vnto them, The Sonne of
man is Lord also of the Sabbath day.
6 ¶ *[2] It came to passe also on another
Sabbath, that he entred into the Synagogue,
and taught, and there was a man, whose right
hand was dried vp.
7 And the Scribes and Pharises watched
him, whether he would heale on the Sabbath
day, that they might finde an accusation *against*
him.
8 But he knew their thoughts, and sayd
to the man which had the withered hand, Arise
and stand vp in the mids. And hee arose, and
stood vp.
9 Then saide Iesus vnto them, I will aske
you a question. Whether is it lawfull on the
Sabbath dayes to doe good, or to doe euill? to
saue life, or to [b] destroy?
10 And he beheld them all in compasse, and
said vnto the man, Stretch foorth thine hand.
And he did so, and his hand was restored againe
as whole as the other.
11 Then they were filled full of madnesse,
and communed one with another, what they
might doe to Iesus.
12 ¶ [3] And it came to passe in those dayes,
that he went into a mountain to pray, and spent
the night in prayer to God.
13 And when it was day, * hee called his
disciples, and of them hee chose twelue which
also he called Apostles.
14 (Simon whom he named also Peter, and
Andrew his brother, Iames and Iohn, Philip
and Bartlemew:
15 Matthew and Thomas: Iames *the sonne*
of Alpheus, and Simon called Zelous:
16 Iudas Iames *brother*, and Iudas Iscariot,
which also was the traitour.)
17 Then hee came downe with them, and
stood in a plaine place with the companie of
his disciples, and a great multitude of people out of all Iudea, and Hierusalem, and from
the [c] sea coast of Tyrus and Sydon, which
came to heare him, and to be healed of their
diseases:
18 And they that were vexed with foule
spirits, and they were healed.
19 And the whole multitude sought to
touch him: for there went vertue out of him,
and healed them all.
20 ¶ *[4] And he lifted vp his eyes vpon his
disciples, and saide, Blessed *be* yee poore: for
yours is the kingdome of God.
21 *Blessed are ye that hunger now: for ye
shalbe satisfied: *blessed *are* ye that weepe now
for ye shall laugh.
22 * Blessed are ye when men hate you,
and when they [d] separate you, and reuile *you*,
and put out your name as euil, for the Sonne of
mans sake.
23 Reioyce yee in that day, and [e] be glad:
for behold, your reward *is* great in heauen: for
after this maner their fathers did to the Prophets.
24 *But woe *be* to you *that are* rich: for ye
haue [f] receiued your consolation.
25 Woe *be* to you that are full: for ye shal
hunger. Woe *be* to you that now laugh: for ye
shall waile and weepe.
26 Woe *be* to you when all men speake wel
of you: for so did their fathers to the false prophets.
27 ¶ *[5] But I say vnto you which heare,
Loue your enemies: doe well to them which
hate you.
28 Blesse them that curse you, and pray for
them which hurt you.
29 *And vnto him that smiteth thee on the
one cheeke, offer also the other: *and him that
taketh away thy cloke, forbid not *to take thy*
coat also.
30 Giue to euery man that asketh of thee:
and of him that taketh away the *things that be*
thine, aske them not againe.
31 *And as ye would that men should doe
to you, so doe ye to them likewise.
32 *For if ye loue them which loue you,
[g] what thanke shall ye haue? for euen the sinners loue those that loue them.
33 And if ye doe good for them which doe
good for you, what thanke shall ye haue? for
euen the sinners doe the same.

* Matth.12.1. marke 2.23.

1 Christ sheweth against the superstitious, who sticke in euery trifle, that the Lawe of the very Sabbath, was not giuen to be kept without exception: much lesse that the saluation of man should consist in the outward keeping of it.

a Epiphanius noteth well in his treatise, where he confuteth Ebion, that the time when the disciples plucked the eares of corne, was in the feast of vnleauened bread. Now, whereas in those feasts, which were kept many dayes together, as the feast of Tabernacles, and the Passouer, their first day, and the last were of like solemnitie, Leui.23. Luke fitly calleth the last day, the second Sabbath, though Theophylact vnderstandeth it of any other of them, that followed the first.

* 1.Sam.21.6.

* Exod.29 33. leuit 8.31. and 24.9.

* Matth.12.19. marke 3.1.

2 Charitie is the rule of all ceremonies.

b Who so helpeth not his neighbour when he can, he killeth him.

3 In that that Christ vseth earnest and long prayer, in chusing twelue of his owne companie, to the office of the Apostleshippe, hee sheweth howe religiously wee ought to behaue our selues in the choise of Ecclesiasticall persons.

* Chap.9.1. matth.10.1. mar.13.3. and 6.7.

c From all the sea coast, which is called Syrophenicia.

* Matth.5.3.

4 Christ teacheth against all Philosophers, and especially the Epicures, that the chiefest felicitie of man is laid vp in no place, here in earth, but in heauen, and that persecution for righteousnesse sake, is the right way vnto it.

* Esa.65.13.

* Esai.61.3.

* Matth.5.11.

d Cast you out of their Synagogues, as Iohn expoundeth it 16.2. which is the sharpest punishment the Church hath, if so be the Elders iudge rightfully, and by the word of God.

e Leape (as cattell doe, which are prouender pricked) for exceeding ioy.

* Amos 6.1.

f That is, you reape now of your riches, all the commoditie and blessing you are euer like to haue, and therefore you haue not to looke for any other reward, Matth.6.2.

* Esai.65.13.

* Matth.5.44.

5 Christian charitie, which differeth much from the worldly, doth not only not reuenge iniuries, but comprehendeth euen our most grieuous enemies, and that for our Fathers sake, which is in heauen: so farre is it, from seeking it owne profit in well doing.

* Matth.5.39.

* 1 Cor.6 7.

* Matth.7.12.

* Matth.5.46.

g What is there in this your worke, that is to be accounted of? for if you looke to haue commoditie by louing, seeke those commodities, which are commodities in deed: loue your enemies, and so shall you shew to the world that you looke for those commodities which come from God.

34 * And if yee lend *to them* of whome ye
hope to receiue,what thanke shall ye haue? for
euen the sinners lend to sinners, to receiue the
like.
35 Wherefore loue ye your enemies, and
doe good, and lend, [h] looking for nothing a-
gaine, and your reward shall be great, and yee
shalbe the children of * the most High: for he
is kind vnto the vnkind, and to the euill.
36 Be ye therefore mercifull, as your father
also is mercifull.
37 ¶ * [6] Iudge not, and ye shall not be iudged: condemne not, and ye shall not be condemned: forgiue,and ye shalbe forgiuen.
38 Giue, *and it shall be giuen vnto you:
* a good measure, [k] pressed downe, shaken together and running ouer shall men giue into
your bosome: for with what measure ye mete,
with the same shall men mete to you againe.
39 [7] And hee spake a parable vnto them,
* Can the blind lead the blinde? shall they not
both fall into the ditch?
40 * The disciple is not aboue his master:
but whosoeuer *will be* a perfect disciple, shalbe
as his master.
41 ¶ * [8] And why seest thou a mote in thy
brothers eye, and considerest not the beame
that is in thine owne eye?
42 Either how canst thou say to thy brother, Brother, let me pull out the mote that is
in thine eye, when thou seest not the beame
that is in thine owne eye? Hypocrite, cast out
the beame out of thine owne eye first,and then
shalt thou see perfectly to pull out the mote
that is in thy brothers eye.
43 ¶ * [9] For it is not a good tree that bringeth forth euill fruit: neither an euill tree, that
bringeth forth good fruit.
44 * For euery tree is knowen by his owne
fruit: * for neither of thornes gather men figs,
nor of bushes gather they grapes.
45 A good man out of the good treasure of
his heart bringeth forth good, and an euill man
out of the euill treasure of his heart bringeth
foorth euill: for of the abundance of the heart
his mouth speaketh.
46 ¶ * But why call ye me Lord,Lord,and
doe not the things that I speake?
47 [10] Whosoeuer commeth to me,and heareth my words,and doeth the same, I will shew
you to whom he is like:
48 He is like a man which built an house,
and digged deepe, and laid the foundation on
a rocke: and when the waters arose, the flood
beat vpon the house, and could not shake it:
for it was grounded vpon a rocke.
49 But he that heareth and doeth not,is like
a man that built an house vpon the earth without foundation, against which the flood did
beate, and it fell by and by: and the fall of that
house was great.

Matth.5.42. deut.15.8.

h When you will lend, doe it onely to benefit and pleasure withall, and not for hope, to receiue the principall againe.

Matth.5.45.

Matth.7.1.

6 Brotherly reprehensions must not proceed of curiositie nor churlishnes nor malice,but they must be iust,moderate and louing.

i He speaketh not here of ciuill iudgements,and therefore by the word,forgiue,is meant that good nature,which the Christians vse in suffring and pardoning wrongs.

Matth.7.2. marke 4.24.

k These are borowed kindes of speeches, taken from them which vse to measure dry things, as corne and such like,who vse a franke kinde of dealing therein, & thrust it downe and shake it together,and presse it and heape it.

7 Vnskilful reprehenders hurt both themselues and other: for such as the master is,such is the scholler.

Matth.5.15.

Matth.10.24. iohn 13.16.and 15.20.

Matth.7.3.

8 Hypocrites which are very seuere reprehenders of other, are very quicke of spight to spie other mens fauls, but very blinde to see their owne.

Matth.7.17.

9 He is a good man,not that is skilfull to reprehend other,but he that proueth his vprightnesse both in word and deed.

Matth.12.33.

Matth.7.16.

Matth 7.21. rom.2.13. iames 1.21.

10 Affliction doeth at the length discerne true godlines from false and fained.

CHAP. VII.

1 *Of the Centurions seruant.* 9 *The Centurions faith.* 11
The widowes sonne raised from death at Nain. 19 *Iohn*
sendeth his disciples to Christ. 33 *His peculiar kinde of li-*
uing. 37 *The sinfull woman washeth Iesus feet.*

WHen * [1] he had ended all his sayings in
the audience of the people,he entred
into Capernaum.
2 And a certaine Centurions seruant was
sicke and ready to die, which was deare vnto
him.
3 And when he heard of Iesus,he sent vnto him the Elders of the Iewes,beseeching him
that he would come, and heale his seruant.
4 So they came to Iesus,and besought him
instantly, saying that hee was worthy that hee
should doe this for him:
5 For he loueth,*said they*, our nation, and
he hath built vs a Synagogue.
6 Then Iesus went with them: but when
he was now not farre from the house, the Centurion sent friends to him, saying vnto him,
Lord, trouble not thy selfe: for I am not worthy that thou shouldest enter vnder my roofe:
7 Wherefore I thought not my selfe worthy to come vnto thee: but say the word, and
my seruant shalbe whole.
8 For I likewise am a man set vnder authoritie,and haue vnder me souldiers,and I say vnto one, Goe, and hee goeth: and to another,
Come,and he commeth:and to my seruant,Do
this, and he doeth it.
9 When Iesus heard these things, he marueiled at him, and turned him, and saide to
the people that followed him, I say vnto you,
I haue not found so great faith no not in Israel.
10 And when they that were sent, turned
backe to the house, they found the seruant that
was sicke, whole.
11 [2] And it came to passe the day after, that
he went into a citie called [a] Nain, and many of
his disciples went with him, and a great multitude.
12 Now when he came neere to the gate of
the citie, behold, there was a dead man caried
out, *who was* the onely begotten sonne of his
mother, which was a widowe, and much people of the citie was with her.
13 And when the Lord sawe her, hee had
compassion on her, and said vnto her, Weepe
not.
14 And hee went and touched the coffin
(and they that bare him,stood still) and he said,
Yong man,I say vnto thee, Arise.
15 And he that was dead, sate vp, and began to speake, and he deliuered him to his mother.
16 Then there came a feare on them all, and
they glorified God, saying, A great Prophet
is risen among vs,and God hath visited his people.
17 And this rumour of him went foorth
throughout all Iudea, and throughout all the
region round about.

Matth.8.5.

1 Christ admonisheth the Iewes,by setting before them the example of the Centurion,that for their obstinacie andrebellion,he will goe to the Gentiles.

2 Christ auoucheth openly his power ouer death.

a Nain is the name of a towne in Galilee,which was situate on the other side of Kison, which falleth into the sea of Galilee.

18 [3] And

3 Iohn ſendeth from the priſon his vnbeleeuing diſciples, to Chriſt himſelfe, to be confirmed.

18 [3]And the Diſciples of Iohn ſhewed him
of all theſe things.
19 So Iohn called vnto him two certaine
men of his diſciples, and ſent them to Ieſus,
ſaying, Art thou he that ſhould come, or ſhall
we waite for another?
20 And when the men were come vnto
him, they ſaid, Iohn Baptiſt hath ſent vs vnto
thee, ſaying, Art thou he that ſhould come, or
ſhall we waite for another?

b When Iohns Diſciples came to Chriſt.

21 And [b] at that time he cured many of their
ſickneſſes, and plagues, and of euill ſpirits, and
vnto many blind men he gaue ſight freely.
22 And Ieſus anſwered, and ſaid vnto them,
Goe your wayes, and ſhew Iohn what things
yee haue ſeene and heard: that the blind ſee,
the halt goe, the lepers are cleanſed, the deafe
heare, the dead are raiſed, *and* the poore receiue
the Goſpel.
23 And bleſſed is he, that ſhal not be offended in me.

4 That which the Prophets ſhewed long before, Iohn ſheweth at hand: and Chriſt himſelfe doeth preſent it daily vnto vs in the Goſpel, but for the moſt part in vaine, for that many ſeeke nothing elſe, but fooliſh toyes and vaine glorie.

24 [4]And when the meſſengers of Iohn were
departed, he began to ſpeake vnto the people,
of Iohn, What went ye out into the wilderneſſe
to ſee? A reede ſhaken with the wind?
25 But what went yee out to ſee? A man
clothed in ſoft raiment? behold, they which are
gorgeouſly apparelled, and liue delicately, are
in Kings courts.
26 But what went yee forth to ſee? A Prophet? yea, I ſay to you, and greater then a
Prophet.

* *Mala. 3.1.*

27 This is hee of whom it is written, * Behold, I ſend my meſſenger before thy face,
which ſhall prepare thy way before thee.
28 For I ſay vnto you, there is no greater Prophet then Iohn, among them that are
begotten of women: neuertheleſſe, hee that is
the leaſt in the kingdome of God, is greater
then he.

c Said that hee was iuſt, good, faithfull, and mercifull.

29 Then all the people that heard, and the
Publicanes [c] iuſtified God, being baptized with
the baptiſme of Iohn.

d To their owne hurt.

30 But the Phariſes and the expounders of
the Law deſpiſed the counſell of God [d] againſt
themſelues, and *were* not baptized of him.

* *Matth. 11.16.*

5 What way ſoeuer God followeth in offering vs the Goſpel, the moſt part of men procure offences vnto themſelues: yet notwithſtanding ſome Church is gathered together.

31 * [5]And the Lord ſaid, Whereunto ſhall
I liken the men of this generation? and what
thing are they like vnto?
32 They are like vnto little children ſitting
in the market place, and crying one to another,
and ſaying, We haue piped vnto you, and yee
haue not daunced: wee haue mourned to you,
and yee haue not wept.
33 For Iohn Baptiſt came, neither eating
bread, nor drinking wine: and yee ſay, He hath
the deuill.
34 The Sonne of man is come, and eateth
and drinketh: and yee ſay, Behold, a man *which*
is a glutton, and a drinker of wine, a friend of
Publicanes and ſinners:
35 But wiſedome is iuſtified of all her children.

6 Proud men depriue themſelues of the benefits of the preſence of Chriſt, euen when he is at home with them in their houſes, which the humble and baſe doe enioy.

36 ¶ [6] And one of the Phariſes deſired
him that hee would eate with him: and hee
went into the Phariſes houſe, and ſate downe
at table.
37 And behold, a woman in the citie, which
was a ſinner, when ſhee knew that Ieſus ſate at
table in the Phariſes houſe, ſhe brought a boxe
of oyntment.

* *Marke 15.42. Iohn 20.11.*

38 * And ſhee ſtood at his feete behind him
weeping, and beganne to waſh his feete with
teares, and did wipe them with the haires of her
head, and kiſſed his feete, and anoynted them
with the oyntment.

7 Raſhneſſe is the fellow of pride.

e The Phariſe reſpecteth the Law, which holdeth them defiled that touch the defiled.

39 [7] Now when the Phariſe which bade
him, ſaw it, hee ſpake within himſelfe, ſaying,
If this man were a Prophet, hee would ſurely
haue knowen who, and what maner of woman this is which toucheth him: [e] for ſhee is a
ſinner.

8 To loue Chriſt, is a ſure and perpetuall witneſſe of remiſſion of ſinnes

f That is, ſaith Theophylact, ſhee hath ſhewed her faith abundantly: and Baſil in his Sermon of Baptiſme ſaith, Hee that oweth much, hath much forgiuen him, that he may loue much more: And therefore Chriſts ſaying is ſo plaine by the ſimilitude, that it is a wonder to ſee the enemies of the trueth, draw and racke this place ſo fondly, to eſtabliſh their meritorious workes: for the greater ſumme a man hath forgiuen him, the more he loueth him that hath beene ſo gratious to him: And this woman ſheweth by dueties of loue, how great the benefit was ſhe had receiued: and therfore the charitie that is here ſpoken of, is not to be taken for the cauſe, but as a ſigne: for Chriſt ſaith not as the Phariſes did, that ſhee was a ſinner, but beareth her witneſſe that the ſinnes of her life paſt are forgiuen her.

40 [8]And Ieſus anſwered, and ſaid vnto him,
Simon, I haue ſomewhat to ſay vnto thee. And
he ſaid, Maſter, ſay on.
41 There was a certaine lender which had
two debters: the one ought fiue hundreth
pence, and the other fiftie:
42 When they had nothing to pay, he forgaue them both: Which of them therefore, tell
me, will loue him moſt?
43 Simon anſwered, and ſaid, I ſuppoſe that
he, to whom he forgaue moſt. And he ſaid vnto him, Thou haſt truely iudged.
44 Then he turned to the woman, and ſaid
vnto Simon, Seeſt thou this woman? I entred
into thine houſe, and thou gaueſt me no water
to my feete: but ſhee hath waſhed my feete
with teares, and wiped them with the haires of
her head.
45 Thou gaueſt me no kiſſe: but ſhee, ſince
the time I came in, hath not ceaſed to kiſſe my
feete.
46 Mine head with oyle thou diddeſt not
anoynt: but ſhee hath anoynted my feete with
oyntment.
47 Wherefore I ſay vnto thee, Many ſinnes
are forgiuen her: [f] for ſhee loued much. To
whom a little is forgiuen, he doeth loue a little.
48 And he ſaid vnto her, Thy ſinnes are forgiuen thee.
49 And they that ſate at table with him, began to ſay within themſelues, Who is this that
euen forgiueth ſinnes?

g He confirmeth the benefit which he had beſtowed, with a bleſſing.

50 And hee ſaid to the woman, Thy faith
hath ſaued thee: [g] goe in peace.

CHAP. VIII.

2 Women that miniſter vnto Chriſt of their ſubſtance. 4 The parable of the ſower. 16 The candle. 19 Chriſts mother and brethren. 22 He rebuketh the winds. 26 Of Legion. 37 The Gadarens reiect Chriſt. 41 Iairus daughter healed. 43 The woman deliuered from the iſſue of blood. 52 Weeping for the dead.

AND it came to paſſe afterward, that hee
himſelfe went through euery citie and
towne, preaching and publiſhing the kingdome of God, and the twelue *were* with him,

2 And certaine women, which were hea-
led of euill spirits, and infirmities, *as* * Marie
which was called Magdalene, out of whome
went seuen deuils.
3 And Ioanna the wife of Chuza Herods
steward, and Susanna, and many other which
ministred vnto him of their substance.
4 * [1] Now when much people were gathered together, and were come vnto him out of
all cities, he spake by a parable.
5 A sower went out to sow his seede, and
as he sowed, some fell by the wayes side, and it
was troden vnder feete, and the foules of heauen deuoured it vp.
6 And some fell on the stones, and when it
was sprung vp, it withered away, because it lacked moystnesse.
7 And some fell among thornes, and the
thornes sprang vp with it, and choked it.
8 And some fell on good ground, and
sprang vp, and bare fruit, an hundreth fold. And
as he said these things, he cried, Hee that hath
eares to heare, let him heare.
9 Then his disciples asked him, demaun-
ding what parable that was.
10 And hee said, Vnto you it is giuen to
know the [a] secrets of the kingdome of God, but
to other in parables, that when * they see, they
should not see, & when they heare, they should
not vnderstand.
11 * The parable is this, The seede is the
word of God.
12 And they that are beside the way, are
they that heare: afterward commeth the deuil,
and taketh away the word out of their hearts,
lest they should beleeue, and be saued.
13 But they that are on the stones, *are they*
which when they haue heard, receiue the word
with ioy: but they haue no rootes: which for
a while beleeue, but in the time of tentation
goe away.
14 And that which fell among thornes,
are they which haue heard, and after [b] their
departure are choked with cares and with riches, and voluptuous liuing, and [c] bring foorth
no fruit.
15 But that *which fell* in good ground, are
they which with an [d] honest and good heart
heare the word, [e] and keepe it, and bring forth
fruit with patience.
16 ¶ * [2] No man when hee hath lighted a
candle, couereth it vnder a vessell, neither putteth it vnder the bed, but setteth it on a candlesticke, that they that enter in, may see the
light.
17 * For nothing is secret, that shall not bee
euident: neither any thing hid, that shall not be
knowen, and come to light.
13 [3] Take [f] heede therefore how yee heare:
for * whosoeuer hath, to him shall bee giuen:
and whosoeuer hath not, from him shall bee
taken euen that [g] which it seemeth that hee
hath.

* *Marke* 16.9.
* *Matth.* 13.3. *marke* 4.1.
1 The selfe same Gospel is sowen euery where, but not with like fruit: and that through the onely fault of men themselues.
a Those things are called secret, which may not be vttered: for the word vsed here, is as much as we say in our tongue, to hold a mans peace
* *Esai.* 6.9. *matth.* 13.14. *marke* 4.12. *iohn* 12.40. *actes* 28.26. *rom.* 11.8.
* *Matth.* 13.18. *marke* 4.15.
b That is, so soone as they haue heard the word, they goe about their businesse.
c They bring not foorth perfect and full fruit to the ripening: or, they begin, but they bring not to an end
d Which seeketh not onely to seeme such one, but is so in deede: so that this word, Honest, respecteth the outward life, and the word Good, is referred to the good gifts of the minde.
e With much adoe, for the deuill and the flesh fight against the spirit of God, which is a new ghuest.
* *Chap.* 11.33. *matth.* 5.15. *marke* 4.21.
2 That that euery man hath receiued in priuate, he ought to bestow to the vse and profite of all men.
* *Matth.* 10.26. *marke* 4.22. *chap* 12.2.
3 Heauenly gifts are lost with niggardlinesse: and increase with liberalitie.
f That is, with what minds you come to heare the word, and how you behaue your selues, when you haue heard it.
* *Matth* 13.12. *and* 15.19. *marke* 4.25. *chap.* 20.26.
g Either to himselfe, or to other, or to both: for there are none so proud as these fellowes, if it were possible to see that, that they cloke: neither are there that deceiue the simple more then they do.

19 ¶ * [4] Then came to him his mother and
his brethren, and could not come neere to him
for the preasse.
20 And it was told him *by certaine* which
said, Thy mother and thy brethren stand without, and would see thee.
21 But hee answered, and said vnto them,
My mother and my brethren are these which
heare the word of God, and doe it.
22 ¶ * [5] And it came to passe on a certaine
day, that hee went into a ship with his disciples, and he said vnto them, Let vs goe ouer vnto the other side of the lake. And they lanched
foorth.
23 And as they sayled, he fell [h] asleepe, and
there came downe a storme of wind on the lake,
and [i] they were filled with water, and were in
ieopardie.
24 And they went to him, and awoke him,
saying, Master, Master, we perish. And he arose,
and rebuked the wind, and the waues of water:
and they ceased, and it was calme.
25 And hee said vnto them, Where is your
faith? and they feared, and wondred among
themselues, saying, Who is this that commandeth both the windes and water, and they o-
bey him!
26 ¶ * So they sailed vnto the region of the
Gadarenes, which is ouer against Galile.
27 [6] And as he went out to land, there met
him a certaine man out of the citie, which had
deuils long time, and he ware no garment, neither abode in house, but in the graues.
28 And when he saw Iesus, hee cried out,
and fell downe before him, and with a lowde
voice said, What haue I to doe with thee, Iesus
the Sonne of God the most high? I beseech
thee torment me not.
29 For hee commaunded the foule spirit
to come out of the man: (for oft times hee had
caught him: therefore hee was bound with
chaines, and kept in fetters: but hee brake the
bands, [k] and was caried of the deuill into wildernesses.)
30 And Iesus asked him, saying, What is
thy name? and hee said, Legion, because many
deuils were entred into him.
31 And they besought him, that he would
not command them to goe out into the deepe.
32 And there was there by, an heard of many swine, feeding on an hill: and the *deuils* besought him, that he would suffer them to enter
into them. So he suffered them.
33 Then went the deuils out of the man,
and entred into the swine: and the heard was
caried with violence from a steepe downe place
into the lake, and was choked.
34 When the heardmen saw what was done,
they fled: and when they departed, they told it
in the citie and in the countrey.
35 Then they came out to see what was
done, and came to Iesus, and found the man
out of whom the deuils were departed, sitting
at

* *Matth.* 12.46. *marke* 3.32.
4 There is no knot of flesh and blood among men so nigh and straight, as the band which is between Christ, and them who imbrace him with a true faith.
* *Matth.* 8.23. *marke* 4.36.
5 It is expedient for vs sometime to come into extreme danger, as though Christ passed not for vs, that we may haue a better triall, both of his power, and also of our weaknes.
h Iesus fell on sleepe, and it appeareth that hee was very fast on sleepe, because they called him twise before he awoke.
i Not the disciples, but the ship.
* *Matth.* 8.18. *marke* 5.1.
6 Christ sheweth by casting out a Legion of deuils by his word onely, that his heauenly vertue was appointed to deliuer men from the slauerie of the deuill: but foolish men will not for the most part, redeeme this so excellent grace freely offered vnto them, with the least losse of their pelting pelfe.
k By force and violence, as a horse when he is spurred.

at the feete of Iesus, clothed, and in his right
minde: and they were afraid.
36 They also which sawe it, tolde them by
what meanes hee that was possessed with the
deuill was healed.
37 Then the whole multitude of the countrey about the Gadarens, besought him that he
would depart from them: for they were taken
with a great feare, and he went into the ship,
and returned.
38 Then the man, out of whom the deuils were departed, besought him that hee
might bee with him: but Iesus sent him away,
saying,
39 Returne into thine owne house, and
shewe what great things God hath done to
thee. So hee went his way, and preached
[l] throughout all the citie, what great things
Iesus had done vnto him.
40 ¶ And it came to passe, when Iesus
was come againe, that the people [m] receiued
him: for they all waited for him.
41 ¶ *7 And beholde, there came a man
named Iairus, and hee was the ruler of the
Synagogue, who fell downe at Iesus feete,
and besought him that he would come into his
house.
42 For he had but a daughter onely, about
twelue yeeres of age, and shee lay a dying (and
as he went, the people thronged him.
43 And a woman hauing an issue of blood
twelue yeeres long, which had spent all her
[n] substance vpon physicians, and could not bee
healed by any:
44 When she came behinde *him*, she touched the hemme of his garment, and immediately her issue of blood stanched.
45 Then Iesus said, Who is it that hath touched me? When euery man denied, Peter said
and they that were with him, Master, the multitude thrust thee, and tread on thee, and sayest
thou, Who hath touched me?
46 And Iesus sayd, So mee one hath touched mee: for I perceiue that vertue is gone
out of mee.
47 When the woman saw that she was not
hidde, she came trembling, and fell downe before him, and tolde him before all the people,
for what cause shee had touched him, and how
she was healed immediately.
48 And hee sayd vnto her, Daughter, be of
good comfort: thy faith hath saued thee: goe
in peace.)
49 While hee yet spake, there came one
from the ruler of the Synagogues house, which
sayd to him, Thy daughter is dead: disease not
the master.
50 When Iesus heard it, hee answered
him, saying, Feare not: beleeue onely, and shee
shall be saued.
51 And when hee went into the house, hee
suffered no man to goe in with him, saue Peter, and Iames, and Iohn, and the father and
mother of the mayde.
52 And all wept, and [o] sorowed for her: but
hee sayd, Weepe not: for she is not dead, but
sleepeth.
53 And they laught him to scorne, knowing that she was dead.
54 So hee thrust them all out, and tooke
her by the hand, and cried, saying, Maide, arise.
55 And her spirit came againe, and shee
[p] rose straightway: and he commanded to giue
her meate.
56 Then her parents were astonied: but he
commanded them that they should tell no man
what was done.

l To wit, the citie of the Gadarens: & though Marke say that he preached it in Decapolis, they dissent not, for Plinie recordeth lib. 5. cap. 18 that Gadara is a towne of Decapolis: so that Decapolis was partly on this side Iordan, and partly on the other side.
m The multitude was glad he was come againe, and reioyced greatly.
**Matth. 9. 18. marke 5. 22.*
7 Christ sheweth by a double miracle, that he is Lord both of life and death.
n All that she had to liue vpon.
o The word signifieth to beate and strike, and is transferred to the mournings and lamentations, that are at burials, at which times men vse such kinde of behauiour.
p The corps was layd out, and the wench receiued life, and rose out of the bed, that all the world might see, she was not onely restored to life, but also voide of all sicknesse.

CHAP. IX.

1 The Apostles are sent to preach. 7. and 19 The common peoples opinion of Christ. 12 Of the fiue loaues and two fishes. 20 The Apostles confession. 24 To lose the life. 35 Wee must heare Christ. 37 The possessed of a spirit. 46 Strife among the Apostles for the Primacie. 49 One casting out deuils in Christes Name. 52 The Samaritanes will not receiue Christ. 55 Reuenge forbidden. 57 59 61 Of three that would follow Christ, but on diuers conditions.

THen *1 called he his twelue disciples together, and gaue them power and authoritie ouer all deuils, and to heale diseases.
2 * And he sent them forth to preach the
kingdome of God, and to cure the sicke.
3 And he sayd to them, *Take nothing
to your iourney, neither staues, nor scrippe, neither bread, nor siluer, neither haue two coates
apiece.
4 And whatsoeuer house yee enter into,
there [a] abide, and thence depart.
5 And how many soeuer will not receiue
you, when ye goe out of that citie, * shake off
the very dust from your feete for a testimony
against them.
6 And they went out, and went through
euery town preaching the Gospel, and healing
euery where.
7 ¶ *2 Now Herod the Tetrarch heard of
all that was done by him: and he [b] doubted, because that it was sayd of some, that Iohn was
risen againe from the dead:
8 And of some, that Elias had appeared:
and of some, that one of the old Prophets was
risen againe.
9 Then Herod sayd, Iohn haue I beheaded: who then is this of whome I heare such
things? and he desired to see him.
10 ¶ *3 And when the Apostles returned
they tolde him what great things they had
done. *Then he tooke them to him, and went
aside into a [c] solitary place, *neere* to the citie
called Bethsaida.
11 But when the people knew it, they followed him: and he receiued them, and spake
vnto them of the kingdome of God, and healed
them that had neede to be healed.

**Matth 10. 1. marke 3. 13. and 6. 7.*
1 The twelue Apostles are sent forth at the onely commandement of Christ, and furnished with the power of ye holy Ghost: both that none of the Israelites might pretend ignorance, and also that they might be better prepared to their generall ambassie.
**Matth. 10. 7.*
**Matth. 10. 9. marke 6. 8.*
a When you depart out of any citie, depart from thence, where you first tooke vp your lodging: so that in few words, the Lord forbiddeth them to change their lodgings: for this publishing of the Gospel, was as it were a thorow passage, that none of Iudea might pretend ignorance, as though he had not heard that Christ was come.
**Chap. 10. 11. matth. 10. 14. marke 6. 11. actes 13. 51.*
**Matth. 14. 1. marke 6. 14.*
2 So soone as the world heareth tidings of the Gospel, it is diuided into diuers opinions, and the tyrants especially are afraide.
b He stucke as it were fast in the myre. **Marke 6 30.* 3 They shall lacke nothing that follow Christ, no not in the wildernesse. **Matth 14. 13. marke 6. 32.* *c The worde signifieth a desert: note this was not in the towne Bethsaida, but part of the fields belonging to the towne.*

*Matth.14.15. marke 6.35. iohn 6.5.

d This is vnperfectly spoken, and therefore we must vnderstand some thing, as thus, we cannot giue them to eate, vnlesse we goe and buy, &c.

12 *And when the day began to weare away, the twelue came, and said vnto him, Send the people away, that they may goe into the townes and villages round about, and lodge, and get meate: for we are here in a desart place.

13 But hee said vnto them, Giue yee them to eate. And they said, Wee haue no more but fiue loaues and two fishes,[d] except wee should goe and buy meate for all this people.

14 For they were about fiue thousand men. Then he said to his disciples, Cause them to sit downe by fifties in a companie.

15 And they did so, and caused all to sit downe.

e He gaue God thankes for these loaues and fishes, and withall prayed him to feede this so great a multitude with so small a quantitie, and to be short, that this whole banket might be to the glorie of God.

16 Then hee tooke the fiue loaues, and the two fishes, and looked vp to heauen, and [e] blessed them, and brake, and gaue to the disciples, to set before the people.

17 So they did all eate, and were satisfied: and there was taken vp of that remained to them, twelue baskets full of broken meate.

*Matth 16.13. marke 8.27.

4 Although the world be tossed vp and downe, betwixt diuers errours, yet we ought not to contemne the trueth, but be so much the more desirous to know it, and be more constant to confesse it.

f Alone from the people.

18 ¶ *4 And it came to passe, as hee was [f] alone praying, his disciples were with him: and he asked them, saying, Whom say the people that I am?

19 They answered, and said, Iohn Baptist: and others said, Elias: and some say, that one of the old Prophets is risen againe.

20 And hee said vnto them, But whom say yee that I am? Peter answered, and said, That Christ of God.

5 Christ himselfe attained to the heauenly glory, by the crosse and inuincible patience.

*Matth 17.22. marke 8.31.

21 And he warned and commanded them, that they should tell that to no man,

22 [5] Saying, *The sonne of man must suffer many things, and bee reprooued of the Elders, and of the hie Priests and Scribes, and be slaine, and the third day rise againe.

*Chap.14.27. matth.10.38.and 15.24 mar.8.34

g Euen as one day followeth an other, so doeth one crosse follow another, and the crosse is by the figure Metonymie, taken for the miseries of this life: for to be hanged, was the sorest and cruellest punishment, that was amongst the Iewes.

23 ¶ *And he said to them all, If any man will come after me, let him denie himselfe, and take vp his crosse [g] daily, and follow me.

*Chap.17.33. matth.10 39 and 16.25.ioh 12.25

24 *For whosoeuer will saue his life, shall lose it: and whosoeuer shall lose his life for my sake, the same shall saue it.

*Matth.16.26. marke 8.36.

25 *For what auantageth it a man, if hee winne the whole world, and destroy himselfe, or lose himselfe?

*Chap.12.9. matth.10.33. marke 8.38. 2.tim.2.12.

26 *For whosoeuer shall bee ashamed of me, and of my words, of him shall the Sonne of man be ashamed, when hee shall come in his glory, and *in the glory* of the Father, and of the holy Angels.

*Matth.16.28. marke 9.1.

27 *And I tel you of a suretie, there be some standing here, which shall not taste of death, till they haue seene the kingdome of God.

*Matth.17.2. marke 9.2.

6 Lest the disciples of Christ should be offended at the debasing himselfe in his flesh, he teacheth them that it is voluntarie, shewing therewithall for a space, the brightnesse of his glory

28 *6 And it came to passe about an eight dayes after those words, that hee tooke Peter and Iohn, and Iames, and went vp into a mountaine to pray.

29 And as hee prayed, the fashion of his countenance was changed, and his garment *was* white and glistered.

30 And behold, two men talked with him, which were Moses and Elias;

31 Which appeared in glory, and told of his [h] departing, which he should accomplish at Hierusalem.

h What death he should die in Hierusalem.

32 But Peter and they that were with him, were heauie with sleepe, and when they awoke, they saw his glory, and the two men standing with him.

33 And it came to passe, as they departed from him, Peter said vnto Iesus, Master, it is good for vs to bee here: let vs therefore make three tabernacles, one for thee, and one for Moses, and one for Elias, and wist not what he said.

34 Whiles hee thus spake, there came a cloud and ouershadowed them, and they feared when they were entring into a cloud.

35 *And there came a voice out of the cloud, saying, This is that my beloued Sonne, heare him.

*2.Pet.1.17.

36 And when the voice was past, Iesus was found alone: and they kept it close, and told no man in [i] those dayes any of those things which they had seene.

i Vntill Christ was risen againe from the dead.

37 ¶ 7 And it came to passe on the next day, as they came downe from the mountaine, much people met him.

7 Christ is offended with nothing so much, as with incredulitie, although he beare with it for a time.

38 *And behold, a man of the companie cried out, saying, Master, I beseech thee, behold my sonne: for he is all that I haue.

*Matth.17.14. marke 9.17.

39 And loe, a spirit taketh him, and suddenly he crieth, and he teareth him, and he fometh, and hardly departeth from him, when hee hath [k] bruised him.

k As it fareth in the falling sicknesse.

40 Now I haue besought thy disciples to cast him out, but they could not.

41 Then Iesus answered, and said, O generation faithlesse, and crooked, how long now shall I bee with you, and suffer you? bring thy sonne hither.

42 And whiles hee was yet comming, the deuill rent him, and tare him: and Iesus rebuked the vncleane spirit, and healed the child, and deliuered him to his father.

43 ¶ 8 And they were all amased at the mighty power of God: and while they all wondred at all things, which Iesus did, he said vnto his disciples,

8 We haue no cause to promise our selues rest and quietnesse in this world, seeing that they themselues which seemed to fawne vpon Christ, doe shortly after crucifie him.

44 [l] Marke these words diligently: *for it shall come to passe, that the Sonne of man shall be deliuered into the hands of men.

l Giue diligent eare vnto them, and when you haue once heard them, see that you keepe them.

45 But they vnderstood not that word: for it was hid from them, *so* that they could not perceiue it: and they feared to aske of him that word.

*Matth.17.22. marke 9.31.

46 ¶ *9 Then there arose a disputation among them, which of them should bee the greatest.

*Matth.18.1. marke 9.35.

9 The ende of ambition is ignominie: but the ende of modest obedience is glorie.

47 When Iesus saw the thoughts of their hearts, he tooke a little child, and set by him,

48 And said vnto them, Whosoeuer receiueth this little child in my Name, receiueth me: and whosoeuer shall receiue me, receiueth him that sent me: for he that is least among you all, he shall be great.

49 ¶ *10 And

49 ¶ * [10] And Iohn anfwered and fayd,
Mafter, wee fawe one cafting out deuils in thy
Name, and we forbade him, becaufe he followeth *thee* not with vs.
50 Then Iefus faid vnto him, Forbid ye *him*
not: for he that is not againft vs, is with vs.
51 ¶ [11] And it came to paffe, when the
dayes were accomplifhed, that he fhould be receiued vp, hee [m] fetled himfelfe fully to goe to
Hierufalem,
52 And fent meffengers before him: and
they went and entred into a towne of the Samaritans, to prepare him *lodging*.
53 But they would not receiue him, becaufe his behauiour was as though hee would
goe to Hierufalem.
54 [12] And when his difciples, Iames and
Iohn fawe it, they faid, Lord, wilt thou that we
command, that fire come downe from heauen,
and confume them, euen as * Elias did?
55 But Iefus turned about, and rebuked
them, and fayd, Yee knowe not of what [n] fpirit
yee are.
56 For the Sonne of man is not come to
deftroy mens liues, but to faue them. Then
they went to another towne.
57 ¶ [13] And it came to paffe, that as they
went in the way, * a certaine man fayd vnto
him, I will follow thee, Lord, whitherfoeuer
thou goeft.
58 And Iefus fayd vnto him, The foxes
haue holes, and the birds of the heauen neftes,
but the Sonne of man hath not whereon to lay
his head.
59 [14] But he faid vnto another, Follow mee.
And the fame fayd, Lord, fuffer me firft to goe
and burie my father.
60 And Iefus fayd vnto him, Let the dead
burie [o] their dead: but goe thou, and preach
the kingdome of God.
61 [15] Then another fayde, I will followe
thee, Lord: but let me firft goe bid them farewell, which are at mine houfe.
62 And Iefus fayd vnto him, No man that
putteth his hand to the plough, and looketh
backe, is apt to the kingdome of God.

*Marke 9.38.
10 Extraordinary things, are neither rafhly to be allowed, nor condemned.
11 Chrift goeth willingly to death.
m *Word for word he hardened his face: that is, hee refolued with himfelfe to die, and therefore ventured vpon his iourney, and caft away all feare of death, and went on.*
12 Wee muft take heed of the immoderatenes of zeale & fond imitation, euen in good caufes, that whatfoeuer we doe, we do it to Gods glory, and the profit of our neighbour.
* 2.King.1.10, 12, 13.
n *So fpeake the Hebrewes, that is, you knowe not what will, minde, and counfell you are of: fo the gifts of Gods are called the fpirit, becaufe they are giuen of Gods Spirit, and fo are they that are contrary to them, which proceede of the wicked fpirit, as the fpirit of couetoufneffe, of pride, and madneffe.*
13 Such as followe Chrift, muft prepare themfelues to fuffer all difcommodities.
*Matth.8.19.
14 The calling of God ought to be preferred, without all controuerfie, before all dueties that we owe to men.
o *Who notwithftanding that they liue in this fraile life of man, yet are ftrangers from the true life, which is euerlafting and heauenly.*
15 Such as follow Chrift, muft at once renounce all worldly cares.

CHAP. X.

1 *The feuentie difciples.* 10 *The vnthankefull cities charged with impietie.* 17 *The difciples returning home, are warned to bee humble.* 30 *Who is our neighbour.* 38 *Of Martha and her fifter Marie.*

AFter * [1] thefe things, the Lord appointed other feuentie alfo, and fent them
two and two before him, into euery citie and
place, whither hee himfelfe fhould come.
2 And he fayd vnto them, * The haruest *is*
great, but the labourers *are* fewe: pray therefore the Lord of the haruest to fend foorth labourers into his haruest.
3 [2] Goe your wayes: behold, I fend you
fоorth as lambes among wolues.
4 Beare no bag, neither fcrip, nor fhooes,
and * falute [a] no man by the way.
5 * And into whatfoeuer houfe ye enter,
firft fay, Peace *be* to this houfe.
6 And if the fonne of peace be there, your
peace fhall reft vpon him, if not, it fhall turne to
you againe.
7 And in that houfe [c] tarie ftill, eating and
drinking fuch things as by them *fhall hee fet*
before you: * for the labourer is worthie of his
wages. Goe not from houfe to houfe.
8 * But into whatfoeuer citie yee fhall enter, if they receiue you, [d] eate fuch things as
are fet before you,
9 And heale the ficke that are there, and
fay vnto them, The kingdome of God is come
neere vnto you.
10 [3] But into whatfoeuer citie ye fhall enter, if they will not receiue you, goe your waies
out into the ftreetes of the fame, and fay,
11 Euen the very * duft which cleaueth on
vs of your citie, we wipe off againft you: notwithftanding knowe this, that the kingdome of
God was come neere vnto you.
12 For I fay to you, that it fhall bee eafier
in that day for them of Sodome, then for that
citie.
13 * Woe *be* to thee, Chorazin: woe *be* to
thee, Beth-faida: for if the miracles had beene
done in Tyrus and Sidon, which haue beene
done in you, they had a great while agone repented, fitting in fackecloth and afhes.
14 Therefore it fhal be eafier for Tyrus, and
Sidon, at the iudgement, then for you.
15 And thou, Capernaum, which art exalted to heauen, fhalt be thruft downe to hell.
16 ¶ * He that heareth you, heareth mee:
and he that defpifeth you, defpifeth me: and he
that defpifeth me, defpifeth him that fent me.
17 ¶ [4] And the feuentie turned againe with
ioy, faying, Lord, euen the deuils are fubdued
to vs [e] through thy Name.
18 And hee fayd vnto them, I fawe Satan,
like lightning, [f] fall downe from heauen.
19 Beholde, I giue vnto you power to
tread on Serpents, and Scorpions, and ouer
all the power of the enemie, and nothing fhall
[g] hurt you.
20 Neuertheleffe, in this reioyce not, that
the fpirits are fubdued vnto you: but rather
reioyce, becaufe your names are written in
heauen.
21 ¶ [5] That fame houre reioyced Iefus in
the fpirit, and fayd, I confeffe vnto thee, Father, Lord of heauen and earth, that thou haft
hidde thefe things from the [h] wife and vnder-
ftanding, and hath reuealed them to babes:

*Marke 10.1.
1 The feuentie are fent as the fecond forewarners of the comming of Chrift.
*Matth 9.37.
*Matth.10.16.
2 The faithfull minifters of the worde are in this world, as lambes among wolues: but if they bee diligent to doe their duetie, he that fent them will alfo preferue them.

*2 King.4.29.
a *This is fpoken after the manner of a figure, which men vfe when they put downe more in wordes then is meant: vfuall among the Hebrewes, when they command a thing to bee done fpeedilie without delay, as 2.King.4.29. for otherwife courteous and gentle falutations, are poynts of Chriftian dueties: as for the calling, it was but for a feafon.*
*Matth.10.12. marke 6.10.
b *So fpeake the Hebrewes: that is, hee that fauoureth the doctrine of peace and imbraceth it.*
c *Take vp your lodging in that houfe, which ye firft enter into, that is, be not carefull for commodious lodging, as men doe which purpofe to tarie long in a place: for here is not inftituted that folemne preaching of the Gofpel, which was vfed afterward, when the Churches were fetled: but thefe are fent abroad to all the coafts of Iudea, to giue them to vnderftand, that the laft Iubile is at hand.*
*Deut 24.14. matth.10.10. 1.tim.5.18.
*Matth.10.11.
d *Content your felues with that meate that is fet before you.*
3 God is a moft feuere reuenger of the mifterie of his Gofpel.
*Chap. 9.5. actes 13.51. and 18.6.
* Matth.11.21.
* Matth.10.40. iohn 13.20.
4 Neither the gift of miracles, neither what elfe foeuer excellent gift, but onely our election giueth vs occafion of true ioy. And the only publifhing of the Gofpel is the deftruction of Satan.
e *For Chriftes difciples vfed no abfolute authoritie, but wrought fuch miracles, as they did by calling vpon Chriftes Name.*
f *Paul placeth the deuill and his angels, in the ayre, as Ephef.6.12. and hee is fayd to bee caft downe from thence by force, when his power is abolifhed by the voyce of the Gofpel.*
g *Shall doe you wrong.*
5 The Church is contemptible, if wee behold the outward face of it, but the wifedome of God is not fo marueilous in any thing, as in it.
h *Of this world.*

euen so, Father, because it so pleased thee. ||
22 [6] All things are giuen mee of my Father: and no man knoweth who the Sonne is,
but the Father: neither who the Father is,
saue the Sonne, and he to whom the Sonne wil
reueale him.
23 ¶ [7] And he turned to his disciples, and
sayd secretly, *Blessed *are* the eyes, which
see that yee see.
24 For I tell you that many Prophets and
Kings haue desired to see those things, which
yee see, and haue not seene *them*: and to heare
those things which yee heare, and haue not
heard *them*.
25 ¶ * [8] Then beholde, [i] a certaine Law-
yer stoode vp, and tempted him, saying, Master, What shall I doe to inherite eternall life?
26 And he sayd vnto him, What is written
in the Lawe? how readest thou?
27 And hee answered, and sayde, * Thou
shalt loue thy Lord God with all thine heart,
and with all thy soule, & with all thy strength,
and with all thy thought, * and thy neighbour
as thy selfe.
28 Then hee sayd vnto him, Thou hast answered right: this doe, and thou shalt liue.
29 [9] But hee willing [k] to iustifie himselfe,
sayde vnto Iesus, Who is then my neighbour?
30 And Iesus answered, and sayd, A certaine man went downe from Hierusalem to Iericho, and fell among theeues, and they robbed him of his raiment, and wounded him, and
departed, leauing him halfe dead.
31 Now so it fell out, that there came down
a certaine Priest that same way, and when hee
sawe him, he passed by on the other side.
32 And likewise also a Leuite, when hee
was come neere to the place, went and looked
on him, and passed by on the other side.
33 Then a certaine Samaritane, as he iourneyed, came neere vnto him, and when he sawe
him, he had compassion on him,
34 And went to him, and bound vp his
wounds, and powred in oyle and wine, and put
him on his owne beast, and brought him to an
Inne, and made prouision for him.
35 And on the morrow when he departed,
hee tooke out two pence, and gaue them to the
hoste, and sayd vnto him, Take care of him, and
whatsoeuer thou spendest more, when I come
againe, I will recompence thee.
36 Which nowe of these three, thinkest
thou, was neighbour vnto him that fell among
the theeues?
37 And he sayd, He that shewed mercie on
him. Then said Iesus vnto him, Goe, and doe
thou likewise.
38 ¶ [10] Now it came to passe, as they went,
that he entred into a certaine towne, and a certaine woman named Martha, receiued him into her house.
39 And she had a sister called Marie, which

|| Then he turned to his disciples, and sayd, *Is read in some copies.*

6 Whosoeuer seeketh the Father without the Sonne, wandreth out of the way.

7 The differēce of the old Testament and newe consisteth in the measure of reuelation.

**Matth.*13.16.

**Matth.*22.35. *marke* 12.28.

8 Faith doeth not take away, but establish the doctrine of the Lawe.

i One of them, that professed himselfe to bee learned in the rites and Lawes of Moses.

**Deut.*6.5.

**Leuit.*19.18.

9 All they are comprehended in the name of our neighbour by the Lawe, whomsoeuer we may helpe.

k That is, to vouch his righteousnes, or shewe that he was iust, that is voide of all faults: and Iames 5. vseth the word of iustification in this sense.

10 Christ careth not to be entertained delicately, but to bee heard diligently, that is it, which he especially requireth.

also sate at Iesus feete, and heard his preaching.
40 But Martha was cumbred about much
seruing, and came to him, and sayd, Master,
doest thou not care that my sister hath left
mee to serue alone? bid her therefore that shee
helpe mee.
41 And Iesus answered, and sayd vnto her,
Martha, Martha, thou carest, and art troubled a-
bout many things:
42 But one thing is needefull, Marie hath
chosen the good part, which shall not be taken
away from her.

CHAP. XI.

1 He teacheth his Apostles to pray. 14 The dumbe deuill driuen out. 27 A woman of the companie lifteth vp her voyce. 29 The Iewes require signes. 37 Hee being feasted of the Pharise, reproueth the outward shew of holinesse.

AND so it was, that as hee was praying in
a certaine place, when he ceased, one of
his disciples sayd vnto him, Lorde, teach vs to
pray, as Iohn also taught his disciples.
2 * And he said vnto them, When ye pray,
say, [1] Our Father which art in heauen, halowed
be thy Name: Thy kingdome come: Let thy
will be done, euen in earth, as *it is* in heauen:
3 Our dayly bread giue vs [a] for the day:
4 And forgiue vs our sinnes: for euen wee
forgiue euery man that is indebted to vs: And
leade vs not into temptation: but deliuer vs
from euill.
5 ¶ [2] Moreouer he said vnto them, Which
of you shall haue a friend, and shall goe to him
at midnight, and say vnto him, Friend, lend me
three loaues?
6 For a friend of mine is come out of the
way to mee, and I haue nothing to set before
him:
7 And he within should answere, and say,
Trouble mee not: the doore is now shut, and
my children are with me in bed: I cannot rise
and giue them to thee.
8 I say vnto you, Though he would not
rise and giue him, because he is his friend, yet
doubtlesse because of his [b] importunitie, hee
would rise and giue him as many as he needed.
9 * And I say vnto you, Aske, and it shall
be giuen you: seeke, and ye shall find: knocke,
and it shall be opened vnto you.
10 * For euery one that asketh, receiueth:
and he that seeketh, findeth: and to him that
knocketh, it shall be opened.
11 * If a sonne shall aske bread of any of
you that is a father, will hee giue him a stone?
or if *he aske* a fish, will hee for a fish giue him
a serpent?
12 Or if he aske an egge, will he giue him
a scorpion?
13 If ye then which are euill, can giue good
gifts vnto your children, how much more shall
your heauenly Father giue the holy Ghost to
them, that desire him?
14 ¶ * Then he cast out a deuill which was
dumbe:

**Matth.*6.9.

1 A forme of true prayer.

a That is, as much as is needefull for vs this day, whereby we are not debarred to haue an honest care for the maintenance of our liues, but that carping care, which killeth a number of men, is cut off and restrained.

2 We must pray with faith.

b Word for word, impudencie: but that impudencie which is spoken of here, is not to bee found fault withal, but is very commendable before God, for he liketh well of such importunitie.

**Matth.*7.7. *and* 21.22. *mar.* 11.24. *iohn* 14.13. *and* 16.23. *iames* 1.5.

**Matth.*7.8.

**Matth.*7.9.

**Matth.*9.32. *and* 12.22.

dumbe: and when the deuill was gone out, the
dumbe ſpake, and the people wondered.
15 [3] But ſome of them ſayd, * He caſteth
out deuils through Beelzebub the chiefe of the
deuils.
16 And others tempted him, ſeeking of him
a ſigne from heauen.
17 [4] But he knew their thoughts, and ſayd
vnto them, * Euery kingdome diuided againſt
it ſelfe, ſhall be deſolate, and an houſe *diuided*
againſt an houſe, falleth.
18 So if Satan alſo bee diuided againſt
himſelfe, how ſhall his kingdome ſtand, becauſe yee ſay that I caſt out deuils [c] through
Beelzebub?
19 If I through Beelzebub caſt out deuils,
by whome doe your children caſt them out?
Therefore ſhall they be your Iudges.
20 But if I by the [d] finger of God caſt out
deuils, doubtleſſe the kingdome of God is
come vnto you.
21 When a ſtrong man armed keepeth his
[e] palace, the things that hee poſſeſſeth, are in
peace.
22 But when a ſtronger then he, commeth
vpon him, and ouercommeth him: hee taketh
from him all his armour wherin he truſted, and
diuideth his ſpoiles.
23 [5] He that is not with me, is againſt me:
and he that gathereth not with me, ſcattereth.
24 * [6] When the vncleane ſpirit is gone
out of a man he walketh through drie places,
ſeeking reſt: and when hee findeth none, hee
ſaith, I will returne vnto mine houſe whence
I came out.
25 And when hee commeth, he findeth it
ſwept and garniſhed.
26 Then goeth hee, and taketh to him ſeuen other ſpirits worſe then himſelfe: and they
enter in, and dwell there: * ſo the laſt ſtate of
that man is worſe then the firſt.
27 ¶ [7] And it came to paſſe as he ſaid theſe
things, a certaine woman of the company lifted vp her voice, and ſayd vnto him, Bleſſed *is*
the wombe that bare thee, and the paps which
thou haſt ſucked.
28 But he ſayd, Yea, rather bleſſed *are* they
that heare the word of God, and keepe it.
29 ¶ * [8] And when the people were gathered thicke together, he began to ſay, This is a
wicked generation: They ſeeke a ſigne, and
there ſhal no ſigne be giuen them, but the ſigne
of * Ionas the Prophet.
30 For as Ionas was a ſigne to the Nineuites: ſo ſhall alſo the Sonne of man be to this
generation.
31 * The Queene of the South ſhall riſe
in iudgement, with the men of this generation, and ſhall condemne them: for ſhee came
from the vtmoſt parts of the earth to heare the
wiſedome of Solomon, and beholde, a greater
then Solomon *is* here.
32 The men of Nineue ſhall riſe in iudge-

3 An example of horrible blindnes, and ſuch as cannot be healed, when as vpon an euill conſcience, and pretended malice, the power of God is blaſphemed.
* *Matth 9.34. and 12.24. marke 3.22.*
4 The true way to know the true Chriſt from the falſe, is this, that the true Chriſt hath no accord or agreement with Satan: And it remaineth that after wee knowe him, we acknowledge him.
* *Matth. 12.25. mar. 3.24.*
c *By the name and power of Beelzebub.*
d *That is, by the power of God: ſo it is ſayd, Exod. 8.19.*
e *The word ſignifieth properly an open and voide roome before an houſe, and ſo by tranſlation is taken for Noble mens houſes.*
5 Againſt indifferent men, and ſuch as loue to haue a meane, which ſeeke means to reconcile Chriſt and Satan together.
* *Matth. 12.43.*
6 He that doeth not continue, is in worſe caſe, then he that neuer begun.
* *Hebr 6.4. 2 pet. 2.20.*
7 Chriſt ſeeketh not praiſe in him ſelfe, but in our ſaluation.
* *Mat. 12.38,39.*
8 They that are fond deſirers of miracles, in ſtead of miracles ſhall receiue puniſhment.
* *Ionas 1.12.*
* *1. King. 10.1. 2. chron. 9.1.*

ment with this generation, and ſhal condemne
it: for they * repented at the preaching of Ionas: and behold, a greater then Ionas *is* here.
33 ¶ * [9] No man when hee hath lighted a
candle, putteth it in a priuie place, neither vnder a buſhell: but on a candleſticke, that they
which come in, may ſee the light.
34 * The light of the bodie is the eye:
therefore when thine eye is ſingle, then is thy
whole body light: but if thine eye be euil, then
thy bodie is darke.
35 Take heede therefore, that the light
which is in thee, be not darkeneſſe.
36 If therefore thy whole bodie *ſhall bee*
light, hauing no part darke, then ſhall all bee
light, euen as when a candle doeth light thee
with the brightneſſe.
37 ¶ [10] And as hee ſpake, a certaine Phariſe
beſought him to dine with him: and hee went
in, and ſate downe at table.
38 And when the Phariſe ſaw it, he marueiled that he had not firſt waſhed before dinner.
39 * And the Lord ſayd to him, In deed ye
Phariſes make cleane the outſide of the cup,
and of the platter: but the inward part is full
of rauening and wickedneſſe.
40 Ye fooles, did not hee that made that
which is without, make that which is within
alſo?
41 Therefore, giue almes [f] of thoſe things
which you haue, and behold, all things ſhall be
cleane to you.
42 [11] But woe *be* to you, Phariſes: for yee
[g] tithe the mint and the rue, and [h] all manner
herbes, and paſſe ouer [i] iudgement, and the loue
of God: theſe ought yee to haue done, and
not to haue left the other vndone.
43 * [12] Woe *bee* to you, Phariſes: for yee
loue the vppermoſt ſeats in the Synagogues,
and greetings in the markets.
44 [13] Woe *be* to you, Scribes and Phariſes
hypocrites: for yee are as graues which appeare not, and the men that walke ouer them,
perceiue not.
45 ¶ [14] Then anſwered one of the Lawyers, and ſaid vnto him, Maſter, thus ſaying
thou putteſt vs to rebuke alſo.
46 And he ſayd, Woe *be* to you alſo, yee
Lawyers: * for ye lade men with burdens grieuous to be borne, and ye your ſelues touch not
the burdens with one of your fingers.
47 [15] Woe *be* to you: * for ye build the ſepulchres of the Prophets, and your fathers killed them.
48 Truely [k] yee beare witneſſe, and allow
the deeds of your fathers: for they killed them,
and ye build their ſepulchres.

* *Ionas 3.5.*
* *Chap. 8.16. matth. 5.15. marke 4.21.*
9 Our mindes are therefore lightned with the knowledge of God, that we ſhould giue light vnto others, and therefore our chiefeſt labour ought to be to pray for that light.
* *Matth. 6.22.*
10 The ſeruice of God cōſiſteth not in outward cleanlineſſe, and deuiſed rites or ceremonies, but in the ſpirituall righteouſneſſe of the heart and charitie.
* *Matth. 23.25.*
f *That is, according to your abilitie: as who would ſay, in ſtead of your extortion, which hindered you, that you could not eate cleanly, vſe charitie, and accordingly as your abilitie ſhall ſerue you, bee good to the poore, and ſo ſhall that, that is within the platter, be ſanctified though the platter be vnwaſhed.*
11 It is the propertie of hypocrites, to ſtand ſtoutly for little trifles, and let paſſe greater matters.
g *You decide by Gods Law that the tenth part is due to be payd.*
h *Of all kinde of herbes ſome, as Auguſtine expoundeth it in his enchiridion to Laurence, cap. 99. where he ſheweth in like ſort how that place of Paul, 1. Tim. 2.4. God will haue all men to be ſaued, is to be expounded after the ſame maner.*
i *That is to ſay, that that is right and reaſon to do for this worde Iudgement, conteineth the commandements of the ſecond table, and the other words, the loue of God, containe the firſt.*
* *Chap. 20.46. matt. 23.6. mar. 12.38,39.*

12 Hypocriſie and ambition are commonly ioyned together. 13 Hypocrites deceiue men with an outward ſhew. * *Mat. 23.27.* 14 Hypocrites are very ſeuere againſt other men, but thinke all things lawfull to themſelues. * *Mat. 23.4 acts 15.10.* 15 Hypocrites honour thoſe ſaints when they are dead, whom they moſt cruelly perſecute, when they are aliue. * *Matt 23.29.* k *When you perſecute Gods ſeruants, like mad men, euen as your fathers did, though you colour it with a pretence of godlines, yet notwithſtanding, in that you beautifie the ſepulchres of the Prophets, what do you elſe but glory in your fathers crueltie, and ſet vp monuments (as it were) in glory & triumph of its*

49 There-

49 Therefore sayd the wisedome of God, I
will send them Prophets and Apostles, and of
them they shall slay and [l] persecute away,
50 That the blood of all the Prophets,
[m] shed from the foundation of the world, may
be required of this generation,
51 From the blood of * Abel vnto the blood
of * Zacharias, which was slaine betweene the
altar and the Temple: verely I say vnto you, it
shall be required of this generation.
52 [16] Woe *be* to you Lawyers: for ye haue
[n] taken away the key of knowledge: yee entred not in your selues, and them that came in,
ye forbade.
53 [17] And as hee sayd these things vnto
them, the Scribes and Pharises began to vrge
him sore, and to [o] prouoke him to speake of
many things,
54 Laying waite for him, and seeking to
catch some thing of his mouth, whereby they
might accuse him.

l They shall so vexe them and trouble them, that at length they shal banish them.
m That you may be called to an account for it, yea, and be punished, for the sheding of that blood of the Prophets.
**Gene.4.8.*
**2.Chro.24.21.*
16 They haue of long time chiefly hindered the people from entring into the knowledge of God, which ought to be the doore keepers of the Church.
n You haue hidden and taken away, so that it cannot bee found any where.
17 The more the world is reprehended, the worse it is, and yet must wee not betray the trueth. *o They proposed many questions to him, to draw some thing out of his mouth, which they might traiterously carpe at.*

CHAP. XII.

1 The leauen of the Pharises. 5 Who is to be feared. 8 To confesse Christ. 17 The parable of the rich man whose land was very fertile. 22 Not to care for earthly things, 31 but to seeke the kingdome of God. 39 The thiefe in the night. 51 Debate for the Gospels sake.

IN * [1] the meane time, there gathered together [a] an innumerable multitude of people,
so that they trode one another: and hee began
to say vnto his disciples first, Take heede to
your selues of the leauen of the Pharises, which
is hypocrisie.
2 *For there is nothing couered, that shall
not be reuealed: neither hid, that shall not bee
knowen.
3 Wherefore whatsoeuer ye haue spoken
in darkenesse, it shall be heard in the light: and
that which ye haue spoken in the eare, in secret
places, shall be preached on the houses.
4 * [2] And I say vnto you, my friendes, bee
not afraid of them that kill the body, and after
that are not able to doe any more.
5 But I will [b] forewarne you, whome yee
shall feare: feare him which after hee hath killed, hath power to cast into hell: yea, I say vnto you, him feare.
6 Are not fiue sparrowes bought for two
farthings, *and* yet not one of them is forgotten
before God?
7 *Yea, and all the haires of your head are
numbred: feare not therefore: yee are more of
value then many sparrowes.
8 * [3] Also I say vnto you, Whosoeuer shall
confesse me before men, him shall the Sonne of
man confesse also before the Angels of God,

**Matth.16.5. marke 8.14.*
1 The faithfull teachers of Gods word, which are appointed by him for his people, must both take good heed of them, which corrupt the puritie of doctrine with goodly gloses, and also take paines through the help of God, to set forth sincere doctrine, openly & without feare.
a Word for word, ten thousand of people, a certaine number for an vncertaine.
**Mat.10.26. marke 4.22.*
**Mat.10.28.*
2 Although hypocrites haue princes to execute their crueltie, yet there is no cause why we should be afraid of them, the least iote that may be, seeing they can do nothing, but what pleaseth God, and God will not any thing that may be against the saluation of his elect. *b He warneth them of dangers that presently hang ouer their heads, for those that come vpon the sudden, doe make the greater wound.* * *1.Sam.14.45. actes 27.35.* * *Chap.9.26. matth.10.32. marke 8.38. 2.tim.1.12.* 3 Great is the reward of a constant confession: and horrible is the punishment of the denying of Christ, yea impossible to be called backe againe shall the punishment bee, if vpon set purpose, both with mouth and heart we blaspheme a knowen trueth.

9 But hee that shall denie me before men,
shall be denied before the Angels of God.
10 * And whosoeuer shall speake a word a-
gainst the Sonne of man, it shall bee forgiuen
him: but vnto him, that shal blaspheme the holy Ghost, it shall not be forgiuen.
11 * [4] And when they shall bring you vnto
the Synagogues, and vnto the rulers and Princes, take no thought how, or what thing yee
shall answere, or what ye shall speake.
12 For the holy Ghost shall teach you in
the same houre what ye ought to say.
13 [5] And one of the companie saide vnto
him, Master, bid my brother diuide the inheritance with me.
14 And he sayd vnto him, Man, who made
me a iudge, or a diuider ouer you.
15 Wherefore hee sayd vnto them, Take
heed, and beware of [c] couetousnes: for though
a man haue abundance, *yet* his life [d] standeth not
in his riches.
16 [6] And he put forth a parable vnto them,
saying, The [e] ground of a certaine rich man
brought foorth fruits plenteously.
17 Therefore hee [f] thought with himselfe,
saying, What shall I doe, because I haue no
roome, where I may lay vp my fruits?
18 And he sayd, This will I doe, I will pull
downe my barnes, and build greater, & therein
will I gather all my fruits, and my goods.
19 And I will say to my soule, Soule, thou
hast much goods layd vp for many yeres: liue
at ease, eate, drinke, and [g] take thy pastime.
20 But God sayd vnto him, O foole, this
night will they fetch away thy soule from
thee: then whose shall those things bee which
thou hast prouided?
21 So *is* hee that gathereth riches [h] to himselfe, and is not rich in God.
22 [7] And he spake vnto his disciples, Therefore I say vnto you, * Take no thought for your
life, what yee shall eate: neither for your bodie, what ye shall put on.
23 The life is more then meate: and the
bodie *more* then rayment.
24 Consider the rauens: for they neither
sowe nor reape: which neither haue storehouse
nor barne, and *yet* God feedeth them: how
much more are ye better then foules?
25 And which of you with taking thought
can adde to his stature one cubite?
26 If yee then bee not able to doe the
least thing, why take ye thought for the remnant?
27 Consider the lilies how they grow: they
labour not, neither spin they: yet I say vnto
you, that Salomon himselfe in all his royaltie
was not clothed like one of these.
28 If then God so clothe the grasse which

**Matth.12.31. marke 3.28. 1.iohn 5.15.*
**Matth.10.19. marke 13.11.*
4 It is a great and hard conflict to confesse the trueth, yet hee that can doe all things, and is almighty, will not be wanting to the weakest which striue and contend in his appointed time.
5 Christ would not for three causes be a iudge to diuide an inheritance. First, for that hee would not foster vp and cherish the fleshly opinion that the Iewes had of Messias: Secondly, for that he would distinguish the ciuill gouernance, from the Ecclesiastical: Thirdly, to teach vs to beware of them which abuse the shew of the Gospel, and also the name of ministers, to their owne priuate commodities.
c By couetousnesse is meant, that greedie desire to get, commonly with other mens hurt.
d God is the authour and preseruer of mans life, goods are not.
6 There are none more mad, then rich men, which hang vpon their riches.
e Or rather countrey, for here is set forth a man that possesseth not a piece of ground onely, but an whole countrey, as they doe, which ioyne house to house, and fielde to fielde, Esai. 5.8.
f Made his reckoning with himselfe, which is the propertie of couetous churles which spend their life in those trifles.
g Bee merrie and make good cheare. *h Caring for no man but for himselfe, and minding to trust in himselfe.*
7 An earnest thinking vpon the prouidence of God, is a present remedie against most foolish, and pining carefulnesse of men, for this life. * *Matth.6.25. 1.pet.5.7. psal.55.22.*

is to day in the field, and to morow is cast into
the ouen, how much more *will he clothe* you,
O ye of little faith?
29 Therefore aske not what yee shall eate,
or what ye shall drinke, neither [i] hang you in
suspense.
30 For all such things the people of the
world seeke for: and your father knoweth that
ye haue neede of these things.
31 [8] But rather seeke yee after the kingdome of God, and all these things shall be cast
vpon you.
32 [9] Feare not, little flocke: for it is your
Fathers pleasure, to giue you the kingdome.
33 ¶ *[10] Sell that ye haue, and giue [k] almes:
make you bagges, which waxe not olde, a
treasure that can neuer faile in heauen, where
no thiefe commeth, neither moth corrupteth.
34 For where your treasure is, there will
your hearts be also.
35 ¶ *[11] Let your loines be girt about, and
your lights burning,
36 And yee your selues like vnto men that
waite for their master, when hee will returne
from the wedding, that when hee commeth
and knocketh, they may open vnto him immediatly.
37 Blessed *are* those seruants, whome the
Lord when hee commeth shall finde waking:
verely I say vnto you, hee will gird himselfe a-
bout, and make them to sit downe at table, and
will come foorth and serue them.
38 And if he come in the second watch, or
come in the third watch, and shall finde them
so, blessed are those seruants.
39 * Now vnderstand this, that if the good
man of the house had knowen at what houre
the thiefe would haue come, hee would haue
watched, and would not haue suffred his house
to be digged through.
40 [12] Be ye also prepared therefore: for the
Sonne of man will come at an houre when yee
thinke not.
41 Then Peter said vnto him, Master, tel-
lest thou this parable vnto vs, or euen to all?
42 And the Lord said, Who is a faithfull
steward and wise, whom the master shall make
ruler ouer his houshold, to giue them their
[l] portion of meat in season?
43 Blessed *is* that seruant, whom his master
when he commeth, shall finde so doing.
44 Of a trueth I say vnto you, that he will
make him ruler ouer all that he hath.
45 But if that seruant say in his heart, My
master doeth deferre his comming, and shall
begin to smite the seruants, and maidens, and
to eate, and drinke, and to be drunken,
46 The master of that seruant will come
in a day when he thinketh not, and at an houre
when hee is not ware of, and will cut him
off, and giue him his portion with the vnbeleeuers.
47 ¶ And that seruant that knew his ma-

i A metaphore taken of things that hang in the aire, for they that are carefull for this wordly life, and hang vpon the arme of man, haue alwayes wauering and doubtfull mindes, swaying sometimes this way, and sometimes that way.

8 They shall lacke nothing, which are carefull for the kingdome of heauen.

9 It is a foolish thing, not to looke for small things, at his hands, which giueth vs freely the greatest things.

* *Mat.6.20.*

10 A godly bountifulnes is a ready way to get true riches.

k This is the figure Metonymie, for by this word, Almes, is meant that compassion, and friendlinesse of an heart, that tendreth the miserie and poore estate of a man, and sheweth forth it selfe by some gift, and hath the name giuen it in the Greeke tongue, of mercy and compassion: and therefore he is said to giue almes, who parteth with some thing to another, and giueth to the poore, shewing thereby that he pitieth their poore estate.

* *1.Pet.1.13.*

11 The life of the faithfull seruants of God, in this world is a certaine watchfull peregrination, hauing the light of the word going before it.

* *Matth.24.43. reuel.16.15. and 3.3.*

12 None haue more neede to watch, then they that haue some degree of honor in the houshold of God.

l That is, euery moneth such measure of corne as was appointed them.

sters will, and prepared not himselfe, neither
did according to his will, shalbe beaten with
many *stripes*.
48 But hee that knewe it not, and yet did
commit things worthy of stripes, shalbe beaten with fewe *stripes*: for vnto whomsoeuer
much is giuen, of him shalbe much required,
and to whom men much commit, [m] the more
of him will they aske.
49 ¶ [13] I am come to put fire on the earth,
and what is my desire, if it be already kindled?
50 Notwithstanding I must bee baptized
with a baptisme, and how am I grieued, till it
be ended?
51 * Thinke yee that I am come to giue
peace on earth? I tell you, nay, but rather debate.
52 For from hencefoorth there shalbe fiue
in one house diuided, three against two, and
two against three.
53 The father shall be diuided against the
sonne, and the sonne against the father: the
mother against the daughter, and the daughter against the mother: the mother in law a-
gainst her daughter in law, and the daughter in
law against her mother in law.
54 ¶ * [14] Then sayde hee to the people,
When yee see a cloud [n] rise out of the West,
straightway yee say, a showre commeth: and
so it is.
55 And when *ye see* the South winde blow,
ye say, that it will be hote: and it commeth to
passe.
56 Hypocrites, ye can discerne the face of
the earth, and of the skie: but why discerne ye
not this time?
57 [15] Yea, and why iudge ye not of your
selues what is right?
58 ¶ * While thou goest with thine aduersarie to the ruler, as thou art in the way, giue
diligence in the way, that thou mayest be deliuered from him, lest he draw thee to the iudge,
and the iudge deliuer thee to the [o] iayler, and
the iayler cast thee into prison.
59 I tell thee, thou shalt not depart thence,
till thou hast payed the vtmost mite.

m More then of him, to whom so much was not giuen.

13 The Gospel is the only cause of peace betwixt the godly: and so is it the occasion of great trouble among the wicked.

* *Matt.10.34.*

* *Matt.16.2.*

14 Men which are very quick of sight in earthly things, are blind in those things, which pertaine to the heauenly life, and that through their owne malice.

n Which appeareth, and gathereth it selfe together in that part of the ayre.

15 Men that are blinded with the loue of themselues, and therefore are detestable & stubburne, shall beare the reward of their folly.

* *Matt.5.25.*

o To him that had to demand and gather the amerciaments, which they were condemned vnto, that had wrongfully troubled men: moreouer, the magistrates officers make them which are condemned, pay that, that they owe, yea and oftentimes if they be obstinate, they doe not only take the costs and charges of them, but also imprison them.

CHAP. XIII.

2 Of the Galileans, 2 and those that were slaine vnder Siloam. 6 The figtree that bare no fruite. 11 The woman vexed with the spirit of infirmitie, that is, with a disease brought on her by Satan, is healed. 19 The parable of the graine of mustard seede. 21 Of leauen. 23 How fewe shall be saued. 32 Herode that foxe.

There [1] were certaine men present at the
same season, that shewed him of the Galileans, whose blood [a] Pilate had mingled with
their sacrifices.
2 And Iesus answered, and said vnto them,
Suppose yee, that these Galileans were greater
sinners then all the *other* Galileans, because
they haue suffered such things?
3 I tell you, nay: but except yee amend
your liues, ye shall all likewise perish.

1 We must not reioyce at the iust punishment of others, but rather be instructed thereby to repentance.

a Pontius Pilate was gouernour of Iudea, almost ten yeeres, and about the fourth yeere of his gouernment, which might be about the fifteenth yeere of Tiberius reigne, Christ finished the worke of our redemption by his death.

4 Or thinke you that those eighteene, vpon whome the tower in [b] Siloam fell, and slew
them, were sinners aboue all men that dwell in
Ierusalem?
5 I tell you, nay: but except yee amend
your liues, ye shall all likewise perish.
6 ¶ [2] He spake also this parable, A certaine
man had a figge tree planted in his vineyard:
and hee came and sought fruite thereon, and
found none.
7 Then said hee to the dresser of his vineyard, Behold, this three yeeres haue I come
and sought fruit of this figtree, and find none:
cut it downe: why keepeth it also the ground
[c] barren?
8 And hee answered, and said vnto him,
Lord, let it alone this yeere also, till I digge
round about it, and dung it.
9 And if it beare fruite, *well*: if not, then
after thou shalt cut it downe.
10 ¶ [3] And hee taught in one of the Synagogues on the Sabbath day.
11 And behold, there was a woman which
had a [d] spirit of infirmity eighteene yeeres, and
was bowed together, and could not lift vp *her
selfe* in any wise.
12 When Iesus sawe her, hee called her to
him, and said to her, Woman, thou art [e] loosed
from thy disease.
13 And hee laid his hands on her, and immediatly shee was made straight againe, and
glorified God.
14 [4] And the [f] ruler of the Synagogue answered with indignation, because that Iesus
healed on the Sabbath *day*, and said vnto the
people, There are sixe dayes in which men
ought to worke: in them therefore come and
be healed, and not on the Sabbath day.
15 Then answered him the Lord, and said,
Hypocrite, doeth not each one of you on the
Sabbath *day* loose his oxe or his asse from the
stall, and leade him away to the water?
16 And ought not this daughter of Abraham, whom Satan had bound, loe, eighteene
yeeres, be loosed from this bond on the Sabbath day?
17 And when hee said these things, all his
aduersaries were ashamed: but all the people
reioyced at all the excellent things, that were
done by him.
18 ¶ * Then said hee, What is the kingdome of God like? or whereto shall I compare it?
19 [5] It is like a graine of mustard seede,
which a man tooke and sowed in his garden,
and it grewe, and waxed a great tree, and the
foules of the heauen made nestes in the branches thereof.
20 ¶ * And againe he said, Whereunto shall
I liken the kingdome of God?
21 It is like leauen, which a woman tooke,
and hidde in three peckes of floure, till all was
leauened.

b To wit, in the place, or riuer: for Siloam was a small riuer, from whence the conduits of the citie came, whereof Iohn 9.7. and Esay 8. 6. and therefore it was a tower or a castle, built vpon the conduit side, which fell downe suddenly and killed some.

2 Great & long suffering is the patience of God, but yet so that at length he executeth iudgement.

c Maketh the ground barren in that part, which otherwise were good for vines.

3 Christ came to deliuer vs from the hand of Satan.

d Troubled with a disease which Satan brought.

e For Satan had the woman bound, as if she had beene in chaines, in so much that for eighteene yeeres space, she could not hold vp her head.

4 A liuely image of hypocrisie, & reward thereof.

f One of the rulers of the Synagogue, for it appeareth by Marke 5.22. and Actes 13.15. that there were many rulers of the Synagogue.

** Mat.13.31. marke 4.31.*

5 God beginneth his kingdome with small beginnings, that the vnlooked for proceeding of it, may better set forth his power.

** Mat.13.33.*

22 ¶ * [6] And hee went through all cities
and townes, teaching, and iourneying towards
Ierusalem.
23 Then said one vnto him, Lord, *are there*
few that shalbe saued? And he said vnto them,
24 * Striue to enter in at the strait gate: for
many, I say vnto you, will seeke to enter in,
and shall not be able.
25 When the good man of the house is risen vp, and hath shut to the doore, and ye begin
to stand without, and to knocke at the doore,
saying, Lord, Lord, open to vs, and hee shall
answere and say vnto you, I knowe you not
whence ye are,
26 [7] Then shall yee begin to say, Wee haue
eaten and drunke in thy presence, and thou
hast taught in our streetes.
27 * But he shall say, I tell you, I know you
not whence yee are: depart from me, all yee
workers of iniquitie.
28 [8] There shall be weeping and gnashing
of teeth, when ye shall see Abraham and Isaac,
and Iacob, and all the Prophets in the kingdome of God, and your selues thrust out at
doores.
29 Then shall come *many* from the [g] East,
and from the West, and from the North, and
from the South, and shall sit at Table in the
kingdome of God.
30 * And behold, there are last, which shall
be first, and there are first, which shalbe last.
31 [9] The same day there came certaine Pharises, and said vnto him, Depart, and go hence:
for Herod will kill thee.
32 Then said hee vnto them, Goe yee and
tell that [h] Foxe, Behold, I cast out deuils, and
will heale still [i] to day, and to morow, and the
third day I shall be [k] perfected.
33 [10] Neuerthelesse, I must walke to day,
and to morow, and the day following: for it
cannot be that a Prophet should perish out of
Hierusalem.
34 * O Hierusalem, Hierusalem, which killest the Prophets, and stonest them that are sent
to thee, how often would I haue gathered thy
children together, as the henne *gathereth* her
[l] brood vnder *her* wings, and ye would not!
35 Behold, your house is left vnto you desolate: and verely I tell you, ye shall not see me
vntill *the time* come that ye shall say, Blessed *is*
he that commeth in the Name of the Lord.

** Mat.9.35. marke 6.6.*

6 Against them which had rather erre with many, then goe right with a few, and by that meanes through their own slownesse, are shut out of the kingdom of God.

** Matt.7.13.*

7 He is in vaine in the Church, which is not of the Church, which thing the cleannesse of life sheweth.

** Marke 7.23. and 25.41. psal.6.8.*

8 The casting off of the Iewes, and the calling of the Gentiles is foretold.

g From all the quarters of the world, and these are foure of the chiefest.

** Matt.19.30. and 20.16. marke 10.31.*

9 We must goe forward in the case of our calling, through the middest of terrors, whether they be true or fained.

h That deceitfull & trecherous mã.

i That is, a small time, and Theophylact. sayth, it is a prouerbe: or else, by To day, we may vnderstand the time that now is, and by to morow, the time to come, meaning thereby, all the time of his ministerie and office.

k To wit, when the sacrifice for sinne is ended.

10 There are no where more cruell enemies of the godly, then they which are within the Sanctuary & Church it selfe: but God seeth it, & will in his time haue an account of it.

** Matth.23.37.*

l Word for word, the nest: now the brood of chickens is the nest.

CHAP. XIIII.

2 The dropsie healed on the Sabbath. 8 The chiefe places at banquets. 12 The poore must bee called to our feasts. 16 Of those that were bid to the great Supper. 23 Some compelled to come in. 28 One about to build a tower.

AND [1] it came to passe that when hee was
entred into the house of [a] one of the
chiefe Pharises on the Sabbath *day*, to eate
bread, they watched him.

1 The Law of the very Sabbath ought not to hinder the offices of charitie.

a Either one of the Elders, whom they called the Sanhedrin, or one of the chiefe of the Synagogue: for all the Pharises were not chiefe men of the Synagogue, Iohn 7.48. for this word Pharise was the name of a sect, though it appeare by the whole historie that the Pharises were in great credite.

2 And behold, there was a certaine man before him, which had the dropsie.

3 Then Iesus answering, spake vnto the Lawyers and Pharises, saying, Is it lawfull to heale on the Sabbath *day?*

4 And they helde their peace. Then hee tooke him, and healed him, and let him goe,

5 And answered them, saying, Which of you *shall haue* an asse, or an oxe fallen into a pit, and will not straightway pull him out on the Sabbath day?

6 So they could not answere him againe to those things.

2 The reward of pride is ignominie: and the reward of true modestie is glory.

7 ¶ [2] He spake also a parable to the guests, when he marked how they chose out the chiefe roomes, and said vnto them,

8 When thou shalt be bidden of any man to a wedding, set not thy selfe downe in the chiefest place, lest a more honourable man then thou, be bidden of him,

9 And he that bade both him and thee, come, and say to thee, Giue this man roome, and thou then begin with shame to take the lowest roome.

* *Prou.25.5.*

10 * But when thou art bidden, goe and sit downe in the lowest roome, that when he that bade thee, commeth, hee may say vnto thee, Friend, sit vp higher: then shalt thou haue worship in the presence of them that sit at table with thee.

* *Chap.18.14. matth.23.12.*

11 * For whosoeuer exalteth himselfe, shall be brought lowe, and he that humbleth himselfe, shall be exalted.

3 Against them which lauish out their goods either ambitiously or for hope of recompence, whereas Christian charitie respecteth onely the glory of God, and the profit of our neighbour.
* *Prou.3.27. tob.4.7.*

12 ¶ [3] Then said he also to him that had bidden him, * When thou makest a dinner, or a supper, call not thy friends, nor thy brethren, neither thy kinsmen, nor the rich neighbours, lest they also bid thee againe, and a recompense be made thee.

13 But when thou makest a feast, call the poore, the maimed, the lame, *and* the blinde,

14 And thou shalt be blessed, because they cannot recompense thee: for thou shalt be recompensed at the resurrection of the iust.

15 ¶ Now when one of them that sate at table heard these things, he said vnto him, Blessed *is* he that eateth bread in the kingdome of God.

* *Matth.22.1. reuel.19.9.*

4 The most part euen of them to whom God hath reueiled himselfe are so mad, that such helpes as they haue receiued of God, they willingly turne into lets and hinderances.

b As of set purpose, and a thing agreed vpon before: for though they alledge seuerall causes, yet all of them agree in this, that they haue their excuses, that they may not come to Supper.

16 Then said he to him, * A certaine man made a great supper, and bade many,

17 And sent his seruants at supper time to say to them that were bidden, Come: for all things are now ready.

18 [4] But they all with [b] one *minde* began to make excuse: The first said vnto him, I haue bought a Farme, and I must needs goe out and see it: I pray thee haue me excused.

19 And another said, I haue bought fiue yoke of oxen, and I goe to proue them: I pray thee, haue me excused.

20 And another said, I haue married a wife, and therefore I cannot come.

21 So that seruant returned, and shewed his master these things. Then was the good man of the house angry, and said to his seruant, Goe out quickly into the [c] streets and lanes of the citie, and bring in hither the poore, and the maimed, and the halt, and the blinde.

c Wide and broad quarters.

22 And the seruant said, Lord, it is done as thou hast commanded, and yet there is roome.

23 Then the master said to the seruant, Goe out into the high wayes, and hedges, and compell them to come in, that mine house may be filled.

24 For I say vnto you, that none of those men which were bidden, shall taste of my supper.

25 [5] Now there went great multitudes with him, and he turned and said vnto them,

5 Euen those affections, which are of themselues worthy of prayse and commendation, must be ruled and ordered, that godlinesse may haue the vpper hand and preeminence.
* *Matth 10.37.*
d If the matter stand betweene God and him, as Theophylact saith: and therefore these words are not spoken simply, but by comparison.

26 * If any man come to me, and [d] hate not his father, and mother, and wife, and children, and brethren, and sisters: yea, and his owne life also, he cannot be my disciple.

* *Chap 9.29. matth.16.24. mar.8.34.*
6 The true followers of Christ must at once build and fight, and therefore be ready and prepared to suffer all kinde of miseries.

27 * [6] And whosoeuer beareth not his crosse, and commeth after mee, cannot be my disciple.

28 For which of you minding to build a towre, [e] sitteth not downe before, and counteth the cost, whether he haue sufficient to performe it,

e At home, and casteth all his costs, before hee begin the worke.

29 Lest that after he hath laid the foundation, and is not able to performe it, all that behold it, begin to mocke him,

30 Saying, This man began to builde, and was not able to make an end?

31 Or what King, going to make warre against another King, sitteth not downe first and taketh counsell, whether he be able with tenne thousand, to meet him that commeth against him with twentie thousand?

32 Or els while he is yet a great way off, he sendeth an ambassage, and desireth peace.

33 So likewise, whosoeuer he be of you, that forsaketh not all that he hath, he cannot be my disciple.

* *Matth.5.13. mar.9.50.*
7 The disciples of Christ must be wise, both for themselues, and for other: otherwise they become the foolishest of all.

37 * [7] Salt is good: but if salt haue lost his sauour, wherewith shall it be salted?

35 It is neither meet for the land, nor yet for the dunghill, but men cast it out. He that hath eares to heare, let him heare.

CHAP. XV.

4 The parable of the lost sheepe, 8 Of the groat, 11 And of the prodigall sonne.

|| *Or, drew neere.*
1 We must not despaire of them, which haue gon out of the way, but according to the example of Christ, wee must take great paines about them.
a Some Publicanes and sinners came to Christ from all quarters
* *Matth.18.12.*

Then || resorted vnto [1] him [a] all the Publicanes and sinners to heare him.

2 Therefore the Pharises and Scribes murmured, saying, Hee receiueth sinners, and eateth with them.

3 Then spake he this parable to them, saying,

4 * What man of you hauing an hundreth sheepe, if he lose one of them, doeth not leaue ninetie and nine in the wildernesse, and goe after that which is lost, vntill he finde it?

5 And when he hath found it, hee laieth it on his shoulders with ioy.

6 And when he commeth home, he calleth
together his friends, and neighbours, ſaying
vnto them, Reioyce with me: for I haue found
my ſheepe which was loſt.
7 I ſay vnto you, that likewiſe ioy ſhall be
in heauen for one ſinner that conuerteth, *more*
then for ninetie and nine iuſt men, which need
none amendment of life.
8 Either what woman hauing ten groats,
if ſhe loſe one groat, doeth not light a candle,
and ſweepe the houſe, and ſeeke diligently till
ſhe finde it?
9 And when ſhe hath found it, ſhe calleth
her friends, and neighbours, ſaying, Reioyce
with me: for I haue found the groat which I
had loſt.
10 Likewiſe I ſay vnto you, there is ioy
in the preſence of the Angels of God, for one
ſinner that conuerteth.
11 ¶ [2] He ſaid moreouer, A certaine man
had two ſonnes.
12 And the yonger of them ſaid to his father, Father, giue me the portion of the goods
that falleth to me. So he diuided vnto them *his*
ſubſtance.
13 So many dayes after, when the yonger
ſonne had gathered all together, he tooke his
iourney into a farre countrey, and there he waſted his goods with riotous liuing.
14 Now when he had ſpent all, there aroſe
a great dearth throughout that land, and he began to be in neceſſitie.
15 Then hee went and claue to a citizen of
that countrey, and he ſent him to his farme, to
feed ſwine.
16 And he would faine haue filled his belly
with the huſks, that the ſwine ate: but no man
gaue *them* him.
17 [3] Then he came to himſelfe, and ſaide,
How many hired ſeruants at my fathers haue
bread inough, and I die for hunger?
18 I will riſe and goe to my father, and ſay
vnto him, Father, I haue ſinned againſt [b] heauen and before thee,
19 And am no more worthy to be called thy
thy ſonne: make me as one of thy hired ſeruants.
20 So he aroſe and came to his father, and
when he was yet a great way off, his father ſaw
him, and had compaſſion, and ranne and fell on
his necke, and kiſſed him.
21 [4] And the ſonne ſaid vnto him, Father,
I haue ſinned againſt heauen, and before
thee, and am no more worthy to bee called thy
ſonne.
22 Then the father ſaide to his ſeruaunts,
Bring forth the beſt robe, and put it on him,
and put a ring on his hand, and ſhooes on his
feet,
23 And bring the fat calfe, and kill him,
and let vs eat, and be merrie:
24 For this my ſonne was dead, and is aliue
againe: and he was loſt, but he is found. And
they began to be merrie.
25 [5] Now the elder brother was in the field,
and when he came & drew neere to the houſe,
he heard melodie and dancing,
26 And called one of his ſeruants, and aſked what thoſe things meant.
27 And hee ſaide vnto him, Thy brother
is come, and thy father hath killed the fatte
Calfe, becauſe hee hath receiued him ſafe and
ſound.
28 Then he was angry, and would not goe
in: therefore came his father out and entreated
him.
29 But hee anſwered and ſaide to his father, Loe, theſe many yeeres haue I done thee
ſeruice, neither brake I at any time thy commandement, and yet thou neuer gaueſt me a
Kidde that I might make merrie with my
friends.
30 But when this thy ſonne was come,
which hath deuoured thy goods with harlots,
thou haſt for his ſake killed the fat Calfe.
31 And he ſaid vnto him, Sonne, thou art
euer with me, and all that I haue, is thine. It
was meet that we ſhould make merrie, and be
glad: for this thy brother was dead, and is aliue
againe: and he was loſt, but he is found.

2 Men by their voluntarie falling from God, hauing ſpoyled themſelues of the benefites which they receiued of him, caſt themſelues headlong into infinite calamities: but God of his ſingular goodneſſe, offering himſelfe freely to them, whom he called to repentance, through the greatneſſe of their miſerie wherewith they were tamed, doth not onely gently receiue them, but alſo enricheth them with farre greater gifts & bleſſeth them with the chiefeſt bliſſe.

3 The beginning of repentance is the acknowledging of the mercie of God, which ſtirreth vs to hope well.

b Againſt God, becauſe he is ſaid to dwell in heauen.

4 In true repentance there is a feeling of our ſinnes, ioyned with ſorow and ſhame, from whence ſpringeth a confeſſion, after which followeth forgiueneſſe.

5 Such as truely feare God, deſire to haue all men to be their fellowes.

CHAP. XVI.

1 The parable of the ſteward accuſed to his maſter. 13 To ſerue two maſters. 16 The Law & the Prophets. 19 Of Diues and Lazarus.

And he ſaid alſo vnto his diſciples, [1] There
was a certain rich man, which had a ſteward, and he was accuſed vnto him, that he waſted his goods.
2 And he called him, and ſaide vnto him,
How *is it* that I heare this of thee? Giue an accounts of thy ſtewardſhip: for thou mayeſt be
no longer ſteward.
3 Then the ſteward ſaid within himſelfe,
What ſhall I doe? for my maſter taketh away
from me the ſtewardſhip. I cannot dig, *and* to
beg I am aſhamed.
4 I knowe what I will doe, that when I am
put out of the ſtewardſhip, they may receiue
me into their houſes.
5 Then called hee vnto him euery one of
his maſters debters, & ſaid vnto the firſt, How
much oweſt thou vnto my maſter?
6 And hee ſaid, An hundred meaſures of
oyle. And he ſaid vnto him, Take thy writing,
and ſit downe quickly, and write fiftie.
7 Then ſaide he to another, How much
oweſt thou? and he ſaid, An hundred meaſures
of wheat. Then he ſaid to him, Take thy writing, and write foureſcore.
8 And the Lord commended [a] the vniuſt
ſteward, becauſe he had done wiſely. Wherefore the [b] children of this world are in their generation wiſer then the children of light.
9 And I ſay vnto you, Make you friends

1 Seeing that men oftentimes purchaſe friendſhip to themſelues, by other mens coſts, it is ſhame for vs, if with a free and liberall beſtowing of the goods which the Lord hath giuen vs, to that purpoſe we doe not pleaſe him, nor procure ẏ good wil of our neighbours, ſeeing that by this only meanes, riches, which are often times occaſions of ſinne, are turned to another end and purpoſe.

a This parable doeth not approue the ſtewards naughtie dealing, for it was very theft: but parables are ſet forth, to ſhew a thing couertly, and as it were, vnder a figure to repreſent the trueth, though it agree not thorowly with the matter it ſelfe: ſo that Chriſt meaneth by this parable, to teach vs, that worldly men are more heedie in the affaires of this world, then the children of God are carefull for euerlaſting life. *b Men that are giuen to this preſent life, contrary to whome the children of light are ſet: S. Paul calleth thoſe ſpirituall, and the other carnall.*

with the riches [c] of iniquitie, that when ye shall
want, they may receiue you into euerlasting
[d] habitations.
10 [2] He that is faithfull in the least, he is also faithfull in much: and he that is vniust in the
least, is vniust also in much.
11 If then ye haue not bene faithfull in the
wicked riches, who will trust you in the [e] true
treasure?
12 And if ye haue not bene faithfull in [f] another mans *goods*, who shal giue you that which
is yours?
13 * [3] No seruant can serue two masters: for
either he shall hate the one, and loue the other:
or els he shall leane to the one, and despise the
other. Ye cannot serue God and riches.
14 All these things heard the Pharises also
which were couetous, and they scoffed at him.
15 [4] Then he sayd vnto them, Ye are they,
which iustifie your selues before men: but God
knoweth your hearts: for that which is highly
esteemed among men, is abomination in the
sight of God.
16 * [5] The Law and the Prophets *endured*
vntill Iohn: and since that time the Kingdome
of God is preached, and euery man presseth into it.
17 * Nowe it is more easie that heauen and
earth should passe away, then that one title of
the Law should fall.
18 ¶ * Whosoeuer putteth away his
wife, and marrieth another, committeth adulterie: and whosoeuer marrieth her [g] that is
put away from her husband, committeth adulterie.
19 ¶ [6] There was a certain rich man, which
was clothed in [h] purple and fine linen, and fared
well and delicately euery day.
20 Also there was a certaine begger named Lazarus, which was laide at his gate full of
sores,
21 And desired to bee refreshed with the
crummes that fell from the rich mans table: yea, and the dogges came and licked his
sores.
22 And it was so that the begger died, and
was caried by the Angels into Abrahams bosome. The rich man also died, and was buried.
23 And being in hell in torments, [i] he lift vp
his eyes, and saw Abraham afarre off, and Lazarus in his bosome.
24 Then he cried, and said, Father Abraham
haue mercy on me, & send Lazarus that he may
dip the tip of his finger in water, and coole my
tongue: for I am tormented in this flame.
25 But Abraham sayd, Son, remember that
thou in thy life time receiuedst thy pleasures,
and likewise Lazarus paines: now therefore is
he comforted, and thou art tormented.

c This is not spoken of goods that are euill gotten, for God will haue our bountifulnesse to the poore, proceed and come from a good fountaine: but he calleth those riches of iniquitie, which men vse naughtily.
d To wit, the poore Christians: for they are the inheritours of these Tabernacles. Theo.
2 We ought to take heed, that for abusing our earthly function and duetie, we be not depriued of heauely gifts: for howe can they vse spirituall gifts aright, who abuse worldly things?
e That is, heauenly and true riches: which are contrary to worldly and flitting substance.
f In worldly goods, which are called other mens, because they are committed to our credit.
* *Matth.6.24.*
3 No man can loue God & riches together.
4 Our sinnes are not hidden to God, although they be hidden to men, yea although they be hidden to them, whose sinnes they are.
* *Matth.11.12.*
5 The Pharises despised the excellencie of the new Couenant, in respect of the old, being ignorant of the perfect righteousnes of the Lawe, and how false expounders they were of the Law Christ declareth by the seuenth Commandement.
* *Matth.5.18.*
* *Matth.5.32.& 19.9.1.cor.7.11*
g They that gather by this place, that a man cannot be maried againe after that he hath put away his wife for adulterie, while she liueth, reason fondly: for Christ speaketh of those diuorces, which the Iewes vsed, of which sort we can not take the diuorcement for adulterie, for adulterers were put to death by the Law.
6 The end of the pouertie and miserie of the godly shall be euerlasting ioy: as the end of the riotousnesse and cruell pride of the rich shall be euerlasting miserie, without all hope of mercie. *h Very gorgeously and sumptuously, for purple garments were costly, and this fine linnen, which was a kind of linnen that came out of Achaia, was as deare as gold. i Heauenly & spirituall things are expressed and set forth vnder colours, & resemblances fit for our senses.*

26 Besides all this, betweene you & vs there
is a great gulfe set, so that they which would go
from hence to you, cannot: neither can they
come from thence to vs.
27 [7] Then he said, I pray thee therefore, father, that thou wouldest send him to my fathers house,
28 (For I haue fiue brethren) that hee may
testifie vnto them, lest they also come into this
place of torment.
29 Abraham said vnto him, They haue Moses and the Prophets: let them heare them.
30 And he said, Nay, Father Abraham: but
if one came vnto them from the dead, they will
amend their liues.
31 Then he said vnto him, If they heare not
Moses and the Prophets, neither will they bee
perswaded, though one rise from the dead a-
gaine.

7 Seeing that we haue a most sure rule to liue by, layed forth vnto vs in the word of God, rashly & vainely doe men seeke for other reuelations.

CHAP. XVII.

1 Offences. 3 We must forgiue him that trespasseth against vs. 10 We are vnprofitable seruants. 11 Of the ten lepers. 20 Of the comming of the kingdome of heauen. 33 False Christes. 36 After what manner Christs comming shall bee.

Then said he to his disciples, * [1] It cannot be
auoyded, but that offences will come, but
woe *be* to him by whom they come.
2 It is better for him that a great milstone
were hanged about his necke, and that he were
cast into the sea, then that he should offend one
of these litle ones.
3 ¶ [2] Take heed to your selues: if thy brother trespasse against thee, rebuke him: and if
he repent, forgiue him.
4 * And though he sinne against thee seuen times in a day, & seuen times in a day turne
againe to thee, saying, It repenteth mee, thou
shalt forgiue him.
5 ¶ [3] And the Apostles said vnto the Lord,
Increase our faith.
6 And the Lord said, * If ye had faith, *as*
much as is [a] a graine of mustard seed, and should
say vnto this mulbery tree, Plucke thy selfe vp
by the rootes, and plant thy selfe in the sea, it
should euen obey you.
7 ¶ [4] Who is it also of you, that hauing a
seruant plowing, or feeding cattell, would say
vnto him by and by, when he were come from
the field, Goe, and sit downe at table?
8 And would not rather say to him, Dresse
wherewith I may sup, and gird thy selfe, and
serue me, till I haue eaten and drunken, and afterward eat thou, and drinke thou?
9 Doeth he thanke that seruant, because he
did that which was commaunded vnto him? I
trowe not.
10 [5] So likewise ye, when ye haue done all
those things, which are commanded you, say,
Wee are vnprofitable seruants: we haue done
that which was our duetie to doe.
11 ¶ [6] And so it was when he went to Hierusalem, that he passed through the middes of
Samaria, and Galile.

* *Matth.18.7. marke 9.42.*
1 The Church is of necessitie subiect to offences, but the Lord will not suffer them vnpunished, if any of ÿ least be offended.
2 Our reprehensions must be iust, and proceed of loue and charitie.
* *Matth.18.21.*
3 God will neuer be vtterly lacking to the godly, (although be not so perfitly with them, as they would) euẽ in those difficulties, which can not be ouercome by mans reason.
* *Matth.17.20.*
a If you had no more faith, but the quantitie of the graine of mustard seede.
4 Seeing that God may chalenge vnto himselfe of right, both vs and all that is ours, he can be debter vnto vs for nothing, although we labour manfully euen vnto death.
5 The most perfit keeping of the Law, which we can performe, deserueth no reward.
6 Christ doeth well euen vnto such, as will be vnthankeful, but the benefits of God profit them only to saluation, which are thankefull.

12 And as he entred into a certaine towne,
there met him ten men that were lepers, which
stood afarre off.
13 And they lift vp their voyces and sayd,
Iesus, Master, haue mercie on vs.
14 And when he sawe *them*, hee saide vnto
them, *Goe, shew your selues vnto the Priests.
And it came to passe, that as they went, they
were cleansed.
15 Then one of them, when he sawe that
he was healed, turned backe, and with a loude
voyce praysed God,
16 And fell downe on his face at his feete,
and gaue him thanks: and hee was a Samaritane.
17 And Iesus answered, and said, Are there
not ten cleansed? but where *are* the nine?
18 There is none found that returned to
giue God prayse, saue this stranger.
19 And he said vnto him, Arise, go thy way,
thy faith hath saued thee.
20 ¶ [7] And when he was demaunded of
the Pharises, when the kingdome of GOD
should come, he answered them, and said, The
kingdome of God commeth not with [b] obseruation.
21 Neither shall men say, Loe here, or loe
there: for beholde, the kingdome of God is
[c] within you.
22 [8] And he saide vnto the disciples, The
dayes will come, when yee shall desire to see
[d] one of the dayes of the Sonne of man, and ye
shall not see it.
23 *[9] Then they shall say to you, Beholde
here, or behold there: *but* goe not thither, neither follow them.
24 For as the lightning that lighteneth out
of the one *part* vnder heauen, shineth vnto the
other *part* vnder heauen, so shall the Sonne of
man be in his day.
25 But first he must suffer many things, and
be reproued of this generation.
26 * [10] And as it was in the dayes of Noe,
so shall it bee in the dayes of the Sonne of
man.
27 They ate, they dranke, they married
wiues, and gaue in mariage vnto the day that
Noe went into the Arke: and the flood came,
and destroyed them all.
28 *Likewise also, as it it was in the dayes
of Lot: they ate, they dranke, they bought,
they sold, they planted, they built.
29 But in the day that Lot went out of Sodom, it rained fire and brimstone from heauen,
and destroyed them all.
30 After these *ensamples* shall it be in the
day when the Sonne of man is reueiled.
31 [11] At that day he that is vpon the house,
and his stuffe in the house, let him not come
downe to take it out: and he that is in the field
likewise, let him not turne backe to that he left
behind.
32 *Remember Lots wife.

*Leuit 14.2.
7 The kingdom of God is not marked of many although it be most present before their eyes: because they foud y perswade themselues, that it is ioyned with outward pompe.
b With any outward pompe and shew of maiestie, to be knowen by: for there were otherwise many plaine and euident tokens whereby men might haue vnderstood, that Christ was the Messias, whose kingdome was so long looked for: but he speaketh in this place of those signes which the Pharises dreamed of, which looked for an earthly kingdome of Messias.
c You looke about for Messias, as though hee were absent, but he is amongst you in the midst of you.
8 We often times neglect those things when they be present, which we afterward desire when they are gone, but in vaine.
d The time will come, that you shall seeke for the Sonne of man, with great sorow of heart, and shall not finde him.
**Matth. 24.23. mar. 13.21.*
9 Christ forewarneth vs, that false Christs shal come and that his glory shall suddenly bee spread farre and wide thorow the world, after that the ignominie of the crosse is put out and extinguished.
**Gen. 7.5. mar. 24.38. 1. pet. 3 20.*
10 The world shalbe taken vnawares with the sudden iudgement of God: and therfore the faithfull ought to watch continually.
**Gen. 19.24.*
11 We must take good heed, that neither distrust, nor the inticements of this world, nor any respect of friendship hinder vs the least that may be.
**Gene. 19.26.*

33 *Whosoeuer wil seeke to saue his soule,
shall loose it: and whosoeuer shall loose it, shall
[e] get it life.
34 *I tell you, in that night there shall be
two in one bed: the one shall be receiued, and
the other shall be left.
35 Two women shall bee grinding together, the one shall be taken, and the other shall
be left.
36 Two shalbe in the field: one shall be receiued, and another shall be left.
37 [12] And they answered, and saide to him,
Where Lord? And he said vnto them, *Wher-
soeuer the body *is*, thither shall also the Eagles
be gathered together.

CHAP. XVIII.

2 The parable of the vnrighteous iudge and the widowe. 10 Of the Pharise and the Publicane. 15 Children are of the kingdome of heauen. 22 To sell all and giue to the poore. 28 The Apostles forsake all. 31 Christ foretelleth his death. 35 The blind man receiueth sight.

AND [1] he spake also a parable vnto them,
to this end, that they *ought alwayes to
pray, and not to [a] waxe faint,
2 [b] Saying, There was a iudge in a certaine
citie, which feared not God, neither reuerenced
man.
3 And there was a widowe in that citie,
which came vnto him, saying, Doe me iustice
against mine aduersarie.
4 And he would not of a long time: but
afterward he said with himselfe, Though I feare
not God, nor reuerence man,
5 Yet because this widow troubleth mee,
I will doe her right, lest at the last she come and
[c] make me wearie.
6 And the Lord said, Heare what the vnrighteous iudge saith.
7 Now shall not God auenge his elect,
which cry day and night vnto him, yea, though
[d] he suffer long for them?
8 I tell you he will auenge them quickly:
but when the Sonne of man commeth, shal he
find faith on the earth?
9 ¶ [2] He spake also this parable vnto certaine which trusted in themselues that they
were iust, and despised other.
10 Two men went vp into the Temple to
pray: the one a Pharise, & the other a Publican.
11 [3] The Pharise stood and prayed thus
with himselfe, O God, I thanke thee, that I am
not as other men, extortioners, vniust, adulterers, or euen as this Publicane.
12 I fast twise in the weeke: I giue tithe of
all that euer I possesse.
13 But the Publicane standing [e] a farre off
would not lift vp so much as his eyes to heauen,
but smote his brest, saying, O God, be mercifull
to me a sinner.
14 I tell you, this man departed to his

**Chap. 9 24. matth. 10.39. marke 8.35. iohn 12.25.*
e That is, shall saue it, so Matthew expoundeth it: for the life that is here spoken of, is euerlasting saluation.
**Matth. 24.41.*
12 The onely way to continue is to cleaue to Christ.
**Matth. 24.28.*
1 God wil haue vs to continue in prayer, not to wearie vs, but to exercise vs, therfore we must so striue with impatience, that long delay cause vs not to breake off the course of our prayers.
**Rom. 12.12. 1. thes. 5 17.*
a Yeeld to afflictions, and aduersities, as they doe which are out of heart.
b He doeth not compare things that are equall together, but the lesse with the greater: If a man get his right at a most vnrighteous iudges hands, much more shall the prayers of the godly preuaile before God.
c Word for word, beate me downe with her blowes, and it is a metaphore taken of wrestlers, who beate their aduersaries with their fists or clubs: so doe they that are importunate bear the iudges eares with their crying out, euen as it were with blowes.
d Though hee seeme slowe in reuenging the iniuries done to his.
2 Two things especially make our prayers void & of none effect: confidence of our owne righteousnes, and the contempt of other: & an humble heart is contrarie to both these. 3 Although we confesse, that whatsoeuer we haue, we haue it of God, yet are we despised of God, as proud and arrogant, if we put neuer so litle trust in our owne works before God. *e Farre from the Pharise in lower place.*

house

* Chap. 14.11. matth. 23.12.

house iustified rather then the other: * for euery man that exalteth himselfe, shall be brought
lowe, and he that humbleth himselfe, shall be
exalted.

* Matth. 19.13. marke 10.13.
f The children were tender and yong, in that they were brought, which appeareth more euidently in that, that they were infants: which is to be marked against them that are enemies to the baptizing of children.
4 To iudge or thinke of Christ after the reason of the flesh, is the cause of infinite corruptions.
5 The children also of the faithfull are comprehended in the free couenant of God.
g Them that caried the children, whom the disciples droue away.
6 Childe-like innocencie is an ornament of Christians.
* Matth. 19.16. marke 10.17.
* Exod. 20.13.
7 The intisement of riches carieth away many from the right way.

15 ¶ * f They brought vnto him also babes
that he should touch them. 4 And when his disciples saw it, they rebuked them.
16 5 But Iesus g called them vnto him, and
said, Suffer the babes to come vnto me, and forbid them not: for of such is the kingdome of
God.
17 6 Verely I say vnto you, whosoeuer receiueth not the kingdome of God as a babe, he
shall not enter therein.
18 * Then a certaine ruler asked him, saying, Good Master, what ought I to doe, to inherit eternall life?
19 And Iesus saide vnto him, Why callest
thou me good? none is good, saue one, *euen*
God.
20 Thou knowest the commaundements,
* Thou shalt not commit adulterie: Thou shalt
not kill: Thou shalt not steale: Thou shalt not
beare false witnesse: Honour thy father and
thy mother.
21 7 And he said, All these haue I kept from
my youth.
22 Now when Iesus heard that, he said vnto him, Yet lackest thou one thing. Sell all that
euer thou hast, and distribute vnto the poore,
and thou shalt haue treasure in heauen, & come
follow me.
23 But when he heard those things, he was
very heauy: for he was marueilous rich.

8 To be both rich and godly, is a singular gift of God.

24 8 And when Iesus saw him very sorowfull, he said, With what difficultie shall they
that haue riches, enter into the Kingdome of
God!
25 Surely it is easier for a Camell to goe
through a needles eye, then for a rich man to
enter into the kingdome of God.
26 Then said they that heard it, And who
then can be saued?
27 And he said, The things which are vnpossible with men, are possible to God.

* Matth. 19.27. marke 10.28.

28 ¶ * Then Peter said, Loe, we haue left
all, and haue followed thee.

9 They become the richest of al, which refuse not to be poore for Christes sake.

29 9 And he saide vnto them, Verily I say
vnto you, there is no man that hath left house,
or parents, or brethren, or wife, or children for
the kingdome of Gods sake,
30 Which shall not receiue much more in
this world, and in the world to come life euerlasting.

* Matth 20.17. marke 10.32.
10 As sure and certaine as persecution is, so sure is the glory which remaineth for the conquerours.

31 ¶ * 10 Then Iesus tooke vnto him the
twelue, and said vnto them, Behold, we goe vp
to Ierusalem, and all things shall be fulfilled to
the Sonne of man, that are written by the Prophets.
32 For he shall be deliuered vnto the Gentiles, and shall be mocked, and shalbe spiteful-
ly entreated, and shall be spitted on.
33 And when they haue scourged him, they
will put him to death: but the third day he shal
rise againe.

h Hereby we see how ignorant the disciples were.

34 But they vnderstood h none of these
things, and this saying was hidde from them,
neither perceiue they the things, which were
spoken.

* Matth 20.29. marke 10.46.
11 Christ sheweth by a visible myracle, that he is the light of the world.

35 ¶ * 11 And it came to passe, that as hee
was come neere vnto Iericho, a certaine blind
man sate by the way side, begging.
36 And when he heard the people passe by,
he asked what it meant.
37 And they saide vnto him, that Iesus of
Nazareth passed by.
38 Then he cryed, saying, Iesus the sonne
of Dauid, haue mercie on me.

12 The more stops and lets that Satan layeth in our way, euen by them which professe Christs Name, so much the more ought we to goe forward.

39 12 And they which went before, rebuked
him that he should hold his peace, but he cried
much more, O Sonne of Dauid, haue mercie
on me.
40 And Iesus stood still, and commaunded
him to be brought vnto him. And when he was
come neere, he asked him,
41 Saying, What wilt thou that I doe vnto
thee? And he said, Lord, that I may receiue my
sight.
42 And Iesus saide vnto him, Receiue thy
sight: thy faith hath saued thee.
43 Then immediatly he receiued his sight,
and followed him, praysing God: and all the
people, when they sawe *this*, gaue prayse to
God.

CHAP. XIX.

2 Zaccheus the Publicane. 13 Ten pieces of money deliuered to seruants to occupie withall. 29 Iesus entreth into Ierusalem. 41 He foretelleth the destruction of the Citie with teares. 45 He casteth the sellers out of the Temple.

1 Christ preuenteth them with his grace especially, which seemed to be furthest from it.
a The ouerseer and head of the Publicanes, which were there together: for the Publicanes were diuided into companies, as we may gather by many places of Cicero his Orations.
2 The world forsaketh the grace of God, and yet is vnwilling that it should be bestowed vpon other.
3 The example of true repentance, is knowen by the effect.
b By falsly accusing any man: and this agreeth most fitly to the master of the customers person: for commonly they haue this trade among them when they robbe and spoyle the Common-wealth, they haue nothing in their mouthes, but the profit of the Common-weale, and vnder that colour they play the theeues, in so much that if men reproooue and goe about to redresse their robberie and spoyling, they cry out, the Common-weale is hindered.

NOw 1 when Iesus entred & passed through
Iericho,
2 Behold, there was a man named Zaccheus, which *was* the a chiefe receiuer of the tribute, and he was rich.
3 And he sought to see Iesus, who he should
be, and could not for the preasse, because hee
was of a low stature.
4 Wherefore he ranne before, and climed
vp into a wilde fig tree, that he might see him:
for he should come that *way*.
5 And when Iesus came to the place, hee
looked vp, and saw him, and said vnto him, Zaccheus, come downe at once: for to day I must
abide at thine house.
6 Then he came downe hastily, and receiued him ioyfully.
7 2 And when they all saw it, they murmured, saying, that he was gone in to lodge with a
sinfull man.
8 3 And Zaccheus stood forth, and said vnto the Lord, Beholde, Lord, the halfe of my
goods I giue to the poore: and if I haue taken
from any man by b forged cauillation, I restore
him foure fold.

9 Then Iesus said to him, This day is saluation come vnto this house, forasmuch as hee
is also become the [c] sonne of Abraham.
10 * For the Sonne of man is come to seek,
and to saue that which was lost.
11 [4] And whiles they heard these things,
he continued and spake a parable, because hee
was neere to Ierusalem, and because also they
thought that the kingdome of God should
shortly appeare.
12 He said therefore, * A certaine Noble
man went into a farre countrey, to receiue for
himselfe a kingdome and *so* to come againe.
13 [5] And he called his ten seruants, and deliuered them ten pieces of money, and said vn-
them, Occupie till I come.
14 Now his citizens hated him, and sent
an ambassage after him, saying, Wee will not
haue this man to reigne ouer vs.
15 And it came to passe, when he was come
againe, and had receiued his kingdome, that he
commanded the seruants to be called to him, to
whom he gaue his money, that he might know
what euery man had gained.
16 Then came the first, saying, Lord, [d] thy
piece hath increased ten pieces.
17 And he said vnto him, Well, good seruant: because thou hast bene faithfull in a very little thing, take thou authoritie ouer tenne
cities.
18 And the second came, saying, Lord, thy
piece hath increased fiue pieces.
19 And to the same he said, Be thou also *ruler* ouer fiue cities.
20 [6] So the other came, and said, Lord, behold thy piece, which I haue laid vp in a napkin:
21 For I feared thee, because thou art a strait
man: thou takest vp, that thou laiest not down,
and reapest that thou didst not sow.
22 Then he said vnto him, Of thine owne
mouth will I iudge thee, O euill seruant. Thou
knowest that I am a strait man, taking vp that
I layed not downe, and reaping that I did not
sowe.
23 Wherefore then gauest not thou my money into the [e] banke, that at my comming I
might haue required it with vantage?
24 And he said to them that stood by, Take
from him that piece, and giue it him that hath
ten pieces.
25 (And they said vnto him, Lord, he hath
ten pieces.)
26 * For I say vnto you, that vnto all them
that haue, it shall be giuen, and from him that
hath not, euen that he hath, shall be taken from
him.
27 Moreouer, those mine enemies, which
would not that I should reigne ouer them,
bring hither, and slay them before me.
28 ¶ And when he had thus spoken, [f] hee
went forth before, ascending vp to Hierusalem.

c Beloued of God, one that walketh in the steps of Abrahams faith: and we gather that saluation came to that house, because they receiued the blessing as Abraham had, for all of the houshold were circumcised.
* *Matth. 18.11.*
4 We must patiently wait for the iudgement of God, which shall be reueiled in his time.
* *Matth. 25.14.*
5 There are three sorts of men in ye Church the one sort fall from Christ, whom they see not: the other, which according to their vocation, bestowe the gifts, which they haue receiued of God, to his glory with great paines and diligence: the third liue idlely, and doe no good As for the first, the Lord when he commeth will iustly punish the in his time: the other he will blesse, according to the paines which they haue taken: and as for the slouthfull and idle persons he will punish them as the first.
d This was a piece of money, which the Grecians vsed, and was in value about an hundred pence, which is about ten crownes.
6 Against them which spend their life idlely in deliberating and otherwise in contemplation.
e To the bankers and changers.
* *Chap. 8.18. matth. 13.12. and 25.29. marke 4.25.*
f The disciples staggered and stayed at the matter, but Christ goeth on boldly though death were before his eyes.

29 * [7] And it came to passe, when hee was
come nere to Bethphage, and Bethania, besides
the mount which is called *the mount* of Oliues,
he sent two of his disciples,
30 Saying, Goe ye to the towne which is
before *you*, wherein, assoone as ye are come, ye
shal finde a Colt tied, whereon neuer man sate:
loose him, and bring him *hither*.
31 And if any man aske you, why ye loose
him, thus shall yee say vnto him, Because the
Lord hath need of him.
32 So they that were sent, went their way,
and found it as he had said vnto them.
33 And as they were loosing the Colt, the
owners thereof said vnto them, Why loose ye
the Colt?
34 And they said, The Lord hath need of
him.
35 ¶ * So they brought him to Iesus, and
they cast their garments on the Colt, and set
Iesus thereon.
36 And as he went, they spread their clothes
in the way.
37 And when he was come neere to the going downe of the mount of Oliues, the whole
multitude of the disciples began to reioyce, and
to prayse God with a loude voyce, for all the
great works that they had seene,
38 Saying, Blessed *be* the King that commeth in the Name of the Lord: peace in heauen, and glory in the highest *places*.
39 [8] Then some of the Pharises of the company said vnto him, Master, rebuke thy disciples
40 But he answered, and said vnto them, I
tell you, that if these should hold their peace,
the stones would crie.
41 ¶ * [9] And when he was come neere, hee
beheld the Citie, and wept for it,
42 [g] Saying, O [h] if thou haddest euen know-
en [i] at the least in this [k] thy day those things,
which *belong* vnto thy [l] peace! but nowe are
they hid from thine eyes.
43 For the dayes shall come vpon thee, that
thine enemies shall cast a trench about thee,
and compasse thee round, and keepe thee in on
euery side,
44 And shal make thee euen with the ground,
and thy children which are in thee, and they
shall not leaue in thee a stone vpon a stone, because thou knewest not [m] that season of thy visitation.
45 ¶ * [10] He went also into the Temple, and
began to cast out them that solde therein, and
them that bought,
46 Saying vnto them, It is written, * Mine
house is the house of prayer, but ye haue made
it a denne of theeues.
47 And he taught dayly in the Temple. And
the high Priests and the Scribes, and the chiefe
of the people sought to destroy him.
48 But they could not find what they might
doe to him: for all the people hanged vpon him
when they heard him.

* *Matth. 21.1. marke 11.1.*
7 Christ sheweth in his owne person, that his kingdome is not of this world.
* *Matth 27.7. iohn 12.14.*
8 When they linger which ought to be the chiefest Preachers and setters foorth of the kingdome of God, he wil raise vp other extraordinarily in despite of them.
* *Chap. 21.6. matth. 24.1. marke 13.1.*
9 Christ is not simply delighted with the destruction, no not of the wicked.
g Christ breaketh off his speech, which sheweth partly how he was mooued with compassion for the destruction of the citie, that was like to ensue: and partly to vpbraid them for their treachery and stubburnnesse against him, such as hath not lightly bene heard of.
h At leastwise thou, O Hierusalem, to whom this message was properly sent.
i If after the slaying of so many Prophets, and so oft refusing me the Lord of the Prophets now especially, in this my last comming to thee, thou hadst had any regard to thy selfe.
k The fit and commodious time is called the day of this Citie.
l That is, those things wherein thy happines standeth.
m That is, this very instant, wherein God visited thee.
* *Matth 21.13.*
10 Christ sheweth after his entrie into Hierusalem by a visible signe, that it is his office inioyned him of his Father to purge the Temple
* *Marke 11.17. isa. 56.7.*
* *Ierem. 7.11.*

CHAP.

CHAP. XX.

From whence Iohns baptisme was. 9 The wickednesse of the Priests is noted by the parable of the vineyard and the husbandmen. 21 To giue tribute to Cesar. 27 Hee conuinceth the Sadduces denying the resurrection. 41 How Christ is the Sonne of God.

*Matt.21.23. marke 11.27.
1 The Pharises being ouercome with the trueth of Christs doctrine, mooue a question about his outward calling, and are ouercome by the witnesse of their own conscience.

AND *[1] it came to passe, that on one of
those dayes, as hee taught the people in
the Temple, and preached the Gospel, the hie
Priests and the Scribes came vpon him with
the Elders,
2 And spake vnto him, saying, Tell vs by
what authority thou doest these things, or who
is he that hath giuen thee this authoritie?
3 And he answered, and said vnto them, I
also will aske you one thing: tell me therefore:
4 The baptisme of Iohn, was it from heauen, or of men?
5 And they reasoned within themselues,
saying, If we shall say, From heauen, hee will
say, Why then beleeued yee him not?
6 But if we shall say, Of men, all the people will stone vs: for they be perswaded that
Iohn was a Prophet.
7 Therfore they answered, that they could
not tell whence it *was*.
8 Then Iesus said vnto them, Neither tell
I you, by what authoritie I doe these things.
9 ¶ *[2] Then began hee to speake to the
people this parable, A certaine man planted a
vineyard, & let it foorth to husbandmen: and
went into a strange countrey, for a great time.
10 And at the time conuenient hee sent a
seruant to the husbandmen, that they should
giue him of the fruite of the vineyard: but the
husbandmen did beat him, and sent him away
emptie.
11 Againe he sent yet another seruant: and
they did beate him, and foule intreated him,
and sent him away emptie.
12 Moreouer hee sent the third, and him
they wounded, and cast out.
13 Then said the Lorde of the vineyard,
What shal I do? I will send my beloued sonne:
it may be that they will doe reuerence, when
they see him.
14 But when the husbandmen sawe him,
they reasoned with themselues, saying, This is
the heire: come, let vs kill him, that the inheritance may be ours.
15 So they cast him out of the vineyard, and
killed him. What shall the Lord of the vineyard therefore doe vnto them?
16 Hee will come and destroy these husbandmen, and will giue out his vineyard to others. But when they heard it, they said, God
forbid.
17 ¶ And he beheld them, and said, What
meaneth this then that is written, *The stone
that the builders refused, that is made the head
of the corner?
18 Whosoeuer shall fall vpon that stone,
shall be broken: and on whomsoeuer it shall
fall, it shall grinde him to powder.

*Matt.21.33. marke 12.1. isai. 5.1. iere.2.21.
2 It is no new thing to haue them the chiefest enemies of Christ and his seruants, which are conuersant in the very Sanctuarie of Gods holy place: but at length they shall not escape vnpunished.

*Psal.118.22. isai 28.16. actes 4.11. rom.9.33. 1.pet.2.8.

19 Then the high Priests, and the Scribes
the same houre went about to lay handes on
him: (but they feared the people) for they
perceiued that hee had spoken this parable against them.
20 *[3] And they [a] watched *him*, and sent
foorth [b] spies, which should faine themselues
iust men, [c] to take him in his talke, and to deliuer him vnto the power and [d] authoritie of the
gouernour.
21 And they asked him, saying, Master, we
knowe that thou sayest, and teachest aright,
neither doest thou accept [e] mans person, but
teachest the way of God truely.
22 Is it lawfull for vs to giue Cesar tribute
or no?
23 But he perceiued their [f] craftinesse, and
said vnto them, Why tempt ye me?
24 Shewe me a penie. Whose image and
superscription hath it? They answered, and
said, Cesars.
25 Then he said vnto them, *Giue then vnto Cesar the things which are Cesars, and to
God those which are Gods.
26 And they could not reprooue his saying
before the people: but they marueiled at his
answere, and helde their peace.
27 *[4] Then came to him certaine of the
Sadduces (which deny that there is any resurrection) and they asked him,
28 Saying, Master, *Moses wrote vnto vs,
If any mans brother die hauing a wife, and hee
die without children, that his brother should
take *his* wife, & raise vp seed vnto his brother.
29 Now there were seuen brethren, and
the first tooke a wife, and he died without children.
30 And the second tooke the wife, and hee
died childlesse.
31 Then the third tooke her: and so likewise the seuen died, and left no children.
32 And last of all the woman died also.
33 Therefore at the resurrection, whose
wife of them shall shee be? for seuen had her
to wife.
34 Then Iesus answered, and said vnto
them, The [g] children of this world marrie
wiues, and are married.
35 But they which shalbe counted worthy
to enioy that world, and the resurrection from
the dead, neither marrie wiues, neither are
married.
36 For they can die no more, forasmuch as
they are equall vnto the Angels, and are the
sonnes of God, since they are the [h] children of
the resurrection.
37 And that the dead shall rise againe, euen
*Moses shewed it besides the bush, when hee
said, The Lord *is* the God of Abraham, and the
God of Isaac, and the God of Iacob.
38 For hee is not the God of the dead, but
of them which liue: for all [i] liue vnto him.
39 Then certaine of the Scribes answered,

*Matth.22.16. marke 12.13.
3 The last refuge that false prophets haue to destroy the true Prophets, is to lay sedition and treason to their charge.
a *A fit time to take him in.*
b *Whom they had deceitfully hired.*
c *That they might take some holde in his talke, & thereby forge some false accusation against him.*
d *Put him to death.*
e *Thou art not mooued by fauour of any man: and by person he meaneth outward circumstances, which if a man haue respect vnto, he will not iudge alike of them that are indeed alike.*
f *Craftinesse is a certeine diligence and wittinesse to doe euill, gotten by much vse and great practise in matters.*
*Rom.13.7.
*Matth.22.23. marke 12.18.
5 The resurrection of the flesh is auouched against the Sadduces.
*Deut.25.5.
g *They are called here in this place, the children of this world, which liue in this world: and not they, that wholly are giuen to the world, as before chap. 16.8. which are contrarie to the children of light.*
h *That is, men partakers of the resurrection: for as we say truely that they shall liue in deed, which shall enioy euerlasting blisse, so doe they rise in deed, which rise to life, though if this word, resurrection, be taken generally, it belongeth also to the wicked, which shall rise to condemnation, which is not properly life, but death.*
*Exod.3.6.
i *That is, before him: a notable saying, the godly do not die, though they die here on earth.*

red, and said, Master, thou hast well said.
40 And after that, durst they not aske him
any thing at all.

* Matth. 22. 44. marke 12. 35.
5 Christ is so the sonne of Dauid according to the flesh, that he is also his Lorde (because he is the euerlasting Sonne of God) according to the spirit.
* Psal. 110. 1.

41 * [5] Then said hee vnto them, How say
they that Christ is Dauids sonne?
42 And Dauid himselfe sayth in the booke
of the Psalmes, * The Lord said vnto my Lord,
Sit at my right hand,
43 Till I shal make thine enemies thy footstoole.
44 Seeing Dauid called him Lord, how is
he then his sonne?

* Chap. 11. 43. matth. 23. 6. marke 12. 38.
6 We must auoid the example of the ambitious and couetous pastours.
k This is spoken by the figure Metonymie, houses, for the goods and substance.

45 ¶ Then in the audience of all the people he said vnto his disciples,
46 * [6] Beware of the Scribes, which willingly go in long robes, and loue salutations in the
markets, and the highest seates in the assemblies, and the chiefe roomes at feasts:
47 Which deuoure widowes [k] houses, and
in shew make long prayers: these shall receiue
greater damnation.

CHAP. XXI.

1 The widowes liberalitie aboue her riches. 5 Of the time of the destruction of the Temple, 19 and Hierusalem. 25 The signes going before the last iudgement.

* Marke 12. 42.
1 The poore may exceed in bountie and liberalitie, euen the richest, according to Gods iudgement.

AND * [1] as he beheld, he saw the rich men,
which cast their gifts into the treasurie.
2 And he saw also a certaine poore widow
which cast in thither two mites:
3 And he said, Of a trueth I say vnto you,
that this poore widow hath cast in more then
they all.
4 For they all haue of their superfluitie
cast into the offerings of God: but shee of her
penurie hath cast in all the liuing that she had.

* Chap. 19. 43. matth. 24. 1. marke 13. 1.
2 The destruction of the Temple is foretold, that that true spirituall building may be built vp, whose head builders must and ought to be circumspect.
a These were things that were hanged vpon wals and pillars.
* Ephes. 5. 6. 2. thess. 2. 3.
b Vsing my Name.

5 * [2] Now as some spake of the Temple,
how it was garnished with goodly stones, and
with [a] consecrate things, he said,
6 Are these the things that ye looke vpon?
the dayes will come wherein a stone shall not
be left vpon a stone, that shall not be throwen
downe.
7 Then they asked him, saying, Master,
but when shal these things be? and what signe
shall there *be* when these things shall come to
passe?
8 * And he said, Take heed, that ye be not
deceiued: for many will come [b] in my Name,
saying, I am *Christ*, and the time draweth nere:
follow ye not them therefore.

3 The true Temple of God is built vp euen in the middest of incredible tumults, and most sharpe miseries, through inuincible patience, so that the ende thereof cannot be but most happie.
* Mat. 24. 7. marke 13. 8.

9 [3] And when ye heare of warres and seditions, be not afraid: for these things must first
come, but the end followeth not by and by.
10 Then said hee vnto them, Nation shall
rise against nation, and kingdome against kingdome,
11 * And great earthquakes shall be in diuers places, and hunger, and pestilence, and
fearefull things, and great signes shall there be
from heauen.
12 But before all these, they shall lay their
handes on you, and persecute *you*, deliuering
you vp to the assemblies, and into prisons, and
bring you before Kings and rulers for my
Names sake.
13 And this shall turne to you, for [c] a testimoniall.

c This shalbe the end of your troubles and afflictions, they shalbe witnesses both before God and man as well of the treacherous and cruell dealing of your enemies, as also of your constancie: A noble saying, that the afflictions of the godly and holy men pertaine to the witnesse of the trueth.
* Chap. 12. 12. matth. 10. 19. marke 13. 11.
* Matth. 10. 30.
d Though you are compassed about on all sides with many miseries, yet notwithstanding be valiant and couragious, and beare out these things manfully.
* Dan. 9. 27. matt. 24. 15. marke 13. 14.
4 The finall destruction of the whole citie is foretolde.

14 * Lay it vp therefore in your hearts, that
ye cast not before hand, what ye shall answere.
15 For I will giue you a mouth, and wisedome, where against all your aduersaries shall
not be able to speake, nor resist.
16 Yea, ye shalbe betrayed also of your parents, and of your brethren, and kinsemen, and
friends, and *some* of you shal they put to death.
17 And ye shall be hated of all men for my
Names sake.
18 * Yet there shall not one haire of your
heads perish.
19 By your patience [d] possesse your soules.
20 ¶ * [4] And when yee see Hierusalem besieged with souldiers, then vnderstand that the
desolation thereof is neere.
21 Then let them which are in Iudea, flee
to the mountaines: and let them which are in
the mids thereof, depart out: and let not them
that are in the countrey, enter therein.
22 For these be the dayes of vengeance, to
fulfill all things that are written.
23 But woe *be* to them that be with childe,
and to them that giue sucke in those dayes: for
there shall be great distresse in this land, and
[e] wrath ouer this people.
24 And they shall fall on the [f] edge of the
sword, and shall be led captiue into all nations,
and Hierusalem shall be troden vnder foote of
the Gentiles, vntill the time of the Gentiles be
fulfilled.

e By wrath those things are meant, which God sendeth when he is displeased.
f Word for word, mouth: for the Hebrewes call the edge of a sword, the mouth, because the edge biteth.
* Isa. 13. 10. ezek. 32. 7. matt. 24. 29. mar. 13. 24.
g When the times are expired, appointed for the saluation of the Gentiles, and punishment of the Iewes: And so he passeth from the destruction of Hierusalem, to the history of the latter iudgement.
5 After diuers tempests, the Lord wil at the length plainely appeare to deliuer his Church.
* Rom. 8. 27.
6 We must be sober and watchful both day and night for the Lords comming, that we be not taken at vnwares.

25 * [g] Then there shalbe signes in the sunne,
and in the moone, and in the starres, and vpon
the earth trouble among the nations with perplexitie: the sea and the waters shall roare.
26 [5] And mens hearts shall faile them for
feare, and for looking after those things which
shall come on the world: for the powers of
heauen shall be shaken.
27 And then shall they see the Sonne of
man come in a cloud, with power and great
glory.
28 And when these things begin to come
to passe, then looke vp, and lift vp your heads:
* for your redemption draweth neere.
29 [6] And hee spake to them a parable, Behold, the figge tree, and all trees,
30 When they now shoote foorth, ye seeing them, know of your owne selues, that summer is then neere.
31 So likewise ye, when ye see these things
come to passe, know yee that the kingdome of
God is neere.
32 Verely I say vnto you, This age shall not
passe, till all *these* things be done:
33 Heauen and earth shall passe away, but
my words shall not passe away.
34 * Take heede to your selues, lest at any
time your hearts be oppressed with surfetting
and

* Rom. 13. 13.

and drunkennesse, and cares of this life, and
lest that day come on you at vnwares.
35 For as a snare shall it come [h] on all them
that dwell on the face of the whole earth.
36 Watch therefore, and pray continually, that yee may bee counted worthy to escape all these things that shall come to passe,
and that yee may [i] stand before the Sonne of
man.
37 ¶ Now in the day time hee taught in
the Temple, and at night he went out, and a-
bode in the mount that is called *the mount* of
Oliues.
38 And all the people came in the morning to him, to heare him in the Temple.

h On all men wheresoeuer they be.

i You may so appeare, that you will abide the countenance and sentence of the Iudge without feare.

CHAP. XXII.

3 Iudas selleth Christ. 7 The Apostles prepare the Passe-ouer. 24 They striue who shall bee chiefest. 31 Satan desireth them. 35 Christ sheweth that they wanted nothing. 42 Hee prayeth in the mount. 44 Hee sweateth blood 50 Malchus eare cut off and healed. 57. 58. 60. Peter denyeth Christ thrise. 63 Christ is mocked and stroken. 69 He confesseth himselfe to be the Sonne of God.

NOwe * the [1] feast of vnleauened bread
drew nere, which is called the Passeouer.
2 And the high Priests and Scribes sought
how they might kill him: for they feared the
people.
3 * [2] Then entred Satan into Iudas, who
was called Iscariot, and was of the number of
the twelue.
4 And hee went his way, and communed
with the high Priests and [a] captaines, how hee
might betray him to them.
5 So they were glad, and agreed to giue
him money.
6 And he consented and sought opportunitie to betray him vnto them, when the people were [b] away.
7 ¶ * [3] Then came the day of vnleauened bread, when the Passeouer [c] must bee sacrificed.
8 And hee sent Peter and Iohn, saying,
Goe and prepare vs the [d] Passeouer, that wee
may eate it.
9 And they said vnto him, Where wilt
thou, that we prepare *it?*
10 Then he said vnto them, Behold, when
yee be entred into the citie, there shall a man
meete you, bearing a pitcher of water: follow
him into the house that he entreth in,
11 And say vnto the good man of the house,
The Master sayth vnto thee, where is the lodging where I shall eate my Passeouer with my
disciples?
12 Then hee shall shewe you a great high
chamber trimmed: there make it readie.
13 So they went, and found as hee had said
vnto them, and made readie the Passeouer.
14 * [4] And when the [e] houre was come,
hee sate downe, and the twelue Apostles with
him.
15 Then he said vnto them, I haue earnestly desired to eate this Passeouer with you, before I [f] suffer.
16 For I say vnto you, Henceforth I will
not eate of it any more, vntill it be fulfilled in
the kingdome of God.
17 And he tooke the cup, and gaue thanks,
and sayde, Take this, and diuide it among
you,
18 For I say vnto you, I will not drinke
of the fruite of the vine, vntill the kingdome
of God be come.
19 * [5] And hee tooke bread, and when hee
had giuen thankes, hee brake it, and gaue to
them, saying, This is my body, which is giuen
for you: doe this in remembrance of me.
20 Likewise also after supper *he tooke* the
cup, saying, This [g] cup *is* [h] that new Testament
in my blood, which is shed for you.
21 * [6] Yet behold, the [i] hand of him that
betrayeth me, is with me at the table.
22 [7] And truely the Sonne of man goeth as
it is appointed: but woe *be* to that man, by
whom he is betrayed.
23 Then they began to enquire among
themselues which of them it should be, that
should doe that.
24 ¶ * [8] And there arose also a strife among
them, which of them should seeme to be the
greatest.
25 But he said vnto them, The Kings of the
Gentiles reigne ouer them, and they that beare
rule ouer them, are called [k] bountifull.
26 But ye *shall* not *be* so: but let the greatest among you be as the least: and the chiefest
as he that serueth.
27 For who is greater, hee that sitteth at
table, or hee that serueth? Is not hee that sitteth at table? And I am among you as hee that
serueth.
28 [9] And ye are they which haue continued
with me in my tentations.
29 Therefore I appoint vnto you a kingdome, as my Father hath appointed vnto me,
30 * That yee may eate and drinke at my
table in my kingdome, and sit on seates, and
iudge the twelue tribes of Israel.
31 ¶ [10] And the Lord said, Simon, Simon,
behold, * Satan hath desired you, [l] to winow
you as wheate.
32 [11] But I haue prayed for thee, that thy
faith faile not: therefore when thou art conuerted, strengthen thy brethren.
33 * [12] And hee said vnto him, Lord, I am
readie to goe with thee into prison, and to
death.
34 But hee said, I tell thee Peter, the cocke

* Matth. 26. 1. marke 14. 1.
1 Christ is taken vpon the day of the Passeouer, rather by the prouidence of his Father, then by the will of men.
* Matth. 26. 14. marke 14. 10.
2 God by his wonderfull prouidence, causeth him to be the minister of our saluation, who was the authour of our destruction.
a They that had the charge of keeping the Temple, which were none of the Priests and Bishops, as appeareth by the 52. vers. of this Chap.
b Without tumult, vnwitting to the people which vsed to follow him: and therefore in deed they watched their time, when they knew he was alone in the garden.
* Mat. 26. 17. marke 14. 13.
3 Christ teacheth his disciples by a manifest miracle, that although he be going to be crucified, yet nothing is hidde from him: and therefore that he goeth willingly to death.
c By the order appointed by the Law.
d The lambe which was the figure of the Passeouer: And this is spoken by the figure Metonymie, which is very vsuall in the matter of the Sacraments. * Matth. 26. 20. marke 14. 17. 4 Christ hauing ended the Passeouer according to the order of the Law, forewarneth them that this shall be his last banket with them, after the maner and necessitie of this life. *e The euening and twilight, at what time this supper was to be kept.*

f I am put to death.
* Matth. 26. 26. marke 14. 22. 1. cor. 11. 24.
5 Christ establisheth his newe Couenant, and his communicating with vs with new signes.
g Here is a double Metonymie: for first the vessell is taken for that which is conteined in the vessell, as the cup, for the wine, which is within the cuppe. Then the wine is called the Couenant or Testament, whereas indeed it is but the signe of the Testament, or rather of the blood of Christ, whereby the Testament was made: neither is it a vaine signe, although it be not all one with the thing that it representeth
h This word, that, sheweth the excellencie of the Testament, and answereth to the place of Ieremie, Chap. 31. 31. where the newe Testament is promised.
* Matth. 26. 21. marke 14. 18. psalm. 41. 9.
6 Christ sheweth againe that hee goeth to death willingly, although he be not ignorant of Iudas treason.
i That is, his practise, so vse the Ebrewes to speake, as 2. King. 14. 19. Is not the hand of Ioab in this matter?
7 Although the decree of Gods prouidẽce come necessarily to passe, yet it excuseth not the fault of the instruments.
* Mat. 20. 25. marke 10. 42.
8 The Pastours are not called to rule but to serue.
k Haue great titles, for so it was the custome to honour Princes with some great titles.
9 Such as are partakers of the afflictions of Christ shall also be partakers of his kingdome.
* Mat. 19. 28.
10 We must alwayes thinke vpon the wait that Satan layeth for vs.

* 1. Pet. 5. 8. *l To tosse you and scatter you, and also to cast you out.* 11 It is through the prayers of Christ, that the elect doe neuer vtterly fall away from the faith: and that for this cause, that they should stirre vp one another. * Matt. 26. 34. mark. 1. 39. iohn 13. 38. 12 Christ sheweth that faith differeth much from a vaine securitie, in setting before vs the grieuous example of Peter.

shall

ſhall not crow this day, before thou haſt thrice denyed that thou kneweſt me.

35 ¶ And hee ſayd vnto them, * When I ſent you without bagge, and ſcrippe, and ſhooes, lacked yee any thing? And they ſaid, Nothing.

36 [m] Then hee ſaid to them, But now hee that hath a bagge, let him take it, and likewiſe a ſcrip: and hee that hath none, let him ſell his coate, and buy a ſword.

37 For I ſay vnto you, That yet the ſame which is written, muſt be performed in mee, * Euen with the wicked was he numbred: for doubtleſſe thoſe things which *are written* of me, haue an end.

38 And they ſaid, Lord, behold, here are two ſwords. And hee ſaid vnto them, It is enough.

39 ¶ * And he came out, and went (as hee was woont) to the mount of Oliues: and his diſciples alſo followed him.

40 * [13] And when hee came to the place, hee ſayd to them, Pray, leſt yee enter into tentation.

41 [14] And he was drawen aſide from them about a ſtones caſt, and kneeled downe, and prayed,

42 Saying, Father, if thou wilt, take away this cup from me: neuertheleſſe, not my will, but thine be done.

43 And there appeared an Angel vnto him from heauen, comforting him.

44 But being in an [n] agonie, hee prayed more earneſtly: and his ſweate was like [o] drops of blood, trickling downe to the ground.

45 [15] And he roſe vp from prayer, and came to *his* diſciples, and found them ſleeping for heauineſſe.

46 And he ſaid vnto them, Why ſleepe ye? riſe and pray, leſt ye enter into tentation.

47 ¶ * [16] And while hee yet ſpake, Behold a company, and he that was called Iudas one of the twelue, went before them, and came neere vnto Ieſus to kiſſe him.

48 And Ieſus ſaid vnto him, Iudas, betrayeſt thou the Sonne of man with a kiſſe?

49 [17] Now when they which were about him, ſawe what would follow, they ſayd vnto him, Lord, ſhall we ſmite with ſword?

50 And one of them ſmote a ſeruant of the hie Prieſt, and ſtrooke off his eare.

51 Then Ieſus anſwered, and ſaid, Suffer *them* thus farre: and hee touched his eare, and healed him.

52 [18] Then Ieſus ſaid vnto the high Prieſts, and captaines of the Temple, and the Elders which were come to him, Be ye come out as

** Matth. 10.9.*

m All this talke is by way of an allegorie, as if hee ſaid, O my friends and fellow ſouldiours, you haue liued hitherto as it were in peace: but now there is a moſt ſharpe battell at hand to be fought, and therefore you muſt lay all other things aſide, and thinke vpon furniſhing your ſelues in armour. And what this armour is, he ſhewed by his owne example, when he prayed afterward in the garden, and reprooued Peter for ſtriking with the ſword.

** Eſai 53.12.*

** Matth. 26 36. marke 14.32. iohn 18.1.*

** Matt. 26.41. marke 14.38.*

13 Chriſt hath made death acceptable vnto vs, by ouercomming in our name, all the horrors of death which had ioyned with them, the curſe of God.

14 Prayers are a ſure ſuccour againſt the moſt perillous aſſaults of our enemies.

n This agonie ſheweth that Chriſt ſtroue much, and was in great diſtreſſe: for Chriſt ſtroue not onely with the feares of death, as other men vſe to doe, for ſo many Martyrs might ſeeme more conſtant then Chriſt, but with the fearefull iudgement of his angry Father, which is the fearefulleſt thing in the world: and the matter was for that hee tooke the burden of all our ſinnes vpon himſelfe.

o Theſe doe not onely ſhewe that Chriſt was true man, but other things alſo which the godly haue to conſider of, wherein the ſecret of the redemption of all mankinde is conteined in the Sonne of God his debaſing himſelfe to the ſtate of a ſeruant: ſuch things, as no man can ſufficiently declare. 15 Men are vtterly ſluggiſh, euen in their greateſt dangers, vntill Chriſt ſtirre them vp. * *Matth. 26. 47. marke 14.43. iohn 18.3.* 16 Chriſt is willingly betrayed and taken, that by his obedience hee might deliuer vs, which were guiltie for the betraying of Gods glorie. 17 That zeale which carieth vs out of the bounds of our vocation, pleaſeth not Chriſt. 18 Euen the very feare of them which tooke Chriſt, prooueth partly their euill conſcience, and partly alſo that all theſe things were done by Gods prouidence.

vnto a thiefe with ſwords and ſtaues?

53 When I was daily with you in the Temple, yee ſtretched not foorth the hands againſt me: but this is your very houre, and the [p] power of darkeneſſe.

54 ¶ * Then tooke they him, and led him, and brought him to the high Prieſts houſe. [19] And Peter followed afarre off.

55 * And when they had kindled a fire in the middes of the hall, and were ſet downe together, Peter alſo ſate downe among them.

56 And a certaine maid beheld him as hee ſate by the fire, and hauing wel looked on him, ſaid, This man was alſo with him.

57 But hee denied him, ſaying, Woman, I know him not.

58 And after a little while, another man ſawe him, and ſaid, Thou art alſo of them. But Peter ſaid, Man, I am not.

59 And about the ſpace of an houre after, a certaine other affirmed, ſaying, Verely euen this man was with him: for hee is alſo a Galilean.

60 And Peter ſaid, Man, I know not what thou ſayeſt. And immediatly while hee yet ſpake, the cocke crewe.

61 Then the Lord turned backe, and looked vpon Peter, and Peter remembred the word of the Lord, how he had ſaid vnto him, * Before the cocke crowe, thou ſhalt denie me thrice.

62 And Peter went out, and wept bitterly.

63 ¶ [20] * And the men that helde Ieſus, mocked him, and ſtroke him.

64 And when they had blindfolded him, they ſmote him on the face, and asked him, ſaying, Prophecie who it is that ſmote thee.

65 And many other things blaſphemouſly ſpake they againſt him.

66 * [21] And aſſoone as it was day, the Elders of the people, and the hie Prieſts and the Scribes came together, and led him into their councill,

67 Saying, Art thou that Chriſt? tell vs. And he ſaid vnto them, If I tell you, yee will not beleeue it.

68 And if alſo I aske you, you will not anſwere me, nor let me goe.

69 Hereafter ſhall the Sonne of man ſit at the right hand of the power of God.

70 Then ſayd they all, Art thou then the ſonne of God? And he ſaid to them, Yee ſay, that I am.

71 Then ſaid they, What neede wee any further witneſſe? for we our ſelues haue heard it of his owne mouth.

p The power that was giuen to darkeneſſe to oppreſſe the light for a ſeaſon.

** Mat. 26.58.*

19 We haue to behold in Peter an example both of the fragilitie of mans nature, and of the ſingular goodneſſe of God towards his elect.

** Mat. 26.58, 69. marke 14.66. iohn 18.25.*

** Mat. 26.34. iohn 13.38.*

20 Chriſt bare the ſhame that was due to our ſinnes.

** Mat. 26.67. marke 14.65.*

** Matth. 27.1. marke 15.1. iohn 18.28.*

21 Chriſt is wrongfully condemned of blaſphemie before the hie Prieſts iudgement ſeate, that we might be quit before God from the blaſphemie which we deſerued.

CHAP. XXIII.

1 Hee is accuſed before Pilate. 7 He is ſent to Herode, 11 He is mocked. 24 Pilate yeeldeth him vp to the Iewes requeſt. 27 The women bewaile him. 33 He is crucified. 39 One of the theeues reuileth him: 43 The other is ſaued by faith. 45 He dyeth. 53 He is buried.

Then

1 Christ, who is now ready to suffer for the sedition which we raised in this world, is first of all pronounced guiltlesse, that it might appeare that he suffered not for his owne sinnes (which were none) but for ours.

THen [1] the whole multitude of them arose, and led him vnto Pilate.

2 And they began to accuse him, saying, Wee haue found this man [a] peruerting the nation, * and forbidding to pay tribute to Cesar, saying, That he is Christ a King.

a Corrupting the people, and leading them into errours.

* Matt.22.21. marke 12.17.

3 * And Pilate asked him, saying, Art thou the King of the Iewes? And he answered him, and said, Thou sayest it.

* Matt.27.11. marke 15.2. iohn 18.33.

4 Then said Pilate to the high Priests, and to the people, I finde no fault in this man.

5 But they were the more fierce, saying, Hee mooueth the people, teaching throughout all Iudea, beginning at Galile, euen to this place.

2 Christ is a laughing stocke to Princes, but to their great smart.

6 [2] Now when Pilate heard of Galile, hee asked whether the man were a Galilean.

7 And when hee knewe that hee was of [b] Herodes iurisdiction, hee sent him to Herod, which was also at Hierusalem in those dayes.

b This was Herod Antipas the Tetrarch, in the time of whose gouernance, which was almost the space of 22 yeeres, Iohn the Baptist preached and was put to death, and Iesus Christ also died and rose againe, and the Apostles began to preach, and diuers things were done at Hierusalem almost seuen yeeres after Christs death. This Herod was sent into banishment to Lyons, about the second yeere of Caius Cesar.

8 And when Herod saw Iesus, he was exceedingly glad : for he was desirous to see him of a long season, because he had heard many things of him, and trusted to haue seene some signe done by him.

9 Then questioned he with him of many things : but he answered him nothing.

10 The high Priests also and Scribes stood foorth, and accused him vehemently.

11 And Herod with his [c] men of warre, despised him, and mocked him, & arayed him in white, and sent him againe to Pilate.

c Accompanied with his Nobles and soldiers which followed him from Galile.

12 [3] And the same day Pilate and Herode were made friends together : for before they were enemies one to another.

3 The hatred of godinesse ioyneth the wicked together.

13 ¶ [4] Then Pilate called together the hie Priests and the [d] rulers, and the people,

4 Christ is quit the second time, euen of him, of whom he is condemned, that it might appeare, how he being iust, redeemed vs which were vniust.

d Those whom the Iewes called the Sanhedrin.

14 * And said vnto them, Ye haue brought this man vnto mee, as one that peruerted the people : and behold, I haue examined him before you, and haue found no fault in this man, of those things whereof ye accuse him :

* Matt.27.23. marke 15.14. iohn 18.34.

15 No, nor yet Herod : for I sent you to him : and loe, nothing worthy of death is done of him.

16 [5] I will therefore chastise him, and let him loose.

5 The wisdome of the flesh, of two euils chuseth the lesse, but God curseth such counsels.

17 (For of necessitie hee must haue let one loose vnto them at the feast.)

18 Then all the multitude cryed at once, saying, Away with him, and deliuer vnto vs Barabbas :

19 Which for a certaine insurrection made in the citie, and murther, was cast in prison.

20 Then Pilate spake againe to them, willing to let Iesus loose.

21 But they cryed, saying, Crucifie, crucifie him.

22 [6] And he said vnto them the third time, But what euill hath hee done? I finde no cause of death in him : I will therefore chastise him, and let him loose.

6 Christ is quit the third time, before he was cōdemned once, that it might appeare, how that our sinnes were condemned in him.

23 But they were instant with loud voices, and required that hee might be crucified : and the voices of them and of the high Priests preuailed.

24 So Pilate gaue sentence, that it should be as they required.

25 And he let loose vnto them him that for insurrection and murther was cast into prison, whom they desired, and deliuered Iesus to doe with him what they would.

26 ¶ * [7] And as they ledde him away, they caught one Simon of Cyrene, comming out of the field, and on him they laid the crosse, to beare it after Iesus.

* Matth.27.32. marke 15.21.

7 An example of the outragiousnesse and disorder of soldiers.

27 [8] And there followed him a great multitude of people, and of women, which women bewailed and lamented him.

8 The triumph of the wicked hath a most horrible end.

28 But Iesus turned backe vnto them, and said, Daughters of Hierusalem, weepe not for me, but weepe for your selues, and for your children.

29 For behold, the dayes will come, when men shall say, Blessed *are* the barren, and the wombes that neuer bare, and the paps which neuer gaue sucke.

30 Then shall they beginne to say to the mountaines, * Fall on vs, and to the hilles, Couer vs.

* Isa 2.19. hose. 10.8. reuel.6.16.

31 * For if they do these things to a [e] greene tree, what shall be done to the drie?

* 1.Pet.4.17.

e As if he said, If they doe thus to me that am fruitfull and alwayes flourishing, and who liue for euer by reason of my Godhead, what will they doe to you, that are vnfruitfull and void of all liuely righteousnesse?

32 * And there were two others, which were euill doers, ledde with him to be slaine.

* Matth.27.38. marke 15.27. iohn 19.18.

33 [9] And when they were come to the place, which is called Caluarie, there they crucified him, and the euill doers : one at the right hand, and the other at the left.

9 Christ became accursed for vs vpon the crosse, suffering the punishment which they deserued that would be Gods.

34 [10] Then said Iesus, Father, forgiue them : for they know not what they doe. And they parted his raiment and cast lots.

10 Christ in praying for his enemies, sheweth that hee is both the Sacrifice & the Priest.

35 And the people stood, and beheld : and the rulers mocked him with them, saying, Hee saued others : let him saue himselfe, if he be that Christ, the [f] Chosen of God.

f Whom God loueth more then all other.

36 The souldiours also mocked him, and came and offered him vineger,

37 And said, If thou bee the King of the Iewes, saue thy selfe.

38 [11] And a superscription was also written ouer him, in Greeke letters, and in Latine, and in Ebrew, THIS IS THAT KING OF THE IEVVES.

11 Pilate at vnwares is made a preacher of the kingdome of Christ.

39 ¶ [g] And [12] one of the euill doers, which were hanged, railed on him, saying, If thou be that Christ, saue thy selfe and vs.

g Therefore either we must take that spoken by Synecdoche, which Matthew sayth, or that both of them mocked Christ. But one of them at the length overcome with the great patience of God, brake forth into that confession worthy all memorie.

12 Christ in the middest of the humbling of himselfe vpon the crosse, sheweth in deed that he hath both power of life to saue the beleeuers, & of death to reuenge the rebellious.

40 But the other answered, and rebuked him, saying, Fearest thou not God, seeing thou art in the same condemnation?

41 Wee are in deede righteously *here* : for wee receiue things worthy of that wee haue done : but this man hath done nothing [h] amisse.

h More then hee ought.

42 And hee said vnto Iesus, Lord, remember mee, when thou commest into thy kingdome.

43 Then

43 Then Ieſus ſaid vnto him, Verely I ſay
vnto thee, to day ſhalt thou be with me in [i] Paradiſe.

44 ¶ [13] And it was about the ſixt houre:
and there was a darkeneſſe ouer all the land,
vntill the ninth houre.

45 [14] And the Sunne was darkened, and
the vaile of the Temple rent thorow the
middes.

46 And Ieſus cryed with a loud voice, and
ſaid, * Father, into thine hands I commend
my ſpirit. And when he thus had ſaid, he gaue
vp the ghoſt.

47 ¶ [15] Now when the Centurion ſaw what
was done, he glorified God, ſaying, Of a ſuretie this man was iuſt.

48 And all the people that came together
to that ſight, beholding the things which were
done, ſmote their breaſts, and returned.

49 [16] And all his acquaintance ſtood afarre
off, and the women that followed him from
Galile, beholding theſe things.

50 ¶ * [17] And behold, there was a man named Ioſeph, which was a counſeller, a good
man and a iuſt.

51 He did not conſent to the counſell and
deede of them, *which was* of Arimathea, a citie
of the Iewes: who alſo himſelfe waited for the
kingdome of God.

52 He went vnto Pilate, and asked the bodie of Ieſus,

53 And tooke it downe, and wrapped it in
a linnen cloth, and laide it in a tombe hewen
out of a rocke, wherein was neuer man yet
layd.

54 And that day was the Preparation, and
the Sabbath [k] drew on.

55 [18] And the women alſo that followed
after, which came with him from Galile, beheld the ſepulchre, and how his body was laid.

56 And they returned, and prepared odors,
and ointments, and reſted the Sabbath *day* according to the commandement.

i God made the viſible paradiſe in the Eaſt part of the world: but that which wee behold with the eyes of our minde is the place of euerlaſting ioy and ſaluation, through the goodneſſe and mercie of God, a moſt pleaſant reſt of the ſoules of the godly, and moſt quiet and ioyfull dwelling.

13 Chriſt being euen at the point of death, ſheweth himſelfe to bee God Almightie euen to the blinde.

14 Chriſt entreth ſtoutly into the very darkeneſſe of death, for to ouercome death euen within his moſt ſecret places.

* *Pſal. 31.6.*

15 Chriſt cauſeth his very enemies to giue honourable witneſſe on his ſide, ſo oft as it pleaſeth him.

16 Chriſt gathereth together, and defendeth his little flocke, in the midſt of the tormentours.

* *Matth. 27.57. marke 15.43. iohn 19.38.*

17 Chriſt thorow his famous buriall, confirmeth the trueth both of his death, and reſurrection, by the plaine and euident witneſſe of Pilate.

k Word for word, dawning, and now beginning: for the light of the former day drew toward the going downe, and that was the day of preparation for the Feaſt, which was to bee kept the day following. 18 Chriſt being ſet vpon by the deuill and all his inſtruments, and being euen in deaths mouth, ſetteth weake women in his fore-ward, minding ſtraightway to triumph ouer theſe terrible enemies, without any great endeauour.

CHAP. XXIIII.

1 The women come to the ſepulchre. 9 They report that which they heard of the Angels, vnto the Apoſtles. 13 Chriſt doeth accompany two going to Emmaus. 27 Hee expoundeth the Scriptures vnto them. 39 Hee offereth himſelfe to his Apoſtles to be handled. 49 Hee promiſeth the holy Ghoſt. 51 He is caried vp into heauen.

NOw the * [1] firſt *day* of the weeke [a] early
in the morning, they came to the ſepulchre, and brought the odours, which they had
prepared, and certaine *women* with them.

2 And they found the ſtone rolled away
from the ſepulchre,

* *Marke 16.1. iohn 20.1.*

1 Poore ſilly women euen beſide their expectation are choſen to be the firſt witneſſes of the reſurrection, that there might bee no ſuſpition either of deceit or violence. *a Verie earely, as Marke ſayth: or as Iohn ſayth, while it was yet darke, that is, when it was yet ſcarce the dawning of the day.*

3 And went in, but found not the body of
the Lord Ieſus.

4 And it came to paſſe, that as they were
amazed thereat, behold, two men ſuddenly
ſtood by them in ſhining veſtures.

5 And as they were afraid, and bowed
downe their faces to the earth, they ſayd to
them, Why ſeeke yee him that liueth, among
the dead?

6 He is not here, but is riſen: remember
* how he ſpake vnto you, when hee was yet in
Galile,

7 Saying, that the Sonne of man muſt be
deliuered into the hands of ſinfull men, and be
crucified, and the third day riſe againe.

8 And they remembred his words,

9 [2] And returned from the Sepulchre, and
tolde all theſe things vnto the eleuen, and to
all the remnant.

10 Now it was Mary Magdalene, and Ioanna, and Mary the *mother* of Iames, and other
women with them, which tolde theſe things
vnto the Apoſtles.

11 But their words ſeemed vnto them, as a
fained thing, neither beleeued they them.

12 * [3] Then aroſe Peter, and ranne vnto
the Sepulchre, and [b] looked in, and ſawe the
linen clothes laid by themſelues, and departed wondering in himſelfe at that which was
come to paſſe.

13 ¶ * [4] And behold, two of them went
that ſame day to a towne which was from Hieruſalem about threeſcore furlongs, called Emmaus.

14 And they talked together of all theſe
things that were done.

15 And it came to paſſe, as they communed together, and reaſoned, that Ieſus himſelfe
drew neere, and went with them.

16 [c] But their eyes were holden, that they
could not know him.

17 And he ſaid vnto them, What manner
of communications are theſe that ye haue one
to another as ye walke and are ſad?

18 And [d] the one (named Cleopas) anſwered, and ſaid vnto him, Art thou onely a ſtranger in Hieruſalem, and haſt not knowen the
things that are come to paſſe therein in theſe
dayes?

19 And hee ſaid vnto them, What things?
And they ſaid vnto him, Of Ieſus of Nazareth, which was a Prophet, mightie in deede
and in word before God, and all people,

20 [5] And how the hie Prieſts, and our rulers deliuered him to be condemned to death,
and haue crucified him.

21 But we truſted that it had beene he that
ſhould haue deliuered Iſrael, and as touching
all theſe things, to day is the third day, that
they were done.

* *Chap. 9.22. mat. 17.23. marke 9.31.*

2 The cowardly and daſtardly minde of the diſciples is vpbraided by the ſtout courage of women (ſo wrought by Gods great mercies) to ſhewe that the kingdome of God conſiſteth in an extraordinarie power.

* *Iohn 20.6.*

3 Chriſt vſeth the incredulitie of his diſciples, to the fuller ſetting forth of the trueth of his reſurrection, leaſt they ſhould ſeeme to haue beleeued that too lightly, which they preached afterward to all the world.

b As it were holding downe his head, and bowing his necke, looked diligently in.

* *Marke 16.12.*

4 The reſurrection is prooued by two other witneſſes, which ſaw it, and that it was no forged thing framed of purpoſe in their owne braines, all the circumſtances doe declare.

c Were holden backe and ſtayed, God ſo appointing it, no doubt: and therefore his body was not inuiſible, but their eyes were dimmed.

d Some of the olde fathers thinke that the other diſciple was this our Euangeliſt, but Epiphanius writing againſt the Saturnilians, ſayth it was Nathanael, but all theſe are vncertainties 5 It appeareth by the conferring of the forewarnings of the Prophets, that all thoſe things are true and certaine which the Euangeliſts haue put downe in writing of Chriſt.

22 Yea, and certaine women among vs
made vs aſtonied, which came earely vnto the
ſepulchre,
23 And when they found not his body, they
came, ſaying, that they had alſo ſeene a viſion
of Angels, which ſaid, that he was aliue.
24 Therefore certaine of them which were
with vs, went to the ſepulchre, and found it
euen ſo as the women had ſaid, but him they
ſaw not.
25 Then hee ſaid vnto them, O fooles and
ſlow of heart to beleeue all that the Prophets
haue ſpoken!
26 Ought not Chriſt to haue ſuffered theſe
things, and to enter into his glory?
27 And he began at Moſes, & at all the Prophets, & interpreted vnto them in all the Scriptures the things which were *written* of him.
28 And they drewe neere vnto the towne
which they went to, but he made as though he
would haue gone further.
29 But they conſtrained him, ſaying, Abide
with vs: for it is towards night, and the day is
farre ſpent. So he went in to tarie with them.
30 And it came to paſſe, as he ſate at table
with them: hee tooke the bread, and bleſſed,
and brake it, and gaue it to them.
31 Then their eyes were opened, and they
knew him: and he was[e] no more ſeene of them.
32 And they ſaid betweene themſelues,
Did not our hearts burne within vs, while hee
talked with vs by the way, and when hee opened to vs the Scriptures?
33 And they roſe vp the ſame houre, and returned to Hieruſalem, and found the eleuen gathered together, & them that were with them,
34 Which ſaid, The Lord is riſen in deede,
and hath appeared to Simon.
35 Then they told what things *were* done
in the way, and how he was knowen of them in
[f] breaking of bread.
36 ¶ * [6] And as they ſpake theſe things, Ieſus himſelfe ſtood in the mids of them, and ſaid
vnto them, Peace *be* to you.

e Suddenly taken away and therfore we may not imagine that he was there in ſuch a body as could not bee ſeene, but beleeue in deede that hee changed his place.
f When he brake bread, which that people vſed, as the Iewes vſe yet at this day at the beginning of their meales, and ſay a prayer.
* *Marke* 16.14. *iohn* 20 19.
6 The Lord himſelfe ſheweth by certaine and neceſſarie ſignes, that he was riſen againe, and that in the ſame body which he tooke vpon him.

37 But they were abaſhed and afraid, ſuppoſing that they had ſeene a ſpirit.
38 Then hee ſaid vnto them, Why are yee
troubled? and wherefore doe [g] doubts ariſe in
your hearts?
39 Behold mine hands and my feete: for it
is I my ſelfe: handle me, and ſee: for a ſpirit hath
not fleſh and bones, as yee ſee me haue.
40 And when he had thus ſpoken, he ſhewed them *his* hands and feete.
41 And while they yet beleeued not for ioy,
and wondered, hee ſaid vnto them, Haue yee
here any meate?
42 And they gaue him a piece of a broyled
fiſh, and of an hony combe.
43 And hee tooke it, and did eate before
them.
44 [7] And he ſaid vnto them, Theſe are the
words, which I ſpake vnto you while I was yet
with you, that all muſt bee fulfilled which are
written of me in the Law of Moſes, and in the
Prophets, and in the Pſalmes.
45 Then opened hee their vnderſtanding,
that they might vnderſtand the Scriptures,
46 And ſaid vnto them, Thus is it written,
and thus it behoued Chriſt to ſuffer, and to riſe
againe from the dead the third day,
47 And that repentance, and remiſſion of
ſinnes ſhould bee preached in his Name among
all nations, [h] beginning at Hieruſalem.
48 Now yee are witneſſes of theſe things.
49 And behold, I doe ſend the * promiſe of
my Father vpon you: but tarie yee in the citie
of Hieruſalem, [i] vntill ye be endued with power from on hie.
50 [8] Afterward he led them out into Bethania, and lift vp his hands, and bleſſed them.
51 And it came to paſſe, that as hee bleſſed
them, * he departed from them, and was caried vp into heauen.
52 And they worſhipped him, and returned to Hieruſalem with great ioy,
53 And were continually in the Temple,
praiſing, and lauding God, Amen.

g Diuers and doubtfull thoughts which fall oft into mens heads, when any ſtrange thing falleth out, whereof there is no great likelyhood.
7 The preaching of the Goſpel, which was promiſed to the Prophets, and performed in his time, is committed vnto the Apoſtles: the ſumme whereof is, Repentance and remiſſion of ſinnes.
h The Apoſtles who are the preachers of the Goſpel begiming at Hieruſalem.
* *Iohn* 15.26. *actes* 1.4.
i Vntill the holy Ghoſt come downe from heauen vpon you.
8 Chriſt aſcendeth into heauen, and departing bodily from his diſciples, filleth their hearts with the holy Ghoſt.
* *Marke* 16.19. *actes* 1.9.

THE HOLY GOSPEL OF IESVS CHRIST, ACCORDING TO IOHN.

CHAP. I.

1 That word begotten of God before all worlds, 2 and which was euer with the Father, 14 is made man. 6.7 For what end Iohn was sent from God: 16 His preaching of Christs office: 19. 20 The record that hee bare giuen out vnto the Priests. 40 The calling of Andrew, 41 of Peter, 43 Philip, 45 and Nathanael.

N [1] the [a] beginning [b] was
[c] that Word, and that Word
was [d] with God, and that
[e] Word was God.
2 This same was in the
beginning with God.
3 * [2] All [f] things were made by it, and
[g] without it [h] was made nothing that was made.
4 [i] In it [k] was life, and that life was [l] the
light of men.
5 [3] And that light shineth in the darknes,
and the darknesse [m] comprehended it not.
6 ¶ * [4] There was a man sent from God,
whose name *was* Iohn.
7 *This* same came for a witnesse, to beare
witnesse of that light, that all men [n] through
him might beleeue.
8 Hee was not [o] that light, but *was sent* to
beare witnesse of that light.
9 [5] This was [p] that true light, which ligh-
teth euery man that commeth into the world.
10 [q] He was in the world, and the world was
* made by him: and the world knew him not.
11 He came [r] vnto his owne, and his owne
receiued him not.
12 [6] But as many as receiued him, to them
he gaue [f] prerogatiue to be the sonnes of God,
euen to them that beleeue in his Name.

1 The Sonne of God is of one, and the selfe same eternitie or euerlastingnesse, and of one and the selfe same essence or nature with the Father.

a From the beginning, as the Euangelist saith, 1. Epistle 1.1 as though he said, that the Word began not then to haue his being, when God began to make all that was made: for the Word was euen then when all things that were made, began to be made, and therefore he was before the beginning of all things.

b Had his being.

c This word That, pointeth out vnto vs a peculiar and choise thing aboue all other, and putteth a difference betweene this Word, which is the Sonne of God, and the Lawes of God, which otherwise are also called the word of God.

13 Which are borne not of blood, nor of
the [t] will of the flesh, nor of the will of man,
but of God.
14 * [7] And that Word was made [u] flesh,
and [x] dwelt among vs, (and wee * sawe the
[y] glory thereof, [z] as the glory of the onely begotten *Sonne* of the Father) [a] full of grace and
trueth.
15 ¶ [8] Iohn bare witnesse of him, and cried,
saying, This was he of whom I said, Hee that
commeth [b] after me, was [c] before me: for hee
was better then I.
16 * [9] And of his fulnesse haue all wee receiued, and [d] grace for grace.
17 For the Law was giuen by Moses, but
grace, and trueth came by Iesus Christ.
18 [10] * No man hath seene God at any
time: that onely begotten Sonne, which is
in the [e] bosome of the Father, hee hath [f] declared him.
19 ¶ [11] Then this is the record of Iohn,
when the Iewes sent Priests and Leuites from
Hierusalem to aske him, Who art thou?
20 And he [g] confessed and [h] denied not, and
said plainely, I * am not that Christ.
21 And they asked him, What then? Art
thou Elias? And he said, [i] I am not. Art thou
[k] that Prophet? And he answered, No.
22 Then said they vnto him, Who art thou,
that we may giue an answere to them that sent
vs? What sayest thou of thy selfe.

t Of that grosse and corrupt nature of man, which is thorowout the Scripture, set as enemy to the spirit.

** Matth. 1.16.*

7 That sonne who is God from euerlasting tooke vpon him mans nature, that one and the selfe same might be both God and man, which manifestly appeared to many witnesses, that saw him, amongst whom he was conuersant, and vnto whom by sure & vndoubted arguments he shewed both his natures.

u That is, man: so that the part is taken for the whole, by the figure Synecdoche: for he tooke vpon him all our whole nature, that is to say, a true body, and a true soule.

x For a season, and when that was ended, he went vp into heauen: for the word which he vseth, is taken from tents: and yet notwithstanding, his absence from vs in body is not such, but that he is alwayes present with vs, though not in flesh, yet by the vertue of his spirit.

d This word With, pointeth out the distinction of persons to vs. *e This word (Word) is the first in order in the sentence, & is that which the learned call (Subiectum) and this word (God) is the latter in order, and the same which the learned call (predicatum)* ** Col. 1.16.* 2 The sonne of God declareth that same his euerlasting Godhead, both by the creating of all things, and also by the preseruing of them, and especially by the excellent gifts of reason and vnderstanding, wherewith hee hath beautified man aboue all other creatures. *f Paul expoundeth this place, Coloss 1.15. and 16 verses.* *g That is, as the Father did worke, so did the Sonne worke with him: for he was fellow worker with him.* *h Of all those things which were made, nothing was made without him.* *i That is, by him: and it is spoken after the maner of the Hebrewes, meaning thereby that by his force and working power, all life commeth to the world.* *k To wit, euen then, when all things are made by him, for else he would haue said, Life is in him, and not life was.* *l That force of reason and vnderstanding, which is kindled in our minds to acknowledge him, the authour of so great a benefit.* 3 The light of men is turned into darknesse, but yet so, that there is clearenesse enough to make them without excuse. *m They could not perceiue nor reach vnto it, to receiue any light of it, no, they did not so much as acknowledge him.* ** Matth. 3.1. marke 1.4. luke 3.1.* 4 There is another more full manifestation of the Sonne of God, to the consideration whereof men are in good time stirred vp, euen to Iohns voice, who is as it were the herault of Christ. *n Through Iohn.* *o That light which we spake of, to wit, Christ, who onely can lighten our darknesse.* 4 When as the Sonne of God saw, that men did not acknowledge him by his workes, although they were endued with vnderstanding (which he had giuen to them all) hee exhibited himselfe vnto his people to be seene of them with their corporall eyes: yet neither so did they acknowledge him, nor receiue him *p Who onely and properly deserueth to bee called the light, for he shineth of himselfe and boroweth light of none.* *q The person of the Word, was made manifest euen at that time when the world was made.* ** Heb. 11.3.* *r The Word shewed himselfe againe, when hee came in the flesh.* 6 The Sonne being shut out of the most of his people, and acknowledged but of a few, doeth regenerate them by his owne vertue and power, and receiueth them into that honour which is common to all the children of God, that is, to bee the sonnes of God. *f Hee vouchsafed to giue them this prerogatiue to take them to be his children.*

** Matth. 17.2. 2. pet 1.17.* *y The glory which he speaketh of here is that manifestation of Christ his maiestie, which was as it were laide open before our eyes, when the Sonne of God appeared in the flesh.* *z This word (as) doeth not in this place betoken a likelinesse, but the trueth of the matter, for his meaning is this, that wee saw such a glory, as beseemed and was meete for the true and onely begotten Sonne of God, who is Lord and King ouer all the world.* *a Hee was not onely a partaker of grace, and trueth, but was full of the very substance of grace and trueth.* 8 Iohn is a faithfull witnes of the excellencie of Christ. *b That is, He before whom I am sent to prepare him the way: so that these words are referred to the time of his calling, and not of his age, for Iohn was sixe moneths older then he.* *c This sentence hath in it a turning of the reason as we call it, as who should say, a setting of that first which should be last, and that last which should be first: for in plaine speech this it is, Hee that commeth after me, is better then I am, for he was before me. The like kind of turning the reason we find in Luke 7.47 Many sinnes are forgiuen her, because shee loued much, which is thus much to say, Shee loued much, because many sinnes are forgiuen her.* ** Colos. 1.19 and 29.* 9 Christ is the most plentifull fountaine of all goodnesse, but then hee powred out his gifts most bountifully, when as hee exhibited and shewed himselfe to the world. *d That is, grace vpon grace, as a man would say, graces heaped one vpon another.* 10 The true knowledge of God proceedeth onely from Iesus Christ. ** 1. Timo. 6. 16. 1. iohn 4 12.* *e Who is neerest to his father, not onely in respect of his loue towards him, but by the bond of nature, and for that vnion or onenesse that is betweene them, whereby the Father and the Sonne are one.* *f Reuealed him and shewed him vnto vs, whereas before hee was hid vnder the shadowes of the Law, so that the quicknesse of the sight of our minds was not able to perceiue him: for whosoeuer seeth him, seeth the Father also.* 11 Iohn is neither the Messias, nor like to any of the other Prophets, but is the herault of Christ who is now present. *g Hee did acknowledge him, and spake of him plainely and openly.* *h This rehearsing of the one and the selfe same thing, though in diuers words, is vsed much of the Hebrewes, and it hath great force, for they vse to speake one thing twise, to set it out more certainely and plainely.* ** Actes 13.25.* *i The Iewes thought that Elias should come againe before the dayes of Messias, and they tooke the ground of that their opinion out of Mala. 4.5. which place is to be vnderstood of Iohn, Matth. 11.14. And yet Iohn denieth that hee is Elias, answering them in deed according as they meant.* *k They inquire of some great Prophet, and not of Christ, for Iohn denied before that he is Christ, for they thought that some great Prophet should be sent like vnto Moses, wresting to that purpose that place of Deut. 18.15. which is to be vnderstood of all the companie of the Prophets and ministers, which haue beene and shall be to the end, and especially of Christ who is the head of all Prophets.*

23 Hee said, I am * the voice of him that
crieth in the wildernesse, Make straight the
way of the Lord, as said the Prophet Esaias.
24 [12] Now they which were sent, were of
the Pharisees.
25 And they asked him, and said vnto him,
[l] Why baptizest thou then, if thou be not that
Christ, neither Elias, nor that Prophet?
26 Iohn answered them, saying, I baptize
with water: but there is one [m] among you,
whom yee know not.
27 * He it is that commeth after me, which
was before mee, whose shoe latchet I am not
worthy to vnloose.
28 These things were done in Bethabara
beyond Iordan, where Iohn did baptize.
29 ¶ [13] The next day Iohn seeth Iesus comming vnto him, and saith, Behold [n] that Lambe
of God, which [o] taketh away the [p] sinne of the
world.
30 This is he of whom I said, After me commeth a man, which was before me: for hee was
better then I.
31 And [q] I knew him not: but because hee
should bee declared to Israel, therefore am I
come, baptizing with water.
32 [14] So Iohn bare record, saying, I beheld
* that Spirit come downe from heauen, like a
doue, and it abode vpon him,
33 And I knew him not: but hee that sent
me to baptize with water, he said vnto me, Vpon whom thou shalt see the Spirit come down,
and tarie still on him, that is hee which baptizeth with the holy Ghost.
34 And I saw, and bare record that this is
[r] that Sonne of God.
35 ¶ [15] The next day Iohn stood againe,
and two of his disciples.
36 [16] And he beheld Iesus walking by, and
said, Behold that Lambe of God.
37 [17] And the two disciples heard him
speake, and followed Iesus.
38 Then Iesus turned about, and saw them
follow, and said vnto them, What seeke yee?
And they said vnto him, Rabbi (which is to
say by interpretation, Master) [s] where dwellest thou?
39 Hee said vnto them, Come, and see.
They came and saw where hee dwelt, and a-
bode with him that day: for it was about the
[t] tenth houre.
40 Andrew, Simon Peters brother, was
one of the two which had heard it of Iohn, and
that followed him.
41 The same found his brother Simon first,
and said vnto him, We haue found that Messias,
which is by interpretation, that [u] Christ.

Isa 40.3. matth.3.3. luke 3.4.

12 Christ is the authour of baptisme, and not Iohn: and therefore the force thereof consisteth not in Iohn, who is the minister, but wholy in Christ the Lord.

l Hereby we may proue that the Iewes knew there should be some change in religion vnder Messias.

m Whom all the world seeth, and euen amongst you.

** Matth.3.11. marke 1.7 luk.3.16. actes 1.5. and 11.16. and 19.4.*

13 The body and trueth of all the sacrifices of the Law, to make satisfaction for the sinne of the world, is in Christ.

n This word (that) which is added, hath great force in it, not onely to set foorth the worthinesse of Christ, and so to separate him from the Lambe, which was a figure of him, and from all other sacrifices of the Law, but also to bring into our minds the Prophecies of Esai and others.

o This word of the present time, signifieth a continuall act, for the Lambe hath this vertue proper vnto him, and for euer to take away the sinnes of the world.

p That is, that roote of sinnes, to wit, our corruption, and so consequently the fruites of sinne, which are commonly called in the plural number, sinnes.

q I neuer knew him by face before.

14 Christ is proued to be the Sonne of God, by the comming downe of the holy Ghost, by the fathers voice, and by Iohns testimonie.

** Matth.3.16. marke 1.10. luke 3.22.*

r This word (That) pointeth out vnto vs some excellent thing, and maketh difference betweene Christ and other, whom Moses and the Prophets commonly call the sonnes of God, or the sonnes of the most High. 15 Iohn gathereth disciples not to himselfe, but to Christ. 16 Christ is set before vs to follow, not as a vaine shadow, but as our Mediatour. 17 In this first gathering of the disciples, we haue shewed vnto vs, that the beginning of saluation is from God, who calleth vs vnto his Sonne by the ministerie of his seruants: whom (so preuenting vs) we must also heare, and follow him home, that being instructed by him, wee may also instruct others. *s Where is thy lodging? t The night grewe on. u That is, annoynted, and king after the maner of the Iewish people.*

42 And he brought him to Iesus. And Iesus
beheld him, and said, Thou art Simon the sonne
of Iona: thou shalt bee called Cephas, which is
by interpretation, a stone.
43 ¶ The day following, Iesus would goe
into Galile, and found Philip, and said vnto
him, Follow me.
44 Now Philip was of Bethsaida, the citie
of Andrew and Peter.
45 [18] Philip found Nathanael, and sayd
vnto him, Wee haue found him of whome
* Moses did write in the Law, and the * Prophets, Iesus that sonne of Ioseph, that was of
Nazareth.
46 Then Nathanael said vnto him, Can there
any good thing come out of Nazareth? Philip
said to him, Come, and see.
47 [20] Iesus saw Nathanael comming to him,
and said of him, Behold indeede an Israelite, in
whom is no guile.
48 [21] Nathanael said vnto him, Whence
knewest thou mee? Iesus answered, and
sayd vnto him, Before that Philippe called
thee, when thou wast vnder the figge tree, I
saw thee.
49 Nathanael answered, and said vnto him,
Rabbi, thou art that Sonne of God: thou art
that King of Israel.
50 Iesus answered, and said vnto him, Because I said vnto thee, I saw thee vnder the figtree, beleeuest thou? thou shalt see greater
things then these.
51 And he said vnto him, Verily, verily I say
vnto you, hereafter shall yee see heauen open,
and the Angels of God * [x] ascending, and descending vpon that Sonne of man.

18 The good indeuours euen of the vnlearned, God doeth so allow, that he maketh them masters to the learned.

** Gene.39.10. deut.18.18.*

** Isai.4.2. and 40.10. and 45.8. iere.23.5 and 33.14. ezech.34.23. and 37.24. dan. 9.24.*

19 We must especially take heede of false presumptions, which shut vp against vs the entrance to Christ.

20 Simple vprightnesse discerneth the true Israelites from the false.

21 The end of miracles is to set before vs Christ the Almightie, and also the onely authour of our saluation, that we may apprehend him by faith.

** Gene.28.12.*

x By these words, the power of God is signified which should appeare in his ministerie by the angels seruing him, as the head of the Church.

CHAP. II.

1 Christ turneth water into wine, 11 which was the beginning of his miracles. 12 He goeth downe to Capernaum, 13 from thence he goeth vp to Hierusalem, 14 and casteth the merchandise out of the Temple 19 Hee foretelleth that the Temple, that is, his body shall be destroyed of the Iewes. 23 Many beleeue in him, seeing the miracles which he did.

AND [1] the [a] third day, there was a marriage
in Cana *a towne* of Galile, and the mother
of Iesus was there.
2 And Iesus was called also, and his disciples vnto the marriage.
3 [2] Now when the wine failed, the mother of Iesus sayd vnto him, They haue no
wine.
4 Iesus sayd vnto her, Woman, what
haue I to doe with thee? mine [b] houre is not
yet come.
5 His mother said vnto the seruants, Whatsoeuer he saith vnto you, doe it.
6 And there were set there, sixe [c] water-
pots of stone, after the maner of the purifying
of the Iewes, conteining two or three [d] firkins
a piece.

1 Christ declaring openly in an assembly by a notable miracle that he hath power ouer the nature of things, to feede mans body, leadeth the minds of all men, to his spirituall and sauing vertue and power.

a After the talke which hee had with Nathanael, or after that hee departed from Iohn, or after that he came into Galile.

2 Christ is carefull enough of our saluation, and therefore hath no neede of others to put him in mind of it. *b Mine appointed time. c These were vessels appointed for water, wherein they washed themselues. d Euery firkin conteined an hundred pound, at twelue ounces the pound: Whereby we gather that Christ holpe them with a thousand and eight hundred pounds of wine.*

7 And Iesus said vnto them, Fill the wa-
terpots with water. Then they filled them vp
to the brimme.
8 Then he said vnto them, Draw out now
and beare vnto the gouernour of the feast. So
they bare it.
9 Now when the gouernour of the feast
had tasted the water that was made wine, (for
he knew not whence it was: but the seruants,
which drew the water, knew) the gouernour of
the feast called the bridegrome,
10 And said vnto him, All men at the beginning set foorth good wine, and when men
haue [e] well drunke, then that which is worse:
but thou hast kept backe the good wine vntill now.
11 This beginning of miracles did Iesus in
Cana *a towne* of Galile, and shewed foorth his
glory: and his disciples beleeued on him.
12 After that, hee went downe into Capernaum, he and his mother, and his [f] brethren, and
his disciples: but they continued not many
dayes there.
13 [3] For the Iewes Passeouer was at hand.
Therefore Iesus went vp to Hierusalem.
14 [4] And he found in the Temple those that
sold oxen, and sheepe, and doues, and changers
of money sitting *there*.
15 Then he made a scourge of small cordes,
and draue them all out of the Temple with the
sheepe and oxen, and powred out the changers
money, and ouerthrew the tables,
16 And said vnto them that sold doues,
Take these things hence: make not my fathers
house, an house of merchandise.
17 And his disciples remembred, that it was
written, * The [g] zeale of thine house hath eaten
me vp.
18 [5] Then answered the Iewes, and said vn-
him, What [h] signe shewest thou vnto vs, that
thou doest these things?
19 Iesus answered, and said vnto them,
* Destroy this Temple, and in three dayes I
will raise it vp againe.
20 Then said the Iewes, Fourtie and sixe
yeeres was this Temple a building, and wilt
thou reare it vp in three dayes?
21 But hee spake of the [i] temple of his
bodie.
22 Assoone therefore as hee was risen from
the dead, his disciples remembred that he thus
said vnto them: and they beleeued the Scripture, and the word that Iesus had said.
23 Now when hee was at Hierusalem at
the Passeouer in the feast, many beleeued in his
Name, when they sawe his miracles which
hee did.
24 [6] But Iesus did not commit himselfe vnto them, because he knew them all,
25 [7] And had not need that any should testifie of man: for he knew what was in man.

e Word for word, are drunken: Now this speach, to be drunken, is not alwayes taken in euill part in the Hebrew tongue, but signifieth sometime such store, and plentifull vse of wine, as doth not passe measure, as Gene. 43. 34.
f That is, his Cousins.
3 Christ being made subiect to the Law for vs, satisfieth the Lawe of the Passeouer.
4 Christ being ordeined to purge ÿ Church, doth with great zeale begin his office both of Priest and Prophet.
* *Psal. 69. 9.*
g Zeale in this place is taken for a wrathfull indignation and displeasure of the minde, conceiued of some naughtie and euill dealing towards them whom wee loue well.
5 Against them which so binde God to an ordinarie calling which they them selues most shamefully abuse, that they will not admit an extraordinarie, which God confirmeth from heauen (and they although in vaine would haue it extinguished) vnlesse it be sealed with outward and bodily miracles.
h With what miracle doest thou confirme it, that we may see that heauenly power and vertue, which giueth thee authoritie to speake and doe thus?
* *Matth. 26 61. and 27. 40. marke 14. 58. and 15. 29.*
i That is, of his body.
6 It is not good crediting them, which stand onely vpon miracles
7 Christ is the searcher of hearts, and therfore true God.

CHAP. III.

1 Christ teacheth Nicodemus the very principles of Christian regeneration. 14 The serpent in the wildernesse. 23 Iohn baptizeth, 27 And teacheth his, that hee is not Christ.

THere [1] was now a man of the Pharises, named Nicodemus, a [a] ruler of the Iewes.
2 This *man* came to Iesus by night, and
said vnto him, Rabbi, we know that thou art a
[b] teacher come from God: for no man could
doe these miracles that thou doest, [c] except
God were with him.
3 [2] Iesus answered, and said vnto him,
Verily, verily I say vnto thee, Except a man be
borne againe, hee cannot [d] see the [e] kingdome
of God.
4 Nicodemus said vnto him, How [f] can
a man be borne which is olde? can he enter into
his mothers wombe againe, and be borne?
5 Iesus answered, Verily, verily I say vnto
thee, except that a man bee borne of water and
of the Spirit, hee cannot enter into the kingdome of God.
6 That which is borne of the flesh, is
[g] flesh: and that which is borne of the Spirit,
is spirit.
7 Maruaile not that I said vnto thee, Yee
must be borne againe.
8 The wind bloweth where it [h] listeth, and
thou hearest the sound therof, but canst not tell
whence it commeth, and whither it goeth: so is
euery man that is borne of the Spirit.
9 [3] Nicodemus answered, and said vnto
him, How can these things be?
10 Iesus answered, and said vnto him, Art
thou a teacher of Israel, and knowest not these
things?
11 Verily, verily I say vnto thee, We speake
that we know, and testifie that wee haue seene:
but yee receiue not our [i] witnesse.
12 If when I tell you earthly things, yee beleeue not, how should yee beleeue, if I shall tell
you of heauenly things?
13 For no [k] man [l] ascendeth vp to heauen,
but he that hath descended from heauen, [m] that
Sonne of man which [n] is in heauen.
14 * And as Moses lift vp the serpent in
the wildernesse, so must that Sonne of man bee
lift vp,
15 That whosoeuer beleeueth in him, should
not perish, but haue eternall life.
16 * [5] For God so loued the world, that he

1 There are none sometimes more vnlearned, then the learned: but as well the learned as the vnlearned must desire wisedome of Christ onely.
a A man of great estimation, and a ruler amongst the Iewes.
b We know that thou art sent from God to teach vs.
c But he in whom some part of the excellencie of God appeareth. And if Nicodemus had knowen Christ aright, he would not onely haue said that God was with him, but in him, as Paul doeth, 2. Cor. 1. 19.
2 The beginning of Christianitie consisteth in this, that we know our selues not onely to be corrupt in part, but to be wholy dead in sinne: so that our nature hath neede to be created anew, as touching the qualities therof: which can bee done by no other vertue, but by the diuine and heauenly, whereby wee were first created
d That is, goe in, or enter, as he expounded himselfe afterward, vers. 5.
e The Church: for Christ sheweth in this place, how we come to be citizens, and to haue ought to doe in the citie of God.
f How can I that am old, be borne againe? for he answereth, as if Christ his words belonged to none but to him.
g That is, fleshly, to wit, wholy vncleane and vnder the wrath of God: and therefore this word (Flesh) signifieth the corrupt nature of man: contrarie to which is the (Spirit) that is, the man ingrafted into Christ through the grace of the holy Ghost, whose nature is euerlasting and immortall, though the strife of the flesh remaineth. *h With free and wandring blasts as it listeth.* 3 The secret mysterie of our regeneration which cannot bee comprehended by mans capacitie, is perceiued by faith, and that in Christ onely, because that hee is both God on earth, and man in heauen, that is to say, in such sort man, that he is God also, and therefore almightie: and in such sort God, that he is man also, and therefore his power is manifest vnto vs. *i You handle doubtfull things and such as you haue no certaine authour for, and yet men beleeue you: but I teach those things that are of a trueth and well knowen, and you beleeue me not.* *k Onely Christ can teach vs heauenly things, for no man ascendeth, &c.* *l That is, hath any spirituall light and vnderstanding, or euer had, but onely that Sonne of God, which came downe to vs.* *m Whereas he is said to haue come downe from heauen, that must be vnderstood of his Godhead, and of the maner of his conception: for Christ his birth vpon the earth was heauenly, and not earthly, for hee was conceiued by the holy Ghost.* *n That which is proper to the diuinitie of Christ, is here spoken of whole Christ, to giue vs to vnderstand that hee is but one person wherein two natures are vnited, and this kind of speach men call, the communicating of properties.* * *Numb. 21. 9. chap. 12. 32.* * *1. Iohn 4. 9.* 5 Nothing else but the free loue of the Father, is the beginning of our saluation, and Christ is he in whom our righteousnesse and saluation is resident: and faith is the instrument or meane whereby we apprehend it, and life euerlasting is that which is set before vs to apprehend.

hath giuen his only begotten Sonne, that whosoeuer beleeueth [o] in him, should not perish,
but haue euerlasting life.
17 *[6] For God sent not his Sonne into the
world, that he should [p] condemn the world, but
that the [q] world through him might be saued.
18 Hee that beleeueth in him, is not condemned: but he that beleeueth not, is condemned already, because he hath not belieued in the
Name of that onely begotten Sonne of God.
19 *[7] And this is the [r] condemnation, that
the light came into the world, and men loued
darknesse rather then that light, because their
deedes were euill.
20 For euery man that euill doeth, hateth
the light, neither commeth to the light, lest his
deedes should be reproued.
21 But he that [s] doeth trueth, commeth to
the light, that his deedes might be made manifest, that they are wrought [t] according to God.
22 ¶ After these things came Iesus and his
disciples into the land of Iudea, and there taried
with them, and * baptized.
23 And Iohn also baptized in Enon besides
Salim, because there was much water there:
and they came, and were baptized.
24 For Iohn was not yet cast into prison.
25 [8] Then there arose a question betweene
Iohns disciples and the Iewes, about purifying.
26 And they came vnto Iohn, and said vnto
him, Rabbi, he that was with thee beyond Iorden, to whom * thou barest witnesse, behold,
he baptizeth, and all men come to him.
27 Iohn answered and said, A man [u] can receiue nothing, except it bee giuen him from
heauen.
28 Yee your selues are my witnesse, that * I
said, I am not that Christ, but that I am sent before him.
29 Hee that hath the bride, is the bridegrome: but the friend of the bridegrome which
standeth and heareth him, reioyceth greatly,
because of the bridegromes voice. This my ioy
therefore is fulfilled.
30 He must increase, but I *must* decrease.
31 He that is come from an high, is aboue
all: he that is of the earth, is of the [x] earth, and
[y] speaketh of the earth: hee that is come from
heauen, is aboue all.
32 And what hee hath [z] seene and heard,
that he testifieth: but [a] no man receiueth his testimonie.
33 Hee that hath receiued his testimonie,
hath sealed that * God is true.
34 For hee whom God hath sent, speaketh
the words of God: for God giueth *him* not the
spirit by measure,
35 The Father loueth the sonne, and hath
* b giuen all things into his hand.
36 * Hee that beleeueth in the Sonne, hath
euerlasting life, and hee that obeyeth not the

o It is not all one to beleeue in a thing, and to beleeue of a thing, for we may not beleeue (in any thing) saue onely in God, but we may beleeue (of any thing) whatsoeuer, saith Nazianzene in his Oration of the spirit.
* *Chap.9.39. and 12.47.*
6 Not Christ, but the despising of Christ doeth contemne.
p That is, to be the cause of condemning of the world, for in deede sinnes are the cause of death, but Christ shall iudge the quicke and the dead.
q Not onely the people of the Iewes, but whosoeuer shal beleeue in him.
* *Chap.1.9.*
7 Onely wickednesse is the cause, why men refuse the light that is offered them.
r That is, the cause of condemnation, which sticke fast in men, vnlesse through God his great benefit they be deliuered from it.
s That is, he that leadeth an honest life, and voide of all craft & deceit.
t That is, with God, God as it were going before.
* *Chap.4.1.*
8 Satan inflameth the disciples of Iohn with a fond emulation of their master, to hinder the course of the Gospel: but Iohn being mindfull of his office, doeth not onely breake off their endeuours, but also taketh occasion therby, to giue testimonie of Christ, how that in him onely the Father hath set foorth life euerlasting.
* *Chap.1.34.*
u What meane you to goe about to better my state? this is euery mans lot and portion, that they cannot better themselues one iote.
* *Chap.1.20*
x Is nothing else but man, a piece of worke made of the slyme of the earth.
y Sauoureth of nothing, but corruption, ignorance, dulnesse, &c.
z What he knoweth fully and perfectly. *a That is, very few.* *Rom.3.4. *Matth.11.27. *b Committed them to his power and will.* *Abac.2.4. 1.Iohn 5.10.

Sonne, shall not [c] see life, but the wrath of God
abideth on him.

CHAP. IIII.

6 Iesus being wearie, asketh drink of the woman of Samaria. 21 He teacheth the true worship. 26 Hee confesseth that he is the Messias. 32 His meate. 39 The Samaritanes beleeue in him. 46 He healeth the Rulers sonne.

NOw [1] when the Lord knew, how the Pharises had heard, that Iesus made * and
baptised moe disciples then Iohn.
2 (Though Iesus himselfe baptized not:
but his disciples)
3 He left Iudea, and departed againe into
Galile.
4 And he must needs go thorow Samaria.
5 [2] Then came he to a citie of Samaria called
Sychar, neere vnto the possession that * Iacob
gaue to his sonne Ioseph.
6 And there was Iacobs well. Iesus then
wearied in the iourney, sate [a] thus on the well:
it was about the [b] sixt houre.
7 There came a woman of Samaria to
drawe water: Iesus said vnto her, Giue mee
drinke.
8 For his disciples were gone away into
the citie, to buy meate.
9 Then said the woman of Samaria vnto
him, How is it, that thou being a Iew, askest
drinke of me, which am a woman of Samaria?
for the Iewes [c] meddle not with the Samaritans.
10 Iesus answered and said vnto her, If thou
knewest that [d] gift of God, and who it is that
saith to thee, Giue me drinke, thou wouldest
haue asked of him, and hee would haue giuen
thee [e] water of life.
11 The woman said vnto him, Sir, thou hast
nothing to draw with, and the well is deepe:
from whence then hast thou that water of life?
12 Art thou greater then our father Iacob,
which gaue vs the well, and he himselfe dranke
thereof, and his sonnes, and his cattell?
13 Iesus answered, and said vnto her,
Whosoeuer drinketh of this water, shall thirst
againe:
14 But whosoeuer drinketh of the water
that I shall giue him, shall neuer bee more a-
thirst: but the water that I shall giue him, shall
bee in him a well of water, springing vp into e-
uerlasting life.
15 The woman said vnto him, Sir, giue me
of that water, that I may not thirst, neither
come hither to draw.
16 Iesus said vnto her, Goe, call thine husband, and come hither.
17 The woman answered, and said, I haue
no husband. Iesus said vnto her, Thou hast well
said, I haue no husband.
18 For thou hast had fiue husbands, and he
whom thou now hast, is not thine husband:
that saidst thou truely.
19 The woman said vnto him, Sir, I see that
thou art a Prophet.

c Shall not enioy.
1 This measure is to be kept in doing of our dutie, that neither by feare we be terrified from going forward, neither by rashnesse procure or plucke dangers vpon our heads.
* *Chap 3.22.*
2 Christ leauing the proud Pharises, communicateth the treasures of euerlasting life with a poore sinful woman and stranger, refelling the grosse errours of the Samaritanes, and defending the true seruice of God, which was deliuered to the Iewes, but yet so, that hee calleth both of them backe to himselfe, as one whom onely all the fathers, and also all the ceremonies of the Law, did regard, and had a respect vnto.
* *Gene.33.19. and 48.22. Iosh.24.32.*
a Euen as he was wearie, or because he was wearie.
b It was almost noone.
c There is no familiaritie nor friendship between the Iewes, and the Samaritanes.
d By this word (That) we are giuen to vnderstand, that Christ speaketh of some excellent gift, that is to say, euen of himselfe, whom his father offered to this woman.
e This euerlasting water, that is to say, the exceeding loue of God, is called liuing, or of life, to make a difference betweene it, and the water that should be drawen out of a well: and these metaphores are very much vsed of the Iewes, Iere.2.13. Ioel 3.18. Zach.13.1.

20 [3] Our fathers worshipped in this [f] mountaine, and ye say, that in * Ierusalem is the place
where men ought to worship.
21 Iesus said vnto her, Woman, beleeue
me, the houre commeth, when yee shall neither
in this mountaine, nor at Hierusalem worship
the Father.
22 Yee worship that which yee * know not:
we worship that which we know: for saluation
is of the Iewes.
23 But the houre commeth, and now is,
when the true worshippers shall worship the
Father in [g] spirit, and trueth: for the father requireth euen such to worship him.
24 * God is a [h] spirit, and they that worship
him, must worship him in spirit and trueth.
25 The woman said vnto him, I know well
that Messias shall come which is called Christ:
when he is come, he will tell vs all things.
26 Iesus said vnto her, I am he, that speake
vnto thee.
27 ¶ And vpon that, came his disciples, and
marueiled that he talked with a woman: yet no
man said vnto him, What askest thou? or why
talkest thou with her?
28 The woman then left her water-pot,
and went her way into the citie, and said to the
men,
29 Come, see a man which hath told me all
things that euer I did: is not he that Christ?
30 Then they went out of the citie, and
came vnto him.
31 ¶ In the meane while, the Disciples
prayed him, saying, Master, eate.
32 [4] But he said vnto them, I haue meate to
eate that yee know not of.
33 Then said the disciples betweene themselues, Hath any man brought him meate?
34 Iesus said vnto them, My meate is that
I may doe the will of him that sent mee, and finish his worke.
35 [5] Say not yee, There are yet foure moneths, and *then* commeth haruest? Behold, I
say vnto you, Lift vp your eyes, and looke on
the regions: * for they are white already vnto
haruest.
36 [6] And he that reapeth, receiueth reward,
and gathereth fruit vnto life eternall, that both
he that soweth, and he that reapeth, might reioyce together.
37 For herein is the [i] saying true, that one
soweth, and another reapeth.
38 I sent you to reape that, whereon yee
bestowed no labour: other men laboured, and
yee are entred into their labours.
39 [7] Now many of the Samaritanes of that
citie beleeued in him, for the saying of the woman which testified, He hath told me all things
that euer I did.
40 Then when the Samaritanes were come
vnto him, they besought him, that hee would
tarie with them: and he abode there two dayes.

3 All the religion of superstitious people, standeth for the most part vpon two pillars, but very weake, that is to say, vpon the examples of the fathers peruerted, & a foolish opinion of outward things: against which errours we haue to set the word and nature of God.
f The name of this mountaine is Garizim, whereupon Sanabaletta the Cuthite built a Temple by Alexander of Macedonie his leaue, after the victorie of Issica: and made there Manasses his sonne in law, high Priest. Iose. bo. 11.
* *Deut. 12. 6.*
* *2 King 17. 29.*
g This word (spirit) is to be taken here, as it is set against that commandement which is called carnall, Hebr. 7 16. as the commandement is considered in it selfe: and so hee speaketh of (Truth) not as wee set it against a lie, but as we take it in respect of the outward ceremonies of the Law, which did onely shadow that which Christ performed indeede.
* *2 Cor. 3. 27.*
h By the word (Spirit) he meaneth the nature of the Godhead, and not the third person in the Trinitie.
4 We may haue care of our bodies, but yet so, that we preferre willingly and freely the occasion which is offered vs to enlarge the kingdome of God, before all necessities of this life whatsoeuer.
5 When the spirituall corne is ripe, we must not linger, for so the children of this world would condemne vs.
* *Matth. 9. 37. luke 10 2.*
6 The doctrine of the Prophets was as it were a sowing time: and the doctrine of the Gospel, as the haruest: and there is an excellent agreement betweene them both, and the ministers of them both.
i That prouerbe.
7 The Samaritanes doe most ioyfully imbrace that, which the Iewes most stubbornely reiected.

41 And many moe beleeued because of his
owne word.
42 And they said vnto the woman, Now we
beleeue, not because of thy saying: for we haue
heard him our selues, and know that this is in
deede that Christ the Sauiour of the world.
43 ¶ [8] So two dayes after hee departed
thence, and went into [k] Galile.
44 For Iesus himselfe had * testified, that
a Prophet hath none honour in his owne countrey.
45 Then when hee was come into Galile,
the Galileans receiued him, which had seene all
the things that hee did at Hierusalem at the
feast: for they went also vnto the feast.
46 [9] And Iesus came againe into * Cana *a
towne* of Galile, where hee had made of water,
wine. And there was a certaine [l] ruler whose
sonne was sicke a Capernaum.
47 When he heard that Iesus was come out
of Iudea into Galile, he went vnto him, and besought him that he would goe down, and heale
his sonne: for he was euen ready to die.
48 Then said Iesus vnto him, Except yee
see signes and wonders, yee will not beleeue.
49 The ruler said vnto him, Sir, goe downe
before my sonne die.
50 Iesus said vnto him, Goe thy way, thy
sonne liueth: & the man beleeued the word that
Iesus had spoken vnto him, and went his way.
51 And as hee was now going downe, his
seruants met him, saying, Thy sonne liueth.
52 Then inquired he of them the houre when
hee began to amend. And they said vnto him,
Yesterday the seuenth houre the feuer left him.
53 Then the father knew, that it was the
same houre in the which Iesus had said vnto
him, Thy sonne liueth. And he beleeued, and
all his houshold.
54 This second miracle did Iesus againe,
after he was come out of Iudea into Galile.

CHAP. V.

2 One lying at the poole, 5 is healed of Christ on the Sabbath. 10 The Iewes that rashly find fault with that his deed, 17 he conuinceth with the authoritie of his Father. 19. 20 He proueth his diuine power by many reasons, 45 and with Moses testimonie.

After * that, there was a feast of the Iewes,
and Iesus went vp to Ierusalem.
2 [1] And there is at Hierusalem by the place
of the sheepe, a [a] poole called in Ebrew [b] Be-
thesda, hauing fiue porches.
3 In the which lay a great multitude of
sicke folke, of blind, halte, and withered, way-
ting for the mouing of the water.
4 For an Angel went downe at a certaine
season into the poole, and troubled the water:
whosoeuer then first, after the stirring of the
water, stepped in, was made whole of whatsoeuer disease he had.
5 And a certaine man was there, which had
beene diseased eight and thirtie yeeres.
6 When Iesus saw him lie, and knew that
he

8 The despisers of Christ depriue themselues of his benefite: yet Christ prepareth a place for himselfe.
k Into the townes and villages of Galile, for he would not make abode in his countrey of Nazareth, because they despised him, and where (as the other Euangelists write) the efficacie of his benefits was hindered through their marueilous stiffeneckednesse.
* *Matth. 13. 57. marke 6. 4. luke 4. 24.*
9 Although Christ be absent in body, yet he worketh mightily in the beleeuers, by his word
* *Chap. 2 1, 12.*
l Some of Herods countreys, for though Herod was not a King, but a Tetrarch, yet the loftie name onely except, he was a King, or at least the people called him a King.
* *Leuit 23. 3. deut. 16. 1.*
1 There is no disease so old, which Christ can not heale.
a Whereof cattell dranke, and vsed to be plunged in, whereof there could not be but great store at Hierusalem.
b That is to say, the house of powring out, because great store of water was powred out into that place.

hee now long time had been diseased, he sayd
vnto him, Wilt thou be made whole?
7 The sicke man answered him, Sir I haue
no man, when the water is troubled, to put mee
into the poole: but while I am comming, another steppeth downe before me.
8 Iesus sayd vnto him, Rise: take vp thy
bed and walke.
9 And immediately the man was made
whole, and tooke vp his bed, and walked: and
the same day was the Sabbath.
10 [2] The Iewes therefore sayd to him that
was made whole, It is the Sabbath *day*: *it is
not lawfull for thee to cary thy bed.
11 He answered them, Hee that made mee
whole, he sayd vnto me, Take vp thy bed and
walke.
12 Then asked they him, What man is that
which sayd vnto thee, Take vp thy bedde, and
walke?
13 And hee that was healed, knewe not
who it was: for Iesus had conueyed himselfe a-
way from the multitude that was in that place.
14 And after that, Iesus found him in the
Temple, and sayd vnto him, Beholde, thou art
made whole: sinne no more, lest a worse thing
come vnto thee.
15 ¶ The man departed and tolde the
Iewes that it was Iesus, which had made him
whole.
16 And therefore the Iewes did persecute
Iesus, and sought to slay him, because hee had
done these things on the Sabbath *day*.
17 [3] But Iesus answered them, My Father worketh hitherto, and I worke.
18 *Therfore the Iewes sought the more
to kill him: not onely because he had broken
the Sabbath: but sayd also that God was [c] his
Father, and made himselfe equall with God.
19 Then answered Iesus, and sayd vnto
them, Verely verely I say vnto you, The Sonne
can doe nothing [d] of himselfe, saue that hee
[e] seeth the Father doe: for whatsoeuer things
hee doeth, the same things doeth the Sonne
[f] in like maner.
20 For the Father loueth the Sonne, and
sheweth him all things, whatsoeuer hee himselfe doeth, and he will shew him greater works
then these, that ye should marueile.
21 [4] For likewise as the Father raiseth vp the
dead, and quickneth them, so the Sonne quickneth whom hee will.
22 For the Father [g] iudgeth [h] no man,
but hath committed all iudgement vnto the
Sonne,
23 Because that all men should honour
the Sonne, as they honour the Father: hee that
honoureth not the Sonne, the same honoureth

2 True religion is not more cruelly assaulted by any means, then by the pretence of religion it selfe.

Iere.17.22.

3 The worke of God was neuer the breach of the Sabbath, but the works of Christ are the works of the Father, both because they are one God, and also because the Father doth not work but in the Sonne.

**Chap 7.19.*

c That is, his onely and no mans else, which they gather by that, that hee sayth, (And I worke) applying this word (worke) to himselfe, which is proper to God, and therefore maketh himselfe equall to God

d Not only without his Fathers authoritie, but also without his mightie working and power.

e This must bee understoode of Christ his person, which consisteth of two natures, and not simply of his Godhead: so then he sayth that his Father mooueth and gouerneth him in all things, but yet not withstanding when he saith he worketh with his Father, he voucheth his Godhead.

f In like sorte, ioyntly and together. Not for that the Father doeth some things, and then the Sonne worketh after him and doeth the like, but because the might and power of the Father & the Sonne doe worke equally and ioyntly together.

4 The Father maketh no man partaker of euerlasting life, but in Christ, in whō onely also hee is truely worshipped.

g This worde (Iudgeth) is taken by the figure Synecdoche, for all gouernement.

h These are not so to be taken, as though they simply denied that God gouerned the worlde, but as the Jewes imagined it, which separate the Father from the Sonne, whereas in deed, the Father doth not gouerne the worlde, but onely in the person of his Sonne, being made manifest in the flesh: so sayth hee afterward verse 30. that hee came not to doe his owne will: that his doctrine is not his owne, chap.7.16. that the blinde man and his parents sinned not, &c. chap.9.3.

not the Father which hath sent him.
24 [5] Verely, verely I say vnto you, he that
heareth my worde, and beleeueth him that
sent mee, hath euerlasting life, and shall not
come into condemnation, but hath passed from
death vnto life.
25 [6] Verely, verely I say vnto you, the
houre shall come, and nowe is, when the dead
shall heare the voice of the Sonne of God: and
they that heare it, shall liue.
26 For as the Father hath life in himselfe,
so likewise hath he giuen to the Sonne to haue
life in himselfe,
27 And hath giuen him [i] power also to execute iudgement, in that hee is [k] the Sonne
of man.
28 [7] Marueile not at this: for the houre
shal come, in the which al that are in the graues,
shall heare his voice.
29 [8] And they shall come [l] foorth, *that
haue done good vnto the [m] resurrection of life:
but they that haue done euill, vnto the resurrection of condemnation.
30 [9] I can [n] doe nothing of mine owne
selfe: [o] as I heare, I iudge: and my iudgement is
iust, because I seeke not mine owne will, but
the will of the Father who hath sent me.
31 If I *should beare witnesse of my selfe,
my witnesse were not [p] true.
32 *There is another that beareth witnesse
of mee, and I knowe that the witnesse, which
he beareth of me, is true.
33 *[10] Yee sent vnto Iohn, and hee bare
witnesse vnto the trueth.
34 But I receiue not the record of man:
neuerthelesse these things I say, that ye might
be saued.
35 He was a burning and a shining candle:
and yee would for [q] a season haue reioyced in
his light.
36 But I haue greater witnesse then the
witnesse of Iohn: for the works which the Father hath giuen mee to finish, the same works
that I doe, beare witnesse of mee, that the Father sent me.
37 And the *Father himselfe, which hath
sent me, beareth witnesse of mee. Ye haue not
heard his voice at any time, *neither haue yee
seene his shape.
38 And his word haue you not abiding in
you: for whō he hath sent, him ye beleeue not.
39 *Search the Scriptures: for in them ye
thinke to haue eternall life, and they are they
which testifie of me.
40 But yee will not come to mee, that yee
might haue life.
41 I receiue not the praise of men.
42 But I knowe you, that yee haue not the
[r] loue of God in you.
43 I am come in my Fathers Name, and yee
receiue mee not: if another shall come in his
owne name, him will ye receiue.
44 How can yee beleeue, which receiue
*honour

5 The Father is not worshipped but by his Sonnes worde apprehended by faith, which is the onely way that leadeth to eternall life.

6 Wee are all dead in sinne, & cannot be quickned by any other meanes, then by ỹ word of Christ apprehended by faith.

i That is, hie and soueraigne power to rule and gouern all things, in so much that he hath power of life and death.

k That is, he shall not onely iudge the world as hee is God, but also as he is man, he receiued this of his father to bee iudge of the world.

7 All shall appeare before the iudgement seate of Christ at length to be iudged.

8 Faith and infidelitie shall bee iudged by their fruits.

l Of their graues.

**Matth 25.41.*

m To that resurrection which hath life euerlasting following it: against which is set the resurrection of condemnation, that is, which condemnation followeth.

9 The Father is the author and approuer of all things which Christ doth.

n Looke vers.22.

o As my Father directeth me, who dwelleth in me.

**Chap 8.14.*

p Faithfull, that is, worthy to bee credited, looke chap.8.14.

**Matth.3.17.*

**Chap.1.27.*

10 Christ is declared to be the only Sauiour by Iohns voice, and infinite miracles, and by the testimonies of all the Prophets. But the world notwithstanding being addicted to false prophets, and desirous to seeme religious, seeth none of all these things.

q A little while.

**Matth.3.17. and 17.5.*

**Deut.4.12.*

**Act.17.11.*

r Loue toward God.

*Chap.12.43.

f This denial doth not put away that which is here said, but correcteth it, as if Christ said, the Iewes shall haue no sorer accuser then Moses.

*Gen.3.15 and 22.18.and 49.10.deut.18.15.

* honour one of another,and seeke not the honour that commeth of God alone?
45 f Doe not thinke that I will accuse you
to my Father: there is one that accuseth you,
euen Moses,in whom ye trust.
46 For had ye beleeued Moses, yee would
haue beleeued me: for he wrote of me.
47 But if ye beleeue not his writings, how
shall yee beleeue my words?

CHAP. VI.

5 Fiue thousand are fedde with fiue loaues and two fishes. 15 Christ goeth apart from the people. 17 As his disciples were rowing, 19 he commeth to them walking on the water. 29 He reasoneth of the true, 27 and euerlasting 35 bread of life. 41. 52 The Iewes murmure, 60 and many of the disciples 66 depart from him. 69 The Apostles confesse him to be the Sonne of God.

a Not that hee cut ouer the lake of Tiberias, but by reason of the large creekes, his sailing made his iourney the shorter: therefore he is sayd to haue gone ouer the sea, when as he passed ouer from one side of the creeke to the other.

*Leuit.23.7. deut.16.1.

* Matt.14.16. marke 6.37. luke 9.13.

1 They that folow Christ, doe sometime hunger, but they are neuer destitute of helpe.

AFter these things, Iesus went his way
a ouer the sea of Galile,which is Tiberias.
2 And a great multitude followed him,be-
cause they saw his miracles, which hee did on
them that were diseased.
3 Then Iesus went vp into a mountaine,
and there he sate with his disciples.
4 Now the Passeouer,a*feast of the Iewes,
was neere.
5 *1 Then Iesus lift vp *his* eyes, and seeing that a great multitude came vnto him, hee
said vnto Philip, Whence shall we buy bread,
that these might eate?
6 (And this he sayd to proue him: for he
himselfe knew what he would doe.)
7 Philip answered him,Two hundreth pe-
nieworth of bread is not sufficient for them,
that euery one of them may take a little.
8 Then said vnto him one of his disciples,
Andrew,Simon Peters brother,
9 There is a little boy here, which hath
fiue barley loaues,and two fishes: but what are
they among so many?
10 And Iesus sayd, Make the people sit
downe. (Now there was much grasse in that
place.) Then the men sate downe, in number,
about fiue thousand.
11 And Iesus tooke the bread, and gaue
thankes,and gaue to the disciples,and the disciples to them that were set downe: and likewise
of the fishes as much as they would.
12 And when they were satisfied, he sayd,
vnto his disciples, Gather vp the broken meate
which remaineth,that nothing be lost.
13 Then they gathered it together, and
filled twelue baskets with the broken meate of
the fiue barley loaues, which remained vnto
them that had eaten.
14 Then the men,when they had seene the
miracle that Iesus did, sayd, this is of a trueth
that Prophet that should come into the world.
15 2 When Iesus therefore perceiued that
they would come, and take him to make him a
King, hee departed againe into a mountaine
himselfe alone.
16 ¶3 When euen was now come, his disciples went downe into the sea,

2 Christ is not only not delited, but also greatly offended with a preposterous worship.

3 The godly are often in perill and danger, but Christ commeth to them in time, euen in the mids of the tempests & bringeth them to the hauen.

17 * And entred into a ship, and went ouer
the sea, b towardes Capernaum: and now it
was darke, and Iesus was not come to them.
18 And the Sea arose with a great winde
that blew.
19 And when they had rowed about fiue
and twenty, or thirtie furlongs, they saw Iesus
walking on the sea,and drawing neere vnto the
ship: so they were afraid.
20 But he sayd vnto them, It is I: bee not
afraid.
21 Then c willingly they receiued him into
the ship,and the ship was by and by at the land,
whither they went.
22 ¶ The day following,the people which
stoode on the other side of the sea, sawe that
there was none other ship there saue that one,
whereinto his disciples were entred, and that
Iesus went not with his disciples in the ship,
but that his disciples were gone alone,
23 And that there came other ships from
Tiberias neere vnto the place where they ate
the bread,after the Lord had giuen thankes.
24 Now when the people sawe that Iesus
was not there, neither his disciples, they also
tooke shipping, and came to Capernaum, seeking for Iesus.
25 And when they had found him on the o-
ther side of the sea, they sayd vnto him, Rabbi,
when camest thou hither?
26 4 Iesus answered them,and sayd,Verely,
verely I say vnto you, ye seeke me not because
ye sawe the miracles, but because yee ate of the
loaues,and were filled.
27 d Labour not for the meate which perisheth, but for the meate that endureth vnto e-
uerlasting life, which the Sonne of man shall
giue vnto you: for him hath * God the Father
e sealed.
28 Then sayd they vnto him, What shal we
doe,that we might worke the f works of God?
29 5 Iesus answered, and said vnto them,
* g This is the worke of God,that yee beleeue
in him,whom he hath sent.
30 6 They sayd therefore vnto him, What
signe shewest thou then, that we may see it,and
beleeue thee? what doest thou worke?
31 Our fathers did eate Manna in the desert, as it is * written, Hee gaue them bread
from heauen to eate.
32 7 Then Iesus sayd vnto them, Verely,
verely I say vnto you, Moses gaue you not
h that bread from heauen,but my Father giueth
you that true bread from heauen.
33 For the bread of God is he which commeth downe from heauen,and giueth life vnto
the worlde.

*Matth.14.25. marke 6.47.

b In Mark 6.45 they are willed to goe before to Bethsaida, for Bethsaida was in the way to Capernaum.

c They were afraid at the first, but when they knew his voyce, they became new men, and tooke him willingly into the ship, whom they shunned and fled from before.

4 They that seek the kingdome of heauen, lacke nothing: notwithstanding the Gospel is not the foode of the bellie, but of the minde.

d Bestowe your labour and paine.

*Chap.1.32. matth.3.17. and 17.3.

e That is, whom God the Father had distinguished from all other men by planting his owne vertue in him, as though hee had sealed him with his seale, that he might be a liuely paterne and representer of him: and that more is, installed him to this office, to reconcile vs men to God, and bring vs to euerlasting life, which is only proper to Christ.

f Which please God: for they thinke that euerlasting life hangeth vpon the condition of fulfilling the Law: therefore Christ calleth them backe to faith.

5 Men torment themselues in vaine, when they goe about to pleased God without faith.

*1.Iohn 3.23.

g That is, this is the worke that God requireth, that you beleeue in me, and therefore hee calleth them backe to faith.

6 The spirituall vertue of Christ is contemned of them that are desirous of earthly miracles.

*Exod.16.14.numb.11.7.psal 78.25. 7 Christ, who is the true and onely author and giuer of eternall life, was signified vnto the Fathers in Manna. *h Hee denieth that Manna was that true heauenly bread, and saith that hee himselfe is that true bread, because he feedeth to the true and euerlasting life. And as for that, that Paul, 1.Cor.10. calleth Manna spirituall foode, it maketh nothing against this place, for hee ioyneth the thing signified with the signe: but in this whole disputation, Christ dealeth with the Iewes after their owne opinion and conceit of the matter, and they had no further consideration of the Manna, but in that it fed the bellie,*

34 Then

34 Then they sayd vnto him, Lord, euermore giue vs this bread.
35 And Iesus sayd vnto them, I am that
bread [i] of life: he that commeth to mee, shall
not hunger, and he that beleeueth in mee, shall
neuer thirst.
36 But I sayd vnto you, that yee also haue
seene me, and beleeue not.
37 [8] All that the Father giueth me, shall
come to me: and him that commeth to mee, I
cast not away.
38 For I came downe from heauen, not to
doe mine [k] owne will: but his will which hath
sent me.
39 And this is the Fathers will which hath
sent me, that of all which hee hath giuen mee, I
should lose nothing, but should raise it vp a-
gaine at the last day.
40 And this is the will of him that sent me,
that euery man which [l] seeth the Sonne, and
beleeueth in him, should haue euerlasting life:
and I will raise him vp at the last day.
41 [9] The Iewes then murmured at him because he saide, I am that bread which is come
downe from heauen.
42 And they sayd, * Is not this Iesus that
sonne of Ioseph, whose father and mother we
knowe? how then sayth hee, I came downe
from heauen?
43 Iesus then answered, and said vnto them,
Murmure not among your selues.
44 No man can come to me, except the Father which hath sent me, drawe him: and I will
raise him vp at the last day.
45 It is written in the * [m] Prophets, And
they shall bee all [n] taught of God. Euery man
therefore that hath heard, and hath learned of
the Father, commeth vnto me:
46 * Not that any man hath seene the Father, [o] saue hee which is of God, he hath seene
the Father.
47 Verely, verely I say vnto you, hee that
beleeueth in me hath euerlasting life.
48 [10] I am that bread of life.
49 * Your fathers did eate Manna in the
wildernesse, and are dead.
50 [p] This is that bread, which commeth
downe from heauen, that hee which eateth of
it, should not die.
51 [11] I am that [q] liuing bread, which came
downe from heauen: if any man [r] eate of this
bread, he shall liue for euer: and the bread that
I will giue, is my flesh, which I will giue for the
life of the world.
52 [12] Then the Iewes stroue among themselues, saying, How can this man giue vs *his*
flesh to eate?
53 Then Iesus sayde vnto them, Verely,
verely I say vnto you, Except ye eate the flesh
of the Sonne of man, and drinke his blood, yee
haue [s] no life in you.
54 Whosoeuer * eateth my flesh, and drinketh my blood, hath eternall life, and I will
raise him vp at the last day.
55 For my flesh is meate in deede, and my
blood is drinke in deede.
56 He that eateth my flesh, and drinketh
my blood, dwelleth in me, and I in him.
57 As [t] that liuing Father hath sent mee, so
liue I by the [u] Father, and hee that eateth mee,
euen he shall liue by mee.
58 This is that bread which came downe
from heauen: not as your fathers haue eaten
Manna, and are dead. Hee that eateth of this
bread shall liue for euer.
59 These things taught he in the Synagogue,
as he taught in Capernaum.
60 [13] Many therefore of his disciples (when
they heard this) sayd, This is an hard saying:
who can heare it?
61 But Iesus knowing in himselfe, that
his disciples murmured at this, sayd vnto them,
Doth this offend you?
62 *What* then if yee should see the Sonne
of man ascend vp * where he was before?
63 [14] It is the [x] spirit that quickeneth: the
flesh profiteth nothing: the words that I speak
vnto you, are spirit and life.
64 But there are some of you that beleeue
not: for Iesus knewe from the beginning,
which they were that beleeued not, and who
should betray him.
65 And hee sayd, Therefore sayd I vnto
you, that no man can come vnto me, except it
be giuen vnto him of my Father.
66 [15] From that time, many of his disciples
went backe, and walked no more with him.
67 Then sayd Iesus vnto the twelue, Will
ye also goe away?
68 Then Simon Peter answered him, Master, to whom shall we go? thou hast the words
of eternall life:
69 And wee beleeue and knowe that thou
art that Christ the Sonne of the liuing God.
70 [16] Iesus answered them, Haue not I
* chosen you twelue, and one of you is a deuil?
71 Now hee spake it of Iudas Iscariot the
sonne of Simon: for hee it was that should betray him, though he was one of the twelue.

i Which haue life, and giue life.

8 The gift of faith proceedeth from the free election of the Father in Christ, after which followeth necessarily euerlasting life: Therefore faith in Christ Iesus is a sure witnesse of our election, & therefore of our glorification, which is to come.

k Looke aboue, Chap. 5. verse 22.

l Seeing and beleeuing are ioyned together: for there is another kind of seeing which is generall, which the deuils haue, for they see: but here he speaketh of that kind of seeing, which is proper to the elect.

9 Flesh cannot perceiue spiritual things, & therefore the beginning of our saluation commeth from God, who changeth our nature, so that wee being inspired of him, may abide to be instructed and saued by Christ.

*Matth. 13.55.

* *Isa. 54.13. ier. 31.33.*

m In the booke of the Prophets, for the old Testament was diuided by them into three seuerall parts, into the Law, the Prophets, and the holy writ.

n To wit, they shall be children of the Church, for so the Prophet Esai expoundeth it, chap. 54.13. that is to say, ordained to life, Acts 13.48 and therefore the knowledge of the heauenly trueth is the gift and worke of God, and standeth not in any power of man.

**Matth. 11.17.*

s If Christ be present, life is present, but when Christ is absent, then is death present.

* *1. Cor. 11.27.*

t In that that Christ is man, hee receiueth that power, which quickneth and giueth lefe to them that are his, of his Father: and hee addeth this word (That) to make a difference betweene him and all other fathers.

u Christ his meaning is, that though hee bee man, yet his flesh can giue light, not of the owne nature, but because that flesh of his liueth by the Father, that is to say, doeth sucke and drawe out of the Father, that power which it hath to giue life.

13 The reason of man cannot comprehend the vniting of Christ and his members: therefore let it worship & reuerence that which is better then it selfe.

**Chap. 3.13*

14 The flesh of Christ doeth therefore quicken vs, because that he that is man, is God: which mystery is only comprehended by faith, which is the gift of God, proper only to the elect.

x Spirit, that is, that power which floweth from the Godhead, causeth the flesh of Christ, which otherwise were nothing but flesh, both to liue in it selfe, and to giue life to vs.

15 Such is the malice of men that they take occasion of their owne destruction, euen of the very doctrine of saluation, vnlesse it be a few, which beleeue through the singular gift of God. 16 The number of the professors of Christ is very small among them also there bee some hypocrites, and worse then all other. * *Matth. 26.16.*

o If the Son onely hath seene the Father, then it is hee onely that can teach and instruct vs truely. 10 The true vse of Sacraments is to ascend from them to the thing it selfe, that is, to Christ: by the partaking of whom onely, wee get euerlasting life. * *Exod. 16.15.* *p Hee pointed out himselfe when hee speaketh these words.* 11 Christ being sent from the Father, is the selfe same vnto vs for the getting and keeping of euerlasting life, that bread and flesh, yea, meate and drinke, are to the vse of this transitorie life. *q Which giueth life to the worlde.* *r That is to say, whosoeuer is partaker of Christ in deede, who is our foode.* 12 Flesh cannot put a difference betweene fleshly eating, which is done by the helpe of the teeth, and spirituall eating, which consisteth in faith: and therefore it condemneth that which it vnderstandeth not: yet notwithstanding, the trueth must be preached and taught.

CHAP. VII.

2 Christ, after his cousins were gone vp to the feast of Tabernacles, 10 goeth thither priuily. 12 The peoples sundrie opinions of him. 14 Hee teacheth in the Temple. 32 The Priests command to take him. 41 Strife among the multitude about him, 47 and betweene the Pharises and the officers that were sent to take him, 50 and Nicodemus.

After

AFter these things, Iesus walked in Galile,
and would not walke in Iudea: for the
Iewes sought to kill him.
2 Now the Iewes *[a] feast of the Tabernacles was at hand.
3 [1] His brethren therefore sayd vnto him,
Depart hence, and goe into Iudea, that thy disciples may see thy workes that thou doest.
4 For there is no man that doth any thing
secretly, and he himselfe seeketh to be famous.
If thou doest these things, shew thy selfe to the
worlde.
5 For as yet his [b] brethren beleeued not in
him.
6 [2] Then Iesus said vnto them, My time is
not yet come: but your time is alway ready.
7 The world cannot hate you: but mee it
hateth, because I testifie of it, that the workes
thereof are euill.
8 Goe ye vp vnto this feast: I will not goe
vp yet vnto this feast: *for my time is not yet
fulfilled.
9 ¶These things he sayd vnto them, and
abode still in Galile.
10 [3] But assoone as his brethren were gone
vp, then went he also vp vnto the feast, not o-
penly, but as *it were* priuily.
11 Then the Iewes sought him at the feast,
and sayd, Where is he?
12 And much murmuring was there of
him among the people. Some sayd, Hee is a
good man: other sayd, Nay: but he deceiueth
the people.
13 Howbeit no man spake [c] openly of him
for feare of the Iewes.
14 [4] Nowe when the [d] halfe the feast was
done, Iesus went vp into the Temple and
taught.
15 And the Iewes marueiled, saying, How
knoweth this man the Scriptures, seeing that
he neuer learned!
16 [5] Iesus answered them, and sayd, [e] My
doctrine is not mine, but his that sent me.
17 If any man will doe his will, hee shall
knowe of the doctrine, whether it be of God, or
whether I speake of my selfe.
18 [6] He that speaketh of himselfe, seeketh
his owne glorie: but he that seeketh his glorie
that sent him, the same is true, and no vnrighteousnesse is in him.
19 *[7] Did not Moses giue you a Lawe, and
yet none of you keepeth the Law? Why goe ye
about to kill me?
20 The people answered, and sayd, Thou
hast a deuill: who goeth about to kill thee?
21 [8] Iesus answered, and sayd to them, I

*Leuit.23.34.
a This feast was so called, because of the boothes and tents which they pight of diuers kindes of boughs, and sate vnder them, seuen dayes together, all which time the feast lasted.
1 The grace of God commeth not by inheritance, but it is a gift that commeth other wayes: whereby it commeth to passe, that oftentimes the children of God suffer more affliction by their own kinsfolkes, then by strangers.
b His kinsfolkes: for so vse the Hebrewes to speake.
3 We must not follow the foolish desires of our friends.
*Chap 8.20.
3 An example of horrible confusion in the very bosome of the Church. The Pastors oppresse the people with terrour and feare: the people seeke Christ, when he appeareth not: when he offereth himselfe, they neglect him. Some also that knowe him, condemne him rashly: a very fewe thinke well of him, and that in secret.
c Or, boldly and freely: For the chiefe of the Iewes sought nothing so much, as to bury his fame and name.
4 Christ striueth with goodnesse against the wickednesse of the worlde: in the meane season the most part of men take occasion of offence euen by that same, whereby they ought to haue been stirred vp to embrace Christ.
d About the fourth day of the feast.
5 Therefore are there fewe to whom ẏ Gospel fauoureth very well, because the studie of godlines is very rare. *e Looke aboue chap. 5.ver.22. and he speaketh this after the opinion of the Iewes, as if he said, My doctrine is not mine, that is, it is not his whom you take to be a man as other are, and therfore set light by him, but it is his that sent me.* 6 The true doctrine of saluation differeth from the false in this, that the same setteth foorth the glorie of God, and this by puffing vp men, darkneth the glory of God. *Exod.24.3. 7 None do more confidently boast themselues to be the defenders of the Law of God, then they that doe most impudently breake it. *Chap.5.12. 8 The Sabbath day (which is here set before vs for a rule of all ceremonies) was not appointed to hinder, but to further & practise Gods works; amongst which the loue of our neighbour is the chiefest.

haue done one worke, and ye all maruell.
22 *Moses therefore gaue vnto you circumcision, (not because it is of Moses, but of
the *fathers) and yee on the Sabbath *day* circumcise a man.
23 If a man on the Sabbath receiue circumcision, that the [f] Law of Moses should not bee
broken, be yee angry with mee, because I haue
made a man euery whit whole on the Sabbath *day*.
24 *[9] Iudge not [g] according to the appearance, but iudge righteous iudgement.
25 ¶[10] Then sayde some of them of Hierusalem, Is not this he, whom they goe about
to kill?
26 And behold, hee speaketh openly, and
they say nothing to him: doe the rulers knowe
in deede, that this is in deed that Christ?
27 [11] Howbeit we knowe this man whence
he is: but when that Christ commeth, no man
shall knowe whence he is.
28 ¶[12] Then cried Iesus in the Temple
as he taught, saying, Yee both knowe me, and
knowe whence I am: yet am I not come of my
selfe, but he that sent mee is true, whome yee
knowe not.
29 But I knowe him: for I am of him, and
he hath sent me.
30 [13] Then they sought to take him, but
no man layd hands on him, because his houre
was not yet come.
31 Now many of the people beleeued in
him, and sayd, When that Christ commeth,
will hee doe moe miracles then this man hath
done?
32 [14] The Pharises heard that the people
murmured these things of him, and the Pharises, and high Priestes sent officers to take
him.
33 Then sayd Iesus vnto them, Yet am I a
little while with you, and then goe I vnto him
that sent me.
34 *Ye shall seeke me, and shall not finde
me, and where I am, can ye not come.
35 Then sayde the Iewes among themselues, Whither will he goe, that we shall not
finde him? Will hee goe vnto them that are
[h] dispersed among the Grecians, and teach
the Grecians?
36 What saying is this that hee sayd, Yee
shall seeke mee, and shall not finde *mee*? and
where I am, cannot ye come?
37 [15] Now in the [i] last *and* *great day of the
feast, Iesus stood and cryed, saying, If any man
thirst, let him come vnto me, and drinke.
38 He that beleeueth in me, *as sayth the
[k] Scripture, out of his belly shall flowe riuers of
water of life.

*Leuit.12.3.
*Gen.17.10.
f That is to say, if the law of circumcision which Moses gaue be of so great account amongst you, that you doubt not to circumcise vpon the Sabbath, doe you rightly reprooue me for healing a man throughly?
*Deut.1.16.
9 Wee must iudge according to the trueth of things, lest the persons of men doe turne vs and carrie vs away.
g By the shewe that I make: for I seeme to be but an abiect and rascall of Galile, and a carpenters sonne, whom no man maketh account of: but marke the matter it selfe wel, and iudge the tree by the fruit.
10 Many doe marueil that the endeuours of the enemies of God haue no successe: yet in the meane season, they doe not acknowledge the vertue and power of God.
11 Men are very wise to procure stops and stayes to themselues.
12 The trueth of Christ doeth not hang vpon the iudgement of man.
13 The wicked cannot do what they lust, but what God hath appointed.
14 As the kingdome of God increaseth, so increaseth the rage of his enemies, till at the length they in vaine seeke for those blessings absent, which they despised when they were present.
*Chap.13.33.
h Word for word, (to the dispersion of the Gentiles or Grecians) and vnder the name of the Grecians he vnderstandeth the Iewes which were dispersed amongst the Gentiles, 1.Pet.1.1.
15 There are two principles of our saluation: the one to be thorowly touched wit a true feeling of our extreme pouertie: the other, to seeke in Christ onely (whom we catch hold on by faith) the abundance of all good things. *i The last day of the feast of Tabernacles, that is, the eight day was as high a day as the first.* *Leu.23.36. *Deut.18.15. *k This is not read word for word in any place, but it seemeth to bee taken out of many places where mention is made of the giftes of the holy Ghost, as Ioel 2.Esai.44 but especially in Esai.55.*

39 (*This spake hee of the Spirit, which
they that beleeued in him, should receiue: for
the[l] holy Ghost was not yet *giuen*, because that
Iesus was not yet [m] glorified.)
40 [16] So many of the people, when they
heard this saying, sayd, *Of a trueth this is that
Prophet.
41 Other sayde, This is that Christ: and
some sayd, But shall that Christ come out of
Galile?
42 *Sayeth not the Scripture, that that
Christ shall come of the seede of Dauid, and
out of the towne of Beth-leem, where Dauid
was?
43 So was there dissension among the people for him.
44 And some of them would haue taken
him, but no man layd hands on him.
45 [17] Then came the officers to the high
Priests and Pharises, and they sayd vnto them,
Why haue ye not brought him?
46 The officers answered, Neuer man spake
like this man.
47 Then answered them the Pharises, Are
ye also deceiued?
48 [18] Doth any of the rulers, or of the Pharises beleeue in him?
49 But this people, which knowe not the
Lawe, are cursed.
50 Nicodemus sayd vnto them, (*he that
came to Iesus by night, and was one of them.)
51 Doeth our Lawe iudge a man before it
heare him, *and knowe [n] what he hath done?
52 They answered, and sayd vnto him, Art
thou also of Galile? Search and looke: for out
of Galile ariseth no Prophet.
53 [19] And euery man went vnto his owne
house.

*Ioel 2.28. acts 2.17.
l What is meant by the holy Ghost, he expressed a little before, speaking of the Spirit which they that beleeued in him should receiue. So that by the name of holy Ghost, are meant the vertues and mightie workings of the holy Ghost.
m That is, those things were not yet seene and perceiued, which were to shew and set foorth the glory of the onely begotten.
16 There is contention euen in the Church it selfe about the chiefe poynt of religion: neither hath Christ any more cruell enemies then those that occupie the seate of trueth: yet cannot they doe what they would.
**Deut. 18.15.*
**Mich.5.2. matth.2 5.*
17 God from heauen scorneth such as are his Sonnes enemies.
18 False pastors are so fond and foolish, that they esteeme the Church of God according to the multitude and outward shew.
**Chap.3.2.*
**Deut.17.8. and 19.15.*
n What he hath committed, who is accused.
19 There is no counsell against the Lord.

CHAP. VIII.

3 *The woman taken in adulterie,* 11 *hath her sinnes forgiuen her.* 12 *Christ is the light of the world.* 19 *The Pharises aske where his father is.* 39 *The sonnes of Abraham.* 42 *The sonnes of God.* 44 *The deuill the father of lying.* 56 *Abraham saw Christs day.*

AND Iesus went vnto the mount of O-
liues,
2 And early in the morning came againe
into the Temple, and all the people came vnto him, and he sate downe and taught them.
3 [1] Then the Scribes and the Pharises
brought vnto him a woman taken in adultery,
and set her in the mids,
4 And sayd vnto him, Master, wee found
this woman committing adultery, euen in the
very act.
5 *Now Moses in our Lawe commanded,
that such should be stoned: what sayest thou
therefore?
6 And this they sayd to tempt him, that
they might haue whereof to accuse him. But
Iesus stouped downe, and with his finger wrote
on the ground.
7 [2] And while they continued asking him,
he lift himselfe vp, and sayd vnto them, *Let
him that is among you without sinne, cast the
first stone at her.
8 And againe he stouped down, and wrote
on the ground.
9 And when they heard it, being accused by their owne conscience, they went out
one by one, beginning at the eldest, euen to the
last: so Iesus was left alone, and the woman
standing in the mids.
10 [3] When Iesus had lift vp himselfe againe,
and saw no man, but the woman, he sayd vnto
her, Woman, where are those thine accusers?
hath no man condemned thee?
11 Shee sayd, No man, Lorde. And Iesus
sayd, Neither do I condemne thee: goe and sin
no more.
12 [4] Then spake Iesus againe vnto them,
saying, I *am that light of the world: hee that
followeth mee, shall not walke in darkenesse,
but shall haue that light of life.
13 [5] The Pharises therefore sayd vnto him,
[a] Thou bearest record of thy selfe: thy record is
not true.
14 *Iesus answered, and sayd vnto them,
[b] Though I beare record of my selfe, *yet* my record is true: for I knowe whence I came, and
whither I goe: but yee cannot tell whence I
come, and whither I goe.
15 Yee iudge after the flesh: I [c] iudge no
man.
16 And if I also iudge, my iudgement is
true: for I am not alone, but I and the Father,
that sent me.
17 And it is also written in your Law, *that
the testimonie of two men is true.
18 [d] I am one that beare witnesse of my
selfe, and the Father that sent me, beareth witnesse of mee.
19 [6] Then sayd they vnto him, Where is
that Father of thine? Iesus answered, Ye neither know mee, nor that Father of mine. If ye
had knowen me, ye would haue knowen that
Father of mine also.
20 These wordes spake Iesus in the [e] treasurie, as he taught in the Temple, and no man
layd hands on him: [7] for his houre was not yet
come.
21 [8] Then sayd Iesus againe vnto them, I
goe my way, and ye shall seeke me, and shall die
in your sinnes. Whither I go, can ye not come.
22 Then sayd the Iewes, will hee kill himselfe, because he sayth, Whither I goe, can yee
not come?
23 And he sayd vnto them, Ye are from beneath, I am from aboue: ye are of this worlde, I
am not of this world.
24 I sayd therefore vnto you, That ye shall

1 Whiles the wicked goe about to make a snare for good men, they make a snare for themselues.
**Leuit.20.10.*
2 Against hypocrites which are very seuere iudges against other men, and flatter themselues in their owne sinnes.
**Deut.17.7.*

3 Christ would not take vpon him the ciuill magistrates office: he contented himselfe to bring sinners to faith and repentance.
4 The world, which is blind in it selfe, cannot come to haue any light but in Christ onely.
**Cha.1.5. & 9.5.*
5 Christ is without all exceptiō, the best witnesse of the trueth, for he was sent by his Father for that purpose, and was by him approoued to the world by infinite miracles.
a Thou bearest witnesse of thy selfe, which thing by all mens opinions is naught, and for a man to commend himselfe is very discommendable.
**Chap.5.31.*
b That which hee denied afore, Chap. 5.31. must be taken by a maner of granting, for in that place he framed himselfe somwhat to the humor of his hearers which acknowledged nothing in Christ but his humanitie, and therfore he was content they should set light by his owne witnesse, vnlesse it were otherwise confirmed. But in this place, he standeth for the maintenance of his Godhead, & prayseth his Father, who is his witnesse, and agreeth with him.
c I doe now onely teach you, I condemne no man: but yet if I lust to doe it, I might lawfully doe it, for I am not alone, but my Father is with me.
**Deut.17.6. and 19.15. matth.18 16. 2.cor.13.1. hebr.10.28.*
d The Godhead is plainely distinguished from the manhood, else there were not two witnesses: for the partie accused is not taken for witnesse. 6 No man can know God, but in Christ onely. *e This was some place appointed for the gathering of the offerings.*
7 We liue and die at the pleasure of God, and not of men: therefore this one thing remayneth that we goe forward constantly in our vocation. 8 Because that men doe naturally abhorre heauenly things, no man can bee a fit disciple of Christ, vnlesse the Spirit of God frame him: in the meane season notwithstanding, the worlde must of necessitie perish, because it refused the life that it offered vnto it.

die

die in your ſinnes : for except ye beleeue, that
I am he, ye ſhall die in your ſinnes.
25 [9] Then ſayd they vnto him, Who art
thou? And Ieſus ſaid vnto them, Eue[f] the ſame
thing that I ſaid vnto you from the beginning.
26 [10] I haue many things to ſay, and to
iudge of you : but he that ſent me, is true, and
the things that I haue heard of him, thoſe ſpeak
I to the world.
27 [11] They vnderſtood not that he ſpake to
them of the Father.
28 Then ſayd Ieſus vnto them, When yee
haue lift vp the Sonne of man, then ſhall yee
knowe that I am he, and that I doe nothing of
my ſelfe, but as my Father hath taught mee, *ſo*
I ſpeake theſe things.
29 For he that ſent me is with me : the Father hath not left me alone, becauſe I do alwaies
thoſe things that pleaſe him.
30 ¶ As he ſpake theſe things, many beleeued in him.
31 [12] Then ſayd Ieſus to the Iewes which
beleeued in him, If ye continue in my worde,
ye are verely my diſciples,
32 And ſhal knowe the trueth, & the trueth
ſhall [g] make you free.
33 [h] They anſwered him, We be [i] Abrahams
ſeede, and were neuer bond to any man : why
ſayeſt thou then, Ye ſhall be made free?
34 Ieſus anſwered them, Verely, verely I
ſay vnto you, that whoſoeuer committeth ſin,
is the * ſeruant of ſinne.
35 And the ſeruant abideth not in the houſe
for euer : but the Sonne abideth for euer.
36 If that Sonne therefore ſhall make you
fre☙, ye ſhall be free in deede.
37 [13] I knowe that ye are Abrahams ſeede,
but ye ſeeke to kill mee, becauſe my word hath
no place in you.
38 I ſpeake that which I haue ſeene with
my Father : and yee doe that which yee haue
ſeene with your father.
39 They anſwered, and ſayd vnto him, A-
braham is our father. Ieſus ſayd vnto them, If
ye were Abrahams children, yee would do the
workes of Abraham.
40 But now ye go about to kill me, a man
that haue tolde you the trueth, which I haue
heard of God : this did not Abraham.
41 Ye doe the workes of your father. Then
ſayd they to him, We are not borne of fornication : we haue one Father, which is God.
42 Therefore Ieſus ſayd vnto them, If God
were your Father, then would yee loue me : for
I proceeded foorth, and came from God, neither came I of my ſelfe, but he ſent me.
43 Why doe ye not vnderſtand my [k] talke?
becauſe ye can not heare my word.
44 * Yee are of your father the deuill, and
the luſts of your father yee will doe : hee hath
beene a murtherer from the [l] beginning, and
[m] abode not in the [n] trueth, becauſe there is no
trueth in him. When hee ſpeaketh a lie, then

9 He ſhall at length knowe who Chriſt is, which will diligently heare what he ſayth.
f That is, I am Chriſt, and the Sauiour, for ſo I told you from the beginning that I was.
10 God is the reuenger of Chriſts doctrine deſpiſed.
11 Euen the cōtempt of Chriſt maketh for his glory : which thing his enemies ſhall feele at length to their great ſmart.
12 The true diſciples of Chriſt continue in his doctrine, that profiting more and more in the knowledge of the trueth, they may be deliuered from the moſt grieuous burden of ſinne, into the true libertie of righteouſnes and life.
g From the ſlauerie of ſinne.
h Some of the multitude, not they that beleeued: for this is not the ſpeach of men that conſent vnto him, but of men that are againſt him.
i Borne and begotten of Abraham.
*Rom.6.20. 1.pet.2.19.
13 Our wicked maners declare, that wee are plainely borne of a deuiliſh nature: But we are changed, and made of the houſhold of God according to the couenant which he made with Abraham by Chriſt onely, apprehended & layd hold on by faith : which faith is knowen by a godly and honeſt life.
k Or, language: as though he ſayd, you doe no more vnderſtand what I ſay, then if I ſpake in a ſtrange and vnknowen language to you.
*1.Iohn 3.8.
l From the beginning of the world: for as ſoone as man was made, the deuill caſt him headlong into death.
m That is, continued not conſtantly, or remained not
n That is, in faithfulnes and vprightnes, that is, he kept not his creation.

ſpeaketh he of his [o] owne : for hee is a liar, and
the [p] father thereof.
45 And becauſe I tell you the trueth, ye beleeue me not.
46 [14] Which of you can rebuke mee of
ſinne? and if I ſay the trueth, why doe ye not
beleeue me?
47 * Hee that is of God, heareth Gods
words: ye therefore heare them not, becauſe ye
are not of God.
48 [15] Then anſwered the Iewes, and ſayd
vnto him, Say we not well, that thou art a Samaritane, and haſt a deuill?
49 Ieſus anſwered, I haue not a deuill, but
I honour my Father, and yee haue diſhonou-
red me.
50 And I ſeeke not mine owne praiſe : but
there is one [q] that ſeeketh it, and iudgeth.
51 [16] Verely, verely I ſay vnto you, If a man
keepe my word, he ſhall neuer [r] ſee death.
52 [17] Then ſayde the Iewes to him, Now
knowe wee that thou haſt a deuill. Abraham is
dead, and the Prophets : and thou ſayeſt, If
a man keepe my word, hee ſhall neuer taſte of
death.
53 Art thou greater then our father Abraham, which is dead? and the Prophets are dead :
whom makeſt thou thy ſelfe?
54 [18] Ieſus anſwered, If I honour my ſelfe,
mine honour is [ſ] nothing worth : it is my Father that honoureth me, whom ye ſay that he is
your God.
55 [19] Yet yee haue not knowen him : but I
knowe him, and if I ſhould ſay, I knowe him
not, I ſhould bee a liar like vnto you : but I
know him, and keepe his word.
56 [20] Your father Abraham [t] reioyced to ſee
my [u] day, and he [x] ſaw it, and was glad.
57 Then ſayd the Iewes vnto him, Thou
art not yet fiftie yeere olde, and haſt thou ſeene
Abraham?
58 Ieſus ſayd vnto them, Verely, verely I ſay
vnto you, before Abraham was, I [y] am.
59 [21] Then tooke they vp ſtones to caſt at
him, but Ieſus hid himſelfe, and went out of
the Temple : And hee paſſed thorow the mids
of them, and ſo went his way.

o Euen of his owne head, and of his owne braine or diſpoſition.
p The author thereof.
14 Chriſt did throughly execute the office that his Father inioyned him.
* 1.Iohn 4.6.
15 The enemies of Chriſt make their brauery for a while, but the Father will appeare at his time to reuenge the reproch that is done vnto him in the perſon of his ſonne.
q That is, that wil reuenge both your deſpiſing of me, and of him.
16 The onely doctrine of the Goſpel apprehended by faith, is a ſure remedy againſt death.
r That is, he ſhall not feele it : for euen in the midſt of death, the faithfull ſee life.
17 Againſt them which abuſe the glory of the Saints, to darken Chriſts glory.
18 There is nothing further off from all ambition then Chriſt, but his Father hath ſet him aboue all things.
ſ This is ſpoken by maner of a grant : as if he had ſaid, be it ſo, let this report which I giue of my ſelfe, be of no force: yet there is another that glorifieth me, that is, that honoureth my Name.
19 There is no right knowledge of God, without Chriſt, neither any right knowledge of Chriſt without his word.
20 The vertue of Chriſt ſhewed it ſelfe thorow all former ages in the fathers, for they ſaw in the promiſes, that he ſhould come, and did very ioyfully lay holde on him with a liuely faith. *t Was very deſirous.* *u A day is a ſpace that a man liueth in, or doeth any notable acte, or ſuffereth any great thing.* *x With the eyes of faith, Heb.11.13.* *y Chriſt as he was God, was before Abraham : and hee was the Lambe ſlaine from the beginning of the world.* 21 Zeale without knowledge, breaketh out at length into a moſt open madneſſe : and yet the wicked cannot doe what they luſt.

CHAP. IX.

1 Chriſt giueth ſight on the Sabbath day to him that was borne blinde : 13 Whome, after hee had long reaſoned againſt the Phariſes, 22. 35 and was caſt out of the Synagogue, 36 Chriſt endueth with the knowledge of the euerlaſting light.

AND [1] as Ieſus paſſed by, hee ſawe a man
which was blind from his birth.
2 And his diſ^ciples aſked him, ſaying,
Maſter, who did ſinne, this man, or his parents,
tha he was borne blind?

1 Sin is the beginning euen of all bodily diſeaſes, & yet doth it not folow, ẏ God alway reſpecteth their ſinnes whō he moſt ſharply puniſheth.

3 Ieſus

a Christ reasoneth here, as his disciples thought, which presuppose that there come no diseases but for sinnes onely: wherupon he answereth that there was another cause of this mans blindnesse, and that was, that God his worke might be seene.
2 The works of Christ are as it were a light, which lighten the darkenes of the world.
b By (day) is meant the light, that is, the lightsome doctrine of the heauenly trueth: and by night is meant the darkenesse which commeth by the obscuritie of the same doctrine.
**Chap.1.9 and 8 12. and 12.35.*
3 Christ healing the man borne blind, by taking the signe of clay, and afterward the signe of the fountaine of Siloam (which signifieth Sent) sheweth that as he at the beginning made man, so doeth he againe restore both his body and soule: and yet so, that he himselfe commeth first of his owne accord to heale vs.
4 A true image of all men, who as they are of nature blinde, doe neither themselues receiue the light that is offered vnto them, nor suffer it in other, and yet make a great adoe amongst themselues.
c This is an Hebrew kinde of speach, for they call a mans eyes shut, when they cannot receiue any light: And therefore they are said to haue their eyes opened, which of blinde men are made to see.
5 Religion is not assaulted by any meanes more, then by pretence of religion: but the more it is pressed downe, the more it riseth vp.

3 Iesus answered, [a] Neither hath this man
sinned, nor his parents, but that the workes of
God should be shewed on him.
4 [2] I must worke the workes of him that
sent me, while it is [b] day: the night commeth
when no man can worke.
5 As long as I am in the world, *I am the
light of the world.
6 [3] Assoone as he had thus spoken, he spat
on the ground, & made clay of the spettle, and
anoynted the eyes of the blind with the clay,
7 And said vnto him, Go wash in the poole
of Siloam (which is by interpretation, Sent.)
He went his way therefore, and washed, and
came againe seeing.
8 [4] Now the neighbours and they that had
seene him before, when he was blind, said, Is
not this he that sate and begged?
9 Some said, This is he: and other saide,
He is like him: but he himselfe said, I am he.
10 Therfore they said vnto him, How were
thine eyes [c] opened?
11 He answered, and said, The man that is
called Iesus, made clay, and anoynted mine
eyes, and said vnto me, Goe to the poole of Siloam,
and wash. So I went and washed, and receiued
sight.
12 Then they said vnto him, Where is he?
He said, I cannot tell.
13 ¶They brought to the Pharises him that
was once blinde.
14 And it was the Sabbath *day*, when Iesus
made the clay, and opened his eyes.
15 Then againe the Pharises also asked him,
how he had receiued sight. And he said vnto
them, He layed clay vpon mine eyes, and I washed,
and doe see.
16 [5] Then said some of the Pharises, This
man is not of God, because he keepeth not the
Sabbath *day*. Others said, How can a man that
is a sinner, doe such miracles? and there was a
dissension among them.
17 Then spake they vnto the blinde againe,
What sayest thou of him, because he hath opened
thine eyes? And he said, Hee is a Prophet.
18 Then the Iewes did not beleeue him
(that he had bene blind, and receiued his sight)
vntill they had called the parents of him that
had receiued sight.
19 And they asked them, saying, Is this your
sonne, whom ye say was borne blind? How
doeth he now see then?
20 His parents answered them, and saide,
We know that this is our sonne, and that hee
was borne blind:
21 But by what meanes he now seeth, we
know not: or who hath opened his eyes, can
we not tell: he is old enough: aske him: hee
shall answere for himselfe.
22 These words spake his parents, because
they feared the Iewes: for the Iewes had ordeined
already, that if any man did confesse that
he was Christ, he should be *excommunicate* out
of the Synagogue.
23 Therefore said his parents, He is old ynough:
aske him.
24 Then againe called they the man that
had bene blind, and said vnto him, [d] Giue glory
vnto God: we know that this man is a [e] sinner.
25 Then he answered, and said, Whether
he be a sinner or no, I cannot tell: one thing I
know, that I was blind, and now I see.
26 Then said they to him againe, What did
he to thee? How opened he thine eyes?
27 He answered them, I haue told you already,
and yee haue not heard it: wherefore
would ye heare it againe? will yee also be his
disciples?
28 [6] Then reuiled they him, and said, Be thou
his disciple: we be Moses disciples.
29 We knowe that God spake with Moses:
but this man we know not from whence
he is.
20 The man answered and said vnto them,
Doubtlesse, this is a marueilous thing, that yee
know not whence he is, and yet he hath opened
mine eyes.
31 Now we knowe that God heareth not
sinners: but if any man be a worshipper of God
and doeth his will, him heareth he.
32 Since the world began, was it not heard,
that any man opened the eyes of one that was
borne blind.
33 If this man were not of God, he could
haue done nothing.
34 They answered & said vnto him, [f] Thou
art altogether borne in sinnes, and doest thou
teach vs? so they cast him out.
35 [7] Iesus heard that they had cast him out:
and when he had found him, he said vnto him,
Doest thou beleeue in the Sonne of God?
36 He answered, and said, Who is he, Lord,
that I might beleeue in him?
37 And Iesus saide vnto him, Both thou
hast seene him, and hee it is that talketh with
thee.
38 Then he said, Lord, I beleeue, and worshipped
him.
39 [8] And Iesus said, I am come vnto [g] iudgment
into this world, that they [h] which see
not, might see: and that they *which see, might
be made blinde.
40 And some of the Pharises which were
with him, heard these things, and said vnto him,
Are we blind also?
41 Iesus said vnto them, If ye were blinde,
ye should not haue sinne: but now ye say, We
see: therefore your sinne remaineth.

d A solemne order, whereby men were constrained in olde time to acknowledge their fault before God, as if they should say, Consider thou art before God, who knoweth the whole matter, and therefore see thou reuerence his Maiestie, and doe him this honour rather to confesse the whole matter openly then to lie before him, Iosh.7.19. 1.Sam.6.5.
e He is called a sinner in the Hebrew tongue, which is a wicked man, and maketh as it were an art of sinning.
6 Proud wickednesse must needs at length breake forth, which in vaine lieth hid vnder a zeale of godlinesse.
f Thou art naught euen from thy cradle, and as we vse to say, there is nothing in thee but sinne.
7 Most happy is their state, which are cast furthest out of the Church of ẏ wicked (which proudly boast themselues of the name of the Church) that Christ may come neerer to them.
8 Christ doeth lighten all them by the preaching of the Gospel, which acknowledge their own darkenesse, but such as seeme to themselues to see cleerely enough, those he altogether blindeth: of which sort are they oftentimes, which haue the highest place in the Church.
*g With great power and authoritie, to doe what is righteous, and iust: as if he said, these men take vpon them to gouerne the people of God after their own lust, as though they saw all things, and no man but they: but I wil rule farre otherwise then these men doe: for whome they account for blinde men, them will I lighten, and such as take themselues to be wisest, them will I drowne in most grosse darkenesse of ignorance. h In these words (of seeing and not seeing) there is a secret taunting & checke to the Pharises: for they thought all men blinde but themselues. * Chap.3.17. and 12.47.*

CHAP. X.

1 *Christ prooueth that the Pharises are the euill shepheards,*
8 *and by many reasons that himselfe* 11.14 *is the good shepheard:*

shepheard: 19 And thereof dissension ariseth. 31 They
take vp stones, 39 and goe about to take him, but hee
escapeth.

Verely, [1] verely I say vnto you, He that entreth not in by the doore into the sheep-
fold, but climeth vp another way, he is a thiefe
and a robber.
2 But he that goeth in by the doore, is the
shepheard of the sheepe.
3 To him the [a] Porter openeth, and the
sheepe heare his voyce, and he calleth his owne
sheepe by name, and leadeth them out.
4 And when he hath sent foorth his owne
sheepe, he goeth before them, and the sheepe
follow him: for they know his voyce.
5 And they will not follow a stranger, but
they flee from him: for they knowe not the
voyce of strangers.
6 This [b] parable spake Iesus vnto them:
but they vnderstood not what things they were
which he spake vnto them.
7 Then said Iesus vnto them againe, Verely, verely I say vnto you, I am that doore of the
sheepe.
8 [2] All, that [c] euer came before mee, are
theeues and robbers: but the sheepe did not
heare them.
9 [3] I am that doore: by me if any man enter in, he shall be saued, and shall [d] goe in, and
goe out, and find pasture.
10 The thiefe commeth not, but for to steale,
and to kill, and to destroy: I am come that they
might haue life, and haue it in abundance.
11 * I am that good sheepheard: that good
sheepheard giueth his life for his sheepe.
12 But an hireling, and he which is not the
sheepheard, neither the sheepe are his owne,
seeth the Woolfe comming, and he leaueth the
sheepe, and fleeth, and the Woolfe catcheth
them, and scattereth the sheepe.
13 So the hireling fleeth, because hee is an
hireling, and careth not for the sheepe.
14 I am that good sheepheard, and knowe
mine, and am knowen of mine.
15 As the Father [e] knoweth me, so knowe
I the Father: and I lay downe my life for *my*
sheepe.
16 [4] Other sheepe I haue also, which are
not of this folde: them also must I bring, and
they shall heare my voyce: and * there shall be
[f] one sheepefold, *and* one shepheard.
17 [5] Therefore doeth my Father loue mee,
because * [g] I lay downe my life, that I might
take it againe.
18 No man taketh it from mee, but I lay
it downe of my selfe: I haue power to lay it
downe, and haue power to take it againe: this

1 Seeing that by Christ onely we haue accesse to the Father, there are neither other true shepheards, then those which come to Christ themselues and bring other thither also, neither is any to be thought the true sheepefold, but that which is gathered to Christ.
a In those dayes they vsed to haue a seruant alwayes sitting at the doore, and therefore he speaketh after the maner of those dayes.
b This word (parable) which the Euangelist vseth here, signifieth a darke kinde of speech, when words are taken from their naturall meaning, to signifie another thing to vs.
2 It maketh no matter, how many, neither how old the false teachers haue bene.
c These large termes must be applied to the matter he speaketh of. And therefore when he calleth himselfe the doore, he calleth all them theeues and robbers which take vpon them this name of Doore, which none of the Prophets can, for they shewed the sheepe that Christ was the doore.
3 Onely Christ is the true Pastor, and that only is the true Church, which acknowledgeth him to be properly their onely Pastor: To him are opposite theeues which feed not the sheepe, but kill them: and hirelings also, which forsake the flock in time of danger, because they feed it onely for their owne profit and gaines.
d That is, shall liue safely: So vse the Iewes to speake, as Deut. 26.6. and yet there is a peculiar alluding to the shepheards office. * *Isai. 40.11. ezek. 34.23.* *e Loueth me, alloweth me.* 4 The calling of the Gentiles. **Ezek. 37.22.* *f The certaine marke of the Catholique Church throughout all the world, which hath one head, that is, Christ, the onely keeper, and onely sheepheard of it.* 5 Christ is by the decree of the Father, the onely true sheepeheard of the true Church, for he willingly gaue his life for his sheepe, and by his owne power rose againe to life. * *Isai. 53.7.* *g Hee speaketh in the time that now is, because Christs whole life, was as it were a perpetuall death.*

* commandement haue I receiued of my Father.
19 ¶ [6] Then there was a dissension againe
among the Iewes for these sayings,
20 And many of them said, He hath a deuill, and is madde: why heare ye him?
21 Other said, These are not the words of
him that hath a deuill: can the deuill open the
eyes of the blinde?
22 And it was at Hierusalem the *feast of the*
[h] *Dedication*, and it was winter.
23 [7] And Iesus walked in the Temple, in
Salomons porch.
24 Then came the Iewes round about him,
and saide vnto him, How long doest thou
make vs doubt? If thou be that Christ, tell vs
plainely.
25 [8] Iesus answered them, I told you, and
ye beleeue not: the works that I doe in my Fathers Name, they beare witnesse of me.
26 [9] But ye beleeue not: [i] for ye are not of
my sheepe, as I said vnto you.
27 My sheepe heare my voyce, and I know
them, and they follow me,
28 And I giue vnto them eternall life, and
they shall neuer perish, neither shall any plucke
them out of mine hand.
29 My Father which gaue *them* me, is greater then all, and none is able to take them out of
my Fathers hand.
30 I and my Father are one.
31 * [10] Then the Iewes again tooke vp stones
to stone him.
32 Iesus answered them, Many good works
haue I shewed you from my [k] Father: for which
of these works doe ye stone me?
33 The Iewes answered him, saying, For
the good worke we stone thee not, but for blasphemie, and that thou being a man, makest thy
selfe God.
34 Iesus answered them, Is it not written in
your Law, * I said, Ye are gods?
35 If he called them gods, vnto whom the
word of God was *giuen*, and the Scripture cannot be [l] broken,
36 Say ye of him, whom the Father hath sanctified, and sent into the world, Thou blasphe-
mest, because I said, I am the Sonne of God?
37 If I doe not the works of my Father, beleeue me not.
38 But if I doe, then though ye beleeue not
me, *yet* beleeue the works, that ye may knowe
and beleeue, that the Father *is* in me, and I in
him.
39 [11] Againe they went about to take him:
but he escaped out of their hands,
40 And went againe beyond Iordan, into
the place where Iohn first baptized, and there
abode.
41 And many resorted vnto him, and said,
Iohn did no miracle: but all things that Iohn
spake of this man, were true.
42 And many beleeued in him there.

* *Acts 2.24.*
6 The Gospel discouereth hypocrisie, & therefore the world must needs rage when it commeth forth.
h The feast of the Dedication was instituted by Iudas Maccabeus and his brethren, after the restoring of Gods true religion, by the casting out of Antiochus his garison, 1. Mac. 4. 59.
7 The vnbeleeuers and proud men accuse the Gospel of darknesse, which darkenesse in deed, is within themselues.
8 The doctrine of the Gospel is proued from heauen by two witnesses: both by the puritie of the doctrine, and by miracles.
9 It is no marueile that there doe but a fewe beleeue, seeing that all men are by nature vntamed beasts: yet notwithstanding God hath his, which he turneth into sheepe, and committeth them vnto his Sonne, and preserueth them against the crueltie of all wilde beasts.
i He giueth a reason why they beleeue not, to wit, because they are none of his sheepe.
* *Chap. 8.59.*
10 Christ proueth his dignitie by diuine works
k Through my Fathers authoritie and power.
* *Psalme 82.6.*
l Voyd and of none effect.
11 Christ fleeth danger, not of mistrust, nor for feare of death, nor that hee would be idle, but to gather a Church in another place.

CHAP.

CHAP. XI.

1 Christ, to shewe that he is 25 the life and the resurrecti-
on, 14 commeth to Lazarus being dead, 17. 34 and
buried, 43 and raiseth him vp. 47 As the Priests were
consulting together, 49 Caiaphas 50 prophesieth that
one must die for the people. 56. 57 They commaund to
seeke Christ out, and to take him.

1 Christ in restoring the stinking carkase of his friend to life, sheweth an example both of his mighty power, & also of his singular good wil toward men: which is also an image of the resurrection to come.
a Where his sisters dwelt.
** Chap.12.3. matth.26.7.*
b That is to say, sent for the purpose to kill him.

AND [1] a certaine man was sicke, *named* Lazarus of Bethania, the [a] Towne of Mary,
and her sister Martha.
2 (And it was that * Mary which anoynted the Lord with oyntment, and wiped his
feete with her haire, whose brother Lazarus
was sicke.)
3 Therefore *his* sisters sent vnto him, saying, Lord, behold, he whome thou louest, is
sicke.
4 When Iesus heard it, he said, This sickenesse is not vnto [b] death, but for the glorie of
God, that the Sonne of God might be glorified thereby.
5 ¶ Now Iesus loued Martha and her sister, and Lazarus.

2 In that, that God seemeth sometimes to linger in helping of vs, he doeth it both for his glorie, and for our saluation, as the falling out of the matter in the ende, plainely prooueth.
3 This onely is the sure and right way to life to follow God boldly without feare, who calleth vs and shineth before vs in the darkenes of this world.
** Chap.7.30. and 8.59. and 10.33.*
c All things are fitly wrought and brought to passe in their season.
d The Iewes vsed a milder kinde of speach, and called death a sleepe, whereupon in other languages the place of buriall where the dead are laid waiting for the resurrection, is called a sleeping place.

6 [2] And after he had heard that hee was
sicke, yet abode he two dayes still in the same
place where he was.
7 Then after that said he to his disciples,
Let vs goe into Iudea againe.
8 [3] The disciples saide vnto him, Master,
the Iewes lately sought to * stone thee, and
doest thou goe thither againe?
9 Iesus answered, Are there not [c] twelue
houres in the day? If a man walke in the day,
he stumbleth not, because he seeth the light of
this world.
10 But if a man walke in the night, he stumbleth, because there is no light in him.
11 These things spake he, and after, he said
vnto them, Our friend Lazarus [d] sleepeth: but
I goe to wake him vp.
12 Then said his disciples, Lord, if he sleepe,
he shall be safe.
13 Howbeit, Iesus spake of his death: but
they thought that he had spoken of the naturall sleepe.
14 Then said Iesus vnto them plainely, Lazarus is dead.
15 And I am glad for your sakes, that I was
not there, that ye may beleeue: but let vs goe
vnto him.
16 Then said Thomas (which is called Didymus) vnto his fellowe disciples, Let vs also
goe, that we may die with him.
17 ¶ Then came Iesus, and found that hee
had lien in the graue foure dayes already.
18 (Now Bethania was neere vnto Hierusalem, about fifteene furlongs off.)

4 God who is the maker of nature, doeth not condemne naturall affections, but sheweth that they ought to be examined by the rule of faith.

19 [4] And many of the Iewes were come to
Martha and Mary to comfort them for their
brother.
20 Then Martha, when she heard that Iesus
was comming, went to meet him: but Marie
sate still in the house.
21 Then said Martha vnto Iesus, Lord, if
thou hadst bene here, my brother had not bene
dead.
22 But now I know also, that whatsoeuer
thou askest of God, God will giue it thee.
23 Iesus said vnto her, Thy brother shall
[e] rise againe.
24 Martha said vnto him, I knowe that hee
shall rise againe * in the resurrection at the last
day.
25 Iesus said vnto her, I am the resurrection
and the life: * he that beleeueth in me, though
he were dead, *yet* shall he liue.
26 And whosoeuer liueth, and beleeueth in
me, shall neuer die: Beleeuest thou this?
27 She said vnto him, Yea, Lord, I beleeue
that thou art that Christ that Sonne of God,
which should come into the world.
28 ¶ And when she had so said, shee went
her way, and called Mary her sister secretly, saying, The Master is come, and calleth for thee.
29 And when she heard it, she arose quickly, and came vnto him.
30 For Iesus was not yet come into the
towne, but was in the place where Martha
met him.
31 The Iewes then which were with her
in the house, and comforted her, when they
saw Mary, that shee rose vp hastily, and went
out, followed her, saying, Shee goeth vnto the
graue, to weepe there.
32 Then when Mary was come where Iesus
was, and saw him, she fell downe at his feet, saying vnto him, Lord, if thou hadst beene here,
my brother had not bene dead.
33 [5] When Iesus therefore saw her weepe,
and the Iewes *also* weepe which came with her,
he [f] groned in the spirit, and was troubled in
himselfe,
34 And said, Where haue yee layed him?
They said vnto him, Lord, come and see.
35 *And* Iesus wept.
36 Then said the Iewes, Behold, how he loued him.
37 And some of them said, * Could not he,
which opened the eyes of the blind, haue made
also, that this man should not haue died?
38 Iesus therefore againe groned in himselfe, and came to the graue. And it was a caue,
and a stone was laid vpon it.
39 Iesus said, Take ye away the stone. Martha the sister of him that was dead, saide vnto
him, Lord, he stinketh already: for he hath bin
dead foure dayes.
40 Iesus said vnto her, Said I not vnto thee,
that if thou diddest beleeue, thou shouldest see
the glory of God?
41 Then they tooke away the stone *from the*
place where the dead was layed. And Iesus lift
vp his eyes, and said, Father, I thanke thee, because thou hast heard me.
42 I know that thou hearest me alwaies, but
because of the people that stand by, I saide it,
that they may beleeue, that thou hast sent me.

e That is, shall recouer life againe.
** Chap.5.29. luke 14.14.*
** Chap.6.35.*
5 Christ tooke vpon him together with our flesh, all affections of man (sin onely excepted) and amongst the especially mercy, and compassion.
f These are tokens that he was greatly mooued, but yet they were without sinne: and these affections are proper to mans nature.
** Chap.9.6.*

6 The last point of hard & yronlike stubburnnesse is this, to proclaime open warre against God, and yet ceaseth not to make a pretence both of godlines, and of the profit of the cōmon wealth.

g The Iewes called the councill Sanhedrin: and the word that Iohn vseth, is Synedri.

h That is, take away from vs by force: for at that time, though the high Priests authoritie was greatly lessened and decayed, yet there was some kind of gouernement left among the Iewes.

7 The raging and mad companie of the false church perswade themselues that they cannot be in safetie, vnlesse hee be taken away, who onely vpholdeth the Church. And so likewise iudgeth the wisedome of the flesh in worldly affaires, which is gouerned by the spirit of giddinesse or madnesse.

* *Chap.* 18.14.

8 Christ doeth sometimes so turne ẏ tongues, euen of the wicked, that euen in cursing, they blesse.

i For they were not gathered together in one countrey, as the Iewes were, but to be gathered from all quarters, from the East to the West.

9 We may giue place to the rage of the wicked, when it is expedient so to doe, but yet in such sort, that wee swarue not from Gods vocation.

43 As he had spoken these things, he cryed
with a loud voyce, Lazarus, come forth.
44 Then he that was dead, came foorth,
bound hand and foot with bands, and his face
was bound with a napkin. Iesus said vnto them,
Lose him, and let him goe.
45 ¶ Then many of the Iewes, which came
to Mary, and had seene the things which Iesus
did, beleeued in him.
46 [6] But some of them went their way to
the Pharises, and told them what things Iesus
had done.
47 Then gathered the high Priests, and the
Pharises a [g] councill, and said, What shall wee
doe? For this man doeth many miracles.
48 If we let him thus alone, all men will beleeue in him, and the Romanes will come and
[h] take away both our place, and the nation.
49 [7] Then one of them *named* Caiaphas,
which was the high Priest that same yeere, said,
vnto them, Ye perceiue nothing at all,
50 *Nor yet doe you consider that it is expedient for vs, that one man die for the people,
and that the whole nation perish not.
51 [8] This spake he not of himselfe: but being high Priest that same yeere, he prophesied
that Iesus should die for that nation:
52 And not for that nation onely, but that
he should gather together in one the children
of God, which [i] were scattered.
53 Then from that day forth they consulted
together to put him to death.
54 [9] Iesus therefore walked no more openly
among the Iewes, but went thence vnto a
countrey neere to the wildernesse, into a citie
called Ephraim, and there continued with his
disciples.
55 ¶ And the Iewes Passeouer was at hand,
and many went out of the country vp to Hierusalem before the Passeouer, to purifie themselues.
56 Then sought they for Iesus, and spake
among themselues, as they stood in the Temple, What thinke ye, that he commeth not to
the feast?
57 Now both the high Priests and the Pharises had giuen a commandement, that if any
man knew where he were, he shoul shew it, that
they might take him.

CHAP. XII.

2 As Christ is at supper with Lazarus, 3 Mary anointeth his feet. 5 Iudas findeth fault with her. 7 Christ defendeth her. 10 The Priestes would put Lazarus to death. 12 As Christ commeth to Hierusalem, 18 The people meete him. 20 The Grecians desire to see him. 42 The chiefe Rulers that beleeue in him, but for feare doe not confesse him, 44 he exhorteth to faith.

* *Chap.* 26.7. *marke* 14.3.

THen * Iesus, sixe dayes before the Passeouer, came to Bethania, where Lazarus
was, who died, whome he had raised from the
dead.
2 There they made him a supper, and Martha serued: but Lazarus was one of them that
sate at the table with him.
3 Then tooke Mary a pound of ointment
of Spikenard very costly, and anointed Iesus
feet, and wiped his feet with her haire, and the
house was filled with the sauour of the oyntment.
4 Then said one of his disciples, *euen* Iudas Iscariot Simons *sonne*, which should betray
him:
5 [1] Why was not this ointment solde for
three hundreth pence, and giuen to the poore?
6 Now he said this, not that hee cared for
the poore, but because he was a thiefe, and *had
the bagge, and bare that which was giuen.
7 [2] Then said Iesus, Let her alone: against
the day of my burying she kept it.
8 For the poore alwayes ye haue with you,
but me ye shall not haue alwayes.
9 [3] Then much people of the Iewes knew
that he was there: and they came, not for Iesus
sake onely, but that they might see Lazarus also, whom he had raised from the dead.
10 The high Priestes therefore consulted,
that they might put Lazarus to death also,
11 Because that for his sake many of the
Iewes went away, and beleeued in Iesus.
12 ¶ *On the morowe a great multitude
that were come to the feast, when they heard
that Iesus should come to Hierusalem,
13 Tooke branches of Palme trees, & went
forth to meet him, and cried, Hosanna, Blessed
is the King of Israel that commeth in the Name
of the Lord.
14 And Iesus found a yong asse, and sate
thereon, as it is written.
15 * Feare not, daughter of Sion: beholde,
thy King commeth sitting on an asses colt.
16 But his disciples vnderstood not these
things at the first: but when Iesus was glorified, then remembred they, that these things
were written of him, and that they had done
these things vnto him.
17 The people therefore that was with him,
bare witnesse that he called Lazarus out of the
graue, and raised him from the dead.
18 Therefore met him the people also,
because they saide that hee had done this miracle.
19 [4] And the Pharises said among themselues, Perceiue ye how ye preuaile nothing?
Behold, the world goeth after him.
20 ¶ Now there were certaine Greekes among them that [a] came to worshippe at the
feast.
21 And they came to Philip, which was of
Bethsaida in Galile, and desired him, saying,
Sir, we would see that Iesus.
22 Philip came and told Andrewe: and againe Andrew and Philip tolde Iesus.
23 And Iesus answered them, saying, The
houre is come, that the Sonne of man must be
glorified.
24 [5] Verely, verely I say vnto you, Except the wheat corne fall into the ground and
[b] die,

1 An horrible example in Iudas of a minde blinded with couetousnesse, and yet pretending godlinesse.

* *Chap.* 13.29.

2 This extraordinarie anointing which was for a signe, is so allowed of God, that he witnesseth how he will not be worshipped with outward pompe, or costly seruice, but with almes.

3 When the light of the Gospel sheweth it selfe, some are found to be curious, and others (which least ought) to be open enemies: others in a rage honour him, whom they will straightway fall from: and very fewe doe so reuerently receiue him as they ought: Notwithstanding Christ beginneth his spirituall kingdome in the mids of his enemies.

* *Matth.* 21.8. *marke* 11.8. *luke* 19.35.

* *Zech.* 9.9.

4 Euen they which go about to oppresse Christ, are made instruments of his glory.

a After the solemne custome: the Grecians were first so called by the name of the country of Greece, where they dwelt: but afterward, all that were not of the Iewes religion, but worshipped false gods and were also called Heathens, were called by this name.

5 The death of Christ is as it were a sowing, which seemeth to be a dying to the corne, but in deed is the cause of a farre greater haruest: and such as is the condition of the head, so shall it be of the members.

[b] die, it bideth alone: but if it die, it bringeth forth much fruit.

25 *He that loueth his life, ſhall loſe it, and he that hateth his life in this world, ſhall keepe it vnto life eternall.

26 *If any man ſerue me, let him followe me: for where I am, there ſhall alſo my ſeruant be: and if any man ſerue me, him will my Father honour.

26 [6] Now is my ſoule troubled: and what ſhall I ſay? Father, ſaue me from this [c] houre: but therefore came I vnto this houre.

28 Father, [d] glorifie thy Name. Then came there a voyce from heauen, *ſaying*, I haue both glorified it, and will glorifie it againe.

29 Then ſaid the people that ſtood by, and heard, that it was a thunder: other ſaide, An Angel ſpake to him.

30 [7] Ieſus anſwered, and ſaid, This voyce came not becauſe of me, but for your ſakes.

31 Now is the iudgement of this world: now ſhall the prince of this world be caſt out.

32 *And I, if I were [e] lift vp from the earth, will draw [f] all men vnto me.

33 Now this ſaid he, ſignifying what death he ſhould die.

34 The people anſwered him, Wee haue heard out of the *Law, that that Chriſt bideth for euer: and how ſayeſt thou, that that Sonne of man muſt be lift vp? Who is that Sonne of man?

35 [8] Then Ieſus ſaid vnto them, Yet a little while is *the light with you: walke while yee haue that light, leſt the darkeneſſe come vpon you: for he that walketh in the darke, knoweth not whither he goeth.

36 While ye haue the light, beleeue in that light, that ye may be the [g] children of the light. Theſe things ſpake Ieſus, and departed, and hid himſelfe from them.

37 ¶ [9] And though hee had done ſo many miracles before them, *yet* beleeued they not on him,

38 That the ſaying of Eſaias the Prophet might be fulfilled, that he ſaid, *Lord, who beleeued our report? and to whom is the [h] arme of the Lord reueiled?

39 Therefore could they not beleeue, becauſe that Eſaias ſaith againe,

40 *He hath blinded their eyes, and hardened their heart, that they ſhould not ſee with *their* eyes, nor vnderſtand with *their* heart, and ſhould be conuerted, and I ſhould heale them.

41 Theſe things ſaid Eſaias when he ſaw his glory, and ſpake of him.

42 [10] Neuertheleſſe, euen among the chiefe rulers, many beleeued in him: but becauſe of the Phariſes they did not confeſſe him, leſt they

b A wheate corne dieth when it is changed by vertue of the ground, and becommeth a root of a fruitfull blade.

* *Matth.* 10.39. *and* 16.25. *marke* 8.35. *luke* 9.24. *and* 17.33.

* *Chap.* 17.34.

6 Whiles Chriſt went about to ſuffer all the puniſhment which is due to our ſinnes, and whileſt his diuinitie did not yet ſhew his might and power ſo farre, as this ſatisfaction might bee throughly wrought, now when he is ſtriken with the great feare of the curſe of God, he crieth and prayeth, and deſireth to be releaſed: yet nowithſtanding he preferreth the will and glory of his Father before all things, whoſe obedience the Father alloweth euen from heauen

c To wit, of death that is now at hand.

d So then the Fathers glory is Chriſt his glory.

7 Chriſt foretelleth to the deafe, the maner of his death, the ouercomming of the deuil and the world, and in concluſion his triumph.

* *Chap.* 3.14.

e Chriſt vſed a word, which hath a double meaning, for it ſignifieth either to lift vp, or to rid out of the way: for his meaning was to put them in minde of his death, but the Iewes ſeeme to take it another way.

f Chryſoſt and Theophyl. referre this word All, to all nations: that is, not to the Iewes onely.

* *Pſal.* 89.36. *and* 110.4. *and* 117.2. *iſai.* 40.8. *ezech.* 37.25.

8 Vnmeaſurable is the mercie of God, but an horrible iudgement followeth, if it be contemned.

* *Chap.* 1.9.

ſhould be *caſt* out of the Synagogue.

43 *For they loued the praiſe of men, more then the prayſe of God.

44 [11] And Ieſus cryed, and ſaid, He that beleeueth in me, beleeueth [i] not in me, but in him that ſent me.

45 And hee that ſeeth mee, ſeeth him that ſent me.

46 I *am come a light into the world, that whoſoeuer beleeueth in me, ſhould not abide in darkeneſſe.

47 *And if any man heare my words, and beleeue not, I iudge him not: for I came not to iudge the world, but to ſaue the world.

48 He that refuſeth me, and receiueth not my words, hath one that iudgeth him: *the word that I haue ſpoken, it ſhall iudge him in the laſt day.

49 For I haue not ſpoken of my ſelfe: but the Father which hath ſent me, hee gaue me a commandement what I ſhould ſay, and what I ſhould ſpeake.

50 And I know that his commaundement is life euerlaſting: the things therefore that I ſpeake, I ſpeake *them* ſo as the Father ſaid vnto me.

* *Chap* 5.44.

11 The ſumme of the Goſpel, and therefore of ſaluation, which Chriſt witneſſed in the midſt of Hieruſalem by his crying out, is this: to reſt vpon Chriſt through faith as the onely Sauiour appoynted and giuen vs of the Father.

i This word, Not, doeth not take any whit of this from Chriſt which is here ſpoken of, but is in way of correction rather, as if he ſaid He that beleeueth in me, doeth not ſo much beleeue in me, as in him that ſent me. So is it in Marke 9.37.

* *Chap.* 3.19. *and* 9.39.

* *Chap.* 3.17.

* *Mar.* 16.16.

CHAP. XIII.

4 Chriſt riſing from Supper, 15 to commend humilitie to his Apoſtles, waſheth their feet. 21 He noteth the traitor Iudas 26 with an euident token. 34 Hee commendeth charitie. 37. 39 He foretelleth Peter of his deniall.

NOw *[1] before the feaſt of the Paſſeouer, when Ieſus knewe that his houre was come, that he ſhould depart out of this world vnto the Father, foraſmuch as hee loued his [a] owne which were in the world, vnto the end he loued them.

2 And when ſupper was done (and that the deuill had now put in the heart of Iudas Iſcariot, Simons *ſonne*, to betray him)

3 Ieſus knowing that the Father had giuen all things into his [b] handes, and that hee was come forth from God, and went to God,

4 He [c] riſeth from ſupper, and layeth aſide *his vpper* garments, and tooke a towell, and girded himſelfe.

5 After that, he powred water into a baſen, and began to waſh the diſciples feete, and to wipe them with the towell, wherewith hee was girded.

6 Then came he to Simon Peter, who ſaid to him, Lord, doeſt thou waſh my feet?

7 Ieſus anſwered and ſaid vnto him, What I doe, thou knoweſt not now: but thou ſhalt know it hereafter.

8 Peter ſaid vnto him, Thou ſhalt neuer waſh my feet. Ieſus anſwered him, If I waſh thee not, thou ſhalt haue [d] no part with me.

9 Simon Peter ſaid vnto him, Lord, not my feet onely, but alſo the hands & the head.

10 Ieſus ſaide to him, Hee that is waſhed, needeth not, ſaue to waſh *his* feet, but is cleane euery

* *Mat.* 26.2. *mar.* 14.1 *luke* 22.1.

1 Chriſt no leſſe certaine of the victorie, then of the combate which was at hand, vſing the ſigne of waſhing the feete, doeth partly thereby giue an example of ſingular modeſtie, and his great loue toward his Apoſtles in this notable acte, being like very ſhortly to depart from them: and partly witneſſeth vnto them, that it is he only which waſheth away the filth of his people, and that by litle & litle in their time and ſeaſon.

a Them of his houſhold, that is, his Saints.

b Into his power.

c In that he is ſaid to riſe, it argueth that there was a ſpace betweene the ceremonie of the Paſſeouer, and this waſhing of feet, at what time it ſeemeth that the ſupper was inſtituted.

d Vnleſſe thou ſuffer me to waſh thee, thou ſhalt haue no part in the Kingdome of heauen.

g That is, partakers of light. 9 Faith is not of nature, but of grace. * *Iſai.* 53.1. *rom.* 10.16 *h The arme of the Lord, is the Goſpel, which is, the power of God to ſaluation to all that beleeue leeue: And therefore the arme of the Lord is not reueiled to them, whoſe hearts the Lord hath not opened.* * *Iſai.* 6.9. *matth.* 13.14. *marke* 4.12. *luke* 8.10. *acts* 28.26. *rom.* 11.8. 10 Such as beleeue, are not onely fewe in number, if they bee compared with the vnbeleeuers, but alſo the moſt of thoſe fewe (yea and that eſpecially the chiefeſt) doe feare men more then God.

euery whit: and ye are * cleane,but not all.
11 For he knewe who ſhould betray him:
therefore ſaid he,Ye are not all cleane.
12 ¶ So after he had waſhed their feet, and
had taken his garments, and was ſet downe a-
gaine, he ſaid to them, Knowe ye what I haue
done to you?
13 Ye call me Maſter, and Lord, and ye ſay
well: for *ſo* am I.
14 If I then your Lord, and Maſter, haue
waſhed your feete, ye ought alſo to waſh one
anothers feet.
15 For I haue giuen you an example,that ye
ſhould doe, euen as I haue done to you.
16 Verely,verely I ſay vnto you, *The ſeruant is not greater then his maſter, neither the
‖ ambaſſadour greater then he that ſent him.
17 If ye know theſe things, bleſſed are ye,
if ye doe them.
18 ¶ [2] I ſpeake not of you all: I know whom
I haue choſen: but *it is* that the Scripture might
be fulfilled, *He that eateth bread with mee,
hath lift vp his heele againſt me.
19 From hencefoorth tell I you before it
come, that when it is come to paſſe,yee might
beleeue that I am hee.
20 * Verely, verely I ſay vnto you, If I
ſend any, he that receiueth him, receiueth me,
and he that receiueth me, receiueth him that
ſent me.
21 When Ieſus had ſaid theſe things, hee
was troubled in the Spirit, and [e] teſtified, and
ſayd, Verely, verely I ſay vnto you, that one of
you ſhall betray me.
22 *Then the diſciples looked one on another, doubting of whom he ſpake.
23 Now there was one of his diſciples,
which [f] leaned on Ieſus boſome, whome Ieſus
loued.
24 To him beckened therefore Simon Peter, that he ſhould aske who it was of whome
he ſpake.
25 He then, as he leaned on Ieſus breaſt,
ſaid vnto him, Lord, who is it?
26 Ieſus anſwered, Hee it is, to whome I
ſhall giue a ſop,when I haue dipt it: and he wet
a ſoppe, and gaue it to Iudas Iſcariot, Simons
ſonne.
27 And after the ſoppe, Satan entred into
him,Then ſaid Ieſus vnto him,That thou doeſt,
doe quickly.
28 But none of them that were at table,
knew,for what cauſe he ſpake it vnto him.
28 For ſome of them thought becauſe Iudas
had the bagge, that Ieſus had ſaid vnto him,
Buy thoſe things that we haue need of againſt
the feaſt: or that he ſhould giue ſome thing to
the poore.
30 Aſſoone then as he had receiued the ſop,
he went immediatly out, and it was night.
31 ¶ [3] When he was gone out, Ieſus ſaide,
[g] Now is the ſonne of man glorified, and God
is glorified in him.

*Chap.15.20. matth.10.24. luke 6 40.
‖ *The word ſignifieth an Apoſtle, which is any one that is ſent from another.*
2 The betraying of Chriſt was not caſuall, or a thing that happened by chance, but the Father ſo ordeined the cauſe of our ſaluation, to reconcile vs vnto himſelfe in his Sonne,and the Sonne did willingly and voluntarily obey the Father.
* *Pſal.*41.9.
* *Matth* 10.40. *luke* 10.16.
e He affirmed it openly and ſoothed it.
* *Matth.*26.21. *marke* 14 18. *luke* 22.21.
f Iohn his leaning was ſuch, that ſitting downe in his bed, his head was toward Ieſus his head: ſo that it was an eaſie matter for him to touch Ieſus his boſome: for it is certaine that in old time men vſed not to ſit at the table, but to lie downe on the one ſide.
3 We haue to conſider the glorifying of Chriſt in his ignominie
g This verſe and the next following,are a moſt plaine and euident teſtimonie of the diuinitie of Chriſt.

32 If God be glorified in him, God ſhall
alſo glorifie him in himſelfe, and ſhall ſtraightway glorifie him.
33 [4] Little children, yet a little while am I
with you: ye ſhall ſeeke me, but as I ſaide vnto
the *Iewes, Whither I goe,can ye not come:
alſo to you ſay I now,
34 *A new commaundement giue I vnto
you, that ye loue one another: as I haue loued
you, that ye alſo loue one another.
35 By this ſhall all men know that yee are
my diſciples, if ye haue loue one to another.
36 [5] Simon Peter ſaid vnto him, Lord,whi-
ther goeſt thou? Ieſus anſwered him,Whither
I goe, thou canſt not follow me now: but thou
ſhalt follow me afterward.
37 Peter ſaid vnto him, Lord,why can I not
follow thee now? * I will lay downe my life
for thy ſake.
38 Ieſus anſwered him, Wilt thou lay
downe thy life for my ſake? Verely,verely I ſay
vnto thee, The Cocke ſhall not crowe,till thou
haue denied me thriſe.

4 The eternall glory ſhall flow by litle and litle from the head into the members. But in the meane time,we muſt take good heed, that wee paſſe ouer the race of this life in brotherly loue.
* *Chap.*7.34. *Leuit.*19 18. *matth.*22.39. *chap.*15.12. 1.*iohn* 4.21.
5 An heauy example of raſh truſt and confidence.
* *Matth.*26.33. *marke* 14.29. *luke* 22.33.

CHAP. XIIII.

1 He comforteth his diſciples, 2. 7 declaring his diuinitie and the fruit of his death, 16 promiſing the comforter, 17 euen the holy ſpirit, 26 whoſe office he ſetteth out. 27 He promiſeth peace.

LEt [1] not your heart be troubled:ye beleeue
in God, beleeue alſo in me.
2 In my Fathers houſe are many dwelling
places: if it were not ſo, [a] I would haue tolde
you: I goe to [b] prepare a place for you.
3 [2] And if I goe to prepare a place for you,
I will come againe, and receiue you vnto my
ſelfe, that where I am,there may ye be alſo.
4 [3] And whither I goe, ye knowe, and the
way ye know,
5 Thomas ſaid vnto him, Lord, we know
not whither thou goeſt: howe can wee then
know the way?
6 Ieſus ſaid vnto him, I am [d] that way,and
that trueth, and that life. No man commeth
vnto the Father,but by me.
7 [e] If ye had knowen me, ye ſhould haue
knowen my Father alſo: and from henceforth
ye know him, and haue ſeene him.
8 Philip ſaid vnto him, Lord, ſhew vs *thy*
Father, and it ſufficeth vs.
9 Ieſus ſaid vnto him, I haue bene ſo long
time with you, and haſt thou not knowen me?
Philip, he that hath ſeene me, hath ſeene my
Father: how then ſayeſt thou, Shewe vs *thy*
Father?

1 He beleeueth in God that beleeueth in Chriſt and there is no other way to con[illegible]rme our mindes in greateſt diſtreſſes.
a That is,if it were not ſo as I tell you,to wit, vnleſſe there were place enough not onely for me,but for you alſo, in my Fathers houſe, I would not thus deceiue you with a vaine hope,but I would haue tolde you ſo plainely.
b All this ſpeach is by the way of an allegorie,whereby the Lord comforteth his owne, declaring to them his departure into heauen, which is, not to reigne there alone, but to goe before and prepare a place for them.
2 Chriſt went not away from vs, to the end to forſake vs, but rather that hee might at length take vs vp with him into heauen. *c Theſe words are to be referred to the whole Church, and therefore the Angels ſaide to the diſciples when they were aſtoniſhed,what ſtand you gazing vp into heauen? This Ieſus ſhall ſo come as you ſaw him go vp, Acts* 1.11.*and in all places of the Scripture, the full comfort of the Church is referred to that day when God ſhall be all in all, and is therefore called the day of redemption.* 3 Chriſt onely is the way to true and euerlaſting life, for he it is in whome the Father hath reueiled himſelfe *d This ſaying ſheweth vnto vs both the nature,the will and office of Chriſt. e It is plaine by this place,that to know God,and to ſee God, is all one: Now whereas he ſayd before,that no man ſawe God at any time, that is to be vnderſtood thus,without Chriſt,or were it not through Chriſt,no man could euer ſee,nor ſaw God at any time: for as Chryſoſtom ſaith, the Sonne is a very ſhort and eaſie ſetting forth of the fathers nature to vs.*

10 [4] Belee-

10 [4] Beleeuest thou not, that I am in the
Father, and the Father is in me? The wordes
that I speake vnto you, I speake not of my selfe:
but the Father that dwelleth in me, hee doeth
the workes.
11 Beleeue me, that I *am* in the Father, and
the Father *is* in me: at the least, beleeue me for
the very workes sake.
12 [5] Verely, verely I say vnto you, Hee that
beleeueth in me, the workes that I doe, he shall
doe also, and [f] greater then these shall he doe:
for I goe vnto my Father.
13 * And whatsoeuer ye aske in my Name,
that will I do, that the Father may be glorified
in the Sonne.
14 If yee shall aske any thing in my Name,
I will doe it.
15 [6] If ye loue me, keepe my commandements.
16 And I will pray the Father, and hee shall
giue you another comforter, that he may abide
with you for euer,
17 *Euen* the [g] Spirit of trueth whome the
[h] world cannot receiue, because it seeth him
not, neither knowe him: but ye know him: for
he dwelleth with you, and shalbe in you.
18 I will not leaue you fatherlesse: *but* I
will come to you.
19 Yet a little while, and the world shall see
me no more, but ye shal see me: because I liue,
ye shall liue also.
20 At that day shall ye know that I am [i] in
my Father, and you in me, and I in you.
21 He that hath my commandements, and
keepeth them, is hee that loueth me: and hee
that loueth me, shall be loued of my Father:
and I will loue him, and will [k] shew mine owne
selfe to him.
22 [7] Iudas said vnto him (not Iscariot) Lord,
what is the cause that thou wilt shewe thy selfe
vnto vs, and not vnto the world?
23 Iesus answered, and said vnto him, If
any man loue me, he will keepe my word, and
my Father will loue him, and we will come vnto
him, and will dwell with him.
24 He that loueth me not, keepeth not my
wordes, and the word which ye heare, is not
mine, but the Fathers which sent me.
25 [8] These things haue I spoken vnto you,
being present with you.
26 * But the comforter, which is the holy
Ghost, whom the Father will send in my name,
he shall teach you all things, & bring all things
to your remembrance, which I haue told you.
27 [9] Peace I leaue with you: my peace I
giue vnto you: not as the world giueth, giue
I vnto you. Let not your hearts be troubled,
nor feare.
28 [10] Yee haue heard how I sayd vnto you,

4 The maiestie of God sheweth it selfe most euidently, both in Christs doctrine and deeds.
5 The approouing of the vertue of Christ is not included within his owne person, but it is spread thorow the body of his whole Church.
f That is, not only doe them, but I can also giue other men power to doe greater.
* *Chap.16 23. mat.7.7. marke 11.24. iam.1.5.*
6 He loueth Christ aright which obeyeth his commandement: and because the same is accompanied with an infinite sort of miseries, although he be absent in bodie, yet doeth hee comfort his with the present vertue of the holy Ghost, whom the world despiseth, because it knoweth him not.
g The holy Ghost is called the Spirit of trueth, of the effect which he worketh, because he inspireth the trueth into vs, whereas otherwise hee hath trueth in himselfe.
h Worldly men.
i The Sonne is in the Father after such sort, that hee is one of one selfesame substance with the Father, but he is in his disciples in a certaine respect as an aider and helper of them.
k I will shew my selfe to him, and be knowen of him, as if he sawe me with his eyes: but this shewing of himselfe is not bodily, but spirituall, yet so plaine as none can be more.
7 We must not aske why the Gospel is reueiled to some rather then to other, but we must rather take heed, that we embrace Christ who is offered vnto vs, and that we truly loue him, that is to say, that we giue our selues wholy to his obedience.
8 It is the office of the holy Ghost to imprint in the mindes of the elect, in their times and seasons, that which Christ once spake. * *Chap.15.26.* 9 All true felicitie commeth to vs by Christ alone. 10 So farre is it, that we should be sory for the departing of Christ from vs according to the flesh, that we should rather reioyce for it, seeing that all the blessing of the members dependeth vpon the glorifying of the head.

I goe away, and will come vnto you. If ye loued
me, ye would verely reioyce, because I said
I goe vnto the Father: for the Father is [l] greater
then I.
29 And now haue I spoken vnto you, before
it come, that when it is come to passe, yee
might beleeue.
30 [11] Hereafter will I not speak many things
vnto you: for the prince of this world commeth,
and hath [m] nought in me.
31 But *it is* that the world may know that
I loue *my* Father: and as the Father hath commanded
me, so I doe. Arise, let vs goe hence.

l This is spoken, in that that he is Mediatour, for so the Father is greater then hee, in as much as the person to whom request is made, is greater then hee that maketh the request.
11 Christ goeth to death not vnwillingly, but willingly, not as yeelding to the deuill, but obeying his Fathers decree.
m As who would say, Satan will by and by set vpon me with all the might he can, but hee hath no power ouer me, neither shall hee finde any such thing in me as he thinketh he shall.

CHAP. XV.

1 By the parable of the vine, 2 and the branches, 5.6. he declareth how the disciples may beare fruite. 12. 17 He commendeth mutuall loue. 18 He exhorteth them to beare afflictions patiently, 20 by his owne example.

I [1] Am that true vine, and my Father is that
husbandman.
2 * Euerie branch that beareth not fruite
in me, he taketh away: and euery one that beareth
fruit, he purgeth it, that it may bring forth
more fruite.
3 * Now are ye cleane through the word,
which I haue spoken vnto you.
4 Abide in me, and I in you: as the branch
cannot beare fruite of it selfe, except it abide in
the vine, no more can yee, except yee abide
in me.
5 I am the vine: yee *are* the branches: hee
that abideth in me, and I in him, the same bringeth
foorth much fruite: for without me can
yee doe nothing.
6 * If a man abide not in mee, hee is cast
foorth as a branch, and withereth: and men gather
them, and cast *them* into the fire, and they
burne.
7 * [2] If yee abide in me, and my words abide
in you, aske what yee will, and it shall be
done to you.
8 [a] Herein is my Father glorified, that ye
beare much fruit, and be made my disciples.
9 [3] As the father hath loued me, so haue I
loued you: [b] continue in that my loue.
10 If ye shall keepe my commandements,
ye shall abide in my loue, as I haue kept my Fathers
commandements, and abide in his loue.
11 These things haue I spoken vnto you,
that my ioy might remaine in you, and that
your ioy might be full.
12 * This is my commandement, that yee
loue one another, as I haue loued you.
13 Greater loue then this hath no man,
when any man bestoweth his life for his
friends.
14 Ye are my friends, if ye doe whatsoeuer
I command you.

1 Wee are of nature drie and fit for nothing, but the fire: Therefore that we may liue and be fruitfull, wee must first bee graffed into Christ, as it were into a vine, by the Fathers hand: and then be daily fined with a continuall meditation of the word, and the crosse: otherwise it shall not auaile any man at all to haue beene graffed, vnlesse hee cleaue fast vnto the vine, and so draw iuyce out of it.
* *Matt.15.13.*
* *Chap.13.10.*
* *Colos.1.23.*
* *1.Iohn 3.22.*
2 He abideth in Christ, which resteth in his doctrine, and therefore bringeth forth good fruit: And the Father will denie such an one nothing.
a As who would say, Herein shall my Father be glorified, and herein also shall you be my disciples, if you bring foorth much fruite.
3 The loue of the Father towardes the Sonne, and of the Sonne towards vs, and ours toward God and our neighbour, are ioyned together with an vnseparable knot: and there is nothing more sweete and pleasant then it is. Now this loue sheweth it selfe by the effects: a most perfect example whereof, Christ himselfe exhibiteth vnto vs. *b That is, in that loue, wherewith I loue you: which loue is on both parts.* * *Chap. 13.34. 1.thess. 4.9. 1.iohn 3.11, and 4.21.*

15 [4] Hence-

15 [4] Hencefoorth call I you not seruants:
for the seruant knoweth not what his master
doeth: but I haue called you friends: for all
things that I haue heard of my Father, haue I
made knowen to you.
16 [5] Yee [c] haue not chosen me, but I haue
chosen you, and ordeined you, * that yee goe
and bring foorth fruite, and that your fruite remaine, that whatsoeuer ye shall aske of the Father in my Name, he may giue it you.
17 These things command I you, that yee
loue one another.
18 [6] If the world hate you, yee know that
it hated me before you.
19 If ye were of the world, the world would
loue his owne: but because ye are not of the
world, but I haue chosen you out of the world,
therefore the world hateth you.
20 Remember the worde that I sayd vnto
you, * The seruant is not greater then his master. * If they haue persecuted me, they will
persecute you also: if they haue kept my word,
they will also keepe yours.
21 [7] But * all these things will they doe vnto you for my Names sake, because they haue
not knowen him that sent me.
22 [d] If I had not come and spoken vnto
them, they should not haue had sinne: but now
haue they no cloke for their sinne.
23 Hee that hateth me, hateth my Father
also.
24 If I had not done workes among them
which none other man did, they had no had
sinne: but now haue they both seene, and haue
hated both me and my Father.
25 But *it is* that the word might be fulfilled, that is written in their [e] Law, * They hated
me without a cause.
26 [8] But when that Comforter shall come,
* whom I will send vnto you from the Father,
euen the Spirit of trueth, which proceedeth of
the Father, he shall testifie of me.
27 And yee shall witnesse also, because yee
haue beene with me from the beginning.

4 The doctrine of the Gospel (as it is vttered by Christes owne mouth) is a most perfect and absolute declaration of the counsell of God, which pertaineth to our saluation and is committed vnto the Apostles.
5 Christ is the authour and preseruer of the ministerie of the Gospel, euen to the worlds ende, but the ministers haue aboue all things neede of prayer and brotherly loue.
c *This place teacheth vs plainly, that our saluation commeth from the onely fauour and gracious goodnesse of the euerlasting God towards vs, and of nothing that we doe or can deserue.*
* *Mat.*18.18.
6 It ought not onely not to feare, but rather confirme the faithfull ministers of Christ, when they shall be hated of the world as their Master was.
* *Chap.*13.16. *matth.*10.24.
* *Matth.*24.9.
7 The hatred that the world beareth against Christ, proceedeth of the blockishnesse of the mind, which notwithstanding is voluntarie blind, so that the world can pretend no excuse to colour their fault.
* *Chap.*16.4.
d *As who would say, If I had not come, these men would not haue stucke to haue said still before Gods iudgement seat, that they are religious, and void of sinne: but seeing I came to them, and they cleane refuse me, they can haue no cloke for their wickednesse.* e *Sometime by this word Law, are meant the fiue bookes of Moses, but in this place, the whole Scripture: for the place alledged is in the Psalmes.* * *Psalm.*35.19.
8 Against the rage of the wicked, we shall stand surely by the inward testimonie of the holy Ghost: But the holy Ghost speaketh no otherwise, then hee spake by the mouth of the Apostles. * *Chap.*14.26. *luke* 24.49.

CHAP. XVI.

1 *Hee foretelleth the disciples of persecution.* 7 *Hee promiseth the Comforter, and declareth his office.* 21 *Hee compareth the affliction of his, to a woman that trauaileth with childe.*

1 These [1] things haue I said vnto you, that
ye should not be offended.
2 They shall excommunicate you: yea,
the time shall come, that whosoeuer killeth
you, will thinke that he doeth God seruice.
3 And these things will they doe vnto
you, because they haue not knowen the Father, nor me.
4 * But these things haue I tolde you, that
when the houre shall come, yee might remember that I told you them. And these things said
I not vnto you from the beginning, because I
was with you.
5 But now I goe my way to him that sent
me, and none of you asketh me, Whither goest thou?
6 But because I haue said these things vnto you, your hearts are full of sorow.
7 [2] Yet I tell you the trueth, It is expedient for you that I goe away: for if I goe
not away, the Comforter will not come vnto
you: but if I depart, I will sende him vnto
you.
8 [3] And when he is come, he will [a] reproue
the [b] world of sinne, and of righteousnesse, and
of iudgement.
9 Of sinne, because they beleeued not
in me.
10 Of [c] righteousnesse, because I go to my
Father, and ye shall see me no more.
11 Of [d] iudgement, [e] because the prince of
this world is iudged.
12 [4] I haue yet many things to say vnto
you, but ye cannot beare them now.
13 Howbeit, when he is come which is the
Spirit of trueth, he wil lead you into all trueth:
for he shall not speake of himselfe, but whatsoeuer he shall heare, shall he speake, and he will
shew you the things to come.
14 [5] Hee shall glorifie me: for hee shall receiue of mine, and shall shew it vnto you.
15 All things that the Father hath, are
mine: therefore said I, that hee shall take of
mine, and shew it vnto you.
16 [6] A [f] little *while*, and ye shall not see me:
and againe a little *while*, and ye shall see mee:
[g] for I goe to the Father.
17 Then said *some* of his disciples among
themselues, What is this that he sayth vnto vs,
A little *while*, and yee shall not see me, and a-
gaine, a little *while*, and yee shall see me, and,
For I goe to the Father?
18 They said therefore, What is this that
he sayth, A little *while*? we know not what he
sayth.
19 Now Iesus knewe that they would aske
him, and said vnto them, Doe yee enquire a-
mong your selues, of that I said, A little *while*,
and yee shall not see mee: and againe, a little
while, and ye shall see me?
20 Verely, verely I say vnto you, that yee
shall weepe and lament, and the world shall
reioyce: and yee shall sorow, but your sorow
shalbe turned to ioy.
21 A woman when shee trauaileth hath

1 The ministers of the Gospel must look for all maner of reproches, not only of them which are open enemies, but euen of them also which seeme to be of the same houshold, and the very pillars of the Church.
* *Chap.*15.21.

2 The absence of Christ according to the flesh, is profitable to the Church that we may wholly depend vpon his spirituall power.
3 The Spirit of God worketh so mightily by the preaching of the word, that hee constraineth the world, will it, nill it, to confesse it owne vnrighteousnesse and Christes righteousnesse and almightinesse.
a *He will so reprooue the world, that the worldlings shall be able to pretend no excuse.*
b *He respecteth the time that followed his ascension, when as all gainsayers were manifestly reprooued, through the powring out of the holy Ghost vpon the Church: So that the very enemies of Christ were reprooued of sinne, in that they were constrained to confesse that they were deceiued, in that they beleeued not, and therefore they said to Peter, Actes 1. Men and brethren, what shall we doe?*
c *Of Christ himselfe: for when the world shall see, that I haue powred out the holy Ghost, they shall be constrained to confesse that I was iust, and was not condemned of my Father, when I went out of this world.*
d *Of that authoritie and power, which I haue both in heauen and earth.*
e *That is, because they shall then vnderstand and know in deede, that I haue ouercome the deuill, and doe gouerne the world, when all men shall see, that they set themselues against you in vaine, for I will arme you with that heauenly power, whereby you may destroy euery high thing which is lifted vp against the knowledge of God, 2. Corinth.*10.12. 4 The doctrine of the Apostles proceeded from the holy Ghost, and is most perfite. 5 The holy Ghost bringeth no new doctrine, but teacheth that which was vttered by Christes owne mouth, and imprinteth it in our mindes. 6 The grace of the holy Ghost is a most liuely glasse, wherein Christ is truely beholden with the most sharpe sighted eyes of faith, and not with the bleared eyes of the flesh: whereby wee feele a continuall ioy euen in the middest of sorowes. f *When a little time is once past.* g *For I passe to eternall glory, so that I shall be much more present with you then I was before: for then you shall feele in deede what I am, and what I am able to doe.*

sorow,

sorow, because her houre is come: but assoone
as shee is deliuered of the childe, shee remembreth no more the anguish, for ioy that a man
is borne into the world.
22 And yee now therefore are in sorow:
but I will see you againe, and your hearts shall
reioyce, and your ioy shall no man take from
you.
23 And in that day shall yee aske me nothing. *Verely, verely I say vnto you, Whatsoeuer ye shall aske the Father in my Name, he
will giue it you.
24 Hitherto haue yee asked nothing in my
Name: aske, and ye shall receiue, that your ioy
may be full.
25 [7] These things haue I spoken vnto you
in parables: but the time will come, when I
shall no more speake to you in parables: but I
shall shew you plainely of the Father.
26 [8] At that day shall ye aske in my Name,
and I say not vnto you, that I will pray vnto the
Father for you:
27 For the Father himselfe loueth you, because yee haue loued me, *and haue beleeued
that I came out from God.
28 I am come out from the Father, & came
into the world: againe I leaue the world, and
goe to the Father.
29 [9] His disciples said vnto him, Loe, now
speakest thou plainely, and thou speakest no
parable.
30 Now know wee that thou knowest all
things, and needest not that any man should
aske thee. By this wee beleeue that thou art
come out from God.
31 Iesus answered them, Doe you beleeue
now.
32 *[10] Behold, the houre commeth, and is
alreadie come, that yee shall be scattered euerie man into his owne, and shall leaue me a-
lone: but I am not alone: for the Father is
with me.
33 [11] These things haue I spoken vnto
you, that [h] in me yee might haue peace: in the
world yee shall haue affliction, but be of good
comfort: I haue ouercome the world.

*Chap.14.13. mat.7.7. and 21.22 mar. 11.24. luk.11.9. iames 1.5.

7 The holy Ghost, which was powred vpon the Apostles after the Ascension of Christ, instructed both them in all the chiefest mysteries and secrets of our saluation, and also by them the Church, and will also instruct it to the end of the world.

8 The summe of the worship of God, is the inuocation of the Father in the Name of the Sonne the Mediatour, who is already heard for vs, for whom he both abased himselfe, and is now also glorified.

*Chap.17.8.

9 Faith and foolish securitie differ very much.

*Matt.26.31. marke 14.27.

10 Neither the wickednesse of the world, neither the weakenesse of his owne can diminish any thing of the vertue of Christ.

11 The suretie and stay of the Church dependeth only vpon the victorie of Christ.

h That in me you might be throughly quieted. For by (peace) is meant in this place, that quiet state of mind which is cleane contrarie to disquietnesse and heauinesse.

CHAP. XVII.

1 Christ prayeth that his glory together with his Fathers may be made manifest. 9 He prayeth for his Apostles, 20 And for all beleeuers.

THese [1] things spake Iesus, and lift vp his
eyes to heauen, and said, [2] Father, that
houre is come: glorifie thy Sonne, that thy
Sonne may also glorifie thee,
2 *As thou hast giuen him power *ouer*
[a] all flesh, that he should giue eternall life to all
them that thou hast giuen him.
3 And this is life eternall, that they know
thee *to be* the [b] onely very God, and whome
thou hast sent, Iesus Christ.
4 I haue glorified thee on the earth: I haue
finished the worke which thou gauest me to
doe.
5 And now glorifie me, thou Father, with
thine owne selfe, with the glorie which I had
with thee before the world was.
6 [3] I haue declared thy Name vnto the men
which thou gauest me out of the world: [c] thine
they were, and thou [d] gauest them mee, and
they haue kept thy word.
7 *Now they know that all things whatsoeuer thou hast giuen me, are of thee.
8 For I haue giuen vnto them the words
which thou gauest me, and they haue receiued
them, and haue knowen surely that I came out
from thee, and haue beleeued that thou hast
sent me.
9 I pray for them: I pray not for the world,
but for them which thou hast giuen mee: for
they are thine.
10 And all mine are thine, and thine are
mine, and I am glorified in them.
11 And now I am no more in the world,
but these are in the world, and I come to thee.
Holy Father, keepe them in thy Name, *euen*
them whom thou hast giuen mee, that they
may be [e] one as we *are*.
12 While I was with them in the world, I
kept them in thy Name: those that thou gauest me, haue I kept, and none of them is lost,
but the childe of perdition, that the *scripture
might be fulfilled.
13 And now come I to thee, and these
things speake I in the world, that they might
haue my ioy fulfilled in themselues.
14 I haue giuen them thy word, and the
world hath hated them, because they are not
of the world, as I am not of the world.
15 [4] I pray not that thou shouldest take
them out of the world, but that thou keepe
them from euill.
16 They are not of the world, as I am not
of the world.
17 [f] Sanctifie them with thy trueth: thy
word is trueth.
18 [5] As thou diddest send me into the world,
so haue I sent them into the world.
19 And for their sakes sanctifie I my selfe,
that they also may be sanctified through the
[g] trueth.
20 [6] I pray not for these alone, but for them

1 Iesus Christ the euerlasting hie Priest, being ready straightwayes to offer vp himselfe, doth by solemne praiers consecrate himselfe to God the Father, as a Sacrifice, and vs together with himselfe. Therefore this prayer was from the beginning, is, and shall be to the end of the world, the foundation and ground of the Church of God. 2 Hee first declareth, that as hee came into the world to the end that the Father might shewe in him, being apprehended by faith, his glory in sauing his elect, so hee applyed himselfe to that onely: and therefore desireth of the Father, that hee would blesse the worke which he had finished. *Matth.28.18. *a Ouer all men.*

b He calleth the Father the onely very God, to set him against all false gods, and not to shut out himselfe and the holy Ghost, for straightwayes he ioyneth the knowledge of the Father and the knowledge of himselfe together, and according to his accustomed manner setteth foorth the whole Godhead in the person of the Father: So is the Father alone said to be King, immortall, wise, and dwelling in light which no man can attaine vnto, inuisible, Rom.16.27. 1.tim.1.17.

3 First of all he prayeth for those his disciples by whom he would haue the rest to be gathered together, and commendeth them vnto the Father, (hauing once reiected the whole company of the reprobate) because he receiued them of him, into his custodie, and for that they embracing his doctrine, shall haue so many and so mightie enemies, that there is no way for them to be in safetie, but by his helpe onely.

c Hee sheweth hereby that euerlasting election and choise, which was hidden in the good will and pleasure of God, which is the groundworke of our saluation.

d He sheweth how that euerlasting and hidden purpose of God is declared in Christ, by whom we are iustified and sanctified, if we lay hold on him by faith, that at length we may come to the glory of the election.

*Chap.16.27.

e He prayeth that his people may peaceably agree and be ioyned together in one, that as the Godhead is one, so they may be of one minde and one consent together. *Psal.109.7.

4 Hee sheweth what manner of deliuerance hee meaneth, not that they should be in no danger, but that they beeing preserued from all, might prooue by experience that the doctrine of saluation is true, which they receiued at his mouth to deliuer to other. *f That is, make them holy: and that is said to be holy, which is dedicated and made proper to God onely.* 5 Hee addeth moreouer, that the Apostles haue a vocation common with him, and therefore that they must be holden vp by the selfe same vertue to giue vp themselues wholly to God, whereby hee beeing first, did consecrate himselfe to the Father. *g The true and substantiall sanctification of Christ, is set against the outward purifyings.* 6 Secondarily, hee offereth to God the Father all his, that is, how many soeuer shall beleeue in him by the doctrine of the Apostles: that as hee cleaueth vnto the Father, receiuing from him all fulnesse, so they being ioyned with him, may receiue life from him, and at length being together beloued in him, may also with him enioy euerlasting glory.

also

also which shall beleeue in me, through their
word,

21 That they all may be one, as thou, O
Father, *art* in me, and I in thee: *euen* that they
may be also in vs, that the world may beleeue
that thou hast sent me.

22 And the glory that thou gauest me, I
haue giuen them, that they may be one, as wee
are one.

23 I in them, and thou in me, that they may
be made perfite in one, and that the world may
know that thou hast sent me, and hast loued
them, as thou hast loued me.

24 * Father, I will that they which thou
hast giuen mee, be with me euen where I am,
that they may behold that my glorie, which
thou hast giuen mee: for thou louedst me before the foundation of the world.

25 O righteous Father, the world also hath
not knowen thee, but I haue knowen thee, and
these haue knowen, that thou hast sent me.

26 [7] And I haue declared vnto them thy
Name, and will declare it, that the loue where-
with thou hast loued me, may be in them, and
I in them.

*Chap.12.26.

7 He communicateth with his by little and little, the knowledge of the Father, which is most ful in Christ the Mediatour, that they may in him be beloued of the Father, with the selfe-same loue wherwith he loueth the Sonne.

CHAP. XVIII.

2 By Christs power, whom Iudas betrayeth, 6 the souldiers are cast downe to the ground. 13 Christ is led to Annas, and from him to Caiaphas. 22. 23 His answere to the officer that smote him with a rod. 28 Being deliuered to Pilate, 36 he declareth his kingdome.

WHen [1] Iesus had spoken these things,
hee went foorth with his disciples o-
uer the brooke * Cedron, where was a garden,
into the which he entred, and his disciples.

2 And Iudas which betrayed him, knew
also the place: for Iesus oft times resorted thither with his disciples.

3 * [2] Iudas then, after hee had receiued a
band of men and officers of the high Priests,
and of the Pharises, came thither with lanterns
and torches, and weapons.

4 [3] Then Iesus, knowiug all things that
should come vnto him, went foorth and said
vnto them, Whome seeke yee?

5 They answered him, Iesus of Nazareth.
Iesus said vnto them, I am hee. Now Iudas also which betrayed him, stood with them.

6 Assoone then as he had said vnto them,
I am hee, they went away backwards, and fell
to the ground.

7 Then hee asked them againe, Whome
seeke yee? And they said, Iesus of Nazareth.

8 [4] Iesus answered, I said vnto you, that I
am hee: therefore if ye seeke me, let these goe
their way.

9 *This was* that the word might be fulfilled which he spake, *Of them which thou gauest me haue I lost none.

10 [5] Then Simon Peter hauing a sword,
drew it, and smote the hie Priests seruant, and
cut off his right eare. Now the seruants name
was Malchus.

1 Christ goeth of his owne accord into a garden, which his betrayer knew, to be taken: that by his obedience he might take away the sinne that entred into the world by one mans rebellion, and that in a garden.
*Mat.26.36. marke 14.32. luke 22.39.
*Mat.26.47. marke 14.43. luke 22.47.
2 Christ who was innocent, was taken as a wicked person, that we which are wicked might be let goe as innocent.
3 Christs person (but not his vertue) was bound of the aduersaries, when and how he would.
4 Christ doeth not neglect the office of a good pastour, no not in his greatest danger.
*Chap.17.12.
5 We ought to conteine the zeale we beare to God, within the bounds of our vocation.

11 Then said Iesus vnto Peter, Put vp thy
sword into the sheath: shall I not drinke of the
cup which *my* Father hath giuen me?

12 Then the band and the captaine, and the
officers of the Iewes tooke Iesus and bound
him,

13 [6] And led him away to * Annas first (for
hee was father in law to Caiaphas, which was
the hie Priest that same yeere.)

14 * And Caiaphas was he, that gaue counsell to the Iewes, that it was expedient that one
man should die for the people.

15 ¶ [7] * Now Simon Peter followed Iesus, and another disciple, and that disciple was
knowen of the hie Priest: therefore he went in
with Iesus into the hall of the hie Priest:

16 But Peter stood at the doore without.
Then went out the other disciple which was
knowen vnto the hie Priest, and spake to her
that kept the doore, and brought in Peter.

17 Then said the maid that kept the doore,
vnto Peter, Art not thou also one of this mans
disciples? He said, I am not.

18 And the seruants and officers stood
there, which had made a fire of coles: for it
was colde, and they warmed themselues. And
Peter also stood among them, and warmed
himselfe.

19 ¶ ([8] The hie Priest then asked Iesus of
his disciples, and of his doctrine.

20 Iesus answered him, I spake openly to
the world: I euer taught in the Synagogue and
in the Temple, whither the Iewes resort continually, and in secret haue I said nothing.

21 Why askest thou me? aske them which
heard me what I said vnto them: behold, they
know what I said.

22 When he had spoken these things, one
of the officers which stood by, smote Iesus
with *his* rodde, saying, Answerest thou the hie
Priest so?

23 Iesus answered him, If I haue euill spoken, beare witnesse of the euill: but if I haue
well spoken, why smitest thou me?

24 ¶ * Nowe Annas had sent him bound
vnto Caiaphas the hie Priest.)

25 * [9] And Simon Peter stood and warmed
himselfe, and they said vnto him, Art not thou
also of his disciples? Hee denyed it, and said, I
am not.

26 One of the seruants of the hie Priest, his
cousin whose eare Peter smote off, sayd, Did
not I see thee in the garden with him?

27 Peter then denyed againe, and immediatly the cocke crew.

28 ¶ * [10] Then led they Iesus from [a] Caiaphas into the common hall. Now it was morning, and they themselues went not into the
common hall, lest they should be * defiled, but
that they might eate the Passeouer.

29 Pilate then went out vnto them, & said,
What accusation bring ye against this man?

30 They answered, and said vnto him, If

6 Christ is brought before an earthly high Priest to be condemned for our blasphemies, that we might be quitted of the euerlasting high Priest himselfe.
* Luke 3.2.
*Chap.11.50.
7 A liuely example of the fragilitie of man euen in the best, when they be once left to themselues.
*Matt.26.58. marke 14.54. luke 22.54.
8 Christ defendeth his cause but slenderly, not that hee would withdraw himselfe from death, but to shew that he was condemned as an innocent.
*Matth.26.57. luke 22.54.
*Matth.26.69. marke 14.59. luke 22.55.
9 After that men haue once fallen, they cannot onely not lift vp themselues by their owne strength, but also they fall more and more into worse, vntil they be raised vp againe, by a new vertue of God.
*Matth.27.2. marke 15.1. luke 23.1.
10 The sonne of God is brought before the iudgement seate of an earthly and prophane man, in whom there is found much lesse wickednes, then in the princes of the people of God: A liuely image of the wrath of God against sinne, and therewithall of his great mercie, & last of all, of his most seuere iudgement against the stubburne contemners of his grace when it is offered vnto them.
a From Caiaphas house.
*Actes 10.28. and 11.3.

hee were not an euill doer, we would not haue
deliuered him vnto thee.
31 Then said Pilate vnto them, Take yee
him, and iudge him after your owne Lawe.
Then the Iewes said vnto him, b It is not lawfull for vs to put any man to death.

b For iudgements of life and death were taken from them fortie yeeres before the destruction of the Temple.

32 *It was* that the word of Iesus * might be
fulfilled which he spake, c signifying what death
he should die.

* *Matth.20.19.*
c For Christ had foretold that he should be crucified.

33 * So Pilate entred into the common hall
againe, and called Iesus, and said vnto him, Art
thou the King of the Iewes?

* *Matth.17.11. marke 15.2. luke 23.3.*

34 Iesus answered him, Sayest thou that of
thy selfe, or did other tell it thee of me?
35 Pilate answered, Am I a Iewe? Thine
owne nation, and the hie Priests haue deliuered thee vnto me. What hast thou done?

11 Christ auoucheth his spirituall kingdome, but reiecteth a worldly.

36 11 Iesus answered, My kingdome is not
of this world: if my kingdome were of this
world, my seruants would surely fight, that I
should not be deliuered to the Iewes: but now
is my kingdome not from hence.
37 Pilate then said vnto him, Art thou a
King then? Iesus answered, Thou sayest that I
am a King: for this cause am I borne, and for
this cause came I into the world, that I should
beare witnesse vnto the trueth: euery one that
is of the trueth heareth my voice.

12 It was requisit that Christ should be pronounced innocent, but notwithstanding (in that that hee tooke vpon him our person) was to be condemned as a most wicked man.

38 12 Pilate said vnto him, d What is trueth?
And when he had said that, he went out againe
vnto the Iewes, and said vnto them, I finde in
him no cause at all.

d He speaketh this disdainfully and scoffingly, and not by way of asking a question.

39 * But you haue a custome, that I should
deliuer you one loose at the Passeouer: will ye
then that I loose vnto you the King of the
Iewes?

* *Matth.27.15. marke 15.6. luke 23.17.*

40 * Then e cryed they all againe, saying,
Not him, but Barabbas: now this Barabbas
was a murtherer.

* *Actes 3.14.*
e Word for word, made a great and foule voice.

CHAP. XIX.

1 Pilate, when Christ was scourged, 2 and crowned with thorne, 4 was desirous to let him loose: 8 but beeing ouercome with the outrage of the Iewes, 16 Hee deliuereth him to be crucified. 26 Iesus committeth his mother to the disciple. 30 Hauing tasted vineger, hee dyeth. 34 And beeing dead, his side is pearced with a speare. 40 He is buried.

* *Matth.27.27. marke 15.16.*
1 The wisdome of the flesh, chuseth of two euils the least, but God curseth that same wisedome.

THen * Pilate tooke Iesus and 1 scourged
him.
2 And the souldiers platted a crowne of
thornes, and put it on his head, and they put
on him a purple garment,
3 And said, Haile King of the Iewes. And
they smote him with *their* roddes.

2 Christ is again quitted by that same mouth wherewith he was afterward condemned.

4 2 Then Pilate went foorth againe, and
said vnto them, Behold, I bring him foorth to
you, that ye may know, that I finde no fault in
him at all.
5 Then came Iesus forth wearing a crowne
of thornes, and a purple garment. And *Pilate*
said vnto them, Behold the man.
6 Then when the hie Priests and officers
saw him, they cryed, saying, a Crucifie, crucifie *him*. Pilate said vnto them, Take ye him and
crucifie *him*: for I finde no fault in him.

a They will haue him crucified, whom by an olde custome of theirs, they should haue stoned and hanged vp as conuict of blasphemie: but they desire to haue him crucified after the maner of the Romanes.

7 The Iewes answered him, Wee haue a
law, and by our law he ought to die, because he
made himselfe the Sonne of God.
8 ¶ 3 When Pilate then heard that word,
he was the more afraid,
9 And went againe into the common hall,
and said vnto Iesus, Whence art thou? But Iesus gaue him none answere.

3 Pilates conscience fighteth for Christ, but straightway it yeeldeth, because it is not vpholden with the singular vertue of God.

10 Then said Pilate vnto him, Speakest
thou not vnto mee? Knowest thou not that I
haue power to crucifie thee, and haue power
to loose thee?
11 Iesus answered, Thou couldest haue no
power at all against mee, except it were giuen
thee from aboue: therefore he that deliuered
me vnto thee, hath the greater sinne.
12 From thencefoorth Pilate sought to
loose him, but the Iewes cryed, saying, If thou
deliuer him, thou art not Cesars friend: *for*
whosoeuer maketh himselfe a King, speaketh
against Cesar.
13 ¶ 4 When Pilate heard this word, hee
brought Iesus foorth, and sate downe in the
iudgement seate, in a place called, The Pauement, and in Hebrew, b Gabbatha.

4 Pilate condemneth himselfe first, with the same mouth wherewith hee afterward condemneth Christ.
b Gabbatha signifieth an hie place, as iudgement seates are.

14 And it was the preparation of the Passeouer, and about the sixt houre: and he said vnto
the Iewes, Behold your King.
15 But they cryed, Away with him, away
with him, crucifie him. Pilate said vnto them,
Shall I crucifie your King? The high Priests
answered, We haue no King but Cesar.
16 5 Then deliuered he him vnto them, to
be crucified. And they tooke Iesus, and ledde
him away.

5 Christ fasteneth Satan, sinne and death to the crosse.

17 * And he bare his owne crosse, and came
into a place named *of dead mens* skulles, which
is called in Hebrew, Golgotha:

* *Matth.27.31. marke 15.25. luke 23.26.*

18 Where they crucified him, and two o-
ther with him, on either side one, and Iesus in
the middes.
19 ¶ 6 And Pilate wrote also a title, and put
it on the Crosse, and it was written, IESVS
OF NAZARETH THE KING OF THE
IEVVES.

6 Christ sitting vpon the throne of the crosse, is openly written euerlasting king of all people, with his owne hand, whose mouth condemned him for vsurping a kingdom.

20 This title then read many of the Iewes:
for the place where Iesus was crucified, was
neere to the citie: and it was written in Hebrew, Greeke and Latine.
21 Then said the high Priests of the Iewes
to Pilate, Write not, The king of the Iewes, but
that he said, I am king of the Iewes.
22 Pilate answered, What I haue written,
I haue written.
23 ¶ 7 Then the * souldiers, when they
had crucified Iesus, tooke his garments (and
made foure parts, to euery souldier a part) and
his coate: and the coate was without seame
wouen from the top throughout.

7 Christ signifieth by the diuisiō of his garments amongst the bloodie butchers, (his coate except, that had no seam) that it shall come to passe, that he wil shortly diuide his benefits, and enrich his very enemies throwout ẏ world: but so notwithstanding that the treasure of his Church shall remaine whole.
* *Matth.27.35. marke 15.24.*

24 Therefore they sayd one to another,
Let vs not diuide it, but cast lots for it, whose
it shall be. *This was* that the Scripture might be
fulfilled,

fulfilled, which ſayth, *They parted my garments among thnm, and on my coate did caſt lots. So the ſouldiers did theſe things indeed.

25 ¶ [8] Then ſtood by the croſſe of Ieſus his mother, and his mothers ſiſter, Mary *the wife of* Cleophas. and Mary Magdalene.

26 And when Ieſus ſawe his mother, and the diſciple ſtanding by, whom hee loued, hee ſaid vnto his mother, Woman, behold thy ſonne.

27 Then ſaid he to the diſciple, Behold thy mother: & from that houre the diſciple tooke her home vnto him.

28 ¶ [9] After, when Ieſus knew that all things were performed, that the *Scripture might be fulfilled, he ſaid, I thirſt.

29 And there was ſet a [c] veſſell full of vineger: and they filled a ſponge with vineger, and put it about an Hyſope *ſtalke*, and put it to his mouth.

30 Now when Ieſus had receiued of the vineger, hee ſaid, It is finiſhed, and bowed his head, and gaue vp the ghoſt.

31 [10] The Iewes then (becauſe it was the Preparation, that the bodies ſhould not remaine vpon the croſſe on the Sabbath *day*: for that Sabbath was an high day) beſought Pilate that their legges might bee broken, and that they might be taken downe.

32 Then came the ſouldiers and brake the legges of the firſt, and of the other which was crucified with *Ieſus*.

33 But when they came to Ieſus, and ſawe that hee was dead alreadie, they brake not his legges.

34 [11] But one of the ſouldiers with a ſpeare [d] pearced his ſide, and foorthwith came there out blood and water.

35 And he that ſaw it, bare record, and his record is true: and hee knoweth that he ſayth true, that ye might beleeue it.

36 For theſe things were done, that the Scripture ſhould be fulfilled, *Not a bone of him ſhall be broken.

37 And againe another Scripture ſayth, *They ſhall ſee him whom they haue thruſt through.

38 *[12] And after theſe things, Ioſeph of Arimathea (who was a diſciple of Ieſus, but ſecretly for feare of the Iewes) beſought Pilate that he might take downe the bodie of Ieſus. And Pilate gaue him licence. He came then and tooke Ieſus bodie.

39 And there came *alſo Nicodemus (which firſt came to Ieſus by night) & brought of myrrhe and aloes mingled together about an hundreth pound.

40 Then tooke they the bodie of Ieſus, and wrapped it in linnen clothes with the odours, as the manner of the Iewes is to burie.

41 And in that place where Ieſus was crucified, was a garden, and in the garden a newe ſepulchre, wherein was [e] neuer man yet laid.

42 There then laide they Ieſus, becauſe of the Iewes preparation *day*, for the ſepulchre was neere.

*Pſal. 22.18.

8 Chriſt is a perfect example of all righteouſneſſe, not only in the keeping of the firſt, but alſo of the ſecond Table.

9 Chriſt when he hath taken the vineger, yeeldeth vp the Ghoſt, drinking vp in deed that moſt bitter and ſharpe cup of his Fathers wrath in our name.

*Pſal. 96.22.

c Galatinus witneſſeth out of the booke called Sanhedrin, that the Iewes were woont to giue them that were executed, vineger mixed with frankincenſe to drinke, to make their braines ſomewhat troubled: ſo charitably the Iewes prouided for the poore mens conſcience, which were executed.

10 The body of Chriſt which was dead for a ſeaſon (becauſe it ſo pleaſed him) is wounded, but the leaſt bone of it is not broken: and ſuch is the ſtate of his myſticall bodie.

11 Chriſt being dead vpon the croſſe, witneſſeth by a double ſigne, that hee onely is the true ſatisfaction, and the true waſhing for the beleeuers.

d This wound was a moſt manifeſt witnes of the death of of Chriſt: for the water that iſſued out by this wound, gaue vs plainely to vnderſtand, that the weapon pierced the very ſkinne that compaſſeth the heart, which is the veſſell that conteineth that water, and that being once wounded, that creature which is ſo pearced, and ſtriken, cannot chuſe but die.

*Exod. 12.46. numb. 9.12.

*Zach. 12.10.

*Matth. 27.57. marke. 15.42. luke 23.50.

12 Chriſt is openly buried, and in a famous place, Pilate writing and ſuffering it, and that by men which did fauour Chriſt, in ſuch wiſe, that yet before that day, they neuer openly followed him: ſo that by his buriall, no man can iuſtly doubt either of his death, or reſurrection.

*Chap. 3.2.

CHAP. XX.

1 Marie bringeth word that Chriſt is riſen: 3 Peter and Iohn 4 runne to ſee it. 15 Ieſus appeareth to Marie, 19 and to the diſciples that were together in the houſe. 25 Thomas, before faithleſſe, 29 now beleeueth.

NOwe *[1] the firſt *day* of the weeke came Mary Magdalene, earely when it was yet darke, vnto the ſepulchre, and ſawe the ſtone taken away from the tombe.

2 Then ſhe ranne, and came to Simon Peter, and to the other diſciple whom Ieſus loued, and ſaid vnto them, They haue taken away the Lord out of the ſepulchre, and wee know not where they haue laid him.

3 Peter therfore went forth, and the other diſciple, and they came vnto the ſepulchre.

4 So they ranne both together, but the other diſciple did outrunne Peter, and came firſt to the ſepulchre.

5 And he ſtouped downe, and ſaw the linnen clothes lying: yet went he not in.

6 Then came Simon Peter following him, and went into the ſepulchre, and ſaw the linnen clothes lie,

7 And the kerchiefe that was vpon his head, not lying with the linnen clothes, but wrapped together in a place by it ſelfe.

8 Then went in alſo the other diſciple, which came firſt to the ſepulchre, and hee ſaw it, and beleeued.

9 For as yet they knew not the Scripture, That he muſt riſe againe from the dead.

10 And the diſciples went away againe vnto their owne home.

11 ¶ *But Mary ſtood [a] without at the ſepulchre weeping: and as ſhe wept, ſhe bowed her ſelfe into the ſepulchre,

12 [2] And ſaw two Angels in [b] white, ſitting, the one at the head, and the other at the feete, where the bodie of Ieſus had layen.

13 And they ſaid vnto her, Woman, why weepeſt thou? She ſaid vnto them, They haue taken away [c] my Lord, and I know not where they haue laid him.

14 [3] When ſhee had thus ſaid, ſhee turned her ſelfe backe, and ſawe Ieſus ſtanding, and knew not that it was Ieſus.

15 Ieſus ſayth vnto her, Woman, why weepeſt thou? whom ſeekeſt thou? Shee ſuppoſing that he had beene the gardener, ſaid vnto him, Sir, if thou haſt borne him hence, tell me where thou haſt laid him, and I will take him away.

16 Ieſus ſayth vnto her, Marie. She turned her ſelfe and ſaid vnto him, Rabboni, which is to ſay, Maſter.

17 [4] Ieſus ſayth vnto her, Touch me not: for I am not yet aſcended to my Father: but

e That no man might cauill at his reſurrection, as though ſome other that had bin buried there, had riſen. Theophyl.

*Marke 16.1. luke 24.1.

1 Marie Magdalene, Peter and Iohn, are the firſt witneſſes of the reſurrection: and ſuch as cannot iuſtly be ſuſpected, for that they themſelues could ſcarcely be perſwaded of it, ſo farre it is off, that they ſhould inuent it of ſet purpoſe.

*Matth. 28.1. marke 16.5.

a That is, without the caue, which the ſepulchre was cut out of.

2 Two Angels are made witneſſes of the Lords reſurrection.

b In white clothing.

c Mary ſpake as the common people vſe to ſpeake: for they ſpeake of a dead carkeiſe, as they doe of a whole man.

3 Ieſus witneſſeth by his preſence, that he is truely riſen.

4 Chriſt which is riſen, is not to be ſought in this world, according to the fleſh, but in heauen by faith whither he is gone before vs

goe

goe to my [d] brethren, and ſay vnto them, I aſcend vnto [e] my Father, and to your Father, and
to my God, and your God.
18 Marie Magdalene came and told the diſciples that ſhee had ſeene the Lord, and that he
had ſpoken theſe things vnto her.
19 ¶ *[5] The ſame day then at night, which
was the firſt *day* of the weeke, and when the
[f] doores were ſhut where the diſciples were
aſſembled for feare of the Iewes, came Ieſus
and ſtood in the mids, and ſaid to them, Peace
be vnto you.
20 And when hee had ſo ſayd, hee ſhewed
vnto them *his* hands, and his ſide. Then were
the Diſciples glad when they had ſeene the
Lord.
21 * Then ſaid Ieſus to them againe, Peace
bee vnto you: as my Father ſent mee, ſo ſend
I you.
22 And when he had ſaid that, he breathed
on them, and ſaid vnto them, Receiue the holy Ghoſt.
23 [6] Whoſoeuers ſinnes yee remit, they are
remitted vnto them: *and* whoſoeuers ſinnes ye
retaine, they are retained.
34 ¶ [7] But Thomas one of the twelue called Didymus, was not with them when Ieſus came.
25 The other diſciples therefore ſaid vnto
him, We haue ſeene the Lord: but he ſaid vnto
them, Except I ſee in his hands the print of the
nailes, and put my finger into the print of the
nailes, and put mine hand into his ſide, I will
not beleeue it.
26 ¶ And eight dayes after, againe his diſciples were within, and Thomas with them. *Then*
came Ieſus, when the doores were ſhut, and
ſtood in the mids, and ſaid, Peace *be* vnto you.
27 After ſaid he to Thomas, Put thy finger
here, and ſee mine hands, and put foorth thine
hand, and put it into my ſide, and be not faithleſſe, but faithfull.
28 Then Thomas anſwered, and ſaid vnto
him, *Thou art* my Lord, and my God.
29 [8] Ieſus ſaid vnto him, Thomas, becauſe
thou haſt ſeene me, thou beleeueſt: bleſſed *are*
they that haue not ſeene, and haue beleeued.
30 ¶ *[9] And many other ſignes alſo did Ieſus in the preſence of his diſciples, which are
not written in this booke.
31 But theſe things are written, that yee
might beleeue, that Ieſus is that Chriſt that
Sonne of God, and that in beleeuing yee might
haue life through his Name.

d By his brethren, he meaneth his diſciples: for in the next verſe following, it is ſaid, that Mary told his diſciples.
e He calleth God his father, becauſe he is his Fathor naturally in the Godhead, and he ſaith your Father, becauſe he is our Father by grace, through the adoption of the ſonnes of God: that is, by taking vs of his free grace to bee his ſons, Epiphanius
*Mar.16.14 *luk.* 24.36 1.cor.15.5
5 Chriſt in that that he preſented himſelfe before his diſciples ſuddenly through his diuine power, when the gates were ſhut, doth fully aſſure them both of his reſurrection, and alſo of their Apoſtleſhip, inſpiring them with the holy Ghoſt who is the directour of the miniſterie of the Goſpel.
f Either the doores opened to him of their owne accord, or the very wals themſelues were a paſſage to him.
* *Matth.28.18.*
6 The publiſhing of the forgiueneſſe of ſinnes by faith in Chriſt, and the ſetting forth and denouncing the wrath of God in retaining the ſinnes of the vnbeleeuers, is the ſumme of the preaching of the Goſpel.
7 Chriſt draweth out of the vnbeliefe of Thomas, a certaine and ſure teſtimonie of his reſurrection.
8 True faith dependeth vpon the mouth of God, & not vpon fleſhly eyes.
* *Chap.21.25.*
9 To beleeue in Chriſt the ſonne of God and our onely Sauiour, is the end of the doctrine of the Goſpel and eſpecially of the hiſtorie of the reſurrection.

CHAP. XXI.

1 Ieſus appeareth to his diſciples as they were a fiſhing, 6. 7 whom they knew by a miraculous draught of fiſhes. 15 He committeth the charge of the ſheepe to Peter, 18 and foretelleth him of the maner of his death.

AFter theſe things, [1] Ieſus ſhewed himſelfe
againe to his diſciples at the ſea of Tiberias: and thus ſhewed he *himſelfe*.

1 In that, that Chriſt here is not onely preſent but alſo eateth with his Diſciples, hee giueth a moſt full aſſurance of his Reſurrection.

2 There were together Simon Peter, and
Thomas, which is called Didymus, and Nathanael of Cana in Galile, and the *ſonnes* of Zebedeus, and two other of his diſciples.
3 Simon Peter ſaid vnto them, I goe a fiſhing. They ſaid vnto him, Wee alſo will goe
with thee. They went their way and entred into a ſhip ſtraightway, and that night caught
they nothing.
4 But when the morning was now come,
Ieſus ſtood on the ſhore: neuertheleſſe the diſciples knew not that it was Ieſus.
5 Ieſus then ſaid vnto them, Sirs, haue yee
any meate? They anſwered him, No.
6 Then he ſaid vnto them, Caſt out the net
on the right ſide of the ſhip, and yee ſhall find.
So they caſt out, and they were not able at all
to draw it, for the multitude of fiſhes.
7 Therefore ſaid the diſciple whom Ieſus
loued, vnto Peter, It is the Lord. When Simon
Peter heard that it was the Lord, he girded his
[a] coate to him (for he was naked) and caſt himſelfe into the ſea.
8 But the other diſciples came by ſhip (for
they were not farre from land, but about two
hundreth cubites) and they drew the net with
fiſhes.
9 Aſſoone then as they were come to land,
they ſaw hoate coales, and fiſh laide thereon,
and bread.
10 Ieſus ſaid vnto them, Bring of the fiſhes
which yee haue now caught.
11 Simon Peter ſtepped foorth and drew
the net to land, full of great fiſhes, an hundreth,
fiftie and three: and albeit there were ſo many,
yet was not the net broken.
12 Ieſus ſaid vnto them, Come, *and* dine.
And none of the Diſciples durſt aske him,
Who art thou? ſeeing they knew that hee was
the Lord.
13 Ieſus then came and tooke bread and
gaue them, and fiſh likewiſe.
14 This is now the third time that Ieſus
ſhewed himſelfe to his diſciples, after that hee
was riſen againe from the dead.
15 ¶ [2] So when they had dined, Ieſus ſaid
to Simon Peter, Simon *the ſonne* of Iona, loueſt
thou me more then theſe? Hee ſaid vnto him,
Yea Lord, thou knoweſt that I loue thee. Hee
ſaid vnto him, Feede my lambes.
16 Hee ſaid to him againe the ſecond time,
Simon *the ſonne* of Iona, loueſt thou me? He ſaid
vnto him, Yea Lord, thou knoweſt that I loue
thee. He ſaid vnto him, Feede my ſheepe.
17 He ſaid vnto him the [b] third time, Simon
the ſonne of Iona, loueſt thou me? Peter was ſo-
rie becauſe he ſaid to him the third time, Loueſt
thou me? and ſaid vnto him, Lord, thou knoweſt all things: thou knoweſt that I loue thee.
Ieſus ſaid vnto him, Feede my ſheepe.
18 [3] Verily, verily I ſay vnto thee, When
thou waſt yong, thou [c] girdedſt thy ſelfe, and
walkedſt whither thou wouldeſt: but when

a It was a linnen garment, which could not let his ſwimming.
2 Peter by this triple confeſsion is reſtored into his former degree from whence he fell by his triple denial: and therewithall is aduertiſed, that he is in deede a paſtour, which ſheweth his loue to Chriſt, in feeding his ſheepe.
b It was meete that he that had denied him thriſe ſhould confeſſe him thriſe, that Peter might neither doubt of the forgiueneſſe of his ſo grieuous a ſinne, nor of his reſtoring to the office of the Apoſtleſhip.
3 The violent death of Peter is foretold.
c They that tooke farre iourneyes, eſpecially in the Eaſt countrey and in thoſe places where the people vſed long garments, had neede to be girded and truſſed vp.

thou ſhalt be old, thou ſhalt ſtretch forth thine
hands, and another ſhall [d] gird thee, and leade
thee whither thou wouldeſt [e] not.
19 And this ſpake hee ſignifying by [f] what
death hee ſhould glorifie God. And when hee
had ſaid this, he ſaid to him, Follow me.
20 [4] Then Peter turned about, and ſawe
the diſciple whome Ieſus loued, following,
which had alſo * leaned on his breſt at ſupper,
and had ſaid, Lord, which is hee that betrayeth thee?
21 When Peter therefore ſaw him, he ſaid
to Ieſus, Lord, what ſhall this man *doe?*
22 Ieſus ſaid vnto him, If I will that hee
tarie till I come, what is it to thee? followe
thou me.
23 Then went this word abroad among the
brethren, that this diſciple ſhould not die. Yet
Ieſus ſaid not to him, He ſhall not die: but, If I
will that he tarie till I come, what is it to thee?
24 [5] This is that diſciple, which teſtifieth of
theſe things, and wrote theſe things, and wee
know that his teſtimonie is true.
25 * Now there are alſo many other things
which Ieſus did, the which if they ſhould bee
written euery one, I ſuppoſe the world could
not conteine the bookes that ſhould bee written, Amen.

d Hee meant that kind of girding which is vſed toward captiues, when they are bound faſt with cordes and chaines, as who would ſay, Now thou girdeſt thy ſelfe as thou thinkeſt beſt, to goe whither thou liſteſt, but the time will be, when thou ſhalt not gird thee with a girdle, but another ſhall bind thee with chaines, and carie thee whither thou wouldeſt not. *e Not that Peter ſuffered ought for the trueth of God againſt his will, for we reade that he came with ioy and gladneſſe, when hee returned from the Councell where he was whipped, but becauſe this will commeth not from the fleſh, but from that gift of the Spirit which is giuen vs from aboue, therefore he ſheweth there ſhould be a certaine ſtriuing and conflict or repugnancie, which alſo is in vs, in all our ſufferances as touching the fleſh.* *f That is, that Peter ſhould die by a violent death.* 4 We muſt take heede, that whiles wee caſt our eyes vpon other, we neglect not that which is inioyned vs. * *Chap. 13.23.*

5 The hiſtorie of Chriſt is true and warily written: not for the curioſitie of men, but for the ſaluation of the godly. * *Chap. 20.30.*

THE ACTES OF THE HOLY APOSTLES, WRIT-TEN BY LVKE THE EVANGELIST.

CHAP. I.

1 Luke tieth this hiſtorie to his Goſpel. 9 Chriſt being taken into heauen, 10 the Apoſtles 11 being warned by the Angels, 12 returne, 14 and giue themſelues to prayer. 15 By Peters motion, 18 into Iudas the traytours place, Matthias is choſen.

I Haue made the [1] former treatiſe, O Theophilus, of all
that Ieſus beganne to [a] doe
and teach,
2 Vntill the day that hee
was taken vp, after that hee
through the holy Ghoſt, had giuen commaundements vnto the Apoſtles, whome hee
had choſen:
3 [2] To whom alſo hee preſented himſelfe
aliue after that he had ſuffred, by many [b] infallible tokens, being ſeene of them by the *ſpace* of
fortie dayes, & ſpeaking of thoſe things which
appertaine to the kingdome of God.
4 * And when he had [c] gathered *them* together, hee commanded them that they ſhould
not depart from Hieruſalem, but to waite for
the promiſe of the Father, * which *ſaid he,* yee
haue heard of me.
5 * For Iohn in deede baptized with water, but yee ſhall bee baptized [d] with the holy
Ghoſt within theſe few dayes.
6 [3] When they therefore were come together, they asked of him, ſaying, Lord, wilt
thou at his time [e] reſtore the kingdome to
Iſrael?
7 And he ſaid vnto them, It is not for you
to know the times, or the [f] ſeaſons, which the
father hath put in his owne power,
8 * But ye ſhall receiue power of the holy
Ghoſt, when hee ſhall come on you: and yee
ſhall be witneſſes vnto me both in Hieruſalem
and in all Iudea, and in Samaria, and vnto the
vttermoſt part of the earth.
9 * [4] And when he had ſpoken theſe things,
while they beheld, he was taken vp: for a cloud
tooke him vp out of their ſight.
10 And while they looked ſtedfaſtly toward heauen, as hee went, behold, two men
ſtood by them in white apparell,
11 Which alſo ſaid, Yee men of Galile,
why ſtand yee gazing into heauen? This Ieſus which is taken vp [g] from you into heauen,
ſhall ſo come, as yee haue ſeene him goe into
heauen.
12 ¶ Then returned they vnto Hieruſalem
from the mount that is called *the mount* of O-
liues, which is neere to Hieruſalem, being from
it a Sabbath [h] *dayes* iourney.
13 [5] And when they were [i] come in, they
went vp into an vpper chamber, where abode
both Peter and Iames, and Iohn, and Andrew,
Philip, and Thomas, Bartlemew, and Matthew,
Iames *the ſonne* of Alpheus, and Simon Zelotes,
and Iudas Iames *brother.*
14 Theſe all [k] continued with [l] one accord
in [m] prayer and ſupplication with the [n] women,
and Marie the mother of Ieſus, and with his
[o] brethren.
15 ¶ [6] And in thoſe dayes Peter ſtood vp

1 A paſſing ouer from the hiſtorie of the Goſpel, that is, from the hiſtorie of the ſayings and doings of Chriſt, vnto the Acts of the Apoſtles.
a The actes of Ieſus are the miracles and doings which ſhewed his Godhead, and his moſt perfit holineſſe and examples of his doctrine.
2 Chriſt did not ſtraightwayes aſcend into heauen after his reſurrection, becauſe he would throughly proue his reſurrection, and with his preſence confirme his Apoſtles in the doctrine, which they had heard.
b He calleth thoſe infallible tokens, which are otherwiſe termed neceſſarie: now in that, that Chriſt ſpake, and walked, and ate, and was felt of many, theſe are ſure ſignes and tokens that he truely roſe againe. * *Luke 24.49.* *c They were diſperſed here and there, but hee gathereth them together that they might altogether be witneſſes of his reſurrection.* * *Iohn 14.25. mat. 3.11. mar. 1 8. luk 3.16. chap. 2.1. and 11.16. and 19.4.* *d Either of the Father, or of me: ſo that either the Father or Chriſt, is ſet here againſt Iohn, as the holy Ghoſt is againſt the water, as things anſwereable the one to the other.* 3 We muſt fight before we triumph: and we ought not curiouſly to ſearch after thoſe things, which God hath not reueiled. *e To the olde and ancient ſtate.*

f That is, the fit occaſions that ſerue to doing of matters which the Lord hath appointed to bring things to paſſe in.
* *Chap. 2.2.*
* *Luke 24.51.*
4 After that Chriſt hath promiſed the full vertue of the holy Ghoſt, wherewith he would gouerne his church, although he ſhould be abſent in body, he tooke vp his body from vs into the heauenly tabernacles, there to continue vntil the latter day of iudgement, as the Angels witneſſe.
g That is, out of your ſight.
h About two mile.
5 Eccleſiaſticall aſſemblies to heare the word, and to make common prayer, were firſt inſtituted and kept in priuate houſes by the Apoſtles.
i They went into the houſe, which the Church had choſen at that time to be a receite for the whole aſſembly.
k The Greeke word ſignifieth an inuincible conſtancie, & ſteadineſſe.

l It is to good purpoſe, that this concord is mentioned: for thoſe prayers are moſt acceptable to God, which are made with agreeing minds and wils. *m The diſciples prayed for the ſending of the holy Ghoſt, and alſo to be deliuered from preſent dangers, wherewith they were beſet.* *n For it was behoueable, to haue the wiues confirmed, who were afterward to bee partakers of the dangers with their husbands.* *o With his kinſfolkes.* 6 Peter is made the mouth and interpreter of the whole companie of the Apoſtles, either by ſecret reuelation of the holy Ghoſt, or by expreſſe iudgement of the congregation.

in the mids of the disciples, and said (now the
number of [p] names that were in one place were
about an hundreth and twentie.)
16 [7] Yee men *and* brethren, this Scripture
must needes haue beene fulfilled, which the
*holy Ghost by the mouth of Dauid spake be-
fore of Iudas, which was * guide to them that
tooke Iesus.
17 For hee was numbred with vs, and had
obtained fellowship in this ministration.
18 Hee therefore hath [q] purchased a field
with the reward of iniquitie: and when *hee
had [r] throwen downe himselfe headlong, hee
brast asunder in the mids, and all his bowels
gushed out.
19 And it is knowen vnto all the inhabitants of Hierusalem, in so much, that the field is
called in their owne language, Aceldama, that
is, The field of blood.
20 For it is written in the booke of Psalmes,
* Let his habitation bee voide, and let no man
dwell therein: * also, Let another take his
[s] charge.
21 [8] Wherefore of these men which haue
companied with vs, all the time that the Lord
Iesus was [t] conuersant among vs,
22 Beginning from the Baptisme of Iohn
vnto the day that hee was taken vp [u] from vs,
must one of them bee made a witnesse with vs
of his resurrection.
23 [9] And they [x] presented two, Ioseph called Barsabas, whose surname was Iustus, and
Matthias.
24 And they prayed, saying, Thou Lord,
which knowest the hearts of all men, shewe
whether of these two thou hast chosen,
25 That he may take the [y] roome of this ministration and Apostleship, from which Iudas
hath [z] gone astray, to goe to his owne place.
26 Then they gaue forth their lots: and the
lot fell on Matthias, and he was by a common
consent counted with the eleuen Apostles.

p Because men are commonly billed and enrolled by their names.
7 Peter preuenteth the offence that might bee taken of the falling away of Iuday the betrayer, shewing that all things which came vnto him, were foretold by God.
* *Psal.41.9.*
* *Iohn 13 27.*
q Luke considered not Iudas his purpose, but that that followed of it, and so we vse to say, that a man hath procured him selfe harme, not that his will and purpose was so, but in respect of that which followed.
* *Matth.27 5.*
r The Greeke words signifie thus much, and Iudas fell downe flat and was rent in sunder in the mids, with a marueilous huge noyse.
* *Psal.69 26.*
* *Psal 109.7.*
s His office and ministerie: Dauid wrote these words against Doeg the Kings heardman: And these words, Shepheard, Sheepe, and Flocke, are put ouer to the Church office and ministerie, so that the Church and the offices are called by these names.
8 The Apostles deliberate vpon nothing, but first they consult and take aduisement by Gods word: and againe they doe nothing that concerneth and is behoueable for the whole body of the Congregation, without making the Congregation priuie vnto it. *t Word for word, went in and out, which kind of speech betokeneth as much in the Hebrew tongue, as the exercising of a publique and painefull office, when they speake of such as are in any publique office, Deut.31.2.1.Chron.27.1. u From our companie.* 9 The Apostles must be chosen immediatly from God: and therefore after prayers, Matthias is chosen by lot, which is as it were, Gods owne voice. *x Openly, and by the voices of all the whole companie. y That he may be fellow and partaker of this ministerie. z Departed from, or fallen from: And it is a Metaphore taken from the way: For Callings are signified by the name of wayes, with the Hebrewes.*

CHAP. II.

1 The Apostles 4 filled with the holy Ghost 8 speake with diuers tongues: 13 They are thought to bee drunke, 15 but Peter disprooueth that: 34 He teacheth that Christ is the Messias: 37 And seeing the hearers astonied, 38 he exhorteth them to repentance.

AND [1] when the day of Pentecost was
[a] come, they were [b] all with one accord
in one place.
2 And suddenly there came a sound from
heauen, as of a rushing *and* mightie wind, and it
filled all the house where they sate.
3 And there appeared vnto them clouen
tongues, like fire, and it sate vpon each of them.
4 And they were all filled with the holy
Ghost, & began to speake with [c] other tongues,
as the [d] Spirit gaue them vtterance.
5 And there were dwelling at Hierusalem
Iewes, men that feared God, of euery nation
vnder heauen.
6 Now when this was noysed, the multitude came together, and were astonied, because
that euery man heard them speake his owne
language.
7 And they wondered all, and marueiled,
saying among themselues, Behold, are not all
these which speake, of Galile?
8 [e] How then heare wee euery man our
owne language, wherein we were borne?
9 Parthians, and Medes, and Elamites, and
the inhabitants of Mesopotamia, and of Iudea,
and of Cappadocia, of Pontus, and Asia,
10 And of Phrygia, and Pamphylia, of E-
gypt, and of the parts of Libya, which is beside
Cyrene, and strangers of Rome, and [f] Iewes,
and Proselites,
11 Creetes, and Arabians: we heard them
speake in our owne tongues the wonderfull
workes of God.
12 [2] They were all then amazed, and doubted, saying one to another, What may this be?
13 And others [g] mocked, and said, They are
full of new wine.
14 ¶ But Peter standing with the Eleuen,
[h] lift vp his voice, and said vnto them, Yee men
of Iudea, *and* yee all that inhabite Hierusalem,
bee this knowen vnto you, and hearken vnto
my words.
15 For these are not drunken, as yee suppose, since it is but the [i] third houre of the day.
16 But this is that, which was spoken by
the [k] Prophet * Ioel,
17 [3] And it shall bee in the last dayes, saith
God, I wil powre out my spirit vpon [l] all [m] flesh,
and your sonnes, and your daughters shall prophecie, and your yong men shall see visions,
and your old men shall dreame dreames.
18 And on my seruants, and on mine hand-
maides I will powre out of my spirit in those
dayes, and they shall prophecie.
19 And I will shew wonders in heauen a-
boue, and tokens in the earth beneath, blood,
and fire, and vapour of smoke.
20 The Sunne shall bee turned into darke-

1 The Apostles being gathered together on a most solemne feast day in one place, that it might euidently appeare to all the world, that they had all one office, one Spirit, one faith, are by a double signe from heauen authorised, and anoynted with all the most excellent gifts of the holy Ghost, and especially with an extraordinarie and necessarie gift of tongues. *a Word for word, was fulfilled: that is, was begun, as Luke 2. 21. For the Hebrewes say, that a day, or a yeere is fulfilled or ended, when the former dayes or yeeres are ended, and the other begun, Iere.25.12 And it shall come to passe, that when seuentie yeeres are fulfilled, I will visite, &c. For the Lord did not bring home his people, after the seuentieth yeere was ended, but in the seuentieth yeere: Now the day of Pentecost, was the fiftieth day after the feast of the Passeouer. b The twelue Apostles, which were to bee the Patriarkes as it were of the Church.*

c He calleth them other tongues, which were not the same which the Apostles vsed commonly, and Marke calleth them newe tongues
d Hereby wee vnderstand, that the Apostles vsed not now one tongue, and then an other by haphazard at all aduenture, or as fantasticall men vse to doe, but with good consideration of their hearers: and to be short, that they speake nothing, but as the holy Ghost gouerned their tongues.
e Not that they spake with one voice, and many languages were heard, but that the Apostles spake with strange tongues: for else the miracle had rather beene in the hearers whereas now it is in the speakers, Nazianzen in his oration of Whitsunday.
f By Iewes, hee meaneth them that were both Iewes by birth, and Iewes by profession of religion though they were borne in other places: and they were Proselytes, which were Gentiles borne, and imbraced the Iewish religion.
2 Gods word pearceth some so, that it driueth them to seeke out the trueth, and it doeth so choke other, that it forceth them to be witnesses of their owne impudencie.
g The word which he vseth here signifieth such a kind of mocking which is reprochfull and contumelious: And by this reprochfull mocking we see, that there is no miracle so great and excellent, which the wickednesse of man dareth not speake euill of. h Peter his holinesse is to be marked, wherein the grace of the holy Ghost is to bee seene, euen straight after the beginning. i After the sunne rising, which may bee about seuen or eight of the clocke with vs. k There is nothing that can dissolue questions and doubts, but testimonie taken out of the Prophets: for mens reasons may be ouerturned, but Gods voice cannot bee ouerturned.
* *Ioel 2.28.esai.24 3.* 3 Peter setting the trueth of God against the false accusations of men, sheweth in himselfe and in his fellowes, that that is fulfilled which Ioel spake before concerning the full giuing of the holy Ghost in the latter dayes: which grace also is offered to the whole Church, to their certaine and vndoubted destruction, which doe condemne it. *l All without exception, both vpon the Iewes and Gentiles. m That is, men.*

nesse, and the Moone into blood, before that
great and terrible day of the Lord come.
21 [4] And it shall bee, that whosoeuer shall
[n] call on the Name of the Lord, shall be saued.
22 [5] Yee men of Israel, heare these words,
Iesus of Nazareth, a man [o] approoued of God
among you with great workes and wonders,
and signes, which God did by him in the mids
of you, as yee your selues also know:
23 Him, *I say*, being deliuered by the determinate counsell, and [p] foreknowledge of God,
after you had taken with wicked [q] hands, you
haue crucified and [r] slaine.
24 [6] Whom God hath raised vp, and loosed
the [ſ] sorrowes of death, because it was vnpossible that he should be holden of it.
25 For Dauid saith concerning him, * I
beheld the Lord alwayes before mee: for
hee is at my right hand, that I should not bee
shaken.
26 Therefore did mine heart reioyce, and
my tongue was glad, and moreouer also my
flesh shall rest in hope,
27 Because thou wilt not [t] leaue my soule
in graue, neither wilt suffer thine holy one to
see corruption.
28 Thou hast [u] shewed mee the wayes of
life, and shalt make mee full of ioy with thy
countenance.
29 Men *and* brethren, I may boldly speake
vnto you of the Patriarke Dauid, * that hee is
both dead and buried, and his sepulchre remaineth with vs vnto this day.
30 Therefore, seeing he was a Prophet, and
knew that God had * [x] sworne with an oath to
him, that of the fruit of his loynes hee would
raise vp Christ concerning the flesh, to set him
vpon his throne,
31 Hee knowing this before, spake of the
resurrection of Christ, that * his soule should
not be left in graue, neither his flesh should see
corruption.
32 [7] This Iesus hath God raised vp, whereof we are all witnesses.
33 Since then that he by the [y] right hand of
God hath beene exalted, and hath receiued of
his Father the promise of the holy Ghost, hee
hath shed foorth this which yee now see and
heare.
34 For Dauid is not ascended into heauen,
but he saith, * The Lord said to my Lord, Sit at
my right hand,
35 Vntill I make thine enemies thy footestoole.
36 Therefore, let all the house of Israel
know for a suretie, that God hath [z] made him
both Lord, and Christ, this Iesus, *I say*, whom
yee haue crucified.
37 Now when they heard it, they were
pricked in their hearts, and said vnto Peter and
the other Apostles, Men *and* brethren, what
shall we doe?
38 [8] Then Peter said vnto them, Amend
your liues, and be baptized euery one of you in
the Name of Iesus Christ for the remission of
sinnes: and yee shall receiue the gift of the holy Ghost.
39 For the [a] promise *is made* vnto you, and
to your children, and to all that are afarre off,
euen as many as the Lord our God shall call.
40 [9] And with many other words hee besought and exhorted *them*, saying, Saue your
selues from this froward generation.
41 [10] Then they that gladly receiued his
word, were baptized: and the same day there
were added *to the Church* about three thousand soules.
42 [11] And they continued in the Apostles
doctrine, and [b] fellowship, and [c] breaking of
bread, and prayers.
43 ¶ [12] And feare came vpon euery soule,
and many wonders and signes were done by
the Apostles.
44 [13] And all that beleeued, were in one
place, and had all things common.
45 And they sold their possessions and
goods, and parted them to all men, as euery
one had need.
46 [14] And they continued dayly with one
accord in the Temple, and breaking bread at
home, did eate their meate together with gladnesse and singlenesse of heart,
47 Praising God, and had fauour with all
the people: and the Lord added to the Church
from day to day, such as should be saued.

4 The chiefest vse of all the gifts of the holy Ghost is to bring men to saluation by faith.
n This word, Call on, signifieth in holy Scriptures, an earnest praying and crauing for help at Gods hand.
5 Christ being innocent, was by Gods prouidence crucified of wicked men.
o Who is by those workes which God wrought by him, so manifestly approoued and allowed of, that no man can gainesay him
p Gods euerlasting knowledge going before, which can neither be separated from his determinate counsell, as the Epicures say, neither yet bee the cause of euill: for God in his euerlasting and vnchangeable counsell, appointed the wicked act of Iudas to an excellent end: and God doth that well, which the instruments doe ill.
q Gods counsell doeth not excuse the Iewes, whose hands were wicked
r The fact is said to be theirs, by whose counsell and egging forward it is done.
6 Christ (as Dauid foretold) did not onely rise againe, but also was in the graue voide of all corruption.
ſ The death that was full of sorrow both of body and mind: therefore when death appeared conquerour and victorer ouer those sorrowes, Christ is rightly said to haue ouercome those sorowes of death when as being dead, he ouercame death, to liue for euer with his Father.
* *Psal. 16.9.*
t Thou wilt not suffer me to remaine in graue.
u Thou hast opened me the way to the true life.
* *1. King. 2. 10. chap 13.36.*
* *Psal. 132.11.*
x Had sworne solemnely.
* *Psal. 16.10. chap. 13 35.*
7 Peter witnesseth that Iesus Christ is the appointed euerlasting King, which hee proueth manifestly by the gifts of the holy Ghost and the testimonie of Dauid. *y Might and power of God.* * *Psal. 110.1.* *z Christ is said to be made, because he was aduanced to that dignitie, and therefore it is not spoken of his nature, but of his estate and high dignitie.*

8 Repentance and remission of sinnes in Christ, are two principles of the Gospl and therefore of our saluation: and they are obtained by the promises apprehended by faith, and are ratified in vs by Baptisme, wherewith is ioyned the vertue of the holy Ghost.
a The word that is vsed here, giueth vs to vnderstand that it was a free gift.
9 He is truely ioyned to the Church, which separateth himselfe from the wicked.
10 A notable example of the vertue of the holy Ghost: but such as are of age, are not baptised, before they make confession of their faith.
11 The markes of the true Church are the doctrine of the Apostles, the duties of charitie, the pure and simple administration of the Sacraments, and true inuocation vsed of all the faithfull.
b Communicating of goods, and all other dueties of charitie, as is shewed afterward. *c The Iewes vsed thinne loaues, and therfore they did rather brake them then cut them: So by breaking of bread, they vnderstood that liuing together, and the banquets which they vsed to keepe. And when they kept their loue feasts, they vsed to celebrate the Lords Supper, which euen in these dayes began to be corrupted, and Paul amendeth it, 1. Cor. 11.* 12 So oft as the Lord thinketh it expedient, he bridleth the rage of strangers, that the Church may bee planted, and haue some refreshing. 13 Charitie maketh all things common concerning the vse, according as necessitie requireth. 14 The faithfull came together at the beginning with great fruit, not onely to the hearing of the word, but also to meate.

CHAP. III.

1 Peter going into the Temple with Iohn, 2 healeth the creeple. 9 To the people gathered together to see the miracle, 12 hee expoundeth the mysterie of our saluation through Christ, 14 accusing their ingratitude, 19 and requiring their repentance.

Nowe [1] Peter and Iohn went vp together into the Temple, at the ninth houre
of prayer.
2 And a certaine man which was a creeple
from his mothers wombe, was caried, whome
they laid dayly at the gate of the Temple called
Beautifull, to aske almes of them that entred into the Temple.
3 Who seeing Peter and Iohn, that they
would enter into the temple, desired to receiue
an almes.
4 And Peter earnestly beholding him with
Iohn, said, Looke on vs.
5 And he [a] gaue heed vnto them, trusting
to receiue some thing of them.
6 Then said Peter, Siluer and gold haue I
none,

1 Christ, in healing a man that was borne lame, and well knowen to all men, both in place and time very famous, by the hands of his Apostles, doeth partly confirme them which beleeued, and partly also calleth other to beleeue.
a Both with heart and eyes.

none, but such as I haue, that giue I thee: In
the Name of Iesus Christ of Nazareth, rise vp
and walke.
7 And he tooke him by the right hand, and
lift *him* vp, and immediatly his feete and ankle
bones receiued strength.
8 And he leaped vp, stood, and walked, and
entred with them into the Temple, walking
and leaping, and praising God.
9 And all the people saw him walke, and
praising God.
10 And they knew him, that it was he which
sate for the almes at the Beautifull gate of the
Temple, and they were amased, and sore astonied at that, which was come vnto him.
11 ¶And as the creeple which was healed,
[b] held Peter and Iohn, all the people ranne a-
mased vnto them in the porch which is called
Salomons.
12 [2] So when Peter saw it, he answered vnto the people, Yee men of Israel, why maruaile
yee at this? or why looke yee so stedfastly on
vs, as though by our owne power or godlinesse, we had made this man goe?
13 The God of Abraham, and Isaac, and Iacob, the *God of our fathers hath glorified his
Sonne Iesus, whom yee betrayed, and denied in
the presence of Pilate, when he had iudged him
to be deliuered.
14 But yee denied the Holy one and the
Iust, and desired a murtherer to be giuen you,
15 And killed the Lord [c] of life, whome
God hath raised from the dead, whereof we are
witnesses.
16 And his Name hath made this man sound,
whom yee see and know, through faith in his
Name: [d] and the faith which is by him, hath giuen to him this perfit health of his whole body
in the presence of you all.
17 [3] And nowe brethren, I knowe that
through ignorance yee did it, as *did* also your
gouernours.
18 But those things which God before had
shewed [e] by the mouth of all his Prophets, that
Christ should suffer, he hath thus fulfilled.
19 Amend your liues therefore, and turne,
that your sinnes may bee put away, when the
time of refreshing shal come from the presence
of the Lord.
20 And hee shall send Iesus Christ, which
before was preached vnto you,
21 [f] Whom the heauen must containe vntill
the time that all things be restored, which God
had spoken by the mouth of all his holy Prophets since the world began.
22 *For Moses said vnto the fathers, The
Lord your God shall raise vp vnto you [g] a Prophet, *euen* of your brethren, like vnto me: yee
shall heare him in all things, whatsoeuer he shal
say vnto you.
23 For it shall bee that euery person which
shall not heare that Prophet, shall be destroyed
out of the people.

b Either because he loued them, who had healed him: or because he feared that if he once let them goe out of his sight, he should be lame againe.

2 Miracles are appointed to conuince the vnbeleeuers, and therefore they doe wickedly abuse them, who standing amased, either at the miracles themselues or at the instruments & meanes which it pleaseth God to vse, take an occasion to establish idolatry and superstition, by that which God hath prouided for ẏ knowledge of his true worship, that is, Christianitie.

* *Chap 5.30.*

c Who hath life in himselfe, and giueth life to other.

d Because he beleeued on him being raised from the dead, whose Name he heard of by vs.

3 It is best of all to receiue Christ so soone as he is offered vnto vs: but such as haue neglected so great a benefit through mans weaknesse, haue yet repentance for a mean: As for the ignominie of the crosse, we haue to set against that, the decree and purpose of God, foretold by the Prophets, of Christ, how that first of all hee should be crucified here vpon earth, and then hee should appeare from heauen the iudge and restorer of all things, that all beleeuers might be saued, and all vnbeleeuers vtterly perish.

e Though there were many Prophets, yet he speaketh but of one mouth, to shew vnto vs the consent and agreement of the Prophets.

f Or, be taken vp into heauen.

* *Deut. 18.15. chap. 7.37.*

g This promise was of an excellent and singular Prophet.

24 Also all the Prophets [h] from Samuel, and
thenceforth as many as haue spoken, haue likewise foretold of these dayes.
25 [4] Yee are the [i] children of the Prophets,
and of the couenant, which God hath made
vnto our fathers, saying to Abraham, *Euen
in thy seede shall all the kinreds of the earth bee
blessed.
26 First vnto you hath God [k] raised vp his
Sonne Iesus, and him hee hath sent to blesse
you, in turning euery one of you from your
iniquities.

h At what time the kingdome of Israel was established.

4 The Iewes that beleeued are the first begotten in the kingdome of God.

i For whome the Prophets were specially appointed.

* *Gene. 12.3. gala. 3.8.*

k Giuen to the world, or raised from the dead, and aduanced to his kingdome.

CHAP. IIII.

1 Peter and Iohn, 3 are taken and brought before the Councell. 7 and 19 They speake boldly in Christs cause. 24 The disciples pray vnto God. 32 Many sell their possessions. 36 Of whom Barnabas is one.

1 AND [1] as they spake vnto the people, the
Priests and the [a] Captaine of the Temple,
and the Sadduces came vpon them,
2 Taking it grieuously that they taught
the people, and preached in Iesus *Name* the resurrection from the dead.
3 And they laide hands on them, and put
them in hold, vntill the next day: for it was
now euentide.
4 Howbeit, many of them which heard the
word, beleeued, and the [b] number of the men
was about fiue thousand.
5 ¶And it came to passe on the morrow
that their [c] rulers and Elders, and Scribes, were
gathered together at Ierusalem,
6 And Annas the chiefe Priest, and Caiaphas, and Iohn, and Alexander, and as many as
were of the [d] kinred of the hie Priests.
7 [2] And when they had set them before
them, they asked, By what power, or in what
[e] Name haue yee done this?
8 Then Peter full of the holy Ghost, said
vnto them, Yee Rulers of the people, and Elders of Israel,
9 [3] For as much as wee this day are examined of the good deede *done* to the impotent man, *to wit*, by what meanes hee is made
whole,
10 [4] Bee it knowen vnto you all, and to all
the people of Israel, that by the Name of IE-
SVS CHRIST of Nazareth, whom yee haue
crucified, whome God raised againe from the
dead, *euen* by him doth this man stand here before you, whole.
11 *This is the stone cast aside of you builders, which is become the head of the corner.
12 Neither is there saluation in any other:
for among men there is [f] giuen none other
[g] Name [h] vnder heauen, whereby wee must
be saued.

1 None are commonly more diligent or bolder enemies of the Church, then such as professe themselues to be head builders: but the more they rage, the more constantly the faithfull seruants of God doe continue.

a The Iewes had certaine garrisons for the garde and saftie of the Temple and holy things Matth 26.65. These garisons had a Captaine, such as Eleazarus Ananias the hie Priests sonne was in the time of the warre that was in Iudea being a very impudent and proud yong man, Ioseph. lib. 2. of the taking of Iudea.

b While they thought to diminish the number, they increased them.

c These were they that made the Sanhedrim, which were all of the tribe of Iuda, vntill Herod vsed that crueltie against Dauids stocke.

d Of whome the high Priests were wont to be chosen and made, the execution of the yeerely office being now changed.

2 Against such as bragge of a succession of persons, without a succession of doctrine, and by that means beate downe the true ministers of the word, so farre foorth as they are able.

e By what authoritie.

3 The Woolues which succeede true Pastours, pleade their owne cause and not Gods, neither the Churches.

4 He is in deede a true sheepheard, that teacheth his sheepe to hang vpon Christ onely, as vpon one that is not dead, but hath conquered death, and hath all rule in his owne hands.

* *Psal. 118.22. esai. 28.16 matth 21.42 marke 12.10. luke 20.17. roma. 9.33. 1. peter 2.7.*

f Of God.

g There is no other man, or no other power and authoritie whatsoeuer: which kind of speech being vsuall among the Iewes, rose vpon this, that when wee are in danger, we call vpon them at whose hands we looke for helpe.

h Any where: and this setteth foorth vnto vs the largenesse of Christs kingdome.

13 [5]Now when they saw the boldnesse of
Peter and Iohn, and vnderstood that they were
vnlearned men and without [i]knowledge, they
marueiled, and knew them, that they had bene
with Iesus:
14 And beholding also the man which was
healed standing with them, they had nothing
to say against it.
15 Then they commanded them to goe a-
side out of the Councill, and [k]conferred among
themselues,
16 [6]Saying, What shall wee doe to these
men? for surely a manifest signe is done by
them, *and it is* openly knowen to all them that
dwell in Hierusalem: and we cannot denie it.
17 But that it bee noised no further among
the people, let vs threaten and charge them,
that they speake hencefoorth to no man in this
Name.
18 So they called them, and commaunded
them, that in no wise they should speake or
teach in the Name of Iesus.
19 [7]But Peter and Iohn answered vnto
them, and sayd, Whether it bee right in the
sight of God, to obey you rather then God,
iudge yee.
20 For wee cannot but speake the things
which we haue seene and heard.
21 [8]So they threatned them, and let them
goe, and found nothing how to punish them,
because of the people: for all men praised God
for that which was done.
22 For the man was aboue fourtie yeeres
olde, on whome this miracle of healing was
shewed.
23 [9]Then assoone as they were let goe, they
came to their fellowes, and shewed all that the
hie Priests and Elders had said vnto them.
24 [10]And when they heard it, they lift vp
their voices to God with one accord, and said,
O Lord, thou art the God which hast made the
heauen, and the earth, the sea, and all things
that are in them,
25 Which by the mouth of thy seruant Dauid hast said, *Why did the Gentiles rage, and
the people imagine vaine things?
26 The Kings of the earth assembled, and
the Rulers came together against the Lord, and
against his Christ.
27 For doubtlesse, against thine holy Sonne
Iesus, whom thou haddest anointed, both Herod and Pontius Pilate, with the Gentiles
and the [l]people of Israel gathered themselues
together,
28 To [m]doe whatsoeuer [n]thine hand, and
thy counsel had determined before to be done.
29 And now, O Lord, behold their threatnings, and graunt vnto thy seruants with all
boldnesse to speake thy word,

5 The good libertie and boldnesse of the seruants of God doeth yet thus much good, that such as lay hid vnder a vizard of zeale, doe at length betray themselues to be in deede wicked men.
i *The word vsed here, is Idiot, which being spoken in comparison had to a Magistrate, betokeneth a priuate man: but when we speake of sciences and studies, it signifieth one that is vnlearned: and in accompt of honour and estimation, it importeth one of base degree, and no estimation.*
k *Laide their heads together.*
6 He that flattereth himselfe in ignorance, commeth at length to doe open wickednesse, and that against his owne conscience.
7 We must so obey men to whom we are subiect, that especially and before all things we obey God.
8 So farre off are the wicked from doing what they list, that contrariwise God vseth euen that to the setting forth of his glorie, which he giueth them leaue to doe.
9 The Apostles communicate their troubles with the Congregation.
10 We ought neither to bee afraid of the threatnings of our enemies, neither yet foolishly contemne their rage and madnesse against vs: but we haue to set against their force and malice, an earnest thinking vpon the power and good will of God (both which we doe manifestly behold in Christ) and so flee to the aide and succour of our Father.
* *Psal. 2.1.*
l *Although the people of Israel was but one people, yet the plurall number is here vsed, not so much for the twelue tribes, euery one of which made a people, as for the great multitude of them, as though many nations had assembled themselues together, as Iudges 5.14.*
m *The wicked execute Gods counsell, though they thinke nothing of it, but they are not therefore without fault.*
n *Thou haddest determined of thine absolute authoritie and power.*

30 So that thou stretch foorth thine hand,
that healing, and signes, and wonders may bee
done by the Name of thy holy Sonne Iesus.
31 [11]And when as they had prayed, the
place was shaken where they were assembled
together, and they were all filled with the holy Ghost, and they spake the word of God
boldly.
32 [12]And the multitude of them that beleeued, were of [o]one heart, and of one soule: neither any of them said, that any thing of that
which he possessed, was his owne, but they had
all things *common.
33 And with great power gaue the Apostles
witnesse of the resurrection of the Lord Iesus:
and great grace was vpon them all.
34 [13]Neither was there any among them,
that lacked: for as many as were possessours of
lands or houses, sold them, and brought the
price of the things that were sold,
35 And laid it downe at the Apostles feete,
and it was distributed vnto euery man, according as he had need.
36 Also Ioses which was called of the Apostles, Barnabas (that is by interpretation the
sonne of consolation) being a Leuite, *and* of the
countrey of Cyprus,
37 Whereas hee had land, solde it, and
brought the money, and laide it downe at the
Apostles feete.

11 God witnesseth to his Church by a visible signe, that it is he that will establish it, by shaking the powers both of heauen and earth.
12 An example of the true Church, wherein there is consent as well in doctrine as in charitie one toward another: And the Pastours deliuer true doctrine both sincerely, and constantly.
o *They agreed both in counsell, will, and all purposes.*
* *Chap. 2.44.*
13 True charitie helpeth the necessitie of the poore with his owne losse: but so that all things be done well and orderly.

CHAP. V.

1 Ananias, for his deceite in keeping backe part of the price, 5 falleth downe dead, 20 and likewise Sapphira his wife. 12 Through diuers the Apostles miracles, 24 the faith is increased. 18 The Apostles that were imprisoned, 19 are deliuered by an Angell, 26 and being before the Synode of the Priests, 36 through Gamaliels counsell they are kept aliue, 40 and beaten: 41 they glorifie God.

BVt [1]a certaine man named Ananias, with
Sapphira his wife, sold a possession,
2 And [a]kept away *part* of the price, his
wife also being of counsell, and brought a certaine part, and laide it downe at the Apostles
feete.
3 Then said Peter, Ananias, why hath Sa-
tan [b]filled thine heart, that thou shouldest [c]lie
vnto the holy Ghost, and keepe away *part* of
the price of this possession?
4 Whiles it remained, appertained it not
vnto thee? and after it was sold, was it not in
thine owne power? how is it that thou hast
[d]conceiued this thing in thine heart? thou hast
not lied vnto men, but vnto God.
5 Now when Ananias heard these words,
hee fell downe, and gaue vp the ghost. Then
great feare came on all them that heard these
things.
6 And the yong men rose vp, and tooke
him vp, and caried *him* out, and buried *him*.
7 And it came to passe about the space of
three houres after, that his wife came in, ignorant of that which was done.
8 And Peter said vnto her, Tell mee, sold
yee

1 Luke sheweth by contrarie examples, how great a sinne hypocrisie is, especially in them which vnder a false pretence and cloake of zeale would seeme to shine and be chiefe in the Church.
a *Craftily tooke away.*
b *Fully possessed.*
c *For when they had appointed that farme or possession for the Church, they stucke not at it to keepe away a part of the price, as though they had had to doe with men, and not with God, and therefore he saith afterward that they temped God.*
d *Hereby is declared an aduised and purposed deceite, and the fault of the man in admitting the deuils suggestions.*

yee the land for so much? And she sayd, Yea,
for so much.
9 Then Peter sayd vnto her, Why haue
ye agreed together to [e] tempt the spirit of the
Lord? behold, the feete of them which haue
buried thine husband, *are* at the [f] doore, and
shall carie thee out.
10 Then she fell downe straightway at his
feete, and yeelded vp the ghost: and the yong
men came in, and found her dead, and caried
her out, and buried her by her husband.
11 [2] And great feare came on al the Church,
and on as many as heard these things.
12 Thus by the handes of the Apostles
were many signes and wonders shewed among
the people (and they were all with one accord
in Solomons porch.
13 And of the other durst no man ioyne
himselfe to them: neuerthelesse the people
[g] magnified them.
14 Also the number of them that beleeued
in the Lord, both of men and women, grew
more and more)
15 Insomuch that they brought the sicke
into the streetes, and layd them on beds and
couches, that at the least way the shadowe of
Peter, when he came by, might shadowe some
of them.
16 There came also a multitude out of the
cities round about vnto Hierusalem, bringing
sicke folkes, and them which were vexed with
vncleane spirits, who were all healed.
17 ¶ [3] Then the chiefe Priest rose vp, and
all they that were with him (which was the
[h] sect of the Sadduces) and were full of indignation,
18 And layd hands on the Apostles, and
put them in the common prison.
19 [4] But the Angell of the Lord, by night
opened the prison doores, and brought them
foorth, and sayd,
20 [5] Goe your way, and stand in the Temple, and speake to the people all the [i] wordes
of this life.
21 [6] So when they heard it, they entred into the Temple early in the morning, & taught.
And the chiefe Priest came, and they that
were with him, and called the councill together, and all the Elders of the children of Israel,
and sent to the prison, to cause them to bee
brought.
22 But when the officers came and found
them not in the prison, they returned and
tolde it,
23 Saying, Certeinly wee found the prison shut as sure as was possible, and the keepers standing without, before the doores:
but when we had opened, wee found no man
within.
24 Then when the *chiefe* Priest, and the
captaine of the Temple, and the hie Priests
heard these things, they doubted of them
whereunto this would growe.

e Looke how oft men doe things with an euill conscience, so oft they pronounce sentence against themselues, & as much as in them lieth, prouoke God to anger, as of set purpose, minding to trie whether he be iust and almighty or no.
f Are at hand.
2 The Lord by his marueilous vertue brideleth some, that they may not hurt the Church: othersome he keepeth in his awe and feare: and other some he allureth vnto him.
g Highly praised them.
3 The more that the Church increaseth, ẏ more increaseth the rage of Satan, & therefore they proceed from threatnings to prisoning.
h The word which is vsed here, is Heresie, which signifieth a choice, and so is taken for a right forme of learning, or faction, or studie and course of life, which the Latines call a sect: at the first this word was indifferently vsed, but at length it came to be taken onely in euill part, wherupon came the name of Heretike which is taken for one that goeth astray from sound and wholesome doctrine after such sort, that he setteth light by the iudgement of God and his Church, and continueth in his opinion, and breaketh the peace of the Church.
4 Angels are made seruants of the seruants of God.
5 God doeth therefore deliuer his, that they may more stoutly prouoke his enemies.
i Words, whereby the way vnto life is shewed.
6 God mocketh his enemies attempts from aboue.

25 [7] Then came one and shewed them,
saying, Beholde, the men that yee put in prison, are standing in the Temple, and teach
the people.
26 [8] Then went the captaine with the officers, and brought them without violence (for
they feared the people lest they should haue
bene stoned)
27 And when they had brought them, they
set them before the Councill, and the chiefe
Priest asked them,
28 [9] Saying, Did not wee straightly command you, that yee should not teach in this
Name? and behold, ye haue filled Hierusalem
with your doctrine, and ye would [k] bring this
mans blood vpon vs.
29 [10] Then Peter and the Apostles answered, and sayd, Wee ought rather to obey God
then men.
30 [11] The *God of our fathers hath raysed vp Iesus, whome ye slew, and hanged on
a tree.
31 Him hath God lift vp with his right
hand, *to bee* a Prince and a Sauiour, to giue
repentance to Israel, and forgiuenes of sinnes.
32 [12] And we are his witnesses concerning
these things which wee say: yea, and the holy
Ghost, whom God hath giuen to them that o-
bey him.
33 Now when they heard it, they [l] brast
for anger, and consulted to slay them.
34 [13] Then stood there vp in the Councill a certaine Pharise named Gamaliel, a Doctor of the Lawe, honoured of all the people,
and commanded to put the Apostles foorth a
little space,
35 And sayd vnto them, Men of Israel, take
heede to your selues, what yee intend to doe
touching these men.
36 [14] For before these times, rose vp Theu-
das [m] boasting himselfe, to whome resorted a
number of men, about a foure hundreth, who
was slaine: and they all which obeyed him,
were scattered, and brought to nought.
37 After this man, arose vp Iudas of Galile, in the dayes of the tribute, and drew away
much people after him: he also perished, and
all that obeyed him, were scattered abroad.
38 And now I say vnto you, [n] Refraine your
selues from these men, and let them alone: for
if this counsel, or this worke be of [o] men, it will
come to nought:
39 But if it be of God, ye cannot destroy it,
lest ye be found euen fighters against God.
40 And to him they agreed, and called the
Apostles: and when they had beaten them,
they cōmanded that they should not speake in
the Name of Iesus, and let them goe.
41 [15] So they departed from the Councill,

7 The more openly that Christs vertue sheweth it selfe, the more increaseth the madnes of his enemies which conspire against him.
8 Tyrāts which feare not God, are constrained to feare his seruants.
9 It is the propertie of tyrants to set out their owne commandements as right and reason, be they neuer so wicked.
k Make vs guilty of murdering that man whom yet they will not vouchsafe to name.
10 Wee ought to obey no man, but so farre forth as obeying him we may obey God.
11 Christ is appointed and in deed declared Prince and preseruer of his Church in despight of his enemies.
**Chap. 3. 13.*
12 It is not sufficient for vs, that there is a right ende, but we must also according to our vocation goe on forward till wee come vnto it.
l This betokeneth that they were in a most vehement rage, and marueilously disquieted in minde, for it is a borrowed kinde of speach taken from them which are harrishly cut in sunder with a saw.
13 Christ findeth defenders of his cause, euen in the very rout of his enemies, so oft as hee thinketh it needfull.
14 In matters of religion wee must take good heede, that wee attempt nothing vnder a colour of zeale, beside our vocation.
m To be of some fame.
n He disswadeth his fellowes from murdering the Apostles, neither doth he thinke it good to referre the matter to the Romane Magistrate, for the Iewes could abide nothing worse, then to haue the tyrannie of the Romanes confirmed. *o If it bee counterfeite and deuised.* 15 The Apostles accustomed to suffer and beare wordes, are at length inured to beare stripes, and yet so, that by that meanes they become stronger.

cill, reioycing, that they were counted worthy to suffer rebuke for his Name.
42 And dayly in the [p]Temple, and from
house to house they ceased not to teach, and
preach Iesus Christ.

p Both publikely and priuately.

CHAP. VI.

2 The Apostles 3 appoint the office of Deaconship 5 to seuen chosen men: 8 Of whom Steuen, full of faith, is one: 12 He is taken, 13 and accused as a transgressour of Moses Lawe.

AND [1] in those dayes, as the number of the
disciples grew, there arose a murmuring
of the [a]Grecians toward the Hebrewes, because their widowes were neglected in the
[b]dayly ministring.
2 [2]Then the twelue called the multitude
of the disciples together, and sayd, It is not
[c]meete that we should leaue the word of God
to serue the [d]tables.
3 [3]Wherefore brethren, looke yee out a-
mong you seuen men of honest report, and full
of the holy Ghost, and of wisedome, which we
may appoint to this businesse.
4 And wee will giue our selues continually
to prayer, and to the ministration of the word.
5 And the saying pleased the whole multitude: & they chose Steuen, a man full of faith
and of the holy Ghost, and *Philip, and Pro-
chorus, and Nicanor, and Timon, and Parme-
nas, and Nicolas a Proselite of Antiochia,
6 [4]Which they set before the Apostles: and
they prayed, and [e]layd their hands on them.
7 [5]And the word of God increased, and
the number of the disciples was multiplied in
Hierusalem greatly, and a great companie of
the Priests were obedient to the [f]faith.
8 ¶ [6]Now Steuen full of faith and [g]po-
wer, did great wonders and miracles among
the people.
9 [7]Then there arose certaine of the [h]Syna-
gogue, which are called Libertines, and Cyre-
nians, and of Alexandria, and of them of Cilicia, and of Asia, and disputed with Steuen.
10 [8]But they were not able to resist the wisdome, and the Spirit by the which he spake.
11 Then they suborned men, which sayd,
We haue heard him speake blasphemous words
against Moses, and God.
12 [9]Thus they mooued the people and
the Elders, and the Scribes: and running vpon him, caught him, and brought him to the
Councill,

1 When Satan hath assailed the Church without, and that to small purpose & in vaine, he assaileth it within, with ciuil dissension & strife betwixt themselues: But the Apostles take occasion thereby to set order in the Church.

a Of their parts, which of Grecians became religious Iewes.

b In the bestowing of almes according to their necessitie.

2 The office of preaching the word, and dispensing ẏ goods of the Church, are different one from another, and not rashly to be ioyned together, as the Apostles doe here institute: And the Apostles doe not chuse so much as the Deacons without the consent of the Church.

c It is such a matter, as we may in no wise accept of it.

d Banquets: though by the name of tables, other offices are also meant, which are annexed to it, such as pertaine to the care of the poore.

3 In chusing of Deacons (and much more of Ministers) there must be examination both of their learning and maners of life.

**Chap. 21.8.*

4 The ancient Church did with laying on of hands, as it were consecrate to the Lord, such as were lawfully elected. *e This ceremonie of laying on of hands, came from the Iewes, who vsed this order both in publike affaires, and offering of sacrifices, and also in priuate prayers and blessings, as appeareth, Gen. 28 and the Church obserued this ceremonie, 1. Tim. 5.22. acts 8.17. but here is no mention made either of creame, or shauing, or rasing, or crossing, &c.* 5 An happie ende of temptation. *f This is the figure Metonymia, meaning by faith, the doctrine of the Gospel which ingendreth faith* 6 God exerciseth his Church first with euill words and slanders, then with imprisonments, afterward with scourgings, and by these meanes prepareth it in such sort, that at length hee causeth it to encounter with Satan and the world, euen to bloodshed and death, and that with good successe. *g Excellent and singular gifts.* 7 Schooles and Vniuersities were of old time addicted to false pastors, and were the instruments of Satan, to blowe abroad and defend false doctrines. *h Of the companie and Colledge, as it were.* 8 False teachers, because they wil not be ouercome, flee from disputations to manifest and open slandering & false accusations. 9 The first bloodie persecution of the Church of Christ, begun and sprang from a Councel of Priests, by the Suggestion of the Vniuersitie doctors.

13 [10]And set foorth false witnesses, which
saide, This man ceaseth not to speake blasphemous wordes against this holy place, and the
Law.
14 For wee haue heard him say, That this
Iesus of Nazareth shall destroy this place, and
shall change the ordinaunces, which Moses
gaue vs.
15 And as all that sate in the Councill, looked stedfastly on him, they [i]saw his face as *it had*
bene the face of an Angel.

10 An example of caullers or false accusers, which gather false conclusions of things that are well vttered and spoken.

i Hereby it appeareth, that Steuen had an excellent and goodly countenance, hauing a quiet and setled mind, a good conscience, and sure perswasion that his cause was iust: For seeing hee was to speake before the people, God beautified his countenance, to the end that with the very beholding of him, the Iewes mindes might be pearced and amased.

CHAP. VII.

1 Steuen pleading his cause, sheweth that God chose the Fathers, 20 before Moses was borne, 47 and before the Temple was built: 44 And that all outward ceremonies were ordeined according to the heauenly paterne. 54 The Iewes gnashing their teeth, 59 stone him.

THEN [1] sayde the chiefe Priest, Are these
things so?
2 [2]And he said, Ye men, brethren, and Fathers, hearken. *That God of [a]glory appeared
vnto our father Abraham, while he was in [b]Me-
sopotamia, before he dwelt in Charran,
3 And sayde vnto him, Come out of thy
countrey, and from thy kindred, and come into
the land which I shall shew thee.
4 Then came hee out of the lande of the
Chaldeans, and dwelt in Charran. And after
that his father was dead, *God* brought him
from thence into this land, wherein yee now
dwell,
5 And he gaue him none inheritance in it,
no, not the [c]bredth of a foot: yet he [d]promised
that hee would giue it to him for a possession,
and to his seed after him, when as yet he had no
childe.
6 But God spake thus, that his *seede
should be a soiourner in a strange land: and that
they should keepe it in bondage, and entreat it
euill [e]foure hundred yeeres.
7 But the nation to whom they shall bee
in bondage, will I iudge, saieth God: and after
that, they shall come forth and serue me in this
place.
8 *Hee gaue him also the Couenant of
Circumcision: and so *Abraham* begat *Isaac,
and circumcised him the eight day: and Isaac
begate *Iacob, and Iacob the twelue *Patriarkes.
9 [3]And the Patriarkes mooued with enuie, solde *Ioseph into Egypt: but God was
[f]with him,
10 And deliuered him out of all his affli-

1 Steuen is admitted to plead his cause, but to this end & purpose that vnder a cloke and colour of Law, he might be condemned.

2 Steuen witnesseth vnto the Iewes, that he acknowledgeth the true fathers, & the onely true God: & sheweth moreouer that they are more ancient then the Temple, with all that seruice appointed by the Law, and therefore they ought to lay another foundation of true religion, that is to say, the free couenant ẏ God made with the fathers.

**Gen. 12.4.*

a That mighty God full of glory and maiestie.

b When he saith afterward, vers. 4 that Abraham came out of Caldea, it is euident that Mesopotamia conteined Caldea which was neere vnto it, and bordering vpon it, and so writeth Plinius, Booke 6. chap. 27.

c Not so much ground as to set his foote vpon.

d The promise of the possession was certaine, and belonged to Abraham, though his posteritie enioyed it a great while after his death: and this is the figure Synecdoche. *Gen. 15.13. *e There are reckoned foure hundred yeeres, from the beginning of Abrahams progenie, which was at the birth of Isaac: and foure hundred and thirtie yeeres which are spoken of by Paul, Gal. 3.17. from the time that Abraham and his father departed together out of Vr of the Caldeans.* *Gen. 17.9. *Gen. 21.3. *Gen. 25.24. *Gen. 29.33. and 30.5. and 35.23. 3 Steuen reckoneth vp diligently the horrible mischiefs of some of the Fathers, to teach the Iewes that they ought not rashly to rest in the authoritie or examples of the Fathers. *Gene. 37.28. *f By this kinde of speach, is meant the peculiar fauour that God sheweth men: for hee seemeth to bee away from them, whome hee helpeth not: and on the other side, hee is with them whom hee deliuereth out of whatsoeuer great troubles.*

ctions,

ctions, and * gaue him [g] fauour and wisedome in the sight of Pharao king of Egypt, who made him gouernour ouer Egypt, and *ouer* his whole house.

*Gen.41.37.
g Gaue him fauour in Pharaohs sight for his wisedome.

11 ¶ Then came there a famine ouer all the land of Egypt and Chanaan, and great affliction, that our fathers found no sustenance.

12 But when * Iacob heard that there was corne in Egypt, he sent our fathers first:

*Gen.42.1.

13 * And at the second time, Ioseph was knowen of his brethren, and Iosephs kinred was made knowen vnto Pharao.

*Gen.45.4.

14 Then sent Ioseph, and caused his father to be brought, and all his kinred, euen threescore and fifteene soules.

15 So * Iacob went downe into Egypt, and he * died, and our fathers,

*Gen.46.5.
*Gen.49.33.

16 And were [h] remoued into Sychem, and were put in the sepulchre, that Abraham had bought * for money of the sonnes of Emor, *sonne* of Sychem.

h The Patriarkes the sonnes of Iacob, though there be mention made of no moe then Ioseph, Iosh.24.32.
*Gen.23.16.

17 But when the time of the promise drew neere, which God had sworne to Abraham, the people * grew and multiplied in Egypt,

*Exod.1.7.

18 Till another King arose, which knew not Ioseph.

19 The same [i] dealt subtilly with our kinred, and euill intreated our fathers, and made them to cast out their yong children, that they should not remaine aliue.

i He deuised a subtill inuention against our stocke, in that hee commanded all the males to be cast out.

20 * The same time was Moses borne, and was [k] acceptable vnto God, which was nourished vp in his fathers house three moneths.

*Exod.2.2.
k That child was borne through Gods mercifull goodnesse and fauour, to bee of a goodly and faire countenance.

21 And when hee was cast out, Pharaohs daughter tooke him vp, and nourished him for her owne sonne.

22 And Moses was learned in all the wisedome of the Egyptians, and was mightie in wordes and in deedes.

23 Now when hee was full fortie yeere olde, it came into his heart to visite his brethren, the children of Israel.

24 * And when he sawe one *of them* suffer wrong, he defended him, and auenged his quarell that had the harme done to him, and smote the Egyptian.

*Exod.2.11.

25 For hee supposed his brethren would haue vnderstood, that God by his hand should giue them deliuerance: but they vnderstood it not.

26 * And the next day, he shewed himselfe vnto them as they stroue, and would haue set them at one againe, saying, Sirs, yee are brethren: why doe ye wrong one to another?

*Exod.2.13.

27 But hee that did his neighbour wrong, thrust him away, saying, Who made thee a Prince, and a Iudge ouer vs?

28 Wilt thou kill mee, as thou diddest the Egyptian yesterday?

29 Then fled Moses at that saying, and was a stranger in the land of Madian, where he begate two sonnes.

30 And when fourtie yeeres were expired, there appeared to him in the * wildernesse of mount Sina, an [l] Angel of the Lord in a flame of fire, in a bush.

*Exod.3.2.
l Now he calleth the Sonne of God an Angel, for hee is the Angel of great counsell, and therefore straight wayes after hee sheweth him, saying to Moses, I am the God of thy Fathers, &c.

31 And when Moses saw it, he wondred at the sight: and as he drewe neere to consider it, the voice of the Lord came vnto him, *saying*,

32 I am the God of thy fathers, the God of Abraham, and the God of Isaac, and the God of Iacob. Then Moses trembled, and durst not beholde it.

33 Then the Lord sayd to him, Put off thy shooes from thy feete: for the place where thou standest is holy ground.

34 I haue seene, I haue seene the affliction of my people, which is in Egypt, and I haue heard their groning, and am come downe to deliuer them: and now come, and I will send thee into Egypt.

35 This Moses whome they forsooke, saying, Who made thee a Prince and a iudge? the same God sent for a Prince, and a deliuerer by the [m] hand of the Angel, which appeared to him in the bush.

m By the power.

36 Hee * brought them out, doing wonders, and miracles in the land of Egypt, and in the red sea, and in the wildernesse * fortie yeeres,

*Exod.7,8,9.10, 11,14.chapters.
*Exod.16.1.

37 [4] This is that Moses, which sayd vnto the children of Israel, * A Prophet shal the Lord your God raise vp vnto you, *euen* of your brethren, like vnto me: him shall ye heare.

4 He acknowledgeth Moses for the Lawgiuer, but so, that he prooueth by his owne witnesse, that the Law had respect to a more perfect thing, that is to say, to the propheticall office which tended to Christ, the head of all Prophets.
*Deut.18.15, chap.3.22.

38 * This is he that was in the Congregation, in the wildernesse with the Angel, which spake to him in mount Sina, and with our Fathers, who receiued the liuely Oracles to giue vnto vs.

*Exod.19.2.

39 To whom our Fathers would not obey, but refused, and in their hearts turned backe againe into Egypt:

40 Saying vnto Aaron, * Make vs gods that may goe before vs: for we knowe not what is become of this Moses that brought vs out of the land of Egypt.

*Exod.32.1.

41 And they made a [n] calfe in those dayes, and offered sacrifice vnto the idole, and reioyced in the workes of their owne hands.

n This was the superstition of the Egyptians idolatrie: for they worshipped Apis a strange and marueilous calfe, and made goodly images of kine, Herod. lib.2.

42 Then God turned himselfe away, and [o] gaue them vp to serue the [p] host of heauen, as it is written in the booke of the Prophets, * O house of Israel, haue yee offered to mee slaine beasts and sacrifices by the space of fortie yeres in the wildernesse?

o Being destitute and voide of his spirit, hee gaue them vp to Satan, and wicked lusts, to worship starres.
p By the hoste of heauen here, hee meaneth not the Angels, but the Moone and Sunne, and other starres, Deut.17.3.
*Amos 5.25.

43 And yee [q] tooke vp the Tabernacle of Moloch, and the starre of your god Remphan, figures, which ye made to worship them: therfore I wil carie you away beyond Babylon.

q You tooke it vpon your shoulders and caried it.

44 [5] Our fathers had the Tabernacle of [r] witnes, in the wildernes, as he had appointed, speaking vnto * Moses, that he should make it according to the fashion that he had seene.

5 Moses in deed erected a Tabernacle, but that was to call them backe to that forme which he had seene in the mountaine.
r That is of the couenant.
*Exod.25.40. hebr.8.5.

45 * Which *Tabernacle* also our Fathers [s] receiued, and brought in with Iesus into the [t] possession of the Gentiles, which God

*Iosh.3.14.
s Deliuered from hand to hand.
t By the figure Metonymia, for the countreys which the Gentiles possessed.

draue

draue out [u] before our Fathers, vnto the dayes
of Dauid:-
46 *Who found fauour before God, and
desired that he might find a Tabernacle for the
God of Iacob.
47 *[6] But Solomon built him an house.
48 Howbeit the most High * dwelleth
not in Temples made with hands, as saith the
Prophet,
49 *Heauen *is* my throne, and earth *is* my
footstoole: what house will ye build for mee,
sayth the Lord? or what place is it that I should
rest in?
50 Hath not mine hand made all these
things?
51 *[7] Yee stiffenecked and of [x] vncircumcised hearts and eares, yee haue alwayes resisted the holy Ghost: as your Fathers *did*, so
doe you.
52 Which of the Prophets haue not your
fathers persecuted? and they haue slaine them,
which shewed before of the comming of that
Iust, of whom yee are now the betrayers and
murtherers,
53 *Which haue receiued the Lawe by the
[y] ordinance of Angels, and haue not kept it.
54 [8] But when they heard these things,
their hearts brast for anger, and they gnashed
at him with *their* teeth.
55 [9] But hee being full of the holy Ghost,
looked stedfastly into heauen, and sawe the
glory of God, and Iesus [z] standing on the
right hand of God,
56 And sayd, Beholde, I see the heauens
open, and the Sonne of man standing at the
right hand of God.
57 [10] Then they gaue a shout with a loud
voice, and stopped their eares, and [a] ran vpon
him violently all at once,
58 And cast him out of the citie, and stoned
him: and the [b] witnesses layd downe their
clothes at a yong mans feete, named Saul.
59 And they stoned Steuen, who called on
God, and sayd, Lord Iesus, receiue my spirit.
60 [11] And hee kneeled downe, and cried
with a loud voice, Lord, *lay not this sinne to
their charge. And when hee had thus spoken,
hee [d] slept.

u God draue them out, that they should yeeld vp the possession of those countreys to our Fathers, when they entred into the land.
*2 Sam 7.2. psal. 132.5.
*1. Chron. 17. 12. 1. king. 6. 2.
6 Salomon built a Temple, according to Gods commandement, but not with any such condition, that the Maiestie of God should be inclosed therein.
*Chap. 17. 24.
*Esai. 66. 1.
*Ierem. 9. 26. ezek. 44. 9.
7 Steuen mooued with the zeale of God, at length iudgeth his owne iudges.
x They are of vncircumcised hearts, which lie drowned still in the sinnes of nature, and sticke fast in them: for otherwise all the Iewes were circumcised as touching the flesh, and therefore there were two kinds of circumcision, Rom. 2. 28.
*Exod. 19. 16. gal. 3. 19.
y By the ministerie of Angels.
8 The more Satan is pressed, the more hee brasteth out into an open rage.
9 The neerer that the Martyrs approch to death, the neerer they, beholding Christ, doe rise vp euen into heauen.
z Ready to confirme him in the confession of the truth, and to receiue him to him.
10 The zeale of hypocrites and superstitious people, breaketh out at length into most open madnesse.

a This was done in a rage and furie, for at that time the Iewes could put no man to death by lawe, as they confesse before Pilate, saying, that it was not lawfull for them to put any man to death, and therefore it is reported by Ioseph lib. 20. that Ananus a Sadduce slew Iames the brother of the Lorde, and for so doing, was accused before Albinus the president of the countrey. b It was appointed by the Lawe, that the witnesses should cast the first stones, Deut. 17. 7. 11 Faith and charitie neuer forsake the true seruants of God, euen to the last breath. *c The word which hee vseth here, noteth out such a kinde of imputing or laying to ones charge, as remaineth firme and steady for euer, neuer to be remitted. d Looke 1. Thess. 4. 13.*

CHAP. VIII.

2 The Godly make lamentation for Steuen. 3 Saul maketh hauocke of the Church. 5 Philip preacheth Christ at Samaria. 9 Simon Magus 18 his couetousnesse reprooued. 26 Philip 27 commeth to the Ethiopian Eunuch, 38 and baptiseth him.

AND [1] Saul consented to his death, and
at that time, there was a great persecution against the Church which was at Hierusalem, and they were all scattered abroad thorow the regions of Iudea and of Samaria, except the Apostles.
2 [2] Then *certaine* men fearing God, [a] caried Steuen amongst them *to bee buried*, and
made great lamentation for him.
3 [3] But Saul made hauocke of the
Church, and entred into euery house, and drew
out both men and women, and put them into
prison.
4 Therefore they that were scattered a-
broad, went to and fro preaching the word.
5 ¶ [4] Then came Philip into the citie of
Samaria, and preached vnto them.
6 And the people gaue heede vnto those
things which Philip spake, with one accord,
hearing and seeing the miracles which he did.
7 For vncleane spirits crying with a loud
voice, came out of many that were possessed *of
them*: and many taken with palsies, and that
halted, were healed.
8 And there was great ioy in that citie.
9 [5] And there was before in the citie a certaine man called Simon, which vsed [b] witchcraft, and [c] bewitched the people of Samaria,
saying that he himselfe was some great man.
10 To whom they gaue heed from the least
to the greatest, saying, This man is that great
power of God.
11 And they gaue heede vnto him, because
that of long time he had bewitched them with
sorceries.
12 But assoone as they beleeued Philip,
which preached the things that concerned the
kingdome of God, and the Name of Iesus
Christ, they were baptized both men and
women.
13 [6] Then Simon himselfe beleeued also
and was baptized, and continued with Philip,
and wondred when hee sawe the signes and
great miracles which were done.
14 ¶ [7] Now when the Apostles, which
were at Hierusalem, heard say, that Samaria
had receiued the word of God, they sent vnto
them Peter and Iohn,
15 Which when they were come downe,
prayed for them, that they might receiue the
[d] holy Ghost.
16 (For as yet he was fallen downe on none
of them, but they were baptized onely in the
Name of the Lord Iesus.)
17 Then layd they their hands on them,
and they receiued the holy Ghost.
18 [8] And when Simon sawe, that through
laying on of the Apostles hands the holy Ghost
was giuen, he offered them money,
19 Saying, Giue me also this power, that
on whomsoeuer I lay the hands, he may receiue
the holy Ghost.
20 [9] Then said Peter vnto him, Thy money

1 Christ vseth the rage of his enemies to the spreading forth and enlarging of his kingdome.
2 The godly mourne for Steuen after his death, and bury him, shewing therein an example of singular faith and charitie: but no man prayeth to him.
a Amongst all the dueties of charitie which the godly vse, there is no mention made of shrining vp of relikes.
3 The dispersiō or scattering abroad of ÿ faithfull, is the ioyning together of Churches.
4 Philip who was before a Deacon in Hierusalem, is made of God extraordinarily an Euangelist.
5 Christ ouercommeth Satan so oft as he listeth, and carieth him about as it were in a triumph, in the sight of them whom he deceiued and bewitched.
b The word which is vsed in this place was at the first taken in good part, and is borowed out of the Persians language, who call their wise men by that name, but afterward it was taken in euill part.
c He had so allured the Samaritans with his witchcrafts, that as blind and mad harebraines they were wholly addicted to him.
6 The wicked and the very reprobate are constrained oftentimes to taste of the good gift of God, but they cast it vp againe forthwith.
7 Peter, not chiefe but as an ambassador sent from the whole company of the Apostles, & Iohn his companion, according to the authority which was committed vnto them, confirme and build vp the Churches of Samaria, whose foundatiō had been layd afore by Philip.
d Those excellent gifts, which are necessary, especially for them that were to bee appointed rulers and gouernours of the Church. 8 Ambition and couetousnesse doe at length plucke the hypocrites out of their dennes. 9 They are the successors of Simon Magus, and not of Simon Peter, which either buy or sell holy things.

perish

perish with thee, because thou thinkest that
the gift of God may bee obtained with money.
21 Thou hast neither part nor fellowship
in this [e] businesse: for thine heart is not [f] right
in the sight of God.
22 [10] Repent therefore for this thy wickednesse, and pray God, that if it be possible, the
thought of thine heart may be forgiuen thee.
23 For I see that thou art the [g] gall of bitternesse, and in the [h] bond of iniquitie.
24 Then answered Simon, and sayd, Pray
ye to the Lord for me, that none of these things
which ye haue spoken come vpon me.
25 ¶ So they, when they had testified and
preached the word of the Lord, returned to
Hierusalem, and preached the Gospel in many
townes of the Samaritanes.
26 [11] Then the Angel of the Lord spake vnto Philip, saying, Arise, and goe toward the
South vnto the way that goeth downe from
Hierusalem vnto Gaza, which is waste.
27 And he arose and went on: and behold,
a certaine Eunuch of Ethiopia, Candaces the
Queene of the Ethiopians [i] chiefe Gouernour,
who had the rule of all her treasure, and came to
Hierusalem to worship:
28 And as he returned sitting in his charet,
he read Esaias the Prophet.
29 Then the Spirit said vnto Philip, Goe
neere and ioyne thy selfe to yonder charet.
30 And Philip ran thither, and heard him
reade the Prophet Esaias, and sayd, But vnderstandest thou what thou readest?
31 And he sayd, How can I, except I had
[k] a guide? And he desired Philip that he would
come vp and sit with him.
32 [12] Now the place of the Scripture which
he read, was this, * He was led as a sheepe to the
slaughter, and like a Lambe dumbe before his
shearer, so opened he not his mouth.
33 In his [l] humilitie his iudgement hath bene
exalted: but who shal declare his [m] generation?
for his life is taken from the earth.
34 Then the Eunuch answered Philip,
and sayd, I pray thee, of whom speaketh the
Prophet this? of himselfe, or of some other
man?
35 Then Philip opened his mouth, and began at the same Scripture, and preached vnto
him Iesus.
36 And as they went on their way, they
came vnto a certaine water, and the Eunuch
sayd, See, here *is* water: what doeth let mee to
be baptized?
37 [13] And Philip sayd vnto him, If thou beleeuest with all thine heart, thou mayest. Then
he answered, and sayd, [n] I beleeue that that Iesus Christ is that sonne of God.

e In this doctrine which I preach.
f Is not vpright in deed and without dissembling.
10 Wee must hope well euen of the vilest sinners, so long and so farre forth as we may.
g He calleth the inward malice of the heart, and that venemous and deuilish wickednesse wherwith the Magician was wholly replenished, the gall of bitternesse: and he is said to be in the gall, as though he were wholly ouerwhelmed with gall, and buried in it.
h Intangled in the bonds of iniquitie.
11 Christ who calleth freely whom he listeth, doth now vse Philip who thought on no such matter, to instruct & baptize the Eunuch at vnawares, and by this meanes extendeth the limits of his kingdome euen into Ethiopia.
i A man of great wealth and authoritie with Candaces. Now this word Candaces is a common name to all the Queenes of Ethiopia
k To shew me the way how to vnderstand it.
12 Those things which seeme most to come by chance or fortune (as men terme it) are gouerned by the secret prouidence of God.
*Esai.53.7.
l The Hebrewe text readeth it thus, out of a narrow straite, and out of iudgement was he taken: where by the narrowe straite, hee meaneth the graue & the very bands of death, and by iudgement, the punishment which was layd vpon him, and that miserable state which Christ tooke vpon him for our sakes, in bearing his Fathers wrath.

m How long his age shall last: for Christ hauing once risen from the dead, dieth no more, Rom. 6.9. 13 Profession of faith is requisite in baptizing of them which are of yeeres, and therefore it is euident that we are not then first ingraffed into Christ, when wee are baptized, but being already ingraffed, are then confirmed. *n The summe of the confession which is necessary for baptisme.*

38 Then he commanded the charet to stand
still: and they went downe both into the water, both Philip and the Eunuch, and he baptized him.
39 And assoone as they were come vp out
of the water, the Spirit of the Lord caught a-
way Philip, that the Eunuch saw him no more:
so he want on his way reioycing.
40 But Philip was found at Azotus, and
he walked to and fro preaching in all the cities,
til he came to Cesarea.

CHAP. IX.

2 Saul going toward Damascus, is striken downe to the ground of the Lord: 10 Ananias is sent 18 to baptize him. 23 The laying wait of the Iewes 25 hee escapeth, being let downe through the wall. 23 Peter cureth Aeneas of the palsie, 36 and by him Tabitha being dead 40 is restored to life.

AND [1] * Saul yet [a] breathing out threatnings
and slaughter against the disciples of the
Lord, went vnto the hie Priest,
2 And desired of him letters to Damascus
to the Synagogues, that if hee found any that
were of that [b] way (either men or women) hee
might bring them bound vnto Hierusalem.
3 Now as hee iourneyed, it came to passe
that as he was come neere to Damascus, * suddenly there shined round about him a light
from heauen.
4 And he fell to the earth and heard a voice,
saying to him, Saul, Saul, why persecutest
thou mee?
5 And he sayd, Who art thou, Lord? And
the Lord said, I am Iesus whom thou persecutest: it is [c] hard for thee to kicke against pricks.
6 He *then* both trembling and astonied,
said, Lord, what wilt thou that I doe? And the
Lord said vnto him, Arise and go into the citie,
and it shall be told thee what thou shalt doe.
7 The men also which iourneyed with
him, [d] stood amased, hearing *his* [e] voyce, but
seeing no man.
8 And Saul arose from the ground, and
opened his eyes, *but* sawe no man. Then led
they him by the hand, and brought him into
Damascus,
9 Where hee was three dayes without
sight, and neither ate nor dranke.
10 And there was a certaine disciple at Damascus named Ananias, and to him sayd the
Lord in a vision, Ananias. And he sayd, Behold,
I am *here* Lord.
11 Then the Lord sayd vnto him, Arise, and
goe into the street which is called Straight, and
seeke in the house of Iudas after one called Saul
of [f] Tarsus: for behold, hee prayeth.
12 (And hee sawe in a vision a man named
Ananias comming in *to him*, and putting his
hands on him, that he might receiue his sight.)
13 Then Ananias answered, Lord, I haue
heard by many of this man, how much euill he
hath done to thy saints at Hierusalem.

1 Saul (who is also Paul) persecuting Christ most cruelly, who did as it were flee before him, falleth into his hands, and is ouercome: and with a singular example of the goodnesse of God in stead of punishment which hee iustly deserued for his cruelty, is not onely receiued to fauour, but is also euen by the mouth of God appointed an Apostle, and is confirmed by the ministerie and witnesse of Ananias.
*Rom.9.3. gal.1.13.
a This is a token that Sauls stomacke boyled and cast out great threatnings to murther the disciples.
b Any trade of life which a man taketh himselfe vnto, the Iewes call a way.
*Chap.22.6. 1.cor.15.8.
c This is a prouerbe, which is spoken of them that through their stubbornnesse hurt themselues.
d Stood still and could not goe one step forward, but abode amased as if they had been very stones.
e They heard Pauls voyce: for afterward it is said in flat termes, that they heard not his voice that spake: as beneath chap.22.9. But other goe about to set these places at one which seeme to be at a iarre, after this sort, to wit, that they heard a sound of a voice, but no perfect voice. *f Tarsus was a citie of Cilicia neere vnto Anchiala, which two cities Sardanapalus is said to haue built in one day.*

14 More-

14 Moreouer here hee hath authoritie of
the hie Priestes, to binde all that call on thy
Name.
15 Then the Lord said vnto him, Goe thy
way: for hee is a [g] chosen vessell vnto mee, to
beare my Name before the Gentiles, and
Kings, and the children of Israel.
16 For I will [h] shew him, how many things
he must suffer for my Names sake.
17 Then Ananias went his way, and entred
into [i] that house, and put his hands on him, and
sayd, Brother Saul, the Lord hath sent me (*euen*
Iesus that appeared vnto thee in the way as
thou camest) that thou mightest receiue thy
sight, and be filled with the holy Ghost.
18 And immediately there fell from his eyes
as *it had been* scales, and suddenly hee receiued
sight, and arose, and was baptized,
19 And receiued meate, and was strengthened. So was Saul certaine dayes with the disciples which were at Damascus.
20 [2] And straightway hee preached Christ
in the Synagogues, that hee was that Sonne
of God,
21 So that all that heard him, were amased, and sayd, Is not this he, that made hauocke
of them which called on this Name in Hierusalem, and came hither for that intent, that hee
should bring them bound vnto the hie Priests?
22 [3] But Saul encreased the more in
strength, and confounded the Iewes which
dwelt at Damascus, [k] confirming that this
was that Christ.
23 [4] And after that many dayes were fulfilled, the Iewes tooke counsell together, to
kill him.
24 But their laying awaite was knowen of
Saul: now they * watched the gates day and
night, that they might kill him.
25 [5] Then the disciples tooke him by night,
and put him through the wall, and let him
downe by a rope in a basket.
26 [6] And when Saul was come to Hierusalem, he assayed to ioyne himselfe with the disciples: but they were all afraid of him, and beleeued not that he was a disciple.
27 But Barnabas tooke him, and brought
him to the Apostles, and declared to them, how
he had seene the Lord in the way, and that he
had spoken vnto him, and how hee had spoken
boldly at Damascus in the Name of Iesus.
28 [7] And he was conuersant [l] with them at
Hierusalem,
29 And spake boldly in the Name of the
Lord Iesus, and spake and disputed against the
[m] Grecians: but they went about to slay him.
30 [8] But when the brethren knewe it, they
brought him to Cesarea, and sent him forth to
Tarsus.
31 [9] Then had the Churches rest through

g To beare my name in.

h I will shew him plainely.

i Into Iudas his house.

2 Paul beginneth straightwaies to execute the office which was enioyned him, neuer consulting with flesh and blood.

3 Paul striueth not with his owne authority alone, but with the testimonies of the Prophets.

k By conferring places of the Scripture together, as cunning craftesmen doe, when they make vp any thing, they vse to gather all parts together, to make them agree fitly one with an other.

4 Paul who was before a persecuter, hath now persecution layd before him sefe, but yet a farre off.

* *2.Cor.11.32.*

5 Wee are not forbidden to auoid and eschew the dangers and conspiracies that the enemies of God lay for vs, so that wee swarue not from our vocation.

6 In auncient time, no man was rashly or lightly receiued into the number of and amongst the sheepe of Christ, much lesse to be a Pastour.

7 The constant seruants of God must looke for danger after danger: yet God watcheth for them.

l With Peter and Iames, for he saith that he saw none of the Apostles but them, Gal.1.18,19. *m Looke chap.6.1*

8 The ministers of the word may change their place by the aduise and counsell of the Congregation and Church.

2 The end of persecutions is the building of the Church, so that we will patiently waite for the Lord.

all Iudea, and Galile, aud Samaria, and were
[n] edified and walked in the feare of the Lorde,
and were multiplied by the comfort of the holy
Ghost.
32 [10] And it came to passe, as Peter walked
throughout all *quarters*, hee came also to the
Saints which dwelt at Lydda.
33 And there he found a certaine man named Aeneas, which had kept his couch eight
yeeres, and was sicke of the palsie.
34 Then sayd Peter vnto him, Aeneas,
Iesus Christ maketh thee whole: arise, and
trusse thy couch together. And hee arose immediately.
35 And all that dwelt at [o] Lydda and Saron, saw him, and turned to the Lord.
36 [11] There was also at Ioppa a certaine *woman*, a disciple named Tabitha (which by interpretation is called Dorcas) she was full of
good workes and almes which she did.
37 And it came to passe in those dayes, that
she was sicke and died: and when they had washed her, they layd her in an vpper chamber.
38 Now forasmuch as Lydda was neere
to Ioppa, and the disciples had heard that Peter was there, they sent vnto him two men,
desiring that he would not delay to come vnto
them.
39 Then Peter arose and came with them:
and when hee was come, they brought him into the vpper chamber, where all the widowes
stood by him weeping, and shewing the coats
and garments which Dorcas made, while shee
was with them.
40 But Peter put them all foorth, and kneeled downe, and prayed, and turned him to the
bodie, and sayd, Tabitha, Arise. And she opened her eyes, and when she saw Peter, sate vp.
41 Then he gaue her the hand and lift her
vp, and called the Saints and widowes, and restored her aliue.
42 And it was knowen throughout all Ioppa, and many beleeued in the Lord.
43 And it came to passe that he taried many
dayes in Ioppa with one Simon a Tanner.

n This is a borrowed kinde of speach, which signifieth establishment & increase.

10 Peters Apostleship is confirmed by healing of the man that was sicke of the palsie.

o Lydda was a citie of Palestina, and Saron a champion countrey, and a place of good pasturage, betweene Cesarea of Palestine and the mountain Tabor, and the lake of Genazareth, which extendeth it selfe in great length beyond Ioppa.

11 Peter declareth euidently by raising vp a dead body through the Name of Christ, that hee preacheth the glad tidings of life.

CHAP. X.

1 Cornelius, 4 at the Angels commandement, 5 sendeth for Peter: 11 Who also by a vision, 15. 20 is taught not to despise the Gentiles: 34 Hee preacheth the Gospel to Cornelius and his houshold: 45 Who hauing receiued the holy Ghost, 47 are baptized.

FVrthermore [1] there was a certaine man in
Cesarea called Cornelius, a captaine of the
band called the Italian *band*,
2 A [a] deuoute man, and one that feared God with [b] all his houshold, which gaue
much almes to the people, and prayed God
continually.
3 He saw in a vision euidently (about the
ninth houre of the day) an Angel of God comming in to him, & saying vnto him, Cornelius.
4 But when he looked on him, hee was a-

1 Peter consecrateth the first fruits of the Gentiles to God by the meanes of two miracles.

a So that he worshipped one God, and was no Idolater, neither could be voide of faith in Christ, because hee was a deuoute man: but as yet hee knew not that hee was come.

b This is a great commendation to the man, that he laboured to haue all his houshold and familiar friends and acquaintance to be religious, and godly.

fraid,

fraid, and said, [c] What is it, Lord? and he sayd
vnto him, Thy prayers and thine almes are
[d] come vp into [e] remembrance before God.
5 Now therefore send men to Ioppa, and
call for Simon, whose surname is Peter.
6 He lodgeth with one Simon a Tanner,
whose house is by the sea side: he shall tell thee
what thou oughtest to doe.
7 And when the Angel which spake vnto
Cornelius, was departed, he called two of his
seruants and a souldier that feared God, one
of them that waited on him,
8 And told them all things, and sent them
to Ioppa.
9 On the morow as they went on their
iourney, and drew neere vnto the citie, Peter
went vp vpon the house to pray, about the sixt
houre.
10 Then waxed he an hungred, and would
haue eaten: but while they made *some thing* ready, he fell into a [f] trance.
11 And he saw heauen opened, and a certaine vessell come down vnto him, as *it had bene*
a great sheete, knit at the [g] foure corners, and
was let downe to the earth.
12 Wherein were [h] all maner of [i] foure footed beasts of the earth, and wilde beastes, and
[k] creeping things, and foules of the heauen.
13 And there came a voyce to him, Arise,
Peter: kill, and eate.
14 [2] But Peter sayd, Not so, Lord: for I
haue neuer eaten any thing that is polluted, or
vncleane.
15 And the voyce *spake* vnto him againe
the second time, The things that God hath
purified, [l] pollute thou not.
16 This was so done thrise: and the vessell
was drawen vp againe into heauen.
17 ¶ Now while Peter doubted in himselfe
what this vision which he had seene, meant,
beholde, the men which were sent from Cornelius, had inquired for Simons house, and
stood at the gate,
18 And called, and asked, whether Simon,
which was surnamed Peter, were lodged there.
19 And while Peter thought on the vision,
the Spirit said vnto him, Behold, three men
seeke thee.
20 Arise therefore, and get thee downe,
and goe with them, and doubt nothing: for I
haue sent them.
21 ¶ Then Peter went downe to the men,
which were sent vnto him from Cornelius, and
said, Behold, I am he whom ye seeke: what is
the cause wherefore ye are come?
22 And they said, Cornelius the captaine,
a iust man, and one that feareth God, and of
good report among all the nation of the Iewes,
was warned from heauen by an holy Angel,
to send for thee into his house, and to heare thy
words.
23 Then called hee them in, and lodged
them, and the next day, Peter went forth with

c What wilt thou with me Lord? for he setleth himselfe to heare.

d This is a borowed kinde of speech, which the Hebrewes vse very much, taken from sacrifices and applied to prayers: for it is said of whole burnt sacrifices, that the smoke and sauour of them goeth vp into Gods nostrils, so doe our prayers, as a sweet smelling sacrifice which the Lord taketh great pleasure in.

e That is, in so much that they will not suffer God as it were to forget thee: for so doeth the Scripture vse often times to prattle with vs as nurses doe with litle children, when they frame their tongues to speake.

f For though Peter stand not amazed as one that is tongue tied, but talketh with God and is instructed in his mysteries, yet his minde was farre otherwise then it was wont to be, but shortly returned to the old bent.

g So that it seemed to be a foure-square sheet.

h Here is this word (All) which is generall, plainely put for an indefinite and vncertaine, that is to say, for some of all sorts, not for all of euery sort.

i That is, such as were meet for mens vse.

k What is meant by these creeping things, Looke Leuit. 11.

2 Peter profiteth dayly in the knowledge of the benefice of Christ, yea, after that he had receiued the holy Ghost.

l Doe not thou hold them as vnprofitable.

them, and certaine brethren from Ioppa accompanied him.
24 ¶ And the day after, they entred into
Cesarea. Now Cornelius waited for them, and
had called together his kinsemen, and speciall
friends.
25 [3] And it came to passe as Peter came in,
that Cornelius met him, and fell downe at his
feete, and worshipped him.
26 But Peter tooke him vp, saying, Stand
vp: for euen I my selfe am a man.
27 And as he talked with him, he came in,
and found many that were come together.
28 And he said vnto them, Ye know that it
is an vnlawfull thing for a man that is a Iewe, to
company, or come vnto any of other nations:
but God hath shewed me, that I should not
call any man polluted, or vncleane.
29 Therefore came I vnto you without saying nay, when I was sent for. I aske therefore,
for what intent haue ye sent for me?
30 Then Cornelius said, Foure dayes agoe,
about [m] this houre, I fasted, and at the ninth
houre I praied in mine house, and behold, a man
stood before me in bright clothing,
31 [4] And said, Cornelius, thy prayer is heard,
and thine almes are had in remembrance in the
sight of God.
32 [5] Send therefore to Ioppa, and call for
Simon, whose surname is Peter (hee is lodged
in the house of Simon a Tanner by the sea side)
who when he commeth shall speake vnto thee.
33 Then sent I for thee immediatly, & thou
hast well done to come. Now therefore are we
all here present before God, to heare all things
that are commanded thee of God.
34 [6] Then Peter opened *his* mouth, and said,
Of a trueth I perceiue, that [n] *God is no ac-
cepter of persons.
35 But in euery nation he that [o] feareth him,
& worketh righteousnes, is accepted with him.
36 Ye [p] know the word which God hath
sent to the children of Israel, preaching peace
by Iesus Christ, which is Lord of all:
37 [7] *Euen* the worde which came through
all Iudea, *beginning in Galile, after the baptisme which Iohn preached.
38 *To wit*, how God [q] annointed Iesus of
Nazareth with the holy Ghost, and with power: who went about doing good, and healing
all that were oppressed of the deuill: for God
was with him.
39 And we are witnesses of all things which
he did both in the lande of the Iewes, and in
Hierusalem, whom they slew, hanging him on
a tree.
40 Him God raised vp the third day, and
caused that he was shewed openly:
41 Not to all the people, but vnto the wit-

3 Religious adoration or worship agreeth only to God: but ciuill worship is giuen to the Ministers of ÿ word although not without danger.

m He meaneth not the selfe same houre, but the like, that is, about nine of the cloke the other day, as it was then nine when he spake to Peter.

4 Cornelius faith sheweth forth it selfe by prayer and charitie.

5 As faith commeth by hearing so it is nourished and groweth vp by the same.

6 Distinction of nations is taken away by ÿ comming of Christ: And it is euidently seene by faith and righteousnesse, who is agreeable to him or whom he accepteth.

n That God iudgeth not after the outward appearance.

* *Deut* 10.17. 2.*chron*.19.7. *iob*.34.19. *rom*. 2. 11. *gal*. 2. 6. *ephe*. 6. 9. *colos*. 3. 25. 1. *pet*. 1. 17.

o By the feare of God the Hebrewes vnderstood the whole seruice of God, whereby we perceiue that Cornelius was not void of faith, no more then they were which liued before Christs time: and therefore they deale foolishly which build preparatiue workes and free will, vpon this place.

p God gaue the Israelites to vnderstand, that whosoeuer liueth godly, is acceptable to God, of what nation soeuer hee be, for he preached peace to men through Iesus Christ, who is Lord not of one nation only, that is, of the Iewes, but of all.

7 The summe of the Gospel (which shalbe made manifest at the latter day, when Christ himselfe shall sit as Iudge both of the quicke and dead) is this, that Christ promised to the Fathers, & exhibited in his time with the mighty power of God, (which was by all meanes shewed) and at length crucified to reconcile vs to God, did rise againe the third day, that whosoeuer beleeueth in him should be saued through the remission of sinnes. * *Luke* 4. 14.

q The stile is taken from an olde custome of the Iewes, who vsed to anoint their kings & Priests, whereupon it grew, to call them anointed vpon whom God bestoweth gifts and vertues.

neſſes [r] choſen before of God, *euen* to vs which
did eat and drinke with him, after he aroſe from
the dead.
42 And he commanded vs to preach vnto
the people, and to teſtifie, that it is he that is
ordeined of God a Iudge of quicke and dead.
43 To him alſo giue all the *Prophets witneſſe, that through his Name all that beleeue
in him, ſhall receiue remiſſion of ſinnes.
44 [8] While Peter yet ſpake theſe words, the
holy Ghoſt fell on all them which heard the
word.
45 So they of the circumciſion which beleeued, were aſtonied, as many as came with
Peter, becauſe that on the Gentiles alſo was
powred out the gift of the holy Ghoſt.
46 For they heard them ſpeake with tongues,
and magnifie God. Then anſwered Peter,
47 [9] Can any man forbid water, that theſe
ſhould not be baptized, which haue receiued
the holy Ghoſt, as well as we?
48 So he commanded them to be baptized
in the Name of the Lord. Then prayed they
him to tarie certaine dayes.

r This chuſing of the Apoſtles is properly giuen to God: for though God be preſident in the lawfull election of Miniſters, yet there is in this place a ſecret oppoſition & ſetting of Gods chuſing and mens voyces the one againſt the other, for the Apoſtles are immediatly appoynted of God, and the Church miniſters by means.

**Ier.* 31.34. *mica.* 7.18. *chap.* 15.9.

8 The ſpirit of God ſealeth that in the heart of ỹ hearers, which the Miniſter of ỹ word ſpeaketh by the commandement of God, as it appeareth by the effects.

9 Baptiſme doth not ſanctifie or make them holy which receiue it, but ſealeth vp & confirmeth their ſanctification.

CHAP. XI.

2 Peter being accuſed for going to the Gentiles, 5 defendeth himſelfe. 22 Barnabas is ſent to Antiochia, 26 Where the diſciples are called Chriſtians: 28 And there Agabus foretelleth a famine to come.

NOw [1] the Apoſtles and the brethren that
were in Iudea, heard that the Gentiles
had alſo receiued the word of God.
2 And when Peter was come vp to Hieruſalem, they of the circumciſion contended a-
gainſt him,
3 Saying, Thou wenteſt in to men vncircumciſed, and haſt eaten with them.
4 Then Peter began, and expounded *the
thing* in order to them, ſaying,
5 I was in the citie of Ioppa, praying, and
in a trance I ſawe *this* viſion, A certaine veſſell
comming downe as *it had bene* a great ſheet, let
downe from heauen by the foure corners, and
it came to me.
6 Toward the which when I had faſtened
mine eyes, I conſidered, and ſaw foure footed
beaſts of the earth, and wilde beaſts, and creeping things, and foules of the heauen.
7 Alſo I heard a voyce, ſaying vnto me, A-
riſe, Peter: ſlay and eate.
8 And I ſaid, God forbid, Lord: for nothing polluted or vncleane hath at any time entred into my mouth.
9 But the voyce anſwered me the ſecond
time from heauen, The things that God hath
purified, pollute thou not.
10 And this was done three times, and all
were taken vp againe into heauen.
11 Then behold, immediatly there were
three men already come into the houſe where
I was, ſent from Ceſarea vnto me.
12 And the Spirit ſaide vnto mee, that I
ſhould go with them, without doubting: moreouer, theſe ſixe brethren came with me: and we
entred into the mans houſe.

1 Peter being without cauſe reprehended of the vnskilful and ignorant, doeth not obiect that he ought not to be iudged of any, but openly giueth an accoũt of his doing.

13 And he ſhewed vs, how he had ſeene an
Angel in his houſe, which ſtood and ſaide to
him, Send men to Ioppa, and call for Simon,
whoſe ſurname is Peter.
14 Hee ſhall ſpeake wordes vnto thee,
whereby both thou and all thine houſe ſhall be
ſaued.
15 And as I beganne to ſpeake, the holy
Ghoſt fell on them, * euen as vpon vs at the beginning.
16 Then I remembred the worde of the
Lord, how he ſaid, * Iohn baptized with water, but yee ſhall bee baptized with the holy
Ghoſt.
17 Foraſmuch then as God gaue them a
like gift, as *he did* vnto vs, when we beleeued
in the Lord Ieſus Chriſt, who was I, that I
could let God?
18 [2] When they heard theſe things, they
held their peace, and glorified God, ſaying,
Then hath God alſo to the Gentiles granted
repentance vnto life.
19 ¶ [3] And they which were * ſcattered a-
broad becauſe of the affliction that aroſe about
Steuen, went throughout till they came vnto
Phenice and Cyprus, and [a] Antiochia, preaching the word to no man, but vnto the Iewes
onely.
20 [4] Now ſome of them were men of Cyprus and of Cyrene, which when they were
come into Antiochia, ſpake vnto the Grecians,
and preached the Lord Ieſus.
21 And the hande of the Lord was with
them, ſo that a great number beleeued and turned vnto the Lord.
22 [5] Then tidings of thoſe things came
vnto the eares of the Church, which was in
Hieruſalem, and they ſent forth Barnabas, that
he ſhould goe vnto Antiochia.
23 Who when he was come and had ſeene
the grace of God, was glad, and exhorted all,
that with purpoſe of heart they would continue in the Lord.
24 For he was a good man, and full of the
holy Ghoſt, and faith, and much people ioyned themſelues vnto the Lord.
25 ¶ [6] Then departed Barnabas to Tarſus
to ſeeke Saul:
26 And when he had found him, he brought
him vnto Antiochia: and it came to paſſe that
a whole yeere they were conuerſant with the
Church, and taught much people, inſomuch
that the diſciples were firſt called Chriſtians in
Antiochia.
27 [7] In thoſe dayes alſo came Prophets from
Hieruſalem vnto Antiochia.
28 And there ſtood vp one of them named
Agabus, and ſignified by the Spirit, that there
ſhould be great famin thorowout all the world,
which alſo came to paſſe vnder Claudius Ceſar.

**Chap.* 2.4.

**Chap.* 1.5. *and* 19.4. *math.* 3.11. *marke* 1.8. *luk.* 3.16. *iohn* 1.26.

2 Such as aske a queſtion of the trueth which they know not ought to be quietly heard, and muſt alſo quietly yeeld to the declaration thereof.

3 The ſcattering abroad of Hieruſalem, is the cauſe of the gathering together of many other Churches.

* *Chap.* 8.1.

a He ſpeaketh of Antiochia which was in Syria and bordered vpon Cilicia.

4 The Church of Antioch, the new Hieruſalem of the Gentiles was extraordinarily called.

5 The Apoſtles doe not raſhly condemne an extraordinary vocation, but yet they iudge it by the effects.

6 There was no contention amongſt the Apoſtles either of vſurping, or of holding places and degrees.

7 God doeth ſo wrappe vp his Church with the wicked, in his ſcourges and plagues which he ſendeth vpon the earth, that notwithſtanding he prouideth for it conueniently.

29 [8] Then the disciples euery man according to his abilitie, purposed to send [b] succour
vnto the brethren which dwelt in Iudea.
30 Which thing they also did, and sent it
to the Elders, by the hand of Barnabas & Saul.

8 All Congregations or Churches make one body.
b That is, that thereof the Deacons might succour the poore: for it behoued to haue all these things done orderly and decently, and therefore it is saide, that they sent these things to the Elders, that is, to the gouernours of the Church.

CHAP. XII.

2 Herod killeth Iames with the sword: 4 And imprisoneth Peter, 8 whom the Angel deliuereth. 20 Herod being offended with them of Tyrus, 21 is pacified: 22 And taking the honour due to God, to himselfe, 23 he is eaten with wormes, and so dieth.

NOw [1] about that time, [a] Herod the king
stretched forth *his* hands to vexe certaine
of the Church,
2 And he [b] killed Iames the brother of
Iohn with the sword.
3 [2] And when hee sawe that it pleased the
Iewes, he proceeded further, to take Peter also (then were the dayes of vnleauened bread.)
4 [3] And when he had caught him, hee put
him in prison, and deliuered him to foure qua-
ternions of souldiers to be kept, intending after the Passeouer to bring him foorh to the
people.
5 [4] So Peter was kept in prison, but earnest prayer was made of the Church vnto God
for him.
6 And when Herod would haue brought
him out vnto the people, the same night slept
Peter betweene two souldiers, bound with
two chaines, and the keepers before the doore,
kept the prison.
7 * And behold, the Angel of the Lord
came vpon them, and a light shined in the
[c] house, and he smote Peter on the side, and
raised him vp, saying, Arise quickely. And his
chaines fell off from *his* hands.
8 And the Angel said vnto him, Gird thy
selfe, and binde on thy sandales. And so he did.
Then he said vnto him, Cast thy garment a-
bout thee, and follow me.
9 So *Peter* came out, and followed him,
and knewe not that it was true, which was
done by the Angel, but thought he had seene a
vision.
10 Now when they were past the first and
the second watch, they came vnto the yron gate
that leadeth vnto the citie, which opened to
them by it owne accord, and they went out,
and passed through one street, and by and by
the Angel departed from him.
11 ¶ And when Peter was come to himselfe, he said, Now I know for a trueth, that the
Lord hath sent his Angel, and hath deliuered
me out of the hand of Herod, and from all the
waiting for of the people of the Iewes.
12 [5] And as he considered *the thing*, he came
to the house of Mary, the mother of Iohn,
whose surname was Marke, where many were
gathered together, and prayed.

1 God giueth his Church a truce but for a litle time.
a This name Herod was common to all them that came of the stocke of Herod Ascalonites, whose surname was Magnus: but he that is spoken of here, was nephew to Herod the great, sonne to Aristobulus, and father to that Agryppa who is spoken of afterward.
b Violently, his cause being not once heard.
2 It is an old fashion of Tyrants to procure the fauour of the wicked, with the blood of the godly.
3 The tyrants & wicked make a galous for themselues euen then when they doe most according to their owne will & fantasie.
4 The prayers of the godly ouerturne the counsell of Tyrants, obteine Angels of God, breake the prison, vnloose the chaines, put Satan to flight, and preserue the Church.
* Chap. 5. 19.
c In the prison.
5 Holy meetings in ye night as well of men as women (when they cannot be suffered in the day time) are allowable by the example of the Apostles.

13 [6] And when Peter knocked at the entrie doore, a maide [d] came foorth to hearken,
named Rhode.
14 But when shee knew Peters voyce, shee
opened not the entrie *doore* for gladnesse, but
ran in, & told how Peter stood before the entry
15 But they saide vnto her, Thou art mad.
Yet shee affirmed it constantly, that it was so.
Then said they, It is his Angel.
16 But Peter continued knocking, & when
they had opened it, and sawe him, they were
astonied.
17 [7] And he beckened vnto them with the
hand, to hold their peace, and tolde them how
the Lord had brought him out of the prison.
And he said, Goe shew these things vnto Iames
and to the brethren: and he departed and went
into another place.
18 ¶ [8] Now assoone as it was day, there was
no small trouble among the souldiers, what
was become of Peter.
19 And when Herod had sought for him,
and found him not, he examined the keepers,
& commanded them to be led to be punished.
And he went downe from Iudea to Cesarea,
and *there* abode.
20 [9] Then Herod was angry with them of
Tyrus and Sydon, but they came all with one
accord vnto him, and perswaded Blastus the
kings Chamberlaine, and they desired peace,
because their countrey was nourished by the
kings *land*.
21 And vpon a day appointed, Herod arayed himselfe in royall apparell, and sate on the
iudgement seat, & made an oration vnto them.
22 [10] And the people gaue a shout, *saying*,
The voyce of God, and not of man.
23 [11] But immediatly the Angel of the Lord
smote him, because he [e] gaue not glory vnto
God, so that he was eaten of wormes, & gaue
vp the ghost.
24 [12] And the [f] word of God grewe and
multiplied.
25 So Barnabas & Saul returned from Hierusalem, when they had fulfilled their office,
and tooke with them Iohn, whose surname was
Marke.

6 We obtaine more of God then we dare well hope for.
d Out of the place where they were assembled, but not out of the house.
7 We may somtimes giue place to the rage of the wicked, but yet so that our diligence which ought to be vsed in Gods busines, be not a whit slacked.
8 Euill counsell falleth out in the end to the hurt of the deuisers of it.
9 A miserable and shameful example of the end of the enemies of the Church.
10 The flattery of the people, maketh fooles faine
11 God resisteth the proud.
e Iosephus recordeth, that this king did not represse those flatterers tongues, and therefore at his death he complained and cryed out of their vanitie.
12 Tyrants build vp the Church by plucking it downe.
f They that heard the word of God.

CHAP. XIII.

2 The holy Ghost commandeth that Paul and Barnabas be separated vnto him. 6 At Paphus 8 Elymas the sorcerer 11 is strooken blind: 14 From whence being come to Antiochia, 17 they preach the Gospel, 45 The Iewes vehemently withstanding them.

THere [1] were also in the Church that was
at Antiochia, certaine Prophets and teachers, as Barnabas, and Simeon called Niger,
and Lucius of Cyrene, and Manahen (which
had bin brought vp with [a] Herod the Tetrarch)
and Saul.
2 Now as they [b] ministred to the Lord,
and fasted, the holy Ghost said, Separate mee

1 Paul with Barnabas is againe the second time appoynted Apostle of the Gentiles, not of man, neither by man, but by an extraordinarie commandement of the holy Ghost.

a The same was Antipas, which put Iohn Baptist to death b Whiles they were busie doing their office, that is, as Chrysostome expoundeth it, while they were preaching.

Barnabas and Saul, for the worke whereunto I
haue [c] called them.
3 [2] Then fasted they and prayed, and laid
their hands on them, and let them goe.
4 [3] And they, after they were sent foorth
of the holy Ghost, came downe vnto [d] Seleucia, and from thence they sailed to Cyprus.
5 And when they were at Salamis, they
preached the word of God in the Synagogues
of the Iewes: and they had also Iohn to *their*
minister.
6 So when they had gone throughout
the Ile vnto Paphus, they found a certaine sorcerer, a false Prophet, being a Iew, named Bar-
iesus.
7 Which was with the Deputie Sergius
Paulus, a prudent man. Hee called vnto him
Barnabas and Saul, and desired to heare the
word of God.
8 [4] But Elymas, the sorcerer (for so is his
name by interpretation) withstood them, and
sought to turne away the deputie frō the faith.
9 Then Saul (which also *is called* Paul)
beeing full of the holy Ghost, set his eyes on
him,
10 [5] And said, O full of all subtiltie and all
[e] mischiefe, the childe of the deuill, *and* enemie of all righteousnesse, wilt thou not cease to
peruert the straight wayes of the Lord?
11 Now therefore beholde, the [f] hande of
the Lord *is* vpon thee, and thou shalt be blind,
and not see the sunne for a season. And immediatly there fell on him a mist and a darkenesse,
and he went about, seeking some to leade him
by the hand.
12 Then the Deputie when hee sawe what
was done, beleeued, and was astonied at the
doctrine of the Lord.
13 [6] Now when Paul and they that were
with him were departed by ship from Paphus,
they came to Perga *a citie* of Pamphylia: then
Iohn departed from them, & returned to Hierusalem.
14 But when they departed from Perga,
they came to Antiochia *a citie* of [g] Pisidia, and
went into the Synagogue on the Sabbath day,
and sate downe.
15 [7] And after the lecture of the Lawe and
Prophets, the rulers of the Synagogue sent vnto them, saying, Ye men and brethren, if ye
[h] haue any word of exhortation for the people,
say on.
16 [8] Then Paul stood vp and beckened with
the hand, and said, Men of Israel, and ye that
feare God, hearken.
17 Then God of this people of Israel chose
our fathers, and [i] exalted the people when they
dwelt in the land of * Egypt, & with an * [k] high
arme brought them out thereof.
18 And about the time of * fourtie yeeres,
suffered he their maners in the wildernesse.
19 And he destroyed seuen nations in the
land of Chanaan, and * diuided their lande to
them by lot.
20 Then afterward he gaue vnto them * Iudges about [l] foure hundred and fiftie yeeres, vnto *the time of* Samuel the Prophet.
21 So after that, they desired a * King, and
God gaue vnto them * Saul the sonne of Cis,
a man of the tribe of Beniamin *by the space* of
[m] fortie yeeres.
22 And after hee had taken him away, hee
raised vp * Dauid to be their King, of whom
hee witnessed, saying, I haue found Dauid *the*
sonne of Iesse, a man after mine owne heart,
which will do all things that I will.
23 [9] Of this mans seed hath God * according to *his* promise raised vp to Israel, the Sauiour Iesus:
24 When * Iohn had first preached [n] before his comming the baptisme of repentance
to all the people of Israel.
25 And when Iohn had fulfilled *his* course,
he said, * Whom yee thinke that I am, I am not
he: but behold, there commeth one after me,
whose shoe of *his* feete I am not worthie to
loose.
26 [10] Ye men and brethren, children of the
generatiō of Abraham, and whosoeuer among
you feareth God, to you is the word of this saluation sent.
27 [11] For the inhabitants of Hierusalem, and
their rulers, because they knew him not, nor
yet the words of the Prophets, which are read
euery Sabbath *day*, they haue fulfilled them in
condemning him.
28 And though they founde no cause of
death *in him*, * *yet* desired they Pilate to kill
him.
29 And when they had fulfilled all things
that were written of him, they tooke him down
from the tree, and put him in a sepulchre.
30 [12] But God * raysed him vp from the
dead.
31 And he was seene many dayes of them,
which came vp with him from Galile to Hie-
rusalē, which are his witnesses vnto the people.
32 And we declare vnto you, that touching
the promise made vnto the fathers,
33 God hath fulfilled it vnto vs their children, in that he [o] raised vp Iesus, [13] euen as it is
written in the second Psalme, * Thou art my
sonne: this day haue I begotten thee.
34 Now as concerning that he raised him
vp from the dead, no more to returne to cor-

c The Lord is said to call (Whereof this word (Calling) commeth, which is vsual in the Church) when he causeth that to be, which was not, whether you referre it to the matter it selfe, or to any qualitie or thing about the matter: and it groweth of this, because when things begin to be, then they haue some name: as God his mightie power is also declared thereby, who spake the word, and things were made.

2 Fast, and solemne prayers were vsed before the laying on of hands.

3 Paul and his companions doe at the first bring Cyprus to the subiection and obedience of Christ.

d Seleucia was a citie of Cilicia, so called of Seleucus one of Alexanders successours.

4 The deuil maketh ẏ conquest of Christ more glorious, in that that he setteth himselfe against him.

5 The sorcerer which was stricken of Paul with a corporall punishment (although extraordinarily) sheweth an example to lawfull magistrates, how they ought to punish them which wickedly and obstinately hinder the course of the Gospel.

e He noteth out such a fault, as who so hath it, runneth headlong & with great desire to all kind of wickednesse with the least motion in the world.

f His power which he sheweth in striking and beating downe his enemies.

6 An example in one and the selfe same companie both of singular constancie, and also of great weakenesse.

g This putteth a difference betwixt it, and Antiochia which was in Syria.

7 In the Synagogue of the Iewes (according to the pattern wherof Christian congregations were instituted) first the Scriptures were read, then such as were learned, were licensed by the rulers of the Synagogue to speake & expound. *h Word for word, If there be any word in you, this is a kind of speech taken from the Hebrewes, whereby is meant that the gifts of Gods grace are in vs, as it were in treasure houses, and that they are not ours, but Gods. In like sort saith Dauid, Thou hast put a new song in my mouth, Psa. 40. 1.*

8 God bestowed many peculiar benefits vpon his chosen Israel, but this especially, that he promised them the euerlasting redeemer. *i Aduanced and brought to honour.*

* *Exod. 1. 9.*
* *Exod. 13. 14.*

k Openly and with maine force, breaking in pieces the enemies of his people.

* *Exod. 16. 1.*
* *Iosua. 14. 1.*
* *Iudges 3. 9.*

l There were from the birth of Isaac vnto the destruction of the Canaanites vnder the gouernance of Iosua foure hundred and seuen and fourtie yeeres, and therefore he addeth in this place this word, About, for there want three yeeres, but the Apostle vseth the whole greater number.

* *1 Sam 8. 5.*
* *1 Sam. 9. 15. and 10. 1.*

m In this space of fortie yeeres, must the time of Samuel be reckoned with the dayes of Saul, for the kingdome did as it were swallow vp his gouernment.

* *1. Sam. 16. 13.*

9 He proueth by the witnes of Iohn, that Iesus is that Sauiour which should come of Dauid.

* *Psal. 89. 21. esai. 11. 1.*
* *Malac. 3. 1. matth. 3. 1. mar. 1. 2. luke 3. 2.*

n Iohn as an Herault, did not shew Christ comming afarre off as the other prophets did, but hard at hand and entred on his iourney.

* *Matth. 3. 11. marke 1. 7. iohn 1. 20.*

10 Christ was promised and sent properly to the Iewes.

11 All things came to passe to Christ, which ẏ Prophets foretold of Messias: so that hereby also it appeareth that he is the true and onely Sauiour: and yet notwithstanding they are not to be excused which did not onely not receiue him, but also persecute him most cruelly although he was innocent.

* *Matth. 27. 22. mar. 15. 13. luke 23. 23. ioh. 19. 6.*

12 We must set the glory of the resurrection against the shame of the crosse, and graue. And the resurrection is proued as well by witnesses which saw it, as by the testimonies of the Prophets. * *Matth. 28 2. mar. 16. 6 luke 24. 6. ioh. 20. 19.* *o For then he appeared plainely and manifestly as that onely Sonne of God, when as he left off his weakenes and came out of the graue, hauing conquered death.* 13 If Christ had taried in death, he had not bene the true Sonne of God, neither had the couenant, which was made with Dauid, bene sure. * *Psal. 2. 7. hebr. 1. 5. and 5. 5.*

ruption,

ruption, he hath saide thus, *I will giue you
the holy things of Dauid, p which are faithfull.
35 [14] Wherefore hee saith also in another
place, *Thou wilt not suffer thine Holy one to
see corruption.
36 Howbeit, Dauid after he had serued his
time by the counsell of God, he *slept, and
was laide with his fathers, and sawe corruption.
37 But he whome God raised vp, sawe no
corruption.
38 [15] Be it knowen vnto you therefore, men
and brethren, that through this man is preached vnto you the forgiuenesse of sinnes.
39 And from q all things, from which yee
could not be iustified by the Law of Moses, by
him euery one that beleeueth, is iustified.
40 [16] Beware therefore lest that come vpon
you, which is spoken of in the Prophets,
41 *Behold ye despisers, and wonder, and
vanish away: for I worke a worke in your daies,
a worke which yee shall not beleeue, if a man
would declare it you.
42 ¶ [17] And when they were come out of
the Synagogue of the Iewes, the Gentiles besought, that they would preach these words to
them the next Sabbath *day*.
43 Now when the congregation was dissolued, many of the Iewes and r Proselytes that
feared God, followed Paul & Barnabas, which
spake vnto them, and exhorted them to continue in the grace of God.
44 And the next Sabbath *day* came almost
the whole citie together to heare the word of
God.
45 [18] But when the Iewes saw the people,
they were full of enuie, and spake against those
things, which were spoken of Paul, contrary-
ing *them*, and railing on *them*.
46 [19] Then Paul and Barnabas spake boldly,
and said, It was necessary that the word of God
should first haue beene spoken vnto you: but
seeing yee put it from you, and s iudge your
selues vnworthie of euerlasting life, loe wee
turne to the Gentiles.
47 For so hath the Lord commaunded vs,
saying, *I haue made thee a light of the Gentiles, that thou shouldest be the saluation vnto
the end of the world.
48 And when the Gentiles heard it, they
were glad, and glorified the word of the Lord:
and as many as were t ordeined vnto eternall
life, beleeued.
49 Thus the word of the Lord was published throughout the whole countrey.
50 [20] But the Iewes stirred *certaine* u deuout
and honorable women, and the chiefe men of
the citie, and raised persecution against Paul

** Esa.55.3.* *p The Grecians call those, holy things, which the Hebrewes call gracious bounties: and they are called Dauids bounties in the passiue signification, because God bestowed them vpon Dauid: Moreouer they are termed faithfull, after the maner of speech which the Hebrewes vse, who terme those things faithfull, which are steadie and sure, such as neuer alter, nor change.*
14 The Lord was so in graue, that he felt no corruption.
** Psal.16.11. chap.2.31.*
** 1.King.2.10. chap.2.29.*
15 Christ was sent to giue them free remission of sinnes which were condemned by the Lawe.
q Whereas the ceremonies of the Lawe could not absolue you from your sinnes, this man doeth absolue you, if you lay holde on him by faith.
16 The benefites of God turne to the vtter vndoing of them that contemne them.
** Habak.1.5.*
17 The Gentiles goe before the Iewes into the kingdome of heauen.
r Which had forsaken their heathenish religion, and embraced the religion set foorth by Moses.
18 The fauour of one selfe same Gospel is vnto the reprobate and vnbeleeuers, death, and to the elect and such as beleeue, life.
19 The Gospel is published to the Gentiles by the expresse commandement of God.
s By this your doing you doe as it were pronounce sentence against your selues, and iudge your selues.
** Esai.49.6.* *t Therefore either all were not appoynted to euerlasting life, or els all should haue beleeued, but because that is not so, it followeth that some certaine were ordeined: and therefore God did not onely foreknowe, but also fore ordeine, that neither faith nor the effects of faith, should be the cause of his ordeining, or appoyntment, but his ordeining the cause of faith.* 20 Such is the craft and subtiltie of the enemies of the Gospel, that they abuse the simplicitie of some which are not altogether euill men, to execute their crueltie. *u Such as imbraced Moses his Law.*

and Barnabas, and expelled them out of their
coastes.
51 [21] But they *shooke off the dust of their
feet against them, and came vnto Iconium.
52 And the disciples were filled with ioy,
and with the holy Ghost.

21 The wickednes of the world cannot let God to gather his Church together, and to foster & cherish it, when it is gathered together. ** Matth.10.14. mar.6.11. luke 9.5. chap.18.6.*

CHAP. XIIII.

1 Paul and Barnabas 5 are persecuted from Iconium. 6 At Lystra Paul 10 healeth a creeple. 13 They are about to doe sacrifice vnto them, 15 but they forbid it. 19 Paul by the persuasion of certaine Iewes, is stoned: 23 From thence passing through diuers Churches, 26 They returne to Antiochia.

AND [1] it came to passe in a Iconium, that
they went both together into the Synagogue of the Iewes, and so spake, that a great
multitude both of the Iewes and of the Grecians beleeued.
2 And the b vnbeleeuing Iewes stirred vp,
and corrupted the mindes of the Gentiles a-
gainst the brethren.
3 [2] So therefore they abode there a long
time, and spake boldly in the Lord, which gaue
testimony vnto the word of his grace, & caused
signes and wonders to be done by their hands.
4 But the multitude of the citie was diuided: and some were with the Iewes, and some
with the Apostles.
5 And when there was an assault made
both of the Gentiles, and of the Iewes with
their rulers, to doe them violence, and to stone
them,
6 They were ware of it, and c fled vnto
Lystra, and Derbe, cities of Lycaonia, and
vnto the region round about,
7 And there preached the Gospel.
8 ¶ [3] Now there sate a certaine man at
Lystra, impotent in his feet, which was a creeple from his mothers wombe, who had neuer
walked.
9 He heard Paul speake: who beholding
him, and perceiuing that he had faith to bee
healed,
10 Said with a loud voice, Stand vpright on
thy feet. And he leaped vp, and walked.
11 Then when the people sawe what Paul
had done, they lift vp their voices, saying in the
speech of Lycaonia, Gods are come downe to
vs in the likenesse of men.
12 And they called Barnabas, Iupiter: and
Paul, Mercurius, because hee was the chiefe
speaker.
13 Then Iupiters Priest, which was before
their citie, brought bulles with garlands vnto
the d gates, and would haue sacrificed with the
people.
14 But when the Apostles, Barnabas and
Paul heard it, they rent their clothes, and ranne
in among the people, crying,
15 [4] And saying, O men, why doe ye these
things? We are euen men subiect to the e like
passions that ye be, and preach vnto you, that
ye should turne from these f vaine things vnto
the

1 We ought to be no lesse constant in preaching of the Gospel, then the peruersenesse of the wicked is obstinate in persecuting of it.
a Iconium was a city of Licaonia.
b Which obeyed not the doctrine.
2 We ought not to leaue our places and giue place to threatnings, neither to open rage, but when there is no other remedie, and that not for our owne quietnesse sake, but that the Gospel of Christ may be spread further abroad.
c It is lawfull sometimes to flee dangers, in time conuenient.
3 It is an olde subtiltie of the deuill, either to cause the faithfull seruants of God to be banished at once, or to be worshipped for idoles: and that chiefly taking occasion by myracles wrought by him.
d Of the house where Paul and Barnabas were.
4 That is also called idolatry, which giueth to creatures, bee they neuer so holy and excellent, that which is proper to the onely One God, that is inuocation, or calling vpon.
e Men, as ye are, and partakers of the selfe same nature of man as you.
f He calleth idols, vaine things, after the maner of the Hebrewes.

the liuing God, * which made heauen and
earth, and the ſea, and all things that in them
are:
16 [5] Who in times paſt [g] *ſuffered all the
Gentiles to walke in their owne wayes.
17 Neuertheles, he left not himſelfe without witneſſe, in that he did good *and* gaue vs
raine from heauen, and fruitfull ſeaſons, filling
our hearts with food, and gladneſſe.
18 And ſpeaking theſe things, ſcarce ap-
peaſed they the multitude, that they had not
ſacrificed vnto them.
19 [6] Then there came certaine Iewes from
Antiochia and Iconium, which when they had
perſwaded the people, *ſtoned Paul, and drewe
him out of the citie, ſuppoſing he had beene
dead.
20 Howbeit, as the diſciples ſtood round a-
bout him, he aroſe vp, and came into the citie,
and the next day he departed from Barnabas to
Derbe.
21 [7] And after they had preached the glad
tidings of the Goſpel to that citie, and had
taught many, they returned to Lyſtra, and to
Iconium, and to Antiochia,
22 [8] Confirming the diſciples hearts, and
exhorting them to continue in the faith, *affirming* that wee muſt through many afflictions
enter into the kingdome of God.
23 [9] And when they had ordeined them Elders by election in euery Church, and prayed,
and faſted, they commended them to the Lord
in whom they beleeued.
24 [10] Thus they went throughout Piſidia,
and came to Pamphylia.
25 And when they had preached the word
in Perga, they came downe to [h] Attalia,
26 And thence ſailed to [i] Antiochia, * from
whence they had bene commended vnto the
grace of God, to the worke, which they had
fulfilled.
27 And when they were come and had gathered the Church together, they rehearſed all
the things that God had done by them, & how
hee had opened the doore of faith vnto the
Gentiles.
28 So there they abode a long time with
the diſciples.

*Gene. 1.1. pſal. 146.5. reuel 14.7.
5 Cuſtome, be it neuer ſo old, doeth not excuſe the idolaters.
* Pſal. 81.13. rom. 24.
g *Suffered them to liue as they liſted, preſcribing and appoynting them no kinde of religion.*
6 The deuill when hee is brought to the laſt caſt, at length rageth openly, but in vaine, euen then when he ſeemeth to haue the vpper hand.
*1.Cor. 11.25.
7 We muſt goe forward in our vocatiõ through a thouſand deaths.
8 It is the office of the miniſters, not onely to teach, but alſo to confirme them that are taught, and prepare them to the croſſe.
9 The Apoſtles committed the Churches which they had planted, to proper and peculiar Paſtours, which they made, not raſhly, but with prayers and faſtings going before: neither did they thruſt them vpon Churches through briberie, or lordly ſuperioritie, but choſe and placed them by the voyce of the congregation.
10 Paul and Barnabas hauing made an end of their peregrination, and being returned to Antiochia, doe render an account of their iourney to the Congregation or Church.

h *Attalia was a ſea city of Pamphylia, neere to Lycia.* i *Antiochia of Syria.* *Chap. 13.3.

CHAP. XV.

1 *Certaine goe about to bring in circumciſion at Antiochia.* 6 *About which matter the Apoſtles conſult.* 19 *& what muſt be done* 23 *they declare by letters.* 39 *Paul and Barnabas* 36 *are at great variance.*

THen [1] came downe [a] certaine from Iudea,
and taught the brethren, *ſaying*, Except ye
be circumciſed after the maner of Moſes, yee
cannot be ſaued.
2 [2] And when there was great diſſenſion,
and diſputation by Paul and Barnabas againſt
them, they ordeined that Paul and Barnabas,
and certaine other of them, ſhould goe vp to
Hieruſalem vnto the Apoſtles and Elders about
this queſtion.
3 Thus [b] beeing brought foorth by the
Church, they paſſed through Phenice and Samaria, declaring the conuerſion of the Gentiles, and they brought great ioy vnto all the
brethren.
4 And when they were come to Hieruſalem, they were receiued of the Church, and
of the Apoſtles and Elders, and they declared
what things God had done by them.
5 But *ſaid they*, certaine of the ſect of the
Phariſes, which did beleeue, roſe vp, ſaying,
that it was needfull to circumciſe them, and to
command *them* to keepe the law of Moſes.
6 [3] Then the Apoſtles and Elders came together to looke to this matter.
7 And when there had bene great diſputation, Peter roſe vp, and ſaide vnto them,
*[4] Ye men and brethren, ye know that a [c] good
while agoe, among vs God choſe out *me*, that
the Gentiles by my mouth ſhould heare the
word of the Goſpel, and beleeue.
8 And God which knoweth the hearts,
bare them witneſſe, in giuing vnto them the
holy Ghoſt euen as *he did* vnto vs.
9 And he put no [d] difference betweene vs
and them, after that * [e] by faith he had purified their hearts.
10 [5] Now therefore, why [f] tempt ye God,
to * lay a yoke vpon the diſciples necks, which
neither our fathers, nor we were able to beare?
11 But we beleeue, through the grace of
the Lord Ieſus Chriſt to be ſaued, euen as they
doe.
12 [6] Then all the multitude kept ſilence, and
heard Barnabas and Paul, which tolde what
ſignes and wonders God had done among the
Gentiles by them.
13 And when they held their peace, [g] Iames
anſwered, ſaying, Men *and* brethren, hearken
vnto me.
14 [7] Simeon hath declared how God firſt
did viſit the Gentiles, to take *of them* a people
vnto his Name.
15 And to this agree the words of the Prophets, as it is written,
16 ¶ * After this I will returne, and will
build againe the tabernacle of Dauid, which is
fallen downe, and the ruines thereof wil I build
againe, and I will ſet it vp,
17 That the reſidue of men might ſeeke after the Lord, and all the Gentiles vpon whome
my Name is called, ſaith the Lord which doeth
all theſe things.
18 From the beginning of the world, God
[h] knoweth all his works.

1 The Church is at length troubled with diſſention within it ſelfe, & the trouble riſeth of the proud and ſtubburne wits of certaine euill men: The firſt ſtrife was concerning the office of Chriſt, whether wee be ſaued by his onely righteouſneſſe apprehended by faith, or we haue neede alſo to obſerue the Lawe. a *Epiphanius is of opinion that this was Cerinthus.* 2 Meetings of Congregations were inſtituted to ſuppreſſe hereſies, whereunto certaine were ſent by common conſent in the name of all.

b *Courteouſly and louingly brought on their way, by the Church, that is, by certaine appoynted by the Church.*
3 The matter is firſt handled, both parts being heard, in the aſſemblie of the Apoſtles and auncients, and after is communicated with the people.
* Chap. 10.20. and 11.13.
4 God himſelfe in calling of the Gentiles which are vncircumciſed, did teach that our ſaluatiõ doeth conſiſt in faith without the worſhip appoynted by the Lawe.
c *Word for word of old time, that is, euen from the firſt time that we were commanded to preach the Goſpel, and ſtraightwayes after that the holy Ghoſt came downe vpon vs.*
d *He put no difference betweene vs and them, as touching the benefit of his free fauour.*
* Chap. 10.43. 1.Cor. 1.2.
e *Chriſt pronounceth them bleſſed which are pure of heart: and here we are plainely taught that men are made ſuch by faith.*
5 Peter paſſing from the ceremonies, to the Lawe it ſelfe in generall, ſheweth that none could be ſaued, if ſaluation were to be ſought for by the Lawe, and not by grace onely in Ieſus Chriſt: becauſe that no man could euer fulfill the Lawe, neither Patriarch nor Apoſtle.
f *Why tempt yee God, as though he could not ſaue by faith?*
* Math. 23.4.
6 A true patterne of a lawful Councill, where Gods trueth onely reigneth.
g *The ſonne of Alpheus, who is alſo called the Lords brother.*

7 Iames confirmeth the calling of the Gentiles out of the word of God, therein agreeing to Peter. * *Amos 9.11.* h *And therefore nothing commeth to paſſe by fortune, but by Gods appoyntment.*

19 [8] Where-

19 [8]Wherefore my ſentence is, that wee
trouble not them of the Gentiles that are turned to God,
20 But that wee ſend vnto them, that they
abſtaine themſelues from [i] filthineſſe of idoles,
and fornication, and that is ſtrangled, and from
blood.
21 For Moſes of old time hath in euery citie them that preach him, ſeeing he is read in
the Synagogues euery Sabbath *day*.
22 [9]Then it ſeemed good to the Apoſtles
and Elders with the whole Church, to ſend
choſen men of their owne companie to Antiochia with Paul and Barnabas: *to wit*, Iudas
whoſe ſurname was Barſabas, and Silas, which
were chiefe men among the brethren,
23 And wrote letters by them after this
maner, THE APOSTLES, and the Elders,
and the brethren, vnto the brethren which are
of the Gentiles in Antiochia, and in Syria, and
in Cilicia, ſend greeting.
24 [10]Foraſmuch as we haue heard, that certaine which [k] went out fron vs, haue troubled
you with words, and [l] cumbred your mindes,
ſaying, Ye muſt be circumciſed and keepe the
Lawe, to whom wee gaue no ſuch commandement,
25 It ſeemed therefore good to vs, when
wee were come together with one accord, to
ſend choſen men vnto you, with our beloued
Barnabas and Paul,
26 Men that haue [m] giuen vp their liues for
the Name of our Lord Ieſus Chriſt.
27 Wee haue therefore ſent Iudas and Silas, which ſhall alſo tell you the ſame things by
mouth.
28 [11] For it ſeemed good to the [n] holy
Ghoſt, and [o] to vs, to lay no more burthen vpon you, then theſe [p] neceſſarie things,
29 [12] *That is*, that yee abſtaine from things
offered to idoles, and blood, and that that is
ſtrangled, and from fornication: from which
if ye keepe your ſelues, ye ſhall doe well. Fare
ye well.
30 [13]Now when they were departed, they
came to Antiochia, and after that they had aſſembled the multitude, they deliuered the E-
piſtle.
31 And when they had read it, they reioyced for the conſolation.
32 And Iudas and Silas beeing Prophets,
exhorted the brethren with many words, and
ſtrengthened them.
33 And after they had taried there a ſpace,
they were let goe in [q] peace of the brethren vnto the Apoſtles.
34 Notwithſtanding Silas thought good

8 In matters indifferent, we may ſo farre beare with the weakneſſe of our brethren, as they may haue time to be inſtructed.

i From ſacrifices, or from feaſts which were kept in Idoles temples.

9 In a lawfull Synode, neither they which are appointed and choſen Iudges, appoint and determine any thing tyrannouſly or vpon a lordlineſſe, neither doeth the common multitude ſet themſelues tumultuouſly againſt them which ſit as iudges by the word of God: as the like order alſo is holden in publiſhing and ratifying thoſe things which haue beene ſo determined and agreed vpon.

10 The Councill of Hieruſalem concludeth, that they trouble mens conſciences which teach vs to ſeeke ſaluation in any other meanes then in Chriſt onely, apprehended by faith, from whence ſoeuer they come, & whomſoeuer they pretend to be author of their vocation.

k From our congregation.

l A borowed kinde of ſpeech taken of them which pull downe that that was built vp: and it is a very vſuall metaphore in the Scriptures, to ſay the Church is built, for the Church is planted and ſtabliſhed.

m Haue greatly hazarded their liues.

11 That is a lawfull Council, which the holy Ghoſt ruleth.

n Firſt they made mention of the holy Ghoſt, that it may not ſeeme to be any mans worke.

o Not that men haue any authoritie of themſelues,

to abide there ſtill.
35 Paul alſo and Barnabas continued in
Antiochia, teaching and preaching with many
other, the word of the Lord.
36 ¶[14]But after certaine dayes, Paul ſayd
vnto Barnabas, Let vs returne, and viſite our
brethren in euery citie, where wee haue preached the word of the Lord, *and ſee* how they
doe.
37 [15] And Barnabas counſelled to take
with them Iohn, called Marke.
38 But Paul thought it not meete to take
him vnto their company, which departed from
them from Pamphylia, and went not with
them to the worke.
39 [16]Then were they ſo [r] ſtirred, that they
departed aſunder one from the other, ſo that
Barnabas tooke Marke, and ſailed vnto Cyprus.
40 And Paul choſe Silas and departed, being commended of the brethren vnto the grace
of God.
41 And he went thorow Syria and Cilicia,
ſtabliſhing the Churches.

r They were in great heat: But herein wee haue to conſider the force of Gods counſell: for by this meanes it came to paſſe, that the doctrine of the Goſpel was exerciſed in many places.

14 Congregations or Churches doe eaſily degenerate, vnleſſe they be diligently ſeene vnto, and therefore went theſe Apoſtles to ouerſee ſuch as they had planted, and for this cauſe alſo Synodes were inſtituted and appointed.

15 A lamentable example of diſcord betweene excellent men and very great friends, yet not for profane or their priuate affaires, neither yet for doctrine.

16 God vſeth the faults of his ſeruants to the profit and building of the Church: yet we haue to take heed, euen in the beſt matters, that we paſſe not meaſure in our heate.

CHAP. XVI.

1 Paul hauing circumciſed Timotheus, 12 being at Philippi, 14 inſtructeth Lydia in the faith. 16 The ſpirit of Diuination 18 is by him caſt out: 20 and for that cauſe 22 they are whipped, 24 and impriſoned. 26 Through an earthquake 27 the priſon doores are opened. 31. 32 The Iayler receiueth the faith.

THen [1] came hee to Derbe and to Lyſtra:
and behold, a certaine diſciple was there,
named *Timotheus, a womans ſonne, which
was a [a] Ieweſſe and beleeued, but his father
was a Grecian.
2 Of whom the brethren which were at
Lyſtra and Iconium, [b] reported well.
3 [2]Therefore Paul would that hee ſhould
goe foorth with him, and tooke and circumciſed him, becauſe of the Iewes, which were in
thoſe quarters: for they knewe all, that his father was a Grecian.
4 [3] And as they went through the cities,
they deliuered them the [c] decrees to keepe, ordeined of the Apoſtles and Elders, which were
at Ieruſalem.
5 And ſo were the Churches ſtabliſhed in
the faith, and increaſed in number daily.
6 ¶[4] Now when they had gone throughout Phrygia, and the region of Galatia, they
were [d] forbidden of the holy Ghoſt to preach
the word in Aſia.
7 Then came they to Myſia, and ſought to
goe into Bithynia: but the Spirit ſuffered them
not.
8 Therefore they paſſed through Myſia,
and came downe to Troas.
9 [5]Where a viſion appeared to Paul in the
night.

1 Paul himſelfe doth not receiue Timothie into the miniſterie without ſufficient teſtimonie, and allowance of the brethren.

*Rõ. 16. 21. phil. 2. 20. 1. theſſ. 3. 2.

a Paul in his latter Epiſtle to Timothie, commendeth the godlines of Timothies mother and grandmother.

b Both for his godlineſſe and honeſtie.

2 Timothie is circumciſed, not ſimply for any neceſſitie, but in reſpect of the time only to win the Iewes.

3 Charitie is to be obſerued in things indifferent, that ſo, regard be had both of the weak, and the quietneſſe of the Church.

c Theſe degrees which he ſpake of in the former Chapter.

4 God appointeth certaine and determinate times to open & ſet forth his truth, ẏ both the election, and the calling may proceed of grace. *d Hee ſheweth not why they were forbidden, but only that they were forbidden, teaching vs to obey, and not to enquire.* 5 They are the miniſters of the Goſpel, by whom he helpeth ſuch as are like to periſh.

but to ſhew the faithfulnes that they vſed in their miniſtery & labor. p This was no preciſe neceſsity, but in reſpect of the ſtate of that time, that the Gentiles and the Iewes might more peaceably liue together with leſſe occaſion of quarell. 12 Charitie is requiſite euen in things indifferent. 13 It is requiſite for all people to know certainly what to hold in matters of faith and religion, and not that the Church by ignorance and knowing nothing, ſhould depend vpon the pleaſure of a fewe. *q This is an Hebrew kinde of ſpeech, which is as much to ſay, as the brethren wiſhed them all proſperous ſucceſſe, and the Church diſmiſſed them with good leaue.*

night. There stood a man of Macedonia, and
prayed him, saying, Come into Macedonia,
and helpe vs.

6 The Saints did not easily beleeue euery vision.

10 [6] And after hee had seene the vision, immediatly we prepared to goe into Macedonia,
being assured that the Lorde had called vs to
preach the Gospel vnto them.

11 Then went wee foorth from Troas, and
with a straight course came to Samathracia,
and the next day to Neapolis,

7 God beginneth his kingdome in Macedonia by the conuersion of a woman, and so sheweth that there is no acceptation of persons in the Gospel.

12 ¶ And from thence to Philippi, which
is the chiefe citie in the parts of Macedonia,
and whose inhabitants came from Rome to
dwell there, and we were in that citie abiding
certaine dayes.

e *Where they were woont to assemble themselues.*

13 [7] And on the Sabbath day, we went out
of the citie, besides a Riuer, where they were
woont to [e] pray: and we sate downe, and spake
vnto the women, which were come together.

8 The Lord only openeth the heart to heare the word which is preached.

14 [8] And a certaine woman named Lydia,
a seller of purple, of the citie of the Thyatiri-
ans, which worshipped God, heard *vs*: whose
heart the Lord opened, that she attended vnto
the things, which Paul spake.

9 An example of a godly huswife.

15 [9] And when she was baptized, and her
houshold, she besought vs, saying, If yee haue
iudged me to be faithfull to the Lord, come into mine house, and abide *there*: and shee constrained vs.

10 Satan transformeth himselfe into an Angel of light, and coueteth to enter by vndermining, but Paul openly letteth him, and casteth him out.

f *This is a proper note of Apollo, which was woont to giue answeres to them that asked him.*

16 [10] And it came to passe that as we went
to prayer, a certaine maide hauing a spirit of
[f] diuination, met vs, which gate her masters
much vantage with diuining.

17 Shee followed Paul and vs, and cryed,
saying, These men are the seruants of the
most high God, which shew vnto you the way
of saluation.

g *Paul made no haste to this miracle, for he did all things as he was led by the Spirit.*

18 And this did shee [g] many dayes: but
Paul being grieued, turned about, and said to
the spirit, I command thee in the Name of Iesus Christ, that thou come out of her. And hee
came out the same houre.

11 Couetousnes of lucre & gaines is an occasion of persecuting the trueth. In the meane season, God sparing Timothie, calleth Paul and Silas, as the stronger to battell.

19 [11] Now when her masters sawe that the
hope of their gaine was gone, they caught Paul
and Silas, and drew them into the market place
vnto the Magistrates,

12 Couetousnes pretendeth a desire of common peace and godlinesse.

20 [12] And brought them to the gouernors,
saying, These men which are Iewes, trouble
our citie,

13 It is an argument of the deuill, to vrge the authoritie of ancesters without any distinction.

21 [13] And preach ordinances, which are not
lawfull for vs to receiue, neither to obserue,
seeing we are Romanes.

14 An example of euill Magistrates, to obey the furie and rage of the people.

22 [14] The people also rose vp together a-
gainst them, and the gouernours rent their
clothes, and commaunded *them* to be beaten
with rods.

h *Because hee would be more sure of them, hee set them fast in the stockes.*

23 And when they had beaten them sore,
they cast *them* into prison, commanding the
Iayler to keepe them surely.

24 Who hauing receiued such commandement, cast them into the inner prison, and made
their feete [h] fast in the stockes.

15 The prayers of the godly doe shake both heauen and earth.

25 [15] Now at midnight Paul & Silas prayed,
and sung Psalmes vnto God: and the prisoners
heard them.

26 And suddenly there was a great earthquake: so that the foundation of the prison was
shaken: and by and by all the doores opened,
and euery mans bands were loosed.

16 The mercifull Lord, so oft as he listeth, draweth men to life euen through the middest of death & whereas iustly they deserued great punishment, he sheweth them great mercie.

27 [16] Then the keeper of the prison waked
out of his sleepe, and when hee saw the prison
doores open, he drew out his sword and would
haue killed himselfe, supposing the prisoners
had beene fled.

28 [17] But Paul cryed with a loud voice, saying, Doe thy selfe no harme: for wee are all
heere.

17 In meanes, which are especially extraordinarie, we ought not to moue our foot forward, vnlesse that God goe before vs.

29 Then he called for a light, and leaped in,
and came trembling, and fell downe before
Paul and Silas,

30 And brought them out, and sayd, Sirs,
what must I doe to be saued?

31 And they said, Beleeue in the Lord Iesus Christ, and thou shalt be saued, and thine
houshold.

32 And they preached vnto him the word
of the Lord, and to all that were in the house.

18 God with one selfe same hand woundeth and healeth when it pleaseth him.

33 [18] Afterward hee tooke them the same
houre of the night, and washed *their* stripes,
and was baptized with all that belonged vnto
him, straightway.

34 And when hee had brought them into
his house, hee set meate before them, and reioyced that hee with all his houshold beleeued
in God.

19 Shame and confusion is in processe of time the reward of wicked and vniust Magistrates.

35 [19] And when it was day, the gouernours
sent the sergeants, saying, Let those men goe.

10 We must not render iniury for iniurie, and yet notwithstanding it is lawfull for vs to vse such helps as God giueth vs, to bridle the outragiousnesse of the wicked, that they hurt not other in like sort.

39 Then the keeper of the prison tolde
these words vnto Paul, *saying*, The gouernours
haue sent to loose you: now therefore get you
hence, and goe in peace.

37 [20] Then said Paul vnto them, After that
they haue beaten vs openly vncondemned,
which are Romanes, they haue cast vs into
prison, and now would they put vs out priuily? nay verely: but let them come and bring
vs out.

21 The wicked are not mooued with the feare of God, but with the feare of men: and by that meanes also God prouideth for his, when it is needfull.

38 [21] And the sergeants tolde these words
vnto the gouernours, who feared when they
heard that they were Romanes.

39 Then came they and prayed them, and
brought them out, and desired them to depart
out of the citie.

22 We may eschew dangers, so that we neuer neglect our duetie.

40 [22] And they went out of the prison, and
entred into *the house of* Lydia: and when they
had seene the brethren, they comforted them,
and departed.

CHAP. XVII.

1 Paul at Thessalonica 3 preaching Christ, 6. 7 is entertained of Iason: 10 He is sent to Berea: 15 from thence comming to Athens, 19 in Mars streete 23 he preacheth the liuing God to them vnknowen, 34 and so many are conuerted vnto Christ.

1 The casting out of Silas and Paul was the sauing of many other.

NOw [1] as they passed through Amphipo-
lis, and Apollonia, they came to Thessalonica, where was a Synagogue of the Iewes.

2 And

2 And Paul, as his manner was, went in
vnto them, and three Sabbath *dayes* diſputed
with them by the Scriptures,
3 [2]Opening, and alleadging that Chriſt
muſt haue ſuffered, and riſen againe from the
dead: and this is Ieſus Chriſt, whom, *ſaid he,*
I preach to you.
4 And ſome of them beleeued, and ioyned in companie with Paul and Silas: alſo of
the Grecians that feared God a great multitude, and of the chiefe women not a few.
5 [3] But the Iewes which beleeued not,
mooued with enuie, tooke vnto them certaine
[a]vagabonds *and* wicked fellowes, and when
they had aſſembled the multitude, they made
a tumult in the citie, and made aſſault againſt
the houſe of Iaſon, and ſought to bring them
out to the people.
6 But when they found them not, they
drewe Iaſon and certaine brethren vnto the
heads of the city, crying, Theſe are they which
haue ſubuerted the ſtate of the [b]world, and
here they are,
7 Whom Iaſon hath receiued, and theſe
all doe againſt the decrees of Ceſar, ſaying that
there is another King one Ieſus.
8 Then they troubled the people, and the
heads of the city, whẽ they heard theſe things.
9 Notwithſtanding when they had receiued ſufficient [c]aſſurance of Iaſon and of the o-
ther, they let them goe.
10 [4]And the brethren immediatly ſent a-
way Paul and Silas by night vnto Berea, which
when they were come thither, entred into the
Synagogue of the Iewes.
11 [5]Theſe were alſo more [d]noble men then
they which were at Theſſalonica, which receiued the worde with all readineſſe, and ſearched the Scriptures daily, whether thoſe
things were ſo.
12 Therefore many of them beleeued, and
of honeſt women, which were Grecians, and
men not a fewe.
13 ¶ [6]But when the Iewes of Theſſalonica
knew, that the word of God was alſo preached
of Paul at Berea, they came thither alſo, and
mooued the people.
14 [7]But by and by the brethren ſent away
Paul to goe as *it were* to the ſea: but Silas and
Timotheus abode there ſtill.
15 [8] And they that did conduct Paul,
[e]brought him vnto Athens: and when they
had receiued a commandement vnto Silas and
Timotheus, that they ſhould come to him at
once, they departed.
16 ¶ [9]Now while Paul waited for them at
Athens, his ſpirit was [f] ſtirred in him, when he
ſaw the citie ſubiect to [g] idolatrie.

2 Chriſt is therfore the Mediatour, becauſe he was crucified and roſe againe: much leſſe is he to be reiected becauſe the croſſe is ignominious.

3 Although the zeale of the vnfaithfull ſeeme neuer ſo goodly, yet at length it is found to haue neither truth nor equity: But yet the wicked cannot doe what they liſt, for euen among themſelues God ſtirreth vp ſome, whoſe helpe he vſeth to the deliuerance of his.

a Certaine companions which doe nothing but walke the ſtreetes, wicked men, to be hired for euery mans money to doe any miſchiefe, ſuch as we commonly call the raſcals and very ſinkes and dunghill knaues of all townes and cities.

b Into what countrey and place ſoeuer they come, they cauſe ſedition and tumult.

c When Iaſon had put them in good aſſurance that they ſhould appeare.

4 That is indeed the wiſdom of the Spirit, which alwayes ſetteth the glory of God before it ſelfe as a marke whereunto it directeth it ſelfe and neuer ſwarueth from it.

5 The Lord ſetteth out in one moment, and in one people diuers examples of his vnſearchable wiſdome to cauſe them to feare him.

d He compareth the Iewes with the Iewes.

6 Satan hath his, who are zealous for him, and that euen ſuch, as leaſt of al ought.

7 There is neither counſell, nor furie, nor madnes againſt the Lord.

8 The ſheepe of Chriſt doe alſo watch for their paſtours health and ſafetie, but yet in the Lord.

e It is not for naught that the Iewes of Berea were ſo commended, for they brought Paul ſafe from Macedonia to Athens, and there is in diſtance betwixt thoſe two, all Theſſalia, and Bœotia, and Attica. 9 In comparing the wiſedome of God with mans wiſedome, men ſcoffe and mocke at that which they vnderſtand not: And God vſeth the curioſitie of fooles to gather together his elect. *f He could not forbeare. g Slauiſhly giuen to idolatrie: Pauſanias writeth that there were more idols in Athens then in all Grecia, yea they had altars dedicated to Shame, and Fame, and Luſt, whom they make goddeſſes.*

17 Therefore he diſputed in the Synagogue
with the Iewes, and with them that were religious, and in the market daily with [h] whomſoeuer he met.
18 [10]Then certaine Philoſophers of the E-
picures, and of the Stoikes, diſputed with him,
and ſome ſaid, What will this [i] babler ſay? O-
thers *ſaid,* Hee ſeemeth to be a ſetter foorth of
ſtrange gods (becauſe he preached vnto them
Ieſus, and the reſurrection.)
19 And they tooke him, and brought him
into [k]Mars ſtreete, ſaying, May we not know,
what this newe doctrine, whereof thou ſpea-
keſt, is?
20 For thou bringeſt certain ſtrange things
vnto our eares: wee would knowe therefore,
what theſe things meane.
21 [11]For all the Athenians, and ſtrangers
which dwelt there, gaue themſelues to nothing
elſe, but either to tell, or to heare ſome newes.
22 [12]Then Paul ſtood in the mids of Mars
ſtreete, and ſaid, Yee men of Athens, I perceiue that in all things yee are too [l] ſuperſtitious.
23 For as I paſſed by, and beheld your [m] de-
uotions, I found an altar wherein was written, VNTO THE [n]VNKNOVVEN GOD.
Whom ye then ignorantly worſhip, him ſhew
I vnto you.
24 [13]God that made the world, and all
things that are therein, ſeeing that hee is Lord
of heauen and earth,* dwelleth not in temples
made with hands,
25 *Neither is worſhipped with mens
hands, as though hee needed any thing, ſeeing
he giueth to all life, and breath, and all things,
26 [14]And hath made of [o] one blood all
mankinde, to dwell on all the face of the earth,
and hath aſsigned the ſeaſons which were ordeined before, and the bounds of their habitation,
27 That they ſhould ſeeke the Lord, if ſo
be they might haue [p] groped after him, and
found *him,* though doubtleſſe he be not farre
from euery one of vs.
28 For in him wee liue, and mooue, and
haue our being, as alſo certaine of your owne
Poets haue ſayd, For wee are alſo his generation.
29 *Foraſmuch then, as we are the generation of God, wee ought not to thinke that the
Godhead is like vnto golde, or ſiluer, or ſtone
[q]grauen by arte and the inuention of man.
30 [15]And the time of this ignorance God

h Whomſoeuer Paul met with, that would ſuffer him to talke with him, he reaſoned with him, ſo throughly did he burne with the zeale of Gods glory.

10 Two ſectes eſpecially of the Philoſophers, do ſet themſelues againſt Chriſt: the Epicures, which make a mock and ſcoffe at all religion: and the Stoikes, which determine vpon matters of religion according to their owne braines.

i Word for word, ſeede gatherer: a borrowed kind of ſpeech taken of birds which ſpoile corne, and is ap-plyed to them which without all arte bluſter out ſuch knowledge as they haue gotten by hearing this man and that man.

k This was a place called as you would ſay, Mars hill, where the Iudges ſate, which were called Areopagitæ, vpon weightie affaires, which in old time arrained Socrates, and afterward condemned him of impietie.

11 The wiſdom of man is vanitie.

12 The idolaters themſelues miniſter moſt ſtrong and forcible arguments againſt their own ſuperſtitiõ.

l To ſtand in too peeuiſh and ſeruile a feare of your gods.

m Whatſoeuer men worſhip for religions ſake, that we call deuotion.

n Pauſanias in his Atticis maketh mention of the altar which the Athenians had dedicated to vnknowen gods: and Laertius in his Epimenides maketh mention of an altar that had no name intituled.

13 It is a moſt fooliſh and vaine thing to compare the Creator with the creature, to limit him within a place which can bee comprehended in no place, and to thinke to allure him with gifts, of whom all men haue receiued al things whatſoeuer they haue: And theſe are the fountaines of all idolatrie. * *Chap.7.48.* * *Pſal.50.8.* 14 God is wonderfull in all his workes, but eſpecially in the worke of man: not that wee ſhould ſtand amaſed at his workes, but that we ſhould lift our eyes to the workman. *o Of one ſtocke and one beginning. p For as blinde men wee could not ſeeke out God but onely by gropingwiſe, before the true light came and lightened the world.* * *Eſai 40.19.* *q Which ſtuffe, as golde, ſiluer, ſtones, are cuſtomably grauen as a mans wit can deuiſe, for men will not worſhippe that groſſe ſtuffe as it is, vnleſſe by ſome arte it haue gotten ſome ſhape vpon it.* 15 The oldneſſe of the errour doeth not excuſe them that erre, but it commendeth and ſetteth foorth the patience of God: who notwithſtanding will be a iuſt Iudge to ſuch as contemne him.

regarded not: but now he admoniſheth all men
euery where to repent,
31 Becauſe he hath appointed a day in the
which he will iudge the world in righteouſnes,
by that man whom he hath appointed,*whereof*
he hath giuen an [r] aſſurance to all men, in that
he hath raiſed him from the dead.
32 [16] Now when they heard of the reſurrection from the dead, ſome mocked, and other
ſaid, We will heare thee againe of this thing.
33 And ſo Paul departed from among
them.
34 Howbeit certaine men claue vnto Paul,
and beleeued: among whome was alſo Denys
Areopagita, and a woman named Damaris,
and other with them.

r By declaring Chriſt to be the Iudge of the world through the reſurrection from the dead.

16 Men to ſhew forth their vanitie, are diuerſly affected and mooued by one ſelfe ſame Goſpel, which notwithſtanding ceaſeth not to be effectuall in the elect.

CHAP. XVIII.

1 As Paul at Corinth 6 taught the Gentiles, 9 the Lord comforteth him. 12 He is accuſed before Gallio, 16 but in vaine: 18 From thence hee ſaileth to Syria, 19 and ſo to Epheſus. 23 At Galatia and Phrygia hee ſtrengtheneth the diſciples. 24 Apollos beeing more perfectly inſtructed by Aquila, 28 preacheth Chriſt with great efficacie.

After [1] theſe things, Paul departed from
Athens, and came to Corinthus,
2 And found a certaine Iewe named * A-
quila, borne in Pontus, lately come from Italie, and his wife Priſcilla, (becauſe that [a] Claudius had commanded all Iewes to depart from
Rome) and he came vnto them.
3 And becauſe he was of the ſame craft, he
abode with them and wrought (for their craft
was to make tents)
4 [2] And hee diſputed in the Synagogue e-
uery Sabbath *day*, and [b] exhorted the Iewes,
and the Grecians.
5 Now when Silas and Timotheus were
come from Macedonia, Paul, [c] forced in ſpirit, teſtified to the Iewes that Ieſus was the
Chriſt.
6 [3] And when they reſiſted and blaſphemed, hee * ſhooke his raiment, and ſaid vnto
them, Your [d] blood *be* vpon your owne head:
I am cleane: from hencefoorth will I goe vnto
the Gentiles.
7 So he departed thence, and entred into
a certaine mans houſe, named Iuſtus, a wor-
ſhipper of God, whoſe houſe ioyned hard to
the Synagogue.
8 And * Criſpus the chiefe ruler of the
Synagogue, beleeued in the Lord with all his
houſhold: and many of the Corinthians hearing it, beleeued and were baptized.
9 [4] Then ſaid the Lord to Paul in the night
by a viſion, Feare not, but ſpeake and hold not
thy peace.
10 For I am with thee, and no man ſhall
lay *hands* on thee to hurt thee: for I haue much
people in this citie.

1 The true miniſters are ſo farre from ſeeking their owne profite, that they do willingly depart from their right, rather then the courſe of the Goſpel ſhould be hindered in the leaſt wiſe that might be.

* *Rom. 16.3.*

a Suetonius recordeth, that Rome baniſhed the Iewes, becauſe they were alwayes at diſquiet, and that by Chriſtes meanes.

2 The trueth ought alwayes to be freely vttered, yet notwithſtanding the doctrine may be ſo moderated, as occaſion of the profite that the people take thereby ſhall require.

b Exhorted ſo that he perſwaded, and ſo the word ſignifieth.

c Was very much grieued in minde: whereby is ſignified the great earneſtneſſe of his minde, which was greatly mooued: for Paul was ſo zealous, that hee cleane forgate himſelfe, and with a wonderfull courage gaue himſelfe to preach Chriſt.

3 Although we haue aſſayed all meanes poſſible, and yet in vaine, we muſt not leaue off from our worke, but forſake the rebellious, and goe to them that be more obedient. * *Chap. 13.51. mat. 10.14.* *d This is a kinde of ſpeech taken from the Hebrewes, whereby he meaneth that the Iewes are cauſe of their owne deſtruction, and as for him, that he is without fault in forſaking them and going to other nations.* * *1. Cor. 1.14.* 4 God doth auouch and maintaine the conſtancie of his ſeruants.

11 So he [e] continued there a yeere and ſixe
moneths, and taught the word of God among
them.
12 ¶ [5] Nowe when Gallio was deputie of
[f] Achaia, the Iewes aroſe with one accord a-
gainſt Paul, and brought him to the iudgement
ſeate,
13 Saying, This fellow perſwadeth men
to worſhip God otherwiſe then the Lawe appointeth.
14 And as Paul was about to open his
mouth, Gallio ſaid vnto the Iewes, If it were
a matter of wrong, or an euill deede, O yee
Iewes, I would according to [g] reaſon maintaine you.
15 But if it be a queſtion of [h] wordes and
[i] names, and of your Lawe, looke yee to it
your ſelues: for I will bee no iudge of thoſe
things.
16 And he draue them from the iudgement
ſeate.
17 Then tooke all the Grecians Soſthenes
the chiefe ruler of the Synagogue, and beat
him before the iudgement ſeat: but Gallio cared nothing for thoſe things.
18 [6] But when Paul had taried there yet a
good while, hee tooke leaue of the brethren,
and ſailed into Syria (and with him Priſcilla
and Aquila) after that [k] he had ſhorne his head
in [l] Cenchrea: for he had a * vow.
19 Then he came to Epheſus, and left them
there: but he entred into the Synagogue, and
diſputed with the Iewes.
20 [7] Who deſired him to tarie a longer time
with them: but he would not conſent,
21 But bade them farewell, ſaying, I muſt
needes keepe this feaſt that commeth, in Ieruſalem: but I will returne againe vnto you,
* [m] if God will. So he ſailed from Epheſus.
22 ¶ And when hee came downe to Ceſarea, he went vp *to Ieruſalem*: and when he had
ſaluted the Church, hee went downe vnto Antiochia.
23 Now when hee had taried *there* a while,
hee departed, and went through the countrey
of Galatia and Phrygia by order, ſtrengthe-
ning all the diſciples.
24 [8] And a certaine Iewe, named * Apollos, borne at Alexandria, came to Epheſus, an
eloquent man, and [n] mightie in the Scriptures.
25 The ſame was inſtructed in the way of
the Lorde, and hee ſpake feruently in the
Spirit, and taught diligently the things of
the Lord, and knewe but the baptiſme of Iohn
onely.
26 And hee began to ſpeake boldly in the
Synagogue. Whom when * Aquila and Priſcilla had heard, they tooke him vnto them, and
expounded vnto him the [o] way of God more
perfectly.

e Word for word, ſate, whereupon they in former time, tooke the name of their Biſhops ſeate: but Paul ſate, that is, continued teaching the word of God: and this kinde of ſeate belongeth nothing to them, which neuer ſawe their ſeates with a minde to teach in them.

5 The wicked are neuer wearie of euill doing, but the Lord mocketh their endeauours marueilouſly.

f That is, of Grecia, yet the Romanes did not call him Deputie of Grecia, but of Achaia, becauſe the Romanes brought the Grecians into ſubiection, by the Achaians, which in thoſe dayes were Princes of Grecia, as Pauſanias recordeth.

g As much as in right I could.

h As if a man haue not ſpoken well, as the caſe of your religion ſtandeth.

i For this prophane man thinketh that the controuerſie of religion, is but a braule about words, and for no matter of ſubſtance.

6 Paul is made all to all, to winne all to Chriſt.

k That is, Paul.

l Cenchrea was an hauen of the Corinthians.

* *Numb. 16.18. chap. 21.24.*

7 The Apoſtles were caried about not by the will of man, but by the leading of the holy Ghoſt.

* *1. Cor. 4.19. iames 4.15.*

m So we ſhould promiſe nothing without this clauſe, for wee know not what the day following will bring foorth.

8 Apollos, a godly and learned man, refuſeth not to profit in the ſchoole of a baſe and abiect handicraftſman, and alſo of a woman; and ſo becommeth an excellent miniſter of the Church. * *1. Cor. 1.12.* *n Very well inſtructed in the knowledge of the Scriptures.* * *Rom. 16.3.* *o The way that leadeth to God.*

27 And when hee was minded to goe into
Achaia, the brethren exhorting him, wrote to
the disciples to receiue him: and after hee was
come thither, he holpe them much which had
beleeued through [p] grace.
28 For mightily he confuted publikely the
Iewes, with great vehemencie, shewing by the
Scriptures, that Iesus was that Christ.

p Through Gods gracious fauour, or by those excellent gifts which God had bestowed vpon him.

CHAP. XIX.

1 Certaine disciples at Ephesus, 3 hauing onely receiued Iohns baptisme, 2 and knewe not the visible giftes of the holy Ghost wherewith God had beautified his sonnes kingdome, 5 are baptized in the Name of Iesus. 13 The Iewish exorcists 16 are beaten of the deuill. 19 Coniuring bookes are burnt. 24 Demetrius 29 raiseth sedition against Paul.

And [1] it came to passe, while Apollos was
at Corinthus, that Paul when hee passed
thorow the vpper coasts, came to Ephesus, and
found certaine disciples,
2 And said vnto them, Haue yee receiued
the [a] holy Ghost since ye beleeued? And they
said vnto him, Wee haue not so much as heard
whether there be an holy Ghost.
3 [2] And hee said vnto them, Vnto [b] what
were ye then baptized? And they said, Vnto
[c] Iohns baptisme.
4 Then said Paul, * Iohn verely baptized
with the baptisme of repentance, saying vnto
the people, that they should beleeue in him
which should come after him, that is, in Christ
Iesus.
5 And when they heard it, they were baptized
in the Name of the Lord Iesus.
6 So Paul laid his hands vpon them, and
the holy Ghost came on them, and they spake
the tongues and prophecyed.
7 And all the men were about twelue.
8 ¶ Moreouer hee went into the Synagogue,
and spake boldly for the space of three
moneths, disputing & exhorting to the things
that *appertaine* to the kingdome of God.
9 [3] But when certaine were hardened, and
disobeyed, speaking euill of the [d] way *of God*
before the multitude, he departed from them,
and separated the disciples, and disputed daily
in the schoole of one [e] Tyrannus.
10 And this was done by the space of two
yeeres, so that all they which dwelt in Asia,
heard the word of the Lord Iesus, both Iewes
and Grecians.
11 And God wrought no small miracles
by the hands of Paul,
12 So that from his body were brought
vnto the sicke, kerchiefs, or handkerchiefs, and
the diseases departed from them, and the euill
spirits went out of them.
13 [4] Then certaine of the vagabond Iewes,
[f] exorcists, tooke in hand to name ouer them
which had euill spirits, the Name of the Lord
Iesus, saying, Wee adiure you by Iesus, whom
Paul preacheth.
14 (And there were certaine sons of Sceua
a Iew, the Priest, *about* seuen which did this)

1 Paul being nothing offended at the rudenesse of the Ephesians, planteth a Church amongst them.

a Those excellent giftes of the holy Ghost, which were in those dayes in the Church.

2 Iohn did only begin to instruct the disciples whom Christ should make perfite.

b In what doctrine then are you taught and instructed?

c To be baptized into Iohns baptisme, is to professe the doctrine which Iohn preached and sealed with his baptisme.

**Cha.1.5.& 2.2. and 11.16.matt. 3.11. mark.1.8. luke 3.16.iohn 1.26.*

3 For a man to separate himselfe and others from infidels which are vtterly desperate, it is not to diuide the Church, but rather to vnite it, and make it one.

d By this word, Way, the Hebrewes vnderstand any kinde of life, and here it is taken for Christianitie.

e This was a mans proper name.

4 Satan is constrained to giue witnesse against himselfe.

f So were they called which cast out deuils by coniuring them in the Name of God: and in the beginning of the Church, they which had the gift of working miracles, and laid their handes on them that were possessed with deuils, were also so called.

15 And the euill spirit answered, and said,
Iesus I acknowledge, and Paul I knowe: but
who are yee?
16 And the man in whom the euill spirit
was, ranne on them, and ouercame them, and
[g] preuailed against them, so that they fled out
of that house naked, and wounded.
17 And this was knowen to all the Iewes
and Grecians also, which dwelt at Ephesus,
and feare came on them all, and the Name of
the Lord Iesus was magnified,
18 [5] And many that beleeued, came and
[h] confessed, and shewed their workes.
19 Many of them also which vsed curious
artes, brought their bookes, and burned them
before all men: and they counted the price of
them, and found it fiftie thousand *pieces* of
siluer.
20 So the word of God grew mightily, and
preuailed.
21 ¶ [6] Now when these things were accomplished,
Paul purposed by the [k] Spirit to
passe through Macedonia and Achaia, and to
goe to Hierusalem, saying, After I haue beene
there, I must also see Rome.
22 So sent he into Macedonia two of them
that ministred vnto him, Timotheus and Erastus,
but he remained in Asia for a season.
23 [7] And the same time there arose no small
trouble about that way.
24 For a certaine man named Demetrius
a siluer smith, which made siluer [l] Temples of
Diana, brought great gaines vnto the craftesmen,
25 Whom hee called together, with the
workemen of like things, and said, Sirs, yee
know that by this craft we haue our goods:
26 Moreouer yee see and heare, that not alone
at Ephesus, but almost throughout all Asia
this Paul hath perswaded, and turned away
much people, saying, That they be not gods
which are made with hands.
27 So that not onely this thing is dangerous
vnto vs, that this our [m] portion shall bee
reproued, but also that the temple of the great
goddesse Diana should bee nothing esteemed,
and that it would come to passe that her magnificence,
which all Asia and the world worshippeth,
should be destroyed.
28 Now when they heard it, they were full
of wrath, and cryed out, saying, Great *is* Diana
of the Ephesians.
29 And the whole citie was full of confusion,
and they rushed into the common place
with one assent, and caught * Gaius, and * Aristarchus,
men of Macedonia, and Pauls companions
of his iourney.
30 And when Paul would haue entred in
vnto the people, the disciples suffered him not.
31 [8] Certaine also of the chiefe of Asia
which were his friends, sent vnto him, desiring
him that he would not present himselfe in the
Common place.

g He preuailed against them, though they stroue neuer so much.

5 Coniuring and sorcerie is condemned by open testimonie, and by the authoritie of the Apostle.

h Confessed their errours, and detested them openly, being terrified with the feare of the iudgement of God: and what is this to earshrift?

i They that make the least value of it, recken it to be about eight hundred pounds English.

6 Paul is neuer wearie.

k By the motion of Gods Spirit: therefore we may not say that Paul ranne hand ouer head to death, but as the Spirit of God led him.

7 Gaine cloked with a shewe of religion, is the verie cause wherfore idolatrie is stoutly and stubburnly defended.

l These were certaine counterfeit temples with Dianas picture in them, which they bought that worshipped her.

m As if he said, If Paul goe on thus as he hath begun, to confute the opinion which men haue of Dianas image, all this our gaine will come to nought.

**Rom.16.23. 1.cor.1.14.*

** Coloss.4.10.*

8 There ought to be in all Christians, and especially in the ministers, an inuincible constancie, which may not by any stormes or assaults be ouercome, which notwithstanding must suffer it selfe modestly to be gouerned by wisedome.

32 Some

9 Instead of reason, the idolaters are sufficiently contented with their owne madnesse & outcries, and those are the greatest defences that they haue.

10 An example of a politike man who redeemeth peace and quietnesse with lies, which Paul would neuer haue done.

n The Ephesians beleeued superstitiously, that the image of Diana came downe from heauen to them.

o Haue ought to accuse any mã of.

p For there are certaine dayes appointed for ciuill causes & matters of iudgement, and the Deputies sit.

q By the Deputies are meant also the Deputies substitutes, that is, such as did sit for them.

r He speaketh of a lawfull assembly not onely to except against the disordered hurly burly of the people, but also against all meeting and comming together which was not by order: for there were certaine dayes appointed to call people together in.

32 Some therefore cryed one thing, and
some another: for the assembly was out of order, and the more part knewe not wherefore
they were come together.
33 And *some* of the company drew foorth
Alexander, the Iewes thrusting him forwards.
Alexander then beckened with the hand, and
would haue excused the matter to the people.
34 [9]But when they knewe that hee was a
Iewe, there arose a shout almost for the space
of two houres, of all men, crying, Great *is* Diana of the Ephesians.
35 [10]Then the Towne-clarke when he had
stayed the people, sayd, Yee men of Ephesus,
what man is it that knoweth not how that the
citie of the Ephesians is a worshipper of the
great goddesse Diana, and of *the image*, which
[n]came downe from Iupiter?
36 Seeing then that no man can speake against these things, yee ought to be appeased,
and to doe nothing rashly.
37 For yee haue brought hither these men,
which haue neither committed sacriledge, neither doe blaspheme your goddesse.
38 Wherefore, if Demetrius and the craftsmen which are with him, haue a [o]matter against any man, the [p]lawe is open, and there
are [q]Deputies: let them accuse one another.
39 But if ye inquire any thing concerning
other matters, it may be determined in a [r]lawfull assembly.
40 For we are euen in ieopardie to be accused of this dayes sedition, for as much as there
is no cause, whereby we may giue a reason of
this concourse of people.
41 And when he had thus spoken, hee let
the assembly depart.

CHAP. XX.

1 Paul appointeth to goe to Macedonia: 7 In Troas preaching vntill midnight, 9 Eutychus fell downe dead out of a window, 10 he raiseth him to life: 15 At Miletum, 17 hauing called the Elders of Ephesus together, 23 hee declareth what things shall come vpon himselfe, 28 and others.

1 Paul departeth from Ephesus by the consent of the Church, not to be idle or at rest, but to take paines in another place.

a For after so great trouble, there was need of a long exhortatiõ.

2 A froward zeale is the guider and instructer to murders: and we are not debarred by the wisdome of God to preuent the endeauours of wicked men.

NOw [1]after the tumult was appeased, Paul
called the disciples vnto him, and embraced them, and departed to go into Macedonia.
2 And when hee had gone through those
parts, and had exhorted them with [a]many
words, he came into Grecia.
3 [2]And hauing taried *there* three moneths,
because the Iewes laid wait for him, as hee was
about to saile into Syria, hee purposed to returne through Macedonia.
4 And there accompanied him into Asia,
Sopater of Berea, and of them of Thessalonica,
Aristarchus, and Secundus, and Gaius of Derbe, and Timotheus, and of them of Asia, Tychicus, and Trophimus.
5 These went before, and taried vs at
Troas.
6 And we sailed foorth from Philippi, after the dayes of vnleauened bread, and came
vnto them to Troas in fiue dayes, where we abode seuen dayes.
7 [3]And the [b]first day of the weeke, the
disciples being come together to breake bread,
Paul preached vnto them, ready to depart on
the morow, and continued the preaching vnto
midnight.
8 [4]And there were many lights in an vpper chamber, where they were gathered together.
9 And there sate in a window a certaine
yong man named Eutychus, fallen into a dead
sleepe: and as Paul was long preaching, hee
ouercome with sleepe, fell downe from the
third loft, and was taken vp dead.
10 But Paul went downe, and laid himselfe
vpon him, and embraced him, saying, Trouble
not your selues: for his life is in him.
11 Then when *Paul* was come vp againe,
and had broken bread, and eaten, hauing spoken a long while till the dawning of the day,
he so departed.
12 And they brought the boy aliue, and
they were not a little comforted.
13 ¶ Then we went before to ship, and sailed vnto *the citie* Assos, that we might receiue
Paul there: for so had he appointed, and would
himselfe goe afoote.
14 Now when he was come vnto vs to Assos, and we had receiued him, we came to Mitylenes.
15 And we sailed thence, and came the next
day ouer against Chios, and the next day wee
arriued at Samos, and taried at Trogyllium:
the next day we came to Miletum.
16 [5]For Paul had determined to saile by Ephesus, because hee would not spend the time
in Asia: for he hasted to be, if he could possible,
at Hierusalem at the day of Pentecost.
17 ¶ Wherefore from [c]Miletum, hee sent
to Ephesus, & called the Elders of the Church.
18 [6]Who when they were come to him, he
said vnto them, Yee knowe from the first day
that I came into Asia, after what manner I haue
beene with you at all seasons,
19 Seruing the Lorde with all modestie,
and with many teares, and tentations, which
came vnto me by the layings awaite of the
Iewes,
20 And how I kept [d]backe nothing that
was profitable, but haue shewed you, & taught
you openly and throughout euery house,
21 Witnessing both to the Iewes, and to
the Grecians the repentance toward God, and
faith toward our Lord Iesus Christ.
22 [7]And now behold, I goe [e]bound in the
Spirit vnto Hierusalem, and know not what
things shall come vnto me there,
23 Saue that the holy Ghost witnesseth in
euery citie, saying, that bonds and afflictions
abide me.
24 But I passe not at all, neither is my life
deare vnto my selfe, so that I may fulfill my
course

3 Assemblies in the night time cannot be iustly condemned, neither ought, whẽ the cause is good.

b Word for word, the first day of the Sabbath, that is, vpon the Lords day: so that by this place, and by 1.Cor.16.2. it is not amisse gathered, that in those dayes the Christians were woont to assemble themselues solemnly together vpon that day.

4 The deuill minding to trouble the Church with a great offence, giueth Paul a singular occasion to confirme the Gospel.

5 Paul an earnest and diligent follower of Christ, making haste to his bonds without any ceasing or stopping in his race, doeth first of all as it were make his testament, wherein he giueth an account of his former life, defendeth the doctrine which he taught, and exhorteth the Pastors of the Church to perseuere and goe forward with continuance in their office.

c According as the situation of these places is set forth, that distance betweene Ephesus and Miletum, was about 400. furlongs, which maketh almost fiftie dutch miles.

6 A liuely image of a true Pastor.

d I refrained not to speake, neither dissembled in any respect whatsoeuer, either for feare or lucres sake.

7 He testifieth that he goeth to his bonds by the commandement of God.

e He calleth that motion of the holy Ghost, which inforced him to take his iourney to Hierusalem, the bond of the Spirit, whom he followed with all his heart.

course with ioy, and the ministration which I
haue receiued of the Lord Iesus, to testifie the
Gospel of the grace of God.
25 And now behold, I know that hencefoorth ye all, through whom I haue gone preaching the kingdome of God, shall see my face
no more.
26 Wherfore I take you to record this day,
that I am [f] pure from the blood of all men.
27 [8] For I haue kept nothing backe, but
haue shewed you all the counsell of God.
28 Take heede therefore vnto your selues,
and all the flocke, whereof the holy Ghost hath
made you ouerseers, to [g] feede the Church of
God, which [h] hee hath purchased with [i] that
his owne blood.
29 [9] For I know this, that after my departing shal grieuous wolues enter in among you,
not sparing the flocke.
30 Moreouer of your owne selues shall
men arise speaking peruerse things, to [k] draw
disciples after them.
31 Therefore watch, and remember, that
by *the space* of three yeres I ceased not to warne
euery one, both night and day with teares.
32 [10] And now brethren, I commend you
to God, and to the word of his grace, which is
able to build further, and to giue you an [l] inheritance among all them, which are sanctified.
33 [11] I haue coueted no mans siluer, nor
golde, nor apparell.
34 Yea, ye know that these hands haue ministred vnto my * necessities, and to them that
were with me.
35 I haue shewed you all things, how that
so labouring, ye ought [m] to support the weake,
and to remember the words of the Lord Iesus,
how that hee said, It is a blessed thing to giue,
rather then to receiue.
36 And when he had thus spoken, he kneeled downe, and prayed with them all.
37 [12] Then they wept all abundantly, and
fell on Pauls necke, and kissed him,
38 Being chiefly sory for the words which
hee spake, That they should see his face no
more. And they accompanied him vnto the
shippe.

f If you doe perish, yet there shall be no fault in me, Looke chap.18.6.
8 The doctrine of the Apostles is most perfite and absolute.
g To keepe it, to feede and gouerne it.
h A notable sentence for Christs Godhead: which sheweth plainely in his person, how that by reason of the ioyning together of the two natures in his owne person, that which is proper to one is spoken of the other, being taken in the deriuatiue, and not in the primatiue: which in old time the godly fathers tearmed, a communicating or fellowship of proprieties, that is to say, a making common of that to two, which belongeth but to one.
i This word, That, sheweth the excellencie of this blood.
9 A prophecie of pastours that should straightway degenerate into wolues, against such as boast and brag onely of a succession of persons.
k This is great miserie, to want the presence of such a shepheard, but greater to haue wolues enter in.
10 The power of God, and his free promises reueiled in his word, are the props and vpholders of the ministerie of the Gospel.
l As children, and therefore of free loue and good will.
11 Pastors must before all things beware of couetousnesse. * *1.Cor.4.13. 1.thess.2.9. 2.thess.3.8.*
m As it were by reaching out the hand to them, which otherwise are about to slippe and fall away, and so to stay them. 12 The Gospel doeth not take away naturall affections, but ruleth and bridleth them in good order.

CHAP. XXI.

1 Paul goeth toward Hierusalem: 8 at Cesarea he talketh with Philip the Euangelist. 10 Agabus foretelleth him of his bonds. 17 After he came to Hierusalem, 26 and into the Temple, 27 the Iewes laide handes on him: 32 Lysias the captaine taketh him from them.

AND [1] as we lanched forth, and were departed from them, wee came with a straight
course vnto Coos, and the day following vnto
the Rhodes, and from thence vnto Patara.
2 And wee found a shippe that went ouer
vnto Phenice, and went aboard, and set foorth.
3 And when wee had discouered Cyprus,
wee left it on the left hand, and sailed toward
Syria, and arriued at Tyrus: for there the ship
vnladed the burden.
4 And when we had found disciples, wee
taried there seuen dayes. And they tolde Paul
through the [a] Spirit, that he should not goe vp
to Hierusalem.
5 But when the dayes were ended, wee
departed and went our way, and they all accompanied vs with *their* wiues and children,
euen out of the citie: and wee kneeling downe
on the shore, prayed.
6 Then when we had embraced one another, we tooke ship, and they returned home.
7 And when we had ended the course from
Tyrus, wee arriued at Ptolemais, and saluted
the brethren, and abode with them one day.
8 And the next day, Paul and we that were
with him, departed, and came vnto Cesarea:
and wee entred into the house of * Philip the
Euangelist, which was one of the [b] seuen *Deacons*, and abode with him.
9 Now hee had foure daughters virgines,
which did [c] prophecie.
10 And as wee taried there many dayes,
there came a certaine Prophet from Iudea, named Agabus.
11 And when he was come vnto vs, he tooke
Pauls girdle, and bound his owne handes and
feete, and said, Thus sayth the holy Ghost, So
shall the Iewes at Hierusalem binde the man
that oweth this girdle, and shall deliuer him
into the hands of the Gentiles.
12 And when wee had heard these things,
both we and other of the same place besought
him that he would not goe vp to Hierusalem.
13 Then Paul answered, and said, What
doe ye weeping and breaking mine heart? For
I am readie not to bee bound onely, but also
to die at Hierusalem for the Name of the Lord
Iesus.
14 [2] So when hee would not be perswaded,
we ceased, saying, The wil of the Lord be done.
15 And after those dayes we trussed vp our
fardels, and went vp to Hierusalem.
16 There went with vs also *certaine* of the
disciples of Cesarea, and brought with them
one Mnason of Cyprus, an olde disciple, with
whom we should lodge.
17 And when wee were come to Hierusalem, the brethren receiued vs gladly.
18 And the next day Paul went in with vs
vnto Iames: and all the Elders were there assembled.
19 [3] And when he had embraced them, he
told by order all things, that God had wrought
among the Gentiles by his ministration.
20 [4] So when they heard it, they glorified
God, and said vnto him, Thou seest, brother,
how many thousand Iewes there are which beleeue, and they are all zealous of the Law:

1 Not onely men simply, but euen our friends, and such as are endued with the Spirit of God, doe sometimes goe about to hinder the course of our vocation: but it is our part to goe forward without all stopping or staggering, after that we are sure of our calling from God.
a They foretolde through the Spirit what dangers hanged ouer Pauls head: and this they did as Prophets: but of a fleshly affection they frayed him from going to Hierusalem.
* *Chap.6.5.*
b He speaketh of the seuen Deacons which he mentioned before, Chap.6.
c They had a peculiar gift of foretelling things to come.
2 The will of God bridleth all affections in them which earnestly seeke the glory of God.
3 God is to be praised, who is the Authour of all good sayings and deeds.
4 In things indifferent (of which sort were not the traditions of the Pharises, but the ceremonies of the Law, vntill such time as Christian libertie was more fully reueiled to the Iewes) charitie willeth vs to conforme or apply our selues willingly so farre as wee may, to our brethren which doe not stubburnly and maliciously resist the trueth, but are not throughly instructed, especially if the question be of a whole multitude.

21 Now they are informed of thee, that thou teachest all the Iewes, which are among the Gentiles, to forsake Moses, and sayest that they ought not to circumcise their sonnes, neither to liue *after* the customes.

22 What is then *to be done?* the multitude must needs come together : for they shal heare that thou art come.

23 Doe therefore this that wee say to thee. We haue foure men, which haue made a vow,

24 Them take, and [d] purifie thy selfe with them, and [e] contribute with them, that they may * shaue their heads : & all shall know, that those things, whereof they haue been informed concerning thee, are nothing, but that thou thy selfe also walkest and keepest the Law.

d That is, consecrate thy selfe : for hee speaketh not here of the vncleane, but of such as be subiect to the vow of the Nazarites.

e That it may be knowen, that thou wast not onely present at the vow, but also a chiefe man in it : and therefore it is said afterwards, that Paul declared the dayes of purification : for although the charges for the Nazarites offerings were appointed, yet they might adde somewhat vnto them, Num.6.21.

** Chap.18.18. numb.6.18.*

25 For as touching the Gentiles, which beleeue, we haue written, and determined that they obserue no such thing, but that they keep themselues from things offered to idoles, and from blood, and from that that is strangled, and from fornication.

26 Then Paul tooke the men, and the next day was purified with them, and entred into the Temple, [f] declaring the accomplishment of the dayes of the purification, vntill that an offring should be offered for euery one of them.

f The Priests were to be aduertised of the accomplishment of the dayes of the purification, because there were sacrifices to be offered the same day, that their vow was ended.

27 [5] And when the seuen dayes were almost ended, the Iewes which were of Asia (when they sawe him in the Temple) mooued all the people, and laid hands on him,

5 A preposterous zeale is the cause of great confusion, and great mischiefes.

28 Crying, Men of Israel, helpe : this is the man that teacheth all men euery where against the people, and the Law, and this place : moreouer, he hath brought Grecians into the Temple, and hath polluted this holy place.

29 For they had seene before Trophimus an Ephesian with him in the citie, whome they supposed that Paul had brought into the Temple.

30 Then all the citie was mooued, and the people ranne together : and they tooke Paul, and drew him out of the Temple, and foorthwith the doores were shut.

31 [6] But as they went about to kill him, tidings came vnto the chiefe captaine of the band, that all Hierusalem was on an vproare.

6 God findeth some euen amongst the wicked and profane themselues, to hinder the endeuours of the rest.

32 Who immediatly tooke souldiers and Centurions, and ranne downe vnto them : and when they sawe the chiefe captaine and the souldiers, they left beating of Paul.

33 Then the chiefe captaine came neere and tooke him, and commanded him to bee bound with two chaines, and demanded who he was, and what he had done.

34 And one cryed this, another that, among the people. So when hee could not know the certaintie for the tumult, he commanded him to be led into the castle.

35 And when he came vnto the grieces, it was so that he was borne of the souldiers, for the violence of the people.

36 For the multitude of the people followed after, crying, Away with him.

37 And as Paul should haue beene led into the castle, he said vnto the chiefe captaine, May I speake vnto thee? Who said, Canst thou *speake* Greeke?

38 Art not thou the [g] Egyptian who before these dayes raised a sedition, and led out into the wildernesse foure thousand men that were murtherers?

g Touching this Egyptian which assembled thirtie thousand men, reade Ioseph.booke 2.chap.12.

39 Then Paul said, Doubtlesse, I am a man which am a Iewe, and citizen of Tarsus, a famous citie in Cilicia, and I beseech thee, suffer me to speake vnto the people.

40 And when hee had giuen him licence, Paul stood on the grieces, and beckened with the hand vnto the people : and when there was made great silence, hee spake vnto them in the Hebrew tongue, saying,

CHAP. XXII.

1 Paul yeeldeth a reason of his faith, 22 and the Iewes heare him a while. 32 But so soone as they cryed out, 24 hee is commanded to be scourged and examined, 27 and so declareth that he is a citizen of Rome.

YE men, brethren and fathers, heare my defence now towards you.

2 (And when they heard that he spake in the Hebrew tongue to them, they kept the more silence, and he said)

3 [1] I am verely a man, *which am* a Iewe, borne in Tarsus in Cilicia, but brought vp in this citie at the [a] feete of Gamaliel, and instructed according to the perfect manner of the Lawe of the Fathers, and was zealous toward God, as ye all are this day.

1 Paul making a short declaration of his former life, prooueth both his vocation and doctrine to be of God.

a That is, his daily hearer : the reason of this speech is this, for that they which teach, sit commonly in the higher place, speaking to their schollars which sit vpon fourmes beneath : and therefore he sayth, at the feete of Gamaliel.

4 And I persecuted this way vnto the death, binding and deliuering into prison both men and women.

5 As also the chiefe Priest doeth beare me witnesse, and all the companie of the Elders, of whom also I receiued letters vnto the brethren, and went to Damascus to bring them which were there, bound vnto Hierusalem, that they might be punished.

6 ¶ And so it was, as I iourneyed and was come neere vnto Damascus about noone, that suddenly there shone from heauen a great light round about me.

7 So I fell vnto the earth, and heard a voice, saying vnto mee, Saul, Saul, why persecutest thou me?

8 Then I answered, Who art thou, Lord? And hee said to me, I am Iesus of Nazareth, whom thou persecutest.

9 Moreouer they that were with me, saw in deed a light and were afraid : but they heard not the voice of him that spake vnto me.

10 Then I said, What shall I doe, Lord? And the Lord said vnto me, Arise, and goe into Damascus : and there it shall be tolde thee of all things, which are appointed for thee to doe.

11 So when I could not see for the glory of that light, I was led by the hand of them that were with me, and came into Damascus.

12 And

12 And one Ananias a godly man, as perteining to the Law, hauing good report of all
the Iewes which dwelt there,
13 Came vnto me, and stood, and said vnto
me, Brother Saul, receiue thy sight: and that
same houre I looked vpon him.
14 And hee said, The God of our fathers
hath appointed thee, that thou shouldest know
his will, and shouldest see that Iust one, and
shouldest heare the voice of his mouth.
15 For thou shalt be his witnesse vnto all
men, of the things which thou hast seene and
heard.
16 Now therefore why tariest thou? Arise,
and be baptized, and wash away thy sinnes, in
calling on the Name of the Lord.
17 ¶ And it came to passe, that when I was
come againe to Hierusalem, and prayed in the
Temple, I was in a trance,
18 And saw him saying vnto mee, Make
haste, and get thee quickly out of Hierusalem:
for they will not receiue thy witnesse concerning me.
19 Then I said, Lord, they know that I pri-
soned, and beat in euery Synagogue them that
beleeued in thee.
20 And when the blood of thy martyr
Steuen was shed, I also stood by, and consented vnto his death, and kept the clothes of
them that [b] slewe him.
21 Then hee said vnto mee, Depart: for I
will send thee farre hence vnto the Gentiles.
22 ¶ [2] And they heard him vnto this word,
but then they lift vp their voices, and said, A-
way with such a fellow from the earth: for it is
not meet that he should liue.
23 And as they [c] cryed and cast off their
clothes, and threw dust into the aire,
24 [3] The chiefe captaine commanded him
to be led into the castle, and bade that he should
be scourged & examined, that he might know
wherefore they cryed so on him.
25 [4] And as they bound him with thongs,
Paul said vnto the Centurion that stood by, Is
it lawfull for you to scourge one that is a Romane, and not condemned?
26 Now when the Centurion heard it, hee
went and tolde the chiefe captaine, saying,
Take heede what thou doest: for this man is a
Romane.
27 Then the chiefe captaine came, and said
to him, Tell me, art thou a Romane? And he
said, Yea.
28 And the chiefe captaine answered, With
a great summe obtained I this freedome. Then
Paul said, But I was so borne.
29 Then straightway they departed from
him, which should haue examined him: and
the chiefe captaine also was afraid, after hee
knewe that hee was [d] a Romane, and that he
had bound him.
30 On the next day, because he would haue
knowen the certaintie wherefore he was accused of the Iewes, he loosed him from *his* bonds,
and commanded the high Priests and all their
Councill to come *together*: and hee brought
Paul, and set him before them.

b This is properly spoken: for Steuen was murdered of a sort of cut-throats, not by order of iustice, but by open force: for at that time the Iewes could not put any man to death by Law.

2 Stout and stubborne pride will neither it selfe embrace the trueth, neither suffer other to receiue it.

c The description of a seditious hurly burly, and of an harebrained and mad multitude.

3 The wisdome of the flesh doth not consider what is iust, but what is profitable, and therewithall measure the profite, according as it appeareth presently.

4 There is no cause why we may not vse those lawfull meanes which God giueth vs, to repell, or put away an iniury.

d Not by nation, but by the law of the citie.

CHAP. XXIII.

1 *As Paul pleadeth his cause,* 2 *Ananias commaundeth them to smite him.* 7 *Dissention among his accusers.* 11 *God encourageth him.* 14 *The Iewes laying waite for Paul* 20 *is declared to the chiefe captaine:* 27 *He sendeth him to Felix the Gouernour.*

AND [1] Paul beheld earnestly the Council,
and said, Men *and* brethren, I haue in all
good conscience serued God vntill this day.
2 [2] Then the hie Priest Ananias commanded them that stood by, to smite him on the
mouth.
3 [3] Then said Paul to him, God [a] will smite
thee, thou [b] whited wall: for thou sittest to
iudge me according to the Lawe, and [c] transgressing the Lawe, commandest thou me to be
smitten?
4 And they that stood by, said, Reuilest
thou Gods hie Priest?
5 [4] Then said Paul, I knewe not brethren,
that hee was the high Priest: for it is written,
* Thou shalt not speake euill of the ruler of thy
people.
6 [5] But when Paul perceiued that the one
part were of the Sadduces, and the other of the
Pharises, hee [c] cryed in the Councill, Men *and*
brethren, * I am a Pharise, the sonne of a Pharise: I am accused of the hope and resurrection
of the dead.
7 [6] And when he had said this, there was a
dissension betweene the Pharises and the Sadduces, so that the multitude was diuided.
8 [7] * For the Sadduces say that there is no
resurrection, neither [d] Angel, nor spirit: but
the Pharises confesse both.
9 [8] Then there was a great crie: and the
[e] Scribes of the Pharises part rose vp, & stroue,
saying, Wee finde none euill in this man: but
if a Spirit or an Angel hath spoken vnto him,
let vs not fight against God.
10 [9] And when there was a great dissension,
the chiefe captaine, fearing lest Paul should
haue been pulled in pieces of them, commanded the souldiers to goe downe, and take him
from among them, and to bring him into the
castle.
11 Now the night following, the Lord
stood by him, & said, Be of good courage, Paul:
for as thou hast testified of me in Hierusalem,
so must thou beare witnesse also at Rome.
12 [10] And when the day was come, certaine of the Iewes made an assembly, & bound
themselues [f] with a curse, saying, that they

1 Paul, against the false accusations of his enemies, setteth a good conscience, for proofe whereof, he repeateth the whole course of his life.

2 Hypocrites are constrained at length to betray themselues by their intemperancie.

3 It is lawfull for vs to complaine of iniuries, and to summon the wicked to the iudgment seat of God, so that we doe it without hatred, and with a quiet and peaceable minde.

a It appeareth plainely by the Greeke phrase, that Paul did not curse the high Priest, but onely pronounce the punishment of God against him.

b This is a vehement and sharpe speech, but yet not reprochfull: For the godly may speake roundly, and yet be void of the bitter affection of a sharpe and angry minde.

c For the Lawe commandeth the Iudge to heare the person that is accused patiently, and to pronounce the sentence aduisedly.

4 Wee must willingly and from the heart giue honour to Magistrates, although they be tyrants.

* *Exod. 22.17.*

5 We may lawfully sometimes set the wicked together by the eares, that they may leaue off to assault vs, so that it be with no hinderance of the trueth.

* *Chap. 24.22.* * *phil. 3.5.*

6 The concord of the wicked is weake, although they conspire together to oppresse the trueth. 7 It is an old heresie of the Sadduces, to denie the substance of Angels and soules, and therewithall the resurrection of the dead. * *Matt. 22.23.* *d Natures that want bodies.* 8 The Lord when it pleaseth him, findeth defenders of his cause, euen amongst his enemies. *c The Scribes office was a publike office, and the name of the Pharises, was the name of a sect.* 9 God will not forsake his to the ende. 10 Such as are caried away with a foolish zeale, thinke that they may lie & murder, and do whatsoeuer mischiefe they list. *f They cursing & banning themselues, promised,*

would neither eate nor drinke, till they had killed Paul.

13 And they were more then fortie, which had made this conſpiracie.

14 And they came to the chiefe Prieſts and Elders, and ſaid, Wee haue bound our ſelues with a ſolemne curſe, that we will eat nothing, vntill we haue ſlaine Paul.

15 Now therefore, yee and the [g] Councill ſignifie to the chiefe captaine, that hee bring him foorth vnto you to morow, as though you would knowe ſome thing more perfectly of him, and we, or euer he come neere, will be readie to kill him.

g Ye and the Senate requiring the ſame to be done, leſt that the Tribune ſhould thinke that it was demanded of him at ſome priuate mans ſute.

16 But when Pauls ſiſters ſonne heard of their laying a wait, he went, and entred into the caſtle, and tolde Paul.

17 [11] And Paul called one of the Centurions vnto him, and ſaid, Take this young man hence vnto the chiefe captaine: for hee hath a certaine thing to ſhew him.

11 The wiſdome of the Spirit muſt be ioyned with ſimplicitie.

18 So hee tooke him, and brought him to the chiefe captaine, and ſaid, Paul the priſoner called mee vnto him, and prayed mee to bring this young man vnto thee, which hath ſome thing to ſay vnto thee.

19 Then the chiefe captaine tooke him by the hand, and went apart with him alone, and asked him, What haſt thou to ſhew me?

20 And he ſaid, The Iewes haue conſpired to deſire thee, that thou wouldeſt bring foorth Paul to morow into the Councill, as though they would inquire ſomewhat of him more perfectly:

21 But let them not perſwade thee: for there lie in waite for him of them, more then fortie men, which haue bound themſelues with a curſe, that they will neither eate nor drinke, till they haue killed him: and now are they readie, and waite for thy promiſe.

22 [12] The chiefe captaine then let the yong man depart, after hee had charged him to vtter it to no man, that hee had || ſhewed him theſe things.

12 There is no counſell againſt the Lord and his ſeruants.
|| Greeke, that thou haſt ſhewed theſe things to me.

23 And hee called vnto him two certaine Centurions, ſaying, Make ready two hundred ſouldiers, that they may goe to Ceſarea, and horſemen threeſcore and tenne, and two hundred with dartes, at the third houre of the night.

24 And let them make readie an horſe, that Paul being ſet on, may bee brought ſafe vnto Felix the Gouernour.

25 And he wrote an Epiſtle in this maner:

26 [13] Claudius Lyſias vnto the moſt noble Gouernour Felix ſendeth greeting.

13 Lyſias is ſuddenly made by the Lord, Pauls patrone.

27 As this man was taken of the Iewes, and ſhould haue beene killed of them, I came vpon them with the gariſon, and reſcued him, perceiuing that he was a Romane.

28 And when I would haue knowen the cauſe, wherefore they accuſed him, I brought him foorth into their Councill.

29 *There* I perceiued that hee was accuſed of queſtions of their Law, but had no crime worthy of death, or of bonds.

30 And when it was ſhewed me, how that the Iewes laide waite for the man, I ſent *him* ſtraightway to thee, and commaunded his accuſers to ſpeake before thee the things that they had againſt him. Farewell.

31 Then the ſouldiers as it was commanded them, tooke Paul, & brought him by night to Antipatris.

32 And the next day, they left the horſemen to goe with him, and returned vnto the caſtle.

33 Now when they came to Ceſarea, they deliuered the Epiſtle to the Gouernour, and preſented Paul alſo vnto him.

34 So when the Gouernour had read it, he asked of what prouince he was: and when he vnderſtood that he was of Cilicia,

35 I will heare thee, ſaid hee, when thine accuſers alſo are come, and commanded him to be kept in Herods iudgement hall.

CHAP. XXIIII.

2 Tertullus accuſeth Paul: 10 He anſwereth for himſelfe. 21 Hee preacheth Chriſt to the Gouernour and his wife. 27 Felix hopeth, but in vaine, to receiue a bribe, 28 who going from his office, leaueth Paul in priſon.

NOw [1] after fiue dayes, Ananias the high Prieſt came downe with the Elders, and *with* Tertullus a certaine oratour, which appeared before the Gouernour againſt Paul.

1 Hypocrites, when they can not doe what they would doe by force and deceit, at length they goe about to compaſſe it by a ſhew of Lawe.

2 And when he was called foorth, Tertullus began to accuſe *him*, ſaying, Seeing that wee haue obtained great quietneſſe [a] through thee, and that many [b] worthy things are done vnto this nation through thy prouidence,

3 Wee acknowledge it wholly, and in all places moſt noble Felix, with all thankes.

4 But that I bee not tedious vnto thee, I pray thee, that thou wouldeſt heare vs of thy curteſie a fewe words.

5 Certainely wee haue found this man a [c] peſtilent fellow, and a moouer of ſedition among all the Iewes throughout the world, and a [d] chiefe maintainer of the ſect of the [e] Nazarites:

6 And hath gone about to pollute the temple: therefore wee tooke him, and would haue iudged him according to our Law:

7 But the chiefe captaine Lyſias came vpon vs, and with great violence tooke him out of our hands,

8 Commanding his accuſers to come to thee: of whom thou mayeſt (if thou wilt enquire) know all theſe things whereof wee accuſe him.

9 And the Iewes likewiſe [f] affirmed, ſaying that it was ſo.

10 [2] Then Paul, after that the Gouernour had beckened vnto him that he ſhould ſpeake,

a Pelix ruled that prouince with great crueltie and couetouſneſſe, and yet Ioſephus recordeth that he did many worthy things, as that hee tooke Eleazar the captaine of certaine cut-throats, and put that deceiuing wretch the Egyptian to flight, which cauſed great troubles in Iudea.

b Hee vſeth a word which the Stoikes defined to be a perfite duety and behauiour.

c Word for word, a plague.

d As you would ſay, a ringleader, or enſigne bearer.

e So they called the Chriſtians, ſcoffingly, of the townes name where they thought that Chriſt was borne, whereupon it came, that Iulian the Apoſtate called him Galilean.

f Confirmed Tertullus his ſaying. 2 Tertullus by the deuils rhetorique beginning with flatterie, maketh an end with lies: but Paul vſing heauenly eloquence, and but a ſimple beginning, caſteth off from himſelfe the crime of ſedition, wherewith hee was burdened, with a ſimple deniall.

anſwered,

answered, I doe the more gladly answere for
my selfe, for as much as I knowe that thou
hast beene of [g] many yeeres a Iudge vnto this
nation,
11 Seeing that thou mayest knowe, that
there are but twelue dayes since I came vp to
worship in Hierusalem.
12 And they neither found me in the Temple disputing with any man, neither making
vproare among the people, neither in the Synagogues, nor in the citie.
13 Neither can they [h] prooue the things,
whereof they now accuse me.
14 [3] But this I confesse vnto thee, that after the way (which they call [i] heresie) so worship I the God of my Fathers, beleeuing all
things which are written in the Lawe and the
Prophets,
15 And haue hope towards God, that the
resurrection of the dead, which they themselues looke for also, shall be both of iust and
vniust.
16 And herein I endeuour my selfe to haue
alway a cleare conscience toward God and toward men.
17 * Now after many yeeres, I came and
brought almes to my nation and offerings.
18 At [k] what time, certaine Iewes of [l] Asia
found me purified in the Temple, neither with
multitude, nor yet with tumult.
19 Who ought to haue been present before
thee, & accuse *me*, if they had ought against me.
20 Or let these themselues say, if they haue
found any vniust thing in me, while I stood in
the [m] Councill,
21 Except *it be* for this one voice, that I
cried standing among them, Of the resurrection of the dead am I accused of you this day.
22 [5] Now when Felix heard these things,
he deferred them, and said, When I shall more
[n] perfectly knowe the things which concerne
this way, by the comming of Lysias the chiefe
captaine, I will decide your matter.
23 [6] Then hee commanded a Centurion to
keepe Paul, and that hee should haue ease, and
that he should forbid none of his acquaintance
to minister vnto him, or to come vnto him.
24 ¶ And after certaine dayes, came Felix
with his wife [o] Drusilla, which was a Iewesse,
and he called foorth Paul, and heard him of the
faith in Christ.
25 And as hee disputed of righteousnesse
and temperance, & of the iudgement to come,
Felix trembled, and answered, Goe thy way for
this time, and when I haue conuenient time, I
will call for thee.
26 He hoped also that money should haue
beene giuen him of Paul, that he might loose
him: wherefore hee sent for him the oftener,
and communed with him.

g Paul pleaded his cause two yeres before Felix departed out of the prouince, Chap. 27. but he had gouerned Trachonite, and Batauea, and Galaunite, before that Claudius made him gouernour of Iudea: Iosephus in the historie of the Iewes warre, lib 2. cap. 11.
h They cannot lay foorth before thee, and prooue by good reason.
3 Paul goeth in the case of religion, from a state coniecturall to a state of qualitie, not onely not denying that religion which was obiected against him, but also prouing it to be true, to be heauenly and from God, and to be the oldest of all religions.
i Here this word, Heresie, or Sect, is taken in good part.
4 Paul in conclusion telleth the thing which was done truely, which Tertullus had before diuers wayes corrupted.
k And while I was busie about those things.
l Hereby it appeareth that these of Asia were Paul his enemies, and those that stirred vp the people against him.
m Whither the Tribune brought me.
5 The Iudge suspendeth his sentence, because the matter is doubtfull.
n Felix could not iudge whether hee had done wickedly in the matters of his religion or no, vntill hee had better vnderstanding of that way which Paul professed: and as for other matters touching the sedition, hee thinketh good to deferre it till he heare Lysias, and therefore he gaue Paul somewhat more libertie.
6 God is a most faithfull keeper of his seruants, and the force of the trueth is wonderfull, euen amongst men which are otherwise profane.
o This Drusilla was Agrippa his sister, of whom Luke speaketh afterward, a very harlot and licentious woman, and being the wife of Azizus king of the Emesens, who was circumcised, departed from him, and went to this Felix the brother of one Pallas, who was sometime Nero his bondman.

27 [7] When two yeeres were expired, Por-
cius Festus came into Felix roume: and *Felix*
willing to [p] get fauour of the Iewes, left Paul
bound.

7 In a naughtie minde, that is guiltie to it selfe, although sometime there be some shewe of equitie, yet by and by it will be extinguished: but in the meane season we haue neede of patience, and that continually.
p For whereas he had behaued himselfe very wickedly in the prouince, had it not beene for fauour of his brother Pallas, he should haue died for it: so that we may gather hereby, why he would haue pleasured the Iewes.

CHAP. XXV.

1 Festus succeeding Felix, 6 commaundeth Paul to bee brought foorth. 11 Paul appealeth vnto Cesar. 14 Festus openeth Pauls matter to king Agrippa, 23 and bringeth him before him, 27 that hee may vnderstand his cause.

WHen [1] Festus was then come into the
Prouince, after three dayes he went
vp from Cesarea, vnto Hierusalem.
2 Then the high Priest, and the chiefe of
the Iewes appeared before him against Paul:
and they besought him,
3 And desired fauour against him, that he
would send for him to Hierusalem: and they
laid wait to kill him by the way.
4 But Festus answered, that Paul should
be kept at Cesarea, and that he himselfe would
shortly depart *thither*.
5 Let them therefore, said hee, which a-
mong you are able, come downe with vs: and
if there be any wickednesse in the man, let them
accuse him.
6 ¶ [2] Nowe when hee had taried among
them no more then ten dayes, he went downe
to Cesarea, and the next day sate in the iudgement seate, & commanded Paul to be brought.
7 And when hee was come, the Iewes
which were come from Hierusalem, stood a-
bout him, and laid many and grieuous complaints against Paul, whereof [a] they could make
no plaine proofe,
8 Forasmuch as he answered, that hee had
neither offended any thing against the lawe of
the Iewes, neither against the temple, nor a-
gainst Cesar.
9 [3] Yet Festus willing to get fauour of the
Iewes, answered Paul and said, Wilt thou goe
vp to Hierusalem, and there be iudged of these
things before me?
10 Then said Paul, I stand at Cesars iudgement seate, where I ought to be iudged: to the
Iewes I haue done no wrong, as thou very
well knowest.
11 For if I haue done wrong, or committed any thing worthy of death, I refuse not to
die: but if there be none of these things wherof they accuse me, no man, to pleasure them,
can deliuer me to them: I appeale vnto Cesar.
12 Then when Festus had spoken with the
Councill, hee answered, Hast thou appealed
vnto Cesar? vnto Cesar shalt thou goe.
13 ¶ [4] And after certaine dayes, King [b] A-
grippa and Bernice came downe to Cesarea to
salute Festus.
14 And when they had remained there many dayes, Festus declared Pauls cause vnto
the

1 Satans ministers are subtill and diligent in seeking all occasions: but God who watcheth for his, hindreth all their counsels easily.
2 We may repell an iniurie iustly, but not with iniurie.
a They could not prooue them certainly and with vndoubted reasons.
3 God doth not onely turne away the counsell of the wicked, but also turneth it vpon their owne heads.
4 Festus, thinking no such thing, euen before kings, bringing to light the wickednesse of the Iewes, and Pauls innocencie, doth maruelously confirme the Church of God.
b This Agrippa was Agrippa his sonne, whose death Luke spake of before, and Bernice was his sister.

the King, saying, There is a certaine man left
in prison by Felix.
15 Of whom when I came to Hierusalem,
the high Priestes and Elders of the Iewes informed me, and desired to haue iudgement a-
gainst him.
16 To whom I answered, that it is not the
manner of the Romanes for fauour to [c] deliuer
any man to the death, before that he which is
accused, haue the accusers before him, and
haue place to defend himselfe, concerning
the crime.

c The Romanes vse not to deliuer any man to be punished before, &c.

17 Therefore when they were come hither,
without delay the day following I sate on the
iudgement seate, and commanded the man to
be brought foorth.
18 Against whom when the accusers stood
vp, they brought no crime of such things as I
supposed:
19 [5] But had certaine questions against him
of their owne [d] superstition, and of one Iesus
which was dead, whome Paul affirmed to be
aliue.
20 And because I doubted of such maner
of question, I asked him whether hee would
goe to Hierusalem, and there bee iudged of
these things.
21 But because he appealed to be reserued
to the examination of Augustus, I commanded him to bee kept, till I might send him to
Cesar.
22 [6] Then Agrippa said vnto Festus, I would
also heare the man my selfe. To morow, said
he, thou shalt heare him.
23 And on the morow when Agrippa was
come and Bernice with great [e] pompe, and
were entred into the Common hall with the
chiefe captaines and chiefe men of the citie,
at Festus commaundement Paul was brought
foorth.

5 The profane and wicked take an occasion to condemne the true doctrine, by reason of priuate controuersies and contentions of men betwixt themselues: but the truth neuerthelesse abideth in the meane season safe and sure.
d This profane man calleth the Iewish religion, superstition, and that before King Agrippa, but no marueile: for the rulers of prouinces by reason of the maiestie of the empire of Rome, vsed to preferre themselues before Kings.
6 That is fulfilled in Paul, which the Lord before had told to Ananias of him, Chap. 9. 15.
e Gorgeously like a Prince.

24 And Festus said, King Agrippa, and all
men which are present with vs, yee see this
man, about whome all the multitude of the
Iewes haue called vpon me, both at Hierusalem, and here, crying, that he ought not to liue
any longer.
25 Yet I haue found nothing worthy of
death, that he hath committed: neuerthelesse,
seeing that hee hath appealed to Augustus, I
haue determined to send him.
26 Of whome I haue no certaine thing to
write vnto my [f] lord: wherfore I haue brought
him foorth vnto you, and specially vnto thee,
King Agrippa, that after examination had, I
might haue somewhat to write:
27 For me thinketh it vnreasonable to send
a prisoner, and not to shewe the causes which
are *laid* against him.

f To Augustus. Good princes refused this name at the first, to wit, to be called Lords, but afterward they admitted it, as we read of Traiane.

CHAP. XXVI.

2 Paul in the presence of Agrippa, 4 declareth his life from his childhood, 16 and his calling, 22 with such efficacie of wordes, 28 that almost hee perswaded him to Christianitie: 30 But he and his companie depart, doing nothing in Pauls matter.

THen Agrippa said vnto Paul, Thou art
permitted to speake for thy selfe. So Paul
stretched foorth the hand, and answered for
himselfe.
2 [1] I thinke my selfe happy, king Agrippa, because I shall answere this day before
thee of all the things whereof I am accused of
the Iewes,
3 Chiefly, because thou hast knowledge
of all customs, and questions which are among
the Iewes: wherefore I beseech thee to heare
me patiently.
4 [2] As touching my life from *my* childhood, and what it was from the beginning a-
mong mine owne nation at Hierusalem, know
all the Iewes,
5 Which [a] knew me heretofore, euen from
my [b] Elders (if they would testifie) that after
the [c] most strait sect of our religion, I liued a
Pharise.
6 [3] And now I stand and am accused for
the hope of the promise made of God vnto our
fathers.
7 Whereunto our twelue tribes instantly
seruing *God* day and night, hope to come: for
the which hopes sake, O king Agrippa, I am
accused of the Iewes.
8 [4] Why should it be thought a thing incredible vnto you, that God should raise a-
gaine the dead?
9 I also verely thought in my selfe, that I
ought to doe many contrary things against the
Name of Iesus of Nazareth.
10 *Which thing I also did at Hierusalem:
for many of the Saints I shut vp in prison, hauing receiued authoritie of the high Priests,
and when they were put to death, I gaue *my*
[d] sentence.
11 And I punished them throughout all
the Synagogues, and [e] compelled them to blaspheme, and being more madde against them,
I persecuted them, euen vnto strange cities.
12 At which time, euen as I went to *Damascus with authoritie, and commission from
the hie Priests,

1 To haue a skilfull iudge, is a great and singular gift of God.
2 Paul diuideth the history of his life into two times: for the first he calleth his aduersaries witnesses: for the latter, the Fathers and Prophets.
a What I was, and where, and how I liued.
b That my parents were Pharises.
c The sect of the Pharises was the most exquisite amongst all the sects of the Iewes, for it was better then all the rest.
3 There are three chiefe and principall witnesses of true doctrine, God, the true Fathers, and the consent of the Church.
4 He prooueth the resurrection of the dead, first by the power of God, then by the resurrection of Christ, whereof he is a sufficient witnesse.
* *Chap. 8. 3.*
d I consented to and allowed of their doing: for he was not a Iudge.
e By extreme punishment.
* *Chap. 9. 2.*

13 At midday, O king, I saw in the way a
light from heauen, passing the brightnesse of
the Sunne, shine round about me, and them
which went with me.
14 So when we were all fallen to the earth,
I heard a voice speaking vnto mee, and saying
in the Hebrew tongue, Saul, Saul, why persecutest thou me? It is hard for thee to kicke a-
gainst prickes.
15 Then I said, Who art thou, Lord? And
he said, I am Iesus whom thou persecutest.
16 But rise and stand vpon thy feete: for I
haue appeared vnto thee for this purpose, to
appoint thee a Minister and a witnesse, both of
the things which thou hast seene, and of the
things in the which I will appeare vnto thee,
17 Deliuering thee from this people, and
from the Gentiles, vnto whom I now send thee,

18 [5] To

5 The ende of the Gospel is to saue them which are brought to the knowledge of Christ, and are iusti ed and sanctified in him, being laid hold on by faith.
6 Paul alledgeth God to be authour of the office of his Apostleship, and his grace, as a witnesse.
* *Chap.9.22,26. and 13.4.*

18 [5] To open their eyes, that they may
turne from darkenesse to light, and from the
power of Satan vnto God, that they may receiue forgiuenesse of sinnes, and inheritance a-
mong them, which are sanctified by faith in
me.
19 [6] Wherefore, King Agrippa, I was not
disobedient vnto the heauenly vision,
20 *But shewed first vnto them of Damascus, and at Hierusalem, and throughout all the
coasts of Iudea, and *then* to the Gentiles, that
they should repent and turne to God, and doe
works worthy amendment of life.
21 For this cause the Iewes caught me in
the * Temple, and went about to kill me.
22 [7] Neuertheles, I obteined helpe of God,
and continue vnto this day, witnessing both to
[f] small and to great, saying none other things,
then those which the Prophets and Moses did
say should come,
23 *To wit*, that Christ should [g] suffer, and
that hee should bee the [h] first that should rise
from the dead, & should shew [i] light vnto this
people, and to the Gentiles.
24 [8] And as he thus answered for himselfe,
Festus said with a loud voyce, Paul, thou art
besides thy selfe: much learning doeth make
thee mad.
25 But he saide, I am not madde, O noble
Festus, but I speake the wordes of trueth and
sobernesse.
26 For the king knoweth of these things,
before whome also I speake boldely: for I am
perswaded that none of these things are hidden from him: for this thing was not done in a
[k] corner.
27 [9] O King Agrippa, beleeuest thou the
Prophets? I know that thou beleeuest.
28 Then Agrippa saide vnto Paul, Almost
thou perswadest me to become a Christian.
29 Then Paul said, [l] I would to God that
not only thou, but also all that heare me to day,
were both almost, and altogether such as I am,
except these bonds.
30 [10] And when hee had thus spoken, the
King rose vp, and the Gouernour, and Bernice,
and they that sate with them.
31 And when they were gone apart, they
talked betweene themselues, saying, This
man doeth nothing worthy of death, nor of
bonds.
32 Then said Agrippa vnto Festus, This
man might haue bene loosed, if he had not appealed vnto Cesar.

* *Chap.21.30.*
7 Christ is the end of the Law and the Prophets.
f To euery one.
g That Christ should not be such a king as the Iewes dreamed of, but one appoynted to beare our miseries, and the punishment of our sinnes.
h The first of them, which are raised from the dead.
i Life, yea and that a most blessed life which shall be endlesse: and this is set against darkenesse, which almost in all tongues signifieth sometime death, and sometime miserie and calamitie.
8 The wisedome of God is madnesse to fooles, yet notwithstanding we must boldly auouch the trueth.
k Secretly and priuily.
9 Paul as it were forgetting himselfe that he stood a prisoner to defend his cause forgetteth not the office of his Apostleship.
l I would to God that not onely almost, but throughly and altogether, both thou and all that heare me this day, might bee made as I am, my bonds onely except.
10 Paul is solemnly quit, and yet not dismissed.

CHAP. XXVII.

1 *Paul* 7. 9 *foretelleth the perill of the voyage,* 11 *but he is not beleeued.* 14 *They are tossed to and fro with the tempest,* 22. 41 *and suffer shipwracke:* 34 *Yet all safe and sound* 44 *escape to land.*

1 Paul with many other prisoners, & through the midst of many deaths, is brought to Rome, but yet by Gods owne hand as it were, and set foorth and commended vnto the world with many singular testimonies.

NOW [1] when it was concluded, that wee
should saile into Italy, they deliuered
both Paul, and certaine other prisoners vnto a
Centurion named Iulius, of the band of Augustus.
2 And * we entred into a shippe of Adra-
myttium, purposing to saile by the coastes of
Asia, and lanched foorth, and had Aristarchus
of Macedonia, a Thessalonian, with vs.
3 And the next day we arriued at Sidon:
and Iulius courteously intreated Paul, and gaue
him libertie to goe vnto his friends, that they
might refresh him.
4 And from thence we launched, and sailed hard by Cyprus, because the windes were
contrary.
5 Then sailed we ouer the sea, by Cilicia,
and Pamphylia, and came to Myra *a citie* in
Lycia.
6 And there the Centurion found a shippe
of Alexandria, sailing into Italy, and put vs
therein.
7 And when wee had sailed slowly many
dayes, and scarce were come against Gnidum,
because the winde suffered vs not, wee sailed
hard by Candie, neere to [a] Salmone,
8 And with much adoe sailed beyond it,
and came vnto a certaine place called the Faire
hauens, neere vnto the which was the citie
Lasea.
9 [2] So when much time was spent, and sailing was now ioperdous, because also the [b] Fast
was now passed, Paul exhorted *them*,
10 And said vnto them, Sirs, I see that this
voyage will be with hurt and much damage,
not of the lading, and shippe onely, but also of
our liues.
11 [3] Neuerthelesse the Centurion beleeued
rather the gouernour and the master of the
shippe, then those things which were spoken
of Paul.
12 And because the hauen was not commodious to winter in, many tooke counsell
to depart thence, if by any meanes they might
attaine to Phenice, *there* to winter, which
is an hauen of Candie, and lieth toward the
Southwest, and by West, and Northwest and
by West.
13 And when the Southerne winde blewe
softly, they supposing to attaine their purpose,
loosed neerer, and sailed by Candie.
14 But anon after, there arose by [c] it a stor-
mie wind called [d] Euroclydon.
15 And when the ship was caught, & could
not resist the wind, we let her goe, and were caried away.
16 And wee ranne vnder a litle Ile named
Clauda, and had much adoe to get the boat.
17 Which they tooke vp and vsed all helpe,
vndergirding the ship, fearing lest they should
haue fallen into Syrtes, and they strake saile, and
so were caried.
18 [4] The next day when wee were tossed
with an exceeding tempest, they lightned the
shippe.

* *2.Cor.11.15.*
a Which was an high hill of Candie.
2 Gods prouidence taketh not away the causes which God vseth as meanes, but rather ordereth and disposeth their right vse euen then when he openeth an extraordinarie issue.
b This is meant of the Iewes fast which they kept in the feast of expiation, as wee reade, Leuit.23.27 which fell in the seuenth moneth which we call October, and is not good for nauigation or sailing.
3 Men cast themselues willingly into an infinite sort of dangers, when they chuse to follow their own wisedome, rather then God, speaking by ye mouth of his seruants.
c By Candie, from whose shore our ship was driuen by that meanes.
d Northeast wind.
4 The end proueth that none prouide worse for themselues, then they which commit themselues to be gouerned onely by their owne wisedome.

19 And

19 And the third day wee caſt out with our
owne hands the tackling of the ſhip.
20 And when neither ſunne nor ſtarres in
many dayes appeared,and no ſmall tempeſt lay
vpon vs, all hope that we ſhould be ſaued, was
then taken away.
21 [5]But after long abſtinence, Paul ſtood
foorth in the mids of them, and ſaid, Sirs, ye
ſhould haue hearkned to me,and not haue looſed from Candie: ſo ſhould ye haue gained this
hurt and loſſe.
22 But now I exhort you to bee of good
courage : for there ſhal be no loſſe of any mans
life among you, ſaue of the ſhip onely.
23 For there ſtood by me this night the angel of God, whoſe I am, and whom I ſerue,
24 Saying, Feare not, Paul : for thou muſt
be brought before Ceſar : and loe, God hath
giuen vnto thee freely all that ſaile with thee.
25 [6]Wherefore, ſirs, be of good courage :
for I beleeue God that it ſhall bee ſo as it hath
bene told me.
26 Howbeit, we muſt be caſt into a certaine
Iland.
27 [7]And when the fourteenth night was
come, as we were caried to and fro in the [e]A-
driaticall *Sea* about mid-night, the ſhipmen
deemed that ſome Countrey [f]approched vnto
them,
28 And ſounded, and found it twentie fa-
thoms : and when they had gone a litle further,
they ſounded againe, and found fifteene fa-
thoms.
29 Then fearing leſt they ſhould haue fallen into ſome rough places, they caſt foure ankers out of the ſterne, and wiſhed that the day
were come.
30 [8]Now as the mariners were about to flee
out of the ſhip, and had let done the boat into
the Sea vnder a colour as though they would
haue caſt ankers out of the foreſhip,
31 [9]Paul ſaide vnto the Centurion and the
ſouldiers, Except theſe abide in the ſhip, ye can
not be ſafe.
32 Then the ſouldiers cut off the ropes of
the boat, and let it fall away.
33 [10]And when it began to be day, Paul exhorted them all to take meate, ſaying, This is
the fourteenth day that ye haue taried, and continued faſting, receiuing nothing:
34 Wherefore I exhort you to take meate :
for this is for your ſafegard : for there ſhall not
an [g]haire fall from the head of any of you.
35 And when he had thus ſpoken, he tooke
bread and gaue thanks to God, in preſence of
them all, and brake it, and began to eate.
36 Then were they all of good courage, and
they alſo tooke meat.
37 Now we were in the ſhip in all two hundreth threeſcore and ſixteene ſoules.
38 And when they had eaten enough, they
lightened the ſhip, and caſt out the wheat into
the Sea.

5 God ſpareth the wicked for a time, for his elect and choſens ſake.

6 The promiſe is made effectual through faith.

7 We attaine and come to the promiſed and ſure ſaluation through the midſt of tempeſts & death it ſelfe.

e For Ptolome writeth, that the Adriaticall ſea beateth vpon the Eaſt ſhoare of Cicilia.

f That they drew neere to ſome countrey.

8 There is none ſo foule an acte, whereunto diſtruſt and an euil conſcience do not enforce men.

9 Although the perfourming of Gods promiſes doeth not ſimply depend vpon ſecond cauſes, yet they make themſelues vnworthy of Gods bountifulneſſe, which doe not embrace thoſe meanes which God offereth them, either vpon raſhneſſe or diſtruſt.

10 When the world trembleth, the faithfull alone be not only quiet, but confirme others by their example.

g This is a prouerbe which the Hebrewes vſe, whereby is meant, that they ſhall be ſafe, and not one of them periſh.

39 [11]And when it was day, they knew not
the countrey, but they ſpied a certaine [h]creeke
with a banke, into the which they were minded (if it were poſſible) to thruſt in the ſhip.
40 So when they had taken vp the ankers,
they committed *the ſhip* vnto the ſea, and looſed the rudder bonds, and hoiſed vp the maine
ſaile to the winde, and drew to the ſhoare.
41 And when they fell into a place, where
[i]two Seas met, they thruſt in the ſhippe : and
the forepart ſtucke faſt, and could not be mooued, but the hinder part was broken with the
violence of the waues.
42 [12]Then the ſouldiers counſell was to kill
the priſoners, leſt any of them, when hee had
ſwomme out, ſhould flee away.
43 [13]But the Cẽturion willing to ſaue Paul,
ſtayed them from *this* counſell, and commanded that they that could ſwimme, ſhould caſt
themſelues firſt into the Sea, and goe out to
lande.
44 [14]And the other, ſome on boards, and
ſome on certaine *pieces* of the ſhippe : and ſo it
came to paſſe, that they came all ſafe to land.

11 Then are tempeſts moſt of all to be feared and looked for, when the Port or hauen is neereſt.

h A creeke is a ſea within land, as the Adriaticall ſea, and the Perſian ſea.

i So is Iſthmus called, becauſe the Sea toucheth it on both ſides.

12 There is no where more vnfaithfulneſſe and vnthankfulnes then in vnbeleeuers.

13 God findeth euen amongſt his enemies them, whoſe help he vſeth to preſerre his.

14 The goodneſſe of God ouercommeth mans malice.

CHAP. XXVIII.

2 The Barbarians courteſie towards Paul and his companie. 3 A viper on Pauls hand : 6 Hee ſhaketh it off without harme : 3 Publius 9 and others are by him healed. 11 They depart from Melita, 16 and come to Rome. 17 Paul openeth to the Iewes 20 the cauſe of his comming : 22 He preacheth Ieſus 30 two yeeres.

AND when they were come ſafe, then
they knew that the Ile was called [a]Me-
lita.
2 And the Barbarians ſhewed vs no little
kindneſſe :for they kindled a fire, and receiued
vs euery one, becauſe of the preſent ſhowre,
and becauſe of the cold.
3 [1]And when Paul had gathered a number of ſticks, and layed them on the fire, there
came a viper out of the heat, and leapt on his
hand.
4 [2]Now when the Barbarians ſawe the
worme hang on his hand, they ſaide among
themſelues, This man ſurely is a murtherer,
whome, though he hath eſcaped the ſea, yet
[b]Vengeance hath not ſuffered to liue.
5 But hee ſhooke off the worme into the
fire, and felt no harme.
6 Howbeit they waited when hee ſhould
haue [c]ſwolne, or fallen downe dead ſuddenly :
[3]but after they had looked a great while, and
ſawe no inconuenience come to him, they
changed their mindes, and ſaid, That he was a
God.
7 [4]In the ſame quarters, the chiefe man
of the Ile (whoſe name was Publius) had poſ-
ſeſſions : the ſame receiued vs, and lodged vs
three dayes courteouſly.
8 And ſo it was, that the father of Publius lay ſicke of the feuer, and of a bloodie flixe:
to whom Paul entred in, and when he prayed,
he

a That is it, which at this day we call Malta.

1 The godly are ſure to haue danger vpon danger, but they haue alwayes a glorious iſſue.

2 Although aduerſitie be the puniſhment of ſinne, yet ſeeing that God in puniſhing of men doth not alwaies reſpect ſinne, they iudge raſhly, which either doe not wait for the end, or doe iudge and eſteeme of men, according to proſperitie or aduerſitie.

b Right & reaſon.

c The Greeke word ſignifieth to be inflamed or to ſwell : moreouer Dioſcorides in his 6. booke, chap. 38. witneſſeth that the biting of a viper, cauſeth a ſwelling of the body, and ſo ſaith Nicander, in his remedies againſt poyſons.

3 There is nothing more vnconſtant euery way, then they which are ignorant of true religion.

4 It neuer yet repented any man, that receiued the ſeruant of God, were he neuer ſo miſerable & poore

he laid *his* hands on him, and healed him.
9 [5] When this then was done, other also
in the Ile, which had diseases, came to him, and
were healed,
10 [6] Which also did vs great honour: and
when we departed, they laded vs with things
necessarie.
11 ¶ [7] Now after three moneths we departed in a ship of Alexandria, which had win-
tred in the Ile, whose [d] badge was Castor and
Pollux.
12 And when we arriued at Syracuse, wee
taried *there* three dayes.
13 And from thence we fet a compasse, and
came to Rhegium: and after one day, the South
winde blewe, and we came the second day to
Putioli:
14 [8] Where we found brethren, and were
desired to tarie with them seuen dayes, and so
we went toward Rome.
15 ¶ [9] And from thence, when the brethren heard of vs, they came to meete vs at the
[e] Market of Appius, and at the Three tauernes,
whom when Paul sawe, he thanked God, and
waxed bold.
16 So when we came to Rome, the Centurion deliuered the prisoners to the generall
Captaine: but Paul was suffered to dwell by
[f] himselfe with a souldier that kept him.
17 [10] And the third day after, Paul called
the chiefe of the Iewes together: and when
they were come, he said vnto them, Men *and*
brethren, though I haue committed nothing
against the people, or Lawes of the fathers, *yet*
was I deliuered prisoner from Hierusalem into
the hands of the Romanes.
18 Who when they had examined mee,
would haue let me goe, because there was no
cause of death in me:
19 [11] But when the Iewes spake contrary,
I was constrained to appeale vnto Cesar,
not because I had ought to accuse my nation of.
20 For this cause therefore haue I called
for you, to see *you*, and to speake with *you*:
for that hope of Israels sake, I am bound with
this chaine.
21 Then they said vnto him, Wee neither
receiued letters out of Iudea concerning thee,
neither came any of the brethren that shewed
or spake any euill of thee.
22 But we will heare of thee what thou
thinkest: for as concerning this sect, we know
that euery where it is spoken against.
23 [12] And when they had appointed him a
day, there came many vnto him into *his* lodging, to whom hee expounded [g] testifying the
kingdome of God, and perswading them those
things that concerne Iesus, both out of the
Law of Moses, and out of the Prophets, from
morning to night.
24 [13] And some were perswaded with the
things which were spoken, and some beleeued
not.
25 Therefore when they agreed not among
themselues, they departed, after that Paul had
spoken one worde, *to wit*, Well spake the
holy Ghost by Esaias the Prophet vnto our fathers,
26 [14] Saying, * Goe vnto this people, and
say, By hearing ye shall heare, and shall not
vnderstand, and seeing ye shal see, and not perceiue.
27 For the heart of this people is waxed
fatte, and their eares are dull of hearing, and
with their eyes haue they [h] winked, lest they
should see with *their* eyes, and heare with *their*
eares, and vnderstand with *their* heart, and
should returne that I might heale them.
28 [15] Be it knowen therefore vnto you, that
this saluation of God is sent to the Gentiles,
and they shall heare it.
29 [16] And when he had saide these things,
the Iewes departed, and had great reasoning a-
mong themselues.
30 [17] And Paul remained two yeeres full in
an house hired for himselfe, and receiued all
that came in vnto him,
31 Preaching the kingdome of God, and
teaching those things which concerne the Lord
Iesus Christ, with all boldnes of speech, without let.

5 Although Paul were a captiue, yet the vertue of God was not captiue.
6 God doeth well to strangers for his childrens sake.
7 Idoles do not defile the saints, which do in no wise consent vnto them.
d So they vsed to decke the forepart of their ships, whereupon their ships were called by such names.
8 God boweth and bendeth the hearts euen of prophane men, as it pleaseth him to fauour his.
9 God neuer suffereth his to be afflicted, aboue their strength.
e Appius way, was a pauement made by Appius the blind, with the helpe of his souldiers, long and broad, and runneth out toward the sea, and there were three tauernes in it.
f Not in a common prison, but in a house which he hired for himselfe.
10 Paul in euery place remembreth himselfe to be an Apostle.
11 We may vse the meanes which God giueth vs, but so, that we seeke the glory of God, and not our selues.
12 The Lawe and the Gospel agree well together.
g By good reasons, and proued that the kingdome of God foretold them by the Prophets, was come.
13 The Gospel is a fauour of life to them that beleeue, and a fauour of death to them that be disobedient.
14 The vnbeleeuers doe willingly resist the trueth, and yet not by chance.
* *Esai.6.9.matth.*13.14 *marke* 4.12.*luke* 8.10. *iohn* 12.40. *rom.*11.8.
h They made as though they saw not that which they saw against their willes: yea they did see, but they would not see.
15 The vnbeliefe of the reprobate & castawayes cannot cause the trueth of God to be of none effect.
16 Not the Gospel, but the contempt of the Gospel is the cause of strife and debate.
17 The word of God cannot be bound.

THE

THE EPISTLE OF THE APOSTLE PAVL TO THE ROMANES.

CHAP. I.

1 He first sheweth on what authoritie his Apostleship standeth. 15 Then he commendeth the Gospel, 16 by which God setteth out his power to those that are saued 17 by faith, 21 but were guiltie of wicked vnthankefulnesse to God. 26 For which his wrath was worthily powred on the, 39 so that they ranne headlong to all kinde of sinnes.

PAVL [1] a [a] seruant
of IESVS CHRIST,
called *to be* an [b] Apostle, * [c] put apart *to*
preach the Gospel of
God,
2 (Which hee
had promised afore
by his Prophets in
the holy Scriptures.)
3 [3] Concerning his [d] Sonne Iesus Christ
our Lord (which was [e] made of the seede of
Dauid [f] according to the flesh,
4 And [g] declared [h] mightily *to be* the Sonne
of God, touching the Spirit of sanctification
by the resurrection from the dead)
5 [i] By whome we haue receiued [k] grace
and Apostleship (that [l] obedience might be giuen vnto the faith) for his Name [m] among all
the Gentiles,
6 Among whom ye be also the [n] called of
Iesus Christ:
7 To all *you* that bee at Rome beloued of
God, called *to be* Saints: [o] Grace *be* with you,
and peace from God our Father, and *from* the
Lord Iesus Christ.
8 [4] First I thanke my God through Iesus
Christ for you all, because your faith is [p] published throughout the [q] whole world.
9 For God is my witnesse (whome I serue
in my [r] spirit in the [s] Gospel of his Sonne) that
without ceasing I make mention of you
10 Alwayes in my prayers, beseeching that
by some meanes, one time or other I might
haue a prosperous iourney by the will of God,
to come vnto you.
11 For I long to see you, that I might bestowe among you some spirituall gift, that you
might be strengthened:
12 That is, that [t] I might be comforted together with you, through *our* mutuall faith,
both yours and mine.
13 Now my brethren, I would that yee
should not be ignorant, how that I haue often
times purposed to come vnto you (but haue
bene let hitherto) that I might haue some fruit
also among you, as I *haue* among the other
Gentiles.
14 I am debter both to the Grecians, and to
the Barbarians, both to the wise men and to the
vnwise.
15 Therefore as much as in me is, I am readie to preach the Gospel to you also that are at
[u] Rome.
16 For I am not ashamed of the Gospel of
Christ: [5] for it is the [x] power of God vnto saluation to euery one that beleeueth, to the Iew
first, and also to the [y] Grecian.
17 [6] For by it the righteousnesse of God is
reueiled from [z] faith to faith: [7] as it is written:
* The iust shall liue by faith.
18 [8] For the wrath of God is reueiled from
heauen against [a] all vngodlinesse, and vnrighteousnesse of men, which withhold the [b] trueth
in vnrighteousnesse.
19 [9] Forasmuch as that, which may be know-
en of God, is manifest in [c] them: for God hath
shewed it vnto them.
20 For the inuisible things of him, that is,
his eternall power and Godhead are seene by
the creation of the world, being [d] considered
in *his* works, to the intent that they should be
without excuse:
21 Because that when they knew God, they
[e] glorified him not as God, neither were thankfull, but became [f] vaine in their thoughts, and
their foolish heart was full of darkenesse.
22 When they [g] professed themselues to be

1 The first part of the Epistle conteining a most profitable Preface vnto verse 6.
2 He mouing the Romanes to giue diligent eare vnto him, in that he sheweth that he commeth not in his owne name, but as Gods messenger vnto the Gentiles, entreateth with them of the waightiest matter that is, promised long since of God, by many fit witnesses, and nowe at the length performed in deed.
a Minister, for this word Seruant is not taken in this place as set against this word Freemen, but declareth his ministerie and office.
b Whereas he said before in a generall terme, that he was a Minister, now hee commeth to a more speciall name, and saith he is an Apostle, and that he tooke not vpon him this office of his owne head, but being called of God, and therefore in this his writing to the Romanes, doeth nothing but his duety
* *Actes* 13.1.

t Though Paul were neuer so excellent, yet by teaching the Church, he might be instructed by it.
u He meaneth all them that dwell at Rome, though some of them were not Romanes, Looke the ende of the Epistle.
5 The second part of the Epistle vnto the beginning of the 9. chapter. Now the whole end and purpose of the disputation is this: that is to say, to shewe that there is but one way to attaine vnto saluation (which is set foorth vnto vs of God in the Gospel, without any difference of nations) and that is Iesus Christ apprehended by faith.
x God his mightie and effectuall instrument to saue men by.
y When this word, Grecian, is set against this word Iew, then doeth it signifie a Gentile.
6 The confirmation of the former proposition: we are taught in the Gospel, that we are iustified before God by faith, which increaseth daily: and therfore also saued.
z From faith which increaseth dayly.
7 The proofe as well of the first as of the second proposition, out of Abakuk, who attributeth & giueth vnto faith, both iustice and life before God.

c Appointed of God to preach the Gospel. 3 By declaring the summe of the doctrine of the Gospel, he stirreth vp the Romanes to good consideration of the matter wherof he entreateth: So then he sheweth that Christ (who is the very substance & summe of the Gospel) is the onely Sonne of God the Father, who as touching his humanitie, is made of the seed of Dauid, but touching his diuine and spirituall nature, whereby he sanctified himselfe, is begotten of the Father from euerlasting, as by his mightie resurrection manifestly appeareth. *d This is a plaine testimonie of the person of Christ, that he is but one, and of his two natures, and their properties. e Which tooke flesh of the Virgine, Dauid his daughter. f As he is man: for this Word, Flesh, by the figure Synecdoche, is taken for man. g Shewed and made manifest. h The diuine and mightie power is set against the weakenesse of the flesh, for that ouercame death. i Of whome. k This marueilous liberall and gracious gift, which is giuen me, the least of all the Saints, to preach, &c.* Ephesians 3.8. *l That men through faith might obey God. m For his Namessake. n Which through Gods goodnesse are Christes. o Gods free good will: by peace, the Hebrewes meane a prosperous successe in all things.* 4 Hee procureth their fauourable patience, in that hee reckoneth vp their true commendation, and his true Apostolique good will toward them, confirmed by taking God himselfe to witnesse. *p Because your faith is such, that it is commended in all Churches. q In all Churches. r Very willingly and with all my heart. s In preaching his Sonne.*

* *Abakuk.* 2.4. 8 Another confirmation of that principall question: All men being considered in themselues, or without Christ, are guiltie both of vngodlinesse & also vnrighteousnes, and therefore are subiect to condemnation: Therefore must they needes seeke righteousnes in some other. *a Against all kindes of vngodlinesse. b By trueth Paul meaneth all the light that is left in man since his fall, not as though they being led thereby were able to come into fauour with God, but that their owne reason might condemne them of wickednesse both against God and man.* 9 Their vngodlines he proueth hereby, that although all men haue a most cleere & euident glasse wherein to behold the euerlasting and almightie nature of God, euen in his creatures, yet haue they fallen away from those principles to most foolish & fond deuises of their owne braines, in constituting and appointing the seruice of God. *c In their hearts. d Thou seest not God, and yet thou acknowledgest him as God by his works, Cic. e They did not honour him with that honour and seruice which was meet for his euerlasting power & Godhead. f As if he said, became so mad of themselues. g Or, thought themselues.*

wise,

wise, they became fooles.
23 For they turned the glory of the [h] incorruptible God to the similitude of the image
of a corruptible man, and of birds, and foure
footed beasts, and of creeping things.
24 [10] Wherefore [i] also God [k] gaue them vp
to their hearts lusts, vnto vncleannes, to defile
their owne bodies betweene themselues:
25 Which turned the trueth of God vnto
a lie, and worshipped and serued the creature,
forsaking the Creatour, which is blessed for e-
uer, Amen.
26 For this cause God gaue them vp vnto
vile affections: for euen their womẽ did change
the naturall vse into that which is against nature.
27 And likewise also the men left the naturall vse of the woman, and burned in their lust
one toward another, and man with man
wrought filthinesse, and receiued in themselues such [l] recompense of their errour, as was
meet.
28 [11] For as they regarded not to acknowledge God, *euen so* God deliuered them vp
vnto a [m] reprobate minde, to doe those things
which are not conuenient,
29 Being full of all vnrighteousnesse, fornication, wickednesse, couetousnesse, maliciousnesse, full of enuie, of murther, of debate,
of deceit, taking all things in the euill part,
whisperers,
30 Backebiters, haters of God, doers of
wrong, proude, boasters, inuenters of euill
things, disobedient to parents, without vnderstanding, [n] couenant breakers, without naturall affection, such as can neuer bee appeased,
mercilesse.
31 Which men, though they knewe the
[o] Law of God, how that they which commit
such things are worthy of death, *yet* not onely doe the same, but also [p] fauour them that
doe them.

h For the true God they tooke another.
10 The vnrighteousnes of men he setteth forth first in this, that euen against nature following their lusts, they defiled themselues one with another, by the iust judgement of God.
i The contempt of religion is the fountaine of all mischiefe.
k As a iust iudge
l A meet reward for their deserts.
11 He prooueth the vnrighteousnesse of man by a large rehearsal of many kindes of wickednesse, from which (if not from all, yet at the least from many of them) no man is altogether free.
m Into a mad & froward minde, whereby it commeth to passe, that the conscience being once put out, and hauing almost no more remorse of sinne, men runne headlong into all kind of mischiefe.
n Vnmindfull of their couenants and bargaines.
o By the lawe of God he meaneth that which the Philosophers called the Lawe of nature, and the Lawyers themselues termed the Lawe of nations.
p Are fellowes and partakers with them in their wickednesse, and beside that, commend them which doe amisse.

CHAP. II.

1 He bringeth all before the iudgement seat of God. 12 The excuse that the Gentiles might pretend 14 Of ignorance, he taketh quite away. 17 He vrgeth the Iewes with the written Law, 23 In which they boasted: 27 And so maketh both Iewe and Gentile alike.

THerefore [1] thou art inexcusable, O man,
whosoeuer thou art that condemnest: for
in that thou condemnest another, thou condemnest thy selfe: for thou that condemnest,
doest the same things.
2 But we [a] know that the iudgement of
God is according to [b] trueth, against them
which commit such things.
3 And thinkest thou this, O thou man,
that condemnest them which doe such things,
and doest the same, that thou shalt escape the
iudgement of God?
4 [2] Or despisest thou the riches of his bountifulnesse, and patience, and long sufferance,
not knowing that the bountifulnesse of God
leadeth thee to repentance?
5 But thou, after thine hardnesse, and
heart that cannot repent, * [c] heapest vp as a
treasure vnto thy selfe wrath against the day of
wrath, and of the declaration of the iust iudgment of God,
6 [3] * Who will reward euery man according to his works:
7 *That is*, to them which through patience in well doing, seeke [d] glory, and honour,
and immortalitie, euerlasting life:
8 But vnto them that are contentious and
disobey the [e] trueth, and obey vnrighteousnes,
shalbe [f] indignation and wrath.
9 Tribulation and anguish *shalbe* vpon the
soule of euery man that doeth euil: of the Iew
first, and *also* of the Grecian.
10 But to euery man that doeth good, *shall
be* glory, and honour, and peace: to the Iewe
first, and *also* to the Grecian.
11 For there is no [g] respect of persons with
God.
12 [4] For as many as haue sinned without the
Lawe, shall perish also without the Law: and
as many as haue sinned in the Lawe, shall bee
iudged by the Lawe,
13 [5] (For the hearers of the Lawe *are* not
righteous before God: but the doers of the
Lawe shalbe [h] iustified.
14 [6] For when the Gentiles which haue [i] not
the Law, doe by [k] nature, the things *conteined*
in the Lawe, they hauing not a Law, are a Law
vnto themselues,
15 Which shewe the effect of the Lawe
[l] written in their hearts, their conscience also
bearing witnesse, and their thoughts accusing
one another, or excusing,)
16 [7] At that day, when God shall iudge the
secrets of men by Iesus Christ, according to
[m] my Gospel.
17 ¶ [8] Behold, thou art called a Iew, and
restest in the Law, and gloriest in God,
18 And knowest *his* will, and [n] ‖ triest the
things that dissent from it, in that thou art instructed by the Law:
19 And perswadest thy selfe that thou art a
guide of the blind, a light of them which *are* in
darkenesse,

2 A vehement & grieuous crying out against them that please themselues because they see more thẽ other doe, and yet are no whit better then others are.
*Iames. 5. 3.
c Whilest thou giuest thy selfe to pleasures, thinking to increase thy goods, thou shalt find Gods wrath.
3 The ground of the former disputation, That both the Iewes and Gentiles haue altogether need of righteousnesse.
**Psal. 62. 12. mat. 16. 27. reuel. 22. 12.*
d Glory which followeth good works, which he laieth not out before vs, as though there were any that could attaine to saluation by his owne strength, but, by laying this condition of saluation before vs, which no man can performe, to bring men to Christ, who alone iustifieth the beleeuers, as he himselfe concludeth, chap. 3. 21. 22. following.
e By trueth, hee meaneth that knowledge which we haue of nature
f Gods indignation against sinners, which shall quickly be kindled.
g God doeth not measure men either by their blood or by their countrey, either to receiue them or to cast them away.
4 He applieth that generall accusation of mankind particularly both to the Gentiles, and to the Iewes.
5 He preuenteth an obiection which might be made by ẏ Iewes whom the Lawe doth not excuse, but condemne, because that not the hearing of the Lawe, but the keeping of the Law doeth iustifie.

1 He conuinceth them which would seeme to be exempt out of the number of other men, because they reprehend other mens faults, and saith, that they are least of all to be excused, for if they were well and narrowly searched (as God surely doeth) they themselues would bee found guiltie in those things which they reprehend, and punish in other: so that in condemning other, they pronounce sentence against themselues. *a Paul alledgeth no places of Scripture, for hee reasoneth generally against all men: but he bringeth such reasons as euery man is perswaded of in his minde, so that the deuill himselfe is not able to plucke them cleane out. b Considering and iudging things aright, and not by any outward shewe.*

h Shall be pronounced iust before Gods iudgment seate: which is true indeed if any such could be found that had fulfilled the Law: but seing Abraham was not iustified by the Law, but by faith, it followeth that no man can be iustified by works. 6 He preuenteth an obiection which might be made by the Gentiles, who although they haue not the Law of Moses, yet they haue no reason why they may excuse their wickednes, in that they haue somewhat written in their hearts in stead of a Law, as men, that forbid and punish some things as wicked, and command & commend other some as good. *i Not simply, but in comparison of the Iewes. k Command honest things, and forbid dishonest. l This knowledge is a naturall knowledge.* 7 God deferreth many iudgements, which notwithstanding he will execute at their conuenient time by Iesus Christ, with a most strait examination, not onely of words and deedes, but of thoughts also, be they neuer so hidden or secret. *m As my doctrine witnesseth, which I am appoynted to preach.* 8 Hee prooueth by the testimonie of Dauid, and the other Prophets, that God bestowed greatest benefits vpon the Iewes, in giuing them also the Law, but that they are the most vnthankful & vnkindest of all men. *n Canst try & discerne what things swarue from Gods will.* ‖ Or, allowest the things ẏ are excellent.

o The way to teach and frame other in the knowledge of the trueth *p As though he said, that the Iewes vnder a colour of an outward seruing of God, chalenged all to themselues, when as in deed, they did nothing lesse then obserue the Law.* **Esai.51.5. ezek.36.20.*

9 He precisely preuenteth their obiection, which set an holinesse in circumcision, and the outward obseruation of the Lawe: So that he sheweth that the outward circumcision, if it be separated from the inward, doeth not onely not iustifie, but also condemne them that are indeed circumcised, of whom it requireth that, which it signifieth, that is to say, cleannesse of the heart and the whole life according to the commandement of the Law, so that if there be a man vncircumcised according to the flesh, who is circumcised in heart, he is farre better and more to be counted of, then any Iewe that is circumcised according to the flesh onely.

20 An instructer of them which lacke discretion, a teacher of the vnlearned, which hast
the [o] forme of knowledge, and of the trueth in
the [p] Law.
21 Thou therefore, which teachest another, teachest thou not thy selfe? thou that
preachest, A man should not steale, doest thou
steale?
22 Thou that sayest, A man should not
commit adulterie, doest thou commit adulterie? thou that abhorrest idoles, committest
thou sacriledge?
23 Thou that gloriest in the Lawe,
through breaking the Law, dishonourest thou
God?
24 For the Name of God is blasphemed
among the Gentiles through you, *as it is
written,
25 [9] For circumcision verely is profitable, if
thou doe the Law: but if thou be a transgressour of the Law, thy circumcision is made vncircumcision.
26 Therefore, if the [q] vncircumcision keepe
the ordinances of the Law, shal not his [r] vncircumcision be counted for circumcision?
27 And shall not [s] vncircumcision which is
by nature, (if it keepe the Lawe) condemne
thee which by the [t] letter and circumcision *art*
a transgressour of the Lawe?
28 For he is not a Iewe, which is one [u] outward: neither is that circumcision, which is
outward in the flesh:
29 But he is a Iewe which is one within,
and the circumcision *is* of the heart, in the [x] spirit, not in the letter, whose praise is not of men,
but of God.

q This is the figure Metonymie, for, if the vncircumcised. r The state and condition of the vncircumcised. s He which is vncircumcised by nature and blood. t Paul vseeth often times to set the letter against the Spirit: but in this place, the circumcision which is according to the letter, is the cutting off of the foreskinne, but the circumcision of the Spirit, is the circumcision of the heart, that is to say, the spirituall end of the ceremonie, is true holinesse and righteousnesse, whereby the people of God is knowen from prophane and heathenish men. u By the outward ceremonie onely. x Whose force is inward, and in the heart.

CHAP. III.

1 He giueth the Iewes some 2 preferment, for the couenants sake, 4 but yet such, as wholly dependeth on Gods mercy. 9 That both Iewes and Gentiles are sinners, 11 he proueth by Scripture: 19 and shewing the vse of the Law, 28 he concludeth that we are iustified by faith.

1 The first meeting with or preuenting an obiection of the Iewes: what then haue the Iewes no more preferment then the Gentiles? yes, that haue they, saith the Apostle, on Gods behalfe, for he committed the tables of the couenant to them, so that the vnbeliefe of a few, cannot cause the whole nation without exception to be cast away of God, who is true, and who also vseth their vnworthines to commend and set forth his goodnesse.

What [1] is then the preferment of the
Iew? or what is the profit of circumcision?
2 Much euery maner of way: for [a] chiefly, because vnto them were of credit committed the [b] oracles of God.
3 For what, though some did not [c] beleeue? shall their vnbeliefe make the [d] faith of
God without effect?
4 God forbid: yea, let God be true and
euery man a lyar, as it is written, That thou
mightest be [e] iustified in thy words, and ouercome, [f] when thou art iudged.
5 [2] Now if our [g] vnrighteousnesse commend the righteousnesse of God, what shall we
say? Is God vnrighteous which punisheth?
(I speake as [h] a man.)
6 God forbid: else how shall God iudge
the world?
7 [3] For if the [i] veritie of God hath more a-
bounded through my lie vnto his glory, why
am I yet condemned as a sinner?
8 And (as we are blamed, and as some affirme, that we say) why do we not euill, that
good may come *thereof*? whose damnation is
iust.
9 [4] What then? are wee more excellent?
No, in no wise: for we haue already prooued,
that all, both Iewes and Gentiles are [k] vnder
sinne,
10 As it is written, *There is none righteous, no not one.
11 There is none that vnderstandeth: there
is none that seeketh God.
12 They haue all gone out of the way:
they haue bene made altogether vnprofitable:
there is none that doeth good, no not one.
13 *Their throte is an open sepulchre: they
haue vsed their tongues to deceit: *the poison
of aspes *is* vnder their lips.
14 *Whose mouth is full of cursing and
bitternesse.
15 *Their feete are swift to shed blood.
16 Destruction and calamitie *are* in their
wayes,
17 And the [l] way of peace they haue not
knowen.
18 *The feare of God is not before their
eyes.
19 [5] Now wee know that whatsoeuer the
[m] Lawe sayeth, it saith it to them which are
vnder the Lawe, that [6] euery mouth may bee
stopped, and all the world bee [n] subiect to the
iudgement of God.
20 Therefore by the [o] workes of the Lawe
shal no [p] flesh be [q] iustified in his [r] sight: for by
the Law *commeth* the knowledge of sinne.
21 [7] But now is the righteousnesse of God
made manifest without the Law, hauing witnesse of the Law and of the Prophets,
22 [8] *To wit*, the righteousnesse of God by

f Forasmuch as thou shewedst foorth an euident token of thy righteousnesse, constancie and faith, by preseruing him who had broken his couenant.

2 An other preuention issuing out of the former answer: that the iustice of God is in such sort commended and set foorth by our vnrighteousnesse, that therefore God forgetteth not that hee is the Iudge of the world, & therefore a most seuere reuenger of vnrighteousnesse.

g Trecherie, and all the fruits thereof. *h Therefore I speake not these words in mine owne person, as though I thought so, but this is the talke of mans wisedome, which is not subiect to the will of God.*

3 A third obiection, which addeth somewhat to the former, If sinnes doe turne to the glory of God, they are not only not to be punished, but we ought rather to giue our selues to them: which blasphemie Paul contending to curse and detest, pronounceth iust punishment against such blasphemers.

i The trueth and constancie.

4 Another answere to the first obiection: that the Iewes, if they be considered in themselues, are no better then other men are: as it hath bene long since pronounced by the mouth of the Prophets.

a The Iewes state and condition was chiefest. b Wordes. c Brake the couenant. d The faith that God gaue. e That thy iustice might be plainely seene.

k Are guiltie of sinne. **Psal.14 1,3 & 53.1,3.* **Psal.5.10.* **Psal.143.3.* **Psal.10.7.* **Esai.59.7.* *l An innocent and peaceable life.* **Psal.36 1.* 5 He proueth that this grieuous accusation which is vttered by Dauid & Esaias, doth properly concerne the Iewes. *m The Law of Moses.* 6 A conclusion of all the former disputation, from the 18.ver.of the 1 chapter. Therefore saith the Apostle, No man can hope to be iustified by any Lawe, whether it be that general Law, or the particular law of Moses, & therfore to be saued: seeing it appeareth (as we haue already proued) by comparing the Law and mans life together, that all men are sinners, and therefore worthy of condemnation in the sight of God. *n Be found guiltie before God. o By that, that the Law can by vs be performed. p Flesh is here taken for man, as in many other places, and furthermore hath here greater force: for it is put to shew the contrarietie betwixt God and man: as if you would say, Man who is nothing els but a piece of flesh defiled with sinne, and God who is most pure and most perfect in himselfe. q Absolued before the iudgment seate of God. r A secret setting of the righteousnesse which is before men, be they neuer so iust, against the iustice which can stand before God: now there is no righteousnesse can stand before God, but the righteousnesse of Christ onely.* 7 Therefore saith the Apostle, Lest that men should perish, God doeth now exhibit that which he promised of old, that is to say, a way whereby we may be instified and saued before him without the Law. 8 The matter, as it were, of this righteousnesse is Christ Iesus apprehended by faith, and for this ende offered to all people, as without him all people are shut out from the kingdome of God.

the faith of [f] Iesus Christ, vnto all, and vpon all
that beleeue.
23 For there is no difference : for all haue
sinned, and are depriued of the [t] glory of God,
24 [9] And are iustified [u] freely by his grace,
through the redemption that is in Christ Iesus,
25 [10] Whom God hath set foorth *to be* a reconciliation through faith in his [x] blood to declare his righteousnesse, by the forgiuenesse of
the sinnes that [y] are passed,
26 Through the [z] patience of God to shew
at [a] this time his righteousnesse, that hee might
be [b] iust, and a [c] iustifier of him which is of the
[d] faith of Iesus.
27 [11] Where is then the reioycing? It is excluded. By what [e] Law? of workes? Nay: but
by the Law of faith.
28 Therefore wee conclude, that a man
is iustified by faith, without the workes of the
Lawe.
29 [12] *God*, is he the God of the [f] Iewes only, and not of the Gentiles also? Yes, euen of
the Gentiles also.
30 For it is one God, who shall iustifie
[g] circumcision of faith, and vncircumcision
through faith.
31 [13] Doe we then make the Law of [h] none
effect through faith? God forbid: yea, we [i] establish the Law.

f Which we giue to Iesus Christ, or which resteth vpon him. *t By the glorie of God, is meant that marke which we all shoot at, that is, euerlasting life, which standeth in that we are made partakers of the glory of God.* 9 Therefore this righteousnes touching vs, is altogether freely giuen, for it standeth vpon those things which we haue not done our selues, but such as Christ hath suffered for our sakes, to deliuer vs from sinne. *u Of his free gift, and meere liberalitie.* 10 God then is the authour of that free iustification, because it pleased him: and Christ is hee, which suffered punishment for our sinnes, and in whom wee haue remission of them: and the meane whereby we apprehend Christ, is faith. To bee short, the ende is the setting foorth of the goodnesse of God, that by this meanes it may appeare, that he is mercifull in deede, and constant in his promises, as he that freely, and of meere grace, iustifieth the beleeuers. *x This name of blood, calleth vs backe to the figure of the olde sacrifices, the trueth and substance of which sacrifices is in Christ. y Of those sinnes which we committed, when we were his enemies. z Through his patience, and suffering nature. a To wit, when Paul wrote this. b That he might be found exceeding true and faithfull. c Making him iust and without blame, by putting Christs righteousnesse vnto him. d Of the number of them which by faith lay hold vpon Christ: contrarie to whome are they, which looke to bee saued by circumcision, that is by the Law.* 11 An argument to prooue this conclusion, that we are iustified by faith without workes, taken from the ende of iustification. The end of iustification is the glory of God alone: therefore we are iustified by faith without workes: for if wee were iustified either by our owne workes onely, or partly by faith, and partly by workes, the glory of this iustification should not bee wholly giuen to God. *e By what doctrine? now the doctrine of workes hath this condition ioyned with it, if thou doest: and the doctrine of faith, hath this condition, if thou beleeuest.* 12 Another argument of an absurditie: if iustification depended vpon the Law of Moses, then should God bee a Sauiour to the Iewes onely. Againe, if he should saue the Iewes after one sort, and the Gentiles after another, he should not be one and like him else. Therefore he will iustifie both of them after one selfe same maner, that is to say, by faith. Moreouer, this argument must be ioyned to that which followeth next, that his conclusion may be firme and euident. *f God is said to be their God, after the maner of the Scripture, whom he loueth and tendreth. g The circumcised.* 13 The taking away of an obiection: yet is not the Law taken away therefore, but is rather established, as it shall bee declared in his proper place. *h Vaine, voide, to no purpose, and of no force. i We make it effectuall and strong.*

CHAP. IIII.

1 *Hee prooueth that which he said before of faith, by the example of Abraham, 3.6 and the testimonie of the Scripture: and ten times in the chapter hee beateth vpon this word Imputation.*

WHat [1] shall wee say then, that Abraham our father hath found concerning the [a] flesh?
2 [2] For if Abraham were iustified by
workes, hee hath wherein to reioyce, but not
with God.
3 [3] For what saith the Scripture? Abraham beleeued God, and it was counted to him
for righteousnesse.

1 A new argument of great weight, taken from the example of Abraham the father of all beleeuers: And this is the proposition, If Abraham be considered in himselfe by his workes, he hath deserued nothing wherein to reioyce with God. *a By works, as appeareth in the next verse.* 2 A preuenting of an obiection. Abraham may well reioyce, & extoll himselfe amongst men, but not with God. 3 A confirmation of the proposition: Abraham was iustified by imputation of faith, therefore freely without any respect of his workes,

4 [4] Now to him that [b] worketh, the wages is not [c] counted by fauour, but by debt:
5 But to him that worketh not, but beleeueth in him that [d] iustifieth the vngodly, his
faith is counted for righteousnes.
6 [5] Euen as Dauid declareth the blessed-
nes of the man, vnto whom God imputeth
righteousnes without workes, *saying*,
7 Blessed *are* they, whose iniquities are
forgiuen, and whose sinnes are couered.
8 Blessed *is* the man, to whom the Lord
imputeth not sinne.
9 [6] *Came* this [e] blessednesse then vpon the
circumcision *onely*, or vpon the vncircumcision
also? For we say, that faith was imputed vnto
Abraham for righteousnes.
10 [7] How was it then imputed? when he was
circumcised, or vncircũcised? not when he was
circumcised, but when he was vncircumcised.
11 [8] After he receiued the [f] signe of circumcision, *as* the [g] seale of the righteousnesse of the
faith which he had, when he was vncircumcised, [9] that hee should be the father of all them
that beleeue, not being circumcised, that righteousnesse might be imputed to them also,
12 [10] And the father of circumcision, not
vnto them onely which are of the circumcision, but vnto them also that walke in the steps
of the faith of our father Abraham, *which he
had* when he was vncircumcised.
13 [11] For the promise that he should be the
[h] heire of the world, was not *giuen* to Abraham,
or to his seed, through the [i] Lawe, but through
the righteousnesse of faith.
14 [12] For if they which are of the [k] Law, *be*
heires, faith is made voyd, and the promise is
made of none effect.
15 [13] For the Law causeth wrath: for where
no Law is, there *is* no transgression.
16 [14] Therefore *it is* by faith, that *it might
come* by grace, and the promise might be sure
to all the [l] seede, [15] not to that only which is of
the Law: but also to that which is of the faith
of Abraham, who is the father of vs all,
17 (As it is written, I haue made thee a

4 The first proofe of the confirmation, taken of cõtraries: to him ẏ deserueth any thing by his labour, the wages is not counted by fauour, but by debt: but to him that hath done nothing but beleeueth in him which promiseth freely, faith is imputed. *b To him that hath deserued any thing by his worke. c Is not reckoned nor giuen him. d That maketh him, which is wicked in himselfe, iust in Christ.* 5 Another proofe of the same confirmation: Dauid putteth blessednesse in free pardon of sinnes, therefore iustification also. 6 A new proposition: that this maner of iustification belongeth both to vncircumcised, and also to the circumcised: as is declared in the person of Abraham. *e This saying of Dauid, wherein he pronounceth thẽ blessed.* 7 He prooueth that it belongeth to the vncircumcised (for their was no doubt of the circumcised in this sort: Abraham was iustified in circumcision, therefore this iustification belongeth also to the vncircumcised. Nay it doeth not apperteine to the circumcised, in respect of the circumcision, much lesse are the vncircumcised shut out for their vncircumcision. 8 A preuenting of an obiection: Why then was Abraham circumcised, if hee were already iustified? That the gift of righteousnesse (saith he) might be confirmed in him. *f Circumcision, which is a signe: as we say the Sacrament of Baptisme, for Baptisme which is a Sacrament. g Circumcision, was called before, a signe, in respect of the outward ceremony: now Paul sheweth the force and substance of that signe, that is, to what end it is vsed, to wit, not onely to signifie, but also to seale vp the righteousnesse of faith, whereby we come to possesse Christ himselfe: for the holy Ghost worketh that inwardly in deed, which the Sacraments being ioyned with the word, doe represent.* 9 An applying of the example of Abraham to the vncircumcised beleeuers, whose father also he maketh Abraham. 10 An applying of the same example, to the circumcised beleeuers, whose father Abraham is, but yet by faith. 11 A reason why the seed of Abraham is to be esteemed by faith, because that Abraham himselfe through faith was made partaker of that promise, whereby he was made the father of al nations. *h That all the nations of the world should be his children: or by the world may be vnderstood the land of Canaan. i For workes that hee had done, or vpon this condition, that he should fulfill the Law.* 12 A double confirmation of that reason: the one is that the promise cannot be apprehended by the law, and therfore it should be frustrate: the other, that the condition of faith should bee ioyned in vaine to that promise which should be apprehended by workes. *k If they be heires which haue fulfilled the Law.* 13 A reason of the first confirmation. why the promise cannot be apprehended by the Law: because that the law doth not reconcile God and vs, but rather denounceth his anger against vs, forsomuch as no man can obserue it. 14 The conclusion of this argument: The saluation & iustification of ẏ posteritie of Abraham (that is, of the Church which is gathered together of all people) proceedeth of faith which laieth hold on the promise made vnto Abraham, and which promise, Abraham himselfe first of all laid hold on. *l To all the beleeuers.* 15 That is to say, not onely of them which beleeue and are also circumcised according to the Law, but of them also which without circumcision, and in respect of faith onely, are counted amongst the Children of Abraham,

16 This fatherhood is spirituall, depending onely vpon the vertue of God, who made the promise.
m Before God, that is by a spirituall kindred, which hath place before God, and maketh vs acceptable to God.
n Who restoreth to life.
o With whome those things are already, which as yet are not indeed, as he that can with a word make what he will of nothing.
17 A description of true faith wholly resting in the power of God, and his good will, set footh in the example of Abraham.
p Very strong and constant.
q Voide of strength, and vnmeete to get children.
r Acknowledged and praised God, as most gracious and true.

[16] father of many nations) *euen* before [m] God
whom he beleeued, who [n] quickneth the dead,
and [o] calleth those things which bee not, as
though they were.
18 [17] Which *Abraham* aboue hope, beleeued
vnder hope, that he should be the father of
many nations: according to that which was
spoken *to him,* So shall thy seed be.
19 And hee [p] not weake in the faith, considered
not his owne body, which was nowe
[q] dead, being almost an hundred yeere old, neither
the deadnesse of Saraes wombe.
20 Neither did hee doubt of the promise of
God through vnbeliefe, but was strengthened
in the faith, and gaue [r] glory to God,
21 Being [s] fully assured that hee which had
promised, was able to doe it.
22 And therefore it was imputed to him for
righteousnesse.
23 [18] Now it is not written for him onely,
that it was imputed to him for righteousnesse,
24 But also for vs, to whom it shalbe imputed
for righteousnesse, which beleeue in him that
raised vp Iesus our Lord from the dead.
25 Who was deliuered *to death* for our
[t] sinnes, and is risen againe for our iustification.

s A description of true faith. 18 The rule of iustification is alwayes one, both in Abraham, and in all the faithfull: that is to say, faith in God, who after that there was made a full satisfaction for our sins in Christ our mediatour, raised him from the dead, that we also being iustified, might be saued in him. *t To pay the ransome for our sinnes.*

CHAP. V.

1 Hee amplifieth 2 Christs righteousnesse, which is laide hold on by faith, 5 who was giuen for the weake, 8 and sinfull. 14 He compareth Christ with Adam, 17 Death with Life, 20 and the Law with Grace.

1 Another argument taken of the effectes: we are iustified with that, which truely appeaseth our conscience before God: but faith in Christ doeth appease our conscience and not the Law, as it was before said, therefore by faith we are iustified and not by the Law.
* Ephes.2.18.
2 Whereas quietnesse of conscience is attributed to faith it is to be referred to Christ, who is the giuer of faith it selfe, and in whom faith it selfe is effectuall.

THen being [1] iustified by faith, wee haue
peace toward God through our Lord Iesus
Christ,
2 [2] By whom also through faith, wee haue
[a] had this accesse vnto this grace, [b] wherein we
[c] stand, [3] and [d] reioyce vnder the hope of the
glory of God.
3 [4] Neither *that* onely, but also wee * reioyce
in tribulations, [5] knowing that tribulation
bringeth forth patience,
4 And patience experience, and experience
hope,
5 [6] And hope maketh not ashamed, because
the [e] loue of God is shed abroad in our
hearts by ye holy Ghost, which is giuen vnto vs.
6 [7] For Christ, when wee were yet of no
strength, at *his* [f] time died for the * vngodly.
7 [8] Doubtlesse one will scarce die [g] for a
righteous man: but yet for a good man it may
be that one dare die.
8 But God [h] setteth out his loue towards
vs, seeing that while wee were yet [i] sinners,
Christ died for vs.
9 Much more then, being now iustified by
his blood, wee shall bee saued from [k] wrath
through him.
10 For if when we were enemies, wee were
reconciled to God by the death of his Sonne,
much more being reconciled, we shall be saued
by his life.
11 [9] And not onely *so,* but wee also reioyce
in God through our Lord Iesus Christ, by
whom we haue now receiued the atonement.
12 [10] Wherefore, as by [l] one man [m] sinne
entred into the world, and death by sinne, and
so death went ouer all men: [n] in whom all men
haue sinned.
13 [11] For vnto the time [o] of the Lawe was
sinne in the world, but sinne is not [p] imputed,
while there is no law.
14 [12] But death reigned from Adam to Moses,
euen ouer [q] them also that sinned not after
the like [r] maner of the transgression of Adam,
[13] which was the figure of him that was to come.
15 [14] But yet the gift is not so, as is the offence:
for if through the offence of [s] that one,
many bee dead, much more the grace of God,
and the gift by grace, which is by one man Iesus
Christ, hath abounded vnto many.
16 [15] Neither is the gift *so* as *that which entred*
in by one that sinned: for the fault *came* of one
offence vnto condemnation: but the gift *is* of
many offences to [t] iustification.
17 [16] For if by the offence of one, death
reigned through one, much more shall they
which receiue that abundance of grace, and of
that gift of that righteousnesse, [u] reigne in life
through one, *that is,* Iesus Christ.

a We must here know, that we haue yet still the same effect of faith. *b By which grace, that is, by which gracious loue and good will, or that state whereunto we are graciously taken.* *c We stand stedfast.* 3 A preuenting of an obiection against them, which beholding the daily miseries and calamities of the Church, thinke that the Christians dreame, when they brag of their felicitie: to whom the Apostle answereth, that their felicitie is laide vp vnder hope in another place: which hope is so certaine and sure, that they doe no lesse reioyce for that happinesse, then if they did presently enioy it. *d Our minds are not only quiet and setled, but also we are maruelously glad, and conceiue great ioy for that heauenly inheritance, which waiteth for vs.* 4 Tribulation it selfe giueth vs diuers and sundry wayes occasions to reioyce, much lesse doeth it make vs miserable. * *Iam 1.2.* 5 Afflictions accustome vs to patience, and patience assureth vs of the goodnesse of God, and this experience confirmeth and fostereth our hope, which neuer deceiueth vs. 6 The ground of hope is an assured testimonie of the conscience, by the gift of the holy Ghost, that wee are beloued of God, and this is nothing else but that which wee call faith, whereof it followeth, that through faith our consciences are quieted *e Wherewith hee loueth vs.* 7 A sure comfort in aduersity, that our peace and quietnesse of conscience bee not troubled: for hee that so loued them that were of no strength and while they were yet sinners, that he died for them, how can he neglect them being now sanctified and liuing in him?

f In time fit and conuenient which the Father had appointed.
* *Hebr.9.15. 1.pet.3.18.*
8 An amplifying of the loue of God toward vs, so that we cannot doubt of it, who deliuered Christ to death for the vniust, and for them of whom he could receiue no commoditie, and (that more is) for his very enemies. How can it be then that Christ being now aliue, should not saue them from destruction, whom by his death hee iustifieth and reconcileth?
g In the stead of some iust man.
h He setteth out his loue vnto vs, that in the midst of our afflictions, we may know assuredly, he will bee present with vs.
i While sinne reigned in vs.
k From affliction and destruction.
9 Hee now passeth ouer to the other part of Iustification, which consisteth in the free imputation of the obedience of Christ: so that to the remission of sinnes, there is added moreouer and besides, the gift of Christs righteousnesse imputed or put vpon vs by faith, which swalloweth vp that vnrighteousnesse which flowed from Adam into vs, and all the fruites thereof: so that in Christ wee doe not onely cease to be vniust, but we begin also to bee iust. 10 From Adam in whom all haue sinned, both guiltinesse and death (which is the punishment of the guiltinesse) came vpon all. *l By Adam, who is compared with Christ, like to him in this, that both of them make those which are theirs, partakers of that they haue: but they are vnlike in this, that Adam deriueth sinne into them that are his, euen of nature, and that to death: but Christ maketh them that are his, partakers of his righteousnesse by grace, and that vnto life.* *m By sinne, is meant that disease which is ours by inheritance, & men commonly call it originall sinne: for so he vseth to call that sinne in the singular number, whereas if hee speake of the fruits of it, hee vseth the plurall number, calling them sinnes.* *n That is, in Adam.* 11 That this is so, that both guiltinesse and death began not after the giuing and transgressing of Moses Law, it appeareth manifestly by that, that men died before that Law was giuen: for in that they died, sinne, which is the cause of death, was then: and in such sort, that it was also imputed: wherupon it foloweth that there was then some Law, the breach whereof was the cause of death. *o Euen from Adam to Moses.* *p Where there is no Law made, no man is punished as faultie and guiltie.* 12 But that this Law was not the vniuersall Law, and that that death did not proceede from any actuall sinne of euery one particularly, it appeareth hereby, that the very infants which neither could euer know nor transgresse that naturall Law, are notwithstanding dead as well as Adam. *q Our infants.* *r Nor after that sort as they sin that are of moe yeres, following their lusts: but yet the whole posteritie was corrupted in Adam when as he wittingly and willingly sinned.* 13 Now that first Adam answereth the latter, who is Christ, as it is afterward declared. 14 Adam and Christ are compared together in this respect, that both of them doe giue and yeeld to theirs, that which is their own: but herein first they differ, that Adam by nature hath spread his fault to the destruction of many, but Christs obedience hath by grace ouerflowed many. *s That is, Adam.* 15 Another inequalitie consisteth in this, that by Adams one offence men are made guiltie, but the righteousnesse of Christ imputed vnto vs freely, doth not onely absolue vs from that one fault, but from all other. *t To the sentence of absolution, wherby we are quiet and pronounced righteous.* 16 The third difference is, that the righteousnesse of Christ, being imputed, vnto vs by grace, is of greater power to bring life, then the offence of Adam is to addict his posteritie to death. *u Be partakers of true and euerlasting life.*

17 Therefore to be short, as by one mans offence, the guiltinesse came on all men to make them subiect to death: so on the contrarie side, the righteousnesse of Christ, which by Gods mercie is imputed to all beleeuers, iustified them, that they may become partakers of euerlasting life.
x *Not onely because our sinnes are forgiuen vs, but also because the righteousnesse of Christ is imputed to vs.*

18 [17] Likewise then as by the offence of one,
the fault came on all men to condemnation, so
by the Iustifying of one, *the benefit abounded*
toward all men to the [x] iustification of life.
19 [18] For as by one mans [y] disobedience
[z] many were made sinners, so by that obedience of that one shall many also bee made
righteous.
20 [19] Moreouer the Law [a] entred thereupon that the offence should abound: neuerthelesse, where sinne abounded, *there* grace [b] a-
bounded much more:
21 That as sinne had reigned vnto death, so
might grace also reigne by righteousnesse vnto
eternall life through Iesus Christ our Lord.

18 The ground of this whole comparison is this, that these two men are set as two stockes or rootes, so that out of the one, sinne by nature, out of the other, righteousnesse by grace doth spring forth vpon others. y *So then, sinne entreth not into vs onely by following the steps of our forefather, but we take corruption of him by inheritance.* z *This word, Many, is set against this word, a few.* 19 A preuenting of an obiection: why then did the Law of Moses enter thereupon? that men might be so much the more guiltie, and the benefit of God in Christ Iesus be so much the more glorious. a *Besides that disease which all men were infected withall by being defiled with one mans sinne, the Law entred.* b *Grace was powred so plentifully from heauen, that it did not onely counteruaile sinne, but aboue measure passed it.*

CHAP. VI.

1 *He commeth to sanctification, without which, that no man putteth on Christs righteousnesse, he prooueth,* 4 *by an argument taken of Baptisme,* 12 *and thereupon exhorteth to holinesse of life,* 16 *briefly making mention of the Law transgressed.*

1 Hee passeth now to another benefit of Christ, which is called sanctification or regeneration.
a *In that corruption, for though the guiltinesse of sinne, be not imputed to vs, yet the corruption remaineth still in vs: the which Sanctification that followeth Iustification, killeth by little and little.*
2 The benefite of Iustification and Sanctification, are alwayes ioyned together inseparably, and both of them proceede from Christ by the grace of God: Now Sanctification is the abolishing of sinne, that is, of our naturall corruption, into whose place succeedeth the cleannesse and purenesse of nature reformed.

WHat [1] shall we say then? Shall we continue still in [a] sinne, that grace may a-
bound? God forbid.
2 [2] How shall we, that are [b] dead to sinne,
liue yet therein?
3 [3] Know yee not, that *all we which haue
beene baptized into [c] Iesus Christ, haue beene
baptized into his death?
4 *We are buried then with him by baptisme into his death, that like as Christ was raised vp from the dead [d] to the glory of the father,
so [e] we also should * walke in newnesse of life.
5 [4] * For if we be planted with him to the
[f] similitude of his death, euen so shall we [g] bee
to the similitude of his resurrection,
6 Knowing this, that our [h] old man is crucified with [i] him, that the [k] body of sinne might
bee destroyed, that hencefoorth we should not
[l] serue sinne.
7 [5] For he that is dead, is freed from sinne.
8 Wherefore, if we bee dead with Christ,
we beleeue that we shall liue also with him.
9 Knowing that Christ being raised from
the dead, dieth no more: death hath no more
dominion ouer him.
10 For in that hee died, hee died [m] once to
sinne: but in that he liueth, he liueth to [n] God.
11 Likewise thinke yee also, that yee are
dead to sinne, but are aliue to God in Iesus
Christ our Lord.
12 [6] Let not sinne [o] reigne therfore in your
mortall body, that yee should obey it in the
lusts thereof:
13 Neither [p] giue yee your [q] members *as*
[r] weapons of vnrighteousnesse vnto sinne: but
giue your selues vnto God, as they that are a-
liue from the dead, and *giue* your members *as*
weapons of righteousnesse vnto God.
14 [7] For sinne shall not haue dominion o-
uer you: for yee are not vnder the Law, but vnder grace.
15 [8] What then? shall we sinne, because we
are not vnder the Law, but vnder grace? God
forbid.
16 *Know ye not, that to whomsoeuer yee
giue your selues as seruants to obey, his seruants yee are to whom yee obey, whither it be
of sinne vnto death, or of obedience vnto righteousnesse?
17 [9] But God *bee* thanked, that yee haue
bene the seruants of sinne, but ye haue obeyed
from the heart vnto the [s] forme of the doctrine,
whereunto yee were deliuered.
18 Being then made free from sinne, yee
are made the seruants of righteousnesse.
19 I speake after the maner of man, because
of the infirmitie of your flesh: for as yee haue
giuen your members seruants to vncleannesse
and to iniquitie, to *commit* iniquitie, so nowe
giue your members seruants vnto righteousnesse in holinesse.
20 For when ye were the seruants of sinne,
yee were [t] freed from righteousnesse.
21 [10] What fruit had ye then in those things,
whereof yee are now ashamed? For the [u] ende
of those things *is* death.
22 But now being freed from sinne, and
made seruants vnto God, yee haue your fruite
in holinesse, and the end, euerlasting life.
23 [11] For the wages of sinne is death: but
the gift of God *is* eternall life, through Iesus
Christ our Lord.

l *The end of sanctification which we shoot at, and shall at length come to, to wit, when God shall be all in all.*
5 He prooueth it by the effects of death, vsing a comparison of Christ the head with his members.
m *Once for all.*
n *With God.*
6 An exhortation to contend and striue with corruption and all the effectes thereof.
o *By reigning, S. Paul meaneth that chieftie and high rule, which no man striueth against, and if any doe, yet it is in vaine.*
p *To sinne, as to a Lord or tyrant.*
q *Your mind and all the powers of it.*
r *As instruments to commit wickednesse withall.*
7 He granteth, that sinne is not yet so dead in vs that it is vtterly extinct: but he promiseth victory to them that contend manfully, because we haue the grace of God giuen vs which worketh so that the Law is not now in vs the power & instrument of sinne.
8 To be vnder the Law and vnder sinne signifie all one, in respect of them which are not sanctified, as on the contrary side to be vnder grace and righteousnesse, agree to them that are regenerate. Now these are contraries, so that one cannot agree with the other: Therefore let righteousnesse expell sinne.
* Iohn 8.34. 2.pet.2.19.
9 By nature we are slaues to sin and free from righteousnesse, but by the grace of God we are made seruants to righteousnes, and therefore free from sinne.

b *They are said of Paul to be dead to sinne, which are in such sort made partakers of the vertue of Christ, that that naturall corruption is dead in them, that is, the force of it is put out, and it bringeth not foorth his bitter fruites: And on the other side, they are said to liue to sinne, which are in the flesh, that is, whom the spirit of God hath not deliuered from the slauerie of the corruption of nature.* 3 There are three parts of this Sanctification: to wit, the death of the olde man or sinne, his buriall, and the resurrection of the new man, descending into vs from the vertue of the death, buriall, and resurrection of Christ, of which benefit our baptisme is a signe and pledge. * *Gal.3.27.* c *To the end that growing vp in one with him, we should receiue his strength, to quench sinne in vs, and to make vs new men.* * *Col.2.12.* d *That Christ himselfe being discharged of his infirmitie and weaknesse, might liue in glory with God for euer.* e *And wee which are his members rise for this end, that being made partakers of the selfe same vertue, we should begin to leade a new life, as though wee were already in heauen.* * *Ephes.4.23.colos.3.8.hebr.12 1.1.Pet.2.1.* 4 The death of sinne and the life of righteousnesse, or our ingraffing into Christ, and growing vp into one with him, cannot bee separated by any meanes, neither in death nor life: whereby it followeth, that no man is sanctified, which liueth still to sinne, and therefore is no man made partaker of Christ by faith, which repenteth not and turneth not from his wickednesse: for as hee said before, the Lawe is not subuerted but established by faith. * *1.Cor.6.14.2.tim.2.11.* f *In so much as by meanes of the strength which commeth from him to vs, wee so die to sinne, as hee is dead.* g *For we become euery day more perfite then other: for we shall neuer bee perfectly sanctified, as long as we liue here.* h *All our whole nature, as we are conceiued and borne into this world with sinne, which is called olde, partly by comparing that olde Adam with Christ, and partly also in respect of the deformation of our corrupt nature, which we change with a new.* i *Our corrupt nature is attributed to Christ, not in deed, but by imputation.* k *That naughtinesse which sticketh fast in vs.*

s *This kind of speach hath a force in it: for he meaneth thereby that the doctrine of the Gospel is like vnto a certaine mould which we are cast into, to be framed and fashioned like vnto it.* t *Righteousnesse had no rule ouer you.* 10 An exhortation to the study of righteousnesse and hatred of sinne, the contrary ends of both being set downe before vs. u *The reward or payment.* 11 Death is the punishment due to sinne, but wee are sanctified freely, vnto life euerlasting.

CHAP. VII.

2 *Hee declareth what it is, to bee no more vnder the Lawe,* 2 *by an example taken of the Lawe of marriage:* 7. 12 *And lest the Law should seeme faultie,* 14 *hee prooueth, that our sinne is the cause* 13 *that the same is an occasion*

of death, 17 which was giuen vs, vnto life: 21 He setteth out the battell betweene the flesh and the spirit.

KNow [1] yee not brethren, (for I speake
to them that know the Lawe) that the
Lawe hath dominion ouer a man as long as he
liueth?
2 *For the woman which is in subiection
to a man, is bound by the Lawe to the man,
while he liueth: but if the man bee dead, shee is
deliuered, from the Law of the man.
3 So then, if while the man liueth, shee taketh another man, shee shall be [a] called an * a-
dulteresse: but if the man bee dead, shee is free
from the Lawe, so that shee is not an adulteresse, though shee take another man.
4 [2] So yee, my brethren, are dead also to
the Law by the body of Christ, that ye should
bee vnto another, *euen* vnto him that is raised
vp from the dead, that we should bring foorth
[c] fruit vnto [d] God.
5 [3] For when we [e] were in the flesh, the [f] affections of sinnes, which were by the [g] Lawe,
had [h] force in our members, to bring forth fruit
vnto death.
6 But now wee are deliuered from the
Law, he [i] being dead [k] in whom wee were [l] holden, that we should serue in [m] newnesse of Spirit, and not in the oldnesse of the [n] letter.
7 [4] What shall wee say then? *Is* the Lawe
sinne? God forbid. Nay, I knew not sinne, but
by the Law: for I had not knowen [o] lust, except
the Law had said, * Thou shalt not lust.
8 But sinne tooke an occasion by the commaundement, and wrought in mee all maner
of concupiscence: for without the Law sinne
is [p] dead.
9 [5] For I once was aliue, without the
[q] Law: but when the commaundement [r] came
sinne reuiued,
10 But I [s] died: and the same commandement which was *ordeined* vnto life, was found
to be vnto me vnto death.
11 For sinne tooke occasion by the commandement, and deceiued mee, and thereby
slewe *me*.
12 [6] Wherefore the Law *is* * holy, and that
[t] commandement *is* holy and iust and good.
13 [7] Was that then which is good, [u] made
death vnto mee? God forbid: but sinne that it
might [x] appeare sinne, wrought death in me by
that which is good, that sinne might be [y] out of
measure sinfull by the commandement.
14 [8] For we know that the Law is spirituall,
but I am carnall, sold vnder sinne.
15 [9] For I [10] allow not that which I doe: for
what I [11] would, that do I not: but what I hate,
that doe I.
16 If I doe then that which I would not, I
consent to the Law that *it is* good.
17 Now then, it is no more I, that doe it,
but [z] sinne that dwelleth in me.
18 [12] For I know, that in me, that is, in my
flesh dwelleth no good thing: for to wil is present with mee: but I find [a] no meanes to performe that which is good:
19 For I doe not the good thing, which I
would, but the euill, which I would not, that
doe I.
20 Now if I doe that I would not, it is no
more I that doe it, but the sinne that dwelleth
in mee.
21 [13] I find then that when I would doe
good, I am thus yoked, that euill is present
with mee.
22 For I delite in the Law of God concerning the [b] inner man:
23 But I see another Lawe in my mem-

1 By propounding the similitude of mariage, he compareth the state of man both before and after regeneration together. The law of matrimonie, saith he, is this, that so long as the husband liueth, the marriage abideth in force, but if hee be dead, the woman may marrie againe.

* 1.Cor.7.39.

a That is, shee shall be an adulteresse, by the consent and iudgement of all men.

* Matth.5.32.

2 An application of the similitude thus So, saith he, doth it fare with vs: for now we are ioyned to the Spirit, as it were to the second husband, by whom we must bring foorth new children: wee are dead in respect of the first husband, but in respect of the latter, we are as it were raised from the dead.

b That is, in the body of Christ, to giue vs to vnderstand, how straite and neere that fellowship is betwixt Christ and his members.

c He calleth the children, which the wife hath by her husband, fruit.

d Which are acceptable to God.

s In sinne, or by sinne.

6 The conclusion: That the Law of it selfe is holy, but all the fault is in vs which abuse the Law.

* 1.Tim 1.8.

t Touching not coueting.

7 The proposition, that the Law is not the cause of death, but our corrupt nature being therewith not onely discouered, but also stirred vp: and tooke occasion thereby to rebel, as which the more that things are forbidden it, the more it desireth them, and from hence commeth guiltinesse, and occasion of death.

u Beareth it the blame of my death?

x That sinne might shew it selfe to be sinne, and bewray it selfe to be that, which it is in deede.

y As euill as it could, shewing all the venoume it could.

8 The cause of this matter, is this because that the Lawe requireth a heauenly purenesse, but men such as they be borne, are bondslaues of corruption, which they willingly serue.

3 A declaration of the former saying: for the concupiscences (saith he) which the Law stirred vp in vs were in vs, as it were a husband, of whome wee brought foorth very deadly and cursed children: But now since that husband is dead, and so consequently being deliuered from the force of that killing Law, we haue passed into the gouernance of the Spirit, so that we bring forth now, not those rotten and dead, but liuely children. *e When we were in the state of the first mariage, which he calleth in the next verse following, the oldnesse of the letter. f The motions that egged vs to sinne, which shew their force euen in our minds. g He saith not, of the Law, but by the Law, because they spring of sinne which dwelleth within vs, and take occasion to worke thus in vs, by reason of the restraint that the Law maketh, not that the fault is in the law but in our selues. h Wrought their strength. i As if he said, The bond which bound vs, is dead, and vanished away, insomuch that sinne which held vs, hath not now wherewith to hold vs. k For this husband is within vs. l Satan is an vniust possessour, for hee brought vs in bondage of sinne and himselfe, deceitfully: and yet notwithstanding so long as we are sinners, we sinne willingly. m As becommeth them, which after the death of their old husband are ioyned to the Spirit: as whom the Spirit of God hath made new men. n By the letter, he meaneth the Law, in respect of that old condition: for before that our will bee framed by the holy Ghost, the Law speaketh but to deafe men, and therefore it is dumbe and dead to vs, as touching the fulfilling of it.* 4 An obiection: What then? are the Law and sinne all one, and do they agree together? nay saith he: Sinne is reproued and condemned by the Law. But because sinne cannot abide to bee reprooued, and was not in a maner felt, vntill it was prouoked and stirred vp by the Law, it taketh occasion thereby to bee more outragious, and yet by no fault of the Law. *o By the word, Lust, in this place he meaneth not euill lusts themselues, but the fountaine from whence they spring, for the very heathen Philosophers themselues condemned wicked lusts, though somewhat darkely, But as for this fountaine of them, they could not so much as suspect it, and yet it is the very seate of that naturall and vncleane spot and filth. * Exod.20.17 deut 5.21. p Though sinne be in vs, yet it is not knowen for sinne, neither doth it so rage, as it rageth after that the Law is knowen.* 5 He setteth himselfe before vs for an example, in whom al men may behold, first what they are of nature before they earnestly thinke vpon the Law of God: to wit, blockish, and heady to sinne and wickednesse, without all true sence and feeling of sinne, then what maner of persons they become, when their conscience is reproued by the testimonie of the Law, to wit, stubburne and more enflamed with the desire of sinne, then euer they were before. *q When I knew not the Lawe, then mee thought I liued in deed: for my conscience neuer troubled me, because it knew not my disease. r When I beganne to vnderstand the commaundement.*

9 Hee setteth himselfe being regenerate, before vs, for an ensample, in whom may easily appeare the strife of the Spirit and the flesh, and therefore of the Law of God, and our wickednes. For since that the Law in a man not regenerate bringeth forth death onely, therefore in him, it may easily be accused: but seeing that in a man which is regenerate, it bringeth foorth good fruit, it doth better appeare that euill actions proceed not from the Law but from sinne, that is, from our corrupt nature: And therefore the Apostle teacheth also what the true vse of the Law is, in reprouing sinne in the regenerate, vnto the end of the chapter: as a little before (to wit, from the seuenth verse vnto this fifteenth) he declared the vse of it in them which are not regenerate. 10 The deedes of my life, saith he, answere not, nay they are contrarie to my will: Therefore by the consent of my will with the Law, and repugnancie with the deedes of my life, it appeareth euidently, that the Law and a right ruled will doe perswade one thing, but corruption which hath her seate also in the regenerate, an other thing. 11 It is to bee noted, that one selfe same man is said to will and not to will, in diuers respects: to wit, hee is said to will, in that, that hee is regenerate by grace: and not to will, in that, that he is not regenerate, or in that, that he is such an one as hee was borne. But because the part which is regenerate, at length becommeth conquerour, therefore Paul susteining the part of the regenerate, speaketh in such sort as if the corruption which sinneth willingly, were something without a man: although afterward he graunteth that this euill is in his flesh, or in his members. *z That naturall corruption, which cleaueth fast euen to them that are regenerate, and not cleane conquered.* 12 This vice, or sinne, or law of sinne, doeth wholly possesse those men which are not regenerate, and hindreth them or holdeth them backe that are regenerate. *a This doeth in deede agree to that man, whome the grace of God hath made a new man: for where the spirit is not, how can there be any strife there?* 13 The conclusion: As the Law of God exhorteth to goodnesse, so doeth the Law of sinne (that is, the corruption wherein we are borne) force vs to wickednesse: but the Spirit, that is, our mind, in that that it is regenerate, consenteth with the Law of God: but the flesh, that is, the whole naturall man, is bondslaue to the Law of sinne. Therefore to bee short, wickednesse and death are not of the Lawe, but of sinne, which reigneth in them that are not regenerate: for they neither will, nor doe good, but will, and doe euill: but in them that are regenerate, it striueth against the Spirit or lawe of the mind, so that they cannot neither liue so well as they would, or bee so voide of sinne as they would. *b The inner man, and the new man are all one, and are answerable and set as contrarie to the old man, neither doeth this word, Inner man, signifie mans minde and reason, and the olde man, the powers that are vnder them, as the Philosophers imagine, but by the outward man is meant whatsoeuer is either without or within a man from top to toe, so long as that man is not borne a new by the grace of God.*

c The Law of the mind in this place, is not to be vnderstood of the mind as it is naturally, and as our mind is from our birth, but of the mind which is renewed by the Spirit of God.

bers, rebelling against the Law of my [c] minde,
and leading me captiue vnto the Law of sinne,
which is in my members.
24 [14] O [d] wretched man that I am, who shal
deliuer me from the body of this death!
25 I [e] thanke God through Iesus Christ
our Lord. Then I [f] my selfe in my minde serue
the Lawe of God, but in my flesh the lawe of
sinne.

14 It is a miserable thing to be yet in part subiect to sinne, which of it owne nature maketh vs guiltie of death: but wee must crie to the Lord, who will by death it selfe at length make vs conquerours as we are alreadie conquerours in Christ. *d Wearied with miserable and continuall conflicts.* *e Hee recouereth himselfe, and sheweth vs that he resteth onely in Christ.* *f This is the true perfection of them that are borne anew, to confesse that they are imperfit.*

CHAP. VIII.

1 He concludeth that there is no condemnation to them, who are grafted in Christ through his spirit, 3 howsoeuer they be as yet burdened with sinnes: 9 for they liue through that Spirit, 14 whose testimonie 15 driueth away all feare, 28 and relieueth our present miseries.

1 A conclusion of all the former disputation, from verse 16. chap. 1 euen to this place: Seeing that we, being iustified by faith in Christ, doe obtaine remission of sinnes and imputation of righteousnesse, and are also sanctified, it followeth hereof, that they that are grafted into Christ by faith, are out of all feare of condemnation.

NOw [1] then there *is* no condemnation to
them that are in Christ Iesus, which
[2] walke not after the [a] flesh but after the spirit.
2 [3] For the [b] Law of the Spirit of [c] life, *which
is* in [d] Christ Iesus, hath [e] freed mee from the
Law of sinne and of death.
3 [4] For, (that that was [f] impossible to the
Law, in as much as it was weake, because of the
[g] flesh) God sending his owne Sonne, in the similitude of [h] sinfull flesh, and for [i] sinne, [k] condemned sinne in the flesh,
4 That that [l] righteousnesse of the Lawe
might bee fulfilled [5] in vs, which walke not after the flesh, but after the Spirit.
5 [6] For they that are after the [m] flesh, sauour
the things of the flesh: but they that are after
the Spirit, the things of the Spirit.

2 The fruites of the Spirit, or effectes of sanctification which is begun in vs, doe not ingraft vs into Christ, but doe declare that wee are grafted into him. *a Follow not the flesh for their guide: for hee is not said to liue after the flesh, that hath the holy Ghost for his guide, though sometimes hee step awry.* 3 A preuenting of an obiection: seeing that the vertue of the Spirit which is in vs, is so weake, how may wee gather thereby, that there is no condemnation to them that haue that vertue? Because saith hee, that vertue of the quickening spirit which is so weake in vs, is most perfect and most mightie in Christ, and being imputed vnto vs which beleeue, causeth vs to bee so accompted of, as though there were no reliques of corruption and death in vs. Therefore hitherto, Paul disputed of remission of sinnes, and imputation of fulfilling the Law, and also of sanctification which is begunne in vs: but now he speaketh of the perfit imputation of Christs manhood, which part was necessarily required to the full appeasing of our consciences: For our sinnes are defaced by the blood of Christ, and the guiltinesse of our corruption is couered with the imputation of Christs obedience, and the corruption it selfe (which the Apostle calleth sinfull sinne) is healed in vs by little and little, by the gift of sanctification: but yet lacketh besides that, another remedie, to wit, the perfect sanctification of Christs owne flesh, which also is to vs imputed. *b The power and authoritie of the Spirit, against which, is set the tyrannie of sinne.* *c Which mortifieth the olde man, and quickneth the newe man.* *d To wit, absolutely and perfectly.* *e For Christs sanctification being imputed to vs, perfiteth our sanctification which is begunne in vs.* 4 Hee vseth no argument here, but expoundeth the mysterie of sanctification, which is imputed vnto vs: for because saith hee, that the vertue of the Law was not such (and that by reason of the corruption of our nature) that it could make man pure and perfit, and for that it rather kindled the disease of sinne, then did put it out and extinguish it, therefore God clothed his Sonne with flesh like vnto our sinfull flesh, wherein he vtterly abolished our corruption, that being accompted throughly pure and without fault in him apprehended and laide hold on by faith, wee might bee found to haue fully that singular perfection which the Lawe requireth, and therefore that there might bee no condemnation in vs. *f Which is not proper to the Law, but commeth by our fault.* *g In man not borne anew, whose disease the Lawe could point out, but it could not heale it.* *h Of mans nature which is corrupt through sinne, vntill hee sanctified it.* *i To abolish sinne in our flesh.* *k Shewed that sinne hath no right in vs.* *l The very substance of the Lawe of God might bee fulfilled, or that same which the Law requireth, that we may bee found iust before God: for if with our iustification, there bee ioyned that sanctification which is imputed to vs, wee are iust, according to that perfit forme which the Lord requireth.* 5 Hee returneth to that which hee said, that the sanctification which is begunne in vs, is a sure testimonie of our ingraffing into Christ, which is a most plentifull fruite of a godly and honest life. 6 A reason why to walke after the flesh, agreeth not to them which are grafted in Christ, but to walke after the spirit, agreeth and is meete for them: Because saith he, that they which are after the flesh, sauour the things of the flesh, but they that are after the Spirit, the things of the Spirit. *m They that liue as the flesh leadeth them.*

6 [7] For the wisedome of the flesh *is* death:
but the wisdome of the Spirit *is* life and peace.
7 [8] Because the wisedome of the flesh *is*
enimitie against God: [9] for it is not subiect to
the Law of God, neither in deed can be.
8 [10] So then they that are in the flesh, can
not please God.
9 [11] Now ye are not in the flesh, but in the
Spirit, because the Spirit of God dwelleth in
you: but if any man hath not the Spirit of
Christ, the same is not his.
10 [12] And if Christ bee in you, the [n] body is
dead, because of sinne: but the Spirit *is* life for
righteousnesse sake.
11 [13] But if the Spirit of him that raised vp
Iesus from the dead, dwell in you, hee that raised vp Christ from the dead, shall also quicken
your mortall bodies, by his Spirit that [o] dwelleth in you.
12 [14] Therefore brethren, wee are debters
not to the flesh, to liue after the flesh:
13 [15] For if yee liue after the flesh, yee shall
die: but if ye mortifie the deeds of the body by
the Spirit, yee shall liue.
14 [16] For as many as are led by the Spirit of
God, they are the sonnes of God.
15 [17] For yee haue not receiued the [p] Spirit
of bondage, to [q] feare againe: but yee haue receiued the Spirit of [r] adoption, whereby wee
crie Abba, Father.
16 The same Spirit beareth witnesse with
our spirit, that we are the children of God.
17 [18] If *we be* children, *we are* also [s] heires,
euen the heires of God, and heires annexed
with Christ: [19] if so be that we suffer with him,
that we may also be glorified with him.
18 [20] For I [t] count that the afflictions of this
present time *are* not worthy of the glorie,
which shall be shewed vnto vs.

7 Hee prooueth the consequent: because that whatsoeuer the flesh fauoureth, that engendereth death: and whatsoeuer the Spirit fauoureth, that tendeth to ioy and life euerlasting. 8 A reason and proofe why the wisedome of the flesh is death, because saith hee, it is the enemy of God. 9 A reason why the wisedome of the flesh is enemie to God, because it neither will neither can be subiect to him, and by flesh hee meaneth a man not regenerate. 10 The conclusion. Therefore they that walke after the flesh, cannot please God: whereby it followeth, that they are not grafted into Christ. 11 Hee commeth to the others, to wit, to them which walke after the Spirit, of whom we haue to vnderstand contrarie things, to the former: and first of all, he defineth what it is to be in the Spirit, or to bee sanctified: to wit, to haue the Spirit of God dwelling in vs. Then he declareth, that sanctification is so ioyned and knit to our graffing in Christ, that it can by no meanes bee separated. 12 He confirmeth the faithfull against the reliques of flesh and sinne, graunting that they are yet (as appeareth by the corruption which is in them) touching one of their parts (which he calleth the body, that is to say, a lumpe) which is not yet purged from this earthly filthinesse and death: but therewithal willing them to doubt nothing of the happie successe of this combate, because that euen this little sparke of the Spirit, (that is, of the grace of regeneration) which appeareth to bee in them by the fruites of righteousnesse, is the seede of life. *n The flesh, or all that, which as yet sticketh fast in the clefts of sinne and death.* 13 A confirmation of the former sentence. You haue the selfe same Spirit which Christ hath: Therefore at length it shall doe the same in you, that it did in Christ, to wit, when all infirmities being vtterly laide aside, and death ouercome, it shall cloth you with heauenly glory. *o By the vertue and power of it, which shewed the same might first in our head, and daily worketh in his members.* 14 An exhortation to oppresse the flesh daily more and more by the vertue of the Spirit of regeneration, because (saith he) you are debters vnto God, for so much as you haue receiued so many benefites of him. 15 An other reason of the profit that ensueth: for such as striue and fight valiantly shall haue euerlasting life. 16 A confirmation of this reason: for they bee the children of God, which are gouerned by his spirit, therefore shall they haue life euerlasting. 17 Hee declareth and expoundeth by the way, in these two verses by what right this name, to bee called the children of God, is giuen to the beleeuers, because saith hee, they haue receiued the grace of the Gospel, wherein God sheweth himselfe, not (as before in the publishing of the Law) terrible and fearefull, but a most benigne and louing father in Christ, so that with great boldnesse wee call him Father, the holy Ghost sealing this adoption in our hearts by faith. *p By the Spirit, is ment the holy Ghost whom we are said to receiue, when hee worketh in our minds.* *q Which feare it stirred vp in our minds by the preaching of the Lawe.* *r Which sealeth our adoption in our minds, and therefore openeth our mouthes.* 18 A proofe of the consequent of the confirmation: because that he which is the sonne of God, doth enioy God with Christ. *s Partakers of our fathers goods, and that freely, because we are children by adoption.* 19 Now Paul teacheth by what way the sonnes of God doe come to that felicitie, to wit, by the crosse, as Christ himselfe did: and therewithall openeth vnto them fountaines of comfort: as first that wee haue Christ a companion and fellow of our afflictions: secondly that we shalbe also his fellowes in that euerlasting glory. 20 Thirdly that this glory which we looke for, doth a thousand parts surmount the miserie of our afflictions. *t All being well considered, I gather.*

19 [21] For the feruent deſire of the [u] creature waiteth when the ſonnes of God ſhall bee reueiled.

20 Becauſe the creature is ſubiect to [x] vanitie, not of it [y] owne will, but by reaſon [z] of him, which hath ſubdued it vnder [a] hope.

21 Becauſe the creature alſo ſhall be deliuered from the [b] bondage of corruption into the glorious libertie of the ſonnes of God.

22 For wee know that euery creature groneth with vs alſo, & [c] trauaileth in paine together vnto this preſent.

23 [22] And not onely *the creature*, but wee alſo which haue the firſt fruites of the Spirit, euen wee doe ſigh in our [d] ſelues, waiting for the adoption, *euen* * [e] the redemption of our bodie.

24 [23] For we are ſaued by hope: but [f] hope that is ſeene, is not hope: for how can a man hope for that he ſeeth?

25 But if we hope for that we ſee not, wee doe with patience abide for it.

26 [24] Likewiſe the Spirit alſo [g] helpeth our infirmities: for wee know not what to pray as wee ought: but the Spirit it ſelfe maketh [h] requeſt for vs with ſighes, which can not bee expreſſed.

27 But he that ſearcheth the hearts, knoweth what is the [i] meaning of the Spirit: for hee maketh requeſt for the Saints, [k] according to *the will of* God.

28 [25] Alſo wee knowe that [l] all things worke together for the beſt vnto them that loue God, euen to them that are called of *his* [m] purpoſe.

29 For thoſe which he knew before, he alſo predeſtinate to be made like to the image of his ſonne, that hee might be the firſt borne among many brethren.

30 Moreouer whome hee [n] predeſtinated, them alſo he called, and whom he called, them alſo he iuſtified, and whom he iuſtified, them he alſo glorified.

31 [26] What ſhall wee then ſay to theſe things? If God bee on our ſide, who *can bee* againſt vs?

32 Who ſpared not his owne Sonne, but gaue him for vs all *to death*, how ſhall hee not with him [o] giue vs all things alſo?

33 [27] Who ſhall lay any thing to the charge of Gods choſen? *it is* [p] God that iuſtifieth,

34 Who ſhall condemne? *it is* Chriſt which is dead, yea or rather which is riſen againe, who is alſo at the right hand of God, and maketh requeſt alſo for vs.

35 Who ſhall ſeparate vs from the loue of [q] Chriſt? ſhall tribulation or anguiſh, or perſecution, or famine, or nakedneſſe, or perill, or ſword?

36 As it is written, * For thy ſake are wee killed all day long: we are counted as ſheepe for the ſlaughter.

37 [r] Neuertheleſſe, in all theſe things wee are more then conquerours through him that loued vs.

38 For I am perſwaded that neither death, nor life, nor Angels, nor principalities, nor powers, nor things preſent, nor things to come,

39 Nor height, nor depth, nor any other creature ſhall bee able to ſeparate vs from the loue of God, which is in Chriſt Ieſus our Lord.

21 Fourthly, he plainly teacheth vs that we ſhall certainely bee renued from that confuſion and horrible deformation of the whole world, which cannot be continuall, as it was not at the beginning: But as it had a beginning by the ſinne of man for whom it was made by the ordinance of God, ſo ſhall it at length be reſtored with the elect.

u *All this world.* x *Is ſubiect to a vaniſhing and flitting ſtate.* y *Not by their naturall inclination.* z *That they ſhould obey the Creators commandment, whom it pleaſed to ſhew by their fickle ſtate, how greatly he was diſpleaſed with man.* a *God would not make the world ſubiect to euerlaſting curſe, for the ſinne of man, but gaue it hope that it ſhould be reſtored.* b *From the corruption which they are now ſubiect to, they ſhall be deliuered and changed into that bleſſed ſtate of incorruption, which ſhall be reuealed, when the ſonnes of God ſhall be aduanced to glory.* c *By this word is meant, not onely exceeding ſorrow, but alſo the fruit that followeth of it.* 22 Fiftly, if the reſt of the world looke for a reſtoring, groning as it were for it, and that not in vaine, let it not grieue vs alſo to ſigh, yea, let vs bee more certainely perſwaded of our redemption to come, for as much as we haue the firſt fruits of the Spirit. d *Euen from the bottome of our hearts.* * *Luke* 21 28. e *That laſt reſtoring, which ſhall be the accompliſhment of our adoption.* 23 Sixtly, hope is neceſſarily ioyned with faith: ſeeing then that wee beleeue thoſe things which we are not yet in poſſeſsion of, and hope reſpecteth not the thing that is preſent, we muſt therefore hope and patiently waite for that which we beleeue ſhall come to paſſe. f *This is ſpoken by the figure Metonomie: Hope, for that which is hoped for.* 24 Seuenthly, There is no cauſe why we ſhould faint vnder the burden of afflictions, ſeeing that prayers miniſter vnto vs a moſt ſure helpe: which cannot bee fruſtrate, ſeeing they proceede from the ſpirit of God which dwelleth in vs. g *Beareth our burden, as it were, that we faint not vnder it.* h *Prouoketh vs to prayers, and telleth vs as it were within, what we ſhall ſay, and how we ſhall grone.* i *What ſobs and ſighs proceede from the inſtinct of his Spirit.* k *Becauſe he teacheth the godly to pray according to Gods will.* 25 Eightly, wee are not afflicted, either by chance or to our harme, but by Gods prouidence for our great profit: who as hee choſe vs from the beginning, ſo hath he predeſtinate vs to be made like to the image of his Sonne: and therefore will bring vs in his time, being called and iuſtified, to glory, by the croſſe. l *Not onely afflictions, but whatſoeuer elſe.* m *Hee calleth that, Purpoſe, which God hath from euerlaſting appointed with himſelfe according to his good will and pleaſure.* n *He vſeth the time paſt, for the time preſent, as the Hebrewes vſe, who ſometime ſet downe the thing that is to come, by the time that is paſt, to ſignifie the certaintie of it: and hee hath alſo a regard to Gods continuall working.* 26 Ninthly, we haue no cauſe to feare that the Lord will not giue vs whatſoeuer is profitable for vs, ſeeing that hee hath not ſpared his owne Sonne to ſaue vs.

o *Giue vs freely.* 27 A moſt glorious and comfortable concluſion of the whole ſecond part of this Epiſtle, that is of the treatiſe of iuſtification. There are no accuſers that wee haue neede to bee afraid of before God, ſeeing that God himſelfe abſolueth vs as iuſt: and therefore much leſſe neede wee to feare damnation, ſeeing that we reſt vpon the death and reſurrection, the Almightie power and defence of Ieſus Chriſt. Therefore what can there bee ſo waightie in this life, or of ſo great force and power, that might feare vs, as though wee might fall from the loue of God, wherewith he loueth vs in Chriſt? Surely nothing, ſeeing that it is in it ſelfe moſt conſtant and ſure, and alſo in vs being confirmed by ſtedfaſt faith. p *Who pronounceth vs not onely guiltleſſe, but alſo perfitly iuſt in his Sonne.* q *Wherewith Chriſt loueth vs.* * *Pſalme* 44.22. r *Wee are not onely not ouercome with ſo great and many miſeries and calamities, but alſo more then conquerours in all of them.*

CHAP. IX.

1 He anſwereth an obiection, that might bee brought on the Iewes behalfe, 7 and telleth of two ſortes of Abrahams children, 15 and that God worketh all things in this matter according to his will, 20 euen as the potter doeth. 24. 30 Hee prooueth aſwell the calling of the Gentiles, 31 as alſo the reiecting of the Iewes, 25. 27 by the teſtimonies of the Prophets.

I Say [1] the trueth in Chriſt, I lie not, my conſcience bearing me witneſſe in the holy Ghoſt,

2 That I haue great heauineſſe, and continuall ſorrow in mine heart.

3 For I would wiſh my ſelfe to bee [a] ſeparated from Chriſt, for my brethren that are my kinſemen according to the [b] fleſh,

4 Which are the Iſraelites, to whom *pertaineth* the adoption, and the [c] glorie, and the * [d] Couenaunts, and the giuing of the [e] Lawe, and the [f] ſeruice *of God*, and the [g] promiſes.

5 Of whom *are* the fathers, and of whom concerning the fleſh, Chriſt *came*, who is [2] God ouer all, bleſſed for euer, Amen.

6 * [3] Notwithſtanding it cannot bee that the Word of God ſhould take none effect: for all they are not [h] Iſrael, which are of Iſrael:

1 The third part of this Epiſtle, euen to the twelfth Chapter, wherein Paul aſcendeth to the higher cauſes of faith: and firſt of all, becauſe hee purpoſed to ſpeake much of the caſting off of the Iewes, hee vſeth an inſinuation, declaring by a double or triple oath, and by witneſsing of his great deſire towards their ſaluation, his ſingular loue towards them, and therewithall graunting vnto them all their prerogatiues. a *The Apoſtle loued his brethren ſo entirely, that if it had beene poſsible, hee would haue beene ready to haue redeemed the caſting away of the Iſraelites, with the loſſe of his owne ſoule for euer: for this word, Separate, betokeneth as much in this place.* b *Being brethren by fleſh, as of one nation and countrey.* c *The Arke of the couenant, which was a token of Gods preſence.* * *Chap.* 2.17. *epheſ.* 2.12. d *The tables of the couenant, and this is ſpoken by the figure Metonymia.* e *Of the iudiciall Law.* f *The ceremoniall Law.* g *Which were made to Abraham and to his poſteritie.* 2 A moſt manifeſt teſtimonie of the Godhead and diuinitie of Chriſt. * *Chap.* 2.28. 3 He entreth into the handling of predeſtination, by a kind of preuenting an obiection: How may it be, that Iſrael is caſt off, but that therewithall we muſt alſo make the couenant which God made with Abraham and his ſeed, fruſtrate and void? He anſwereth therefore, that Gods word is true, although that Iſrael bee caſt off: for the election of the people of Iſrael is ſo generall and common, that notwithſtanding the ſame God chuſeth by his ſecret councel, ſuch as it pleaſeth him. So then this is the propoſition and ſtate of this treatiſe: The grace of ſaluation is offered generally in ſuch ſort, that notwithſtanding it, the efficacie thereof pertaineth onely to the elect. h *Iſrael in the firſt place, is taken for Iacob: and in the ſecond, for the Iſraelites.*

7 Neither

7 Neither *are they* all children, becauſe
they are the ſeede of Abraham: *[4] but, In [i] I-
ſaac ſhall thy ſeede be called:
8 [5] That is, they which are the children of
the [k] fleſh, are not the children of God: but
the * children of the [l] promiſe, are counted for
the ſeede.
9 [6] For this is a word of promiſe, * In this
ſame time wil I come, & Sara ſhal haue a ſonne.
10 [7] Neither *he* onely *felt this*, but alſo * Re-
becca, when ſhe had conceiued by one, *euen* by
our father Iſaac.
11 For yet *the children* were borne, and
when they had neither done good nor euill
(that the [m] purpoſe of God might [8] remaine according to election, not by workes, but by him
that calleth)
12 [9] It was ſayd vnto her, * The elder ſhall
ſerue the yonger.
13 As it is writen, * I haue loued Iacob, and
haue hated Eſau.
14 [10] What ſhall we ſay then? Is there [n] vnrighteouſneſſe with God? God forbid.
15 [11] For hee ſayth to Moſes, * I will [o] haue
mercie on him, to whome I will ſhew mercie:
and will haue [p] compaſſion on him, on whom I
will haue compaſſion.
16 [12] So then *it is* not in him that [q] willeth,
nor in him that runneth, but in God that ſheweth mercie.
17 [13] For the [r] Scripture ſaith vnto Pharao,
* For this ſame purpoſe haue I [ſ] ſtirred thee
vp, that I might [14] ſhew my power in thee, and
that my Name might be declared throughout
all the earth.
18 [15] Therefore he hath mercie on whome
he [t] will, and whom he will he hardeneth.
19 [16] Thou wilt ſay then vnto me, Why
doeth he yet complaine? for who hath reſiſted
his will?
20 [17] But, O man, who art thou which
pleadeſt againſt God? [18] ſhall the * thing [u] formed ſay to him that formed it, Why haſt thou
made me thus?
21 * [19] Hath not the potter power of the
clay to make of the ſame lumpe one [20] veſſel to
[x] honour, and another vnto [21] diſhonour?
22 [22] *What* and if God would, to ſhew his
wrath, and to make his power knowen, ſuffer
with long patience the [y] veſſels of wrath, prepared to [23] deſtruction?
23 And that he might declare the [z] riches of
his glory vpon the veſſels of mercie, which hee
hath prepared vnto glory?
24 [24] Euen vs whom he hath called, not of

*Gen. 21. 12. heb. 11. 18.
4 The firſt proofe is taken from the example of Abrahams owne houſe, wherin Iſaac only was accoũted the ſonne, and that by Gods ordinance: although that Iſmael alſo was borne of Abraham, & circumciſed before Iſaac.
i Iſaac ſhall bee thy true and naturall ſonne, and therefoore heire of the bleſsing.
5 A general application of the former proofe or example.
k Which are borne of Abraham by the courſe of nature.
*Gal 4. 28.
l Which are borne by vertue of the promiſe.
6 A reaſon of that application: Becauſe that Iſaac was borne by the vertue of the promiſe, and therfore he was not choſen, nay, he was not at al, but by the free will of God: whereby it followeth, that the promiſe is the fountaine of predeſtination, and not the fleſh, from which promiſe the particular election proceedeth, that is, that the elect are borne elect, and not that they be firſt borne, and then after elected, in reſpect of God who doth predeſtinate. * Gen. 18. 10. 7 Another forcible proofe taken from the example of Eſau & Iacob, which were both borne of the ſame Iſaac, which was the ſonne of promiſe of one mother, and at one birth, and not at diuers as Iſmael and Iſaac were: and yet notwithſtanding, Eſau being caſt off onely Iacob was choſen: and that before their birth, that neither any goodneſſe of Iacobs, might bee thought to bee the cauſe of his election, neither any wickedneſſe of Eſaus, of his caſting away. * *Gen. 25. 21.* *m Gods decree which proceedeth of his meere good will, whereby it pleaſeth him to chuſe one, and refuſe the other.* 8 Paul ſayth not, *might be made*, but *being made might remaine*. Therefore they are deceiued which make foreſeene faith the cauſe of election, and foreknowen infidelitie the cauſe of reprobation. 9 Hee prooueth the caſting away of Eſau by that, that he was made ſeruant to his brother: and prooueth the chuſing of Iacob, by that, that hee was made Lorde of his brother, although his brother was the firſt begotten. And leſt that any man might take this ſaying of God, and referre it to externall things, the Apoſtle ſheweth out of Malachi, who is a good interpreter of Moſes, that the ſeruitude of Eſau was ioyned with the hatred of God, and the Lordſhip of Iacob, with the loue of God. * *Geneſ. 25. 23.* * *Malach. 1. 2.* 10 The firſt obiection, If God doeth loue or hate vpon no conſideration of worthineſſe or vnworthineſſe, then is hee vniuſt, becauſe hee may loue them which are vnworthy, and hate them that are worthy. The Apoſtle deteſteth this blaſphemie, and afterward anſwereth it ſeuerally, poynt by poynt. *n Mans wit knoweth no other cauſes of loue or hatred, but thoſe that are in the perſons, and thereupon this obiection riſeth.* 11 Hee anſwereth firſt touching them which are choſen to ſaluation: in the chuſing of whom he denieth that God may ſeeme vniuſt, although hee chuſe and predeſtinate to ſaluation them that are not yet borne, without any reſpect of worthineſſe: becauſe he bringeth not the choſen to the appointed ende, but by the meanes of his mercie, which is a cauſe next vnder predeſtination. Now mercie preſuppoſeth miſerie, and againe, miſerie preſuppoſeth ſinne or voluntary corruption of mankinde, and corruption preſuppoſeth a pure and perfect creation. Moreouer, mercie is ſhewed by her degrees: to wit, by calling, by faith, by iuſtification and ſanctification, ſo that at length wee come to glorification, as the Apoſtle will ſhewe afterward. Now all theſe things orderly following the purpoſe of God, doe clearely prooue that hee can by no meanes ſeeme vniuſt in louing and ſauing his. * *Exodus 33. 19.* *o I will bee mercifull and fauourable to whome I liſt to bee fauourable.* *p I will haue compaſsion on whomſoeuer I liſt to haue compaſsion.* 12 The concluſion of the anſwere: Therefore GOD is not vniuſt in chuſing and ſauing of his free goodneſſe, ſuch as it pleaſeth him: as hee alſo anſwered Moſes when hee prayed for all the people. *q By Will hee meaneth the thought and endeuour of heart, and by running, good workes, to neither of which hee giueth the prayſe, but onely to the mercie of God.* 13 Now hee anſwereth concerning the reprobate, or them whome God hateth being not yet borne, and hath appointed to deſtruction, without any reſpect of vnworthineſſe. And firſt of all hee prooueth this to be true, by alleaging the teſtimonie of God himſelfe, touching Pharao, whome hee ſtirred vp to this purpoſe, that hee might bee glorified in his hardening and iuſt puniſhing. *r God ſo ſpeaketh vnto Pharao in the Scripture, or, the Scripture bringeth in God, ſo ſpeaking to Pharao.*

*Exod. 9. 16.
ſ Brought thee into this world.
14 Secondly, he bringeth the end of Gods counſell, to ſhew that there is no vnrighteouſneſſe in him. Now this chiefeſt ende is, not properly & ſimply the deſtruction of the wicked, but Gods glorie which appeareth in their rightfull puniſhment.
15 A concluſion of the full anſwere to ye firſt obiection: therfore ſeeing God doth not ſaue them whom he freely choſe according to his good will and pleaſure, but by iuſtifying & ſanctifying them by his grace, his coũſell in ſauing them cannot ſeeme vniuſt. And againe, there is no vniuſtice in the euerlaſting counſell of God, touching the deſtruction of them whom hee liſteth to deſtroy, for that he hardeneth before he deſtroyeth: Therefore the third anſwere for the maintenance of Gods iuſtice in the euerlaſting counſell of reprobation, conſiſteth in this word Hardening: which notwithſtanding he concealed in the former verſe, becauſe the hiſtory of Pharao was wel knowen. But the force of the word is great, for hardening which is ſet againſt Mercie, preſuppoſeth the ſame things that mercy did, to wit, a voluntary corruption, wherein the reprobate are hardened: and againe, corruption preſuppoſeth a perfect ſtate of creation. Moreouer, this hardening alſo is voluntary, for God ſo hardeneth being offended with corruption, that he vſeth their owne will whom he hardeneth, to the executing of that iudgement. Then follow the fruits of hardening, to wit, vnbeliefe and ſinne, which are the true and proper cauſes of the condemnation of the reprobate. Why doeth he then appoint to deſtruction? becauſe he will: why doth he harden? becauſe they are corrupt: why doth he condemne? becauſe they are ſinners. Where is then vnrighteouſnes? Nay, if hee ſhould deſtroy all after this ſort, to whom ſhould he doe iniurie? *t Whom it pleaſed him to appoint, to ſhew his fauour vpon.* 16 Another obiection, but onely for the reprobate, riſing vpon the former anſwere. If God doe appoint to euerlaſting deſtruction, ſuch as he liſteth, and if that cannot be hindered nor withſtanded, that hee hath once decreed, how doeth he iuſtly condemne them, which periſh by his will? 17 The Apoſtle doth not anſwere that it is not Gods will, or that God doeth not either reiect or elect according to his pleaſure, which thing the wicked call blaſphemie, but hee rather granteth his aduerſary both the antecedents, to wit, that it is Gods will, and that it muſt of neceſſitie ſo fall out, yet hee denieth that God is therefore to bee thought an vniuſt reuenger of the wicked: for ſeeing it appeareth by manifeſt proofe that this is the will of God, and his doing, what impudencie is it for man, which is but duſt and aſhes, to diſpute with God, and as it were to call him into iudgement? Now if any man ſay that the doubt is not ſo diſſolued & anſwered, I anſwere, that there is no ſurer demonſtration in any matter, becauſe it is grounded vpon this principle, That the will of God is the rule of righteouſneſſe. 18 An amplification of the former anſwere, taken from a compariſon, whereby alſo it appeareth that Gods determinate counſell is ſet of Paul the higheſt of all cauſes: ſo that it dependeth not vpon any reſpect of the ſecond cauſes, but doth rather frame and direct them. * *Eſa. 45. 9.* *u This ſimilitude agreeth very fitly in the firſt creation of mankinde.* * *Ierem. 18. 6.* 19 Alluding to the creation of Adam, hee compareth mankind not yet made, (but in the Creators minde) to a lumpe of clay: whereof afterward God made, and doth dayly make, according as he purpoſed from euerlaſting, both ſuch as ſhould be elect, and ſuch as ſhould be reprobate, as alſo this word, Making, declareth. 20 Whereas in the obiection propounded, mention was onely made of veſſels to diſhonour, yet he ſpeaketh of the other alſo in this anſwere, for that he proueth ye Creator to be iuſt in either of them, as the rule of contraries requireth. *x To honeſt vſes.* 21 Seeing then, that in ye name of diſhonor, the ignominy of euerlaſting death is ſignified, they ſpeake with Paul, which ſay, that ſome are made of God to moſt iuſt deſtructiõ: & they that are offẽded with this kind of ſpeach bewray their own folly. 22 The ſecõd anſwere is this, that God, moreouer and beſides that he doth iuſtly decree whatſoeuer he doth decree, vſeth that moderation in executing of his decrees, as declareth his ſingular lenitie euen in the reprobate, in that, that hee ſuffreth them a long time, and permitteth them to enioy many and ſingular benefits, vntill at length he iuſtly condemne them: and that to good end and purpoſe, to wit, to ſhew himſelfe to be an enemie and reuenger of wickednes, that it may appeare what power he is of by theſe ſeuere iudgments, & finally by compariſon of contraries to ſet forth in deed, how great his mercie is towards ye elect. *y By veſſels, the Hebrewes vnderſtand al kinds of inſtruments.* 23 Therefore againe, we may ſay with Paul that ſome men are made of God the Creator to deſtruction. *z The vnmeaſurable and marueilous greatneſſe.* 24 Hauing eſtabliſhed the doctrine of the eternall predeſtination of God on both parts, that is, as well of the reprobate, as of the elect, he commeth now to ſhew the vſe of it, teaching vs that we ought not to ſeeke the teſtimonie of it in the ſecret counſel of God, but by the vocation which is made manifeſt, and ſet foorth in the Church, propounding vnto vs, the example of the Iewes and Gentiles, that the doctrine may be better perceiued.

a He sayth not, that all and euery one of the Iewes are called, but some of the Iewes, and some of the Gentiles.

25 Our vocation or calling, is free, & of grace, euen as our predestination is: & therfore there is no cause why either our owne vnworthinesse, or the vnworthinesse of our ancesters should cause vs to think that we are not the elect & chosen of God, if we be called of him, and so embrace through faith the saluatiō that is offered vs.

* *Hose.2.23. 1.pet.2.10.*

* *Hose.1.10.*

26 Contrariwise, Neither any outward generall calling, neither any worthinesse of our ancesters, is a sufficient witnes of election, vnlesse by faith & beliefe wee answere Gods calling: which thing came to passe in the Iewes, as the Lord had forewarned.

**Isa.20.21.*

b God purposeth to bring the vnkinde and vnthankefull people to an extreame fewnesse.

the [a] Iewes onely, but also of the Gentiles,
25 [25] As hee also sayth in Osee, *I will call
them, My people, which were not my people:
and her, Beloued, which was not beloued.
26 And it shall be in the place where it was
sayd vnto them, * Yee are not my people, that
there they shall be called, The children of the
liuing God.
27 [26] Also Esaias crieth concerning Israel,
* Though the number of the children of Israel
were as the sand of the sea, *yet* shall *but* a remnant be saued.
28 For he will make his account, and gather
it into a [b] short summe with righteousnesse:
for the Lord will make a short account in the
earth.
29 *And as Esaias sayde before, Except
the Lord of [c] hostes had left vs a [d] seede, wee
had been made as Sodom, and had been like to
Gomorrha.
30 [27] What shall wee say then? That the
Gentiles which followed [e] not righteousnesse,
haue attained vnto righteousnesse, euen the
righteousnesse which is of faith.
31 [28] But Israel which followed the Lawe
of righteousnesse, could not attaine vnto the
Lawe of righteousnesse.
32 Wherefore? Because *they sought it* not
by faith, but as *it were* by the [f] workes of the
Lawe: for they haue stumbled at the stumbling stone,
33 As it is written, *Behold, I lay in Sion a stumbling stone, and a rocke to make men
fall: and euery one that beleeueth in him shall
not be ashamed.

**Isa.1.9.* *c Armies, by which word the chiefest power that is, is giuen to God.* *d Euen as very few.* 27 The declaration and manifestation of our election, is our calling, apprehended by faith, as it came to passe in the Gentiles. *e So then the Gentiles had no workes to prepare and procure Gods mercie before hand: and as for that the Gentiles attained to that which they sought not for, the mercie of God is to be thanked for it: and in that the Iewes attaine not to that which they sought after, they can thanke none for it but themselues, because they sought it not aright.* 28 The pride of men is the cause that they contemne vocation, so that the cause of their damnation neede not to be sought for any other where but in themselues. *f Seeking to come by righteousnesse, they followed the law of righteousnesse.* **Psal.118.22. isa.8.14. and 28.16. 1.pet.2.6.*

CHAP. X.

1 *Hee handleth the effects of election,* 3 *that some refuse, and some embrace* 4 *Christ, who is the end of the Lawe.* 15 *Hee sheweth that Moses foretold the calling of the Gentiles,* 20 *and Esaias the hardening of the Iewes.*

1 Purposing to set forth in the Iewes an example of marueilous obstinacie he vseth an insinuation.

2 The first entrance into the vocation vnto saluation, is to renounce our owne righteousnesse; the next is to imbrace that righteousnesse by faith, which God freely offereth vs in the Gospel.

Brethren, [1] mine hearts desire and praier to
God for Israel is, that they might be saued.
2 For I beare them record, that they haue
the zeale of God, but not according to knowledge.
3 [2] For they, [a] being ignorant of the righteousnes of God, and going about to [b] stablish
their owne righteousnes, haue not submitted
themselues to the righteousnes of God.
4 * [3] For Christ *is* the [c] end of the Lawe for
righteousnesse vnto [d] euery one that beleeueth.
5 [4] For Moses *thus* describeth the righteousnesse which is of the Law, *That the man
which doeth these things, shall liue thereby.
6 But the righteousnesse which is of faith,
speaketh on this wise, * [e] Say not in thine
heart, Who shall ascend into heauen? (that is
to bring Christ from aboue:)
7 Or, Who shall descend into the deepe?
(that is to bring Christ againe from the dead)
8 [5] But what sayth it? * The [f] worde is
neere thee, *euen* in thy mouth, & in thine heart.
This is the word of faith which we preach.
9 [6] For if thou shalt [g] confesse with thy
mouth the Lord Iesus, & shalt beleeue in thine
heart, that [h] God raised him vp from the dead,
thou shalt be saued:
10 For with the heart man [i] beleeueth vnto
righteousnesse, and with the mouth man confesseth to saluation.
11 [7] For the Scripture sayth, *Whosoeuer
[k] beleeueth in him, shall not be ashamed.
12 For there is no difference betweene the
Iew and the Grecian: for hee that is Lord ouer
all, is rich vnto all, that call on him.
13 * [8] For whosoeuer shall call vpon the
Name of the Lord, shall be saued.
14 But howe shall they call on him, in
whom they haue not beleeued? [9] and how shal
they beleeue in him, of whom they haue not
heard? and how shall they heare without a
preacher?
15 And how shall they preach, except they
bee sent? as it is written, *Howe beautifull
are the feete of them which bring glad tidings
of peace, and bring glad tidings of good
things!
16 [10] But they haue not [l] all obeyed the
Gospel: for Esaias sayth, * Lord, who hath beleeued our report?
17 [11] Then faith is by hearing, and hearing by the [m] word of God.
18 [12] But I demand, Haue they not heard?
* No doubt their sound went out through all
the earth, and their words into the ends of the
world.

d Not onely to the Iewes, but also to the Gentiles.

4 That the Law regardeth and tendeth to Christ, that is a manifest proofe, for that it propoundeth such a condition as can be and is fulfilled of none but of Christ onely: which being imputed vnto vs by faith, our conscience is quieted, so that now no man can aske, Who can ascend vp into heauen, or bring vs from hell, seeing the Gospel teacheth that both of these is done by Christ and that for their sakes, which with true faith embrace him which calleth them.

**Leuit 18.5. ezek.20.11. galat.3.12.*

**Deut 30.12.*

e Think not with thy selfe, as men that are staggering vse to doe.

5 Vocation commeth by the word preached.

**Deut.30.14.*

f By the worde, Moses vnderstood the law which the Lord published with his owne voice: and Paul applied it to the preaching of the Gospel, which was the perfection of the Law.

6 That is in deed true faith which is setled not onely in the head, but also in the heart of man whereof also we giue testimonie, by our outward life, and which tendeth to Christ as to our alone and onely Sauiour, euen as he setteth foorth himselfe in his word.

a The ignorance of the Lawe which we ought to knowe, excuseth none before God, especially it excuseth not them that are of his houshold. *b Ignorance hath alway pride ioyned with it.* * *Gal.3.24.* 3 The proofe: The Law it selfe hath respect vnto Christ, that such as beleeue in him should be saued. Therefore the calling to saluation by the workes of the Lawe, is vaine and foolish: but Christ is offered for saluation to euery beleeuer. *c The ende of the Lawe is to iustifie them that keepe the Lawe: but seeing wee doe not obserue the Lawe through the fault of our flesh, we attaine not vnto this end: but Christ salueth this disease, for he fulfilled the Law for vs.*

g If thou professe plainely, sincerely, and openly, that thou takest Iesus onely to be thy Lord and Sauiour. *h The Father, who is sayd to haue raysed the Sonne from the dead: and this is not spoken to shut out the diuinitie of the Sonne, but to set forth the Fathers counsell touching our redemption in the resurrection of the Sonne.* *i Faith is sayd to iustifie, and furthermore seeing the confession of the mouth is an effect of faith, and confession is the way to come to saluation, it followeth that faith is also sayd to saue.* 7 Now he prooueth the other part which he propoundeth afore in the fourth verse, to wit, that Christ calleth whomsoeuer he listeth without any difference, and this he confirmeth by a double testimonie. **Isai.28.16.* *k To beleeue in God, is to yeeld and consent to God his promise of our saluation by Christ, and that not onely in generall, but when we knowe that the promises pertaine to vs, whereupon riseth a sure trust.* **Ioel 1.38.* 8 True calling vpon the name of God is the testimonie of true faith, and true faith, of true vocation or calling, and true calling of true election. 9 That is, true faith, which seeketh God in his worde, and that preached: according as God hath appointed in the Church. * *Isaias 52.7. nahum 1.15.* 10 Wheresoeuer faith is, there is also the word, but not contrariwise, wheresoeuer the word is, there is faith also: for many refuse and reiect the word. *l He speaketh this because of the Iewes.* * *Isa.53.1. ioh.12.38.* 11 A conclusion of the former gradation: we must ascend from faith to our vocation, as by our vocation, wee came to the testimonie of our election. *m By Gods commaundement.* 12 An obiection: If calling bee a testimony of election, were not the Iewes called? why should I not grant that, saith the Apostle, seeing that there is no nation which hath not beene called? much lesse can I say, that the Iewes were not called. **Psal.19.3.*

19 [13] But I demaund, Did not Iſrael knowe
God? Firſt Moſes ſayth, * I will prouoke you to
enuie by a [n] nation that is not *my* nation, and by
a fooliſh *nation* I will anger you.
20 * And Eſaias is [o] bold, and ſayth, I was
found of them that ſought mee not, and haue
been made manifeſt to them that asked not after mee.
21 And vnto Iſrael he ſayth, * All the day
long haue I ſtretched forth mine hande vnto a
diſobedient and gaineſaying people.

13 The defender and maintainer of the Iewes cauſe, goeth on ſtill to aske, whether ÿ Iewes alſo knew not God which caled them. Eſai (ſaith the Apoſtle) denieth it: and witneſſeth that the Goſpel was tranſlated from them to the Gentiles, becauſe the Iewes neglected it. And therewithall the Apoſtle teacheth, that that outward and vniuerſall calling, which is ſet foorth by the creation of the world, ſufficeth not to the knowledge of God: yea, and that the particular alſo which is by the word of God, is of it ſelfe of ſmall or no efficacie, vnleſſe it be apprehended or layd on by faith, by the gift of God: otherwiſe by vnbeleefe it is made vnprofitable, and that by the onely fault of man, who can pretend no ignorance. *Deut. 32. 21. *n Hee calleth all prophane people, a nation that is no nation, as they are not ſayd to liue but to die, which are appointed for euerlaſting condemnation.* *Iſa. 65. 1. *o Speaketh without feare.* *Iſa. 65. 2.

CHAP. XI.

1 Leaſt the caſting off of the Iewes ſhould bee limited according to the outward appearance, 4 he ſheweth that Elias was in times paſt deceiued: 16 and that, ſeeing they haue an holy roote, 23 many of them likewiſe ſhall bee holy. 18. 24 Hee exhorteth the Gentiles to be humble, 33 and crieth out, that Gods iudgements are vnſearchable.

I Demaund then, [1] Hath God caſt away his
people? God forbid: for [2] I alſo am an Iſ-
raelite, of the ſeede of Abraham, of the tribe of
Beniamin.
2 [3] God hath not caſt away his people,
which he [a] knew before. [4] Knowe ye not what
the Scripture ſayth of Elias, how he communeth with God againſt Iſrael, ſaying,
3 * Lord, they haue killed thy Prophets,
and digged downe thine altars: and I am left
alone, and they ſeeke my life?
4 But what ſayth the anſwere of God to
him? * I haue [b] reſerued vnto my ſelfe ſeuen
thouſand men, which haue not bowed the knee
to [c] Baal.
5 Euen ſo then at this preſent time is
there a remnant according to the [d] election of
grace.
6 [5] And if *it be* of grace, it is [e] no more of
workes: or elſe were grace no more grace: but
if it be of workes, it is no more grace: or elſe
were worke no more worke.
7 What then? Iſrael hath not obtained
that hee ſought, but the election hath obtained
it, and the reſt haue been [f] hardened,
8 [6] According as it is written, * God hath
giuen them the ſpirit of [g] ſlumber: eyes that
they [h] ſhould not ſee, & eares that they ſhould
not heare vnto this day.
9 And Dauid ſayth, * [i] Let their table bee
made a ſnare, and a net, and a ſtumbling block,
euen for a recompence vnto them.
10 Let their eyes be darkened that they ſee
not, and bow downe their backe alwayes.
11 [7] I demaund then, Haue they ſtumbled,
that they ſhould fall? God forbid: but through
their fall, ſaluation *commeth* to the Gentiles,
to prouoke them to follow them.
12 Wherefore if the fall of them *be* the [k] riches of the world, and the diminiſhing of them
the riches of the Gentiles, how much more
ſhall their [l] abundance *be?*
13 [8] For *in that* I ſpeake to you Gentiles, in
as much as I am the Apoſtle of the Gentiles,
[m] I magnifie mine office,
14 *To trie* if by any meanes I might prouoke them of my fleſh to follow them, & might
ſaue ſome of them.
15 For if the caſting away of them *bee* the
reconciling of the world, what *ſhall* the receiuing *be*, [n] but life from the dead?
16 [9] For if the [o] firſt fruits *bee* holy, ſo *is* the
whole lumpe: and if the roote [p] be holy, ſo *are*
the branches.
17 * [10] And though ſome of the branches
be broken off, and thou being a wild Oliue tree,
waſt graft in [q] for them, and made [r] partaker of
the roote and fatneſſe of the Oliue tree:
18 [ſ] Boaſt not thy ſelfe againſt the branches: and if thou boaſt thy ſelfe, thou beareſt
not the roote, but the roote thee.
19 Thou wilt ſay then, The branches are
broken off, that I might be graft in.
20 Well, through vnbeliefe they are broken off, and thou ſtandeſt by faith: bee not

1 Now the Apoſtle ſheweth how this doctrine is to bee applied to others, abiding ſtill in his propounded cauſe. Therfore he teacheth vs, that all the Iewes in particular, are not caſt away, and therfore we ought not to pronoũce raſhly of priuate perſons, whether they be of the number of the elect or not. 2 The firſt proofe: I am a Iewe, and yet elected, therefore we may & ought fully reſolue vpon our election, as hath been before ſaid: but of another mans we cannot be ſo certainely reſolued, and yet ours may cauſe vs to hope well of others. 3 The ſecond proofe: Becauſe that God is faithfull in his league or couenant, although men be vnfaithfull: ſo then, ſeeing that God hath ſaid, that he will be the God of his vnto a thouſand generations, wee muſt take heed, that we thinke not that the whole race and ofspring is caſt off, by reaſon of the vnbeliefe of a few, but rather that we hope well of euery member of the Church, becauſe of Gods league and couenant. *a Which he loued and choſe from euerlaſting.* 4 The third proofe taken from the anſwere that was made to Elias: euen then alſo, when there appeared openly to the face of the world no elect, yet God knew his elect and choſen, and of them alſo great ſtore and number. Whereupon this alſo is concluded, that we ought not raſhly to pronounce of any man as of a reprobate, ſeeing that the Church is often times brought to that ſtate, that euen the moſt watchfull and ſharpe ſighted paſtors, thinke it to be cleane extinct and put out. *1. *Kin.* 19. 10. *1. *King.* 19. 18. *b He ſpeaketh of remnants and reſerued people which were choſen from euerlaſting, and not of remnants that ſhould be choſen afterward: for they are not choſen, becauſe they were not idolaters: but therefore they were not idolaters, becauſe they were choſen and elect.* *c Baal ſignifieth as much as Maſter, or Patron, or one in whoſe power another is, which name the idolaters at this day giue their idoles, naming them Patrons, and Patroneſſes, or Ladies.* *d The election of grace is, not whereby men choſe grace, but whereby God choſe vs of his grace and goodneſſe.* 5 Although that all bee not elect and choſen, yet let them that are elected, remember that they are freely choſen: and let them that ſtubbornely refuſe the grace and free mercie of God, impute it vnto themſelues. *e This ſaying beateth downe flat to the ground all the doctrine of all kindes and manner of workes, whereby our iuſtifiers of themſelues doe teach, that workes are either wholly or partly the cauſe of our iuſtification.*

f Looke Matt. 3. 5. 6 And yet this hardneſſe of heart commeth not but by Gods iuſt decree and iudgement, and yet without fault, when as he ſo puniſheth the vnthankefull by taking from them all ſence and perceiuerance, and by doubling their darkeneſſe, that the benefits of God which are offered vnto them, doe redound to their iuſt deſtruction. **Iſa.* 6. 9. *and* 29. 10. *mat.* 13. 14. *ioh.* 12. 40. *acts* 28. 26. *g A very dead ſleepe, which taketh away all ſenſe.* *h That is, eyes vnfit to ſee.* **Pſal.* 69. 23. *i As vnhappie birds are entiſed to death by that which is their ſuſtenance, ſo did that onely thing turne to the Iewes deſtruction, out of which they ſought life, to wit, the law of God, for the prepoſterous zeale whereof, they refuſed the Goſpel.* 7 God appointed this caſting off of the Iewes, that it might be an occaſion to call the Gentiles: and againe might turne this calling of the Gentiles, to bee an occaſion to reſtore the Iewes, to wit, that they being inflamed & prouoked by emulation of the Gentiles, might themſelues at length imbrace the Goſpel. And hereby we may learne, that the ſeueritie of God ſerueth as well to the ſetting foorth of his glory, as his mercie doth, and alſo that God prepareth himſelfe a way to mercie, by his ſeuerity: ſo that we ought not raſhly to deſpaire of any man, nor proudly triumph ouer other men, but rather prouoke them to an holy emulation, that God may be glorified in them alſo. *k By riches, hee meaneth the knowledge of the Goſpel to euerlaſting life: and by the world, all nations diſperſed throughout the whole world.* *l Of the Iewes, when the whole nation without exception ſhall come to Chriſt.* 8 Hee witneſſeth by his owne example, that hee goeth before all other in this behalfe. *m I make noble and famous.* *n It ſhall come to paſſe that when the Iewes come to the Goſpel, the world ſhall as it were quicken againe, and riſe vp from death to life.* 9 The nation of the Iewes being conſidered in their ſtocke and roote, that is, in Abraham, is holy, although that many of the branches bee cut off. Therefore in iudging of our brethren, wee muſt not ſticke in their vnworthineſſe, to thinke that they are at once all caſt off, but wee ought to conſider the roote of the couenant, and rather goe backe to their Anceſters which were faithfull, that we may knowe that the bleſſing of the couenant reſteth in ſome of their poſteritie, as wee alſo finde proofe hereof in our ſelues. *o He alludeth to the firſt fruits of thoſe loaues, by the offering whereof all the whole croppe of corne was ſanctified, and they might vſe the reſt of the yeere following with good conſcience.* *p Abraham.* * *Jerem.* 11. 6. 10 There is no cauſe why the Gentiles which haue obtained mercie, ſhould triumph ouer the Iewes which contemne the grace of God, ſeeing they are graffed into the Iewes anceſters. But let them rather take heede, that that alſo bee not found in them which is worthily condemned in the Iewes. And hereof alſo this generall doctrine may bee gathered and taken, that wee ought to bee ſtudious of Gods glory, euen in reſpect of our neighbours: ſo farre ought wee to bee from bragging and glorying, for that, that wee are preferred before other by a ſingular grace. *q In place of thoſe boughes which are broken off.* *r It is againſt the common courſe of husbandrie, that the barren iuice of the impe is changed with the iuice of the good tree.* *ſ We may reioyce in the Lord, but ſo that wee deſpiſe not the Iewes, whom we ought rather to prouoke to that good ſtriuing with vs.*

high minded, but [t] feare.
21 For if God spared not the [u] naturall branches, *take heede* lest he also spare not thee.
22 [11] Behold therefore the [x] bountifulnesse
and seueritie of God: toward them which haue
fallen, seueritie: but toward thee, bountifulnes,
if thou continue in *his* [y] bountifulnesse: or else
thou shalt also be cut off.
23 [12] And they also, if they abide not still in
vnbeliefe, shall be graffed in: for God is able to
graffe them in againe.
24 For if thou wast cut out of the Oliue
tree, which was wilde by [z] nature, and wast
graffed contrary to nature in a [a] right Oliue
tree, how much more shall they that are by nature be graffed in their owne Oliue tree?
25 [13] For I would not, brethren, that yee
should be ignorant of this secret (lest ye should
be arrogant in your [b] selues) that partly obstinacie is come to Israel, vntill the fulnesse of the
Gentiles be [c] come in.
26 And so all Israel shall bee saued, as it is
written, *The deliuerer shall come out of Sion, and shall turne away the vngodlinesse from
Iacob.
27 And this is my couenant to them, *When
I shall take away their sinnes.
28 [14] As concerning the [d] Gospel, *they are*
enemies for your sakes: but as touching the
[e] election, they are beloued for the fathers sake.
29 [15] For the gifts and calling of God are
without repentance.
30 [16] For euen as yee in times past haue not
beleeued God, yet haue now obtained mercie
through their vnbeliefe:
31 Euen so now haue they not beleeued by
the mercie *shewed* vnto you, that they also
may obtaine mercie.
32 For God hath shut vp [f] all in vnbeliefe,
that he might haue mercie on all.
33 [17] O the deepenesse of the riches, both
of the wisedom, and knowledge of God! how
vnsearchable are his [g] iudgements, and his
wayes past finding out!
34 *[18] For who hath knowen the minde of
the Lord? or who was his counsellour?
35 Or who hath giuen vnto him [i] first, and
he shall be recompensed?
36 For of him, and through him, and for
[k] him are all things: to him *bee* glory for euer.
Amen.

t See that thou stand in awe of God modestly and carefully. *u He calleth them naturall, not because they had any holinesse of nature, but because they were borne of them whom the Lord set apart for himselfe from other nations, by his league & couenāt which hee freely made with them.* 11 Seeing the matter it selfe declareth, that election cōmeth not by inheritance (although the fault bee in men, and not in God, why the blessing of God is not perpetual) wee must take good heed that that be not foūd in our selues, which we think blame worthy in others, for ỹ election is sure, but they that are truely elect and ingrafted, are not proud in themselues with contempt of other, but with due reuerence to God, and loue towards their neighbour, run to the marke which is set before them. *x The tender and louing heart.* *y In that state which God his bountifulnes hath aduanced thee vnto: and wee must marke here, that he speaketh not of the election of euery priuate man, which remaineth stedfast for euer, but of the election of the whole nation.* 12 Many are now for a season cut off, that is, are without the roote, which in their time shall bee grafted in: and againe there are a great sort, which after a sort, and touching the outward shew seeme to be ingraffed, which notwithstanding through their owne fault afterward are cut off, and cleane cast away: Which thing is especially to be considered in nations and peoples, as in the Gentiles and Iewes. *z Understand nature, not as it was first made, but as it was corrupted in Adam, and so deriued from him to his posterity.* *a Into the people of the Iewes, which God had sanctified of his meere grace: & he speaketh of the whole nation, not of any one part.* 13 The blindnesse of the Iewes is neither so vniuersall that the Lord hath no elect in that nation, neither shall it be continuall: for there shall be a time wherein they also (as the Prophets haue forewarned) shall effectually embrace that, which they doe now so stubbornely for the most part reiect and refuse *b That ye be not proud within your selues.* *c Into the Church.* *Esai 59 20. *Esai 27.9. 14 Againe, that he may ioyne the Iewes and Gentiles together as it were in one body, and especially may teach what duety the Gentiles owe to the Iewes, he beateth this into their heads, that the nation of the Iewes is not vtterly cast off without hope of recouerie. *d Forasmuch as they receiue it not.* *e In that, that God respecteth not what they deserue, but what hee promised to Abraham.* 15 The reason or proofe: because the couenant made with that nation of life euerlasting, cannot be frustrate and vaine. 16 Another reason: Because that although they which are hardened, are worthily punished, yet hath not this stubbornnesse of the Iewes so come to passe properly for an hatred to that nation, but that an entrie might bee as it were opened to bring in the Gentiles, and afterward the Iewes being inflamed with emulation of that mercie which is shewed to the Gentiles, might themselues also be partakers of the same benefite, and so it might appeare that both Iewes and Gentiles are saued onely by the free mercie and grace of God, which could not haue been so manifest, if at the beginning God had brought all together into the Church, or if hee had saued the nation of the Iewes without this interruption. *f Both Iewes and Gentiles.* 17 The Apostle crieth out as astonished with this wonderfull wisedome of God, which hee teacheth vs, to bee religiously reuerenced, and not curiously and prophanely to bee searched beyond the compasse of that that God hath reuealed vnto vs.

g The course that he holdeth in gouerning all things both generally and particularly. *h The order of his counsels and doings.* *Iob 41.2. esai. 42.13. 1.cor.2.16. 18 He brideleth three maner of wayes, the wicked boldnes of man: First, because that God is aboue all most wise, and therefore it is very absurd, and plainely godlesse to measure him by our follie. Moreouer, because he is debter to no man, and therefore no man can complaine of iniurie done vnto him. Thirdly, because all things are made for his glorie, and therefore we must referre all things to his glory, much lesse may we contend and debate the matter with him. *i This saying ouerthroweth the doctrine of foreseene works and merits.* *k To wit, for God, to whose glory all things are referred, not onely things that were made, but especially his new workes which he worketh in his elect.*

CHAP. XII.

1 Hee exhorteth 2 to that worship which is acceptable to God: 9 to loue vnfained, 14. 20 euen towards our enemies.

I Beseech [1] you therefore brethren, [a] by the
mercies of God, that ye [b] giue vp your [c] bodies a [d] liuing sacrifice, holy, acceptable vnto
God, *which is* your [e] reasonable seruing of God.
2 [2] And fashion not your selues like vnto
this world, but be yee changed by the renewing of your [f] minde, that yee may * prooue
what that good, and acceptable, and perfect wil
of God is.
3 [3] For I [g] say through the grace that is
giuen vnto mee, to euery one that is among
you, that no man [h] presume to vnderstand a-
boue that which is meete to vnderstand, but
that hee vnderstand according to [i] sobrietie, as
God hath dealt to euery man the * measure of
[k] faith.
4 [4] For as we haue many members in one
body, and all members haue not one office.
5 So wee being many, are one bodie in
Christ, and euery one, one anothers members.
6 *[5] Seeing then that wee haue gifts that
are diuers, according to the grace that is giuen
vnto vs, whether *wee haue* prophesie, *let vs*

1 The fourth part of this Epistle, which after the finishing of the chiefe points of Christian doctrine, consisteth in declaring of precepts of Christian life. And first of all he giueth generall precepts and grounds: the chiefest whereof is this, that euery man consecrate himselfe wholly to the spirituall seruice of God, and doe as it were sacrifice himselfe, trusting to the grace of God. *a By this preface he sheweth that Gods glory is the vtmost end of all our doings.* *b In times past the sacrifices were presented before the altar: but now the altar is euery where.* *c Your selues: in times past, other bodies then our owne, now our owne must bee offered.* *d In time past, dead sacrifices were offered, but now wee must offer such as haue the spirit of life in them.* *e Spirituall.* 2 The second precept is this, That wee take not other mens opinions or maners for a rule of life, but that wee wholly renouncing this world, set before vs as our marke, the wil of God as is manifested and opened vnto vs in his word. *f Why then there is no place left for reason, which the heathen Philosophers place as a Queen in a Castell, nor for mans free will, which the Popish Schoolemen dreame on, if the minde must bee renewed, Looke Ephes.1.18. and 2.3. and 4.17. and Coloss.1.21.* * Ephes.5.17 1.thess.4.3. 3 Thirdly, he admonisheth vs very earnestly, that euery man keepe himselfe within the bounds of his vocation, and that euery man bee wise according to the measure of grace that God hath giuen him. *g I charge.* *h That he please not himselfe too much, as they doe, which perswade themselues they knowe more then in deed they doe.* *i Wee shall be sober, if we take not that vpon vs, which we haue not, and if we bragge not of that we haue.* * 1.Cor 12.11. ephes.4.7. *k By faith he meaneth the knowledge of God in Christ, and the gifts which the holy Ghost powreth vpon the faithfull.* 4 There is a double reason of the precept going afore: the one is, because God hath not committed euery thing to be done of euery man: and therefore hee doeth backewardly, and not onely vnprofitably, but also to the great disprofit of others, wearieth himselfe and others, which passeth the bounds of his vocation: the other is for that this diuersitie and inequalitie of vocations and giftes, redoundeth to our commoditie: seeing that the same is therfore instituted and appointed, that we should bee bound one to another. Whereupon it followeth, that no man ought to bee grieued thereat, seeing that the vse of euery priuate gift is common. * 1.Pet.4.10. 5 That which he spake before in generall, hee applieth particularly to the holy functions, wherein men offend with greater danger. And he diuideth them into two sorts: to wit, into Prophets and Deacons: and againe he diuideth the Prophets into Doctors and Pastours. And of Deacons he maketh three sorts: to wit, the one to be such as are (as it were) treasures of the Church cofers, whom hee calleth properly Deacons: the other to be the gouernours of the discipline, who are called Seniours or Elders: the third, to bee such as properly serued in the helpe of the poore, of which sort the companie of widowes were.

prophesie according to the [l] portion of faith :
7 Or an office, *let vs waite* on the office : or
he that [m] teacheth, on teaching:
8 Or he that [n] exhorteth, on exhortation :
he that [o] distributeth, *let him doe it* * with simplicitie : he that [p] ruleth, with diligence: he that
[q] sheweth mercie, with cherefulnesse.
9 [6] *Let* loue *bee* without dissimulation,
* Abhorre that which is euill, and cleaue vnto
that which is good.
10 * Bee affectioned to loue another with
brotherly loue. In giuing honour goe one before another.
11 Not slothfull to doe seruice : feruent in
spirit, [r] seruing the Lord,
12 [7] Reioycing in hope, patient in tribulation, * continuing in prayer,
13 * [s] Distributing vnto the [t] necessities
of the Saints : * giuing your selues to hospitalitie.
14 * Blesse them which persecute you :
blesse, *I say*, and curse not.
15 Reioyce with them that reioyce, and
weepe with them that weepe.
16 Be of like affection one towards another : * bee not high minded : but make your
selues equall to them of the [u] lower sort: bee
not [x] wise in your selues.
17 * Recompence to no man euill for euill :
procure things honest in the sight of all men.
18 * If it be possible, as much as in you is,
haue peace with all men.
19 Dearely beloued, * auenge not your
selues, but giue place vnto wrath : for it is written, * Vengeance is mine : I will repay, sayth
the Lord.
20 * Therfore, if thine enemie hunger, feed
him : if he thirst, giue him drinke : for in so doing, thou shalt heape [y] coals of fire on his head.
21 Be not ouercome of euill, but ouercome
euill with goodnesse.

l That euery man obserue the measure of that which is reuealed vnto him. *m Whose office is onely to expound the Scriptures.* *n Who in other places is called the Pastour.* *o To wit, the almes, that he distribute them faithfully, and without respect of person.* * *Matth. 6.2. 2.cor.9.7.* *p The Elders of the Church.* *q They that are busied about tending on the poore, must doe it with cheerefulnesse, lest they adde sorrowe to sorrow.*

6 Now he commeth to the dueties of the second Table, which he deriueth from charitie, which is as it were the fountaine of them all. And he defineth Christian charitie by sinceritie, hatred of euill, earnest studie of good things, good affection to helpe our neighbour, and whose finall end is the glory of God. * *Amos 5.15.* * *Ephes 4.2. 1.pet.2.17.* *r This piece is wel put in, for it maketh difference betweene Christian dueties, and Philosophicall dueties.*

7 He reckoneth vp diuers other vertues together which are effects, to wit, hope, patience in tribulation, equanimitie, continuance in prayer, liberalitie, toward the Saints, hospitalitie, moderatiō of mind euen in helping our enemies, a selfe same feeling with others as well in aduersitie as prosperitie, modestie, endeuour to maintaine honest concord so nigh as we may with all men, which cannot be extinguished by any mans iniuries. * *1.Pet. 5.8.* * *Luke 18.1. 1.cor 16.1.* *s A true rule of charitie, when we are no lesse touched with other mens wants, then with our owne, and hauing that feeling, helpe them as much as we can.* *t Not vpon pleasures and needelesse dueties, but vpon necessarie vses* * *Heb.13.2. 1.pet.4.13.* * *Matt.5.44* * *Prou 3.7. isai.5.11.* *u There is nothing that doeth so much breake concord as ambition, when as euery man lotheth a base estate, and seeketh ambitiously to be aloft.* *x Be not puffed vp with opinion of your owne wisedome.* * *Prou.20 23.matth.5.39. 2.cor.8 11. 1 pet.3.9.* * *Heb.12.14.* * *Eccles.2.18 mat.5 39.* * *Deut. 32.35.hebr.10.30.* * *Prou.25.22.* *y After this sort doth Salomon point out the wrath of God that hangeth ouer a man.*

CHAP. XIII.

1 Hee willeth that wee submit our selues to Magistrates : 8 To loue our neighbours : 13 To liue vprightly, 14 and to put on Christ.

* *Titus 3.1. 1.pet.1.13.*

Let * [1] euery [a] soule bee subiect vnto the
higher [2] powers : [3] for there is no power
but of God : and the powers that bee, are [b] ordained of God.
2 Whosoeuer therefore resisteth the power, resisteth the ordinance of God : and they
that resist, shall receiue to themselues condemnation.
3 [4] For Magistrates are not to bee feared
for good workes, but *for* euill. [5] Wilt thou then
be without feare of the power? doe well : so
shalt thou haue praise of the same.
4 For hee is the minister of God for thy
wealth, [6] but if thou doe euill, feare : for he beareth not the sword for nought: for he is the minister of God to [c] take vengeance on him that
doeth euill.
5 [7] Wherefore ye must be subiect, not because of wrath onely, but [d] also for conscience
sake.
6 [8] For, for this cause yee pay also tribute :
for they are Gods ministers, applying themselues for the same thing.
7 * Giue to all men therefore their duetie :
tribute, to whom *yee owe* tribute : custome, to
whom custome : feare, to whom [e] feare: honor,
to whom *ye owe* [f] honour.
8 [9] Owe nothing to any man, but to loue
one another : [10] for he that loueth another, hath
fulfilled the [g] Law.
9 For this, * Thou shalt not commit adulterie, Thou shalt not kill, Thou shalt not steale,
Thou shalt not beare false witnesse, Thou
shalt not couet : and if there be any other commaundement, it is [h] briefly comprehended in
this saying, *euen* in this. * Thou shalt loue thy
neighbour as thy selfe.
10 Loue doeth not euill to his neighbour :
therefore is loue the * fulfilling of the Law.
11 [11] And that, considering the season, that
it is now time that we should arise from sleepe:
for now is our saluation neerer, then when we
beleeued it.
12 The night is past, and the day is [i] at hand,
let vs therefore cast away the workes [k] of darknesse, and let vs put on the armour of light,
13 So that wee walke honestly, as in the
day : not in * gluttonie, and drunkennesse, neither in chambering and wantonnesse, nor in
strife and enuying.
14 * But [l] put yee on the Lord IESVS
CHRIST, and take no thought for the
flesh, to *fulfill* the lusts of it.

1 Now he sheweth seuerally, what subiects owe to their magistrates, to wit, obedience : from which he sheweth that no man is free : and in such sort, that it is not onely due to the higest Magistrate himselfe, but also euen to the basest, which hath any office vnder him. *a Yea, though an Apostle, though an Euangelist, though a Prophet : Chrysostome. Therefore the tyrannie of the Pope ouer all kingdomes must downe to the ground.* 2 A reason taken of the nature of the thing it selfe : For to what purpose are they placed in higher degree, but that the inferiours should be subiect vnto them? 3 Another argument of great force : Because God is authour of this order : so that such as are rebels, ought to knowe, that they make warre with God himselfe : wherefore they cannot but purchase to themselues great miserie and calamitie.

b Be distributed for some are greater, some smaller. 4 The third argument taken from the ende wherefore they were made, which is most profitable : for that God by this meanes preserueth the good and brideleth the wicked : by which words, the Magistrates themselues are put in minde of that duetie which they owe to their subiects. 5 An excellent way to beare this yoke, not onely without griefe, but also with great profit. 6 God hath armed the Magistrate euen with a reuenging sword. *c By whom God reuengeth the wicked.* 7 The conclusion : We must obey the Magistrate, not onely for feare of punishment, but much more because that (although the Magistrate hath no power ouer the conscience of man, yet seeing he is Gods minister) he cannot be resisted by any good conscience. *d So farre as lawfully wee may: for if vnlawfull things be commanded vs, we must answere as Peter teacheth vs, It is better to obey God, then men.* 8 He reckoneth vp the chiefest things wherein consisteth the obedience of subiects. * *Matth.22.11.* *e Obedience, and that from the heart.* *f Reuerēce, which (as reason is) we must giue to the Magistrate.*

9 He sheweth how very fewe iudgements neede to be executed, to wit, if we so order our life as no man may iustly require any thing of vs, besides that onely, that wee owe one to another, by the perpetuall law of charitie. 10 Hee commendeth Charitie, as an abridgement of the whole Law. *g Hath not onely done one commandement but performed generally that which the Law commandeth.* * *Exod.20.14. deut.5.18.* *h For the whole Lawe commaundeth nothing else, but that wee loue God, and our neighbour. But seeing Paul speaketh here of the dueties we owe one to another, wee must restraine this worde, Lawe, to the second Table.* * *Leuiticus 19 18. matth.22.39. marke 12.31.galat.5.14. iam 2.8.* * *1.Timoth.1.1.* 11 An application taken of the circumstance of the time : which also it selfe putteth vs in minde of our duetie, seeing that this remaineth, after that the darkenesse of ignorance and wicked affections by the knowledge of Gods trueth bee driuen out of vs, that wee order our life according to that certaine and sure rule of all righteousnesse and honestie, being fully grounded vpon the vertue of the Spirit of Christ. *i In other places wee are sayd to bee in the light, but yet so, that it appeareth not as yet what we are, for as yet wee see but as it were in the twilight.* *k That kinde of life which they leade, that flee the light.* * *Luke 21.34.* * *Galathians 5.16. 1.peter 2.11.* *l To put on Christ, is to possesse Christ, to haue him in vs, and vs in him.*

CHAP.

CHAP. XIIII.

1 Hee willeth that we so deale with the weake in faith, 15 that through our fault they bee not offended. 10 And on the other side hee commaundeth them not rashly to iudge of the stranger: 19 That within the bonds of edification 20 and charitie, 22 Christian libertie may consist.

HIm [1] that is weake in the faith, [a] receiue
vnto you, *but* not for [b] controuersies of
disputations.
2 [2] One [c] beleeueth that he may eate of all
things: and another, which is weake, eateth
herbes.
3 [3] Let not him that eateth, despise him
that eateth not: and let not him which eateth
not, condemne him that eateth: for [4] God hath
receiued him.
4 *[5] Who art thou that condemnest another mans seruant? he standeth or falleth to his
owne master: yea, he shall be established: for
God is able to make him stand.
5 [6] This man esteemeth one day aboue another day, and another man counteth euerie
day alike: [7] let [d] euery man bee fully perswaded in his mind.
6 [8] He that [e] obserueth the day, obserueth
it to the Lord: and he that obserueth not the
day, obserueth it not to the [f] Lord. Hee that
[g] eateth, eateth to the Lord: [9] for hee giueth
God thankes: and hee that eateth [h] not, eateth
not to the Lord, and giueth God thankes.

1 Now hee sheweth how wee ought to behaue our selues toward our brethren in matters and things indifferent, offending in the vse of them, not of malice, or damnable superstition, but for lacke of knowledge of the benefite of Christ. And thus hee teacheth that they are to bee instructed gently and patiently, and so that we applie our selues to their ignorance in such matters according to the rule of charitie.
a Doe not for a matter or thing which is indifferent, and such as you may doe or not doe, shun his company, but take him to you
b To make him by your doubtfull and vncertaine disputations goe away more in doubt then hee came, or start backe with a troubled conscience. 2 Hee propoundeth for an example, the difference of meats, which some thought was necessarily to bee obserued as a thing prescribed by the Lawe (not knowing that it was taken away) where as on the contrary side such as had profited in the knowledge of the Gospel, knew well that this schoolemastership of the Lawe was abolished. *c Knoweth by faith.* 3 In such a matter, saith the Apostle, let neither them which knowe their libertie, proudly despise their weake brother, neither let the vnlearned crabbedly or frowardly condemne that, that they vnderstand not. 4 The first reason: Because that seeing both he that eateth, and he that eateth not, is notwithstanding the member of Christ, neither he which eateth not, can iustly bee contemned, neither hee which eateth, bee iustly condemned: Now the first proposition is declared in the sixt verse following. **Iam. 4,12.* 5 Another reason which hangeth vpon the former: why the ruder and more vnlearned ought not to be condemned of the more skilfull, as men without hope of saluation: Because, sayth the Apostle, he that is ignorant to day, may be indued to morrow with further knowledge, so that he may also stand sure: Therefore it belongeth to God, and not vnto man, to pronounce the sentence of condemnation. 6 Another example of the difference of dayes according to the Lawe. 7 He setteth against this contempt, and hastie or rash iudgements, a continuall desire to profit, that the strong may bee certainely perswaded of their libertie of what maner and sort it is, and how they ought to vse it: and againe the weake may dayly profite, least either they abuse the gift of God, or these please themselues in their infirmitie. *d That hee may say in his conscience, that hee knoweth and is perswaded by Iesus Christ, that nothing is vncleane of it selfe, and this perswasion must bee grounded vpon the word of God* 8 A reason taken from the nature of indifferent things, which a man may with good conscience doe, and omit: for seeing that the difference of dayes and meates was appointed by God, how could they which as yet vnderstood not the abrogating of the Law, and yet otherwise acknowledged Christ as their Sauiour, with good conscience neglect that which they knew was commaunded of God? And on the contrary side, they that knew the benefite of Christ in this behalfe, did with good conscience neither obserue dayes nor meats, Therefore sayth the Apostle verse 10. Let not the strong condemne the weake for these things, seeing that the weake brethren are brethren notwithstanding. Now if any man would drawe this doctrine to these our times and ages, let him knowe that the Apostle speaketh of such things indifferent, as they, which thought them not to be indifferent, had a ground in the Lawe, and were deceiued by simple ignorance, and not of malice, (for to such the Apostle yeelded not, no not for a moment) nor superstition, but of a religious feare of God. *e Obserueth precisely.* *f God shall iudge whether he doe well or no: And therefore you should rather striue about this, how euerie one of you may be allowed of God, then to thinke vpon other mens doings.* *g Hee that maketh no difference of meates.* 9 So the Apostle sheweth that hee speaketh of the faithfull, both strong and weake: But what if we haue to doe with infidels? Then must we here take heede of two things as also is declared in the Epistle to the Corinthians. The one is, that we count not their superstition among things indifferent, as they did which sate downe to meate in Idols temples: the other is, that then also when the matter is indifferent (as to buy a thing offered to Idols, in the butchers shambles, and to eate it at home or in a priuate banquet) wee wound not the conscience of our weake brother. *h Hee that toucheth not meates which he taketh to be vncleane by the Lawe.*

7 [10] For none of vs liueth to [i] himselfe, neither doth anie die to himselfe,
8 For whether we liue, wee liue vnto the
Lord: or whether wee die, wee die vnto the
Lord: whether we liue therefore, or die, we are
the Lords.
9 For Christ therfore died and rose againe,
and reuiued, that he might be Lord both of the
dead and the quicke.
10 [11] But why doest thou condemne thy
brother? or why doest thou despise thy brother? *for we shall all appeare before the iudgement seat of Christ.
11 For it is written, * I [k] liue, sayth the
Lord, and euery knee shall bow to me, and all
tongues shall [l] confesse vnto God.
12 So then euery one of vs shall giue accounts of himselfe to God.
13 [12] Let vs not therefore iudge one another any more: but vse *your* iudgement rather
in [m] this, that no man put an occasion to fall, or
a stumbling blocke before *his* brother.
14 [13] I knowe, and am perswaded through
the [n] Lord Iesus, that there is nothing vncleane
of it [o] selfe: but vnto him that iudgeth any
thing to be vncleane, to him *it is* vncleane.
15 But if thy brother bee grieued for the
meate, now walkest thou not charitably: *[14] destroy not him with thy meate, for whome
[15] Christ died.
16 [16] Cause not your commoditie to bee e-
uill spoken of.
17 [17] For the kingdom of God is not meate
nor drinke, but righteousnesse, and peace, and
ioy in the holy Ghost.
18 For whosoeuer in [p] these things serueth
Christ is acceptable vnto God, and is approoued of men.
19 [18] Let vs then follow those things which
concerne peace, and wherewith one may e-
difie another.
20 Destroy not the worke of God for meats
sake: * all things in deed are pure: but *it is* e-
uill for the man which eateth with offence.

10 We must not sticke, sayth hee, in the meate it selfe, but in the vse of the meate, so that he is iustly to bee reprehended that liueth so, that hee casteth not his eyes vpon God, For both our life and our death is dedicated to him, and for this cause Christ hath properly died, and not simplie that we might eate this meate or that.
i Hath respect to himselfe onely, which the Hebrewes vtter after this sort, Doeth well to his owne soule.
11 The conclusion: wee must leaue to God his right, and therefore in matters, which according as the conscience is affected, are either good or euil, the strong must not despise their weake brethren, much lesse condemne them. But this consequent cannot be taken of equall force in the contrary, to wit, that the weake should not judge the strong because the weake doe not knowe, that they which doe not obserue a day and eat, obserue it not to the Lord, and eat to the Lord, as the strong men knowe that the weak which obserue a day and eate not, obserue the day to the Lord, and eat not to ẏ Lord.
**2 Cor. 1.10.*
**Isai. 45.23 Philip. 2.10.* *k This is a forme of an othe, proper to God onely, for he and none but he liueth, and hath his being of himselfe.* *l Shall acknowledge mee for God.* 12 After that he hath concluded what is not to be done, he sheweth what is to be done: to wit, we must take heede that wee doe not vtterly cast downe with abusing our libertie our brother which is not yet strong. *m He rebuketh by the way these malicious iudgers of others which occupie their heads about nothing, but to finde fault with their brethrens life, whereas they should rather bestowe their wits vpon this, that they doe not with their disdainefulnesse either cast their brethren cleane downe, or giue them some offence.* 13 The preuenting of an obiection: It is true that the schoolemastership of the Lawe is taken away by the benefite of Christ, to such as knowe it, but yet notwithstanding we haue to consider in the vse of this libertie, what is expedient, that we may haue regard to our weake brother, seeing that our libertie is not lost thereby. *n By the Spirit of the Lord Iesus, or by the Lord Iesus, who I am sure brake downe the wall at his comming.* *o By nature.* **1 Corinth. 8.11.* 14 It is the part of a cruell minde to make more account of meate, then of our brothers saluation. Which thing they doe, that presume to eate with the offence of any brother, and so giue him occasion to goe backe from the Gospel. 15 An other argument: Wee must followe Christs example: who was so farre from destroying the weake with meate, that he gaue his life for them. 16 Another argument: for that by this meanes the libertie of the Gospel is euill spoken of, as though it openeth the way to attempt any thing whatsoeuer, and boldeneth vs to all things. 17 A generall reason, and the ground of all the other arguments: The kingdom of heauen consisteth not in these outward things, but in the studie of righteousnesse and peace, and comfort of the holy Ghost. *p Hee that liueth peaceably, and doeth righteously, through the holie Ghost.* 18 A generall conclusion: The vse of this libertie, yea, and our whole life, ought to be referred to the edifying of one another, insomuch that we esteeme that thing vnlawfull by reason of the offence of our brother, which is of it selfe pure and lawfull. **Titus 1.5.*

21 **It is* good neither to eate flesh, nor to
drinke wine, nor any thing whereby thy brother stumbleth, or is offended, or made weake,

22 [19] Hast thou [q] faith? haue it with thy
selfe before God: blessed *is* hee that condemneth not himselfe in that thing which hee
[r] alloweth.

23 For he that [f] doubteth, is condemned if
hee eate, because *he eateth* not of faith: and
whatsoeuer is not of faith, is sinne.

* 2.Cor.8.13.
19 He giueth a double warning in these matters: one, which pertaineth to the strong, that hee which hath obtained a sure knowledge of this libertie, keepe that treasure to the end he may vse it wisely and profitably, as hath beene said: the other which respecteth the weake, that they doe nothing rashly by other mens example with a wauering conscience, for that cannot bee done without sinne, whereof we are not perswaded by the word of God, that he liketh and approueth it. *q Hee shewed before, verse 14. what hee meaneth by faith, to wit, for a man to be certaine and out of doubt in matters and things indifferent.* r *Embraceth.* f *Reasoneth with himselfe.*

CHAP. XV.

1 *The stronger must employ their strength to strengthen the weake,* 3 *by Christes example,* 7 *who receiueth* 8 *not onely the Iewes,* 10 *but also the Gentiles.* 11 *The cause why he wrote this Epistle.*

WEe [1] which are strong, ought to beare
the infirmities of the weake, and not
to [a] please our selues.

2 *Therfore* let euery man please his neighbour in that that is [b] good to edification.

3 [2] For Christ also would not please himselfe, but as it is written, *The rebukes of them
which rebuke thee, fell on me.

4 [3] For whatsoeuer things are written
[c] aforetime, are written for our learning, that
wee through patience, and comfort of the
[d] Scriptures might haue hope.

5 [4] Now the God of patience and consolation, giue you that yee be * like minded one
towards another, according to Christ Iesus,

6 That yee with one minde, *and* with one
mouth may praise God, euen the Father of our
Lord Iesus Christ.

7 Wherefore receiue yee one another, as
Christ also [e] receiued vs to the glory of God.

8 [5] Now I say, that Iesus Christ was a minister of the [f] circumcision, for the [g] trueth
of God, to confirme the promises *made* vnto
the Fathers.

9 [6] And let the Gentiles praise God for
his mercy, as it is written, *For this cause I will
[h] confesse thee among the Gentiles, and sing
vnto thy Name.

10 And againe he saith, *Reioyce, ye Gentiles, with his people.

11 And againe, * Praise the Lord, all yee
Gentiles, and laud ye him, all people together.

12 And againe Esaias sayth, *There shall

1 Now the Apostle reasoneth generally of tolerating or bearing with the weake by all meanes, so farre foorth as may be for their profite.
a And despise others.
b For his profite and edification.
2 A confirmation taken of the example of Christ, who suffered all things, to bring not only the weake, but also his most cruell enemies, ouercomming them with patience, to his Father.
* *Psal.69.10.*
3 The preuenting of an obiection: Such things as are cited out of the examples of the ancients, are propounded vnto vs to this end and purpose, that according to the example of our Fathers, wee should in patience and hope beare one with another.
c By Moses and the Prophets.
d The Scriptures are sayd to teach and comfort, because God vseth them to teach and comfort his people withall. 4 We must take an example of patience, of God: that both the weake and the strong, seruing God with a mutuall consent, may bring one another to God, as Christ also receiued vs vnto himselfe, although we were neuer so vnworthie. * *1.Corinth.1.10.* e *He did not disdaine vs, but receiued vs of his owne accord, to make vs partakers of Gods glory.* 5 An applying of the example of Christ to the Iewes, whome hee vouchsafed this honour for the promises which hee made vnto their Fathers, although they were neuer so vnworthie, that hee executed the office of a Minister amongst them with marueilous patience: therefore much lesse ought the Gentiles despise them for certaine faults, whome the Sonne of God so much esteemed f *Of the circumcised Iewes, for as long as hee liued, hee neuer went out of their quarters.* g *That God might be seene to be true.* 6 An applying of the same to the Gentiles, whome also the Lorde of his incomprehensible goodnesse had regard of, so that they are not to bee contemned of the Iewes, as strangers. **Psalm.18.50.* h *I will openly professe, and set foorth thy Name.* **Deut.32.43.* **Psal.117.1.* **Esai 11.10.*

be a root of Iesse, and he that shall rise to reigne
ouer the Gentiles, in him shall the Gentiles
trust.

13 [7] Now the God of [i] hope fill you with
[k] all ioy, and peace in beleeuing, that ye may a-
bound in hope, through the power of the holy
Ghost.

14 [8] And I my selfe am also perswaded of
you, my brethren, that [l] ye also are full of goodnesse, and filled with all knowledge, and are a-
ble to admonish one another.

15 Neuerthelesse, brethren, I haue somewhat boldly after a sort written vnto you, as
one that putteth you in remembrance, through
the grace that is giuen me of God,

16 That I should be the minister of Iesus
Christ toward the Gentiles, ministring the
Gospel of God, that the [m] offering vp of the
Gentiles might be acceptable, being sanctified
by the holy Ghost.

17 [9] I haue therefore whereof I may reioyce in Christ Iesus in those things which *pertaine* to God.

18 For I dare not speake of any thing, which
[n] Christ hath not wrought by me, *to make* the
Gentiles obedient in word and deede,

19 With the [o] power of signes and woonders, by the power of the Spirit of God: so
that from Hierusalem, and round about vnto
Illyricum, I haue caused to abound the Gospel
of Christ.

20 Yea, so I enforced my selfe to preach
the Gospel, not where Christ was named, lest
I should haue built on another mans foundation,

21 But as it is written, *To whom hee was
not spoken of, they shall see *him*, and they that
heard not, shall vnderstand *him*.

22 *[10] Therefore also I haue beene oft let
to come vnto you:

23 But now seeing I haue no more place in
these quarters, and also haue * beene desirous
many yeeres agoe to come vnto you,

24 When I shall take my iourney into
Spaine, I will come to you: for I trust to see
you in my iourney, and to be brought on my
way thitherward by you, after that I haue been
somewhat filled with your *company*.

25 But now goe I to Hierusalem, to [p] minister vnto the Saints.

26 For it hath pleased them of Macedonia
and Achaia, to make a certaine distribution vnto the poore Saints which are at Hierusalem.

27 [11] For it hath pleased them, & their debters are they: * for if the Gentiles be made partakers of their spirituall things, their duety is
also to [q] minister vnto them in carnall things.

7 He sealeth vp as it were all the former treatise with prayers, wishing all that to be giuen them of the Lord, that hee had commanded them.
i In whome we hope.
k Abundantly and plentifully.
8 The conclusion of the epistle, wherein he first excuseth himselfe, that hee hath written somewhat at large vnto them, rather to warne them, then to teach them, and that of necessity, by reason of his vocation, which bindeth him peculiarly to the Gentiles
l Of your owne accord, and of your selues.
m By the offering vp of the Gentiles, he meaneth the Gentiles themselues, whom he offered to God as a sacrifice.
9 He commendeth his Apostleship highly by the effects but yet so, that moreouer and besides that he speaketh all things truely, he giueth all the glory to God as the only author: and doeth not properly respect himselfe, but this rather, that men might lesse doubt of the trueth of the doctrine which he propoundeth vnto them.
n Christ was so with me in all things, and by all meanes, that if I would neuer so faine, yet I can not say, what he hath done by me to bring the Gentiles to obey the Gospel.
o In the first place this word, Power, signifieth the force and working of the woonders in pearcing mens mindes: and in the latter, it signifieth Gods mightie power which was the worker of those wonders.
* *Isa 52.15.*
* *Chap.1.11.*
10 Hee writeth at large to the Romanes, and that familiarly, his singular good will towards them, and the state of his affaires, but so, that he swarueth not a iote from the end of Apostolicall doctrine: for hee declareth nothing but that which appertaineth to his office, and is godly: and commending by a little digression as it were, the liberalitie of the Churches of Macedonia, he promiseth them modestly to follow their godly deed. * *1.Thes.1.17.* p *Doing his duety for the Saints, to carie them that money which was gathered for their vses.* 11 Almes are voluntarie, but yet such as wee owe by the lawe of charitie. * *1.Cor.6.11.* q *To serue their turnes.*

28 When I haue therefore performed this,
and haue [r] sealed them this [s] fruit, I will passe
by you into Spaine.
29 [11] And I know when I come, that I shall
come to you with abundance of the blessing of
the Gospel of Christ.
30 Also brethren, I beseech you for our
Lord Iesus Christes sake, and for the [t] loue of
the spirit, that ye would striue with me by praiers to God for me,
31 That I may bee deliuered from them
which are disobedient in Iudea, and that my
seruice which I haue to do at Hierusalem, may
be accepted of the Saints,
32 That I may come vnto you with ioy
by the will of God, and may with you be refreshed.
33 Thus the God peace *be* with you all.
Amen.

CHAP. XVI.

1 He commendeth Phebe. 3 He sendeth greetings to many, 17 and warneth to beware of them which are the causes of diuision.

I [1] Commend vnto you Phebe our sister,
which is a seruant of the Church of Cenchrea:
2 That ye receiue her in the [a] Lord, as it
becommeth Saints, and that yee assist her in
whatsoeuer businesse she needeth of your aid:
for she hath giuen hospitalitie vnto many, and
to me also.
3 Greete * Priscilla, and Aquila my fellow helpers in Christ Iesus,
4 (Which haue for my life laid downe
their owne necke. Vnto whom not I only giue
thankes, but also all the Churches of the Gentiles.)
5 Likewise *greete* the [b] Church that is in
their house. Salute my beloued Epenetus,
which is the [c] first fruites of Achaia in Christ.
6 Greete Mary which bestowed much
labour vpon vs.
7 Salute Andronicus and Iunia my cousins and fellow prisoners, which are notable a-
mong the Apostles, and were in [d] Christ before me.
8 Greet Amplias my beloued in the Lord.
9 Salute Vrbanus our fellowe helper in
Christ, and Stachys my beloued.
10 Salute Apelles approued in Christ. Salute them which are of Aristobulus *friends*.
11 Salute Herodian my kinseman. Greete
them which are of the *friends* of Narcissus,
which are in the Lord.
12 Salute Tryphena and Tryphosa, which
women labour in the Lord. Salute the beloued
Persis, which *woman* hath laboured much in
the Lord.
13 Salute Rufus chosen in the Lord, and
his mother and mine.
14 Greete Asyncritus, Phlegon, Hermas,
Patrobas, Mercurius, and the brethren which
are with them.
15 Salute Philologus and Iulias, Nereas
and his sister, and Olympas, and all the Saints
which are with them.
16 Salute one another with an * holy [e] kisse.
The Churches of Christ salute you.
17 ¶ [2] Now I beseech you, brethren, [f] marke
them diligently which cause diuision and offences, contrary to the doctrine which ye haue
learned, and * auoid them.
18 For they that are such, serue not the
Lord Iesus Christ, but their owne bellies, and
with [g] faire speech and flattering deceiue the
hearts of the simple.
19 [3] For your obedience is come abroad a-
mong all: I am glad therefore of you: but yet
I would haue you [h] wise vnto that which is
good, and [i] simple concerning euill.
20 [4] The God of peace shall tread Satan
vnder your feet shortly. The grace of our Lord
Iesus Christ *be* with you.
21 * [5] Timotheus my helper, and Lucius,
and Iason, and Sosipater my kinsemen, salute
you.
22 I Tertius, which [k] wrote out this Epistle, salute you in the Lord.
23 Gaius mine hoste and of the whole
Church saluteth you. Erastus the steward of
the citie saluteth you, and Quartus a brother.
24 [6] The grace of our Lord Iesus Christ *be*
with you all, Amen.
25 * [7] To him now that is of power to establish you according to my Gospel, and preaching of Iesus Christ, * by the reuelation of the
[l] mysterie, which was kept secret since the
world began:
26 (But now is opened, and [m] published
among all nations by the Scriptures of the Prophets, at the commandement of the euerlasting God for the obedience of faith)
27 To God, *I say*, onely wise, bee praise
through Iesus Christ for euer. Amen.

Written to the Romanes from Corinthus, *and sent* by Phebe, seruant of the Church, which is at Cenchrea.

r Performed it faithfully, and sealed it as it were with my ring.
s This money which was gathered for the vse of the poore: which almes is very fitly called fruite.
11 He promiseth them through þe blessing of God, not to come emptie vnto them: and requiring of them the duty of prayers, he sheweth what thing we ought chiefly to rest vpon in all difficulties and aduersities.
t For that mutuall coniunction, wherwith the holy Ghost hath tied our hearts and mindes together.

1 Hauing made an end of the whole disputation, he commeth now to familiar commendations and salutations, and that to good consideration and purpose, to wit, that the Romanes might know, who are most to be honored and made accompt of amongst them: and also whom they ought to set before them to follow: & therefore he attributeth vnto euery of them peculiar and singular testimonies.
a For Christes sake, which is proper to the Christians, for the heathen Philosophers haue resemblances of the same vertues.
* *Actes 18.3.*
b The companie of the faithfull, for in so great a citie as that was, there were diuers companies.
c For he was the first of Achaia that beleeued in Christ: and this kind of speech is an allusion to the ceremonies of the Law.
d Ingraffed by faith.

* *1.Cor.16.20. 2.cor.13.12. 1.pet.5.14.*
e He calleth that an holy kisse, which proceedeth from an heart that is full of that holy loue: now this is to be referred to the maner vsed in those dayes.
2 As by namely describing them which were worthy of commendation, hee sufficiently declared whom they ought to heare & follow, so doeth he now paint out vnto them whom they ought to take heed of, yet he nameth them not, for that it was not needfull.
f Warily and diligently, as though you should scout out for your enemies in a watch tower.
* *2.Iohn.10.*
g The word which he vseth, signifieth a promising which performeth nothing, and if thou hearest any such, thou mayest assure thy selfe that he that promiseth thee, is more carefull of thy matters, then of his owne.
3 Simplicitie must be ioyned with wisdome.
h Furnished with the knowledge of the trueth and wisedome, that you may embrace good things, and eschew euill, beware of the deceits and snares of false prophets, and resist them openly: and this place doeth plainly destroy the Papists faith of credite, whereby they maintaine it to be sufficient for one man to beleeue as another man beleeueth, without further knowledge or examination what the matter is, or what ground it hath: vsing these daily speeches, We beleeue as our fathers beleeued, and we beleeue as the Church beleeueth.
i As men that know no way to deceiue, much lesse do deceiue in deed.
4 We must fight with a certaine hope of victorie.
* *Acts 16.1. phil.2.19.*
5 He annexeth salutations, partly to renue mutuall friendship, & partly to the end that this Epistle might bee of some weight with the Romanes, hauing the confirmation of so many that subscribed vnto it.
k Wrote it as Paul vttered it.
6 Now taking his leaue of them this third time, he wisheth that vnto them, whereupon dependeth all the force of the former doctrine.
* *Eph.3.20.*
7 Hee setteth foorth the power and wisedome of God with great thankesgiuing, which especially appeare in the Gospel, and maketh mention also of the calling of the Gentiles, to confirme the Romanes in the hope of this saluation.
* *Ephes.3.9. col.1.26. 2.tim.1.10. titus 1.2.*
l That secret and hidden thing, that is to say, the calling of the Gentiles.
m Offered and exhibited to all nations to be knowen.

THE

THE FIRST EPISTLE OF PAVL TO THE CORINTHIANS.

CHAP. I.

1 After the salutation, 10 which in effect is an exhortation, 12 he reprehendeth the Corinthians sectes and diuisions, 17 and calleth them from pride to humilitie: 20 For, ouerthrowing all wordly wisedome, 23, 25 he aduanceth onely the preaching of the crosse.

PAul [1] called *to be* an [2] Apostle
of Iesus Christ, through the
will of God, and *our* brother
[3] Sosthenes,
2 [4] Vnto the Church of
God, which is at Corinthus,
to them that are * [5] sanctified in [a] Christ Iesus,
* Saints by [b] calling * with all that [c] call on the
Name of our Lord Iesus Christ in euery place,
both their *Lord*, and ours:
3 [6] Grace *be* with you, and peace from
God our Father, and *from* the Lorde Iesus
Christ.
4 [7] I thanke my God alwayes on your behalfe for the grace of God, which is giuen you
in Iesus Christ,
5 That in all things yee are made rich in
him, [8] in [d] all kinde of speech, and in all knowledge:
6 [9] As the testimonie of Iesus Christ hath
beene [e] confirmed in you:
7 So that ye are not destitute of any gift:
* [10] waiting for the [f] appearing of our Lord Iesus Christ,
8 * [11] Who shall also confirme you vnto
the end, that ye may be [g] blamelesse, in the day
of our Lord Iesus Christ.

1 The inscription of the Epistle, wherein he chiefly goeth about to procure the good will of the Corinthians towards him, yet notwithstanding so, that alwayes he letteth them to wit, that he is the seruant of God and not of men.
2 If he be an Apostle, then hee must be heard, although hee sometime reprehend them sharpely, seeing he hath not his owne cause in hand, but is a messenger that bringeth the commaundements of Christ.
3 Hee ioyneth Sosthenes with himselfe, that this doctrine might be confirmed by two witnesses.
4 It is a Church of God, althogh it hath great faults in it, so that it obey them which admonish them.

9 *God is [h] faithfull, by whom yee are
called vnto the fellowship of his Sonne Iesus
Christ our Lord.
10 [12] Now I beseech you, brethren, by the
Name of our Lord Iesus Christ, that [13] yee all
speake one thing, and that there be no dissentions among you: but be ye [i] knit together in
one mind and in one iudgement.
11 [14] For it hath beene declared vnto mee,
my brethren, of you by them that are of the
house of Cloe, that there are contentions a-
mong you.
12 Now [k] this I say, that euery one of you
sayth, I am Pauls, and I am * Apollos, and I am
Cephas, and I am Christs.
13 [15] Is Christ diuided? was [16] Paul crucified for you? either were yee [17] baptized into
the name of Paul?
14 [18] I thanke God, that I baptized none
of you, but * Crispus and Gaius,
15 Lest any should say, that I had baptized
into mine owne name.
16 I baptized also the houshold of Stephanas: furthermore know I not, whether I baptized any other.
17 [19] For *Christ* sent me not to baptize, but
to preach the Gospel, [20] not with * [l] wisedome

* *1.Thess.5.24.* *h True and constant, who doeth not onely call vs, but giueth vs the gift of perseuerance also.*
12 Hauing made an end of the preface, he commeth to the matter it selfe, beginning with a most graue obtestation, as though they should heare Christ himselfe speaking, and not Paul.
13 The first part of this Epistle, wherein his purpose is, to call backe the Corinthians to brotherly concord, and to take away all occasion of discord. So then this first part concerneth the taking away of schismes. Now a schisme is when men which otherwise agree and consent together in doctrine, doe yet separate themselues one from another.

* *Actes 15.9. 1.thess. 4.7.* 5 A true definition of the Catholique Church which is one. *a The Father sanctifieth vs, that is to say, separateth vs from the wicked, in giuing vs to his Sonne, that hee may be in vs, and wee in him.* * *Roman. 1.7. ephes. 1.1. coloss. 1.22. 2.tim. 1.9. titus 2.13.* *b Whome God of his gracious goodnesse and meere loue hath separated for himselfe: or whome God hath called to holinesse: the first of these two expositions, sheweth from whence our sanctification commeth: and the second sheweth to what ende it tendeth.* * *2.Timoth. 1.22.* *c Hee is sayd properly to call on God, who cryeth vnto the Lord when hee is in danger, and craueth helpe at his handes, and by the figure Synecdoche it is taken for all the seruice of God: and therefore to call vpon Christes Name, is to acknowledge and take him for very God.* 6 The foundation and the life of the Church, is Christ Iesus giuen of the Father. 7 Going about to condemne many vices, hee beginneth with a true commendation of their vertues, lest he might seeme after to descend to chiding, beeing mooued with malice or enuie: yet so, that hee referreth all to God, as the authour of them, and that in Christ, that the Corinthians might be more ashamed to prophane and abuse the holy giftes of God. 8 Hee toucheth that by name, which they most abused. *d Seeing that whiles wee liue heere, wee know but in part, and prophecie in part, this word (All) must be restrained to the present state of the faithfull: but by Speech hee meaneth not a vaine kinde of babling, but the gift of holy eloquence, which the Corinthians abused.* 9 He sheweth that the true vse of these giftes consisteth herein, thet the mightie power of Christ might thereby be set foorth in them, that hereafter it might euidently appeare, how wickedly they abused them to glory and ambition. *e By those excellent giftes of the holy Ghost.* * *Titus 2.11. philip. 3.20.* 10 Hee sayeth by the way, that there is no cause why they should please themselues so much in those giftes which they had receiued, seeing that those were nothing in comparison of them which are to bee looked for. *f Hee speaketh of the last comming of Christ.* * *1.Thess. 3.13. and 5.23.* 11 Hee testifieth that he hopeth well of them hereafter, that they may more patiently abide his reprehension afterward. And yet together therewithall sheweth, that as well the beginning as the accomplishing of our saluation, is onely the worke of God. *g Hee calleth them blamelesse, not whom man neuer found fault with, but with whom no man can iustly find fault, that is to say, them which are in Christ Iesus, in whom there is no condemnation. See Luke 1.6.*

i Knit together, as a body that consisteth of all his parts fitly knit together. 14 Hee beginneth his reprehension and chiding by taking away of an obiection: for that hee vnderstood by good witnesses, that there were many factions among them. And therewithall he openeth the cause of dissentions, because that some did hang on one doctour, some on another, and some were so addicted to themselues, that they neglected all doctours and teachers, calling themselues the disciples of Christ onely, shutting foorth their teachers. *k The matter I would say to you, is this.* * *Actes 18.24.* 15 The first reason why schismes ought to be eschewed: because Christ seemeth by that meanes, to be diuided and torne in pieces, who cannot be the head of two diuers and disagreeing bodies, being himselfe one. 16 Another reason: Because they cannot without great iniurie to God, so hang of men as of Christ: which thing no doubt they doe, which allow whatsoeuer some man speaketh, euen for his persons sake: as these men allowed one selfe same Gospel being vttered of one man, and did lothe it being vttered of another man. So that these factions were called by the names of their teachers. Now Paul setteth downe his owne name, not onely to grieue no man, but also to shewe that hee pleadeth not his owne cause. 17 The third reason taken of the forme and end of Baptisme, wherein wee make a promise to Christ, calling on also the Name of the Father, and the holy Ghost. Therefore although a man doe not fall from the doctrine of Christ, yet if hee hang vpon some certaine teachers, and despise others, hee forsaketh Christ: for if he hold Christ his only master, he would heare him, teaching by whomsoeuer. 18 He protesteth that hee speaketh so much the more boldly of these things, because that through Gods prouidence, hee is void of all suspition of chalenging disciples vnto himselfe, and taking them from others. Whereby wee may vnderstand, that not the schollars onely, but the teachers also are here reprehended, which gathered themselues flockes apart. * *Actes 18.8.* 19 The taking away of an obiection: that he gaue not himselfe to baptize many amongst them: not for the contempt of baptisme, but because hee was chiefly occupied in deliuering the doctrine, and committed them that receiued his doctrine to others to be baptized, whereof he had store. And so hee declared sufficiently how farre he was from all ambition: whereas on the other side, they, whom he reprehendeth, as though they gathered disciples vnto themselues and not vnto Christ, bragged most ambitiously of numbers, which they had baptized. 20 Now he turneth himselfe to the doctors themselues, which pleased themselues in braue and ambitious eloquence, to the end that they might drawe more disciples after them. Hee confesseth plainely that hee was like vnto them, opposing grauely, as it became an Apostle, his example against their peruerse iudgements: So that this is another place of this Epistle, touching the obseruing of a godly simplicitie both in words and sentences in teaching of the Gospel. * *Chap. 2.13. 1 pet. 1.16.* *l With eloquence: which Paul casteth off from him not onely as not necessarie, but also as flat contrary to the office of his Apostleship: and yet had Paul this kinde of eloquence, but it was heauenly, not of man, and void of painted wordes.*

of words, lest the [21] crosse of Christ should be
made of none effect.
18 For that [m] preaching of the crosse is to
them that perish, foolishnesse: but vnto vs,
which are saued, it is the * [n] power of God.
19 [22] For it is written, * I will destroy the
wisedome of the wise, and will cast away the
vnderstanding of the prudent.
20 Where is the wise? where is the [o] Scribe?
where is the [p] disputer of this world? hath not
God made the wisedome of this world foolishnesse?
21 [23] For seeing the [q] world by wisedome
knewe not God in the [r] wisedome of *God*, [24] it
pleased God by the [s] foolishnesse of preaching
to saue them that beleeue:
22 * [25] Seeing also that the Iewes require
a signe, and the Grecians seeke after wisdome.
23 But wee preach Christ crucified: vnto
the Iewes euen a stumbling blocke, and vnto
the Grecians, foolishnesse:
24 But vnto them which are called, both of
the Iewes and Grecians, *we preach* Christ, the
power of God, and the wisedome of God.
25 For the foolishnesse of God is wiser
then men, and the weakenesse of God is stronger then men.
26 [26] For brethren, you see your [t] calling,
how that not many wise men [u] after the flesh,
not many mightie, not many noble *are called*.
27 But God hath chosen the foolish things

21 The reason why he vsed not the pompe of wordes, and painted speech: because it was Gods will to bring the world to his obedience by that way, whereby the most idiots amongst men might vnderstand, that this worke was done of God himselfe without the arte of man. Therefore as saluation is set foorth vnto vs in the Gospel by the crosse of Christ, then which nothing is more contemptible, and more farre from life, so God would haue the manner of the preaching of the crosse, most different from those meanes, with which men doe vse to draw and entise other, either to heare or beleeue: therefore it pleased him by a certaine kinde of most wise folly, to triumph ouer the most foolish wisdome of the world, as he had said before by Esay, that hee would. And hereby we may gather, that both these doctors which were puffed vp with ambitious eloquence, and also their hearers, strayed farre away from the ende and marke of their vocation. *m The preaching of Christ crucified, or the kinde of speech which wee vse.* *Roman. 1.16. *n It is that wherein hee declareth his marueilous power in sauing his elect, which would not so euidently appeare, if it hanged vpon any helpe of man, for so, man might attribute that to himselfe, which is proper onely to the crosse of Christ.* 22 The Apostle prooueth, that this ought not only not to seem strange, seeing that it was foretolde so long before, but declareth further, that God is woont to punish the pride of the world in such sort, which so pleaseth it selfe in it owne wisedome: and therefore that that is vaine, yea a thing of nothing, and such as God reiecteth as vnprofitable, which they so carefully laboured for, and made so great accompt of. *Esai 29.14. *o Where art thou, O thou learned fellow, and thou that spendest thy dayes in turning thy bookes? p Thou that spendest all thy time in seeking out the secret things of this world, and in expounding all hard questions: and thus triumpheth he against all the men of this world, for there was not one of them that could so much as dreame vpon this secret and hidden mysterie.* 23 Hee sheweth that the pride of men was worthily punished of God, because they would not behold God, as meete was they should, in the most cleare glasse of the wisedome of the world, which is the workemanship of the world. *q By the world he meaneth all men which are not borne anew, but remaine as they were, when they were first borne. r In the workemanship of this world, which hath the marueilous wisedome of God engraued in it, so that euery man may behold it.* 24 The goodnesse of God is woonderfull, for while hee goeth about to punish the pride of this world, hee is very prouident and carefull for the saluation of it, and teacheth men to become fooles, that they may bee wise to God. *s So hee calleth the preaching of the Gospel, as the enemies supposed it: but in the meane season hee taunteth them very sharpely, who had rather charge God with folly, then acknowledge their owne, and craue pardon for it.* * Matth. 12.38. 25 A declaration of that which hee said: that the preaching of the Gospel, is foolish. It is foolish, sayeth hee, to them whome God hath not endued with new light, that is to say, to all men being considered in themselues: for the Iewes require miracles, and the Grecians arguments, which they may comprehend by their wit and wisedome: and therefore they doe not onely not beleeue the Gospel, but also they mocke at it. Notwithstanding in this foolish preaching, there is the great vertue and wisedome of God, but such as those onely which are called doe perceiue: God shewing most plainely, that euen then when madde men thinke him most foolish, hee is farre wiser then they are: and that he surmounteth all their might and power, when hee vseth most vile and abiect things, as it hath appeared in the fruite of the preaching of the Gospel. 26 A confirmation taken of those things which came to passe at Corinth, where the Church especially consisted of the basest and common people, insomuch that the philosophers of Greece were driuen to shame when they sawe that they could doe nothing with their wisedome and eloquence, in comparison of the Apostles, whom notwithstanding they called idiots and vnlearned. And herewithall doth he beat downe their pride: for God did not preferre them before those noble and wise men because they should be proud, but that they might be constrained euen whether they would or not, to reioyce in the Lord, by whose mercy, although they were the most abiects of all, they had obteined in Christ, both this wisedome, and all things necessarie to saluation. *t What way the Lord hath taken in calling you. u After that kinde of wisedome which men make accompt of, as though there were none else: who because they are carnall, know not spirituall wisedome.*

of the world to confound the wise, and God
hath chosen the weake things of the world, to
confound the mightie things,
28 And vile things of the world & things
which are despised, hath God chosen, and
things which [x] are not, to bring to [y] nought
things that are,
29 That no [z] flesh should reioyce in his
presence.
30 But yee are [a] of him in Christ Iesus,
[27] who of God is made vnto vs wisedome and
righteousnes, and sanctification, and redemption,
31 That, according as it is written, * [b] He
that reioyceth, let him reioyce in the Lord.

x Which in mans iudgement are almost nothing. y To shewe that they are vaine and vnprofitable, and nothing worth. See Rom. 3.31. z Flesh, is oft, as we see, taken for the whole man: and he vseth this word Flesh, very fitly, to set the weake and miserable condition of man, and the maiestie of God, one against the other. a Whom he cast downe before, now he lifteth vp, yea, higher then all men: yet so, that hee sheweth them, that all their worthinesse is without themselues, that is, standeth in Christ, and that of God. 27 Hee teacheth that especially and aboue all things, the Gospel ought not to bee contemned, seeing it conteineth the chiefest things that are to be desired, to wit, true wisedome, the true way to obtaine righteousnesse, the true way to liue honestly and godly, the true deliuerance from all miseries and calamities. * *Ierm. 9.24. 2. corinth. 10.17 b Let him yeeld all to God and giue him thankes: and so by this place is mans free will beaten downe, which the Papists so dreame of.*

CHAP. II.

1 Hee setteth downe a platforme of his preaching, 4 which was base in respect of mans wisedome, 7. 13 but noble in respect of the spirituall power and efficacie, 14 and so concludeth, that flesh and blood cannot rightly iudge thereof.

AND [1] I, brethren, when I came to you,
came not with * excellencie of words, or
of wisedome, shewing vnto you the [a] testimonie of God.
2 For I [b] esteemed not to know any thing
among you, saue Iesus Christ, and him crucified.
3 * And I was among you in [c] weaknesse,
and in feare, and in much trembling.
4 Neither *stood* my word, and my preaching in the * entising speech of mans wisedome, [2] but in plaine [d] euidence of the Spirit
and of power.
5 [3] That your faith should not bee in the
wisedome of men, but in the power of God.
6 [4] And we speake wisdome among them
that are [e] perfect: not the wisedome of this
world, neither of the [f] princes of this world,
which come to nought.
7 [5] But wee speake the wisedome of God
in a [g] mysterie, *euen* the hid *wisedome*, [6] which
God had determined before the world, vnto
our glory.

1 He returneth to the 17. verse of the former chapter, that is to say, to his owne example: confessing that he vsed not among them either excellencie of words or entising speech of mans wisdome, but with great simplicitie of speech both knew and preached Iesus Christ crucified, humble and abiect, as touching the flesh. * *Chap. 1.17. a The Gospel. b I purposed not to professe any knowledge but the knowlede of Christ and him crucified.* * *Actes 18.1. c He setteth weaknesse, against excellencie of words, and therefore ioyneth with it feare and trembling, which are companions of true modestie, not such feare and trembling as terrifie the conscience, but such as are contrary to vanitie and pride.* * *Chap. 1.17. 2. pet. 1.16.* 2 Hee turneth that now to the commendation of his ministerie, which he had granted to his aduersaries: for his vertue and power which they knewe well enough, was so much the more excellent, because it had no worldly helpe ioyned with it. *d By plaine euidence he meaneth such a proofe, as is made by certaine and necessary reasons.* 3 And he telleth the Corinthians, that he did it for their great profite, because they might thereby know manifestly that the Gospel was from heauen. Therefore hee priuily rebuketh them, because that in seeking vaine ostentation, they willingly depriued themselues of the greatest helpe of their faith. 4 Another argument taken of the nature of the thing, that is, of the Gospel, which is true wisedome, but knowen to them only which are desirous of perfection: and is vnsauorie to them which otherwise excell in the world, but yet vainely and fraily. *e Those are called perfect here, not which had gotten perfection alreadie, but such as tend to it, as Philip. 3.15. so that perfect, is set against weake. f They that are wiser, richer, or mightier then other men are.* 5 Hee sheweth the cause why this wisdome cannot be perceiued of those excellent worldly wits: to wit, because indeed it is so deep, that they cannot attaine vnto it. *g Which men could not so much as dreame of.* 6 He taketh away an obiection: If it be so hard, when and how is it knowen? God saith he, determined with himselfe from the beginning, that which his purpose was to bring forth at this time out of his secrets, for the saluation of men,

7 He taketh away another obiection: why then, how commeth it to passe, that this wisedome was so reiected of men of highest authoritie, that they crucified Christ himselfe? Paul answereth: because they knew not Christ such as he was.

8 [7]Which none of the princes of this world
hath knowen: for had they knowen it, they
would not haue crucified the [h] Lorde of
glory.
9 [8]But as it is written, *The things which
eye hath not seene, neither eare hath heard,
neither came into [i] mans heart, *are*, which
God hath prepared for them that loue him.
10 [9]But God hath reueiled *them* vnto vs
by his Spirit: for the spirit [k] searcheth al things,
yea, the deepe things of God.
11 [10]For what man knoweth the things of
a man, saue the [l] spirit of a man, which is in
him? euen so the things of God knoweth no
man, but the Spirit of God.
12 Now wee haue receiued not the [m] spirit
of the world, but the Spirit which is of God,
[11]that wee might [n] knowe the things that are
giuen vs of God.
13 [12]Which things also wee speake, not in
the * words which mans wisedome teacheth,
but which the holy Ghost teacheth, [o] comparing spirituall things with spirituall things.
14 [13]But the [p] naturall man perceiueth not
the things of the Spirit of God: for they are
foolishnesse vnto him: neither can hee know
them, because they are [q] spiritually discerned.
15 [14]But hee that is spirituall, [r] discerneth
all things: yet [15]hee himselfe is iudged of [s] no
man.
16 *[16]For who hath knowen the minde of
the Lord, that hee might [t] instruct him? But
we haue [u] the mind of Christ.

h That mightie God, full of true maiestie and glory: Now this place hath in it a most euident proofe of the Diuinitie of Christ, and of his ioyning of the two natures in one, which hath this in it, that that which is proper to the manhood alone, is vouched of the Godhead ioyned with the manhood: which kinde of speech, is called of the old Fathers, A making common of things belonging to some one, with other to whom they doe not belong.

8 Another obiection: But how could it be that those wittie men could not perceiue this wisedome? Paul answereth: Because wee preach those things which passe all mans vnderstanding. * *Esai 64.4* *i Man cannot so much as thinke of them, much lesse conceiue of them with his senses* 9 A question: If it surmount the capacitie of men, how can it bee vnderstood of any man, or how can you declare and preach it? by a peculiar lightning of Gods Spirit, wherewith whosoeuer is inspired, hee can enter euen into the very secrets of God. *k There is nothing so secret and hidden in God, but the Spirit of God pearceth into it.* 10 Hee setteth that foorth by a similitude, which hee spake of the inspiration of the Spirit. As the force of mans wit searcheth out things pertaining to man, so doeth our minde by that power of the holy Ghost, vnderstand heauenly things. *l The minde of man which is endued with the ablenesse to vnderstand and iudge.* *m The Spirit which we haue receiued, doeth not teach vs things of this world, but lifteth vs vp to God, and this place teacheth vs against the Papists, what faith is, from whence it commeth, and what force it is of.* 11 That which hee spake generally, hee restraineth now to those things which God hath opened vnto vs of our saluation in Christ: lest that any man should separate the Spirit from the preaching of the word and Christ: or should thinke that those fantasticall men are gouerned by the Spirit of God, which wandering besides the word, thrust vpon vs their vaine imaginations for the secrets of God. *n This word (know) is taken here in his proper sense, for true knowledge, which the Spirit of God worketh in vs.* 12 Now hee returneth to his purpose, and concludeth the argument which hee began verse 6. and it is thus: The wordes must be applyed to the matter, and the matter must be set foorth with words which are meete and conuenient for it: now this wisedome is spirituall and not of man, and therefore it must be deliuered by a spirituall kinde of teaching, and not by entising wordes of mans eloquence, that the simple, and yet woonderfull maiestie of the holy Ghost may therein appeare. * *Chap.1.17. 2.pet.1.16.* *o Applying the words vnto the matter, to wit, that as we teach spirituall things, so must our kind of teaching be spirituall.* 13 Againe he preuenteth an offence or stumbling blocke: How commeth it to passe, that so few allow these things? This is not to be marueiled at, sayth the Apostle, seeing that men in their naturall powers (as they tearme them) are not endued with that facultie whereby spirituall things are discerned (which facultie commeth another way) and therefore they account spirituall wisedome as folly: and it is as if he should say, It is no marueile that blinde men cannot iudge of colours, seeing that they lacke the light of their eyes, and therefore light is to them as darknesse. *p The man that hath no further light of vnderstanding, then that which he brought with him, euen from his mothers wombe, as Iude defineth it, Iude 19.* *q By the vertue of the holy Ghost.* 14 Hee amplifieth the matter by contraries. *r Vnderstandeth and discerneth.* 15 The wisedome of the flesh, sayth Paul, determineth nothing certainly, no not in it owne affaires, much lesse can it discerne strange, that is, spirituall things. But the Spirit of God, wherewith spirituall men are endued, can bee deceiued by no meanes, and therefore be reprooued of no man. *s Of no man: for when the Prophets are iudged of the Prophets, it is the Spirit that iudgeth, and not the man.* * *Esai 40.13. rom. 11.34.* 16 A reason of the former saying: for hee is called spirituall, which hath learned that by the vertue of the Spirit, which Christ hath taught vs. Now if that which we haue learned of that Master, could be reprooued of any man, he must needs be wiser then God: whereupon it followeth, that they are not onely foolish, but also wicked, which thinke that they can deuise some thing that is either more perfect, or that they can teach the wisedome of God a better way then they knewe or taught, which vndoubtedly were indued with Gods Spirit.

t Lay his head to his, and teach him what he should do. *u We are endued with the Spirit of Christ, who openeth vnto vs those secrets, which by all other meanes are vnsearchable, and also all trueth whatsoeuer.*

CHAP. III.

1 Hee yeeldeth a reason why he preached small matters vnto them: 4 Hee sheweth how they ought to esteeme of ministers. 6 The ministers office. 10 A true forme of edifying. 16 Hee warneth the Corinthians, that they be not drawen away to profane things, 18 through the proud wisedome of the flesh.

And [1] I could not speake vnto you, brethren, as vnto spirituall men, but as vnto
[a] carnall, *euen* as vnto babes in Christ.
2 I gaue you milke to drinke, and not
[b] meate: for yee were not yet [c] able *to beare it*,
neither yet now are ye able.
3 For ye are yet carnall: for whereas *there*
is among you enuying, and strife, and diuisions,
are ye not carnall, and walke as [d] men?
4 For when one sayth, I am Pauls, and
another, I am Apollos, are ye not carnall?
5 [2] Who is Paul then? and who is Apollos, but the ministers by whom yee beleeued,
and as the Lord gaue to euery man?
6 [3] I haue planted, Apollos watered, but
God gaue the increase.
7 So then, neither is he that planteth, any
thing, neither he that watereth, but God that
giueth the increase.
8 And he that planteth, and he that watereth, are one: * and euery man shall receiue
his wages according to his labour.
9 For we together are Gods [e] labourers:
ye are Gods husbandrie, *and* Gods building.
10 According to the grace of God giuen
to me, as a skilfull master builder, I haue laid
the foundation, and another buildeth thereon:
[4] but let euery man take heed how he buildeth
vpon it.

1 Hauing declared the worthinesse of heauenly wisedome, and of the Gospel, and hauing generally condemned ẏ blindnesse of mans minde, now at length he applyeth it particularly to the Corinthians, calling them carnall, that is, such in whom as yet the flesh preuaileth against the Spirit. And he bringeth a double testimonie of it: first, for that he had prooued them to be such, in so much that he dealt with them no otherwise then with ignorant men, and such as are almost babes in the doctrine of godlinesse, and secondly, because they shewed in deede by these dissentions, which sprang vp by reason of the ignorance of the vertue of the Spirit, and heauenly wisedome, that they had profited very litle or nothing. *a He calleth them carnall, which are as yet ignorant, and therefore to expresse it the better, he termeth them babes.* *b Substantiall meat, or strong meat.* *c To be fed by me with substantiall meat: therefore as the Corinthians grewe vp in age, so the Apostle nourished them by teaching, first with milke, then with strong meat, which difference was only but in the maner of teaching.* *d By the square and compasse of mans wit and iudgement.* 2 After that hee hath sufficiently reprehended ambitious teachers, and their foolish esteemers, now he sheweth how the true ministers are to be esteemed, that we attribute not vnto them more or lesse then we ought to doe. Therfore he teacheth vs, that they are they by whom wee are brought to faith and saluation, but yet as the ministers of God, and such as do nothing of themselues, but God so working by them as it pleaseth him to furnish them with his gifts. Therefore wee haue not to marke or consider what minister it is that speaketh, but what is spoken: and we must depend only vpon him which speaketh by his seruants. 3 Hee beautifieth the former sentence, with two similitudes: first comparing the company of the faithfull, to a field which God maketh fruitfull, when it is sowed & watered through the labor of his seruants: next, by comparing it to an house, which in deed the Lord buildeth, but by the hands of his workemen, some of whom he vseth in laying the foundation, others in building of it vp. Now, both these similitudes tend to this purpose, to shew that all things are wholly accomplished by Gods onely authoritie and might, so that we must onely haue an eye to him. Moreouer, although that God vseth some in the better part of the worke, we must not therfore contemne other, in respect of them, and much lesse may we diuide or set them apart, (as these factious men did) seeing that all of them labor in Gods businesse, and in such sort, that they serue to finish one selfe same worke, although by a diuers maner of working, insomuch that they need one anothers helpe. * *Psal.62.12. gal.6.5.* *e Seruing vnder him: Now they which serue vnder another, doe nothing of their owne strength, but as it is giuen them of grace, which grace maketh them fit to that seruice. Looke chap.15.10. and 2.cor.3.6. and all the increase that commeth by their labour, doth so proceed from God, that no part of the praise of it may be giuen to the vnder seruant.* 4 Now hee speaketh to the teachers themselues, which succeeded him in the Church of Corinth, and in their person to all that were after or shalbe Pastors of Congregations, seeing that they succeed into the labour of the Apostles, which were planters & chiefe builders. Therfore he warneth them first, that they perswade not themselues that they may build after their owne fantasie, that is, that they may propound and set foorth any thing in the Church, either in matter, or in kinde of teaching, different from the Apostles which were the chiefe builders.

5 Moreouer, hee ſheweth what this foundation is, to wit, Chriſt Ieſus, from whence they may not turne away one iote in the building vp of this building.

6 Thirdly hee ſheweth, that they muſt take heede that the vpper part of the building be anſwerable to the foundation, that is, that admonitions, exhortations, and whatſoeuer pertaineth to the edifying of the flocke, be anſwerable to the doctrine of Chriſt, as well in the matter as in forme: which doctrine is compared to golde, ſiluer, and precious ſtones: of which matter, Eſaias alſo and Iohn in the Reuelation build the heauenly citie. And to theſe are oppoſite, wood, hay, ſtubble, that is to ſay, curious and vaine queſtions or decrees: and beſides to be ſhort, all that kinde of teaching which ſerueth to oſtentation. For falſe doctrines, whereof he ſpeaketh not here, are not ſaid properly to

11 [5] For other foundation can no man
lay, then that which is laide, which is Ieſus
Chriſt.
12 [6] And if any man build on this foundation,
golde, ſiluer, precious ſtones, timber, hay,
or ſtubble,
13 [7] Euery mans worke ſhalbe made manifeſt:
for the day ſhall declare it, becauſe it ſhall
bee reueiled by the fire: and the fire ſhall trie
euery mans worke of what ſort it is.
14 If any mans worke, that hee hath built
vpon, abide, he ſhall receiue wages.
15 If any mans worke burne, he ſhall loſe,
but [8] he ſhall be ſaued himſelfe: neuertheleſſe
yet as it were by the fire.
16 * [9] Know ye not that ye are the Temple
of God, and that the Spirit of God dwelleth
in you?
17 If any man [f] deſtroy the Temple of
God, him ſhall God deſtroy: for the Temple
of God is holy, which ye are.
18 [10] Let no man deceiue himſelfe: If any
man amongſt you ſeeme to bee wiſe in
this world, let him be a foole, that hee may be
wiſe.
19 For the wiſedome of this world is fooliſhneſſe
with God: for it is written, * Hee
[g] catcheth the wiſe in their owne craftineſſe.
20 * And againe, The Lord knoweth that
the thoughts of the wiſe be vaine.
21 [11] Therfore let no man [h] reioyce in men:
for all things are [i] yours.
22 Whether it be Paul, or Apollos, or Cephas,
or the [12] world, or life, or death: whether
they be things preſent, or things to come, *euen*
all are yours,
23 And ye Chriſts, and Chriſt Gods.

be built vpon this foundation, vnleſſe peraduenture in ſhewe onely. 7 Hee teſtifieth, as in deede the trueth is, that all are not good builders, no not ſome of them which ſtand vpon this one and onely foundation: but howſoeuer this worke of euill builders, ſayeth hee, ſtand for a ſeaſon, yet ſhall it not alwayes deceiue, becauſe that the light of the trueth appearing at length, as day, ſhall diſſolue this darkeneſſe, and ſhewe what it is. And as that ſtuffe is tryed by the fire, whether it bee good or not, ſo will God in his time, by the touch of his Spirit and word, trie all buildings, and ſo ſhall it come to paſſe, that ſuch as bee found pure and ſound, ſhall ſtill continue ſo, to the praiſe of the workeman; but they that are otherwiſe, ſhall bee conſumed and vaniſh away, and ſo ſhall the workeman bee fruſtrate of the hope of his labour, which pleaſed himſelfe in a thing of naught. 8 Hee taketh not away hope of ſaluation from the vnskilfull and fooliſh builders, which holde faſt the foundation, of which ſort were thoſe Rhetoricians rather then Paſtours, of Corinth: but hee addeth an exception, that they muſt notwithſtanding ſuffer this tryall of their worke, and alſo abide the loſſe of their vaine labours. * *Chap.6.19. 2.corinth.6.16.* 9 Continuing ſtill in the metaphore of building, hee teacheth vs that this ambition is not onely vaine, but alſo ſacrilegious: for hee ſayeth that the Church is as it were the Temple of God, which God hath as it were conſecrated vnto himſelfe by his Spirit. Then turning himſelfe to theſe ambitious men, hee ſheweth that they profane the Temple of God, becauſe thoſe vaine artes wherein they pleaſe themſelues ſo much, are as he teacheth, ſo many pollutions of the holy doctrine of God, and the puritie of the Church. Which wickedneſſe ſhall not be ſuffered vnpuniſhed. *f Defileth it and maketh it vncleane, being holy: and ſurely they doe defile it, by Paul his iudgement, which by fleſhly eloquence defile the puritie of the Goſpel.* 10 Hee concludeth by the contrarie, that they profeſſe pure wiſedome in the Church of God, which refuſe and caſt away all thoſe vanities of men: and if they be mocked of the world, it is ſufficient for them that they be wiſe according to the wiſedome of God, and as hee will haue them to bee wiſe. * *Iob 5.13.* *g Be they neuer ſo craftie, yet the Lord will take them when he ſhall diſcouer their trecherie.* * *Pſal.44.11.* 11 He returneth to the propoſition of the 2. verſe, firſt warning the hearers, that henceforward they eſteeme not as Lords, thoſe whome God hath appointed to bee Miniſters and not Lords of their ſaluation: which thing they doe, that depend vpon men, and not vpon God that ſpeaketh by them. *h Pleaſe himſelfe.* *i Helpes, appointed for your benefite.* 12 Hee paſſeth from the perſons to the things themſelues, that his argument may bee more forcible: yea, hee aſcendeth from Chriſt to the Father, to ſhew that we reſt our ſelues no not in Chriſt himſelfe, in that that he is man, but becauſe he carieth vs vp euen to the Father, as Chriſt witneſſeth of himſelfe euery where that he was ſent of his Father, that by this band we may be all knit with God himſelfe.

CHAP. IIII.

1 Bringing in the definition of a true Apoſtle, 7 he ſheweth that humilitie ought rather to bee an honour then a ſhame vnto him. 9 He bringeth in proofe, whereby it may euidently appeare, 10 that he neither had care of glory, 11 nor of his belly. 17 He commendeth Timothie.

1 Let [1] a [a] man ſo thinke of vs, as of the Miniſters
of Chriſt, and diſpoſers of the ſecrets
of God:
2 [2] And as for the reſt, it is required of the
diſpoſers, that euery man be found faithfull.
3 [3] As touching me, I paſſe very little to
be iudged of you, [4] or of mans [b] iudgement:
no, [5] I iudge not mine owne ſelfe.
4 For I know nothing by my ſelfe, yet am
I not thereby iuſtified: but hee that iudgeth
me, is the [c] Lord.
5 [6] Therefore * iudge nothing before the
time, vntill the Lord come, who will lighten
things that are hid in darkeneſſe, and make the
counſels of the heart manifeſt: and then ſhall
euery man haue [d] praiſe of God.
6 [7] Now theſe things, brethren, I haue figuratiuely
applyed vnto mine owne ſelfe and
Apollos, for your ſakes, that yee might learne
[e] by vs, that no man preſume aboue that which
is written, that one ſwell not againſt another
for any mans cauſe.
7 [8] For who ſeparateth thee? and what
haſt thou, that thou haſt not receiued? if thou
haſt receiued it, why reioyceſt thou, as though
[f] thou hadſt not receiued it?
8 [9] Now yee are full: now yee are made
rich: ye reigne as kings without vs, and would
to God yee did reigne, that wee alſo might
reigne with you.
9 For I thinke that God hath ſet foorth vs
the laſt Apoſtles, as men appointed to death:
for wee are made a [g] gaſing ſtocke vnto the
world, and to the Angels, and to men.
10 Wee *are* fooles for Chriſtes ſake, and

1 He concludeth the duety of the hearers towards their Miniſters: that they eſteeme them not as Lords: and yet notwithſtanding that they giue eare vnto them, as to them that are ſent from Chriſt, ſent I ſay to this end and purpoſe, that they may receiue as it were at their hands, the treaſure of ſaluation which is drawen out of the ſecrets of God.

a Euery man.

2 Laſt of all, he warneth the miniſters, that they alſo behaue themſelues not as Lords, but as faithfull ſeruants, becauſe they muſt render an accompt of their ſtewardſhip vnto God.

3 Becauſe in reprehending others, hee ſet himſelfe for an example, he vſeth a preoccupation or preuenting of an obiection, and vſing the grauitie of an Apoſtle, he ſheweth that he careth not for the contrarie iudgements that they haue of him, in that they eſteemed him as a vile perſon, becauſe hee did not ſet foorth himſelfe as they did. And hee bringeth good reaſons why hee was nothing mooued with the iudgements which they had of him. 4 Firſt, becauſe that that which men iudge in theſe caſes of their owne braines, is no more to bee accompted of, then when the vnlearned doe iudge of wiſedome. *b Word for word, Day, after the manner of the ſpeech of the Cilicians.* 5 Secondly, ſayth hee, how can yee iudge how much or how little I am to be accompted of, ſeeing that I my ſelfe which knowe my ſelfe better then you doe, and which dare profeſſe that I haue walked in my vocation with a good conſcience, dare not yet notwithſtanding challenge any thing to my ſelfe: for I know that I am not vnblameable, all this notwithſtanding: much leſſe therefore ſhould I pleaſe my ſelfe as you doe. *c I permit my ſelfe to the Lords iudgement.* 6 A third reaſon proceeding of a concluſion, as it were, out of the former reaſons. It is Gods office to eſteeme euery man according to his value, becauſe hee knoweth the ſecrets of the heart, which men for the moſt part are ignorant of. Therefore this iudgement pertaineth not to you. * *Matth.7.1.* *d One could not bee praiſed aboue the reſt, but the other ſhould be blamed: and hee mentioneth praiſe rather then diſpraiſe, for that the beginning of this ſore was this, that they gaue more to ſome men, then meete was.* 7 Hauing reiected their iudgement, hee ſetteth foorth himſelfe againe as a ſingular example of modeſtie, as one which concealing in this Epiſtle thoſe factious teachers names, doubted not to put downe his owne name and Apollos in their place, and tooke vpon him as it were their ſhame: ſo farre was hee from preferring himſelfe to any. *e By our example, which choſe rather to take other mens faults vpon vs, then to carpe any by name.* 8 Hee ſheweth a good meanes to bridle pride: firſt if thou conſider how rightly thou exempteſt thy ſelfe out of the number of others, ſeeing thou art a man thy ſelfe: againe, if thou conſider that although thou haue ſome thing more then other men haue, yet thou haſt it not but by Gods bountifulneſſe. And what wiſe man is hee that will bragge of anothers goodneſſe, and that againſt God? *f There is nothing then in vs of nature, that is worthie of commendation: but all that we haue, we haue it of grace, which the Pelagians and halfe Pelagians will not confeſſe.* 9 Hee deſcendeth to a moſt graue mocke, to cauſe thoſe ambitious men to bluſh euen againſt their willes. *g Hee that will take a right view how like Paul and the Pope are, who lyingly boaſteth that he is his ſucceſſour, let him compare the delicatts of the Popiſh court, with Saint Pauls ſtate as wee ſee it here.*

ye *are* wise in Christ: we *are* weake, and yee
are strong: yee *are* honourable, and wee *are*
despised.
11 Vnto this houre we both hunger, and
thirst, and are naked, and are buffeted, and haue
no certaine dwelling place,
12 * And labour, working with our owne
hands: we are reuiled, and *yet* we blesse: wee
are persecuted, *and* suffer it.
13 * We are euill spoken of, and we pray:
we are made as the [h] filth of the world, the off-
skouring of all things, vnto this time.
14 [10] I write not these things to shame you,
but as my beloued children I admonish you.
15 For though ye haue tenne thousand in-
structers in Christ, yet *haue ye* not many fathers: for in Christ Iesus I haue begotten you
through the Gospel.
16 Wherefore, I pray you be ye followers
of me.
17 For this cause haue I sent vnto you Timotheus, which is my beloued sonne, & faithfull in the Lord, which shal put you in remembrance of my [i] wayes in Christ, as I teach euery where in euery Church.
18 [11] Some are puffed vp as though I would
not come vnto you.
19 But I will come to you shortly, * if the
Lord will, and will know, not the [k] wordes of
them which are puffed vp, but the power.
20 For the kingdom of God *is* not in word,
but in power.
21 [12] What will ye? shall I come vnto you
with a rod, or in loue, and in the [l] spirit of meek-
nesse?

*Actes 20.34. 1.thess. 2.9. 2.thess. 3.8.
*Matth. 15.44. luke 23.34. actes 7.60.
h Such as by sweeping is gathered together.
10 Moderating the sharpnesse of his mocke, hee putteth them in minde to remember of whom they were begotten in Christ, and that they should not doubt to follow him for an example, although he seeme vile according to the outward shew in respect of others, yet mightie by the efficacie of Gods Spirite, as they had triall thereof in themselues.
i What way and rule I follow euery where in teaching the Churches.
11 Last of all he descendeth also to Apostolique threatnings, but yet chiding them as a father, lest by their disorder he be constrained to come to punish some amongst them.
*Actes 19.21. iames 4.15.
k By wordes, he meaneth their painted and coloured kinde of eloquence, against which he setteth the vertue of the Spirit. 12 A passing ouer to another part of this Epistle, wherein he reprehendeth most sharply a very hainous offence, shewing the vse of ecclesiastical correction. *l Meekly affected toward you.*

CHAP. V.

1 That they haue winked at him who committed incest with his mother in Lawe, 2. 6 he sheweth should cause them rather to be ashamed, then to reioyce. 10 Such kinde of wickednesse is to be punished with excommunication, 12 lest other be infected with it.

It is [1] heard certainely *that there is* fornication among you: and such fornication as is
not once named among the Gentiles, that one
should haue his fathers wife.
2 [2] And ye are puffed vp and haue not rather sorowed, that hee which hath done this
deed, might be put from among you.
3 [3] For I verely as absent in body, but present in [a] spirit, haue determined already as
though I were present, that he that hath thus
done this thing,
4 When ye are gathered together, and my
spirit, in the [b] Name of our Lord Iesus Christ,
that such one, *I say,* [4] by the power of our Lord
Iesus Christ,
5 [5] Bee [c] deliuered vnto Satan, for the
[6] destruction of the flesh, that the spirit may be
saued in the day of the Lord Iesus.
6 [7] Your reioycing [d] is not good: knowe
ye not that a little leauen leaueneth the whole
lumpe?
7 [8] Purge out therefore the olde leauen,
that ye may be a newe [e] lumpe, as ye are vnleauened: for Christ our [f] Passeouer is sacrificed
for vs.
8 Therefore let vs keepe the [g] feast, not
with old leauen, neither in the leauen of maliciousnesse and wickednesse: but with the vnleauened bread of synceritie and trueth.
9 [9] I wrote vnto you in an Epistle, that ye
should not companie together with fornicatours,
10 And not [h] altogether with the fornicatours of this world, or with the couetous, or
with extortioners, or with idolaters: for then
ye must goe out of the world.
11 But now I haue written vnto you, that
ye companie not together: if any that is called
a brother, be a fornicatour, or couetous, or an
idolater, or a railer, or a drunkard, or an extorti-
oner, with such one eat not.
12 [10] For what haue I to doe, to iudge them
also which are without? doe ye not iudge them
which are within?
13 But God iudgeth them that are without: Put away therefore from among your
selues that wicked man.

1 They are greatly to be reprehended which by suffering of wickednesse, set forth the church of God to bee mocked & scorned of infidels.
2 There are none more proud then they that least know themselues.
3 Excommunication ought not to be committed to one mans power, but must be done by the authoritie of the whole Congregation, after the matter is diligently examined.
a In minde, thought and will. b Calling vpon Christ his Name. 4 There is no doubt but that iudgement is ratified in heauen, wherein Christ himselfe sitteth as Iudge. 5 The excommunicate is deliuered to the power of Satan, in that, that he is cast out of the house of God. *c What it is to bee deliuered to Satan, the Lord himselfe declareth when he saith, Let him be vnto thee as an Heathen and Publicane, Matth. 18.17. that is to say, to bee disfranchised and put out of the right and libertie of the Citie of Christ, which is the Church, without which Satan is lord and master.*

6 The end of excommunication is not to cast away the excommunicate, that he should vtterly perish, but that he may be saued, to wit, that by this meanes his flesh may be tamed, that hee may learne to liue to ye Spirit. 7 Another end of excommunication is, that other be not infected, and therefore it must of necessitie be reteined in the Church, that the one be not infected by the other. *d Is naught, and not grounded vpon good reason, as though you were excellent, and yet there is such wickednesse found amongst you.* 8 By alluding to the ceremonie of the Passeouer, he exhorteth them to cast out that vncleane person from among them. In times past, saith he, it was not lawfull for them which did celebrate the Passeouer, to eat vnleauened bread: Insomuch that he was holden as vncleane and vnworthy to eat the Passeouer, whosoeuer had but tasted of leauen. Now we all our whole life must bee as it were the feast of vnleauened bread, wherein all they that are partakers of that immaculate Lambe which is slaine, must cast out both of themselues, and also out of their houses and Congregations all impuritie. *e By lumpe he meaneth the whole body of the Church, euery member whereof must be vnleauened bread, that is, be renewed in Spirit, by plucking away the old corruption. f The Lambe of the Passeouer. g Let vs leade our whole life, as it were a continuall feast, honestly, and vprightly.* 9 Now hee speaketh more generally: and that which he spake before of the incestuous person, he sheweth that it pertaineth to others, which are knowen to be wicked and such as through their naughtie life are a slander to the Church, which ought also by lawfull order bee cast out of the communitie of the Church. And making mention of eating of meat, either hee meaneth those feasts of loue whereat the Supper of the Lord was receiued, or else their common vsage & maner of life: which is rightly to be taken, lest any man should thinke, that either Matrimonie were broken by excommunication, or such dueties hindred and cut off thereby, as we owe one to another: children to their parents, subiects to their rulers, seruants to their masters, and neighbour to neighbour, to winne one another vnto God. *h If you should vtterly absteine from such mens companie, you should goe out of the world: therefore I speake of them which are in the very bosome of the Church, which must be called home by discipline, and not of them which are without, with whome we must labour by all meanes possible, to bring them to Christ.* 10 Such as are false brethren, ought to be cast out of the Congregation, as for them which are without, they must be left to the iudgement of God.

CHAP. VI.

1 Hee inueyeth against their contentions in lawe matters, 6 wherewith they vexed one another vnder iudges that were infidels, to the reproch of the Gospel, 9 and then sharpely threatneth fornicatours.

Dare [1] [a] any of you, hauing busines against
another, bee iudged [b] vnder the vniust,
[2] and not vnder the Saints?
2 [3] Doe ye not know, that the Saints shall
iudge the world? If the world then shall bee

1 The third question is of ciuill iudgements. Whether it be lawfull for one faithfull to draw another faithfull before the iudgment seat of an infidell? He answereth that is not lawfull for offence sake, for it is not euil of it selfe. *a As if he said, Are you become so impudent, that you are not ashamed to make the Gospel a laughing stocke to prophane men? b Before the vniust.* 2 He addeth that hee doeth not forbid that one neighbour may goe to law with another, if neede so require, but yet vnder holy iudges. 3 He gathereth by a comparison that the faithfull cannot seeke to infidels to be iudged, without great iniurie done to the Saints, seeing that God himselfe will make the Saints iudges of the world, and of the deuils, with his Sonne Christ: much more ought they to judge these light & small causes which may be by equitie, and good conscience determined.

iudged by you, are ye vnworthy to iudge the
ſmalleſt matters?
3 Knowe yee not that we ſhall iudge the
Angels? how much more things that perteine
to this life?
4 [4] If then ye haue [c] iudgements of things
perteining to this life, ſet vp them which are
[d] leaſt eſteemed in the Church.
5 [5] I ſpeake it to your ſhame. Is it ſo that
there is not a wiſe man among you? no not one,
that can iudge betweene his brethren?
6 But a brother goeth to lawe with a brother, and that vnder the infidels.
7 [6] Now therefore there is altogether [e] infirmitie in you, in that ye goe to law one with
another: [7] * why rather ſuffer ye not wrong?
why rather ſuſteine ye not harme?
8 * Nay, ye your ſelues do wrong, and doe
harme, and that to your brethren.
9 Know ye not that the vnrighteous ſhall
not inherit the kingdome of God? [8] Bee not
deceiued: neither fornicatours: nor idolaters,
nor adulterers, nor wantons, nor buggerers,
10 Nor theeues, nor couetous, nor drun-
kards, nor railers, nor extortioners ſhall inherit the kingdome of God.
11 And ſuch were * ſome of you: but yee
are waſhed, but yee are ſanctified, but yee are
iuſtified in the [f] Name of the Lord Ieſus, and
by the ſpirit of our God.
12 ¶ * [9] [g] All things are lawfull vnto mee,
but all things are not profitable. I may doe all
things, but I will not bee brought vnder the
[h] power of any thing.
13 [10] Meats *are ordeined* for the bellie, and
the bellie for the meates: but God ſhall deſtroy both it, and them. Nowe the bodie *is*
not for fornication, but for the Lord, and the
Lord for the body.
14 And God hath alſo raiſed vp the Lord,
and * ſhall raiſe vs vp by his power.
15 [11] Knowe ye not, that your bodies are
the members of Chriſt? ſhall I then take the
members of Chriſt, and make them the members of an harlot? God forbid.
16 [12] Doe ye not know, that he which cou-
pleth himſelfe with an harlot, is one body? * for
[i] two, ſaith he, ſhall be one fleſh.
17 But he that is ioyned vnto the Lord, is
one ſpirit.
18 [13] Flee fornication, euery ſinne that a
man doeth, is without the body: but hee that
committeth fornication, ſinneth againſt his
owne bodie.
19 [14] Know ye not, that * your bodie is the
Temple of the holy Ghoſt, *which is* in you,
whom ye haue of God? and [15] ye are not your
owne.
20 * For ye are bought for a price: therefore glorifie God in your body, and in your
ſpirit: for they are Gods.

4 The concluſion, wherein hee preſcribeth a remedie for this miſchiefe: to wit, if they ende their priuate affaires betweene themſelues by choſen aribiters out of ye Church: for which matter and purpoſe, the leaſt of you, ſaith he, is ſufficient. Therefore he condemneth not iudgement ſeats, but ſheweth what is expedient for the circumſtance of the time, and that without any diminiſhing of the right of the Magiſtrate: for he ſpeaketh not of iudgmēts, which are practiſed betwixt the faithfull and the infidels, neither of publike iudgements, but of controuerſies which may be ended by priuate arbiters.

c Courts and places of iudgements.

d Euen the moſt abiect among you.

5 He applieth the generall propoſition to a particular, alwayes calling thē backe to this, to take away from them that falſe opinion of their owne excellencie from whence all theſe miſchiefs ſprang. 6 Now he goeth further alſo, & although by granting thē priuate biters, out of the congregation of the faithful, he do not ſimply condemne, but rather eſtabliſh priuate iudgments, ſo that they be exerciſed without offence, yet he ſheweth that if they were ſuch as they ought to bee, and as it were to be wiſhed, they ſhould not need to vſe that remedie neither. *e A weakenes of mind which is ſaid to be in them, that ſuffer themſelues to be ouercome of their luſts, and it is a fault that ſquareth greatly from temperancie and moderation: ſo that he nippeth them which could not put vp an iniurie done vnto them.* 7 This perteineth chiefly to the other part of the reprehenſion, to wit, that they went to lawe euen vnder infidels, whereas they ſhould rather haue ſuffered any loſſe, then to haue giuen that offence. But yet this is generally true, that we ought rather to depart from our right, then trie the vttermoſt of the lawe haſtily, and vpon an affection to reuenge an iniurie. But the Corinthians cared for neither, and therefore he ſaith that they muſt repent, vnleſſe they will be ſhut out of the inheritance of God. * *Matth.5.39. luke 6.29 rom.12 19.* * *1 Theſ.4 6.* 8 Now he prepareth himſelfe to paſſe ouer to the fourth Treatiſe of this Epiſtle, which concerneth matters indifferent, debating this matter firſt, how men may well vſe women or not: which queſtion hath three branches, fornication, matrimonie, and a ſingle life. As for fornication, he vtterly condemneth it. And mariage hee commandeth to ſome, as a good and neceſſarie remedie for them, to other he leaueth it free: And other ſome hee diſſwadeth from it, not as vnlawfull, but as diſcommodious, and that not without exception. As for ſingleneſſe of life (vnder which alſo I comprehend virginitie) hee inioyneth it to no man: yet he perſwadeth men vnto it, but not for it ſelfe, but for another reſpect, neither all men, nor without exception. And being about to ſpeake againſt fornication, he beginneth with a generall reprehenſion of thoſe vices, wherewith that rich and riotous Citie moſt abounded: warning and teaching them earneſtly, that repentance is vnſeparably ioyned with forgiuenes of ſinnes, & ſanctification with iuſtification. * *Titus 3.3.* *f In Ieſus.* * *Chap.10.23.* 9 Secondly, hee ſheweth that the Corinthians doe ſimply offend in matters indifferent: Firſt, becauſe they abuſed them: next, becauſe they vſed indifferent things, without any diſcretion, ſeeing the vſe of thē ought to be brought to the rule of charitie: & that he doth not vſe them aright, which immoderately abuſeth them, and ſo becommeth a ſlaue vnto them. *g Whatſoeuer: but this generall word muſt bee reſtrained to things that are indifferent.* *h Hee is in ſubiection to things that are indifferent, whatſoeuer he be that thinketh he may not be without them: which is a flattering kind of ſlauerie vnder a colour of libertie, which ſeiſeth vpon ſuch men.* 10 Secondarily, becauſe they counted many things for indifferent, which were of themſelues vnlawfull, as fornication, which they numbred amongſt meere naturall and lawfull deſires, as well as meat and drinke: Therefore the Apoſtle ſheweth, that they are vtterly vnlike: for meats ſaith he, were made for the neceſſarie vſe of mans life which is not perpetuall: For both meats, and all this maner of nouriſhng, are quickely aboliſhed. But we muſt not ſo thinke of the vncleannes of fornication, for which the bodie is not made, but on the contrary ſide is ordeined to pureneſſe, as appeareth by this, that it is conſecrated to Chriſt, euen as Chriſt alſo is giuen vs of his Father, to quicken our bodies with that vertue, wherewith he alſo roſe againe.

* *Rom.6.5.*

11 A declaratiō of the former argument by contraries, and the applying of it.

12 A proofe of the ſame argument: A harlot and Chriſt are cleane contrary, ſo are the fleſh and the Spirit: therefore he that is one with an harlot, (which is done by carnall copulation of their bodies) cannot be one with Chriſt, which vnitie is pure and ſpirituall.

* *Gene.2.24. matth.19 5. marke 10.8. ephe.5.31.*

i Moſes doeth not ſpeake theſe words of fornication, but of mariage: but ſeeing that fornication is the corruption of mariage, and both of them is a carnall and fleſhly copulation, we cannot ſay that the Apoſtle abuſeth his teſtimonie. Againe, Moſes hath not this word (Two) but it is very well expreſſed both here and in Matthew 19.5. becauſe he ſpeaketh onely but of man and wife: whereupon the opinion of them that vouch it to be lawfull to haue many wiues, is beaten downe: for hee that companieth with many, is ſundred as it were into many parts. 13 Another argument why fornication is to be eſchewed, becauſe it defileth the body with a peculiar kinde of filthineſſe. 14 The third argument: Becauſe a fornicatour is ſacrilegious, for that our bodies are conſecrate to God. * *Chap.3.17. 2.corinth.6.16.* 15 The fourth argument: Becauſe we are not our owne men, to giue our ſelues to any other, much leſſe to Satan and the fleſh, ſeeing that God himſelfe hath bought vs, and that with a great price, to the end that both in body and ſoule, we ſhould ſerue to his glorie. * *Chap.7.23. 1.pet.1.18.*

CHAP. VII.

1 Entreating here of mariage, 4 which is a remedie againſt fornication, 10 And may not bee broken, 18. 20 hee willeth euery man to liue contented with his lot. 25 Hee ſheweth what the ende of virginitie ſhould bee, 45 and who ought to marrie.

NOw [1] concerning the things [a] whereof
ye wrote vnto me, It *were* [b] good for a
man not to touch a woman.
2 Neuertheleſſe, to auoid fornication, let
euery man haue his wife, and let euery woman
haue her owne husband.
3 * [2] Let the husband giue vnto the wife
[c] due beneuolence, and likewiſe alſo the wife
vnto the husband.
4 [3] The wife hath not the power of her
owne body, but the husband: and likewiſe alſo the husband hath not the power of his owne
body, but the wife.
5 Defraude not one another, [4] except *it*
be with conſent for a time, that yee may [d] giue
your ſelues to faſting and prayer, and againe
come together, that Satan tempt you not for
your incontinencie.

1 He teacheth concerning mariage, that although a ſingle life hath his cōmodities, which he will declare afterwards, yet that mariage is neceſſary for the auoiding of fornication: but ſo that neither one man may haue many wiues, nor any wife many husbands.

a Touching thoſe matters whereof you wrote vnto me.

b Commodious, and (as we ſay) expedient. For mariage bringeth many griefes with it, and that by reaſon of the corruption of our firſt eſtate. * *1.Pet.3.7.* 2 Secondly, hee ſheweth that the parties maried, muſt with ſingular affection, entirely loue one the other. *c The word (due) conteineth all kinde of beneuolence, though hee ſpeake more of one ſort then of the other, in that that followeth.* 3 Thirdly, he warneth them, that they are each in others power, as touching the body, ſo that you may not defraud one another. 4 He addeth an exception, vnleſſe the one abſtaine from the other by mutuall conſent, that they may the better giue themſelues to prayer, wherein notwithſtanding, he warneth them to conſider what is expedient, leſt by this long breaking off as it were from mariage, they be ſtirred vp to incontinencie. *d Doe nothing els.*

6 [5] But

6 [5] But I speake this by permission, not by
commandement.
7 For I [e] would that all men were euen as
I my selfe *am*: but euery man hath his proper
gift of God, one after this maner, and another
after that.
8 [6] Therefore I say vnto the [f] vnmaried,
and vnto the widowes, It is good for them if
they abide euen as I *doe*.
9 But if they cannot abstaine, let them marrie: for it is better to marrie then to [g] burne.
10 *[7] And vnto the married, I command,
not I, but the Lord, Let not the wife depart
from her husband.
11 But and if she depart, let her remaine
vnmaried, or be reconciled vnto her husband,
and let not the husband put away *his* wife.
12 [8] But to the remnant I speake, *and* not
the Lord, If any brother haue a wife, that beleeueth not, if shee be content to dwell with
him, let him not forsake her.
13 And the woman which hath an husband
that beleeueth not, if he be content to dwell
with her, let her not forsake him,
14 [9] For the vnbeleeuing husband is [h] sanctified to the [i] wife, and the vnbeleeuing wife
is sanctified to the [k] husband, else were your
children vncleane: but now are they [l] holy.
15 [10] But if the vnbeleeuing depart, let him
depart: a brother or a sister is not in subiection
in [m] such things: [11] but God hath called vs in
peace.
16 For what knowest thou, O wife, whether thou shalt saue thine husband? Or what
knowest thou, O man, whether thou shalt saue
thy wife?
17 [12] But as God hath distributed to euery
man, as the Lorde hath [n] called euery one, so
let him walke: and so ordaine I in all Churches.
18 [13] Is any man called being circumcised?
let him not [o] gather *his vncircumcision:* is any

5 Fifthly he teacheth that mariage is not simply necessary for all men, but for the which haue not the gift of continencie, and this gift is by a peculiar grace of God.
e I wish.
6 Sixtly, he giueth ŷ selfe same admonition touching the second mariage, to wit, that a single life is to be allowed, but for such as haue the gift of continencie: otherwise they ought to marrie againe, that their conscience may be at peace.
f This whole place is flat against them which condemne second mariages.
g So to burne with lust, that either the will yeeldeth to the temptation, or els we cannot call vpon God with a quiet conscience.
* *Matth.5.32. and 19.9. marke 10.11, 12. luke 16. 18.*
7 Seuenthly, he forbiddeth contentions & publishing of diuorces (for he speaketh not here of ŷ fault of whoredome, which was then death euen by the law of the Romanes also) whereby he affirmeth that the band of mariage is not dissolued, and that from Christ his mouth
8 Eightly, he affirmeth, that those mariages which are alreadie contracted betweene a faithfull, and an vnfaithfull or infidell, are firme: so that the faithfull may not forsake the vnfaithfull. 9 He answereth an obiection: But the faithfull is defiled by the societie of the vnfaithfull. The Apostle denieth that, and proueth that the faithfull man with good conscience may vse the vessell of his vnfaithfull wife, by this, that their children which are borne of them, are accounted holy (that is, conteined within the promise) for it is said to all the faithfull, I will be thy God, and the God of thy seed. *h The godlinesse of the wife is of more force, to cause their coupling together to be accounted holy, then the infidelitie of the husband is, to prophane the mariage. i The infidell is not sanctified or made holy in his owne person, but in respect of his wife, he is sanctified to her. k To the faithfull husband. l This place destroyeth the opinion of them, that would not haue children to be baptized, and their opinion also, that make Baptisme the very cause of saluation. For the children of the faithfull are holy, by vertue of the couenant, euen before Baptisme, and Baptisme is added as the seale of that holinesse.* 10 He answereth to a question: what if the vnfaithfull forsake the faithfull? then is the faithfull free, saith he, because he is forsaken of the vnfaithfull. *m When any such thing falleth out.*
11 Lest any man vpon pretence of this libertie should giue an occasion to the vnfaithfull to depart, he giueth to vnderstand, that mariage contracted with an infidell, ought peaceably to be kept, that if it be possible the infidell may be wonne to ŷ faith,
12 Taking occasion by that which he saide of the bondage and libertie of matrimonie, he digresseth to a generall doctrine concerning the outward state and condition of mans life, as Circumcision and vncircumcision, seruitude and libertie: warning euery man generally to liue with a contented minde in the Lord, what state or condition soeuer he be in, because, that those outward things, as to be circumcised or vncircumcised, to be bond or free, are not of the substance (as they terme it) of the kingdome of heauen. *n Hath bound him to a certaine kind of life.* 13 Notwithstanding hee giueth vs to vnderstand, that in these examples all are not of like sort: because that Circumcision is not simply of it self to be desired, but such as are boũd may desire to be free. Therefore herein onely they are equall, that the kingdome of God consisteth not in them, and therefore these are no hinderance to obey God. *o He is said to gather his vncircumcision, who by the helpe of a Chirurgian, recouereth an vpper skin: which is done by drawing the skinne with an instrument, to make it to couer the nut. Celsus in his 7. Booke and 25 Chapter.*

called vncircumcised? let him not bee circumcised.
19 Circumcision is nothing, and vncircumcision is nothing, but the keeping of the commandements of God.
20 * Let euery man abide in the same vocation wherein he was called.
21 Art thou called *being* a seruant? [p] care
not for it: but yet if thou mayest bee free,
vse it rather.
22 For he that is called in the [q] Lord, *being*
a seruant, is the Lords free man: likewise also
hee that is called *being* free, is Christs seruant.
23 *[14] Ye are bought with a price: bee not
the seruants of men.
24 [15] Brethren, let euery man, wherein hee
was called, therein abide with [r] God.
25 [16] Now concerning virgins, I haue no
commandement of the Lorde: but I giue mine
[f] aduise, as [t] one that hath obteined mercy of
the Lord to be faithfull.
26 I suppose then [u] this to bee good for the
[x] present necessitie: *I meane* that it is good for a
man so to be.
27 Art thou bound vnto a wife? seeke not
to bee loosed: art thou loosed from a wife?
seeke not a wife.
28 But if thou takest a wife, thou sinnest
not: and if a virgine marie, she sinneth not: neuerthelesse, such shal haue trouble in the [y] flesh:
but I [z] spare you.
29 And this I say, brethren, because the time
is [a] short, hereafter that both they which haue
wiues, be as though they had none:
30 And they that [b] weepe, as though they
wept not: and they that reioyce, as though they
reioyced not: & they that buy, as though they
possessed not:
31 And they that vse this [c] world, as though
they vsed it not: for the [d] fashion of this world
goeth away.
32 And I would haue you without care.
The vnmaried careth for the things of the Lord
how he may please the Lord.
33 But he that is maried, [e] careth for the
things of the world, how he may please *his* wife
34 There is difference also betweene a virgine and a wife: the vnmaried woman careth
for the things of the Lord, that she may be holy, both in body and in [f] spirit: but she that is
maried, careth for the things of the world, how
she may please her husband.
35 And this I speake for your owne [g] com-

* *1.Tim.6.1.*
p As though this calling were too vnworthy a calling for Christ.
q He that is in state of a seruant, and is called to be a Christian.
* *Chap.6.20. 1.pet.1.18.19.*
14 He sheweth the reason of the vnlikenesse, because that hee that desired to be circumcised, maketh himselfe subiect to mans tradition, and not to God. And this may bee much more vnderstood of superstitions, which some doe foolishly account for things indifferent.
15 A repetition of the generall doctrine.
r So purely and from the heart, that your doings may be approued before God.
16 He enioyneth virginitie to no man, yet he perswadeth and praiseth it for an other respect, to wit, both for the necessitie of the present time, because the faithfull could scarce abide in any place, and vse the commodities of this present life, & therefore such as were not troubled with families, might be the readier, and also for the cares of this life, which mariage draweth with it of necessitie, so that they cannot but haue their minds distracted: and this hath place in women especially.
f The circumstances considered, this I counsell you.
t It is I that speake this which I am minded to speake: and the trueth is, I am a man, but yet worthy credit, for I haue obteined of the Lord to be such an one. u To remaine a virgin. x For the necessitie which the Saints are dayly subiect vnto, who are continually tossed vp & downe, so that their estate may seeme most vnfit for mariage, were it not that the weakenesse of the flesh enforced them to it. y By the (Flesh) he vnderstandeth what things soeuer belong to this present life, for mariage bringeth with it many discommodities: so that he bendeth more to a sole life, not because it is a seruice more agreeable to God then mariage is, but for those discommodities, which (if it were possible) he would wish all men to be void of, that they might giue themselues to God only. z I would your weakenes were prouided for. a For we are now in the latter end of the world. b By weeping, the Hebrewes vnderstand all aduersitie, and by ioy, all prosperitie c Those things which God giueth vs here. d The guise and shape, and fashion: whereby he sheweth vs, that there is nothing in this world that continueth. e They that are maried, haue their wits drawen hither and thither, & therefore if any man haue the gift of continencie, it is more cõmodious for him to liue alone: but they that are maried may care for the things of the Lord also. Clem. Strom. 3. f Minde. g He meaneth that he will enforce no man, either to marie or not to marrie, but to shew them barely what kind of life is most commodious.

moditie,

17 Now he turneth himselfe to the parents, in whose power & authoritie their children are, warning them that according to the former doctrine they consider what is meet and conuenient for their children, that they neither depriue them of the necessary remedie against incontinencie, nor constraine them to mariage, whereas neither their will doth leade them, nor any necessitie vrgeth them. And againe he praiseth virginitie, but of it selfe, and not in all.

moditie, not to tangle you in a snare, but that
ye follow that, which is honest, and that ye may
cleaue fast vnto the Lord without separation.
36 [17] But if any man thinke that it is vncomely for his virgine, if she passe the floure of *her*
age, and need so require, let him doe what hee
will, he [h] sinneth not : let them be maried.
37 Neuerthelesse, he that standeth firme in
his [i] heart, that he hath no [k] neede, but hath
power ouer his owne will, and hath so decreed
in his heart, that he will keepe his virgine, hee
doeth well.
38 So then he that giueth her to mariage,
doeth well, but he that giueth her not to mariage, doeth [l] better.
39 [18] The wife is bound by the [m] Lawe, as
long as her husband *liueth : but if her husband be dead, shee is at libertie to marrie with
whom she will, onely in the [n] Lord.
40 But she is more blessed, if she so abide,
in my iudgement : *and I thinke that I haue also the Spirit of God.

b He doeth well: for so he expoundeth it. ver. 38. i Resolued himselfe. k That the weaknesse of his daughter inforceth him not, or any other matter, but that he may safely keepe her a virgin still. l Prouideth more commodiously for his children, and that not simply, but by reason of such conditions as are before mentioned. 18 That which he spake of a widower, he speaketh now of a widow, to wit, that she may mary again, so that she doe it in the feare of God : and yet he dissembleth not, but saith, that if she remaine still a widow, she shall be void of many cares. *m By the Law of mariage.* * *Rom. 7. 1. n Religiously, and in the feare of God.* * *1. Thess. 4. 8.*

CHAP. VIII.

1 From this place vnto the end of the tenth Chapter, he willeth them not to be at the Gentiles prophane banquets. 18 He restraineth the abuse of Christian libertie, 11 and sheweth that knowledge must be tempered with charitie.

1 He entreth to entreat of another kinde of things indifferent, to wit, of things offered to idoles, or the vse of flesh so offered and sacrificed. And first of all he remoueth all those things which the Corinthians pretended in vsing things offered to idoles without any respect. First of all they affirmed that this difference of meats was for the vnskilfull men, but as for them, they knewe well enough the benefit of Christ, which causeth all these things

AND [1] as touching things sacrificed vnto
idoles, wee knowe that wee [a] all haue
knowledge : knowledge [b] puffeth vp, but loue
[c] edifieth.
2 Now, if any man thinke that he knoweth any thing, he knoweth nothing yet as hee
ought to know.
3 But if any man loue God, the same is
knowen of him.
4 [2] Concerning therefore the eating of
things sacrificed vnto [d] idoles, we know that an
idole *is* [e] nothing in the world, and that there *is*
none other God but one.
5 For though there be that are called gods,
whether in heauen, or in earth (as there be many gods, and many lords)
6 Yet vnto vs there *is* but one God, *which
is* that Father, [f] of whome are all things, and
wee [g] in him : and * [h] one Lord Iesus Christ,
[i] by whom *are* all things, and we by him.
7 [3] But euery man hath not that knowledge : for [4] many hauing [k] conscience of the
idole, vntill this houre, eate as a thing sacrificed vnto the idole, and so their conscience being weake, is defiled.
8 [5] But meat maketh vs not acceptable to
God, for neither if we eate, haue we the more :
neither if we eat not, haue we the lesse.
9 But take heede lest by any meanes this
power of yours be an occasion of falling, to
them that are weake.
10 [6] For if any man see thee which hast
knowledge, sit at table in the idols temple, shal
not the conscience of him which is weake, be
boldned to eate those things which are sacri-
ficeh to idoles?
11 [7] And through thy knowledge shall the
* weake brother perish, for whom Christ died.
12 [8] Now when ye sinne so against the brethren, and wound their weake conscience, yee
sinne against Christ.
13 * [9] Wherefore if meat offend my brother, I will eate no flesh while the world standeth, that I may not offend my brother.

to be cleane to them that are cleane. Be it so saith Paul: be it that we are all sufficiently instructed in the knowledge of Christ, I say notwithstanding that we must not simply rest in this knowledge. The reason is, that vnlesse our knowledge be tempered with charitie, it doeth not onely not auaile, but also doeth much hurt, because it is the mistresse of pride: nay it doth not so much as deserue the name of godly knowledge, if it be separate from the loue of God, & therefore from the loue of our neighbour. *a This generall word is to bee abridged as appeareth, ver. 7 for there is a kinde of taunt in it, as we may perceiue by the next verse. b Ministreth occasion of vanitie and pride : because it is void of charitie. c Instructeth our neighbour.* 2 The application of that answere to things offered to idoles : I grant, saith he, that an idole is indeede a vaine imagination, and that there is but one God and Lord, and therefore that meat can not be made either holy or prophane by the idole : but it followeth not therefore that a man may without respect vse those meats as any other. *d This word (Idole) in this place is taken for an image which is made to represent some godhead, that worship might bee giuen vnto it : whereupon came the word (Idolatrie) that is to say, Image seruice. e Is a vaine dreame. f When the Father is distinguished from the Sonne, hee is named the beginning of all things. g Wee haue our being in him.* * *Ioh. 13. 13. chap. 12. 3. h But as the Father is called Lord, so is the Sonne, God : therefore this word (One) doeth not respect the persons, but the natures.*

i This word (By) doeth not signifie the instrumentall cause, but the efficient: for the Father & the Sonne worke together, which is not so to be taken, that we make two causes, seeing they haue both but one nature, though they be distinct persons. 3 The reason why that followeth not, is this: because there are many men which doe not knowe that which you know. Now the iudgement of outward things depend not only vpon your conscience, but vpon the conscience of them that beholde you, and therefore your actions must be applied not only to your knowledge, but also to the ignorance of your brethren. 4 An applying of the reason: There are many which cannot eate of things offered to idoles, but with a wauering conscience because they thinke them to be vncleane : therfore if by thy example they enterprise to doe that which inwardly they thinke displeaseth God, their conscience is defiled with this eating, and thou hast bin the occasion of this mischiefe. *k By conscience of the idole, he meaneth the secret iudgement that they had within themselues, whereby they thought all things vncleane, that were offered to idoles, and therefore they could not vse them with good conscience. For this force hath conscience, that if it be good, it maketh things indifferent good, and if it be euill, it maketh them euill.* 5 A preuenting of an obiection : Why then shall we therefore be depriued of our libertie ? Nay saith the Apostle, you shall lose no part of Christianitie although you abstaine for your brethrens sake, as also if you receiue the meat, it maketh you no whit the more holy, for our comendation before God consisteth not in meates : but to vse our libertie with offence of our brethren, is an abuse of libertie, the true vse thereof is cleane contrary, to wit, so to vse it, as in vsing of it we haue consideration of our weake brethren. 6 Another plaine explication of the same reason, propounding the example of the sitting downe at the table in the idoles temple, which thing the Corinthians did euil account of among things indifferent, because it is simply forbidden for the circumstance of the place, although offence doe cease, as it shalbe declared in his place. 7 An amplification of the argument taken both of comparison & contraries : Thou wretched man, saith he, pleasing thy selfe with thy knowledge which indeed is none (for if thou haddest true knowledge, thou wouldest not sit downe to meat in an idols temple) wilt thou destroy thy brother hardening his weake conscience by this example to doe euill, for whose saluation Christ himselfe hath died ? * *Rom. 14. 15.* 8 Another amplification : Such offending of our weake brethren, redoundeth vnto Christ, and therefore let not these men thinke that they haue to doe onely with their brethren. * *Rom. 14. 21.* 9 The conclusion, which Paul conceiueth in his owne person, that he might not seeme to exact that of other, which hee will not be first subiect to himselfe. I had rather (saith he) abstaine for euer from all kinde of flesh, then giue occasion of sinne to any of my brethren, much lesse would I refuse in any certaine place or time for my brothers sake not to eate flesh offered to idoles.

CHAP. IX.

1 He declareth, that from the libertie which the Lord gaue him, 15 hee willingly abstained, 18. 22 lest in things indifferent he should offend any. 24 He sheweth that our life is like vnto a race.

AM [1] I not an Apostle ? am I not free ?
[2] haue I not seene Iesus Christ our Lord ?
are ye not [a] my worke in the Lord ?
2 If I be not Apostle vnto other, yet doubtlesse I am vnto you : for yee are the [b] seale of
mine Apostleship in the Lord.

1 Before he proceedeth any further in his purposed matter of things offered to idols, he would shew the cause of all this mischiefe, and also take it away : to wit, that the Corinthians thought themselues not bound to depart from a iote of their libertie for any mans pleasure. Therefore hee propoundeth himselfe for an example, and that in a matter almost necessary. And yet he speaketh seuerally of both, but first of his owne person. If (saith he) you alledge for your selues, that you are free, and therefore will vse your libertie, am I not also free, seeing I am an Apostle ? 2 He proueth his Apostleship by the effects, in that he was appoynted of Christ himselfe, & the authoritie of his function was sufficiently confirmed to him amongst them by their conuersion. And all these things he setteth before their eyes, to make them ashamed for that they would not in the least wise that might be, debase themselues for the weaks sake, wheras ẏ Apostle himselfe did all that he could to win them to God, when they were vtterly reprobate and without God. *a By the Lord. b As a seale whereby it appeareth sufficiently that God is the authour of my Apostleship.*

3 [3] My

3 Hee addeth this by the way, as if he should say, So farre it is oft, that you may doubt of my Apostleship, that I vse to refute thē which cal it into controuersie, by opposing those things which the Lord hath done by mee amongst you.
c Which like iudges examine me & my doings.
4 Now touching the matter it selfe, he saith, Seeing that I am free, and truely an Apostle, why may not I (I say not, eate of all things offered to Idoles,) but be maintained by my labours, yea and keepe my wife also, as the residue of the Apostles lawfully doe, as by name, Iohn and Iames, the Lords cousins, and Peter himselfe?
d Vpon the expense of the Church?
e One that is a Christian and a true beleeuer?
f Not liue by the works of our hands?
5 That he may not seem to burden the Apostles, he sheweth that it is iust that they doe, by an argument of comparison, seeing that souldiers liue by their wages, and husbandmen by the fruits of their labours, and shepheards by that that commeth of their flocks,
g Vseth to goe a warfare?
6 Secondly, he bringeth forth

3 [3] My defence to them that [c] examine me,
is this,
4 [4] Haue wee not power to [d] eate and to
drinke?
5 Or haue we not power to leade about a
wife being a [e] sister, as well as the rest of the
Apostles, and as the brethren of the Lord, and
Cephas?
6 Or I onely and Barnabas, haue not wee
power [f] not to worke?
7 [5] Who [g] goeth a warfare any time at his
owne cost? who planteth a vineyard, and eateth
not of the fruit therof? or who feedeth a flocke
and eateth not of the milke of the flocke?
8 [6] Say I these things [h] according to man?
saith not the Lawe the same also?
9 For it is written in the Lawe of Moses,
* Thou shalt not moosell the mouth of the oxe
that treadeth out the corne: doeth God take
care for [i] Oxen?
10 Either saith he it not altogether for our
sakes? For our sakes no doubt it is written, that
he which eareth, should eare in hope, & that he
that thresheth in hope, should be partaker of
his hope.
11 * [7] If wee haue sowen vnto you spirituall things, *is it* a great thing if we reape your
carnall things?
12 [8] If others with you be partakers of *this*
[k] power, *are* not we rather? neuerthelesse, we
haue not vsed this power, but suffer all things,
that wee should not hinder the Gospel of
Christ.
13 [9] Doe ye not know, that they which minister about the * holy things, eat of the [l] things
of the Temple? and they which waite at the
Altar, are [m] partakers with the Altar?
14 So also hath the Lord ordeined, that
they which preach the Gospel, should liue [n] of
the Gospel.
15 But I haue vsed none of these things:
[10] neither wrote I these things, that it should
be so done vnto me: for it were better for me to
die, then that any man should make my reioycing vaine.

16 For though I preach the Gospel, I haue
nothing to reioyce of: for necessitie is laid vpon me, and woe is vnto me, if I preach not the
Gospel.
17 For if I doe it willingly, I haue a reward,
but if I doe it against my will, *notwithstanding*
the dispensation is committed vnto me.
18 What is my reward then? verely that
when I preach the Gospel, I make the Gospel
of Christ [o] free, that I abuse not my authoritie
in the Gospel.
19 For though I be free from all men, yet
haue I made my selfe seruant vnto all men, that
I might winne the moe.
20 * And vnto the Iewes, I become as a
Iewe, that I may winne the Iewes: to [illegible]m
that are vnder the [p] Lawe, as *thoug*[illegible] *were* vnder the Law, that I may w[illegible]ne them that are
vnder the Law.
21 To them that are without Lawe, as
though I were without Lawe, (when I am not
without Lawe as perteining to God, but *am* in
in the Lawe through Christ) that I may winne
them that are without Lawe:
22 To the weake I become as weake, that I
may winne the weake: I am made all things
to [q] all men, that I might by all meanes saue
some.
23 And this I doe for the Gospels sake, that
I might be partaker thereof with [r] you.
24 [11] Knowe ye not, that they which runne
in a race, runne all, yet one receiueth the price?
so runne that ye may obtaine.
25 And euery man that prooueth maste-
ries, [s] abstaineth from all things: and they *doe*
it to obteine a corruptible crowne: but we for
an vncorruptible.
26 I therefore so runne, not as vncertainely:
so fight I, not as one that beateth the aire.
27 But I beat downe my [t] bodie, and bring
it into subiection, lest by any meanes after that
I haue preached to other, I my selfe should bee
[u] reproued.

o By taking nothing of them to whom I preach it.
** Acts 16.3. gal 2.3*
p The word (law) in this place, must be restrained to the ceremoniall Law.
q In matters that are indifferent, which may be done or not done with a good conscience: as if hee said, I changed my selfe into all fashions, that by all meanes I might saue some.
r That both I a[illegible] they to wh[illegible] [illegible] the Gospel, may receiue fruit by the Gospel.
11 He bringth in another cause of this mischiefe, to wit, that they were giuen to gluttonie, for there were solemne banquets of sacrifices, and the riot of the Priestes was alwayes too much celebrated and kept. Therefore it was hard for them which were accustomed to riotousnesse, especially when they pretended the libertie of the Gospel, to be restrained frō these banquets: but contrariwise the Apostle calleth them by a pleasant similitude, and also by his owne example, to sobrietie and mortification of the flesh, shewing that they cannot be fit to run or wrestle (as thē the games of Isthmies were) which pamper vp their bodies: and therefore affirming that they can haue no reward, vnlesse they take another course & trade of life. *s Vseth a most exquisite diet. t The olde man which striueth against the Spirit. u This word (Reproued) is not set as contrary to the word (Elect) but as contrary to the word (Approued) when we see one by experience not to be such an one as he ought to be.*

the authoritie of Gods institution by an argument of comparison. *h Haue I no better ground then the common custome of men? * Deut. 25.4 1.tim.5 18. i Was it Gods proper drift to prouide for Oxen, when he made this Lawe? for otherwise there is not the smallest thing in the world, but God hath a care of it. * Rom. 15.27.* 7 An assumption of the arguments with an amplification, for neither in so doing doe wee require a reward meet for our deserts. 8 Another argument of great force: other are nourished amongst you, therefore it was lawfull for me, yea rather for me then any other: and yet I refused it, and had rather still suffer any discommoditie, then the Gospel of Christ should be hindered. *k The word signifieth right and interest, whereby hee giueth vs to vnderstand that the Ministers of the word must of right & duetie be found of the Church.* 9 Last of all, he bringeth forth the expresse Lawe concerning the nourishing of the Leuites: which priuiledge notwithstanding he will not vse. ** Deut. 18.1. l This is spoken by the figure Metonymie, for, those things that are offered in the Temple. m Are partakers with the altar in diuiding the sacrifice. n Because they preach the Gospel. It followeth by this place, that Paul gate no liuing, neither would haue any other man get, by any cōmoditie of Masses, or any other such superstitious trumperies.* 10 He taketh away occasion of suspition by the way, that it might not be thought ẏ he wrote this as though he chalenged his wages, that was not payed him. Nay, saith he, I had rather die, then not to continue in this purpose to preach the Gospel freely. For I am bound to preach the Gospel, seeing that the Lord hath inioyned me this office: but vnlesse I doe it willingly and for the loue of God, nothing is to be allowed that I doe. If I had rather that the Gospel should bee euill spoken of, then that I should not require my wages, then would it appeare that I tooke these paines not so much for the Gospels sake, as for my gaines and aduantages. But I say, this were not to vse, but abuse my right and libertie: Therefore not onely in this thing, but also in all other (as much as I could) I am made all things to all men, that I might winne them to Christ, and might together with them be wonne to Christ.

CHAP. X.

1 If God spared not the Iewes, neither will hee spare those who are of like condition, 3. 4 touching the outward signes of his grace. 14 That it is absurd, that such should be partakers of the table of the deuils, who are partakers of the Lords Supper. 24 To haue consideration of our neighbour in things indifferent.

Moreouer, [1] brethren, I would not that
ye should be ignorant, that all our [a] fathers were vnder * that cloude, and all passed
thorow that * sea,

1 He setteth out that which hee sayd, laying before them an example of ẏ horrible iudgement of God against them which had in effect the selfe same pledges of the same adoption & saluation that we haue: & yet notwithstanding when they gaue themselues to idols feasts, perished in the wildernesse, being horribly and manifoldly punished. Now, moreouer and besides that these things are fitly spoken against them which frequented idoles feasts, the same also seeme to bee alleaged to this ende and purpose, because many men are thus minded, that those things are not of such great weight, that God will bee angry with them if they vse them, so that they frequent Christian assemblies and bee baptized, and receiue the Communion, and confesse Christ. *a Paul speaketh thus in respect of the Couenant, and not in respect of the persons, sauing in generall. * Exod. 13.21. num. 9.18. * Exodus. 14.22.*

2 [2] And were all [b] baptized vnto [c] Moses,
in that cloud, and in that sea,
3 * And did all eate the [d] same spirituall
[e] meat,
4 * And did all drinke the same spirituall
drinke (for they dranke of the spirituall Rocke
that [f] followed them : and the Rocke was
[g] Christ.)
5 But with many of them God was not
pleased : for they were * ouerthrowen in the
wildernesse.
6 [3] Now these things are our [h] ensamples,
to the intent that we should not lust after euill
things, * as they also lusted.
7 Neither be ye idolaters as *were* some of
them, as it is written, * The people sate downe
to eate and drinke, and rose vp to play.
8 Neither let vs commit fornication, as
some of them committed fornication, and fell
in one * day three and twentie thousand.
9 Neither let vs tempt [i] Christ, as some
of them also tempted *him*, and * were destroyed of Serpents.
10 Neither murmure ye, as some of them
* also murmured, and were destroyed of the
destroyer.
11 Now all these things came vnto them
for ensamples, and were written to admonish
vs, vpon whome the [k] endes of the world are
come.
12 [4] Wherefore, let him that thinketh hee
standeth, take heed lest he fall.
13 There hath no tentation taken you, but
such as appertaine to [l] man : and God is faithfull, which will not suffer you to be tempted a-
boue that you bee able, but will euen [m] giue
the issue with the tentation, that ye may be a-
ble to beare it.
14 Wherefore my beloued, flee from idolatrie.
15 [5] I speake as vnto them which haue vnderstanding : iudge ye what I say.
16 The cup of [n] blessing which we blesse,
is it not the [o] comunion of the blood of Christ?
The bread which we breake, is not the communion of the body of Christ ?
17 For we that are many, are one bread and
one body, because wee are all partakers of one
bread.
18 Beholde Israel, *which is* after the [p] flesh :
are not they which eat of the sacrifices [q] partakers of the altar ?
19 What say I then? that the idole is any
thing? or that that which is sacrificed to idoles,
is any thing ?
20 *Nay*, but that these things which the
Gentiles sacrifice, they sacrifice to deuils, and
not vnto God : and I would not that ye should
haue [r] fellowship with the deuils.
21 Ye cannot drinke the cup of the Lord,
and the [s] cup of the deuils. Ye cannot be partakers of the Lords Table, and of the table of the
deuils.
22 Doe we prouoke the Lord to anger? are
we stronger then he?
23 * [6] [t] All things are lawfull for me, but all
things are not expedient : all things are lawfull
for me, but all things edifie not.
24 Let no man seeke his owne, but euery
man anothers wealth.
25 [7] Whatsoeuer is sold in the [u] shambles, eat
ye, and aske no question for conscience sake.
26 * For the earth *is* the Lords, and [x] all that
therein is.
27 If any of them which beleeue not, call
you *to a feast*, and if yee will goe, whatsoeuer is
set before you, eat, asking no question for conscience sake.
28 But if any man say vnto you, This
is sacrificed vnto idoles, eate it not, because
of him that shewed it, and for the conscience
(for the earth *is* the Lordes, and all that therein is)
29 And the conscience, I say, not thine, but
of that other : [8] for why should my libertie bee
condemned of another mans conscience ?
30 For if I through *Gods* [y] benefit be partaker, why am I euill spoken of, for that wherfore
I giue thanks?
31 * [9] Whether therefore ye eate or drinke,
or whatsoeuer yee doe, doe all to the glory of
God.
32 Giue none offence, neither to the Iewes,
nor to the Grecians, nor to the Church of
God :
33 Euen as I please all men in all things, not
seeking mine owne profit, but *the profit* of many, that they might be saued.

2 In effect the Sacraments of the olde fathers were al one with ours, for they respected Christ onely who offered himselfe vnto them in diuers shadowes. *b All of them were baptized with the outward signe, but not in deede, wherewith God cannot bee charged, but they themselues. c Moses being their guide.* * *Exod. 16. 15.* *d The same that we doe. e Manna, which was a spirituall meat to the beleeuers, which in faith lay hold vpon Christ who is the true meat.* * *Exod. 17. 6. numb. 20 10. and 22. 16.* *f Of the Riuer & running Rocke, which followed the people. g Did sacramentally signifie Christ, so that together with the signe, there was the thing signified, and the trueth it selfe : for God doeth not offer a bare signe, but the thing signified by the signe, together with it, which is to be receiued with faith.* * *Numbers 26. 65.* 3 An amplifiing of the example against them which are caried away with their lusts beyond the bounds which God hath measured out. For this is the beginning of all euill, as of idolatrie (which hath gluttonie a companion vnto it) fornication, rebelling against Christ, murmuring, & such like, which God punished most sharply in that old people, to the end that we which succeed them, and haue a more full declaration of the will of God, might by that meanes take better heed. *h Some reade figures : which signified our Sacraments : for circumcision was to the Iewes a seale of righteousnesse, to vs a liuely paterne of Baptisme, and so in the other Sacraments.* * *Numb 11 4. and 26 64. psal. 106. 14.* * *Exod. 33. 6.* * *Num. 25. 9.* *i To tempt Christ, is to prouoke him to a combate as it were, which those men doe, who abuse the knowledge that he hath giuen them, and make it to serue for a cloake for their lustes and wickednesse.* * *Numb. 21 6. psal. 106. 14.* * *Numb. 14. 37. iudg. 8. 24.* *k This our age, is called the end, for it is the shutting vp of all ages.* 4 In conclusion, he descendeth to the Corinthians themselues, warning them that they please not themselues, but rather that they preuent the subtilties of Satan. Yet he vseth an insinuation, & comforteth them, that he may not seeme to make them altogether like to those wicked idolaters & contemners of Christ, which perished in the wildernesse. *l Which commeth of weakenes. m He that would haue you tempted for your profits sake, will giue you an issue to escape out of the tentation.* 5 Now returning to those Idoles feasts, that hee may not seeme to dally at all: first he promiseth that he wil vse no other reasons, then such as they knew very well themselues. And he vseth an Induction borowed of the agreement that is in the things themselues. The holy banquets of the Christians are pledges, first of all, of the communitie that they haue with Christ, and next, one with another. The Israelites also doe ratifie in the sacrifices, their mutuall coniunction in one selfe same religion : therefore so doe the idolaters also ioyne themselues with their Idoles or deuils rather, (for idoles are nothing) in those solemne banquets, whereupon it followeth, that that table is a table of deuils, and therefore you must eschew it : For you cannot be partakers of the Lord and of idoles together, much lesse may such banquets be accounted for things indifferent. Will ye then striue with God? and if yee doe, thinke you that you shall get the vpper hand ? *n Of thankesgiuing : whereupon, that holy banquet was called Eucharist, that is a thankesgiuing. o A most effectuall pledge and note of our knitting together with Christ, and ingraffing to him.*

p That is, as yet obserue their ceremonies. q Are consenting and guiltie both of that worship and sacrifice. r Haue any thing to doe with the deuils or enter into that societie which is begun on the deuils name. s The heathen and prophane people were wont to shut vp & make an ende of their feasts which they kept to the honour of their gods, in offering meate offrings & drinke offerings to them, with banquets and feastings. * *Chap. 6. 12.* 6 Comming to another kinde of things offered to idoles, he repeateth that generall rule, that in the vse of things indifferent, we ought to haue consideration not of our selues onely, but of our neighbours, and therefore there are many things which of themselues are lawfull, which may be euill done of vs, because of offence to our neighbour. *t Looke afore chap. 6. 13.* 7 An applying of the rule to the present matter : Whatsoeuer is sold in the shambles, you may indifferently buy it as it were at the Lords hand, and eate it either at home with the faithful, or being called home to the vnfaithfuull, to wit, in a priuate banket : but yet with this exception, vnlesse any man be present which is weake, whose conscience may be offended by setting meats offered to idoles before them: for then you ought to haue consideration of their weakenesse. *u The flesh that was sacrificed, was vsed to be sold in the shambles, and the price returned to the Priests.* * *Psal. 24. 1.* *x All those things whereof it is full.* 8 A reason : for we must take heed that our libertie be not euil spoken of, & that the benefit of God which we ought to vse with thanksgiuing be not changed into impiety, & that through our fault, if we chuse rather to offend the conscience of the weake, then to yeeld a litle of our libertie in a matter of no importance, & so giue occasion to the weake to iudge in such sort of vs, & of Christian liberty. And the Apostle taketh these things vpon his owne person, that the Corinthians may haue so much the lesse occasion to oppose any thing against him. *y If I may through Gods benefit eat this meat, or that meat, why should I through my fault, cause that benefit of God to turne to my blame?* * *Col. 3. 17.* 9 The cōclusion: We must order our liues in such sort, ẏ we seeke not our selues, but Gods glory, & so the saluation of as many as we may: wherin the apostle sticketh not to propoūd himselfe to the Corinthians (euen his own flocke) as an example, but so that he calleth them back to Christ, vnto whō he himselfe hath regard.

CHAP. XI.

1 Hee blameth the Corinthians for that in their holy assemblies, 4 men do pray hauing their heads couered, 6 and women bare headed, and because their meetings tended to euill, 21 who mingled prophane bankets with the holy Supper of the Lord, 23 which he requireth to be celebrated according to Christs institution.

* 2 *Thess.* 3.9.
1 The fifth treatise of this Epistle concerning the right ordering of publike assemblies, conteining three points, to wit, of the comely apparell of men and women, of the order of the Lords Supper, and of the right vse of spirituall gifts. But going about to reprehend certaine things, he beginneth notwithstanding with a generall praise of them, calling those particular lawes of comelinesse and honestie, which belong to the Ecclesiasticall policie, traditions: which afterward they called Canons.
2 Hee setteth downe God, in Christ our Mediatour, for the ende and marke not onely of doctrine, but also of Ecclesiasticall comelines. Then applying it to the question proposed, touching the comely apparell both of men and women in publike assemblies, hee declareth that the woman is

BE * yee followers of me, euen as I am of
Christ.
2 [1] Now brethren, I commend you, that
yee remember all my things,and keepe the ordinances, as I deliuered them to you.
3 [2] But I will that yee know, that Christ is
the * head of euery man: and the man is the
womans head: and God is [a] Christs head.
4 [3] Euery [b] man praying or prophecying
hauing *any thing* on *his* head, dishonoureth
his head.
5 [4] But euery woman that prayeth or prophecieth bare headed, dishonoureth her head,
[5] for it is euen one very thing, as though shee
were shauen.
6 Therefore if the woman bee not couered,let her also bee shorne: and if it bee shame
for a woman to be shorne or shauen, let her be
couered.
7 [6] For a man ought not to couer *his* head:
for as much as hee is the * image and glorie of God: but the woman is the glorie of
the man.
8 [7] For the man is not of the woman, but
the woman of the man.
9 * [8] For the man was not created for
the womans sake: but the woman for the
mans sake.
10 [9] Therefore ought the woman to haue
[c] power on *her* head, because of the [10] Angels.
11 [11] Neuerthelesse,neither is the man without the woman, neither the woman without
the man [d] in the Lord.
12 For as the woman is of the man, so is
the man also by the woman: but all things are
of God.
13 [12] Iudge in your selues, Is it comely
that a woman pray vnto God vncouered?
14 Doeth not nature it selfe teach you,
that if a man haue long haire, it is a shame vnto him?
15 But if a woman haue long haire, it is a
praise vnto her: for her haire is giuen her for a
[e] couering.
16 [13] But if any man lust to be contentious,
wee haue no such custome, neither the Churches of God.
17 ¶ [14] Now in this that I declare, I praise
you not, that yee come together, not with profit, but with hurt.
18 [15] For first of all, when yee come together in the Church, I heare that there are dissentions amon you: and I beleeue it *to be true*
in some part.
19 [16] For there must bee heresies euen a-
mong you, that they which are [f] approoued a-
mong you, might be knowen.
20 When yee come together therefore
into one place, *this* is [g] not to eat the Lords
Supper.
21 For euery man when they should eate,
taketh his owne supper [h] afore, and one is hungrie, and another is drunken.
22 [17] Haue yee not houses to eate and to
drinke in? despise yee the Church of God, and
shame them that haue not? what shall I say
to you? shall I prayse you in this? I prayse
you not.
23 [18] For I haue receiued of the Lord that
which I also haue deliuered vnto you, *to wit*,
That the Lord Iesus in the night when hee was
betrayed, tooke bread:
24 * And when he had giuen thankes, hee
brake it, and said, Take, eate: This is my body,
which is [i] broken for you: this doe yee in remembrance of me.
25 After the same maner also *hee tooke* the
cup, when he had supped, saying, This cup is
the New Testament in my blood: this doe as
oft as yee drinke it, in remembrance of me.
26 For as often as yee shall eate this bread,
and drinke this cup, yee shew the Lords death
till he come.
27 [19] Wherefore, whosoeuer shall eate this
bread, and drinke the cup of the Lord [k] vnwor-

12 He vrgeth the argument taken from the common sense of nature.
e To be a couering for her, and such a couering, as should procure another.
13 Against such as are stubbornely contentious, we haue to oppose this, that the Churches of God are not contentious.
14 He passeth now to the next Treatise concerning the right administration of the Lords supper. And the Apostle vseth this sharper preface, that the Corinthians might vnderstand, that whereas they obserued generally the Apostles commandements, yet they foully neglected them in a matter of greatest importance.
15 To celebrate the Lords Supper aright, it is requisite that there be not onely consent of doctrine, but also of affections, that it be not prophaned.
16 Although that schismes and heresies proceed from the deuill, and are euill, yet they come not by chance, nor without cause, & they turne to the profit of the elect.
f Whom experience hath taught to be of sound religion and godlinesse.
g This is an vsuall kind of speach whereby the Apostle denieth that flatly, which many did not well.
h Eateth his meate and tarieth not till other come.
17 The Apostle thinketh it good to take away the loue feastes, for their abuse, although they had beene a long time, and with commendation vsed in Churches, and were appointed and instituted by the Apostles.
18 We must take a true forme of keeping the Lords Supper, out of the institution of it, the parts whereof are these, touching the Pastours, to shew foorth the Lords death by preaching his word: to blesse the bread and the wine by calling vpon the Name of God, and together with prayers to declare the institution thereof, and finally to deliuer the bread broken to be eaten, and the cup receiued to bee drunke with thankesgiuing. And touching the flocke, that euery man examine himselfe, that is to say, to prooue both his knowledge, and also faith, and repentance: to shew foorth the Lords death, that is, in true faith to yeeld vnto his word and institution: and last of all, to take the bread at the Ministers hand, and to eate it and to drinke the wine, and giue God thankes: This was Pauls and the Apostles maner of ministring. * *Matth.* 26. 16. *marke* 14 22. *luke* 22.19. *i This word (Broken) noteth out vnto vs Christ his maner of death, for although his legges were not broken, as the theeues legges were, yet was his body very sore tormented, and torne, and bruised.* 19 Whosoeuer contemne the holy Sacraments, that is, vse them not aright, are guiltie not of the bread and wine, but of the thing it selfe, that is, of Christ, and shall bee grieuously punished for it. *k Otherwise then meete is such mysteries should be handled.*

one degree beneath the man by the ordinance of God, and that the man is so subiect to Christ, that the glorie of God ought to appeare in him for the preeminence of the sexe. * *Ephesians* 5.23. *a In that, that Christ is our Mediatour.* 3 Hereof hee gathereth, that if men doe either pray or preach in publike assemblies, hauing their heades couered (which was then a signe of subiection) they did as it were, spoyle themselues of their dignitie, against Gods ordinance. *b It appeareth, that this was a politike Lawe seruing onely for the circumstances of the time that Paul liued in, by this reason, because in these our dayes for a man to speake bare headed in an assembly, is a signe of subiection.* 4 And in like sort hee concludeth, that women which shew themselues in publike and Ecclesiasticall assemblies without the signe and token of their subiection, that is to say, vncouered, shame themselues. 5 The first argument taken from the common sense of man, for so much as nature teacheth women, that it is dishonest for them to come abroad bare headed, seeing that shee hath giuen them thicke and long haire, which they doe so diligently trimme and decke, that they can in no wise abide to haue it shauen. 6 The taking away of an obiection: Haue not men also haire giuen them? I graunt, saith the Apostle, but there is another matter in it: For man was made to this ende and purpose, that the glorie of God should appeare in his rule and authoritie: but the woman was made, that by profession of her obedience, shee might more honour her husband. * *Genesis* 1 26. *and* 5.1. *and* 9 6. *colossians* 3.10. 7 He prooueth the inequalitie of the woman, by that, that the man is the matter whereof woman was first made. * *Genesis* 2.22. 8 Secondly, by that, that the woman was made for man, and not the man for the womans sake. 9 The conclusion: Women must bee couered, to shew by this externall signe, their subiection. *c A couering which is a token of subiection.* 10 What this meaneth, I doe not yet vnderstand. 11 A digression which the Apostle vseth, least that which hee spake of the superioritie of men, and lower degree of women, in consideration of the policie of the Church, should bee so taken as though there were no measure of this inequalitie. Therefore hee teacheth that men haue in such sort the preeminence, that God made them not alone, but women also: and woman was so made of man, that men also are borne by the meanes of women, and this ought to put them in minde to obserue the degree of euery sexe in such sort, that mutuall coniunction may be cherished. *d By the Lord.*

thily, shall bee guiltie of the body and blood of
the Lord.
28 *[20] Let [l] euery man therefore examine
himselfe, and so let him eate of this bread, and
drinke of this cup.
29 For he that eateth and drinketh vnwor-
thily, eateth and drinketh his owne damnation, *because* he [m] discerneth not the Lords body.
30 [21] For this cause many *are* weake, and
sicke among you, and many sleepe.
31 For if we would [n] judge our selues, we
should not be iudged.
32 But when we are iudged, we are chastened of the Lord, because wee should not be
condemned with the world.
33 [22] Wherefore, my brethren, when yee
come together to eate, tary one for another.
34 [23] And if any man bee hungry, let him
eate at home, that ye come not together vnto
condemnation. [24] Other things will I set in order when I come.

* 2.Cor.13.5.
20 The examination of a mans selfe, is of necessitie required in the Supper, and therefore they ought not to be admitted vnto it, which cannot examine themselues: as children, furious and mad men, also such as either haue no knowledge of Christ, or not sufficient, although they professe Christian religion and others such like.
l This place beateth downe the faith of credite, or vnwrapped faith, which the Papists maintaine.
m Hee is sayd to discerne the Lords body, that hath consideration of the worthinesse of it, and therefore commeth to eate of this meate with great reuerence. 21 The prophaning of the body and blood of the Lord in his mysteries, is sharpely punished of him, and therefore such a mischiefe ought diligently to bee preuented by iudging and correcting of a mans selfe. *n Trie and examine our selues, by faith and repentance, separating our selues from the wicked.* 22 The Supper of the Lord is a common action of the whole Church and therefore there is no place for priuate suppers. 23 The Supper of the Lord was instituted not to feede the belly but to feede the soule with the communion of Christ, and therefore it ought to bee separated from common bankets. 24 Such things as pertaine to order, as place, time, forme of prayers, and other such like, the Apostle tooke order for in Congregations, according to the consideration of times, places and persons.

CHAP. XII.

1 To draw away the Corinthians from contention and pride, he sheweth that spirituall gifts are therefore diuersly bestowed, 7 that the same being ioyntly to ech other imployed, 12 wee may growe vp together into one body of Christ in such equall proportion and measure, 20 as the members of mans body.

Now [1] concerning spiritual *gifts*, brethren,
I would not haue you [a] ignorant.
2 [2] Ye know that ye were [b] Gentiles, and
were caried away vnto the dumme Idols, as ye
were led.
3 [3] Wherefore, I declare vnto you, that no
man *speaking by the Spirit of God calleth Iesus * [c] execrable: also no man can say that Iesus is the Lord, but by the holy Ghost.
4 [4] Now there are diuersities of gifts, but
the [d] same Spirit.
5 And there are diuersities of administra-
tions, but the same Lord.
6 And there are diuersities of [e] operations,
but God is the same which worketh all in all.
7 But the manifestation of the Spirit is
[f] giuen to euery man, to [g] profit withall.
8 [5] For to one is giuen by the Spirit the
word of [h] wisedome: and to an other the word
of knowledge, by the same Spirit:
9 And to another *is giuen* faith by the same
Spirit: and to another the gifts of healing, by
the same Spirit:
10 And to another the [i] operations of great
works: and to another, [k] prophecie: and to a-
nother, the [l] discerning of spirits: and to another diuersities of tongues: and to another, the
interpretation of tongues.
11 *And all these things worketh one and
the selfe same Spirit, distributing to euery man
seuerally [6] as he will.
12 [7] For as the body is one, and hath many
members, and all the members of the body,
which is one, though they bee many, *yet* are *but*
one body: [8] euen so is [m] Christ.
13 For by one Spirit wee are all baptized into [n] one body, whether *we bee* Iewes
or Grecians, whether *we bee* bond or free,
and haue beene all made to [o] drinke into one
Spirit.
14 [9] For the body also is not one member,
but many.
15 [10] If the foote would say, Because I am
not the hand, I am not of the body, is it therefore not of the body?
16 And if the eare would say, Because I am
not the eye, I am not of the body, is it therefore
not of the body?
*17 [11] If the whole body *were* an eye, where
were the hearing? If the whole *were* hearing,
where *were* the smelling?
18 But now hath God disposed the members euery one of them in the body at his own
pleasure.
19 For if they were all one member, where
were the body?
20 But now *are* there many members, yet
but one body.

1 Now hee entreth into ye third part of this treatise touching the right vse of spirituall giftes, wherein hee giueth the Corinthians plainely to vnderstand that they abused them: for they that excelled bragged ambitiously of them, and so robbed God of the praise of his giftes: and hauing no consideration of their brethren, abused them to a vaine ostentation, and so robbed the Church of the vse of those giftes. On the other side the inferiour sort enuied the better, and went about to make a departure, so that all that body was as it were scattered and rent in pieces. So then he going about to remedie these abuses willeth them first to consider diligently, that they haue not these gifts of themselues, but from the free grace and liberalitie of God, to whose glory they ought to bestow them all. *a Ignorant to what purpose these gifts are giuen you.* 2 He reproueth the same by comparing their former state with that wherein they were at this time indued, with those excellent gifts. *b As touching Gods seruice and the couenant, meere strangers.* 3 The conclusion: Know you therefore that you cannot so much as mooue your lips to honour Christ withall, but by the grace of the holy Ghost. * *Marke 9.39.* * *Iohn.13.13. chap.8.6 phil.2.11.* *c Doth curse him, or by any meanes whatsoeuer diminish his glorie.* 4 In the second place, he layeth another foundation, to wit, that these gifts are diuers, as the functions also are diuers and their offices diuers, but that one selfe same Spirit, Lord and God is the giuer of all these gifts, and that to one end, to wit, for the profit of all. *d The Spirit is plainely distinguished from the gifts.* *e So Paul calleth that inward force which commeth from the holy Ghost, & maketh men fit to wonderful things.*

f The holy Ghost openeth and sheweth himselfe freely in giuing of these giftes.
g To the vse and benefite of the Church.
5 He declareth this manifold diuersitie, and reckoneth vp the chiefest giftes, beating that into their heads, which he said before, to-wit, that all these things proceeded from one selfe same Spirit.
h Wisedome is a most excellent gift, very requisite, not onely for them which teach, but also for them that exhort and comfort, which thing is proper to the Pastours office: as the word of knowledge agreeth to the Doctours.
i By operation hee meaneth those great workings of Gods mightie power, which passe and excell amongst his miracles, as the deliuerie of his people Israel by the hand of Moses: that which hee did by Elias against the Priests of Baal, in sending downe fire from heauen to consume his sacrifice: and that which hee did by Peter, in the matter of Ananias and Saphira.
k Foretelling of things to come.
l Whereby false prophets are knowen from true, wherein Peter passed Philip in discouering Simon Magus, Actes 8.20. * *Rom.12.3. ephes.4.7.*
6 Hee addeth moreouer somewhat else, to wit, that although that these giftes are vnequall, yet they are most wisely diuided, because the will of the Spirit of God is the rule of this distribution. 7 Hee setteth foorth his former saying by a similitude taken from the body: This saith hee, is manifestly seene in the body, whose members are diuers, but yet so knit together, that they make but one body. 8 The applying of the similitude. So must we also thinke, saith hee, of the mysticall body of Christ: for all we that beleeue, whether we bee Iewes or Gentiles, are by one selfe same Baptisme, ioyned together with our head, that by that meanes, there may bee framed one body compact of many members: and wee haue drunke one selfe same spirit, that is to say, a spirituall feeling, perceiuerance and motion common to vs all out of one cup. *m Christ ioyned together with his Church.* *n To become one body with Christ.* *o By one quickning drinke of the Lords blood, we are made partakers of his onely Spirit.* 9 Hee amplifieth that which followed of the similitude: as if hee should say, The vnitie of the body is not onely not let by this diuersitie of members, but also it could not bee a body, if it did not consist of many, and those diuers members. 10 Now hee buildeth his doctrine vpon the foundations which hee hath laide: and first of all hee continueth in his purposed similitude, and afterward hee goeth to the matter barely and simply. And first of all hee speaketh vnto them which would haue separated themselues from those whome they enuied, because they had not such excellent gifts as they: now this is, saith he, as if the foote should say, it were not of the bodie, because it is not the hand, or the eare, because it is not the eye. Therefore all parts ought rather to defend the vnitie of the bodie, being coupled together to serue one the other. 11 Againe speaking to them, hee sheweth them that if that should come to passe which they desire, to wit, that all should bee equall one to another, there would followe a destruction of the whole bodie, yea and of themselues: for it could not bee a bodie, vnlesse it were made of many members knit together, and diuers one from the other. And that no man might finde fault with this diuision as vnequall, hee addeth that God himselfe hath coupled all these together. Therefore all must remaine coupled together, that the body may remaine in safetie.

21 [12] And

12 Now on the other side, hee speaketh vnto them which were indued with more excellent gifts, willing them not to despise the inferiours as vnprofitable, and as though they serued to no vse: for God saith hee, hath in such sort tempered this inequalitie, that the more excellent and beautifull members can in no wise lacke the more abiect and such as we are ashamed of, and that they should haue more care to see vnto them and to couer them: that by this meanes the necessitie which is on both parts, might keepe the whole body in peace and concord: that although if each part be considered apart, they are of diuers degrees and conditions, yet because they are ioyned together, they haue a communitie both in commodities and discommodities.

21 [12] And the eye cannot say vnto the hand,
I haue no neede of thee: nor the head againe to
the feete, I haue no neede of you.
22 Yea, much rather those members of the
body, which seeme to be [p] more feeble, are necessarie.
23 And vpon those *members* of the body,
which wee thinke most vnhonest, but we more
[q] honestie on: and our vncomely *parts* haue
more comelinesse on.
24 For our comely *parts* neede it not: but
God hath tempered the body together, and
hath giuen the more honour to that *part* which
lacked,
25 Lest there should be any diuision in the
body: but that the members should haue the
same [r] care one for another.
26 [13] Therefore if one member suffer, all
suffer with it: if one member be had in honour,
all the members reioyce with it.
27 Now yee are the body of Christ, and
members for *your* [s] part.
28 *And God hath ordeined some in the
Church: *as* first Apostles, secondly Prophets,
thirdly teachers, then them that doe miracles:
after that, the gifts of healing, [t] helpers, [u] gouernours, diuersitie of tongues.
29 Are all Apostles? are all Prophets? are all
teachers?
30 Are all doers of miracles? haue all the
gifts of healing? doe all speake with tongues?
doe all interpret?
31 [14] But desire you the best gifts, and I wil
yet shew you a more excellent way.

p *Of the smallest and vilest offices, and therefore smally accounted of, of the rest.* q *We more carefully couer them.* r *Should bestow their operations and offices to the profit and preseruation of the whole body.* 13 Now he applieth this same doctrine to the Corinthians without any allegorie, warning them that seeing there are diuers functions and diuers gifts, it is their duetie, not to offend one against another, either by enuie or ambition, but rather that they being ioyned together in loue and charitie one with another, euery one of them bestow to the profit of all, that which he hath receiued according as his ministerie doth require. s *For all Churches wheresoeuer they are dispersed through the whole world, are diuers members of one body.* * *Ephe. 4. 11.* t *The offices of Deacons.* u *He setteth foorth the order of Elders, which were the maintainers of the Churches discipline.* 14 Hee teacheth them that are ambitious and enuious, a certaine holy ambition and enuie, to wit, if they giue themselues to the best gifts, and such as are most profitable to the Church, and so if they contend to excell one another in loue, which farre passeth all other gifts.

CHAP. XIII.

1 *Hee sheweth that there are no gifts so excellent, which in Gods sight are not corrupt, if Charitie bee away:* 4 *and therefore he digresseth vnto the commendation of it.*

1 He reasoneth first of Charitie, the excellencie whereof he first sheweth by this, that without it, all other gifts are as nothing before God: which thing he prooueth partly by an induction, and partly also by an argument taken of the end, wherefore those gifts are giuen. For, to what purpose are those gifts but to Gods glory, and the profit of the Church as is before prooued? so that those giftes without Charitie, haue no right vse.

THough [1] I speake with the tongues of
men and [a] Angels, and haue not loue, I
am *as* sounding brasse, or a [b] tinckling cymball.
2 And though I had the *gift* of prophecie,
and knew all secrets and all knowledge, yea if I
had all [c] faith, so that I could remooue * mountaines, and had not loue, I were nothing.
3 And though I feede the poore with all
my goods, and though I giue my bodie, that
I bee burned, and haue not loue, it profiteth
me nothing.

a *A very earnest kind of amplifying a matter, as if hee said, If there were any tongues of Angels, and I had them, and did not vse them to the benefit of my neighbour, it were nothing else but a vaine and pratling kind of babbling.* b *That giueth a rude and no certaine sound.* c *By faith hee meaneth the gift of doing miracles, and not that faith which iustifieth, which can not be voide of Charitie as the other may.* * *Matth. 17. 20.*

4 [2] Loue [d] suffereth long: it is bountifull:
loue enuieth not: loue doeth not boast it selfe:
it is not puffed vp:
5 It doeth [e] no vncomely thing: it seeketh
not her owne things: it is not prouoked to anger: it thinketh not euil:
6 It reioyceth not in iniquitie, but [f] reioyceth in the trueth:
7 It suffereth all things: it beleeueth all
things: it hopeth all things: it endureth all
things.
8 [3] Loue doth neuer fall away, though that
prophecyings bee abolished, or the tongues
cease, or [g] knowledge vanish away.
9 [4] For we know in [h] part, and wee prophecie in part.
10 But when that which is perfect, is come,
then that which is in part, shall be abolished.
11 [5] When I was a child, I spake as a child,
I vnderstood as a child, I thought as childe:
but when I became a man, I put away childish
things.
12 [6] For [i] now we see through a glasse darkly: but then *shall we see* face to face. Now I
know in part: but then shall I know euen as I
am knowen.
13 [7] And now abideth faith, hope & loue, *e-
uen* these three: but the chiefest of these *is* loue.

2 Hee describeth the force and nature of charitie, partly by a comparison of contraries, and partly by the effects of it selfe: whereby the Corinthians may vnderstand, both how profitable it is in the Church, and how necessarie: and also how farre they are from it, and therefore how vainely & without cause they are proud. d *Word for word, deferreth wrath.* e *It is not contumelious.* f *Reioyceth at righteousnesse in the righteous. For the Hebrewes meane by trueth, righteousnesse.* 3 Againe hee commendeth the excellencie of charitie in that, that it shall neuer be abolished in the Saints, whereas the other gifts which are necessarie for the building vp of the Church, so long as wee liue here, shall haue no place in the world to come. g *The way to get knowledge by prophecying.* 4 The reason: Because we are now in that state that we haue neede to learne daily, and therefore we haue need of those helpes, to wit, of the gift of tongues, and knowledge, & also of them that teach them. But to what purpose serue they then, when we haue obtained and gotten the full knowledge of God, which serue now but for them, which are imperfit and goe by degrees to perfection? k *We learne imperfectly.* 5 He setteth forth that, that he said, by an excellent similitude, comparing this life to our infancie, or childhood, wherein wee stagger and stammer rather then speake, and thinke and vnderstand childish things, and therefore haue neede of such things as may forme and frame our tongue and minde: but when we become men, to what purpose should wee desire that stammering, those childish toyes, and such like things, whereby our childhood is framed by little and little? 6 The applying of the similitude of our childhood to this present life, wherein wee darkely behold heauenly things, according to the small measure of light which is giuen vs, through the vnderstanding of tongues, and hearing the teachers and ministers of the Church: of our mans age and strength, to that heauenly and eternall life, wherein when wee behold God himselfe present, and are lightened with his full and perfect light, to what purpose should wee desire the voice of man, and those worldly things which are most imperfect? But yet then, shall all the Saints bee knit both with God, and betweene themselues with most feruent loue, and therefore Charitie shall not bee abolished, but perfected, although it shall not bee shewed foorth and entertained by such maner of dueties as peculiarly and onely belong to the infirmitie of this life. i *All this must bee vnderstood by comparison.* 7 The conclusion: As if the Apostle should say, Such therefore shall bee our condition then: but now wee haue three things, and they remaine sure if wee bee Christes, as without which, true religion cannot consist, to wit, faith, hope, and charitie. And among these, Charitie is the chiefest because it ceaseth not in the life to come as the rest doe, but is perfected and accomplished. For seeing that faith and hope tend to things which are promised and are to come, when wee haue presently gotten them, to what purpose should wee haue faith and hope? but yet there at length shall wee truely and perfectly loue both God, and one another.

CHAP. XIIII.

1 *He commendeth the gift of prophecying:* 7 *and by a similitude taken of the musicall instruments,* 12 *hee teacheth the true vse of interpreting the Scriptures:* 17 *he taketh away the abuse:* 34 *and forbiddeth women to speake in the Congregation.*

FOllow [1] after loue, and couet spiritual *gifts*,
and rather that yee may [a] prophecie.

1 Hee inferreth now of that he spake before: Therefore seeing charitie is the chiefest of all, before all things set it before you as chiefe and principall: and so esteeme those things as most excellent, which profite the greater part of men: (as prophecie, that is to say, the gift of teaching and applying the doctrine: which was contemned in respect of other giftes, although it bee the chiefest and most necessarie for the Church) and not those which for a shew seeme to bee marueilous, as the giftes of tongues, when a man was suddenly indued with the knowledge of many tongues, which made men greatly amazed and yet of it selfe was not greatly to any vse, vnlesse there were an interpreter. a *What prophecie is, he sheweth in the third verse.*

2 He reprehendeth their peruerſe iudgement touching the gift of tongues. For why was it giuen? to wit, to the intent that the myſteries of God might be ỹ better knowen to a greater ſort. Thereby it is euident that prophecie, whereunto the gift of tongues ought to ſerue, is better then this: and therefore the Corinthians did iudge amiſſe, in that they made more accompt of the gift of tongues then of prophecying: because forſooth ỹ gift of tongues was a thing more to be bragged of. And hereupon followed another abuſe of the gift of tongues, in that the Corinthians vſed tongues in the congregation without an interpreter. Which thing although it might be done to ſome profit of him that ſpake them, yet hee corrupted the right vſe of that gift because there came therby no profit to the hearers: and common aſſemblies were inſtituted and appointed not for any priuate mans commoditie, but for the profit of ỹ whole company.

b A ſtrange language which no man can vnderſtand without an interpreter.

c By that inſpiration which he hath receiued of the Spirit, which notwithſtanding he abuſeth, when he ſpeaketh myſteries which none of the companie can vnderſtand.

d Which may further men in the ſtudy of godlineſſe.

e The companie.

2 [2]For he that ſpeaketh a *ſtrange* [b] tongue,
ſpeaketh not vnto men, but vnto God: for no
man heareth *him*: howbeit in the [c] ſpirit hee
ſpeaketh ſecret things.
3 But he that prophecieth, ſpeaketh vnto
men to [d] edifying, and to exhortation, and to
comfort.
4 He that ſpeaketh *ſtrange* language, edifieth himſelfe: but he that prophecieth, edifieth
the [e] Church.
5 I would that yee all ſpake *ſtrange* languages, but rather that yee prophecied: for
greater is hee that prophecieth, then hee that
ſpeaketh *diuers* tongues, except he expound it,
that the Church may receiue edification.
6 And now, brethren, if I come vnto you
ſpeaking *diuers* tongues, what ſhall I profite
you, except I ſpeake to you, either by reuelation, or by knowledge, or by prophecying, or
by doctrine?
7 [3] Moreouer things without life which
giue a ſound, whether *it be* a pipe or an harpe,
except they make a diſtinction in the ſounds,
how ſhall it bee knowen what is piped or
harped?
8 And alſo if the trumpet giue an vncertaine ſound, who ſhall prepare himſelfe to
battell?
9 So likewiſe you, by the tongue, except
yee vtter words that haue [f] ſignification, how
ſhall it bee vnderſtood what is ſpoken? for yee
ſhall ſpeake in the ayre.
10 [4] There are ſo many kinds of voices (as
it commeth to paſſe) in the world, and none of
them is dumme.
11 Except I know then the power of the
voice, I ſhall bee vnto him that ſpeaketh a barbarian, and he that [g] ſpeaketh ſhall be a barbarian vnto me.
12 [5] Euen ſo, foraſmuch as yee couet ſpirituall *gifts*, ſeeke that yee may excell vnto the
edifying of the Church.
13 Wherfore let him that ſpeaketh a *ſtrange*
tongue, [h] pray that he may interprete.
14 [6] For [i] if I pray in a *ſtrange* tongue, my
[k] ſpirit prayeth: but mine vnderſtanding is
[l] without fruit.
15 What is it then? I will pray with the ſpirit, but I will pray with the [m] vnderſtanding
alſo: I will ſing with the ſpirit, but I will ſing
with the vnderſtanding alſo.
16 [7] Elſe, when thou bleſſeſt with the [n] ſpirit, how ſhall hee that [o] occupieth the roome
of the vnlearned, ſay [p] Amen, at thy giuing of
thankes, ſeeing hee knoweth not what thou
ſayeſt?
17 For thou verily giueſt thankes well, but
the other is not edified.
18 [8] I thanke my God, I ſpeake languages
more then yee all.
19 Yet had I rather in the Church to ſpeake
[q] fiue words with mine vnderſtanding, that I
might alſo inſtruct others, then ten thouſand
words in a *ſtrange* tongue.
20 [9] Brethren, be not *children in vnderſtanding, but as concerning maliciousneſſe be children, but in vnderſtanding bee of a ripe age.
21 In the [r] Law it is written, *By men of
other tongues, and by other languages will I
ſpeake vnto this people: yet ſo ſhall they not
heare me, ſaith the Lord.
22 [10] Wherefore *ſtrange* tongues are for a
ſigne, not to them that beleeue, but to them
that beleeue not: but prophecying *ſerueth* not
for them that beleeue not, but for them which
beleeue.
23 [11] If therefore when the whole Church
is come together in one, and all ſpeake *ſtrange*
tongues, there come in they that are [ſ] vnlearned, or they which beleeue not, will they not
ſay, that yee are out of your wits?
24 But if all prophecie, and there come in
one that beleeueth not, or one vnlearned, he is
rebuked of all men, and is iudged of all,
25 And ſo are the ſecrets of his heart made
manifeſt, and ſo hee will fall downe on his face
and worſhip God, and ſay plainely that God is
in you in deede.
26 [12] What is to bee *done* then, brethren?
when ye come together, *according as* euery one
of you hath a Pſalme, *or* hath doctrine, *or* hath
a tongue, *or* hath reuelation, *or* hath interpretation, let all things be done vnto edifying.
27 [13] If any man ſpeake a *ſtrange* tongue, *let
it be* by two, or at the moſt, by three, and that
by courſe, and let one interprete.
28 But if there bee no interpreter, let him
keepe ſilence in the Church, *which ſpeaketh
languages*, and let him ſpeake to himſelfe, and
to God.
29 [14] Let the Prophets ſpeake two, or three,
and let the other iudge.

7 An other reaſon: Seeing that the whole congregation muſt agree to him that ſpeaketh, and alſo witneſſe this agreement, How ſhall they giue their aſſent or agreement which know not what is ſpoken?

n Onely, without all conſideration of the hearers.

o Hee that ſitteth as a priuate man.

p So then one vttered the prayers, and all the companie anſwered, Amen.

8 He propoundeth himſelfe for an example, both that they may be aſhamed of their fooliſh ambition, and alſo that he may eſchew all ſuſpition of enuie.

q A very fewe words.

9 Now hee reprooueth them freely for their childiſh folly, which ſee not how this gift of tongues which was giuen to the profit of the Church, is turned by their ambition into an inſtrument of curſing, ſeeing that the ſame alſo is contained amongſt the puniſhments wherwith God puniſhed the ſtubburnneſſe of his people, that hee diſperſed them amongſt ſtrangers whoſe language they vnderſtood not.

*Matth. 28 3.

r By the Law he vnderſtandeth all the whole Scripture.

*Iſa 18.11.

10 The concluſion: Therefore ỹ gift of tongues ſerueth to puniſh the vnfaithfull and vnbeleeuers, vnleſſe it be referred to prophecie (that is to ſay, to the interpretation of Scripture) and that that which is ſpoken be by that meanes vnderſtood of the hearers.

3 Hee ſetteth foorth that which hee ſaid by a ſimilitude, which hee borroweth and taketh from inſtruments of muſicke, which although they ſpeake not perfitly, yet they are diſtinguiſhed by their ſounds, that they may bee the better vſed. *f That doe fitly vtter the matter it ſelfe.* 4 Hee prooueth that interpretation is neceſſarily to bee ioyned with the gift of tongues, by the manifold varietie of languages, inſomuch that if one ſpeake to another without an interpreter, it is as if hee ſpake not. *g As the Papiſtes in all their Sermons, and they that ambitiouſly powre out ſome Hebrew or Greeke words in the Pulpit before the vnlearned people, thereby to get them a name of vaine learning.* 5 The concluſion: if they will excell in thoſe ſpirituall giftes, as it is meete, they muſt ſeeke the profit of the Church, and therefore they muſt not vſe the gift of tongues, vnleſſe there bee an interpreter to expound the ſtrange and vnknowen tongue, whether it bee himſelſe that ſpeaketh, or another interpreter. *h Pray for the gift of interpretation.* 6 A reaſon: Becauſe it is not ſufficient for vs to ſpeake ſo in the congregation, that wee our ſelues doe worſhip God in ſpirit, that is according to the gift which wee haue receiued, but wee muſt alſo bee vnderſtood of the companie, leaſt that bee vnprofitable to other, which wee haue ſpoken. *i If I pray, when the Church is aſſembled together, in a ſtrange tongne. k The gift and inſpiration which the ſpirit giueth mee, doeth his part, but onely to my ſelfe. l No fruite commeth to the Church by my prayers. m So that I may be vnderſtood of other, and may inſtruct other.*

11 An other argument: The gift of tongues without prophecie is not onely vnprofitable to the faithfull, but alſo doeth very much hurt: as well to them as to the vnfaithfull which ſhould be won in the publike aſſemblies. For by this meanes it commeth to paſſe, that the faithful ſeeme to other to be mad, much leſſe can the vnfaithfull be inſtructed thereby. *ſ Looke Acts 4.13.* 12 The concluſion. The edifying of the congregation is a rule and ſquare of the right vſe of all ſpirituall giftes. 13 The maner how to vſe the gift of tongues. It may be lawfull for one or two, or at the moſt for three, to vſe ỹ gift of tongues, one after another in an aſſembly, ſo that there be ſome to expound the ſame: but if there be none to expound, let him that hath that gift, ſpeake to himſelf alone. 14 The maner of prophecying: Let two or three propound, and let the other iudge of that that is propounded, whether it be agreeable to the word of God or no: If in this examination the Lord giue any man ought to ſpeake, let them giue him leaue to ſpeake. Let euery man be admitted to prophecie, ſeuerally and in his order, ſo farre forth as it is requiſite for the ediſying of the Church: Let them be content to be ſubiect each to others iudgement.

30 And

30 And if any thing be reueiled to another
that sitteth by, let the first hold his peace.
31 For yee may all prophecie one by one,
that all may learne, and all may haue comfort.
32 And the [t] spirits of the Prophets are subiect to the Prophets.
33 For God is not *the authour* of confusion,
but of peace, as *we see* in all the Churches of the
Saints.
34 [15] * Let your women keepe silence in the
Churches: for it is not permitted vnto them to
speake, but *they ought* to be subiect, as also * the
Law saith.
35 And if they will learne any thing, let
them aske their husbands at home: for it is a
shame for a woman to speake in the Church.
36 [16] Came the word of God out from you?
either came it vnto you onely?
37 If any man thinke himselfe to be a Prophet, or [u] spirituall, let him acknowledge, that
the things that I write vnto you, are the commandements of the Lord.
38 [17] And if any man bee ignorant, let him
be ignorant:
39 [18] Wherfore, brethren, couet to prophecie, and forbid not to speake languages.
40 Let all things bee done honestly, and
by order.

t The doctrine which the Prophets bring, which are inspired with Gods spirit. 15 Women are commaunded to be silent in publike assemblies, and they are commaunded to aske of their husbands at home. * *1.Tim.2.12.* * *Gene.3.16.* 16 A generall conclusion of the treatise of the right vse of spirituall gifts in assemblies: with a sharpe reprehension, lest the Corinthians might alone seeme to themselues to be wise. *u Skilful in knowing and iudging spirituall things.* 17 The Church ought not to care for such as be stubburnely ignorant, and will not abide to be taught, but to goe forward notwithstanding, in those things which are right. 18 Prophecie ought simply to be retained and kept in Congregations, the gift of tongues is not to be forbidden, but all things must be done orderly.

CHAP. XV.

1 *The Gospel that Paul preached.* 3 *The death and resurrection of Christ.* 8 *Paul saw Christ.* 9 *He had persecuted that Church, whereof afterward he was made a minister.* 12 *Christ first rose againe, and we all shall rise by him.* 26 *The last enemie, death.* 29 *To be baptized for dead.* 32 *At Ephesus Paul fought with beasts.* 35 *How the dead are raised.* 45 *The first Adam. The last Adam.* 47 *The first and second man.* 51 *We shal all be changed, wee shall not all sleepe.* 55 *Deaths sting,* 57 *victorie.* 58 *Constancie and stedfastnesse.*

Moreouer [1] * brethren, I declare vnto
you the Gospel, which I preached vnto
you, which yee haue also receiued, and wherein
yee [a] continue,
2 And whereby yee are saued, if yee keepe
in memorie, after what maner I preached it vnto you, [b] except yee haue beleeued in vaine.
3 For first of all, I deliuered vnto you that
which I receiued, how that Christ died for our
sinnes, according to the * Scriptures,
4 And that hee was buried, and that hee
arose the third day, according to the * Scriptures,
5 * And that he was seene of Cephas, then
of the [c] twelue.
6 After that, hee was seene of moe then
fiue hundreth brethren at [d] once: whereof many remaine vnto this present, and some also are
asleepe.
7 After that, he was seene of Iames: then
of all the Apostles.
8 * [2] And last of all he was seene also of me,
as of one borne out of due time.
9 * For I am the least of the Apostles, which
am not meete to be called an Apostle, because I
persecuted the Church of God.
10 * But by the grace of God, I am that I
am: and his grace which is in mee, was not in
vaine: but I laboured more aboundantly then
they all: yet not I, but the grace of God which
is with me.
11 Wherefore, whether it were I, or they,
so we preach, and so haue ye beleeued.
12 ¶ [3] Now if it be preached, that Christ is
risen from the dead, how say some among you,
that there is no resurrection of the dead?
13 [4] For if there bee no resurrection of the
dead, then is Christ not risen:
14 [5] And if Christ bee not risen, then is our
preaching vaine, and your faith is also vaine.
15 And we are found also false witnesses of
God: for we haue testified of God, that he hath
raised vp Christ: whom he hath not raised vp, if
so be the dead be not raised.
16 [6] For if the dead bee not raised, then is
Christ not raised.
17 And if Christ be not raised, your faith is
vaine: [7] yee are [e] yet in your sinnes.
18 [8] And so they which are asleepe in Christ
are perished.
19 [9] If in this life onely wee haue hope in
Christ, we are of all men the most miserable.
20 [10] But now is Christ risen from the dead,
[11] *and* was made the * [f] first fruites of them
that slept.
21 [12] For since by man *came* death, by man
came also the resurrection of the dead.
22 For as in Adam all die, euen so in Christ
shall all be [g] made aliue,
23 [13] But euery man in his * owne order: the
first fruits *is* Christ, afterward, they that are of
Christ, at his comming *shall rise againe.*

1 The sixt treatise of this Epistle, concerning the resurrection: and he vseth a transition, or passing ouer from one matter to another, shewing first that he bringeth no new thing, to the end that the Corinthians might vnderstand that they had begun to swarue from the right course: and next that he goeth not about to intreate of a trifling matter, but of another chiefe point of the Gospel, which if it be taken away, their faith must needes come to nought. And so at the length hee beginneth this treatise at Christs resurrection, which is the ground and foundation of ours, and confirmeth it first by the testimonie of the Scriptures and by the witnesse of the Apostles, and of more then fiue hundreth brethren, and last of all by his owne. * *Gala.1.11.* *a In the profession whereof you continue yet.* *b Which is very absurd, and cannot bee, but that they that beleeue must reape the fruite of faith.* * *Isa.53.5. 1.pet.2.24.* * *Ionas 2.1.* * *Iohn 20 19.* *b Of those twelue picked and chosen Apostles, which were commonly called twelue, though Iudas was put out of the number.* *d Not at seuerall times, but together and at one instant.*

* *Actes 9 5.* 2 He maintaineth by the way, the authoritie of his Apostleship, which was requisite to be in good credite among the Corinthians, that this Epistle might bee of force and waight amongst them. In the meane season hee compareth himselfe in such sort after a certaine diuine art with certaine other, that he maketh himselfe inferiour to them all. * *Ephe.3 8.* * *Ephe.3.7.* 3 The first argument to proue that there is a resurrection from the dead: Christ is risen againe, therefore the dead shall rise againe. 4 The second by an absurditie, if there be no resurrection of the dead, then is not Christ risen againe. 5 The proofe of that absurditie, by other absurdities: If Christ be not risen againe, the preaching of the Gospel is in vaine, and the credite that you gaue vnto it, is vaine, and wee are lyars. 6 He repeateth the same argument taken of an absurditie, purposing to shew how faith is in vaine, if the resurrection of Christ be taken away. 7 First, seeing death is the punishment of sinne, in vaine should we beleeue that our sinnes were forgiuen vs, if they remaine: but they doe remaine, if Christ rose not from death. *e They are yet in their sins, which are not sanctified, nor haue obtained remission of their sins.* 8 Secondly, vnlesse that this be certain that Christ rose againe, all they which died in Christ are perished. So then what profite commeth of faith? 9 The third argument which is also taken from an absurditie: for vnlesse there bee another life, wherein such as trust and beleeue in Christ shall bee blessed, they were the most miserable of all creatures, because in this life they are the most miserable. 10 A conclusion of the former argument: Therefore Christ is risen againe. 11 He putteth the last conclusion for the first proposition of the argument that followeth. Christ is risen againe: Therefore shall we the faithfull (for of them hee speaketh) rise againe. Then followeth the first reason of this consequent: for Christ is set foorth vnto vs to bee considered of, not as a priuate man apart and by himselfe, but as the first fruites: And hee taketh that which was knowen to all men, to wit, that the whole heape is sanctified in the first fruites. * *Coloss.1.18. reuelat.1.5.* *f Hee alludeth to the first fruites of corne, the offering whereof sanctified the rest of the fruites.* 12 An other confirmation of the same consequent: for Christ is to bee considered as opposite to Adam, that as from one man Adam, sinne came ouer all, so from one man Christ, life commeth vnto all: that is to say, that all the faithfull, as they die, because by nature they were borne of Adam, so because in Christ they are made the children of God by grace, they are quickened and restored to life by him. *g Shall rise by the vertue of Christ.* 13 Hee doeth two things together: for hee sheweth that the resurrection is in such sort common to Christ with all his members, that notwithstanding hee farre passeth them, both in time (for hee was the first that rose againe from the dead) and also in honour, because that from him and in him is all our life and glorie. Then by this occasion hee passeth to the next argument. * *1.Thessalonians 4 13.*

24 [14] Then *shall be* the [h] end, when hee hath
deliuered vp the kingdome to God, euen the
Father, when he hath put downe [i] all rule, and
all authoritie and power.
25 For he must reigne, * till he hath put all
his enemies [k] vnder his feete.
26 The [l] last enemie that shal be destroyed,
is death.
27 * For hee hath put downe all things
vnder his feete. (And when hee saith that all
things are subdued *to him*, it is manifest that
he is excepted, which did put downe all things
vnder him)
28 And when all things shall bee subdued
vnto him, [m] then shall the Sonne also himselfe
be subiect vnto him, that did subdue all things
vnder him, that [n] God may be all in all.
29 [15] Else what shall they doe which are
baptized [o] for dead? if the dead rise not at all,
why are they then baptized for dead?
30 [16] Why are wee also in ieopardie euery
houre?
31 By our [p] reioycing which I haue in
Christ Iesus our Lord, I die daily.
32 [17] If I haue fought with beastes at E-
phesus [q] after the maner of men, what ad-
uantageth it me, if the dead bee not raised vp?
*[18] let vs [r] eate and drinke: for to morrow wee
shall die.
33 [19] Be not deceiued: euill speakings corrupt good maners.
34 Awake to liue righteously, and sinne
not: for some haue not the knowledge of God,
I speake this to your shame.
35 [20] But some man will say, How are the
dead raised vp? and with what body come they
foorth?

14 The fourth argument wherwith also he confirmeth the other, hath a most sure ground, to wit, because that God must reigne. And this is the maner of his reigne, that the Father will bee shewed to bee King in his Sonne who was made man, to whom all things are made subiect (the promiser onely except) to the ende that the Father may afterward triumph in his Sonne the conquerour. And he maketh two parts of this reigne and dominion of the Sonne wherein the Fathers glorie consisteth: to wit, the ouercomming of his enemies (whereof some must be depriued of all power, as Satan and all the wicked, be they neuer so proud and mightie, and other must be vtterly abolished, as death) and a plaine and full deliuerie of the godly from all enemies, that by this meanes God may fully set forth the body of the Church cleauing fast vnto their head Christ, his kingdome and glory, as a King in his subiects. Moreouer he putteth the first degree of his kingdome in the resurrection of the Sonne, who is the head: and the perfection, in the full coniunction of the members with the head, which shalbe in the latter day. Now all these tend to this purpose, to shew that vnlesse the dead doe rise againe, neither the Father can bee King aboue all, neither Christ the Lord of all: for neither should the power of Satan and death bee ouercome, not the glory of God be full in his Sonne, nor his sonnes in his members. h *The shutting vp and finishing of all things.* i *All his enemies which shall be spoyled of all the power they haue.* *Psal 110 1. acts 2.34 heb. 1.13. and 10.13. k *Christ is considered here, as he appeared in the forme of a seruant, in which respect he ruleth the Church as head, and that because this power was giuen him of his Father.* l *The shutting vp of the argument, which is taken from the whole to the part: for if all his enemies shall be put vnder his feete, then must it needs be that death also shall be subdued vnder him.* *Psal. 8 6. heb. 2.8. m *Not because the Sonne was not subiect to his Father before, but because his body, that is to say, the Church which is here in distresse, and not yet wholly partaker of his glory, is not yet fully perfect, and also because the bodies of the Saints which be in the graues, shall not be glorified vntill the resurrection: but Christ as hee is God, hath vs subiect to him as his Father hath, but as he is Priest, he is subiect to his Father together with vs. August. booke* 1. *chap.* 8. *of the Trinitie.* n *By this hie kind of speech, is set foorth an incomprehensible glory which floweth from God, and shall fill all of vs, as we are ioyned together with our head, but yet so, that our head shall alwayes reserue his preeminence.* 15 The fift argument taken of the end of Baptisme, to wit, because that they which are baptized, are baptized for dead: that is to say, that they may haue a remedy against death, because that baptisme is a token of regeneration. o *They that are baptized to this end and purpose, that death may bee put out in them, or to rise againe from the dead, whereof baptisme is a seale.* 16 The sixt argument: Vnlesse there be a resurrection of the dead, why should the Apostles so daily cast themselues into danger of so many deaths? p *As though he said, I die daily, as all the miseries I suffer can well witnesse, which I may truely boast of that I haue suffered amongst you.* 17 The taking away of an obiection: But thou Paul didst ambitiously, as commonly men are wont to doe, when thou didst fight with beasts at Ephesus: that is very like, saith Paul: for what could that aduantage me, were it not for the glory of eternall life which I hope for? q *Not vpon any godly motion, nor casting mine eyes vpon God, but caried away with vaine glory, or a certaine headinesse.* *Isa. 22.13. 18 The seuenth argument which dependeth vpon the last: If there be no resurrection of the dead, why doe wee giue our selues to any thing else, saue to eating and drinking? r *These are speaches that Epicures vse.* 19 The conclusion with a sharpe exhortation, that they take heed of the naughtie companie of certaine: from whence he sheweth that this mischiefe sprang: warning them to bee wise with sobrietie vnto righteousnesse. 20 Now that hee hath prooued the resurrection, he discouereth their doltishnesse, in that they scoffingly demaunded, how it could be that the dead could rise againe, and if they did rise againe, they asked mockingly, what maner of bodies they should haue. Therefore he sendeth these fellowes, which seemed to themselues to be marueilous wise and wittie, to be instructed of poore rude husbandmen.

36 [21] O foole, that which thou sowest, is
not quickned, except it die.
37 And that which thou sowest, thou sowest not that body that shall bee, but bare corne,
as it falleth, of wheat, or of some other.
38 [22] But God giueth it a body at his pleasure, euen to euery seede his owne body.
39 All flesh *is* not the same flesh, but there
is one flesh of men, another flesh of beasts, and
another of fishes, and another of birds.
40 There *are* also heauenly bodies, and
earthly bodies: but the glory of the heauenly
is one, and *the glory* of the earthly *is* another.
41 There is another glory of the sunne, another glory of the moone, and another glory of
the starres: for one starre differeth from *another*
starre in glory.
42 [23] So also *is* the resurrection of the dead.
The body is [s] sowen in corruption, *and* is raised
in incorruption.
43 It is sowen in [t] dishonour, *and* is raised
in glory: it is sowen in weaknesse, *and* is raised
in [u] power.
44 [24] It is sowen a naturall body, *and* is raised a spirituall body: there is a naturall body,
and there is a spirituall body.
45 [25] As it is also written, The [x] first man
* Adam was made a liuing soule: and the last
Adam *was made* a [y] quickning Spirit.
46 [26] Howbeit that *was* not first which is
spirituall: but that *which is* naturall, and afterward that *which is* spirituall.
47 The first man *is* of the earth, [z] earthly:
the second man *is* the Lord from [a] heauen.
48 [27] As *is* the earthly, such *are* they that are
earthly: and as *is* the heauenly, such *are* they
also that are heauenly.
49 And as wee haue borne the [b] image of

21 Thou mightest haue learned either of these, saith Paul, by daily experience: for seedes are sowen, and rot, and yet notwithstanding so farre it is off that they perish, that contrariwise they grow vp farre more beautifull: and wheras they are sowen naked and drie, they spring vp greene from death by the vertue of God: and doeth it seeme incredible to thee that our bodies should rise from corruption, and that indued with a farre more excellent qualitie? 22 We see a diuersitie both in one and the selfe same thing which hath now one forme and then another, and yet keepeth it owne kind, as it is euident in a graine which is sowen bare, but springeth vp farre after another sort: and also in diuers kinds of one selfe same sort, as amongst beasts: and also among things of diuers sorts, as the heauenly bodies and the earthly bodies: which also differ very much one from another. Therefore there is no cause why wee should reiect either the resurrection of the bodies, or the changing of them into a better state, as a thing impossible, or strange. 23 Hee maketh three maner of qualities of the bodies being raised: Incorruption, to wit, because they shall bee sound and altogether of a nature that can not bee corrupt: Glorie, because they shall bee adorned with beautie and honour: Power, because they shall continue euerlasting, without meate, drinke, and all other helpes, without which this fraile life cannot keepe it selfe from corruption. s *Is buried, and man is hid as seede in the ground.* t *Voide of honour, voide of glorie and beautie.* u *Freed from the former weakenesse, whereas it is subiect to such alteration and change that it cannot mainetaine it selfe without meate and drinke and such other like helpes.* 24 Hee sheweth perfitely in one word this change of the qualitie of the body by the resurrection, when hee saith, that of a naturall body, it shall become a spirituall body: which two qualities being cleane different the one from the other he straightway expoundeth, and setteth foorth diligently. 25 That is called a naturall body which is quickned and maintained by a liuing soule onely such as Adam was, of whom all wee are borne naturally: and that is said to bee a spirituall, which together with the soule is quickned with a farre more excellent vertue, to wit, with the Spirit of God, which descendeth from Christ the second Adam into vs. x *Adam is called the first man: because hee is the roote as it were from whence wee spring, and Christ is the latter man: because he is the beginning of all them that are spirituall, and in him wee are all comprehended.* * Genesis 2.7. y *Christ is called a Spirit, by reason of that most excellent nature, that is to say, God who dwelleth in him bodily, as Adam is called a liuing soule, by reason of the soule which is the best part in him.* 26 Secondly hee willeth the order of this double state or qualitie to bee obserued, that the naturall was first, Adam being created of the clay of the earth: and the spirituall followeth and came vpon it, to wit, when as the Lord being sent from heauen, indued our flesh, which was prepared and made fit for him, with the fulnesse of the Godhead. z *Wallowing in durt, and wholly giuen to an earthly nature.* a *The Lord is said to come downe from heauen by that kind of speach, whereby that which is proper to one is vouched of another.* 27 Hee applieth both the earthly naturalnesse of Adam (if I may so say) to our bodies, so long as they are naturally conuersant vpon earth, to wit, in this life, and in the graue: and also the Spiritualtie of Christ to the same our bodies, after they are risen againe: and hee saith that that goeth before, and this shall followe. b *Not a vaine and false image, but such an one as had the trueth with it in deede.*

the earthly, so shall wee beare the image of the heauenly.

28 The conclusion: We cannot be partakers of the glory of God vnlesse we put off all that grosse and filthy nature of our bodies subiect to corruption, that the same body may be adorned with incorruptible glory.

50 [28] This I say, brethren, that [c] flesh and blood cannot inherite the kingdome of God, neither doeth corruption inherite incorruption.

c Flesh and blood are taken here for a liuing bodie, which cannot attaine to incorruption, vnlesse it put off corruption.

29 Hee goeth further, declaring that it shall come to passe that they which shall be found aliue in the latter day, shall not descend into that corruption of the graue, but shall be renewed with a sudden change, which change is very requisite: and that the certaine enioying of the benefite and victorie of Christ, is deferred vnto that latter time.

51 [29] Beholde, I shew you a [d] secret thing, Wee shall not all sleepe, but wee shall all bee changed,

d A thing that hath been hid, and neuer knowen hitherto, and therefore worthy that you giue good eare vnto it.

52 In [e] a moment, in the twinkling of an eie at the last *trumpet: for the trumpet shal blow, and the dead shall bee raised vp incorruptible, and we shalbe changed.

53 For this corruptible must put on incorruption, and this mortall *must* put on immortalitie.

54 So when this corruptible hath put on incorruption, & this mortall hath put on immortalitie, then shall be brought to passe the saying that is written, *Death is swallowed vp into victory.

55 O death where *is* thy sting? O graue where *is* thy victory?

56 The sting of death *is* sinne: and the strength of sinne *is* the Law.

57 * But thanks *be* vnto God, which hath giuen vs victorie through our Lorde Iesus Christ.

58 [30] Therefore my beloued brethren, bee yee stedfast, vnmooueable, abundant alwayes in the worke of the Lorde, forasmuch as ye knowe that your labour is not in vaine in the [f] Lord.

e He sheweth that the time shall be very short. *Matth.24.31.1.thess.4.16. *Ose.13 14 hebr.2.14. *1.Iohn 5.5. 30 An exhortation taken of the profit that ensueth, that seeing they vnderstand that the glory of the other life is layd vp for faithfull workemen, they continue and stand fast in the trueth of the doctrine of the resurrection of the dead. *f Through the Lords helpe and goodnesse working in vs.*

CHAP. XVI.

1 Hee exhorteth them to helpe the poore brethren of Hierusalem: 10 Then he commendeth Timothy, 13 and so with a friendly exhortation, 19 and commendations, endeth the Epistle.

1 Collections in old time were made by the Apostles appointment the first day of the week, on which day the maner was then to assemble themselues.

Concerning [1] the gathering for the Saints, as I haue ordained in the Churches of Galatia, so doe yee also.

2 Euery [a] first *day* of the weeke, let euery one of you put aside by himselfe, and lay vp as *God* hath [b] prospered him, that then there be no gatherings when I come.

a Which in times past was called Sunday, but now is called the Lords day

b That euery man bestow according to the abilitie that God hath blessed him with.

3 And when I am come, whomsoeuer ye shall allow by [c] letters, them wil I send to bring your liberalitie vnto Hierusalem.

4 [2] And if it be meete that I goe also, they shall goe with mee.

c Which you shall giue them to carrie. 2 The residue of the Epistle is spent in writing of familiar matters, yet so that all things be referred to his purposed marke, that is to say, to the glory of God, and the edifying of the Corinthians.

5 Now I will come vnto you, after I haue gone through Macedonia (for I will passe through Macedonia)

6 And it may be that I will abide, yea, or winter with you, that yee may bring me on my way, whithersoeur I goe.

7 For I will not see you now in my passage, but I trust to abide a while with you, if the Lord permit.

8 And I will tarie at Ephesus vntill Pentecost.

9 For a great doore and [d] effectual is opened vnto me: and there are many aduersaries.

d Very fit and conuenient to do great things by.

10 ¶ Now if Timotheus come, see that he be [e] without feare with you: for he worketh the worke of the Lord, euen as I *doe*.

e Without anie iust occasion of feare.

11 Let no man therefore despise him: but conuey him forth [f] in peace, that he may come vnto me, for I looke for him with the brethren.

f Safe and sound and that with all kinde of curtesie.

12 As touching *our* brother Apollos, I greatly desired him, to come vnto you with the brethren: but his minde was not at all to come at this time: howbeit he will come when he shall haue conuenient time.

13 ¶ Watch ye: stand fast in the faith: quite you like men, *and* be strong.

14 Let all your things be done in loue.

15 Now brethren, I beseech you (ye knowe the house of [g] Stephanas, that it is the first fruits of Achaia, and that they haue [h] giuen themselues to minister vnto the Saints:)

g Stephanas is the name of a man and not of a woman.

h Giuen themselues wholly to the ministery.

16 That yee bee [i] obedient euen vnto such, and to all that helpe with vs and labour.

i That you honor and reuerence them, be obedient to them, and bee content to be ruled by them, as meet is you should, seeing they haue bestowed themselues and their goods to helpe you withall.

17 I am glad of the comming of Stephanas, and Fortunatus, and Achaicus: for they haue supplied the want of you.

18 For they haue comforted my [k] spirit and yours: [l] acknowledge therefore such men.

k Mine heart.

l Take them for such men as they are in deede.

19 The Churches of Asia salute you: Aquila and Priscilla with the Church that is in their house, salute you greatly in the Lord.

20 All the brethren greet you. Greete yee one another with an * holy kisse.

*Rom.16.16. 2.cor.13.12. 1.pet.5.14.

21 The salutation of *mee* Paul with mine owne hand.

22 If any man loue not the Lord Iesus Christ, let him be had in execration [m] marana-tha.

m By these words, is betokened the seuerest kinde of curse and excommunication that was amongst the Iewes: and the words are as much to say, as our Lord commeth: So that his meaning may be this, Let him be accursed euen to the comming of the Lord, that is to say to his deaths day, euen for euer.

23 The grace of our Lord Iesus Christ *bee* with you.

24 My loue *be* with you all in Christ Iesus, Amen.

The first *Epistle* to the Corinthians, written from Philippi, *and sent* by Stephanas, and Fortunatus, and Achaicus, and Timotheus.

THE

THE SECOND EPISTLE OF PAVL TO THE CORINTHIANS.

CHAP. I.

1 He beginneth with the prayse of afflictions, 8 declaring what he hath suffered in Asia, 10 and how happily God assisted him. 17 He sayth it was not vpon any lightnesse that he came not according to his promise.

1 See the declaration of such salutations, in the former Epistles.

PAVL [1] an Apostle of Iesus
Christ, by the will of God,
and *our* brother Timotheus,
to the Church of GOD,
which is at Corinthus, with
all the Saintes which are
in all Achaia:

2 Grace *be* with you, and peace from God
our Father, and *from* the Lord Iesus Christ.

3 *[2] [a] Blessed *bee* God, euen the Father of
our Lord Iesus Christ, the Father of [b] mercies,
and the God of all comfort,

4 Which comforteth vs in all our tribulation, [3] that we may be able to comfort them
which are in any affliction by the comfort
wherewith wee our selues are comforted of
God.

5 For as the [c] sufferings of Christ abound
in vs, so our consolation aboundeth through
Christ.

6 [4] And whether wee bee afflicted, *it is* for
your consolation and saluation, which is
[d] wrought in the induring of the same suffrings
which we also suffer: or whether wee be comforted, *it is* for your consolation and saluation.

7 And our hope is stedfast concerning you,
in as much as wee knowe that as yee are partakers of the sufferings, so *shall yee be* also of the
consolation.

8 [5] For, brethren, we would not haue you
ignorant of our affliction, which came vnto vs
in Asia, how wee were pressed out of measure
passing strength, so that we altogether [e] doubted euen of life.

9 Yea, wee receiued the sentence of death
in [f] our selues, because wee should not trust in
our selues, but in God, which raiseth the dead.

10 Who deliuered vs from so [g] great a death,
and doeth deliuer *vs:* in whom wee trust, that
yet hereafter he will deliuer *vs,*

**Ephes.* 1.3. 1.*pet.* 1.3.

2 He beginneth after this maner with thankesgiuing, which notwithstanding (otherwise then he was wont) he appplieth to him selfe: beginning his Epistle, with the seting forth of the dignity of his Apostleship, constrained (as it should seeme) by their importunitie which tooke an occasion to despise him, by reason of his miseries. But he answereth, that he is not so afflicted but that his cōforts doe exceed his afflictions, shewing the ground of them, euen the mercie of God the Father in Iesus Christ.

a To him bee prayse and glory giuen.

b Most mercifull.

3 The Lord doth comfort vs to this ende and purpose, that we may so much the more surely comfort others.

c The miseries which we suffer for Christ, or which Christ suffereth in vs.

11 *[6] So that ye labour together in prayer
for vs, [7] that for the gift *bestowed* vpon vs for
many, thankes may be giuen by many persons
for vs.

12 [8] For our reioycing is this, the testimonie of our conscience, that in simplicitie and
godly [h] purenesse, *and* not in fleshly wisedome,
but by the [i] grace of God we haue had our conuersation in the world, and most of all to you
wards.

13 For wee write [k] none other things vnto
you, then that yee reade, or else that yee acknowledge, and I trust yee shall acknowledge
vnto the [l] end.

14 Euen as ye haue acknowledged vs partly, that wee are your [m] reioycing, euen as yee
are ours, in the [n] day of *our* Lord Iesus.

15 And in this confidence was I minded
first to come vnto you, that ye might haue had
a [o] double grace,

16 And to passe by you into Macedonia,
and to come againe out of Macedonia vnto
you, and to be led forth toward Iudea of you.

17 [9] When I therefore was thus minded,
did I vse lightnesse? or minde I those things
which I mind, according to the [p] flesh, that with
me should be, [q] Yea, yea, and Nay, nay?

18 [10] Yea, God is [r] faithfull, that our word
toward you was not Yea, and Nay.

19 [11] For the Sonne of God Iesus Christ,
who was preached among you by vs, *that is,*
by me, and Siluanus, and Timotheus, [s] was not
Yea, and Nay: but in [t] him it was Yea.

20 [12] For all the promises of God in him *are*
Yea, and are in [u] him Amen, vnto the glory of
God through [x] vs.

21 [13] And it is God which stablisheth vs
with you in Christ, and hath anointed vs.

22 Who hath also sealed vs, and hath giuen
the [y] earnest of the spirit in our hearts.

**Rom.* 15.30.

6 That he may not seeme to boast himselfe, he atttributeth all to God, and therewith also confesseth that he attributeth much to the prayers of the faithfull.

7 The end of the afflictions of the Saints, is the glory of God, and therefore they ought to be precious vnto vs.

8 Secondly he putteth away an other slander, to wit, that he was a light man, and such a one as was not lightly to be credited, seeing that hee promised to come vnto them, and came not. And first hee speaketh of the simplicitie of his minde, and sinceritie, which they knew both by his voyce when he was present, and they ought to acknowledge it also in his letters, being absent: and moreouer he protesteth that he will neuer be otherwise.

h With clearenesse, and holy and true plainenesse of mind, as God himselfe can witnes.

i Trusting to that very wisedome, which God of his free goodnesse hath giuen mee from heauen.

k He sayth, hee writeth barely and simplie: for he that writeth in coloured sort, is rightly sayd to write otherwise then we reade: and this he sayth the Corinthians shall truely knowe and like of very well. *l Perfectly.* *m Pauls reioycing in the Lord was, that hee had wonne the Corinthians: and they themselues reioyced that such an Apostle was their instructer, and taught them so purely and sincerely.* *n When he shall sit as iudge.* *o Another benefite.* 9 He putteth away their slaunder and false report by denying it, and first of all in that that diuers went about to perswade the Corinthians, that in the preaching of the Gospel, Paul agreed not to himselfe: for this was the matter and the case. *p As men doe which will rashly promise any thing, and change their purpose at euery turning of an hand.* *q That I should say and vnsay a thing?* 10 He calleth God to witnesse aud for Iudge, of his constancie in preaching and teaching one selfe same Gospel. *r True, and of whose faithfull witnesse it were horrible wickednesse to doubt.* 11 Hee ioyneth also with himselfe, his fellowes as witnesses with whom he fully consented in teaching one selfe same thing, to wit, one selfe same Christ. *s Was not diuers and wauering.* *t That is, in God.* 12 Last of all he declareth the summe of his doctrine, to wit, that all the promises of saluation are sure and ratified in Christ. *u Christ is set forth to exhibite and fulfill them also most assuredly, and without all doubt.* *x Through our ministerie.* 13 Hee attributeth the praise of this constancie, onely to the grace of God, through the holy Ghost, and therewithall concludeth, that they cannot doubt of his faith and his fellowes, without doing iniurie to the Spirit of God, seeing that they themselues doe knowe all this to be true. *y An earnest, is whatsoeuer is giuen to confirme a promise.*

4 Hee denieth that either his afflictions wherewith he was often afflicted, or the consolations which he receiued of God, may iustly bee despised, seeing that the Corinthians both ought and might take great occasion to bee confirmed by either of them. *d Although saluation bee giuen vs freely, yet because there is a way appointed vs whereby we must come to it, which is the race of an innocent and vpright life, which wee must runne, therefore we are said to worke our saluation, Philip.2.12. And because it is God onely that of his free good will worketh all things in vs, therefore is hee sayd to worke the saluation in vs by those selfe same things by which wee must passe to euerlasting life, after that wee haue once ouercome all incumbrances.* 5 Hee witnesseth that he is not only not ashamed of his afflictious, but that he desireth also to haue all men knowe the greatnesse of them, and also his deliuery from them, although it be not yet perfect. *e I knewe not at all what to doe, neither did I see by mans helpe which way to saue my life.* *f I was resolued within my selfe to die.* *g From these great dangers.*

23 [14]Now, I call God for a record vnto my [z]soule, that to spare you, I came not as yet vnto Corinthus.

24 [15]Not that we haue dominion ouer your faith, but we are helpers of your [a]ioy: for by faith ye stand.

14 Now comming to the matter, he sweareth that he did not onely, not lightly alter his purpose of comming to them, but rather that hee came not vnto them for this cause, that hee might not bee constrained to deale more sharply with them being present, then he would. *z Against my selfe, and to the danger of mine owne life.* 15 Hee remoueth all suspition of arrogancie, declaring that hee speaketh not as a Lord vnto them, but as a seruant, appointed of God to comfort them. *a Hee setteth the ioy and peace of conscience, which God is author of, against tyrannous feare, and therewithall sheweth the ende of the Gospel.*

CHAP. II.

1 He excuseth his not comming vnto them, 2 and priuily reprehendeth them. 4 He sheweth that such is his affection toward them, 5 that hee neuer reioyceth but when they are merrie. 6 Perceiuing the adulterer (whom he commanded to be deliuered vp to Satan) to repent, he requesteth that they forgiue him. 31 He mentioneth his going into Macedonia.

BVt I determined thus in my selfe, that I would not come againe to you in [a]heauinesse.

2 For if I make you sorie, who is he then that should make me glad, but the same which is made sorie by me?

3 And I wrote this same thing vnto you, lest when I came, I should take heauinesse of them, of whom I ought to reioyce: this [b]confidence haue I in you all, that my ioy is the *ioy* of you all.

4 For in great affliction, and anguish of heart I wrote vnto you with many teares: not that ye should be made sorie, but that ye might perceiue the loue which I haue, specially vnto you.

5 [1]And if any hath caused sorrowe, the same hath not made [c]mee sorie, but [d]partly (lest I should more [e]charge *him*) you all.

6 It is sufficient vnto the same man, that he was rebuke of many.

7 So that now contrariwise yee ought rather to [f]forgiue *him*, and comfort *him*, lest the same should bee swallowed vp with ouer much heauinesse.

8 Wherefore, I pray you, that you would [g]confirme your loue towards him.

9 For this cause also did I write, that I might knowe the proofe of you, whether yee would be obedient in all things.

10 To whome yee forgiue any thing, *I forgiue* also: for verely if I forgaue any thing, to whom I forgaue it, for your sakes *forgaue I it* in the [h]sight of Christ,

11 Lest Satan should circumuent vs: for we are not ignoraut of his [i]enterprises.

12 ¶ [2]Furthermore, when I came to Troas *to preach* Christs Gospel, and a doore was opened vnto me of the Lord,

13 I had no rest in my spirit, because I found not Titus my brother, but tooke my leaue of them, and went away into Macedonia.

a Causing griefe amongst you, which he should haue done, if hee had come to them before they had repented them. *b For I trusted that you would take that out of the way forthwith which you knew I was discontented with, considering how you are perswaded that my ioy is your ioy.* 1 Hee passeth to another part of this Epistle: which notwithstanding is put amongst the first, whereunto he returneth afterward: and he handleth the releasing and vnloosing of the incestuous person, because hee seemed to haue giuen sufficient testimony of his repentance: shewing the true vse of excommunication, to wit, that it proceede not of hatred, but of loue, and so end, lest if we keepe no measure, wee serue Satan the deuill. *c As if hee sayd, All that sorrow is so cleane wiped away, as though he had neuer felt it.* *d As for mee (saith Paul) I haue no more to doe with him.* *e Lest I should ouercharge him, who is burdened enough of himselfe, which I would bee glad were taken from him.* *f That whereas before you punished him sharply, you would now forgiue him.* *g That at my entreatie, you would declare by the consent of the whole Church, that you take him againe for a brother.* *h Truely, and from the heart.* *i Of his mischieuous counsel and deuilish will.* 2 He returneth to the confirmation of his Apostleship, & bringeth forth the testimonies, both of his labours, and also of Gods blessing.

14 Now thankes *be* vnto God, which alwayes maketh vs to triumph in Christ, and maketh manifest the [k]sauour of his knowledge by vs in euery place.

15 [3]For wee are vnto God the sweete sauour of Christ, in them that are saued, and in them which perish.

16 To the one *we are* the sauour of death, vnto death: and to the other the sauour of life, vnto life: [4]and who is sufficient for these things?

17 *For wee are not as many, which make [l]merchandise of the word of God: but as of sinceritie, but as of God in the sight of God speake we in Christ.

k He alludeth to the oynting of the Priests, and the incense of the sacrifices. 3 He denieth ye ought should be taken away frō the dignity of his Apostlship, because they sawe euidently that it was not receiued with like successe in euery place, nay rather very many reiected and detested him, seeing that hee preacheth Christ not onely as a Sauiour of them that beleeue, but also as a iudge of them that contemne him. 4 Againe, he putteth away all suspicion of arrogancie, attributing all things that he did, to the vertue of God, whom he serueth sincerely, and without all dishonest affection: whereof he maketh them witnesses, euen to the 6. verse of the next Chapter. **Chap. 4.2.* *l We doe not handle it craftily & couetously, or lesse sincerely then we ought: & he vseth a metaphore, which is taken from hucksters, which vse to play the false harlots with whatsoeuer commeth into their hands.*

CHAP. III.

1 Hee desireth no other commendation, 3 Then their continuing in the faith. 6 He is a Minister, not of the letter, but of the Spirit. 8 Hee sheweth the difference of the Lawe and the Gospel. 13 That the brightnesse of the Lawe doeth rather dimme the sight then lighten it: 18 But the Gospell doeth make manifest Gods countenance vnto vs.

DOe we begin to praise our selues againe? or neede we, as some other, epistles of recommendations vnto you, or *letters* of recommendation from you?

2 Ye are our epistle, written in our hearts, which is vnderstood, and read of all men,

3 In that ye are [a]manifest, to bee the Epistle of Christ, [b]ministred by vs, and written, not with inke, but with the Spirit of the [c]liuing God, [1]not in tables of stone, but in fleshly tables of the heart.

4 And such[d] trust haue we through Christ to God:

5 Not that we are sufficient of our selues, to thinke any thing, as of our selues: but our [e]sufficiencie *is* of God,

6 [2]Who also hath made vs able ministers of the new Testament, not of the [f]letter, but of the Spirit: for the letter killeth, but the Spirit giueth life.

7 If then the ministration of death *written* with letters [g]and ingrauen in stones, was [h]glorious, so that the children of Israel could not behold the face of Moses, for the glory of his countenance (which *glory* is done away.)

a The Apostle frameth his speach wisely, that by little and little, hee may come from the commendation of the person, to the matter it selfe. *b Which I tooke paines to write as it were.* *c By the way, he setteth the vertue of God, against the inke wherewith epistles are commonly written, to shew that it was wrought by God.* 1 He alludeth by the way, to the comparison of the outward ministerie of the priesthood of Leui, with the ministerie of the Gospel, and the Apostolicall ministerie, which he handleth afterward more fully. *d This boldnesse we shew, and thus gloriously may we boast of the worthinesse and fruit of our ministery.* *e In that we are fit and meete to make other men partakers of so great a grace.* 2 He amplifieth his ministerie and his fellowes: that is to say, the ministery of the Gospell comparing it with the ministerie of the Lawe, which he considereth in the person of Moses, by whom the Lawe was giuen: against whom he setteth Christ the Authour of the Gospel. Now this comparison is taken from the very substance of the ministery. The Lawe is as it were a writing of it selfe, dead, and without efficacie: but the Gospel, and new Couenant, as it were the verie vertue of God it selfe, in renewing, iustifying, and sauing of men. The Law propoundeth death, accusing all men of vnrighteousnesse: The Gospel offereth and giueth righteousnesse and life. The gouernance of the Lawe serued for a time to the promise: the Gospel remaineth to the ende of the worlde. Therefore what is the glorie of that in comparison of the maiestie of this? *f Not of the Lawe, but of the Gospel.* *g Imprinted and ingrauen: so that by this place we may plainely perceiue, that the Apostle speaketh not of the ceremonies of the Lawe, but euen of the ten commaundements.* *h This word, Glory, betokeneth a brightnesse, and a maiestie which was bodily in Moses, but spiritually in Christ.*

8 How shall not the [i]ministration of the
Spirit be more glorious?
9 For if the ministerie of condemnation
was glorious, much more doth the ministration
of [k]righteousnes exceede in glory.
10 For euen that which was glorified, was
not glorified in this point, *that is*, as touching
the exceeding glory.
11 For if that which should bee [l]abolished,
was glorious, much more shall that which remaineth, be glorious.
12 [3]Seeing then that we haue such trust, we
vse great boldnesse of speach.
13 *[4]And *we are* not as Moses, *which* put
a vaile vpon his face, that the children of Israel
should not looke vnto the [m]end of that which
should be abolished.
14 Therfore their minds are hardened: for
vntill this day remaineth the same couering
vntaken away in the reading of the old Testament, which *vaile* in Christ is put away.
15 But euen vnto this day, when Moses
is read, the vaile is layd ouer their hearts.
16 Neuerthelesse, when their *heart* shall be
turned to the Lord, the vaile shal be takē away.
17 Now the [n]Lord is the * Spirit, & where
the Spirit of the Lord *is*, there *is* libertie.
18 [5]But wee all behold as in a mirrour the
glory of the Lorde with open face, and are
changed into the same image, from glory to
glory, as by the Spirit of the Lord.

i Whereby God offereth, yea, and giueth the Spirit, not as a dead thing, but a quickening Spirit, working life. *k To wit, of Christ, which being imputed to vs as our owne, wee are not onely not cōdemned, but also we are crowned as righteous.* *l The Law, yea, and the ten commandements them selues, together with Moses, is abolished, if we consider the ministery of Moses apart by it selfe.* 3 He sheweth wherin standeth this glory of the preaching of the Gospel, to wit, in that that it setteth foorth plainely and euidently, that which the Law shewed darkely, for it sent them that heard it to bee healed of Christ, which was to come, after that it had wounded them. *Exod. 34. 34.* 4 Hee expoundeth by the way the allegory of Moses his couering, which was a token of the darkenesse and weaknesse that is in men, which were rather dulled by the bright shining of the Lawe then lightened: which couering was taken away by the comming of Christ, who lighteneth the hearts, and turneth them to the Lord, that we may bee brought from the slauery of this blindnesse, and set in the libertie of the light by the vertue of Christs Spirit. *m Into the very bottome of Moses his Ministerie.* *n Christ is that Spirit, which taketh away that couering, by working in our hearts, whereunto also the Lawe it selfe called vs, though in vaine, because it speaketh to dead men, vntill the Spirit quickeneth vs.* *John 4. 14.* 5 Going forwards in the allegorie of the couering, he compareth the Gospel to a glasse, which although it bee most bright and sparkeling, yet doeth it not onely not dasell their eyes, which looke in it as the Law doeth, but also transformeth them with it beames, so that they also be partakers of the glorie and shining of it, to lighten others: as Christ sayd vnto his, You are the light of the world, whereas he himselfe was the onely light. Wee are also commanded in another place, to shine as candles before the world, because we are partakers of Gods Spirit. But Paul speaketh here properly of the ministers of the Gospel, as it appeareth both by that that goeth before, and that that commeth after, and that, setting them his owne example and his fellowes.

CHAP. IIII.

1 *Hee sheweth that hee hath so laboured in preaching the Gospel,* 4 *that such are euen blinded of Satan, who doe not perceiue the brightnesse thereof,* 7 *that the same is caried in earthen vessels,* 10 *Who are subiect to many miseries,* 16 *and therefore hee exhorteth them by his owne example to bee couragious,* 17 *and contemne this present life.*

1 THerefore, [1]seeing that we haue this ministery, as wee haue receiued mercie, wee
[a]faint not:
2 But haue cast from vs the [b]cloakes of
shame, and walke not in craftinesse, neither
handle wee the word of God [c]deceitfully: but
in declaration of the trueth we approoue our
selues to euery mans conscience in the sight
of God.

1 Now hee plainely witnesseth that both hee and his fellowes (through the mercie of God) doe their vocation and duety vprightly and sincerely, neglecting all dangers. *a Though wee are broken in pieces with miseries and calamities, yet we yeelde not.* *b Subtiltie and all kinde of deceite which men hunt after, as it were dennes and lurking holes, to couer their shamelesse dealings withall.* *c This is that in the former Chapter hee called, making merchandise of the word of God.*

3 [2]If our Gospel bee then hid, it is hid to
them that are lost.
4 In whom the God of this world hath
blinded the mindes, *that is*, of the infidels, that
the [d]light of the glorious Gospel of Christ,
which is the [e]image of God, should not shine
vnto them.
5 [3]For wee preach not our selues, but
Christ Iesus the Lord, and our selues your seruants for [f]Iesus sake.
6 For God * [g]that commanded the light
to shine out of darkenesse, *is he* which hath shined in our hearts, to giue the [h]light of the
knowledge of the glory of God in the face of
Iesus Christ.
7 [4]But we haue this treasure in earthen vessels, [5]that the excellencie of that power might
be of God, and not of vs.
8 We are afflicted on euery side, yet *are
we* not in distresse: we are in doubt, but yet we
despaire not.
9 *Wee are* persecuted, but not forsaken:
cast downe, but we perish not.
10 [6]Euery where we beare about in our bodie the [i]dying of the Lord Iesus, that the life
of Iesus might bee also made manifest in our
bodies.
11 For we which [k]liue, are alwayes deliuered vnto death for Iesus sake, that the life
also of Iesus might bee made manifest in our
[l]mortall flesh:
12 [7]So then death worketh in vs, and life
in you.
13 [8]And because we haue the same [m]spirit
of faith, according as it is written, * I beleeued, and therefore haue I spoken, wee also beleeue, and therefore speake,
14 Knowing that hee which hath raised vp
the Lord Iesus, shall raise vs vp also by Iesus,
and shall set vs with you.
15 [9]For all things are for your sakes, [n]that
the most plenteous grace by the thankesgiuing of many, may redound to the prayse of
God.
16 Therefore we faint not, [10]but though

2 An obiection: Many heare the Gospel, and yet are no more lightned thereby, then by the preaching of the Lawe. He answereth, The fault is in the men themselues, whose eyes Satan plucketh out, who ruleth in this world. And yet notwithstanding doeth hee and his fellowes set forth the most cleare light of the Gospel to be seene and vpholden, seeing that Christ whom onely they preach, is he in whom onely God will bee knowen, and as it were seene. *d The light of plaine and lightsome preaching, which telleth forth the glory of Christ.* *e In whome the Father setteth forth himselfe to be seene and beholden.* 3 Hee remooueth according to his accustomed maner, all suspicion of ambition, auouching that he teacheth faithfully, but as a seruant, and witnessing that all this light which he and his fellowes giue to other, proceedeth from the Lord. *f To preach this selfe same Iesus to you.* *Gen. 1. 3.* *g Which made onely with his word.* *h That being lightned of God, we should in like sort giue that light to others.* 4 He taketh away a stumbling blocke, by which was darkened amongst some the bright shining of the ministery of the Gospel, to wit, because the Apostles were the most miserable of all men. Paul answereth, that hee and his fellowes are as it were, earthen vessels, but yet there is in them a most precious treasure. 5 He bringeth marueilous reasons, why the Lord doeth so afflict his chiefest seruants, to the end, saith hee, that all men may perceiue that they stand not by any mans vertue, but by the singular vertue of God, in that they die a thousand times, but neuer perish. 6 An amplification of the former sentence, wherein he compareth his afflictions to a dayly death, & the vertue of the Spirit of God in Christ, to life, which oppresseth that death. *i So Paul calleth that miserable estate and condition, that the faithfull, but especially the ministers are in.* *k Which liue that life, to wit, by the Spirit of Christ, amongst so many & so great miseries.* *l Subiect to that miserable condition.* 7 A very cunning conclusion: as if he would say, Therefore to be short we die that you may liue by our death, for that they ventured into all those dangers for the building of the Churches sake, and they ceased not to confirme all the faithfull with the examples of their patience. 8 He declareth the former sentence, shewing that hee and his fellowes die in a sort, to purchase life to others, but yet notwithstanding they are partakers of the same life with them: because they themselues doe first beleeue that, which they propound to other to beleeue, to wit, that they also shall be saued together with them in Christ. *m The same faith, by the inspiration of the same Spirit.* *Psal. 116. 10.* 9 Hee sheweth how this constancie is preserued in them, to wit, because they respect Gods glory, and the saluation of the Churches committed vnto them. *d When it shall please God to deliuer me, and restore me to you, that exceeding benefit which shall be powred vpon mee shall in like sort redound to the glory of God, by the thankesgiuing of many.* 10 Hee addeth as it were a triumphant song, how that hee is outwardly afflicted, but inwardly he profiteth dayly: and passeth not at all for all the miseries that may be susteined in this life, in comparison of that most constant and eternal glory.

our

our outward man perish, yet the inward man is o renewed dayly.

17 For our p light affliction which is but for a moment, causeth vnto vs a farre more excellent *and* an eternall waight of q glory:

18 While wee looke not on the things which are seene, but on the things which are not seene: for the things which are seene, *are* temporall: but the things which are not seene, *are* eternall.

o Gathereth new strength that the outward man bee not ouercome with the miseries which come freshly one vpon the necke of another, being maintained and vpholden with the strength of the inward man.

p Afflictions are not called light, as though they were light of themselues, but because they passed away quickely, when as in deede our whole life is of no great long continuance. *q Which remaineth for euer firme and stable, and can neuer be shaken.*

CHAP. V.

1 Hee continueth in the same argument, 6 touching the certaine hope of saluation 8 through faith, 12 not to prayse himselfe, 14 seeing hee hath God and his Church before his eyes, 17 and esteemeth nothing, but newnesse of life in Christ.

1 Taking occasion by the former comparison, hee compareth this miserable bodie as it is in this life, to a frail and brittle tabernacle, against which he setteth the heauenly tabernacle, so terming that sure and euerlasting condition of this same bodie glorified in heauen, in so much saith he, that we are not only not addicted to this tabernacle, but also doe with sobbes and sighs desire rather that tabernacle. And so this place also concerning the glory to come, is put within the treatise of the dignitie of the ministerie as the other was, whereof we spake in the beginning of the second chapter.

FOr 1 wee know that if our earthly house of this tabernacle bee destroyed, wee haue a building *giuen* of God, *that is*, an house not made with hands, *but* eternall in the heauens.

2 For therefore wee sigh, desiring to bee a clothed with our house, which is frō b heauen.

3 2 Because that if we be clothed, we shall not be found * naked.

4 For in deede wee that are in this tabernacle, sigh & are burdened, because we would not be vnclothed, but would be clothed vpon, that mortalitie might be swallowed vp of life.

5 And hee that hath c created vs for this thing, *is* God, who also hath giuen vnto vs the earnest of the Spirit.

6 3 Therefore wee are alway d bold, though we knowe that whiles we are at home in the body, we are absent from the Lord.

7 (For wee walke by e faith, and not by sight.)

8 Neuerthelesse, we are f bold, and loue rather to remoue out of the body, and to dwel with the Lord.

9 Wherefore also wee g couet, that both dwelling at home, and remoouing from home, we may be acceptable to him.

10 * 4 For wee must all h appeare before the iudgement seate of Christ, that euery man may receiue the things which are *done* in his bodie according to that he hath done, whether *it bee* good or euill.

11 5 Knowing therefore that i terrour of the Lord, we perswade men, and we are made manifest vnto God, and I trust also that wee are made manifest in your consciences.

12 6 For we praise not our selues againe vnto you, but giue you an occasion to reioyce of vs, that yee may haue *to answere* against them, which reioice in the k face, and not in the heart.

13 7 For whether we be out of our wit, *wee are it* to God: or whether wee bee in our right minde, *we are it* vnto you.

14 8 For that loue of Christ l constraineth vs,

15 Because wee thus iudge, that if m one bee dead for all, then were all dead, and he died for all, that they which liue, should not henceforth n liue vnto themselues, but vnto him which died for them, and rose againe.

16 9 Wherefore, henceforth knowe we no man after the flesh, 10 yea though wee had knowen Christ after the flesh, yet now henceforth knowe we *him* no more.

17 11 Therefore if any man *bee* in Christ, *let him be* a o new creature. * Olde things are passed away: beholde, all things are become newe.

18 12 And all things *are* of God, which hath reconciled vs vnto himselfe by Iesus Christ, and hath giuen vnto vs the ministerie of reconciliation.

19 For God was in Christ, and reconciled the world to himselfe, not imputing their sins vnto them, and hath p committed to vs the word of reconciliation.

20 Now then are we ambassadors for Christ: as though God did beseech *you* through vs, wee pray you in Christs stead, that ye be reconciled to God.

21 For he hath made him *to bee* q sinne for vs, which r knew no sinne, that we should bee made the s righteousnesse of God in him.

5 Now he passeth ouer, and taking occasion of the former sentence, returneth to the former chap. verse 16. confirming his owne sinceritie and his fellowes.

i That terrible iudgement.

6 Hee remoueth all suspition of pride, by a new reason, because it is behoueable, not for his part but for theirs, that his Apostleship be counted sincere against the vaine ostentation of a few others.

k In outward disguising, and that coloured shew of mans wisedome and eloquence, and not in true godlines, which is sealed in the heart.

7 The meaning is: Euen when I am mad (as some men think of me) whilest I seeme as a foole to boast my selfe, I doe it for your profite, no lesse then when I preach the Gosple simply vnto you.

8 He goeth forward in putting away all suspicion of desire of estimation and boasting: for ý loue of Christ, saith he, compelleth vs hereunto, that seeing he died for vs all, which were dead when as we liued to our selues (that is, while we were yet giuen to these earthly affections) we in like sort should consecrate our whole life, which we haue receiued of him, to him (to wit) being indued with the holy Ghost, to this end and purpose, that we should meditate vpon nothing but that which is heauenly. *l Possesseth vs wholly.* *m Hee speaketh here of sanctification, whereby it commeth to passe that Christ liueth in vs.* *n Looke Roman chapter 6 and 7.* 9 Hee sheweth what is is, not to liue to our selues but to Christ, to wit, to knowe no man according to the flesh, that is to say, to be conuersant amongst men as not to care for those worldly and carnall things, as they doe which respect a mans stocke, his countrey, forme, glory, riches, and such like, wherein men commonly dote and wearie themselues. 10 An amplification, This is, sayth hee, so true, that wee doe not now thinke carnally of Christ himselfe, who hath now left the worlde, and therfore must be considered of vs, spiritually. 11 An exhortation for euery man which is renewed with the spirit of Christ, to meditate heauenly things, and not earthly. *o As a thing made anew of God, for though a man be not newly created when God giueth him the spirit of regeneration, but onely his qualities are changed, yet notwithstanding it pleased the holy Ghost to speake so, to teach vs that wee must attribute all things to the glory of God: not that we are stockes and blockes, but because God createth in vs, both the will to will well, and the power to doe well.* * *Esai.43.19. reuelat.21.5.* 12 Hee commendeth the excellencie of the ministerie of the Gospel, both by the authoritie of God himselfe, who is the author of that ministerie, and also by the excellencie of the doctrine of it: for it announceth atonement with God, by free forgiuenesse of our sinnes, and iustification offered vnto vs in Christ, and that so louingly and liberally, that God himselfe doth after a sort pray men by the mouth of his ministers to haue consideration of themselues, and not to despise so great a benefit. And when he so sayth, he plainely reprehendeth them which falsly challenged to themselues the name of Pastors. *p Vsed our labour and trauaile.* *q A sinner, not in himselfe, but by imputation of the guilt of all our sinnes to him.* *r Who was cleane voyde of sinne.* *s Righteous before God, and that with righteousnesse, which is not essentiall to vs, but being essentiall in Christ, God imputeth it to vs through faith.*

a He calleth the glorie of immortalitie, which we shall be as it were clothed with, a garment. *b Heauenly, not that the substance of it is heauenly, but for the glorie of it.* 2 An exposition of the former saying: We doe not without cause desire to be clad with the heauenly house, that is, with that euerlasting and immortall glory, as with a garment: for when we depart hence, we shall not remaine naked, hauing once cast off the couering of this bodie, but we shall take our bodies againe, which shall put on as it were another garment besides: and therefore we sigh not for the wearinesse of this life, but for the desire of a better life: Neither is this desire in vaine, for we are made to that life, the pledge whereof we haue, euen the Spirit of adoption. * *Reuel.16.15.* *c He meaneth that first creation, to giue vs to vnderstand, that our bodies were made to this ende, that they should be clothed with heauenly immortalitie.* 3 Hee inferreth vpon that sentence that went next before, thus, Therefore seeing that we knowe by the Spirit, that wee are strangers so long as wee are here, wee patiently suffer this tariance (for we are now so with God, that we behold him but by faith, and are therefore now absent from him) but so that we aspire and haue a longing alwayes to him: therefore also we behaue our selues so, that we may be acceptable to him, both while wee liue here, and when we goe from hence to him. *d Hee calleth them (bold) which are alwayes resolued with a quiet and setled mind to suffer what danger soeuer, nothing doubting but their end shall bee happie.* *e Faith, of those things which wee hope for, and not hauing God presently in our viewe.* *f And yet wee are in such sort bolde and doe so passe on our pilgrimage with a valiant and quiet mind, that yet notwithstanding wee had rather depart hence to the Lorde.* *g And seeing it is so, wee striue to liue so, that both in this our pilgrimage here we may please him, and that at length we may bee receiued home to him.* * *Rom.14.10.* 4 That no man might thinke it to pertaine to all, which hee spake of that heauenly glory, hee addeth, that euery one shall first render an account of his pilgrimage, after that hee is departed from hence. *h Wee must all appeare personally, and enquirie shall be made of vs, that all may see, how we haue liued.*

CHAP.

CHAP. VI.

1 Hee exhorteth them to leade their liues as it becommeth Christians, 5 neither to be dismayed in tribulation, 9 nor puffed vp with glory: 14 to auoyde all vncleanenesse, 16 considering that they are the temples of the liuing God.

1 Men doe not onely neede the ministerie of the Gospel, before they haue receiued grace that they may be partakers of it, but also after they haue receiued grace that they may continue in it.
2 In that that grace is offered, it is of the grace of God, who hath appointed times & seasons to all things, that wee may take occasion when it is offred.
* *Esai 49.8.*
a Which I of my free mercie and loue towards thee liked of and appointed: at which time God powred out that his marueilous loue vpon vs.
3 He sheweth the Corinthians a paterne of a true minister in his owne example and Timotheus and Syluanus, to the end, that (as he purposed from the beginning) he might procure authority to himselfe and his like.
b Declare and shew indeede.
* *1.Cor.4.1.*
4 He first of all reckoneth vp those things, which are neither alwayes in the ministers, nor without exception, vnlesse it be according to the affection of the minde, patience onely except, which also is one of ẏ vertues which ought to be alwaies in a good minister.
c In tossing to and fro, finding no place of rest and quietnesse.

SO [1] wee therefore as workers together beseech *you*, that ye receiue not the grace of
God in vaine.
2 [2] For hee sayth, * I haue heard thee in a
time [a] accepted, and in the day of saluation haue
I succoured thee: beholde now the accepted
time, behold now the day of saluation.
3 [3] We giue no occasion of offence in any
thing, that *our* ministery should not bee reprehended.
4 But in all things we [b] approue our selues
as * the ministers of God, [4] in much patience,
in afflictions, in necessities, in distresses,
5 In stripes, in prisons, in [c] tumults, in labours,
6 [5] By watchings, by fastings, by puritie,
by knowledge, by long suffering, by kindnesse,
by the holy Ghost, by loue vnfained,
7 By the [d] word of trueth, by the [e] power
of God, by the [f] armour of righteousnesse on
the right hand, and on the left,
8 By honour, and dishonour, by euil report,
and good report, as deceiuers, and *yet* true:
9 As vnknowen, and *yet* knowen: as dying, and beholde, wee liue: as chastened, and
yet not killed:
10 As sorrowing, and *yet* alway reioycing:
as poore, and *yet* make many rich: as hauing
nothing, and *yet* possessing all things.
11 [6] O Corinthians, our mouth is [g] open
vnto you: our heart is made large.
12 Yee are not [h] kept strait in vs, but ye are
kept streight in your owne [i] bowels.
13 Nowe for the same recompence, I
speake as to *my* children, Be you also inlarged.
14 [7] Be not vnequally yoked with the infidels: for * what fellowship hath righteousnes
with vnrighteousnesse? and what communion
hath light with darkenesse?
15 And what concord hath Christ with
Belial? or what [k] part hath the beleeuer with
the Infidell?
16 And what agreement hath the Temple of God with idols? * for ye are the Temple
of the [l] liuing God: as God hath sayd, * I will
[m] dwell among them, and walke there: and I
will be their God, and they shall be my people.
17 * Wherefore come out from among
them, and separate your selues, sayth the Lord,
and touch none vncleane thing, and I will receiue you.
18 * And I will bee a Father vnto you, and
yee shall be my sonnes and daughters, sayth the
Lord almightie.

m God dwelleth with vs, because Christ is become God with vs.
* *Isai 52.11.*
* *Iere. 31.1.*

CHAP. VII.

1 Lest by ouermuch vrging them hee should dismay their tender minds, 2 he proueth that all that he sayd, 4 proceeded of the great good will hee bare vnto them: 8 and therefore they should not bee offended that hee made them sorie, 10 and brought them to repentance not to bee repented of.

SEeing then we haue these promises, dearely
beloued, let vs cleanse our selues from all
filthinesse of the [a] flesh and spirit, and finish *our*
sanctification in the feare of God.
2 [1] [b] Receiue vs: we haue done wrong to
no man: we haue corrupted no man: we haue
defrauded no man.
3 I speake it not to *your* [c] condemnation:
for I haue sayd before, that ye are in our hearts,
to die and liue together.
4 I vse great boldnesse of speach toward
you: I reioyce greatly in you: I am filled with
comfort, and am exceeding ioyous in all our
tribulation.
5 For when we were come into Macedo-
nia, our flesh had no rest, but we were troubled
on euery side, fightings without, and terrours
within.
6 But God, that comforteth the [d] abiect,
comforted vs at the [e] comming of Titus:
7 And not by his comming onely, but also
by the consolation wherewith he was comforted of you, when hee told vs your great desire,
your mourning, your feruent mind to me ward
so that I reioyced much more.
8 [2] For though I made you sorie with a
letter, I repent not, though I did repent: for
I perceiue that the same Epistle made you sory,
though *it were* but for a season.
9 I now reioice, not that ye were sory, but
that ye sorrowed to [f] repentance: for yee sorrowed godly, so that in nothing yee were hurt
by vs.
10 For [g] godly sorrow causeth repentance
vnto saluation, not to be repented of: but the
worldly sorrow causeth death.
11 For behold this thing that ye haue been
godly sory, what great care it hath wrought in
you: yea, what clearing of your selues: yea,
what indignation: yea, *what* feare: yea, *how*
great desire: yea, *what* a zeale: yea, *what* reuenge: in all things yee haue shewed your
selues, that ye are pure in this matter.

a Both of bodie and soule, that by this meanes the sanctification may be perfect consisting in both the parts thereof.
1 He returneth againe from that admonition to his owne person, opposing the testimonies both of his faithfulnes and also of his continuall good will towards them.
b Let mee haue some place amongst you, that I may teach you.
c To condemne you of vnkindnes or treacherie.
d Whose hearts are cast downe, and are very farre spent.
e With those things which Titus tolde me of you at his comming, to wit, how fruitfully you reade ouer my letters, moreouer and besides that I am exceedingly refreshed with his presence.
2 An obiection: But thou hast hādled vs roughly: the Apostle answereth that hee vsed not this roughnes without griefe. And he addeth moreouer, ẏ he is also glad now that he draue them to that sorrow, although it was against his will, since it was so profitable vnto them: for there is a sorrow not only praise worthy, but also necessary, to wit, whereby repentāce groweth by certaine degrees, for the which repentance hee praysteth them highly. And this is the fifth part of this Epistle.

place of rest and quietnesse. 5 Secondly hee reckoneth vp such vertues as are necessarie, and ought alwayes be in them, and whereby as by good armour, all lets and hinderances may be ouercome. *d Preaching of the Gospel.* *e Power to worke miracles, and to bring vnder the wicked.* *f Vprightnesse.* 6 Going about to rebuke them, he sayth first, that hee dealeth with them sincerely and with an open and plaine heart, and therewithall complaineth that they doe not the like in louing againe their Father. *g The opening of the mouth and heart, betokeneth a most earnest affection in him that speaketh, as it fareth commonly with them that are in some great ioy.* *h You are in my heart, as in an house, and that no narrow or straite house, for I haue opened my whole heart to you, but you are inwardly strait laced to mee ward.* *i After the manner of the Hebrewes, heee calleth those tender affections which rest in the heart, bowels.* 7 Now he rebuketh them boldly, for that they became fellowes with infidels in outward idolatrie, as though it were a thing indifferent. And this is the fourth part of this Epistle, the conclusion whereof is, that such as the Lord hath vouchsafed the name of his Children, must keepe themselues pure, not onely in mind, but also in bodie, that they may wholly bee holy vnto the Lord. * *Eccles. 13. 18.* *k What can there bee betweene them?* * *1.Cor. 3.16. and 6.19.* *l Hee setteth the liuing God against Idoles.* * *Leuit. 26.11.*

f Insomuch that that sorrow did you much good towards the amending of your lewdnesse and sinnes. *g Godly sorrow is when wee are not terrified with the feare of punishment, but because wee feele wee haue offended God our most mercifull father. Contrarie to this there is another sorrow, that onely feareth punishment, or when a man is vexed for the losse of some worldly goods: the fruit of the first is repentance, the fruit of the second is desperation, vnlesse the Lord helpe speedily.*

12 Where-

12 Wherefore, though I wrote vnto you, I did it not for his cauſe that had done the wrong, neither for his cauſe that had the iniurie, but that our care toward you in the [h] ſight of God might appeare vnto you.

h It was not coloured nor counterfeit, but ſuch as I dare ſtand to before God.

13 Therefore we were comforted, becauſe yee were comforted: but rather wee reioyced much more for the ioy of Titus, becauſe his ſpirit was refreſhed by you all.

14 For if that I haue boaſted any thing to him of you, I haue not beene aſhamed: but as I haue ſpoken vnto you all things in trueth, euen ſo our boaſting vnto Titus was true.

15 And his inward affection is more abundant toward you, when he remembreth the obedience of you all, *and* how with feare and trembling ye receiued him.

16 I reioyce *therefore*, that I may put my confidence in you in all things.

CHAP. VIII.

1 Hee exhorteth them, by the example of the Macedonians, 9 and alſo euen of Chriſt himſelfe, 14 to be liberall towards the Saints. 16 For which purpoſe, he ſheweth that Titus, 18 and another brother came vnto them.

WEe [1] doe you alſo to wit, brethren, of the [a] grace of God beſtowed vpon the Churches of Macedonia,

2 Becauſe in [b] great triall of affliction their ioy abounded, and their moſt extreme pouerty abounded vnto their rich liberalitie.

3 For to *their* power (I beare record) yea, and beyond their power, they were [c] willing,

4 And prayed vs with great inſtance, that wee would receiue the [d] grace, and fellowſhip of the miniſtring which is toward the Saints.

5 [2] And *this they did*, not as we looked for: but gaue their owne ſelues, firſt to the Lord, and *after* vnto vs by the will of God,

6 That we ſhould exhort Titus, that as he had begun, ſo hee would alſo accompliſh the ſame grace among you alſo.

7 Therefore, as ye abound in euery thing, in faith and word, and knowledge, and in all diligence, and in your loue towards vs, *euen ſo ſee* that ye abound in this grace alſo.

8 [3] This ſay I not by commandement, but becauſe of the [e] diligence of others: therefore prooue I the [f] naturalneſſe of your loue.

9 [4] For ye know the grace of our Lord Ieſus Chriſt, that hee being rich, for your ſakes became poore, that yee through his pouertie might be made rich.

10 [5] And I ſhewe *my* mind herein: for this is expedient for you, which haue begun not to doe onely, but alſo to [g] will, a yeere agoe.

1 The ſixt part of this Epiſtle conteining diuers exhortations to ſtirre vp the Corinthians to liberalitie, wherewith the pouertie of the Church of Hieruſalem might be holpen in time conuenient. And firſt of all he ſetteth out before them the example of the Churches of Macedonia, which otherwiſe were brought by great miſery to extreme pouertie, to the ende that they ſhould follow them.
a The benefite that God beſtowed vpon the Churches.
b For thoſe manifold afflictions wherewith the Lord tried them, did not only not quaile their ioyfull readineſſe, but alſo made it much more excellent and famous.
c Of their owne accord they were liberall.
d He calleth that, Grace, that other men would haue called a burden. And this verſe is to be expounded by the ſixt verſe.
2 Hee amplifieth the forwardneſſe of the Macedonians, in this, that they alſo deſired Paul to ſtirre vp the Corinthians to accompliſh the giuing of almes, by ſending againe of Titus vnto them. 3 Thirdly, hee warneth them, that they deceiue not their expectation which they haue conceiued of them. *e At the requeſt of the Macedonians. f Then appeareth the naturalneſſe of our loue, when as indeede, and that frankely and freely, wee helpe our brethren euen for Chriſt his ſake.* 4 The fourth argument taken from the example of Chriſt. 5 Hee taketh good heede that hee ſeeme not to wreſt it out of them by conſtraint, for vnleſſe it be voluntarie, God doeth not accept it. *g Not onely to doe, but alſo to doe willingly: for hee noteth out a readie willingneſſe, without any inforcement by any other men, much leſſe came it of ambition and vaine glory.*

11 Now therefore performe to doe it alſo, that as *there was* a readineſſe to will, euen ſo ye may performe it of that which ye haue.

12 [6] For if there bee firſt a willing minde, it is accepted according to that a man hath, and not according to that he hath not.

13 [7] Neither *is it* that other men ſhould be eaſed, and you grieued: but vpon [h] like condition, at this time your abundance *ſupplyeth* their lacke:

14 That alſo their abundance may be for your lacke, that there may be equalitie:

15 As it is written, * He that *gathered* much, had nothing ouer, and hee that *gathered* little, had not the leſſe.

16 [8] And thankes *be* vnto God, which hath put in the heart of Titus the ſame care for you.

17 Becauſe hee accepted the exhortation, yea, he was ſo carefull that of his owne accord he went vnto you.

18 And we haue ſent alſo with him the brother, whoſe praiſe *is* [i] in the Goſpel thorowout all the Churches.

19 (And not ſo onely, but is alſo choſen of the Churches to bee a fellow in our iourney, concerning this [k] grace that is miniſtred by vs vnto the glory of the ſame Lord, and *declaration* of your prompt minde)

20 Auoiding this, that no man ſhould blame vs in this [l] abundance that is miniſtred by vs,

21 * Prouiding for honeſt things, not only before the Lord, but alſo before men.

22 And wee haue ſent with them our brother, whom wee haue oft times prooued to be diligent in many things, but now much more diligent, for the great confidence, which *I haue* in you.

23 Whether *any doe enquire* of Titus, *he is* my fellow and helper to you ward: or of our [m] brethren, they are meſſengers of the Churches, *and* the [n] glory of Chriſt.

24 Wherefore ſhew toward them, and before the [o] Churches the proofe of your loue, and of the reioycing that we haue of you.

6 Againſt ſuch as vſe to excuſe themſelues, becauſe they are not rich, as though it were onely proper to rich men to helpe the poore.
7 Chriſtian liberalitie is mutuall, that proportion may be obſerued.
h That like as now in your abundance you helpe others, which are poore, with ſome part of your goods, ſo ſhould others in like ſort beſtow ſome of theirs vpon you.
* Exod. 16. 18.
8 He commendeth Titus and his two companions for many cauſes both that their credite might not be ſuſpected, as though he had ſent them ſlily to ſpoile the Churches, & alſo that they might be ſo much the readier to contribute.
i In the preaching of the Goſpel.
k Theſe almes which are beſtowed for the reliefe of the Church of Hieruſalem.
l In this plentifull liberalitie of the Churches, which is committed to our truſt.
* Rom. 12. 17.
m Titus his two companions.
n By whom the glory of Chriſt is ſet foorth.
o All Churches ſhall be witneſſes of this your godly dealing, in whoſe preſence you are, for ſo much as you ſee the meſſengers whom they haue choſen by all their conſents, and ſent them vnto you.

CHAP. IX.

1 Why, albeit hee thinke well of their readie willes, 3 yet earneſtly exhorteth them, 4 he yeeldeth a reaſon. 6 He compareth almes to ſeede ſowing, 13 which God doth repay with great gaines.

FOr [1] as touching the miniſtring to the Saints, it is ſuperfluous for me to write vnto you.

2 For I knowe your readineſſe of minde, whereof I boaſt my ſelfe of you vnto them of Macedonia, *and ſay*, that Achaia was prepared a yere agoe, & your zeale hath prouoked many.

3 Now haue I ſent the brethren, leſt our reioycing ouer you ſhould be in vaine in this behalfe, that yee (as I haue ſaid) be readie:

1 Hee wiſely meeteth with the ſuſpicion which the Corinthians might conceiue, as though the Apoſtle in vrging them ſo carefully ſhould doubt of their good will. Therfore he witneſſeth that he doeth it not to teach them that they ought to helpe the Saints, ſeeing that he had become ſuretie for them to the Macedonians, but only to ſtirre them vp which were running of themſelues, to the end that all things might both be in a better readineſſe, and alſo be more plentifull.

4 Left if they of Macedonia come with
me, and finde you vnprepared, wee (that wee
may not fay, you) fhould be afhamed in this
my [a] conftant boafting.
5 Wherefore, I thought it neceffarie to
exhort the brethren to come before vnto you,
and to finifh your beneuolence appointed a-
fore, that it might be readie, *and come* as of beneuolence, and not as of [b] niggardlineffe.
6 [2] This yet *remember*, that he which foweth fparingly, fhall reape alfo fparingly, and he
that foweth liberally, fhall reape alfo liberally.
7 As euery man [c] wifheth in his heart, *fo*
let him giue, not * [d] grudgingly, or of [e] neceffi-
tie: * for God loueth a cheerefull giuer.
8 And God is able to make [f] all grace to
abound toward you, that ye alwayes hauing all
fufficiencie in all things, may abound in [g] euery good worke,
9 (*As it is written, Hee hath fparfed a-
broad and hath giuen to the poore: his beneuolence remaineth for [h] euer.
10 Alfo he that findeth feede to the fower,
will minifter likewife bread for food, and multiply your feede, and increafe the fruits of your
beneuolence,)
11 That on all parts yee may be made rich
vnto all liberalitie, which caufeth through vs
thankfgiuing vnto God.
12 [3] For the miniftration of this feruice not
only fupplieth the neceffities of the Saints, but
alfo abundantly caufeth many to giue thankes
to God,
13 (Which by the [k] experiment of this miniftration praife God for your [l] voluntarie fub-
miffion to the Gofpel of Chrift, and for your
liberall diftribution to them, and to all men)
14 And in their prayer for you, to long after you greatly, for the abundant grace of
God in you.
15 [m] Thankes therefore *be* vnto God for
his vnfpeakeable gift.

a The word which he vfeth, fignifieth fuch a ftaiedneffe and fetledneffe of mind as cannot be mooued with any terrour or feare.
b As from couetous men.
2 Almes muft be giuen neither niggardly, nor with a loathfull minde, or hardly: but a franke and free almes is compared to a fowing which hath a moft plentifull haruelt of moft abundant bleffing following it.
c Determineth and appointeth freely with himfelfe.
*Rom. 12.8.
d With a fparing and niggardly heart.
e Againft his will, as loth to be euill reported of.
*Ecclef. 35.10.
f All God his bountifull liberalitie.
g To helpe others by all meanes poffible, in doing them good in their neceffities.
*Pfal. 112.9.
h Is euerlafting: Now Dauid fpeaketh of a man that feareth God, and loueth his neighbour, who fhall neuer want (fayth hee) to giue to others.
i There is none fo good an inheritance to the godly, as bountifulnes is.
3 An other excellent and double fruit of liberalitie towards the Saints, is this: that it giueth occafion to praife God, and that our faith alfo is thereby made manifeft. *k By this proofe of your liberalitie in this helping and fuccouring of them. l In fhewing with one confent, that you acknowledge that onely Gofpel, which you haue willingly fubmitted your felues vnto, declaring thereby, that you agree with the Church of Hierufalem. m Left by this great commendation and praife, the Corinthians fhould be puffed vp, he fhutteth vp this exhortation, with this exclamation.*

CHAP. X.

2 He fheweth with what confidence, 4 with what weapons, 6 and with what reuenge he is armed againft the cauillations of the wicked, 7 and that, when hee is prefent, his deedes haue no leffer power, 11 then his words haue force, when he is abfent.

Now [1] I Paul my felfe befeech you by the
meekeneffe, and [a] gentleneffe of Chrift,
which when I am prefent among you *am* bafe,
but am bold toward you being abfent:

1 He returneth to the defence of his Apoftlefhip, but fo that he vfeth his authoritie therein: for he warneth them earneftly and grauely, vfing alfo terrible threatnings, to fhew themfelues fuch as are apt to be inftructed. And he refelleth certaine proud men which made no better account of him, then of a bragging Thrafo, in that hee vfed to be fharpe againft them when hee was abfent, becaufe they faw no great maieftie in him after the maner of men, and befides had prooued his lenitie, notwithftanding that in his abfence, he had written to them fharpely. Therefore firft of all he profeffeth that he was gentle and moderate, but after the example of Chrift: but if they continue ftill to defpife his gentleneffe, he protefteth vnto them that hee will fhewe in deede how farre they are deceiued, which make that account of the office of an Apoftle, that they doe of worldly offices, that is, according to the outward appearance. *a That nature which is enclined to mercie, rather then to rigour of iuftice.*

2 And *this* I require you, that I neede not
to be bolde when I am prefent, with that fame
confidence, wherewith I thinke to be bolde a-
gainft fome, which efteeme vs as though wee
walked [b] according to the flefh.
3 [2] Neuertheleffe, though we walke in the
flefh, yet we doe not warre after the flefh.
4 (For the weapons of our warrefare are
not [c] carnall, but mightie through [d] God, to
caft downe holdes)
5 Cafting downe the imaginations, and
euery high thing that is exalted againft the
knowledge of God, [3] and bringeth into capti-
uity euery thought to the obedience of Chrift,
6 And hauing readie the vengeance a-
gainft all difobedience, when your obedience
is fulfilled.
7 [4] Looke ye on things after the [e] appearance? If any man truft in himfelfe that hee is
Chriftes, let him confider this againe of [f] himfelfe, that as hee *is* Chriftes, euen fo *are* wee
Chriftes.
8 For though I fhould boaft fomewhat
more of our authoritie, which the Lord hath
giuen vs for edification, and not for your deftruction, I fhould haue no fhame.
9 *This I fay*, that I may not feeme as *it*
were to feare you with letters.
10 For the letters, fayth [g] hee, are fore and
ftrong, but his bodily prefence is weake, and
his fpeech is of no value.
11 Let fuch one thinke this, that fuch as
wee are in word by letters, when wee are abfent, fuch *will we be* alfo in deed, when wee are
prefent.
12 [5] For wee [h] dare not make our felues of
the number, or to compare our felues to them,
which praife themfelues: but they vnderftand
not that they meafure themfelues with [i] themfelues, and [k] compare themfelues with themfelues.
13 But wee will not reioyce of things,
which are not within *our* [l] meafure, *but according to the meafure of the line, whereof
God hath diftributed vnto vs a meafure to attaine euen vnto you.
14 For wee ftretch not our felues beyond
our meafure, as though wee had not attained
vnto you: for euen to you alfo haue we come
in preaching the Gofpel of Chrift,
15 Not boafting of things which are [m] without *our* meafure: *that is*, of other mens labors:
and we hope, when your faith fhall increafe, to
be magnified by you according to our line a-
bundantly,
16 And to preach the Gofpel in thofe *re-*

b As though I had no other aide and helpe then that which outwardly I feeme to haue: and therefore Paul fetteth his flefh, that is, his weake condition and ftate, againft his fpirituall and Apoftolike dignitie.
2 Secondly, he witneffeth, that although he be like vnto other men, yet hee commeth furnifhed with that ftrength, which no holds of man can match, whether they refift by craft and deceit, or by force and might, becaufe he warrefareth with diuine weapons.
c Are not fuch as men get them authoritie withall one of another, and doe great acts.
d Stand vpon that infinite power of God.
3 An amplification of this fpirituall vertue, which in fuch fort conquereth the enemies, be they neuer fo craftie and mightie, that it bringeth fome of them by repentance vnto Chrift, and iuftly reuengeth others that are ftubbornly obftinate, feparating them from the other which fuffer themfelues to be ruled.
4 He beateth into their heads that fame matter, with great weight of words and fentences.
e Do ye iudge of things according to the outward fhewe?
f Not being tolde of it by me.
g He noteth out fome one that was the feeds-man of this fpeech.
5 Being conftrained to refell the foolifh brags of certaine ambitious men: he witneffeth, that they are able to bring nothing, but that they falfly perfwade themfelues of themfelues: and as for himfelfe, although he brag of excellent things, yet he will not paffe the bounds which God hath meafured him out, according whereunto he came euen vnto them in preaching the Gofpel of Chrift, and trufteth that hee fhall goe further, when they haue fo profited that hee fhall not neede to tary any longer amongft them to inftruct them. And hereunto is added an amplification, in that hee neuer fucceeded other men in their labours. *h This is fpoken after a taunting fort. i Vpon a vaine perfwafion that they haue of themfelues, they take vpon them they care not what. k They contemne another, and meafure all their doings onely by themfelues. l Of thofe things which God hath not meafured to me.* *Ephef. 4.7. *m As though God had diuided the whole world among the Apoftles, to be husbanded.*

gions which *are* beyond you: not to reioyce in
[n] another mans line, *that is*, in the things that
are prepared alreadie.
17 *[6] But let him that reioyceth, reioyce
in the Lord.
18 For hee that praiseth himselfe is not allowed, but he whom the Lord praiseth.

n In countreys which other men haue prepared and husbanded with the preaching of the Gospel.
* *Iere.9.24. 1.cor.1 31.*
6 He somewhat mitigateth that which he spake of himselfe, and therewith also prepareth the Corinthians to heare other things, witnessing that hee seeketh nothing else but to approoue himselfe to God, whose glory he only seeketh.

CHAP. XI.

2 He testifieth, that for the great loues sake he beareth to the Corinthians, hee is compelled 5 to vtter his owne prayses: 9 And that hee bestowed his labour on them without any reward, 15 that the false apostles should not surpasse him in any thing, 22 whom hee farre excelled in those things which are praise worthy indeede.

Would [1] to God, yee could suffer a little my foolishnesse, and in deed, ye
suffer me.
2 For I am iealous ouer you with [a] godly
iealousie: for I haue prepared you for one husband, to [b] present you *as* a pure virgine to
Christ:
3 But I feare lest as the * serpent beguiled
Eue through his subtiltie, so your mindes
should be [c] corrupt from the simplicitie that is
in [d] Christ.
4 [2] For if hee that commeth, preacheth
[e] another Iesus whom wee haue not preached:
or if yee receiue another spirit whom yee haue
not receiued: either another Gospel, which ye
haue not receiued, ye might well haue suffered *him*.
5 Verely I suppose that I was not inferiour to the very chiefe Apostles.
6 [3] And though *I be* [f] rude in speaking,
yet *I am* not *so* in knowledge, but among you
we haue been made manifest to the vttermost,
in all things.
7 [4] Haue I committed an offence, because
I abased my selfe, that yee might be exalted,
and because I preached to you the Gospel of
God freely?
8 I robbed other Churches, and tooke
wages *of them* to doe you seruice.
9 And when I was present with you, and
had need,* I was not slothful to the hinderance
of any man: for that which was lacking vnto
me, the brethren which came from Macedonia
supplied, & in all things I kept [5] and will keepe
my selfe, that I should not be grieuous to you.

1 He granteth that after a sort he playeth the foole in this vaunting of things, but he addeth that hee doeth it against his will for their profite, because he seeth them deceiued by certaine vaine and craftie men, through the craft and subtiltie of Satan.
a He speaketh as a woer, but yet as one that seeketh them not for himselfe, but for God.
b To marry you together.
* *Gen 3.4.*
c This place is to be marked against them, which lothe that plaine and pure simplicitie of the Scriptures, in comparison of the colours and paintings of mans eloquence.
d Which is meete for them that are in Christ.
2 He sheweth that they deceiue themselues, if they looke to receiue of any other man, either a more excellent Gospel, or more excellent gifts of the holy Ghost.
e A more perfect doctrine of Iesus Christ.
3 He refuteth the slanders of those Thrasoes. I grant, sayth hee, that I am not so eloquent an Oratour, but yet they cannot take away the knowledge of the Gospel from me, whereof you haue had good proofe, and that euery maner of way. *f Paul lacked not of that kinde of eloquence which is meet for a man, and fit for the Gospel, but hee willingly wanted that painted kinde of speech, which too many now adayes hunt after and follow.* 4 Another slander, to wit, that hee was a rascall, and liued by the labor of his owne hands. But herein, saith the Apostle, what can you lay against me, but that I was content to take any paines for your sakes, and when I lacked, to trauaile for my liuing with mine owne hands in part, & partly also when pouertie constrained me, I chose rather otherwise to seeke my sustenance, then to be any burden to you, although I preached the Gospel vnto you? * *Chap.12.13.* 5 An amplification: So farre is he from being ashamed of this acte, that he hath also resolued with himselfe to doe no otherwise hereafter amongst them, to the intent that it may alwayes be truely said, that he taught in Achaia for nothing: not that hee disdaineth the Corinthians, but that these Thrasoes may neuer finde the occasion which they haue alreadie sought for, and he in the meane season, may set some thing before them to follow, that at length they may truely say, that they are like to Paul.

10 The [g] trueth of Christ is in me, that this
reioycing shall not be [h] shut vp against me in
the regions of Achaia.
11 Wherefore? because I loue you not?
God knoweth.
12 But what I doe, that I will doe: that I
may cut away occasion from them which desire occasion, that they may be found like vnto
vs in that wherein they [i] reioyce.
13 [6] For such false apostles are deceitfull
workers, and transforme themselues into the
Apostles of Christ.
14 And no marueile: for Satan himselfe is
transformed into an Angel of [k] light.
15 Therefore it is no great thing, though
his ministers transforme themselues, as though
they were the ministers of righteousnes, whose
end shalbe according to their workes.
16 [7] I say againe, Let no man thinke that
I am foolish, or else take me euen as a foole,
that I also may boast my selfe a little.
17 That I speake, I speake it not after the
Lord: but as *it were* foolishly in this *my* great
boasting,
18 Seeing that many reioyce after the flesh,
I will reioyce also.
19 For ye suffer fooles gladly, because that
ye are wise.
20 [8] For ye suffer, euen if a man bring you
into bondage, if a man deuoure *you*, if a man
take *your goods*, if a man exalt himselfe, if a man
smite you on the face.
21 I speake as concerning the [l] reproch,
as though that wee had beene [m] weake: but
wherein any man is bold (I speake foolishly)
I am bold also.
22 They are Hebrewes, * so am I: they
are Israelites, so am I: they are the seede of A-
braham, so am I:
23 They are the Ministers of Christ (I
speake as a foole) I am [n] more: in labors more
abundant: in stripes aboue measure: in prison
more plenteously: in [o] death oft.
24 Of the Iewes [p] fiue times receiued I
fortie *stripes* saue one.
25 I was [q] thrice * beaten with roddes:
I was * once stoned: I suffered thrice * shipwracke: night and day haue I beene in the
deepe Sea.
26 In iourneying *I was* often, in perils of
waters, in perils of robbers, in perils of mine
owne nation, in perils among the Gentiles,
in perils in the Citie, in perils in wildernesse,
in perils in the Sea, in perils among false brethren,

g This is a forme of an othe, as if he said, Let me not be thought to haue any trueth in me.
h Shalbe alwayes open to me.
i Pauls aduersaries sought all occasions they could to be equall to him. And therefore seeing they had rather eate vp the Corinthians, then preach to them for nothing, they sought another occasion, to wit, to make Paul to take some thing: which thing if hee had done, then hoped they by that meanes to be equall to him: for they made such a shewe of zeale and knowledge, and set it foorth with such a glosing kinde of eloquence, that some of them euen despised Paul: but he sheweth that all this is nothing but colours and painting.
6 Nowe at length he painteth out these fellowes in their colours, forewarning, that it will come to passe, that they will at length betray themselues, what countenance soeuer they make to the zeale that they haue of Gods glory.
k By light is meant the heauenly glory, whereof the Angels are partakers.
7 He goeth forward boldly, and vsing a vehement ironie or kind of taunting, desireth the Corinthians to pardon him, if for a time hee contend as a foole before them being wise, with those iolly fellowes touching those externall things, to wit, touching his stocke, his ancestors and valiant actes.
8 Before hee commeth to the matter, he toucheth the Corinthians, who perswading themselues to bee very wise men, did not marke in the meane season, that those false apostles abused their simplicitie for aduantage. *l As if hee sayd, In respect of that reproch which they doe vnto you (I speake it) which surely is as euill, as if they did beat you.* *m Paul is called weake, in that hee seemeth to the Corinthians a vile and abiect man, a beggarly artificer, a most wretched and miserable idiot, whereas notwithstanding therein Gods mightie power was made manifest.* * *Philip.3.5.* *n Paul being honourable indeede, defendeth his ministery openly, not for his owne sake, but because hee sawe his doctrine come into hazard.* *o In danger of present death.* *p Hee alludeth to that that is written, Deut 25.3. and moreouer this place sheweth vs, that Paul suffered many things which Luke passed ouer.* *q Of the Romane Magistrates.* * *Actes 16.23.* * *Actes 14.19.* * *Actes 27.14.*

27 In wearinesse and [r] painfulnesse, in watching often, in hunger and thirst, in fastings often, in colde and nakednesse.
28 [9] Beside the things which are outward,
I am combred daily, *and haue* the care of all the
Churches.
29 Who is weake, and I am not weake?
who is offended, and I burne not?
30 [10] If I must needs reioyce, I will reioyce
of mine infirmities.
31 The God, euen the Father of our Lord
Iesus Christ, which is blessed for euermore,
knoweth that I lie not.
32 In * Damascus the Gouernour of the
people vnder king Aretas, laid watch in the
Citie of the Damascens, and would haue
caught me,
33 But at a window was I let downe in a
basket through the wall, and escaped his hands.

r Painefulnesse is a troublesome sickenesse, as when a man is wearie and would rest, he is constrained to fall to new labour.

9 Hee addeth this in conclusion further, that the Corinthians might be ashamed to despise him, vpon whose care, almost all Churches depended, as it was plainely seene by experience.

10 Hee turneth that against the aduersaries, which they obiected against him: as if hee should say, They alleadge my calamities, to take away my authoritie from me: but if I would boast my selfe, I would take no better argument: and God himselfe is my witnesse that I deuise and forge nothing. * *Actes 9.24.*

CHAP. XII.

1 He doeth euen vnwillingly make rehearsall 3 of the heauenly visions, 4 that were reueiled vnto him: 6 for which though hee might indeed glory, yet he will not, 10 being priuie of his owne infirmities: 11 but they driue him to this kinde of folly, 20 in that they giue eare to certaine vaineglorious persons, who draw them from Christ.

IT [1] is not expedient for me no doubt to reioyce: for I will come to visions and reuelations of the Lord.
2 I knowe a man [a] in Christ aboue fourteene yeeres agone, (whether *he were* in the
body, I cannot tell, or out of the body, I can
not tell: God knoweth) which was taken vp
into the [b] third heauen.
3 And I knowe such a man (whether in
the body, or out of the body, I cannot tell:
God knoweth)
4 How that he was taken vp into [c] Paradise, and heard words which [d] cannot be spoken, which are not [e] possible for man to vtter.
5 [2] Of such a man will I reioyce: of my
selfe will I not reioyce, except it be of mine infirmities.
6 For though I would reioyce, I should
not be a foole, for I will say the trueth: but I
refraine, lest any man should think of me aboue
that he seeth in me, or that he heareth of me.
7 [3] And lest I should be exalted out of
measure through the abundance of reuelations, there was giuen vnto me [f] a pricke in the
flesh, the messenger of [g] Satan to buffet me, because I should not be exalted out of measure.
8 For this thing I besought the Lorde
[h] thrice, that it might depart from me.
9 And hee said vnto me, My grace is sufficient for thee: for my power is made perfect
through weakenesse. [4] Very gladly therefore
will I reioyce rather in mine infirmities, that
the power of Christ may [i] dwell in me.
10 Therefore I take [k] pleasure in infirmities, in reproches, in necessities, in persecutions, in anguish for Christes sake: for when I
am weake, then am I strong.
11 I was a foole to boast my selfe: ye haue
compelled mee: [5] for I ought to haue beene
commended of you: for in nothing was I inferiour vnto the very chiefe Apostles, though
I be nothing.
12 The [l] signes of an Apostle were wrought
among you with all patience, with signes, and
wonders, and great workes.
13 For what is it, wherein ye were inferiours vnto other Churches, * except that I haue
not beene [m] slothfull to your hinderance? forgiue me this wrong.
14 Behold, the third time I am readie to
come vnto you, and yet will I not be slothfull
to your hinderance: for I seeke not yours, but
you: for the children ought not to lay vp for
the fathers, but the fathers for the children.
15 And I will most gladly bestow, and will
be bestowed for your soules: though the more
I loue you, the lesse I am loued.
16 [6] But be it that I charged you not: yet
forasmuch as I was craftie, I tooke you with
guile.
17 Did I pill you by any of them whom I
sent vnto you?
18 I haue desired Titus, and with him I haue
sent a brother: did Titus pill you of any thing?
walked we not in the selfe same spirit? *walked
we* not in the same steppes?
19 [7] Againe, thinke yee that we excuse our
selues vnto you? wee speake before God in
[n] Christ. But *we doe* all things, dearely beloued,
for your edifying.
20 [8] For I feare lest when I come, I shall not
finde you such as I would: and that I shall be
found vnto you such as ye would not, and lest
there be strife, enuying, wrath, contentions,
backebitings, whisperings, swellings, *and* discord.
21 *I feare* lest when I come againe, my God
abase me among you, and I shall bewaile many of them which haue sinned alreadie, and
haue not repented of the vncleannesse and fornication, and wantonnesse which they haue
committed.

1 He goeth forward in his purpose, and because those bragging mates boasted of reuelations, he reckeneth vp those things which lift him vp aboue the common capacitie of men: but he vseth a preface, and excuseth himselfe aduisedly.

a I speake this in Christ, that is, be it spoken without vaineglory, for I seeke nothing but Christ Iesus only.

b Into the highest heauen: for wee neede not to dispute subtilly vpon the word (Third) but yet this place is to be marked against them, which would make heauen to be euery where.

c So the Grecians name that which we call a Parke, that is to say, a place where trees are planted, and wild beasts kept, by which name they that translated the old Testament out of Hebrew into Greeke, called the garden Eden, whereinto Adam was put straight after his creation, as a most delicate and pleasant place And hereupon grewe it, that that blessed seat of the glory of God is called by that name. *d Which no man is able to vtter.* *e Which the Saints themselues are not by any meanes able to expresse, because it is God himselfe. Thus doeth Clemens Alexandrinus expound this place, Strom. 5.* 2 To remooue all suspition of ambition, he witnesseth that he braggeth not of those things as of his own, but as out of himselfe, and yet notwithstanding faineth nothing, lest by this occasion other men should attribute vnto him more then indeed hee is: and therefore he had rather glory in his miseries. 3 An excellent doctrine: why God will haue euen his best seruants to be vexed of Satan, and by all kinde of temptations: to wit, lest they should be too much puffed vp, and also that they may be made perfite by that continuall exercise. *f He meaneth concupiscence, that sticketh fast in vs, as it were a pricke, insomuch as it constrained Paul himselfe being regenerate, to cry out, I doe not that good that I would, &c. And he calleth it a pricke, by a borowed kind of speech taken from thornes, or stumpes, which are very dangerous and hurtfull for the feet, if a man walke through woods that are cut downe.*

g Which stirreth those lustes on fire.

h Oft.

4 He concludeth, that he wil onely set his miseries against the vaine brags of the false apostles, and therewith also excuseth himselfe, for that by their importunitie, he was constrained to speake so much of those things as he did: to wit, because that if his Apostleship were subuerted, his doctrine must needs fall.

i That I might feele the vertue of Christ more and more: For the weaker that our Tabernacles are, the more doeth Christes vertue appeare in them.

k I doe not only take them patiently, and with a good heart, but also I take great pleasure in them.

5 Againe hee maketh the Corinthians witnesses of those things whereby God had sealed his Apostleship amongst them, and againe he declareth by certaine arguments how farre he is from all couetousnesse, and also how he is affectioned towards them.

l The arguments whereby it may well appeare, that I am indeed an Apostle of Iesus Christ.

* *Chap. 11.9.*

m I was not slothfull in getting my liuing with mine owne hands, that I might not bee burdensome to you.

6 Hee putteth away another most grieuous slander, to wit, that he did subtilly and by others, make his gaine and profite of them.

7 Hee concludeth that hee writeth not these things vnto them, as though he needed to defend himselfe, for he is guiltie of nothing: but because it is behooueable for them to doubt nothing of his fidelitie, who instructed them. *n As it becommeth him to speake truely and sincerely, that professeth himselfe to be in Christ, that is to say, to be a Christian.* 8 Hauing confirmed his authoritie vnto them, hee rebuketh them sharpely, and threatneth them also like an Apostle, shewing that he will not spare them hereafter, vnlesse they repent, seeing that this is the third time that he hath warned them.

CHAP.

CHAP. XIII.

1 Comming the third time, 2 hee denounceth the sharper vengeance towards them, 5 who haue a perfect triall of the power of Christ in his Apostleship: 10 At length hee prayeth for their repentance, 11 and wisheth them prosperitie.

LOe this *is* the third time that I come vnto
you. * In the mouth of two or three witnesses shall euery word stand.
2 I tolde you before, and tell you before:
as though I had bene present the second time,
so write I now being absent to them which
heretofore haue sinned, and to all others, that
if I come againe, I will not spare,
3 [1] Seeing that yee seeke experience of
Christ, that speaketh in me, which toward you
is not weake, but is [a] mightie in you.
4 For though he was crucified concerning
[b] *his* infirmitie, yet liueth he through the power of God. And we no doubt are weake in him,
but we shall liue with him, through the power
of God toward you.
5 * [2] Prooue your selues whether yee are
in the faith: examine your selues: know yee
not your owne selues, how that Iesus Christ
is in you, except ye be reprobates?
6 [3] But I trust that ye shall know that wee
are not reprobates.
7 Now I pray vnto God that ye doe none
euill, not that wee should seeme approoued,
but that yee should doe that which is honest:
though we be as [c] reprobates.
8 For we cannot *doe* any thing against the
trueth, but for the trueth.
9 For wee are glad when wee are weake,
and that ye are strong: this also wee wish for,
euen your [d] perfection.
10 Therefore write I these things being
absent, lest when I am present, I should vse
sharpenesse, according to the power which the
Lord hath giuen me, to edification, and not to
destruction.
11 [4] Finally brethren, fare ye well: be perfect: be of good comfort: be of one minde:
liue in peace, and the God of loue and peace
shalbe with you.
12 [5] Greete one another with an * holy
kisse. All the Saints salute you.
13 The grace of our Lord Iesus Christ, and
the loue of God, and the communion of the
holy Ghost be with you all, Amen.

¶ The second *Epistle* to the Corinthians, written from Philippi, a citie in Macedonia, *and sent* by Titus and Lucas.

* *Deut.* 19.15. *matth.* 18.16. *iohn* 8.17. *heb.* 10.28.

1 A most sharpe reprehension, for that, while they despise the Apostles admonitions, they tempt Christes owne patience: and also while they contemne him as wretched and miserable, they lay nothing herein against him, which is not common to him with Christ.

a And will be most mightie to be reuenged of you, when neede shall be.

b As touching that base forme of a seruant which he tooke vpon him when hee abased himselfe. * 1.*Corinth.* 11.28. 2 Hee confirmeth that which hee spake of the vertue of God appearing in his ministerie, and hee gathereth by the mutuall relation betweene the peoples faith, and the Ministers preaching, that they must either reuerence his Apostleship, vpon whose doctrine their faith is grounded, or they must condemne themselues of infidelitie, and must confesse themselues not to be of Christes body.

3 He mitigateth that sharpnesse, trusting that they will shewe themselues towards their faithfull Apostle, apt and willing to be taught: adding this moreouer, that hee passeth not for his owne fame and estimation, so that they may serue to their saluation, which is the onely marke that he shooteth at.

c In mens iudgement.

d That all things may be in good order amongst you, and the members of the Church restored into their place, which haue beene shaken and out of place.

4 A briefe exhortation, but yet such an one as comprehendeth all the parts of a Christian mans life.

5 He saluteth them familiarly, and in conclusion wisheth well vnto them. 1.*Cor.* 16.20.

THE EPISTLE OF THE APOSTLE PAVL TO THE GALATIANS.

CHAP. I.

1 Straight after the salutation, 6 hee reprehendeth the Galatians for reuolting 9 from his Gospel, 15 which hee receiued from God, 17 before he had communicated with any of the Apostles.

PAVL [1] an Apostle (not
[a] of men, neither by
[b] man, * but by [c] Iesus
Christ, and God the Fa-
ther which hath raised
him from the dead)
2 And all the bre-
thren which are with
me, vnto the Churches of Galatia:
3 Grace *bee* with you, and peace from
God the Father, and *from* our Lorde Iesus
Christ,
4 [2] Which gaue himselfe for our sinnes,
that hee might deliuer vs * from this present
euill [d] world, according to the will of God
euen our Father,
5 To whom *be* glory for euer and euer,
Amen.
6 [3] I marueile that ye are so soone [e] remoued away vnto another Gospel, from him that
had called you in the grace of Christ,
7 [4] Which is not another *Gospel*, saue that
there be some which trouble you, and intend
to [f] peruert the Gospel of Christ.
8 But though that wee, or an Angel from
heauen preach vnto you otherwise, then that
which we haue preached vnto you, let him be
[g] accursed.
9 As we said before, so say I now againe,
If any man preach vnto you otherwise, then
that ye haue receiued, let him be accursed.

1 A salutation comprehending in fewe wordes the summe of the Apostles doctrine, and also besides, straightway from the beginning, shewing the grauitie meet for the authoritie of an Apostle, which he had to maintaine against the false Apostles.

a He sheweth who is the author of the ministerie generally: for here in the whole ministerie agreeth, that whether they bee Apostles, or Shepheards, or Doctours, they are appointed of God.

b Hee toucheth the instrumentall cause: for this is a peculiar prerogatiue to the Apostles, to bee called immediatly from Christ. * *Titus* 1.3. *c Christ no doubt is man, but hee is God also, and head of the Church, and in this respect to bee exempted out of the number of men.* 2 The summe of the true Gospel is this, that Christ by his only offering saueth vs being chosen out of the world, by the free decree of God the Father. * *Luke* 1.74.

d Out of that most corrupt state which is without Christ.

3 The first part of the Epistle, wherein he witnesseth that he is an Apostle, nothing inferiour to those chiefe disciples of Christ, and wholy agreeing with them, whose names the false apostles did abuse. And he beginneth with chiding, reprouing them of lightnesse, for that they gaue eare so easily vnto them which peruerted them and drew them away vnto a new Gospel.

e Hee vseth the passiue voice to cast the fault vpon the false apostles, and he vseth the time that now is to giue them to vnderstand, that it was not alreadie done, but in doing. 4 He warneth them in time to remember that there are not many Gospels, and therfore whatsoeuer these false apostles pretend which had the Law, Moses, and the Fathers, in their mouthes, yet they are in deede so many corruptions of the true Gospel, insomuch that hee himselfe, yea, and the very Angels themselues (and therefore much more these false apostles) ought to be holden accursed, if they go about to change the lest iote that may be in the Gospel that hee deliuered to them before. *f For there is nothing more contrary to faith or free iustification, then iustification by the Law, or by deseruing.* *g Looke Rom.* 9.3.

10 [5]For now preach I [h] mans *doctrine*, or
Gods? or goe I about to please men? for if I
should yet please men, I were not the seruant
of Christ.
11 * [6] Now I certifie you, brethren, that
the Gospel which was preached of mee, was
not after man.
12 For neither receiued I it of man, neither was I taught it, but by the [i] reuelation of
Iesus Christ.
13 [7]For ye haue heard of my conuersation
in time past, in the Iewish religion, how that
* I persecuted the Church of God extremely,
and wasted it,
14 And profited in the Iewish religion a-
boue many of my companions of mine owne
nation, and was much more zealous of the
[k] traditions of my Fathers.
15 But when it pleased God (which had
[l] separated me from my mothers wombe, and
called *me* by his grace)
16 To reueile his Sonne [m] in mee, that I
should preach him * among the Gentiles, immediatly [8] I communicated not with [n] flesh
and blood:
17 Neither came I againe to Hierusalem to
them which were Apostles before mee, but I
went into Arabia, and turned againe vnto Damascus.
18 Then after three yeeres I came againe
to Hierusalem to visite Peter, and abode with
him fifteene dayes.
19 And none other of the Apostles saw I,
saue Iames the Lords brother.
20 Nowe the things which I write vnto
you, behold, *I witnesse* [o] before God, that I
lie not.
21 After that, I went into the coasts of Syria and Cilicia: for I was vnknowen by face
vnto the Churches of Iudea, which were in
Christ.
22 But they had heard onely *some say*, Hee
which persecuted vs in time past, now preacheth the [p] faith which before he destroyed.
23 And they glorified God for me.

5 A confirmation taken both from the nature of the doctrine it selfe, and also from the manner which hee vsed in teaching: for neither saith hee, did I teach those things which pleased men, as these men doe which put part of saluation in externall things, and workes of the Lawe, neither went I about to procure any mans fauour. And therefore the matter it selfe sheweth that that doctrine which I deliuered vnto you, is heauenly.
h Hee toucheth the false apostles, who had nothing but men in their mouthes, and he, though he would derogate nothing from the Apostles, preacheth God, and not men.
* *1.Cor.15.1.*
6 A second argument to proue that his doctrine is heauenly, because he had it from heauen, from Iesus Christ himselfe, without any mans helpe, wherein hee excelleth them whome Christ taught here on earth, after the maner of men.
i This place is to be vnderstood of an extraordinarie reuelation, for otherwise the Sonne alone reuealed his Gospel by his Spirit, although by the ministerie of men, which Paul shutteth out here. 7 Hee prooueth that hee was extraordinarily taught of Christ himselfe, by the historie of his former life, which the Galathians themselues knewe well enough: for sayeth hee, it is well knowen in what schoole I was brought vp, euen from a childe, to wit, amongst the deadly enemies of the Gospel. And that no man may cauill and say, that I was a schollar of the Pharisees in name onely, and not in deede, no man is ignorant howe that I excelled in Pharisaisme, and was suddainly made of a Pharise, an Apostle of the Gentiles, so that I had no space to bee instructed of men. * *Actes 9.1.* *k Hee calleth them the traditions of his Fathers, because hee was not onely a Pharise himselfe, but also had a Pharise to his father.* *l Hee speaketh of Gods euerlasting predestination, whereby hee appointed him to bee an Apostle, whereof hee maketh three degrees; the euerlasting counsell of God, his appointing from his mothers wombe, and his calling. here is no mention at all, wee see, of workes foreseene.* *m To mee, and thus is a kinde of speech which the Hebrewes vse, whereby this is giuen vs to vnderstand, that this gift commeth from God.* * *Ephes.3.8.* 8 Because it might bee obiected, that in deede hee was called of Christ in the way, but afterward was instructed of the Apostles and others, whose names (as I sayde before) the false apostles abused to destroy his Apostleship, as though hee deliuered another Gospel then the true Apostles did, and as though hee were not of their number, which are to bee credited without exception: therefore Paul answereth, that hee began straightway after his calling to preach the Gospel at Damascus and in Arabia, and was not from that time in Hierusalem but onely fifteene dayes, where hee sawe onely Peter and Iames, and afterwards, hee began to teach in Syria and Cilicia, with the consent and approbation of the Churches of the Iewes, which knewe him onely by name: so farre off was it, that hee was there instructed of men. *n With any man in the world.* *o This is a kinde of othe.* *p The doctrine of faith.*

CHAP. II.

1 That the Apostles did nothing disagree from his Gospel, 3 hee declareth by the example of Titus being vncircumcised, 11 and also by his auouching the same against Peters dissimulation: 17 And so hee passeth to the handling of our free iustification by Christ, &c.

THen [1] fourteene yeeres after, I went vp
againe to Hierusalem with Barnabas, and
tooke with me Titus also.
2 And I went vp by reuelation, and declared vnto them that Gospel which I preach a-
mong the Gentiles, but particularly to them
that were the chiefe, lest by any means I should
runne, or had runne [a] in vaine:
3 But neither yet Titus which was with
me, though he were a Grecian, was compelled
to be circumcised,
4 To wit, for the [b] false brethren which
were craftily sent in, and crept in priuily to spie
out our libertie, which we haue in Christ Iesus,
that they might bring vs into bondage.
5 To whom we gaue not place by [c] subiection for an houre, that the [d] trueth of the Gospel might continue with [e] you.
6 But by them which seemed to be great,
I was not taught (whatsoeuer they were in time
passed, I am nothing the better, *God accepteth no mans person) for they that are the
chief, did adde nothing to me *aboue that I had.*
7 But contrariwise, when they sawe that
the Gospel ouer the [f] vncircumcision was committed vnto me, as *the Gospel* ouer the circumcision was vnto Peter:
8 (For he that was mightie by Peter in his
Apostleship ouer the circumcision, was also
mightie by me toward the Gentiles)
9 And when Iames, and Cephas, and Iohn,
knewe of the grace that was giuen vnto mee,
which are [g] counted to bee pillars, they gaue
to me and to Barnabas the right [h] hands of fellowship, that wee *should preach* vnto the Gentiles, and they vnto the Circumcision,
10 *Warning* onely that wee should remember the poore: which thing also I was diligent
to doe.
11 ¶And when Peter was come to Antiochia, I withstood him to his [i] face: for hee was
to be condemned.
12 [2] For before that certaine came from
Iames, hee ate with the Gentiles: but when
they were come, hee withdrew and separated
himselfe, fearing them which were of the Circumcision.
13 And the other Iewes played the hypocrites likewise with him, in so much that Bar-

1 Now hee sheweth how he agreeth with the Apostles, with whom he granteth that hee conferred touching his Gospel which he taught among the Gentiles, fourteene yeeres after his conuersion, and they allowed it in such sort, that they constrained not his fellow Titus to be circumcised, although some tormented themselues therein, which traiterously laid wait against him, but in vaine: neither did they adde the least iote that might be to the doctrine which he had preached, but contrariwise they gaue to him and Barnabas the right hands of fellowship and acknowledged them as Apostles appointed of the Lord to the Gentiles.
a Vnfruitfull, for as touching his doctrine, Paul doubteth not of it, but because there were certaine reports cast abroad of him, that he was of another opinion then the rest of the Apostles were, which thing might haue hindered the course of the Gospel, therefore he laboureth to remedie this sore. *b Which by deceit and counterfeit holinesse crept in amongst the faithfull.* *c By submitting our selues to them, and betraying our owne libertie.* *d The true and sincere doctrine of the Gospel, which remained safe from beeing corrupt with any of these mens false doctrines.* *e Vnder the Galatians name, hee vnderstandeth all nations.* * *Deuter.10,17. 2.chron.19 7. iob 34.19. actes 10 34. roman.2.11. ephes.6.9. coloss.3.25. 1 pet.1.17.* *f Among the Gentiles, as Peter had to preach it among the Iewes.* *g Whome alone and onely, these men count for pillars of the Church, and whose name they abuse to deceiue you.* *h They gaue vs their hand in token that wee agreed wholly in the doctrine of the Gospel.* *i Before all men.* 2 Another most vehement proofe of his Apostleship, and also of that doctrine which hee had deliuered concerning free iustification by faith onely, because that for this thing onely hee reprehended Peter at Antioch, who offended herein, in that for a fewe Iewes sakes which came from Hierusalem, he played the Iewe, and offended the Gentiles which had beleeued.

nabas was [k] led away with them by that their
hypocrisie.
14 But when I saw, that they went not the
[l] right way to the [m] trueth of the Gospel, I said
vnto Peter before all men, If thou being a Iew,
liuest as the Gentiles, and not like the Iewes,
why [n] constrainest thou the Gentiles to doe
like the Iewes?
15 [3] We *which are* Iewes [o] by nature, and
not [p] sinners of the Gentiles,
16 Know that a man is not iustified by the
works of the Law, but by the faith [q] of Iesus
Christ, euen we, *I say*, haue beleeued in Iesus
Christ, that we might bee iustified by the faith
of Christ, and not by the works of the Law, because that by the works of the Law, [r] no flesh
shall be iustified.
17 * [4] If then while [s] wee seeke to be made
righteous by Christ, wee our selues are found
sinners, is Christ therfore the minister of sinne?
God forbid.
18 For if I build againe the things that I
haue destroyed, I make my selfe a trespasser.
19 For I through the Lawe am dead to
the [t] Lawe, that I might liue vnto God.
20 I am crucified with Christ, but I liue,
yet not [u] I any more, but Christ liueth in mee:
and in that I now liue in the [x] flesh, I liue by
the faith in the Sonne of God, who hath loued
me, and giuen himselfe for me.
21 [5] I doe not abrogate the grace of God:
for if righteousnes *be* by the Law, then Christ
died without a [y] cause.

k By example rather then by iudgment.
l Word for word, with a right foot, which he setteth against halting & dissembling, which is backeward.
m He calleth the trueth of the Gospel, both the doctrine it selfe, and also the vse of the doctrine, which we call the practise.
n He saith they were constrained, which played the Iewes by Peters example.
3 The second part of this Epistle, the state whereof is this: we are iustified by faith in Christ Iesus without the works of the Lawe. Which thing he propoundeth in such sort, that first of all he meeteth with an obiection, (for I also saith he am a Iewe, that no man may say against me, that I am an enemie to the Law) and afterward, he confirmeth it by the expresse witnes of Dauid.
o Although we be Iewes, yet we preach iustification by faith, because we know vndoubtedly, that no man can be iustified by the Lawe. *p So the Iewes called the Gentiles, because they were strangers from Gods couenant.* *q In Iesus Christ.* *r No man, and in this word (flesh) there is a great vehemencie, whereby is meant that the nature of man is vtterly corrupt.* * *Rom.3.19.* 4 Before he goeth any further, he meeteth with their obiection, which abhorred this doctrine of free iustification by faith, because say they, men are by this meanes withdrawen from the studie of good works. And in this sort is the obiection: if sinners should be iustified through Christ by faith without the Law, Christ should approue sinners, and should as it were exhort them thereunto by his ministerie. Paul answereth that this consequence is false, because that Christ destroyeth sinne in the beleeuers: For so, saith he, doe men flee vnto Christ through the terrour and feare of the Law, that being quit from the curse of the Law and iustified, they may be saued by him, that together therewithall, he beginneth in them by little and little that strength and power of his which destroyeth sinne: to the end that this old man being abolished by the vertue of Christ crucified, Christ may liue in them, and they may consecrate themselues to God. Therefore if any man giue himselfe to sinne after he hath receiued the Gospel, let him not accuse Christ nor the Gospel, but himselfe, for that he destroyeth the worke of God in himselfe. *s Hee goeth from iustification to sanctification, which is another benefit we receiue by Christ, if we lay holde on him by faith.* *t The Law that terrifieth the conscience, bringeth vs to Christ, and he onely causeth vs to die to the Law in deed, because that by making vs righteous, he taketh away from vs the terrour of conscience, and by sanctifying vs, causeth through the mortifying of lust in vs, that it can not take such occasion to sinne by the restraint which the Lawe maketh, as it is before, Rom.7.10,11.* *u The same that I was before.* *x In this mortall body.* 5 The second argument taken of an absurditie: If men may be iustified by the Lawe, then was it not necessarie for Christ to die. *y For there was no cause why he should doe so.*

CHAP. III.

1 He rebuketh them, for suffering themselues to bee drawen from the grace of free iustification in Christ, most liuely set out vnto them. 6 He bringeth in Abrahams example, 10 declaring the effect, 21 and causes of the giuing of the Lawe.

O [1] Foolish Galatians, who hath bewitched
you, that ye should not obey the trueth,
to whom Iesus Christ before was described in
your [a] sight, *and* among you crucified?
2 This onely would I learne of you, Receiued ye the Spirit by the works of the Lawe,
or by hearing of [c] faith *preached*?
3 [2] Are ye so foolish, that after ye haue begun in the Spirit, ye would now be made perfit
by the [d] flesh?
4 [3] Haue yee suffered so many things in
vaine? if so be it be euen in vaine.
5 [4] He therefore that ministreth to you the
Spirit, and worketh miracles among you, *doeth
he it* through the works of the Law, or by the
hearing of faith *preached*?
6 [5] *Yea, rather* as [e] Abraham beleeued
God, and it was * imputed to him for righteousnesse.
7 [6] Knowe yee therefore that they which
are of faith, the same are the children of Abraham.
8 [7] For the Scripture foreseeing, that
GOD would iustifie the Gentiles through
faith, preached before the Gospel vnto Abraham, *saying*, * [8] In thee shall all the Gentiles
be [f] blessed.
9 [9] So then they which bee of faith, are
blessed [g] with faithfull Abraham.
10 [10] For as many as are of the workes of
the Lawe, are vnder the curse: [11] for it is written, * Cursed is euery man that continueth
not in all things, which are written in the book
of the Law, to doe them.
12 [12] And that no man is iustified by the
Law in the sight of God, it is euident: * for the
iust shall liue by faith.
12 [13] And the Lawe is not of faith: but
* the man that shall doe these things, shall liue
in them.
13 [14] Christ hath redeemed vs fro the curse
of the Law, being made a curse for vs, ([15] for it

1 The third reason or argument taken of those gifts of the holy Ghost, wherewith they were indued from heauen after they had heard and beleeued the Gospel by Pauls ministerie: which seeing they were so euident to all mens eyes, that they were as it were liuely images, wherein they might behold the trueth of the doctrine of the Gospel, no lesse then if they had beheld with their eyes Christ himselfe crucified, in whose onely death they ought to haue their trust, he marueileth how it could be that they could be so bewitched by the false apostles.

a Christ was laid before you so notably and so plainly, that you had his liuely image as it were represented before your eyes, as if he had bene crucified before you.
b Those spirituall graces and gifts, which were a seale as it were to the Galatians that the Gospel which was preached to them was true.
c Of the doctrine of faith.
2 The fourth argument mixed with the former, and it is double. If the Lawe be to be ioyned with faith, this were not to goe forward, but backward, seeing that those spirituall gifts which were bestowed vpon you are more excellent then any that could proceed from your selues. And moreouer, it should followe, that the Lawe is better then Christ, because it should perfect & bring to ende that, which Christ began onely.
d By the (flesh) hee meaneth the ceremonies of the Law, against which he setteth the Spirit, that is, the spirituall working of the Gospel.
3 An exhortation by maner of vpbraiding, that they doe not in vaine suffer so many conflicts. 4 He repeateth the third Argument which was taken of the effects, because hee had interlaced certaine other arguments by the way. 5 The fift Argument which is of great force, and hath three grounds. The first, that Abraham was iustified by faith, to wit, by free imputation of righteousnesse according to the promise apprehended by faith, as Moses doeth most plainely witnesse. *e Looke Romanes 4.* * *Gen.15.6. rom.4.3. iames 2.23.* 6 The second, that the sonnes of Abraham must bee esteemed and accounted of by faith. 7 The third, that all people that beleeue, are without exception comprehended in the promise of the blessing. * *Gen.12.3. actes 3.15.* 8 A proofe of the first and second grounds, out of the words of Moses. *f Blessing in this place, signifieth the free promise by faith.* 9 The conclusion of the fift argument: Therefore as Abraham is blessed by faith, so are all his children (that is to say, all the Gentiles that beleeue) blessed, that is to say, freely iustified. *g With faithfull Abraham, and not by faithfull Abraham, to giue vs to vnderstand that the blessing commeth not from Abraham, but from him, by whom Abraham and all his posteritie is blessed.* 10 The sixt argument, the conclusion wherof is also in the former verse taken of contraries, thus, They are accursed which are of the works of the Law, that is to say, which value their righteousnesse by the performance of the Law. Therefore they are blessed which are of faith, this is, they which haue righteousnesse by faith. 11 A proofe of the former sentence or proposition, and the proposition of this argument is this: Cursed is he that fulfilleth not the whole Law. * *Deut.27.26.* 12 The second proposition with the conclusion: But no man fulfilleth the Lawe, Therefore no man is iustified by the Law, or els, All are accursed which seeke righteousnesse by the works of the Law. And there is annexed also this maner of proofe of the second proposition, to wit, Righteousnesse and life are attributed to faith, Therefore no man fulfilleth the Lawe. * *Habakkuk 2.4. rom.1.17. heb.10.38.* 13 Here is a reason shewed of the former consequence: Because the Lawe promiseth life to all that keepe it, and therefore if it be kept, it iustifieth and giueth life. But the Scripture attributing righteousnesse and life to faith taketh it from the Law, seeing that faith iustifieth by imputation, and the Lawe by the performing of the worke. * *Leuit.18.5.* 14 A preuenting of an obiection: How then can they be blessed, whome the Lord pronounceth to bee accursed? Because Christ susteined the curse which the Lawe layed vpon vs, that we might be quit from it. 15 A proofe of the answere by the testimonie of Moses.

is

is written, * [h] Cursed is euery one that hangeth on tree.)

14 [16] That the blessing of Abraham might
come on the Gentiles through Christ Iesus,
that we might receiue the promise of the Spirit
through faith.

15 [17] Brethren, I speak as [i] men do: *though
it be but a mans couenant, when it is [k] confirmed, *yet* no man doeth abrogate it, or addeth
any thing thereto.

16 Now to Abraham and his seede were
the promises made. He saith not, And to the
seeds, as *speaking* of many: but, And to thy
seed, as of one, [18] which is [l] Christ.

17 [19] And this I say, that the couenant that
was confirmed afore of God [m] in respect of
Christ, the [20] Law which was foure hundred
and thirtie yeeres after, can not disanull, that
it should make the promse of none effect.

18 [21] for if the [n] inheritance *be* of the Law,
it is no more by the promise, but God gaue it
freely vnto Abraham by promise.

19 [22] Wherefore then *serueth* the Lawe?
It was added because of the [o] transgressions,
[p] till the seed came, vnto the which the promise was made: [23] & it was [q] ordeined by [r] Angels in the hand of a Mediatour.

20 Now a Mediatour is not *a Mediatour*
of one: [24] but God is one.

*Deut.21.23.
h Christ was accursed for vs, because he bare the curse that was due to vs, to make vs partakers of his righteousnesse.

16 A conclusion of all that was said before in the handling of the fift and sixt reasons, to wit, that both the Gentiles are made partakers of the free blessing of Abraham in Christ, and also that the Iewes themselues, of whose number the Apostle counteth himselfe to be, cannot obtaine that promised grace of the Gospel, which he calleth the Spirit, but onely by faith. And the Apostle doeth seuerally apply the conclusion, both to the one and to the other, preparing himselfe a way to the next argument whereby he declareth, that ye one onely seed of Abraham, which is made of all peoples, can no otherwise be ioyned and grow vp together but by faith in Christ. 17 He putteth forth two generall rules before the next argument, which is the seuenth in order: The one is, that it is not lawfull to breake couenants & contracts which are iustly made, & according to Law, among men, neither may any thing be added vnto them: The other is, that God did so make a couenant with Abraham, that he would gather together his children which consist both of Iewes and Gentiles into one body (as appeareth by that which hath bin said before.) For he did not say, that he would be the God of Abraham & of his seeds, (which thing notwithstanding should haue bin said, if he had many and diuers seedes, as the Gentiles apart, and the Iewes apart) but that he would be the God of Abraham, and of his seede, as of one. *i I will vse an example which is common among you, that you may be ashamed that you giue not so much to Gods couenants, as you do to mans.* * *Heb.9.17.* *k Autenticall, as we call it.* 18 He putteth forth the summe of the seuenth argument, to wit, that both the Iewes and the Gentiles, grow together in one body of the seed of Abraham, in Christ onely, so that all are one in Christ, as it is afterward declared, ver.28. *l Paul speaketh not of Christs person, but of two peoples, which grew together in one, in Christ.* 19 The eight argument taken of comparison, thus: If a mans couenant (being autenticall) be firme and strong, much more Gods couenant. Therefore the Law was not giuen to abrogate the promise made to Abraham which had respect to Christ, that is to say, the end whereof did hang on Christ. *m Which tended to Christ.* 20 An enlarging of that argument, thus: Moreouer and besides that the promise is of it selfe firme and strong, it was also confirmed with the prescription of long time, to wit, of 430. yeeres, so that it could in no wise be broken. 21 An obiection: We grant that the promise was not abrogated by the couenant of the Law, and therefore we ioyne the Law with the promise. Nay, saith the Apostle, these two cannot stand together, to wit, that the inheritance should both be giuen by the Lawe and also by promise, for the promise is free: whereby it followeth, that the Law was not giuen to iustifie, for by that meanes the promise should be broken. *n By this word (inheritance) is meant the right of the seede, which is, that God should be our God, that is to say, that by vertue of the Couenant that was made with faithfull Abraham, we that be faithfull, might by that meanes be blessed of God as well as hee.* 22 An obiection which riseth from the former answere: If the inheritance be not by the Law (at the least part) then why was the Lawe giuen after that the promise was made? Therefore saith the Apostle, to reprooue men of sinne, and so to teach them to looke vnto Christ, in whome at length that promise of sauing all people together, should bee fulfilled, and not that the Lawe was giuen to iustifie men. *o That men might vnderstand, by discouering of their sinnes, that they are saued by the onely grace of God which hee reueiled to Abraham, and that in Christ.* *p Vntill the partition wall was broken downe, and that full seede sprang vp, framed of two peoples, both of Iewes and Gentiles: for by this worde Seede, we may not vnderstand, Christ alone by himselfe, but coupled and ioyned together with his body.* 23 A confirmation of the former answere taken from the manner and forme of giuing the Law: for it was giuen by Angels, striking a great terrour into all, and by Moses a Mediatour comming betweene. Now they that are one, neede no Mediatour, but they that are twaine at the least, and that are at variance one with another. Therefore the Lawe it selfe and the Mediatour, were witnesses of the wrath of God, and not that God would by this meanes reconcile men to himselfe and abolish the promise, or adde the Lawe vnto the promise. *q Commanded and giuen, or proclaimed.* *r By the seruice and ministerie.* 24 A taking away of an obiection, lest any man might say, that sometimes by consent of the parties which haue made a couenant, some thing is added to the couenant, or the former couenants are broken. This, saith the Apostle, commeth not to passe in God, who is alwayes one, and the selfe same, and like himselfe.

21 [25] *Is* the Law then against the promises of
of God? God forbid: For if there had beene a
Law giuen which could haue giuen life, surely
righteousnesse should haue bene by the Law.

22 But the [s] Scripture hath *concluded [t] all
vnder sin, that the [u] promise by the faith of Iesus
Christ should be giuen to them that beleeue.

23 [26] But before faith came, we were kept
vnder the Lawe, *as vnder* a garison, and shut
vp vnto [x] that faith, which should afterward be
reuealed.

24 Wherefore the Law was our schoolemaster *to bring vs* to Christ, that we might be
made righteous by faith.

25 But after that faith is come, wee are no
longer vnder a schoolemaster.

26 [27] For yee are all the sonnes of God by
faith, in Christ Iesus.

27 [28] For all yee that are [y] baptized into
Christ, haue [z] put on Christ.

28 There is neither Iew nor Grecian: there
is neither bond nor free: there is neither male
nor female: for ye are all [a] one in Christ Iesus.

29 And if *ye be* Christs, then are ye Abrahams seed, and heires by promise.

25 The conclusion vttered by a maner of asking a question, and it is that same that was vttered before, verse 17. but proceeding of another rule: so that the argument is new, and is this: God is alwayes like vnto himselfe: Therefore the Law was not giuen to abolish the promises. But it should abolish them if it gaue life, for by that meanes it should iustifie, and therefore it should abolish that iustification, which was promised to Abraham and to his seed by faith Nay it was rather giuen to bring to light the guiltinesse of all men, to the ende that all beleeuers fleeing to Christ promised, might be freely iustified in him. *s By this word, Scripture, he meaneth the Lawe.* * *Rom.3.9.* *t All men, and whatsoeuer commeth from man.* *u In euery one of these words, there lieth an argument against the merits of works: for all these words, promise, faith, Christ, might be giuen, to beleeuers, are against merits, & not one of them can stand with deseruing works.* 26 Now there followeth another handling of the second part of this Epistle; the state whereof was this: Although the Law (that is, the whole gouernement of Gods house according to the Lawe) do not iustifie, is it therefore to be abolished, seeing that Abraham himselfe was circumcised, and his posteritie held still the vse of Moses Lawe? Paul affirmeth that it ought to be abolished, because it was instituted for that ende and purpose, that it should be as it were a schoolemaster, and keeper to the people of God, vntill the promise appeared in deed, that is to say, Christ, and the Gospel manifestly published with great efficacie of the Spirit. *x The cause why we were kept vnder the Lawe, is set downe here.* 27 Because age changeth not the condition of seruants, he addeth that we are free by condition, and therefore, seeing we are out of our childehood, we haue no more need of a keeper and Schoolemaster. 28 Vsing a generall particle, lest the Iewes at the least should not thinke themselues bound with the band of the Law, he pronounceth that Baptisme is common to all beleeuers, because it is a pledge of our deliuerie in Christ, as well to the Iewes as to the Grecians, that by this meanes all may be truely one in Christ, that is to say, that promised seed to Abraham, and inheritours of euerlasting life. *y He setteth Baptisme, secretly against circumcision, which the false apostles so much bragged of.* *z The Church must put on Christ, as it were a garment, and be couered with him, that it may be throughly holy, and without blame.* *a You are all one: and so is this great knot and coniunction signified.*

CHAP. IIII.

1 Being deliuered from the bondage of the Law, 4 by Christs comming, who is the end thereof, 9 it is very absurd to slide backe to beggerly ceremonies: 13 Hee calleth them againe therefore to the puritie of the doctrine of the Gospel, 21 confirming his discourse with a fine allegorie.

THen [1] I say, that the heire as long as he is a
childe, differeth nothing from a seruant,
though he be lord of all,

2 But is vnder tutours and gouernours,
[a] vntill the time appointed of the Father.

3 Euen so, we when wee were children,
were in bondage vnder the [b] rudiments of the
world.

1 He declareth that by another double similitude, which he said before concerning the keeper and schoolemaster: For he saith, that the Law (that is, the whole gouernment of Gods house according to the Law) was as it were a tutour or ouerseer appoynted for a time, vntill such time as that protection and ouerseeing which was but for a time, being ended, we should at length come to bee at our owne libertie, and should liue as children, and not as seruants. Moreouer, hee sheweth by the way, that that gouernance of the Lawe, was as it were an A B C, and as certaine principles, in comparison of the doctrine of the Gospel. *a This is added because he that is alwayes vnder a tutour or gouernour, may hardly be counted a freeman.* *b The Law is called rudiments, because that by the Lawe God instructed his Church as it were by rudiments, and afterward powred out his holy Spirit most plentifully in the time of the Gospel.*

2 He vttereth and declareth many things at once, to wit, that this tutourship was ended at his time: that curious men may leaue to aske, why ẏ schoolemastership lasted so long. And moreouer, that we are not sons by nature, but by adoption, and that in the Son of God, who therefore tooke vpon him our flesh, that wee might be made his brethren.

c The time is said to be full, when all parts of it are past and ended, and therefore Christ could not haue come either sooner or later.

d He calleth Marie a woman, in respect of the sexe, & not as the word is vsed in a contrary sence to a virgine, for she remained a virgine still.

* *Romanes 8. 15.*

e The adoption of the sonnes of God, is from euerlasting, but is reueiled and shewed in the time appointed for it.

3 He sheweth that we are in such sort free & set at liberty, that in the meane season we must be gouerned by the Spirit of Christ, which reigning in our hearts, may teach vs the true seruice of the Father. But this is not to serue, but rather to enioy true libertie, as it becommeth sonnes and heires.

4 [2]But when the [c] fulnesse of time was come, God sent foorth his Sonne made of a [d] woman, *and* made vnder the Law,

5 That hee might redeeme them which were vnder the Law, that wee * might receiue the [e] adoption of the sonnes.

6 [3] And because ye are sonnes, God hath [f] sent forth the [g] Spirit of his Sonne into your hearts, which crieth, Abba, Father.

7 Wherefore, thou art no more a [h] seruant, but a sonne: now if *thou be* a sonne, *thou art* also the [i] heire of God through Christ.

8 [4] But euen then, when ye knew not God, ye did seruice vnto them, which by nature are not Gods:

9 But now, seeing ye know God, yea, rather are knowen of God, how turne ye againe vnto impotent & [k] beggerly rudiments, whereunto *as* from the beginning ye will be in bondage [l] againe?

10 Ye obserue dayes, and moneths, & times and yeeres.

11 I am in feare of you, lest I haue bestowed on you labour in vaine.

12 [5] Be ye as I (for I am euen as you) brethren, I beseech you: ye haue not hurt me at all.

13 And ye knowe how through [m] infirmitie of the flesh, I preached the Gospel vnto you at the first.

14 And the [n] triall of me which was in my flesh, ye despised not, neither abhorred: but ye receiued me as an Angel of God, *yea,* as [o] Christ Iesus.

15 [p] What was then your felicitie? for I beare you record, that if it had bene possible, ye would haue plucked out your owne eyes, and haue giuen them vnto me.

16 Am I therefore become your enemie, because I tell you the trueth?

17 They are ielous ouer you [q] amisse: yea, they would exclude you, [r] that ye should altogether loue them.

18 But it is a good thing to loue [ſ] earnestly alwayes in a good thing, and not onely when I am present with you.

19 My little children, of whom I trauaile in birth againe, vntill Christ be formed in you.

20 And I would I were with you now, that I might [t] change my voyce: for I am in doubt of you.

21 [6] Tell me, yee that [u] will be vnder the Lawe, doe ye not heare the Lawe?

22 For it is written, that Abraham had two sonnes, * one by a seruant, and * one by a free woman.

23 But hee which was of the seruant was borne after the [x] flesh: and he which was of the free woman, *was borne* by [y] promise.

24 By the which things another thing is meant: for [z] these *mothers* are the [a] two testaments, the one which is Agar of mount [b] Sina, which gendreth vnto bondage.

25 (For Agar *or* Sina is a mountaine in Arabia, and it [c] answereth to Hierusalem which now is) and [d] she is in bondage with her children.

26 But Hierusalem, which is [e] aboue, is free: which is the mother of vs all.

27 [7] For it is written, * Reioyce thou barren that bearest no children: breake forth, and cry, thou that trauailest not: for the [f] desolate hath many moe children, then she which hath an husband.

28 * Therefore, brethren, we are after the [g] maner of Isaac, children of the [h] promise.

29 But as then he that was borne after the [i] flesh, persecuted him that *was borne* after the [k] Spirit, euen so *it is* now.

30 But what saith the Scripture? * Put out the seruant and her sonne: for the sonne of the seruant shall not be heire with the sonne of the free woman.

31 [8] Then brethren, we are not children of the seruant, but of the free woman.

t Vse other words among you.

6 Because the false apostles vrged this, that vnlesse the Gentiles were circumcised, Christ could profit the nothing at all, and this dissension of them which beleeued of the circumcision, against them which beleeued of the vncircumcision, was full of offence: the Apostle, after diuers argumẽts whereby he hath refuted their errour, bringeth forth an allegorie, wherein he saith, the holy Ghost did shadow out vnto vs, all these mysteries: to wit, ẏ it should come to passe, that two sorts of sonnes, should haue Abraham a father common to them both: but not with like successe: for as Abraham begate Ishmael by the common course of nature, of Agar his bondmaid and a stranger, and begate Isaac of Sara a free woman, by the vertue of ẏ promise, and by grace onely, and the first was not onely not heire, but also persecuted the heire: So there are two couenants, and as it were two sonnes borne to Abraham of those two couenants, as it were of two mothers. The one was made in Sina, without the land of promise, according to which couenant Abrahams children according to the flesh were begotten: to wit, the Iewes, which seeke righteousnesse by that couenant, that is, by the Lawe: but they are not heires, nay they shall at length be cast out of the house, as they that persecute the true heires. The other was made in that high Hierusalem, or in Sion (to wit, by the sacrifice of Christ) which begetteth children of promise, to wit, beleeuers, by the vertue of the holy Ghost, which children (as Abraham) doe rest themselues in the free promise, and they onely by the right of children shalbe partakers of the fathers inheritance, and those seruants shall be shut out. *u That desire so greatly.* * *Gene.16.15.* * *Gen.21.1.* *x As all men are, and by the common course of nature.* *y By vertue of the promise, which Abraham laid hold on for himselfe & his true seed, for otherwise Abraham and Sara were past begetting and bearing of children.* *z These doe represent and shadowe foorth.* *a They are called two couenants, one of the old Testament, and another of the New: which were not two in deed, but in respect of the times, and the diuersitie of the gouernement.* *b He maketh mention of Sina, because that couenant was made in that mountaine, of which mountaine Agar was a shadowe.* *c Looke how the case standeth betwixt Agar and her children, euen so standeth it betweene Ierusalem and hers.* *d That is, Sina.* *e Which is excellent, and of great account.* 7 He sheweth that in this allegorie, he hath followed the steps of Esay, who foretold that the Church should be made and consist of the children of barren Sara, that is to say, of them which onely spiritually should bee made Abrahams children by faith, rather then of fruitfull Agar, euen then foreshewing the casting off of the Iewes, and calling of the Gentiles. * *Esa.54.1.* *f She that is destroyed and wasted.* * *Rom.8.9.* *g After the maner of Isaac, who is the first begotten of the Heauenly Hierusalem, as Ismael is of the slauish Synagogue.* *h That seede vnto which the promise belongeth.* *i By the common course of nature.* *k By the vertue of Gods promise and after a spirituall manner.* * *Gen.21.10.* 8 The conclusion of the former allegorie, that we by no meanes procure and call backe againe the slauerie of the Law, seeing that the children of the bondmaid shall not be heires.

f By that that followeth he gathereth that that went before: for if wee haue his Spirit, we are his sonnes, and if we are his sonnes, then are we free. *g The holy Ghost, who is both of the Father, and of the Sonne: but there is a peculiar reason why hee is called the Spirit of the Sonne, to wit, because the holy Ghost sealeth vp our adoption in Christ, and maketh vs a full assurance of it.* *h The word, seruant, is not taken here for one that liueth in sinne, which is proper to the infidels, but for one that is yet vnder the ceremonies of the Law, which is proper to the Iewes.* *i Partaker of his blessings.* 4 Hee applieth the former doctrine to the Galatians, with a peculiar reprehension: for in comparison of them, the Iewes might haue pretended some excuse as men that were borne and brought vp in that seruice of the Lawe. But seeing that the Galatians were taken and called out of idolatrie to Christian libertie, what pretence might they haue to go backe to those impotent and beggerly rudiments? *k They are called impotent and beggerly ceremonies, being considered apart by themselues without Christ: and againe, for that by that meanes they gaue good testimonie that they were beggers in Christ, when as notwithstanding, for men to fall backe from Christ to ceremonies, is nothing els, but to cast away riches, and to followe beggerie.* *l By going backeward.* 5 Hee mitigateth and qualifieth those things, wherein he might haue seemed to haue spoken somewhat sharpely, wery artificially and diuinely, declaring his good will toward them in such sort, that the Galatians could not but either bee vtterly desperate when they reade these things, or acknowledge their owne lightnesse with teares, and desire pardon. *m Many afflictions.* *n Those dayly troubles wherewith the Lord tried mee amongst you.* *o For my ministeries sake.* *p What a talke was there abroad in the world amongst men, how happy you were?* *q For they are ielous ouer you for their owne commoditie.* *r That they may conuey all your loue from me, to themselues.* *ſ Hee setteth his owne true and good loue, which was earnestly bent toward them, against the naughtie vicious loue of the false apostles.*

CHAP. V.

1 Hauing declared that we came of the free woman, he sheweth the price of that freedome, 13 and how wee should vse the same, 16 that we may obey the Spirit, 19 and resist the flesh.

Stand

STand fast therefore in the libertie wherewith Christ hath made vs free, and be not
intangled againe with the yoke of bondage.
2 [1] * Behold, I Paul say vnto you, that if
ye be [a] circumcised, Christ shall profit you nothing.
3 For I testifie againe to euery man, which
is circumcised, that hee is bound to keepe the
whole Law.
4 Ye are * [b] abolished from Christ: who
soeuer are [c] iustified by the Lawe, ye are fallen
from grace.
5 [2] For we through the [d] Spirit waite for
the hope of righteousnesse through faith.
6 [3] For in Iesus Christ neither circumcision auaileth any thing, neither [4] vncircumcision,
[5] but [e] faith, which worketh by loue.
7 [6] Ye did run well: who did let you, that
ye did not obey the trueth?
8 [7] *It is* not the perswasion of [f] him that
calleth you.
9 * [8] A litle leauen doeth leauen the whole
lumpe.
10 [9] I haue trust in you through the Lord,
that ye will be none otherwise minded: but he
that troubleth you, shall beare *his* condemnation whosoeuer he be.
11 [10] And brethren, if I yet preach circumcision, why doe I yet suffer persecution? Then
is the slander of the crosse abolished.
12 [11] Would to God they were euen cut
off, which doe [g] disquiet you.
13 For brethren, ye haue bene called vnto
libertie: [12] onely vse not *your* libertie as an occasion vnto the flesh, but by loue serue one a-
nother.
14 [13] For [h] all the Lawe is fulfilled in one
worde, which is this, * Thou shalt loue thy
neighbour as thy selfe.
15 [14] If ye bite and deuoure one another,
take heed lest ye be consumed one of another.
16 [15] Then I say, * Walke in the Spirit, and
ye shall not fulfill the lusts of the flesh.
17 For the [i] flesh lusteth against the Spirit,
and the Spirit against the flesh: and these are
contrary one to another, so that ye cannot doe
the same things that ye would.
18 And if ye be led by the Spirit, ye are not
vnder the Law.
19 [16] Moreouer the works of the flesh are
manifest, which are adulterie, fornication, vncleannesse, wantonnesse,
20 Idolatrie, witchcraft, hatred, debate,
emulations, wrath, contentions, seditions, heresies,
21 Enuie, murthers, drunkennes, gluttonie, and such like, whereof I tell you before, as
I also haue told you before, that they which do
such things, shall not inherit the kingdome of
God.
22 But the [k] fruit of the Spirit is loue, ioy,
peace, long suffering, gentlenesse, goodnesse,
faith,
23 Meekenesse, temperancie: [17] against
such there is no Law.
24 For they that are Christs, haue crucified
the flesh with the affections and the lusts.
25 If we [l] liue in the Spirit, let vs also walke
in the Spirit.
26 [18] Let vs not be desirous of vaine glory,
prouoking one another, enuying one another.

1 Another obtestation wherin he plainely witnesseth that iustification of works, and iustification of faith cannot stand together, because no man can be iustified by the Law, but he that doeth fully and perfectly fulfill it. And he taketh the example of circumcision, because it was the ground of all the seruice of the Law, and was chiefly vrged of the false Apostles. * *Acts 15.1.* *a Circumcision is in other places called the seale of righteousnesse, but here we must haue consideration of the circumstance of the time, for now had Baptisme come in the place of circumcision. And moreouer Paul reasoneth according to the opinion that his enemies had of it, which made circumcision a piece of their saluation.* * *1.Cor.1.17.* *b That is, as hee himselfe expoundeth it afterward, yee are fallen from grace.* *c That is, seeke to be iustified by the Law, for in deed no man is iustified by the Law.* 2 Hee priuily compareth the new people with the old: for it is certaine that they also did ground all their hope of iustification and life in faith, and not in circumcision, but so, that their faith was wrapped in the externall and ceremonial worship: but our faith is bare and content with spirituall worship. *d Through the Spirit which ingendreth faith.* 3 He addeth a reason, for that now, circumcision is abolished, seeing that Christ is exhibited vnto vs with full plentie of Spirituall circumcision. 4 He maketh mention also of vncircumcision, lest the Gentiles should please themselues in it, as the Iewes doe in circumcision. 5 The taking away of an obiection: If all that worship of the Law be taken away, wherein then shall we exercise our selues? In charitie, saith Paul: for faith whereof we speake, cannot be idle, nay it bringeth forth daily fruits of charitie. *e So is true faith distinguished from counterfeit faith: for charitie is not ioyned with faith as a fellow cause, to helpe forward our iustification with faith.* 6 Againe he chideth the Galatians, but with an admiration, and therewithall a praise of their former race, to the ende that he may make them more ashamed. 7 He playeth the part of an Apostle with them, and vseth his authoritie, denying that that doctrine can come from God, which is contrary to his. *f Of God.* * *1.Cor 5.6.* 8 Hee addeth this, that he may not seeme to contend vpon a trifle, warning them diligently (by a similitude which he boroweth of leauen, as Christ himselfe also did) not to suffer the puritie of the Apostolicall doctrine to be infected with the least coruption that may bee. 9 He mitigateth the former reprehension, casting the fault vpon the false apostles, against whom he denounceth the horrible iudgement of God. 10 Hee willeth them to consider how that he seeketh not his owne profit in this matter, seeing that he could eschew the hatred of men, if he he would ioyne Iudaisme with Christianitie. 11 An example of a true Pastour inflamed with the zeale of Gods glory, and loue of his flocke. *g For they that preach the Law, cause mens consciences alwayes to tremble.* 12 The third part of this Epistle, shewing that the right vse of Christian libertie consisteth in this, that being deliuered & set at libertie from the slauerie of sinne and the flesh, and being obedient to the spirit, we should serue vnto anothers saluation through loue. 13 He propoundeth the loue of our neighbour, as a marke whereunto all Christians ought to referre all their actions, and thereunto he citeth the testimonie of the Law. *h This particle (All) must be restrained to the second Table* * *Leuit. 19.18. matth.22.39. mar.12.31. rom.13.9 iam.2,8.* 14 An exhortation to the dueties of charitie, by the profit that ensueth thereof, because that no men prouide worse for themselues, then they that hate one another.

15 He acknowledgeth the great weakenes of the godly, for ẏ they are but in part regenerate; but he willeth them to remember that they are indued with the Spirit of God, which hath deliuered them frō the slauerie of sinne, and so of the Lawe, so far forth as it is the vertue of sinne, that they should not giue themselues to lusts. * *Rom.13.14. 1.pet.2.11.* *i For the flesh dwelleth euen in the regenerate man, but the Spirit reigneth, although not without great strife, as is largely set forth, Rom.7.* 16 He setteth out that particularly, which he spake generally, reckoning vp some chiefe effects of the flesh, and opposing them to the fruits of the spirit, that no man may pretend ignorance. *k Therefore they are not the fruits of free will, but so farre forth as our will is made free by grace.* 17 Lest that any man should obiect, that Paul playeth the Sophister, as one who vrging the Spirit, vrgeth nothing but that which the Law commandeth, he sheweth that he requireth not that literall and outward obedience, but spirituall, which proceedeth not from the Lawe, but from the Spirit of Christ, which doeth beget vs againe, and must and ought to be the ruler and guider of our life. *l If we be in deede indued with the quickening Spirit, which causeth vs to die to sinne, and liue to God, let vs shew it in our deeds, that is, by holinesse of life.* 18 He addeth peculiar exhortations according as he knew the Galatians subiect to diuers vices: and first of all he warneth them to take heed of ambition, which vice hath two fellowes, backebiting and enuie, out of which two it cannot be, but many contentions must needs arise.

CHAP. VI.

1 Now hee entreateth particularly of charitie toward such as offend, 6 toward the ministers of the word, 10 and those that are of the houshold of faith: 11 Not like vnto such who haue a counterfeit Zeale of the Law, 13 glorying in the mangling of the flesh, 14 and not in the crosse of Christ.

BRethren, [1] if a man be [a] suddenly taken in
any offence, ye which are [b] spirituall, [c] restore such one with the [d] spirit of meekenesse,
[2] considering thy self, lest thou also be tempted.
2 [3] Beare ye one anothers burden, and so
fulfill the [e] Law of Christ.
3 For if any man seeme to himselfe, that
he is somewhat, when he is nothing, he deceiueth himselfe in his imagination.
4 But let euery man prooue his owne
worke: & then shall he haue reioycing in himselfe onely and not in another.
5 * [4] For euery man shall beare his owne
burden.

1 He condemneth importunate rigour because that brotherly reprehensions ought to be moderated & tempered by the spirit of meeknes *a Through the malice of the flesh and the deuill.* *b Which are vpholden by the vertue of Gods Spirit* *c Labour to fill vp that that is wanting in him.* *d This is a kinde of speech which the Hebrewes vse, giuing to vnderstand thereby, that all good gifts come from Gad.* 2 He toucheth the sore: for they cōmōly are most seuere iudges, which forget their own infirmities. 3 He sheweth ẏ this is the end of reprehensions, to raise vp our brother which is fallen, and not proudly to oppresse him. Therfore euery one must seeke to haue cōmendation of his owne life by approuing of himselfe, & not by reprehendiug others. *e Christ, in plaine & flat words, calleth the cōmandement of charitie, his cōmandement.* * *1.Cor.3.8.* 4 A reason, wherfore men ought to haue ẏ greatest eye vpon thēselues, because that euery man shalbe iudged before God, according to his owne life, & not by cōparing himselfe with other men.

6 [5] Let

5 It is meet that masters should bee found by their schollers, so farre forth as they are able.
f *Of whatsoeuer he hath according to his abilitie.*
* 1.*Cor* 9.7.
6 He commendeth liberalitie towards ỹ poore, and first of all chideth them which were not ashamed to pretend this & that, and all because they would not help their neighbours, as though they could deceiue God: and afterward compareth almes to a spirituall sowing which shall haue a most plẽtifull haruest, so that it shall be very profitable:

6 [5] Let him that is taught in the worde,
make him that hath taught him, partaker of
[f] all *his* * goods.
7 [6] Be not deceiued: God is not mocked:
for whatsoeuer a man soweth, that shall he also reape.
8 For he that soweth to his [g] flesh, shall
of the flesh reape corruption: but he that soweth to the spirit, shall of the spirit reape life e-
uerlasting.
9 * [7] Let vs not therefore be weary of well
doing: for in due season we shall reape, if we
faint not.
10 [8] While we haue therefore time, let vs
doe good vnto all men, but specially, vnto
them, which are of the houshold of faith.
11 ¶ [9] Yee see how large a letter I haue
written vnto you with mine owne hand.
12 As many as desire to make a [h] faire shew
in [i] the flesh, they constraine you to be circumcised, onely beause they would not suffer persecution for the [k] crosse of Christ.
13 For they themselues which are circumcised keepe not the Lawe, but desire to haue
you circumcised, that they might reioyce in
[l] your flesh.
14 [10] But God forbid that I should [m] reioice,
but in the crosse of our Lord Iesus Christ,
whereby the world is crucified vnto me, and I
vnto the world.
15 For in Christ Iesus neither circumcision
auaileth any thing, nor vncircumcision, but a
new creature.
16 And as many as walke according to this
rule, peace *shalbe* vpon them, and mercie, and
vpon the [n] Israel of God.
17 [11] From henceforth let no man put me
to busines: for I beare in my body the [o] marks
of the [p] Lord Iesus.
18 [12] Brethren, the grace of our Lord Iesus
Christ *be* with your [q] spirit, Amen.

¶ Vnto the Galatians written
from Rome.

k *For the preaching of him that was crucified.*
l *That they haue entangled you in Iudaisme, and yet he harpeth on the forme of circumcision.*
10 He sticketh not to compare himselfe with them, shewing that on the contrary part he reioyceth in those afflictiõs which he suffereth for Christes sake, and as he is despised of the world, so doeth he in like sort esteem the world as naught: which is the true circumcision of a true Israelite.
m *When Paul vseth this worde in good sense or part, it signifieth to rest a mans selfe wholy in a thing, and to content himselfe therewith.*
n *Upon the true Israel, whose praise is of God & not of men, Rom.* 2.19.

and compareth couetous nigardlinesse to a carnall sowing, whereof nothing can bee gathered but such things as fade away, and perish by and by. *g* *To the commodities of this present life.* * 2.*Thess*.3.13. 7 Against such as are liberall at the beginning, but continue not, because the haruest seemeth to be deferred very long, as though the seed time and the haruest were at one instant. 8 They that are of the houshold of faith, that is, such as are ioyned with vs in the profession of one selfe same religion ought to be preferred before all other, yet so notwithstanding that our liberalitie extend to all. 9 The fourth and last part of the Epistle, wherein hee returneth to his principall end and purpose: to wit, that the Galatians should not suffer themselues to be led out of the way by the false apostles: and he painteth out those false apostles in their colours, reprouing them of ambition, as men that doe not that which they do, for any affection and zeale they haue to the Law, but onely for this purpose, that they may purchase themselues fauour amongst their owne sort, by the circumcision of the Galatians. *h* *He setteth a faire shew against the trueth.* *i* *In keeping of ceremonies.*

11 Continuing still in the same metaphore, he opposeth his miseries & the marks of those stripes which he bare for Christ sake against the skar of the outward circumcision, as a true marke of his Apostleship. *o* *Markes which are burnt into a mans flesh, as they vsed in olde time, to marke their seruants that had run away from them.* *p* *For it importeth much, whose marks wee beare: for the cause maketh the Martyr, and not the punishment.* 12 Taking his farewell of them, he wisheth them grace, and the spirit against the deceits of the false apostles, which laboured to beat those outward things into their braines. *q* *With your mindes and hearts.*

THE EPISTLE OF PAVL TO THE EPHESIANS.

CHAP. I.

1 *After the salutation,* 4 *he entreateth of the free election of God,* 5 *and adoption,* 7. 13 *from whence mans saluation floweth as from the true naturall fountaine: and because so high a mysterie cannot be vnderstood,* 16 *he prayeth that the full* 20 *knowledge of Christ may by God be reuealed vnto the Ephesians.*

1 The inscription and salutation, whereof we haue spoken in the former Epistles.
* 1.*Cor*.1.2.
a *This is the definition of the Saints, shewing what they are.*
* 1.*Cor*.1.3. 1.*pet*.1.3.
2 The first part of the Epistle, wherin he handleth all the parts of our saluation, propounding the example of the Ephesians, and

PAVL [1] an Apostle of IESVS
CHRIST by the wil of God,
to the * Saints, which are at
Ephesus, and to the [a] faithfull
in Christ Iesus.
2 Grace *be* with you, and
peace from God our Father, and *from* the Lord
Iesus Christ.
3 * [2] Blessed *be* God, [3] and the Father of
our Lord Iesus Christ, [4] which hath blessed vs
with [b] all spiritual blessing in [c] heauenly things
in [5] Christ,
4 [6] As he hath chosen vs in [d] him, before
the foundation of the world, [7] that we [e] should
[f] be holy, and without blame [g] before him in
loue:
5 [8] Who hath predestinate vs, to be adopted through Iesus Christ [h] in himselfe, according to the good pleasure of his will,
6 [9] To the [i] praise of the glory of his grace,
[10] wherewith he hath made vs freely accepted
in *his* beloued.
7 [11] By whom we haue redemption through
his blood, *euen* the forgiuenesse of sinnes, according to his rich grace:
8 [12] [k] Whereby he hath bin aboundant toward vs in [l] all wisedome and vnderstanding,

7 Hee expoundeth the next finall cause, which he maketh double, to wit, sanctification, and iustification, whereof he will speake hereafter. And hereby also two things are to be noted, to wit, that holines of life cannot be separate from the grace of election: and again, what purenesse soeuer is in vs, is the gift of God who hath freely of his mercie chosen vs.

vsing diuers exhortations, & beginning after his maner with thanksgiuing. 3 The efficient cause of our saluation is God, not considered confusedly and generally, but as the father of our Lord Iesus Christ. 4 The next finall cause, and in respect of vs, is our saluation, all things being bestowed vpon vs which are necessarie to our saluation, which kind of blessing is heauenly and proper to the elect. *b* *With all kinde of gracious and bountifull goodnesse which is heauenly indeed & from God onely.* *c* *Which God our Father gaue vs from his high throne from aboue: or because the Saints haue those gifts bestowed on them, which belong properly to the Citizens of heauen.* 5 The matter of our Saluation is Christ, in whom onely we are indued with spirituall blessing and vnto saluation. 6 He declareth the efficient cause, or by what meanes God the Father saueth vs in his Sonne: Because saith he, hee chose vs from euerlasting in his Sonne. *d* *To be adopted in him.*

e *Then God did not chuse vs, because we were, or otherwise should haue bene holy but to the end we should be holy.* *f* *Being clothed with Christs righteousnesse.* *g* *Truely and sincerely.* 8 An other plainer exposition of the efficient cause, and also of eternall election, whereby God is said to haue chosen vs in Christ, to wit, because it pleased him to appoynt vs out when we were not yet borne, whom he would make to be his children by Iesus Christ: so that there is no reason here of our election to be sought, but in the free mercie of God, neither is faith which God foresaw, the cause of our predestination, but the effect. *h* *God respecteth nothing, either that present is, or that is to come, but himselfe onely.* 9 The vttermost & chiefest finall cause is the glory of God the Father, who saueth vs freely in his Sonne *i* *That as his bountifull goodnesse deserueth all praise, so also it should be set forth and published.* 10 Another finall cause more neere, is our iustification, while that he freely accounted vs for iust, in his Sonne. 11 An expounding of the materiall cause, how we are made acceptable to God in Christ, for it is he onely whose sacrifice by the mercie of God is imputed vnto vs, for forgiuenesse of sinnes 12 Now he commeth at length to the formal cause, that is to say to vocation or preaching of the Gospel, whereby God executeth that eternall counsell of our free reconciliation and saluation in Christ. And putting in place of the Gospel all wisdome & vnderstanding, he sheweth how excellent it is. *k* *By which gracious goodnesse and bountifulnes.* *l* *In perfit and sound wisedome.*

9 And

9 And hath opened vnto vs the [m] mystery
of his will [13] according to his good pleasure,
which he had purposed in him.
10 [14] That in the dispensation of the fulnes
of the times, he might [n] gather together in one
all things, both which are in heauen, and which
are in earth, *euen* in Christ:
11 [15] In whom also we are chosen when we
were predestinate according to the purpose of
him, which worketh [o] all things after the counsell of his owne will,
12 That we, which [p] first trusted in Christ,
should be vnto the praise of his glory:
13 [16] In whom also yee *haue trusted*, after
that ye heard the [q] worde of trueth, *euen* the
Gospel of your saluation, wherin also after that
ye beleeued, ye were [r] sealed with the holy
[ſ] Spirit of promise,
14 Which is the earnest of our inheritance,
for the [t] redemption of that libertie purchased
vnto the praise of his glory.
15 [17] Therefore also after that I heard of the
faith, which ye haue in the Lord Iesus, and loue
toward all the Saints,
16 I cease not to giue thankes for you, making mention of you in my prayers,
17 [18] That the GOD of our Lord Iesus
Christ, the Father of [u] glory, might giue vnto
you the spirit of wisedome, and reuelation
through the [x] acknowledging of him,
18 That the eyes of your vnderstanding
may be lightened, that ye may knowe what the
[y] hope is of his calling, and what the riches of
his glorious inheritance *is* in the Saints,
19 [19] And what is the exceeding greatnesse
of his power toward vs which beleeue, *according to the working of his mightie power,
20 [20] Which he wrought in Christ, when
he raised him from the dead, and set him at his
[z] right hand in heauenly *places*,
21 Farre aboue all principality, and power,
and might, and domination, and euery [a] name,
that is named, not in this world onely, but also in that that is to come,
22 [21] And hath made all things subiect vnder his feet, and hath giuen him ouer all things
to be the [b] head of the Church,
23 Which is his body, *euen* the [c] fulnesse of
him that filleth all in all things.

m For vnlesse the Lord had opened vnto vs that mysterie, we could neuer haue so much as dreamed of it our selues.

13 Not onely the election, but also the vocation proceedeth of meere grace.

14 The Father exhibited and gaue Christ, who is the head of all the elect vnto the world, at that time which was conuenient according as he most wisely disposed all times from euerlasting. And Christ is he, in whom all the elect from the beginning of the world, (otherwise wandering and separated from God) are gathered together: of which somewere then in heauen, when he came into the earth, (to wit, such as by faith in him to come, were gathered together) and other being found vpon the earth, were gathered together of him, and the rest are daily gathered together.

n The faithfull are said to be gathered together in Christ, because they are ioyned together with him through faith, and become as it were one man.

15 He applieth seuerally the benefit of vocation to the beleeuing Iewes, going backe to the very fountaine, that euen they also may not attribute their saluation, neither to themselues, nor to their stocke, nor any other thing, but to the onely grace and mercie of God, both because they were called, and also because they were first called. *o All things are attributed to the grace of God without exception, and yet for all that, wee are not stocks, for he giueth vs grace both to will, and to be able to doe those things that are good, Phil. 2.13. p He speaketh of the Iewes.* 16 Now he maketh the Ephesians (or rather all the Gentiles) equall to the Iewes, because that notwithstanding they came last, being called by the same Gospel, they embraced faith, and were sealed vp with the same spirit, which is the pledge of election, vntill the inheritance it selfe be seene, that in them also the glory of God might shine forth & be manifested. *q That word which is trueth in deed, because it commeth from God. r This is a borowed kinde of speech taken of a seale, which being put to any thing, maketh difference betweene those things that are autenticall, and others that are not. ſ With that Spirit, which bringeth not the Lawe, but the promise of free adoption. t Full and perfect.* 17 Hee returneth to the former gratulation, concluding two things together of those things that went before: the first is, that all good things come to vs from God the Father in Christ, and by Christ, that for them he may be praised of vs. The second is, that all those things (which he bringeth to two heads, to wit, faith and charitie) are increased in vs by certaine degrees, so that we must desire increase of his grace, from whome wee haue the beginning, and of whom we hope for the ende. 18 The causes of faith, are God the Father lightning our minds with his holy spirit, that we may embrace Christ opened vnto vs in the Gospel, to the obteining of euerlasting life, and the setting forth of Gods glory. *u Full of maiestie. x For it is not enough for vs to haue knowen God once, but we must know him euery day more and more. y What blessings they are which he calleth you to hope for, whom he calleth to Christ.* 19 The excellencie of faith is declared by the effects, because the mightie power of God is set foorth and shewed therein. * Chap 3.7 col.2.12. 20 The Apostle willeth vs to beholde in our most glorious Christ with the eyes of faith that most excellent power and glory of God, whereof all the faithfull are partakers, although it be as yet very darke in vs, by reason of the ignominie of the crosse, and the weakenesse of the flesh. *z To be set on Gods right hand, is to be partaker of the soueraigntie which he hath ouer all creatures. a Euery thing whatsoeuer it be, or aboue all things, be they of neuer such power or excellencie.*

21 That wee should not think that the excellent glory of Christ is a thing wherwith we haue nought to doe, he witnesseth, that he was appoynted of God the Father, Head of all the Church, and therefore the body must be ioyned to this head, which otherwise would be a maimed thing without the members: which notwithstanding is not of necessitie (seeing that the Church is rather quickened and susteined by the holy vertue of Christ, so far off is it, that he needeth the fulnesse thereof) but of the infinite good will and pleasure of God, who vouchsafeth to ioyne vs to his Sonne. *b In so much that there is nothing but is subiect to him. c For the loue of Christ is so great towards the Church, that though he doe fully satisfie all with all things, yet he esteemeth himselfe but a maimed and vnperfect head, vnlesse he haue the Church ioyned to him as his body.*

CHAP. II.

1 The better to set out the grace of Christ, hee vseth a comparison, calling them to minde, 5 that they were altogether cast-awayes and aliants, 8 That they are saued by grace, 13 and brought neere, 16 by reconciliation through Christ, 17 published by the Gospel.

AND [1] * you *hath he quickened*, that were
[a] dead in [2] trespasses and sinnes,
2 [3] Wherein, in times past ye walked, [4] according to the course of this world, *and* [b] after
the prince that ruleth in the ayre, *euen* the spirit, that now [5] worketh in the [c] children of disobedience,
3 [6] Among whom wee also had our conuersation in time past in the lusts of our [d] flesh,
in fulfilling the wil of the flesh, & of the mind,
and [7] were by nature the [e] children of wrath, as
well as [f] others.
4 [8] But God which is rich in mercy, through
his great loue wherewith he loued vs,
5 Euen when wee were dead by sinnes,
hath quickened vs together in Christ, *by whose*
grace ye are saued,
6 And hath raised vs vp [g] together, and
made vs sit together in the heauenly *places* in
Christ Iesus,
7 That he might shewe in the ages to come
the exceeding riches of his grace through his
kindnesse toward vs in Christ Iesus.
8 For by [h] grace ye are saued through faith,
& that not of your selues: *it is* the gift of God,

1 He declareth againe the greatnesse of Gods good will by comparing that miserable state wherein we are borne, with that dignitie whereunto we are aduanced by God the Father in Christ, So that he describeth that condition in such sort, that he saith, that touching spirituall motions we are not onely borne halfe dead, but wholy and altogether dead. * *Coloss 2.13. a Looke Rom. 6.2. So then he calleth them dead, which are not regenerate: for as the immortalitie of them which are damned is no life: so this knitting together of body & soule, is properly no life, but death in them which are not ruled by the Spirit of God.* 2 He sheweth the cause of death, to wit, sinnes. 3 Hee prooueth by the effects that all were spiritually dead. 4 He proueth this euill to bee vniuersall, in so much as all are slaues of Satan. *b At the pleasure of the prince.* 5 Men are therefore slaues to Satan, because they are willingly rebellious against God. *c They are called the children of disobedience, which are giuen to disobedience.* 6 After that he hath seuerally condemned the Gentiles, he confesseth that the Iewes amongst whom he numbreth himselfe, are not a whit better. *d By the name of flesh in the first place, hee meaneth the whole man, which he diuideth into two parts: into the flesh, which is the part that the Philosophers terme without reason, and into the thought, which they call reasonable: so that hee leaueth nothing in man halfe dead, but concludeth that the whole man is of nature the sonne of wrath.* 7 The Conclusion: All men are borne subiect to the wrath and curse of God. *e Men are saide to bee the children of wrath passiuely, that is to say guiltie of euerlasting death by the iudgement of God, who is angry with them. f Prophane people which knewe not God.* 8 Now hereof followeth another member of the comparison declaring our excellencie, to wit, that by the vertue of Christ we are deliuered from that death, and made partakers of eternall life, to the ende that at length wee may reigne with him. And by diuers and sundry meanes hee beateth this into their heads, that the efficient cause of this benefit is the free mercie of God: and Christ himselfe is the materiall cause: and faith is the instrument, which also is the free gift of God: and the ende is Gods glory. *g To wit, as he addeth afterwards, in Christ, for as yet this is not fulfilled in vs, but onely in our head by whose Spirit we haue begun to die to sinne, and liue to God, vntill that worke be fully brought to an ende: but yet the hope is certaine, for wee are as sure of that we looke for, as we are of that we haue receiued already. h So then, Grace, that is to say, the gift of God, and faith, doe stand one with another, to which two these are contrarie, To be saued by our selues, or by our workes. Therefore what meane they which would ioyne together things of so contrary nature?*

9 [9]Not of workes, least any man should boast himselfe.

10 For we are [i]his workmanship created in Christ Iesus vnto good workes, which God hath ordeined that we should walke in them.

11 [10]Wherefore remember that yee being in time past Gentiles in the flesh, *and* [k]called vncircumcision of them, which are [l]called circumcision in the flesh, made with hands,

12 That yee were, *I say*, at that time [m]without Christ, and were [n]aliants from the commonwealth of Israel, and were *strangers from the couenants of promise, and had no hope, and *were* without God in the world.

13 [11]But now in Christ Iesus, yee which once were farre off, are made neere by the blood of Christ.

14 [12]For he is our peace, which hath made of both one, and hath broken the stoppe of the partition wall,

15 *In abrogating through his flesh the hatred, *that is*, the Law of commaundements *which standeth* in ordinances, for to make of twaine one newe man in himselfe, *so* making peace,

16 And that he might reconcile both vnto God in [o]one body by *his* crosse, and [p]slay hatred therby,

17 [13]And came, and preached peace to you which were a farre off, and to them that were neere.

18 For [q]through him we both haue an entrance vnto the Father by one Spirit.

19 [14]Now therefore yee are no more strangers & forreiners: but citizens with the Saints, and of the houshold of God,

20 [15]And are built vpon the foundation of the Apostles and Prophets, Iesus Christ himselfe being the [r]chiefe corner stone,

21 In whome all the building [s]coupled together, groweth vnto an holy Temple in the Lord.

22 In whom yee also are built together to be the habitation of God by the Spirit.

9 He taketh away expresly and namely from our workes the praise of iustification, seeing that the good workes themselues are the effects of grace in vs.
i He speaketh here of grace, and not of nature: therefore be the workes neuer so good, looke what they are, they are it of grace.
10 Applying the former doctrine to the Gentiles, he sheweth that they were not onely as the Iewes by nature, but also after an especiall sort, strangers and without God: therefore they ought so much the rather remember that saue so great a benefit of God.
k You were called no otherwise then Gentiles, that all the world might witnesse of your vncleannesse.
l Of the Iewes which were knowen from you by the marke of circumcision, the marke of the couenant.
m He beginneth first with Christ, who was the ende of all the promises.
n You had no right or title to the common wealth of Israel.
** Rom. 9.4.*
11 Christ is the onely bond of the Iewes and Gentiles, whereby they be reconciled to God.
12 As by the ceremonies and worship appointed by the Law, the Iewes were diuided from the Gentiles, so now Christ, hauing broken downe the partition wall, ioyneth them both together, both in himselfe, and betwixt themselues, and to God. Whereby it followeth, that whosoeuer establisheth the ceremonies of the Law, maketh the grace of Christ voide and of none effect. ** Colos. 2.14* *o Hee alludeth to the sacrifices of the Law, which represented that true and onely Sacrifice.* *p For hee destroyed death by death, and fastened it as it were to the crosse.* 13 The preaching of the Gospel, is an effectuall instrument of this grace, common as well to the Iewes as to the Gentiles. *q Christ is the gate as it were, by whom wee come to the Father, and the holy Ghost, is as it were our lodes man who leadeth vs.* 14 The conclusion: The Gentiles are taken into the fellowship of saluation, and hee describeth the excellencie of the Church, calling it the citie and house of God. 15 The Lord committed the doctrine of saluation, first to the Prophets, and then to the Apostles, the end whereof, and matter as it were and substance, is Christ. Therefore that is in deede the true and Catholique Church, which is builded vpon Christ by the Prophets and Apostles, as a spirituall temple consecrated to God. *r That is the head of the building, for the foundations are as it were heads of the building.* *s So that God is the workeman not onely of the foundation, but also of the whole building.*

CHAP. III.

1 He declareth that therefore he suffered many things of the Iewes, 3 because hee preached the mystery touching the saluation of the Gentiles, 8 at Gods commaundement. 13 After he desired the Ephesians not to faint for his afflictions: 14 And for this cause hee prayeth vnto God, 18 That they they may vnderstand the great loue of Christ.

For [1]this cause, I Paul *am* the [a]prisoner of Iesus Christ for you Gentiles,

2 If ye haue heard of the dispensation of the grace of God, which is giuen me to you ward,

3 *That is*, that *God* by reuelation hath shewed this mysterie vnto me (as I wrote aboue in few words,

4 Whereby when ye read, yee may know mine vnderstanding in the mysterie of Christ)

5 Which in [b]other ages was not opened vnto the sonnes of men, as it is now reueiled vnto his holy Apostles and Prophets by the Spirit,

6 That the Gentiles should bee inheriters also, and of the same body, and partakers of his promise in Christ by the Gospel,

7 Whereof I am made a minister by the gift of the grace of God giuen vnto me through the effectuall working of his power.

8 Euen vnto mee the least of all Saints is this grace giuen, that I should preach among the Gentiles the vnsearchable riches of Christ,

9 And to make cleare vnto all men what the fellowship of the mysterie is, which from the beginning of the world hath beene hid in God, who hath created all things by Iesus Christ,

10 [2]To the intent, that now vnto principalities and powers in heauenly *places*, might bee knowen by the Church the [c]manifold wisedome of God,

11 According to the [d]eternall purpose which he wrought in Christ Iesus our Lord:

12 By whom wee haue boldnesse and entrance with confidence by faith in him.

13 Wherefore I desire that yee faint not at my tribulations for your sakes, which is your glorie.

14 [3]For this cause I bow my knees vnto the Father of our Lord Iesus Christ,

15 (Of whom is named the whole [e]family in heauen and in earth)

16 That he might graunt you according to the [f]riches of his glorie, that ye may be strengthened by his spirit in the [g]inner man,

17 That Christ my dwell in your hearts by faith:

18 That yee, being rooted and grounded in [h]loue, may bee able to comprehend with all Saints, [i]what is the breadth, and length, and depth and height:

19 And to know the [k]loue of Christ, which [l]passeth knowledge, that yee may bee filled with all [m]fulnesse of God.

1 He maintaineth his Apostleship against the offence of the crosse, whereon also he taketh an argument to confirme himselfe, affirming that he was not onely appointed an Apostle by the mercie of God, but was also particularly appointed to the Gentiles to call them on euery side to saluation, because God had so determined it from the beginning although he deferred a great while the manifestation of that his counsell.
a These words, the prisoner of Iesus Christ, are taken passiuely, that is to say I Paul am cast into prison for maintaining the glory of Christ.
b He meaneth not that none knew the calling of the Gentiles before, but because very fewe knew of it, and they that did know it, as the Prophets, had it reueiled vnto them very darkely and vnder figures.
2 The vnlooked for calling of the Gentiles, was as it were a glasse to the heauenly Angels wherein they might behold the marueilous wisedome of God.
c God neuer had but one way onely, to saue men by: but it had diuers fashions & formes.
d Which was before all beginnings.
3 He teacheth by his owne example, that the efficacie of the doctrine dependeth vpon the grace of God, and therefore we ought to ioyne prayers with the preaching and hearing of the word: which are needfull not onely to them which are yonglings in religion, but euen to the oldest also, that they growing vp more and more by faith in Christ being confirmed with all spirituall giftes, may bee grounded and rooted in the knowledge of that immeasurable loue, wherewith God the Father hath loued vs in Christ, seeing that the whole family, whereof part is already receiued into heauen, and part is yet here on earth, dependeth vpon that adoption of the heauenly Father, in his onely Sonne. *e All that whole people, which had but one houshold Father, and that is the Church which is adopted in Christ.* *f According to the greatnesse of his mercie.* *g Looke Romanes 7.22.* *h Wherewith God loueth vs, which is the roote of our election.* *i How perfite that worke of Christ is in euery part.* *k Which God hath shewed vs in Christ.* *l Which passeth all the capacitie of mans wit, to comprehend it fully in his mind: for otherwise who so hath the spirit of God perceiueth so much (according to the measure that God hath giuen him) as is sufficient to saluation.* *m So that we haue aboundantly in vs, whatsoeuer things are requisite to make vs perfit with God.*

4 He breaketh foorth into a thankesgiuing, whereby the Ephesians also may be confirmed to hope of any thing of God.

20 [4] Vnto him therefore that is able to doe
exceeding aboundantly aboue all that we aske
or thinke, according to the power that worketh in vs,
21 *Be* praise in the Church by Christ Iesus,
throughout all generations for euer, Amen.

CHAP. IIII.

These three last chapters conteine precepts of maners. 1 Hee exhorteth them to mutuall loue. 7 Sundrie giftes are therefore bestowed of God, 16 That the Church may bee built vp. 18 He calleth them from the vanitie of the infidels, 25 from lying, 29 and from filthy talking.

1 Another part of the Epistle, conteining precepts of Christian life, the summe whereof is this, that euery man behaue himselfe as it is meete for so excellent grace of God.

a *By this is meant the generall calling of the faithfull, which is this, to be holy as our God is holy.*

2 Secondly, he commendeth meekenesse of the minde, which is shewed foorth by bearing one with another.

b *Looke Matth. 18.25.*

3 Thirdly hee requireth perfit agreement, but yet such as is knit with the band of the holy Ghost.

4 An argument of great waight, for an earnest intertaining of brotherly loue and charitie one with another, because wee are made one body as it were of one God and Father, by one Spirit, worshipping one Lord with one faith, and consecrated to him with one Baptisme, and hope of one selfe same

I Therefore, [1] being a prisoner in the Lord,
pray you that yee walke worthy of the [a] vocation whereunto yee are called,
2 [2] With all humblenesse of minde, and
meekenesse, with [b] long suffering, supporting
one another through loue,
3 [3] Endeuouring to keepe the vnitie of the
Spirit in the bond of peace.
4 [4] There *is* one body, and one Spirit, euen
as yee are called in one hope of your vocation.
5 *There is* one Lord, one Faith, one Baptisme,
6 One God and Father of all, which is [c] a-
boue all, and [d] through all, and [e] in you all.
7 [5] But vnto euery one of vs is giuen
grace, according to the measure of the [f] gift
of Christ.
8 Wherefore he saith, When he ascended
vp on hie, he led [g] captiuitie captiue, and gaue
gifts vnto men.
9 (Now, in that he ascended, what is it but
that he had also descended first into the [h] lowest parts of the earth?
10 Hee that descended, is euen the same
that ascended, farre aboue all heauens, that hee
might [i] fill [k] all things.)
11 [6] He therfore gaue some *to be* [l] Apostles,
and some [m] Prophets, and some [n] Euangelists,
and some [o] Pastours, and Teachers,
12 [7] For the repairing of the Saints, for the
worke of the ministerie, *and* for the edification
of the [p] body of Christ,
13 [8] Till wee all meete together (in the
[q] vnitie of faith and that acknowledging of the
Sonne of God) vnto a perfit man, *and* vnto the
measure of the [r] age of the fulnesse of Christ,
14 [9] That we hencefoorth be no more children, [10] wauering and caried about with euery
wind of doctrine, by the [s] deceite of men, and
[t] with craftinesse, whereby they lay in waite to
deceiue.
15 [11] But let vs follow the trueth in loue,
and in all things grow vp into him, which is
the head, *that is*, Christ.
16 By whome all the body being coupled,
and knit together by euery ioynt, for the furniture *thereof* (according to the [u] effectuall power, *which is* in the measure of euery part) receiueth [x] increase of the body, vnto the edifying
of it selfe in [y] loue.
17 [12] This I say therefore and testifie in
the Lord, that yee hencefoorth walke not
as * other Gentiles walke, in [z] vanitie of their
minde,
18 Hauing their vnderstanding darkened,
and being strangers from the [a] life of God
through the ignorance that is in them, because
of the hardnesse of their heart:
19 Which being [b] past feeling, haue giuen
themselues vnto wantonnesse, to worke all vncleannesse, *euen* with [c] greedinesse.
20 [13] But yee haue not so learned Christ,
21 If so bee yee haue heard him, and
haue beene taught by him, [d] as the trueth is
in Iesus,
22 * *That is*, that yee cast off, concerning the conuersation in time past, [e] that
olde man, which is corrupt through the deceiueable lusts,
23 And bee renewed in the [f] Spirit of your
minde,
24 And put on the new man, which [g] after
God is created [h] vnto righteousnesse, and [i] true
holinesse.
25 [14] Wherefore cast off lying, and speake
euery man trueth vnto his neighbour: for wee
are members one of another.

q *In that most neere coniunction which is knit and fastened together by faith.*

r *Christ is said to grow vp to full age, not in himselfe, but in vs.*

9 Betwixt our childhood (that is to say, a very weake state, while as wee doe yet altogether wauer) and our perfit age, which we shall haue at length in another world, there is a meane, to wit, our youth, and steady going forward to perfection.

10 Hee compareth them which rest not themselues vpon the word of God, to little boates which are tossed hither and thither with the doctrines of men as it were with contrarie winds, and therewithall forewarneth them that it commeth to passe not onely by the lightnesse of mans braine, but also by the craftinesse of certaine, which make as it were an art of it.

s *With those vncertaine chances which tosse men to and fro.*

t *By the deceite of those men which are very well practised in deceiuing of other.*

11 By earnest affection of the trueth and loue, we grow vp into Christ: for he

glory, whereunto wee are called. Therefore whosoeuer breaketh charitie, breaketh all these things asunder. c *Who onely hath the chiefe authoritie ouer the Church.* d *Who only powreth forth his prouidence, through all the members of the Church.* e *Who onely is ioyned together with vs in Christ.* 5 Hee teacheth vs, that we in deede are all one body, and that all good giftes proceede from Christ onely, who reigneth in heauen hauing mightily conquered all his enemies (from whence hee heapeth all giftes vpon his Church:) but yet notwithstanding these gifts are diuersly and sundry wayes diuided according to his will and pleasure, and therefore euery man ought to bee content with that measure that God hath giuen him, and to bestow it to the common profit of the whole body. f *Which Christ hath giuen.* g *A multitude of captiues.* h *Downe to the earth, which is the lowest part of the world.* i *Fill with his giftes.* 6 First of all hee reckoneth vp the Ecclesiasticall functions, which are partly extraordinarie and for a season, as Apostles, Prophets, Euangelists, and partly ordinarie and perpetuall, as Pastors and Doctors. l *The Apostles were those twelue vnto whom Paul was afterward added, whose office was to plant Churches throughout all the world.* m *The Prophets office was one of the chiefest, which were men of marueilous wisedome, and some of them could foretell things to come.* n *These the Apostles vsed as fellowes in the execution of their office, being not able to answere all places themselues.* o *Pastours are they which gouerne the Church, and Teachers are they which gouerne the schooles.* 7 He sheweth the end of Ecclesiasticall functions, to wit, that by the ministerie of men all the Saints may so grow vp together, that they may make one mystical body of Christ. p *The Church.* 8 The vse of this ministerie is perpetuall so long as we are in this world, that is, vntill that time that hauing put off the flesh, and throughly and perfitly agreeing betwixt our selues, we shall bee ioyned with Christ our head. Which thing is done by that knowledge of the Son of God increasing in vs, and he himselfe by little and little growing vp in vs vntill we come to be a perfit man, which shall bee in the world to come, when God shall be all in all.

(being effectuall by the ministerie of his word, which as the vitall spirit doth so quicken the whole body, that it nourisheth all the limmes thereof according to the measure and proportion of each one) quickneth and cherisheth his Church, which consisteth of diuers functions, as of diuers members, and preserueth the proportion of euery one. And thereof it followeth that neither this body can liue without Christ, neither can any man grow vp spiritually, which separateth himselfe from the other members u *Of Christ who in maner of the soule, quickneth all the members.* x *Such increase as is meete the body should haue.* y *Charitie is the knitting of the limmes together.* 12 He descendeth to the fruites of Christian doctrine, and reasoneth first vpon the principles of maners and actions, setting downe a most graue comparison betweene the children of God, and them, which are not regenerate: For in these men, all the powers of the minde are corrupted, and their minde is giuen to vanitie, and their senses are darkened with most grosse mistinesse, and their affections are so accustomed by little and little to wickednesse, that at length they runne headlong into all vncleannesse, being vtterly destitute of all iudgement. * *Rom. 1.21.* z *If the noblest parts of the soule bee corrupted, what is man but corruption onely?* a *Whereby God liueth in them.* b *Voide of all iudgement.* c *They stroue to passe one another, as though there had beene some gaine to bee gotten by it.* 13 Here followeth the contrarie part touching men which are regenerate by the true and liuely knowledge of Christ, which haue other principles of their doing farre different, to wit, holy and honest desires, and a minde cleane changed by the vertue of the holy Ghost, from whence proceede also like effects, as a iust and holy life in deede. d *As they haue learned, which acknowledge Christ in deed, and in good earnest.* * *Col. 3.8.* e *Your selues.* f *Where there ought to haue beene the greatest force of reason, there is the greatest corruption of all which wasteth all things.* g *After the image of God.* h *The effect and end of the new creation* i *Not fained nor counterfeit.* 14 He commendeth seuerally certaine peculiar Christian vertues, and first of all he requireth truth, (that is to say sincere maners) condemning all deceite and dissembling, because we are borne one for another.

26 [15] Be

26 [15] Be [k] angrie, but sinne not: let not the
sunne goe downe [l] vpon your wrath,
27 Neither giue place to the deuill.
28 [16] Let him that stole, steale no more: but
let him rather labour, and worke with his hands
the thing which is [m] good, that he may haue to
giue vnto him that needeth.
29 [17] Let no [n] corrupt communication proceede out of your mouthes: but that which is
good to the vse of edifying, that it may minister [o] grace vnto the hearers.
30 [18] And grieue not the holy Spirit of
God, by whome yee are sealed vnto the day of
redemption.
31 Let all bitternesse, and anger, and wrath,
crying, and euill speaking bee put away from
you, with all maliciousnesse.
32 Bee yee courteous one to another, and
tender hearted, freely forgiuing one another,
[19] euen as God for Christes sake, freely forgaue you.

15 He teacheth vs how to bridle our anger in such sort, that, although it bee hote, yet that it breaketh not out, and that it be straightwayes quenched before we sleepe: least Satan taking occasion to giue vs euill counsell through the wicked counseller, destroy vs.
k If it so fall out, that you be angrie, yet sin not: that is, bridle your anger, & do not wickedly put that in execution, which you haue wickedly conceiued.
l Let not the night come vpon you in your anger, that is, make an atonement quickly, for all matters.
16 He descendeth from the heart, to the hands, condemning theft: and because the men which giue themselues to this wickednesse, vse to pretend pouertie, he sheweth that labour is a good remedie against pouertie, which God blesseth in such sort, that they which labour haue alwayes some ouerplus to helpe other, so farre is it from this, that they are constrained to steale other mens goods. *m By labouring in things that are holy, and profitable to his neighbour.* 17 He bridleth the tongue also, teaching vs so to temper our talke, that our hearers mindes bee not onely not destroyed, but also instructed. *n Word for word, rotten.* *o By force, hee meaneth that, whereby men most profit to the going on forward in godlinesse and loue.* 18 A generall precept against all excesse of affections which dwell in that part of the mind, which they call, Angrie, and hee setteth against them the contrarie meanes. And vseth a most vehement preface, how we ought to take heede that wee grieue not the holy Spirit of God through our immoderatenesse and intemperancie, who dwelleth in vs to the end, to moderate all our affections. 19 An argument taken from the example of Christ, most graue and vehement, both for pardoning of those iniuries which haue beene done vnto vs by our greatest enemies, and much more for hauing consideration of the miserable, and vsing moderation and gentle behauiour towards all men.

CHAP. V.

2 Lest in those vices which hee reprehended, they should set light by his admonitions, 5 Hee terrifieth them by denouncing seuere iudgements, 8 and stirreth them forward. 15 Then hee descendeth from generall lessons of maners, 21 to the particular dueties of wiues 25 and husbands.

BE yee therefore followers of God, as deare
children.
2 * And walke in loue, euen as Christ hath
loued vs, and hath giuen himselfe for vs, *to bee*
an offering and a sacrifice of a sweete smelling
sauour to God.
3 * [1] But fornication, and all vncleannesse,
or couetousnesse, let it not bee once named a-
mong you, as it becommeth Saints,
4 Neither filthinesse, neither foolish talking, neither [a] iesting, which are things not
comely, but rather giuing of thankes.
5 [2] For this yee knowe, that no whore-
monger, neither vncleane person, nor couetous person, which is an [b] idolater, hath any
inheritance in the kingdome of Christ, and
of God.
6 * Let no man deceiue you with vaine
words: for, for such things commeth the wrath
of God vpon the children of disobedience.

* *Iohn* 15.34. *and* 15.12. 1.*iohn* 3.23.
* *Chap.* 4.29. *coloss.* 3.5. 1.*thes.* 2.17.
1 Now he commeth to another kind of affections, which is in that part of the mind, which men call couetous or desirous: and he reprehendeth fornication, couetousnes, and iesting, very sharpely.
a Iestes which men cast one at an other: that no lightnesse be seene, nor euill example giuen, nor any offence mooued by euill words or backbiting.
2 Because these sinnes are such that the most part of men count them not for sinnes, hee awaketh the godly to the ende they should so much the more take heede to themselues from them as most hurtfull plagues. *b A bondslaue to idolatrie, for the couetous man thinketh that his life standeth in his goods* * *Matth.* 24.4.*marke* 13.5.*luke* 21.8. * 2.*Thes.* 2.3.

7 [3] Be not therfore companions with them.
8 For ye were once darknesse, but are now
[c] light in the Lord: walke as children of light,
9 (For the fruit of the [d] Spirit *is* in all goodnesse, and righteousnesse and trueth)
10 Approouing that which is pleasing to
the Lord.
11 And haue no fellowship with the vnfruitfull workes of darkenesse, but euen [e] reprooue them rather.
12 For it is shame euen to speake of the
things which are done of them in secret.
13 But all things when they are reprooued
of the light, are manifest: for it is light that maketh all things manifest.
14 Wherefore [f] hee saith, Awake thou that
sleepest, and stand vp from the [g] dead, & Christ
shall giue thee light.
15 [4] Take heede therefore that yee walke
circumspectly, not as fooles, but as * wise,
16 [h] Redeeming the season: for the [i] dayes
are euill.
17 * Wherefore, be yee not vnwise, but vnderstand what the will of the Lord is.
18 [5] And be not drunken with wine, wherein is [k] excesse: but be fulfilled with the Spirit,
19 Speaking vnto your selues in psalmes
and hymnes, and spirituall songs, singing, and
making melody to the Lord in your [l] hearts,
20 Giuing thankes alwayes for all things
vnto God euen the father, in the Name of our
Lord Iesus Christ,
21 [6] Submitting your selues one to another
in the feare of God.
22 ¶ * [7] Wiues, submit your selues vnto
your husbands, [8] as vnto the Lord.
23 * [9] For the husband is the wiues head,
euen as Christ is the head of the Church, [10] and
the same is the sauiour of *his* body.
24 [11] Therefore as the Church is in subiection to Christ, euen so *let* the wiues *bee* to their
husbands in euery thing.
25 ¶ * [12] Husbands, loue your wiues, e-
uen as Christ loued the Church, and gaue him
selfe for it,
26 [13] That he might [m] sanctifie it, and cleanse
it by the washing of water through the [n] word,

3 Because wee are not so ready to any thing, as to follow euill examples, therefore the Apostle warneth the godly to remember alwayes, that the other are but as it were darknesse, and that they themselues are as it were light. And therefore the other commit all villanies (as men are wont in the darke) but they ought not onely not to follow their examples, but also (as the propertie of the light is) reproue their darkenesse, and to walke so (hauing Christ that true light going before them) as it becommeth wise men.
c The faithfull are called light, both because they haue the true light in them which lighteneth them, and also because they giue light to other, insomuch, that their honest conuersation reprooueth the life of wicked men.
d By whose force we are made light in the Lord.
e Make them open to all the world, by your good life.
f The Scripture, or God in the Scripture.
g Hee speaketh of the death of sinne.
4 The worse and more corrupt that the maners of this world are, the more watchfull ought we to be against all occasions, and respect nothing but the will of God.
* *Coloss.* 4.5.
h This is a metaphore taken from the merchants: who preferre the least profit that may bee before all their pleasures. *i The times are troublesome and sharpe.* * *Rom.* 12.2. 1.*thes* 4.3. 5 He setteth the sober and holy assemblies of the faithfull, against the dissolute banquets of the vnfaithfull, in which ye praises of the only Lord must ring, be it in prosperitie or aduersitie. *k All kind of riot, ioyned with all maner of filthinesse and shamefulnesse* *l With an earnest affection of the heart, and not with the tongue only.* 6 A short repetition of the end wherunto all things ought to be referred, to serue one another for Gods sake. * *Colo.* 3.18 *tit.* 2.5. 1.*pet* 3.1. 7 Now he descendeth to a family, diuiding orderly all ye parts of a family. And he saith that the dutie of wiues consisteth herein, to be obedient to their husbands. 8 The first argument, for they cannot be disobedient to their husbands, but they must resist God also, who is the authour of this subiection * 1 *Cor.* 11.3. 9 A declaration of the former saying: Because God hath made the man head of the woman in matrimonie, as Christ is the head of the Church. 10 Another argument; Because the good estate of the wife dependeth of the man, so that this submission is not only iust, but also very profitable: as also the saluation of the Church is of Christ, although farre otherwise. 11 The conclusion of the wiues dueties towards their husbands. * *Colos.* 3.19. 12 The husbands duetie towards their wiues, is to loue them as themselues, of which loue, the loue of Christ toward his Church is a liuely paterne. 13 Because many men pretend the infirmities of their wiues to excuse their owne hardnesse and crueltie, the Apostle willeth vs to marke what maner of Church Christ gate, when he ioyned it to himselfe, and how hee doeth not onely not lothe all her filth, and vncleannesse, but cease not to wipe the same away with his cleannesse, vntill he wholly purged it. *m Make it holy.* *n Through the promise of free iustification and sanctification in Christ, receiued by faith.*

27 That hee might make it vnto himselfe a glorious Church,[o] not hauing spot or wrinkle, or any such thing: but that it should bee holy and without blame.

28 [14] So ought men to loue their wiues, as their owne bodies: he that loueth his wife, loueth himselfe.

29 For no man euer yet hated his [p] owne flesh, but nourisheth and cherisheth it, euen as the Lord *doeth* the Church.

30 For we are members of his body, [q] of his flesh, and of his bones.

31 * For this cause shall a man leaue father and mother, and shall [r] cleaue to his wife, and they twaine shall be one flesh.

32 [15] This is a great secret, but I speak concerning Christ, and concerning the Church.

33 [16] Therefore euery one of you, *doe yee so:* let euery one loue his wife, euen as himselfe, and *let* the wife *see* that shee feare her husband.

o The Church as it is considered in it selfe, shall not be without wrinkle, before it come to the marke it shooteth at: for while it is in this life, it runneth in a race: but if it be considered in Christ, it is cleane and without wrinckle.

14 Another argument: Euery man loueth himselfe, euen of nature: therefore hee striueth against nature that loueth not his wife. hee prooueth the consequent, first by the mysticall knitting of Christ and the Church together, and then by the ordinance of God, who saith, that man and wife are as one, that is, not to be deuided. *p His owne body.* *q He alludeth to the making of the woman, which signifieth our coupling together with Christ, which is wrought by faith, but is sealed in the Sacrament of the Supper.* *Gen.2.24 mat.19.5.mar.10.7.1 cor.6.16.* *r Looke Mat 19 5* 15 That no man might dreame of naturall coniunction or knitting of Christ and his Church together (such as the husbands and the wiues is) he sheweth that it is secret, to wit, spirituall and such as farre differeth from the common capacitie of man: as which consisteth by the vertue of the Spirit, and not of the flesh by faith, and by no naturall band. 16 The conclusion both of the husbands duetie toward his wife, and of the wiues toward her husband.

CHAP. VI.

1 He sheweth the dueties of children, 5 seruants, 9 and masters: 10 Then hee speaketh of the fierce battell that the faithfull haue, 12 and what weapons we must vse in the same: 21 In the end he commendeth Tychicus.

1 Children, [1] * obey your parents [2] in the [a] Lord: [3] for this is right.

2 * [4] Honour thy father & mother [5] (which is the first commandement with [b] promise.)

3 That it may bee well with thee, and that thou maiest liue long on earth.

4 [6] And yee, fathers, prouoke not your children to wrath: but bring them vp in instruction and [c] information of the Lord.

5 [7] * Seruants, be obedient vnto them that are *your* masters, [8] according to the flesh, with [d] feare and trembling in singlenesse of your hearts as vnto Christ,

6 Not with seruice to the eye as men pleasers, but as the seruants of Christ, [9] doing the will of God from the heart,

7 With good will, seruing the [e] Lord, and not men.

1 He commeth to another part of a family, and sheweth that the duetie of the children toward their parents, consisteth in obedience vnto them. ** Coloss.3 20.* 2 The first argument: because God hath so appointed: whereupon it followeth also that children are so farre forth bound to obey their parents, as they may not swarue from the true worship of God. *a For the Lord is authour of all fatherhood, and therefore we must yeeld such obedience as hee will haue vs.* 3 The second argument: because this obedience is most iust. ** Exod.20.12. deut.5.16 eccles.3.9. matth 15.4. marke 7.10.* 4 A proofe of the first argument. 5 The third argument taken of the profit that ensueth thereby: Because the Lord vouchsafed this commaundement amongst all the rest of a speciall blessing. *b With a speciall promise: for otherwise the second commandement hath a promise of mercie to a thousand generations, but that promise is generall.* 6 It is the duetie of fathers to vse their fatherly authoritie moderately and to Gods glorie. *c Such informations and precepts as being taken out of Gods booke, are holy and acceptable to him.* 7 Now he descendeth to the third part of a family, to wit, to the duetie both of the masters, and of the seruants. And hee sheweth that the duetie of seruants consisteth in an heartie loue and reuerence to their masters. ** Coloss 3.22.titus 2.9.1.pet.2.18.* 8 Hee mitigateth the sharpenesse of seruice, in that they are spiritually free notwithstanding the same, and yet that spirituall freedome taketh not away corporall seruice: insomuch that they cannot bee Christes, vnlesse they serue their masters willingly and faithfully, so farre foorth as they may with safe conscience *d With carefull reuerence: for slauish feare is not allowable, much lesse in Christian seruants.* 9 To cut off occasion of all pretences, hee teacheth vs that it is Gods will that some are either borne or made seruants, and therefore they must respect Gods will although their seruice bee neuer so hard. *e Being mooued with a reuerence to Godward, as though yee serued God himselfe.*

8 [10] And know yee that whatsoeuer good thing any man doth, that same shall he receiue of the Lord, whether *he be* bond or free.

9 [11] And yee masters doe the same things vnto them, putting away threatning: & know that euen your master also is in heauen, neither is there * [f] respect of person with him.

10 ¶ [12] Finally, my brethren, bee strong in the Lord, and in the power of his might.

11 Put on the whole armour of God, that yee may bee able to stand against the assaults of the deuill.

12 [13] For wee wrestle not against flesh and [g] blood, but against * [h] principalities, against powers, *and* against the worldly gouernors, *the princes* of the darknes of this world, against spiritual wickednesses, *which are* in the hie places.

13 [14] For this cause take vnto you the whole armour of God, that yee may bee able to resist in the [i] euill day, and hauing finished all things, stand fast.

14 Stand therefore, and your loynes girded about with veritie, and hauing on the brest plate of righteousnesse,

15 And your feete shod with the [k] preparation of the Gospel of peace.

16 Aboue all, take the shield of Faith, wherewith yee may quench all the fierie darts of the wicked.

17 And take the helmet of saluation, and the sword of the Spirit, which is the word of God.

18 And pray alwayes with all maner prayer and supplication in the [l] Spirit: and watch therunto with all perseuerance and supplication for all Saints,

19 And for me, that vtterance may bee giuen vnto me, that I may open my mouth boldly to publish the secret of the Gospel.

20 Whereof I am the ambassador in bonds, that therein I may speake boldly, as I ought to speake.

21 ¶ [15] But that yee may also knowe mine affaires, *and* what I doe, Tychicus *my* deare brother and faithfull minister in the Lord, shall shew you of all things,

22 Whom I haue sent vnto you for the same purpose, that yee might know mine affaires, and that he might comfort your hearts.

23 Peace *bee* with the brethren, and loue with faith from God the Father, and *from* the Lord Iesus Christ.

24 Grace *be* with all them which loue our Lord Iesus Christ, to *their* [m] immortalitie, Amen.

¶ Written from Rome vnto the Ephesians, *and sent* by Tychicus.

10 Although they serue vnkind and cruell masters, yet the obedience of seruants is no lesse acceptable to God, then ỹ obedience of them that are free. 11 It is the duetie of masters to vse the authoritie that they haue ouer their seruants, modestly and holily, seeing that they in an other respect haue a common master which is in heauen, who will iudge both the bond and the free. ** Deut.10.17. 2.chro.16.7.iob. 34.19.act.10.34 rom.2.11 gala 2. 6.coloss 3.25. 1 pet.1.17.* *f Either of freedome or bondage.* 12 He concludeth the other part of this Epistle, with a graue exhortation, that all be ready and fight constantly, trusting to spirituall weapons, vntill their enemies be cleane put to flight And first of all he warneth vs to take the armour of God, wherewith onely our enemy may be dispatched. 13 Secondly he declareth that our chiefest and mightiest enemies are inuisible, that we may not thinke that our chiefest conflict is with men. *g. Against men, which are of a fraile and brittle nature, against which are set spirituall subtilties, more mightie then the other by a thousand parts.* ** Chap.2.2.* *h He giueth these names to the euill angels, by reason of the effects which they worke: not that they are able to doe the same of themselues, but because God giueth them the bridle.* 14 He sheweth that these enemies are put to flight with the onely armour of God, to wit, with vprightnesse of conscience, a godly and holy life, knowledge of the Gospel, faith, and to be short, with the word of God, and vsing daily earnest prayer for the health of the Church, and especially for the constancie of the true, godly & valiant ministers of the word. *i Looke Chap.5.16.* *k That the preparation of the Gospel may bee as it were shooes to you: and it is very fitly called the Gospel of peace, for that, seeing we haue to goe to God through most dangerous rankes of enemies, this may encourage vs to goe on manfully, in that ye know by the doctrine of the Gospel, that we take our iourney to God who is at peace with vs.* *l That holy prayers may proceede from the holy spirit.* 15 A familiar and very amiable declaration of his state, together with a solemne prayer, wherewith Paul is wont to ende his Epistles. *m To life euerlasting.*

THE EPISTLE OF PAVL TO THE PHILIPPIANS.

CHAP. I.

3 Hauing testified his godly and tender affection towards the Philippians, 12 hee intreateth of himselfe, and his bonds: 22 And pricketh him forward by his owne example, 27 and exhorteth them to vnitie 28 and patience.

PAVL [1] and Timotheus
the seruants of IESVS
CHRIST, to all the
Saints in Christ Iesus
which are at Philippi,
with the [a] Bishops, and
Deacons:
2 Grace *be* with you,
and peace from God our Father, and *from* the
Lord Iesus Christ.
3 I thanke my God, *hauing* you in perfect
memorie,
4 (Alwayes in all my prayers for all you,
praying with gladnesse.)
5 Because of the [b] fellowship which yee
haue in the Gospel, from the [c] first day vnto now.
6 And I am perswaded of this same thing,
that hee that hath begunne *this* good worke
in you, will performe it vntill the [d] day of Iesus Christ.
7 As it becommeth me, so to iudge of you
all, because I haue you in remembrance, that
both in my [e] bands, and in *my* defence and confirmation of the Gospel you all were partakers
of my [f] grace.
8 [2] For God is my record, how I long after you all from the very heart roote in Iesus
Christ.
9 [3] And this I pray, that your loue may a-
bound, yet more and more in knowledge, and
in all iudgement,
10 That ye may allow those things which
are best, that yee may be pure, and without offence vntill the day of Christ,
11 Filled with the [g] fruites of righteousnes,
which are by Iesus Christ vnto the glory and
praise of God.
12 ¶ [4] I would yee vnderstood, brethren,
that the things which *haue come* vnto me, are
turned rather to the furthering of the Gospel,
13 So that my bands [h] in Christ are famous
throughout all the [i] iudgement hall, and in all
other *places*,
14 In so much that many of the brethren in
the Lord are boldned through my bands, and
dare more frankly speake the [k] word.
15 Some preach Christ euen through enuie
and strife, and some also of good will.
16 The one part preacheth Christ of contention *and* not [l] purely, supposing to adde
more affliction to my bands.
17 But the others of loue, knowing that I
am set for the defence of the Gospel.
18 [5] What then? yet Christ is preached
all maner of wayes, whether *it be* vnder a [m] pretence, or sincerely: and I therein ioy: yea and
will ioy.
19 For I know that this shall turne to my
saluation through your praier, and by the helpe
of the Spirit of Iesus Christ,
20 [6] As I feruently looke for, and hope, that
in nothing I shall be ashamed, but that with all
confidence, as alwayes, so now Christ shall bee
magnified in my body, whether *it bee* by life or
by death.
21 For Christ *is* to me both in life, and in
death aduantage.
22 [7] And whether to liue in the [n] flesh
were profitable for mee, and what to chuse I
know not.
23 For I am distressed betweene both, desiring to be loosed and to be with Christ, which
is best of all.
24 Neuerthelesse, to abide in the flesh, *is*
more needfull for you.
25 And this am I sure of, that I shall abide,
and with you all continue, for your furtherance
and ioy of *your* faith,
26 That yee may more aboundantly reioyce in IESVS CHRIST for me, by my comming to you againe.
27 [8] Onely let your conuersation bee,
as it becommeth the Gospel of Christ, that
whether I come and see you, or else bee absent, I may heare of your matters that yee
[o] continue in one Spirit, *and* in one minde,
fighting together through the faith of the
Gospel.
28 [9] And in nothing feare your aduersaries,
which is to them a token of perdition, and to
you of saluation, and that of God.

1 The marke whereat hee shooteth in his Epistle, is to confirme the Philippians by all meanes possible, not onely not to faint, but also to goe forward. And first of all he commendeth their former doings, to exhort them to goe forward: which thing he saith he hopeth fully they will doe, and that by the testimonie of their liuely charitie, but in the meane season he referreth all things to the grace of God.

a By the Bishops are meant both the Pastours, which haue the dispensation of the word, and the Elders that gouerne: and by Deacons, are meant those that were stewards of the treasurie of the Church, and had to looke vnto the poore.

b Because that you also are made partakers of the Gospel.

c Euer since I knew you.

d The spirit of God will not forsake you vnto the very latter ende, vntill your mortall bodies shall appeare before the iudgement of Christ to bee glorified.

e A true proofe of a true knitting together with Christ.

f Hee calleth his bands grace, as though he had receiued some singular benefit.

2 He declareth his good will towards them, therewithall shewing by what meanes chiefly they may be confirmed, to wit, by continuall prayer.

3 He sheweth what thing we ought chiefly desire, to wit, first of all that we may increase in the true knowledge of God (so that we may be able to discerne things that differ one from another) and also in charitie, that euen to the end we may giue our selues to good workes in deede, to the glorie of God by Iesus Christ.

g If righteousnesse be the tree, and good workes the fruites, then must the Papists needes be deceiued, when they say that workes are the cause of righteousnesse.

4 Hee preuenteth the offence that might come by his persecution, whereby diuers tooke occasion to disgrace his Apostleship. To whom he answereth, that God hath blessed his imprisonment in such wise, that hee is by that meanes become more famous, and the dignitie of the Gospel by this occasion is greatly enlarged, although not with like affection in all men, yet in deede.

h For Christs sake.

i In the Emperours court.

k The Gospel is called the word, to set foorth the excellencie of it.

l Not with a pure minde: for otherwise their doctrine was pure.

5 He sheweth by setting foorth his owne example, that the end of our afflictions is true ioy, and that through the vertue of the Spirit of Christ, which he giueth to them that aske it.

m Vnder a goodly colour and shew: for they make Christ a cloke for their ambition and enuie.

6 We must continue euen to the end, with great confidence, hauing nothing before our eyes but Christes glorie onely whether we liue or die.

7 An example of a true shepheard, who maketh more accompt how he may profit his sheepe, then he doth of any commoditie of his own whatsoeuer.

n To liue in this mortall body.

8 Hauing set downe those things before in maner of a preface, he descendeth now to exhortations, warning them first of all, to consent both in doctrine and minde, and afterward, that being thus knit together with those common bands, they continue through the strength of faith to beare all aduersitie in such sort, that they admit nothing vnworthie the profession of the Gospel.

o The word signifieth to stand fast in, and it is proper to wrestlers, that stand fast and shrinke not a foote.

9 Wee ought not to be discouraged but rather encouraged by the persecutions which the enemies of the Gospel imagine and practise against vs: seeing that they are certaine witnesses from God himselfe both of our saluation, and of the destruction of the wicked.

 29 [10] For

29 [10] For vnto you it is giuen for Christ, that
not onely yee should beleeue in him, but also
suffer for his sake,
30 [11] Hauing the same fight, which yee saw
in me, and now heare *to be* in me.

10 He proueth that his saying, that persecution is a token of our saluation, because it is a gift of God to suffer for Christ, which gift he bestoweth vpon his owne, as he doeth the gift of faith. 11 Now he sheweth for what purpose he made mention of his afflictions.

CHAP. II.

1 Hee exhorteth them aboue all things 3 to humilitie, 6 and that by the example of Christ. 19 Hee promiseth to send Timotheus shortly vnto them, 26 and excuseth the long tarying of Epaphroditus.

IF [1] *there bee* therefore any consolation in
[a] Christ, if any comfort of loue, if any fellowship of the Spirit, if any [b] compassion and
mercie,
2 Fulfill my ioy, that yee be like minded,
hauing the [c] same loue, being of one accord,
and of one iudgement,
3 That nothing *be done* through contention or vaine glorie, but that in meekenesse of
minde euery man esteeme other better then
himselfe.
4 Looke not euery man on his owne
things, but euery man also on the things of o-
ther men.
5 [2] Let the same minde be in you that was
euen in Christ Iesus,
6 Who being in the [d] forme of God,
[e] thought it no robbery to be [f] equal with God:
7 But he made himselfe of [g] no reputation,
and tooke on him the [h] forme of a seruant, and
was made like vnto men, and was found in
shape as a man.
8 He humbled himselfe, & became obedient vnto the death, euen the death of the crosse.
9 [3] Wherefore also God hath highly exalted him, and giuen him a [i] Name aboue euery
name,
10 That at the Name of Iesus should [k] euery knee bowe, *both* of things in heauen, and
things in earth, and things vnder the earth,
11 And that [l] euery tongue should confesse
that Iesus Christ *is* the Lord, vnto the glorie of
God the Father.
12 [4] Wherefore my beloued, as yee haue
alwayes obeyed me, not as in my presence onely, but now much more in mine absence, *so*
[m] make an end of your own saluation with feare
and trembling.
13 [5] For it is God which worketh in you,
both [n] the will and the deede, *euen* of *his* good
pleasure.

1 A most earnest request to remoue all those things, whereby that great and speciall consent and agreement is commonly broken, to wit, contention and pride, whereby it commeth to passe that they separate themselues one from another.
a Any Christian comfort.
b If any feeling of inward loue.
c Like loue.
2 He setteth before them a most perfit example of all modestie and sweete conuersation, Christ Iesus, whom we ought to follow with all our might: who abased himselfe so farre for our sakes, although he be aboue all, that he tooke vpon him the forme of a seruant, to wit, our flesh, willingly subiect to all infirmities, euen to the death of the crosse.
d Such as God himselfe is, and therefore God, for there is none in all parts like to God but God himselfe.
e Christ that glorious and euerlasting God knew that hee might rightfully and lawfully not appeare in the base flesh of man, but remaine with Maiestie meete for God: yet he chose rather to debase himselfe. *f If the Sonne be equall with the Father, then is there of necessitie an equalitie, which Arrius that Heretike denieth: and if the Sonne bee compared to the Father, then is there a distinction of persons, which Sabellius that Heretike denieth.* *g He brought himselfe from all things, as it were to nothing.* *h By taking our manhood vpon him* 3 He sheweth the most glorious euent of Christs submission, to teach vs that modestie is the true way to true praise and glory. *i Dignitie and renoume, and the matter with it.* *k All creatures shall at length be subiect to Christ.* *l Euery nation.* 4 The conclusion: We must goe on to saluation with humilitie and submission by the way of our vocation. *m He is said to make an end of his saluation, which runneth in the race of righteousnesse.* 5 A most sure and grounded argument against pride, for that we haue nothing in vs praise worthy, but it commeth of the free gift of God, and is without vs, for we haue no abilitie or power, so much as to will well, (much lesse to doe well) but onely of the free mercie of God. *n Why then we are not stockes, but yet we doe not will well of nature, but only because God hath made of our naughty will a good will.*

14 [6] Doe all things without * murmuring
and reasonings,
15 [7] That yee may bee blamelesse, and
pure, *and* the sonnes of God without rebuke
in the middes of a naughtie and crooked nation, among whome yee shine as * lights in the
world,
16 Holding foorth the [o] word of life, [8] that
I may reioyce in the day of Christ, that I haue
not runne in vaine, neither haue laboured
in vaine.
17 Yea, and though I bee offered vp vpon
the [p] sacrifice, and seruice of your faith, I am
glad, and reioyce with you all.
18 For the same cause also be yee glad, and
reioyce with me.
19 * [9] And I trust in the Lord Iesus, to send
* Timotheus shortly vnto you, that I also may
be of [q] good comfort, when I know your state.
20 For I haue no man like minded, who wil
faithfully care for your matters.
21 * For [r] all seeke their owne, *and* not that
which is Iesus Christs.
22 But yee know the proofe of him, that as
a sonne with the father, he hath serued with me
in the Gospel.
23 Him therefore I hope to send, assoone
as I know how it will goe with me,
24 And trust in the Lord, that I also my selfe
shall come shortly.
25 But I supposed it necessarie to send *my*
brother Epaphroditus vnto you, my companion in labour, and fellow souldier, euen your
messenger, and he that ministred vnto me such
things as I wanted.
26 For he longed after all you, and was full
of heauinesse, because yee had heard that hee
had beene sicke.
27 And no doubt hee was sicke, very neere
vnto death: but God had mercie on him, and
not on him onely, but on me also, lest I should
haue sorrow vpon sorrow.
28 I sent him therefore the more diligently, that when yee should see him againe, yee
might reioyce, and I might bee the lesse sorrowfull.
29 Receiue him therefore in the Lord with
all gladnesse, and make much of such:
30 Because that for the [s] worke of Christ,
he was neere vnto death, and regarded not his
life, to fulfill that seruice which was lacking on
your part toward me.

6 He describeth modestie by the contrary effects of pride, teaching vs, that it is farre both from all malicious and close or inward hatred, and also from open contentions and brawlings.
* 1.Pet.4 9.
7 To be short, hee requireth a life without fault, and pure, that being lightned with the word of God, they may shine in the darkenesse of this world.
* *Matth.5.14.*
o The Gospel is called the word of life, because of the effects which it worketh.
8 Againe hee pricketh them forward, setting before them his true Apostolike care that he had of them: comforting them moreouer to the end they should not bee sorie for the greatnesse of his afflictions, no not although hee should die to make perfite their oblation with his blood, as it were with a drinke offering.
p As if he said, I brought you Philippians to Christ, my desire is, that you present your selues a liuely sacrifice to him, and then shall it not grieue me to be offered vp as a drinke offering, to accomplish this your spirituall offering.
9 Moreouer, he confirmeth their mindes both by sending backe Epaphroditus vnto them, whose fidelitie towards them, and great paines in helping him, hee commendeth: and also promising to send Timothie shortly vnto them, by whose presence they shall receiue great commoditie, and hoping also to come himselfe shortly vnto them, if God will. * *Actes 16.1.* *q May bee confirmed in my ioy of minde.* * *1.Cor 10.24.* r *The most part.* *s He calleth it here the worke of Christ, to visite Christ, being poore and in bands in the person of Paul.*

CHAP. III.

2 Hee refuteth the vaine boastings of the false Apostles, 7 and setteth Christ against them. 10 Hee setteth out the force and nature of faith, 15 that laying all things aside, they may be partakers of the crosse of Christ, 18 the enemies whereof he noteth out.

Moreouer,

MOreouer, [1] my brethren, reioyce in
the Lord. [2] It grieueth me not to write
the [a] same things to you, and for you it is a sure
thing.
2 Beware of dogges: beware of euill workers: beware of the [b] concision.
3 [3] For wee are the circumcision which
worship God in the spirit, and reioyce in
Christ Iesus, and haue no confidence [c] in the
flesh:
4 [4] Though I might also haue confidence
in the flesh. If any other man thinketh that he
hath whereof he might trust in the flesh, much
more I,
5 Circumcised the eight day, of the kinred
of Israel, of the tribe of Beniamin, * an Ebrew
of the Ebrewes, * by the Lawe a Pharise.
6 Concerning zeale, I persecuted the
Church: touching the righteousnesse which
is in the Lawe, I was vnrebukeable.
7 But the things that were [d] vantage vnto
me, the same I counted losse for Christs sake.
8 Yea, doubtlesse I thinke [e] all things but
losse for the excellent knowledge sake of
Christ Iesus my Lord, for whom I haue counted all things losse, and doe iudge *them* to bee
dung, that I might [f] winne Christ,
9 And might bee found in [g] him, *that is*,
[h] not hauing mine owne righteousnesse, which
is of the Lawe, but that which is through the
faith of Christ: *euen* the righteousnesse which
is of God through faith,
10 [5] That I may [i] knowe him, and the vertue of his resurrection, and the [6] fellowship of
his afflictions, and be made conformable vnto
his death,
11 If by any meanes I might attaine vnto
the [k] resurrection of the dead:
12 Not as though I had already attained
to it, either were alreadie perfect: but I follow,
if that I may comprehend *that* for whose sake
also I am [l] comprehended of Christ Iesus.
13 Brethren, I count not my selfe, that I
haue attained *to it*, but one thing *I doe:* I forget that which is behind, and indeuour my selfe
vnto that which is before,
14 And follow hard toward the marke, for
the price of the high calling of God in Christ
Iesus.

1 A conclusion of those things which haue been before sayd, to wit, that they goe forward chearefully in the Lord.
2 A preface to the next admonition that followeth, to take good heede and beware of false apostles, which ioyne circumcision with Christ, (that is to say, iustification by workes, with free iustification by faith) and beate into mens heads the ceremonies which are abolished, for true exercises of godlinesse and charity. And he calleth them dogges, as prophane barkers, and euill workemen, because they neglected true workes and did not teach the true vse of them. To bee short, hee calleth them Concision, because in vrging Circumcision, they cut off themselues and others from the Church.
a Which you haue oftentimes heard of me.
b He alludeth to circumcision, of the name whereof whiles they boasted, they cut asunder the Church.
3 Hee sheweth that we ought to vse true circumcision, to wit, the circumcision of the heart, that cutting off all wicked affections by the vertue of Christ, we may serue God in purity of life.
c In outward things which pertaine nothing to the soule.
4 He doubteth not to preferre himselfe euen according to the flesh, before those peruerse hote vrgers of the Lawe, that all men may knowe, that hee doeth with good iudgement of minde, lightly esteeme of all those outward things: forsomuch as he lacketh nothing, which hath Christ, nay, the confidence of our workes cannot stand with the free iustification in Christ by faith. * *2.Corint. 11.22.* * *Actes 23.6.* *d Which I accounted for vantage.* *e Hee shutteth out all workes, as well those that goe before, as those that come after faith.* *f That in their place I might get Christ, and of a poore man become rich: so farre off am I from losing any thing.* *g In Christ: for they that are found without Christ, are subiect to condemnation.* *h That is, to bee in Christ, to bee found not in a mans owne righteousnesse, but clothed with the righteousnesse of Christ imputed to him.* 5 This is the end of righteousnesse by faith touching vs, that by the vertue of his resurrection we may escape from death. *i That I may feele him in deede and haue a triall of him.* 6 The way to that eternall saluation is to follow Christ his steps by afflictions and persecutions, vntill wee come to Christ himselfe, who is our marke whereat we shoote, and receiue that reward whereunto God calleth vs in him. And the Apostle setteth these true exercises of godlinesse against those vaine ceremonies of the Lawe, wherein the false apostles put the summe of godlinesse. *k To life euerlasting, which followeth the resurrection of the Saints.* *l For we runne not but so farre forth as we are layed hold on of Christ, that is, as God giueth vs strength, and sheweth vs the way.*

15 [7] Let vs therefore as many as bee [m] perfect, be thus minded: and if yee bee otherwise
minded, God shall reueale euen the same vnto
you.
16 Neuerthelesse, *in that* whereunto wee
are come, let vs proceede by one rule, that wee
may minde one thing.
17 Brethren, be followers of me, and looke
on them, which walke so, as yee haue vs for an
ensample.
18 [8] * For many walke, of whom I haue told
you often, and now tell you weeping, *that they
are* the enemies of the Crosse of Christ:
19 Whose [n] ende *is* damnation, whose god
is their belly, and *whose* [o] glory *is* to their shame,
which minde earthly things.
20 [9] But our conuersation is in heauen,
from whence also we looke for the * Sauiour,
euen the Lord Iesus Christ,
21 Who shall change our vile bodie, that it
may be fashioned like vnto his glorious body,
according to the working, whereby hee is able
euen to subdue all things vnto himselfe.

7 The conclusion of this exhortation standing vpon three members: The one is, that such as haue profited in the trueth of this doctrine, should continue in it. The second is, that if there be any which are yet ignorant and vnderstand not these things, and doubt of the abolishing of the Lawe, they should cause no trouble, and should be gently borne withall, vntill they also be instructed of the Lord. The third is, that they esteeme the false apostles, by their fruits: wherein he doubteth not to set forth himselfe for an example
m He sayd before that he was not perfect. So that in this place he calleth them perfect, which haue somewhat profited in the knowledge of Christ and the Gospel, whom he setteth against the rude and ignorant, as he expoundeth himselfe in the next verse following 8 He painteth out the false apostles in their colours, not vpon malice or ambition, but with sorrowe and teares, to wit, because that being enemies of the Gospel (for that is ioyned with affliction) they regard nothing els, but the commodities of this life: that is to say, that flowing in peace, and quietnes and all worldly pleasures, they may liue in great estimation amongst men, whose miserable end he forewarned them of. * *Rom. 16.17.* *n Reward.* *o Which they hunt after at mens handes.* 9 Hee seteth against these fellowes, true Pastours which neglect earthly things, and aspire to heauen onely, where they knowe, that euen in their bodies they shall be clothed with that eternall glory, by the vertue of God. * *1.Cor. 1.7. titus 2.13.*

CHAP. IIII.

1 *From particular exhortations,* 4 *hee commeth to generall.* 10 *He sayth that hee tooke such ioy in their readinesse to liberality,* 12 *that hee will patiently beare the want.*

THerefore, [1] my brethren, beloued and
longed for, *my* ioy and my [a] crowne, so
continue in the [b] Lord, ye beloued.
2 [2] I pray Euodias, and beseech Syntyche,
that they be of one accord in the Lord.
3 Yea, and I beseech thee, faithfull yoke
fellow, help those *women*, which laboured with
mee in the Gospel, with Clement also, and
with other my fellow labourers, whose names
are in the * [c] booke of life.
4 [3] Reioyce in the [d] Lord alway, againe I
say, Reioyce.
5 [4] Let your [e] patient minde bee knowen
vnto all men. [5] The Lord *is* at hand.
6 [6] Bee nothing carefull, but in all things
let your requests be shewed vnto God in prayer, and supplication with [f] giuing of thankes.

1 A rehearsall of the conclusion: That they manfully continue, vntill they haue gotten the victory, trusting to the Lords strength.
a Mine honour.
b In that concord, whereof the Lord is the band.
2 Hee also calleth on some by name, partly because they needed priuate exhortation, and partly also to stirre vp other to bee more prompt and ready.
* *Reu. 3.5. and 10.6. and 21.27.*
c God is sayd after the maner of men, to haue a booke, wherein the names of his elect are written, to whom hee will giue euerlasting life. Ezekiel calleth it the writing of the house of Israel, and the secret of the Lord, Chap. 13.9. 3 He addeth particular exhortations: and the first is, that the ioy of the Philippians bee not hindered by any afflictions that the wicked imagine and worke against them. *d So is the ioy of the world distinguished from our ioy.* 4 The second is, that taking all things in good part, they behaue themselues moderately with all men. *e Your quiet and setled minde.* 5 The taking away of an obiection: Wee must not be disquieted through impatience, seeing that God is at hand to giue vs remedie in time against all our miseries. 6 The third is, that we be not too carefull for any thing, but with sure confidence giue God thankes, and craue of him, whatsoeuer wee haue neede of, that with a quiet conscience wee may wholly and with all our hearts submit our selues to him. *f So Dauid began very oft with teares, but ended with thankesgiuing.*

7 And the [g] peace of God which passeth all
vnderstanding, shall preserue your [h] hearts and
mindes in Christ Iesus.

8 [7] Furthermore, brethren, whatsoeuer
things are true, whatsoeuer things [i] *are* honest,
whatsoeuer things *are* iust, whatsoeuer things
are pure, whatsoeuer things *are* worthie loue,
whatsoeuer things *are* of good report, if there
be any vertue, or if there *be* any praise, thinke
on these things,

9 Which ye haue both learned and receiued, and heard, and seene in mee: those things
doe, and the God of peace shall be with you.

10 [8] Now I reioyce also in the Lord greatly,
that now at the last your care for me springeth
afresh, wherein notwithstanding ye were carefull, but ye lacked opportunitie.

11 I speake not because of [k] want: for I
haue learned in whatsoeuer state I am, therewith to be content.

12 And I can bee [l] abased, & I can abound:
euery where in all things I am [m] instructed,
both to bee full, and to bee hungry, and to a-
bound, and to haue want.

13 I am able to *doe* all things through the
helpe of Christ, which strengtheneth me.

g That great quietnesse of minde, which God onely giueth in Christ.
h He diuideth the mind into the heart, that is, into that part which is the seat of the wil and affections, and into the higher part, whereby we vnderstand and reason of matters.
7 A general conclusion, that as they haue been taught both in word and example, so they frame their liues to to the rule of all holinesse and righteousnesse.
i Whatsoeuer things are such as doe beautifie and set you out with a holy grauitie.
8 He witnesseth that their liberalitie was acceptable to him, wherewith they did helpe him in his extreme pouertie: but yet so moderating his words, that he might declare himselfe voyde of all suspicion of dishonestie, and that hee hath a minde contented both with prosperitie and aduersitie, and to be short, that he reposeth himselfe in the onely will of God. *k As though I passed for my want. l Hee vseth a generall word, and yet hee speaketh but of one kinde of crosse, which is pouertie, for commonly pouertie bringeth all kindes of discommoditie with it. m This is a metaphore taken from holy things or sacrifices, for our life is like a sacrifice.*

14 Notwithstanding yee haue well done,
that ye did communicate to mine affliction.

15 [9] And yee Philippians knowe also that in
the [n] beginning of the Gospel, when I departed
from Macedonia, no Church communicated
with mee, concerning the matter of giuing and
receiuing, but ye onely.

16 For euen *when I was* in Thessalonica,
yee sent once, and afterward againe for my
necessitie,

17 [10] Not that I desire a gift: but I desire the
fruit which may further your reckoning.

18 Now I haue receiued all, and haue plentie: I was euen filled, after that I had receiued
of Epaphroditus that which *came* from you, an
[o] odour that smelleth sweete, a sacrifice acceptable and pleasant to God.

19 And my God shall fulfill all your necessities through his riches, with glory in Iesus
Christ.

20 Vnto God euen our Father *bee* prayse
for euermore. Amen.

21 Salute all the Saints in Christ Iesus. The
brethren which are with me, greete you.

22 All the Saints salute you, and most of
all they which are of [p] Cesars houshold.

23 The grace of our Lord Iesus Christ *bee*
with you all, Amen.

9 He witnesseth that he remembreth also their former benefits, and againe putteth away sinistrous suspicion of immoderate desire, in that that he receiued nought of any else.
n At the beginning, when I preached the Gospel amongst you.
10 He witnesseth againe, that he alloweth well of their benefite, not so much for his owne sake as for theirs, because they gaue it not so much to him, as they offered it to God as a sacrifice, whereof the Lord himselfe will not be forgetfull.
o Hee alludeth to the sweete smelling sauours that were offered in the old Lawe.
p Such as belong to the Emperour Nero.

¶ Written to the Philippians from Rome, *and sent* by Epaphroditus.

THE EPISTLE OF Paul to the Colossians.

CHAP. I.

1 *After the salutation,* 4 *hee prayseth them the more, to make them attentiue vnto him.* 7 *Hee reporteth the testimonie of the doctrine which they heard of Epaphras.* 13 *Hee magnifieth Gods grace towards them,* 20 *and sheweth that all the parts of our saluation consist in Christ alone.*

PAVL an Apostle of Iesus
Christ, by the [a] will of God,
and Timotheus *our* brother,

2 To them which are at
[b] Colosse, Saints, and faithful brethren in Christ: Grace
be with you, and peace from God our Father,
and *from* the Lord Iesus Christ.

3 [1] Wee giue thankes to God euen the
[c] Father of our Lord Iesus Christ, alway praying for you:

4 Since wee heard of your faith in Christ
Iesus, and of *your* loue toward all Saints,

5 For the [d] hopes sake, which is layed vp for
you in heauen, whereof you haue heard before
by the worde of trueth, *which is* the Gospel,

6 Which is come vnto you, euen as *it is*
vnto all the world, and is fruitfull, as *it is* also
among you, from the day that yee heard and
truely knew the grace of God,

a By the free bountifulnesse of God.
b Colosse is situated in Phrygia, not farre from Hierapolis and Laodicea, on that side that they bend toward Lycia and Pamphylia.
1 He commendeth the doctrine that was deliuered them by Epaphras, and their readinesse in receiuing it.
c Wee cannot otherwise consider of God to our saluation, but as hee is Christs Father, in whom we are adopted.
d For the glory that is hoped for.

7 As yee also learned of Epaphras our
deare fellow seruant, which is for you a faithfull minister of Christ:

8 [2] Who hath also declared vnto vs your
loue in the [e] Spirit.

9 For this cause wee also, since the day
we heard *of it*, cease not to pray for you, and to
desire that yee might bee fulfilled with knowledge of [f] his will in all wisedome, and spirituall
vnderstanding,

10 That yee might walke worthie of the
Lorde, and please *him* in all things, being
fruitfull in all good workes, and increasing in
the knowledge of God,

11 [3] Strengthened with all might through
his glorious power, vnto all patience, and long
suffering with [g] ioyfulnesse,

12 [4] Giuing thankes vnto the [5] Father,
which hath made vs meete to be partakers of

2 He declareth his good will towards them, telling them that they must not still remaine at one stay, but go on further both in the knowledge of the Gospel, and also in the true vse of it.
e Your spirituall loue, or your loue which commeth from the Spirit.
f Gods will.
3 The gift of continuance is not of vs, but it proceedeth from the vertue of God, which he doeth freely giue vs.
g It must not bee vnwilling, and as it were drawen out of vs by force, but proceede from a merrie and ioyfull minde. 4 Hauing ended the preface, he goeth to the matter it selfe, that is to say, to an excellent description (although it be but short) of whole Christianitie, which is fitly diuided into three treatises: for first of all he expoundeth the true doctrine according to the order of the causes, beginning from this verse to the 21. And from thence he beginneth to applie the same to the Colossians with diuers exhortations to the sixt verse of the second Chapter. And last of all in the third place, euen to the 3. Chapter, he refuteth the corruptions of true doctrine. 5 The efficient cause of our saluation is the onely mercie of God the Father, who maketh vs meete to be partakers of eternall life, deliuering vs from the darkenesse wherein wee were borne, & bringing vs to the light of the knowledge of the glory of his Sonne,

the

the inheritance of the Saints in [h] light,
13 Who hath deliuered vs from the power
of darkenesse, and hath translated vs into the
kingdome * of his deare Sonne,
14 [6] In whom we haue redemption through
his blood, *that is*, the forgiuenesse of sinnes,
15 [7] Who is the * image of the inuisible
God, [i] the first begotten of euery creature.
16 *For by him were all things created,
which are in heauen, and which are in earth,
things visible and inuisible: whether *they bee*
[k] Thrones, or Dominions, or Principalities, or
Powers, all things were created by him, and
for him,
17 And he is before all things, and in him
all things consist.
18 [8] And hee is the head of the body of the
Church: hee is the beginning, * *and* the [l] first
begotten of the dead, that in al things he might
haue the preeminence.
19 *For it pleased *the Father*, that in him
should [m] all fulnesse dwell,
20 [9] And through peace made by that blood
of that his crosse, to recōcile to himself through
him, through him, *I say*, [n] all things, both which
are in earth, and which *are* in heauen.
21 [10] And you which were in times past
strangers and enemies, because *your* mindes
were set in euill workes, hath [o] hee now also
reconciled,
22 In that bodie of his [p] flesh through
death, to make you holy and vnblameable and
without fault in his sight,
23 [11] If yee continue grounded and stablished in the faith, and be not moued away from
the hope of the Gospel, whereof ye haue heard,
and which hath been preached to [q] euery creature which is vnder heauen, [12] whereof I Paul
am a minister.
24 Now reioyce I in my suffrings for [r] you,
and fulfill the [s] rest of the afflictions of Christ
in my flesh, for his bodies sake, which is the
Church,

h In that glorious and heauenly kingdome.

*Matth. 3.17. and 17.5. 2 pet.1.17.

6 The matter it selfe of our saluatiō, is Christ the Sonne of God, who hath obtained remission of sinnes for vs, by the offering vp of himselfe.

7 A liuely description of the person of Christ, whereby wee vnderstand, that in him onely God sheweth himselfe to bee seene: who was begotten of the Father before any thing was made, that is, from euerlasting by whom also all things that are made, were made without any exception, by whom also they doe consist, and whose glory they serue.

*Hebr. 1.3.

i Begotten before any thing was made: and therefore the euerlasting Sonne of the euerlasting Father.

*Iohn 1.3.

k He setteth forth the Angels with glorious names, that by the comparison of most excellent spirits, wee may vnderstand how farre passing the excellencie of Christ is, in whom onely we haue to content our selues, and let goe all Angels.

8 Hauing gloriously declared the excellent dignitie of the person of Christ, he describeth his office and function, to wit, that he is that same to the Church, that the head is to the body, that is to say, the prince and gouernour of it, and the very beginning of true life, as who rising first from death is the author of eternall life, so that he is aboue all, in whom onely there is most plentifull abundance of all good things, which is powred out vpon the Church. *Reue.1.5. 1.cor 15.20. l Who so rose againe that he should die no more, and who raiseth other from death to life by his power.* *Ioh. 1.14. cha.2 9. *m Most plentifull abundance of all things pertaining to God.* 9 Now he teacheth how Christ executed that office which his Father enioyned him, to wit, by suffering the death of the crosse (which was ioyned with the curse of God) according to his decree, that by this sacrifice he might reconcile to his Father all men, as well them which beleeued in him to come, and were already vnder this hope gathered into heauen, as them which should vpon the earth beleeue in him afterward. And thus is iustification described of the Apostle, which is one and the chiefest part of the benefite of Christ. *n The whole Church.* 12 Sanctification is another worke of God in vs by Christ, in that that he restored vs (which hated God extreamly & were wholly and willingly giuen to sinne) to his gracious fauour in such sort, that hee therewithall purifieth vs with his holy Spirit, and consecrateth vs to righteousnes. *o The Sonne. p In that fleshly body, to giue vs to vnderstand that his body was not a fantasticall bodie, but a true body.* 11 The second treatise of this part of the Epistle, wherein he exhorteth the Colossians not to suffer themselues by any meanes to be moued from this doctrine, shewing and declaring that there is no where any other true Gospel. *q To all men: whereby we learne that the Gospel was not shut vp within the corners of Iudea alone.* 12 He purchaseth authoritie to this doctrine by his Apostleship, and taketh a most sure proofe thereof, of his afflictions, which hee suffereth for Christ his Name, to instruct the Churches with these examples of patience. *r For your profite and commoditie. s The afflictions of the Church are sayd to bee Christs afflictions, by reason of that fellowship and knitting together that the body and the head haue the one with the other, not that there is any more neede to haue the Church redeemed, but that Christ sheweth his power in the dayly weakenesse of his, and that for the comfort of the whole body.*

25 [13] Whereof I am a minister, according
to the dispensation of God, which is giuen me
vnto you-ward, to fulfill the word of God,
26 * *Which is* the mysterie hid since the
world began, and from *all* ages, but now is
made manifest vnto his [t] Saints,
27 To whom God [u] would make knowen
what is the riches of his glorious mystery a-
mong the Gentiles, which *riches* is Christ in
you, the hope of glory,
28 [14] Whom we preach, admonishing euery
man, and teaching euery man in [x] all wisedom,
that wee may present euery man perfect in
Christ Iesus,
29 Whereunto I also labour and striue, according to his working which worketh in mee
mightily.

13 He bringeth another proofe of his Apostleship, to wit, that God is the Authour of it, by whom also he was appointed peculiarly Apostle of the Gentiles, to the end that by this meanes, that same might be fulfilled by him, which the Prophets foretold of the calling of the Gentiles.

*Rom.16 25. ephes.3.9. 2.tim. 1.10. titus 1.2. 1 pet.1.20.

t Whom he chose to sanctifie vnto himselfe in Christ: moreouer he sayth that the mystery of our redemption was hidden since the world began, except it were reuealed vnto a fewe, who also were taught it extraordinarily. u Thus Paul brideleth the curiositie of men. 14 He protesteth that he doeth faithfully execute his Apostleship in euery place, bringing men vnto Christ onely through the Lordes plentifull blessing of his labours. *x Perfect and sound wisedome, which is perfect in it selfe, and shall in the ende make them perfect that followe it.*

CHAP. II.

4 Hee condemneth, as vaine, whatsoeuer is without Christ, 11 entreating specially of circumcision, 16 of abstinence from meats, 18 and of worshipping of Angels. 20 That wee are deliuered from the traditions of the Lawe through Christ.

FOr I [1] would yee knew what great fighting
I haue for your sakes, and for them of Laodicea, and for as many as haue not seene my
[a] person in the flesh,
2 [2] That [b] their hearts might bee comforted, and they knit together in loue, and in all riches of the [c] full assurance of vnderstanding, to
knowe the mysterie of God, euen the Father,
and of Chist:
3 In whome are hid all the treasures of
[d] wisedome and knowledge.
4 [3] And this I say, lest any man should beguile you with [e] entising words:
5 *For though I bee absent in the flesh,
yet am I with you in the spirit, reioycing and
beholding your [f] order, and your [g] stedfast faith
in Christ.
6 As yee haue therefore [h] receiued Christ
Iesus the Lord, *so* walke in him,
7 Rooted and built in him, and stablished
in the faith, as ye haue been taught, abounding
therein with thankesgiuing.
8 [4] Beware lest there bee any man that
[i] spoile you through philosophie, and vaine deceit, [5] through the traditions of men, [6] according to the [k] rudiments of the world, [7] and not
after Christ.

1 The taking away of an obiection. In ÿ that he visited not the Colossians, nor the Laodiceans, he did it not of any negligence, but is so much the more careful for them. *a Me present in bodie.*

2 He cōcludeth shortly ÿ summe of the former doctrine, to wit, that the whole summe of true wisedome, and most secret knowledge of God, consisteth in Christ onely, and that this is the vse of it touching men, that they being knit together in loue, rest themselues happily in the knowledge of so great a goodnes, vntill they come fully to enioy it.

b Whom he neuer sawe. c Of that vnderstanding, which bringeth forth a certaine and vndoubted perswasion in our minds.

d There is no true wisedome without Christ. 3 A passing ouer to the treatise following, against the corruptions of Christianitie. *e With a framed kind of talke made to perswade.* * 1.Cor.5.3. *f The maner of your Ecclesiasticall discipline. g Doctrine. h So then Christ hangeth not vpon mens traditions.* 4 He bringeth all corruptions to three kindes. The first is that which resteth of vaine and curious speculations, and yet beareth a shew of certaine subtill wisedome. *i This is a worde of warre, and it is as much as to driue or carie away a spoile or bootie.* 5 The second, which is manifestly superstitious and vaine, and standeth onely vpon custome and fained inspirations. 6 The third kinde was of them which ioyned the rudiments of the worlde, (that is to say, the ceremonies of the Lawe) with the Gospell. *k Principles and rules, wherewith God ruled his Church, as it were vnder a Schoolemaster.* 7 A generall confutation of all corruptions is this, that that must needes be a false religion, which addeth any thing to Christ.

9 [8] For

9 [8]For in [l]him [m]dwelleth [n]all the fulneſſe of the Godhead[o] bodily.

10 And yee are complete in him, which is the head of all principalitie and power.

11 [9]In whom alſo ye are circumciſed with *circumciſion made without hands, by putting off the [p]ſinfull bodie of the fleſh, through the circumciſion of Chriſt,

12 [10]In that yee are *[q]buried with [r]him through baptiſme,[11] in whom ye are alſo raiſed vp together through the faith of the operation of [ſ] God, which rayſed him from the dead.

13 *[12]And you which were dead in ſinnes, [13]and in the vncircumciſion of your fleſh, hath hee quickned together with him, forgiuing you all *your* treſpaſſes,

14 [14]And putting out the *[t]hand writing of ordinances that was againſt vs, which was contrary to vs, he euen tooke it out of the way, and faſtened it vpon the croſſe,

15 And hath ſpoyled the [u]Principalities, and Powers, and hath [x]made a ſhew of them openly, and hath triumphed ouer them in the [y]ſame *croſſe*.

16 [15]Let no man therfore condemne you in meate or drinke, or in reſpect of an holy day, or of the new moone, or of the Sabbath *dayes*,

17 Which are *but* a ſhadowe of things to come: but the [z]bodie is in Chriſt.

18 [16]Let no man at his pleaſure beare rule ouer you by [a] humbleneſſe of minde, and worſhipping of Angels, [17]aduancing himſelfe in thoſe things which he neuer ſawe, [18] [b]raſhly puſt vp with his fleſhly minde,

19 [19]And holdeth not the [c]head, whereof all the bodie furniſhed and knit together by ioynts and bands, increaſeth with the increaſing of [d]God.

20 [20]Wherefore if yee *bee* dead with Chriſt from the ordinances of the world, why, [e]as though ye liued in the world, are ye burdened with traditions?

21 [21]*As* Touch not, Taſte not, Handle not.

22 [22]Which all periſh with the vſing, [23]*and are* after the commaundements and doctrines of men.

23 [24]Which things haue indeede a ſhew of [f]wiſedome, in [g]voluntary religion and humbleneſſe of minde, and in [h]not ſparing the bodie, which are things of no value, *ſith they pertaine* to the [i]filling of the fleſh.

8 A reaſon: Becauſe onely Chriſt God and man, is moſt perfect, and paſſeth farre aboue all things, ſo that whoſoeuer hath him, may require nothing more. *l By theſe words, is ſhewed a diſtinction of the natures.* *m This worde (Dwelleth) noteth out vnto vs the ioyning together of thoſe natures, ſo that God and Man, is one Chriſt.* *n Theſe words ſet downe moſt perfect Godhead to be in Chriſt.* *o The knitting together of God and man, is ſubſtantiall and eſſentiall.* 9 Now he dealeth preciſely againſt the third kinde, that is to ſay, againſt them which vrged the Iewiſh religion: and firſt of all, hee denieth that wee haue neede of the circumciſion of the fleſh, ſeeing that without it wee are circumciſed within, by the vertue of Chriſt. *Rom.2.29. *p Theſe manie words are vſed to ſhewe what the old man is, whom Paul in other places calleth the bodie of ſinne.* 10 The taking away of an obiection: We neede not ſo much as the externall ſigne which our fathers had, ſeeing that our Baptiſme is a moſt effectuall pledge and witneſſe, of that inward reſtoring and renewing. *Rom.6.4. eph.1.14. *q Looke Rom.6.4.* *r So then all the force of the matter commeth not from the very deede done, that is to ſay, it is not the dipping of vs into the water by a Miniſter, that maketh vs to be buried with Chriſt, as the Papiſts ſay, that euen for the very actes ſake, we become very Chriſtians, but it commeth from the vertue of Chriſt, for the Apoſtle addeth the reſurrection of Chriſt, and faith.* 11 One ende of Baptiſme is the death and buriall of the old man, and that by the mightie power of God onely, whoſe vertue we lay hold on by faith, in the death and reſurrection of Chriſt. *ſ Through faith which commeth from God.* *Epheſ.2.1. 12 Another end of Baptiſme is, that we which were dead in ſinne, might obteine free remiſſion of ſinnes and eternall life, through faith in Chriſt who died for vs. 13 A new argument which lieth in theſe few words, and it is thus: Vncircumciſion was no hinderance to you, why you being iuſtified in Chriſt ſhould not obtaine life, therefore you neede not circumciſion to the attainement of ſaluation. 14 He ſpeaketh now more generally againſt the whole ſeruice of the Lawe, and ſheweth by two reaſons, that it is aboliſhed. Firſt, to what purpoſe ſhould he that hath obtained remiſſion of all his ſinnes in Chriſt, require thoſe helpes of the Law? Secondly, becauſe, that if a man doe rightly conſider thoſe rites, he ſhall find that they were ſo many teſtimonies of our guiltineſſe, wherby we manifeſtly witneſſed as it were by our owne handwritings, that wee deſerued damnation. Therefore did Chriſt put out that handwriting by his comming, and faſtening it to the Croſſe, triumphed ouer all our enemies, were they neuer ſo mighty. Therefore to what ende and purpoſe ſhould we now vſe thoſe ceremonies, as though we were ſtill guiltie of ſinne, and ſubiect to the tyrannie of our enemies? *Epheſians 2.15. *t Aboliſhing the rites and ceremonies.* *u Satan and his angels.* *x As a conquerour made hee a ſhewe of thoſe captiues, and put them to ſhame.* *y The Croſſe was as a chariot of triumph. No conquerour could haue triumphed ſo glorioufly in his chariot, as Chriſt did vpon the croſſe.* 15 The concluſion: wherein alſo hee nameth certaine kindes, as the difference of dayes, and meates, and prooueth by a new argument, that wee are not bound vnto them: to wit, becauſe thoſe things were ſhadowes of Chriſt to come, but we poſſeſſe him now exhibited vnto vs. *z The bodie as a thing of ſubſtance and pith, hee ſetteth againſt ſhadowes.* 16 He diſputeth againſt the firſt kinde of corruptions, and ſetteth downe the worſhipping of Angels for an example: which kinde of falſe religion hee confuteth, firſt, this way: becauſe that they which bring in ſuch a worſhip, attribute that vnto themſelues which is proper onely to God, to wit, authoritie to bind mens conſciences with religion, although they ſeeme to bring in theſe things by humbleneſſe of mind. *a By fooliſh humbleneſſe of minde: for otherwiſe humbleneſſe is a vertue. For theſe Angel worſhippers, blamed ſuch of pride as would goe ſtraight to God, and vſe no other vndermeanes beſide Chriſt.* 17 Secondly, becauſe they raſhly thruſt vpon them for oracles thoſe things which they neither ſaw nor heard, but deuiſed of themſelues. 18 Thirdly, becauſe theſe things haue no other ground whereupon they are built, but onely the opinion of men, which pleaſe themſelues without all meaſure in their owne deuices. *b Without reaſon.*

19 The fourth argument, which is of great weight: becauſe they ſpoyle Chriſt of his dignity, who onely is ſufficient both to nouriſh and alſo to increaſe his whole bodie. *c Chriſt.* *d With the increaſing which commeth from God.* 20 Now laſt of all he fighteth againſt the ſecond kind of corruptions, that is to ſay, againſt mere ſuperſtitions, inuented of men, which partly deceiue the ſimplicitie of ſome with their craftineſſe, and partly with their fooliſh ſuperſtitions and to be laughed at: as when godlineſſe, remiſſion of ſinnes, or any ſuch like vertue, is put in ſome certaine kind of meate, and ſuch like things, which the inuentors of ſuch rites themſelues vnderſtand not, becauſe in deede it is not. And he vſeth an argument taken of compariſon. If by the death of Chriſt who eſtabliſhed a new couenant with his blood, you be deliuered from thoſe externall rites wherewith it pleaſed the Lord to prepare the world, as it were by certaine rudiments, to that full knowledge of true religiō, why would ye be burdened with traditions I wote not what, as though ye were citizens of this world, that is to ſay, as though ye depended vpon this life, and earthly things? now this is the cauſe why before verſe 8. he followed another order then he doth in the confutation: becauſe he ſheweth there by what degrees falſe religions came into the world, to wit, beginning firſt by curious ſpeculations of the wiſe, after which in proceſſe of time ſucceeded groſſe ſupperſtition, againſt which miſchiefes the Lord ſet at length that ſeruice of the Law, which ſome abuſed in like ſort: but in the confutation he began with the aboliſhing of the Lawe ſeruice, that hee might ſhewe by compariſon, that thoſe falſe ſeruices ought much more to be taken away. *e As though your felicitie ſtood in theſe earthly things, and the kingdome of God were not rather ſpirituall.* 21 An imitation in the perſon of theſe ſuperſtitious men, rightly expreſſing their nature and vſe of ſpeach. 22 Another argument: The ſpirituall and inward kingdome of God cannot conſiſt in theſe outward things, and ſuch as periſh with the vſing. 23 The third argument: Becauſe God is not the author of theſe traditions, and therefore they did not binde the conſciences. 24 The taking away of an obiection. Theſe things haue a goodly ſhew, becauſe men by this means, ſeeme to worſhip God with a good minde, and humble themſelues, and neglect the bodie, which the moſt part of men curiouſly pamper vp and cheriſh: but yet notwithſtanding the things themſelues are of no value, for ſo much as they pertaine not to the things that are ſpiritual & euerlaſting, but to the nouriſhment of the fleſh. *f Which ſeeme in deede to be ſome exquiſite thing, and ſo wiſe deuices as though they came from heauen.* *g Hence ſprang the workes of ſupererogation, as the Papiſts terme them, that is to ſay, needeleſſe workes, as though men performed more then is commaunded them: which was the beginning and the very ground, whereon Monkes merites were brought in.* *h A liuely deſcription of Monkerie.* *i Seeing they ſtand in meate and drinke, wherein the kingdome of God doeth not ſtand.*

CHAP. III.

1 *Againſt earthly exerciſes, which the falſe apoſtles vrged,*
2 *he ſetteth heauenly:* 5 *And beginneth with the mortifying of the fleſh,* 8 *whence hee draweth particular exhortations,* 18 *and particular dueties which depend on each mans calling.*

IF [1]yee then [2]bee [a]riſen with Chriſt, [3]ſeeke thoſe things which are aboue, where Chriſt ſitteth at the right hand of God.

2 Set your affections on things which are aboue, & not on things which are on the [b]earth.

3 [4]For yee are dead, [5]and your life is

1 Another part of this Epiſtle, wherein hee taketh occaſion by reaſon of thoſe vaine exerciſes, to ſhew the duety of a Chriſtian life: which is an ordinarie thing with him, after he hath once ſet downe the doctrine it ſelfe. 2 Our renewing or new birth, which is wrought in vs by being partakers of the reſurrection of Chriſt, is the fountaine of all holineſſe, out of which ſundry armes or riuers doe afterwards flowe. *a For if we be partakers of Chriſt, wee are caried as it were into another life where we ſhall neede neither meate nor drinke, for we ſhall be like vnto the Angels.* 3 The end and marke which all the dueties of Chriſtian life ſhoote at, is to enter into the kingdome of heauen, and to giue our ſelues to thoſe things which leade vs thither, that is, to true godlineſſe, and not to thoſe outward and corporall things. *b So he calleth that ſhewe of religion which he ſpake of in the former Chapter.* 4 A reaſon taken of the efficient cauſes and others: you are dead as touching the fleſh, that is, touching the olde nature which ſeeketh after all tranſitory things, and on the other ſide, you haue begun to liue according to the Spirit, therefore giue your ſelues to ſpirituall and heauenly, and not to carnall and earthly things. 5 The taking away of an obiection: whiles wee are yet in this world, wee are ſubiect to many miſeries of this life, ſo that the life that is in vs, is as it were hidden: yet notwithſtanding we haue the beginnings of life and glorie, the accompliſhment whereof which lieth now in Chriſts and in Gods hand, ſhall bee aſſuredly and manifeſtly performed in that glorious comming of the Lord.

hid with Christ in God.
4 When Christ which is our life shall appeare, then shall yee also appeare with him in
glory.
5 [6] *Mortifie therefore your [c] members
which are on the earth, fornication, vncleannesse, the inordinate affection, euill concupiscence,and couetousnesse which is idolatrie.
6 For the which things sake the wrath of
God [d] commeth on the children of disobedience.
7 Wherein ye also walked once, when yee
liued in them.
8 But nowe put yee away euen all these
things, wrath, anger, maliciousnesse, cursed
speaking,filthie speaking,out of your mouth.
9 Lie not one to another, [7] seeing that yee
haue put off the olde man with his works,
10 And haue put on the new, [8] which is renewed in [e] knowledge after the image of him
that created him,
11 [9] Where is neither Grecian nor Iew,
circumcision nor vncircumcision, Barbarian,
Scythian, bond, free: But Christ is all, and
in all things.
12 Now therefore as the elect of God holy and beloued, [f] put on the [g] bowels of mercies,kindnesse, humblenesse of minde, meekenesse,long suffering:
13 Forbearing one another, and forgiuing
one another, if any man haue a quarell to another: euen as Christ forgaue,euen so doe yee.
14 And aboue all these things *put on* loue,
which is the [h] bond of perfectnesse.
15 And let the peace of God [i] rule in your
hearts,to the which yee are called in [k] one bodie,and be ye thankefull.
16 Let the word of Christ dwell in you
plenteously in all wisedome, teaching and admonishing your owne selues, in [l] Psalmes, and
hymnes, and spirituall songs, singing with a
grace in your hearts to the Lord.
17 * And whatsoeuer yee shall doe, in word
or deede, *doe* all in the [m] Name of the Lord
Iesus, giuing thankes to God euen the Father
by him.
18 ¶ *[10] Wiues, submit your selues vnto
your husbands,as it is [n] comely in the Lord.
19 *[11] Husbands loue your wiues, and be
not bitter vnto them.

6 Let not your dead nature be any more effectuall in you, but let your liuing nature be effectuall. Now the force of nature is knowen by the motions. Therfore let the affections of the world die in you, and let the contrary motions which are spirituall, liue. And hee reckoneth vp a great long scroule of vices, and their contrary vertues.
*Ephes. 5 3.
c The motions and lusts that are in vs, are in this place very properly called members, because that the reason and will of man corrupted, doth vse them as the body doth his members.
d Vseth to come.
7 A definition of our new birth taken of the parts thereof, which are the putting off of the olde man, that is to say, of the wickednesse which is in vs by nature, and the restoring, and repairing of the new man, that is to say, of purenesse which is giuen vs by grace: but both of them are but begun in vs in this present life, and by certaine degrees finished, the one dying in vs by little and little, and the other comming to the perfection of another life, by little and little.
8 Newnesse of life consisteth in knowledge which transformeth man to the image of God his maker, that is to say to the sinceritie and purenesse of the whole soule. *e He speaketh of an effectuall knowledge.* 9 He telleth them againe that the Gospel doeth not respect those externall things, but true iustification and sanctification in Christ onely, which haue many fruits, as hee reckoneth them vp here: But commendeth two things especially, to wit, godly concord, and continuall studie of Gods word *f So put on, that ye neuer put off.* *g Those most tender affections of exceeding compassion.* *h Which bendeth and knitteth together all the dueties that passe from man to man.* *i Rule and gouerne all things.* *k You are ioyned together into one bodie through Gods goodnesse, that you might helpe one another, as fellow members.* *l By Psalmes he meaneth all godly songs which were written vpon diuers occasions, and by Hymnes, all such as containe the prayse of God, and by spirituall songs, other more peculiar and artificious songs which were also in prayse of God, but they were made fuller of musicke.* * *1 Corinth. 10.31.* *m Call vpon the Name of Christ, when you doe it, or doe it to Christs prayse and glory.* *Ephes. 5.22.* 10 Hee goeth from precepts which concerne the whole ciuile life of man, to precepts pertaining to euery mans familie, and requireth of wiues subiection in the Lord. *n For those wiues doe not well, that doe not set God in Christ before them in their loue, but this Philosophie knoweth not.* * *1. Pet 3.1.* 11 Hee requireth of husbands, that they loue their wiues, and vse them gently.

20 ¶ *[12] Children, obey your parents in
[o] all things: for that is well pleasing vnto the
Lord.
21 [13] Fathers, prouoke not your children
to anger, lest they be discouraged.
22 ¶ [14] * Seruants, bee obedient vnto
them that are *your* masters according to the
flesh, in all things,not with eye seruice as men
pleasers, but in singlenesse of heart, fearing
God.
23 And whatsoeuer yee doe,doe it heartily,
as to the Lord,and not to men,
24 Knowing that of the Lord yee shall receiue the [p] reward of the inheritance: for yee
serue the Lord Christ.
25 [15] But he that doeth wrong, shall receiue
for the wrong that he hath done: and there is
no respect of persons.

* *Ephes. 6.1.*
12 He requireth of children, that according to Gods commandement they be obedient to their parents.
o In the Lord, & so is it expounded, Ephes. 5.19.
13 Of parents, that that they be gentle towards their children.
14 Of seruants, that fearing God himselfe to whome their obedience is acceptable, they reuerently, faithfully, and from the heart, obey their masters.
* *Ephes. 6.5. titus 2.9. 1. pet. 2.18.*
p For that that you shall haue duely obeyed your masters, the time shall come, that you shall be made sonnes, of seruants, and then shall you knowe this of a suretie, which shall be when you are made partakers of the heauenly inheritance. 15 He requireth of masters, that being mindfull how that they themselues also shall render an account before that heauenly Lord and Master, which will reuenge wrongfull doings without any respect of masters or seruants, they shew themselues iust and vpright with equitie, vnto their seruants.

CHAP. IIII.

2 *He returneth to general exhortations,* 3 *touching prayer, and gracious speach,* 7 *and so endeth with greetings and commendations.*

YE Masters, doe vnto your seruants, that
which is iust, and equall, knowing that ye
also haue a Master in heauen.
2 [1] *[2] Continue in prayer, and watch in
the same with thankesgiuing,
3 [3] * Praying also for vs, that God may
open vnto vs the [a] doore of vtterance, to speake
the mysterie of Christ: wherefore I am also in
bonds,
4 That I may vtter it, as it becommeth
me to speake.
5 ¶ [4] * Walke [b] wisely toward them that
are without,and redeeme the [c] season.
6 [5] *Let* your speach *be* [d] gracious alwayes,
and powdred with [e] salt, that yee may knowe
how to answere euery man.
7 ¶ Tychicus *our* beloued brother and
faithfull minister, and fellow seruant in the
Lord,shall declare vnto you my whole state:
8 Whome I haue sent vnto you for the
same purpose, that he might knowe your state,
and might comfort your hearts,
9 With Onesimus a faithful and a beloued
brother, who is one of you. They shall shew
you of all things here.
10 Aristarchus my prison fellow saluteth
you, and Marcus Barnabas cousin, (touching
whom yee receiued commandements, If hee
come vnto you, receiue him)
11 And Iesus which is called Iustus, which
are of the circumcision. These [f] onely are my
workefellowes vnto the [g] kingdome of God,
which haue been vnto my consolation.
12 Epaphras the seruant of Christ, which
is one of you, saluteth you, and alwayes striueth for you in prayers, that yee may stand
perfect,

1 He addeth certaine general exhortations, & at length endeth his Epistle with diuers familiar and godly salutations.
* *Luke 18.1. 1. thess. 5.17.*
2 Prayers must be continual and earnest.
3 Such as minister the word, must especially be commended to the prayers of the Church.
**Ephes. 6.18. 2. thes. 3.1.*
a An open & free mouth to preach the Gospel.
4 In all parts of our life, we ought to haue good consideration euen of thẽ which are without the Church.
**Ephes. 5.15.*
b Aduisedly and circumspectly.
c Seeke occasion to winne them, although you lose of your owne by it.
5 Our speach & talke must be applied to ỹ profit of the hearers.
d Framed to the profit of your neighbour.
e Against this is set filthy communication, as Ephes. 4.29.
f Why then, Peter was not at that time at Rome.
g In the Gospel,

perfect,and full in all the will of God.
13 For I beare him record, that hee hath a
great zeale for you, and for them of Laodicea,
and them of Hierapolis.
14 * Luke the beloued Physician greeteth
you,and Demas.
15 Salute the brethren which are of Laodicea,and Nymphas, and the Church which is
in his house.
16 And when this Epistle is read of you,
cause that it be read in the Church of the Laodiceans also, and that yee likewise reade the E-
pistle *written* from Laodicea.
17 And say to Archippus, Take heede to
the ministerie, that thou hast receiued in the
Lord, that thou fulfill it.
18 The salutation by the hand of me Paul.
Remember my bands. Grace *bee* with you,
Amen.

*2.Tim.4.11.

¶Written from Rome to the Colossians,*and sent* by Tychicus and Onesimus.

THE FIRST EPISTLE OF PAVL TO THE THESSALONIANS.

CHAP. I.

1 Hee therefore beginneth with thankesgiuing, 4 to put them in minde that whatsoeuer was prayse worthy in them, 11 it came of Gods goodnesse: 8 and that they are ensamples vnto others.

PAVL, and Syluanus, and
Timotheus, vnto the Church
of the Thessalonians, *which
is* in God the Father, and
in the Lord Iesus Christ:
Grace *be* with you, and peace
from God our Father, and *from* the Lord Iesus
Christ.
2 [1] We giue God thankes alwayes for you
all,making mention of you in our prayers
3 [2] Without ceasing, remembring your
effectuall faith, and diligent loue, and the patience of *your* hope in our Lord Iesus Christ, in
the sight of God, euen our Father,
4 Knowing,beloued brethren, that ye are
[a] elect of God.
5 [3] For our Gospel was not vnto you in
word onely, but also in power, and in the holy Ghost, and in [b] much assurance,as ye know
after what manner wee were among you for
your sakes.
6 [4] And ye became followers of vs, and of
the Lord, and receiued the word in much affliction,with [c] ioy of the holy Ghost,
7 So that yee are as ensamples to all that
beleeue in Macedonia and in Achaia.
8 For from you sounded out the word of
the Lord, not in Macedonia and in Achaia only : but your faith also which is toward God,
spread abroad in all quarters, that we need not
to speake any thing.
9 For [d] they themselues shewe of vs what
maner of entring in wee had vnto you, [5] and
how ye turned to God from idoles, to serue the
liuing and true God,
10 And to looke for his sonne from heauen, whom he raised from the dead, *euen* Iesus which deliuereth vs from [e] that wrath to
come.

1 An example of right Christian reioycing, whereby also we learne,that such as haue great gifts in them, are in two sorts brideled,to wit, if they consider that they haue receiued all from God,and that continuãce must be desired at his handes, whereunto also the whole Epistle exhorteth the Thessalonians.

2 Hee commendeth them for three speciall gifts,effectuall faith, continuall loue, and patient hope: to the end they might bee ashamed being indued with such excellent gifts, not to continue in Gods electiõ.

a Word for word, that your election is of God.

3 Another reason why they ought in no wise start backe but continue to the end, because they cannot doubt of this doctrine which hath beene so many wayes cõfirmed vnto them euen from heauen,as they themselues did well knowe. *b Paul sheweth by two things that there followed very great fruit of his preaching,to wit, by these gifts of the holy Ghost, and that certaine assurance which was throughly setled in their minds,as appeared by their willing bearing of the Crosse.* 4 Another reason, because euen to that day they imbraced the Gospel with great chearefulnesse,insomuch that they were an example to all their neigh bours : so that it should be more shame to them to faint in the mid race. *c With ioy which commeth from the holy Ghost.* *d All the beleeuers.* 5 It is no true conuersion to forsake idoles,vnlesse a man therewithall worship the true and liuing God in Christ the onely Redeemer.

e This worde (That) is not put here without cause: and by (wrath) is meant that reuenge and punishment, wherwith the Lord will iudge the world at length in his terrible wrath.

CHAP. II.

1 Hee declareth how faithfully hee preached the Gospel vnto them, 5 seeking neither gaine, 6 nor praise of men: 10 and he proueth the same by their own testimonie: 14 that they did couragiously beare persecutions of their countrey men: 17 that he desireth very much to see them.

FOr [1] yee your selues knowe, brethren, that
our entrance in vnto you was not in vaine,
2 [2] But euen after that we had suffered before, and were shamefully intreated at * Philippi, (as yee knowe) wee were bold in [a] our
God, to speake vnto you the Gospel of God
with much striuing.
3 [3] For our exhortation was not by deceit,
nor by [b] vncleannesse,nor by guile.
4 [4] But as we were [c] allowed of God, that
the Gospel should bee committed *vnto vs*, so
wee speake, not as they that please men, but
God, which [d] approueth our hearts.
5 Neither yet did wee euer vse flattering
words,as ye knowe,nor coloured couetousnes,
God *is* record.
6 [5] Neither sought wee praise of men, neither of you,nor of others,when we might haue
been [e] chargeable, as the Apostles of Christ.
7 But we were [f] gentle among you, euen
as a nource cherisheth her children.
8 [6] Thus being affectioned toward you,
our good will was to haue dealt vnto you, not
the Gospel of God onely, but also our owne
soules,because ye were deare vnto vs.

1 That which he touched before shortly cõcerning his Apostleship,hee handleth now more at large, and to that end and purpose which we spake of.

2 The vertues of a true Pastor are, freely without feare to preach the Gospel,euen in the midst of dangers.

* Acts 16 12.

a Through God his gracious helpe.

3 To teach pure doctrine faithfully and with a pure heart.

b By any wicked and naughty kind of dealing.

4 To approue his conscience to God,being free from all flattery and couetousnes.

c Seeing there is this difference betweene the iudgements of God and the iudgements of men, that when men chuse,they respect the qualities of those things which stand before them, but God findeth the reason of his counsel onely in himselfe, it followeth, that seeing we are not able to thinke a good thought,that whomsoeuer he first chuseth to those callings, hee maketh them able, and doth not finde them able. And therefore in that we are allowed of God, it hangeth vpon his mercie. *d Which liketh and alloweth of them.* 5 To submit himselfe euen vnto the basest,to win them,and to eschew all pride. *e When I might lawfully haue liued vpon the expences of the Church.* *f We were rough, but easie and gentle as a nource, that is neither ambitious nor couetous, but taketh all paines as patiently as is if she were a mother.* 6 To haue the flocke that is committed vnto vnto him in more estimation then his owne life.

9 [7]For ye remember, brethren, * our labour and trauaile : for wee haue trauailed day
and night, because wee would not be chargeable vnto any of you, and preached vnto you
the Gospel of God.
10 [8]Yee *are* witnesses, and God *also*, how
holily, and iustly, and vnblameably wee behaued our selues among you that beleeue.
11 [9]As ye know how that we exhorted you,
and comforted, and besought euery one of
you (as a father his children)
12 [10]That yee * would walke worthy of
God, who hath called you vnto his kingdome
and glory.
13 [11]For this cause also thanke wee God
without ceasing, that when yee receiued the
word of God, which ye heard of vs, ye receiued it not as the word of men, but as it is indeede the word of God, which also worketh
in you that beleeue.
14 [12]For brethren, ye are become followers of the Churches of God, which in Iudea
are in [g] Christ Iesus, because ye haue also suffered the same things of your owne [h] countreymen, euen as they *haue* of the Iewes.
15 [13]Who both killed the Lord Iesus and
their owne Prophets, and haue persecuted vs
away, [14]and God they please not, and are contrary to [i] all men,
16 And forbid vs to preach vnto the Gentiles, that they might be saued, to [k] fulfill their
sinnes alwayes : for the [l] wrath *of God* is come
on them to the vtmost.
17 [15]Forasmuch, brethren, as wee [m] were
kept from you for a season, concerning sight,
but not in the heart, we enforced the more to
see your face with great desire.
18 Therefore wee would haue come vnto
you (I Paul, at lest once or twise) but Satan
hindered vs.
19 For what is our hope or ioy, or crowne
of reioycing ? are not euen you it in the presence of our Lord Iesus Christ at his comming?
20 Yes, ye are our glory and ioy.

7 To depart with his owne right, rather then to bee chargeable to his sheepe.
* *Acts 20 34. 1.cor.4.12. 2.thess.3.8.*
8 To excell other in example of godly life.
9 To exhort and comfort with a fatherly minde and affection.
10 To exhort all men diligently and earnestly to leade a godly life.
* *Eph.4.1. phil. 1.27. col.1.10.*
11 Hauing approoued his ministery, he commendeth againe (to that end and purpose that I spake of) the cheerefulnesse of the Thessalonians which was answerable to his diligence in preaching, and their manly patience.
12 He confirmeth them in their afflictions which they suffered of their owne people, because they were afflicted of their owne countreymen : which came as well (sayth he) to the Churches of the Iewes, as to them : and therefore they ought to take it in good part.
g Which Christ hath gathered together.
h Euen of them which are of the same countrey and the same towne that you are of.
13 He preuenteth an offence which might be taken, for that the Iewes especially aboue all other persecuted the Gospel. That is no new thing, sayth he, seeing they slewe Christ himselfe, and his Prophets, and haue banished me also. 14 Hee foretelleth the vtter destruction of the Iewes, lest any man should be moued by their rebellion. *i For the Iewes would neither enter into the kingdome of God themselues, nor suffer other to enter in. k Vntill that wickednesse of theirs which they haue by inheritance as it were of their fathers, be growen so great, that the measure of their iniquitie being filled, God may come foorth to wrath. l The iudgement of God being angrie, which indeed appeared shortly after in the destruction of the citie of Hierusalem, whither many resorted euen out of diuers prouinces, when it was besieged.* 15 He meeteth with an obiection, why hee came not to them straightwayes being in so great miserie, I desired often times (sayth he) and it lay not in me, but Satan hindred my endeuours, and therefore I sent Timothie my faithfull companion vnto you, because you are most deare to me. *m Were kept asunder from you, and as it were orphanes.*

CHAP. III.

1 *To shewe his affection toward them, he sendeth Timothie vnto them. 6 He is so mooued by the report of their prosperous state, 9 that hee cannot giue sufficient thankes, 11 and therefore he breaketh out into prayer.*

WHerefore since wee could no longer
forbeare, wee thought it good to remaine at Athens alone,
2 * And haue sent Timotheus our brother and minister of God, and our labour fellow in the Gospel of Christ, to stablish you,
and to comfort you touching your faith,
3 That no man should be mooued with
these afflictions : [1]for yee your selues knowe,
that we are appointed thereunto.
4 For verely when wee were with you,
we tolde you before that wee should suffer tribulations, euen as it came to passe, and yee
know it.
5 Euen for this cause, when I could no
longer forbeare, I sent *him* that I might know
of your faith, lest the tempter had tempted
you in any sort, and that our labour had beene
in vaine.
6 [2]But now lately when Timotheus came
from you vnto vs, and brought vs good tidings of your faith and loue, and that yee haue
good remembrance of vs alwayes, desiring to
see vs as we also *doe* you,
7 Therefore, brethren, wee had consolation in you, in all our affliction and necessitie
through your faith.
8 For now are we [a] aliue, if ye stand fast in
the Lord.
9 For what thankes can we recompense to
God againe for you, for all the ioy wherewith
we reioyce for your sakes before our God,
10 Night and day, * praying exceedingly
that we might see your face & might [b] accomplish that which is lacking in your faith ?
11 Now God himselfe euen our Father,
and our Lord Iesus Christ, guide our iourney
vnto you.
12 [3]And the Lord increase you, and make
you abound in loue one toward another, and
toward all men, euen as we *doe* toward you :
13 * To make your hearts stable and vnblameable in holinesse before God euen our
Father, at the comming of our Lorde Iesus
Christ with all his Saints.

* *Actes 16.1.*
1 The will of God, who calleth his on this condition, to bring them to glory by affliction, is a most sure remedy against all afflictions.
2 Because they haue hitherto gone so well forward, he exhorteth them againe to make an end of the rest of the iourney, seeing that therein also they shal do him their Apostle a great pleasure.
a For now you cannot otherwise thinke me safe and in good case, vnlesse you goe forward in religion and faith.
* *Rom.1.10. and 15.23.*
b Paul was constrained through the importunate dealing of the enemies to leaue the building which he had scarce begun : And for that cause he had left Silas and Timotheus in Macedonia, and when Timothie came to Athens to him, he sent him backe againe straightway. So that he desireth to see the Thessalonians, that he may throughly accomplish their faith and religion, that was as yet imperfect.
3 Another part of the Epistle, wherein he speaketh of the duties of a Christian life. And he sheweth that the perfection of a Christian life, consisteth in two things, to wit, in charitie toward all men, and inward puritie of the heart, the accomplishment whereof notwithstanding is deferred to the next comming of Christ, who will then perfite his worke by the same grace, wherewith he begun it in vs. * *Chap.5 23. 1.cor.1.8.*

CHAP. IIII.

1 *He exhorteth them 3 to holinesse, 9 and brotherly loue. 13 He forbiddeth them to sorow after the manner of infidels. 15 He setteth out the history of our resurrection.*

AND [1] furthermore wee beseech you, brethren, and exhort you in the Lord Iesus,
that ye [a] increase more and more, as ye haue receiued of vs, how yee ought to walke, and to
please God.
2 For ye know what commandements we
gaue you by the Lord Iesus.
3 * [2]For this is the will of God *euen* your
[b] sanctification, *and* that yee should abstaine
from fornication,
4 [3]That euery one of you should know,
how to possesse his vessell in holinesse and honour,

1 Diuers exhortations, the ground whereof is this, to be mindfull of those things which they haue heard of the Apostle.
a That ye labour to excell more and more, and daily passe your selues.
* *Rom.12.2. ephes.5.17.*
2 This is the summe of those things which he deliuered them, to dedicate themselues wholly to God. And he condemneth plainely all filthinesse through lust, because it is altogether contrary to the will of God. *b Looke Iohn 17.17.* 3 An other reason, because it defileth the body.

4 The third, because the Saints are discerned from them which know not God, by honestie and puritie.
* 1.Cor.6.8.
5 Secondly, he reprehendeth all violent oppression, and immoderate desire, and sheweth most seuerely as the Prophet of God, that God will reuenge such wickednesse.
* 1.Cor.1.2.
c These commandements which I gaue you.
6 Thirdly, hee requireth a readie minde to all maner of louing kindnesse, and exhorteth them to profite more and more in that vertue.
* *Iohn* 13.34. *and* 15.12. 1.*iohn* 2.8. *and* 4.21.
7 He condemneth vnquiet braines, and such as are curious in matters which appertaine not vnto them.
8 He rebuketh idlenesse and slothfulnesse, which vices whosoeuer are giuen vnto, fall into other wickednesse, to the great offence of the Church.
9 The third part of the Epistle, which is interlaced among the former exhortations (which he returneth vnto afterward) wherein he speaketh of mourning for the dead, and the maner of the resurrection, and of the latter day.
10 Wee must

5 [4] *And* not in the lust of concupiscence,
euen as the Gentiles which know not God:
6 *[5] That no man oppresse or defraud
his brother in any matter: for the Lord *is* auen-
ger of all such things, as we also haue told you
before time and testified.
7 *For God hath not called vs vnto vncleannesse, but vnto holinesse.
8 He therfore that [c] despiseth *these things*,
despiseth not man, but God who hath euen
giuen you his holy Spirit.
9 [6] But as touching brotherly loue, yee
neede not that I write vnto you: * for yee are
taught of God to loue one another.
10 Yea, and that thing verely yee doe vnto
all the brethren which are throughout all Macedonia: but wee beseech you, brethren, that
ye increase more and more,
11 [7] And that ye studie to be quiet, and to
meddle with your owne businesse, [8] and to
worke with your owne handes, as wee commanded you,
12 That ye may behaue your selues honestly toward them that are without, and that nothing be lacking vnto you.
13 ¶ [9] I would not, brethren, haue you ignorant [10] concerning them [11] which are asleep,
that ye sorow not euen as other which haue no
hope.
14 [12] For if wee beleeue that Iesus is dead,
and is risen, euen so them which sleepe in [d] Iesus, will God [e] bring with him.
15 [13] For this say we vnto you by the [f] word
of the Lord, that [g] wee which liue, and are remaining in the comming of the Lord, shall not
preuent them which sleepe.
16 For the Lord himselfe shal descend from
heauen with a [h] shout, *and* with the voice of the
Archangel, and * with the trumpet of God:
and the dead in Christ shall rise first:
17 Then shall we which liue and remaine,
be [i] caught vp with them also in the clouds, to
meete the Lord in the aire: and so shall we e-
uer be with the Lord.
18 Wherefore, comfort your selues one
another with these words.

take heed that we doe not immoderately bewaile the dead, that is, as they vse to doe which thinke that they are vtterly perished. 11 A confirmation: for death is but a sleepe of the body (for he speaketh of the faithfull) vntill the Lord commeth. 12 A reason of the confirmation, for seeing that the head is risen, the members also shall rise, and that by the vertue of God. *m The dead in Christ, which continue in faith whereby they are graffed into Christ, euen to the last gaspe. e Will call their bodies out of their graues, and ioyne their soules to them againe.* 13 The manner of the resurrection shalbe thus. The bodies of the dead shalbe as it were raised out of sleepe at the sound of the trumpet of God. Christ himselfe shall descend from heauen. The Saints (for hee speaketh properly of them) which shall then be found aliue, together with the dead which shall rise, shalbe taken vp into the clouds to meete the Lord, and shalbe in perpetuall glory with him. *f In the Name of the Lord, as though he himselfe spake vnto you. g He speaketh of these things, as though he should be one of them whom the Lord shall finde aliue at his comming, because that time is vncertaine: and therefore euery one of vs ought to be in such a readinesse, as if the Lord were comming at euery moment. h The word which the Apostle vseth here, signifieth properly that encouragement which mariners vse one to another, when they altogether with one shout put forth their oares and rowe together.* * 1.*Cor.* 15.52. *i Suddenly and in the twinkling of an eye.*

CHAP. V.

1 Condemning the curious searching for the seasons of Christs comming, 6 hee warneth them to bee readie daily to receiue him: 11 And so giueth them sundry good lessons.

BVt [1] of the times and [a] seasons, brethren,
ye haue no neede that I write vnto you.
2 For ye your selues know perfectly, that
the day of the Lord shall come, euen as a thiefe
in the night.
3 For when they shall say, Peace and safetie, then shall come vpon them sudden destruction, as the trauaile vpon a woman with child,
and they shall not escape.
4 [2] But ye, brethren, are not in darkenesse,
that that day shall come on you, as *it were* a
thiefe.
5 Ye are all the children of light, and the
children of the day: wee are not of the night,
neither of darkenesse.
6 Therefore let vs not sleepe as doe other,
but let vs watch and be sober.
7 For they that sleepe, sleepe in the night,
and they that are drunken, are drunken in the
night.
8 [3] But let vs which are of the day, be sober, *putting on the brestplate of faith & loue,
and of the hope of saluation for an helmet.
9 [4] For God hath not appointed vs vnto
wrath, but to obtaine saluation by the meanes
of our Lord Iesus Christ,
10 [5] Which died for vs, that whether wee
wake or sleepe, we should liue together with
him.
11 [6] Wherefore exhort one another, and
edifie one another, euen as yee doe.
12 [7] Now wee beseech you, brethren, that
ye [b] acknowledge them which labour among
you, and are ouer you in the [c] Lord, and admonish you,
13 That yee haue them in singular loue for
[d] their workes sake. [8] Be at peace among your
selues.
14 [9] Wee desire you, brethren, admonish
them that are [e] out of order: comfort the feeble minded: beare with the weake: be patient
toward all men.
15 [10] * See that none recompence euill for
euill vnto any man: but euer folow that which
is good, both toward your selues, and toward
all men.
16 [11] Reioyce euermore.
17 * Pray continually.
18 In all things, giue thankes: for this *is*
the [f] will of God in Christ Iesus toward you.
19 [12] Quench not the Spirit.
20 Despise not [g] prophecying.
21 Try all things, *and* keepe that which is
good.

1 The day that God hath appointed for this iudgement, we know not. But this is sure that it shall come vpon men when they looke for nothing lesse.
a Looke Actes 1.7.
2 Returning to exhortations, he warneth vs which are lightened with the knowledge of God, that it is our duety not to liue securely in deliciousnesse, lest we be suddenly taken in a dead sleepe in pleasures: but contrariwise to haue an eye to the Lord, and not suffer our selues to be oppressed with the cares of this world, for that is meet for the darkenesse of the night, and this for the light.
3 Wee must fight with faith and hope, much lesse ought we lie carelesly snorting.
* *Esai* 59.17. *ephes.*6.17.
4 He pricketh vs forwards by setting most certaine hope of victorie before vs.
5 The death of Christ is a pledge of our victorie, for therefore hee died, that wee might be partakers of his life or vertue, yea euen whiles we liue here.
6 Wee must not onely watch our selues, but we are also bound to stirre vp and confirme one another.
7 Wee must haue great consideration of them which are appointed to the ministerie of the word, and gouernment of the Church of God, and doe their duety.
b That you acknowledge and

take them for such as they are, that is to say, men worthy to be greatly accompted of among you. c In those things which perteine to Gods seruice: so is the Ecclesiasticall function distinguished from ciuill authoritie, and true Shepheards from wolues. d So then, where this cause ceaseth, there must the honour cease. 8 The maintenance of mutuall concord, is especially to bee looked vnto. 9 Wee must haue consideration of euery man, and as the disease is, so must the remedie be vsed. *e That keepe not their ranke or standing.* 10 Charitie ought not to bee ouercome with any iniuries. * *Prouerb.* 17.13. *and* 20.22. *matth.* 5.39. *rom.* 12.17. 1.*pet.* 3.9. 11 A quiet and appeased minde, is nourished with continuall prayers, respecting the will of God. * *Luke* 18.1. *f An acceptable thing to God, and such as hee liketh well of.* 12 The sparkes of the Spirit of God that are kindled in vs, are nourished with daily hearing the worde of God: but true doctrine must bee diligently distinguished from false. *g The expounding of the word of God.*

22 [13] Abstaine

22 [13] Abstaine from all [h] appearance of euill.
23 Now the very God of peace [i] sanctifie
you throughout : and *I pray God* that your
whole spirit and soule and body, may be kept
blamelesse vnto the comming of our Lord Iesus Christ.
24 [14] * [k] Faithfull *is hee* which calleth you,
which will also [l] doe it.
25 [15] Brethren, pray for vs.
26 Greete all the brethren with an holy
kisse.
27 I charge you in the Lorde, that this
Epistle bee read vnto all the brethren the
Saints.
28 The grace of our Lord Iesus Christ *be*
with you, Amen.

13 A generall conclusion, that we waiting for the comming of Christ, doe giue our selues to purenesse both in minde, will, and body, through the grace and strength of the Spirit of God. *h Whatsoeuer hath but the very shew of euill, abstaine from it. i Separate you from the world, and make you holy to himselfe through his Spirit, in Christ, in whom only you shall attaine vnto that true peace.* 14 The good will and power of God is a sure confirmation against all difficulties, whereof we haue a sure witnesse in our vocation. * 1.Cor.1 9. *k Alwayes one, and euer like himselfe, who performeth in deed whatsoeuer he promiseth : and an effectuall calling is nothing else but a right declaring and true setting foorth of Gods will : and therefore the saluation of the elect, is safe and sure.*

l Who will also make you perfect. 15 The last part of the Epistle, wherein with most weightie charge he commendeth both himselfe and this Epistle vnto them.

¶ The first *Epistle* vnto the Thessalonians written from Athens.

THE SECOND EPISTLE OF PAVL TO THE THESSALONIANS.

CHAP. I.

3 He commendeth the increase of faith, and charitie, 4 and the patience of the Thessalonians : 6 and describing Gods vengeance against such as oppresse the godly, 10 he teacheth the godly to waite for the last iudgement.

Aul and Siluanus, and Ti-
motheus, vnto the Church
of the Thessalonians, *which*
is in God our Father, and in
the Lord Iesus Christ:
2 Grace *be* with you,
and peace from God our Father, and *from* the
Lord Iesus Christ.
3 * [1] We ought to thanke God alwayes for
you, brethren, as is it meete, because that your
faith [a] groweth exceedingly, and the loue
of euery one of you toward another, aboundeth,
4 So that we our selues reioyce of you in
the Churches of God, because of your patience and faith in all your persecutions and tribulations that ye suffer,
5 * [2] *Which is* a manifest token of the
righteous iudgement of God, that ye may be
counted worthy of the kingdome of God, for
the which ye also suffer.
6 [3] For it is a righteous thing with God,
to recompense tribulation to them that trouble
you,
7 And to you which are troubled, rest
[4] with vs, * [5] when the Lorde Iesus shall shew
himselfe frō heauen with his mightie Angels,
8 In flaming fire, rendering vengeance
vnto them [6] that do not know God, and which
obey not vnto the Gospel of our Lord Iesus
Christ,
9 Which shall bee punished with euerlasting perdition, from the presence of the Lord,
and from the glory of his power,
10 When hee shall come to be glorified in
his Saints, and to be made marueilous in all
them that beleeue ([7] because our testimonie
toward you was beleeued) in that day.
11 [8] Wherefore, we also pray alwayes for
you, that our God may make you worthy of
[b] this calling, and fulfill [c] all the good pleasure
of *his* goodnesse, and the [d] worke of faith with
power,
12 That the Name of our Lorde Iesus
Christ may be glorified in you, and ye in him,
according to the grace of our God, and of the
Lord Iesus Christ.

* 1. Thess.1.2.
1 The first part of the Epistle, wherein he reioyceth that through the grace of God, they haue manfully sustained all the assaults of their enemies, wherein he confirmeth them, moreouer shewing with what gifts they must chiefly fight, to wit, with faith & charitie, which must dayly increase. *a That whereas it grew vp before, it doeth also receiue some increase euery day more and more.* * *Iude 6.* 2 He openeth the fountaine of all true comfort, to wit, that in afflictions which we suffer for righteousnesse sake, we may behold as it were in a glasse the testimonie of that iudgement to come, and the end thereof most acceptable to vs, and most sharpe to his enemies. 3 A proofe: God is iust, therefore he will worthily punish the vniust, and will doe away the miseries of his people. 4 He confirmeth them also by the way, by this means that the condition both of this present state and the state to come, is common to him with them. * 1.*Thes*.4.16. 5 A most glorious description of the second comming of Christ, to be set against all the miseries of the godly, and the triumphs of the wicked. 6 There is no knowledge of God vnto saluation, without the Gospel of Christ.

7 The children of God shall be counted by the faith which they haue in the Gospel, which is preached vnto them by the Apostles. 8 Seeing that we haue the marke set before vs, it remaineth that we goe vnto it. And we goe to it, by certaine degrees of causes: first by the free loue and good pleasure of God, by vertue whereof all other inferiour causes worke : from thence proceedeth the free calling to Christ, and from calling, faith, whereupon followeth both the glorifying of Christ in vs, and vs in Christ. *b By (calling) he meaneth not the very acte of calling, but that selfe same thing whereunto we are called, which is the glory of that heauenly kingdome. c Which he determined long since onely vpon his gracious and mercifull goodnesse towards you. d So then, faith is an excellent worke of God in vs : and we see here plainly that the Apostle leaueth nothing to free will, to make it checkemate with Gods working therein, as the Papists dreame.*

CHAP. II.

2 He sheweth that the day of the Lord shall not come, till there be a departure from the faith, 3 and that Antichrist be reueiled, 8 whose destruction hee setteth out, 15 and thereupon exhorteth to constancie.

NOw [1] wee beseech you, brethren, by the
comming of our Lord Iesus Christ, and
by our [a] assembling vnto him,
2 [2] That yee bee not suddenly mooued
from *your* minde, nor troubled neither by
[b] spirit, nor by [c] worde, nor by [d] letter, as *it*
were from vs, as though the day of Christ were
at hand.
3 Let no man deceiue you by any meanes:
[3] for *that day shall not come*, except there come a

1 The second part of the Epistle, conteining an excellent prophecie of the state of the Church, which shalbe from the Apostles time vnto the latter day of iudgement. *a If we thinke earnestly vpon that vnmeasurable glory, which wee shall be partakers of with Christ, it will be an excellent remedie for vs against wauering and impatience, so that neither the glistering of the world shall allure vs, nor the dreadfull sight of the crosse dismay vs.* 2 Wee must take heede of false prophets, especially in this matter, which goe about to deceiue, and that for the most part, after three sorts: for either they brag of fained propheticall reuelations, or they bring coniectures and reasons of their owne, or vse counterfeit writings. *b By dreames and fables, which men pretend to be spirituall reuelations. c Either by word of mouth, or by bookes written. d Either by forged letter, or falsly glosed vpon.* 3 The Apostle foretelleth that before the comming of the Lord, there shalbe a throne set vp cleane contrarie to Christes glory, wherein that wicked man shall sit, and transferre all things that appertaine to God, to himselfe, and many shall fall away from God to him.

departing first, and that [e] that man of sinne be
disclosed, *euen* the sonne of perdition,
4 Which is an aduersarie, and [f] exalteth
himselfe against all that is called God, or that
is worshipped: [4] so that he doeth sit as God in
the Temple of God, shewing himselfe that he
is God.
5 [5] Remember ye not, that when I was yet
with you, I tolde you these things?
6 And now ye know [g] what withholdeth
that he might be reueiled in his time.
7 [6] For the mysterie of iniquitie doeth alreadie worke: [7] onely hee which now [h] withholdeth, *shall let* till hee be taken out of the
way.
8 [8] And then shall [i] that wicked man be reueiled, * whom the Lord shall [k] consume with
the [l] Spirit of his mouth, and shall abolish with
the brightnesse of his comming.
9 [9] *Euen him* whose comming is by the
effectual working of Satan, with all power, and
signes, and [m] lying wonders,
10 And in all deceiueablenesse of vnrighteousnesse, among them that perish, because
they receiued not the loue of the trueth, that
they might be saued.
11 And therefore God shall send them
[n] strong delusion, that they should beleeue
lyes,
12 That all they might be damned which
beleeued not the trueth, but [o] had pleasure in
vnrighteousnesse.
13 [10] But wee ought to giue thankes alway to God for you, brethren beloued of the
Lord, because that God hath from the beginning chosen you to saluation, through [p] sanctification of the Spirit, and the [q] faith of trueth,
14 Whereunto he called you by our [r] Gospel, to obtaine the glory of our Lorde Iesus
Christ.
15 [11] Therefore, brethren, stand fast and
keepe the instructions, which yee haue beene
taught, either by word, or by our Epistle.
16 Now the same Iesus Christ our Lord,
and our God euen the Father which hath loued vs, and hath giuen vs euerlasting consolation and good hope through grace,
17 Comfort your hearts, and stablish you
in euery word and good worke.

e By speaking of one, he pointeth out the body of the tyrannous and persecuting Church.
f All men know who he is that sayth he can shut vp heauen and open it at his pleasure, and tooke vpon him to be Lord and Master aboue all kings and princes, before whom kings and princes fall downe and worship, honouring that Antichrist as a god.
4 He foretelleth that Antichrist (that is, whosoeuer he be that shall occupie that seate that falleth away from God) shall not reigne without the Church, but in the very bosome of the Church.
5 This prophecie was continually declared to the ancient Church, but it was neglected of them that followed.
g What hindereth and stayeth.
6 Euen in the Apostles time the first foundations of the Apostaticall seate were laid, but yet so that they deceiued men.
7 He foretelleth, that when the Empire of Rome is taken away, the seate that falleth away from God, shall succeede and hold his place, as the old writers, Tertullian, Chrysostome and Hierome doe expound it.
h He which is now in authoritie and ruleth all, to wit, the Romane Empire
8 That wickednesse shall at length be detected by the word of the Lord, and shall vtterly be abolished by Christs comming. *i Word for word, that lawlesse fellow, that is to say, hee that shall tread Gods Law cleane vnder foote.* * *Isai 11.4.* *k Bring to nought.* *l With his word, for the true Ministers of the word are as a mouth, whereby the Lord breatheth out that mightie and euerlasting word, which shall breake his enemies in sunder, as it were an yron rod.* 9 Hee foretelleth, that Satan will bestow all his might and power, and vse all false miracles that hee can to establish that seate, and that with great successe, because the wickednesse of the world doeth so deserue it: yet so, that onely the vnfaithfull shall perish through his deceit. *m Which are partly false, and partly wrought to establish a falshood.* *n A most mightie working to deceiue them.* *o They liked lyes so well, that they had pleasure in them, which is the greatest madnesse that may be.* 10 The elect shall stand stedfast and safe from all these mischiefes. Now election is knowen by these testimonies: Faith is gathered by sanctification: faith, by that that wee accord vnto the trueth. trueth, by calling, through the preaching of the Gospel: from whence wee come at length to a certaine hope of glorification. *p To sanctifie you.* *q Faith which layeth holde not vpon lies, but vpon the trueth of God, which is the Gospel.* *r By our preaching.* 11 The conclusion: It remaineth then that wee continue in the doctrine which was deliuered vnto vs by the mouth and writings of the Apostles, through the free good will of God, which comforteth vs with an inuincible hope, and also in all godlinesse our whole life long.

CHAP. III.

1 Hee desireth them to further the preaching of the Gospel with their prayers, 6 and to withdraw themselues from those, who through idlenesse 11 and curiositie peruert good order: 14 Whom he excludeth from the company of the faithfull.

FVrthermore, [1] brethren, * pray for vs, that
the word of the Lord may haue free passage and be glorified, euen as *it is* with you.
2 And that wee may be deliuered from
[a] vnreasonable and euil men: [2] for all men haue
not faith.
3 But the Lord is faithfull, which will stablish you, and keepe you from [b] euill.
4 [3] And we are perswaded of you through
the Lord, that yee both doe, and will doe the
things which we warne you of.
5 [4] And the Lord guide your hearts to the
loue of God, and the waiting for of Christ.
6 [5] Wee warne you, brethren, in the Name
of our Lord Iesus Christ, that yee withdraw
your selues from euery brother that walketh
inordinately, and not after the instruction
which he receiued of vs.
7 [6] For yee your selues know, * how yee
ought to follow vs: * for wee behaued not our
selues inordinately among you,
8 Neither tooke we bread of any man for
nought: but we wrought with labour and trauaile night and day, because wee would not be
chargeable to any of you.
9 Not because we haue not authority, but
that we might make our selues an ensample vnto you to follow vs.
10 For euen when we were with you, this
wee warned you of, that if there were any,
which would not worke, that he should [c] not
eate.
11 For we heare, that there are some which
walke among [7] you inordinately, and worke
not at all, [8] but are busie bodies.
12 [9] Therefore them that are such, wee
warne and exhort by our Lord Iesus Christ,
that they worke with quietnesse, and eate their
owne bread.
13 [10] And yee, brethren, be not wearie in
well doing.
14 [11] If any man obey not this our saying
in this letter, note him, and haue no [12] companie with him, [13] that he may be ashamed:

1 He addeth now consequently according to his maner, diuers admonitions: The first of them is, that they make prayers for the increase and free passage of the Gospel, and for the safetie of the faithfull ministers of the same.
* *Ephes. 6.19. colos. 4.3.*
a Which haue no care of their duety.
2 It is no marueile that the Gospel is hated of so many, seing that faith is a rare gift of God. Notwithstanding the Church shall neuer be destroyed by the multitude of the wicked, because it is grounded and stayed vpon the faithfull promise of God.
b From Satans snares, or from euill.
3 The second admonition is, that they follow alwayes the doctrine of the Apostles as a rule for their life.
4 Thirdly, he diligently and earnestly admonisheth them of two things which are giuen vs by the onely grace of God, to wit, of charitie, and a watchfull minde to the comming of Christ.
5 Fourthly, he saith, that idle and lazie persons ought not to be relieued of the Church, nay, that they are not to be suffered.
6 Lest he might seeme to deale hardly with them, hee setteth foorth himselfe for an example, who besides his trauaile in preaching laboured with his hands, which hee sayth hee was not simply bound to doe. * *1 Corinth. 11.1.* * *1. Thess. 4 11.* *c What shall we doe then with those idle bellied Monkes, and sacrificing Priests? A Monke (sayth Socrates, booke 8. of his Tripartite historie) which worketh not with hands, is like a thiefe.* 7 How great a fault idlenesse is, hee declareth by that that God created no man in vaine or to no purpose, neither is there any vnto whom hee hath not allotted as it were a certaine standing and roume. Whereupon it followeth, that the order which God hath appointed, is troubled by the idle, yea broken, which is great sinne and wickednesse. 8 He reprehendeth a vice, which is ioyned with the former, whereupon follow an infinite sort of mischiefes: to wit, that there are none more busie in other mens matters, then they which neglect their owne. 9 The Lord commandeth and the Apostles pray in the Name of Christ, first, that no man be idle, and next, that euery man doe quietly and carefully see to doe his duety in that office and calling wherein the Lord hath placed him. 10 We must take heed, that some mens vnworthinesse cause vs not to bee slacke in well doing. 11 Excommunication is a punishment for the obstinate. 12 We must haue no familiaritie nor fellowship with the excommunicate. 13 The end of the excommunication is not the destruction, but the saluation of the sinner, that at lest through shame he may be driuen to repentance.

15 [14] Yet

15 [14] Yet count him not as an enemie, but
admonish him as a brother.
16 [15] Now the Lord himselfe of peace giue
you peace alwayes by all meanes. The Lord *be*
with you all.

14 Wee must so eschew familiaritie with the excommunicate, that wee diligently seeke all occasions and meanes that may bee, to bring them againe into the right way. 15 Prayers are the seales of all exhortations.

17 [16] The salutation of me Paul, with mine
owne hand, which is the token in euery Epistle: so I write,
18 The grace of our Lord Iesus Christ *be*
with you all, Amen.

¶ The second *Epistle* to the Thessalonians,
written from Athens.

16 The Apostle subscribeth his letter with his owne hand, that false letters might not be brought and put in place of true.

THE FIRST EPISTLE OF PAVL TO TIMOTHEVS.

CHAP. I.

Setting foorth a perfect paterne of a true Pastour, whose office especially consisteth in teaching, 4 hee warneth him that vaine questions set apart, hee teach those things, 5 which further charitie and faith: 12 and that his authoritie be not condemned, 14 he sheweth what an one hee is made through the grace of God.

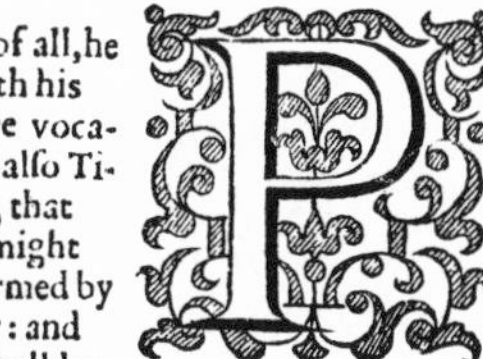

PAVL [1] an Apostle of IESVS
CHRIST, by the || comman-
dement of God our Sauiour,
and of *our* Lord Iesus Christ
our hope,
2 Vnto Timotheus *my*
naturall sonne in the faith: Grace, [a] mercy,
and peace from God our Father, and *from*
Christ Iesus our Lord.
3 [2] As I besought thee to abide still in E-
phesus, when I departed into Macedonia, *so*
doe, that thou mayest warne some, that they
teach none other doctrine,
4 [3] Neither that they giue heed to fables
and [b] genealogies *which are* endlesse, which
breede questions rather then godly edifying,
which is by faith.
5 [4] For * the end of the [c] commandement
is [d] loue out of a pure heart, and of a good conscience, and of faith vnfained.
6 [5] From the which things some haue erred, and haue turned vnto vaine iangling.
7 [6] They would be doctors of the Lawe,
and yet vnderstand not what they speake, neither whereof they affirme.
8 [7] And wee know, that the Law is good,
if a man vse it lawfully,
9 [8] Knowing this, that the Law is not giuen vnto a [e] righteous man, but vnto the lawlesse and disobedient, to the vngodly, and to
[f] sinners, to the vnholy, and to the profane, to
murtherers of fathers and mothers, to man-
slayers,
10 To whoremongers, to buggerers, to
mensteale rs, to lyars, to the periured, and if
there be any other thing, that is contrarie to
wholesome doctrine,
11 [9] *Which is* according to the glorious
Gospel of the blessed God, [10] which is committed vnto me.
12 [11] Therefore I thanke him, which hath
made mee [g] strong, *that is*, Christ Iesus our
Lord: for he counted me faithfull and put me
in *his* seruice:
13 When before I was a [h] blasphemer, and
a persecuter, and an oppressor: but I was receiued to mercie: for I did it ignorantly through
vnbeliefe.
14 But the grace of our Lord was exceeding abundant [12] with faith and loue, which is
in Christ Iesus.
15 [13] This *is* a [i] true saying, & by all meanes
worthy to bee receiued, that * Christ Iesus
came into the world to saue sinners, of whom
I am chiefe.
16 Notwithstanding, for this cause was I
receiued to mercy, that Iesus Christ should first
shew on me all long suffering vnto the ensample of them, which shall in time to come beleeue in him vnto eternall life.
17 [14] Now vnto the king euerlasting, immortall, inuisible, vnto God [k] onely wise, *be*
honour *and* glory, for euer and euer, Amen.
18 [15] This commandement commit I vnto
thee, sonne Timotheus, according to the prophecies, which went before vpon thee, that
thou by [l] them shouldest fight a good fight,
19 Hauing [m] faith and a good conscience,
[16] which some haue put away, and as concerning faith, haue made shipwracke.

1 First of all, he auoucheth his owne free vocation and also Timothies, that the one might be confirmed by the other: and therewithall he declareth the summe of the Apostolicall doctrine, to wit, the mercy of God in Christ Iesus apprehended by faith, the ende whereof is yet hoped for.
|| *Or, ordinance.*
a There is as much difference betwixt mercy and grace, as is betwixt the effect and the cause: for grace is that free good will of God, wherby he chose vs in Christ, and mercy is that free iustificatio which followeth it.
2 This whole Epistle consisteth in admonitions, wherein all the duties of a faithfull Pastour are liuely set out. And the first admonition is this, that no innouation be made either in the Apostles doctrine it self, or in ye maner of teaching it.

9 He setteth against fond and vaine babbling, not onely the Law, but the Gospel also, which condemneth not, but greatly commendeth the wholesome doctrine conteined in the commandements of God, and therefore he calleth it a glorious Gospel, and the Gospel of the blessed God, the vertue whereof these babblers knew not.
10 A reason why neither any other Gospel is to be taught then he hath taught in the Church, neither after any other sort, because there is no other Gospel beside that, which God committed to him.
11 He mainteineth of necessity his Apostleship against some that did carpe at his former life, debasing himselfe euen to hell, to aduance Christs only mercie, wherewith he abolished all those his former doings.
g Which gaue me strength, not only when I had no will to doe well, but also when I was wholly giuen to euill.
h These are the preparatiue works which Paul braggeth of.

3 The doctrine is corrupted not only by false opinions, but also by vaine and curious speculations: the declaration and vtterance whereof can nothing helpe our faith. *b He noteth out one kinde of vaine questions.* 4 The second admonition is, that the right vse and practise of the doctrine must be ioyned with the doctrine. And that consisteth in pure charitie, and a good conscience, and true faith. * *Rom. 13.10.* *c Of the Law.* *d There is neither loue without a good conscience, nor a good conscience without faith, nor faith without the word of God.* 5 That which hee spake before generally of vaine and curious controuersies, he applyeth to them which pretending a zeale of the Law, dwelled vpon outward things, and neuer made an end of babling of foolish trifles. 6 There are none more vnlearned, and more impudent in vsurping the name of holinesse, then foolish sophisticall bablers. 7 The taking away of an obiection: He condemneth not the Law, but requireth the right vse and practise of it. 8 Hee indeed escapeth the curse of the Law, and therefore doeth not abhorre it, who fleeing and eschewing those things which the Law condemneth, giueth himselfe with all his heart, to obserue it: and not he that maketh a vaine babbling of outward and curious matters. *e And such a one is he, whom the Lord hath endued with true doctrine, and with the holy Ghost.* *f To such as make an arte, as it were, of sinning.*

12 He prooueth this change by the effects, for that that he that was a profane man, is become a beleeuer: and hee that did most outragiously persecute Christ, burneth now in loue toward him. 13 Hee turneth the reproch of the aduersaries vpon their owne head, shewing that this singular example of the goodnesse of God, redoundeth to the commoditie of the whole Church. *i Worthy to bee beleeued.* * *Matth. 9.13. marke 2.17.* 14 Hee breaketh out into an exclamation, euen for very zeale of minde, for that hee cannot satisfie himselfe in amplifying the grace of God. *k Looke Iohn 17.3.* 15 The conclusion of both the former fatherly admonitions, to wit, that Timothie striuing manfully against all lets, being called to the ministerie according to many prophecies which went before of him, should both maintaine the doctrine which hee had receiued, and keepe also a good conscience. *l By the helpe of them.* *m Wholesome and sound doctrine.* 16 Whosoeuer keepe not a good conscience, doe lose also by little and little, the gift of vnderstanding: which he prooueth by two most lamentable examples.

* 1.Cor.5.5.

17 Such as fall from God, and his religion, are not to be suffered in the Church, but rather ought to be excommunicated. *n Cast out of the Church, and so delivered them to Satan.* *o That by their smart they might learne what it is to blaspheme.*

20 Of whom is Hymeneus, and Alexander,
*[17] whom I haue [n] deliuered vnto Satan, that
they might [o] learne not to blaspheme.

CHAP. II.

1 Hee exhorteth them to make publike prayers for all men, 4. 5 and that for two causes: 8 And therefore he willeth all men in all places to pray. 9 And declareth in what apparell 11 and with what modestie, women ought to behaue themselues in holy assemblies.

1 Hauing dispatched those things which pertaine to doctrine, he speaketh now in the second place of the other part of the ministerie of the word, to wit, of publike prayers. And first of all, declaring this question, for whome we ought to pray he teacheth that we must pray for all men, and especially for all maner of Magistrates, which thing was at that time somewhat doubted of, seeing that kings, yea, and the most part of magistrates were at that time enemies of the Church.

2 An argument taken of the end: to wit, because that Magistrates are appointed to this ende, that men might peaceably and quietly liue in all godlinesse and honestie, and therefore must we commend them especially to God, that they may faithfully execute so necessarie an office.

I [1] Exhort therefore, that first of all supplications, prayers, intercessions, *and* giuing of thankes be made for all men,

2 For Kings, and for all that are in authority, [2] that we may lead a quiet and a peaceable life, in all godlinesse and [a] honestie.

3 [3] For this is good and acceptable in the sight of God our Sauiour,

4 Who will that all men shalbe saued, and come vnto the acknowledging of the trueth.

5 [4] For there is one God, and one Mediatour betweene God and man, *which is* the [b] man Christ Iesus,

6 Who gaue himselfe a ransome for all men, [5] *to be* that testimonie in due time,

7 * Whereunto I am ordained a Preacher and an Apostle (I speake the trueth in Christ, and lie not) *euen* a teacher of the Gentiles in [c] faith and veritie.

8 [6] I will therefore that the men pray, euery where [d] lifting vp pure handes without [e] wrath, or [f] doubting.

9 *[7] Likewise also the women, that they aray themselues in comely apparell, with shamefastnesse and modestie, not with broided haire, or golde, or pearles, or costly apparell,

10 But (as becommeth women that professe the feare of God) with good workes.

11 Let the woman learne in silence with all subiection.

12 * I permit not a woman to teach, [8] neither to vsurpe authoritie ouer the man, but to be in silence.

a This word conteineth all kinde of duety, which is to be vsed amongst men in all their affaires. 3 Another argument, why Churches or Congregations ought to pray for all men, without any difference of nation, kinde, age, or order: to wit, because the Lord by calling of all sorts, yea sometime those that are greatest enemies to the Gospel, wil haue his Church gathered together after this sort, and therefore prayers to be made for all. 4 God should not else be manifested to be the onely God of all men, vnlesse he should shewe his goodnesse in sauing of all sorts of men: neither should Christ be seene to be the only Mediatour betweene God and all sorts of men, by hauing taken vpon him that nature of man which is common to all men, vnlesse hee had satisfied for all sortes of men, and made intercession for all. *b Christ Iesus which was made man.* 5 A confirmation, because that euen to the Gentiles is the secret of saluation now opened and made manifest, the Apostle himselfe being appointed properly to this office, which he doth faithfully and sincerely execute. * 2.Tim.1.11. *c Faithfully and sincerely: and by faith he meaneth wholesome and sound doctrine, and by trueth, an vpright and sincere handling of it.* 6 He hath spoken of the persons for whom we must pray: and now hee teacheth that the difference of places is taken away: for in times past, one only nation, and in one certaine place, came together to publike seruice: but now Churches or Congregations are gathered together euery where, (orderly and decently) and men come together to serue God publikely with common prayer, neither must wee striue for the nation, or for the purification of the body, or for the place, but for the minde to haue it cleane from all offence, and full of sure trust and confidence. *d Hee putteth the signe for the thing it selfe, the lifting vp of hands for the calling vpon God.* *e Without these griefes and offences of the minde, which hinder vs from calling vpon God with a good conscience.* *f Doubting, which is against faith, Iames 1.6.* * 1.Pet.3.3. 7 Thirdly, he appointeth women to learne in the publike assemblies with silence and modestie, being comely apparelled, without any riot or excesse in their apparell. * 1.Cor.14.34. 8 The first argument, why it is not lawfull for women to teach in the Congregation, because by this meanes, they should be placed aboue men, for they should be their masters: which is against Gods ordinance.

13 [9] For * Adam was first formed, then Eue.

14 * [10] And Adam was not [g] deceiued, but the woman was deceiued, and was in the transgression.

15 [11] Notwithstanding, through bearing of children shee shall be saued, if they continue in faith, and loue, and holinesse with modestie.

9 He prooueth this ordinance of God, whereby the woman is subiect to man, first by that that God made the woman after man, for mans sake.

* Gen.1.27. and 2.7,21.

* Genes.3.6.

10 Then, because that after sinne, God enioyned the woman this punishment, for that the man was deceiued by her. *g Adam was deceiued, but through his wiues means, and therefore she is worthily for this cause subiect to her husband, and ought to be.* 11 Hee addeth a comfort by the way, that their subiection hindereth not but that women may be saued as well as men, if they behaue themselues in those burdens of mariage holily and modestly, with faith and charitie.

CHAP. III.

2 Hee setteth out Bishops, 8 and Christian Deacons, with their wiues, 12 children and family: 15 he calleth the Church the house of God.

1 Hauing dispatched the treatise, as well of doctrine & of the manner of handling of it, as also of publike prayer, he now in the third place commeth to the persons themselues, speaking first of Pastors, and afterward of Deacons, and he vseth a Preface, that the Church may know that these be certaine and sure rules.

2 A bishoprick or the ministerie of the word is not an idle dignitie, but a worke, and that an excellent worke: and therefore a Bishop must be furnished with many vertues both at home and abroad. Wherefore it is requisite before he be chosen, to examine well his learning, his gifts, and ablenesse, and his life.

a Hee speaketh not here of ambitious seeking, then the which there cannot be a worse fault in the Church, but generally of the minde and disposition of man, framed and disposed to helpe and edifie the Church of God, when and wheresoeuer it shall please the Lord.

THis [1] *is* a true saying, [2] If any man [a] desire the office of a Bishop, hee desireth a worthie worke.

2 * A Bishop therfore must be vnreproueable, the husband of [b] one wife, watching, temperate, modest, harberous, apt to teach,

3 Not [c] giuen to wine, no striker, not giuen to filthie lucre, but gentle, no fighter, not couetous,

4 One that can rule his owne house honestly, hauing children vnder obedience with all honestie.

5 For if any cannot rule his owne house, how shall he care for the Church of God?

6 He may not be a yong schollar, lest hee being puffed vp fall into the [d] condemnation of the deuill.

7 Hee must also be well reported of, euen of them which are without, lest he fall into rebuke, and the snare of the deuill.

8 [3] Likewise *must* [e] Deacons *be* graue, not double tongued, not giuen vnto much wine, neither to filthie lucre,

9 * Hauing the [f] mysterie of the faith in pure conscience.

10 And let them first be prooued: then let them minister, if they be found blamelesse.

11 [4] Likewise their wiues *must be* honest, not euill speakers, *but* sober, *and* faithfull in all things.

12 [5] Let the Deacons be the husbands of one wife, and such as can rule their children well, and their owne housholds.

13 For they that haue ministred well, get themselues a good [g] degree, and [h] great libertie in the faith, which is in Christ Iesus.

* Titus 2.6. *b Therefore hee that shutteth out married men from the office of Bishops, onely because they are married, is Antichrist.* *c A common tipler and one that will sit by it.* *d Lest by reason that hee is aduanced to that degree, hee take occasion to be proud, which will vndoe him, and so hee fall into the same condemnation that the deuill himselfe is fallen into.* 3 Likewise the Deacons must first be prooued, that there may be a good triall of their honestie, trueth, sobrietie, minde voide of couetousnesse, that they are well instructed in the doctrine of faith, and to be short, of their good conscience and integritie. *e These are they that had to see to the poore.* * Chap.1.19. *f The doctrine of the Gospel, which is a mysterie in deede: for flesh and blood doe not reueile it.* 4 Regard must be had also, to the Pastours and Deacons wiues. 5 They that haue more wiues then one, at one time, must neither be called to be Ministers, nor to be Deacons. *g Honour and estimation.* *h Bold and assured confidence without feare.*

14 [6] These

6 Paul purposing to adde many peculiar things perteining to the daily office of a Pastour, speaketh first a worde or two concerning his comming to Timothie, that he should be so much the more carefull, lest at his comming he might be reproued of negligence.

14 [6] These things write I vnto thee, trusting to come very shortly vnto thee.
15 But if I tarie long, that thou mayest yet
know, how thou oughtest to behaue thy selfe
in the [7] house of God, which is the Church
of the liuing God, the [i] pillar and ground of
trueth.
16 [8] And without controuersie, great is the
mysterie of godlinesse, *which is*, God is manifested in the flesh, [k] iustified in the Spirit, seene
of Angels, preached vnto the Gentiles, beleeued on in the world, *and* receiued vp in glory.

7 The pastour hath alwayes to thinke, how that he is occupied in the house of the liuing God, wherin the treasure of the trueth is kept. *i To wit, in respect of men: for the Church rested vpon that corner stone, Christ, & is the preseruer of the trueth, but not the mother.* 8 There is nothing more excellent then this trueth, whereof the Church is the keeper and preseruer here among men, the ministerie of the worde being appointed to that ende and purpose: for it teacheth vs the greatest matters that may be thought, to wit, that God is become visible in the person of Christ by taking our nature vpon him, whose Maiestie notwithstanding in so great weakenesse was manifested many wayes, in so much that the sight of it pierced the very Angels, and to conclude, he being preached vnto the Gentiles was receiued of them, and is now placed aboue in glory vnspeakeable. *k The power of the Godhead shewed it selfe so marueilously in that weake flesh of Christ, that though he were a weake man, yet all the world knoweth he was and is God.*

CHAP. IIII.

1 He condemneth aswell false doctrines 3 of mariage and the choise of meats, 7 as also prophane fables: 8 And commendeth the godly exercise, 13 and the daily reading of the Scripture.

1 He setteth against that true doctrine, false opinions, which hee foretelleth that certaine which shall fall away from God and his religion, shall bring in by the suggestion of Satan, and so, that a great number shall giue eare to them.
a From the true doctrine of God.
2 Although heretikes counterfeit holinesse neuer so much, yet haue they no conscience.
b For they will as it were practise the art of disguised persons and players, that we may not thinke they will lie lurking in some one corner or keepe any resemblance of shamefastnesse.

NOw [1] the Spirit speaketh euidently, that
in the latter times some shall depart from
the [a] faith, and shall giue heed vnto spirits of
errour, and doctrines of deuils,
2 [2] Which speake lies through [b] hypocrisie, and haue their [c] consciences burned with an
hote yron,
3 [3] Forbidding to marry, *and commanding*
to absteine from meats [4] which God hath created [5] to be receiued [6] with giuing thankes of
them which beleeue and know the trueth.
4 [7] For euery creature of God *is* good, and
nothing *ought* to be refused, if it bee receiued
with thankesgiuing.
5 [8] For it is [d] sanctified by the [e] worde of
God, and prayer.
6 [9] If thou put the brethren in remembrance
of these things, thou shalt be a good minister of
Iesus Christ, which hast bene nourished vp in
the words of faith, & of good doctrine, which
thou hast continually [f] followed.

c Whose conscience waxed so hard, that there grewe an hard fleshinesse ouer it, and so became to haue a canker in it, and now at length required of very necessitie to be burned with an hote yron. 3 He setteth downe two kindes of this false doctrine, to wit, the Law of sole life, and difference of meats. 4 He prooueth that he iustly called such doctrines deuilish, first, because the teachers of them make lawes of things which are not their owne: for haue they created the meats? 5 Secondly, because they ouerthrow with their decrees, the end wherefore they were created of God, to wit, that we should vse them. 6 Thirdly for that by this meanes they robbe God of his glory, who will be honoured in the vse of them. And herewithall, the Apostle declareth that we must vse the liberalitie of God, soberly, and with a good conscience. 7 He setteth an Apostolicall rule, for taking away the difference of meates, against that false doctrine. 8 He vseth Gods benefits rightly, which acknowledgeth the giuer of them by his word, and calleth vpon him. *d It is so made pure and holy in respect of vs, so that we may vse it with a good conscience, as receiued at the Lords handes.* *e We confesse and acknowledge that God is the maker and giuer of those creatures which we vse. Secondly, that we are of the number of those, who through Christs benefit, haue recouered that right ouer all creatures, which Adam lost by his fall. Thirdly, by our prayers wee craue of the Lord, that we may vse those meates with a good conscience, which wee receiue at his handes. Fourthly, wee make an ende of our eating and drinking, with thankesgiuing and prayer: and so are our meates sanctified to vs.* 9 The Conclusion with an exhortation to Timothie, to propound these things diligently to the Churches, which hee had sucked from the Apostle euen in a manner from the teate. *f Neuer departing from the side of it.*

7 [10] But cast away prophane, & old wiues
fables, [11] and exercise thy selfe vnto [g] godlinesse.
8 [12] For bodily exercise profiteth litle: but
godlinesse is profitable vnto all things, which
hath the promise of the life present, and of that
that is to come.
9 [13] This *is* a true saying, and by all meanes
worthy to be receiued.
10 For therefore we labour and are rebuked, because we trust in the liuing God, which
is the Sauiour of all men, specially of those that
beleeue.
11 These things warne and teach.
12 [14] Let no man despise thy youth, but bee
vnto them that beleeue, an ensample, in word,
in conuersation, in loue, in spirit, in faith *and* in
purenesse.
13 [15] Till I come, giue attendance to reading, to exhortation, *and* to doctrine.
14 Despise not the gift that is in thee, which
was giuen thee by prophecie with the laying
on of the hands of the companie of the Elder-
ship.
15 These things exercise, *and* giue thy selfe
vnto them, that it may be seene how thou pro-
fitest among all men.
16 Take heede vnto thy selfe, and vnto
learning: continue therein: for in doing this
thou shalt both [h] saue thy selfe, and them that
heare thee.

10 He setteth againe true doctrine not onely against that false and apostaticall doctrine, but also against all vaine & curious subtilties
11 It is not onely requisite that the Minister of the word be found in doctrine, but also that his life be godly and religious.
g In the true seruing of God.
12 Godlinesse consisteth in spirituall exercise, and not in outward austerenesse of life, which though it be something to be accounted of, if it bee rightly vsed, yet it is in no wise comparable with godlines. For it profiteth not of it selfe, but through the benefit of another, but this hath the promise both of the life present, and of that that is to come.
13 He goeth a little from his matter, & sheweth that they which giue themselues to godlinesse, although they are afflicted and reproched, are notwithstanding not to be counted miserable as other men are, because they are not afflicted for that cause that other men are, and the end of them both is farre different one from the other. For how can God forsake his, which is bountifull euen towards his enemies? And he willeth that this doctrine be well beaten into their heads. 14 Now hee returneth to that exhortation, shewing which are the true vertues of a Pastor, whereby he may come to be reuerenced although he be but yong, to wit, such speech and life as are witnesses of charitie, zeale, faith, and puritie: but here is no mention made of the crosier staffe, ring, cloake, and such other foolish and childish toyes. 15 The priuate exercise of Pastours, is continuall reading of the Scriptures, whenceout they may drawe water of wholesome doctrine and exhortation, both to themselues and to other. *h Faith is by hearing, and hearing by preaching: and therefore the Ministers of the word are so said to saue themselues and other, for that in them the Lord hath put the worde of reconciliation.*

CHAP. V.

1 Hauing set downe a maner how to rebuke all degrees, 5 he intreateth of widowes, who then were chosen for the seruice of the Church: 17 Then hee commeth to Elders, 23 and speaketh somewhat touching the health of the body.

REbuke [1] not an Elder, but exhort him as
a Father, *and* the yonger men as brethren,
2 The elder women as Mothers, the yonger as sisters, with all purenesse.
3 [2] [a] Honour widowes, which are widowes in deed.
4 [3] But if any widow haue children or nephewes, let them learne first to shew godlines
[4] toward their owne house, and [5] to recompense
their kinred: [6] for that is an honest thing, and
acceptable before God.

1 Of keeping measure in priuate reprehensions according to the degrees of ages and kindes.
2 The Apostle giueth these rules touching the care of widowes.
a Haue care of those widowes which haue need of helpe.
3 Widowes children and nephewes must take care for their parents according to their habilitie. 4 The first reason, because that that which they bestowe vpon theirs, they bestowe it vpon themselues. 5 Another, because nature it selfe teacheth vs to recompense our parents. 6 The third: because this dutifulnesse pleaseth God.

5 [7] And ſhe that is a widow indeed and left
alone, truſteth in God, and continueth in ſup-
plications and praiers night and day.
6 [8] But ſhe that liueth in pleaſure, is dead,
while ſhe liueth.
7 Theſe things therefore warne *them* of,
that they may be blameleſſe.
8 If there bee any that prouideth not for
his owne, and namely for them of his houſe-
hold, he denieth the faith, and is worſe then an
infidell.
9 [9] Let not a widow be taken into the number vnder threeſcore yeere olde, that hath bene
the wife of [b] one husband,
10 And well reported of for good works:
if ſhe haue nouriſhed her children, if ſhe haue
lodged the ſtrangers, if ſhee haue [c] waſhed the
Saints feete, if ſhee haue miniſtred vnto them
which were in aduerſity, if ſhe were continually giuen vnto euery good worke.
11 [10] But [d] refuſe the yonger widowes: for
when they haue begun to wax wanton againſt
Chriſt, they will marry,
12 Hauing damnation, becauſe they haue
broken the firſt faith.
13 [11] And likewiſe alſo being idle, they
learne to goe about from houſe to houſe: yea
they are not onely idle, but alſo pratlers and
buſie bodies, ſpeaking things which are not
comely.
14 [12] I wil therfore that the yonger woman
marry, and beare children, and gouerne the
houſe, *and* giue none occaſion to the aduerſary
to ſpeake euill.
15 For certaine are already turned backe after Satan.
16 [13] If any faithful man, or faithful women
haue widowes, let them miniſter vnto them,
and let not the Church bee charged, that there
may be ſufficient for them that are widowes in
deede.
17 ¶ [14] The Elders that rule well, let them
be had in [e] double honor, [f] ſpecially they which
labour in the word and doctrine,
18 For the Scripture ſaith, * Thou ſhalt not
mouſel the mouth of the oxe that treadeth out
the corne: and, * The labourer is worthy of his
wages.
19 [15] Againſt an Elder receiue none accuſation, but vnder two or three witneſſes.
20 [16] Them that ſin, rebuke openly, that the
reſt alſo may feare.

7 The ſecond rule. Let the Church haue care of ſuch as are widowes in deed, that is to ſay, ſuch as are poore and deſtitute of helpe of their owne friends, and liue godly and religiouſly.
8 The third rule: Let widowes that liue in pleaſure, and neglect the care of their owne familie be holden and accounted as fallers away from God and his religion, and worſe then very Infidels.
9 The fourth rule: Let none vnder threeſcore yeere old, be taken into the number of widowes, to ſerue the Congregations or Churches, and ſuch as are free from all reproch of vnchaſtitie, and are well reported of, for their diligence, charitie, and integritie.
b That hath had no more huſbands, but one at one time.
c This is ſpoken in reſpect of the maner of thoſe countries.
10 The firſt reaſon why yonger widowes are not to be admitted to this miniſterie, to wit, becauſe for the lightnes of their age they will at length ſhake off the burden that Chriſt hath laid vpon them, and thinke rather vpon marying againe: and ſo will forſake the miniſterie wherunto they had bound themſelues.
d Take them not into the Colledge of widowes.
11 Another reaſon: becauſe they are for the moſt part pratlers and buſie bodies, and gadders vp and downe, neglecting their charge and duetie. 12 The fift rule: Let yonger widowes marrie and gouerne their houſes godly. 13 The ſixt rule: Let the faithfull helpe their widowes at their owne charges as much as they can, and let not the Congregation be burdened with theſe expenſes. 14 Now hee giueth rules, and ſheweth how he ought to behaue himſelfe with the Elders, that is to ſay, with the Paſtors, and ſuch as haue the gouernance in the diſcipline of the Church, which is preſident of their companie. The firſt rule: Let the Church or Congregation ſee vnto this eſpecially, as God himſelfe hath commanded, that the Elders that doe their duetie well, bee honeſtly maintained. *e We muſt bee more carefull for them, then for the reſt.* *f There were two kindes of Elders, the one attended vpon the gouernement onely, and looked to the maners of the Congregation, the other did beſide that, attend vpon preaching and prayers, to and for the Congregation.* * *Deuteronomie 25.4. 1.corinthians 9.9.* * *Matthew 10.10. luke 10.7.* 15 The ſecond rule. Let no accuſation be admitted againſt an Elder, but vnder two or three witneeſſes. 16 The third rule, Let the Elders ſo conuicted bee rebuked openly, that they may bee an example to other.

21 ¶ * [17] I charge *thee* before GOD and
the Lord Ieſus Chriſt, and the elect Angels,
that thou obſerue theſe things without preferring one to another, and doe nothing par-
tially.
22 [18] Lay hands [g] ſuddenly on no man, neither bee partaker of other mens ſinnes: keepe
thy ſelfe pure.
23 [19] Drinke no longer water, but vſe a little
wine for thy ſtomacks ſake, and thine often infirmities.
24 [20] Some mens ſinnes are open before
hand, and go before vnto iudgement: but ſome
mens follow after.
25 [21] Likewiſe alſo the good works are manifeſt before hand, and they that are otherwiſe
cannot be hid.

* *Chap.6.13.*
17 The fourth rule. Let ſinceritie be vſed without any preiudice or reſpect of perſons in Eccleſiaſticall proceedings (eſpecially againſt the Elders) becauſe God himſelfe is there preſent, and the Lord Ieſus Chriſt with a multitude of Angels.
18 The fift rule, Let the Miniſter lay hands ſuddenly on no man. Let him not be faultie herein, either by fauouring any mans folly, or peruerſe affection: If ought be done otherwiſe then well of his fellowes, let him keepe his conſcience pure. *g As much as in thee lieth, doe not raſhly admit any whatſoeuer to any Eccleſiaſticall function.* 19 The ſixt rule. Let the Elders haue indifferent conſideration of their health, in the maner of their diet. 20 Becauſe hypocrites ſometimes creepe into the miniſterie, although there be neuer ſo great diligence vſed, the Apoſtle willeth the Paſtours not to be troubled therefore, or ſlacke any whit in their diligence in trying and examining, becauſe the Lord hath appointed a time to diſcouer the faults of ſuch men, and it is our parts to take heede that wee offend not therein. 21 Another comfort belonging to them, which ſometimes are ſlandered and miſreported of.

CHAP. VI.

1 He ſheweth the duetie of ſeruants: 10 and what a miſchieuous euill couetouſneſſe is: 13 and hauing ſpoken ſomewhat of rich men, he once againe forbiddeth Timothie 20 to cumber himſelfe with vaine bablings.

Let [1] as many ſeruants as are vnder the
yoke, count their maſters worthy of all
honour, [2] that the Name of God, and *his* doctrine be not euill ſpoken of.
2 [3] And they which haue beleeuing maſters, let them not deſpiſe them, becauſe they
are brethren, but rather doe ſeruice, becauſe
they are faithfull, and beloued, and [a] partakers
of the benefit. [4] Theſe things teach and exhort.
3 [5] If any man teach otherwiſe, and con-
ſenteth not to the wholeſome wordes of our
Lord Ieſus Chriſt, and to the doctrine, which
is according to godlineſſe,
4 He is puft vp and knoweth nothing, but
doteth about queſtions and [b] ſtrife of wordes,
whereof commeth enuie, ſtrife, railings, euill
ſurmiſings,
5 Froward [c] diſputations of men of corrupt
mindes, & deſtitute of the trueth, which thinke
that gaine is godlineſſe: from ſuch ſeparate thy
ſelfe.

1 He addeth alſo rules for the ſeruants duetie towards their maſters: whereupon no doubt there were many queſtions then moued by them, which tooke occaſion by the Goſpel to trouble the common ſtate. And this is the firſt rule: Let ſeruants that are come to the faith and haue infidels to their maſters, ſerue them notwithſtanding with great fidelity.
2 The reaſon: leſt God ſhould ſeeme by the doctrine of the Goſpel to ſtirre vp men to rebellion and all wickedneſſe.
3 The ſecond rule: Let not ſeruants that are come to the faith, and haue alſo maſters of the ſame profeſſion and religion, abuſe the name of brotherhood, but let them ſo much the rather obey them. *a Let this bee ſufficient, that as touching thoſe things which perteine to euerlaſting life, they are partakers of the ſame good will and loue of God, as their maſters themſelues are.* 4 A generall concluſion, that theſe things ought not onely to be ſimply taught, but muſt with exhortations be diligently beaten into their heads. 5 He condemneth ſeuerely and excommunicateth or caſteth out of the Church as proud men, ſuch as content not themſelues with Chriſts doctrine, (that is to ſay, the doctrine of godlineſſe) but wearie both themſelues and others, in vaine queſtions, (for all other things are vaine) becauſe they content not themſelues in Chriſts doctrine: & as lying deceiuers, becauſe they ſauour or ſound of nothing but vanitie: as mad men, becauſe they trouble themſelues ſo much in matters of nothing: as miſchieuous plagues, for that they cauſe great contentions, and corrupt mens mindes and iudgement: to be ſhort, as prophane and wicked, becauſe they abuſe the precious name of godlineſſe and religion, to filthie lucre. *b Striuings about words, and not about matter: and by words hee meaneth all thoſe things which haue not pith in them, and whereby we can reape no profit.* *c Such as wee ſee in thoſe ſhameleſſe ſchooles of Poperie, which are nothing elſe but vaine babling and prating.*

6 ⁶ But godlinesse is great gaine, if a man
be content with that he hath.
7 ⁷ For we brought nothing into the world,
and it is certaine, that we can cary nothing out.
8 Therefore when we haue food and raiment, let vs therewith be content.
9 ⁸ For they that will be rich, fall into ten-
tation and snares, and into many foolish and
noisome lusts, which drowne men in perdition
and destruction.
10 For the desire of money is the roote of
all euill, which while some lusted after, they
erred from the faith, and [d] pearced themselues
through with many sorowes.
11 ⁹ But thou, O [e] man of God, flee these
things, and follow after righteousnesse, godlinesse, faith, loue, patience, *and* meekenesse.
12 Fight the good fight of faith: lay hold
of eternall life, whereunto thou art also called,
& hast professed a good profession before many witnesses.
13 *¹⁰ I charge thee in the sight of God,
who quickeneth all things, and before Iesus
Christ, which vnder Pontius Pilate * witnessed
a good confession,
14 That thou keepe *this* commandement
without spot, and vnrebukeable, vntill the appearing of our Lord Iesus Christ.
15 Which in due time he shall shewe, that
is [f] *blessed and Prince only, the King of kings,
and Lord of lords.
16 Who onely hath immortality, & dwelleth in the light that none can attaine vnto,
*whome neuer man sawe, neither can see, vnto
whom *be* honour & power euerlasting, Amen.
17 ¹¹ Charge them that are rich in [g] this
world, that they be not high minded, and that
they * trust not in vncertaine riches, but in the
[h] liuing God, (which giueth vs abundantly, all
things to enioy.)
18 That they doe good, *and* be rich in good
workes, *and* be ready to distribute, and communicate,
19 *¹² Laying vp in store for themselues a
good foundation against the time to come, that
they may obteine eternall life.
20 ¹³ O Timotheus, keepe that which is
committed vnto thee, and auoide prophane
and vaine bablings, and oppositions of science
falsly so called,
21 Which while some [i] professe, they haue
erred concerning the faith. Grace *be* with thee,
Amen.

¶ The first *Epistle* to Timotheus, written from Laodicea, which is the chiefest citie of Phrygia Pacaciana.

6 He turneth away fitly the name of gaine and lucre, confessing that godlinesse is great gaine, but farre after another sort, to wit, because it bringeth true sufficiencie.
7 He mocketh their folly, which doe so greedily gape after fraile things, that they can in no wise be satisfied, and yet notwithstanding they can not enioy that excesse.
8 He traieth Timothie from couetousnes after another sort, to wit, becaue it draweth with it an infinite sort of lusts & those very hurtfull, wherewith couetous men doe torment themselues so farre forth that in the end, they cast away from them their faith and saluation.
d Sorow & griefe doe as it were pearce through the mind of man, and are the haruest and true fruits of couetousnesse. 9 A peculiar exhortation to diuers vertues, wherewith it behoueth the Pastours especially to be furnished. *e Whom the Spirit of God ruleth.* * *Chap* 5.21. 10 A most earnest request and charge, to obserue and keepe all the premisses faithfully, with our eyes set vpon the comming of Iesus Christ, whose glory we haue to set against the vaine glistering of this world, and his power against all the terrours of the wicked. * *Matth.*27.11. *iohn* 18.37.

f He heapeth many words together to one purpose: wherby he voucheth the power of God, which if we sticke fast vnto, we shall not be moued out of our standings. *Chap. 1.11. *reue.* 17.14. & 19.16. * *Iohn* 1.18. 11 He addeth for an ouerplus as it were a sharpe admonition to the rich, that they chiefly take heed of two mischiefes, to wit, of pride, and deceitful hope, against which he setteth three excellent vertues, hope in the liuing God, liberalitie towards their neighbour, and gentle conditions. *g In things perteining to this life, with whom those men are compared which are rich in good works.* * *Mar.*4.19. *luke* 12.15. *h Who onely is, & that euerlasting: for he setteth the fraile nature of riches against God.* * *Mat.* 6.2. 12 The praise of liberalitie, by the effects thereof: because it is a sure testimonie of the Spirit of God which dwelleth in vs, and therefore of the saluation that shalbe giuen vs. 13 He rehearseth the chiefest of all the former exhortations, which ought to be deepely imprinted in the mindes of all Ministers of the word, to wit, that they eschew al vaine bablings of Sophistrie, and continue in the simplicitie of sincere doctrine. *i Not onely in word, but also in countenance and gesture: to be short, whiles their behauiour was such that euen when they held their peace, they would make men beleeue, their heads were occupied about nothing but high and weightie matters, euen then they erred concerning the faith.*

THE SECOND EPISTLE OF PAVL TO TIMOTHEVS.

CHAP. I.

5 He commendeth Timotheus faith, 6 and exhorteth him to goe on faithfully in the charge committed vnto him: 8 And that neither for the bonds, 15 nor the reuolting of others, he faint. 11 He triumpheth of his Apostleship. 14 He willeth him to haue care of the thing committed vnto him, 16 and praiseth Onesiphorus.

PAVL an Apostle of Iesus
Christ, by the will of God,
[a] according to the promise of
life which is in Christ Iesus,
2 To Timotheus *my* be-
loued sonne: Grace, mercie
and peace from God the Father, and *from* Iesus
Christ our Lord.
3 ¹ I thanke God, * whom I serue from
mine elders with pure conscience, that without
ceasing I haue remembrance of thee in my
prayers night and day,
4 Desiring to see thee, mindfull of thy
teares, that I may be filled with ioy:
5 When I call to remembrance the vnfained faith that is in thee, which dwelt first in thy
grandmother Lois, and in thy mother Eunice,
and am assured that *it dwelleth* in thee also.
6 ² Wherefore, I put thee in remembrance that thou [c] stirre vp the gift of GOD
which is in thee, by the putting on of mine
hands.
7 For God hath not giuen to vs the Spirit
of [d] feare, but of power, and of loue, and of a
sound mind.
8 ³ Be not therefore ashamed of the testimonie of our Lord, neither of mee [e] his prisoner: but bee partaker of the afflictions of the
[f] Gospel,

a Sent of God to preach that life, which he promised in Christ Iesus. 1 The chiefest marke that hee shooteth at in this Epistle, is to confirme Timothie to continue constantly and manfully euen to the end, setting first before him the great good will he beareth him, and then reckoning vp the excellent gifts which God would as it were haue to be by inheritance in Timothie, and his ancesters, which might so much the more make him bound to God. * *Acts* 22.3. *b From Abraham, Isaac and Iacob: for he speaketh not of Pharisaisme, but of Christianisme.*

2 He warneth vs to set the inuincible power of the Spirit, which God hath giuen vs, against those stormes which may, and doe come vpon vs. *c The gift of God is as it were a certaine liuely flame kindled in our hearts, which the flesh and the deuill goe about to put out: and therefore we on the contrary side must labour as much as we can to foster and keepe it burning.* *d To pearce vs throw, and terrifie vs, as men whom the Lord will destroy.* 3 He prooueth that the ignominie or shame of the crosse is not onely not to be ashamed of, but also that it is glorious and most honourable: first, because the Gospel wherefore the godly are afflicted, is the testimonie of Christ: and secondly because at length the great vertue and power of God appeareth in them. *e For his sake.*

f The Gospel after a sort is said to be afflicted in them that preach it.
g Through the power of God.
4 He sheweth with how great benefits God hath bound vs to maintaine boldly and constantly his glorie which is ioyned with our saluation, and reckoneth vp the causes of our saluation, to wit, that free and eternall purpose of God, to saue vs in Christ which was to come, whereby it should come to passe, that wee should at length be freely called of God by the preaching of the Gospel, to Christ the destroyer of death & author of immortalitie.
* *1 Cor. 1. 2.*
* *Tit. 3. 5.*
h He saith that that grace was giuen vs from euerlasting, vnto which we were predestinate from euerlasting. So that the doctrine of foreseen faith and foreseene works, is cleane contrary to the doctrine which preacheth & teacheth the grace of God.
i Before that course of yeeres,

f Gospel, according to the g power of God,
9 4 Who hath saued vs, and called vs with
an * holy calling, not according to our * works,
but according to his owne purpose and grace,
which was h giuen to vs through Christ Iesus
i before the * world was,
10 But is now made manifest by that appearing of our Sauiour Iesus Christ, who hath abolished death, and hath brought life and immortalitie vnto k light through the Gospel,
11 * 5 Whereunto I am appointed a preacher, and Apostle, & a teacher of the Gentiles,
12 6 For the which cause I also suffer these things, 7 but I am not ashamed: for I knowe whom I haue beleeued, and I am perswaded that he is able to keepe that which I haue committed to him against that day.
13 8 Keepe the true paterne of the wholesome words, which thou hast heard of mee in faith and loue which is in Christ Iesus.
14 9 That worthy thing, which was committed to thee, keep 10 through the holy Ghost, which dwelleth in vs.
15 11 This thou knowest, that all they which are in Asia, be turned from me: of which sort are Phygellus and Hermogenes.
16 The Lord giue mercie vnto the house of Onesiphorus: fore he oft refreshed me, and was not ashamed of my chaine,
17 But when he was at Rome, hee sought me out very diligently, and found *me*.
18 The Lord grant vnto him, that hee may finde mercie with the Lord at that day, and in how many things he hath ministred vnto me at Ephesus, thou knowest very well.

which hath run on euer since the beginning of the world. * *Rom. 16, 25. ephe. 1. 4. col. 1. 16 titus. 1. 2.* *k Hath caused life and immortalitie to appeare.* * *1. Tim. 2. 7.* 5 That is the Gospel which the Apostle preached. 6 He confirmeth his Apostleship by a strange argument, to wit, because the world could not abide it, and therefore it persecuted him that preached it. 7 By setting his owne example before vs, he sheweth vs how it may be, that we shall not be ashamed of the crosse of Christ, to wit, if we be sure that God both can and will keepe the saluation which hee hath as it were laid vp in store by himselfe for vs against that day. 8 Hee sheweth wherein hee ought to be most constant, to wit, both in the doctrine it selfe, the abridgment whereof is faith and charitie, and next in the maner of teaching it, a liuely paterne & shape whereof Timothie knew in the Apostle. 9 An amplification, taken of the dignitie of so great a benefit committed to the ministers. 10 The taking away of an obiection. It is an hard thing to doe it, but the Spirit of God is mightie, who hath inwardly indued vs with his vertue. 11 He preoenteth an offence which arose by the meanes of certaine that fell from God and the religion, and vttereth also their names that they might be knowen of all men But hee setteth against them the singular faith of one man, that one onely good example might counterpoise and weigh downe all euill examples.

CHAP. II.

2 The better to set our perseuerance in the Christian warfare, 3 he taketh similitudes 4 from souldiours, 6 and from husbandmen. 10 He sheweth that his bonds are for the profit of the Saints: 15 Then he warneth Timothie to diuide the word of the trueth aright, 17 to beware of the examples of the wicked, 22 & to doe all things modestly.

1 The conclusion of the former exhortation which hath also added vnto it a declaration, how that they do not keepe that worthy thing that is committed vnto them, which keepe it to themselues, but they rather which do most freely communicate it with other, to the end that many may bee partakers of it, without any mans losse or hinderance. *a When many were by, which can beare witnesse of these things.*

THou 1 therefore, my sonne, bee strong in the grace that is in Christ Iesus.
2 And what things thou hast heard of me, by a many witnesses, the same deliuer to faithful men, which shalbe able to teach other also.
3 2 Thou therefore suffer affliction as a good souldier of Iesus Christ.
4 No man that warreth, entangleth himselfe with the affaires of b *this* life, because hee would please him that hath chosen him to be a souldier.
5 3 And if any man also striue for a Masterie, he is not crowned, except he striue as hee ought to doe.
6 4 The husbandman must labour before he receiue the fruits.
7 5 Consider what I say: & the Lord giue thee vnderstanding in all things:
8 6 Remember that Iesus Christ, *made* of the seed of Dauid, was raised againe from the dead according to my Gospel,
9 7 Wherein I suffer troubles as an euil doer, euen vnto bonds: but the word of God is not bound.
10 Therefore I suffer all things, for the elects sake, that they might also obtaine the saluation which is in Christ Iesus, with eternall glorie.
11 8 *It is* a true saying, For if we be * c dead together *with him*, wee shall also liue together *with him*.
12 If we suffer, we shall also reigne together *with him*: * if we denie *him*, hee also will denie vs.
13 If * we beleeue not, *yet* abideth he faithfull: he cannot denie himselfe.
14 Of these things put them in remembrance, and d protest before the Lord, that they striue not about wordes, which is to no profit, *but* to the peruerting of the hearers.
15 9 Studie to shewe thy selfe approoued vnto God, a workeman that needeth not to be ashamed, diuiding the worde of trueth e aright.
16 f Stay prophane and vaine bablings:
10 for they shall encrease vnto more vngodlinesse.
17 And their word shall fret as a canker: of which sort is Hymeneus and Philetus,
18 Which as concerning the trueth haue erred from the marke, saying that the resur-

2 Another admonition: That the Ministerie of the word is a spirituall warfare, which no man can so trauaile in, that he may please his captaine, vnlesse he forgoe and part with all hinderances which might draw him away from it.
b With affaires of housholde, or other things that belong to other ordinarie businesses.
3 The third admonition: The ministerie is like to a game or iusting, wherein men striue for the victorie, and no man is crowned, vnlesse he striue according to the lawes which are prescribed, be they neuer so hard and painefull.
4 Another similitude tending to the same end, no man may looke for the haruest, vnlesse he first take paines to plow and sow his ground.
5 All these things cannot be vnderstood, and much lesse practised, vnlesse we aske of God and he giue vs vnderstanding.
6 He confirmeth plainely two principles of our faith, which are alwayes assaulted of heretiques, the one whereof (to wit, that Christ is the true Messias, made man of the seed of Dauid) is the ground of our saluation: and the other is the highest part of it, to wit, that hee is risen againe from the dead. 7 The taking away of an obiection: Trueth it is, that hee is kept in prison as an euill doer, yet there is no cause, why therefore some should goe about to derogate credit from his Gospel, seeing that notwithstanding God did blesse his ministerie, nay rather, that example of this his captiuitie and patience, did sundry wayes confirme his Church in the hope of a better life. 8 The fourth admonition: we ought not to contend vpon wordes and questions, which are not onely vnprofitable, but also for the most part hurtfull: but rather vpon this, howe wee may frame our selues to all maner of patience, and to die also with Christ (that is to say, for Christes Name) because that is the plaine way to the most glorious life: as contrariwise the falling away of men can diminish no part of the trueth of God, although by such meanes they procure most certaine destruction to themselues. * *Romanes 6. 5.* *c If we be afflicted with Christ, and for Christ his sake.* * *Matthewe 10. 33. marke 8. 38.* * *Romanes 3. 3. and 9. 6.* *d Call God to witnesse, or as a Iudge: as Moses, Iosbua, Samuel, and Paul himselfe did, actes 20* 9 The fifth admonition: A Minister must not bee an idle disputer, but a faithfull steward in diuiding aright the worde of trueth, in so much that he must stop the mouthes of other vaine bablers. *e By adding nothing to it, neither ouerslipping any thing, neither mangling it, nor renting it in sunder, nor wresting of it: but marking diligently what his hearers are able to beare, and what is fit to edifying.* *f Marke and watch, and see they creepe not on further.* 10 He discouereth the subtiltie of Satan, who beginning with these principles, draweth vs by little and little to vngodlinesse through the meanes of that wicked and prophane babling, still creeping on: which he proueth by the horrible example of them that taught, that the resurrection was already past.

rection is past already, and doe destroy the
faith of certaine.
19 [11] But the foundation of God remaineth
sure, and hath this seale, The Lord knoweth
who are his: and, Let euery one that [g] calleth
on the Name of Christ, depart from iniquitie.
20 [12] Notwithstanding in a great house are
not onely vessels of gold and of siluer, but also
of wood and of earth, * and some for honour,
and some vnto dishonour.
21 If any man therefore [h] purge himselfe
from these, he shall bee a vessell vnto honour,
sanctified, and meet for the Lord, and prepared
vnto euery good worke.
22 [13] Flee from the lusts of youth, and follow after righteousnes, faith, loue, *and* [14] peace,
with them that * call on the Lord with pure
heart,
23 * And put away foolish and vnlearned
questions, knowing that they ingender strife.
24 But the seruaunt of the Lord must not
striue, but *must* be gentle toward all men, apt
to teach, [i] suffering the euill,
25 Instructing them with meekenesse that
are [k] contrary minded, *prouing* if God at any
time will giue them repentance, that they may
acknowledge the trueth,
26 And come to amendment out of that
snare of the deuill, of whom they are taken prisoners, to *doe* his will.

11 A digression, wherein he salueth that offence that rose by their falling away: shewing first, that the elect are out of all danger of any such falling away: secondly, that they are knowen to God, and not to vs: and therefore it is no marueile if we count hypocrites oftentimes for true brethren: but we must take heed that we be not like them, but rather that we be indeede, such as we are said to be.
g That serueth & worshippeth him, and as it were named of him, as faithfull man or Christian.
12 The taking away of an obiection: it is no dishonour to the good man of the house, that he hath not in a great house all vessels of one sort and for one seruice, but we must looke to this, that we be found vessels prepared to honour. * *Romanes 9. 21.* *h By these words is meant the execution of the matter, and not the cause: for in that we purge our selues, it is not to be attributed to any free will that is in vs, but to God, who freely and wholly worketh in vs, a good and an effectuall will.* 13 Returning to the matter from whence hee digressed verse 16. he warneth him to exercise himselfe in weightie matters, and such as pertaine to godlinesse. 14 The sixt admonition, We must aboue all things eschew all bitternesse of minde, both in teaching all men & also in calling them backe which haue gone out of the way. * 1.*Cor.*1.2. * 1.*Tim.*1.4.*and* 4.7. *titus* 3 9. *i To winne them through our patient bearing with them, but not to please them or excuse them in their wickednesse.* *k He meaneth such as doe not yet see the trueth.*

CHAP. III.

1 He foretelleth the dangerous times that are to ensue, 9 but with the certaine hope of victorie, 10 hee encourageth him to the combate, setting out especially the triall of sound doctrine.

This [1] know also, that in the * last dayes
shall come perilous times.
2 For men shall bee louers of their owne
selues, couetous, boasters, proude, cursed speakers, disobedient to parents, vnthankeful, [a] vnholy,
3 Without naturall affection, truce breakers, false accusers, intemperate, fierce, no louers at all of them which are good,
4 Traitours, heady, high minded, louers
of pleasures more then louers of God,
5 Hauing a shew of godlinesse, but haue
denied the power thereof: [2] turne away therefore from such.
6 For of this sort are they which creepe
into houses, and leade captiue simple women
laden with sinnes, and led with diuers lustes.
7 *Which women are* euer learning, and are
neuer able to come to the acknowledging of
the trueth.
8 * And as Iannes and Iambres withstood
Moses, so doe these also resist the trueth, men
of corrupt mindes, reprobate concerning the
faith.
9 [3] But they shall preuaile no longer: for
their madnesse shall be euident vnto all men, as
theirs also was.
10 ¶ [4] But thou hast [b] fully knowen my
doctrine, maner of liuing, purpose, faith, long
suffering, loue, patience,
11 Persecutions, *and* afflictions which
came vnto me at [c] Antiochia, at Iconium, and
at Lystri, which persecutions I suffered: but
from them all the Lord deliuered me,
12 Yea, and all that will liue godly in Christ
Iesus, shall suffer persecution.
13 But the euill men and deceiuers shall
waxe [d] worse and worse, deceiuing, and being
deceiued.
14 But continue thou in the things which
thou hast learned, and which are committed
vnto thee, knowing of whom thou hast learned
them:
15 And that thou hast knowen the holy
Scriptures of a child, which are able to make
thee wise vnto saluation, through the faith
which is in Christ Iesus.
16 * [5] For the whole Scripture *is* giuen by
inspiration of God, and *is* profitable to teach,
to conuince, to correct, *and* to instruct in righteousnesse,
17 That the [e] man of God may be absolute,
being made perfect vnto all good works.

1 The seuenth admonition: we may not hope for a Church in this world without corruption: but there shall be rather great abundance of most wicked men euē in the very bosom of ẏ church, which notwithstanding shall make a shew & countenance of great holinesse, and charitie.
* 1.*Tim* 4.1. 2.*pet.*3 3.*iud.*18
a Which make no account, either of right or honesty.
2 We must not dally with such men as resist the trueth not of simple ignorance, but of a peruerse minde, (which thing appeareth by their fruits which he painteth out here liuely) but we must rather turne away frō them.
* *Exod.*7.11.
3 He addeth a comfort: The Lord will at length plucke off all their vizards.
4 That we be not deceiued by such hypocrites, we must set before vs the vertues of the holy seruants of God, and we must not be afraid of persecution which they suffred willingly, & which alwayes followeth true godlinesse. But we must especially hold fast the doctrine of the Apostles, the summe whereof is this, that we are saued throgh faith in Christ Iesus.
b Thou knowest throughly not onely what I taught and did, but also how I was minded and disposed.
c Which is in Pisidia.
d Their wickednesse shall dayly increase.
* 2.*Pet.*1.20.
5 The eight admonition which is most precious: A Pastour must bee wise by the worde of God onely: wherein we haue perfectly deliuered vnto vs, whatsoeuer perteineth either to discerne, knowe and establish true opinions, and to confute false: and furthermore, to correct euill maners, and to frame good. *e The Prophets and expounders of Gods will, are properly and peculiarly called, Men of God.*

CHAP. IIII.

1 He chargeth him to preach the Gospel with all diligence, 3 in that so miserable a time: 6 That his death is hard at hand, 8 yet so, that as conquerour, he maketh haste to a glorious triumph. 10 He sheweth the cause why he sendeth for Timothie, 11 euen by reason of his present state.

I [1] Charge *thee* therefore before God, and *before* the Lord Iesus Christ, which shal iudge
the quicke and dead at that his appearing, and
in his kingdome,
2 Preach the word: bee instant, in season
and out of season: improue, rebuke, exhort
with all long suffering, and doctrine.
3 [2] For the time will come, when they will
not suffer wholesome doctrine: but hauing
their eares itching, shall after their owne lustes,
get them an heape of teachers,
4 And shal turne their eares from the trueth,
and shalbe giuen vnto [a] fables.
5 [3] But watch thou in all things: suffer aduersitie: do the worke of an Euangelist: [b] cause
thy ministerie to be throughly liked of.

1 The principall and chiefe of all admonitions, being therefore propofed with a most earnest charge, is this: that the word of God be propoūded with a certaine holy importunitie, as necessitie requireth: but so, that a good and true ground of the doctrine be laied, and the vehemencie betempered with all holy meeknes.
2 Faithfull pastours in times past tooke all occasions they could, because men were very prompt & ready to returne to their fables. *a To false and vnprofitable doctrines which the world is now so bewitched withall, that it had rather the open light of the trueth were vtterly put out, then it would come out of darkenesse.* 3 The wickednesse and falling away of the world ought to cause faithfull ministers to be so much ẏ more careful. *b Proue & shew by good & substantiall proofe, that thou art the true minister of God*

6 [4] For

6 [4] For I am now ready to be [c] offered,and
the time of my departing is at hand.
7 I haue fought a good fight, and haue fi-
nifhed my courfe : I haue kept the faith.
8 *For* hencefoorth is laid vp for me the
crowne of righteoufneffe, which the Lord the
righteous iudge fhall giue me at that day : and
not to mee onely, but vnto all them alfo that
loue that his appearing.
9 [5] Make fpeed to come vnto me at once :
10 For Demas hath forfaken me, and hath
[d] embraced this prefent world, and is departed
vnto Theffalonica, Crefcens *is gone* to Galatia,
Titus vnto Dalmatia.
11 *Onely Luke is with me. Take Marke
and bring him with thee : for hee is profitable
vnto me to minifter.
12 And Tychicus haue I fent to Ephefus.
13 The cloke that I left at Troas with Car-
pus, when thou commeft, bring with thee, and
the books, but fpecially the parchments.
14 Alexander the copperfmith hath done
me much euill : the Lord reward him according to his works.
15 Of whom be thou ware alfo : for hee
withftood our preaching fore.

4 He foretelleth his death to be at hand,and fetteth before them an excellent example,both of inuincible conftancie,and fure hope.
c To be offered for a drinke offering : and he alludeth to the powring out of blood or wine which was vfed in facrifices.
5 The laft part of the epiftle,fetting forth grieuous complaints againft certaine, and examples of fingular godlineffe in euery place, and of a mind neuer wearied.
d Contented himfelfe with this world.
**Col.4.10,14.*

16 At my firft anfwering no man affifted
me,but all forfooke me : *I pray God*,that it may
not be laid to their charge.
17 Notwithftanding the Lord affifted me,
and ftrengthened me,that by me the preaching
might be fully beleeued, and that all the Gentiles fhould heare : and I was deliuered out of
the mouth of the [e] lion.
18 And the Lord will deliuer me from euery [f] euill worke, and will preferue me vnto his
[g] heauenly kingdome : to whome *be* praife for
euer and euer, Amen.
19 Salute Prifca and Aquila, & the * houf-
hold of Onefiphorus.
20 Eraftus abode at Corinthus: Trophimus
I left at Miletum ficke.
21 Make fpeed to come before winter, Eu-
bulus greeteth thee, and Pudens, and Linus,
and Claudia,and all the brethren.
22 The Lord Iefus Chrift *be* with thy fpirit : Grace *be* with you, Amen.

¶ The fecond *Epiftle* written from Rome vnto Timotheus, the firft Bifhop elected of the Church of Ephefus,when Paul was prefented the fecond time before the Emperour Nero.

e Of Nero.
f Preferue me pure from committing any thing vnworthy my Apoftlefhip.
g To make mee partaker of his kingdome.
**Chap.1.16.*

THE EPISTLE OF PAVL TO TITVS.

CHAP. I.

6 He fheweth what kind of men ought to be chofen minifters. 10 how vaine bablers mouthes fhould be ftopped : 12 And through this occafion he toucheth the nature of the Cretians, 14 & the Iewes who put holines in outward things.

PAul [1] a [a] feruant of God, and
an Apoftle of Iefus Chrift,ac-
cording to the faith of Gods
[b] elect, [2] and the acknowledging of the trueth, which is
according vnto godlineffe,
2 Vnto the [c] hope of eternall life, which
God that cannot lie, hath [d] promifed before
the * [e] world began :
3 [3] But hath made his word manifeft in due
time through the preaching, which is * committed vnto me, according to the commandement of God our [f] Sauiour :
4 [4] To Titus *my* naturall fonne according
to the common faith, [5] Grace,mercy,*and* peace
from God the Father, and *from* the Lord Iefus
Chrift our Sauiour.
5 [6] For this caufe left I thee in Creta, that
thou fhouldeft continue to redreffe the things

1 He voucheth his Apoftlefhip, (not for Titus, but for ẏ Cretenfes fake) both by the teftimonie of his outward calling,and by his confent wherein he agreeth with all the elect from the beginning of the world.
a A Minifter,as Chrift himfelfe in that that he was a Minifter & head of the Prophets, is called a feruant, Efai.43.10.
b Of thofe whom God hath chofen.
2 The faith wherein all the elect confent,is the true and fincere knowledge of God,tending to this ende,that worfhipping God aright, they may at length obtaine life euerlafting according to the promife of God,who is true,which promife was exhibited in Chrift in due time according to his eternall purpofe. *c Hope is the end of faith.* *d Freely and of his meere liberalitie.* * *Rom.16.25.eph.3.9.col.1.26.2.tim.1.7.1.pet.1.20.* *e Looke 2.Tim.1.9.* 3 This trueth is no other where to be fought,but in the preaching of the Apoftles. * *Galat.1.1.* *f This word (Sauiour) doth not onely fignifie a preferuer of life,but alfo a giuer of life.* 4 The Apoftle mooueth the Cretenfes to heare Titus, by fetting foorth his confent and agreement with them in the faith,and therewithall fheweth by what fpecial note we may diftinguifh true minifters from falfe. 5 There is but one way of faluation, common both to the Paftor and the flocke. 6 The firft admonition to ordeine Elders in euery Church.

that remaine, and fhouldeft ordeine Elders in
euery citie, as I appointed thee,
6 * If any be vnreprooueable, the husband
of one wife,hauing faithfull children,which are
not flandered of riot, neither are [g] difobedient.
7 [7] For a Bifhop muft be vnreproueable,as
Gods [h] fteward, not [i] froward, not angry, nor
giuen to wine, no ftriker, not giuen to filthy
lucre,
8 But harberous, one that loueth good-
neffe, [k] wife, righteous,holy,temperate,
9 [8] Holding faft that faithfull word according to doctrine, [9] that he alfo may be able to
exhort with wholefome doctrine, & conuince
them that fay againft it.
10 [10] For there are many difobedient and
vaine talkers and deceiuers of mindes, chiefly
they of the [l] Circumcifion,
11 Whofe mouthes muft be ftopped,which
fubuert whole houfes, teaching things, which
they ought not, for filthy lucres fake.
12 [m] One of themfelues, *euen* one of their
owne prophets faid, The Cretians *are* alwayes
liars,euill beafts,flow bellies,

**1.Tim.3.2.*
g This word is proper to horfes and oxen,which will not abide the yoke.
7 The fecond admonition : what faults Paftours (whome he comprehended afore vnder the worde Elders) ought to be void of, and what vertues they ought to haue.
h Whome the Lord hath appointed fteward of his gifts.
i Not hard conditioned and euill to pleafe.
k Circumfpect, & of a found iudgement,and of a fingular example of moderation.
8 The third admonition : The Paftour muft hold faft that doctrine,which the Apoftles deliuered,and perteineth to faluation, leauing all curious and vaine matters. 9 The fourth admonition : To apply the knowledge of true doctrine vnto vfe, which confifteth in two things, to wit,in gouerning them which fhew themfelues apt to learne, and confuting the obftinate. 10 An applying of the generall propofition to a particular : The Cretenfes aboue all other need fharpe reprehenfions : both becaufe their mindes are naturally giuen to lies and flouthfulneffe, and becaufe of certaine couetous Iewes, which vnder a colour of godlineffe,ioyned partly certaine vaine traditions, and partly olde ceremonies with the Gofpel. *l Of the Iewes, or rather of thofe Iewes which went about to ioyne Chrift and the Law.* *m Epimenides,who was counted a Prophet amongft them,Looke vpon Laertius,and Cicero in his firft booke of diuination.*

13 This witnesse is true: wherefore conuince them [n] sharply, that they may be found
in the faith,
14 And not taking heed to * Iewish fables
and commandements of men, that turne away
from the trueth.
15 [11] Vnto the pure * *are* all things pure,
but vnto them that are defiled, and vnbeleeuing *is* nothing pure, but euen their [o] mindes
and consciences are defiled.
16 They professe that they know God, but
by workes they denie *him*, and are abominable
and disobedient, and vnto euery good worke
reprobate.

n Roughly and plainely and goe not about the bush with them.
* *1.Tim 1.4.*
11 He sheweth in few words, that puritie consisteth not in any externall worship, and that, that is according to the old Law (as indifference of meates, and washings, and other such things which are abolished) but in the minde and conscience: and whosoeuer teach otherwise, know not what is true religion in deed, and also are nothing lesse then that they would seeme to be. * *Rom. 14.20.* *o If our minds and consciences be vncleane, what cleannesse is there in vs before regeneration?*

CHAP. II.

2 He setteth out the dueties of sundry persons and states, 6 and willeth him to instruct the Church in maners. 11 He draweth an argument from the ende of our redemption, 12 which is, that we liue godly and vprightly.

BVt [1] speake thou the things which become
wholesome doctrine,
2 [2] That the elder men be watchful, graue,
temperate, sound in the faith, in loue, *and* in
patience.
3 The elder women likewise, that they be
in such behauiour as becommeth holinesse, not
false accusers, not subiect to much wine, *but*
teachers of honest things,
4 That they may instruct the yong women
to bee sober minded, that they loue their husbands, that they loue their children,
5 *That they be* temperate, chaste, [a] keeping
at home, good & * subiect vnto their husbands,
that the word of God be not euill spoken of.
6 Exhort yong men likewise, that they be
sober minded.
7 [3] In all things shew thy selfe an example
of good workes with vncorrupt doctrine, with
[b] grauitie, integritie,
8 *And* with the wholesome word, which
cannot be condemned, that he which withstan-
deth, may bee ashamed, hauing nothing concerning you to speake euill of.
9 * [4] Let seruants bee subiect to their masters, and please *them* in all [c] things, not answering againe,
10 Neither pickers, but that they shew all
good faithfulnesse, that they may adorne the
doctrine of God our Sauiour in all things.
11 * [5] For that grace of God, that bringeth
saluation vnto all men, hath appeared,
12 And teacheth vs that wee should denie
vngodlinesse and [d] worldly lustes, and that we
should liue soberly and righteously, and godly
in this present world,
13 [e] Looking for that blessed hope, and appearing of that glory of that mightie God, and
of our Sauiour Iesus Christ,
14 Who gaue himselfe for vs, that he might
redeeme vs from all iniquitie, and purge vs, *to be*
a [f] peculiar people vnto himselfe, zealous of
good workes.
15 These things speake, and exhort, and
conuince with all [g] authoritie. See that no man
despise thee.

1 The fift admonition: The doctrine must not onely be generally pure, but also be applied to all ages and orders of men, according to the diuersitie of circumstances.
2 What are the chiefest vertues for old and yong both men and women: and how they ought to be stirred vp vnto them continually.
a No gadders vp and downe.
* *Ephes. 5.23.*
3 The sixt admonition: That both the Pastours life and doctrine must be found.
b Not such a grauitie as may driue men from comming to the minister, but such as may cause them to come in most reuerent and honest sort.
* *Ephes. 6.5. colos. 3.22. 1.pet. 2 18.*
4 The seuenth admonition, of seruants duetie toward their masters.
c Which may be done without offence to God.
* *1.Cor. 1.2. colos. 1.22.*
5 The eight admonition belonging to all the godly, that seeing God calleth all men to the Gospel, and Christ hath so iustified vs, that he hath also sanctified vs, wee must all of vs giue our selues to true godlinesse, and righteousnesse, setting before vs a sure hope of that immeasurable glory: which thing must in such sort bee beaten into their heads, that the gainesayers also must bee reprooued, by the authoritie of the mightie God.
d Lustes of the flesh, which belong to the present state of this life and world. *e Christ is here most plainely called that mightie God, and his appearance and comming is called by the figure Metonymie, our hope.*
f As it were a thing peculiarly laide vp for himselfe.
g With all authoritie possible.

CHAP. III.

1 He willeth that all generally bee put in minde to reuerence such as be in authoritie: 3 That they remember their former life, and attribute all iustification vnto grace. 9 And if any brabler withstand these things, 10 he willeth that he be reiected.

PVt [1] them in remembrance that they * bee
subiect to the Principalities and powers,
and that they bee obedient, *and* ready to euery
good worke,
2 That they speake euill of no man, that
they be no fighters, *but* soft, shewing all meek-
nesse vnto all men.
3 [2] * For wee our selues also were in times
past vnwise, disobedient, deceiued, seruing the
lusts and diuers pleasures, liuing in maliciousnesse & enuie, hatefull, *and* hating one another.
4 But when that bountifulnesse and that
loue of God our Sauior toward man appeared,
5 *Not by the workes of [a] righteousnesse,
which we had done, but according to his mercie hee saued vs, by the washing of the newe
birth, and the renewing of the [b] holy Ghost.
6 Which hee shedde on vs aboundantly
through Iesus Christ our Sauiour,
7 That wee, being iustified by his grace,
should bee made heires according to the hope
of eternall life.
8 [3] This *is* a true saying, and these things I
will thou shouldest affirme, that they which
haue beleeued God, might be carefull to shew
foorth [c] good workes. These things *are* good
and profitable vnto men.
9 * But stay foolish questions, and genealogies, and contentions, and brawlings about
the Law: for they are vnprofitable and vaine.
10 [4] Reiect him that is an hereticke, after
once or twise admonition,
11 Knowing that he that is such, is peruerted,
and sinneth, being damned of his owne selfe.
12 [5] When I shal send Artemas vnto thee, or
Tychicus, bee diligent to come to me vnto Nicopolis: for I haue determined there to winter.
13 Bring Zenas the expounder of the Law,
and Apollos on their iourney diligently, that
they lacke nothing.
14 And let ours also learne to shew foorth
good workes for necessarie vses, that they bee
not vnfruitfull.
15 All that are with me, salute thee. Greete
them that loue vs in the faith. Grace *be* with
you all, Amen.

¶ To Titus, elect the first Bishop of the Church of the Cretians, written from Nicopolis in Macedonia.

1 He declareth particularly and seuerally that which he said before generally, noting out certaine chiefe and principall dueties, which men owe to men, and especially subiects to their magistrates.
* *Rom. 13.1. 1.pet. 2.13.*
2 He confirmeth againe the former exhortation by propounding the free benefit of our regeneration, the pledge whereof is our baptisme.
* *1.Cor. 6.11.*
* *2.Tim. 1.9.*
a Word for word, of workes which are done in righteousnesse: and this place doth fully refute the doctrine of merites.
b Which the vertue of the holy Ghost worketh.
3 Againe with great earnestnes he beateth into our heads, how that we ought to giue our selues to true godlines and eschew all vaine questions, which serue to nothing but to mooue strife and debate.
c Giue themselues earnestly vnto good workes.
* *1.Tim. 1.4. and 4.7. 2.tim. 2.23.*
4 The ministers of the word, must at once cast off heretikes, that is, such as stubburnely and seditiously disquiet the Church and will giue no eare to Ecclesiasticall admonitions.
5 Last of all, hee writeth a word or two of priuate matters, and commendeth certaine men.

THE EPISTLE OF PAVL TO PHILEMON.

1 Paul handling a base and small matter, yet according to his maner mounteth aloft vnto God. 8 Sending againe to Philemon his vagabound and theeuish seruant, he entreateth pardon for him, and very grauely preacheth of Christian equitie.

PAul a prisoner of Iesus Christ,
and *our* brother Timotheus,
vnto Philemon our deare
friend, and fellow helper,
2 And to *our* deare *sister*
Apphia, and to Archippus
our fellow souldier, and to the Church that is
in thine house:
3 Grace *be* with you, and peace from God
our Father, and *from* the Lord Iesus Christ.
4 I *giue thankes to my God, making
mention alwayes of thee in my prayers,
5 (When I heare of thy loue and faith,
which thou hast toward the Lord Iesus, and toward all Saints.)
6 That the [a] fellowship of thy faith may
bee made effectuall, and that whatsoeuer good
thing is in you through Christ Iesus, may bee
[b] knowen.
7 For wee haue great ioy and consolation
in thy loue, because by thee, brother, the Saints
[c] bowels are comforted.
8 Wherfore, though I be very bold in Christ
to command thee, that which is conuenient,
9 [1] *Yet* for loues sake I rather beseech thee,
though I be as I am, euen Paul aged, and euen
now a prisoner for Iesus Christ.
10 I beseech thee for my sonne *Onesimus,
whom I haue begotten in my bonds,
11 Which in times past was to thee vnprofitable, but now profitable both to thee & to me.
12 Whom I haue sent againe: thou therefore receiue him, that is mine owne [d] bowels.
13 Whom I would haue reteined with me,
that in thy stead hee might haue ministred vnto
me in the bonds of the Gospel.
14 But without thy mind would I doe nothing, that thy benefit should not be as it were
of [e] necessitie, but willingly.
15 It may be that he therfore [f] departed for [g] a
season, that thou shouldst receiue him for euer,
16 Not now as a seruant, but aboue a seruant, *euen as* a brother beloued, especially to
me: how much more then vnto thee, both in
the [h] flesh and in the Lord?
17 If therefore thou count our things common, receiue him as my selfe.
18 If he hath hurt thee, or oweth thee ought,
that put on mine accounts.
19 I Paul haue written *this* with mine owne
hand: I will recompense it, albeit I doe not say
to thee, that thou owest moreouer vnto mee euen thine owne selfe.
20 [i] Yea, brother, let me obteine this pleasure of thee in the Lord: comfort my bowels in
the Lord.
21 Trusting in thine obedience, I wrote vnto thee, knowing that thou wilt doe euen more
them I say.
22 Moreouer also prepare me lodging: for
I trust through your prayers I shall bee freely
giuen vnto you.
23 There salute thee Epaphras my fellow
prisoner in Christ Iesus,
24 Marcus, Aristarchus, Demas, *and* Luke
my fellow helpers.
25 The grace of our Lord Iesus Christ, *bee*
with your spirit, Amen.

¶ Written from Rome to Philemon, *and sent* by Onesimus a seruant.

*1.Thes.1.2. 2.thes.1.3.
a *By fellowship of faith, he meaneth those dueties of charitie which are bestowed vpon the Saints, and flowe forth of an effectuall faith.*
b *That by this meanes al men may perceiue how rich you are in Christ, to wit, in faith, charitie, and all bountifulnesse.*
c *Because thou diddest so dutifully and cheerefully refresh the Saints, that they conceiued inwardly a marueilous ioy: for by this word (Bowels) is meant not onely the inward feeling of wants and miseries that men haue one of anothers state, but also that ioy and comfort which entreth into the very bowels, as though the heart were refreshed and comforted.*
1 An example of a Christian exercise & commendation for an other man.
*Colos 4.9.
d *As mine owne sonne, and as if I had begotten him of mine owne body.*
e *That thou mightest not seeme to haue lent mee thy seruant vpon constraint, but willingly.*
f *Thus he asswageth the harder kind of speach, which is to say, he ranne away.*
g *For a litle time.*
h *Because he is thy seruant, as other seruants are, and because he is the Lords seruant, so that thou must needes loue him both for the Lords sake, and for thine owne sake.*
i *Good brother let me obteine this benefit at thine hand.*

THE EPISTLE TO THE HEBREWES.

THe drift and end of this Epistle, is to shew that Iesus Christ the Sonne of God both God and man is that true eternal & only Prophet, King and high Priest, that was shadowed by the figures of the old law, and is now in deed exhibited: of whom the whole Church ought to be taught, gouerned, & sanctified.

CHAP. I.

1 To shewe that the doctrine which Christ brought, is most excellent, in that it is the knitting vp of all prophecies, 4 hee aduanceth him aboue the Angels: 10 And prooueth by diuers testimonies of the Scripture, that hee farre passeth all other.

AT [1] sundrie times and in diuers maners God spake in the
olde time to *our* fathers by
the Prophets: in these [a] last
dayes hee hath spoken vnto vs
by his [b] Sonne,
2 [2] Whome hee hath made [c] heire of all
things, by whom also he made the [d] worlds,
3 *Who being the [e] brightnes of the glory,
and the ingraued forme of his [f] person, & [g] bearing vp all things by his mighty word, [3] hath by
himselfe purged our sinnes, and [h] sitteth at the
right hand of the maiestie in the highest places,

1 The first part of the generall proposition of this Epistle: the sonne of God is in deed that Prophet or teacher, which hath actually now performed that that God after a sort & in shadowes signified by his Prophets, and hath fully opened his Fathers wil to ŷ world. *a* *So that the former declaration made by the Prophets was not ful, & nothing must be added to this later.* *b* *Which one Son is God & man.*

2 The second part of the same proposition: The same Sonne is appointed of the Father to be our King and Lord, by whom also he made all things: and in whome onely he setteth forth his glory, yea, and himselfe also to be beholden of vs, who beareth vp and susteineth all things by his wil and pleasure. *c* *Possessour and equall compartner of all things with the Father.* *d* *That is, whatsoeuer hath beene at any time, is, or shall be* *Col.1.15. *e* *Hee in whom that glory and Maiestie of the Father shineth, who is otherwise infinite, and cannot be beholden.* *f* *His Fathers person.* *g* *Susteineth, defendeth, and cherisheth.* 3 The third part of the same proposition: The same Sonne executed the office of the hie Priest in offering vp himselfe, and is our onely and most mightie Mediatour in heauen. *h* *This sheweth that the sauour of that his sacrifice is not onely most acceptable to the Father, but also is euerlasting, and furthermore how farre this high Priest passeth all the other high Priests.*

4 [4] And

4 [4] And is made fo much more excellent
then the Angels, in as much as hee hath obteined a more excellent [i] Name then they.
5 [5] For vnto which of the Angels faid hee
at any time, * Thou art my Sonne, [k] this day
begate I thee? [6] and againe, I * will bee his Father, and he fhalbe my Sonne?
6 [7] And [l] againe, when hee bringeth in *his*
firft begotten Sonne into the world, hee faith,
* And let all the Angels of God worfhip him.
7 [8] And of the Angels he faith, * Hee maketh the fpirits his [m] meffengers, and his minifters a [n] flame of fire.
8 But vnto the Sonne *hee faith*, * O God,
thy [o] throne *is* for euer [p] and euer: the fcepter of thy kingdome *is* a [q] fcepter of righteoufneffe.
9 Thou haft loued righteoufneffe and [r] hated iniquitie. Wherefore God, *euen* thy God,
hath [f] anointed thee with the oyle of gladneffe
aboue thy [t] fellowes.
10 [9] And, * Thou Lord, in the beginning
haft [u] eftablifhed the earth, and the heauens are
the workes of thine hands.
11 They fhall perifh, but thou doeft remaine: and they all fhall waxe olde as doeth a
garment.
12 And as a vefture fhalt thou fold them vp,
and they fhall bee changed: but thou art the
fame, and thy yeeres fhall not faile.
13 [10] Vnto which alfo of the Angels faid
he at any time, * Sit at my right hand, till I
make thine enemies thy footftoole?
14 Are they not all [x] miniftring fpirits, fent
foorth to minifter, for their fakes which fhalbe
heires of faluation?

4 Before hee commeth to declare the office of Chrift, he fetteth forth the excellencie of his perfon, and firft of all he fheweth him fo to bee man, that therewithall hee is God alfo
i *Dignitie and honour.*
5.6.7.8.9.10. He prooueth and confirmeth the dignitie of Chrift manifeft in the flefh, by thefe fixe euident teftimonies. wherby it appeareth that he farre paffeth all Angels, infomuch that he is called both Sonne, and God, in verfes 5 6.7. 8.10 13.
* *Pfal.* 2.7. *chap* 5.5.
k *The Father begate the Sonne from euerlafting, but that euerlafting generation was made manifeft and reprefented to the world in his time, and therefore he added this word (To day)*
* 2.*Sam.* 7.14. 1.*chro.* 22.10.
l *The Lord was not content to haue fpoken it once, but he repeateth it in another place.*
* *Pfal.* 97.7.
* *Pfal.* 104.4.
m *Cherub, pfal.* 18.11.
n *Seraph, Efa.* 6.2
* *Pfal.* 45.7. *o* *The throne is proper to Princes and not to feruants.* *p* *For euerlafting, for this doubling of the word increafeth the fignification of it beyond all meafure.* *q* *The gouernement of thy kingdome is righteous.* *r* *This kind of rehearfing which the Iewes vfe by contraries, hath great force in it.* *f* *In that, that the word became flefh, by powring the holy Ghoft vpon him without meafure.* *t* *For he is the head and we are his members.*
* *Pfal.* 102.25. *u* *Madeft the earth firme and fure.* * *Pfal.* 110.1. 1 *cor.* 15.25. *chap.* 10.12,13. *x* *By that name by which wee commonly call Princes meffengers, hee here calleth the fpirits.*

CHAP. II.

1 *Therefore he inferreth that good heede muft bee giuen to Chrifts doctrine:* 9 *And he fetteth him out vnto vs euen as our brother in our flefh, that wee may with a good will yeeld vp our felues wholly vnto him.*

Wherefore [1] wee ought diligently to
giue heede to the things which [a] wee
haue heard, left at any time we [b] runne out.
2 For if the [c] word fpoken by Angels was
ftedfaft, and euery tranfgreffion and difobedience receiued a iuft recompenfe of reward,
3 How fhall we efcape, if wee neglect fo
great faluation, [2] which at the firft beganne to
bee preached by the Lord, and *afterward* was
confirmed vnto vs by [d] them that heard him,
4 * God bearing witneffe thereto, both
with [e] fignes and wonders and with diuers miracles, and gifts of the holy Ghoft, according
to his owne will?
5 [3] For he hath not put in fubiection vnto
the Angels y[e] [f] world to come, wherof we fpeak.
6 [4] But * one in a certaine place witneffed,
faying, [g] What is man, that thou fhouldeft bee
mindfull of him? or the [h] fonne of man, that
thou wouldeft confider him?
7 Thou [i] madeft him a little inferiour to
the Angels: thou crownedft him with [k] glory
and honour, and haft fet him aboue the workes
of thine hands.
8 * Thou haft put all things in fubiection
vnder his feete. And in that hee hath put all
things in fubiection vnder him, he left nothing
that fhould not be fubiect vnto him. [5] But wee
yet fee not all things fubdued vnto him,
9 [6] But we [l] fee Iefus crowned with glory
and honour, * which was made little [m] inferiour to the Angels, [7] through the [n] fuffering of
death, that by Gods grace hee might [o] tafte
death for [8] all men.
10 [9] For it became [p] him, for whom *are* all
thefe things, and by whom *are* all thefe things,
[10] feeing that hee brought many children vnto
glory, [11] that he fhould confecrate the [q] prince
of their faluation through afflictions.
11 [12] For hee that [r] fanctifieth, and they
which are fanctified *are* all of [f] one: wherefore
he is not afhamed to call them brethren,
12 [13] Saying, * I will declare thy Name vnto my brethren: in the mids of the Church will
I fing praifes to thee.

1 Now as it were paufing with himfelfe, and fhewing to what ende and purpofe all thefe things were fpoken, to wit, to vnderftand by the excellencie of Chrift aboue all creatures, that his doctrine, maieftie, and Priefthood, is moft perfect, he vfeth an exhortation taken from a comparifon. *a* *Hee maketh himfelfe an hearer.* *b* *They are faid to let the word runne out, which hold it not faft when they haue heard it.* *c* *The Law which appointed punifhment for the offenders: and which Paul faith was giuen by Angels, Gala.* 3. 19. *and Steuen, Actes* 7.53. 2 If the breach and tranfgrefsion of the word fpoken by Angels was not fuffered vnpunifhed, much leffe fhall it bee lawfull for vs to neglect the Gofpel which the Lord of Angels preached, and was confirmed by the voice of the Apoftles, and with fo many fignes and wonders from heauen, and efpecially with fo great and mightie working of the holy Ghoft. *d* *By the Apoftles.*
* *Marke* 16.20.

e *This is the true ende of miracles. Now they are called fignes, becaufe they appeare one thing, and reprefent another: and they are called wonders, becaufe they reprefent fome ftrange and vnaccuftomed thing: and vertues becaufe they giue vs a glimce of Gods mightie power.*
3 If it were an hainous matter to contemne the Angels which are but feruants, much more hainous is it to contemne that moft mightie King of the reftored world.
f *The world to come, whereof Chrift is Father, Efa.* 9.6. *or the Church, which as a new world, was to be gathered together by the Gofpel.*
4 He fheweth that the vfe of this kingly dignitie confifteth herein, that men might not onely in Chrift recouer that dignitie which they haue loft, but alfo might be throgh him aduanced aboue all things, which dignitie of men Dauid defcribeth moft excellently. * *Pfal.* 8.6. *g* *What is there in man that thou fhouldeft haue fo great regard of him, and doe him that honour?* *h* *Hee calleth all the citizens of that heauenly kingdome as they are confidered in themfelues, before that God giueth them the libertie of that citie in Chrift, Man, and Sonne of man.* *i* *This is the firft honour of the citizens of the world to come, that they are next the Angels.* *k* *For they fhalbe in very great honour when they fhalbe partakers of the kingdom. And he fpeaketh of the thing that fhalbe, as though it were already, becaufe it is fo certaine.* * 1.*Cor.* 15.27 5 An obiection: But where is this fo great rule and dominion? 6 The anfwere: This is already fulfilled in Iefus Chrift our head, who was for a time for our fakes inferiour to the Angels, being made man: but now is aduanced into moft high glorie. *l* *By his vertue and power which appeareth manifeftly in the Church.* * *Phil.* 2.8. *m* *Who abafed himfelfe for a feafon, and tooke vpon him the fhape of a feruant* 7 He fheweth the caufe of this fubiection, to wit, to tafte of death for our fakes, that fo doing the part of a redeemer, he might not onely be our Prophet and King, but alfo our high Prieft. *n* *That he might die.* *o* *Feele death.* 8 Heerein confifteth the force of the argument: for we could not at length be glorified with him, vnleffe he had beene abafed for vs euen all the faithfull. And by this occafion the Apoftle commeth to the other part of the declaration of Chrifts perfon, wherein he prooueth him to be in fuch fort God, that he is alfo man 9 Hee prooueth moreouer by other arguments, why it behoued the Sonne of God who is true God (as hee prooued a little before) to become man notwithftanding, fubiect to all miferies, finne onely except. *p* *God* 10 Firft of all becaufe the Father, to whofe glory all thefe things are to bee referred, purpofed to bring many fonnes vnto glory. And how could he haue men for his fonnes, vnleffe his onely begotten fonne had become brother to men? 11 Secondly, The Father determined to bring thofe fonnes to glory, to wit, out of that ignominie wherein they lay before. Therefore the fonne fhould not haue beene feene plainely to be made man, vnleffe he had beene made like vnto other men, that hee might come to glory by the felfe fame way, by the which he fhould bring other: yea rather, it became him which was Prince of the faluation of other, to be confecrated aboue other, through thofe afflictions, Prophet, King, and Prieft, which are the parts of that principalitie for the faluation of other. *q* *The Chieftaine who as he is chiefeft in dignitie, fo is he firft begotten from among the dead, amongft many brethren* 12 The ground of both the former arguments, for neither fhould we be fonnes through him, neither could he bee confecrate through afflictions, vnleffe hee had beene made man like vnto vs. But becaufe this Sonnehood dependeth not vpon nature onely, for no man is accounted the fonne of God, vnleffe that befides that hee is a fonne of a man, he be alfo Chriftes brother, (which is by fanctification, that is, by becomming one with Chrift, who fanctifieth vs through faith) therefore the Apoftle maketh mention of the fanctifier, to wit, of Chrift, and of them that are fanctified, to wit, of all the faithfull, whome therefore Chrift vouchfafeth to call brethren *r* *He vfeth the time that now is to fhew vs that we are yet ftill going on, and increafing in this fanctification: and by fanctification he meaneth our feparation from the reft of the world, our cleanfing from finne, and our dedication wholly vnto God, all which Chrift alone worketh in vs.* *f* *One, of one felfe fame nature of man.* 13 That which hee taught before of the incarnation of the fanctifier, hee applieth to the propheticall office. * *Pfal* 22.25.

14 He applieth the same to the kingly power of Christ, in deliuering his from the power of the deuill and death.
*Psal.18.2.
t *I will commit my selfe to him, and to his defence.*
*Esa.8.18.
u *This Esai speaketh of himselfe & his disciples but betokening therby all ministers, as also his disciples signifie the whole Church. And therefore seeing Christ is the head of the Prophets & Ministers, these words are more rightly verified of him, then of Esai.*
x *Are made of flesh and blood, which is a fraile and brittle nature.*
*Hose.13.14. 1.cor.15.55.

13 [14] And againe, *I will put my [t] trust in
him. And againe, * [u] Behold, here am I, and
the children which God hath giuen me.
14 Forasmuch then as the children are [x] partakers of flesh and blood, he also himselfe likewise tooke part with them, that hee might destroy *through death, him that had the [y] power
of death, that is, the [z] deuill,
15 And that hee might deliuer all them,
which for feare of [a] death were all their lifetime
subiect to bondage.
16 [15] For hee in no sort tooke on *him* the
[b] Angels *nature*, but he tooke on *him* the [c] seede
of Abraham.
17 [16] Wherefore in [d] all things it behooued
him to be made like vnto his brethren, that hee
might be [e] mercifull, and a [f] faithfull hie Priest in
things concerning God, that hee might make
reconciliation for the sinnes of the people.
18 For in that hee suffered, and was [g] tempted, he is able to succour them that are tempted.

y *The deuill is said to haue the power of death, because he is thee authour of sinne: and from sinne commeth death, and for this cause he eggeth vs daily to sinne.* z *He speaketh of one as of the Prince, ioyning to him secretly all his angels.* a *By (death) thou must vnderstand here, that death which is ioyned with the wrath of God, as it must needes bee, if it be without Christ, then the which there can be nothing deuised more miserable.* 15 He expoundeth those words of flesh and blood, shewing that Christ is true man, and that not by turning his diuine nature, but by taking of mans nature. And he nameth Abraham, respecting the promises made to Abraham in this behalfe. b *The nature of Angels.* c *The very nature of man.* 16 He applieth the same to the Priesthood, for which he should not haue beene fit, vnlesse hee had become man, and that like vnto vs in all things, sinne onely except. d *Not onely as touching nature, but qualities also.* e *That he might be truely touched with the feeling of our miseries.* f *Doing his office sincerely.* g *Was tried and egged to wickednesse by the deuill.*

CHAP. III.

1 *Now hee sheweth how farre inferiour Moses is to Christ,* 5.6 *euen so much as the seruant to the Master: and so he bringeth in certaine exhortations and threatnings taken out of Dauid,* 8 *against such as either stubburnely resist,* 12 *or else are very slow to obey.*

1 Hauing laide the foundation, that is to say, declared and proued both the natures of one selfe same Christ, he giueth him three offices, to wit, the office of a Prophet, King, and Priest, and as touching the office of teaching, and gouerning, compareth him with Moses and Iosuua, vnto the 14. verse of the next Chapter, and with Aaron touching the Priesthood. And he propoundeth that which hee purposeth to speake of, with a most graue exhortation, that all our faith may tend to Christ, as to the onely euerlasting teacher, gouernour, and high Priest.

THerefore, [1] holy brethren, partakers of the
heauenly vocation, consider the [a] Apostle
and high Priest of our [b] profession Christ Iesus:
2 [2] Who was faithfull in him that hath [c] appointed him, [3] euen as *Moses *was* in al his house.
3 [4] For this man is counted worthy of
more glory then Moses, insomuch as he which
hath builded the house, hath more honour
then the house.
4 For euery house is builded of some man,
and he that hath built all things, *is* God.
5 [5] Now Moses verily was faithfull in all
his house, as a seruant, for a witnesse of the
things which should be spoken after.
6 But Christ *is* as the Sonne, ouer his
owne house, [6] whose [d] house we are, if we hold
fast that [e] confidence and that reioycing of that
hope vnto the end.
7 Wherefore, as the holy Ghost saith, *To
day if yee [f] will heare his voice,
8 Harden not your hearts, as in the [g] prouocation, according to the day of the tentation
in the wildernesse,
9 Where your fathers tempted me, prooued
me, and saw my workes fortie yeeres long.
10 Wherefore I was grieued with that generation, and said, They [h] erre euer in *their*
heart, neither haue they knowen my wayes.
11 Therefore I sware in my wrath, If they
shall enter into my rest.
12 [7] Take heed, brethren, least at any time
there be in any of you an euil heart, and vnfaithfull, to depart away from the liuing God.
13 But exhort one another daily, [i] while it
is called to day, lest any of you bee hardened
through the deceitfulnesse of sinne.
14 [8] For we are made partakers of Christ, if
we keepe sure vnto the ende that [k] beginning,
wherewith we are vpholden,
15 [l] So long as it is said, To day if yee heare
his voice, harden not your hearts, as in the
prouocation.
16 For some when they heard, prouoked
him to anger: howbeit, not all that came out of
Egypt by Moses.
17 But with whom was he displeased fortie
yeeres? Was he not displeased with them that
sinned, * whose carkeises fell in the wildernesse?
18 And to whom sware he that they should
not enter into his rest, but vnto them that o-
beyed not?
19 So wee see that they could not enter in,
because of vnbeliefe.

a *The Embassadour or messenger, as Rom. 5. he is called the minister of Circumcision.* b *Of the doctrine of the Gospel which we professe.* 2 He confirmeth his exhortation with two reasons, first of all because Christ Iesus was appointed such an one of God: secondly, because he throughly executed the offices that his Father enioyned him. c *Apostle and high Priest.* 3 Now he commeth to the comparison with Moses, and he maketh them like one of ye other in this, that they were both appointed rulers ouer Gods house, and executed faithfully their office: but by and by after he sheweth that there is great vnlikelinesse in that same similitude. *Num.12.7. 4 The first comparison: The builder of the house is better then ye house it selfe, therfore is Christ better then Moses. The reason of the consequent is this: because ye builder of this house is God, which cannot be attributed to Moses: and therefore Moses was not properly the builder, but a part of the house: but Christ as Lord & God, made all this house. 5 Another comparison: Moses was a faithful seruant in this house, that is, in the Church, seruing the Lord that was to come, but Christ ruleth and gouerneth his house as Lord. 6 Hee applieth the former doctrine to his ende, exhorting all men by the words of Dauid to heare the Sonne himselfe speake, and to giue full credite to his words, seeing that otherwise they cannot enter into that eternall rest. d *To wit, Christs.*

e *He calleth that excellent effect of faith (whereby we crie Abba, that is, Father) confidence, and to confidence he ioyneth hope.*
*Psal.95.8. chap.4.7.
f *So that God was to speake once againe after Moses*
g *In the day that they vexed the Lord, or stroue with him.*
h *They are brutish and mad.*
7 Now weighin the words of Dauid, he sheweth first by this word, *To day*, that we must not neglect the occasion while we haue it: for that word is not to be restrained to Dauids time, but it comprehendeth all that time wherein God calleth vs.
i *While to day lasteth, that is to say, so long as the Gospel is offered to vs.*
8 Now he considereth these words, *If you heare his voice, &c* shewing that they are spoken and meant of the hearing of faith, against which he setteth hardning throgh vnbeliefe.
k *That beginning of trust and confidence: and after the maner of the Hebrewes, he calleth that, beginning, which is chiefest.*
l *So long as this voice soundeth out.*
*Numb.14.37.

CHAP. IIII.

1 *He ioyneth exhortation with threatning, lest they, euen as their fathers were, bee depriued of the rest offered vnto them,* 11 *but that they endeuour to enter into it.* 14 *And so he beginneth to intreate of Christs Priesthood.*

LEt vs feare therefore, least at any time by
forsaking the promise of entring into his
rest, any of you should seeme to be depriued.
2 [1] For vnto vs was the Gospel preached as
also vnto them: but the word that they heard,
profited not them, because it was not [a] mixed
with faith in those that heard it.
3 [2] For we which haue beleeued, doe enter
into rest as hee said *to the other*, * As I haue
sworne in my wrath, If they shall enter into

1 By these words, *His voice*, he sheweth that Dauid ment the preaching of Christ, who was then also preached, for Moses and the Prophets respected none other.

a *Hee compareth the preaching of the Gospel to drinke, which being drunke, that is to say, heard, profiteth nothing, vnlesse it be tempered with faith.* 2 Lest any man should obiect, that those words were meant of the land of Canaan, and of Moses doctrine, and therefore cannot well bee drawen to Christ, and to eternall life, the Apostle sheweth that there are two maner of rests spoken of in the Scriptures: the one of the seuenth day, wherein God is said to haue rested from all his workes: an other said to be that same, whereinto Ioshua led the people: but this rest is not the last rest whereunto we are called: and that he prooueth by two reasons. For seeing that Dauid so long time after, speaking to the people which were then placed in ye land of Canaan, vseth these words, *To day*, and threatneth them still that they shall not enter into the rest of God, which refused then the voice of God that sounded in their eares, we must needes say that hee meant another time then the time of Moses, and another rest then the rest of the land of Canaan: And that is, that euerlasting rest, wherein we begin to liue to God, after that the race of this life ceaseth: as God rested the seuenth day from those his workes, that is to say from making the world. Moreouer the Apostle therewithall signifieth that the way to this rest, which Moses and the land of Canaan, and all that order of the Law did shadow, is opened in the Gospel onely. *Psal.95.11.

my

my rest: although the workes were finished from the foundation of the world.

4 For he spake in a certaine place of the seuenth day on this wise, *And God did rest the seuenth day from all his workes.

5 And in this place againe, If they shall enter into my rest.

6 Seeing therefore it remaineth that some must enter there into, and they to whome it was first preached, entred not therein for vnbeliefes sake:

7 Againe hee appointed in Dauid a certaine day, by To day, after so long a time, saying, as it is said, *This day, if yee heare his voice, hearden not your hearts.

8 For if [b] Iesus had giuen them rest, then would hee not after this haue spoken of another day.

9 There remaineth therefore a rest to the people of God.

10 [c] For he that is entred into his rest, hath also ceased from his owne workes, as God *did* from his.

11 [3] Let vs study therefore to enter into that rest, lest [d] any man fall after the same ensample of disobedience.

12 [4] For the [e] word of God *is* [f] liuely, and mightie in operation, and sharper then any two edged sword, and entreth through, euen vnto the diuiding asunder of the [g] soule and the [h] spirit, and of the ioynts, and the marow, and is a discerner of the thoughts, and the intents of the heart.

13 Neither is there any creature, which is not manifest in [i] his sight: but all things *are* naked and open vnto his eyes, with whome wee haue to doe.

14 [5] Seeing then that wee haue a great hie Priest, which is entred into heauen, *euen* Iesus the Sonne of God, let vs [k] hold fast our profession.

15 [6] For wee haue not an hie Priest, which cannot bee touched with the feeling of our infirmities, but was in all things tempted in like sort, *yet* without sinne.

16 Let vs therefore goe boldly vnto the throne of grace, that wee may receiue mercie, and find grace to helpe in time of neede.

Gene. 2. 2. deut. 5. 14. *Chap. 3. 7.*
b He speaketh of Iosua the sonne of Nun: and as the land of Canaan was a figure of our true rest, so was Iosua a figure of Christ.
c As God rested the seuenth day, so must we rest from our workes, that is, from such as proceede from our corrupt nature.
3 He returneth to an exhortation.
d Lest any man become a like example of infidelitie.
4 An amplification taken from the nature of the word of God, the power whereof is such, that it entreth euen to the deepest and most inward and secret parts of the heart, wounding them deadly that are stubburne, and plainely quickning the beleeuers.
e The doctrine of God which is preached both in the Law and in the Gospel.
f He calleth the word of God liuely, by reason of the effectes it worketh in them to whom it is preached.
g He calleth that the soule, which hath the affections resident in it.
h By the spirit, he meaneth that noblest part which is called the mind.
i In Gods sight.
5 Now he entreth into the comparison of Christs Priesthood with Aarons, and declareth euen in the very beginning the marueilous excellencie of this Priesthood, calling him the Sonne of God, and placing him in the seate of God in heauen, plainely and euidently setting him against Aarons Priests, and the transitorie tabernacle: which comparisons hee setteth foorth afterward more at large. *k And let it not goe out of our hands.* 6 Lest hee might seeme by this great glory of our hie Priest, to stay and stop vs from going vnto him, he addeth straightwayes after, that he is notwithstanding our brother in deede, (as he prooued it also before) and that he accompteth all our miseries his owne, to call vs boldly to him.

CHAP. V.

1 First hee sheweth the duetie of the hie Priest: 5 Secondly, that Christ is appointed of God to bee our hie Priest, 7 and that hee hath fulfilled all things belonging thereunto.

For [1] euery hie Priest is taken from among men, and is ordeined for men, in things pertaining to God, [2] that hee may offer both [a] gifts and [b] sacrifices for sinnes.

2 Which is [c] able sufficiently to haue compassion [d] on them that are ignorant, and that are out of the way, because that he also is [e] compassed with infirmitie,

3 And for the sames sake hee is bound to offer for sinnes, as well for his owne part, as for the peoples.

4 *[3] And no man taketh this honour vnto himselfe, but hee that is called of God, as *was* Aaron.

5 So likewise Christ tooke not to himselfe this honour, to be made the hie Priest, but hee that said vnto him, *Thou art my Sonne, this day begate I thee, *gaue it him.*

6 As hee also in another place speaketh, *Thou art a Priest for euer, after the [f] order of Melchi-sedec.

7 [4] Who in the [g] dayes of his flesh did offer vp prayers and supplications, with strong crying and teares vnto him, that was able to [h] saue him from death, and was also heard in that which he feared.

8 And though hee were the Sonne, yet [i] learned he obedience, by the things which he suffered.

9 [5] And being [k] consecrate, was made the authour of eternall saluation vnto all them that obey him:

10 And is called of God an hie Priest after the order of Melchi-sedec.

11 [6] Of whom we haue many things to say, which are hard to bee vttered, because yee are dull of hearing.

12 [7] For when as concerning the time yee ought to bee teachers, yet haue yee neede againe that we teach you what *are* the first principles of the word of God: and are become such as haue neede of milke, and not of strong meate.

13 For euery one that vseth milke, is inexpert in the [l] word of righteousnesse: for hee is a babe.

14 But strong meate belongeth to them that are of age, which through long custome haue their [m] wittes exercised, to discerne both good and euill.

1 The first part of the first comparison of Christes hie Priesthood, with Aarons: Other hie Priestes are taken from among men, and are called after the order of men.
2 The first part of the second comparison: Others as weake, are made hie Priests, to the end that feeling the same infirmitie in themselues which is in all the rest of the people, they should in their owne and the peoples name offer gifts and sacrifices, which are witnesses of common faith and repentance.
a Offering of things without life.
b Beasts which were killed, but especially in the sacrifices for sinnes and offences.
c Fit and meete.
d On them that are sinfull: for in the Hebrew tongue, vnder ignorance and errour is euery sinne meant, euen that sinne that is voluntarie.
e For that hee himselfe beareth about with him a nature subiect to the same discommodities and vices.
* *1. Chron. 13. 10. and 23. 13.*
3 The third comparison which is whole. The others are called of God, and so was Christ, but in an other order then Aaron: For Christ is called the Sonne, begotten of God, and a Priest for euer after the order of Melchi-sedec.
* *Psal. 2. 7. chap. 1. 5.*
* *Psal. 110. 4. chap. 7. 17.*
f After the likenesse or maner as it is afterward declared.
* *Chap. 7. 15.*
4 The other part of the second comparison: Christ being exceedingly afflicted and exceedingly mercifull asked not for his sinnes, for hee had none, but for his feare, and obteined his request, and offered himselfe for all his. *g While he liued here with vs, in our weake and fraile nature.* *h To deliuer him from death.* *i He learned in deede what it is to haue a Father, whom a man must obey.* 5 The other part of the first comparison. But Christ was consecrate of God the Father as the Authour of our saluation, and an hie Priest for euer, and therefore he is so a man, that notwithstanding he is farre aboue all men. *k Looke Chap. 2. 10.* 6 A digression vntill he come to the beginning of the seuenth Chapter: wherein he partly holdeth the Hebrewes in the diligent consideration of those things which he hath said, and partly prepareth them to the vnderstanding of those things whereof he will speake. 7 An example of an Apostolike chiding. *l In the word which teacheth righteousnes.* *m All their power wherby they vnderstand & iudge.*

CHAP. VI.

1 Hee briefly toucheth the childish slothfulnes of the Hebrewes, 4 and terrifieth them with seuere threatnings: 7 He stirreth them vp to endeuour in time to goe forward: 9 He hopeth well of them: 13 Hee alledgeth Abrahams example: 17 and compareth faith that taketh hold on the word, 19 to an ancre.

THerefore leauing the doctrine of the [a]be-
ginnings of Christ, let vs be led forward
vnto perfection, [1] not laying againe the foundation of repentance from dead workes, and of
faith toward God,
2 Of the doctrine of Baptismes, and laying on of hands, and of the resurrection from
the dead, and of eternall iudgement.
3 And this will we doe if God permit.
4 [2] *For it is [b] impossible that they which
were once lightened, and haue [c] tasted of the
heauenly gift, and were made partakers of the
holy Ghost,
5 And haue tasted of the good word of
God, and of the powers of the world to come,
6 If they fall away, should be renewed a-
gaine by repentance: seeing they [d] crucifie a-
gaine to themselues the Sonne of God, and
make a mocke of him.
7 [3] For the earth which drinketh in the
raine that commeth oft vpon it, and bringeth
foorth herbes meete for them by whome it is
dressed, receiueth blessing of God,
8 But that which beareth thornes and bri-
ers, *is* reprooued: and is neere vnto cursing,
whose end *is* to be burned.
9 [4] But beloued, wee haue perswaded our
selues better things of you, and such as accompanie saluation, though we thus speake.
10 [5] For God *is* not vnrighteous, that hee
should forget your worke, and labour of loue,
which ye shewed toward his Name, in that yee
haue ministred vnto the Saints, & *yet* minister.
11 And wee desire that euery one of you
shew the same diligence, to the full assurance of
hope vnto the end,
12 [6] That ye be not slouthfull, but followers of them, which through faith and patience,
inherite the promises.
13 [7] For when God made the promise to
Abraham, because he had no greater to sweare
by, he sware by himselfe,
14 Saying, * Surely I will [e] abundantly
blesse thee, and multiply thee marueilously.
15 And so after that he had taried patiently,
he enioyed the promise.
16 For men verily sweare by him that is
greater *then themselues*, and an oath for confirmation is among them an end of all strife.
17 So God, willing more [f] abundantly to
shew vnto the heires of promise the stablenesse
of his counsel, bound himselfe by an oath,
18 That by two immutable things, wherein
it is vnpossible that God should lie, wee might
haue strong consolation, which haue our refuge

a The first principles of Christian religion, which we do call the Catechisme.
1 Certaine principles of a Catechisme, which comprehend the summe of the doctrine of the Gospel, were giuen in few words, & briefely to the rude and ignorant, to wit, the profession of repentance and faith in God: the articles of which doctrine, were demanded of them which were not as yet receiued members of the Church, at the dayes appointed for Baptisme: and of the children of the faithfull which were baptized in their infancie, when hands were laide vpon them. And of those articles, two are by name recited: the resurrection of the flesh, and the eternall iudgement.
2 He addeth a vehemencie to his exhortation, and a most sharp threatning of the certaine destruction that shall come to them which fall from God and his religion.
* *Chap.* 10.26. *matth.*12 45. 2.*pet.*2.10.
b He speaketh of a generall backe-sliding and such as doe altogether fall away from the faith, and not of sinnes which are committed through the frailtie of a man against the first and the second Table.
c We must marke the force of this word, for it is one thing to beleeue as Lydia did, whose heart God opened, Acts 16.13.*and another thing to haue some taste.*
d As men that hate Christ, and as though they crucified him againe, make him a mocking stocke to all the world, and that to their owne destruction, as Iulian the Apostata or backslider did. 3 He setteth forth the former threatning with a similitude. 4 He mitigateth and asswageth all that sharpnesse, hoping better of them to whom he writeth. 5 He praiseth them for their charitie, thereby encouraging them to goe forward, and to hold out to the end. 6 He sheweth what vertues chiefly they haue neede of to go forward constantly, and also to profit: to wit, of charitie, and patience: and lest any man should obiect and say, that these things are impossible to be done, he willeth them to set before themselues the examples of their ancesters, and to folow them. 7 An other pricke, to pricke them forward: Because the hope of the inheritance is certaine, if wee continue to the ende, for God hath not onely promised it, but also promised it with an oath. * *Gene.*12.2.*and* 17.4.*and* 22. 17. *e I will heape vp benefits most plentifully vpon thee. f More then was needfull, were it not for the wickednesse of men which beleeue not God, no though he sweare.*

to lay hold vpon that hope that is set before vs,
19 [8] Which *hope* we haue, as an ancre of the
soule, both sure and stedfast, and it entreth into that which is within the vaile,
20 [9] Whither the forerunner is for vs entred
in, *euen* Iesus that is made an hie Priest for euer
after the order of Melchi-sedec.

8 He likeneth hope to an ancre: because that euen as an ancre being cast into the bottome of the sea, stayeth the whole ship, so doth hope also enter euen into the very secret places of heauen. And he maketh mention of the Sanctuarie, alluding to the old Tabernacle, and by this meanes returneth to the comparisons of the Priesthood of Christ with the Leuiticall. 9 He repeateth Dauids words, wherein all those comparisons wherof he hath before made mention, are signified, as he declareth in all ye next Chapter

CHAP. VII.

1 Hee hath hitherto stirred them vp, to marke diligently what things are to bee considered in Melchi-sedec, 15 wherein hee is like vnto Christ. 20 Wherefore the Lawe should giue place to the Gospel.

FOr this [1] Melchi-sedec **was* King of Salem,
the Priest of the most high God, who met
Abraham, as he returned from the slaughter of
the Kings, and [a] blessed him.
2 To whome also Abraham gaue the tithe
of all things: who first is by interpretation king
of righteousnesse: after that, *he is* also King of
Salem, that is, King of peace,
3 [2] Without father, without mother, without kinred, and hath neither beginning of *his*
dayes, neither end of life: but is likned vnto the
Sonne of God, & continueth a Priest for euer.
4 [3] Now consider how great this man *was*,
vnto whom euen the Patriarch Abraham gaue
the tithe of the spoyles.
5 For verily they which are the children
of Leui, which receiue the office of the Priesthood, haue a * commandement to take, according to the Law, tithes of the people (that is,
of their brethren) though they [b] came out of
the loynes of Abraham.
6 But hee whose kinred is not counted a-
mong them, receiued tithes of Abraham, and
blessed him that had the promises.
7 And [c] without all contradiction the lesse
is blessed of the greater.
8 And here men that die, receiue tithes:
but there he *receiueth them*, of whom it is witnessed, that he liueth.
9 [4] And to say as the thing is, Leui also
which receiueth tithes, payd tithes in Abraham.
10 For hee was yet in the loynes of his father *Abraham*, when Melchi-sedec met him.
11 [5] If therefore [d] perfection had beene by

1 Declaring those words, *According to the order of Melchi-sedec*, whereupon that comparison standeth of the Priesthood of Christ with the Leuiticall: first, Melchi-sedec himselfe is considered as the figure of Christ, and these are the heads of that comparison. Melchi sedec was a King and a Priest, and such an one in deede is Christ alone. He was a King of peace & righteousnes, such an one in deede is Christ alone.
* *Gene.* 14.18.
a With a solemne and Priestly blessing
2 An other figure: Melchi-sedec is set before vs to be considered as one without beginning and without ending, for neither his father, nor his mother, nor his ancesters, nor his death are written of: and such an one in deed is the Sonne of God, to wit, an euerlasting Priest: as he is God, without mother wonderfully begotten: as he is man, without father wonderfully conceiued. 3 An other figure: Melchi sedec in consideration of his Priesthood was aboue Abraham: for he tooke tenthes of him, and blessed him as a Priest: Such a one in deede is Christ, vpon whom dependeth euen Abrahams sanctification and all the beleeuers, and whome all men ought to worship and reuerence as the authour of all. * *Numb.*18 21. *b Were begotten of Abraham. c He speaketh of the publike blessing which the Priests vsed.* 4 A double amplification: The first, that Melchi-sedec tooke the tenthes as one immortall (to wit, in respect that hee is the figure of Christ, for his death is in no place made mention of, and Dauid setteth him foorth as an euerlasting Priest) but the Leuiticall Priests, as mortall men, for they succeede one another: the second, that Leui himselfe was tithed in Abraham by Melchi sedec. Therefore the Priesthood of Melchi-sedec (that is, Christes, who is pronounced to bee an euerlasting Priest according to this order) is more excellent then the Leuiticall. 5 The third treatise of this Epistle, wherein after hee hath prooued Christ to bee a King, a Prophet and a Priest, he now handleth distinctly the condition and excellencie of all these offices, shewing that all these were but shadowes in all other, but in Christ they are true and perfect. And he beginneth with the Priesthood, wherewith also the former treatise ended, that by this meanes all the parts and members of the disputation, may better hang together. And first of all he prooueth that the Leuiticall Priesthood was imperfect because another Priest is promised a long time after according to an other order, that is to say, of an other maner of rule and fashion. *d If the Priesthood of Leui could haue made any man perfit.*

the Priesthood of the Leuites (for vnder it the
Law was established to the people) what needed it furthermore, that another Priest should
rise after the order of Melchi-sedec, and not to
be called after the order of Aaron?
12 [6]For if the Priesthood bee changed,
then of necessitie must there be a change of the
[e]Lawe.
13 For hee of whome these things are spoken, pertaineth vnto another tribe, whereof no
man [f]serued at the altar.
14 For it is euident, that our Lord sprung
out of Iuda, concerning the which tribe Moses spake nothing, touching the Priesthood.
15 [7]And it is yet a more euident thing, because that after the similitude of Melchi-sedec,
there is risen vp another Priest,
16 [8]Which is not made *Priest* after the
[g]Law of the carnall commandement, but after the power of the endlesse life.
17 For hee testifieth *thus*, *Thou art a
Priest for euer, after the order of Melchi-
sedec.
18 [9]For the [h]commandement that went a-
fore, is disanulled, because of the weakenesse
thereof, and vnprofitablenesse.
19 For the Law made nothing perfect, but
the bringing in of a better hope *made perfect*,
whereby we drawe neere vnto God.
20 [10]And forasmuch as it is not without
an othe (for these are made Priests without an
othe:
21 But this *is made* with an othe by him
that sayd vnto him, *The Lord hath sworne,
and will not repent, Thou art a Priest for euer,
after the order of Melchi-sedec,)
22 By so much is Iesus made a surety of a
better Testament.
23 [11]And among them many were made
Priests, because they were not suffered to endure, by the reason of death.
24 But this man, because hee endureth e-
uer, hath a Priesthood, which [i]cannot passe
from one to another.
25 Wherefore, hee is [k]able also perfectly
to saue them that come vnto God by him, seeing hee euer liueth, to make intercession for
them.
26 [12]For such an hie Priest it became vs to
haue, *which is* holy, harmelesse, vndefiled, separate from sinners, and made higher then the
heauens:

6 He sheweth how that by the institutiō of the new Priesthood, not onely the imperfection of the Priesthood of Leui was declared, but also that it was changed for this: for these two cannot stand together, because that first appointment of the tribe of Leui, did shut foorth the tribe of Iuda, and made it also inferiour to Leui: and this latter doth place the Priesthood in the tribe of Iuda.
e *Of the institution of Aaron.*
f *Had any thing to doe about the altar.*
7 Lest any man might obiect, that the Priesthood in deede was translated from Leui to Iuda, but yet notwithstanding the same remaineth still, he both weigheth and expoundeth those words of Dauid, *for euer, according to the order of Melchi-sedec*, whereby also a diuers institution of Priesthood is well perceiued.
8 Hee prooueth the diuersity and excellencie of the institution of Melchi-sedecs Priesthood, by this that the Priesthood of the Lawe did stand vpon an outward and bodily anointing: but the sacrifice of Melchisedec is set out to be euerlasting & more spirituall.
g *Not after the ordination, which commaundeth fraile and transitorie things, as was done in Aarons consecration, and all that whole Priesthood.*
* *Psal.* 110.4. *chap.* 5.6.

9 Againe, that no man might obiect that the last Priesthood was added to make a perfect one, by the coupling of them both together, he prooueth that the first was abrogated by the later, as vnprofitable, and that by the nature of them both For how could those corporall and transitorie things sanctifie vs, either of themselues, or being ioyned with another? h *The ceremoniall Lawe.* 10 Another argument, whereby he prooueth that the Priesthood of Christ is better then the Priesthood of Leui, because his was established with an othe, but theirs was not so. **Psal.* 110.4. 11 Another argument tending to the same purpose The Leuiticall Priestes (as mortall men) could not be euerlasting, but Christ, as he is euerlasting, so hath hee also an euerlasting Priesthood, making most effectuall intercession for them which by him come vnto God. i *Which cannot passe away.* k *He is fit and meete.* 12 Another argument: There are required in an hie Priest innocencie and perfect purenesse, which may separate him from sinners, for whom hee offereth. But the Leuiticall hie Priests shall not be found to be such, for they offer first for their owne sinnes: but Christ onely is such a one, and therefore the true and onely hie Priest.

27 Which needeth not dayly as those hie
Priestes to offer vp sacrifice, *first for his owne
sinnes, and then for the peoples: [13]for [l]that
did he [m]once when he offered vp himselfe.
28 For the Lawe maketh men hie Priestes,
which haue infirmitie: but the [n]worde of the
othe [14]that [o]was since the Lawe, *maketh* the
Sonne, who is consecrated for euermore.

**Leuit.* 16.11.
13 Another argument, which notwithstāding he handleth afterward: The Leuiticall Priests offered sacrifice after sacrifice, first for themselues, and then for the people. But Christ offered not for himself, but for other, not sacrifices, but himselfe, not oftentimes, but once. And this ought not to seeme strange, sayth he, forsomuch as they are weake, but this man is consecrated an euerlasting Priest, and that by an othe. l *That sacrifice which he offred.* m *It was so done, that it needeth not to be repeated or offered againe any more.* n *The commandement of God which was bound with an othe.* 14 Another argument taken of the time: Former things are taken away by the later. o *Exhibited.*

CHAP. VIII.

1 *To proue more certainely that the ceremonies of the Lawe are abrogated,* 5 *hee sheweth that they were appointed to serue the heauenly patterne.* 8 *Hee bringeth in the place of Ieremie,* 13 *to proove the amendement of the old couenant.*

NOwe [1]of the things which we haue spoken, *this is* the summe, that we haue such
an high Priest, that sitteth at the right hand of
the throne of the Maiestie in heauens,
2 [2]And is a Minister of the [a]Sanctuarie,
[3]and of that [b]true Tabernacle which the Lord
pight, and not man.
3 [4]For euery hie Priest is ordained to offer both gifts and sacrifices: wherefore it was
of necessitie, that this man should haue somewhat also to offer.
4 [5]For he were not a Priest, if he were on
the earth, seeing there are Priestes that according to the Law offer gifts,
5 Who serue vnto the paterne and shadow
of heauenly things, as Moses was warned by
God, when hee was about to finish the Tabernacle. *See, sayd he, that thou make all things
according to the paterne, shewed to thee in
the mount.
6 [6]But now *our hie Priest* hath obtained
a more excellent office, in as much as hee is the
Mediatour of a better Testament, which is e-
stablished vpon better promises.
7 [7]For if that first *Testament* had been vnblameable, no place should haue been sought
for the second.
8 For in rebuking them he saith, *Behold,
the dayes will come, sayth the Lord, when I
shall make with the [c]house of Israel, and with
the house of Iuda a new Testament:
9 Not like the Testament that I made with
their fathers, in the day that I tooke them by
the hande, to leade them out of the lande of

1 He briefly repeateth that, whereunto all these things are to be referred, to wit, that we haue a farre other hie Priest then those Leuiticall hie Priests are, euen such an one as sitteth at ÿ right hand of the most high God in heauen.
2 They of Leui were hie Priests in an earthly sanctuary, but Christ is in the heauenly.
a *Of heauen.*
3 They of Leui exercised their priesthood in a fraile tabernacle, but Christ beareth about with him a farre other tabernacle, to wit, his body, which God himselfe made to be euerlasting, as it shall afterward bee declared, chapter 9.11.
b *Of his bodie.*
4 He bringeth a reason why it must needes bee that Christ should haue a bodie (which he calleth a Tabernacle which the Lord pight, and not man) to wit, that hee might haue what to offer: for otherwise hee could not be an hie Priest. And the selfe same bodie is both the Tabernacle and the sacrifice. 5 Hee giueth a reason why he sayd that our hie Priest is in the heauenly Sanctuary, and not in the earthly: because, sayth he, if he were now on the earth, he could not minister in the earthly sanctuary, seeing there are yet Leuiticall Priestes which are appointed for him, that is to say, to be paternes of that perfite example. And to what purpose should the paternes serue, when the true and original example is present? **Exo.* 25.40 *acts* 7 44. 6 Hee entreth into the comparison of the olde and transitorie Testament or couenant, being but for a time, whereof the Leuitical Priests were mediators, with the new, the euerlasting Mediatour whereof is Christ, to shew, that this is not only better then that in all respects, but also that that was abrogated by this. 7 He proueth by the testimonie of Ieremie, that there is a second Testament or couenant, and therefore that the first was not perfect. **Ier.* 31.31,32,33,34. *rom.* 11.27. *chap.* 10.16. c *He calleth it an house, as it were one family of the whole kingdome: for whereas the kingdome of Dauid was diuided into two factions, the Prophet giueth vs to vnderstand that through the new Testament they shall be ioyned together againe in one.*

Egypt:

Egypt: for they continued not in my Testament, and I regarded them not, saith the Lord.
10 For this is the Testament that I will
make with the house of Israel, After those
dayes, sayth the Lord, I will put my Lawes in
their minde, and in their heart I will write
them, and I will bee their God, and they shall
be my people,
11 And they shall not teach euery man his
neighbour, and euery man his brother, saying,
Knowe the Lord: for all shall knowe me, from
the least of them to the greatest of them.
12 For I will be mercifull to their vnrighteousnesse, and I will remember their sinnes, and
their iniquities no more.
13 [8] In that he sayth, A new *Testament*, he
hath abrogate the old: now that which is disanulled and waxed olde, is ready to vanish away.

8 The conclusion: Therefore by the later and the new, the first and olde is taken away, for it could not be called new, if it differed not from the olde. And againe, that same is at length taken away, which is subiect to corruption, and therefore imperfect.

CHAP. IX.

2 Comparing the forme of the Tabernacle, 10 and the ceremonies of the Law, 11 vnto the trueth set out in Christ, 15 He concludeth that now there is no more neede of another Priest, 24 Because Christ himselfe hath fulfilled these dueties vnder the new couenant.

THen [1] the first *Testament* had also ordinances of religion, and a [a] worldly Sanctuarie.
2 For the first Tabernacle was made wherein was the candlesticke, and the table, and the
shewbread, which *Tabernacle* is called the
Holy places.
3 And after [b] the second vaile *was* the Tabernacle, which is called the [c] Holiest of all,
4 Which had the golden censer, & the Arke
of the Testament ouerlayd round about with
gold, wherein the golden pot, which had Manna, *was*, and * Aarons rod that had budded, and
the * tables of the Testament.
5 * And ouer the Arke were the glorious
Cherubims, shadowing the [d] mercie seate:
of which things wee will not now speake particularly.
6 [2] Now when these things were thus ordeined, the Priests went alwayes into the first
Tabernacle, and accomplished the seruice.
7 But into the second went the * high
Priest alone, once euery yeere, not without
blood which hee offered for himselfe, and for
the [e] ignorances of the people.
8 [3] Whereby the holy Ghost this signified, that the way into the Holiest of all was
not yet opened, while as yet the first Tabernacle was standing.
9 [4] Which was a figure [f] for that present
time, wherein were offered gifts and sacrifices
that could not make holy, concerning the conscience, him that did the seruice,
10 [5] Which onely stoode in meates and
drinkes, and diuers washings, and carnall
rites, [g] which were enioyned, vntill the time
of reformation.
11 [6] But Christ being come an high Priest
of good things to come, [7] by a [h] greater and a
more perfect Tabernacle, not made with
hands, that is, not of this building,
12 [8] Neither by the blood of [i] goates and
calues: but by his owne blood entred hee in
once into the holy place, and obtained eternal
redemption *for vs*.
13 * [9] For if the blood of bulles and of
goates, and the ashes of an heifer, sprinkling
them that are vncleane, sanctifieth as touching
the [k] purifying of the flesh,
14 How much more shall the * blood of
Christ, which through the eternall Spirit offered himselfe without fault to God, * purge your
conscience from [l] dead workes, to serue the liuing God?
15 [10] And for this cause is he the Mediatour
of the new Testament, that through * death
which was for the redemption of the transgressions *that were* in the former Testament, they
which were called, might receiue the promise
of eternall inheritance.
16 [11] For where a Testament *is*, there must
be the death of him that made the Testament.
17 * For the Testament is confirmed when
men are dead: for it is yet of no force as long as
he that made it, is aliue.
18 [12] Wherfore, neither was the first ordeined without blood.

1 A diuision of the first Tabernacle which he calleth worldly, that is to say, transitorie, and earthly, into two parts, to wit, into the holy places, and the Holiest of all.
a An earthie and a flitting.
b He calleth it the second vaile, not because there were two vailes, but because it was behind the Sanctuarie or the first Tabernacle.
c The holiest Sanctuary.
* *Num.* 7.16.
* 1.*King.* 8.9. 2.*chron.* 5.10.
* *Exod.* 25.21.
d The Hebrewes call the couer of the Arke of the couenant, the mercie seat, whom both the Grecians and we follow.
2 Now he commeth to the sacrifices which he diuideth into those dayly sacrifices, and that yeerely and solemne sacrifice with the which the high Priest onely but once euery yeere entring into the Holiest of all with blood, offered for himselfe and the people.

* *Exod.* 30.10. *leuit.* 16.2. *e For the sinnes, Looke Chap.* 5.2. 3 Of that yeerely rite and the ceremonie, he gathereth that the way was not by such sacrifices opened into heauen, which was shadowed by the Holiest of all: for why did the hie Priest alone enter in thither, shutting out all other, and that to offer sacrifices there both for himselfe, and for others, and after, did shut the Holiest of all againe? 4 An obiection: If the way were not opened into heauen by those sacrifices (that is to say, if the worshippers were not purged by them) why then were those ceremonies vsed? To wit, that men might be called backe to that spiritual example, that is to say, to Christ, who should correct all those things at his comming. *f For that time that that figure had to last.*

5 An other reason why they could not make cleane the conscience of the worshipper, to wit, because they were outward and carnall, or corporal things. *g For they were as you would say, a burden, from which Christ deliuered vs.* 6 Now he entreth into the declaration of the figures, and first of all comparing the Leuiticall high Priest with Christ, (that is to say, the figure with the thing it selfe) he attributeth to Christ the administration of good things to come, that is, euerlasting, which those carnall things had respect vnto. 7 An other comparison of ye first corrupt Tabernacle with the latter, (that is to say, with the humane nature of Christ) which is the true incorruptible Temple of God, whereinto the Sonne of God entred, as the Leuitical high Priests into the other which was fraile and transitory.

h By a more excellent and better. 8 Another comparison of the blood of the sacrifices with Christ. The Leuitical high Priests entring by those their holy places into their Sanctuary, offered corruptible blood for one yeere onely: but Christ entring into that holy body of his, entred by it into heauen it selfe, offering his owne most pure blood for an euerlasting redemption: For one selfe same Christ answereth both to the high Priest, and the Tabernacle, and the sacrifices, and the offerings themselues, as the trueth to the figures, so that Christ is both high Priest and Tabernacle, and Sacrifice, yea, all those both truely and for euer. *i For in this yeerely sacrifice of reconciliation, there were two kindes of sacrifices, the one a goate, the other a heifer, or calfe.* * *Leuit.* 16.14. *numb.* 19.4. 9 If the outward sprinkling of blood and ashes of beasts, was a true and effectual signe of purifying and cleansing, how much more shal the thing it selfe and the trueth being present, which in times past was shadowed by those externall Sacraments, that is to say, his blood, which is in such sort mans blood that it is also the blood of the Sonne of God, and therefore hath an euerlasting vertue of purifying and cleansing, doe it? *k He considereth the signes apart, being separate from the thing it selfe.* * 1.*Peter* 1.19. 1.*Iohn* 1.7. *reuel.* 1.5. * *Luke* 1.74. *l From sinnes which proceede from death, and bring forth nothing but death.* 10 The conclusion of the former argument: therefore seeing the blood of beasts did not purge sinnes, the newe Testament which was before time promised, whereunto those outward things had respect, is now in deede established, by the vertue whereof all transgressions might be taken away, and heauen in deede opened vnto vs: whereof it followeth that Christ shed his blood also for the Fathers, for hee was shadowed by these olde ceremonies, otherwise, vnlesse they had serued to represent him, they had been nothing at all profitable. Therefore this Testament is called the latter, not as concerning the vertue of it, (that is to say, remission of sinnes) but in respect of that time, wherein the thing it selfe was finished, that is to say, wherein Christ was in deede exhibited to the world, and fulfilled all things which were necessarie to our saluation. * *Rom.* 5.6. 1.*pet.* 3 18. 11 A reason why the Testament must be established by the death of ye Mediator, because this Testament hath the condition of a Testament or gift, which is made effectuall by death, and therefore that it might be effectuall, it must needes be that he that made the Testament, should die. * *Gal.* 3.15. 12 There must be a proportion betweene those things which purifie, and those which are purified: Vnder the Lawe all those figures were earthly, The Tabernacle, the booke, the vessels, the sacrifices, although they were the signes of heauenly things. Therefore it was requisite that all those should bee purified with some matter and ceremonie of the same nature, to wit, with the blood of beasts, with water, wooll, hyssope. But vnder Christ all things are heauenly, an heauenly Tabernacle, an heauenly Sacrifice, and heauenly people, an heauenly doctrine, and heauen it selfe is set open before vs for an euerlasting habitation. Therefore all these things are sanctified in like sort, to wit, with that euerlasting offering of the quickening blood of Christ.

m *As the Lord had commanded.*
n *He vsed to sprinkle.*
*Exod.24.8.
o *The similitudes of heauenly things were earthly, and therfore they were to be set forth with earthly things, as with the blood of beasts, and wooll, and hyssope. But vnder Christ all things are heauenly, and therefore they could not be sanctified with the offering of his liuely blood.*
13 Another double comparison: The Leuitical hie Priest entred into the Sāctuary, which was made in deede by the commandement of God, but yet with mens hands, that it might be a paterne of another more excellent, to wit, of the heauenly palace. But Christ entred into heauen it selfe. Againe, he appeared before the Arke, but Christ before God the Father himselfe.
14 Another double comparison: The Leuiticall hie Priest offered other blood, but Christ offered his own: hee euery yeere once iterated his offering: Christ offering himselfe but once, abolished sinne altogether, both of the former ages and of the ages to come.

19 For when Moses had spoken euery precept to the people, [m] according to the Law, he
tooke the blood of calues and of goates, with
water & purple wooll and hyssope, and [n] sprinkled both the booke, and all the people,
20 *Saying, This is the blood of the Testament, which God hath appointed vnto you.
21 Moreouer, he sprinkled likewise the Tabernacle with blood also, and all the ministring
vessels.
22 And almost all things are by the Lawe
purged with blood, and without sheading of
blood is no remission.
23 It was then necessary, that the [o] similitudes of heauenly things should bee purified
with such things: but the heauenly things
themselues *are purified* with better sacrifices
then are these.
24 [13] For Christ is not entred into the holy places that are made with hands, which are
similitudes of the true *Sanctuary*: but *is entred*
into very heauen to appeare now in the sight of
God for vs,
25 [14] Not that he should offer himselfe often, as the hie Priest entred into the holy place
euery yeere with other blood,
26 [15] (For then must hee haue often suffered
since the foundation of the worlde) but now in
the [p] end of the world hath hee been made manifest once, to put away [q] sinne by the sacrifice
of himselfe.
27 And as it is appointed vnto men that they
shal [r] once die, & after that *cōmeth* the iudgmēt:
28 So * Christ was once offered to take a-
way the sinnes of [f] many, [16] and vnto them that
looke for him, shall he appeare the second time
without sinne vnto saluation.

15 An argument to prooue that Christs offering ought not to to be repeated: Seeing that sinnes were to be purged from the beginning of the world, and it is prooued that sinnes cannot be purged, but by the onely blood of Christ: hee must needes haue died oftentimes, since the beginning of the world. But a man can die but once: therefore Christs oblation which was once done in the later dayes, neither could nor can be repeated. Seeing then it is so, surely the vertue of it extendeth both to sinnes that were before, and to sinnes that are after his comming. p *In the later dayes.* q *That whole roote of sinne.* r *He speaketh of the naturall state and condition of man: For as for Lazarus and certaine other that died twise, that was no vsuall thing, but extraordinarie: and as for them that shall be changed, their changing is a kinde of death,* 1.Cor.15.51. *Rom.5.8. 1 pet.3.18. f *Thus the generall promise is restrained to the elect onely: and we haue to seeke the testimonie of our election, not in the secret counsell of God, but in the effects that our faith worketh, and so we must climbe vp from the lowest step to the highest, there to finde such comfort as is most certaine, and shall neuer be moued.* 16 Shortly by the way he setteth out Christ as Iudge, partly to terrifie them, which doe not rest themselues in the onely oblation of Christ once made, and partly to keepe the faithfull in their duetie, that they goe not backe.

CHAP. X.

1 He prooueth that the sacrifices of the Law were vnperfect, 2 because they were yeerely renued: 5 But that the sacrifice of Christ is one, and perpetuall, 6 hee prooueth by Dauids testimonie: 19 Then he addeth an exhortation, 29 and seuerely threatneth them that reiect the grace of Christ. 36 In the end hee prayseth patience, 38 that commeth of faith.

1 He preuenteth a priuie obiection. Why then were those sacrifices offered? The Apostle answereth, first touching the yeerely sacrifice which was the solemnest of all, wherein (sayth he) there was made euery yeere a remembrance againe of all former sinnes. Therefore that sacrifice had no power to sanctifie: for to what purpose should those sinnes which are purged bee repeated againe, and wherefore should new sinnes come to bee repeated euery yeere, if those sacrifices did abolish sinne? a *Of things which are euerlasting, which were promised to the Fathers, and exhibited in Christ.*

FOr [1] the Lawe hauing the shadow of good
things to [a] come, and not the verie image
of the things, can neuer with those sacrifices,
which they offer yeere by yeere continually,
sanctifie the commers thereunto.
2 For would they not then haue ceased to
haue been offered, because that the offerers
once purged, should haue no more conscience
of sinnes?
3 But in those *sacrifices* there *is* a remembrance againe of sinnes euery yeere.
4 For it is vnpossible that the blood of
bulles and goates should take away sinnes.
5 [2] Wherefore when hee [b] commeth into
the world, hee sayth, * Sacrifice and offering
thou wouldest not: but a [c] body hast thou ordeined me.
6 In burnt offerings, and sinne offerings
thou hast had no pleasure.
7 Then I sayd, Loe, I come (In the beginning of the booke it is written of me) that I
should doe thy will, O God.
8 Aboue when hee said, Sacrifice and offering, and burnt offerings, and sinne offerings
thou wouldest not haue, neither hadst pleasure
therein (which are offered by the Law)
9 Then sayd hee, Loe, I come to doe thy
will, O God: he taketh away the [d] first, that he
may stablish the second.
10 By the which will wee are sanctified, *e-
uen* by the offering of the body of Iesus Christ
once *made*.
11 [3] And euery Priest standeth [e] dayly ministring, and oft times offereth one manner of
offering, which can neuer take away sinnes.
12 But this man after he had offered one sacrifice for sinnes, * sitteth for euer at the right
hand of God,
13 [4] And from hencefoorth tarrieth, * till
his enemies be made his footestoole.
14 For with one offering hath he consecrated for euer them that are sanctified.
15 [5] For the holy Ghost also beareth vs record: for after that he had sayd before,
16 * This *is* the Testament that I will make
vnto them after those dayes, sayth the Lorde,
I will put my Lawes in their heart, and in their
mindes I will write them.
17 And their sinnes and iniquities will I remember [f] no more.
18 Now where remission of these things *is*,
there *is* no more offering for [g] sinne.

2 A conclusion following of those things that went before, and comprehending also the other sacrifices. Seeing that the sacrifices of the Lawe could not do it, therefore Christ speaking of himselfe as of our hie Priest manifested in the flesh, witnesseth euidently that God resteth not in the sacrifices, but in the obedience of his Son our hie Priest, in whose obedience he offred vp himselfe once to his Father for vs.
b *The Sonne of God is sayd to come into the world, when he was made man.*
*Psal.40.7.
c *It is word for word in the Hebrew text, Thou hast pearced mine eares through, that is, thou hast made me obedient and willing to heare.*
d *That is, the sacrifices, to establish the second, that is, the will of God.*
3 A conclusion, with the other part of the comparison: The Leuiticall hie Priest repeateth the same sacrifices dayly in his sanctuary: whereupon it followeth that neither those sacrifices, neither those offerings, neither those hie Priests could take away sinnes. But Christ hauing offered one sacrifice once for the sinnes of all men, and hauing sanctified his owne for euer, sitteth at the right hand of the Father, hauing all power in his handes. e *At the altar.* *Chap.1.13. psal.110.1. 1.cor.15.15. 4 Hee preuenteth a priuie obiection, to wit, that yet notwithstanding wee are subiect to sinne and death, whereunto the Apostle answereth, that the full efficacie of Christs vertue hath not yet shewed it selfe, but shall at length appeare when he will at once put to flight all his enemies, with whom as yet we striue. *Chap.1.13. 5 Although there doe yet remaine in vs reliques of sinne, yet the worke of our sanctification which is to bee perfected, hangeth vpon the selfe same sacrifice which neuer shall bee repeated: and that the Apostle prooueth by alleaging againe the testimonie of Ieremie, thus: Sinne is taken away by the new Testament, seeing the Lorde sayth that it shall come to passe, that according to the forme of it, hee will no more remember our sinnes: Therefore we neede now no purging sacrifice to take away that which is already taken away, but wee must rather take paines, that wee may now through faith bee partakers of that sacrifice. *Ierem.31.33. rom.11.27. chap 8.8. f *Why then, where is the fire of Purgatorie, and that Popish distinction of the fault, and the punishment?* g *Hee sayd well, for sinne: for there remaineth another offering, to wit, of thankesgiuing.*

19 [6] Seeing therefore brethren, that by the
blood of Iesus wee may bee bold to enter into
the Holy place,
20 By the new and liuing way, which hee
hath prepared for vs through the vaile, that is,
his [h] flesh:
21 *And seeing we haue* an high Priest, *which
is* ouer the house of God,
22 [7] Let vs drawe neere with a [i] true heart
in assurance of faith, our [k] hearts being pure
from an euill conscience,
23 And washed in our bodies with [l] pure
water, let vs keepe the profession of our hope,
without wauering (for *he is* faithfull that promised)
24 And let vs consider one another, to prouoke vnto loue, and to good workes,
25 Not forsaking the fellowship that wee
haue among our selues, as the maner of some
is: but let vs exhort *one another,* [8] and that so
much the more, because yee see that the day
draweth neere.
26 * For if wee sinne [m] willingly after that
we haue receiued & acknowledged that trueth,
there remaineth no more sacrifice for sinnes,
27 But a fearefull looking for of iudgement,
and violent fire, which shall deuoure the [n] aduersaries.
28 [9] He that despiseth Moses Lawe, dieth
without mercie * vnder two or three witnesses:
29 Of how much sorer punishment suppose ye shall he be worthy, which treadeth vnder foote the sonne of God, and counteth the
blood of the Testament as an vnholy thing,
wherewith he was sanctified, and doth despite
the Spirit of grace?
30 [10] For wee knowe him that hath sayd,
* Vengeance *belongeth* vnto me: I will recompense, saith the Lord. And againe, The Lord
shall [o] iudge his people.
31 It is a fearefull thing to fall into the hands
of the liuing God.
32 [11] Now call to remembrance the dayes
that are passed, in the which, after ye had receiued light, ye endured a great fight in afflictions,
33 Partly while yee were made a [p] gazing
stocke both by reproches and afflictions, and
partly while ye became [q] companions of them
which were so tossed to and fro.
34 For both yee sorrowed with mee for my
bonds, and suffered with ioy the spoyling of
your goods, knowing in your selues how that
yee haue in heauen a better, and an enduring
[r] substance.
35 Cast not away therfore your confidence
which hath great recompence of reward.
36 For yee haue neede of patience, that after ye haue done the will of God, ye might receiue the promise.
37 For yet a very [s] little while, and hee that
shall come, will come, and will not tarie.
38 * [12] Now the iust shal liue by faith: but
if *any* withdrawe himselfe, my soule shall haue
no pleasure in him.
39 But wee are not they which withdrawe
our soules vnto perdition, but *follow* faith vnto the conseruation of the soule.

6 The summe of ÿ former treatise: We are not shut out now of the holy place, as the Fathers were, but wee haue an entrance into the true holy place (that is, into heauen) seeing that we are purged with the blood, not of beasts, but of Iesus, neither as in times past, doth the high Priest shut vs out by setting the vaile against vs, but through the vaile, which is his flesh, he hath brought vs into heauen it selfe, being present with vs, so that we haue now truely an high Priest, which is ouer the house of God.

h So Christs flesh sheweth vs the Godhead as it were vnder a vaile, For otherwise we were not able to abide the brightnesse of it.

7 A most graue exhortation, wherein hee sheweth how that sacrifice of Christ may bee applied to vs: to wit, by faith, which also hee describeth by the consequents, to wit, by sanctification of the Spirit, which causeth vs surely to hope in God, and to procure by all meanes possible one anothers saluation, through the loue that is in vs one towards another.

i With no double and counterfeit heart, but with such an heart as is truely and in deede giuen to God.

k This is it which the Lord saith, Be ye holy, for I am holy.

l With the grace of the holy Ghost.

8 Hauing mentioned the last comming of Christ, he stirreth vp the godly to the meditation of an holy life, and citeth the faithlesse fallers from God to the fearefull iudgement seate of the Iudge, because they wickedly reiected him in whom onely saluation consisteth. * *Chap.6.4.* *m Without any cause or occasion, or shew of occasion.* *n For it is another matter to sinne through the frailtie of mans nature, and another thing to proclaime warre as it were to God as to an enemie.* 9 If the breach of the Lawe of Moses was punished by death, how much more worthie death is it to fall away from Christ? * *Deut.19.15. matth.18.16. iohn 8.17. 2.cor.13.1.* 10 The reason of all these things is, because God is a reuenger of such as despise him: otherwise hee should not rightly gouerne his Church. Now there is nothing more horrible then the wrath of the liuing God. * *Deut 32.35. rom.12. 19.* *o Rule or gouerne* 11 As he terrified the fallers away from God, so doth he now comfort them that are constant and stand strongly, setting before them the successe of their former fights, so stirring them vp to a sure hope of a ful and readie victorie. *p You were brought foorth to be shamed.* *q In taking their miseries, to bee your miseries.*

r Goods and riches.

s He will come within this very little while. * *Hab.2.4. rom.1. 17. gal.3.11.*

12 He commendeth the excellencie of a sure faith by ÿ effect, because it is the only way to life, which sentence he fetteth foorth and amplifieth by setting the contrarie against it.

CHAP. XI.

1 He declareth in the whole chapter, that the Fathers, which from the beginning of the world were approoued of God, attained saluation no other way then by faith, that the Iewes may knowe, that by the same onely, they are knit vnto the Fathers in an holy vnion.

NOw [1] faith is the ground of things, which
are hoped for, and the euidence of things
which are not seene.
2 [2] For by it *our* [a] elders were well reported of.
3 * [3] Through faith wee vnderstand that
the world was ordained by the worde of God,
so that the things which we [b] see, are not made
of things which did appeare.
4 [4] By faith Abel * offered vnto God a
greater sacrifice then Cain, by * the which he
obtained witnesse that he was righteous, God
testifying of his gifts: by the which *faith* also
he being dead, yet speaketh.
5 [5] By faith was * Enoch translated, that
hee should not [c] see death: neither was hee
found: for God had translated him: for before
he was translated, he was reported of, that he
had pleased God.
6 But without faith it is vnpossible to
please *him*: for he that commeth to God, must
beleeue that *God* is, and that hee is a [d] rewarder
of them that seeke him.
7 [6] By faith * Noe being warned of God of
the things which were as yet not seene, moued
with reuerence, prepared the Arke to the sauing of his houshold, through the which *Arke*
he condemned the world, and was made heire
of the righteousnesse, which is by faith.
8 [7] By faith * Abraham when hee was
called, obeyed *God*, to goe out into a place,
which hee should afterward receiue for inheritance, and he went out, not knowing whither
he went.
9 By faith hee abode in the lande of promise, as in a strange countrey, as one that
dwelt in tents with Isaac and Iacob heires with
him of the same promise.
10 For he looked for a citie hauing a [e] foundation, whose builder and maker *is* God.
11 Through faith * Sara also receiued
strength to conceiue seede, and was deliuered
of a childe when she was past age, because shee
iudged

1 An excellent description of faith by the effects, because it representeth things which are but yet in hope, and setteth as it were before our eyes things that are inuisible.

2 Hee sheweth that the Fathers ought to be accounted of by this vertue.

a That is, those Fathers of whom wee came: and whose authority & example ought to mooue vs very much.

* *Gen.1.1. iohn 1.10.*

3 He sheweth the propertie of faith, by setting out vnto vs most piked examples of such as from the beginning of the world excelled in the Church.

b So that the world which we see, was not made of any matter that appeared or was before, but of nothing.

4 Abel. * *Gen.4.4. Matth.23.35.*

5 Enoch. * *Gen.5.24.*

c That he should not die.

d This reward is not referred to our merits, but to the free promise, as Paul teacheth in Abraham the father of all the faithfull, Rom.4.4

6 Noe. * *Gen.6.13.*

7 Abraham and Sara. * *Gen.12.4.*

e This foundation is set against their tabernacles.

* *Gen.17.19. and 21,2.*

f As vnlikely to beare children, as if she had been starke dead.
g In faith, which they had while they liued, and followed, them euen to their graue.
h This is the figure Metonymia, for the things promised.
i For the Patriarchs were wont when they receiued the promises, to professe their religion, by building of altars, and calling on the Name of the Lord.

iudged him faithfull which had promised.
12 And therefore sprang there of one, euen
of one which was [f] dead, *so many* as the starres
of the skie in multitude, and as the sand of the
sea shore which is innumerable.
13 All these died in [g] faith, and receiued
not the [h] promises, but sawe them a farre off,
and beleeued *them*, and [i] receiued *them* thanke-
fully, and confessed that they were strangers
and pilgrims on the earth.
14 For they that say such things, declare
plainely, that they seeke a countrey.
15 And if they had beene mindefull of that
countrey, from whence they came out, they
had leisure to haue returned.
16 But now they desire a better, that is, an
heauenly: wherefore God is not ashamed of
them to be called their God: for hee hath prepared for them a citie.
17 By faith * Abraham offered vp Isaac,
when hee was [k] tried, and hee that had receiued the [l] promises offered his onely begotten
sonne.
18 (To whom it was sayd, * In Isaac shall
thy seede be called.)
19 For hee considered that God was able
to raise *him* vp euen from the dead: from
[m] whence he receiued him also after [n] a sort.
20 [8] By fayth * Isaac blessed Iacob and Esau,
concerning things to come.
21 [9] By faith * Iacob when he was a dying
blessed both the sonnes of Ioseph, and * *leaning*
on the end of his staffe, worshipped *God*.
22 [10] By faith * Ioseph when he died, made
mention of the departing of the children of Israel, and gaue commandement of his bones.
23 [11] * By faith Moses when he was borne,
was hid three moneths of his parents, because
they sawe he was a proper child, neither [o] feared they the * kings commaundement.
24 By faith * Moses when hee was come to
age, refused to be called the sonne of Pharaohs
daughter,
25 And chose rather to suffer aduersity with
the people of God, then to enioy the [p] pleasures
of sinnes for a season,
26 Esteeming the rebuke of Christ greater riches then the treasures of Egypt: for hee
had respect vnto the recompense of the reward.
27 By faith hee forsooke Egypt, and feared not the fiercenes of the king: for he endured, as he that saw him which is inuisible.
28 Through faith he ordeined the * Passeouer and the effusion of blood, least he that destroyed the first borne, should touch them.
29 [12] By faith they * passed through the red
sea, as by drie land, which when the Egyptians
had assayed to doe, they were swallowed vp.
30 [13] By faith the * walles of Iericho fell
downe after they were compassed about seuen
dayes.
31 [14] By fayth the [q] harlot * Rahab peri-

* Gen.22.10.
k Tried of the Lord.
l Although the promises of life were made in that onely begotten sonne Isahac, yet he appointed him to die; and so against hope he beleeued in hope.
* Gen.11.12. rom 9.7.
m From which death.
n For there was not the true and very death of Isaac, but as it were the death, by meanes whereof he seemed also as it were to haue risen againe.
8 Isaac.
* Gen.27 28,39.
9 Iacob.
* Gen.48.15.
* Gen.47.31.
10 Ioseph.
* Gen.50.25.
11 Moses.
* Exod.2.2. acts 7.22.
o They were not afraid to bring him vp.
* Exod.1.16.
* Exod.2.11.
p Such pleasures as hee could not enioy, but he must needes prouoke Gods wrath against him.
* Exod.12.22.
12 The red sea.
* Exod.14.22.
13 Iericho.
* Iosh 6.20.
14 Rahab.
q A notable example of Gods goodnesse.
* Iosh.6.23.

shed not with them which obeyed not, when
* she had receiued the spies [r] peaceably.
32 [15] And what shall I more say? for the
time would be too short for me to tell of * Gedeon, of * Barac, and of * Sampson, and of
* Iephte, also of Dauid, and Samuel, and of
the Prophets?
33 Which through faith subdued kingdomes, wrought righteousnesse, obtained the
[s] promises, stopped the mouthes of lions,
34 Quenched the violence of fire, escaped
the edge of the sword, of weake were made
strong, waxed valiant in battell, turned to
flight the armies of the aliants.
35 The [t] women receiued their dead raysed to life: other also were [u] racked, and would
not be deliuered, that they might receiue a better resurrection.
36 And others haue been tried by mockings
and scourgings, yea, moreouer by bonds and
prisonment.
37 They were stoned, they were hewen a-
sunder, they were tempted, they were slaine
with the sword, they wandred vp and downe in
[x] sheepes skinnes, and in goats skinnes, being
destitute, afflicted, *and* tormented:
38 Whom the world was not worthy of:
they wandered in wildernesses, and mountains,
and dennes, and caues of the earth.
39 [16] And these all through faith obteined
good report, and receiued [y] not the promise,
40 God prouiding a better thing for vs,
that they [z] without vs should not bee made
perfit.

* Iosh 2.1.
r Curteously and friendly, so that she did not onely not hurt them, but also kept them safe.
15 Gedeon, Barac, and other Iudges and Prophets.
* Iudg.6.11.
* Iudg.4.6.
* Iudg 13.24.
* Iudg.11.1. and 127.
s The fruit of the promises.
t He seemeth to meane the story of that woman of Sarepta, whose sonne Elias raysed againe from death, & the Shunammite, whose sonne Eliseus restored to his mother.
u Hee meaneth that persecution which Antiochus wrought.
x In vile and rough clothing, so were the Saints brought to extreme pouertie, and constrained to liue like beasts in wildernesse.
16 An amplification taken of the circumstance of the time; their faith is so much the more to be marueiled at, by how much the promises of things to come were more dark, yet at length were indeede exhibited to vs, so that their faith and ours is as one, as is also their consecration and ours. y But sawe Christ a farre off. z For their saluation did hang vpon Christ, who was exhibited in our dayes.

CHAP. XII.

1 *Hee doeth not onely by the examples of the Fathers before recited, exhort them to patience and constancie,* 3 *but also by the example of Christ.* 11 *That the chastenings of God can not bee rightly iudged by the outward sense of our flesh.*

Wherefore, * [1] let vs also, seeing that we
are compassed with so great a cloud
of witnesses, cast away euery thing that presseth downe, and the sinne that [a] hangeth so fast
on: let vs runne with patience the race that is
set before vs,
2 [2] [b] Looking vnto Iesus the author and fi-
nisher of our faith, who for the [c] ioy that was
set before him, endured the crosse, and despised
the shame, and is set at the right hand of the
throne of God.
4 [3] Consider therefore him that endured
such speaking against of sinners, lest ye should
be wearied and faint in your mindes.
4 [4] Yee haue not yet resisted vnto blood
striuing against sinne.

* Rom.6.4. col.3.8 ephes.4.24. 1 pet.2.1.
1 An applying of the former examples, whereby we ought to be stirred vp to run the whole race, casting away all stoppes and impediments.
a For sinne besiegeth vs on all sides, so that we can not escape out.
2 He setteth before vs, as the marke of this race, Iesus himselfe our captaine, who willingly ouercame all the roughnesse of the same way.

b *As it were vpon the marke of our faith.* c *Whereas he had all kind of blessednesse in his hand and power, yet suffered willingly the ignominie of the Crosse.* 3 An amplification, taken of the circumstance of the person and the things themselues, which he compareth betweene themselues: for how great is Iesus in comparison of vs, and how far more grieuous things did he suffer then we? 4 He taketh an argument of the profit which commeth to vs by Gods chastisements, vnlesse we be in fault. First of all because sinne, or that rebellious wickednesse of our flesh, is by this meanes tamed.

5 [5] And

5 [5]And yee haue forgotten the consolation, which speaketh vnto you as vnto children,
*My sonne, despise not the chastening of the
Lorde, neither faint when thou art rebuked
of him.
6 For whom the Lord loueth, he chasteneth : and he scourgeth euery sonne that he receiueth.
7 If ye endure chastening, God offereth
himselfe vnto you as vnto sonnes : for what
sonne is it whom the father chasteneth not?
8 If therefore yee be without correction,
whereof all are partakers, then are yee bastards,
and not sonnes.
9 [6]Moreouer wee haue had the fathers of
our bodies which corrected vs, and wee gaue
them reuerence : should we not much rather
be in subiection vnto the father of spirits, that
we might liue?
10 [7]For they verely for a few dayes chastened vs after their owne pleasure : but hee *chasteneth vs* for our profit, that wee might bee
partakers of his holinesse.
11 Now no chastening for the present seemeth to be ioyous, but grieuous : but afterward, it bringeth the quiet fruit of righteousnesse, vnto them which are thereby exercised.
12 [8]Wherefore lift vp *your* hands which
[d]hang downe, and *your* weake knees,
13 And make [e]straight steppes vnto your
feete, lest that which *is* halting, be turned out of
the way, but let it rather be healed.
14 *[9]Followe peace with all men, and
holinesse, without the which no man shall see
the Lord.
15 [10]Take heede, that no man fall away
from the grace of God : let no [f]roote of bitternesse spring vp and trouble *you*, lest thereby
many be defiled.
16 [11]Let there bee no fornicator, or prophane person as *Esau, which for one portion
of meate sold his birthright.
17 *For yee knowe how that afterward
also when hee would haue inherited the blessing, he was reiected : for he found no [g]place
to repentance, though hee sought *that blessing* with teares.
18 [12]For ye are not come vnto the *mount
that yee might bee [h]touched, nor vnto burning fire, nor to blackenesse and darkenesse,
and tempest,
19 Neither vnto the sound of a trumpet,
and the voyce of words, which they that heard
it, excused themselues, *that the word should
not be spoken to them any more,
20 (For they were not able to abide that

5 Secondly, because they are testimonies of his fatherly good will towards vs, insomuch that they shew themselues to be bastards, which cannot abide to be chastened of God.
* Prou.3.11.
6 Thirdly, if all men yeeld this right to fathers, to whom next after God wee owe this life, that they may rightfully correct their children, shall we not be much more subiect to that our Father, who is the author of the spirituall and euerlasting life?
7 An amplification of the same argument: Those fathers haue corrected vs after their fancie, for some fraile and transitory profit: but God chasteneth and instructeth vs for our singular profit to make vs partakers of his holinesse: which thing although these our senses do not presently perceiue, yet the end of the matter proueth it.
8 The conclusion: we must goe forward couragiously & keepe alwayes a right course and (as farre foorth as we may (without any staggering or stumbling.
d The description of a man that is out of heart and cleane discouraged.
e Keepe a right course, and so, that you shew example of good life for others to follow.
* Rom 12 18.
9 We must liue in peace and holinesse with all men.
10 We must studie to edifie one another both in doctrine and example of life.
f That no heresie, or backe sliding be an offence.
11 We must eschew fornication, and a prophane minde, that is, such a minde as giueth not to God his due honour, which wickednesse, how seuerely God will at length punish, the horrible example of Esau teacheth vs. *Gen.25.33. *Genes.27.38. *g There was no place left for his repentance: and it appeareth by the effects, what his repentance was, for when he was gone out of his fathers sight, hee threatned his brother to kill him.* 12 Now hee applieth the same exhortation to the Propheticall and Kingly office of Christ compared with Moses, after this sort. If the maiestie of the Lawe was so great, how great thinke you that the glory of Christ and the Gospel is? And this comparison hee declareth also particularly. *Exod 19.16. *h Which might be touched with hands, which was of a grosse & earthly matter.* *Exo.20.19

which was commanded. *yea, though a beast
touch the mountaine, it shal be stoned, or thrust
through with a dart:
21 And so terrible was the [i]sight which
appeared, that Moses said, I feare and quake.)
22 But yee are come vnto the mount Sion,
and to the citie of the liuing God, the celestiall
Hierusalem, and to the companie of innumerable Angels,
23 And to the assembly and congregation
of the first borne, which are written in heauen, and to God the iudge of all, and to the spirits of iust and [k]perfect men,
24 And to Iesus the Mediatour of the new
Testament, and to the blood of sprinkling, that
speaketh better things then that of Abel.
25 [13]See that ye despise not him that speaketh : for if they escaped not which refused
him, that spake on earth : much more shall we
not escape, if we turne away from him that *speaketh* from heauen.
26 [14]Whose voyce then shooke the earth,
and now hath declared, saying, *[l]Yet once
more will I shake, not the earth onely, but also
heauen.
27 And this *word*, Yet once more, signifieth the remoouing of those things which are
shaken, as of things which are made *with hands*,
that the things which are not shaken, may
remaine.
28 [15]Wherefore seeing we receiue a kingdome, which can not bee shaken, let vs haue
grace whereby we may so serue God, that wee
may please him with [m]reuerence and [n]feare.
29 For *euen our God *is* a consuming fire.

* Exod.19.12.
i The shape and forme which hee sawe, which was no counterfeit and forged shape, but a true one.
k So he calleth them that are taken vp into heauen, although one part of them doeth sleepe in the earth.
13 The applying of the former comparison: If it were not lawfull to contemne his word which spake on the earth, how much lesse his voyce which is from heauen?
14 He compareth the stedfast maiestie of the Gospel, wherewith the whole world was shaken, and euen the very frame of heauen was as it were astonished, with the small and vanishing sound of the gouernance by the Law.
*Aggeus 2.7.
l It appeareth euidently in this that the Prophet speaketh of the calling of the Gentiles, that these words must be referred to the kingdome of Christ.
15 A generall exhortation to liue reuerently and religiously vnder the most happie subiection of so mighty a King, who as he blesseth his most mightily, so doth hee most seuerely reuenge the rebellious. And this is the summe of a Christian life, respecting the first table. *m By reuerence is meant that honest shamefastnesse which keepeth them in their dueties. n Religious and godly feare.* * Deut.4.24.

CHAP. XIII.

1 *He giueth good lessons not onely for manners,* 7 *but also for doctrine.*

Let *[1]brotherly loue continue.
2 *Bee not forgetfull to entertaine
strangers : for thereby some haue *receiued
Angels into their houses vnwares.
3 Remember them that are in bonds, as
though ye were bound with them : and them
that are in affliction, as [a]if ye were also *afflicted*
in the body.
4 [2]Mariage *is* honourable among all, and
the bed vndefiled : but whoremongers and adulterers God will iudge.
5 [3]Let your conuersation be without couetousnesse, and be content with those things
that ye haue, for [b]he hath sayd,
6 *I will not faile thee, neither forsake
thee.
7 So that we may boldly say, *The Lord
is mine helper, neither will I feare what [c]man
can doe vnto me.

*Rom.12.10.
1 He commeth to the second table, the summe whereof is charitie, especially toward strangers and such as are afflicted.
*1.Pet.4.9.
*Gen 18.3. and 19.3.
a Bee so much touched, as if their miserie were yours.
2 He commendeth chaste matrimony in all sorts of men, and threatneth vtter destruction from God against whoremongers and adulterers.
3 Couetousnes is condemned, against which is set a contented minde with that which the Lord hath giuen. *b Euen the Lord himselfe.* *Iosh.1.5. *Psal.118.6. *c He setteth man against God.*

8 [4]Remember

8 [4]Remember them which haue the ouersight of you, which haue declared vnto you
the word of God: whose faith follow, considering what hath beene the end of their conuersation, [5]Iesus Christ yesterday, and to day, the
same also *is* for euer.
9 Be not caried about with diuers *and*
strange doctrines: [6]for it is a good thing that
the heart be stablished with grace, *and* not with
[d] meates, which haue not profited them that
haue beene [e]occupied therein.
10 [7]We haue an [f]altar, whereof they haue
no authoritie to eate, which [g] serue in the tabernacle.
11 *For the bodies of those beasts whose
blood is brought into the Holy place by the hie
Priest for sinne, are burnt without the campe.
12 Therefore euen Iesus, that he might sanctifie the people with his owne blood, suffered without the gate.
13 [8]Let vs goe foorth to him therefore out
of the campe, bearing his reproch.
14 *For here haue we no continuing city:
but we seeke one to come.
15 [9]Let vs therefore by him offer the sacrifice of praise alwayes to God, that is, the * fruit
of the lips which confesse his Name.
16 To doe good, and to distribute forget
not: for with such sacrifices God is pleased.
17 [10]Obey them that haue the ouersight of
you, and submit your selues: for they watch
for your soules, as they that must giue accounts, that they may doe it with ioy, and not
with griefe: for that is vnprofitable for you.
18 [11] Pray for vs: for we are assured that we
haue a good conscience in all things, desiring
to liue honestly.
19 And I desire you somewhat the more
earnestly, that ye so doe, that I may be restored
to you more quickely.
20 The God of peace that brought againe
from the dead our Lord Iesus, the great sheepheard of the sheepe, through the blood of the
euerlasting Couenant,
21 Make you [h] perfite in all good workes,
to doe his will, [i] working in you that which is
pleasant in his sight, through Iesus Christ, to
whom *be* praise for euer and euer, Amen.
22 I beseech you also, brethren, suffer the
words of exhortation: for I haue written vnto
you in few words.
23 Know that *our* brother Timotheus is
deliuered, with whom (if he come shortly) I
will see you.
24 Salute all them that haue the ouersight
of you, and all the Saints. They of Italie salute you.
25 Grace *be* with you all, Amen.

¶ Written to the Hebrewes from Italie, *and sent* by Timotheus.

4 We haue to set before vs the examples of valiant Captaines, whom we ought diligently to follow.
5 He repeateth the summe of the doctrine, to wit, the only ground of all precepts of maners, and that is this: That we ought to quiet and content our selues in Christ onely: for there was yet neuer any man saued without the knowledge of him, neither is at this day saued, neither shall be saued hereafter.
6 He toucheth them which mixed an externall worship and especially the difference of meats with the Gospel, which doctrine hee plainly condemneth as cleane repugnant to the benefite of Christ. *d By this one kind which concerneth the difference of cleane and vncleane meats, we haue to vnderstand all the ceremoniall worship.* *e Which obserued the difference of them superstitiously.* 7 He refuteth their errour by an apt and fit comparison. They which in times past serued the Tabernacle, did not eate of the sacrifices whose blood was brought for sinne into the holy place by the hie Priest. Moreouer these sacrifices did represent Christ our offering. Therefore they cannot be partakers of him which serue the Tabernacle, that is, such as stand in the seruice of the Law: but let vs not be ashamed to follow him out of Hierusalem, from whence he was cast out and suffered: for in this also Christ, who is the trueth, answereth that figure, in that he suffered without the gate. *f By the Altar, he meaneth the offerings.* *g Whereof they cannot be partakers, which stubburnly retaine the rites of the Law.* *Leuit. 4. 11. and 6. 30. and 16. 27. 8 He goeth on further in this comparison, and sheweth that this also signified vnto vs, that the godly followers of Christ must as it were goe out of the world bearing his crosse. *Mich. 2. 10. 9 Now that those corporall sacrifices are taken away, he teacheth vs that the true sacrifices of confessiō remaine, which consist partly in giuing of thanks, and partly in liberality, with which sacrifices indeed God is now delighted.

* *Hose 14. 3.*
10 We must obey ẏ warnings and admonitions of our Ministers and Elders, which watch for the saluation of the soules which are committed vnto them.
11 The last part of this Epistle, wherein he commendeth his ministerie to the Hebrewes, and wisheth them continuance and increase of graces from the Lord: and excuseth himselfe in that he hath vsed but fewe words to comfort them, hauing spent the Epistle in disputing: and saluteth certaine brethren familiarly and friendly.
h Make you fit or meete.
i Hence commeth that saying of the Fathers, that God crowneth his workes in vs.

THE [a]GENERALL EPISTLE OF IAMES.

a That is, written to no one man, citie, or countrey, but to all the Iewes generally, being now dispersed.

CHAP. I.

4 *He entreateth of patience,* 6 *of faith,* 10 *and of lowlinesse of minde in rich men.* 13 *That tentations come not of God for our euill,* 17 *because he is the authour of all godlinesse.* 21 *In what manner the word of life must be receiued.*

IAmes a seruant of God, and
of the Lord Iesus Christ, to
the twelue Tribes, which
are [b] scattered abroad, salutation.
2 [1]My brethren, [c]count
it exceeeding ioy, [2] when yee fall into diuers
tentations,
3 * [3] Knowing that the [d] trying of your
faith bringeth foorth patience,
4 [4]And let patience haue *her* perfect
worke, that ye may be perfect and entire, lacking nothing.
5 [5] If any of you lacke [e] wisedome, let
him aske of God, which giueth to all men liberally, and reprocheth no man, and it shall be
giuen him.
6 * But let him aske in faith, and [f] wauer not: [6] for hee that wauereth, is like a waue
of the sea, tost of the wind, and caried away.
7 Neither let that man thinke that he shall
receiue any thing of the Lord.
8 A double minded man *is* vnstable in
[g] all his wayes.

b To all the beleeuing Iewes, of what tribe soeuer they be, and are dispersed thorow the whole world.
1 The first place or part touching comfort in afflictions, wherein we ought not to be cast downe and be faint hearted, but rather reioyce and be glad. *c Seeing their condition was miserable in that scattering abroad, hee doeth well to begin as hee doeth.* 2 The first argument, because our faith is tryed through afflictions: which ought to bee most pure, for so it is behooueable for vs. *Rom. 5. 3. 3 The second, Because patience, a farre passing and most excellent vertue, is by this meanes ingendred in vs. *d That wherwith your faith is tryed, to wit, those manifold tentations.*

4 The third argument proposided in maner of an exhortation, that true & continuall patience may be discerned from fained and for a time. The crosse is as it were the instrument wherewith God doth polish & fine vs. Therefore the worke and effect of afflictions, is the perfecting of vs in Christ.
5 An answere to a priuy obiectiō: It is easily said, but it is not so easily done. He answereth that we need in this case a far other maner of wisedome, then the wisdome of man, to iudge those things best for vs, which are most contrary to the flesh: but yet we shall easily obtaine this gift of wisdome, if we aske it rightly, that is, with a sure confidence of God, who is most bountifull and liberall. *e By wisedome he meaneth the knowledge of that doctrine whereof mention is made before, to wit, wherefore we are afflicted of God, and what fruit we haue to reape of affliction.* *Mat. 7. 7. *marke 11. 24 luke 11. 9. iohn 14. 13. and 16. 23.* *f Why then, what need other Mediatour?* 6 A digression or going aside from his matter, against prayers which are conceiued with a doubting minde, whereas wee haue a certaine promise of God, and this is the second part of the Epistle. *g In all his thoughts and his deeds.*

9 ⁷ Let the brother of [h] lowe degree reioyce in that he is exalted:
10 ⁸ Againe hee that is [i] rich in that hee is
made lowe: ⁹ for as the flower of the grasse,
shall he * vanish away.
11 For *as when* the sunne riseth with heate,
then the grasse withereth, and his flower falleth away, and the goodly shape of it perisheth: euen so shall the rich man wither away in
all his [k] wayes.
12 ¹⁰ * Blessed *is* the man, that endureth
[l] tentation: for when he is tried, he shal receiue
the crowne of life, which the Lord hath promised to them that loue him.
13 ¹¹ Let no man say when hee is [m] tempted, I am tempted of God: ¹² for God cannot
be tempted with euill, neither tempteth he any
man.
14 But euery man is tempted, when hee is
drawen away by his owne concupiscence, and
is enticed.
15 Then when lust hath conceiued, it bringeth forth [n] sinne, and sinne when it is finished,
bringeth foorth death.
16 ¹³ Erre not, my deare brethren.
17 Euery good giuing, and euery perfect
gift is from aboue, and commeth downe from
the [o] Father of lights, with whome is no vari-
ablenesse, neither [p] shadow of turning.
18 ¹⁴ Of his owne [q] will begate hee vs with
the word of trueth, that wee should be as the
[r] first fruits of his creatures.
19 Wherefore my deare brethren, * let e-
uery man be swift to heare, slow to speake, *and*
slow to wrath.
20 For the wrath of man doeth not accomplish the [s] righteousnesse of God.
21 Wherefore lay apart all filthinesse, and
superfluitie of maliciousnesse, *and* receiue with
[t] meekenesse the word that is graffed in you,
which is able to saue your soules.
22 * ¹⁵ And be yee doers of the word, and
not hearers onely, ¹⁶ deceiuing your owne
selues.

7 He returneth to his purpose repeating the proposition, which is, that we must reioyce in the crosse, for it doth not presse vs downe, but exalt vs.
h Who is afflicted with pouerty, or contempt, or with any kind of calamitie.
8 Before hee concludeth, he giueth a doctrine contrary to the former: to wit, how we ought to vse prosperitie, which is plentie of all things: to wit, so, that no man therefore please himselfe, but be so much the more void of pride.
i Who hath all things at his will.
9 An argument taken of the very nature of the things themselues, for that they are most vaine and vncertaine.
* *Esai 40.6. 1.pet.1.24.*
k Whatsoeuer he either purposeth in his minde or doeth.
10 The conclusion: Therefore we must patiently beare the crosse: and he addeth a fourth argument, which comprehendeth the summe of all the former, to wit, because we come by this way to ỳ crowne of life, but yet of grace according to the promise.
* *Iob 5.17.*
l Affliction whereby the Lord tryeth him.
11 The third part of this Epistle, wherein he descendeth from outward tentations, that is, from afflictions whereby God tryeth vs: to inward, that is, to those lustes whereby wee are stirred vp to doe euill. The summe is this: Euery man is the authour of these temptations to himselfe, and not God: for we beare about in our bosomes that wicked corruption, which taketh occasion by what meanes soeuer, to stirre vp euill motions in vs, whence out at length proceed wicked doings, and in conclusion followeth death the iust reward of them. *m When he is prouoked to doe euill.* 12 Here is a reason shewed, why God cannot be the author of euill doing in vs, because he desireth not euill. *n By sinne is meant in this place, actuall sinne.* 13 Another reason taken of contraries: God is the authour of all goodnesse, and so, that he is alwayes like himselfe: how then can hee be thought to be the authour of euill? *o From him who is the fountaine and authour of all goodnesse. p He goeth on in the metaphore: for the sunne by his manifold and sundry kindes of turning, maketh houres, dayes, moneths, yeeres, light and darkenesse.* 14 The fourth part concerning the excellencie and fruite of the word of God, The summe is this: wee must heare the word of God most carefully and diligently, seeing it is the seede, wherewith God of his free fauour and loue hath begotten vs vnto himselfe, picking vs out of the number of his creatures. And the Apostle condemneth two faults, which doe greatly trouble vs in this matter, to wit, for that wee so please our selues, that we had rather speake our selues, then heare God speaking: yea wee snuffe and are angry when wee are reprehended: against which faults, hee setteth a peaceable and quiet mide, and such an one as is desirous of puritie. *q This is it which Paul calleth gracious fauour, and good will, which is the fountaine of our saluation. r As it were an holy kinde of offering, taken out of the residue of man. s That which God appointeth. t By meekenesse, hee meaneth modestie, and whatsoeuer is contrarie to an hautie and proud stomacke.* * *Matth.7.21. rom.2.13.* 15 Another admonition: Therefore is Gods word heard, that wee may frame our liues according to the prescript thereof. 16 Hee addeth reasons, and those most weightie: First, because they that doe otherwise, doe very much hurt themselues.

23 ¹⁷ For if any heare the word, and doe it
not, he is like vnto a man, that beholdeth his
[u] naturall face in a glasse.
24 For when hee hath considered himselfe,
hee goeth his way, and forgetteth immediatly
what manner of one he was.
25 But who so looketh in the perfect lawe
of libertie, and continueth *therein*, he not being a forgetfull hearer, but a doer of the worke,
shalbe blessed in his [x] deed.
26 ¹⁸ If any man among you seeme religious,
and refraineth not his tongue, but deceiueth
his [y] owne heart, this mans religion *is* vaine.
27 ¹⁹ Pure religion and vndefiled before
God, euen the Father, is this, to [z] visite the fatherlesse, and widowes in their aduersitie, *and*
to keepe himselfe vnspotted of the world.

17 Secondly, because they lose the chiefest vse of Gods word, which correct not by it the faults that they know.
u He alludeth to that naturall spot, to which is contrary the puritie whereunto we are borne agrine, the liuely image whereof we behold in the Law.
x Behauing himselfe so: for works doe shew faith.
18 The third admonition: the word of God prescribeth a rule not only to doe well, but also to speake well.

y The fountaine of all brabling, and cursed speaking, and sawcinesse, is this, that men know not themselues. 19 The fourth: the true seruice of God standeth in charitie toward our neighbours (especially such as need others helpe, as the fatherlesse and widowes) and puritie of life. *z To haue a care of them, and to helpe them as much as we can.*

CHAP. II.

1 He sayth, that to haue respect of persons, is not agreeable to Christian faith, 14 which to professe in word is not enough, vnlesse 15 wee shew it also in deeds of mercie and charitie, 21 after the example of Abraham.

My ¹ brethren, haue not the faith of our
[a] glorious Lord Iesus Christ * in respect
of persons.
2 For if there come into your company a
man with a golde ring, and in goodly apparell,
and there come in also a poore man in vile raiment,
3 And ye haue a respect to him that wea-
reth the gay clothing, and say vnto him, Sit
thou here in a [b] goodly place, and say vnto the
poore, Stand thou there, or sit here vnder my
footstoole,
4 Are ye not partiall in [c] your selues, and
are become iudges of euill thoughts?
5 ² Hearken my beloued brethren, hath not
God chosen the [d] poore of this world, *that they
should be* rich in faith, & heires of the kingdom
which he promised to them that loue him?
6 But yee haue despised the poore. ³ Doe
not the rich oppresse you by tyrannie, and
doe not they drawe you before the iudgement
seates?
7 Doe not they blaspheme the worthy
Name after which ye be [e] named?
8 ⁴ But if ye fulfill the [f] royall Law, according to the Scripture, *which sayth*, Thou shalt
loue thy neighbour as thy selfe, ye doe well.
9 But if ye regard the persons, ye commit
sinne, and are rebuked of the Lawe, as trans-
gressours.

1 The first: charitie which proceedeth from a true faith, cannot stand with the accepting of persons: which he proueth plainly by setting foorth their example, who with the reproch or disdaine of the poore, honour the rich.
a For if we knew what Christs glory is, and esteemed it as we ought to doe, there would not be such respect of persons as there is.
* *Leuit.19.15. deut.1.17. and 16.19. prou.24.23.*
b In a worshipfull and honourable place.
c Haue ye not (which ye ought not to doe) by this meanes within your selues iudged one man to be preferred before another?
2 He sheweth, that they are peruerse and naughtie iudges, which preferre the rich before the poore, by that that God on the contrary side preferreth the poore, whome hee hath enriched with true riches, before the rich. *d The needie and wretched, and (if we measure it after the opinion of the world) the veriest abiects of all men.* 3 Secondly, hee prooueth them to be mad men: for that the rich men are rather to be holden execrable and cursed, considering that they persecute the Church, and blaspheme Christ: for he speaketh of wicked and profane rich men, such as the most part of them haue beene alwayes, against whom he setteth the poore and abiect. *e Word for word, which is called vpon of you.* 4 The conclusion: Charitie which God prescribeth cannot agree with the accepting of persons, seeing that wee must walke in the kings hie way. *f The Law is said to be royall and like the kings high way, for that it is plaine and without turnings, and that the Law calleth euery one our neighbour without respect, whom we may helpe by any kinde of duety.*

10 ⁵ For

10 [5] For whosoeuer shall keepe the whole Law, *and* yet faileth in one *point*, hee is guiltie of [g] all.

11 [6] For he that said, Thou shalt not commit adulterie, said also, Thou shalt not kill. Now though thou doest none adulterie, yet if thou killest, thou art a transgressour of the Lawe.

12 [7] So speake ye, and so doe, as they that shalbe iudged by the Law of libertie.

13 For there shalbe condemnation mercilesse to him that sheweth not [h] mercy, and mercy reioyceth against condemnation.

14 [8] What auaileth it, my brethren, though a man sayth hee hath faith, when hee hath no workes? can that faith saue him?

15 [9] For if a brother or a sister be naked and destitute of daily food,

16 And one of you say vnto them, Depart in peace: warme your selues, and fill your bellies, notwithstanding yee giue them not those things, which are needfull to the body, what helpeth it?

17 Euen so the faith, if it haue no workes, is dead in it selfe.

18 But [i] some man might say, Thou hast the faith, and I haue workes: shewe me thy faith out of thy workes, and I will shewe thee my faith by my workes.

19 [10] Thou beleeuest that there is one God: thou doest well: the deuils also beleeue it, and tremble.

20 [11] But wilt thou vnderstand, O thou vaine man, that the faith *which is* without workes, is dead?

21 Was not Abraham our father [k] iustified through workes, * when hee offered Isaac his sonne vpon the altar?

22 Seest thou not that the faith [l] wrought with his workes? and through the workes was the faith made [m] perfect.

23 And the Scripture was [n] fulfilled which saith, * Abraham beleeued God, and it was imputed vnto him for righteousnesse: and hee was called the friend of God.

24 [12] Yee see then how that of workes a man is [o] iustified, and not of [p] faith onely.

5 A new argument to prooue the same conclusion: They doe not loue their neighbours, which neglect some, and ambitiously honour other: for hee doeth not obey God, which cutteth off from the cōmandements of God that that is not so commodious for him, nay he is rather guiltie generally for the breach of the whole Law, although he obserue the residue. *g Not that all sinnes are equall, but because he that breaketh one title of the Law, offendeth the maiestie of the Law giuer.* 6 A proofe: because the Law maker is alwaies the one and selfe same, and the body of the Law cannot be diuided. 7 The conclusion of ÿ whole treatise: we are vpon this condition deliuered from the curse of the Law by the mercie of God, that in like sort we should maintaine and cherish charitie and good will one towards another, and who so doth not so, shall not taste of the grace of God. *h He that is hard and currish against his neighbour, or else helpeth him not, he shall finde God an hard and rough iudge to himselfeward.* 8 The fift place which hangeth very well with the former treatise, touching a true and liuely faith. And the proposition of the place is this: Faith which bringeth not foorth workes, is not that faith whereby we are iustified, but an image of faith: or else this, they are not iustified by faith, which shewe not the effects of faith. 9 The first reason taken of a similitude: If a man say to one that is hungry, Fill thy belly, and yet giueth him nothing, this shall not be true charitie: so if a man say hee beleeueth, and bringeth foorth no workes of his faith, this shall not be a true faith, but a certaine dead thing set out with the name of faith, whereof no man hath to bragge, vnlesse hee will openly incurre reprehension, seeing that the cause is vnderstood by the effects. *i Nay, thus may euery man beate downe thy pride.* 10 Another reason taken of an absurditie: If such a faith were the true faith whereby wee are iustified, the deuils should be iustified, for they haue that, but yet notwithstanding they tremble, and are not iustified therefore, neither is that faith a true faith. 11 The third reason from the example of Abraham, who no doubt had a true faith: but he in offering his sonne, shewed himselfe to haue that faith which was not void of workes, and therefore hee receiued a true testimonie when it was said, that faith was imputed to him for righteousnesse. *k Was he not by his workes knowen and found to be iustified? for he speaketh not here of the causes of iustification, but by what effects wee may know that a man is iustified.* * *Genes.22.10.* *l Was effectuall and fruitfull with good workes.* *m That the faith was declared to be a true faith, and that by workes.* *n Then was the Scripture fulfilled, when it appeared plainely, how truely it was written of Abraham.* * *Genes.15.6. rom.4.3. galat.3.6.* 12 The conclusion: Hee is onely iustified that hath that faith which hath workes following it. *o Is prooued to be iust.* *p Of that dead and fruitlesse faith which you boast of.*

25 [13] Likewise also was not * Rahab the harlot iustified through workes, when she had receiued the messengers, and sent them out another way?

26 [14] For as the body without the spirit is dead, euen so the faith without workes is dead.

13 A fourth reason taken from a like example of Rahab the harlot, who was prooued by her workes that she was iustified by a true faith. * *Iosh.2.1.* 14 The conclusion repeated againe: faith which bringeth not foorth fruits and workes, is not faith, but a dead carkeise.

CHAP. III.

3 To shewe that a Christian man must gouerne his tongue with the bridle of faith and charitie, 9 hee declareth the commodities and mischiefe that ensue thereof: 15 and how much mans wisdome 17 differeth from heauenly.

MY [1] brethren, bee not many masters, [2] knowing that wee [a] shall receiue the greater condemnation.

2 For in many things wee || sinne all. [3] If any man sinne not in word, he is a perfite man, and able to bridle all the body.

3 [4] Behold, wee put bits into the horses mouthes, that they should obey vs, and wee turne about all their body.

4 Behold also the shippes, which though they be so great, & are driuen of fierce windes, yet are they turned about with a very small rudder, whither soeuer the gouernour lusteth.

5 Euen so the tongue is a little member, and boasteth of great things: [5] behold, how great a thing a little fire kindleth.

6 And the tongue is fire, *yea*, a [b] world of wickednesse: so is the tongue set among our members, that it defileth the whole body, and [c] setteth on fire the course of nature, and it is set on fire of hell.

7 For the whole nature of beasts, and of birds, and of creeping things, and things of the sea is tamed, and hath beene tamed of the nature of man.

8 But the tongue can no man tame. *It is* an vnruly euill, full of deadly poison.

9 Therewith blesse we God euen the Father, and therewith curse wee men, which are made after the [7] similitude of God.

10 [8] Out of one mouth proceedeth blessing and cursing: my brethren, these things ought not so to be.

11 Doeth a fountaine send foorth at one place sweete *water* and bitter?

12 Can the figge tree, my brethren, bring foorth Oliues, either a vine figges? so can no fountaine make both salt water and sweete.

13 [9] Who is a wise man and endued with

1 The fixt part or place: Let no man vsurpe (as most men ambitiously doe) authoritie to iudge and censure others rigorously. 2 A reason, Because they prouoke Gods seueritie against themselues, which do so curiously and rigorously condemne others, being themselues guiltie and faultie. *a Vnlesse we surcease from this masterlike and proud finding fault with others.* || *Or, stumble.* 3 The seuenth place, touching the bridling of the tongue, ioyned with the former, so that it is manifest that there is no man which may not iustly be found fault withall, seeing it is a rare vertue to bridle the tongue. 4 He sheweth by two similitudes, the one taken from the bridles of horses, the other from the rudder of ships, how great matters may be brought to passe by the good moderation of the tongue. 5 On the contrary part hee sheweth how great discommodities arise by the intemperancie of the tongue, throughout the whole world, to the end that men may so much the more diligently giue themselues to moderate it. *b An heape of all mischiefes.* *c It is able to set the whole world on fire.* 6 Amongst other faults of the tongue, the Apostle chiefly reprooueth backbiting and speaking euill of our neighbours, euen in them especially which otherwise will seeme godly and religious. 7 Hee denyeth by two reasons, that God can be praised by that man, that vseth cursed speaking, or to backbite: first because man is the image of God, which whosoeuer reuerenceth not, doeth not honour God himselfe. 8 Secondly, because the order of nature which God hath set in things, will not suffer things that are so contrary the one to the other, to stand the one with the other. 9 The eight part which hangeth with the former touching meeknesse of minde, against which he setteth enuie and a contentious mind. And in the beginning he stoppeth the mouth of the chiefe fountaine of all these mischiefes, to wit, a false perswasion of wisedome, whereas notwithstanding there is no true wisdome, but that is heauenly, and frameth our mindes to all kinde of true moderation and simplicitie.

knowledge among you? let him shewe by
good conuersation his workes in meekneſſe of
wiſedome.

d He ſetteth mercie againſt the fierce and cruell nature of man, and ſheweth that heauenly wiſdome bringeth foorth good fruits, for he that is heauenly wiſe, referreth all things to Gods glory, and the profite of his neighbours.

14 But if ye haue bitter enuying and ſtrife
in your hearts, reioyce not, neither be lyars a-
gainſt the trueth.
15 This wiſedome deſcendeth not from a-
boue, but *is* earthly, ſenſuall, and deuiliſh.
16 For where enuying and ſtrife *is*, there *is*
ſedition, and all maner of euill workes.
17 But the wiſedome that *is* from aboue,
is firſt pure, then peaceable, gentle, eaſie to be
intreated, full of [d] mercy and good fruits, without iudging, and without hypocriſie.
18 [10] And the fruite of righteouſneſſe is
ſowen in peace, of them that make peace.

10 Becauſe the world perſwadeth it ſelfe that they are miſerable which liue peaceably and ſimply: on the contrary ſide the Apoſtle pronounceth that they ſhall at the length reape the harueſt of peaceable righteouſneſſe.

CHAP. IIII.

1 *He reckoneth vp the miſchiefes that proceede of the workes of the fleſh,* 7 *hee exhorteth to humilitie,* 8 *and to purge the heart* 9 *from pride,* 10 *backbiting,* 14 *and the forgetfulneſſe of our owne infirmitie.*

1 He goeth on forward in the ſame argument, condemning certaine other cauſes of warres and contentions, to wit, vnbridled pleaſures and immoderate luſtes, by their effects, for ſo much as the Lord doth worthily make them void, ſo that they bring nothing elſe to them in whom they are, but incurable torments.

FRom [1] whence *are* warres and contentions among you? are they not hence, *euen*
of your pleaſures, that fight in your members?
2 Ye luſt, and haue not: ye enuie, and deſire immoderately, and cannot obtaine: yee
fight, and warre, and get nothing, [2] becauſe ye
aske not.
3 Yee aske, and receiue not, becauſe yee
aske amiſſe, that ye might lay the ſame out on
your pleaſures.
4 [3] Yee adulterers and adultereſſes, know
yee not that the amitie of the world is the enimitie of God? Whoſoeuer therefore will be
a friend of the world, maketh himſelfe the e-
nemie of God.
5 [4] Doe ye thinke that the Scripture ſaith
in vaine, The Spirit that dwelleth in vs, luſteth
after enuie?
6 But *the Scripture* offereth more grace,
and therefore ſaith, * God reſiſteth the proud,
and giueth grace to the humble.
7 * [5] Submit your ſelues to God: reſiſt the
deuill, and he will flee from you.
8 Draw neere to God, and hee will drawe
neere to you. Cleanſe your hands, ye ſinners,
and purge your hearts, ye double minded.
9 [6] Suffer afflictions, and ſorow yee, and
weepe: let your laughter be turned into mourning, and *your* ioy into [a] heauineſſe.
10 * Caſt downe your ſelues before the
Lord, and he will lift you vp.

2 He reprehendeth them by name, which are not aſhamed to goe about to make God the miniſter and helper of their luſtes and pleaſures, in asking things which either are of themſelues vnlawfull, or being lawfull, aske them to wicked purpoſes and vſes.

3 Another reaſon why ſuch vnbridled luſts and pleaſures are vtterly to be condemned, to wit, becauſe that hee that giueth himſelfe to ye world, diuorceth himſelfe from God, and breaketh the band of that holy and ſpirituall mariage. 4 The taking away of an obiection: In deede our mindes runne headlong into theſe vices, but wee ought ſo much the more diligently take heede of them: which care and ſtudie ſhall not bee in vaine, ſeeing that God reſiſteth the ſtubborne, and giueth that grace to the modeſt and humble that ſurmounteth all thoſe vices. *Prouerb 3.34. 1.pet.5.5.* * *Epheſ.4.27.* 5 The concluſion: Wee muſt ſet the contrary vertues againſt thoſe vices, and therefore whereas wee obeyed the ſuggeſtions of the deuill, wee muſt ſubmit our mindes to God, and reſiſt the deuill, with a certaine and aſſured hope of victory. To be ſhort, we muſt employ our ſelues to come neere vnto God by puritie and ſinceritie of life. 6 Hee goeth on in the ſame compariſon of contraries, and ſetteth againſt thoſe prophane ioyes an earneſt ſorow of minde, and againſt pride and arrogancie, holy modeſtie. *a By this word the Grecians meane an heauineſſe ioyned with ſhamefaſtneſſe, which is to be ſeene in a caſt downe countenance, and ſetled as it were vpon the ground.* * *1.Pet.5.6.*

11 [7] Speake not euill one of another, brethren. He that ſpeaketh euill of his brother, or
he that condemneth his brother, ſpeaketh euill
of the Lawe, and condemneth the Law: and if
thou condemneſt the Law, thou art not an ob-
ſeruer of the Law, but a Iudge.
12 There is one Lawgiuer, which is able to
ſaue, and to deſtroy. * Who art thou that iud-
geſt another man?
13 [8] Goe to now ye that ſay, To day or to
morow we will goe into ſuch a citie, and continue there a yeere, and buy and ſell, and get
gaine,
14 (And yet ye cannot tell what *ſhallbe* to
morow. For what is your life? It is euen a vapour that appeareth for a little time, and afterward vaniſheth away)
15 For that ye ought to ſay, * If the Lord
will, and, If we liue, we will doe this or that.
16 But now yee reioyce in your boaſtings:
all ſuch reioycing is euill.
17 [9] Therefore, to him that knoweth how
to doe well, and doeth it not, to him it is ſinne.

7 He reprehendeth moſt ſharply another double miſchiefe of pride: the one is, in that the proud and arrogant will haue other men to liue according to their will and pleaſure, & therefore they doe moſt arrogantly condemne whatſoeuer pleaſeth them not: which thing cannot be done without great iniury to our onely Lawmaker, for by this meanes his Lawes are found fault withall, as not circumſpectly enough written, and men chalenge that vnto themſelues which properly belongeth to God alone, in that they lay a Law vpon mens conſciences.

* *Rom.14.4.* 8 The other fault is this: That men doe ſo confidently determine vpon theſe and thoſe matters and buſineſſes, as though that euery moment of their life did not depend of God. * *1.Cor.4.19.* 9 The concluſion of all the former Treatiſe. The knowledge of the will of God, doeth not onely nothing at all profit, vnleſſe the life be anſwerable vnto it, but alſo maketh the ſinnes farre more grieuous.

CHAP. V.

1 *Hee threatneth the rich with Gods ſeuere iudgement, for their pride,* 7 *that the poore hearing the miſerable ende of the rich,* 8 *may patiently beare afflictions,* 11 *as Iob did,* 14 *euen in their diſtreſſes.*

GOe [1] to now, yee rich men: weepe, and
howle for your miſeries that ſhall come
vpon you.
2 Your riches are corrupt, and your garments are motheaten.
3 Your gold and ſiluer is cankred, and the
ruſt of them ſhalbe a witneſſe againſt you, and
ſhall eate your fleſh, as *it were* fire. Yee haue
heaped vp treaſure for the laſt dayes.
4 Behold, the hire of the labourers, which
haue reaped your fields (which is of you kept
backe by fraud) cryeth, and the cryes of them
which haue reaped, are entred into the [a] eares
of the Lord of hoſtes.
5 Yee haue liued in pleaſure on the earth,
and in wantonneſſe. Ye haue [b] nouriſhed your
hearts, as in a [c] day of ſlaughter.
6 Ye haue condemned *and* haue killed the
iuſt, and he hath not reſiſted you.
7 [2] Be patient therefore, brethren, vnto
the comming of the Lord. [3] Behold, the huſ-
bandman waiteth for the precious fruite of the
earth, and hath long patience for it, vntill he receiue the former, and the latter raine.
8 Be yee alſo patient therefore and ſettle
your hearts: for the comming of the Lorde
draweth neere.

1 He denounceth vtter deſtruction to the wicked and prophane rich men, and ſuch as are drowned in their riotouſneſſe, mocking at their fooliſh confidence when as there is nothing in deede more vaine then ſuch things.

a The Lord who is more mightie then ye are, hath heard them.

b Ye haue pampered vp your ſelues.

c The Hebrewes call a day that is appointed to ſolemne banketting, a day of ſlaughter or feaſting.

2 He applyeth that to the poore, which he ſpake againſt the rich, warning them to waite for the Lordes comming patiently, who will reuenge the iniuries which the rich men doe them. 3 The taking away of an obiection: Although his comming ſeeme to linger, yet at the leaſt we muſt follow the huſbandmen, who doe patiently waite for the times that are proper for the fruites of the earth. And againe, God will not deferre the leaſt iote of the time that he hath appointed.

9 [4] [d] Grudge

4 He commendeth Christian patience, for that where as other through impatience vse to accuse one another, the faithfull on the contrary side, complaine not although they receiue iniurie.
d By grudging he meaneth a certain inward complaining which betokeneth impatience.
5 The conclusion: The Lord is at ÿ doore: who will defend his owne, and reuenge his enemies, and therefore we need not to trouble our selues.

9 [4] [d] Grudge not one against another, brethren, lest yee be condemned: [5] behold, the
iudge standeth before the doore.
10 [6] Take, my brethren, the Prophets for
an ensample of suffering aduersitie, and of long
patience, which haue spoken in the Name of
the Lord.
11 Behold, wee count them blessed which
endure. Ye haue heard of the patience of Iob,
and haue knowen what [e] end the Lord *made*.
For the Lord is very pitifull and mercifull.
12 [7] But before all things, my brethren,
* sweare not, neither by heauen, nor by earth,
nor by any other othe: but let [f] your yea, be
yea, and *your* nay, nay, lest ye fall into condemnation.
13 [8] Is any among you afflicted? Let him
pray. Is any merrie? Let him sing.
14 [9] Is any sicke among you? Let him call
for the Elders of the Church, and let them

6 Because most men are woont to obiect, that it is good to repell iniuries by what meanes soeuer, hee setteth against that, the examples of the Fathers whose patience had a most happy end, because God as a most bountifull Father, neuer forsaketh his. *c What end the Lord gaue.* 7 Because euen the best men sometimes through impatience breake out into othes sometimes lesser, sometimes greater, the Apostle warneth vs to detest such wickednesse, and to accustome our tongues to simple and true talke. * *Mat.5 34.* *f That that you haue to say or affirme, speake or affirme it simply, and without an othe: and that that you will deny, deny it simply and flatly.* 8 Hee sheweth the best remedie against all afflictions, to wit, prayers which haue their place both in sorow and ioy. 9 He sheweth peculiarly, to what physicians especially we must goe, when we are diseased, to wit, to the prayers of the Elders, which then also could cure the body, (for so much as the gift of healing was then in force) and take away the chiefest cause of sicknesses & diseases, by obteining for the sicke through their prayers and exhortations, remission of sinnes.

pray for him, and anoint him with * [g] oyle in
the [h] Name of the Lord.
15 And the prayer of faith shall saue the
sicke, and the Lord shall raise him vp: and if
he haue committed [i] sinnes, they shall be forgiuen him.
16 [10] Acknowledge your faults one to another, and pray one for another, that ye may be
healed: [11] for the prayer of a righteous man a-
uaileth much, if it be feruent.
17 * Helias was a man subiect to like passions as we are, and he prayed earnestly that it
might not raine, and it rained not on the earth
for thee yeeres and sixe moneths.
18 And hee prayed againe, and the heauen
gaue raine, and the earth brought foorth her
fruite.
19 [12] Brethren, * if any of you hath erred
from the trueth, and some man hath [k] conuerted him,
20 Let him know that he which hath conuerted the sinner from going astray out of his
way, shall saue a soule from death, and shall
hide a multitude of sinnes.

* *Marke 6.13.*
g This was a signe of the gift of healing: and now seeing we haue the gift no more, the signe is no longer necessarie.
h By calling on the Name of the Lord.
i He hath reason in making mention of sinnes, for diseases are for the most part sent because of sinnes.
10 Because God pardoneth their sinnes which confesse and acknowledge them, and not theirs which iustifie themselues, therefore the Apostle addeth, that wee ought freely to conferre one with another touching those inward diseases, that we may helpe one another with our prayers.
11 He commendeth prayers by the effects that come of them, that all men may vnderstand that there is nothing more effectuall then they are, so that they proceede from a pure minde. * *1.King.17.1. and 18.45. luke 4.25.* 12 The taking away of an obiection: All reprehensions are not condemned, seeing that on the contrary part there is nothing more acceptable to God then to call into the way, a brother that was wandering out of the way. * *Matth.18.15.* *k Hath called him backe from his way.*

THE FIRST EPISTLE GENERALL OF PETER.

CHAP. I.

1 Hee extolleth Gods mercie shewed in Christ which we lay holde on by faith, and possesse through hope: 10 whereof the Prophets foretold. 13 He exhorteth 15 to renounce the world, 23 and their former life, and so wholly yeeld themselues to God.

1 Peter purposing to speake of the dueties of a Christian life, reasoneth first of the principles and beginnings of all Christian actions, rising farre higher then nature, and carying vs also farre aboue the same. For hee sheweth that we which are otherwise of nature sinners, were through the free mercy of God the Father first chosen from euerlasting: then according to that euerlasting decree, were by a certaine second creation made his sonnes in Christ his onely begotten, by whose Spirit wee are inwardly changed, and by whose blood we are also reconciled, to the end, that as Christ himselfe rose againe from the dead, wee also might be receiued into that same heauenly and euerlasting glory. *a Or, according to the purpose of God, who neuer altereth nor changeth the same.* *b That beeing set apart from the rest of this wicked world, through the working of the holy Ghost, they should be consecrated to God, Ephes. 1.5.* *c Euerlasting hope.*

Eter an Apostle of IESVS
CHRIST, to the strangers
that dwell heere and there
throughout Pontus, Gala-
tia, Cappadocia, Asia and
Bithynia,
2 [1] Elect according to the [a] foreknowledge of God the Father vnto [b] sanctification
of the Spirit, through obedience and sprinkling of the blood of Iesus Christ: Grace and
peace be multiplyed vnto you.
3 Blessed *be* God, euen the Father of our
Lord Iesus Christ, which according to his a-
bundant mercy hath begotten vs againe vnto
a [c] liuely hope by the resurrection of Iesus
Christ from the dead,
4 To an inheritance immortall and vndefiled, and that withereth not, reserued in heauen for vs,
5 [2] Which are kept by the power of God
through faith vnto saluation, which is prepared to be shewed in the [d] last time.
6 Wherein yee reioyce, though now for
a season (if neede require) ye are in heauinesse,
through manifold tentations,
7 That the triall of your faith being much
more precious then golde that perisheth
(though it be tryed with fire) might be found
vnto *your* praise, and honour and glory at the
[e] appearing of Iesus Christ:
8 Whom ye haue not seene, and yet loue
him, in whom now, though ye see him not, yet
do you beleeue, and reioyce with ioy vnspeak-
able and glorious,
9 Receiuing the || end of your faith, *euen*
the saluation of *your* soules.
10 [3] Of the which saluation the Prophets
haue enquired and searched, which prophecied
of the grace that should come vnto you,

2 Now he sheweth by what way we come vnto that glory, to wit, through all kinde of afflictions, wherein notwithstanding faith maketh vs so secure, that we are not onely not ouercome with sorow, but also through the beholding of God himselfe (who otherwise is inuisible) with the eyes of faith, are vnspeakably ioyfull: because all such things, as they are but for a time, so are they not applied vnto vs to destroy vs, but as it were by fire to purge vs, and to make vs perfite, that at ÿ length we may obtaine saluation.
d This is that time which Daniel calleth the time of the end, when as that great restoring of all things shall be, which all creatures looke for, Rom.8.19. *e He speaketh of the second comming of Christ.* *|| Or, reward.* 3 He putteth a difference betweene true faith, that is to say, that faith which onely hath an eye to the doctrine of the Prophets and Apostles, and false faith: Afterward hee maketh two degrees of one and the selfe same faith, according to the maner of the diuers reuelations, when as in deed it is but one onely faith. Thirdly, he saith, that the preaching of the Apostles is the fulfilling of the preaching of the Prophets, although the latter end of it be as yet looked for of the very Angels.

11 Searching when or what time the Spirit
which testified before of Christ which was in
them, should declare the sufferings *that should
come* vnto Christ, and the glory that should
follow.
12 Vnto whom it was reuealed, that not vnto themselues, but vnto vs they should minister
the things, which are now shewed vnto you by
them which haue preached vnto you the Gospel by the holy Ghost [f] sent downe frō heauen,
the which things the Angels desire to behold.
13 [4] Wherefore, [g] girde vp the loynes of
your minde: be sober, [5] and trust [h] perfectly on
that grace [6] that is brought vnto you, [7] in the
reuelation of Iesus Christ,
14 [8] As obedient children, not fashioning
your selues vnto the former lustes of your ignorance:
15 But as he which hath called you, is holy,
so be ye holy in * all manner of conuersation,
16 [9] Because it is written, * Be ye holy, for
I am holy.
17 [10] And if yee [i] call him Father, which
without * respect of person iudgeth according
to euery mans worke, passe the time of your
dwelling here in feare,
18 [11] Knowing that ye were not redeemed
with corruptible things, *as* siluer and golde,
from your vaine conuersation, receiued by the
traditions of the fathers,
19 * But with the precious blood of Christ,
as of a Lambe vndefiled, and without spot,
20 [12] Which was * ordained before the
[k] foundation of the world, but was declared in
the last times for your sakes,
21 Which by his meanes do beleeue in God
that raised him from the dead, & gaue him glory, that your faith and hope might be in God.
22 [13] Hauing purified your soules in obey-

f He alludeth to the prophecie of Ioel, which was exhibited vpon the day of Pentecost, in the Apostles, as it were in the first fruites of the holy Ghost, which this same our Peter declareth, Acts 2.6.

4 He goeth from faith to hope, which is in deede a companion that cannot be sundered from faith: and he vseth an argument taken of comparison: We ought not to be wearied in looking for so excellent a thing, which the very Angels wait for with great desire.

g This is a borrowed speech, taken of a common vsage amongst them: for by reason that they wore long garments, they could not trauaile vnlesse they girded vp themselues: and hence it is that Christ said, Let your loines be girded vp.

5 He setteth foorth very briefly, what maner of hope ours ought to be, to wit, continuall, vntill we enioy the thing wee hope for: then, what we haue to hope for, to wit, grace (that is, free saluation) reueiled to vs in the Gospel, and not that, that men doe rashly and fondly promise to themselues. *h Soundly and sincerely.* 6 An argument to stirre vp our mindes, seeing that God doeth not wait till wee seeke him, but causeth so great a benefite to be brought euen vnto vs. 7 He setteth out the ende of faith, lest any man should promise himselfe, either sooner or latter, that full saluation, to wit, the latter comming of Christ, and therewithall warneth vs, not to measure the dignitie of the Gospel according to the present state, seeing that that which we are now, is not yet reueiled. 8 He passeth from faith & hope, to the fruites of them both, which are vnderstood in the name of obedience: And it consisteth in two things, in renouncing our lustes, and liuing godly: which lusts haue their beginning of that blindnesse wherein all men are borne: but holinesse proceedeth from the grace and fauour of God which adopteth vs, and therefore regenerateth vs, that the father and the children may be of one disposition. * *Luke* 1.75. 9 He sheweth that sanctification doeth necessarily follow adoption. * *Leuit.* 11.44. *and* 19.2. *and* 20.7. 10 As before hee distinguished true faith and hope from false, so doeth hee now obedience, setting the quicke and sharpe sight of God, against an outward maske, and earnest reuerence against vaine seueritie. *i If you will be called the sonnes of that father.* * *Deut.* 10.17. *rom.* 2.11. *gal.* 2.6. 11 An exhortation, wherein he setteth foorth the excellencie and greatnesse of the benefite of God the Father in sanctifying vs by the death of his owne Sonne. And he partly setteth the purifyings of the Law against the thing it selfe, that is, against the blood of Christ, and partly also mens traditions, which he condemneth as vtterly vaine and superstitious, be they neuer so olde and ancient. * 1.*Cor.* 6.20. *and* 7.23. *hebr.* 9.14. 1.*iohn* 1.7. *reuelat.* 1.5. 12 The taking away of an obiection: what was done to the world, before that Christ was sent into the world? was there no holinesse before, and was there no Church? The Apostle answereth, that Christ was ordained and appointed to redeeme and deliuer mankinde, before that mankinde was: much lesse was there any Church without him before his comming in the flesh: yet wee are happiest aboue the rest, to whom Christ was exhibited in deede, in this that hee hauing suffered and ouercome death for vs, doeth now most effectually worke in vs by the vertue of his Spirit, to create in vs faith, hope, and charitie. * *Rom.* 16.25. *ephes.* 3.9. *coloss.* 1.26. 2.*tim* 1.10. *titus* 1.2. *k From euerlasting.* 13 He commendeth the practise of obedience, that is, charitie: earnestly beating into their heads againe, that hee speaketh not of any common charitie, and such as proceedeth from that our corrupt nature, but of that whose beginning is the Spirit of God, which purifieth our soules through the word laid holde on by faith, and ingendreth also in vs a spirituall and euerlasting life, as God himselfe is most pure and truely liuing.

ing the trueth through the spirit, to * loue brotherly without faining, loue one another with
a pure heart feruently,
23 Being borne anew, not of mortall seede,
but of immortall, by the word of God, who liueth and endureth for euer.
24 [14] For all * [l] flesh *is* as grasse, and all the
glory of man *is* as the flower of grasse. The
grasse withereth, and the flower falleth away,
25 [15] But the word of the Lord endureth
for euer: and this is the word which is preached among you.

* *Chap.* 2.17. *rom.* 2.10. *ephes.* 4.2.

14 A reason why wee haue need of this heauenly generation, to wit, because that men, be their glory neuer so great, are of nature void of all true and sound goodnesse.

* *Esai* 4.6. *iames* 1.10.

l The word (Flesh) sheweth the weaknesse of our nature, which is chiefly to be considered in the flesh it selfe. 15 Againe lest any man should seeke that spirituall force and vertue in fained imaginations, the Apostle calleth vs backe to the word of God: teaching vs furthermore, that there is no other word of the Lord to be looked for, then this which is preached, in which onely wee must trust.

CHAP. II.

1 Hee exhorteth the new borne in faith, to leade their liues answerable to the same: 6 and lest their faith should stagger, he bringeth in that which was foretolde touching Christ. 11 Then he willeth them to be obedient to Magistrates, 20 and that they patiently beare aduersitie after Christes example.

Wherefore, * [1] laying aside all maliciousnesse, and all guile, and dissimulation, and enuie, and all euill speaking,
2 [2] As [a] new borne babes desire that sincere milke of the word, that yee may growe
thereby,
3 [3] Because ye ‖ haue tasted that the Lord
is bountifull.
4 [4] To whom comming, as vnto a liuing
stone disallowed of men, but chosen of God
and precious,
5 Ye also as liuely stones, be made a spirituall house, [5] an holy * Priesthood to offer vp
spirituall sacrifices acceptable to God by Iesus
Christ.
6 [6] Wherefore also it is conteined in the
Scripture, * Behold, I put in Sion a chiefe corner stone, elect and precious: and he that beleeueth therein, shall not be ashamed.
7 [7] Vnto you therefore which beleeue, it is

* *Rom.* 6.4. *ephe.* 4.23. *colos.* 3.8. *hebr.* 12.1.

1 Hauing laid for the foundation the Spirit of God effectually working by the word, and hauing built thereupon three vertues which are the grounds of all Christian actions, to wit, faith, hope, and charity: now he proceedeth to a generall exhortation, the first member whereof is, that we flee all shew, both of secret and also open malice.

2 The second is, that being newly begotten and borne of the new seede of the vncorrupt word, drawing and sucking greedily the same word as milke, we should more and more as it were grow vp in that spirituall life. And he calleth it, sincere, not onely because it is a most pure thing, but also that we should take heed of them which corrupt it. *a As it becommeth new men.* 3 He commendeth that spiritual nourishment for the sweetnesse and profite of it. ‖ *Or, doe taste.* 4 He goeth on forward in the same exhortation, but vseth another kind of borrowed speech, alluding to the Temple. Therefore hee saith, that the companie of the faithfull is as it were a certaine holy and spirituall building, built of the liuely stones, the foundation whereof is Christ, as a liuely stone susteining all that are ioyned vnto him, with his liuing vertue, & knitting them together with himselfe, although this so great a treasure be neglected of men. 5 Going forward in the same similitude, hee compareth vs now to Priests, placed to this end in that spirituall Temple, that wee should serue him with a spirituall worship, that is, with holinesse and righteousnesse: but as the Temple, so is the Priesthood built vpon Christ, in whom only all our spirituall offerings are accepted. * *Reuel.* 1.6. 6 He prooueth it by the testimonie of the Prophet Esai. * *Esai* 28.16. *rom* 9.33. 7 By setting the most blessed condition of the beleeuers, & the most miserable of the rebellious one against the other, he pricketh forward the beleeuers, & triumpheth ouer the other: and also preuenteth an offence which ariseth hereof, that none doe more resist this doctrine of the Gospel, then they which are chiefest amongst the people of God, as were at that time that Peter wrote these things, the Priests, and Elders, and Scribes. Therefore he answereth first of all, that there is no cause why any man should be astonished at this their stubbornnesse, as though it were a strange matter, seeing wee haue bene forewarned so long before, that it should so come to passe: and moreouer, that it pleased God to create and make certaine to this selfe same purpose, that the Sonne of God might be glorified in their iust cōdemnation. Thirdly, for that the glory of Christ is hereby set foorth greatly, whereas notwithstanding Christ remaineth the sure head of his Church, and they that stumble at him, cast downe and ouerthrow themselues, and not Christ. Fourthly, although they be created to this ende and purpose, yet their fall and decay is not to be attributed to God, but to their owne obstinate stubbornnesse, which commeth betweene Gods decree, and the execution thereof, or their condemnation, and is the true and proper cause of their destruction.

precious:

precious: but vnto them which be disobedient,
the * stone which the builders disalowed, the
same is made the head of the corner,
8 And a * stone to stumble at, and a rocke
of offence, euen *to them* which stumble at the
word, being disobedient, vnto the which thing
they were euen ordeined.
9 [8] But ye are a chosen generation, a royall * Priesthood, an holy nation, a people set at
libertie, that ye should shew forth the vertues
of him that hath called you out of darkenesse
into his maruellous light,
10 * Which in times past were not a people, yet *are* now the people of God: which in
time past were not vnder mercie, but nowe
haue obteined mercie.
11 [9] Dearely beloued, [10] I beseech you, as
strangers and pilgrims, * [11] absteine from flesh-
lie lusts, [12] which fight against the soule,
12 [13] * And haue your conuersation honest
among the Gentiles, that they which speake e-
uill of you as of euill doers, [14] may by *your*
* good works which they shal see, glorifie God
in the day of [b] visitation.
13 [15] * Therefore submit your selues vnto
[c] all maner ordinance of man [16] for the Lords
sake, [17] whether it be vnto the King, as vnto the
superiour,
14 Or vnto gouernours, as vnto them that
are sent of him, [18] for the punishment of euill
doers, and for the praise of them that doe well.
15 [19] For so is the will of God, that by well
doing ye may put to silence the ignorance of
the foolish men,
16 As free, and not as hauing the libertie
for a cloake of maliciousnesse, but as the seruants of God.
17 [20] [d] Honour all men: * loue [e] brotherly

Psal. 118.22. *matth.* 21.42. *actes* 4.11.
* *Esai.* 8.14. *rom.* 9.33.
8 The contrary member, to wit, he describeth the singular excellencie of the elect, and also lest any man should doubt whether he be chosen or not, the Apostle calleth vs backe to the effectuall calling, that is, to the voyce of the Gospel sounding both in our eares and minds by the outward preaching and Sacraments, whereby we may certainely vnderstand that euerlasting decree of our saluation, (which otherwise is most secret and hidden) and that through the onely mercie of God who freely chuseth and calleth vs. Therefore this only remaineth, saith he, that by all meanes possible we set forth so great goodnes of the most mightie God.
* *Exod.* 19.6.
* *Hose* 2.23. *rom.* 9.25.
9 He returneth to that generall exhortation.
10 A reason why we ought to liue holily, to wit, because we are citizens of heauen, and therefore we ought to liue according to the Lawes not of this world, which is most corrupt, but of the heauenly citie, although we be strangers in the world. * *Rom.* 13.14. *gal.* 5.16. 11 Another argument: The children of God liue not according to the flesh, that is, according to that corrupt nature, but according to the spirit. Therfore fleshly motions ought not to beare rule in vs. 12 The third argument: for although those lusts flatter vs, yet they cease not to fight against our saluation. 13 The fourth argument, taken of the profit of so doing: for by this meanes also we prouide for our good name & estimation, whilest we compell them at length to change their minds, which speake euil of vs. * *Chap.* 3.16. 14 The fifth argument, which also is of great force: Because the glory of God is greatly set forth by that meanes, whilest by example of our honest life, euen the most prophane men are brought vnto God, and submit themselues vnto him. * *Mat.* 5.16. *b When God shall haue mercie on them.* 15 That which he spake generally, he now expoundeth by parts, describing seuerally euery mans duetie. And first of all he speaketh of obedience which is due both to the Lawes, and also to the Magistrates both higher and lower. * *Rom.* 13.1. *c By ordinance, is meant the framing and ordering of ciuill gouernement: which he calleth ordinance of man, not because man inuented it, but because it is proper to men.* 16 The first argument: because the Lord is the Authour and reuenger of this policie of men, that is, which is set amongst men: and therefore the true seruants of the Lord must aboue all others be diligent obseruers of this order. 17 Hee preuenteth a cauill which is made by some, that say they will obey Kings and the higher Magistrates, and yet contemne their ministers: as though their ministers were not armed with their authotity which sent them. 18 The second argument taken of the end of this order, which is not onely most profitable, but also very necessary: seeing that by that this meanes vertue is rewarded, and vice punished: wherein the quietnesse and happinesse of this life consisteth. 19 He declareth the first argument more amply, shewing that Christian libertie doeth amongst all things least or not at all consist herein, to wit, to cast off the bridle of Lawes, (as at that time some altogether vnskilfull in the Kingdome of God reported) but rather in this, that liuing holily according to the will of God, we should make manifest to all men, that the Gospel is not a cloake for sinne and wickednesse, seeing we are in such sort free, that yet we are still the seruants of God, and not of sinne. 20 He diuideth the ciuill life of man, by occasion of those things which he spake, into two generall parts: to wit, into those dueties which priuate men owe to priuate men, and especially the faithfull to the faithfull, and into that subiection whereby inferiours are bonnd to their superiours: but so, that Kings be not made equall to God, seeing that feare is due to God, and honour to Kings. *d Bee charitable and duetifull towards all men.* * *Chap.* 1.22. *rom.* 12.10. *e The assemblie and fellowship of the brethren, as Zecharie* 11.14.

fellowship: feare God: honour the King.
18 * [21] Seruants, be subiect to your masters
with all feare, not onely to the good and courteous, but also to the froward.
19 * [22] For this is thanke worthy, if a man
for [f] conscience toward God endure griefe,
suffering wrongfully.
20 For what praise is it, if when ye be buffeted for your faults, yee take it patiently? but
and if when ye doe well, ye suffer *wrong* and
take it patiently, this is acceptable to God.
21 [23] For hereunto ye are called: for Christ
also suffred for you, leauing you an [g] ensample
that ye should follow his steps.
22 * Who did no sinne, neither was there
guile found in his mouth.
23 Who when he was reuiled, reuiled not
againe: when he suffered, hee threatned not,
but [24] committed it to him [25] that iudgeth righteously.
24 * [26] Who his owne selfe bare our sinnes
in his body on the tree, that we being dead to
sinne, should liue in righteousnesse: by whose
stripes ye were healed.
25 For ye were as sheepe going astray: but
are now returned vnto the shepheard and Bishop of your soules.

* *Ephes.* 5.6. *colos.* 3.22.
21 He goeth to the duetie of seruants towards their masters, which he describeth with these bounds, that seruants submit themselues willingly and not by constraint, not onely to the good and courteous, but also to the froward and sharpe masters.
* 2 *Cor.* 7.10.
22 The taking away of an obiection: Indeed the condition of seruants is hard, especially if they haue froward masters: but this their subiection shalbe so much the more acceptable to God, if his will preuaile more with seruants, then the masters iniuries.
f Because he maketh a conscience of it, to offend God, by whose good will and appointment he knoweth this burden is laid vpon him. 23 He mitigateth the grieuousnesse of seruitude, while he sheweth plainely that Christ died also for seruants, that they should beare so much the more patiently this inequalitie betwixt men which are of one selfe same nature: moreouer setting before them Christ that Lord of lords for an ensample, he signifieth that they cannot but seeme too delicate, which shew themselues more grieued in bearing of iniuries, then Christ himselfe who was most iust, and most sharpely of all afflicted, and yet was most patient. *g A borrowed kinde of speech taken of painters and schoolemasters.* * *Esai.* 53.9. 1.*iohn* 3.5. 24 He sheweth them a remedie against iniuries, to wit, that they commend their cause to God, by the example of Christ. 25 Hee seemeth now to turne his speech to masters, which haue also themselues a master and iudge in heauen, who will iustly reuenge their iniuries that are done to seruants, without any respect of persons. * *Esai.* 53.5. *matth* 8.17. 26 He calleth the seruants backe from the consideration of the iniuries which they are constrained to beare, to thinke vpon the greatnesse and the end of the benefit receiued of Christ.

CHAP. III.

1 That christian women should not contemne their husbands though they be infidels, 5 he bringeth in examples of godly women. 8 Generall exhortations, 14 patiently to beare persecutions, 15 and boldly to yeelde a reason of their faith. 18 Christes example.

Likewise * [1] let the wiues bee subiect to their
husbandes, [2] that euen they which obey
not the word, may without the word be wonne
by the conuersation of the wiues,
2 While they behold your pure conuersation, which is with feare.
3 * [3] Whose apparelling, let it not be that
outward, with broided haire, and gold put a-
bout, or in putting on of apparell:
4 But let it bee the [a] hid man of the heart,
which consisteth in the incorruption of a meeke
and quiet spirit, which is [b] before God a thing
much set by.
5 [4] For euen after this maner in time past
did the holy women, which trusted in God tire
themselues, & were subiect to their husbands.

* *Col.* 3.18. *eph.* 5.22.
1 In the third place he setteth forth the wiues dueties to their husbands, commanding them to be obedient.
2 He speaketh namely of them which had husbands that were not Christians, which ought so much the more bee subiect to their husbands, that by their honest and chaste conuersation, they may gaine them to the Lord.
* 1.*Tim.* 2.9.
3 He condemneth the riot and excesse of women, and setteth foorth their true apparelling, such as is precious before God, to wit, the inward and incorruptible, which consisteth in a meeke and quiet spirit. *a Who hath his seat fastened in the heart: so that the hid man is set against the outward decking of the body.* *b Precious in deed and so taken of God.* 4 An argument taken of the example of women, and especially of Sara, which was the mother of all beleeuers.

* Gene.18.12.
5 Because women are of nature fearefull, he giueth them to vnderstand that he requireth of them that subiection, which is not wrung out of them either by force or feare
* 1.Cor.7.3.
6 He teacheth husbands also their dueties, to wit, that the more vnderstanding and wisedome they haue, the more wisely and circumspectly they behaue themselues.
c Doe all the dueties of wedlocke.
d The more wisedome the husband hath, the more circumspectly he must behaue himselfe in bearing those discommodities, which through the womans weakenes oft times cause trouble both to the husband & the wife.
7 The second argument: because the wife notwithstanding that she is weaker by nature then the man, is an excellent instrument of the man, made to farre most excellent vses: whereupon it foloweth, that she is not therefore to be neglected, because shee is weake, but on the contrary

6 As Sara obeyed Abraham, and * called
him Sir: whose daughters ye are, whiles ye do
well, [5] not being afraid of any terrour.
7 * [6] Likewise ye husbands, [c] dwell with
them as men of [d] knowledge [7] giuing [e] honour
vnto the woman, as vnto the weaker [f] vessel,
[8] euen as they which are heires together of the
[g] grace of life, [9] that your prayers be not interrupted.
8 [10] Finally, be yee all of one minde: one
suffer with another: loue as brethren: *be* pitifull: *be* courteous,
9 * [11] Not rendring euill for euill, neither
rebuke for rebuke: but contrariwise, blesse,
[12] knowing that ye are thereunto called, that ye
should be heires of blessing.
10 * [13] For if any man long after life, and to
[h] see good dayes, let him refraine his tongue
from euill, and his lippes that they speake no
guile.
11 * Let him eschew euill, and doe good:
let him seeke peace, and follow after it.
12 For the eyes of the Lord *are* ouer the
righteous, and his eares *are open* vnto their
prayers: and the [i] face of the Lord *is* against
them that doe euill.
13 [14] And who is it that will harme you, if
ye follow that which is good?
14 * Notwithstanding blessed *are ye*, if yee
suffer for righteousnesse sake. [15] Yea, * feare
not their [k] feare, neither be troubled.
15 But [l] sanctifie the Lord GOD in your
hearts: [16] and be ready alwayes to giue an answere
to euery man that asketh you a reason of
the hope that is in you, with meekenesse and
reuerence,
16 Hauing a good conscience, that when

part she ought to be so much the more cared for. *e Hauing an honest care of her.* *f The woman is called a vessell after the maner of the Hebrewes, because the husband vseth her as his fellow and helper, to liue faithfully before God.* 8 The third argument: for that they are equal in that which is the chiefest (that is to say, in the benefit of eternal life) which otherwise are vnequall as touching the gouernance and conuersation at home, and therefore they are not to be despised although they be weake. *g Of that gracious and free benefit, whereby we haue euerlasting life giuen vs.* 9 The fourth argument: All brawlings and chidings must be eschewed, because they hinder prayers and the whole seruice of God, whereunto both the husband and wife are equally called. 10 He turneth to common exhortations, and commendeth concord and whatsoeuer things pertaine to the maintenance of peace and mutuall loue. * *Prou.17.13. and 20.22. matth.5.39. rom.12.17. 1.thess.5.15.* 11 Wee must not onely not recompense iniurie for iniurie, but we must also recõpense them with benefits. 12 An argument taken of comparison: Seeing that we our selues are called of God whome we offend so often, to so great a benefite, (so farre is he from reuenging the iniuries which we doe vnto him,) shall wee rather make our selues vnworthy of so great bountifulnesse, then forgiue one anothers faults? And from this verse to the ende of the Chapter, there is a digression or going from the matter he is in hand with, to exhort vs valiantly to beare afflictions. * *Psal. 34.13.* 13 A secret obiection: But this our patience shall be nothing els but a fleshing and hardening of the wicked in their wickednesse, to make them set vpon vs more boldly and destroy vs. Nay (saith the Apostle by the words of Dauid) to liue without doing hurt, and to follow after peace when it flieth away, is the way to that happie and quiet peace. And if so be any man be afflicted for doing iustly, the Lord marketh all things, and will in his time deliuer the godly, which crie vnto him, and will destroy the wicked. *h Leade a blessed and happie life.* * *Esai.1.16.* *i This worde (Face) after the maner of the Hebrewes, is taken for (anger.)* 14 The second argument: when the wicked are prouoked, they are more wayward: therefore they must rather bee ouercome with good turnes. And if they cannot be gotten by that meanes also, yet notwithstanding we shal be blessed if we suffer for righteousnes sake. * *Matth.5.10.* 15 A most certaine counsell in afflictions, be they neuer so terrible, to be of a constant minde, & to stand fast. But how shall we attaine vnto it? If we sanctifie God in our mindes and hearts, that is to say, if we rest vpon him as one that is Almightie, that loueth mankind, that is good and true indeed. * *Esai.8.12,13.* *k Be not dismaied as they are.* *l Giue him all prayse and glory, and hang onely on him.* 16 He will haue vs, when we are afflicted for righteousnesse sake, to be carefull not for redeeming of our life, either with denying or renouncing the trueth, or with like violence, or any such meanes: but rather to giue an account of our faith boldly, and yet with a meeke spirit, and full of godly reuerence, that the enemies may not haue any thing iustly to obiect, but may rather be ashamed of themselues.

they speake euill of you as of euill doers, they
may bee ashamed, which slander your good
conuersation in Christ.
17 [17] For *it is* better (if the will of God be
so) that ye suffer for well doing, then for euill
doing.
18 * [18] For Christ also hath once suffered
for sinnes, [19] the iust for the vniust, [20] that hee
might bring vs to God, [21] and was put to death
concerning the [m] flesh, but was quickened by
the spirit.
19 [22] By || the which he also went, and preached
vnto the || spirits that *are* in prison,
20 Which were in time passed disobedient,
when [n] once the long suffering of God abode
in the dayes of * Noe, while the Arke was preparing,
wherein fewe, that is, eight [o] soules
were saued in the water.
21 [23] Whereof the baptisme *that* nowe *is*,
answering that figure, (*which is* not a putting
away of the filth of the flesh, but a confident
demanding which a good conscience maketh
to [p] God) saueth vs also [24] by the resurrection
of Iesus Christ,
22 Which is at the right hande of God,
gone into heauen, to whome the Angels, and
Powers, and might are subiect.

17 A reason which standeth vpon two generall rules of Christianitie, which notwithstanding all men allow not of. The one is, if we must needs suffer afflictions, it is better to suffer wrongfully then rightfully: the other is this, because we are so afflicted not by hap, but by the will of our God.
* *Rom.5.6. heb.9.15.*
18 A proofe of either of ỹ rules, by the example of Christ himselfe our chiefe paterne, who was afflicted not for his owne sinnes (which were none) but for ours, and that according to his Fathers decree.
19 An argument taken of comparison: Christ the iust, suffered for vs that are vniust, & shall it grieue vs which are vniust, to suffer for the Iusts cause? 20 An other argument being partly taken of things coupled together, to wit, because Christ bringeth vs to his Father that same way that he went himselfe, and partly from the cause efficient: to wit, because Christ is not onely set before vs for an example to follow, but also he holdeth vs vp by his vertue in all the difficulties of this life, vntill he bring vs to his Father. 21 An other argument taken of the happie ende of these afflictions, wherein also Christ goeth before vs both in example and vertue, as one who suffered most grieuous torments euen vnto death, although but in one part onely of him, to wit, in the flesh or mans nature: but yet became conquerour by the vertue of his diuinitie. *m As touching his manhood, for his body was dead, and his soule felt the sorowes of death.* 22 A secret obiection: Christ in deede might doe this, but what is that to vs? Yes (saith the Apostle) for Christ hath shewed forth his vertue in all ages both to the preseruation of the godly, were they neuer so few and miserable, and to reuenge the rebellion of his enemies, as it appeareth by the history of the flood: for Christ is he which in those dayes (when God through his patience appoynted a time of repentance to the world) was present, not in corporall presence, but by his diuine vertue, preaching repentance, euen by the mouth of Noe himselfe who then prepared the Arke, to those disobedient spirits which are now in prison, waiting for the full recompence of their rebellion, and saued those few, (that is, eight onely persons) in the water. *|| By the vertue of which Spirit, that is to say, of the diuinitie: therefore this word, Spirit, cannot in this place bee taken for the soule, vnlesse we wil say that Christ was raised vp againe & quickned by the vertue of his soule. || He calleth them spirits, in respect of his time, not in respect of the time that they were in the flesh.* *n This worde (once) sheweth that there was a furthermost day appointed, and if that were once past, there should be no more.* * *Gene.6.14. mat.24.38. luke 17.26.* *o Men.* 23 A proportionall applying of the former example to the time which followed the comming of Christ: for that preseruation of Noe in the waters, was a figure of our Baptisme, not as though the materiall water of Baptisme saueth vs, as those waters which bare vp the Arke saued Noe, but because Christ with his inward vertue, which the outward baptisme shadoweth, preserueth vs being washed, so that we may call vpon God with a good conscience. *p The conscience being sanctified, may freely call vpon God.* 24 That selfe same vertue, whereby Christ rose againe, and now being caried vp into heauen hath receiued all power, doeth at this day defend and preserue vs

CHAP. IIII.

1 He bringeth in Christes example, and applieth it 6 to the mortifying of the flesh, especially commending charitie: 12 And so intreateth of patience. 17 That it is necessarie that correction begin at the Church.

Forasmuch [1] then as Christ hath suffered for
vs in the flesh, arme your selues likewise
with the same minde, *which is*, that he which
hath suffered in the flesh, hath ceased from
sinne.
2 That hee henceforward should liue (as

1 Hauing ended his digression and sliding from his matter, now he returneth to the exhortation which he brake off, taking occasion by that which he said touching the death & resurrection of Christ, so defining our sanctification, that to be sanctified, is all one as to suffer in the flesh, that is to say, to leaue off from our wickednesse and vicioulnesse: and to rise againe to God, that is to say, to be renued by the vertue of the holy Ghost, that we may leade the rest of our life which remaineth after the will of God.

much

much time as [a] remaineth in the flesh) not
after the lustes of men, but after the will of
God.
3 *[2]For it is sufficient for vs that we haue
spent the time past of the life, after the [b] lust of
the Gentiles, walking in wantonnesse, lustes,
drunkennesse,in gluttonie,drinkings, and in a-
bominable idolatries.
4 [3]Wherein it seemeth to them [c] strange,
that yee runne not with them vnto the same
excesse of riot: *therefore* speake they euill *of*
you,
5 Which shall giue accounts to him, that
is ready to iudge quicke and dead.
6 [4]For vnto this purpose was the Gospel preached also vnto the dead, that they
might be condemned, according to men in the
flesh, but might liue according to God in the
spirit.
7 [5]Nowe the ende of all things is at
hand. Be ye therefore sober, and watching in
prayer.
8 [6]But aboue all things haue feruent loue
among you: *for loue shall couer the multitude of sinnes.
9 [7]Be ye *harberous one to another, without grudging.
10 [8]*Let euery man as hee hath receiued
the gift, minister the same one to another, [9]as
good disposers of the manifolde graces of
God.
11 [10]If any man speake *let him speake* as
the words of God. If any man minister, *let*
him doe it as of the abilitie which God ministreth, that God in all things may be glorified
through Iesus Christ, to whom is praise & dominion for euer, and euer, Amen.
12 [11]Dearely beloued, thinke it not [d] strange,
[12]concerning the fierie triall, which is among
you to prooue you, as though some strange
thing were come vnto you:
13 [13]But reioyce, in as much as yee are
partakers of Christes sufferings, that when
his glory shall appeare, yee may bee glad and
reioyce.

a So much of this present life as remaineth yet to be passed ouer. *Ephe. 4.22. 2 By putting vs in minde of the dishonestie of our former life led in the filth of sinne, he calleth vs to earnest repentance. *b Wickedly and licenciously after the maner of the Gentiles.* 3 That we be not moued with the enemies peruerse and slanderous iudgments of vs, we haue to set against them that last iudgement of God which remaineth for them: for none, whether they be then found liuing, or were dead before, shal escape it. *c They thinke it a new and strange matter.* 4 A digression: because he made mention of the last generall iudgement. And he preuenteth an obiection, that, seeing Christ came very lately, they may seeme to be excuseable which died before. But this the Apostle denieth: for (saith hee) this selfe same Gospel was preached vnto them also (for he speaketh vnto the Iewes,) and that to the same end that I now preach it vnto you, to wit, that the flesh being abolished and put away (that is to say, that wicked & naughtie corruption which reigneth in men) they should suffer themselues to bee gouerned by the vertue of the Spirit of God. 5 Hee returneth to his purpose, vsing an Argument taken from the circumstance of the time. Because the last ende is at hand, and therefore wee must so much the more diligently watch and pray, with true sobrietie of minde. 6 Hee commendeth charitie of one towards another, because it doeth as it were burie a multitude of sinnes, and therefore preserueth and maintaineth peace and concord: for they that loue one another doe easily forgiue one another their offences. * *Prouerbes* 10.12. 7 Of all the dueties of charitie, he commendeth one, namely which was at that time most necessarie, to wit, hospitalitie, which hee will haue to be voluntarie and most courteous and bountifull. * *Romanes* 12.13. *heb.*13.2. 8 He sheweth the vse of charitie, to wit, that euery man bestowe that gift which he hath receiued, to the profite of his neighbour. * *Rom.* 12.6. *phil.* 2.14. 9 A reason, because that what gift soeuer we haue, wee haue receiued it of God vpon this condition, to bee his disposers and stewards. 10 He reckoneth vp two kindes of these gifts as chiefe, to wit, the office of teaching in the Church, and the other Ecclesiasticall functions, wherein two things especially are to bee obserued: to wit, that the pure word of God be taught, and whatsoeuer is done, bee referred to the glory of God the Father in Christ, as to the proper marke. 11 Because the crosse is ioyned with the sincere profession of religion, the Apostle fitly repeateth that which he touched before, warning vs not to be troubled at persecutions and afflictions, as at a new and strange thing. *d As though some newe thing had befallen you, which you neuer thought of before.* 12 The first reason: because the Lord meaneth not to consume vs with his fire (as it were) but to purge vs of our drosse and make vs perfit. 13 Another reason: Because the afflictions of the godly and the wicked differ very much, and chiefly in three points. First, because the godly communicate with Christ in their afflictions, and therefore shall in their time be partakers also of his glorie,

14 *[14]If ye be railed vpon for the Name
of Christ, blessed *are ye*: for the [e] Spirit of glory, and of God resteth vpon you: *which* on
their part is euill spoken of: but on your part
is glorified.
15 [15]But let none of you suffer as a murtherer, or *as* a thiefe, or an euill doer, or as a busie
bodie in other mens matters.
16 But if *any man suffer* as a Christian, let
him not be ashamed: but let him glorifie God
in this behalfe.
17 [16]For the time *is come*, that iudgement
must begin at the house of God. [17]If it first
begin at vs, what shal the end be of them which
obey not the Gospel of God?
18 *And if the righteous scarcely bee saued, where shall the vngodly and the sinner appeare?
19 [18]Wherefore let them that suffer according to the will of God, commit their soules *to*
him in well doing, as vnto a faithfull Creator.

* *Matth* 5.10. 14 Secondly, because that although the infide's thinke far otherwise, who in afflicting the godly blaspheme God, yet the godly in that they are so railed vpon, are honoured of God with the true spirituall glory, and their adoption is sealed to them by the Spirit of God. *e By Spirit, he meaneth the gifts of the Spirit.* 15 The third difference: for the godly are not afflicted for their euill doings, but for righteousnesse sake as Christians: whereby it commeth to passe that the crosse, seeing it is a testimonie vnto them of faith and righteousnesse, ministreth to them not an occasion of sorow, but of vnspeakeable ioy: now the Apostle propoundeth this third difference vnder the forme of an exhortation. 16 The third reason: Because the Lord of all the world being especially carefull for them of his houshold, doeth therefore chastise them first of all, yet so that he keepeth a measure in his greatest seueritie. And as he hath alwayes vsed to doe heretofore, so doeth he now especially when as he exhibited himselfe in person to his Church. 17 Lest the godly should be offended & stumble at that vaine shadow of felicitie of the wicked, as though God were not the gouernour of the world, for that the wicked are in good case, and the godly in euil, the Apostle teacheth by an argument of a comparison of them together, that God who spareth not his owne, but nourtereth them vnder the crosse, wil at length in his time handle the rebellious and wicked farre otherwise, whom he hath appointed to vtter destruction. * *Prou.*2.31. 18 The conclusion: Seeing the godly are not afflicted by chance, but by the will of God, they ought not to despaire, but goe forward notwithstanding in the way of holinesse & well doing, commending themselues to God their faithfull Creator, that is to say, their Father.

CHAP. V.

1 He warneth the Elders not to vsurpe authoritie ouer the Church, 5 willing the yonger sort to bee willing to bee taught, and to be modest, 8 to be sober and watchfull to resist the cruell aduersarie.

THe [1]Elders which are among you, [2]I beseech which am also an Elder, and a witnesse of the sufferings of Christ, and also a partaker of the glory that shall be reueiled,
2 [3][a]Feede the [4]flocke of God, which [5]de-
pendeth vpon you, [6]caring for it not by constraint, but willingly: not for filthie lucre, but
of a ready minde:
3 Not as though ye were lords ouer *Gods*
[d]heritage, but that yee may be ensamples to
the flocke.
4 [7]And when that chiefe shepheard shal appeare, ye shall receiue an incorruptible crowne
of glory.
5 [8]Likewise yee yonger, submit your
selues vnto the elders, and submit your selues

1 He describeth peculiarly the office of the Elders, that is to say, of them that haue the care of the Church. 2 He vseth a preface touching the circumstance of his owne person: to wit, that he as their companion communeth with them not of maners which he knoweth not, but wherein he is as well experienced as any, and propoundeth vnto them no other condition but that which he himselfe hath susteined before them, and doeth still take the same paines, and also hath one selfe same hope together with them. 3 The first rule: He that is a shepheard let him feede the flocke. *a Hee saith not, offer for the quicke and the dead, and sing patched shreds in a strange tongue, but, (feede)* 4 The second: Let the shepheards consider, that the flocke is not his, but Gods. 5 The third: Let not shepheards inuade other mens flocks, but let them feede that which God hath committed vnto them. 6 Let the shepheards gouerne the Church with the word, and example of godly and vnblameable life, not by constraint but willingly, not for filthie lucre, but of a ready minde, not as lords ouer Gods portion and heritage, but as his ministers. *b Which is the Christian people.* 7 That the shepheards mindes bee not ouercome either with the wickednesse of men, or their crueltie, hee warneth them to cast their eyes continually vpon that chiefe shepheard, and the crowne which is laid vp for them in heauen. 8 Hee commendeth many peculiar Christian vertues, and especially modestie: which admonition all of vs stand in neede of, but especially the yonger sort by reason of the vntowardnesse and pride of that age.

euery

euery man,one to another: * decke your selues
inwardly in lowlines of mind: [9] for * God resisteth the proud,& giueth grace to the humble.
6 Humble * your selues therefore [10] vnder the mightie hand of God, that he may exalt you in due time.
7 * Cast all your care on him: for hee careth for you.
8 [11] Be sober,and watch: for * your aduersarie the deuil as a roaring Lion walketh about,
seeking whom he may deuoure:
9 Whom resist stedfast in the faith, [12] knowing that the same afflictions are accomplished
in your [c] brethren which are in the world.

* *Rom.*12.10.
9 Because pride seemeth to many to be the way vnto the glory of this life, the Apostle witnesseth on the contrary side, that ignominie and shame is the reward of pride, and glory the reward of modestie.
* *Iames* 4.6.
* *Iam* 4.10.
10 Because those proude and loftie spirits threaten the modest and humble, the Apostle warneth vs to set the power of God against the vanitie of proud men, and to hang wholy vpon his prouidence. * *Psal.*55.23. *matth.*6.25.*luke* 12.22. 11 The crueltie of Satan, who seeketh by all meanes to deuoure vs, is ouercome by watchfulnesse and faith. * *Luke* 22.31. 12 The persecutions which Satan stirreth vp, are neither new nor proper to any one man, but from olde and ancient time common to the whole Church, and therefore we must suffer that patiently, wherein we haue such and so many fellowes of our conflicts and cumbates. c *Amongst your brethren which are dispersed throughout the world.*

10 [13] And the God of all grace, which hath
called vs vnto his eternall glory by Christ Iesus,after that ye haue suffered a litle, make you
perfit, confirme, strengthen and stablish *you.*
11 To him *be* glory and dominion for euer
and euer, Amen.
12 [14] By Syluanus a faithfull brother vnto
you, as I suppose, haue I written briefly, exhorting & testifying how that this is the true grace
of God, wherein ye stand.
13 [15] *The Church* that is at [d] Babylon elected
together with you, saluteth you, and Marcus
my sonne.
14 Greete yee one another with the * kisse
of loue. Peace *be* with you all which are in
Christ Iesus, Amen.

13 He sealeth vp as it were with a seale the former exhortation with a solemne prayer, againe willing them to aske encrease of strength at his hands, of whom they had the beginning, and hope to haue the accomplishment: to wit, of God the Father in Christ Iesus, in whom we are sure of the glory of eternall life.
14 Continuance & perseuerance in the doctrine of the Apostles, is the onely ground and foundation of Christian strength: Now the summe of the Apostles doctrine, is saluation freely giuen of God. 15 Familiar salutations. d *In that famous citie of Assyria, where Peter the Apostle of circumcision then was.*
* *Rom.*16.16. 1.*cor.*16.20. 2.*cor.*13.12.

THE SECOND EPISTLE GENERALL OF PETER.

CHAP. I.

3 Hauing spoken of the bountifulnesse of God, 5 and of the vertues of faith, 6 He exhorteth them to holinesse of life. 12 and that his counsell may be the more effectuall, 14 He sheweth that his death is at hand, 16 and that himselfe did see the power of Christ which he opened vnto them.

Simon [1] Peter a seruant and an
Apostle of Iesus Christ,to you
which haue obteined like precious faith with vs by the
[a] righteousnesse of our God,
and our Sauiour Iesus Christ.
2 Grace and peace bee multiplied to you,
[2] through the acknowledging of God, and of
Iesus our Lord,
3 [3] According as his [d] diuine power hath
giuen vnto vs all things that *pertaine* vnto [c] life
and godlinesse, through the [d] acknowledging of him that hath called vs vnto glory and
vertue.
4 [4] Whereby most great and precious promises are giuen vnto vs,that by them ye should
be partakers of the [e] diuine nature, in that yee
flee the corruptiō, which is the [f] world through
[g] lust.
5 [5] Therefore giue euen all diligence ther-

1 A Salutation, wherein he giueth them to vnderstand that he dealeth with them as Christs embassadour, & otherwise agreeth with them in one selfe same faith which is grounded vpon the righteousnes of Iesus Christ, our God and Sauiour.
a *In that that God standing to his promises, shewed himselfe faithfull, and therefore iust vnto vs.*
2 Faith is the acknowledging of God and Christ, from whence all our blessednesse issueth and floweth.
3 Christ setteth foorth himselfe vnto vs plainely in the Gospel, and that by his onely power, and giueth vs all things which are requisite both to eternal life, wherein he hath appointed to glorifie vs, and also to godlines, in that he doth furnish vs with true vertue. b *He speaketh of Christ, whom he maketh God & the only Sauiour.* c *Unto saluation.* d *This is the summe of true religion, to be led by Christ to the Father, as it were by the hand.* 4 An explication of the former sentence, declaring the causes of so great benefits, to wit, God and his free promise, frō whence all these benefits proceed, I say, these most excellent benefits, whereby we are deliuered from the corruption of this world, (that is, from the wicked lusts which we carie about vs) and are made after a sort, like vnto God himselfe. e *By the diuine nature he meaneth not the substance of the Godhead, but the partaking of those qualities, whereby the image of God is restored in vs.* f *In men.* g *For lust is the seat of corruption, and hath his place euen in our very bowels and inmost parts.* 5 Hauing laid the foundation (that is, hauing declared the causes of our saluation, & especially of our sanctification) now he beginneth to exhort vs to giue our minds wholly to the true vse of this grace. And he beginneth with faith, without which nothing can please God, and he warneth vs to haue it full fraught with vertue (that is to say, with good and godly maners) being ioyned with the knowledge of Gods will, without which, there is neither faith, neither any true vertue.

unto: [h] ioyne moreouer vertue with your faith:
and with vertue, knowledge:
6 [6] And with knowledge, temperance: &
with temperance, patience: and with patience,
godlinesse:
7 And with godlinesse, brotherly kindnes:
and with brotherly kindnesse, loue.
8 [7] For if these things be among you, and
abound, they will make you that yee neither
shalbe idle, nor vnfruitfull in the acknowledging of our Lord Iesus Christ:
9 For hee that hath not these things, is
blinde, and [i] can not see farre off, and hath forgotten that he was purged from his old sinnes.
10 [8] Wherefore, brethren, giue rather diligence to make your calling and election sure:
for if ye doe these things, ye shall neuer fall.
11 For by this meanes an entring shall bee
ministred vnto you abundantly into the euerlasting kingdome of our Lord and Sauiour Iesus Christ.
12 [9] Wherefore, I will not be negligent to
put you alwayes in remembrance of these
things, though that ye haue knowledge, and be
stablished in the present trueth.
13 For I thinke it meete as long as I am in
this [k] tabernacle, to stirre you vp by putting
you in remembrance,
14 Seeing I know that the time is at hande
that I must lay downe this my tabernacle, e-
uen as our Lord Iesus Christ hath * shewed
me.
15 I will endeuour therefore alwayes, that
ye also may bee able to haue remembrance of
these things after my departing.

h *Supply also, and support or ayde.*
6 He reckoneth vp certaine and other principall vertues, whereof some pertaine to the first table of the Lawe, others to the last.
7 As those fruits doe spring from the true knowledge of Christ, so in like sort the knowledge it selfe is fostered and groweth by bringing forth such fruits, in so much that he that is vnfruitfull, did either neuer knowe the true light, or hath forgotten the gift of sanctificatiō which he hath receiued.
i *He that hath not an effectuall knowledge of God in him, is blind as touching the kingdome of God, for he can not see things that are afarre off, that is to say, heauenly things.*
8 The conclusion: Therefore seeing our calling and election is approued by those fruits, and is confirmed in vs, and moreouer seeing this is the onely way to the euerlasting kingdome of Christ, it remaineth that we cast our minds wholy that way. 9 An amplifying of the conclusion ioyned with a modest excuse, wherein he declareth his loue towards them, and foretelleth them of his death which is at hand. k *In this body.* * *Iohn* 21.18.

16 * [10] For we followed not deceiueable fables when we opened vnto you the power,and
comming of our Lord Iesus Christ, but with
our eyes we saw his Maiestie:
17 For he receiued of God the Father honour and glory, when there came such a voyce
to him from that excellent glory, * This is my
beloued Sonne,in whom I am well pleased.
18 And this voyce we heard when it came
from heauen, being with him in the Holy
mount.
19 [11] We haue also a most sure word of the
Prophets, [12] to the which ye doe well that yee
take heed,as vnto a light that shineth in a darke
place, vntill the day [l] dawne, and the [m] day star
arise in your hearts.
20 * [13] So that ye first knowe this, that no
prophecie of the [n] Scripture is of any [o] priuate
interpretation.
21 For the prophecie came not in old time
by the will of man : but [p] holy men of God
spake as they were [q] moued by the holy Ghost.

* 1.Cor.1.17. and 2.1.
10 An other amplification taken both of the great certainetie and also excellencie of his doctrine,as whereof our Lord Iesus Christ the Sonne of God is author, whose glory the Apostle himselfe both saw and heard.
* Matth.17.5.
11 The trueth of the Gospel is hereby also manifest,in that it agreeth wholy with the foretellings of the Prophets.
12 The doctrine of the Apostles doeth not shut out the doctrine of the Prophets, for they confirme ech other by ech others testimonies,but the Prophets were as candles which gaue light vnto the blind, vntill the brightnesse of the Gospel began to shine. *l A more full and open knowledge, then was vnder the shadowes of the Law. m That clearer doctrine of the Gospel.* * 2.Tim.3.16. 13 The Prophets are to be read,but so, that we aske of God the gift of interpretation, for he that is the authour of the writings of the Prophets, is also the interpreter of them. *n He ioyneth the Scripture and prophecie together, to distinguish true Prophecies from false. o For all interpretation commeth from God. p The godly interpreters and messengers. q Inspired of God: and these their motions were in very good order, and not such as were the motions of the prophane soothsayers,and foretellers of things to come.*

CHAP. II.

1 Hee foretelleth them of false teachers, 3 whose wicked sleights and destruction he declareth 12 Hee compareth them to bruit beasts, 17 and to welles without water, 20 because they seeke to withdrawe men from God to their old filthinesse.

BVt [1] there were false prophets also among
the [a] people, euen as there shall bee false
teachers among you : which priuily shal bring
in damnable heresies, euen denying the Lord,
that hath bought them, and bring vpon themselues swift damnation.
2 [2] And many shall follow their destructi-
ons, by whom the way of trueth shall be euill
spoken of.
3 [3] And through couetousnesse shall they
with fained words [b] make merchandise of you,
[4] whose condemnation long since resteth not,
and their destruction slumbreth not.
4 For if God spared not the * Angels that
had sinned,but cast them downe into [c] hell,and
deliuered them into [d] chaines of darkenesse,to
be kept vnto damnation:
5 Neither hath spared the [e] old world,but
saued * Noe the eight *person* a [f] preacher of
righteousnesse, and brought in the flood vpon
the world of the vngodly,

1 As in times past there were two kindes of prophets,the one true,the other false,so Peter foretelleth them, that there shalbe some true,and some false teachers in the Church,in so much ẏ Christ himselfe shalbe denied of some, which notwithstanding shal call him redeemer.
a Vnder the Law, while the state and policie of the Iewes was yet standing.
2 There shall not onely bee heresies,but also many followers of them.
3 Couetousnes for the most part is a companion of heresie,and maketh merchandise euen of soules. *b They will abuse you, and sell you as they sell cattell in a faire.* 4 Comfort for the godly : God who cast the Angels that fell away from him, headlong into the darkenesse of hell,at length to be iudged: and who destroyed the old world with the flood, and preserued Noe the eight person : and who burned Sodom, and saued Lot, will deliuer his elect from these errours, and will vtterly destroy those vnrighteous. * *Iob.4.18. iude 6. c So the Grecians called the deepe dungeons vnder the earth, which should be appointed to torment the soules of the wicked in. d Bound them with darkenesse as it were with chaines: and by darkenesse hee meaneth that most miserable state of life that is full of horrour. e Which was before the flood: not that God made a new world, but because the world seemed newe.* * *Gene.7.1. f For he ceased not the space of an hundreth and twentie yeeres to warne the wicked both by worde and deede, what wrath of God hanged ouer their heads.*

6 And * turned the cities of Sodom and
Gomorrhe into ashes, condemned them and
ouerthrew them, and made them an ensample
vnto them that after should liue vngodly,
7 And deliuered iust Loth vexed with the
vncleanly conuersation of the wicked :
8 (For he being righteous, and dwelling
among them, in [g] seeing and hearing, [h] vexed
his righteous soule from day to day with their
vnlawfull deeds.)
9 The Lord [i] knoweth to deliuer the godly out of tentation, and to reserue the vniust
vnto the day of iudgement vnder punishment.
10 [5] And chiefly them that walke after the
flesh,in the lust of vncleannesse,and despise gouernement, *which are* bolde, and stand in their
owne conceit, and feare not to speake euill of
them that are in [k] dignitie.
11 Whereas the Angels which are greater
both in power & might,giue not railing iudgement against them before the Lord.
12 [6] But these, as naturall bruit beasts, led
with sensualitie and [l] made to be taken, and destroyed,speake euil of those things which they
know not, & shall perish through their [m] owne
corruption,
13 And shall receiue the wages of vnrighteousnesse, as they which count it pleasure daily to liue deliciously. ‖ Spots *they are* & blots,
delighting themselues in their deceiuings, [n] in
feasting with you,
14 [7] Hauing eyes full of adulterie, and that
cannot cease to sinne,beguiling vnstable soules:
they haue hearts exercised with couetousnesse,
they are the children of curse :
15 Which forsaking the right way, haue
gone astray, following the way of * Balaam,
the sonne of Bosor, which loued the wages of
vnrighteousnesse.
16 But he was rebuked for his iniquitie :
for the dumbe beast speaking with mans voice,
forbade the foolishnesse of the Prophet.
17 * [8] These are [o] welles without water,*and*
clouds caried about with a tempest, to whome
the [p] blacke darkenesse is reserued for euer.
18 For in speaking [q] swelling wordes of
vanitie,they [r] beguile with wantonnes through
the lusts of the flesh them that were [s] cleane
escaped fro them which are wrapped in errour,
19 Promising vnto them libertie, and are
themselues the * seruants of corruption : for of
whomsoeuer a man is ouercome,euen vnto the
same is he in bondage.

* *Gene.19. 13,24.*
g Which way so euer he looked, & turned his eares
h He had a troubled soule, and being vehemently grieued, liued a painefull life.
i Hath bene long practised in sauing and deliuering the righteous.
5 He goeth to another sort of corrupt men, which notwithstanding are within the bosome of the Church, which are wickedly giuen,and doe seditiously speake euill of the authoritie of Magistrates (which the Angels themselues that minister before God,doe not dispraise.) A true and liuely description of ẏ Romish cleargie (as they call it.)
k Princes and great men,be they neuer so high in authoritie.
6 A liuely painting out of the same persons, wherein they are compared to beasts which are made to snare themselues to destruction,while they giue themselues to fill their bellies: For there is no greater ignorance then is in these men : although they most impudently find fault with those things which they know not : and it shal come to passe that they shall destroy themselues as beasts with those pleasures wherewith they are delighted, and dishonour and defile the companie of the godly.
l Made to this end to be a pray to others : So doe these men willingly cast themselues into Satans snares. m Their owne wicked maners shall bring them to destruction. ‖ Or, litle rocks. n When as by being amongst the Christians in the holy banquets which the Church keepeth, they would seeme by that meanes to be true members of the Church, yet they are in deed but blots of the Church. 7 Hee condemneth those men, as shewing euen in their behauiour and countenance an vnmeasurable lust, as making merchandise of the soules of light persons, as men exercised in all the crafts of couetousnesse, to be short, as men that sell themselues for money to curse the sonnes of God after Balaams example, whome the dumbe beast reprooued. * *Numbers 22.23.* * *Iude 12.* 8 Another note whereby they may be well knowen what manner of men they are,because they haue inwardly nothing but either vtterly vaine or very hurtful, although they make a shew of some great goodnes, yet they shall not escape vnpunished for it, because vnder prence of false libertie, they draw men into most miserable slauerie of sinne. *o Which boast of knowledge and haue nothing in them. p Most grosse darkenes. q They deceiue with vaine and swelling words. r They take them, as fishes are taken with the hooke. s Vnfainedly and in deede, cleane departed from idolatrie.*
* *Iohn 8.34. rom.6.20.*

20 [9] * For

20 [9] [*] For if they, after they haue escaped
from the filthinesse of the world, through the
acknowledging of the Lord, and of the Sauiour Iesus Christ, are yet tangled againe therein, and ouercome, the latter ende is worse with
them then the beginning.

9 It were better to haue neuer knowen the way of righteousnesse, then to turne backe from it to the old filthinesse: and men that doe so, are compared to dogges and swine.
* *Matth. 12.45. hebr. 6.4.*

21 For it had bene better for them, not to
haue acknowledged the way of righteousnesse,
then after they haue acknowledged it, to turne
from the holy commaundement giuen vnto
them.

22 But it is come vnto them, according to
the true Prouerbe, * The dogge is returned to
his owne vomit: and, The sowe that was washed, to the wallowing in the myre.

* *Prou. 26.11.*

CHAP. III.

1 He sheweth that he vttereth the same things againe, 2 because they must often be stirred vp, 4 because dangers hang ouer their heads through certaine mockers. 8 Therefore he warneth the godly that they doe not after the iudgement of the flesh, 12 appoynt the day of the Lord, 14 but that they thinke it alwayes at hand, 15 in which doctrine he sheweth that Paul agreeth with him.

1 This [1] second Epistle I now write vnto you
beloued, wherewith I stirre vp, and warne
your pure mindes,

2 To call to remembrance the words which
were told before of the holy Prophets, and also
the commandement of vs the Apostles of the
Lord and Sauiour.

3 * [2] This first vnderstand, that there shal
come in the last dayes, [a] mockers, which will
walke after their lusts,

4 [3] And say, Where is the promise of his
comming? for since the fathers died, all things
continue alike from the beginning of the creation.

5 [4] For this they willingly know not, that
the heauens were of old, and the [b] earth that
was of the water and by the water, by the word
of God.

6 [5] Wherefore the world that then was, perished, ouerflowed with the [c] water.

7 [6] But the heauens and earth, which are
now, are kept by the same worde in store, and
reserued vnto fire against the day of condemnation, and of the destruction of vngodly men.

8 [7] Dearely beloued, bee not ignorant of
this one thing, that one day *is* with the Lord,
* as a thousand yeeres, and a thousand yeeres
as one day.

1 The remedie against those wicked enemies, both of true doctrine and holinesse, is to bee sought for by the continuall meditation of the writings of the Prophets and Apostles.
* *1. Tim. 4.1. 2. tim. 3.1. iude 18.*
2 He voucheth the second comming of Christ against the Epicures by name.
a Monstrous men, who will seeme wise by their contempt of God, and wicked boldnesse.
3 The reason which these mockers pretend because the course of nature is all one as it was from the beginning, therfore the world was from euerlasting, and shall be for euer.
4 He setteth against them the creation of heauen and earth by the word of God, which these men are willingly ignorant of. *b Which appeared, when the waters were gathered together into one place.* 5 Secondly he setteth, against them the vniuersall flood, which was the destruction, as it were of the whole world. *c For the waters returning into their former place, this world, that is to say, this beautie of the earth which we see, and all liuing creatures which liue vpon the earth, perished.* 6 Thirdly, he pronounceth that it shall not bee harder for God to burne heauen and earth with fire, in that day which is appoynted for the destruction of the wicked (which thing he will also doe) then it was for him in times past to make them with his onely word, and afterward to ouerwhelme them with water. 7 The taking away of an obiection: In that he seemeth to deferre this iudgement a long season, in respect of vs it is true, but not before God, with whome there is no time either long or short.

* *Psal. 90.4.*

9 [8] The Lord of that promise is not slacke
(as some men count slackenesse) [9] but is patient toward vs, and * would haue no man to
perish, but would all men to come to repentance.

10 [10] But the * day of the Lord will come
as a thiefe in the night, in the which the heauens shall passe away with a [d] noyse, and the e-
lements shall melt with heate, and the earth
with the workes that are therein, shall bee
burnt vp.

11 [11] Seeing therefore that all these things
must bee dissolued, what manner persons
ought ye to be in holy conuersation and godlinesse,

12 Looking for, & [e] hasting vnto the comming of that day of God, by which the heauens being on fire, shall bee dissolued, and the
elements shall melt with heate.

13 But wee looke for * new heauens, and a
new earth, according to his promise, [f] wherein
dwelleth righteousnesse.

14 Wherefore, beloued, seeing that yee
looke for such things, be diligent that ye may
be found in him in [g] peace, without spot and
blamelesse.

15 * And suppose that the long suffering of
our Lord is saluation, [12] euen as our beloued
brother Paul according to the wisedome giuen
vnto him, wrote vnto you,

16 As one that in all *his* Epistles speaketh
of these things: [13] among the || which some
things are hard to be vnderstood, which they
that are vnlearned and vnstable, wrest, as they
doe also other Scriptures vnto their owne destruction.

17 Yee therefore beloued, seeing yee
knowe these things before, beware, lest yee
be also plucked away with the errour of the
wicked, and fall from your owne stedfastnesse.

18 But growe in grace, and in the knowledge of our Lord and Sauiour Iesus Christ:
to him *bee* glory both now and euermore. A-
men.

8 The Lorde whill surely come, because hee hath promised: and that neither sooner nor later then he hath promised.
9 A reason why the latter day commeth not out of hand, because God doeth patiently wait till the elect be brought to repentance, that none of them may perish.
* *Ezech. 18.32. and 33.11. 1. tim. 2.4.*
10 A very short description of the last destruction of the world, but in such sort as nothing could be spoken more grauely.
* *Matth. 24.44. 1. thess. 5.2. reuel. 3.3. and 16.15.*
d With the violence as it were of a hissing storme.
11 An exhortation to puritie of life, setting before vs that horrible iudgement of God, both to bridle our wantonnesse, and also to comfort vs, so that wee be found watching, and readie to meet him at his comming.
e Hee requireth patience of vs, yet such patience as is not slouthfull.
* *Esai. 65.17. and 66.22. reue. 21.1.*
f In which heauens.
g That you may trie to your profit, how gentle and profitable hee is.
* *Rom. 2.4.*

12 Pauls Epistles are allowed by the expresse testimonie of Peter. 13 There bee certaine of these things obscure and darke whereof the vnlearned take occasion to ouerthrowe some men that stand not fast, wresting the testimonie of the Scripture to their owne destruction. But this is the remedie against such deceite, to labour that wee may dayly more and more growe vp and increase in the knowledge of Christ. || *That is to say, among the which things: for hee disputeth not here whether Pauls Epistles be plaine or darke, but saith, that amongst those things which Paul hath written of in his Epistles, and Peter himselfe in these two of his owne, there are some things which cannot bee easily vnderstood, and therefore are of some drawen to their owne destruction: and this hee saith to make vs more attentiue and diligent, and not to remooue vs from the reading of holy things, for to what end should they haue written vaine speculations?*

THE FIRST EPISTLE GENERALL OF IOHN.

CHAP. I.

1 He testifieth that hee bringeth the eternall word wherein is life, 5 and light: 9 God will bee mercifull vnto the faithfull, if groning vnder the burden of their sinnes, they learne to flee vnto his mercie.

1 He beginneth with the description of the person of Christ whom he maketh one and not two: and him both God from euerlasting (for he was with the Father from the beginning, and is that eternall life) and also made true man, whom Iohn himselfe & his companions, both heard, and beheld, & handled.

Hat [1] which was from the beginning, which wee haue
[a] heard, which we haue seene
with these our eyes, which
wee haue looked vpon, and
these handes of ours haue
handled of that [b] word of life,
2 (For that life was made manifest, and we
haue seene it, and beare witnesse, and [c] shewe
vnto you that eternall life, which was with the
Father, and was manifest vnto vs.)
3 That, *I say*, which wee haue seene and
heard, declare we vnto you, [2] that yee may also
haue fellowship with vs, and that our fellowship also may bee with the Father, and with his
Sonne IESVS Christ.
4 And these things write wee vnto you,
that that your ioy may be full.
5 [3] This then is the message which wee
haue heard of him, and declare vnto you, that
God * is light, and in him is no darknesse.
6 If we say that wee haue fellowship with
him, and walke in darknesse, we lie, and doe
not truely:
7 But if we walke in the [d] light as hee is in
the light, we haue felowship one with another,
[4] and the * blood of Iesus Christ his Sonne clen-
seth vs from all sinne.
8 [5] * If we say that we haue no sinne, wee
[e] deceiue our selues, and [f] trueth is not in vs.
9 [6] If we acknowledge our sinnes, hee is
[g] faithfull and iust, to [h] forgiue vs our sinnes,
and to cleanse vs from all vnrighteousnesse.
10 [7] If we say we haue not sinned, we make
him [i] a liar, and his [k] word is not in vs.

a I heard him speake, I saw him my selfe with mine eyes, I handled with mine hands him that is very God, being made very man, and not I alone, but others also that were with me. *b That same euerlasting Word by whom all things are made, and in whom onely there is life.* *c Being sent by him: and that doctrine is rightly said to be shewed, for no man could so much as haue thought of it, if it had not beene thus shewed.* 2 The vse of this doctrine is this, that all of vs being coupled and ioyned together with Christ by faith, might become the sonnes of God: in which thing only consisteth all happinesse. 3 Now he entreth into a question, whereby we may vnderstand that we are ioyned together with Christ, to wit, if we bee gouerned with his light, which is perceiued by the ordering of our life. And thus he reasoneth. God is in himselfe most pure light, therefore he agreeth well with them which are lightsome, but with them that are darkesome hee hath no fellowship. ** Iohn 8.12.* *d God is said to be light of his owne nature, and to be in light, that is to say, in that euerlasting infinite blessednesse: and wee are said to walke in light in that the beames of that light doe shine vnto vs in the Word.* 4 A digression or going from the matter he is in hand with, to the remission of sinnes: for this our sanctification which walke in the light, is a testimonie of our ioyning and knitting together with Christ: but because this our light is very darke, we must needes obtaine another benefit in Christ, to wit, that our sinnes may bee forgiuen vs being sprinkled with his blood: and this in conclusion is the prop and stay of our saluation. ** Hebr. 9.28. 1.pet. 1.19. reuela. 1.5.* 5 There is none but needeth this benefite, because there is none that is not a sinner. ** 1.King. 8.46. 2 chron. 6.36. prouerb. 20.9.* *e This place doeth fully refute that perfitnesse of workes of supererogation which the Papists dreame of.* *f So then, Iohn speaketh not thus for modestie sake, as some say but because it is so in deede.* 6 Therefore the beginning of saluation is to acknowledge our wickednesse, and to require pardon of him, who freely forgiueth all sinnes, because he hath promised so to doe, and he is faithfull and iust. *g So then our saluation hangeth vpon the free promise of God, who because he is faithfull and iust, will performe that which he hath promised.* *h Where are then our merites? for this is our true felicitie.* 7 A rehearsall of the former sentence, wherein hee condemned all of sinne without exception: in so much that if any man perswade himselfe otherwise, hee doeth as much as in him lieth, make the word of God himselfe vaine and to no purpose, yea, he maketh God a liar: for to what ende either in times past needed sacrifices, or now Christ and the Gospel, if we be not sinners? *i They doe not onely deceiue themselues but are blasphemous against God.* *k His doctrine shall haue no place in vs; that is, in our hearts.*

CHAP. II.

1 Hee declareth that Christ is our Mediatour and Aduocate, 3 and sheweth that the knowledge of God consisteth in holinesse of life, 12 which apperteineth to all sortes, 14 that depend on Christ alone: 15 Then hauing exhorted them to contemne the world, 18 Hee giueth warning that Antichrists bee auoyded, 24 and that the knowen trueth be stood vnto.

MY [1] little children, these things write I
vnto you, that yee sinne not: and if any
man sinne, we haue an [a] Aduocate with the Father, Iesus Christ the Iust.
2 And hee is the [b] reconciliation for our
sinnes: and not for ours onely, but also for *the
sinnes* of the [c] whole world.
3 [2] And hereby we are sure that we [d] know
him [e] if we keepe his commandements.
4 [3] He that saith, I know him, and keepeth
not his commandements, is a liar, and the truth
is not in him.
5 [4] But hee that keepeth his word, in him
is the [f] loue of God perfect indeed: hereby we
know that we are in [g] him.
6 [5] Hee that saith hee remaineth in him,
ought euen so to walke, as he hath walked.
7 [6] Brethren, I write no new commaundement vnto you, but an old commandement,
which yee haue had from the beginning: this
olde commandement is that word, which yee
haue heard from the beginning.
8 [7] Againe, a new commandement I write
vnto you, that [h] which is true in him, and also
in you: for the darknesse is past, and that true
light now shineth.
9 [8] Hee that saith that he is in that light,
and hateth his brother, is in darknesse, vntill
this time.
10 * He that loueth his brother, abideth in
that light, and there is none occasion of euill
in him.
11 But hee that hateth his brother, is in
darkenesse, and walketh in darkenesse, and

1 It followeth not hereof that we must giue our wicked nature the bridle, or sinne so much the more freely, because our sinnes are clensed away by the blood of Christ, but we must rather so much the more diligently resist sinne. And yet we must not despaire because of our weakenesse, for we haue an aduocate and a purger, Christ Iesus the Iust, and therefore acceptable vnto his Father. *a In that he nameth Christ, he shutteth forth all other.* *b Reconciliation and intercession goe together, to giue vs to vnderstand that he is both aduocate and hie Priest.* *c For men of all sorts, of all ages, and all places, so that this benefite belongeth not to the Iewes onely, of whome hee speaketh as appeareth, verse 7, but also to other nations.* 2 He returneth to the testimonie of our coniunction with God, to wit, to sanctification, declaring what it is to walke in the light, to wit, to keepe Gods commaundements. Whereby it followeth that holinesse doth not consist in those things which men haue deuised, neither in a vaine profession of the Gospel. *d This must bee vnderstood of such a knowledge as hath faith with it, and not of a common knowledge.* *e For the tree is knowen by the fruit.* 3 Holinesse, that is, a life ordered according to the prescript of Gods commandements, how weake soeuer we bee, is of necessitie ioyned with faith, that is, with the true knowledge of the Father in the Sonne. 4 Hee that keepeth Gods commandements loueth God in deede: He that loueth God, is in God, or is ioyned together with God. Therefore hee that keepeth his commandements is in him. *f Wherewith we loue God.* *g He meaneth our coniunction with Christ.* 5 He that is one with Christ, must needes liue his life, that is, must walke in his steps. 6 The Apostle going about to expound the commandement of Charitie one towards another, telleth first that when he vrgeth holinesse, he bringeth no new trade of life (as they vse to doe which deuise traditions one after another) but putteth them in minde of that same law which God gaue in the beginning, to wit, by Moses, at that time that God began to make Lawes to his people. 7 He addeth, that the doctrine indeede is old, but it is now after a sort new both in respect of Christ, and also of vs: in whome hee through the Gospel, engraueth his Law effectually, not in tables of stone, but in our mindes. *h Which thing (to wit, that the doctrine is new which I write vnto you) is true in him, and in you.* 8 Now he commeth to the second table, that is, to charitie one towards another, and denieth that that man hath true light in him, or is in deede regenerate and the sonne of God which hateth his brother: and such an one wandereth miserably in darknesse, bragge hee of neuer so great knowledge of God for that wittingly and willingly he casteth himselfe headlong into hell. ** Chap. 3.14.*

knoweth not whither hee goeth, because that
darkenesse hath blinded his eyes.
12 [9]Little children, [i]I write vnto you, because your sinnes are forgiuen you for his
[k]Names sake.
13 [10]I write vnto you, fathers, because yee
haue knowen him that is from the beginning.
[11]I write vnto you, young men, because yee
haue ouercome that wicked one. [12]I write vnto you, little children, because yee haue know-
en the Father.
14 [13]I haue written vnto you, fathers, because yee haue knowen him, that is from the
beginning. I haue written vnto you, young
men, because yee are strong, and the word of
God abideth in you, and yee haue ouercome
that wicked one.
15 [14]Loue not this [l]world, neither the things
that are in this world. If any man loue this
world, the [m]loue of the father is not in him.
16 For all that is in this world (*as* the lust of
the flesh, the lust of the eyes, and the pride of
life) is not of the Father, but is of this world.
17 [15]And this world passeth away, and the
lust thereof: but hee that fulfilleth the will of
God, abideth euer.
18 [16][n]Little children, [17]it is the last time,
[18]and as yee haue heard that Antichrist shall
come, euen now there are many Antichristes:
whereby we know that it is the last time.
19 [19]They went out from vs, but they were
not of vs: for if they had beene of vs, [o]they
should haue continued with vs. [20]But *this com-*
meth to passe, that it might appeare, that they
are not all of vs.
20 [21]But yee haue an [p]oyntment from that
[q]Holy one, and know all things.
21 [22]I haue not written vnto you, because
yee know not the trueth: but because ye know
it, and that no lie is of the trueth.

9 He returneth againe from the sanctification to remission of sinnes, because that free reconciliation in Christ is the ground of our saluation whereupon afterwards sanctification must be built as vpon a foundation. *i Therefore I write vnto you, because you are of their number whom God hath reconciled to himselfe.* *k For his owne sake: And in that hee nameth Christ he shutteth out all other, whether they be in heauen or earth.* 10 He sheweth that this doctrine agreeth to all ages, and first of all speaking to old men, he sheweth that Christ and his doctrine are passing ancient, and therefore if they be delited with old things, nothing ought to be more acceptable vnto them. 11 He aduertiseth yong men, if they be desirous to shewe their strength, that they haue a most glorious combate set here before them, to wit, Satan the worst enemie, who must be ouercome: willing them to be as sure of the victorie, as if they had already gotten it. 12 Finally, he sheweth to children, that that true Father from whom they haue to looke for all good things, is set forth vnto them in the Gospel. 13 He addeth afterward in like order, as many exhortations: as if he should say, Remember, you Fathers, as I wrote euen now, that the euerlasting Sonne of God is reueiled to vs. Remember yee yong men, that that strength whereby I said that you put Satan to flight, is giuen you by the word of God which dwelleth in you. 14 The world which is full of wicked desires, lusts, or pleasures, and pride, is vtterly hated of our heauenly Father, Therefore the Father and the world cannot bee loued together: and this admonition is very necessarie for greene and flourishing youth. *l He speaketh of the world, as it agreeth not with the will of God, for otherwise God is said to loue the world with an infinite loue, Iohn 3.16. that is to say, those whome hee chose out of the world.* *m Wherewith the Father is loued.* 15 He sheweth how much better it is to obey the Fathers will, then the lusts of the world, by both their natures and vnlike euent. 16 Now, hee turneth himselfe to little children, which notwithstanding are well instructed in the summe of religion, and willeth them by diuers reasons to shake off slouthfulnes, which is too too familiar with that age. *n He vseth this word (Little) not because he speaketh to children, but to allure them the more by vsing such sweete words.* 17 First, because the last time is at hand, so that the matter suffereth no delay. 18 Secondly, because Antichrists, that is, such as fall from God, are already come, euen as they heard that they should come. And it was very requisite to warne that vnheedie and warilesse age of that danger. 19 A digression against certaine offences and stumbling blocks whereat that rude age especially might stumble and be shaken. Therefore that they should not bee terrified with the foule falling backe of certaine, first he maketh plaine vnto men that although such as fall from God and his religion had place in the Church, yet they were neuer of the Church: because the Church is the companie of the elect, which cannot perish, and therefore cannot fall from Christ. *o So then the elect can neuer fall from grace.* 20 Secondly, hee sheweth that these things fall out to the profit of the Church, that hypocrites may be plainely knowen. 21 Thirdly, he comforteth them, to make them stand fast, insomuch as they are anointed of the holy Ghost with the true knowledge of saluation. *p The grace of the holy Ghost, and this is a borrowed kind of speech taken from the oyntings vsed in the Lawe.* *q From Christ who is peculiarly called Holy.* 22 The taking away of an obiection. He wrote not these things as to men which are ignorant of religion, but rather as to them which doe well know the trueth, yea so farre foorth that they are able to discerne trueth from falshood.

22 [23]Who is a liar, but he that denieth that
Iesus is [r]that Christ? the same is that Antichrist
that denieth the Father and the Sonne.
23 [s]Whosoeuer denieth the Sonne, the
same hath not the Father.
24 [24]Let therefore abide in you that same
which yee haue heard from the beginning. If
that which ye haue heard from the beginning,
shall remaine in you, yee also shall continue in
the Sonne, and in the Father.
25 And this is the promise that he hath promised vs, *euen* that eternall life.
26 [25]These things haue I written vnto you,
concerning them that deceiue you.
27 But that [t]anoynting which yee receiued
of him, dwelleth in you: and yee [u]neede not
that any man teach you: but as the same [x]An-
noynting teacheth you of all things, and it is
true, and is not lying, and as it taught you, yee
shall abide in him.
28 [26]And now, little children, abide in him,
that when he shal appeare, we may be bold, and
not be ashamed before him at his comming.
29 [27]If yee know that hee is righteous,
know yee that hee which doeth righteously, is
borne of him.

23 He sheweth now plainely that false doctrine of the Antichrists, to wit, that either they fight against the person of Christ, or his office, or both together and at once. And they that doe so, do in vaine boast and bragge of God, for that in denying the Sonne, the Father also is denied. *r Is the true Messias.* *s They then are deceiued themselues, and also deceiue other, which say that the Turks and other infidels worship the same God that we doe.* 24 The whole preaching of the Prophets and Apostles is contrarie to that doctrine, Therefore it is vtterly to be cast away, and this wholly to be holden, and kept, which leadeth vs to seeke eternall life in the free promise, that is to say, in Christ alone, who is giuen vs of the Father. 25 The same Spirit which indueth the elect with the knowledge of the trueth and sanctifieth them, giueth them therewithall the gift of perseuerance, to continue to the end. *t The Spirit which you haue receiued of Christ, and which hath led you into all trueth.* *u You are not ignorant of those things, and therefore I teach them not as things that were neuer heard of, but call them to your remembrance as things which you doe knowe.* *x He commendeth both the doctrine which they had embraced, and also highly praiseth their faith, and the diligence of such as taught them, yet so, that he taketh nothing from the honour due to the holy Ghost.* 26 The conclusion both of the whole exhortation, and also of the former treatise. 27 A passing ouer to the treatise following, which tendeth to the same purpose, but yet is more ample, and handleth the same matter after another order, for before he taught vs to goe vp from the effects to the cause, and in this that followeth, hee goeth downe from the causes to the effects. And this is the summe of this argument, God is the fountaine of all righteousnesse, and therefore they that giue themselues to righteousnesse, are knowen to be borne of him, because they resemble God the Father.

CHAP. III.

1 Setting downe the inestimable glory of this, that wee are Gods sonnes, 7 he sheweth that newnesse of life must bee testified by good workes, whereof Charitie is a manifest token. 19 Of faith, 22 and praying vnto God.

BEhold, [1][a]what loue the Father hath giuen
to vs, that we should be [b]called the sonnes
of God: [2]for this cause this world knoweth
you not, because it knoweth not him.
2 [3]Dearely beloued, now are wee the
sonnes of God, but yet it is not made manifest
what we shall be: and we know that when hee
shalbe made manifest, we shalbe [c]like him: for
we shall see him [d]as he is.
3 [4]And euery man that hath this hope in
him, purgeth himselfe, euen [e]as he is pure.
4 [5]Whosoeuer [f]committeth sinne, trans-

1 He beginneth to declare this agreement of the Father and the Sonne, at the highest cause, to wit, at that free loue of God towards vs, wherewith he so loueth vs, that also hee adopteth vs to be his children. *a What a gift of how great loue.* *b That we should be the sonnes of God, and so, that all the world may perceiue we are so.* 2 Before he declareth this adoption, he saith two things: the one, that this so great a dignitie, is not to be esteemed according to the iudgement of the flesh, because it is vnknowen to the world, for the world knoweth not God the Father himselfe. 3 The other: This dignitie is not fully made manifest to vs our selues, much lesse to strangers, but we are sure of the accomplishment of it, insomuch that we shall bee like to the Sonne of God himselfe and shall enioy his sight in deede, such as hee is now, but yet notwithstanding this is deferred vntill his next comming. *c Like, but not equall.* *d For now we see as in a glasse, 1.Cor.13.12.* 4 Now he describeth this adoption, (the glory whereof as yet consisteth in hope,) by the effect, to wit, because that whosoeuer is made the Sonne of God, endeuoureth to resemble the Father in puritie. *e This word signifieth a likenesse, but not an equalitie.* 5 The rule of this puritie can from no whence else be taken but from the Law of God, the transgression whereof is that which is called sinne. *f Giueth not himselfe to purenesse.*

gresseth

greſſeth alſo the Law: for [g] ſinne is the tranſ-
greſſion of the Law.
5 [6] And yee know that he was made manifeſt, that hee might * take away our ſinnes,
and in him is no ſinne.
6 Whoſoeuer abideth in him, ſinneth not:
whoſoeuer [h] ſinneth, hath not ſeene him, neither hath knowen him.
7 [7] Little children, let no man deceiue
you: he that doth righteouſneſſe, is righteous,
as he is righteous,
8 [8] Hee that * committeth ſinne, is of the
[i] deuill: for the deuil [k] ſinneth from the [l] beginning: for this purpoſe was made manifeſt that
Sonne of God, that he might looſe the workes
of the deuill.
9 Whoſoeuer is borne of God, ſinneth
not: for his [m] ſeede remaineth in him, neither
can he ſinne, becauſe he is borne of God.
10 [9] In this are the children of God knowen,
and the children of the deuill: whoſoeuer doth
not righteouſneſſe, is not of God, [10] neither he
that loueth not his brother.
11 [11] For this is the meſſage, that yee heard
from the beginning, that * we ſhould loue one
another.
12 [12] Not as * [n] Cain *which* was of that wicked one, and ſlew his brother: [13] and wherefore
ſlew he him? becauſe his owne workes were e-
uill, and his brothers good.
13 Marueile not, my brethren, though this
world hate you.
14 [14] Wee [o] know that we are tranſlated
from death vnto life, becauſe wee loue the brethren: * he that loueth not *his* brother, abideth
in death.
15 [15] Whoſoeuer hateth his brother, is a
manſlayer: and yee know that no manſlayer
hath eternall life abiding in him.
16 * [16] Hereby haue wee perceiued loue,
that hee laide downe his life for vs: therefore
wee ought alſo to lay downe *our* liues for the
brethren.
17 * [17] And whoſoeuer hath this [p] worlds
good, and ſeeth his brother hath neede, and
[q] ſhutteth vp his compaſſion from him, how
dwelleth the loue of God in him?
18 [18] My little children, let vs not loue in
word, neither in tongue *onely*, but in deede
and in trueth.
19 [19] For thereby we know that wee are
of the trueth, [20] and ſhall before him aſſure our
hearts.
20 For [r] if our heart condemne vs, God is
greater then our heart, and knoweth all things.
21 [21] Beloued, if our heart condemne vs not,
then haue we boldneſſe toward God.
22 * [22] And whatſoeuer wee aske we receiue of him, becauſe we keepe his commaundements, and doe thoſe things which are plea-
ſing in his ſight.
23 * This is then his commaundement,
That we beleeue in the Name of his Sonne Ieſus Chriſt, and loue one another as hee gaue
commandement.
24 * For hee that keepeth his commandements, dwelleth in him, and hee in him: and
hereby we know that he abideth in vs, *euen* by
that [ſ] Spirit which he hath giuen vs.

g A ſhort definition of ſinne. 6 An argument taken from the materiall cauſe of our ſaluation: Chriſt in himſelfe is moſt pure, and he came to take away our ſinnes, by ſanctifying vs with the holy Ghoſt. Therefore whoſoeuer is truely partaker of Chriſt, doth not giue himſelfe to ſinne, and contrariwiſe he that giueth himſelfe to ſinne, knoweth not Chriſt. * *Iſa.* 53.6,9,11. 1.*pet.* 2.22,24. *h He is ſaid to ſinne, that giueth not himſelfe to pureneſſe, and in him ſinne reigneth: but ſinne is ſaid to dwell in the faithfull, and not to reigne in them.* 7 An other argument of things coupled together: He that liueth iuſtly, is iuſt, and reſembleth Chriſt that is iuſt, and by that is knowen to be the Son of God. 8 An argument taken of contraries: the deuill is the authour of ſinne, & therfore he is of the deuil, or is ruled by the inſpiration of the deuill, that ſerueth ſinne: and if he be the deuils ſonne, then is he not Gods ſonne: for the deuill and God, are ſo contrary the one to the other, that euen the Sonne of God was ſent to deſtroy the workes of the deuill. Therefore on the contrarie ſide, whoſoeuer reſiſteth ſinne, is the Sonne of God, being borne againe of his ſpirit as of new ſeede, in ſo much, that of neceſsitie he is now deliuered from the ſlauerie of ſinne. * *Iohn* 8.44. *i Reſembleth the deuill, as the child doeth the father, and is gouerned by his Spirit. k He ſaith not ſinned, but, ſinneth, for he doeth nothing elſe but ſinne. l From the very beginning of the world. m The holy Ghoſt is ſo called of the effect hee worketh, becauſe by his vertue and mightie working, as it were by ſeede, we are made new men.* 9 The concluſion: By a wicked life they are knowen which are gouerned by the ſpirit of the deuil: and by a pure life, which are Gods children. 10 He beginneth to commend charitie towards the brethren, as another marke of the ſonnes of God. 11 The firſt reaſon taken of the authoritie of God which giueth the commaundement. * *Iohn* 13.34. *and* 15.12. 12 An amplification taken of the contrary example of Cain which ſlew his brother. * *Gene* 4.8. *n He bringeth forth a very fit and very old example, wherein we may behold both the nature of the Sonnes of God, and the ſonnes of the deuill, and what ſtate and condition remaineth for vs in this world, and what ſhalbe the end of both at length.* 13 A ſhort digreſsion: Let vs not marueile that we are hated of the world for doing our duetie, for ſuch was the condition of Abel who was a iuſt perſon: and who would not rather bee like him then Cain? 14 The ſecond reaſon: Becauſe charitie is a teſtimonie that we are tranſlated from death to life: and therfore hatred towards the brethren is a teſtimonie of death, and whoſoeuer nouriſheth it, doth as it were foſter death in his boſome. *o Loue is a token that we are tranſlated from death to life, foraſmuch as by the effects the cauſe is knowen.* * *Chap.* 2.10. *leuit.* 19.17. 15 A confirmation: Whoſoeuer is a murtherer, is in eternall death: who ſo hateth his brother is a murtherer, therfore he is in death. And therupon followeth the contrary: He that loueth his brother, hath paſſed to life, for indeede we are borne dead. * *Iohn* 15.13. *ephe.* 5.2. 16 Now he ſheweth how farre Chriſtian charitie extendeth, euen ſo farre, that according to the example of Chriſt euery man forget himſelfe, to prouide for and helpe his brethren. * *Luke* 3.11. 17 Hee reaſoneth by compariſons: for if we are bound euen to giue our life for our neighbours, how much more are we bound to helpe our brothers neceſsitie with our goods and ſubſtance? *p Wherewith this life is ſuſtained.*

q Openeth not his heart to him, nor helpeth him willingly & cheerfully. 18 Chriſtian charitie ſtandeth not in words but in deede, & proceedeth from a ſincere affection. 19 He commendeth charitie, by a triple effect: for firſt of all, by it we know that we are in deede the ſonnes of God, as he ſhewed before. 20 Therefore it commeth that we haue a quiet conſcience, as on the contrary ſide he that thinketh that he hath God for a iudge, becauſe he is guiltie to himſelfe, either he is neuer or els very rarely quiet, for God hath a far quicker ſight then we, and iudgeth more ſeuerely. *r If an euill conſcience conuinceth vs, much more ought the iudgement of God condemne vs, who knoweth our hearts better then we our ſelues doe.* 21 A third effect alſo riſeth of the former, that in theſe miſeries we are ſure to bee heard, becauſe we are the ſonnes of God: as we vnderſtand by the grace of ſanctification, which is proper to the elect. * *Matth.* 21.22. *iohn* 15.7. *and* 16.25. *chap.* 5.14. 22 The concluſion. That faith in Chriſt, and loue one towards another are things ioyned together, and therefore the outward teſtimonies of ſanctification muſt and doe anſwere that inward teſtimonie of the Spirit giuen vnto vs. * *Iohn* 6.23 *and* 17.3. * *Iohn* 13.34. *and* 15.10. *ſ He meaneth the Spirit of ſanctification, whereby we are borne anew and liue to God.*

CHAP. IIII.

1 Hauing ſpoken ſomewhat touching the trying of ſpirits: 4 For ſome ſpeake after the world, 5 and ſome after God: 7 He returneth to charitie, 11.19 and by the example of God he exhorteth to brotherly loue.

DEarely [1] beloued, beleeue not euery [a] ſpirit, but trie the ſpirits whether they are
of God: for many falſe prophets are gone out
into this world.
2 [2] Hereby ſhall yee know the Spirit of
God, [b] Euery ſpirit which confeſſeth that [c] Ieſus Chriſt is come in the [d] fleſh, is of God.
3 And euery ſpirit that confeſſeth not that
Ieſus Chriſt is come in the fleſh, is not of God:
but this is the *ſpirit* of Antichriſt, of whom yee
haue heard, how that he ſhould come, and now
already he is in this world.
4 [3] Little children, yee are of God, and
haue ouercome them, for greater is he that is in
you, then he that is in this world.
5 [4] They are of this world, therfore ſpeake
they of this world, & this world heareth them.

1 Taking occaſion by the name of the Spirit, leſt loue and charitie ſhould be ſeparated from the worſhip of God, which chiefly dependeth of his true knowledge, he returneth to that which hee ſpake of in the ſecond chapter touching the taking heede of Antichriſts. And he will haue vs here to take heed of two things, the one is, that ſeeing there be many falſe prophets, we doe not lightly giue credit to euery man: the other is, that becauſe many men teach falſe things, wee ſhould not therefore beleeue any. We muſt then obſerue a meane, that we may bee able to diſcerne the Spirits of God which are altogether to be followed, from impure ſpirits which are to bee eſchewed. *a This is ſpoken by the figure Metonymie, and it is as if he had ſaid, Beleeue not euery one that ſaith that he hath a gift of the holy Ghoſt to doe the office of a Prophet.* 2 Hee giueth a certaine and perpetuall rule to know the doctrine of Antichriſt, to wit, if either the diuine or humane nature of Chriſt, or the true vniting of them together bee denied: or if the leaſt iote that may be, bee derogated from his office who is our onely King, Prophet, and euerlaſting hie Prieſt. *b Hee ſpeaketh ſimply of the doctrine, and not of the perſon. c The true Meſsias. d Is true man.* 3 Hee comforteth the elect with a moſt ſure hope of victorie: but yet ſo, that hee teacheth them that they fight not with their owne vertue, but with the vertue and power of God. 4 Hee bringeth a reaſon why the world receiueth theſe teachers more willingly then the true: to wit, becauſe they breathe out nothing but that which is worldly: which is another note alſo to know the doctrine of Antichriſt by.

6 [5] Wee are of God, *hee that knoweth
God, heareth vs: he that is not of God, heareth
vs not. Hereby know we the [e] spirit of trueth,
and the spirit of errour.
7 [6] Beloued, let vs loue one another: [7] for
loue commeth of God, and euery one that loueth, is borne of God, and knoweth God.
8 He that loueth not, knoweth not God:
[8] for God is [f] loue.
9 *Herein was that loue of God made manifest among vs, because God sent that his onely begotten sonne into this world, that wee
might liue through him.
10 Herein is that loue, not that wee loued
God, but that he loued vs, and sent his Sonne
to be a reconciliation for our sinnes.
11 [9] Beloued, if God so loued vs, wee
ought also to loue one another.
12 *[10] No man hath seene God at any
time. If we loue one another, God dwelleth in
vs, and his loue is [g] perfect in vs.
13 Hereby know we, that we dwel in him,
and he in vs: because hee hath giuen vs of his
Spirit.
14 [11] And wee haue seene, and doe testifie,
that the Father sent that Sonne *to bee* the Sauiour of the world.
15 Whosoeuer [h] confesseth that Iesus is the
Sonne of God, in him dwelleth God, and he in
God.
16 And we haue knowen, and beleeued the
loue that God hath in vs. [12] God is loue, and
he that dwelleth in loue, dwelleth in God, and
God in him.
17 [13] Herein is that loue perfect in vs, that
wee should haue boldnesse in the day of iudgement: for [i] as hee is, euen so are wee in this
world.
18 There is no [k] feare in loue, but perfect loue casteth out feare: for feare hath painefulnesse: and hee that feareth, is not perfect in
loue.
19 [14] We loue him, because he loued vs first.
20 [15] If any man say, I loue God, and hate
his brother, he is a liar: [16] for how can hee that
loueth not his brother whome hee hath seene,
loue God whom he hath not seene?
21 *[17] And this commandement haue we
of him, that hee that loueth God, should loue
his brother also.

5 He testifieth vnto them, that his doctrine and the doctrine of his fellowes, is the assured word of God which of necessitie wee haue boldly to set against all the mouthes of the whole world, and thereby discerne the trueth from falsehood. * Iohn 8.47. e *True Prophets, against whom are false prophets, that is, such as erre themselues, and leade other into errour.* 6 He returneth to the commending of brotherly loue and charitie 7 The first reason: Because it is a very diuine thing, and therefore very meete for the sonnes of God: so that whosoeuer is voide of it, can not be said to know God aright. 8 A confirmation: for it is the nature of God to loue men, whereof wee haue a most manifest proofe aboue all other, in that that of his onely free and infinite good will towards vs his enemies, he deliuered vnto death, not a common man, but that his owne Sonne, yea his onely begotten Sonne, to the end that we being reconciled through his blood might be made partakers of his euerlasting glorie. f *In that he calleth God, Loue, he saith more then if hee had said that he loueth vs infinitely.* * Iohn 3.16. 9 An other reason by comparison: if God so loued vs, shall not we his children loue one another? * Iohn 1.18. 1.tim 6.16. 10 A third reason: Because God is inuisible, therefore by this effect of his spirit, to wit, by charitie, hee is vnderstood, yea and to be not out of vs, but ioyned with vs and in vs, in whome hee is so effectually working. g *Is surely in vs in deede, and in trueth.* 11 Hee vnderlayeth this charitie with another foundation, to wit, faith in Iesus, which ioyneth vs in deede with him, euen as charitie witnesseth that wee are ioyned with him. Furthermore hee testifieth of Christ, as who had seene him with his eyes. h *With such a confession as commeth from true faith, and is accompanied with loue, so that there bee an agreement of all things* 12 A fourth reason: God is the fountaine and welspring of charitie yea charitie it selfe: therefore whosoeuer abideth in it, hath God with him. 13 Againe (as a little before) hee commendeth loue, for that seeing that by our agreement with God in this thing, wee haue a certaine testimonie of our adoption, it commeth thereby to passe that without feare wee looke for that latter day of iudgement, so that trembling, and that torment of conscience is cast out by this loue. i *This signifieth a likenesse, not an equalitie.* k *If we vnderstand by loue, that wee are in God, and God in vs, that wee are sonnes, and that we know God, and that euerlasting life is in vs: he concludeth aright, that we may well gather peace and quietnesse therby* 14 Lest any man should thinke that that peace of conscience proceedeth from our loue as from the cause, he goeth backe to the fountaine, to wit, to the free loue wherewith God loueth vs although wee deserued and doe deserue his wrath. And hereof springeth another double charitie, which both are tokens & witnesses of that first, to wit, that therewithall wee loue God who loued vs first, and then for his sake our neighbours also. 15 As he shewed that the loue of our neighbour cannot bee separate from the loue wherewith God loueth vs, because this last engendereth the other: so he denieth that the other kind of loue wherewith we loue God, can be separate from the loue of our neighbour: whereof it followeth, that they lie impudently, which say they worship God, and yet regard not their neighbours.

16 The first reason taken of comparison, why we cannot hate our neighbour, and loue God, to wit, because that he that cannot loue his brother, whom he seeth, how can he loue God whom hee seeth not? * Iohn 13.34. and 15.12. 17 A second reason, why God cannot be hated and our neighbour loued, because the selfe same Lawmaker commanded both to loue him and our neighbour.

CHAP. V.

1 He sheweth that brotherly loue and faith are things inseparable: 10 And that there is no faith towardes God, but by beleeuing in Christ: 14 Hence proceedeth calling vpon God with assurance, 16 and also that our prayers be auaileable for our brethren.

WHosoeuer [1] beleeueth that Iesus is
that [a] Christ, is borne of God: and e-
uery one that loueth him, which begate, loueth
[b] him also which is begotten of him.
2 [2] In this we know that we loue the children of God, when wee loue God, and keepe
his [c] commandements.
3 [3] For this is the loue of God, that wee
keepe his commandements: [4] and his *commandements are not [d] burdenous.
4 [5] For all that is borne of God, ouercommeth this world: [6] and this is that victorie that
[e] hath ouercome this world, *euen* our [f] faith.
5 *[7] Who is it that ouercommeth this
world, but hee which beleeueth that Iesus is
that Sonne of God?
6 [8] This is that Iesus Christ that came by
water and blood: [9] not by water onely, but by
water and blood: and it is that Spirit, that beareth witnesse: for that Spirit is trueth.
7 For there are three, which beare record
in heauen, the Father, the [h] Word, and the holy Ghost: and these three are [i] one.

1 He goeth on forward in the same argument, shewing how both those loues come into vs, from that loue wherewith God loueth vs, to wit, by Iesus our Mediatour laide hold on by faith, in whome wee are made the children of God, and doe loue the Father of whom we are so begotten, and also our brethren which are begotten with vs. a *Is the true Messias.* b *By one, hee meaneth all the faithfull.* 2 The loue of our neighbour doeth so hang vpon the loue wherewith we loue God, that this last must needes goe before the first: whereof it followeth, that that is not to be called loue, when men agree together to doe euill, neither that, when as in louing our neighbours, we respect not Gods commandements. c *There is no loue where there is no true doctrine.* 3 The reason: for to loue God, is to keepe his commandements, which being so, and seeing that both the loues are commanded of one and the selfe same Lawmaker, (as he taught before) it followeth also, that we doe not loue our neighbours, when we breake Gods commandements. 4 Because experience teacheth vs that there is no abilitie in our flesh, neither yet will to performe Gods commaundements, therefore lest the Apostle should seeme, by so often putting them in minde of the keeping of the commaundements of God, to require things that are impossible, hee pronounceth that the commandements of God are not in such sort grieuous or burdensome, that we can bee oppressed with the burden of them. * Matth. 11.30. d *To them that bee regenerate, that is to say, borne anew, which are led by the Spirit of God, and are through grace deliuered from the curse of the Law.* 5 A reason: Because by regeneration wee haue gotten strength to ouercome the world, that is to say, whatsoeuer striueth against the commandements of God. 6 He declareth what that strength is, to wit, faith. e *Hee vseth the time that is past, to giue vs to vnderstand, that although wee be in the battell, yet vndoubtedly wee shall bee conquerours, and are most certaine of the victorie.* f *Which is the instrumentall cause, and as a meane and hand whereby wee lay hold on him, who in deede doeth performe this, that is, hath and doeth ouercome the world, euen Christ Iesus.* * 1.Corinthians 15.57. 7 Moreouer he declareth two things, the one, what true faith is, to wit that which resteth vpon Iesus Christ the Sonne of God alone: whereupon followeth the other, to wit, that this strength is not proper to faith, but by faith as an instrument is drawen from Iesus Christ the Sonne of God. 8 Hee prooueth the excellencie of Christ, in whom onely all things are giuen vs by sixe witnesses, three heauenly, and three earthly, which wholly and fully agree together. The heauenly witnesses are, the Father who sent the Sonne, the Word it selfe, which became flesh, and the holy Ghost. The earthly witnesses are water, (that is our sanctification) blood, that is, our iustification) the Spirit, (that is, acknowledging of God the Father in Christ by faith) through the testimonie of the holy Ghost. 9 He warneth vs not to separate water from blood (that is sanctification from iustification, or righteousnesse, begunne from righteousnesse imputed) for wee stand not vpon sanctification, but so farre foorth as it is a witnesse of Christs righteousnesse imputed vnto vs: and although this imputation of Christs righteousnesse bee neuer separated from sanctification, yet is it the onely matter of our saluation. g *Our spirit which is the third witnesse, testifieth that the holy Ghost is trueth, that is to say, that that is true which he telleth vs, to wit, that we are the sonnes of God.* h *Looke Iohn 8.14.* i *Agree in one.*

8 And there are three, which beare record
in the earth, the spirit, and the water, and the
blood: and these three agree in one.
9 [10] If wee receiue the witnesse of men,
the witnesse of God is greater: for this is
the witnesse of God, which he testified of his
Sonne.
10 *[11] Hee that beleeueth in that Sonne of
God, hath the witnesse in himselfe: he that beleeueth not God, hath made him a liar, because
he beleeued not the word, that God witnessed
of that his Sonne.
11 [12] And this is that record, *to wit*, that
God hath giuen vnto vs eternall life, and this
life is in that his Sonne.
12 He that hath that Sonne, hath that life:
and hee that hath not that Sonne of God, hath
not that life.
13 [13] These things haue I written vnto you,
that belieue in the Name of that Sonne of God,
that yee may knowe that yee haue eternall
life, and that yee may beleeue in the Name of
that Sonne of God.
14 [14] And this is that assurance, that wee
haue in him, * that if we aske any thing according to his will, he heareth vs.
15 And if wee know that hee heareth vs,
whatsoeuer we aske, we know that wee haue
the petitions, that we haue desired of him.
16 [15] If any man see his brother sinne a
sinne that is not vnto death, let him [l] aske, and
hee shall giue him life for them that sinne not
vnto death. *There is a sinne vnto death: I say
not that thou shouldest pray for it.
17 [16] All vnrighteousnesse is sinne, but there
is a sinne not vnto death.
18 [17] We know that whosoeuer is borne of
God, sinneth not: but hee that is begotten of
God, keepeth himselfe, and that wicked one
toucheth him not.
19 [18] We know that we are of God, and this
whole world lieth in wickednesse.
20 But we know that that Sonne of God is
* come, and hath giuen vs a mind to know him,
which is true: and wee are in him that is true,
that is, in that his Sonne Iesus Christ: this same
is that very [m] God and that eternall life.
21 [19] Little children keepe your selues from
idoles, Amen.

10 He sheweth by an argument of comparison, of what great waight the heauenly testimonie is, that the Father hath giuen of the Sonne, vnto whom agreeth both the Sonne himselfe and the holy Ghost.
k I conclude thus aright: for that testimonie which I said is giuen in heauen, commeth from God, who so setteth foorth his Sonne.
* *Iohn 3.36.*
11 He proueth the surenesse of the earthly witnesses by euery mans conscience hauing that testimonie in it selfe, which conscience he saith cannot be deceiued, because it consenteth to the heauenly testimonie which the Father giueth of the Sonne: for otherwise the Father must needes bee a lyar, if the conscience which accordeth and assenteth to the Father, should lie. 12 Now at length he sheweth what this testimonie is that is confirmed with so many witnesses: to wit, that life or euerlasting felicitie is the meere and onely gift of God, which is the Sonne, and proceedeth from him vnto vs, which by faith are ioyned with him, so that without him, life is no where to be found. 13 The conclusion of the Epistle, wherein he sheweth first of all, that euen they which already beleeue, doe stand in neede of this doctrine, to the end that they may grow more and more in faith: that is to say, to the ende that they may be daily more and more certified of their saluation in Christ, through faith. 14 Because we doe not yet in effect obteine that which wee hope for, the Apostle ioyneth inuocation or prayer with faith, which he will haue to proceede from faith, and moreouer to be conceiued in such sort, that nothing bee asked but that which is agreeable to the will of God: and such prayers can not be vaine.

* *Chap. 3.22.*
15 We haue to make prayers not onely for our selues, but also for our brethren which doe sinne, that their sinnes be not vnto them, to death: and yet hee excepteth that sinne which is neuer forgiuen, or the sinne against the holy Ghost, that is to say, an vniuersall and wilfull falling away from the knowen trueth of the Gospel.
l This is as much as if he said, let him desire the Lord to forgiue him, and he will forgiue him being so desired.
* *Matth. 12.31. marke 3.29.*
16 The taking away of an obiection: In deede all iniquitie is comprehended vnder the name of sinne: but yet we must not despaire therefore, because euery sinne is not deadly, and without hope of remedy. 17 A reason why not all, nay rather why no sinne is mortall to some: to wit, because they bee borne of God, that is to say, made the sonnes of God in Christ, and being indued with his Spirit, they doe not serue sinne, neither are deadly wounded of Satan. 18 Euery man must particularly applie to himselfe the generall promises, that wee may certainely perswade our selues, that whereas all the world is by nature lost, wee are freely made the sonnes of God, by the sending of Iesus Christ his sonne vnto vs, of whome wee are lightned with the knowledge of the true God and euerlasting life. * *Luke 24.45.* *m The diuinitie of Christ is most plainely prooued by this place.* 19 Hee expresseth a plaine precept of taking heede of idoles: which hee setteth against the onely true God, that with this seale as it were he might seale vp all the former doctrine.

THE SECOND EPISTLE OF IOHN.

1 This Epistle is written to a woman of great renowne, 9 who brought vp her children in the feare of God: 6 he exhorteth her to continue in Christian charitie, 7 that shee accompanie not with Antichrists, 10 but auoide them.

THE Elder to the [a] elect
[b] Lady, and her children,
[1] whom I loue in the truth,
and not I onely, but also
all that haue knowen the
trueth,
2 For the truethes
sake which dwelleth in vs,
and shall be with vs for euer:
3 Grace bee with you, mercie and peace
from God the Father, and from the Lord Iesus Christ the sonne of the Father, with [c] trueth
and loue.
4 [2] I reioyce greatly, that I found of thy
children walking in [d] trueth, as we haue receiued a commandement of the Father.
5 And now beseech I thee, Lady, (not as
writing a new commandement vnto thee, but
that same which wee had from the beginning)
that we * loue one another.
6 And this is that loue, that wee should
walke after his commandements. This commandement is, that as yee haue heard from the
beginning, yee should walke in it.
7 [3] For many deceiuers are entred into this
world, which confesse not that Iesus Christ is
come in the flesh. Hee that is such one, is a deceiuer and an Antichrist.
8 [4] [e] Looke to your selues, that we lose not
the things which we haue done, but that wee
may receiue a full reward.
9 Whosoeuer transgresseth, and abideth
not in the doctrine of Christ, hath not God.
He that continueth in the doctrine of Christ, he
hath both the Father and the Sonne.
10 [5] If there come any vnto you, and bring
not this doctrine, * receiue him not to house,
neither bid him, God speede.

a This is no proper name, but to be taken as the word soundeth, that is to say, to the worthy and noble Lady.
b Excellent and honourable Dame.
1 The bond of Christian coniunction or linking together is the true and constant profession of the trueth.
c With true knowledge which hath alwayes loue ioyned with it, and following it.
2 This true professon consisteth both in loue one towards another which the Lord hath commaunded, and also especially in wholesome and sound doctrine, which also is deliuered vnto vs: for the commaundement of God is a sound and sure foundation both of the rule of maners, and of doctrine, and these cannot bee separated the one from the other. *d According as the trueth directeth them.*

* *Iohn 15.12.*
3 Antichristes fighting against the person and office of Christ, were already crept into the Church, in the time of the Apostles.
4 He that maketh shipwracke of doctrine, loseth all.
e Beware, and take good heed.
5 We ought to haue nothing to doe with them that defend peruerse doctrine.
* *Rom. 16.17.*

11 For he that biddeth him, God ſpeede, is partaker of his euill deedes. Although I had many things to write vnto you, yet I would not *write* with paper and ynke: but I truſt to come vnto you, and ſpeake mouth to mouth, that our ioy may be full.

12 The ſonnes of thine elect ſiſter greete thee, Amen.

THE THIRD EPISTLE OF IOHN.

1 Hee commendeth Gaius for hoſpitalitie, 9 and reprehendeth Diotrephes for vaine glory: 10 hee exhorteth Gaius to continue in well doing: 12 and in the end commendeth Demetrius.

He[1] Elder vnto the beloued Gaius, whome I loue in the trueth.

2 Beloued, I wiſh chiefly that thou proſperedſt and faredſt well as thy ſoule proſpereth.

3 For I reioyced greatly when the brethren came, and teſtified of the trueth that is in thee, how thou walkeſt in the trueth.

4 I haue no greater ioy then [a] theſe, *that is*, to heare that my ſonnes walke in veritie.

5 Beloued, thou doeſt [b] faithfully, whatſoeuer thou doeſt to the brethren, & to ſtrangers,

6 Which bare witneſſe of thy loue before the Churches. Whome if thou [c] bringeſt on their iourney as it beſeemeth, according to God, thou ſhalt doe well,

7 Becauſe that for his Names ſake they went forth, and tooke nothing of the Gentiles.

8 Wee therefore ought to receiue ſuch, that we might be [d] helpers to the trueth.

9 [2] I wrote vnto the Church: but Diotrephes which loueth to haue the preeminence among them, receiueth vs not.

10 Wherefore if I come, I will call to your remembrance the deedes which he doth, pratling againſt vs with malicious words, and not therewith content, neither hee himſelfe receiueth the brethren, but forbiddeth them that would, and thruſteth them out of the Church.

11 Beloued, follow not that which is euill, but that which is good: hee that doeth well, is of God: but hee that doeth euill, hath not [e] ſeene God.

12 Demetrius hath good report of all men, and of the trueth it ſelfe: yea, and we our ſelues beare record, and yee know that our recorde is true.

13 I haue many things to write: but I will not with ynke and pen write vnto thee:

14 For I truſt I ſhall ſhortly ſee thee, and wee ſhall ſpeake mouth to mouth. Peace *bee* with thee. The friends ſalute thee. Greete the friends by name.

1 An example of a Chriſtian gratulation.

a Then theſe ioyes. *b As becommeth a beleeuer and a Chriſtian.* *c He commendeth to Gaius, either thoſe ſelfe ſame men whom he had entertained before returning now againe to him, about the affaires of the Church, or elſe ſome other which had like buſineſſe.*

d That we our ſelues may helpe ſomewhat to the preaching of the trueth.

2 Ambition and couetouſneſſe two peſtilent plagues (eſpecially in them which haue any Eccleſiaſticall function) are condemned in Diotrephes perſon.

e Hath not knowen God.

THE GENERALL EPISTLE OF IVDE.

3 Hee warneth the godly to take heed of ſuch men, 4 that make the grace of God a cloke for their wantonneſſe: 5 and that they ſhall not ſcape vnpuniſhed, for the contempt of that grace, 6.7 hee prooueth by three examples: 14 and alledgeth the prophecie of Enoch: 20 Finally hee ſheweth the godly a meane, to ouerthrow all the ſnares of thoſe deceiuers.

IVDE a ſeruant of Ieſus Chriſt, and [a] brother of Iames, to them which are called and ſanctified [b] of God the Father, and [c] reſerued to Ieſus Chriſt:

2 Mercy vnto you, and peace and loue bee multiplied.

3 [1] Beloued, when I gaue all diligence to write vnto you of the [d] common ſaluation, it was needfull for mee to write vnto you to exhort you, that yee ſhould [e] earneſtly contend for *the maintenance of* the faith, which was [f] once giuen vnto the Saints.

4 [2] For there are certaine men crept in, which were before of olde ordeined to this condemnation: [3] vngodly men *they are* which turne the grace of our God into wantonneſſe, and *denie God the onely Lord, and our Lord Ieſus Chriſt.

5 [4] I will therefore put you in remembrance, foraſmuch as yee once knew this, how that the Lord, after that hee had deliuered the people out of Egypt, *deſtroyed them afterward which beleeued not.

6 [5] The *Angels alſo which kept not their firſt eſtate, but left their owne habitation, hee hath reſerued in euerlaſting chaines vnder darkneſſe vnto the iudgement of the great day.

7 As *Sodom and Gomorrhe, and the cities about them, which in like maner as they did, [g] committed fornication, and followed [h] ſtrange fleſh, are ſet foorth for an enſample,

a This is put to make a difference betweene him and Iudas Iſcarioth. *b By God the Father.* *c Set apart by the euerlaſting counſell of God, to be deliuered to Chriſt to be kept.*

1 The end and marke whereat hee ſhooteth in this Epiſtle, is that he confirmeth the godly againſt certaine wicked men both in wholeſome doctrine and good maners. *d Of thoſe things that pertaine to the ſaluation of all of vs.* *e That yee ſhould defend the faith by all the might you can, both by true doctrine and good example of life.* *f Which was once ſo giuen, that it may neuer be changed.*

2 It is by Gods prouidence and not by chance, that many wicked men creepe into the Church. 3 He condemneth this firſt in them, that they take a pretence or occaſion to waxe wanton, by the grace of God: which cannot be, but the chiefe empire of Chriſt muſt bee abrogated, in that ſuch men giue vp themſelues to Satan, as at this day the ſect of Anabaptiſt doth, which they call Libertines. * 2.Pet.2.11. 4 He ſetteth forth the horrible puniſhment of them which haue abuſed the grace of God to follow their owne luſts. *Num.14.37. 5 The fall of the Angels was moſt ſeuerely puniſhed, how much more then will the Lord puniſh wicked and faithleſſe men? * 2.Pet.2.4. * Gen.19.24. *g Following the ſteps of Sodom & Gomorrhe.* *h Thus he couertly ſetteth forth their horrible and monſtrous luſts.*

and

and suffer the vengeance of eternall fire.
8 Likewise notwithstanding, these [i] slee-
pers also defile the flesh, [6] and despise [k] gouernement, and speake euill of them that are
in authoritie.
9 [7] Yet Michael the Archangel, when he
stroue against the deuill, and disputed about
the bodie of Moses, durst not blame him with
cursed speaking, but sayd, The Lord rebuke
thee.
10 [8] But these speake euill of those things,
which they know not: and whatsoeuer things
they knowe naturally, as beasts, which are
without reason, in those things they corrupt
themselues.
11 [9] Woe *be* vnto them: for they haue followed the way of * Cain, and are cast away by
the deceit * of Balaams wages, and perish in
the gainesaying * of Core.
12 [10] These are rockes in your [l] feastes of
charitie when they feast with you, without [m] all
feare, feeding themselues: * cloudes *they are*
without water, caried about of windes, corrupt trees *and* without fruit, twise dead, *and*
plucked vp by the rootes.
13 *They are* the raging waues of the sea, foming out their owne shame: *they are* wandring
starres, to whom is reserued the [n] blacknesse of
darkenesse for euer.
14 And Enoch also the seuenth from Adam,

i Which are so blockish and void of reason as if all their senses and wits were in a most dead sleepe.

6 A other most pernicious doctrine of theirs, in that they take away the authoritie of Magistrates, & speake euill of them as at this day the Anabaptists doe.

k It is a greater matter to despise gouernment then the gouernours, that is to say, the matter it selfe then the persons.

7 An Argument of comparison: Michael one of the chiefest Angels, was content to deliuer Satan, although a most accursed enemie, to the iudgement of God to be punished: and these peruerse men are not ashamed to speake euill of ye powers which are ordained of God.

8 The conclusion: These men are in a double fault, to wit, both for their rash follie in condemning some, and for their impudent and shamelesse contempt of that knowledge, which when they had gotten, yet notwithstanding they liued as bruit beasts, seruing their bellies.

9 He foretelleth their destruction, because they resemble or shew foorth Cains shamelesse malice, Balaams filthie couetousnesse, and to be short, Cores seditious and ambitious head. * *Gen.4.8.* * *Numb.22.21. 2.pet.2.15.* * *Numb.16.1.*

10 Hee rebuketh most sharply with many other notes and markes, both their dishonestie or filthinesse, and their sawcinesse, but especially, their vaine brauerie of wordes and most vaine pride, ioyning therewithall a most graue and heauie threatning out of a most ancient prophesie of Enoch touching the iudgement to come.

l The feastes of charitie, were certaine bankets, which the brethren which were members of the Church kept altogether, as Tertullian setteth them forth in his Apologie, chap.39.

m Impudently, without all reuerence either to God or man. * *2.Pet.2,17.*

n Most grosse darkenesse.

prophesied of such, saying, * Behold, the Lord
[o] commeth with thousands of his Saints,
15 To giue iudgement against all men, and
to rebuke all the vngodly among them of all
their wicked deedes, which they haue vngodly
committed, and of their cruell speakings, which
wicked sinners haue spoken against him.
16 These are murmurers, complainers,
walking after their owne lustes: * whose
mouthes speake proude things, hauing mens
persons in admiration, because of aduantage.
17 [11] But, ye beloued, remember the words
which were spoken before of the Apostles of
our Lord Iesus Christ,
18 How that they tolde you that there
should bee mockers * in the last time, which
should walke after their owne vngodly lusts.
19 [12] These are they that separate themselues from other, naturall, hauing not the
Spirit.
20 But, ye beloued, edifie your selues in your
most holy faith, praying in the holy Ghost,
21 And keepe your selues in the loue of
God, looking for the mercie of our Lord Iesus
Christ, vnto eternall life.
22 [13] And haue compassion of some, in putting difference:
23 And other saue with [p] feare, pulling
them out of the fire, and hate euen that [q] garment which is spotted by the flesh.
24 [14] Now vnto him that is able to keepe
you, that yee fall not, and to present you fault-
lesse before the presence of his glory with ioy,
25 *That is,* to God onely wise, our Sauiour, *bee* glory, and maiestie, and dominion, and
power, both now and for euer, Amen.

* *Reuel.1.7.*

o The present time, for the time to come.

* *Psal.17.10.*

11 The rising vp of such monsters was spoken of before, that we should not be troubled at the newnesse of the matter.

* *1.Tim.4.1. 2.tim 3.1. 2.pet.3 3.*

12 It is the propertie of Antichrists to separate themselues from the godly, because they are not gouerned by the spirit of God: & contrariwise it is the property of Christians to edifie one another through godly prayers, both in faith and also in loue, vntill the mercie of Christ appeare to their full saluation.

13 Amongst them which wander and goe astray, the godly haue to vse this choise, that they handle some of them gently, and that other some being euen in the very flame, they endeuour to saue with seuere and sharpe instruction of the present danger: yet so, that they doe in such sort abhorre ye wicked and dishonest, that they eschew

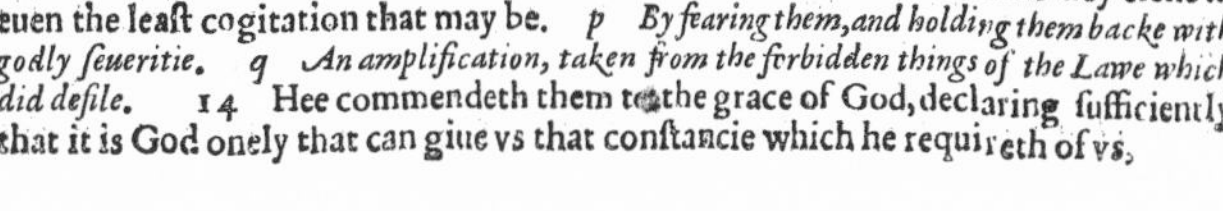

euen the least cogitation that may be.

p By fearing them, and holding them backe with godly seueritie.

q An amplification, taken from the forbidden things of the Lawe which did defile.

14 Hee commendeth them to the grace of God, declaring sufficiently that it is God onely that can giue vs that constancie which he requireth of vs.

THE

THE ORDER OF TIME WHEREVNTO THE CONTENTS OF THIS BOOKE ARE TO BE REFERRED.

The yeere of Christ.

1,&c. *He dragon watcheth the Church of the Iewes, which was ready to trauaile: Shee bringeth foorth, fleeth, and hideth her selfe, whilest Christ was yet vpon the earth.*

34. *The dragon persecuteth Christ ascending into heauen, hee fighteth and is throwen downe: and after persecuteth the Church of the Iewes.*

67. *The Church of the Iewes is receiued into the wildernesse, for three yeeres and an halfe.*

70. *When the Church of the Iewes was ouerthrowen, the dragon inuaded the Catholike Church: all this is in the 12. chap.*

The dragon is bound for a thousand yeeres, chap. 20.

The dragon raiseth vp the beast with seuen heads, and the beast with two heads, which make hauocke of the Church Catholike and her Prophets for 1260. yeeres after the passion of Christ, chap. 13. and 11.

97. *The seuen Churches are admonished of things present, somewhat before the end of Domitian his reigne, and are forewarned of the persecution to come vnder Traiane for tenne yeeres, chap. 2. and 3.*

God by word and signes prouoketh the world, and sealeth the godly, chap. 6. and 7.

He sheweth foorth exemplars of his wrath vpon all creatures, mankinde excepted, chap 8.

1073. *The dragon is let loose after a thousand yeeres, and Gregory the seuenth, being Pope, rageth against Henry the third, then Emperour, chap. 20.*

1217. *The dragon vexeth the world 150. yeeres vnto Gregory the ninth, who writ the Decretals, and most cruelly persecuted the Emperour Fredericke the second.*

The dragon by both the beasts persecuteth the Church, and putteth the godly to death, chap 9.

1295. *The dragon killeth the Prophets after 1260. yeeres, when Boniface the 8. was Pope, who was the author of the sixt booke of the Decretals: hee excommunicated Philip the French King.*

1300. *Boniface celebrateth the Iubile.*

1301. *About this time was a great earthquake, which ouerthrew many houses in Rome.*

1305. *Prophecie ceaseth for three yeeres and a halfe, vntill Benedict the second succeeded after Boniface the 8. Prophecie is reuiued, chap. 11.*

The dragon and the two beasts oppugne Prophecie, chap. 13.

Christ defendeth his Church in word and deede, chap. 14. With threats and armes, chap. 16.

Christ giueth his Church victory ouer the harlot, chap. 17. and 18. Ouer the two beasts, chap. 19. Ouer the dragon, and death, chap. 20.

The Church is fully glorified in heauen with eternall glory, in Christ Iesus, chap. 21. and 22.

THE

THE REVELATION OF SAINT IOHN THE APOSTLE *and Euangelist, with the Annotations* of FRANC. IVNIVS.

CHAP. I.

1 He declareth what kind of doctrine is here handled, 8 euen his that is the beginning and ending: 12 Then the mysterie of the seuen candlestikes and starres 20 is expounded.

THe [1][a]Reuelation of [b]Ie-
sus Christ, which God
gaue vnto him, to shew
vnto his seruants things
which must shortly bee
done: which he sent, &
shewed by his Angel
vnto his seruant Iohn,
2 Who bare record of the word of God,
and of the Testimonie of Iesus Christ, and of all
things that he sawe.
3 Blessed *is he* that readeth, and they that
heare the words of this prophesie, and keepe
those things which are written therin: for the
time is at hand.
4 [2]Iohn to the seuen Churches which are
in Asia, Grace *bee* with you, and peace
[3]from him, [c]Which * is, and Which was,
and Which is to come, and from [4]the
[d]seuen Spirits which are before his Throne,
5 And from Iesus Christ [5]which is that
* faithfull witnesse, *and* * that first begotten of
the dead, and that Prince of the kings of the
earth, vnto him that loued vs, and washed vs
from our sinnes in his * blood,
6 And made vs * Kings and Priestes vnto
God euen his Father, to him, *I say, be* glory, and
dominion for euermore, Amen.
7 Behold, he commeth with * cloudes, and
euery [e]eye shall see him: *yea*, euen they which
pearced him thorow: and all kinreds of the
earth shall waile before him. Euen so, Amen.
8 [6]I * am [f]Alpha and Omega, the beginning and the ending, sayth the Lord, Which is,
and Which was, and Which is to come, *euen*
the Almightie.
9 [7]I Iohn, euen your brother and companion in tribulation, and in the kingdome and
patience of Iesus Christ, was in the yle [g]called
Patmos, for the word of God, and for the witnessing of Iesus Christ.
10 And I was *rauished* in [h]spirit on the
[i]Lords day, and heard behind me a great voice,
as it had been of a trumpet,
11 Saying, I am Alpha and Omega, that first
and that last: and that which thou seest, write
in a booke, & send it vnto the seuen Churches,

1 This Chapter hath two principall parts, the title or inscriptiō, which standeth in stead of an exordium: and a narration going before the whole prophesie of this booke. The inscription is double, generall and particular. The generall containeth the kind of prophesie, the author, end, matter, instruments, and manner of communicating the same, in the first verse: the most religious faithfulnesse of the Apostle as a publike witnesse, verse 2. And the vse of communicating the same, taken from the promise of God, and from the circumstance of the time, verse 3. *a An opening of secret and hid things.* *b Which the Sonne opened to vs out of his Fathers bosome by Angels.* 2 This is the particular or singular inscription, wherein salutation is written vnto certaine Churches by name, which represent the Church Catholike: and the certaintie and trueth of the same is declared, from the Author therof, vnto the 8. verse. 3 That is, from God the Father, eternal, immortal, immutable: whose vnchāgeablenes, Saint Iohn declareth by a forme of speach which is vndeclined. For there is no incongruitie in this place, where, of necessitie the wordes must bee attempred vnto the mysteries, and not the mysteries corrupted or impaired by the wordes. *c By these three times, Is, Was, and Shall bee, is signified this worde Iehouah, which is the proper name of God.* **Exod.3.14.* 4 That is, from the holy Ghost which proceedeth from the Father and the Sonne. This Spirit is one in person according to his subsistencie: but in communication of his vertue, and in demonstration of his diuine workes in those seuen Churches, doeth so perfectly manifest himselfe, as if there were so many Spirits, euery one perfectly working in his owne Church. Wherefore after Chapter 5.6. they are called the seuen hornes and seuen eyes of the Lambe, as much to say, as his most absolute power and wisedome: and Chapter 3.1. Christ is sayd to haue those seuen Spirits of God, and Chap. 4.5. it is sayd, that seuen lampes doe burne before his throne, which also are those seuen Spirits of God. That this place ought to bee so vnderstood, it is thus prooued. For first, grace and peace is asked by prayer of this Spirit, which is a diuine worke, and an action incommunicable in respect of the most high Deitie. Secondly, he is placed betweene the Father and the Sonne, as set in the same degree of dignitie and operation with them, besides, hee is before the throne, as of the same substance with the Father and the Sonne: as the seuen eyes and seuen hornes of the Lambe. Moreouer, these Spirits are neuer sayd to adore God, as all other things are. Finally, that is the power whereby the Lambe opened the booke, and loosed the seuen seales thereof, when none could be found amongst all creatures by whom the booke might be opened, Chap. 5. Of these things long agoe Master Iohn Luide of Oxford wrote learnedly vnto me. Now the holy Ghost is set in order of words before Christ, because there was in that which followeth a long processe of speach to bee vsed concerning Christ.

d These are the seuen spirits, which are afterward Chap. 5. verse 6. called the hornes and eyes of the Lambe, and are now made as a garde waiting vpon God.

5 A most ample and graue commendation of Christ, first from his offices the Priesthood and kingdome: secondly from his benefits, as his loue toward vs, and washing vs with his blood, in this verse, and communication of his kingdome and Priesthood with vs: thirdly, from his eternall glory & power, which is alwaies to be celebrated of vs, verse 6. Finally, from the accomplishmēt of all things once to be effected by him, at his second comming, what time he shall openly destroy the wicked, and shall comfort the godly in the trueth, verse 7. **Psalm.89.38.* **1.Corinth.15.21. coloss.1.18.* **Hebr.9.14. 1.peter 1.19. 1.iohn 1.9.* **1.Peter 2.5.* **Esay 3.14. matth.24.30. iude 14.* *e All men.* 6 A confirmation of the salutation afore going, taken from the wordes of God himselfe: in which hee auoucheth his operation in euery singular creature, the immutable eternitie that is in himselfe, and his omnipotencie in all things: and concludeth in the vnitie of his owne essence, that Trinitie of person which was before spoken of. **Chap.21.6. and 22.13.* *f I am he before whom there is nothing, yea, by whom euery thing that is made, was made, and shall remaine though all they should perish.* 7 The narration, opening the way to the declaring of the authoritie and calling of Saint Iohn the Euangelist in this singular Reuelation, and to procure faith and credit vnto this prophesie. This is the second part of this Chapter, consisting of a proposition, and an exposition. The propositiō sheweth, first who was called vnto this Reuelation, in what place, and how occupied, vers.9. Then at what time, and by what means, namely, by the Spirit and the word, and that on the Lords day, which day euer since the resurrection of Christ, was consecrated for Christians vnto ẏ religion of the Sabboth: that is to say, to be a day of rest, verse 10. Thirdly, who is the authour that calleth him, and what is the summe of his calling. *g Patmos is one of the yles of Sporas, whither Iohn was banished as some write.* *h This is that holy rauishment expressed, wherewith the Prophets were rauished, and being as it were caried out of the worlde, were conuersant with God: and so Ezekiel sayth often, that hee was carried from place to place of the Lordes Spirit, and that the Spirit of the Lorde fell vpon him.* *i Hee calleth it the Lordes day, which Paul calleth the first day of the weeke, 1 Corinthians 16, 2.*

which

which are in Asia,vnto Ephesus,& vnto Smyrna,& vnto Pergamus,& vnto Thyatira, & vnto
Sardis,& vnto Philadelphia, & vnto Laodicea.
12 [8] Then I turned backe to [k] see the voyce
that spake with me : [9] and when I was turned, I
saw seuen golden candlestickes,
13 And in the mids of the seuen candlesticks,one like vnto the Sonne of man, clothed
with a garment downe to the feete, and girded
about the paps with a golden girdle.
14 His head,and haires *were* white as white
wooll,*and* as snow, and his eyes *were* as a flame
of fire,
15 And his feete like fine brasse, burning
as in a furnace: and his voyce, as the sound of
many waters.
16 And hee had in his right hand seuen
starres: and out of his mouth went a sharpe
two edged sword: and his face *shone* as the Sun
shineth in his strength.
17 [10] And when I sawe him,I fell at his feete
as dead : [11] then hee layed his right hand vpon
me,saying vnto me,Feare not: [12] I am the * first
and the last,
18 And am aliue, but I was dead: and behold, I am aliue for euermore, Amen: and I
haue the keyes of hell and of death.
19 [13] Write the things which thou hast seene,
and the things which are, and the things which
shall come hereafter.
20 [14] The mystery of the seuen starres which
thou sawest in my right hand, and the seuen
golden candlesticks,*is this*,The seuen starres are
the [l] Angels of the seuen Churches: and the
seuen candlestickes which thou sawest, are the
seuen Churches.

8 The expositiō, declaring the third and last point of the proposition (for the other points are euident of themselues) wherein is spoken first of the Author of his calling. vnto the 17.verse. Secondly, of the calling it selfe vnto the end of the chapter. And first of al the occasion is noted in this verse, in that Saint Iohn turned himselfe towards the vision: after is set downe the description of the Author,in the verses folowing, 13.14.15.16. *k To see him whose voice I had heard.* 9 The description of the Author, which is Christ: by the candlesticks that stand about him, that is,ẏ Churches that stand before him,and depend vpon his direction, in this verse: by his properties,that he is one furnished with wisedome and dexterity to the atchieuing of great things, verse 13. with ancient grauitie & most exellent sight of the eye verse 14. with strength inuincible and with a mighty word,verse 15. By his operation that he ruleth the ministery of his seruants in the Church, giueth effect thereunto by the sword of his word, and enlightening all things with his countenance,doeth most mightily prouide for euery one by his diuine prouidence,verse 16. 10 A religious feare,that goeth before the calling of the Saints, and their full confirmation to take vpon them the vocation of God. 11 A diuine confirmation of this calling,partly by signe,and partly by word of power. 12 A most elegant description of this calling,contained in three things, which are necessary vnto a iust vocation: first the authoritie of him that calleth, for that he is the beginning and end of all things, in this verse,for that he is eternall and omnipotent,verse 8. Secondly,the summe of his propheticall calling and reuelation, verse 9. Lastly,a declaration of those persons vnto whom this prophecie is by the commandement of God directed in the description thereof, verse 20. *Esay 41.4. 13 The summe of this prophesie, that the Apostle must write whatsoeuer he should see,adding nothing, nor taking away any thing, as verse 2. Hereof there are two parts: one is a narration of those things which are,that is, which then were at that time,contained in the second and third Chapter: the other part is of those things which were to come, conteined in the rest of this booke. 14 That is, the thing which was mysticall signified by the particulars of the vision before going. *l By Angels he meaneth the Ministers of the Church.*

CHAP. II.

1 Iohn is commaunded to write those things which the Lord knew necessary to the Churches of Ephesus, 8 of the Smyrnians, 12 of Pergamus, 18 and of Thyatira, 25 that they keepe those things which they receiued of the Apostles.

VNto [1] the Angel of the Church of Ephesus write, [2] These things saith hee that
holdeth the seuen starres in his right hand, and
walketh in the mids of the seuen golden candlesticks.
2 [3] I know thy workes, and thy labour,&
thy patience, & how thou canst not beare with
them which are euill, and hast examined them
which say they are Apostles,and are not, & hast
found them liars.
3 And thou wast burdened, and hast patience,and for my Names sake hast laboured,and
hast not fainted.
4 Neuerthelesse,I haue *somewhat* [a] against
thee,because thou hast left thy first loue.
5 Remember therfore from whence thou
art fallen, and repent, and doe the first workes:
or else I will come against thee shortly,and will
remooue thy candlesticke out of his place, except thou amend.
6 But this thou hast, that thou hatest the
workes of the Nicolaitanes, which I also hate.
7 [4] Let him that hath an eare, heare what
the Spirit sayeth vnto the Churches: To him
that ouercommeth, will I giue to eate of the
tree of life which is in [5] the mids of the [b] Paradise of God.
8 ¶ [6] And vnto the Angel of the Church
of the [c] Smyrnians,write,These things sayth he
that is first, and last, which was dead and is a-
liue.
9 [7] I know thy workes and tribulation, &
pouertie (but thou art rich) and *I know* the blasphemie of them, which say they are Iewes, and
are not,but *are* the Synagogue of Satan.
10 Feare none of those things, which thou
shalt suffer: behold,it shall come to passe, that
the deuill shall cast some of you into prison,
that yee may be tryed, and yee shall haue [8] tribulation ten dayes: bee thou faithfull vnto the
death,and I will giue thee the crowne of life.
11 [9] Let him that hath an eare, heare what
the Spirit saith to the Churches. He that ouercommeth, shall not bee hurt [10] of the second
death.
12 [11] And to the Angel of the Church,
which is at [d] Pergamus write, This saith hee
which hath that sharpe sword with two edges.
13 [12] I knowe thy workes, and where thou
dwellest, *euen* where Satans throne is, & thou
keepest my Name, & hast not denied my faith,
euen in [e] those dayes when Antipas my faithful
martyr was slaine among you, where Satan
dwelleth.

1 The former part of this book is comprised in a narratiō of those things which then were, as S.Iohn taught vs, Chap.1.19 it belongeth wholly to instruction,and in these two next Chapters, containeth seuen places, according to the number and condition of those Churches which were named before,Chap.1.11.figured verse 12.and distributed most aptly into their Pastors and flockes,verse 10.which verse of that chapter is as it were a passage vnto the first part. Euery one of these seuen places hath three principall members,an Exordium taken from the person of the Author: a proposition,in which is prayse and commendation of that which is good, reprehension of that which is euil: and instruction,contayning either an exhortation alone,or withal a disswasion opposite vnto it,and a conclusion stirring vp vnto attention,by diuine promises And this first place is vnto the Pastors of the Church of Ephesus. 2 The Exordium wherin are contained the speciall prayses of Christ Iesus the Author of this prophesie out of the 6.and 13. verses of the first chapter.

3 The proposition first condemning the Pastor of this Church, verse 2, 3. then reprouing him, verse 4. after informing him,and withall threatning that he will translate the Church to another place,ver. 5. This commination or threat Christ mitigateth by a kinde of correction, calling to minde the particular vertue & piety of ẏ Church,which God neuer leaueth without recompense, ver.6. Concerning the Nicolaitans,see after vpon the 15.verse. *a To deale with thee for.* 4 The conclusion containing a commandement of attention,and a promise of euerlasting life,shadowed out in a figure, of which Gen. 2.9. 5 That is,in Paradise after the maner of the Hebrew phrase. *b Thus Christ speaketh as he is Mediatour.* 6 The second place is vnto the Pastors of the Church of the Smyrnians.The Exordium is taken out of the 17.and 18.verses of the first Chapter. *c Smyrna was one of the cities of Ionia in Asia.* 7 The proposition of prayse is in this verse, and of exhortation ioyned with promise, is in the next verse. 8 That is,of ten yeeres.For so cōmonly both in this booke and in Daniel, yeeres are signified by ẏ name of daies: that God thereby might declare, that the space of time is appointed by him,and the same very short. Now because Saint Iohn wrote this booke in the ende of Domitian the Emperour his reigne, as Iustinus and Ireneus doe witnesse, it is altogether necessary that this should bee referred vnto that persecution which was done by the authority of the Emperour Traian: who began to make hauocke of the Christian Church in the tenth yeere of his reigne,as the Historiographers doe write: and his bloodie persecution continued vntill Adrian the Emperour had succeeded in his place: The space of which time is precisely ten yeres, which are here mentioned. 9 The conclusion, as verse 7. 10 See Chap.20.6. 11 The third place is vnto the Pastors of Pergamus. The exordium is taken out of the 16.verse of the first Chapter. *d Pergamus was the name of a famous citie in olde time in Asia,where the Kings of the Attalians were alwayes resident.* 12 The proposition of praise is in this verse, of reprehension in the two following, and of exhortation ioyned with a conditionall threate,verse 16. Now this Antipas was the Angel or minister of the Church of Pergamus, as Aretas writeth. *e The faith of them of Pergamus is so much the more highly commended, because they remained constant euen in the very heate of persecution.* * Numb.24.14.and 25.1.

14 But I haue a fewe things against thee,
because thou hast there them that maintaine
the doctrine of * Balaam, which taught
Balac to put a stumbling blocke before the
children of Israel, that they should [f] eate of
things sacrificed vnto Idoles, and commit fornication.
15 Euen so hast thou them, that maintaine
the doctrine of the [13] Nicholaitanes, which
thing I hate.
16 Repent thy selfe, or else I will come vnto
thee shortly, and will fight against thee with
the sword of my mouth.
17 [14] Let him that hath an eare, heare what
the Spirit saith vnto the Churches. To him that
ouercommeth, wil I giue to eat [15] of the [g] Manna that is hid, and will giue him a [h] [16] white
stone, and in the stone a new [17] name written,
which no man knoweth sauing hee that receiueth it.
18 ¶ And vnto [18] the Angel of the Church
which is at Thyatira write, These things sayeth
the Sonne of God, which hath his eyes like
vnto a flame of fire, and his feete like fine
brasse.
19 I know [19] thy workes, and thy loue, and
[i] seruice, and faith, and thy patience, and thy
workes, and that *they are* moe at the last, then at
the first.
20 Notwithstanding, I haue a few things a-
gainst thee, that thou sufferest the woman Ie-
zabel, which calleth her selfe a prophetesse, to
teach & to deceiue my seruants, to make them
commit [k] fornication, and to eate meate sacrificed vnto idoles.
21 And I gaue her space to repent of her
fornication, but she repented not.
22 Behold, I will cast her into a bed, and
them that commit fornication with her, into
great affliction, except they repent them of
their workes.
23 And I will kill her children with death:
and all the Churches shall know that I am hee
which * search the reines and hearts: and I will
giue vnto euery one of you according vnto
your workes.
24 And vnto you I say, the rest of them of
Thyatira, As many as haue not this learning,
neither haue knowen the [l] deepenesse of Satan
(as they speake) I will [m] put vpon you none o-
ther burden,
25 But that which ye haue already, holde
fast till I come.

*Num.24.14. and 25.1.

f That which is here spoken of things offred to idoles, is meant of the same kinde which Paul speaketh of, 1.Cor. 10.14.

13 Which follow the footesteps of Balaam, and such as are abandoned vnto all filthinesse, as he shewed in the verse afore going, and is here signified by a note of similitude. And thus also must the sixt verse be vnderstood. For this matter especially Ireneus must be consulted withall.

14 The conclusion, standing of exhortation as before, and of promise.

g Hee alludeth to that sermon which we reade of, Ioh. 6 and to the place wee finde Psalm. 105.40.

h Arethas writeth, that such a stone was wont to be giuen to wrestlers at games, or else that such stones did in old time witnesse the quitting of a man.

15 The bread of life, inuisible, spirituall, and heauenly, which is kept secretly with God, from before all eternitie.

16 Which is a signe and witnes of forgiuenesse and remission of sinnes, of righteousnesse and true holinesse, and of puritie incorrupted, after that the old man is killed.

17 A signe and testimony of newnesse of life in righteousnesse and true holines, by putting on the new man, whome none doth inwardly knowe, saue the spirit of man, which is in himselfe, the praise whereof is not of men, but of God, Romanes 2.28.

18 The fourth place is vnto the Pastours of Thyatira. The Exordium is taken out of the fourteenth and fifteenth verses of the first Chapter.

19 The proposition of prayse is in this verse: of reprehension, for that they tolerated with them the doctrine of vnrighteousnesse and vngodlinesse, is verse 20. the authors whereof, though they were called backe of God, yet repented not, verse 21. whereunto is added a most heauie threatning, verse 2. and 3. of a conditionall promise, and of exhortation to hold fast the trueth is in the two verses following.

i So hee calleth those offices of charitie which are done to the Saints.

k By fornication, is oftentimes in the Scripture Idolatrie meant.

** 1.Samuel 16.7. psalm.7.10. ierem.11.20. and 17.10.*

l Hee poynteth out the bragging of certaine men, which boasted of their deepe, that is, plentifull and common knowledge, which notwithstanding is deuilish.

m I will speake no worse thing against you, being content to haue shewed you what I require to be in you.

26 [20] For hee that ouercommeth and keepeth my works vnto the end, to him will I giue
[21] power ouer nations.
27 [22] * And he shall rule them with a rod of
yron: *and* as the vessels of a potter, shall they
be broken.
28 Euen as I receiued of my Father, so will I
giue him the morning starre.
29 Let him that hath an eare, heare what
the Spirit sayth to the Churches.

20 The conclusion, wherein Christ assureth vnto his seruants the communion of his kingdom and glory, in this verse, and that following: and commandeth an holy attention in the last verse.

21 That is, I will make him a king, by communion with me, and my fellow heire, as it is promised, Matth.19.28. and 25.34. rom.8.17. and 1.cor.6.3. ephes.2.6. and 2.tim.2.12. and apoc.3.21. and 4.4.

22 The brightnesse of greatest glory and honour neerest approaching vnto the light of Christ, who is the Sonne of righteousnesse, and our head. Matth.4. **Psal.2.9.*

CHAP. III.

1 The fift Epistle sent to the Pastours of the Church of Sardis, 7 of Philadelphia, 14 and of the Laodiceans, 16 that they bee not luke warme, 20 but endeuour to further Gods glory.

AND [1] write vnto the Angel of the Church
which is at [a] Sardis, These things saith he
that hath the seuen Spirits of God, and the seuen starres, I knowe thy works: for thou hast a
[b] name that thou liuest, but thou art dead.
2 Bee awake, and strengthen the things
which remaine, that are [c] ready to die: for I
haue not found thy works perfect before God.
3 Remember therefore, how thou hast receiued and heard, and hold fast and repent. *If
therefore thou wilt not watch, I will come on
thee as a thiefe, and thou shalt not know what
houre I will come vpon thee.
4 *Notwithstanding* thou hast a fewe names
yet in Sardis, [3] which haue not defiled their
garments: and they shall walke with mee in
[4] white: for they are [d] worthy.
5 He that ouercommeth, shall be clothed
in white aray, and I will not put out his name
out of the * booke of life, but I will confesse his
name before my Father, and before his Angels.
6 Let him that hath an eare, heare what
the Spirit sayth vnto the Churches.
7 ¶ [6] And write vnto the Angel of the
Church, which is of Philadelphia, These things
sayth he that is Holy, and True, which hath the
[e] key of Dauid, which openeth, & no man shutteth, and shutteth, and no man openeth.
8 [7] I knowe thy works: behold, I haue set
before thee an open doore, and no man can shut
it: for thou hast a little strength, and hast kept
my word, and hast not denied my Name.
9 Behold, I will make them [f] of the Synagogue of Satan, which cal themselues Iewes, &
are not, but doe lie: behold, *I say*, I will make
them that they shall come [8] and worship before
thy feete, and shal know that I haue loued thee.

1 The fift place is vnto the Pastors of Sardis. The exordium is taken out of the 4.& 16. verses of the 1. Chap.

a Sardis is the name of a most florishing & famous citie, where the kings of Lydia kept their courts.

2 The proposition of reproofe is in this verse: of exhortation ioyned with a threatning in the two verses that follow, and of qualification by way of correctiõ, vnto the comfort of ẏ good which yet remained there, verse 4.

b Thou art sayd to liue, but art dead in deed.

c Other things, whose state is such, that they are now going, and vnlesse they be confirmed, will perish forthwith.

**Chap.16.15. 1. thes.5.2. 2.pet. 3.10.*

3 That is, who haue with all religion guarded themselues from sinne and contagion, euen from the very shewe of euil, as S. Iude exhorteth, verse 23.

4 Pure from all spot, and shining with glory. So it is to be vnderstood alwayes hereafter, as in the next verse.

5 The conclusion standing vpõ a promise and a commandement, as before.

d They are meete and fit, to wit, because they are iustified in Christ, as they haue truely shewed it: for he is righteous that worketh righteousnesse: but so as the tree bringeth foorth the fruit, Looke Rom.8.18.

**Chap.20.12. and 21.27. phil.4.3.*

6 The sixt place is vnto the Pastours of Philadelphia. The exordium is taken out of the 18. verse of the 1 chapter.

e All power of rule in commanding and forbidding, in deliuering and punishing. And the house of Dauid is the Church, and the continuall promise of Dauids kingdome belongeth to Christ.

7 The proposition of prayse is in this verse of promises, to bring home againe them that wander, verse 9. and to preserue the godly, verse 10. and of exhortation, verse 11.

f I will bring them to that case.

8 That is, fall down and worship either thee ciuilly, or Christ religiously at thy feet (and thus I had rather take it) whether here in the Church (which seemeth more proper to the argument of this place) or there in the world to come, For Christ verely shall fulfill his word.

10 Be-

g Because thou hast been patient and constant, as I would my seruants should be.
9 The conclusiō, which coteineth a promise and a commandement.
10 That is, the new man shalbe termed after his father, mother, & head Christ.
11 The seuenth place is vnto the pastors of the Church of Laodicea. The exordium is taken out of the 5. ver. of the 1. chapter.
h Amen soundeth as much in the Hebrew tongue, as Truely, or Truth it selfe.
i Of whō all things that are made, haue their beginning.
12 The propositiō of reproofe is in this verse, whereunto is adioined a threatning, ver. 16. with a confirmation declaring the same, ver. 17. and of faith & repentance, ver. 18. 19 whereunto is added a cōditional promise ver. 20.
13 The spiritual misery of men is metaphorically expressed in three points . vnto which are matched as correspōdent, those remedies which are offered, ver 18.
*Prou. 3. 12 hebr. 12. 5.
k Zeale is set against them which are neither hote nor cold.
14 This must be taken after the maner of an allegory, as Iohn 14. 23.
15 The conclusion, consisting of a promise, as Chap. 2. vers. 26 and of an exhortation. Hitherto hath been the first part of the booke of the Apocalypse.

10 Because thou hast g kept the word of my
patience, therefore I will deliuer thee from the
houre of tentation, which will come vpō all the
world to trie them that dwell vpon the earth.
11 Behold, I come shortly: hold that which
thou hast that no man take thy crowne.
12 9 Him that ouercommeth, will I make a
pillar in the Temple of my God, and he shall
goe no more out: 10 and I will write vpon him
the Name of my God, and the name of the citie
of my God, *which is*, the new Hierusalem,
which commeth downe out of heauen from
my God, and *I will write vpon him* my newe
Name.
13 Let him that hath an eare, heare what
the Spirit sayth vnto the Churches.
14 11 And vnto the Angel of the Church of
the Laodiceans write, These things sayth h Amen,
the faithfull and true witnesse, that i beginning
of the creatures of God.
15 12 I knowe thy workes, that thou art
neither colde nor hote: I would thou werest
cold or hote.
16 Therefore, because thou art luke warme
and neither cold nor hote, it will come to passe,
that I shall spue thee out of my mouth.
17 For thou sayest, I am rich and increased
with goods, and haue neede of nothing, and
knowest not how thou art wretched and miserable,
13 and poore, and blinde, and naked.
18 I counsell thee to buy of mee gold tried
by the fire, that thou mayest be made rich: and
white raiment, that thou maiest be clothed, and
that thy filthy nakednesse doe not appeare: and
anoint thine eyes with eye salue, that thou
mayest see.
19 As many as I loue, * I rebuke and chasten:
be k zealous therefore and amend.
20 Behold, I stand at the doore, and knock,
14 If any man heare my voyce, and open the
doore, I wil come in vnto him, and wil sup with
him, and he with me.
21 15 To him that ouercommeth, will I
grant to sit with me in my throne, euen as I ouercame,
and sit with my Father in his throne.
22 Let him that hath an eare, heare what
the Spirit saith vnto the Churches.

CHAP. IIII.

1 Another vision conteining the glory of Gods Maiestie: 8 which is magnified of the foure beasts, 10 and the foure and twentie Elders.

1 AFter 1 this I looked, & behold, a doore was
open in heauen, and the first voice which
I heard, was as it were of a trumpet talking
with me, saying, Come vp hither, & I will shew
thee things which must be done hereafter.
2 And 2 immediately I was *rauished* a in
the spirit, 3 and behold, a throne was set in heauen,
and one sate vpon the throne.
3 4 And hee that sate was to looke vpon,
like vnto a Iasper stone, and a Sardine, and there
was a rainbowe round about the throne, in sight
like to an emeraud.
4 5 And round about the throne *were* foure
and twenty seates, and vpon the seates I sawe
foure and twenty Elders sitting, clothed in
white raiment, and had on their heads crownes
of gold.
5 6 And out of the throne proceeded lightnings,
and thundrings, and voices, and there
were seuen lampes of fire burning before the
throne, which are the seuen Spirits of God.
6 7 And before the throne there was a sea
of glasse like vnto crystall: and in the mids of
the throne, and round about the throne *were*
foure beasts, full of eyes before and behind.
7 And the first beast *was* like a lion, and the
second beast like a calfe, and the third beast had
a face as a man, and the fourth beast *was* like a
flying egle.
8 And the b foure beasts had each one of
them sixe wings about him, and they were full
of eyes within, and they ceased not 8 day nor
night, saying, Holy, holy, holy, Lord God almighty,
Which was, and Which is, and Which
is to come.
9 And when those beasts c gaue glory, and
honour, and thankes to him that sate on the
throne which liueth for euer and euer,
10 9 The foure and twenty Elders fell down
before him that sate on the throne, and worshipped
him that liueth for euermore, and cast
their crownes before the throne, saying,
11 10 Thou art * worthy, O Lord, to receiue
glory, and honour, and power: for thou
hast created all things, and for thy willes sake
they are, and haue been created.

2 The maner of reuelation, as before, 1. 10.
a Looke chap. 1. 10.
3 A description of God the Father, and of his glory in the heauens, framed vnto the maner of men by his office, nature, company, attending, effect, instruments, & euents that followe afterwards. In this verse he is presented in office a Iudge, as Abraham sayd, Gen. 18. which is declared by his throne, as an ensigne of iudgement, and his sitting thereupō.
4 By his nature, in that he is the Father, most glorious in his own person, and with his glory ouershining all other things.
5 By the company attending about him in that, as that most high Iudge, he is accompanied with the most honourable attendance of Prophets and Apostles, both of the olde and new Church, whom Christ hath made to bee Priests & Kings, Chap. 1. 6. and 5. 10.
6 By effects, in that most mightily he speaketh all things by his voyce, & word, as Isa. 29. 3. and with the light of his spirit and prudence peruseth and passeth through all.
7 By instrumēts vsed, in that hee both hath a most ready treasury, & as it were a workhouse excellently furnished with all things, vnto the executing of his will, which things flowe from his commaundement, as repeated, Chap. 15. 2. and hath also the Angels most ready administers of his counsels and pleasure, vnto all parts of the world, continually watching, (in this verse) working by reason otherwise then the instruments without life last mentioned, couragious as lions, mightie as bulles, wise as men, swift as egles, verse 7. most apt vnto all purposes, as furnished with wings on euery part, most piercing of sight, and finally, pure and holy spirits alwayes in continuall motion, verse 8. *b Euery beast had sixe wings.* 8 By euents, in that for all the causes before mentioned, God is glorified both of Angels, as holy, Iudge, omnipotent, eternall, and immutable, verse 8. and also after their example he is glorified of holy men, ver. 9, in signe & in speach, ver. 10, 11. *c God is sayd to haue glory, honour, kingdome, and such like giuen vnto him, when we godly and reuerently set forth that which is properly and only his.* 9 Three signes of diuine honour giuen vnto God, prostration or falling downe, adoration and casting their crownes before God: in which the godly, though made kings by Christ, doe willingly empty themselues of all glory, mooued with a religious respect of the maiestie of God. 10 The summe of their speach: that all glory must be giuen vnto God: the reason, because he is the eternall beginning of all things, from whose onely wil they haue their being, and are gouerned: and finally in all respects are that which they are. *Chap. 5. 12. 11 That is, that thou shouldest challenge the same to thy selfe alone. But as for vs, we are vnworthy, that euen by thy goodnesse we should bee made partakers of this glorie. And hitherto hath been handled the principall cause vnapproachable, which is God.

1 Hereafter followeth the second part of this book, altogether propheticall foretelling those things which were to come, as was said before, Chap. 1. 19. This is diuided into two histories: one common vnto the whole world, vnto the 9. Chapter: and another singular of the Church of God, thence vnto the 22 chapter. and these histories are sayd to be described in seuerall bookes, Chap 5. 1. and 10. 2. Now this verse is as it were a passage from the former part vnto this second: where it is sayd, that the heauen was opened, that is, that heauenly things were vnlocked, and that a voice of a trumpet founded in heauen, to stirre vp the Apostle, and call him to the vnderstanding of things to come. The first historie hath two parts: one of the causes of things done, & of this whole Reuelation, in this and the next Chapter. Another of the acts done in the next foure chapters. The principall causes according to the distinction of persons in the vnitie of the diuine essence, and according to the oeconomie or dispensation thereof, are two: One the beginning, which none can approach vnto, that is, God the Father, of whom is spoken in this chapter. The other, the Sonne, who is the meane cause, easie to be approched vnto, in respect that he is God and man in one person. of whom, Chap. 5.

CHAP. V.

1 The booke sealed with seuen seales, 3 which none could open, 6 that Lambe of God 9 is thought worthy to open, 12 euen by the consent of all the company of heauen.

And

A Nd [1] I saw in the [2] right hand of him that
sate vpon the throne, [3] a booke written
within, and on the backe side sealed with seuen
seales.
2 And I saw a strong Angel which preached with a loud voice, Who is worthy to open
the booke, and to loose the seales thereof?
3 [4] And no man in heauen nor in earth,
neither vnder the earth, was able to open the
booke, neither to looke thereon.
4 Then I wept much, because no man was
found worthy to open, and to reade the booke,
neither to looke thereon.
5 [5] And one of the Elders said vnto mee,
Weepe not: behold, that * [6] Lion which is of
the tribe of Iuda, that root of Dauid, hath obteined to open the booke, and to open the seuen seales thereof.
6 Then I beheld, and loe, [7] in the mids of
the throne, and of the foure beasts, and in the
mids of the Elders stood a Lambe, as though
hee had beene killed, which had seuen hornes,
and seuen eyes, which are the seuen spirits of
God, sent into all the world.
7 [8] And he came, & tooke the booke out of
the right hand of him that sate vpon the throne.
8 [9] And when he had taken the booke, the
foure beasts, and the foure and twentie Elders
fell down before the Lambe, hauing euery one
[10] harpes and golden vials full of odours, which
are the [a] prayers of the Saints,
9 And they sung a [b] newe song, saying,
[11] Thou art worthy to take the booke, and to
open the seales thereof, because thou wast killed, and hast redeemed vs to God by thy blood
out of euery kinred, and tongue, and people,
and nation,
10 And hast made vs vnto our God, *Kings,
and Priests, and we shall reigne on the earth.

1 A passing vnto the second principall cause, which is the Son of God, God and man, the mediatour of all, as the eternall word of God the Father, manifested in the flesh This Chapter hath two parts: one that prepareth the way vnto the Reuelation, by rehearsall of the occasions that did occurre in the first 4. verses. Another, the history of the Reuelation of Christ, thence vnto the end of the Chapter. 2 That is, in the very right hand of God. 3 Heere are shewed the occasions for which the principall cause, and this Reuelation was also necessarie: the same are three, the first a present vision of the book of the counsels of God, concerning the gouernment of this whole world, which booke is said to be laid vp with the Father as it were in his hand: but shut and vnknowen to all creatures, in this verse. The second is a religious desire of the Angels of God to vnderstand the mysteries of this booke, verse 2. whereof see 1 Pet.1.12. The third is a lamentation of S. Iohn and all the godly, moued by the same desire, verse 4. when they saw that it was a thing vnpossible for any creature to effect: which is declared in verse 3. 4 Thus neither of them that are in heauen, nor of them which are in the earth, &c. And this I like better. Now this enumeration of parts, is sufficient to the denying of the whole: For of the creatures, one sort is in heauen, aboue the earth: another in the earth, and another vnder the earth in the sea, as is after declared, verse 13. 5 The second part of this Chapter, in which is set downe the Reuelation of the Sonne, as before was said. This part conteineth first an history of the maner how God prepared S. Iohn to vnderstand this Reuelation, in this verse. Secondly, the Reuelation of the Sonne himselfe, vnto the 7. verse. Thirdly, the accidents of this Reuelatiō, in the rest of the chapter. The maner how, is here described in two sorts: one from without him, by speech, in this verse: another within, by opening the eyes of S. Iohn (which before were held) ẏ he might see, in the verse following. * *Gen.49.9.* 6 That is, the most mighty and most approued Prince: according to the vse of the Hebrew speech. 7 The summe of this Reuelation: Christ the mediator taketh & openeth the booke, ver 6.7 Therfore in this Reuelation is described the person of Christ, in this vers. His fact, in the next verse. The person is thus described: Christ the mediator betweene God, Angels, & men, as the eternall word of God, and our redeemer: as the Lambe of God, standing as slaine, and making intercession for vs by the vertue and merit of his euerlasting sacrifice, is armed with the Spirit of God in his owne person, that is, with the power and wisdome of God effectually vnto the gouernment of this whole world. 8 The fact of Christ the Mediator: that he commeth vnto the throne of the Father, of which, chap.4. and taketh the booke out of his hand to open it. For that he opened it, it is first expressed, chap.6.1.&c. 9 Now folow in the end, the accidents of the Reuelation last spoken of: that all the holy Angels & men did sing vnto him: both the chiefe, verse 9.10 and common order of Angels, verse 11, 12. and of all things created, verse 13. the princes of both sorts agreeing thereunto, verse 14. 10 The symbols or signes of praise, sweete in sauour, and acceptable vnto God, See Chap.8.3. *a Looke chap.8.3.* *b No common song.* 11 That is, composed according to the present matter, the Lambe hauing receiued the book as it were with his feet, & opened it with his horns, as it is said in the Canticle. 12 The song of the Nobles or Princes standing by the throne, consisting of a publication of the praise of Christ, & a confirmation of the same frō his benefits, both which we haue receiued of himselfe (as are the suffering of his death, our redemption vpō the crosse by his blood, in this verse: and our communion with him in Kingdome & Priesthood, which long agoe he hath granted vnto vs with himselfe) & which we hereafter hope to obtaine, as our kingdome to come, in Christ, in the verse following. * *Chap.1.6.1.pet.2.9.*

11 [13] Then I beheld, and I heard the voice
of many Angels round about the throne, and
about the beasts and the Elders, [14] and there
were * [c] ten thousand times ten thousand, and
thousand thousands,
12 Saying with a loud voice, Worthy is the
Lambe that was killed, to [d] receiue power, and
riches, and wisdome, and strength, and honour,
and glory, and praise.
13 [15] And all the creatures which are in heauen, and on the earth, and vnder the earth, and
in the sea, and all that are in them, heard I, saying, Praise, and honour, and glory, and power
be vnto him, that sitteth vpon the throne, and
vnto the Lambe for euermore.
14 [16] And the foure beasts said, Amen, and
the foure and twentie Elders fell downe and
worshipped him that liueth for euermore.

13 The consent of the common order of Angels, answering in melody vnto their Princes ẏ stood by the throne. 14 A number finite, but almost infinite for one infinite in deed, as Dan.7.10. * *Dan.7.10.* *c By this is meant a great number.* *d To haue all praise giuē to him, as to the mightiest and wisest, &c.* 15 The cōsent of all the common multitude of the creatures. 16 A confirmation of the praise before going, frō the contestation of the nobles, expressed in word and signes, as once or twise before this.

CHAP. VI.

1 The Lambe openeth the first seale of the booke, 3 the second, 5 the third, 7 the fourth, 9 the fifth, 12 & the sixth, and then arise, murders, famine, pestilence, outcries of Saints, earthquakes, and diuers strange sights in heauen.

A Fter, [1] I beheld when the Lambe had o-
pened one of the seales, and I heard one
of the foure beasts say, as *it were* the noise of
thunder, Come and see.
2 Therefore [2] I beheld, and loe, there *was* a
white horse, & he that sate on him, had a bow,
and a crowne was giuen vnto him, and he went
forth conquering that he might ouercome.
3 And [3] when hee had opened the second
seale, I heard the second beast say, Come & see.
4 And there went out another horse, *that*
was red, and power was giuen to him that sate
thereon to take peace from the earth, and that
they should kill one another, and there was
giuen vnto him a great sword.
5 [4] And when hee had opened the third
seale, I heard the third beast say, Come and see.
Then I beheld, and loe, a blacke horse, and hee
that sate on him had balances in his hand.
6 And I heard a voice in the middes of the
foure beasts say, A [a] measure of wheat for a peny, & three measures of barley for a peny, [5] and

1 This is the second part of this first historie (which I sayd was common & of the whole world) of the works of God in the gouernment of all things. Of this there are generally 3. members: the foresignifying, the caution, and the execution of all the euils which God powreth out vpon this world, which hath most hardly deserued of him. The foresignifying is set downe in this chapter, the caution for preseruing the Church is in the next chapter, and the execution is described, cha.8.9. In euery part of the foresignifying, there are three branches: the seuerall and expresse calling of S. Iohn, to prepare himselfe to take knowledge of the things that were to be shewed vnto him in the opening of the seales: the signe, and the word expounding the signe: And albeit the expresse calling of S Iohn, be vsed only in foure of the signes, yet the same is also to be vnderstood in the rest that follow. The authour of the foresignifyings is the Lambe, as that word of the Father made the Mediator, opening the seales of the booke. The instruments are the Angels in most of the visions, who expound the signe and the words thereof. Now this first verse containeth an expresse calling of S. Iohn to marke the opening of the first seale 2 The first signe ioyned with declaration, is, that God for the sinnes and horrible rebellion of the world, will inuade the same: and first of all will as afarre off, with his darts of pestilence most suddenly, mightily, and gloriously, beate downe the same as Iudge, and triumph ouer it as conquerour. 3 The second signe ioyned with wordes of declaration (after the expresse calling of S. Iohn as before) is, that God being prouoked vnto wrath by the obstinacie and hard heartednesse of the world, not repenting for the former plague: as setting vpon the same at hand, will kindle the fire of debate amongst men, and will destroy the inhabitants of this world, one by the sword of another. 4 The third signe with declaration, is, that God will destroy the world with famine, withdrawing all prouision: which is by the figure Synecdoche comprehended in wheate, barley, wine, and oyle. *a Hereby is signified what great scarcitie of corne there was, for the word here vsed is a kinde of measure of drie things, which is in quantitie but the eight part of a bushell, which was an ordinary portion to be giuen to seruants for their stint of meate for one day.* 5 I had rather distinguish and reade the words thus, *And the wine and the oyle thou shalt not deale vniustly.* In this sense likewise the wine and the oyle shalbe solde a very little for a peny. Thou shalt not deale vniustly, namely, when thou shalt measure out a very little for a great price: so is the place euident: otherwise that is most true, which the wise man saith, That who so withholdeth the corne, shalbe cursed of the people, Prouerb.11.26.

oyle, and wine hurt thou not.
7 [6] And when hee had opened the fourth
seale, I heard the voice of the fourth beast say,
Come and see.
8 And I looked, and behold, a pale horse,
and his name that sate on him was Death, and
Hell followed after him, and power was giuen
vnto them ouer the fourth part of the earth, to
kill with sword, and with hunger, and with
death, and with the beasts of the earth.
9 [7] And when hee had opened the fifth
seale, I saw vnder the altar the soules of them
that were killed for the word of God, and for
the testimonie which they maintained.
10 And they cryed with a loud voice, saying, How long, Lord, which art holy and true!
doest not thou iudge and auenge our blood on
them that dwell on the earth?
11 And long [8] white robes were giuen vnto
euery one, and it was said vnto them, that they
should rest for a little season vntill their fellow
seruants, and their brethren that should be killed euen as they were, were [b] fulfilled.
12 [9] And I beheld when he had opened the
sixt seale, and loe, there was a great earthquake,
and the Sunne was as blacke as [c] sackecloth of
haire, and the Moone was like blood.
13 And the starres of heauen fell vnto the
earth, as a figge tree casteth her greene figges,
when it is shaken of a mightie winde.
14 And heauen departed away, as a scroule,
when it is rolled, and euery mountaine and yle
were mooued out of their places.
15 [10] And the Kings of the earth, and the
great men, and the rich men, and the chiefe
captaines, and the mighty men, & euery bondman, & euery free man, hid themselues in dens,
and among the rockes of the mountaines,
16 And said to the mountaines and rockes,
[11] * Fall on vs, and hide vs from the presence of
him that sitteth on the throne, and from the
wrath of the Lambe.
17 For the great day of his wrath is come,
and who can stand?

6 The fourth signe ioyned with words of declaration, is, that God will addict the fourth part of the world indifferently, vnto death and hel, or the graue, by all those meanes at once, by which before seuerally and in order he had recalled their minds vnto amendment. Vnto these are also added the wilde and cruell beasts of the earth, out of Leuit. 26.22. Thus doth God according to his wisedome, dispense the treasures of his power, iustly towards all, mercifully towards the good, and with patience or long sufferance towards his enemies.
7 The fift signe is, that the holy Martyrs which are vnder the altar, whereby they are sanctified, that is, receiued into the trust and tuition of Christ (into whose hands they are committed) shall cry out for the iustice of God, in an holy zeale to aduance his kingdome, and not of any priuate perturbation of the minde, in this and the next verse, and that God will, in deed, signe, and word comfort them, vers. 1.
8 As before 3.4.
b Vntill their number be fulfilled.
9 The sixt signe, the narration whereof hath two parts: the signe, and the euent. The signe is, that the earth, heauen, and the things that are in them, for horror of the sinnes of the world vpon those most heauie foretellings of God, and complaints of the Saints shall be shaken most vehemently, trembling in horrible maner, and loosing their light, in this verse: falling from on high, verse 13. withdrawing themselues and flying away for the greatnesse of the trouble, verse 14. So holily doe all creatures depend vpon the wil of God, and content themselues in his glory. *c So they called in old time those wouen works that were of haire.*
10 The euent of the signe aforegoing: that there is no man that shall not be astonished at that generall commotion, flie away for feare and hide himselfe, in this verse, and wish vnto himselfe most bitter death, for exceeding horror of the wrath of God, and of the Lambe, at which before he was astonished. Now this perplexitie is not of the godly but of the wicked, whose portion is in this life, as the Psalmist speaketh, Psal. 17.14. Not that sorow which is according vnto God, which worketh repentance vnto saluation, whereof a man shall neuer repent him, but that wordly sorow that bringeth death, 2.Cor.7.9. as their wishings do declare: for this history of ẏ whole world, is seuered frõ the history of the Church, as I haue shewed before, Cha.4.1. 11 These are words of such as despaire of their escape: of which despaire there are two arguments, the presence of God, and the Lambe prouoked to wrath against the world, in this verse: and the conscience of their owne weakenesse, whereby men feele, that they are no way able to stand in the day of the wrath of God, verse 17. as it is said, Esai 14.27. * *Esai 2.19. hose. 10.8. luke 23.30.*

CHAP. VII.

1 The Angels comming to hurt the earth, 3 are stayed vntill the elect of the Lord 5 of all tribes were sealed. 13 Such as suffered persecution for Christes sake, 16 haue great felicitie, 17 and ioy.

AND [1] after that, I saw foure Angels stand
on the [a] foure corners of the earth, holding the foure windes of the earth, that the
windes should not blow on the earth, neither
on the sea, [2] neither on any tree.
2 [3] And I sawe [4] another Angel come vp
from the East, which had the seale of the liuing
God, and hee cryed with a loud voice to the
foure Angels to whome power was giuen to
hurt the earth, and the sea, saying,
3 Hurt yee not the earth, neither the sea,
neither the trees, till wee haue sealed the seruants of God in their foreheads.
4 And I heard the number of them, which
were sealed, and there *were* sealed [5] an hundred
and foure and fourtie thousand of all the tribes
of the children of Israel.
5 Of the tribe of Iuda were sealed twelue
thousand. Of the tribe of Reuben were sealed
twelue thousand. Of the tribe of Gad were sealed twelue thousand.
6 Of the tribe of Aser were sealed twelue
thousand. Of the tribe of Nephtali were sealed
twelue thousand. Of the tribe of Manasses
were sealed twelue thousand.
7 Of the tribe of Simeon were sealed twelue
thousand. [6] Of the tribe of [b] Leui were sealed
twelue thousand. Of the tribe of Issachar were
sealed twelue thousand. Of the tribe of Zebu-
lun were sealed twelue thousand.
8 Of the tribe of [c] Ioseph were sealed
twelue thousand. Of the tribe of Beniamin
were sealed twelue thousand.
9 After these things I beheld, and loe, a
great multitude, [7] which no man could number, of all nations, and kinreds, and people, and
tongues [8] stood before the throne, and before
the Lambe, clothed with long white robes, and
palmes in their hands.
10 [9] And they cryed with a loud voice, saying, Saluation *commeth* of our God, that sitteth vpon the throne, and of the Lambe.
11 And all the Angels stood round about
the throne, and *about* the Elders, and the foure
beasts, and they fell before the throne on their
faces, and worshipped God,

1 The second member of this part, is a preuenting of danger, as we distinguished the same before, chap. 6.1. ẏ is, of the caution wherby God tooke care before hand and prouided for his, that after the example of the Israelites of old, Exod. 8.23. the faithfull might be exempted from the plagues of this wicked world. This whole place is a certaine interlocution and bringing in for this whole chapter by occasion of the prediction and argument of the sixt seale. For first that euil is preuented in the elect, vnto the 9. verse. Then thankes are giuen by the elect for that cause, verse 10. 11.12. Lastly, the accomplishment of the thing is set forth vnto the end of the Chapter. The first verse is a transition, speaking of the Angels which keepe the inferiour parts from all euill, vntill God doe command. For (as it is excellently figured by Ezek. chap. 11.12.) their faces and their wings are reached vpwards, continually waiting vpon and beholding the countenance of God for their direction, and euery of them goeth into that part that is right before his face: whither soeuer the Spirit shall goe, they goe, they step not out of the way, that is, they depart not so much as a foot breadth from the path commanded them of God. *a On the foure quarters or coasts of the earth.* 2 That is, neither into the aire, into which the tops of trees are aduanced. 3 Now God prouideth against the danger of his elect, by his commandement, verse 2. & 3. and by signe or figure, both for those of the nation of the Iewes, thence vnto the 1. verse, and also of the Gentiles, verse 9. 4 Not onely another, or differing number from the common Angels of God, but also in essence, office and operation exceeding all Angels: that is, Christ Iesus the eternall Angel or word of God, and mediatour of the couenant. So hereafter Chap. 8.3. and 10.15. 5 That is, of the Iewes a number certaine in it selfe before God, and such as may be numbred of vs: for which cause also the same is here set downe as certaine. But of the elect which are of the Gentiles, the number in deede is in it selfe certaine with God, but of vs not possibly to be numbred, as God, Gen. 15.5. and often elsewhere, and Esay figured most excellently, Chap. 49. and 60. This therefore is spoken with respect, when a certaine number is put for one vncertaine. Conferre this with verse 9 *b He skipped Dan, and reckoneth Leui. c Of Ephraim, who was Iosephs other sonne, and had the birthright giuen him, whereof he is called Ioseph.* 6 Here the tribe of Leui is reckoned vp in cõmon with the rest, because all the Israelites were equally made Priests with them in Christ by his Priesthood, Chap. 1.6. & 5.10. and Rom. 12.1. and 1.Pet. 2.9. The name of Dan is not mentioned, because the Danites long before forsaking the worship of God, were fallen away from the fellowship of Gods people, vnto the part of the Gentiles: which euill many ages before, Iacob foresaw, Gen. 49.18. for which cause also there is no mentiõ made of this tribe in the 1. booke of the Chronicles. 7 See before vpon the 4. verse. 8 As Priests, kings, and glorious conquerers by martyrdome: which things are noted by their proper signes in this verse. 9 The praise of God, celebrated first by the holy men, in this verse, then by the heauenly Angels, in the two verses following.

12 Saying,

12 Saying, Amen, Praiſe, and glory, & wiſdome, and thanks, and honour, and power, and
might, *be* vnto our God for euermore, Amen.
13 [10] And one of the Elders ſpake, ſaying
vnto mee, What are theſe which are arayed in
long white robes? and whence came they?
14 And I ſaid vnto him, Lord, thou knoweſt. And he ſaid vnto me, Theſe are they, which
came out of great tribulation, and haue waſhed
their long robes, and haue made their long
robes white in the blood of the Lambe.
15 Therfore are they in the preſence of the
throne of God, and ſerue him [d] day and night
in his Temple, and he that ſitteth on the throne
will dwell [e] among them.
16 *They ſhall hunger no more, neither
thirſt any more, neither ſhall the ſunne light
on them, neither any heat.
17 For the lambe which is in the mids of the
throne ſhall gouerne them, & ſhall leade them
vnto the liuely fountaines of waters, and *God
ſhall wipe away all teares from their eyes.

10 A paſſage ouer vnto the expounding of the viſion, of which the Angel enquireth of S. Iohn to ſtirre him vp withall, in this verſe, and Iohn in the forme of ſpeech, both acknowledgeth his owne ignorance, attributing knowledge vnto the Angel, and alſo in moſt modeſt manner requeſteth the expounding of the viſion.

11 The expoſition of the viſion, wherein the Angel telleth firſt the actes of the Saints, that is, their ſuffrings and worke of faith in Chriſt Ieſus, in this verſ. Secondly their glory: both preſent, which conſiſteth in two things, that they miniſter vnto God, and that God protecteth them, verſe 15. and to come, in their perfect deliuerance from all annoiances, verſe 16. & in participation of al good things which euen the memory of former euils ſhal neuer be able to diminiſh, verſe 17. The cauſe efficient, & which containeth all theſe things, is only one, euen the Lambe of God, the Lord, the Mediatour, and the Sauiour Chriſt Ieſus.

d *He alludeth to the Leuites, which ſerued day and night, for elſe there is no night in heauen.*

e *Or, vpon them, whereby is meant Gods defence and protection, as it were towards them, who are as ſafe, as men in the Lords tents.* *Eſai 49.10. *Eſai 25.8. chap. 21.4.

CHAP. VIII.

1 *After the opening of the ſeuenth ſeale,* 3 *the Saints prayers are offered vp with odours.* 6 *The ſeuen Angels come foorth with trumpets.* 7 *The foure firſt blow, and fire falleth on the earth,* 8 *the ſea is turned inte blood,* 10. 11 *the waters waxe bitter,* 12 *and the ſtarres are darkened.*

AND [1] when hee had opened the ſeuenth
ſeale, there was ſilence in heauen aboue
halfe an houre.
2 [2] And I ſawe the ſeuen Angels, which
[a] ſtood before God, and to them were giuen
ſeuen trumpets.
3 [3] Then another Angel came and ſtood
before the altar, hauing a golden cenſer, and
much odours was giuen vnto him, that hee
ſhould offer with the prayers of all Saints vpon
the golden altar, which is before the throne.
4 And the ſmoke of the odours with the
prayers of the Saints, [b] went vp before God,
out of the Angels hand.
5 And the Angel tooke the cenſer, and filled it with fire of the altar, and caſt it into the
earth, and there were voices, and thunderings,
and lightenings, and earthquake.
6 [4] Then the ſeuen Angels, which had the
ſeuen trumpets, prepared themſelues to blow
the trumpets.
7 [5] So the firſt Angel blew the trumpet,
and there was haile and fire, mingled with
blood, and they were caſt into the earth, and
the third part of trees was burnt, and all greene
graſſe was burnt.
8 [6] And the ſecond Angel blew the trumpet, and as *it were* a great mountaine, burning
with fire, was caſt into the ſea, and the third
part of the ſea became blood.
9 And the third part of the creatures,
which were in the ſea, and had life, died, and the
third part of ſhips were deſtroyed.
10 [7] Then the third Angel blew his trumpet,
and there fell a great ſtarre from heauen, burning like a torch, and it fell into the third part
of the riuers, and into the fountaines of waters.
11 And the name of the ſtarre is called
[8] wormewood: therefore the third part of the
waters became wormwood, & many men died
of the waters, becauſe they were made bitter.
12 [9] And the fourth Angel blew the trumpet, and the third part of the ſunne was ſmit-
ten, and the third part of the moone, and the
third part of the ſtarres, ſo that the third part
of them was darkened: and the day *was ſmit-
ten*, that the third part of it could not ſhine,
and likewiſe the night.
13 And I beheld, and heard one Angel flying thorow the middes of heauen, ſaying with
a loud voice, Woe, woe, woe to the inhabitants
of the earth, becauſe of the ſounds to come of
the trumpet of the three Angels, which were
yet to blow the trumpets.

1 He returneth to the hiſtory of the ſeales of the booke, which the Lambe openeth. The ſeuenth ſeale is the next foreſignification, and a preciſe commandement of the execution of the moſt heauie iudgements of God vpon this wicked world, which foreſignification being vnderſtood by the ſeale, all things in heauen are ſilent, and in horror through admiration, vntill commandement of execution be ſeuerally giuen of God vnto the miniſters of his wrath. So hee paſſeth vnto the third member of which I ſpake before in Chap. 6. verſe 1. which is of the execution of thoſe euils wherewith God moſt iuſtly determined to afflict the world.

2 Now followeth the third branch of the common hiſtory, as euen now I ſaid: which is the execution of the iudgements of God vpon the world. This is firſt generally prepared, vnto the 6. verſe: then by ſeuerall parts expounded according to the order of thoſe that adminiſtred the ſame, vnto the end of the Chapter following. Vnto the preparation of this execution, are declared theſe things: firſt, who were the adminiſters and inſtruments thereof in this verſe. Secondly what is the worke both of the Prince of Angels, giuing order for this execution, thence vnto the 5. verſe, and of his adminiſters in the 6. verſe. The adminiſters of the execution are ſaid to be ſeuen Angels: their inſtruments, trumpets, whereby they ſhould as it were ſound the alarum at the cōmandement of God. They are propounded ſeuen in number, becauſe it pleaſed God not at once to powre out his wrath vpon the rebellious world, but at diuers times, and by piecemeale, and in ſlow order, and as with an vnwilling minde to exerciſe his iudgements vpon his creatures, ſo long called vpon both by word and ſignes, if happily they had learned to repent.

a *Which appeareth before him as his miniſters.*

3 This is that great Emperour, the Lord Ieſus Chriſt, our King and Sauiour, who both maketh interceſſion to God the Father for the Saints, filling the heauenly ſanctuarie with moſt ſweete odour, and offering vp their prayers, as the calues and burnt ſacrifices of their lips, in this verſe: in ſuch ſort as euery one of them (ſo powerfull is that ſweet ſauour of Chriſt, and the efficacie of his ſacrifice) are helde in reconcilement with God and themſelues, made moſt acceptable vnto him, verſe 4. And then alſo out of his treaſurie, and from the ſame ſanctuarie powreth forth vpon the world the fire of his wrath, adding alſo diuine tokens thereunto: and by that meanes (as of olde the heralds of Rome were wont to doe) he proclaimeth warre againſt the rebellious world.

b *Our prayers are nothing worth, vnleſſe that true and ſweet ſauour of that only oblation be eſpecially and before all things with them, that is to ſay, vnleſſe we being firſt of all iuſtified through faith in his Son be acceptable vnto him.*

4 This is the worke of the adminiſters. The Angels the adminiſters of Chriſt, only by ſounding trumpet and voice (for they are only as heralds) doe effectually call foorth the inſtruments of the wrath of God, through his power. Hitherto haue beene things generall. Now followeth the narration of things particular, which the Angels ſixe in number wrought in their order, ſet out in the 19. verſe of the next Chapter, and is concluded with the declaration of the euent which followed vpon theſe things done in the world, and in the 10. and 11. Chap.

5 The firſt execution at the ſound of the firſt Angel, vpon the earth, that is, the inhabitants of the earth (by metonymie) and vpon all the fruits thereof: as the comparing of this verſe with the ſecond member of the 9. verſe doth not obſcurely declare.

6 The ſecond execution vpon the ſea, in this verſe, & all things that are therein, in the next verſe.

7 The third execution vpon the floods and fountaines, that is, vpon all freſh waters, in this verſe: the effect whereof is, that many are deſtroyed with the bitterneſſe of waters, in the verſe following.

8 This is ſpoken by Metaphore, of the name of a moſt bitter herbe, and commonly knowen: vnleſſe perhaps a man following thoſe that note the deriuation of words had rather expound it adiectiuely, for that which by reaſon of bitterneſſe cannot be drunke, or which maketh the liquor into which it is powred, more bitter then that any man can drinke the ſame.

9 The fourth execution vpon theſe lightſome bodies of heauen, which miniſter vnto this inferior world.

10 A lamentable prediction or foretelling of thoſe parts of the diuine execution which yet are behinde: which alſo is a paſſage vnto the argument of the next Chapter. Of all theſe things in a manner Chriſt himſelfe expreſſely foretold in the 21. Chapter of S. Luke, verſe 24. &c. and they are common plagues generally denounced, without particular note of time.

CHAP. IX.

1 *The fift Angel bloweth his trumpet,* 3 *and ſpoiling locuſts come out.* 13 *The ſixt Angel bloweth,* 16 *and bringeth foorth horſemen,* 20 *to deſtroy mankinde.*

AND the fift Angel blew the trumpet, and
I ſaw a [2] ſtarre fall from heauen vnto the

1 The firſt execution vpon the wicked men inhabiting ye earth (as a litle before ye Angel ſaid) wrought by the infernal powers is declared in this place vnto ver. 11. and after the ſixt execution thence vnto ver. 19. And laſtly is ſhewed the common euent that followed the former execution in the world, in the two laſt verſes.

2 That is, ye the Angel of God glittering with glory, as a ſtar fell down from heauen. Whether thou take him for Chriſt, who hath the keyes of hel of himſelfe, & by princely authority, Chap. 1. v. 18. or whether for ſome inferiour Angel, who hath the ſame key permitted vnto him, and occupieth it miniſterially, or by office of his miniſtery, here and Chap. 21. ſo the word *falling* is taken, Gen. 14. 10. and 24. 46. and Hebr. 6. 6.

earth, [3] and to him was giuen the key of the
[a] bottomlesse pit.
2 [4] And he opened the bottomlesse pit, and
there arose the smoke of the pit, as the smoke
of a great fornace, and the sunne, and the aire
were darkened by the smoke of the pit.
3 [5] And there came out of the smoke locusts
vpon the earth, and vnto them was giuen power, as the scorpions of the earth haue power.
4 [6] And it was commanded them that they
should not hurt the grasse of the earth, neither
any greene thing, neither any tree: but onely
those men which haue not the seale of God in
their foreheads.
5 And to them was commanded that they
should not kill them, but that they should be
vexed fiue moneths, & that their paine should
be as the paine that commeth of a scorpion,
when he hath stung a man.
6 *Therefore in those dayes shall men
seeke death, and shall not finde it, and shall desire to die, and death shall flee from them.
7 [7] And the forme of the locusts *was* like
vnto horses prepared vnto battell, and on their
heads *were* as *it were* crownes, like vnto gold,
and their faces *were* like the faces of men.
8 And they had haire as the haire of women, and their teeth were as the teeth of lions.
9 And they had habergeons, like vnto habergeons of yron, and the sound of their
wings *was* like the sound of charets when many horses runne vnto battell.
10 And they had tailes like vnro scorpions,
and there were stings in their tailes, and their
power was to hurt fiue moneths.
11 [8] And they haue a king ouer them, which
is the Angel of the bottomlesse pit, whose
name in Hebrew *is* Abaddon, and in Greeke
he is named Apollyon, *that is, destroying*.
12 [9] One woe is past, *and* behold, yet two
woes come after this.
13 ¶[10] Then the sixt Angel blew the trumpet,[11] & I heard a voice from the [b] foure hornes
of the golden altar, which is before God,
14 Saying to the sixt Angel, which had the
trumpet, [12] Loose the foure Angels, which are
bound in the great riuer Euphrates.
15 [13] And the foure Angels were loosed,
which were prepared at an houre, at a day, at a
moneth, and at a yeere to slay the third part
of men.
16 And the number of horsemen of warre
were twentie thousand times ten thousand:
for I heard the number of them.
17 And thus I saw the horses in a vision, and
them that sate on them, hauing fiery habergi-
ons and of Iacinth, and of brimstone, and the
heads of the horses were as the heads of lions:
and out of their mouthes went foorth fire, and
smoke, and brimstone.
18 Of these three was the third part of men
killed, *that is*, of the fire, and of the smoke, and
of the brimstone, which came out of their
mouthes.
19 For their power is in their mouthes, and

3 The key was giuen to this starre. For those powers of wickednes are thrust downe into hell, and bound with chaines of darknesse, and are there kept vnto damnation, vnlesse God for a time do let them loose, 2.Pet.2.4. Iude 6. and of this book Chap. 21.20. the history of which Chapter hath agreement of time with this present Chapter.

a *By the bottomlesse pit, he meaneth the deepest darknesse of hell.*

4 Vnto this is added, the smoke of the hellish and infernall spirits, all darke, and darkening all things in heauen and in earth. The spirituall darknesses are the causes of all disorder & confusion: For the deuill at a certaine time (whereof verse the fift) sent these darknesses into his kingdome, that he might at once, & with one impression ouerthrow all things, & peruert if it were possible the elect themselues. By this darknesse, all spirituall light, both actiue as of the sunne, & passiue, as of the aire which is lightned by the sunne, is taken away: and this is that which goeth before the spirits: it followeth of the spirits themselues.
5 A description of the malignant spirits inuading the world, taken from their nature, power, forme, & order. From their nature, for that they are like vnto certaine locusts, in quicknesse, subtiltie, hurtfulnesse, number, and such like, in this verse. From their power, for that they are as the scorpions of the earth, of a secret force to do hurt: for our battell is not here with flesh and blood, but with powers, &c. Ephes. 6.12. This place of the power of the deuils, generally noted in this verse, is particularly declared afterwards in the three next verses.
6 Here that power of the deuils is particularly described according to their actions and the effects of the same. Their actions are said to be bounded by the counsell of God: both because they hurt not all men, but only the reprobate (for the godly & elect, in whom there is any part of a better life, God guardeth by his decree) whom Christ shall not haue sealed, in this verse: and also because they neither had all power nor at all times, no not ouer those that are their owne, but limited in maner and time, by the prescript of God, verse 5. So their power to afflict the godly is none, and for the wicked is limited in acte and in effect, by the will of God: for the maner was prescribed vnto them that they should not slay, but torment the wretched world. The time is for fiue moneths, or for an hundred and fifty dayes, that is, for so many yeeres, in which the deuils haue in deed mightily peruerted all things in the world: and yet without that publike and vnpunished license of killing, which afterwards they vsurped when the sixt Angel had blowen his trumpet, as shalbe said vpon verse 13. Now this space is to be accounted from the end of that thousand yeeres mentioned Chap. 20.3. and that is from the Popedome of that *Gregory* the 7. a most monstrous Necromancer, who before was called *Hildebrandus Senensis:* for this man being made altogether of impiety and wickednesse, as a slaue of the deuill, whom he serued, was the most wicked firebrand of the world: he excommunicated the Emperor *Henry* the fourth: went about by all maner of treachery to set vp and put downe Empires and kingdomes as liked himselfe: and doubted not to set *Rodolph* the Swedon ouer the Empire in stead of *Henry* before named, sending vnto him a Crowne, with this verse annexed vnto it: *Petra dedit Petro, Petrus diadema Rodolpho:* that is, The Rocke to Peter gaue the Crowne, and Peter Rodolph doeth renowne. Finally, he so finely bestirred himselfe in his affaires, as he miserably set all Christendome on fire, & conueyed ouer vnto his successors the burning brand of the same: who enraged with like ambitiõ, neuer ceased to nourish that flame, and to enkindle it more & more: whereby Cities, Common-weales, and whole kingdomes set together by the eares amongst themselues by most expert cut-throats, came to ruine, whiles they miserably wounded one another. This terme of an hundred and fifty yeres, taketh end in the time of *Gregory* the 9. or *Hugolinus Anagniensis* (as he was before called) who caused to be compiled by one *Raimond* his Chapleine & confessor, the body of Decretals, and by sufferance of the Kings and Princes, to be published in the Christian world, & established for a Law: For by this sleight at length the Popes arrogated vnto themselues licence to kill whom they would, whiles other were vnwares: and without feare established a butchery out of many of the wicked Canons of the Decretals, which the trumpet of the fift Angel had expresly forbidden, and had hindered vntill this time. The effects of these blody actions are declared vpon the sixt verse: that the miserable world languishing in so great calamities, should willingly run together vnto death, & preferre the same before life, by reason of the grieuousnes of the miseries that oppressed them.
* *Chap. 6.16. esai 2.19. hose. 10.8.*
7 The forme of these hellish spirits and administers, is shadowed out by signes and visible figures in this sort: that they are very expert and swift: that wheresoeuer they are in the world, the kingdome is theirs: that they manage all their affaires with cunning and skill, in this verse: that making shew of mildnesse & tender affection to draw on men withal, they most impudently rage in all mischiefe: that they are most mightie to doe hurt, verse 8 that they are freed from being hurt of any man, as armed with the colour of religion and sacred authoritie of priuiledge: that they fill all things with horror, verse the 9. that they are fraudulent: that they are venimous & extremely noisome, though their power be limited, verse 10 All which things are properly in the infernall powers, and communicated by them vnto their ministers and vassals.

8 The order of powers of maliciousnesse: that they are subiect to one infernall King, whom thou mayest call in English, The Destroyer: who driueth ỹ whole world both Iewes and Gentiles into the destruction that belongeth vnto himselfe. And I cannot tell whether this name haue respect vnto the Etymologicall interpretation of *Hildebrand*, by a figure often vsed in the holy Scripture: which albeit it may otherwise be turned of the Germaines (as the sense of compound words is commonly ambiguous) yet in very deed it signifieth as much as if thou shouldest call him, The firebrand, that is, hee that setteth on fire those that be faithfull vnto him.

9 A passage vnto the next point and the history of the time following.

10 The sixt execution done vpon the world by the tyrannicall powers therof, working in the foure parts of the earth, that is, in most cruell maner executing their tyrannous dominion thorow the whole world: and killing the miserable people without punishment, which before was not lawfull for them to do in that sort, as I shewed vpon the fourth verse. This narration hath two parts: a commandement from God, in the 14. verse, and an execution of the commandement, in the verse following.
11 The Commandement giuen by Christ himselfe, who is gouernour ouer all.
b *He alludeth to the altar of incense, which stood in the Court which the Priests were in, ouer against the Arke of the Couenant, hauing a vaile betwixt them.*
12 As if he should haue said, these hitherto haue bin so bound by power of God, that they could not freely run vpon all men as themselues lusted, but were stayed and restrained at that great flood of Euphrates, that is, in their spirituall Babylon (or this is a Periphrasis of the spirituall Babylon, by the limits of the visible Babylon long since ouerthrowne) that they might not commit those horrible slaughters, which they long breathed after. Now goe to, let loose those foure Angels, that is, administers of the wrath of God, in that number that is conuenient to the slaughtering of the foure quarters of the world: stirre them vp & giue them the bridle, that rushing out of that Babylon of theirs, which is the seat of the wicked ones, they may flie vpon all the world, therein to rage, and most licentiously to practise their tyrannie, as God hath ordeined. This was done when Gregorie the ninth by publique authoritie stablished for Lawe, his owne Decretals, by which hee might freely lay traines for the life of simple men. For who is it that seeth not that the lawes Decretall most of them are snares to catch soules withall? Since that time (O good God) how great slaughters haue there bene? how great massacres? All histories are full of them: and this our age aboundeth with most horrible and monstrous examples of the same.
13 The execution of the commandement is in two points: one, that those butchers are let loose, that out of their tower of ỹ spiritual Babylon they might with furie runne abroad through all the world, as well the chiefe of that crew which are most prompt vnto all assayes, in this verse: as their multitudes, both most copious, of which a number certaine is named for a number infinite, ver. 16. and in themselues by all meanes fully furnished to hide and to hurt, verse the 17. as being armed with fire, smoke and brimstone, as appeareth in the colour of this armour, which dazeleth the eyes to all men, and haue the strength of Lyons to hurt withal, from which (as out of their mouth,) the firie, smokie, and stinking darts of the Pope are shot out, ver. 18. The other points, that these butchers haue effected the Commaundement of God by fraud and violence, in the two verses following.

in their tailes: [14] for their tailes were like vnto
serpents, and had heads wherewith they hurt.
20 [15] And the remnant of the men which
were not killed by the plagues, repented not of
the workes of their hands that they should not
worship deuils, and * idoles of golde, and of
siluer, and of brasse, and of stone, and of wood,
which neither can see, neither heare, nor goe.
21 Also they repented not of their murther, and of their sorcerie, neither of their fornication, nor of their theft.

14 That is, they are harmefull euery way: on what part soeuer thou put thine hand vnto them, or they touch thee, they doe hurt. So the former are called Scorpions, verse 3. 15 Now remaineth the euent (as I said vpon the first verse) which followed of so many and so grieuous iudgements in the most wicked world, namely an impenitent obfirmation of the vngodly in their impietie and vnrighteousnes, though they feele themselues most vehemently pressed with the hand of God: for their obstinate vngodlinesse is shewed in this verse: and their vnrighteousnesse in the verse following. Hitherto hath beene the generall historie of things to be done vniuersally in the whole world: which because it doeth not so much belong to the Church of Christ, is therefore not so expressely distinguished by certeintie of time and other circumstances, but is wouen, as they say, with a slight hand. Also there is none other cause why the historie of the seuenth Angel is passed ouer in this place, then for that the same more properly appertaineth vnto the history of the Church. But this is more diligently set out according to the time thereof, Chapter 11. and 16. as shall appeare vpon those places. *Psal. 115.4. and 135.15.

CHAP. X.

1 Another Angel appeareth clothed with a cloud, 2 holding a booke open, 3 & cryeth out. 8 A voice from heauen commandeth Iohn to take the booke. 10 Hee eateth it.

1 And [1] I saw [2] another mightie Angel come
down from heauen, clothed with a cloud,
and the rainebowe vpon his head, and his face
was as the sunne, and his feete as pillars of fire.
2 And hee had in his hand a [3] little booke
open, and hee put his right foot vpon the sea,
and *his* left on the earth,
3 And cryed with a loud voice, as when a
lion roareth: and when hee had cryed, seuen
thunders vttered their voices.
4 [4] And when the seuen thunders had vttered their voices, I was about to write: but I
heard a voice from heauen, saying vnto mee,
[a] Seale vp those things which the seuen thunders haue spoken, and write them not.
5 And the Angel which I saw stand vpon
the sea, and vpon the earth, [b] lift vp his hand to
heauen,
6 And sware by him that liueth for euermore, which created heauen, and the things
that therein are, and the earth, and the things
that therein are, and the sea, & the things that
therein are, [5] that [c] time should be no more.
7 But in the dayes of the [6] voices of the
seuenth Angel, when hee shall begin to blow
the trumpet, euen the mysterie of God shall be
finished, as he hath declared to his seruants the
Prophets.
8 [7] And the voice which I heard from heauen, spake vnto me againe, and said, Goe, and
take the little booke which is open in the hand
of the Angel, which standeth vpon the sea, and
vpon the earth.
9 So I went vnto the Angel, and said vnto
him, Giue me the little booke. And he said vnto me, Take it, and eate it vp, and it shall make
thy belly bitter, but it shall be in thy mouth as
sweete as honie.
10 Then I tooke the little booke out of the
Angels hand, and ate it vp, and it was in my
mouth as sweete as hony: but when I had eaten it, my belly was bitter.
11 [8] And he said vnto me, Thou must prophecie againe among the people and nations,
and tongues, and to many Kings.

1 Now S. Iohn passeth vnto the other Propheticall historie, which is of the Church of God, as I shewed that this book should be distinguished, Chapter 4 1. This storie reacheth hence vnto the two and twentieth Chapter. And this whole Chapter is but a transition from the common history of the world vnto that which is particulr of the Church. There are in this transition or passage, two preparatiues as it were, vnto this Church storie comprised in this whole chapter. One is the authoritie of Christ reuealing his mysteries and calling his seruant, vnto the seuenth verse. The other is S. Iohn his calling, proper vnto this place, and repeated from before vnto the end of this Chapter. Authoritie is giuen vnto this Reuelation, by these things: first, by the appearing from heauen in this habite and countenance, strong, ready, glorious, surueying all things by his prouidence, & gouerning them by his omnipotencie, verse 1. Secondly, that he brought not by chance, but out of a booke, this open Reuelation, set foorth vnto the eye, to signifie the same vnto the sea, and land, as the Lord ouer all, verse 2. Thirdly that he offered the same not whispering or muttering in a corner (as false prophets do) but crying out with a loud voice vnto them which sleepe, and with a lionish and terrible noise roused vp the secure: the very thunders themselues giuing testimony thereunto, verse 3. Lastly, for that he confirmed all by an othe, verse 5, 6, 7. 2 Christ Iesus, see Chapter 7 verse 2. 3 Namely, a speciall booke of the affaires of Gods Church: For the booke that containeth things belonging vnto the whole world, is said to be kept with the Creator, Chapter 5. verse 1. but the booke of the Church, with the Redeemer: and out of this booke is taken the rest of the history of this Apocalyps 4 A godly care is laudable, but must be ioyned with knowledge Therefore nothing is to be taken in hand but by calling, which must be expected and waited for of the godly. *a Keepe them close.* *b This was a gesture vsed of one that sweareth, which men doe now a dayes vse.* 5 Neither time it selfe, nor the things that are in time: but that the world to come is at hand, which is altogether of eternitie, and beyond all times. *c There shall neuer be anymore time.* 6 Whereof Chap. 11. 15. and 16. 17.

7 The other part of this chap. concerning the particular calling of Saint Iohn to the receiuing of the prophecie folowing, which is enioyned him, first by signe, in three verses, then in plaine words in the last verse. Vnto the setting foorth of the signe belong these things: That Saint Iohn is taught from heauen to demand the booke of the Prophecie in this verse: for these motions and desires God doeth inspire: that demanding the booke, hee is charged to take it in a figuratiue maner, the vse whereof is expounded verse the ninth, (as in the second Chapter of Ezechiel, and the ninth verse,) whence this similitude is borowed: lastly, for that S. Iohn at the commandement of Christ tooke the booke, and found by experience that the same, as proceeding from Christ, was most sweete, but in that it foretelleth the afflictions of the Church, it was most bitter vnto his spirit. 8 A simple and plaine declaration of the signe before going, witnessing the diuine calling of S. Iohn, and laying vpon him the necessitie thereof.

CHAP. XI.

1 The Temple is commanded to be measured. 3 The Lord stirreth vp two witnesses, 7 whom the beast murthereth, 9 and no man burieth them. 11 God raiseth them to life, 12 and calleth them vp to heauen. 13 The wicked are terrified 15 by the trumpet of the seuenth Angel: the resurrection, 18 and iudgement is described.

1 Then [1] was giuen me a reede like vnto a
rod, and the Angel stoood by, saying,
Rise and [2] mete the Temple of God, and the

1 The authority of the intended reuelation being declared, together with the necessity of that calling which was particularly imposed vpon S. Iohn, hereafter followeth the history of the estate of Christ his Church, both conflicting or warfaring, and ouercomming in Christ. For both the true Church of Christ is sayd to fight against that which is falsly so called, ouer the which Antichrist ruleth, Christ Iesus ouerthrowing Antichrist by the spirit of his mouth: and Christ is said to ouercome most gloriously vntill he shall slay Antichrist by the appearance of his comming, as the Apostle excellently teacheth, 2. Thess. 2. 8. So this history hath two parts: One of the state of the Church conflicting with temptations, vnto the 16. Chapter: the other of the state of the same Church obtaining victory, thence vnto the 20. Chapter. The first part hath two members most conueniently distributed into their times, whereof the first containeth an history of the Christian Church for 1260. yeeres, what time the Gospel of Christ was as it were taken vp from amongst men into heauen: the second containeth an history of the same Church vnto the victory perfected. And these two members are briefly, though distinctly, propounded in this Chapter, but are both of them more at large discoursed after in due order. For we vnderstand the state of the Church conflicting, out of Chapters 12. and 13. and of the same growing out of afflictions, out of the 14 15. and 16 Chapters. Neither did S. Iohn at vnwares ioyne together the history of these two times in this Chapter, because here is spoken of prophecie, which all confesse to be but one iust and immutable in the Church, and which Christ commanded to be continuall. The history of the former time reacheth vnto the 14. verse: the latter is set downe in the rest of this Chapter. In the former are shewed these things: the calling of the seruants of God in 4. verses: the conflicts which the faithful must vndergoe in their calling, for Christ and his Church, thence vnto the 10. verse, and their resurrection, and receiuing vp into heauen vnto the fourteenth verse. In the calling of the seruants of God are mentioned two things: the begetting and setling of the Church in two verses, and the education thereof in two verses. The begetting of the Church is here commended vnto S. Iohn by signe, and by speech: the signe is a measuring rod, and the speech a commandement to measure the Temple of God, that is, to reduce the same vnto a new forme: because the Gentiles are already entred into the Temple of Ierusalem, and shall shortly defile and ouerthrow the same vtterly. 2 Either that of Ierusalem, which was a figure of the Church of Christ, or that heauenly exemplar, whereof verse 19. but the first liketh me better, and the things following doe all agree thereunto. The sense therefore is, Thou seest all things in Gods house, almost from the passion of Christ, to be disordered: and that not onely the city of Ierusalem, but also the court of the Temple is trampled vnder foote of the nations, and of profane men whether Iewes or strangers: and that onely the Temple, that is, the body of the Temple, with the altar, and a small company of good men which truly worship God, doe now remaine, whom God doeth sanctifie and confirme by his presence Measure therefore this, euen this true Church, or rather the true type of the true Church, omitting the rest, and so describe all things from me, that the true Church of Christ may be as it were a very little center, and the Church of Antichrist as the circle of the center, euery way in length and breadth compassing about the same, that by way of prophesie thou mayest so declare openly, that the state of the Temple of God, and the faithfull which worship him, that is, of the Church, is much more streight then the Church of Antichrist.

altar, and them that worship therein.
2 [3] But the [a] Court which is without the
Temple [b] cast out, and mete it not: for it is
giuen vnto the [4] Gentiles, and the holy Citie
shall they tread vnder foote, [5] two and fourtie
moneths.
3 But [6] I will giue power vnto my two
witnesses, and they shal [7] prophecie a thousand
two hundreth and threescore dayes clothed in
sackcloth.
4 These [8] are two oliue trees, and two
candlestickes, standing before the God of the
earth.
5 [9] And if any man will hurt them, fire
proceedeth out of their mouthes, and deuou-
reth their enemies: for if any man will hurt
them, thus must he be killed.
6 These haue power to shut heauen, that
it raine not in the dayes of their prophecying,
and haue power ouer waters to turne them into blood, to smite the earth with all manner
plagues as often as they will.
7 [10] And when they haue [c] finished their
testimonie, [11] the beast that commeth out of
the bottomlesse pit, shall make warre against
them, and shall [12] ouercome them, and kill
them.
8 And their corpses shall lie in the [13] streets
of the great citie, which [d] spiritually is called
Sodom, and Egypt, [14] where our Lord also was
crucified.
9 And they of the people and kinreds, and
tongues, and Gentiles shall see their corpses
[15] three dayes and an halfe, and shall not suffer
their carkeises to be buried in graues.
10 And they that dwell vpon the earth,
[16] shall reioyce ouer them and be glad, and shall
send gifts one to another: for these two Prophets [17] vexed them that dwelt on the earth.
11 [18] But after [19] three dayes and an halfe,
[20] the spirit of life *comming* from God, shall enter into them, and they [21] shall stand vp vpon
their feete: and great feare shall come vpon
them which saw them.
12 And they shall heare a great voice from
heauen, saying vnto them, [22] Come vp hither.
And they shall ascend vp to heauen in a cloud,
[23] and their enemies shall see them.
13 [24] And the same houre shal there be a great
earthquake, and the tenth part of the citie shall
fal, and in the earthquake shalbe slaine in number seuen thousand: and the remnant were sore
feared, [25] & [e] gaue glory to the God of heauen.
14 [26] The second woe is past, *and* behold,
the third woe will come anon.

3 As if hee should say, it belongeth nothing vnto thee, to iudge those which are without, 1. Corinth. 15. 12. which be innumerable: looke vnto those of the houshold onely, or vnto the house of the liuing God.

a He speaketh of the outer court, which was called the peoples court, because all men might come into that.

b That is counted to be cast out, which in measuring is refused as profane.

4 To profane persons, wicked and vnbeleeuers, aduersaries vnto the Church.

5 Or a thousand, two hundred and threescore dayes, as is sayd in the next verse: that is, a thousand two hundred and threescore yeeres, a day for a yeere, as often in Ezechiel and Daniel, which thing I noted before 2. 10. The beginning of these thousand two hundreth and threescore yeeres, wee account from the passion of Christ, whereby (the partition wall being broken downe) wee were made of two, one, Ephes. 2.14. I say, one flocke vnder one shepheard, Iohn 10.16. and the ende of these yeeres precisely falleth into the Popedome of Boniface the eight, who a little before the ende of the yeere of Christ, a thousand two hundreth ninety foure, entred the Popedome of Rome, in the feast of Saint Lucie (as *Bergomensis* sayeth) hauing put in prison his predecessour *Cœlestinus*, whome by fraud, vnder colour of Oracle, hee deceiued: for which cause that was well said of him, *Intrauit vt vulpes, regnauit vt leo, mortuus est vt canis.* That is, Hee entred like a foxe, reigned like a lyon, and died like a dogge. For if from a thousand two hundreth ninetie foure yeeres, thou shalt take the age of Christ which hee liued on the earth, thou shalt finde there remaineth iust one thousand two hundreth and threescore yeeres, which are mentioned in this place and many others. 6 I had rather translate it *illud* then *illam*, the Temple then the Citie: for God sayth, I will giue that Temple, and commit it vnto my two witnesses, that is, vnto the ministers of the word, who are fewe in deede, weake and contemptible: but yet two, that is, of such a number as one of them may helpe another, and one confirme the testimonie of another vnto all men, that from the mouth of two or three witnesses euery word may be made good amongst men, 2. Corinth. 13.1. 7 They shall exercise their office enioyned by me by the space of those thousand two hundred and sixtie yeeres, in the middest of afflictions though neuer so lamentable, which is figuratiuely shewed by the mourning garment. 8 That is, the ordinarie and perpetuall instruments of spirituall grace, peace, and light in my Church, which God by his onely power preserued in this Temple. So Zacharie 4.3. 9 The power and efficacie of the holy ministerie, and which is truely Euangelicall, is declared both in earth and in heauen, protecting the administers thereof, and destroying the enemies, in this verse, vertue in deede diuine, most mightily shewing it selfe foorth in heauen, earth and the sea, verse 6. as it is described 2. Corinthians 10.4. according to the promise of Christ, Marke 16.17. And this is the second place (as I sayd before) of the combats which the seruants of God must needes vndergoe in the executing of their calling, and of the things that follow the same combates. In the combats or conflicts are these things to ouercome, in these two verses: to bee ouercome and killed, verse 7. After the slaughter followe these things, that the carkeises of the godly are laide abroad, verse 8. beeing vnburied, are made a matter of scorne, together of cursing and bitter execrations, verse 9. and that therefore gratulations are publiquely and priuately made, verse 10. 10 That is, when they haue spent those thousand two hundreth and sixtie yeeres, mentioned verse 2. and 3. in publishing their testimonie according to their office. *c When they haue done their message.* 11 Of which after, chap. 13. &c. That beast is the Romane Empire, made long agoe of ciuill, Ecclesiasticall: the chiefe head whereof was then Boniface the eight, as I sayd before: who lifted vp himselfe in so great arrogancie, (sayth the authour of *Fasciculus temporum*) that hee called himselfe, Lord of the whole world, as well in temporall causes, as in spirituall: There is an extant of that matter, written by the same Boniface most arrogantly, shall I say, or most wickedly, *Ca. vnam sanctam, extra de maioritate & obedientia.* And in the sixt of the Decretals (which is from the same authour) many things are found of the same argument. 12 Hee shall persecute most cruelly the holy men, and put them to death, and shall wound and pierce through with cursings, both their names and writings. And that this was done to very many godly men, by Boniface and others, the histories doe declare, especially since the time that the odious and condemned name amongst the multitude, first of the brethren Waldonenses or Lugdunenses, then also of the Fraticels, was pretended, that good men might with more approbation be massacred.

13 That is, openly at Rome: where at that time was a most great concourse of people, the yeere of Iubile being then first ordained by Boniface vnto the same ende, in the yeere of Christ 1300. example whereof is read Chap. 1. *Extra, de pœnitentijs & remissionibus.* So by one acte he committed double iniurie against Christ, both abolishing his trueth by the restoring the type of the Iubile, and triumphing ouer his members by most wicked superstition. O religious heart! Now that wee should vnderstand the things of Rome, S. Iohn himselfe is the authour, both after in the 17. Chapter almost throughout, and also in the circumscription now next following, when he sayth, it is that great Citie (as Chap. 17. 18. he calleth it) and is spiritually tearmed Sodom and Egypt: and that spiritually (for that must here againe be repeated from before) Christ was there crucified. For the two first appellations signifie spirituall wickednesses: the latter signifieth the shew and pretence of good, that is, of Christian and sound religion. Sodom signifieth most licentious impietie and iniustice: Egypt, most cruell persecution of the people of God: and Ierusalem signifieth the most confident glorying of that City, as it were in true religion, being yet full of falshood and vngodlinesse. Now who is ignorant that these things doe rather, and more agree vnto Rome, then vnto any other City? The commendations of the City of Rome for many yeeres past, are publikely notorious, which are not for me to gather together. This onely I will say, that he long since did very well see what Rome is, who taking his leaue thereof, vsed these verses:

Roma vale, vidi, satis est vidisse: reuertar
Quum leno, meretrix, scurra, cinædus ero.

Now farewell Rome, I haue thee seene, it was enough to see:
I will returne when as I meane, bawd, harlot, knaue to be

d After a more secret kinde of meaning and vnderstanding. 14 Namely in his members, as also he said vnto Saul, Actes 9 5. 15 That is, for three yeeres and a halfe: for so many yeres Boniface liued after his Iubile, as *Bergomensis* witnesseth. 16 So much the more shal they by this occasion exercise the iolity of their Iubile. 17 The Gospel of Christ is the affliction of the world, and the ministerie thereof, the sauour of death vnto death, to those that perish, 2. Cor. 2.16. 18 The third place, as I noted before, is of the rising againe of the Prophets from the dead, and their carying vp into heauen. For their resurrection is shewed in this verse: their calling and lifting vp into heauen, in the verse following. 19 That is, what time God shall destroy that wicked Boniface. 20 That is, the Prophets of God shall in a sort rise againe, not the same in person (as they say) but in spirit: that is, in the power and efficacie of their ministery, which S. Iohn expressed before, verses 5. and 6. And so the prophesie that is spoken of Elias, is interpreted by the Angel to be vnderstood of Iohn the Baptist, Luke 1.17. For the same Boniface himselfe, who sought to kill and destroy them, was by the fire of Gods mouth (which the holy ministery sheweth & exhibiteth) deuoured & died miserably in prison, by the endeauour of *Satra Columensis* and *Nagaretus* a French knight, whom *Philip* the faire King of France sent into Italy but with a very smal power. 21 That is, the most grieuous heat of afflictions & persecution shal stay for a while, for the great amaze that shal arise vpon that sudden & vnlooked for iudgment of God. 22 They were called by God into heauen, and taken out of this malignant world, into the heauenly Church, which also lyeth hidden here in the earth, to exercise their calling secretly: as of whom this wretched world was vnworthy, Heb. 11.38. For the Church of the wicked is by comparison called the earth, or the world: and the Church of the godly, heauen. So in ancient time amongst the godly Israelites: so amongst the Iewes in the dayes of Manasses and other kings, when the earth refused the heires of heauen, we read that they lay hidden as heauen in the earth. 23 Yet could they not hinder the secret ones of the Lord (as the Psalmist called them, Psal. 83.4.) but that they went on forward in his worke. 24 *Bergomensis* saith, in the yeere of our Lord 1301. this yeere a blasing starre foretelling great calamity to come, appeared in heauen: in which yere vpon the feast of S. Andrew, so great an earthquake arose, as neuer before: which also continuing by times, for many dayes, ouerthrewe many stately houses. This sayth hee of the yeere next following the Iubile: which S. Iohn so many ages before, expressed word for word. 25 They were in deede broken with present astonishment of minde, but did not earnestly repent as they ought to haue done. *e Glorified God by confessing his Name.* 26 He passeth vnto the second history, which is the second part of this Chapter. S. Iohn calleth these the second and third woe, hauing respect vnto Chap. 9. 12.

27 Of whoſe ſounding the trumpet Chriſt expreſly foretold, Chap. 10.7. and this is the ſecond part of this Chapter, containing a generall hiſtorie of the Chriſtian Church, from the time of Boniface, and vnto the conſummation of the victorie declared by voice from heauen. In this hiſtorie there are three branches: a preparation by the ſound of the Angels trumpet: a narration by the voice of heauenly Angels & Elders & a confirmatiō by ſigne

15 [27] And the ſeuenth Angel blew the trumpet, and there were great voices in heauen, ſaying, [28] The kingdomes of the world are our
Lords, and his Chriſts, and he ſhall reigne for
euermore.
16 [29] Then the foure and twentie Elders,
which ſate before God on their ſeats, fell vpon
their faces, and worſhipped God,
17 Saying, We giue thee thanks, Lord God
Almightie, which art, and Which waſt, and
Which art to come: for thou haſt receiued thy
great might, and haſt obtained thy Kingdome.
18 [30] And the Gentiles were angry, and thy
wrath is come, and the time of the dead, that
they ſhould be iudged, and that thou ſhouldeſt
giue reward vnto thy ſeruants the Prophets,
and to the Saints, and to them that feare thy
Name, to ſmall and great, and ſhouldeſt deſtroy them, which deſtroy the earth.
19 Then the Temple of God was [31] opened in heauen, and there was ſeene in his Temple the Arke of his Couenant: and there were
lightnings, and voyces, and thundrings, and
earthquake, and much haile.

28 The narration hath two parts: an acclamation of the heauenly creatures in this verſe, and both an adoration by all the Elders, verſe 16. and alſo a moſt ample thankeſgiuing, ver. 17, 18. The ſence of the acclamation is, Now the Lord is entred on his Kingdome, & hath reſtored his Church in which moſt mightily recouered from the profanation of the Gentiles, he may glorifie himſelfe. Namely that, which the Lord ordeined when firſt he ordeined his Church, that the faith of the Saints doth now behold as accompliſhed. 29 As before, 7.11. This giuing of thanks is altogether of the ſame content with the words going before. 30 A ſpeech of the Hebrew language, as much to ſay, as Gentiles being angry, thine inflamed wrath came vpon them, and ſhewed it ſelfe from heauen, occaſioned by their anger and fury. 31 This is the confirmation of the next prophecy before going by ſignes exhibited in heauen, & that of two ſorts, whereof ſome are viſible, as the paſſing away of the heauen, the opening of the Temple, the Arke of the Couenant appearing in the Temple, and teſtifying the glorious preſence of God, and the lightnings: others apprehended by eare and ſuch dull ſenſe, which beare witneſſe in heauen and earth to the trueth of the iudgements of God.

CHAP. XII.

1 A woman 2 appeareth trauailing with childe, 4 whoſe childe the dragon would deuoure, 7 but Michael ouercommeth him, 9 and caſteth him out, 13 and the more he is caſt downe and vanquiſhed, the more fiercely he exerciſeth his ſubtilties.

1 Hitherto hath bene the generall prophecie, comprehended in 2. parts, as I ſhewed vpon Chap. 11. Now ſhall be declared the firſt part of this prophecie, in this & the next chap. and the latter part in the 14.

AND [1] there appeared a great wonder in
heauen: [2] A woman clothed with the ſun,
and the moone was vnder her feete, and vpon
her head a crowne of twelue ſtarres.
2 And [3] ſhe was with child, & cried traueiling
in birth, and was pained ready to be deliuered.
3 And there appeared another wonder in
heauen: [4] for behold a great red dragon hauing
[5] ſeuen heads, and tenne [6] hornes, and ſeuen
crownes vpon his heads:
4 [7] And his taile drew the third part of the
ſtarres of heauen, and caſt them to the earth.
And the dragon [8] ſtoode before the woman,
which was ready to be deliuered, [9] to deuoure
her childe, when ſhe had brought it forth.
5 [10] So ſhe brought forth a man [11] childe,
which ſhould rule all nations with a rod of y-
ron: and that her child was taken vp vnto God
and to his throne.
6 [12] And the woman fled into the wilderneſſe, where ſhe hath a place prepared of God,
that [13] they ſhould feede her there a thouſand,
two hundreth and threeſcore dayes.
7 And there was a great battell in heauen,
[14] Michael and his Angels fought againſt the
dragon, and the dragon fought and his angels.
8 [15] But they preuailed not, neither was
their [a] place found any more in heauen.
9 And the great dragon, that old ſerpent,
called the deuil and Satan, was caſt out, which
deceiueth all the world: he was *euen* caſt into
the earth, & his angels were caſt out with him.
10 Then I heard a loude voyce in heauen,
ſaying, [16] Now is ſaluation, and ſtrength, and
the Kingdome of our God, and the power of
his Chriſt: for the accuſer of our brethren is
caſt downe, which accuſed them before our
God day and night.
11 But they ouercame him by that blood
of that Lambe, and by that word of their teſtimonie, and they [b] loued not their liues vnto the
death.
12 Therefore reioyce, ye heauens, & ye that

5 Thereby to withſtand thoſe ſeuen Churches ſpoken of, that is, the Catholike Church, and that with kingly furniture and tyrannicall magnificence: ſignified by the crownes ſet vpon his heads, as if the ſame without controuerſie belonged vnto him by the proper right: as alſo he boaſted vnto Chriſt, Mat. 4.9. See after vpon Chap. 13.1.
6 More then are the hornes of the Lambe, or then the Churches are: ſo well furniſhed doeth the tyrant brag himſelfe to be, vnto all maner of miſchiefe.
7 After the deſcription of Satan followeth this action, that is, his battel offred vnto the Church partly to that which is viſible, wherein the wheate is mingled with the chaffe, and the good fiſh with that which is euill: a good part thereof, though in appearance it ſhined as the ſtars ſhine in heauen, he is ſaide to thruſt downe out of heauen,

15. and 16. chapters. Vnto the firſt part, which is of the conflicting or militant Church belong two things. The beginning and the progreſſe of the ſame in conflicts & Chriſtian combats. Of which two the beginning or vp ſpring of the Church is deſcribed in this chapter, and the progreſſe thereof in the Chapter following. The beginning of the Chriſtian Church we define to bee from the firſt moment of the conception of Chriſt, vntil that time wherin this church was as it were weined and taken away from the breſt or milke of her mother: which is the time when the Church of the Iewes with their citie and Temple was ouerthrowen by the iudgement of God. So we haue in this Chapter the ſtory of 69. yeeres and vpwards. The parts of this chap. are three. The firſt, is the hiſtorie of the Conception and bearing in wombe, in 4. verſes. The ſecond, an hiſtorie of the birth from the 5. verſe vnto the 12. The third is, of the woman that had brought forth, vnto the end of the chapter. And theſe ſeuerall parts haue euery one their coufl cts. Therefore in that firſt part are two things contained, one, the conception & bearing in wombe, in two verſes: and another of the lying in wait of the Dragon againſt that ſhould bee brought forth, in the next two verſes. In the firſt point are theſe things, the deſcription of the mother, verſe 1. and the dolors of childe-birth, verſe 2. all ſhewed vnto Iohn from heauen. 2 A type of the true holy Church which then was in the nation of the Iewes. This Church (as is the ſtate of the holy Church Catholique) did in it ſelfe ſhine about with glory giuen of God, troad vnder feet mutabilitie and changeableneſſe, and poſſeſſed the Kingdome of heauen as the heire thereof. 3 For this is that barren woman that brought not forth, of which Eſai 45.1. and Gal 4.27. ſhee cried out for good cauſe, and was tormented at that time, when in the iudgement of all ſhe ſeemed neere vnto death, and in maner ready to giue vp the ghoſt by reaſon of her weakenes & pouertie. 4 That is the deuill or Satan (as is declared ver. 9.) mightie, angry and full of wrath,

& to peruert: for if it were poſſible he would peruert euen the elect, Mat. 24.24. & partly to the elect members of the holy Catholike Church in the ſecond part of this verſe. Many therefore of the members of this viſible Church (ſaith S. Iohn) he ouerthrew and triumphed vpon them. 8 He withſtood that elect Church of the Iewes which was now ready to bring forth the Chriſtian Church, and watched for that ſhe ſhould bring forth. For the whole Church, and whole body is compared vnto a woman: and a part of the Church vnto that which is brought forth, as we haue noted at large vpon Cant. 7.6. 9 Chriſt myſtical (as they cal him) that is, the whole Church, conſiſteth of the perſon of Chriſt as the head, & of the body vnited therunto by the Spirit, ſo is ẏ name of Chriſt taken. 1. cor. 12.12. 10 The 2. hiſtory of this Church deliuered of child: in which firſt ẏ conſideration of the child borne, & of the mother, is deſcribed in 2. verſes: ſecondly the battel of the dragon againſt the yong child, & the victorie obteined againſt him, in 3. verſes folowing: laſt of all is ſung a ſong of victory, vnto the 12. ver. Now S. Iohn in conſideration of the child borne, noteth two things: for he deſcribeth him, and his ſtation or place in this verſe. 11 That is Chriſt the head of the Church ioyned with his Church (the beginning root & foundation wherof is the ſame Chriſt) indowed with kingly power, & taken vp into heauen out of the iawes of Satan (who as a Serpent did bite him vpon the croſſe) that ſitting vpon ẏ celeſtial throne, he might reigne ouer all. 12 The Church of Chriſt which was of the Iewes, after his aſſumption into heauen, hid it ſelfe in the world as in a wildernes, truſting in ẏ onely defence of God, as witneſſeth S. Luke in the Acts of the Apoſtles. 13 Namely the Apoſtles & ſeruants of God ordeined to feed with the word of life, the Church collected both of the Iewes & Gentiles vnles that any man wil take the word *alerent* imperſonally, after the vſe of the Hebrewes, in ſtead of *aleretur*: but I like ẏ firſt better. For he hath reſpect vnto thoſe two Prophets, of whom chap. 11. 3. as for the meaning of the 1290 dayes, looke the ſame place. 14 Chriſt is the Prince of Angels, & head of the Church, who beareth that yron rod, ver. 5. See the notes vpon Daniel, chap. 12.1. In this verſe a deſcription of the battell & of the victorie in the 2. verſes following. The Pſalmiſt had reſpect vnto this battell, Pſal. 68.9 & Paul, Ephe. 4.8. & Col. 2.15. 15 The deſcription of the victorie, by denying of the thing in this verſe, & by affirming the contrary in the next verſe. As that Satan gained nothing in heauen, but was by ẏ power of God thrown downe into ẏ world whereof he is the prince, Chriſt himſelfe & his elect members ſtanding ſtill by the throne of God. *a They were caſt out ſo, that they were neuer ſeene any more in heauen.* 16 The ſong of victorie or triumph containing firſt, a propoſition of the glory of God & of Chriſt ſhewed in that victorie: ſecondly, it containeth a reaſon of the ſame propoſition, taken from the effects, as that the enemie is ouercome in battell, in this verſe, and that the godly are made conquerours (and more then conquerours, Rom 8.37.) verſe 11. Thirdly a concluſion, wherein is an exhortation vnto the Angels, and to the Saints: and vnto the word, a propheſie of great miſerie, and of deſtruction procured by the deuill againſt mankind, leſt himſelfe ſhould ſhortly be miſerable alone, verſe 12. *b He is ſaid in the Hebrew tongue, to loue his life, that eſteemeth nothing more precious then his life: and on the other ſide, he is ſaid not to loue his life, who doubteth not to hazard it, wherſoeuer need requireth.*

17 The third part: an historie of the woman deliuered, consisting of two members, the present battell of Satan against the Christian Church of the Iewish nation, in foure verses: and the battell intended against the seed thereof, that is against the Church of the Gentiles, which is called holy by reason of the Gospel of Christ in the two last verses.

dwell in them. Woe to the inhabitants of the
earth,& of the sea: for the deuil is come downe
vnto you, which hath great wrath, knowing
that he hath but a short time.
13 And when [17] the dragon saw that he was
cast vnto the earth, hee persecuted the woman
which had brought forth the man *childe*.
14 [18] But to the woman were giuen two
wings of a great Eagle, that she might flie into
the wildernes, into her [c] place, where shee is
nourished for a [19] time, and times, and halfe a
time, from the presence of the serpent.
15 [20] And the serpent cast out of his mouth
water after the woman, like a flood, that hee
might cause her to be caried away of the flood.
16 [21] But y earth holpe the woman,& the earth
opened her mouth, & swallowed vp the flood,
which the dragon had cast out of his mouth.
17 [22] Then the dragon was wroth with the
woman, and went and made warre with the
remnant of her seed, which keepe the commandements of God, and haue the testimonie of
Iesus Christ.
18 [23] And I stood on the sea sand.

18 That is, being strengthened with diuine power: & taught by oracle, shee fled swiftly from the assault of the deuill, and from the common destruction of Ierusalem, & went into a solitarie Citie beyond Iordane called Pella, as Eusebius telleth in y 1 chapter of the 3. booke of his Ecclesiasticall historie: which place God had comanded her by Reuelation. c *Into that place which God had appointed for her.* 19 That is, for three yeeres and a halfe: so the same speech is taken Dan 7. 25. This space of time is reckened in maner from that last and most grieuous rebellion of the Iewes, vnto the destruction of the Citie and Temple, for their defection or falling away, began in the twelt yeere of Nero, before the beginning whereof, many foresignes and predictions were shewed from heauen, as Iosephus writeth, lib.7.cap.12, and Hegesippus lib 5.cap.44 amongst which this is very memorable, then in the feast of Pentecost not onely a great sound and noise was heard in the Temple, but also a voyce was heard of many out of the Sanctuary which cried out vnto all, Let vs depart hence. Now three yeeres and a halfe after this defection was begun of the Iewes, and those wonders happened, the Citie was taken by force, the Temple ouerthrowne, and the place forsaken of God: & this compasse of time S Iohn noted in this place. 20 That is, he enflamed the Romanes & Nations that they persecuting the Iewish people with cruell armes, might by the same occasion inuade the Church of Christ, now departed from Ierusalem and out of Iudea. For it is an vsuall thing in Scripture, that the raging tumults of the nations should be compared vnto waters. 21 That is, there was offered in their place other Iewes, vnto the Romanes and Nations raging against that people: and it came to passe thereby that the Church of God was saued whole from that violence, that most raging flood of persecution which the Dragon vomited out being altogether spent in the destruction of those other Iewes. 22 Being set on fire by this meanes, he began to be more mad, and because hee perceiued that his purpose against the Christian Church of the Iewish remnant was come to nought, hee resolued to fall vpon her seed, that is, the Church gathered also by God of the Gentiles, and the holy members of the same. And this is that other branch, as I said vpon the thirteenth verse, in which the purpose of Satan is shewed, ver. 17 and his attempt, verse 18. 23 That is, as a most mightie tempest that he rushed vpon the whole world (whose prince he is) to raise the floods & prouoke the Nations, that they might with their furious bellowes tosse vp and downe, driue here and there, and finally destroy the Church of Christ with the holy members of the same. But the prouidence of God resisted his attempt, that he might fauour the Church of the Gentiles, yet tender and as it were greene. The rest of this storie of the Dragon is excellently prosecuted by the Apostle S Iohn hereafter in the 20. chapter. For here the Dragon endeuouring to doe mischiefe, was by God cast into prison.

CHAP. XIII.

1 *The beast with many heads is described,* 12 *which draweth the most part of the world to idolatrie.* 11 *The other beast rising out of the earth,* 15 *giueth power vnto him.*

AND [1] I saw a beast rise [2] out of the sea, hauing seuen heads, and [3] ten hornes, and
vpon his hornes *were* ten crownes, [4] and vpon
his head [5] the name of blasphemie.
2 And the beast which I sawe was [6] like a
Leopard, and his feete like a beares, and his
mouth as the mouth of a lion: [7] and the dragon gaue him his power and his throne, and
great authoritie.
3 [8] And I sawe one of his heads as *it were*
wounded to death, but his deadly wound was
healed, and all the world wondered *and* followed the beast.
4 And they worshipped the dragon which
gaue the power vnto the beast, and they worshipped the beast, saying, Who is like vnto the
beast! who is able to warre with him!
5 [9] And there was giuen vnto him a mouth,
that spake great things and blasphemies, and

1 The Apostle hauing declared the springing vp of the Christian Church, and the state of the Church from which ours taketh her beginning, doth now passe vnto the story of the progresse thereof, as I shewed in the entrance of the former Chapter. And this historie of the progresse of the Church and the battels thereof, is set downe in this chapter, but distinctly in two parts, one is of y ciuil Romane Empire, vnto ver. 10. Another of the body Ecclesiasticall or propheticall, thence vnto the end of the Chapter. In the former part are shewed these things: First the state of that Empire, in 4 verses: then the acts therof in 3. verses: after the effect: which is exceeding great glory, ver. 8. And last of all is commended the vse: and the instruction of the godly against the euils that shall come from the same, ver. 9.10. The historie of the state, containeth a most ample description of the beast, first entire, ver. 1.2 & then restored after hurt, ver. 3. 4. 2 On the sand whereof stood the deuill practising new tempests against the Church, in the verse next before going: what time the Empire of Rome was endangered by domesticall dissensions, and was mightily tossed, hauing euer and anon new heads, and new Emperours. See in the 17. chapter and verse 8. 3 Hauing the same instruments of power, prouidence, and most expert gouernement which the Dragon is said to haue had, in the 12. chapter and the third verse.

4 We read in the twelft Chapter and 3. verse, that the dragon had 7. crownes set vpon 7. heads becaus y thiefe auoucheth himselfe to be proper Lord and Prince of the world, but this beast is sayd to haue tenne crownes, set vpon seuerall, not heads but hornes: because the beast is beholden for all vnto the Dragon, verse 2. and doeth not otherwise raigne, then by Lawe of subiection giuen by him, namely, that he employ his hornes against the Church of God. The speech is taken from the ancient custome and forme of dealing in such case: by which they that were absolute kings did weare the diadem vpon their heads: but their vassals and such as reigned by grace from them, wore the same vpon their hoods: for so they might commodiously lay downe their diademes whe they came into the presence of their Soueraignes, as also the Elders are said, when they adored God which sate vpon the throne, to haue cast down their crownes before him, Chap 4. ver. 10. 5 Contrary to that which God of olde commanded should be written in the head piece of the high Priest, that is, *Sanctitas Iehouæ*, Holinesse vnto the Lord The name of blasphemie imposed by the Dragon, is (as I thinke) that which S. Paul saith in the second Chapter of his Epistle to the Thessalonians, the fourth verse. *He sitteth as God, and boasteth himselfe to be God.* For this name of blasphemie both the Romane Emperours did then chalenge vnto themselues, as Suetonius and Dion doe report of Caligula and Domitian: and after them the Popes of Rome did with full mouth professe the same of themselues, when they chalenged vnto themselues Soueraintie in holy things; of which kind of sayings the sixt booke of the Decretals, the Clementines, and the Extrauagants, are very ful. For these men were not content with that which Anglicus wrote in his *Poetria*, (the beginning wherof is *Papa stupor mundi*, The Pope is the wonder of the world) *Nec Deus es, nec homo, sed neuter es inter vtrunque.* Thou art not God, ne art thou man, but neuter mixt of both: as the glosse witnesseth vpon the sixt booke: But they were bold to take vnto themselues the very name of God, and to accept it giuen of other: according as almost an hundred and twentie yeres since there was made for Sixtus the fourth, when he should first enter into Rome in his dignitie Papall, a Pageant of triumph, and cunningly fixed vpon the gate of the citie he should enter at, hauing written vpon it this blasphemous verse;

Oraclo vocis mundi moderaris habenas,
Et merito in terris crederis esse Deus.

THAT IS,

By oracle of thine owne voyce, the world thou gouernst all,
And worthily a God on earth men thinke and doe thee call.

These and sixe hundred the like who can impute vnto that modestie whereby good men of olde would haue themselues called the seruants of the seruants of God? Verely either this is a name of blasphemie, or there is none at all. 6 Swift as the Leopard, easily clasping all things, as the Beare doth with his foot, and tearing and deuouring all things with the mouth as doeth the Lion. 7 That is, hee lent the same vnto the beast to vse, when he perceiued that himselfe could not escape, but must needs be taken by the hand of the Angel, and cast into the bottomlesse pit, Chap. 20 yet did not hee abandon the same vtterly from himselfe, but that he might vse it as long as he could. 8 This is the other place that appertaineth to the description of the beast of Rome: that besides that naturall dignitie, and amplitude of the Romane Empire, which was shadowed in the two former verses, there was added this also as miraculous, that one head was wounded as it were, vnto death, and was healed againe, as from heauen, in the sight of all men. This head was Nero the Emperour, in whom the race of the Cæsars fell from the imperiall dignitie, and the gouernment of the Commonweale was translated vnto others: in whose hands the Empire was so cured and recouered vnto health, as he seemed vnto all so much the more deepely rooted and grounded fast, then euer before. And hence followed those effects, which are next spoken of: First an admiration of certaine power, as it were, sacred and diuine, susteining the Empire and gouerning it: Secondly, the obedience & submission of the whole earth, in this verse: Thirdly, the adoration of the Dragon, and most wicked worshipping of deuils confirmed by the Romane Emperours: Lastly, the adoration of the beast himselfe, which grew into so great estimation, as that both the name and worship of a God was giuen vnto him, verse the fourth. Now there were two causes which brought in the minds of men this Religion: the shew of excellencie, which bringeth with it reuerence: and the shew of power inuincible, which bringeth feare. Who is like (say they) vnto the beast? Who shall be able to fight with him? 9 The second member containing an history of the actes of the beast, as I sayd verse 1. The history of them is concluded in two points: the beginning, and the manner of them. The beginning is the gift of the Dragon, who put and inspired into the beast both his impietie against God, and his immanitie and iniustice against all men, especially against the godly and those that were of the houshold of faith, verse the fift. The manner of the actes or actions done, is of two sorts, both impious in minde, and blasphemous in speech against God, his Church and the godly, verse the sixt: and also most cruell and iniurious in deedes, euen such as were done of most raging enemies, and of most insolent and proud conquerours, verse the seuenth.

10 Namely his actions, and maner of dealing. As concerning those two and fourty moneths, I haue spoken of them before in the 12. Chapter, and second ver. 11 That is, the holy Church, the true house of the liuing God. 12 That is, the godly in seuerall who hid themselues from his crueltie. For this bloodie beast surcharged those holy soules most falsly with innumerable accusations for the Name of Christ as we reade in Iustine Martyr, Tertullian, Arnobius, Minutius, Eusebius, Augustine, and others: which examples the latter times followed most diligently, in destroying the flocke of Christ: and we in our owne memorie haue found by experience, to our incredible griefe. Concerning heauen, See in the eleuenth Chapter and in the twelfth verse.

power was giuen vnto him, [10] to doe two and
fourtie moneths.
6 And hee opened his mouth vnto blasphemie against God to blaspheme his Name,
[11] and his tabernacle, [12] and them that dwell in
heauen.
7 And it was giuen him to make warre
with the Saints, and to ouercome them, and
power was giuen him ouer euery kinred, and
tongue, and nation.
8 Therefore all that dwell vpon the earth,
shal worship him, [13] whose names are not written in the Booke of Life of that Lambe,
which was slaine from the beginning of the
world.
9 [14] If any man haue an eare, let him
heare.
10 If any leade into captiuitie, he shall goe
into captiuitie: * if any man kill with a sword,
he must be killed by a sword: here is the patience and the faith of the Saints.
11 [15] And I behelde another beast comming vp out of the earth, [16] which had two
hornes like the Lambe, but hee spake like the
dragon.
12 [17] And he did all that the first beast could
doe before him, and he caused the earth, and
them which dwell therein, [18] to worship the
first beast, whose deadly wound was healed.

13 That is, such as are not from euerlasting elected in Christ Iesus. For this is that Lambe slaine, of which Chapter the fift, verse the sixt. These words I doe with Aretas, distinguish in this maner: *Whose names are not written from the laying of the foundation of the world, in the booke of Life, of the Lambe slaine.* And this distinction is confirmed by a like place hereafter, Chap.17.8. 14 The conclusion of this speech of the first beast, consisting of two parts, An exhortation to attentiue audience, in this verse: and a foretelling, which partly conteineth threatnings against the wicked, & partly comfort for those which in patience and faith shall wait for that glorious comming of our Lord and Sauiour Christ, verse the tenth. * *Gen.9.6. matth.26.52.* 15 The second member of the vision, concerning the Ecclesiasticall dominion, which in Rome succeeded that which was politike, and is in the power of the corporation of false prophets, & of the forgers of false doctrine. Wherefore the same beast, and the bodie or corporation is called of S.Iohn by the name of false prophet, Chap.16.verse 13.and 19.verse 20. The forme of this beast is first described in this verse, then his actes in the verses following: and the whole speech is concluded in the last verse. This beast is by his breed, a sonne of the earth (as they say) obscurely borne, and by little and little creeping vp out of his abiect estate. 16 That is, in shew he resembled the Lambe (for what is more mild or more humble then to bee the seruaunt of the seruants of God?) but in deede he played the part of the Dragon, and of the Wolfe, Matth.7.15. For euen Satan changeth himselfe into an Angel of light, 2 Cor.11.14. and what should his honest disciples and seruants doe? 17 The historie of the acts of this beast conteineth in summe three things, hypocrisie, the witnesse of miracles, and tyrannie: of which the first is noted in this ver, the second in the three verses following: the third in the sixteenth and seuenteenth verses. His hypocrisie is most full of leasing, whereby hee abuseth both the former beast and the whole world: in that albeit hee hath by his cunning, as it were by line, made of the former beast a most miserable σκέλετον or anatomie, vsurped all his authoritie vnto himselfe and most impudently exerciseth the same in the sight and view of him: yet he carieth himselfe so, as if hee honoured him with most high honour, and did in very good trueth cause him to be reuerenced of all men. 18 For vnto this beast of Rome, which of a ciuill Empire is made an Ecclesiasticall hierarchie, are giuen diuine honours, and diuine authoritie so farre, as he is beleeued to be aboue the Scriptures, which the glosse vpon the Decretals declareth by this deuilish verse.

Articulos soluit, synodumque facit generalem.

THAT IS,

He changeth the Articles of faith, and giueth authoritie to generall Councils.

Which is spoken of the Papall power. So the beast is by birth, foundation, seat, and finally substance, one: onely the Pope hath altered the forme and maner thereof, being himselfe the head both of that tyrannicall empire, and also of the false Prophets: for the Empire hath he taken vnto himselfe, and thereunto hath added this cunning deuise. Now these words, *whose deadly wound was cured,* are put here for distinction sake, as also sometimes afterwards: that euen at that time the godly readers of this prophesie might by this signe be brought to see the thing as present: as if it were said, that they might adore this very Empire that now is, whose head we haue seene in our owne memorie to haue bene cut off, and to be cured againe.

13 [19] And he did great wonders, so that hee
made fire to come downe from heauen on the
earth, in the sight of men,
14 And deceiued them that dwell on the
earth by the signes, which were permitted him
to doe in the sight of the beast, saying to them
that dwell on the earth, that they should make
the [20] image of the [21] beast which had the
wound of a sword, and did liue.
15 [22] And it was permitted to him to giue a
[a] spirit vnto the image of the beast, so that the
image of the beast should speake, and should
cause that as many as would not worship the i-
mage of the beast, should be killed.
16 [23] And he made all, both small & great,
rich and poore, free and bond, to receiue [24] a
[b] marke in their right hand or in their foreheads,
17 And that no man might [25] buy or sel, saue
he that had the [26] marke or the name of the
beast, or the number of his name.
18 [27] Here is wisedome. Let him that hath
wit, count the number of the beast: for it is

19 The second point of the things done by the beast, is the credit of great wonders or miracles, and apertaining to the strengthening of this impietie: of which signes some were giuen from aboue, as it is said, that fire was sent downe from heauen by false sorcerie, in this verse. Others were shewed here below in the sight of the beast, to establish idolatry, & deceiue soules: which part Saint Iohn setteth forth, beginning (as they say) at that which is last, in this maner: First, the effect is declared in these words, *He decieueth the inhabitants of the earth.* Secondly, the common manner of working, in two sorts: one of miracles, *For the signes which were giuen him to doe in the presence of the beast:* the other of the wordes added to ye signes, and teaching the idolatrie by those signes, *Saying vnto the inhabitants of the earth, that they should make an image vnto the beast, which &c.* Thirdly, a speciall maner is declared. *That it is giuen vnto him to put life into the image of the beast:* and that such a kinde of quickening, that the same both speaketh by answere vnto those that aske counsell of it, and also pronounceth death against all those that doe not obey nor worship it: all which things oftentimes by false miracles through the procurement and inspiration of the Deuill, haue bene effected and wrought in images. The histories of the Papists are full of examples of such miracles, the most of them faigned, many also done by the deuill in images, as of olde in the Serpent, Genesis the third Chapter, and verse the first. By which examples is confirmed, not the authoritie of the beast, but the trueth of God and these prophesies. 20 That is, images, by *enallage* or change of the number: for the worship of them euer since the second Councell of Nice, hath beene ordeined in the Church by publique credit and authoritie, contrarie vnto the Lawe of God. 21 In the Greeke the word is of the Datiue case, as much to say, as vnto the worship, honour and obeing of the beast: for by this maintenance of images, this pseudo-propheticall beast doeth mightily profit the beast of Rome, of whome long agoe he receiued them Wherefore the same is hereafter very fitly called the image of the beast, for that images haue their beginning from the beast, and haue their forme or maner from the will of the beast, and haue their end and vse fixed in the profite and commoditie of the beast. 22 And of this miracle of the images of the beast, (that is, which the beast hath ordeined to establish idolatrie) which miraculously speake, and giue iudgement, or rather marueilously, by the fraude of the false prophets, the Papists bookes are full fraughted. *a To giue life, as Iannes and Iambres imitated the wonders that Moses wrought.* 23 The third place, is a most insolent tyrannie, as was sayde before, vsurped ouer the persons of men, in this verse: and ouer their goods and actions, in the next verse. For he is saide, both to bring vpon all persons a tyrannous seruitude, that as bondslaues they might serue the beast: & also so to exercise ouer all their goods and actions, a pedler like abuse of indulgences and dispensations (as they terme them) amongst their friends, and against others, to vse most violent interdictions, and to shoote out cursings, euen in naturall and ciuill, priuate and publique contracts, wherein all good faith ought to haue place. 24 That is, their Chrisme, by which in the Sacrament (as they call it) of Confirmation, they make seruile vnto themselues, the persons and doings of men, signing them in their forehead and hands: and as for the signe left by Christ (Of which chapter 7.3.) and the holy Sacrament of Baptisme they make as voide. For whome Christ hath ioyned vnto himselfe by Baptisme this beast maketh challenge vnto them by his greasie Chrisme, which hee doubteth not to preferre before Baptisme, both in authoritie and efficacie. *b The marke of the name of the beast.* 25 That is, haue any traffique or entercourse with men, but they onely which haue this anointing and consecration of Clearkely tonsure, as they call it, Reade Gratian *de Consecratione, distinctione tertia.c.omnes.cap spiritus, &c.* of these matters. 26 Here the false prophets doe require three things, which are set downe in the order of their greatnesse, a character, a name, and the number of the name. The meaning is, that man that hath not their first anoynting and clericall tonsure or shauing: secondly holy orders, by receiuing whereof is communicated the name of the beast: or finally hath not attained that high degree of Pontificall knowledge, and of the Law (as they call it) Canonicall, and hath not as it were made vp in account and cast the number of the mysteries thereof: for in these things consisteth the number of that name of the beast. And this is excellently set foorth in the next verse. 27 That is, in this number of the beast consisteth that Popish wisedome, which vnto them seemeth the greatest of all others. In these words Saint Iohn expoundeth that saying which went before of the number of the beast, what it hath aboue his marke or acconisance and his name. These things, saith Saint Iohn, the marke and the name of the beast doe easily happen vnto any man, but to haue the number of the beast, is wisedome: that is, onely the wise and such as haue vnderstanding, can come by that number: for they must be most illuminate doctours that attaine therunto, as the words following doe declare.

the [28] number of a man, and his number is sixe
hundreth threescore and sixe.

28 How great and of what denomination this number of the beast is by the which the beast accounteth his wisedome, Saint Iohn declareth in these words, Doest thou demaund how great it is? it is so great, that it occupieth the whole man: he is alway learning, and neuer commeth to the knowledge thereof: he must be a man in deede that doeth attaine vnto it. Askest thou of what denomination it is? verily it standeth of sixe throughout, and perfectly riseth of all the parts therof in their seueral denominations (as they terme them:) it standeth of six by vnities, tens, hundreds, &c. so as there is no one part in the learning and order Pontificall, which is not either referred vnto the head, and, as it were, the toppe thereof, or conteined in the same: so fitly doe all things in this hierarchie agree one with another, and with their head. Therefore that cruell beast Boniface the eight, doeth commend by the number of sixe those Decretals which he perfected: in the proœme of the sixt booke. *Which booke* (saith he) *being to be added vnto fiue other bookes of the same volume of Decretals, we thought good to name Sextum the sixt: that the same volume by addition thereof, conteining a senarie, or the number of sixe books (which is a number perfect) may yeelde a perfect forme of managing all things, and perfect discipline of behauiour.* Here therefore is the number of the beast, who powreth from himselfe all his parts, and bringeth them all backe againe vnto himselfe by his discipline in most wise and cunning maner. If any man desire more of this, let him reade the glosse vpon that place. I am not ignorant that other interpretations are brought vpon this place: but I thought it my duetie, with the good fauour of all, and without the offence of any, to propound mine opinion in this point. And for this cause especially, for that it seemed vnto mee neither profitable, nor like to bee true, that the number of the beast, or of the name of the beast should be taken as the common sort of interpreters doe take it. For this number of the beast teacheth, giueth out, imprinteth, as a publique marke of such as be his, and esteemeth that marke aboue all others, as the marke of those whom he loueth best. Now those other expositions seeme rather to be farre remoued from this propertie and condition of that number: whether you respect the name *Latinus*, or *Titan*, or any other. For these the beast doeth not teach, nor giue foorth, nor imprint, but most diligently forbiddeth to be taught, and audaciously denieth: he approoueth not these, but reprooueth them: and hateth them that thinke so of this number, with an hatred greater then that of *Vatinius*.

CHAP. XIIII.

1 The Lambe standeth on mount Sion, 4 with his chaste worshippers. 6 One Angel preacheth the Gospel: 8 another foretelleth the fall of Babylon: 9 the third warneth that the beast be auoyded. 13 A voyce from heauen pronounceth them happy, who die in the Lord. 16 The Lords sickle is thrust into the haruest, 18 and into the vintage.

THen I looked, and loe, a Lambe [1] stood on
mount Sion, and with him [2] an hundreth,
fourtie and foure thousand, hauing his Fathers
[3] Name written in their foreheads.
2 And I heard a voyce from heauen as the
sound of many waters, and as the sound of a
great thunder: and I heard the voyce of harpers,
harping with their harps.
3 And they sung as *it were* a new song before
the throne, and before the foure beastes,
and the Elders: and no man could learne that
song, but the hundreth, fourtie and foure thousand,
which were bought from the earth.
4 These are they which are not defiled with
women: for they are virgins: these followe the
Lambe whithersoeuer hee goeth: these are
bought from men, being the first fruits vnto
God, and to the Lambe.
5 And in their mouthes was found no
guile: for they are without spot before the
throne of God.

1 The historie of the Church of Christ being finished for more then a thousand and three hundreth yeeres at which time Boniface the eight liued as before hath beene said: there remaineth the rest of the historie of the conflicting or militant church, from thence vnto the time of the last victorie in three chapters. For first of all, as the foundation of the whole historie, is described the standing of the Lambe with his armie and retinue in fiue verses, after his worthie actes which he hath done, & yet doth in most mightie maner, whilest he ouerthroweth Antichrist with the spirit of his mouth, in the rest of this chapter, and in the two folowing. Vnto the description of the Lambe, are propounded three things: his situation, place and attendance: for the rest are expounded in the former visions, especially vpon the fift Chapter. 2 As ready girt to doe his office (as acts 5.56) in the midst of the Church, which aforetime mount Sion did prefigure. 3 As before 7.2. This retinue of the Lambe is described first by diuine marke (as before 7.2) in this verse. Then by diuine occupation, in that all and euery one in his retinue most vehemently and sweetly (verse 2.) doe glorifie the Lambe with a speciall song before God & his elect Angels: which song flesh & blood cannot heare, nor vnderstand, ver. 3. Lastly by their deeds done before, and their sanctification in that they were virgins, pure from spirituall and bodily fornication, that is, from impietie and vnrighteousnes, that they folowed the Lambe as a guide vnto all goodnes, and cleaued vnto him: that they are holy vnto him, as of grace redeemed by him: that in trueth & simplicitie of Christ they haue exercised all these things, sanctimonie of life, the direction of the Lambe, a thankfull remembrance of redemption by him: finally (to conclude in a word) that they are blameles before the Lord, ver. 4, 5.

6 ¶ [4] Then I sawe [5] another Angel flie in
the mids of heauen, hauing an euerlasting Gospel
to preach vnto them that dwell on the
earth, and to euery nation, and kinred, and
tongue, and people,
7 [6] * Saying with a loud voyce, Feare God,
and giue glory to him: for the houre of his
iudgement is come: & worship him that made
* heauen and earth, and the sea, and the fountaines
of waters.
8 And there followed another Angel, saying,
* Babylon that great citie is fallen, it is fallen:
for she made all nations to drinke of the
wine of the [a] wrath of her fornication.
9 ¶ And the third Angel followed them,
saying with a loud voyce, [7] If any man worship
the beast and his image, and receiue *his* marke
in his forehead, or on his hand,
10 The same shall drinke of the wine of the
wrath of God, yea, of the pure wine, which is
powred into the cup of his wrath, and he shall
be tormented in fire and brimstone before the
holy Angels, and before the Lambe.
11 And the smoke of their torment shal ascend
euermore: & they shall haue no rest day
nor night, which worship ŷ beast & his image,
& whosoeuer receiueth the print of his name.
12 [8] Here is the patience of Saints: here
are they that keepe the Commandements of
God, and the faith of Iesus.
13 Then I heard a voyce from heauen, saying
vnto me, Write, The dead which die [b] in
the Lord, *are* fully blessed. Euen so saith the
Spirit: for they rest from their labours, and
their [c] works follow them.
14 ¶ [9] And I looked, and beholde, a

4 The other part (as I said on the first verse) is of the acts of the Lambe, the maner whereof is deliuered in two sorts, of his speech and of his facts. His speeches are set forth vnto the 13. ver. of this chapter, and his facts vnto the 16. chapter. In the speech of the Lamb, which is the worde of the Gospel, are taught in this place these things: The seruice of the godly consisting inwardly of reuerence towards God, and outwardly of the glorifying of him: the visible signe of which is adoration, ver. 7. The ouerthrowing of wicked Babylon, ver. 8. and the fall of euery one of the vngodly which worship the beast, ver. 9. 10, 11. Finally the state of the holy seruants of God both present, ver. 11. & to come, most blessed, according to the promise of God, verse 13. 5 This Angel is a type or figure of ŷ good and faithfull seruants of God, whom God especially from that time of Boniface the 8. hath raised vp to ŷ publishing of the Gospel of Christ, both by preaching and by writing. So God first, neere vnto the time of the same Boniface, vsed Peter Cassiodorus an Italian: after, Arnold *de villa noua*, a Frenchman, then Occam, Dante, Petrarch, after that *Iohannes de rupe casa*, a Franciscane: after againe, Iohn Wicklife an Englishman, and so continually one or another vnto the restoring of the trueth, & enlarging of his Church. 6 That is, Babylon is destroied by the sentence & iudgment of God: the execution whereof S. Iohn describeth, chap. 18. And this voyce of the ministers of Christ hath continued since the time that Babylon (which is Rome) hath by deliberate counsell & manifest malice oppugned the light of the Gospel offered from God. * *Psal. 145.6.* * *Acts 14.15.* * *Isa. 21.9. ier. 51.8. chap. 18.2.* *a Of her fornication, whereby God was prouoked to wrath.* 7 That is, shal not worship God alone, but shal transferre his diuine honor vnto this beast, whether he do it with his heart, or counterfeiting in shew. For he (saith Christ) that denieth me before men, him will I deny before my Father & his Angels, Mat. 10.32. And this is that voice of the holy ministery, which at this time is very much vsed of the holy & faithful seruants of God. For hauing now sufficiently found out the publike obstinacie of Babylon, they labour not any longer to thunder out against the same: but to saue some particular members by terror (as S. Iude speaketh) & to plucke them out of the publike flame: or els by vehement commiseration of their estate to lead them away, they set before them eternall death into which they rush vnwares, vnlesse in good time they returne vnto God, but the godly which are of their own flocke, they exhort vnto patience, obedience & faith in the Lord Iesus, & charge them to giue light by their good example, of good life vnto others. 8 The patience, sanctification, & iustification by faith: the consequence whereof are, rest, felicitie, and glory eternal, in the heauenly fellowship of God and his Angels. *b That is, for the Lord.* *c By works, is meant the reward which followeth good works.* 9 The second part of this Chapter, as I said ver. 1. Of the acts and doings of Christ in ouerthrowing of Antichrist & his church by the Spirit of his diuine mouth: seeing that hauing bin called backe by word both publikely & priuately vnto his duetie, & admonished of his most certaine ruine: he yet ceaseth not to maintaine & protect his own adherents, that they may do him seruice: & to afflict the godly with most barbarous persecutions. Of those things wich Christ doth, there are 2. kinds: one common or general in ŷ rest of this chap. another particular against that sauage & rebellious beast & his worshippers, chap. 15, 16. That common kind, is the calamity of wars, spread abroad through ŷ whole earth, & filling all things with blood, & that without respect of any person. This is figured or shadowed out in 2. types, of the haruest & vintage. Since the time ŷ the light of the Gospel began to shine out, & since prophecie or preaching by ŷ grace of God was raised vp again, how horrible wars haue bin kindled in the world? how much humane flesh hath bin throwen to ŷ earth by this diuine reaping? how much blood (alas for woe) hath ouerflowen for these 100. yeres almost? all histories do cry out, & this our age (if euer before) is now in horror by reason of ŷ rage of ŷ sickle which Antichrist calleth for. In this place is the first type, ŷ is of the haruest,

[10] white cloude, and vpon the cloude one ſitting like vnto the Sonne of man, [11] hauing on
his head a golden crowne, and in his hande a
[12] ſharpe ſickle.
15 [13] And another Angel came out of the
Temple, crying with a loud voice to him that
ſate on the cloude, * Thruſt in thy ſickle and
reape : for the time is come to reape : for the
* harueſt of the earth is ripe.
16 And he that ſate on the cloude, thruſt in
his ſickle on the earth, and the earth was reaped.
17 [14] Then another Angel came out of the
Temple, which is in heauen, hauing alſo a
ſharpe ſickle.
18 And another Angel came out from the
altar, which had power ouer fire, and cried
with a loud crie to him that had the ſharpe ſickle, and ſaid, Thruſt in thy ſharpe ſickle, and
gather the cluſters of the vineyard of the
earth : for her grapes are ripe.
19 And the Angel thruſt in his ſharpe ſickle on the earth, and cut downe the vines of the
vineyard of the earth, and caſt them into that
great wine preſſe of the wrath of God.
20 And the wine-preſſe was troden without the citie, [15] and blood came out of the wine
preſſe vnto the horſe bridles, by the ſpace of a
thouſand and ſixe hundreth furlongs.

10 Declaring his fierceneſſe by his colour, like vnto that which is in the white or milke circle of heauen.
11 As one that ſhal reigne from God, and occupie the place of Chriſt in this miſerable execution.
12 That is, a moſt fit & commodious inſtrument of execution, deſtroying all by hewing and thruſting through : for who may ſtand againſt God?
* Ioel 3.13.
* Matth.13.39.
13 Chriſt giueth a commandement in this verſe, and the Angel executeth it in the next verſe.
14 The other type (as I ſayd ver.14.) is the vintage: the maner whereof is one with that which went before, if thou except this, that the grape gathering is more exact in ſeeeking out euery thing, then is the harueſt labour. This is therefore a more grieuous iudgment, both becauſe it ſucceedeth the other, and becauſe it is vnderſtood to be executed with great diligence. 15 That is, it ouerflowed very deepe, and very farre and wide : the ſpeech is hyperbolicall or exceſſiue, to ſignifie the greatneſſe of the ſlaughter. And theſe be thoſe pleaſant fruits forſooth, of the contempt of Chriſt, & deſiring of Antichriſt rather then him, which the miſerable, mad, and blinde world doeth at this time reape.

CHAP. XV.

1 The ſeuen Angels hauing the ſeuen laſt plagues. 3 They that conquered the beaſt, praiſe God. 6 To the ſeuen Angels, 7 ſeuen vials full of Gods wrath are deliuered.

AND [1] I ſaw another ſigne in heauen, great
and marueilous, ſeuen [2] Angels, hauing
the ſeuen laſt plagues : for by them is fulfilled
the wrath of God.
2 [3] And I ſaw [4] as *it were* a glaſſie ſea, mingled with fire, and [5] them that had gotten victorie of the beaſt, and of his image, and of his
marke, and of the number of his name, [6] ſtand
at the glaſſie ſea, hauing the harpes of God,
3 And they ſung [7] the ſong of Moſes the
[a] ſeruant of God, and the ſong of the Lambe,
ſaying, [8] Great and marueilous *are* thy works,
Lord God Almightie : iuſt and true *are* thy
* [b] wayes, King of Saints.
4 * Who ſhall not feare thee, O Lord, and
glorifie thy Name! for thou onely *art* holy, and
all nations ſhall come and worſhip before thee :
for thy iudgements are made manifeſt.
5 [9] And after that I looked, and beholde,
the Temple of the Tabernacle of teſtimonie
was open in heauen.
6 And the ſeuen Angels came out of the
Temple, which had the [10] ſeuen plagues, clothed in [11] pure and bright linnen, and hauing
their breaſts [12] girded with gloden girdles.
7 And one of the [13] foure beaſts gaue vnto
the ſeuen Angels ſeuen golden vials full of the
wrath of God, which liueth for euermore.
8 And the Temple was full of the ſmoke
of the glory of God and of his power, [14] and
no man was able to enter into the Temple, till
the ſeuen plagues of the ſeuen Angels were
fulfilled.

1 This is that other place of the acts of Chriſt, as I noted before 14.14. Now therfore is ſhewed a ſingular worke of the iudgement of God belonging to the ouerthrow of Antichriſt & his forces, of which diuine worke the preparation is deſcribed in this Chapter : & the execution in the next. The preparation is firſt ſet downe generally and in type in this verſe : and is after particularly ſet forth in the reſt of the Chapter. 2 Of which Chap.8.9. in powring forth the plagues of the world : for euen theſe plagues doe for the moſt part agree with thoſe. 3 There are two parts of the narration : one, the confeſſion of the Saints glorifying God, when they ſaw that preparation of the iudgments of God, vnto the 4.verſe, another the vocation, inſtruction, and confirmation of thoſe inſtruments which God hath ordeined for the execution of his iudgements, in foure other verſes. 4 This part of the viſion alludeth vnto that ſea or large veſſell of braſſe, in which the Prieſts waſhed themſelues in the entrance of the Temple : for in the entrance of the heauenly Temple (as it is called verſe 5.) is ſaid to haue beene a ſea of glaſſe, moſt lightſome and cleare, vnto the commoditie of choiſe mixt with fire, that is, as containing the treaſurie of the iudgements of God, which he bringeth forth and diſpenſeth according to his owne pleaſure : for out of the former, the Prieſts were cleanſed of old : and out of this the vngodly are deſtroyed now, chap.4.6. 5 That is, the godly martyrs of Chriſt, who ſhall not giue place euen in miracles vnto that beaſt : of theſe, ſee before, Chap.13.17. and 14.9, 10. 6 Glorifying God, from the particular obſeruation of the weapons and inſtruments of Gods wrath, floting in the ſea of glaſſe. 7 That ſong of triumph, which is, Exod.15.2. *a So is Moſes called for honours ſake, as it is ſet forth, Deu.34.10.*

6 This ſong hath two parts : one a confeſſion, both particular, in this verſe, and generall, in the beginning of the next verſe : another, a narration of cauſes belonging to the confeſſiō, whereof one kinde is eternal in it ſelfe, and moſt preſent vnto the godly, in that God is both holy, & alone God: another kind is future and to come, in that the elect taken out of the Gentiles (that is, out of the wicked ones & vnbeleeuing : as Chap.11.2.) were to bee brought vnto the ſame ſtate of happineſſe, by the magnificencie of the iudgement of God, in the next verſe. * *Pſal.*145.17. *b Thy doings.* * *Iere.*10.7. 9 The ſecond part of the narration (as was noted ver.2.) wherein firſt the authoritie of the whole argument and matter thereof is figured by a forerunning type of a Temple opened in heauen, as Chap.11.19. namely that all thoſe things are diuine and of God, that proceed from thence, in this verſe. Secondly, the adminiſters or executors, come forth out of the Temple, ver.6. Thirdly, they are furniſhed with inſtruments of the iudgements of God, and weapons fit for the maner of the ſame iudgements, ver.7. Finally, they are confirmed by teſtimonie of the viſible glory of God, in the laſt verſe. A like teſtimonie whereunto was exhibited of old in the law, Exod. 40.34. 10 That is, commandements to inflict thoſe ſeuen plagues. Here is the figure called *Metonymia.* 11 Which was in old time a ſigne of the Kingly or princely dignitie. 12 This girding was a ſigne of diligence, and the girdle of golde wat a ſigne of ſinceritie, & truſtineſſe in taking in charge the cōmandements of God. 13 Of theſe before, Chap.4.7. 14 None of thoſe 7. Angels might returne, till he had performed fully the charge committed vnto him, according to the decree of God.

CHAP. XVI.

2 and 17 The Angels powre out the ſeuen vials of Gods wrath giuen vnto them, and ſo diuers plagues ariſe in the world, 18 to terrifie the wicked, 19 and the inhabitants of the great citie.

AND [1] I heard a great voyce out of the
Temple, ſaying to the ſeuen Angels, Goe
your wayes, and powre out the *ſeuen* vials of
the wrath of God vpon the earth.
2 [2] And the firſt went and powred out his
viall vpon the earth : and there fell a noyſome
and a grieuous ſore vpon the men, which had
the [3] marke of the beaſt, and vpon them which
worſhipped his image.
3 [4] And the ſecond Angel powred out his
vial vpon the ſea, & it [a] became as the blood of a
dead man : & euery liuing thing died in the ſea.
4 [5] And the third Angel powred out his

1 In the former Chapter was ſet downe the preparation vnto the worke of God : here is deliuered the execution thereof. And in this diſcourſe of the execution, is a generall commandement, in this verſe, then a particular recitall in order of the execution done by euery of the ſeuen Angels, in the reſt of the chapter. This ſpeciall execution againſt Antichriſt & his crew, doth in maner agree vnto that which was generally done vpon the whole world, chap.8, 9. and belongeth (if my coniecture faile me not) vnto the ſame time. Yet herein they do differ one from another, that this was particularly effected vpon the Princes and ring-leaders of the wickedneſſe of the world, the other generally againſt the whole world being wicked. And therefore theſe iudgments are figured more grieuous then thoſe. 2 The hiſtorie of the firſt Angel, whoſe plague vpon the earth is deſcribed almoſt in the ſame wordes with that ſixt plague of the Egyptians, Exod. 9.9. But it doth ſignifie a ſpirituall vlcer, and that torture or butcherie of conſcience ſeared with an hote yron, which accuſeth the vngodly within, and both by trueth of the word (the light whereof God hath now ſo long ſhewed forth) and by bitternes ſtirreth vp and forceth out the ſword of Gods wrath. 3 See chap 13.16. 4 The hiſtorie of the ſecond Angel, who troubleth and moleſteth the ſeas, that he may ſtirre vp the conſcience of men ſleeping in their wickednes : See Chap.8.8. *a It was turned into rotten and filthy blood, ſuch as is in dead bodies.* 5 The ſtorie of the third Angel ſtriking the riuers, in this verſe, who proclaiming the iuſtice of God, cōmendeth the ſame by a moſt graue compariſon of the ſinnes of men, with the puniſhment of God : which is common to this place, and that which went before. Wherefore alſo this praiſing is attributed to the Angel of the waters, a name common to the ſecond and third Angels, according as both of them are ſaid to be ſent againſt the waters, albeit the one of the ſea, the other of the riuers, in two verſes.

viall vpon the riuers and fountaines of waters,
and they became blood.
5 And I heard the Angel of the waters ſay,
Lord, Thou art iuſt, Which art, and Which
waſt: and holy, becauſe thou haſt iudged theſe
things.
6 For they ſhed the blood of the Saints,
and Prophets, and therefore haſt thou giuen
them blood to drinke: for they are worthy.
7 [6] And I heard another out of the Sanctu-
rie ſay, Euen ſo, Lord God Almightie, true and
righteous are thy iudgements.
8 [7] And the fourth Angel powred out his
viall on the ſunne, and it was giuen to him to
torment men with heat of fire,
9 And men boiled in great heat, and blaſphemed the Name of God, which hath power
ouer theſe plagues, and they repented not to
giue him glory.
10 [8] And the fift Angel powred out his viall vpon the throne of the beaſt, and his kingdome waxed darke, and they gnawed their
tongues for ſorow,
11 And blaſphemed the God of heauen for
their paines, and for their ſores, and repented
not of their works.
12 [9] And the ſixt Angel powred out his viall vpon the great riuer [10] Euphrates, and [11] the
water thereof dried vp, [12] that the way of the
Kings of the Eaſt ſhould be prepared.
13 And I ſaw [13] three vncleane ſpirits [14] like
frogs come out of the mouth of that [15] dragon, and out of the mouth of that [16] beaſt, and
out of the mouth of that [17] falſe prophet.
14 For they are the ſpirits of deuils, working miracles, to goe vnto the kings of the
earth, and of the whole world, to gather them
to the battell of that great day of GOD Almightie.
15 [18] (*Behold, I come as a thiefe. Bleſſed
is he that watcheth, and keepeth his garments,
leſt he walke nakedly, and men ſee his filthines)
16 [19] And they gathered them together
into a place called in Hebrew, [20] Armagedon.
17 ¶ [21] And the ſeuenth Angel powred out
his viall into the [22] aire: and there came a loude
voice out of the Temple of heauen from [23] the
throne, ſaying, [24] It is done.
18 ¶ [25] And there were voyces, and thundrings, and lightnings, and there was a great
earthquake, ſuch as was not ſince men were vpon the earth, euen ſo mightie an earthquake.
19 [26] And the great citie was diuided into
three parts: and the cities of the nations [27] fel:
& that great [28] Babylon came in remembrance
before God, * to giue vnto her the cup of the
wine of the fierceneſſe of his wrath.
20 And euery yle fled away, and the mountaines [29] were not [b] found.
21 [30] And there fel a great haile, like [c] talents,
out of heauen vpon the men, & men blaſphemed God, becauſe of the plague of the haile:
for the plague thereof was exceeding great.

6 A confirmation of the praiſe before going out of the Sanctuary of God, whether immediatly by Chriſt, or by ſome one of his angels, for Chriſt alſo is called another Angel, Chap. 7.2, 3.8. and 12.1.
7 The ſtorie of the fourth Angel, who throweth the plague vpon the heauen & vpon the Sun, of which, Luke 21.26. the effects whereof are noted two. The one peculiar, that it ſhall ſcorch men with heat in this ver. The other proceeding accidentally from the former, that their furie ſhall ſo much ẏ more be enraged againſt God in the next verſe, when yet (O wonderfull mercie and patience of God) all other creatures are firſt ſtriken often and grieuouſly by the hand of God before mankind, by whom he is prouoked: as the things before going doe declare.
8 The ſtorie of the firſt Angel, who ſtriketh the kingdom of the beaſt with two plagues abroad ẇ darkenes, with biles & dolours moſt grieuous, throughout his whole kingdom that thereby he might wound the conſcience of the wicked, and puniſh that moſt peruerſe obſtinacie of the Idolaters: whereof aroſe perturbation, and thence a furious indignation and deſperate madneſſe, raging againſt God and hurtfull vnto it ſelfe. 9 The ſtorie of the ſixt Angel, diuided into his acte, and the euent thereof. The acte is, that the Angel did caſt out of his mouth the plague of a moſt glowing heat, wherewith euen the greateſt floods, and which moſt were wont to ſwell and ouerflow (as Euphrates) were dried vp, by the counſell of God in this verſe. The euent is, that the meere madneſſe wherewith the wicked are enraged that they may ſcorne the iudgements of God, and abuſe them furiouſly to ſerue their owne turne, and to the executing of their owne wicked outrage. 10 The bound of the ſpirituall Babylon, and to the fortreſſes of the ſame, Chap. 9.14. 11 So the Church of the vngodly, and kingdome of the beaſt is ſaid to be left naked, all the defences thereof in which they put their truſt, being taken away from it. 12 That is, that euen they which dwell further off, may with more commoditie make haſte vnto the ſacrifice, which the Lord hath appointed. 13 That is, euery of them bent their whole force, and conſpired that by wonders, worde and worke they might bring into the ſame deſtruction all Kings, Princes and Potentates of the world, curſedly bewitched of them by their ſpirits, and teachers of the vanitie & impunitie of the beaſt that committed fornication with the kings of the earth. And this is a right deſcription of our times. 14 Croking with all importunitie, & continually day and night prouoking and calling forth to armes, as the trumpets & furies of wars, as is declared in the next verſe. 15 That is, the deuil, as chap. 11.3. 16 Wherof, chap. 13.1. 17 That is, of that other beaſt, of which cha. 13.11, for ſo he is called alſo, cha, 19.20. & 20 10 18 A Parentheſis for admonition, in which God warneth his holy ſeruants, who reſt in the expectation of Chriſt, alwayes to addreſſe their minds vnto his comming, and to looke vnto themſelues, that they be not ſhamefully made naked and circumuented of theſe vncleane ſpirits, and ſo they be miſerably vnprepared at the comming of the Lord, ſo Mattth. 24 29 and 25.13. * *Chap 3.3. mat. 24.44. luk. 12 39.* 19 Namely the Angel, who holily according to the commandement of God, was to doe ſacrifice: notwithſtanding that thoſe impure ſpirits doe the ſame wickedly, as ſeruants not vnto God, but vnto the beaſt that hath ſeuen heads.

20 That is, (to ſay nothing of other expoſitions) the mountaine it ſelfe, or mountaine places of Megiddon. Now it is certaine by the holy Scripture, that Megiddon is a citie and territorie in the tribe of Manaſſes, bordering vpon Iſſacar and Aſher, and was made famous by that lamentable ouerthrow of king Ioſias, whereof 2. Reg. 22.30. and 2. Chro. 35.22. and Zach. 12.11. In this mountaine countrey God ſaith by figure or type that the kings of the peoples which ſerue the beaſt ſhal meet together: becauſe the Gentiles did alwayes caſt that lamentable ouerthrow in the teeth of the Church of the Iewes, vnto their great reproch: & therfore were perſwaded, that that place ſhould be moſt fortunate vnto them (as they ſpeake) & vnfortunate vnto the godly. But God here pronounceth, that that reproch of the Church, and confidence of the vngodly, ſhall by himſelfe be taken away, in the ſelfe ſame place where the nations perſwaded themſelues, they ſhould mightily exult and triumph againſt God and his Church. 21 The ſtory of the ſeuenth Angel vnto the end of the chapter, in which firſt is ſhewed by ſigne and ſpeech, the argument of this plague, in this verſe: and then is declared the execution thereof in the verſes following. 22 From whence he might moue the heauen aboue, and the earth beneath. 23 That is, from him that ſitteth on the throne, by the figure called *Metonymia*. 24 That is, Babylon is vndone, as is ſhewed verſe 19. and in the chapters following. For the firſt onſet (as I might ſay) of this denunciation, is deſcribed in this Chapter: and the laſt conteining a perfect victorie, is deſcribed in thoſe that follow. 25 Now is declared the execution (as is ſaid in verſe 27.) and the things that ſhall laſt come to paſſe in heauen and in earth before the ouerthrow of the beaſt of Babylon: both generally, verſe 18. and particularly in the curſed citie, and ſuch as haue any familiaritie therewith, in the laſt verſes. 26 The ſeat or ſtanding place of Antichriſt. 27 Of all ſuch as cleaue vnto Antichriſt, & fight againſt Chriſt. 28 That harlot, of whom in the next chapter following. Now this phraſe, *to come into remembrance*, is after the common vſe of the Hebrewe ſpeech, borrowed from men, and attributed vnto God. * *Iere. 25.15.* 29 That is, were ſeene no more, or were no more extant. A borrowed Hebraiſme. *b Appeared not, which the Hebrewes vtter after this ſort, were not, Gen. 5.24.* 30 The maner of the particular execution, moſt euidently teſtifying the wrath of God by the originall and greatneſſe thereof: the euent whereof is the ſame with that which is Chap. 9.12. and that which hath bene mentioned in this chapter, from the execution of the fourth Angel hitherto, that is to ſay, an incorrigible pertinacie of the world in their rebellion, and an heart that cannot repent, verſe 9 and 11. *c As it were about the weight of a talent, and a talent was threeſcore pound, that is, ſixe hundreeth groats, whereby is ſignified a marueilous and ſtrange weight.*

CHAP. XVII.

1 That great whore is deſcribed, 2 with whom the kings of the earth committed fornication. 6 Shee is drunken with the blood of Saints. 7 The myſterie of the woman, and the beaſt that caried her, expounded. 11 Their deſtruction. 14 The Lambes victorie.

THen [1] there came one of the ſeuen Angels, which had the ſeuen vials, and talked
with me, ſaying vnto me, Come: I will ſhewe
[2] thee the [a] damnation of the great whore that
ſitteth vpon many waters.
2 With whome haue committed fornication the kings of the earth, and the inhabitants
of the earth are drunken with the wine of her
fornication.

1 The ſtate of ẏ Church militant being declared, now followeth the ſtate of the Church ouercōming and getting victorie, as I ſhewed before in the beginning of the 10. chap. This ſtate is ſet forth in 4. chapters. As in the place before going I noted, that in that hiſtorie the order of time was not alwayes exactly obſerued: ſo the ſame is to be vnderſtood in this hiſtory, that it is diſtinguiſhed according to the perſons of which it treateth, and that in the ſeuerall ſtories of the perſons is ſeuerally obſerued in the time thereof. For firſt is deliuered the ſtorie of Babylon deſtroyed in this and the next Chapter (for this Babylon out of all doubt, ſhall perriſh before the two beaſts & the Dragon) Secondly, is deliuered the deſtruction of both the 2 beaſts, Chap. 19. And laſtly of the Dragon, Chap. 18. In the ſtorie of the ſpirituall Babylon, are diſtinctly ſet forth the ſtate thereof in this Chapter, and the ouerthrowe done from God, chap. 18. In this verſe and that which followeth, is a tranſition or paſſage vnto the firſt argument, conſiſting of the particular calling of the Prophet (as often heretofore) and a generall propoſition. 2 That is, that damnable harlot, by a figure called *hyppalage*. For S. Iohn as yet had not ſeene her. Although another interpretation may be borne, yet I like this better. *a The ſentence that is pronounced againſt this harlot.*

3 [3] So

3 [3] So he caried me away into the wildernesse in the Spirit, and I saw a woman sit vpon
a [b] scarlet coloured beast, full of names of blasphemie, which had seuen head and ten hornes.
4 And [4] the woman was arayed [5] in purple
and scarlet, and gilded with gold, and precious
stones, and pearles, and had [6] a cup of gold in
her hand full of abomination, and filthinesse of
her fornication.
5 [7] And in her forehead *was* a name written, A mysterie, [8] that great Babylon that mother of whoredomes, and abominations of the
earth.
6 [9] And I saw the woman drunken with the
blood of Saints, and with the blood of the Martyrs of IESVS, [10] and when I sawe her, I wondred with great maruell.
7 [11] Then the Angel said vnto me, Wherefore maruellest thou? I will shew thee the mysterie of that woman, and of that beast that
beareth her, which hath seuen heads, and ten
hornes.
8 [12] The beast that thou hast seene, [13] was,
and is not, and [14] shall ascend out of the bottomlesse pit, and shall goe into perdition, and
they that dwell on the earth shall wonder
(whose names are not written in the booke of
life from the foundation of the world) [15] when
they behold the beast that was, and is not,
and yet is.
9 [16] Here *is* the minde that hath wisdome.
The [c] seuen heades [17] are seuen mountaines,
whereon the woman sitteth: [18] they are also seuen kings.
10 [19] Fiue are fallen, [20] and one is, [21] and another is not yet come: and when he commeth,
he must continue a long space.
11 [22] And the beast that was, and is not, is
euen [23] the eight, and is [24] one of the seuen,
[25] and shall goe into destruction.
12 [26] And the ten hornes which thou sawest, are [27] ten Kings, which yet haue not receiued a kingdome, but shall receiue power, as
Kings [28] at one houre with the beast.
13 [29] These haue one minde, and shall giue
their power, and authoritie vnto the beast.
14 These shall fight with the [30] Lambe, and
the Lambe shall ouercome them: *for hee is

3 Henceforth is propounded the type of Babylon, and the state thereof, in 4. verses. After, a declaration of the type, in the rest of this chapter. In the type are described two things, the beast (of whom chapter 13.) in the 3. verse, and the woman that sitteth vpon the beast, verse 4.5.6 The beast in processe of time, hath gotten somewhat more then was expressed in the former vision. First in that it is not read before that he was appareled in scarlet, a robe imperiall and of triumph. Secondly, in that this is full of names of blasphemie: the other caried the name of blasphemie onely in his heads. So God did teach that this beast is much increased in impietie and iniustice, and doeth in this last age, triumph in both these more insolently and proudly then euer before. b *A scarlet colour, that is, with a red and purple garment: and surely it was not without cause that the Romish Clergie were so much delighted with this colour.* 4 That harlot, the spiritual Babylon, which is Rome. She is described by her attire, profession, and deeds. 5 In attire most glorious, triumphant, most rich, and most gorgeous. 6 In profession the nourisher of all, in this verse, & teaching her mysteries vnto all, ver. 5. setting forth all things most magnificently: but indeed most pernicious besotting miserable men with her cup, & bringeth vpon them a deadly giddines. 7 Deceiuing with the title of religion, and publike inscription of mysterie: which the beast in times past did not beare. 8 An exposition: in which S. Iohn declareth what maner of woman this is. 9 In maner of deeds: Shee is red with blood, and sheddeth it most licentiously, and therefore is coloured with the blood of the Saints, as on the contrary part, Christ is set foorth imbrued with the blood of his enemies, Esa. 63.1. 10 A passage vnto the second part of this Chapter, by occasion giuen of S. Iohn, as the words of the Angel doe shew in the next verse. 11 The second part or place as I said ver. 1. The enarration of the vision, promised in the verse following. Now there is deliuered first an enarration of the beast and his story, vnto the 14. verse. After, of the harlot, vnto the end of the Chapter. 12 The story of the beast hath a triple description of him. The first is a distinction of this beast from all that euer haue bene at any time: which distinction is conteined in this verse: The second is a delineation or painting out of the beast by things present, by which he might euen at that time bee knowen of the godly: and this delineation is according to his heads, verse 12, 13, 14. This beast is that Empire of Rome, of which I spake Chapter 13.11. according to the mutations and changes whereof, which then had already hapned, the holy Ghost hath distinguished and set out the same. The Apostle distinguisheth this beast from all others in these words: *The beast which thou sawest, was and is not.* For so I expound the words of the Apostle for the euidencie sake, as I will further declare in the notes following. 13 The meaning is, that beast which thou sawest before (Chap. 13.1.) and which yet thou hast now seene, was, (was I say) euen from Iulius Cæsar in respect of beginning, rising vp, station, glory, dominion, maner and stocke, from the house of Iulius: and yet is not now the same, if thou looke vnto the house and stocke: for the dominion of this family was translated vnto another, after the death of Nero from that other vnto a third, from a third vnto a fourth, and so forth, was varied and altered by innumerable changes. Finally, the Empire is one, as it were one beast: but exceedingly varied by kinreds, families, and persons. It was therefore (saith S. Iohn) in the kinred or house of Iulius: and now it is not in that kinred, but translated vnto another. 14 As if he should say, Also this same that is, shal shortly not be: but shal ascend out of the depth, or out of the sea (as was said, Cha. 13 1.) that is, shalbe a new stocke from amongst the nations without difference & shal in the same state go vnto destruction, or run and perish: and so shall successiuely new Princes or Emperours come & goe, arise & fall, the body of the beast remaining still, but tossed with so many and often alterations, as no man can but maruel that this beast was able to stand & hold out, in so many mutations, verely no Empire that euer was tossed with so many changes, and as it were with so many tempests of the sea, euer continued so long. 15 That is, as many as haue not learned the prouidence of God, according to the faith of the Saints, shall maruell at these grieuous and often changes: when they shall consider the selfe same beast, which is the Romane Empire, to haue beene, and not to bee, and to be, and still molested with perpetuall mutation, and yet in the same to stand & continue This in mine opinion, is the most simple exposition of this place, confirmed by the euent of the things themselues. Although the last change also, by which the Empire, that before was ciuill, became Ecclesiasticall, is not obscurely signified in these words, of which two, the first exercised cruelty vpon the bodies of the Saints: the other also vpon their soules. the first by humane order and policy, the other vnder the colour of the law of God, and of Religion, raged and imbrued it selfe with the blood of the godly.

16 An exhortation preparing vnto audience by the same argument, with that of Christ: *He that hath eares to heare let him heare.* Wherefore for mine owne part, I had rather read in this place, *Let there be here a minde, &c.* So the Angel passeth fully vnto the second place of this description. c *Very children know what the seuen hilled citie is, which is so much spoken of, and whereof Virgil thus reporteth.* And compasseth seuen towers in one wall: *that citie it is, which when Iohn wrote these things, had rule ouer the kings of the earth. It was and is not, and yet it remaineth to this day, but it is declining to destruction.* 17 This is the painting out of the beast by things present (as I said before) whereby S. Iohn endeuoured to describe the same, that he might be both knowen of the godly in that age, and be further obserued and marked of posteritie afterwards. This delineation hath one tipe, that is, his heads, but a double description or application of the type: one permanent, from the nature it selfe, the other changeable, by the working of men. The description permanent, is by the seuen hils, in this verse, the other that fleeteth, is from the seuen kings, verse 10, 11. And here it is worthy to be obserued, that one type hath sometime two or more applications, as seemeth good vnto the holy Ghost to expresse, either one thing by diuers types, or diuers things by one type. So I noted before of the seuen spirits, Chapter 1, 4. Now this woman that sitteth vpon seuen hils, is the citie of Rome, called in times past of the Grecians, ἑπτάλοφος. i. of seuen tops or crests and of Varro, *septiceps*. i. of her seuen heads (as here) of seuen heads, and of others, *septem collis*. i. standing vpon seuen hils. 18 The beginning of these Kings or Emperours is almost the same with the beginning of the Church of Christ, which I shewed before Chapter 11.1. Namely from the yeere 25. after the passion of Christ, what time the Temple and Church of the Iewes was ouerthrowen. In which yeere it came to passe by the prouidence of God, that that saying, *The beast was, and is not,* was fulfilled before that destruction of the Iewes immediatly following, came to passe. That was the yeere from the building of the citie of Rome, 809. from which yeere S. Iohn both numbreth the Emperours which hitherto had bene, when he wrote these things, and foretelleth of two other next to come: and with this purpose, that when this particular prediction of foretelling of things to come, should take effect, the trueth of all other predictions in the Church, might bee the more confirmed. Which signe God of olde mentioned in the Law, Deut. 18. and Ieremie confirmeth, Chapter 28.8. 19 Whose names are these: the first, *Seruius Sulpitius Galba*, who was the seuenth Emperour of the people of Rome, the second *Marcus Saluius Otho*, the third *Aulus Vitellius*, the fourth, *Titus Flauius Vespasianus*, the fift. *Titus Vespasianus* his sonne, of his owne name. 20 *Flauius Domitian*, sonne of the first *Vespasian*. For in the latter ende of his dayes Saint Iohn wrote these things, as witnesseth Irenæus, *Lib. 5. aduersus hæreses.* 21 Nerua, The Empire being now translated from the family of *Flauius*. This man reigned only one yere, foure monethes and nine dayes, as the historie writers doe tell. 22 This is spoken by the figure Synecdoche, as much to say, as that head of the beast which was and is not, because it is cut off, and Nerua in so short time extinguished. How many heads there were, so many beastes there seemed to be in one. See the like speech in the third verse of the thirteenth Chapter. 23 Nerua Traianus, who himselfe in diuers respects is called heere the seuenth and the eight. 24 Though in number and order of succession he bee the eighth yet hee is reckoned together with one of these heads, because Nerua and hee were one head. For this man obteined authoritie together with Nerua and was Consul with him, when Nerua left his life. 25 Namely, to molest with persecutions the Churches of Christ, as the Histories doe accord, and I haue briefely noted, Chapter 2.10. 26 The third place of this description, as I said verse 8. is a propheticall prediction of things to come, which the beast should doe, as in the words following Saint Iohn doeth not obscurely signifie, saying, *which haue not yet receiued the kingdome, &c.* For there is an Antithesis or opposition betweene these kings, and those that went before. And first the persons are described in this verse, then their deedes, in the two verses following. 27 That is, arising with their kingdomes out of that Romane beast: at such time as that politicall Empire beganne by the craft of the Popes greatly to fall. 28 Namely, with that second beast, whome wee called before a false Prophet, which beast ascending out of the earth, got vnto himselfe all the authoritie and power of the first beast, and exercised the same before his face, as was said Chapter 14.11, 12. For when the politicall Empire of the West begann to bow downewards, there both arose those ten kings, and the second beast tooke the opportunitie offered, to vsurpe vnto himselfe all the power of the former beast. These kings long agoe, many haue numbred and described to bee ten, and a great part of the euents plainely testifieth the same in this our age. 29 That is, by consent and agreement, that they may conspire with the beast, and depend vpon his becke. Their storie is diuided into three parts, counsels, actes, and euents. The counsellers some of them consist in communicating of iudgements and affections: and some in communicating of power, which they are said to haue giuen vnto this beast, in this verse. 30 With Christ and his Church, as the reason following doeth declare, and heere are mentioned the factes and euents which followed for Christ his sake, and for the grace of God the Father towards those that are called, elected, and are his faithfull ones in Christ. * *Chap. 19.16. 1. tim. 6.15.*

Lord of Lords, and King of Kings: and they
that are on his side, called and chosen, and
faithfull.

15 [31] And hee said vnto me, The waters
which thou sawest, where the whore sitteth,
[32] are people, and multitudes, and nations, and
tongues.

16 And the ten [33] hornes which thou sawest vpon the beast, are they that shall hate the
whore, and shall make her desolate, and naked,
and shall eate her flesh, and burne her with fire.

17 [34] For God hath put in their hearts to fulfill his will, and to doe with one consent for to
giue their kingdome vnto the beast, vntill the
words of God be fulfilled.

18 And that woman which thou sawest, is
that [35] great citie which reigned ouer the kings
of the earth.

31 This is the other member of the enarration, as I said verse 7. belonging vnto the harlot, shewed in the vision, vers. 3. In this history of the harlot, these three things are distinctly propounded, what is her magnificencie, in this verse, what is her fall, and by whom it shall happen vnto her, in the two verses following: and lastly, who that harlot is, in the last verse. This place which by order of nature should haue beene the first, is therefore made the last, because it was more fit to be ioyned with the next Chapter. 32 That is, as vnconstant and variable as are the waters. Vpon this foundation sitteth this harlot as Queene, a vaine person, vpon that which is vaine. 33 The ten Kings, as verse 12. The accomplishment of this fact and euent is daily increased in this our age by the singular prouidence and most mightie gouernement of God. Wherefore the facts are propounded in this verse, and the cause of them in the verses following. 34 A reason rendred from the chiefe efficient cause, which is the prouidence of God, by which alone Saint Iohn by inuersion of order affirmeth to haue come to passe, both that the Kings should execute vpon the harlot that which pleased God, and which he declared in the verse next before going: and also that by one consent and counsell, they should giue their kingdome vnto the beast, &c. verse 13.14. for as these being blinded haue before depended vpon the becke of the beast that lifteth vp the harlot, so it is said, that afterward it shall come to passe, that they shall turne backe, and shall fall away from her, when their hearts shall be turned into better state by the grace and mercie of God. 35 That is, Rome that great Citie, or onely Citie (as Iustinian calleth it) the King and head whereof was then the Emperour, but now the Pope, since that the condition of the beast was changed.

CHAP. XVIII.

2 The horrible destruction of Babylon is set out. 11.16.18. *The merchants of the earth, who were enriched with the pompe and luxuriousnesse of it, weepe and waile:* 20 *But all the elect reioyce for that iust vengeance of God.*

AND [1] after these things, I saw *another* [2] Angel come downe from heauen, hauing
great power, so that the earth was lightened
with his glorie,

2 [3] And hee cried out mightily with a
lowde voice, saying, * It is fallen, it is fallen,
Babylon that great *citie*, and is become the
habitation of deuils, and the hold of all foule
spirits, and a cage of euery vncleane and hatefull bird.

3 For all nations haue drunken of the
wine of the wrath of her fornication, and
the Kings of the earth haue committed fornication with her, and the merchants of the
earth are waxed rich of the abundance of her
pleasures.

4 [4] And I heard another voice from heauen say, [5] Goe out of her, my people, that yee
[6] be not partakers of her sinnes, and that yee receiue not of her plagues.

5 For her sinnes are [a] come vp into heauen, and God hath remembred her iniquities.

6 [7] Reward her, euen as shee hath rewarded you, and giue her double according to her
workes: *and* in the cup that shee hath filled to
you, fill her the double.

7 Inasmuch as shee glorified her selfe, and
liued in pleasure, so much giue yee to her torment and sorrow: for shee saith [b] in her heart, I
sit being a Queene, and am [c] no widow, and
shall [d] see no mourning.

8 Therfore shal her plagues come at [e] one
day, death, and sorrow, and famine, and shee
shall bee burnt with fire: for that God which
condemneth her, is a strong Lord.

9 And [8] the kings of the earth shall bewaile her, and lament for her, which haue committed fornication, and liued in pleasure with
her, when they shall see that smoke of that her
burning,

10 And shall stand afarre off for feare of her
torment, saying, Alas, alas, that great citie Babylon, that mightie citie: for in one houre is
thy iudgement come.

11 [9] And the merchants of the earth shall
weepe and waile ouer her: for no man buyeth
their ware any more.

12 The ware of gold, and siluer, and of precious stone, and of pearles, and of fine linnen,
and of purple, and of silke, and of skarlet, and of
all maner of Thyne wood, and of all vessels of
yuorie, and of al vessels of most precious wood,
and of brasse, and of yron, and of marble,

13 And of cinamom, and odours, and oyntments, and frankincense, and wine, and oyle,
and fine floure, and wheate, and beastes, and
sheepe, and horses, and charets, and seruants,
and soules of men.

14 ([10] And the [f] apples that thy soule lusted
after, are departed from thee, and all things
which were fat and excellent, are departed from
thee, and thou shalt finde them no more.)

15 The merchants of these things which
were waxed rich, shall stand afarre off from her,
for feare of her torment, weeping and wailing,

16 And saying, Alas, alas, that great citie
that was clothed in fine linnen and purple, and
skarlet, and gilded with golde, and precious
stone, and pearles.

1 The second place (as I said before 17. 1.) of the historie of Babylon, is of the wofull fall and ruine of that whore of Babylon. This historicall prediction concerning her, is threefold. The first a plaine and simple foretelling of her ruine, in three verses. The second a figuratiue prediction by the circumstances, thence vnto the 20 verse. The third, a confirmation of the same by signe or wonder, vnto the end of the Chapter.

2 Either Christ the eternall word of God the Father (as often elsewhere) or a created Angel, and one deputed vnto this seruice, but throughly furnished with greatnesse of power, and with light of glory, as the ensigne of power. 3 The prediction or foreshewing of her ruine, conteining both the fall of Babylon, in this verse, and the cause thereof vttered by way of allegorie concerning her spirituall and carnall wickednesse, that is, her most great impietie and vniustice, in the next verse, her fall is first simply declared of the Angel, and then the greatnesse therof is shewed here, by the euents when he saith it shall bee the seate and habitation of deuils, of wilde beastes, and of cursed foules, as of olde Esay 13.21. and often elsewhere. * *Chap.* 14. 8. *esai.* 21. 9. *iere.* 51. 8. 4 The second prediction, which is of the circumstances of the ruine of Babylon: of these there are two kinds: one going before it, as that before hand the godly are deliuered, vnto the ninth verse: the other following vpon her ruine, namely the lamentation of the wicked, and reioycing of the godly, vnto the twentieth verse.

5 Two circumstances going before the ruine, are commanded in this place: one is, that the godly depart out of Babylon: as I mentioned Cha. 12. to haue beene done in time past, before the destruction of Ierusalem: this charge is giuen here and in the next verse. The other is, that euery one of them occupie themselues in their own place, in executing the iudgement of God, as it was commanded the Leuites of olde, Exod. 32.27. and that they sanctifie their hands vnto the Lord, verse 6,7,8. 6 Of this commaundement there are two causes: to auoide the contagion of sinne and to shun the participation of those punishments that belong thereunto. *a He vseth a word which signifieth the following of sinnes one after another, and rising one of another in such sort, that they grow at length to such an heape, that they came vp euen to heauen.* 7 The prouocation of the godly, and the commandement of executing the iudgement of God, stand vpon three causes which are here expressed: the vniust wickednesse of the whore of Babylon, in this verse, her cursed pride opposing it selfe against God, which is the fountaine of all euill actions, verse 7. and her most iust damnation by the sentence of God, verse 8. *b With her selfe.* *c I am full of people and mightie.* *d I shall taste of one.* *e Shortly, and at one instant.* 8 The circumstances following the fall of Babylon, or the consequents thereof (as I distinguished them, verse 4) are two. Namely the lamentation of the wicked, vnto the 19. ver. and the reioycing of the godly, verse 20. This most sorrowful lamentation, according to the persons of them that lament, hath three members: the first whereof is the mourning of the kings and mightie men of the earth, in two verses: The second is, the lamentation of the merchants that trafique by land, thence vnto the 6 verse: The third is, the wailing of those that merchandize by sea, verse 16, 17, 18 In euery of those the cause and maner of their mourning is described in order, according to the condition of those that mourne, with obseruation of that which best agreeth vnto them. 9 The lamentation of those that trade by land, as I distinguished immediatly before. 10 An apostrophe, or turning of the speech by imitation, vsed for more vehemencie, as if those merchants, after the maner of mourners, should in passionate speech speake vnto Babylon, though now vtterly fallen and ouerthrowen. So Esay 12. 9. and in many other places. *f By this is meant that season which is next before the fall of the leafe, at what season fruits ripen, and the word signifieth such fruites as are longed for.*

17 [11]For in one houre so great riches are
come to desolation. And euery shipmaster, and
all the people that occupie ships, and shipmen,
and whosoeuer traffique on the sea, shal stand a
farre off,

18 And crie, when they see that smoke of
that her burning, saying, What *citie was* like
vnto this great citie?

19 And they shall cast dust on their heads,
and crie, weeping, and wailing, and say, Alas,
alas, that great citie, wherein were made rich all
that had ships on the sea by her costlinesse: for
in one houre shee is made desolate.

20 [12]O heauen, reioyce of her, and yee holy
Apostles and Prophets: for God hath punished
her, to be reuenged on her for your sakes.

21 [13]Then a mightie Angel tooke vp a stone
like a great milstone, *and cast it into the Sea,
saying, With such violence shall that great citie
Babylon be cast, and shall be found no more.

22 [14]And the voice of harpers, and musiti-
ans, and of pipers, and trumpetters shall bee
heard no more in thee, and no craftesman, of
whatsoeuer craft *he be*, shall be found any more
in thee: and the sound of a milstone shall bee
heard no more in thee.

23 And the light of a candle shall shine
no more in thee: and the voice of the bridegrome and of the bride shall be heard no more
in thee: for thy merchants were the great men
of the earth: and with thine inchantment were
deceiued all nations.

24 And in her was found the [15]blood of the
Prophets, [16]and of the Saints, and of all that
were slaine vpon the earth.

11 The maner of mourning vsed by them that trade by sea.
12 The other consequent vpon the other ruine of Babylon, is the exultation or reioycing of the godly in heauen and in earth as was noted verse 9.
13 The third prediction, as I said verse 1. standing of a signe, and the interpretation thereof: the interpretation thereof is in two sorts, first by a simple propounding of the thing it selfe, in this verse, and then by declaration of the euents, in the verses following.
* Ierem. 51.63.
14 The euents are two, and one of them opposite vnto the other for amplification sake. There shall be, saith he, in Babylon no mirth nor ioy at al, in this and the next verse, but all heauie and lamentable things, from the bloodie slaughters of the righteous and the vengeance of God comming vpon it for the same.
15 That is shed by bloody massacres, and calling for vengeance. 16 That is, prooued and found out, as if God had appointed a iust enquirie concerning the impietie, vnnaturalnesse, and vniustice of these men.

CHAP. XIX.

1 The heauenly companie praise God for auenging the blood of his seruants on the whore. 9 They are written blessed, that are called to the Lambes supper. 10 The Angel will not be worshipped. 11 The mightie King of kings appeareth from heauen. 19 The battell, 20 wherein the beast is taken, 21 and cast into the burning lake.

AND [1]after these things I heard a great
voice of a great multitude in heauen, saying, [a][2]Hallelu-iah, saluation, and glory, and
honour, and power *be* to the Lord our God.

2 For true and righteous *are* his iudgements: for hee hath condemned that great
whore which did corrupt the earth with her
fornication, and hath auenged the blood of his
seruants *shed* by her hand.

3 And againe they said, [3]Hallelu-iah: and
that her smoke rose vp for euermore.

1 This chapter hath in summe two parts, one transitorie or of passage vnto the things that follow, vnto the 10. verse, another historicall of the victory of Christ gotten against both the beasts, vnto the end of the chapter, which I said was the second historie of this argument, chap. 17. 1.
The transition hath two places, one of praising God for the ouerthrow done vnto Babylon in 4. verses: and another likewise of praise, and Propheticall, for the comming of Christ vnto his kingdome, and his most royall marriage with his Church, thence vnto the tenth verse. The former praise hath three branches, distinguished after the ancient maner of those that sing: προσφώνησις, that is, an inuitation or prouokement in two verses: ἀντιφωνία, a response or answere in the third verse: and συνῳδία, a close or ioyning together in harmonie: all which I thought good of purpose to distinguish in this place, lest any man should with Porphyrius, or other like dogs, obiect vnto Saint Iohn, or the heauenly Church, a childish and idle repetition of speech. *a Praise the Lord.* 2 The proposition of praise with exhortation in this verse, and the cause thereof, in the next verse. 3 The song of the Antiphonie or response, containing an amplification of the praise of God, from the perpetual and most certain testimony of his diuine iudgment as was done at Sodom & Gomarrha, Gen. 19

4 And the foure and twentie Elders, and
the foure beastes fell downe, and worshipped
God that sate on the throne, saying, Amen,
Hallelu-iah.

5 [4]Then a voice came out of the [5]throne
saying, Praise our God, all yee his seruants, and
yee that feare him, both small and great.

6 And I heard [6]like a voice of a great multitude, and as the voice of many waters, and as
the voice of strong thundrings, saying, Hallelu-
iah: for the Lord that God that almightie one
hath reigned.

7 Let vs bee glad and reioyce, and giue
glory to him: for the marriage of the Lambe is
come, and his wife hath [7]made her selfe ready.

8 And to her was graunted, that shee
should bee arayed with [8]pure fine linnen and
shining, for the fine [9]linnen is the [b]righteous-
nesse of Saints.

9 [10]Then he said vnto me, Write, *Blessed *are* they which are called vnto the Lambes
supper. And he said vnto me, These words of
God are true.

10 [11]And I fell before his feete, *to worship him, but he said vnto me, See thou doe it
not: I am thy fellow seruant, and one of thy
brethren, which haue the [c]testimonie of Iesus,
Worship God: for the testimonie of [d]Iesus is
the Spirit of prophesie.

11 [12]And I saw [13]heauen open, and behold
a white horse, and hee that sate vpon him, was
called faithfull and true, and hee iudgeth and
fighteth righteously.

12 And his eyes *were* as a flame of fire, and
on his head *were* many crownes: and hee had a
name written, that no man knew but himselfe.

13 And hee was clothed with a garment
dipt in blood, and his name was called THE
WORD OF GOD.

14 [14]And the hostes which were in heauen,
followed him vpon white horses, clothed with
fine linnen white and pure.

15 [15]And out of his mouth went out a
sharpe sword, that with it he should smite the
heathen: for hee shall *rule them with a rod of
yron: for hee it is that treadeth the wine presse
of the fiercenesse and wrath of Almighty God.

16 [16]And hee hath vpon his garment, and
vpon his thigh a name written, *THE KING
OF KINGS, AND LORD OF LORDS.

4 The second place of praise, as I said verse 1. which first is commaunded from God in this verse: and then is in most ample maner pronounced of the creatures, both because they see that kingdome of Christ, to come, which most they desire, verse 6. also because they see that the Church is called forth to be brought home into the house of her husband by holy marriage, vnto the fellowship of his kingdome, verse 7. 8. Wherefore Saint Iohn is commanded to write into a booke the Epiphonema, or acclamation ioyned with a diuine testimonie, ver. 9.
5 Out of the Temple from God, as 11. 19.
6 Without the Temple in heauen.
7 Namely, vnto that holy marriage, both her selfe in person in this verse, and also furnished of her spouse with marriage giftes princely and diuine, is adorned and prepared in the next verse.
8 As an ensigne of Kingly and Priestly dignitie: which dignitie Christ bestoweth vpon vs, Chapter 1. 6.
9 This is a gift giuen by the husband for mariage sake, and a most choice ornament which Christ bestowed vpon vs, as vpon his spouse.
b Good workes which are liuely testimonies of faith.
* Matth. 22. 2.
10 Namely the Angel, as appeareth by the next verse. 11 The particular historie of this verse is brought in by occasion, and as it were besides the purpose, that S. Iohn might make a publike example of his owne infirmitie, & of the modest sanctimonie of the Angel, who both renounced for himselfe the diuine honours, and recalled all the seruants of God, vnto ẏ worship of him alone: as also 22. 8. * *Chap. 22. 8.* *c Which are commanded to beare witnesse of Iesus.* *d For Iesus is the marke that all the prophesies shoote at.* 12 The second place of this Chapter (as I said verse 1) is of the victorie gotten by Christ against both the beastes: in which first Christ is described as one ready to fight, vnto the 16. verse, then is shewed the battell to be begun, thence vnto the 18. ver, lastly is set forth the victory, vnto the end of the Chapter. In this place doe shine foorth most excellent properties of Christ as our heauenly iudge & reuenger, according to his person, companie, effects and names. 13 Properties belonging to his person, that he is heauenly, iudge, faithful, true, iust, in this verse, searching out all things, ruling ouer all, to bee searched out of none, verse 12. the triumpher, and the very essentiall word of God, verse 13. 14 The companie or retinue of Christ, holy, innumerable, heauenly, iudiciall, royall and pure. 15 The effects of Christ prepared vnto battell, that with his mouth hee striketh the Gentiles, ruleth and destroyeth. * *Psal. 2. 9.* 16 The name agreeing vnto Christ according to the former properties, expressed after the maner of the Hebrewes. * *Chap 17. 14. 1. tim. 6. 15.*

17 [17] And I ſawe an Angel ſtand in the
[18] ſunne, who cried with a lowde voice, ſaying
to all the foules that did flie by [19] the middes of
heauen, Come, and gather your ſelues together vnto the ſupper of the great God,
18 That yee may eat the fleſh of kings, and
the fleſh of high captaines, and the fleſh of
mightie men, and the fleſh of horſes, and of
them that ſit on them, and the fleſh of all free
men, and bond men, and of ſmall and great.
19 [20] And I ſaw the beaſt, and the kings of
the earth, and their hoſts gathered together to
make battell againſt him that ſate on the horſe,
and againſt his armie.
20 But the beaſt [22] was taken, and with him
that falſe prophet that wrought miracles before
him, whereby he deceiued them that receiued
the beaſtes marke, and them that worſhipped
his image. Theſe both were aliue caſt into a
lake of fire burning with brimſtone.
21 And the remnant were ſlaine with the
ſword of him that ſitteth vpon the horſe, which
commeth out of his mouth, and all the fowles
were filled full with their fleſh.

17 The ſecond member, as I ſaid verſe 11. A reprochfull calling forth of his enemies vnto battel: in which not themſelues (for why ſhould they be called foorth of the King of the world, or prouoked being his ſubiects? for that were not comely) but in their hearing, the birds of the ayre are called to eate their carkaſſes. 18 That is, openly, and in ſight of all, as Numb. 25.4. and 2.Sam. 12.11. 19 That is, through this inferiour heauen, and which is neerer vnto vs: an Hebrew phraſe. 20 The third member (as was ſaid verſe 11) of the victorie obtained by Chriſt. Vnto this apperteineth two things: his buckling with the beaſt and his forces, in this verſe: and the euent moſt magnificent, deſcribed after the maner of men, in the verſes following. All theſe things are plaine. 21 Namely, that beaſt with ſeuen heads, of which before, Chapter 13.1. and 17.3. 22 That is, that beaſt with two heads, of which 13.11. Looke more Chapter 16.14.

CHAP. XX.

1 The Angel 2 bindeth Satan for a thouſand yeeres. 8 Being looſed, hee ſtirreth vp Gog and Magog, that is, priuie and open enemies againſt the Saints, 11 but the vengeance of the Lord cutteth off their inſolencie. 12 The bookes are opened, by which the dead are iudged.

AND [1] I ſawe an Angel come downe from
heauen, hauing the key [2] of the bottomleſſe pit, and a great chaine in his hand.
2 And he tooke the dragon that olde ſerpent, which is the deuill and Satan, and hee
bound him [3] a thouſand yeeres:
3 And caſt him into the bottomleſſe pit,
and hee ſhut him vp, and ſealed *the doore* vpon
him, that hee ſhould deceiue the people [4] no
more, till the thouſand yeres were fulfilled: for
after that he muſt be looſed for [5] a little ſeaſon.
4 [6] And I ſaw [a] ſeates: and they ſate vpon them, and [7] iudgment was giuen vnto them,
and *I ſaw* the ſoules of them that were [8] beheaded for the witneſſe of Ieſus, and for the word
of God, and which [9] did not worſhip the beaſt,
neither his image, neither had taken his marke
vpon their foreheads or on their hands: and
they liued, and reigned with Chriſt a thouſand yeere.
5 [10] But the reſt of the dead men [11] ſhall
not liue againe, vntill the thouſand yeeres bee
finiſhed: this is the firſt reſurrection.
6 Bleſſed and holy is hee, that hath part in
the firſt reſurrection: *for* on ſuch the [12] ſecond
death hath no power: but they ſhall bee the
Prieſts of God and of Chriſt, [13] and ſhall reigne
with him a thouſand yeere.
7 [14] And when the [15] thouſand yeeres are
expired, Satan ſhall be looſed out of his priſon,
8 [16] And ſhall goe out to deceiue the people, which are in the foure quarters of the earth:
euen * Gog and Magog, to gather them together to battell, whoſe number *is* as the ſand of
the Sea.
9 And they went vp into the [b] plaine of
the earth, and they compaſſed the tents of the
Saints about, and the beloued citie: but [17] fire
came downe from God out of heauen, and deuoured them.
10 [18] And the deuill that deceiued them,
was caſt into a lake of fire and brimſtone, where
that beaſt and that falſe prophet *are*, and ſhalbe
tormented euen day and night for euermore.
11 [19] And I ſaw a great [20] white throne, and
one that ſate on it, [21] from whoſe face fled away
both the earth and heauen, and their place was
no more found.
12 And I ſaw the dead, both great and ſmall
ſtand before [22] God: and the [23] bookes were o-
pened, *and another booke was opened, which
is *the booke* [24] of life, and the dead were iudged
of thoſe things, which were written in the
bookes, according to their workes.
13 [25] And the ſea gaue vp her dead, which
were in her, and death and hell deliuered vp
the dead, which were in them: and they were

1 Now followeth the third place of the prophetical hiſtorie, which is of the victorie whereby Chriſt ouercame the dragon, as I noted Chap. 7.1. This place muſt neceſſarily bee ioyned with the end of the 12. chapter and be applied vnto the iuſt vnderſtanding thereof. This chapter hath two parts, one of the dragon ouercome, vnto the 10. verſe: the other of the reſurrection and laſt iudgment vnto the end of the chapter. The ſtory of the dragon is doubled: Firſt of the firſt victory, after which he was bound by Chriſt, vnto the 6. ver. The ſecond is of the laſt victory, wherby he was throwen downe into euerlaſting puniſhment, thence vnto the 16. verſe. This firſt hiſtory hapned in the firſt time of the Chriſtian Church, when the dragon throwen downe from heauen by Chriſt, went about to moleſt ẏ new birth of the Church in the earth, Chap. 12.17, 18. For which cauſe I gaue warning, that this ſtory of the Dragon muſt be annexed vnto that place. 2 That is, of hell, whither God threw downe the Angels which had ſinned, and bound them in chaines of darkneſſe to be kept vnto damnation, 2.Pet.2 4. Iud 6. 3 The firſt whereof (continuing this hiſtory with the ende of the ſecond chapter) in the 36. yeere from the paſsion of Chriſt, when the Church of the Iewes being ouerthrowen, Satan aſſayed to inuade the Chriſtian Church gathered of the Gentiles, and to deſtroy part of her ſeede, Chap. 12. 17. The thouſandth yeere falleth preciſely vpon the times of that wicked Hildebrand, who was called Gregorie the ſeuenth, a moſt damnable Necromancer and ſorcerer, whom Satan vſed as an inſtrument when he was looſed out of bonds, thence foorth to annoy the Saints of God with moſt cruel perſecutions, and the whole world with diſſentions, and moſt bloody warres: as Benno the Cardinal reporteth at large. And this is the firſt victory gotten ouer the Dragon in the earth. 4 Namely, with that publike and violent deceite which he attempted before, Chap. 12. and which after a thouſand yeeres (alacke for woe) hee moſt mightily procured in the Chriſtian world. 5 Which being once expired, the ſecond battell and victory ſhall be, of which verſe 7, 8. 6 A deſcription of the common ſtate of the Church of Chriſt in earth in that ſpace of a thouſand yeeres, for which the deuill was in bonds: in which firſt the authoritie, life, and common honour of the godly, is declared, verſe 4. Secondly, newneſſe of life is preached vnto others by the Goſpel, after that ſpace, verſe 5. Finally, he concludeth with promiſes, verſe 6. *a For iudgement was committed to them, as to members ioyned to the head: not that Chriſts office was giuen ouer to them.*

7 This was a type of the authoritie of the good and faithfull ſeruants of God in the Church, taken from the maner of men. 8 Of the Martyrs, which ſuffered in thoſe firſt times. 9 Of the Martyrs which ſuffered after that both the beaſts were now riſen vp, Chap. 15. for there, theſe things are expounded. 10 Whoſoeuer ſhall lie dead in ſinne, and not know the truth of God. 11 They ſhall not be renewed with that newneſſe of the life by the enlightening of the Goſpel of the glorie of Chriſt. For this is the firſt reſurrection, by which ſoules of the dead doe riſe from their death. In the ſecond reſurrection their bodies ſhall riſe againe. 12 That whereby both body and ſoule, that is, the whole man is addicted and deliuered vnto eternall death. So Chap. 2.11. 13 A returne vnto the intended hiſtory, by reſuming the words which are in the end of the fourth verſe. 14 The ſecond hiſtorie, of the latter victory of Chriſt, as was ſaid verſe 1. In which are ſummarily deſcribed the worke, ouerthrow, and eternall puniſhment of Satan. 15 Of which I ſpake, verſe 2. Then therefore ſhall bee giuen vnto him libertie to rage againſt the Church, and to moleſt the Saints for the ſinnes of men: vnto whom the faithfull ſhall haue aſſociated themſelues more then was meete, taſting with them of their impuritie of doctrine and life. 16 The worke or acte of Satan (which is the firſt member, as I diſtinguiſhed in the verſe before going) to deceiue the whole world, euen vnto the vttermoſt nations thereof: to arme them againſt the people of God, in this verſe, and to beſiege and oppreſſe the Church, with his whole ſtrength, in the verſe following. ** Ezechiel 39.2.* *b As if hee ſaid, in ſo much that the whole face of the earth, how great ſoeuer it is, was filled.* 17 The wrath of God, conſuming the aduerſaries, and ouerthrowing all their enterpriſes, Hebr. 10 27. And this is the ſecond member mentioned verſe 7. the ouerthrow of Satan. 18 The third member, eternal deſtruction againſt thoſe that are ouercome: as I noted in the ſame place. 19 The ſecond part of this Chapter, in which is deſcribed the iudge, in this verſe, and the laſt iudgement in the verſe following. 20 That is, a tribunall ſeate moſt Princelike and glorious: for ſo doeth the Greeke word alſo ſignifie. 21 That is, Chriſt, before whom when he commeth vnto iudgement, heauen and earth ſhall periſh for the greatneſſe of his maieſtie, 2.Pet. 3.7, 10. &c. 22 That is, Chriſt the iudge, 2.Cor. 5.10. 23 As it were, his bookes of reckoning or accompts, that is, the teſtimonie of our conſcience, and of our workes, which by no meanes can bee auoided. This is ſpoken after the maner of men. ** Chap. 3.5. and 21.27. philip. 4.3.* 24 The booke of the eternall decree of God, in which God the Father hath elected in Chriſt according to the good pleaſure of his will, thoſe that ſhall bee heires of life. This alſo is ſpoken according to the maner of men. 25 This is a preuention or an anſwere to an obiection: for happily ſome man will ſay, But they are dead, whom the ſea, death and the graue hath conſumed, how ſhall they appeare before the iudge? S. Iohn anſwereth, By reſurrection from death, whereunto all things (howſoeuer repugnant) ſhall miniſter and ſerue at the commandement of God, as Daniel 12.

iudged euery man according to their workes.
41 [26] And death and hell were caſt into the
lake of fire: this is the ſecond death.
15 And whoſoeuer was not found written
in the booke of life, was caſt into the lake of fire.

26 The laſt enemie which is death ſhalbe aboliſhed by Chriſt (that he may no more make any attempt againſt vs,) 1.Cor.15.16. and death ſhall feede vpon the reprobate in hell for euermore, according to the righteous iudgement of God, in the next verſe.

CHAP. XXI.

2 Hee deſcribeth new Hieruſalem deſcending from heauen, 9 the bride the Lambes wife, 12 and the glorious building of the citie, 19 garniſhed with precious ſtones, 22 whoſe Temple the Lambe is.

AND [1] I ſaw *a new heauen, and a newe
earth: for the * firſt heauen, and the firſt
earth were paſſed away, and there was no
more ſea.
2 [2] And I Iohn ſaw the holy citie new Hieruſalem come downe from God out of heauen,
prepared as a bride trimmed for her husband.
3 [3] And I heard a great voice out of heauen, ſaying, Behold, the Tabernacle of God *is*
with men, and hee will dwell with them: and
they ſhall be his people, and God himſelfe ſhal
be their God with them.
4 * And God ſhall wipe away all teares
from their eyes: and there ſhall bee no more
death, neither ſorrow, neither crying, neither
ſhall there bee any more paine: for the firſt
things are paſſed.
5 [4] And he that ſate vpon the throne, ſaid,
*Behold, I make all things new: and hee ſaid
vnto me, Write: for theſe words are faithfull
and true.
6 And he ſaid vnto me, *[5] It is done, I am
Alpha and Omega, the beginning and the end:
I will giue to him that is athirſt, of the well of
the water of life freely.
7 Hee that ouercommeth, ſhall inherit all
things, and I will be his God, and he ſhall bee
my ſonne.
8 But the fearefull and the vnbeleeuing,
and the abominable and murtherers, and whor-
mongers, and ſorcerers, and idolaters, and all
liars ſhall haue their [a] part in the lake, which
burneth with fire and brimſtone, which is the
ſecond death.
9 [6] And there came vnto me one of the ſeuen Angels, which had the ſeuen vials full of
the ſeuen laſt plagues, and talked with me, ſay-

1 Now followeth the ſecond part of the hiſtory prophetical (as I ſaid Chapter 1.and 11.1.) of the future eſtate of the Church in heauen after the laſt iudgement, vnto the fift verſe of the next Chapter. In this are two things briefly declared. The ſtation, ſeate, or place thereof, verſe 1. Then her ſtate and condition, in the verſes following. Before the ſtate of the Church deſcribed, is ſet downe the ſtate of the whole world, that there ſhall be a new heauen, and a new earth, as Eſa.65.7.and 66.12.& 2.Pet. 3.13 and this is the ſeate or place of the Church, in which righteouſneſſe ſhall dwell.

* *Eſa.*65.17. *and* 66.22.

* 2.*Pet*.3.13.

2 The ſtate of this glorious Church, is firſt deſcribed generally, vnto the 8.verſe, and then ſpecially and by parts, in the verſes following. The generall deſcription conſiſteth in a viſion ſhewed afarre off, verſe 2 and in ſpeach ſpoken from heauen. In the generall theſe things are common, that the Church is holy, new, the workemanſhip of God, heauenly, moſt glorious, the ſpouſe of Chriſt, and partaker of his glorie in this verſe. 3 The Church is deſcribed by ſpeach, firſt an Angel, in two verſes, then of God himſelfe, in foure verſes. The Angels ſpeech deſcribeth the glorie of the Church, by the moſt familiar cohabitation of God therewith, by communication of all maner good things according to the couenant, in this verſe: and by remoouing or putting farre away of all euill things, in the verſe following. **Chapter* 7.17. *eſai* 25.8. 4 In the ſpeach of God himſelfe deſcribing the Church, is firſt a certaine exordium, or entrance, verſe 5. Then followeth a magnificent deſcription of the Church, by the preſent and future good things of the ſame, in three verſes following. In the exordium God challengeth vnto himſelfe the reſtoring of all the creatures, of which verſe 1. and witneſſeth the calling of Sint Iohn vnto the writing of theſe things, in this verſe. **Eſay* 43.19. 2.*corinthians* 5.17. **Chapter* 1.8. *and* 22.13. 5 The deſcription of the Church is of three ſortes, by aboliſhing of olde things, by the being of preſent things in God, that is, of things eternall: and by the communication of all good things with the godly, verſe 6. If ſo bee they ſhall ſtriue manfully, verſe ſeuen. But the reprobate are excluded from thence, verſe eight. *a Their lot, and inheritance as it were.* 6 A tranſition vnto the particular deſcribing of the heauenly Church, by the expreſſe calling of Saint Iohn in this verſe, and his rapting vp by the Spirit, in confirmation of the trueth of God in the verſe following.

ing, Come: I will ſhew thee the bride, the
Lambes wife.
10 And he caried me away in the ſpirit to a
great and [7] an high mountaine, and he ſhewed
me [8] that great citie, that holy Hieruſalem, deſcending out of heauen from God,
11 Hauing the glory of God: and her ſhining was like vnto a ſtone moſt precious, as a
iaſper ſtone cleare as chryſtall,
12 [9] And had a great wall and high, and had
[10] twelue gates, and at the gates [11] twelue Angels, and the names writ which are the twelue
tribes of the children of Iſrael:
13 On the Eaſt part *there were* three gates,
and on the North ſide three gates, on the South
ſide three gates, & on the Weſt ſide three gates.
14 And the wall of the citie had [12] twelue
foundations, and in them the names of the
Lambes twelue Apoſtles.
15 [13] And he that talked with me, had a golden reede, to meaſure the citie withall, and the
gates thereof, and the wall thereof.
16 [14] And the citie lay [b] foureſquare, and
the length is as large as the bredth of it, and he
meaſured the citie with the reed, twelue thouſand furlongs: and the length, and the bredth,
and the height of it are equall.
17 And hee meaſured the wall thereof, an
hundred fortie and foure cubites, by the meaſure of man, that is, of the [c] Angel.
18 [15] And the building of the wall of it was
of iaſper: and the citie was pure gold, like vnto
cleare glaſſe.
19 And the foundations of the wall of the
citie were garniſhed with all maner of precious
ſtones: the firſt foundation *was* iaſper: the ſecond of Saphire: the third of a Chalcedonie:
the fourth of an Emeraud:
20 The fift of a Sardonix: the ſixt of a Sar-
dius: the ſeuenth of a Chryſolite: the eight of a
Beril: the ninth of a Topaz: the tenth of a
Chryſopraſus: the eleuenth of a Iacynth: the
twelfth an Amethyſt.
21 And the twelue gates *were* twelue pearls,
and euery gate *is* of one pearle, and the [d] ſtreete
of the citie *is* pure gold, as ſhining glaſſe.
22 And I ſawe no Temple therein: for the
Lord God Almightie and the Lambe are the
Temple of it.
23 * [16] And this citie hath no neede of the
ſunne, neither of the moone to ſhine in it: for
the glory of God did light it: and the Lambe is
the light of it.
24 And the people which are ſaued, ſhall
walke in the light of it: & the kings of the earth
ſhall bring their glory and honour vnto it.

7 He meaneth the place and ſtately ſeate of the Church, ſhadowed out in a mountaine.

8 A type of that Church which is one, ample, or Catholike, holy, celeſtiall, built of God, in this verſe; and glorious in the verſe following. This type propounded generally, is after particularly declared, ve.12.&c.

9 A particular deſcription (as I noted verſe 2.) of the celeſtiall Church, Firſt, by the eſſentiall parts of the ſame, vnder the ſimilitude of a citie, vnto verſe 22. Secondly, by the forreine accidents, vnto the end of the Chapter. Thirdly, by the effects, in the beginning of the next Chapter, the eſſentiall parts are noted the matter and the forme in the whole worke: of theſe the ſuperficies and foundation of the wall are entire parts (as they vſe to be called) which parts are firſt deſcribed in figure, vnto the 14. verſe afterwards more exactly.

10 According to the number of the tribes, of which Chapter 7. For here the outward part is attributed vnto the old Teſtament, and the foundation of the new Teſtament.

11 He meaneth the Prophets, who are the meſſengers of God, and watchmen of the Church.

12 That is, foundation ſtones, according to the number of the gates, as is ſhewed, verſe 19.

13 A tranſition vnto a more exquiſite deſcription of the parts of the Church, by finding out of the meaſure of the ſame, by the Angel that meaſured them. 14 The meaſure and forme moſt equall, in two verſes *b A foureſquare figure hath equall ſides, and outright corners, and therefore the Grecians call by this name thoſe things that are ſteady, and of continuance, and perfect.* *c He addeth this, becauſe the Angel had the ſhape of a man.* 15 The matter moſt precious and glittering, which the preſence of God maketh moſt glorious. *d By ſtreete, hee meaneth the broadeſt place of the citie.* * *Eſa.*60.19. 16 The ſecond forme of particular deſcription (as I ſaid verſ.12.) from forraine and outward accidents which are theſe, Light from God himſelfe, to this verſe: glory from men, ver.24 perfect ſecuritie from al harme, ver.25. Finally ſuch truth & incorruption of glory (ver.26.) as can beare & abide with it, nothing that is inglorious, verſe ye laſt

25 * And the gates of it shall not be shut by
day: for there shall be no night there.
26 And the glory and honour of the Gentiles shalbe brought vnto it.
27 And there shall enter into it none vncleane thing, neither whatsoeuer worketh abomination or lies: but they which are written in
the Lambes * booke of life.

*Esay 60.11.

*Chap.3.5.and 20.12.phil.4.3.

CHAP. XXII.

1 *The riuer of the water of life is shewed,* 2 *and the tree of life:* 6.7 *Then followeth the conclusion of this prophecie,* 8 *where Iohn declareth, that the things herein conteined, are most true:* 13 *And now the third time repeateth these words, All things come from him who is the beginning and the ende.*

AND [1] he shewed me a pure riuer of water
of life, cleare as crystal, proceeding out of
the throne of God, and of the Lambe.
2 In the midst of the streete of it, and of either side of the riuer, was the tree of life, which
bare twelue maner of fruits, and gaue fruit euery moneth: and the leaues of the tree *serued* to
heale the nations with.
3 And there shall bee no more curse, but
the throne of God and of the Lambe shalbe in
it, and his seruants shall serue him.
4 And they shall see his face, and his Name
shalbe in their foreheads.
5 * And there shall be no night there, and
they need no candle, neither light of the sunne:
for the Lord God giueth them light, and they
shall reigne for euermore.
6 [2] And hee said vnto me, These words are
faithful and true: and the Lord God of the holy Prophets sent his Angel to shew vnto his
seruants the things which must shortly bee fulfilled.
7 Behold, I come shortly. Blessed *is* he that
keepeth the words of the prophecie of this
booke.
8 And I am Iohn, which sawe and heard
these things: and when I had heard and seene,
* I fell downe to worship before the feete of
the Angel which shewed me these things.
9 But he said vnto me, See thou *doe it* not:
for I am thy fellow seruant, and of thy brethren
the Prophets, and of them which keepe the
words of this booke: worship God.

10 [3] And hee said vnto me, [4] Seale not the
words of the prophecie of this booke: for the
time is at hand.
11 [5] He that is vniust, let him be vniust still:
and he which is filthy, let him be filthy stil: and
he that is righteous, let him bee righteous still:
and he that is holy, let him be holy still.
12 [6] And behold, I come shortly, and my
reward is with me, * to giue to euery man according as his worke shall be.
13 I am * Alpha and Omega, the beginning
and the end, the first and the last.
14 Blessed *are* they, that doe his Commandements, [7] that their right may bee in the tree
of Life, and may enter in through the gates into the Citie.
15 For without *shall be* dogs & enchanters,
and whoremongers, and murtherers, and idolaters, and whosoeuer loueth or maketh lies.
16 [8] I Iesus haue sent mine Angel, to testifie
vnto you these things in the Churches: I am
the roote and the generation of Dauid, and the
bright morning Starre.
17 And the Spirit and the bride say, Come.
And let him that heareth, say, Come: and let
him that is athirst, come: and * let whosoeuer
will, take of the water of life freely.
18 [9] For I protest vnto euery man that heareth the words of the prophecie of this booke,
If any man shall adde vnto these things, God
shall adde vnto him the plagues that are written in this booke:
19 And if any man shall diminish of the
words of the booke of this prophecie, God
shall take away his part out of the booke of life,
and out of the holy citie, and from those things
which are written in this booke.
20 [10] He which testifieth these things, saith,
Surely I come quickly, Amen. Euen so, come
Lord Iesus.
21 [11] The grace of our Lord Iesus Christ *be*
with you all, AMEN.

1 Here is absolued and finished the description of the celestiall Church (as I shewed before, Chapter 21.12.) by the effects in 5.verses, and then this booke is concluded in the rest of the Chapter. The effects proceeding from God, who dwelleth in ye Church, are these: the euerlasting grace of God, in this verse, the eternall liuing of the godly, as Chapter 2.7. the eternall fruits which the godly bring forth vnto God, themselues and others, verse 2. freedome and immunitie from all euill, God himselfe taking pleasure in his seruants, and they likewise in their God, verse 3. The beholding and sight of God, and sealing of the faithful from all eternitie, verse 4. the light of God and an euerlasting kingdome and glory, verse 5.

*Esay 60.19.

2 This whole booke is concluded and made vp by a confirmation, and a salutation. The confirmation hath three places: The words of the Angel vnto the 15.verse, the words of Christ: verse 16,17. and the obtestation made by Saint Iohn from diuine authoritie, thence vnto the 20.verse. By the speech of the Angel this prophecie is confirmed, vnto the 8.verse, and then he speaketh of the vse of this booke in the verses following. The prophecie is first confirmed by the Angel from the nature thereof, that it is faithfull and true: Secondly, from the nature of the efficient cause, both principall, which is God, and instrumentall, which is the Angel, in this verse. Thirdly, from the promises of God concerning his comming to effect all these things, and concerning our saluation, verse seuen. Fourthly, from the testification of Saint Iohn himselfe, verse eight. The rest of the speech of the Angel tending to the same ende, Saint Iohn interrupted or brake off by his vnaduised acte of worshipping him, in the same verse, which the Angel forbidding, teacheth him that adoration must bee giuen not to him, but onely to God, as for himselfe, that hee is of such nature and office, as hee may not bee adored: which thing also was in like manner done, Chapter 16, verse 10. *Chapter 19.10.*

3 The Angel returneth vnto his former speech: in which he teacheth the vse of this booke both towards our selues, in this and the next verse: and in respect of God for declaration of his trueth, thence vnto the 15.vers. 4 That is, propound this prophecie openly vnto all, & conceale no part of it. The contrary whereunto is commanded Esa 8 6.and Dan.8.26. 5 An obiection preuented. But there will bee some that will abuse this occasion vnto euill, and will wrest this Scripture vnto their owne destruction, as Peter saith. What then? saith the Angel, the mysteries of God must not therefore be concealed, which it hath pleased him to communicate vnto vs. Let them be hurtfull vnto others, let such be more and more vile in themselues, whom this Scripture doeth not please: yet others shalbe further conformed therby vnto righteousnesse, and true holinesse. The care and reformation of these may not be neglected, because of the voluntarie & malicious offence of others. 6 The second place belonging vnto the vse of this booke, as I said verse 10. Also (saith God by the Angel) though there should be no vse of this booke vnto men: yet it shall bee of this vse vnto me, that it is a witnesse of my Trueth vnto my glory, who will come shortly, to giue and execute iust iudgement, in this verse: who haue taught that all these things haue their being in mee, in the 13. verse, and haue denounced blessednesse vnto my seruants in the Church, verse 14. and reprobation vnto the vngodly, verse 15. **Rom. 2.6.* **Chap.1.8. and 21.6. esay 41.44. and 44.6.* 7 The blessednesse of the godly set downe by their title and interest thereunto: and their fruit in the same. 8 The second place of confirmation (as I said) is the speech of Christ ratifying the vocation of Saint Iohn, and the authoritie of his calling and testimonie, both from the condition of his owne person being God and man, in whome all the promises of God are Yea and Amen, 2.Cor.1.20. and also from the testification of other persons, by the acclamation of the holy Ghost, who here is as it were an honourable assistant of the marriage of the Church as the spouse: and of euery of the godly as members: and finally from the thing present, that of their owne knowledge and accord, they are called foorth vnto the participation of the good things of God, verse 17. **Esay 55.1.* 9 The obtestation of S. Iohn (which is the third place of the confirmation, as was noted verse 6.) ioyned with a curse of execration, to preserue the trueth of this booke entire and vncorrupted in two verses. 10 A diuine confirmation or sealing of the obtestation first from Christ auouching the same, & denouncing his comming against all those that shall put their sacrilegious hands hereunto: then from S. Iohn himselfe, who by a most holy praier calleth Christ to take vengeance of them. 11 The salutation Apostolicall, which is the other place of the conclusion, as I said verse 6. and is the end almost of euery Epistle: which we wish vnto the Church, and to all the holy and Elect members thereof, in Christ Iesus our Lord, vntill his comming to iudgement, *Come Lord Iesus* and doe it. Amen, againe Amen.

*Rom.2.6.

*Chap.1.8. and 21.6. esay 41.44. and 44.6.

*Esay 55.1.

THE END.

¶ A briefe